List of Elements with Their Symbols and Atomic Weights

Element	Symbol	Atomic Number	Atomic Weight
Actinium	Ac	89	227.03[a]
Aluminum	Al	13	26.981538
Americium	Am	95	243.06[a]
Antimony	Sb	51	121.760
Argon	Ar	18	39.948
Arsenic	As	33	74.92160
Astatine	At	85	209.99[a]
Barium	Ba	56	137.327
Berkelium	Bk	97	247.07[a]
Beryllium	Be	4	9.012182
Bismuth	Bi	83	208.98038
Bohrium	Bh	107	264.12[a]
Boron	B	5	10.811
Bromine	Br	35	79.904
Cadmium	Cd	48	112.411
Calcium	Ca	20	40.078
Californium	Cf	98	251.08[a]
Carbon	C	6	12.0107
Cerium	Ce	58	140.116
Cesium	Cs	55	132.90545
Chlorine	Cl	17	35.453
Chromium	Cr	24	51.9961
Cobalt	Co	27	58.933200
Copper	Cu	29	63.546
Curium	Cm	96	247.07[a]
Darmstadtium	Ds	110	281.15[a]
Dubnium	Db	105	262.11[a]
Dysprosium	Dy	66	162.50
Einsteinium	Es	99	252.08[a]
Erbium	Er	68	167.259
Europium	Eu	63	151.964
Fermium	Fm	100	257.10[a]
Fluorine	F	9	18.9984032
Francium	Fr	87	223.02[a]
Gadolinium	Gd	64	157.25
Gallium	Ga	31	69.723
Germanium	Ge	32	72.64
Gold	Au	79	196.96655
Hafnium	Hf	72	178.49

Element	Symbol	Atomic Number	Atomic Weight
Hassium	Hs	108	269.13[a]
Helium	He	2	4.002602[a]
Holmium	Ho	67	164.93032
Hydrogen	H	1	1.00794
Indium	In	49	114.818
Iodine	I	53	126.90447
Iridium	Ir	77	192.217
Iron	Fe	26	55.845
Krypton	Kr	36	83.80
Lanthanum	La	57	138.9055
Lawrencium	Lr	103	262.11[a]
Lead	Pb	82	207.2
Lithium	Li	3	6.941
Lutetium	Lu	71	174.967
Magnesium	Mg	12	24.3050
Manganese	Mn	25	54.938049
Meitnerium	Mt	109	268.14[a]
Mendelevium	Md	101	258.10[a]
Mercury	Hg	80	200.59
Molybdenum	Mo	42	95.94
Neodymium	Nd	60	144.24
Neon	Ne	10	20.1797
Neptunium	Np	93	237.05[a]
Nickel	Ni	28	58.6934
Niobium	Nb	41	92.90638
Nitrogen	N	7	14.0067
Nobelium	No	102	259.10[a]
Osmium	Os	76	190.23
Oxygen	O	8	15.9994
Palladium	Pd	46	106.42
Phosphorus	P	15	30.973761
Platinum	Pt	78	195.078
Plutonium	Pu	94	244.06[a]
Polonium	Po	84	208.98[a]
Potassium	K	19	39.0983
Praseodymium	Pr	59	140.90765
Promethium	Pm	61	145[a]
Protactinium	Pa	91	231.03588
Radium	Ra	88	226.03[a]

Element	Symbol	Atomic Number	Atomic Weight
Radon	Rn	86	222.02[a]
Rhenium	Re	75	186.207[a]
Rhodium	Rh	45	102.90550
Roentgenium	Rg	111	272.15[a]
Rubidium	Rb	37	85.4678
Ruthenium	Ru	44	101.07
Rutherfordium	Rf	104	261.11[a]
Samarium	Sm	62	150.36
Scandium	Sc	21	44.955910
Seaborgium	Sg	106	266[a]
Selenium	Se	34	78.96
Silicon	Si	14	28.0855
Silver	Ag	47	107.8682
Sodium	Na	11	22.989770
Strontium	Sr	38	87.62
Sulfur	S	16	32.065
Tantalum	Ta	73	180.9479
Technetium	Tc	43	98[a]
Tellurium	Te	52	127.60
Terbium	Tb	65	158.92534
Thallium	Tl	81	204.3833
Thorium	Th	90	232.0381
Thulium	Tm	69	168.93421
Tin	Sn	50	118.710
Titanium	Ti	22	47.867
Tungsten	W	74	183.84
Uranium	U	92	238.02891
Vanadium	V	23	50.9415
Xenon	Xe	54	131.293
Ytterbium	Yb	70	173.04
Yttrium	Y	39	88.90585
Zinc	Zn	30	65.39
Zirconium	Zr	40	91.224
*b		112	277[a]
*b		113	284[a]
*b		114	289[a]
*b		115	288[a]
*b		116	292[a]
*b		118	294[a]

[a]Mass of longest-lived isotope.

[b]The names of elements have not yet been decided.

D1362427

CUSTOM EDITION FOR THE UNIVERSITY OF MARY WASHINGTON

CHEMISTRY
THE CENTRAL SCIENCE

Theodore L. Brown • H. Eugene LeMay, Jr.
Bruce E. Bursten • Catherine J. Murphy

with contributions from Patrick Woodward

Taken from:

Chemistry: The Central Science
by Theodore L. Brown, H. Eugene LeMay, Jr., Bruce E. Bursten, Catherine J. Murphy,
with contributions from Patrick Woodward

Custom Publishing

New York   Boston   San Francisco
London   Toronto   Sydney   Tokyo   Singapore   Madrid
Mexico City   Munich   Paris   Cape Town   Hong Kong   Montreal

Periodic Table tiles created by Merida Marston for the Department of Chemistry at the University of Mary Washington's Centennial Celebration (1908-2008).

Taken from:

Chemistry: The Central Science
by Theodore L. Brown, H. Eugene LeMay, Jr., Bruce E. Bursten,
Catherine J. Murphy, with contributions from Patrick Woodward
Copyright © 2009 by Pearson Education
Boston, Massachusetts 02116

This special edition published in cooperation with Pearson Custom Publishing.

Printed in the United States of America

10   9   8   7   6   5   4

2008180051

DM

**Pearson
Custom Publishing**
is a division of

www.pearsonhighered.com

ISBN 10: 0-536-88012-3
ISBN 13: 978-0-536-88012-3

To our students, whose enthusiasm and curiosity have often inspired us, and whose questions and suggestions have sometimes taught us.

Brief Contents

Contents

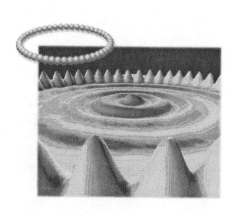

3 Stoichiometry: Calculations with Chemical Formulas and Equations 78

4 Aqueous Reactions and Solution Stoichiometry 118

5 Thermochemistry   164

6 Electronic Structure of Atoms   210

7 Periodic Properties of the Elements   254

8 Basic Concepts of Chemical Bonding   296

9 Molecular Geometry and Bonding Theories   340

13 Properties of Solutions   526

14 Chemical Kinetics   572

15 Chemical Equilibrium   626

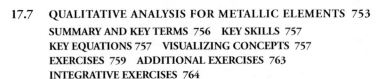

19 Chemical Thermodynamics   800

20 Electrochemistry   842

21 Nuclear Chemistry   892

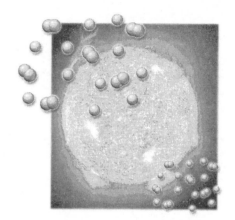

Appendices

Preface

TO THE INSTRUCTOR

Philosophy

This is the eleventh edition of a text that has enjoyed unprecedented success over its many editions. It is fair to ask why there needs to be yet another edition. The answer in part lies in the nature of chemistry itself, a dynamic science in a process of continual discovery. New research leads to new applications of chemistry in other fields of science and in technology. In addition, environmental and economic concerns bring about changes in the place of chemistry in society. We want our textbook to reflect that dynamic, changing character. We also want it to convey the excitement that scientists experience in making new discoveries and contributing to our understanding of the physical world.

In addition, new ideas about how to present chemistry are being offered by teachers of chemistry, and many of these new ideas are reflected in how the textbook is organized and the ways in which individual topics are presented. New technologies and new devices to assist students in learning lead to new ways of presenting learning materials: the Internet, computer-based classroom projection tools, and more effective means of testing, to name just a few. All of these factors impact on how the text and the accompanying supplementary materials are modified from one edition to the next.

Our aim in revising the text has been to ensure that it remains a central, indispensable learning tool for the student. It is the one device that can be carried everywhere and used at any time, and as such, it is a one-stop source of all the information that the student is likely to need for learning, skill development, reference, and test preparation.

We believe that students are more enthusiastic about learning chemistry when they see its importance to their own goals and interests. With this in mind, we have highlighted many important applications of chemistry in everyday life. At the same time, the text provides the background in modern chemistry that students need to serve their professional interests and, as appropriate, to prepare for more advanced chemistry courses.

If the text is to support your role as teacher effectively, it must be addressed to the students. We have done our best to keep our writing clear and interesting and the book attractive and well-illustrated. Furthermore, we have provided numerous in-text study aids for students, including carefully placed descriptions of problem-solving strategies. Together, we have logged many years of teaching experience. We hope this is evident in our pacing and choice of examples.

A textbook is only as useful to students as the instructor permits it to be. This book is loaded with many features that can help students learn and that can guide them as they acquire both conceptual understanding and problem-solving skills. But the text and all the supplementary materials provided to support its use must work in concert with the instructor. There is a great deal for the students to use here, too much for all of it to be absorbed by any one student. You, the instructor, are the guide to a proper use of the book. Only with your active help will the students be able to fully utilize all that the text and its supplements offer. Students care about grades, of course, but with encouragement, they can also care about learning just because the subject matter is interesting. Please consider emphasizing features of the book that can materially enhance student appreciation of chemistry, such as the *Chemistry Put to Work* and *Chemistry and Life* boxes that show how chemistry impacts modern life and its relationship to health and life processes. Learn to use, and urge students to use, the rich Internet resources available. Emphasize conceptual understanding, and place less emphasis on simple manipulative, algorithmic problem solving. Spending less time on solving a variety of gas law problems, for example, can open up opportunities to talk about chemistry and the environment.

Organization and Contents

The first five chapters give a largely macroscopic, phenomenological view of chemistry. The basic concepts introduced—such as nomenclature, stoichiometry, and thermochemistry—provide necessary background for many of the laboratory experiments usually performed in general chemistry. We believe that an early introduction to thermochemistry is desirable because so much of our understanding of chemical processes is based on considerations of energy change. Thermochemistry is also important when we come to a discussion of bond enthalpies. We believe we have produced an effective, balanced approach to teaching thermodynamics in general chemistry. It is no easy matter to walk the narrow pathway between—on the one hand—trying to teach too much at too high a level and—on the other—resorting to oversimplifications. As with the book as a whole, the emphasis has been on imparting *conceptual* understanding, as opposed to presenting equations into which students are supposed to plug numbers.

The next four chapters (Chapters 6–9) deal with electronic structure and bonding. We have largely retained our presentation of atomic orbitals. For more advanced students, *Closer Look* boxes deal with radial probability functions and the nature of antibonding orbitals. In Chapter 7 we have improved our discussion of atomic and ionic radii. The focus of the text then changes to the next level of the organization of matter: the states of matter (Chapters 10 and 11) and solutions (Chapter 13). Also included in this section is an applications chapter on the chemistry of modern materials (Chapter 12), which builds on the student's understanding of chemical bonding and intermolecular interactions. This chapter has again received substantial revision, in keeping with the rapid pace of change in technology. It has been reorganized to emphasize a classification of materials based on their electronic bonding characteristics. This chapter provides an opportunity to show how the sometimes abstract concept of chemical bonding impacts real world applications. The modular organization of the chapter allows you to tailor your coverage to focus on those materials (semiconductors, polymers, biomaterials, nanotechnology, etc.) that are most relevant to your students.

The next several chapters examine the factors that determine the speed and extent of chemical reactions: kinetics (Chapter 14), equilibria (Chapters 15–17), thermodynamics (Chapter 19), and electrochemistry (Chapter 20). Also in this section is a chapter on environmental chemistry (Chapter 18), in which the concepts developed in preceding chapters are applied to a discussion of the atmosphere and hydrosphere.

After a discussion of nuclear chemistry (Chapter 21), the final chapters survey the chemistry of nonmetals, metals, organic chemistry, and biochemistry (Chapters 22–25). Chapter 22 has been shortened slightly. Chapter 23 now contains a modern treatment of band structure and bonding in metals. A brief discussion of lipids has been added to Chapter 25. These final chapters are developed in a parallel fashion and can be treated in any order.

Our chapter sequence provides a fairly standard organization, but we recognize that not everyone teaches all the topics in exactly the order we have chosen. We have therefore made sure that instructors can make common changes in teaching sequence with no loss in student comprehension. In particular, many instructors prefer to introduce gases (Chapter 10) after stoichiometry or after thermochemistry rather than with states of matter. The chapter on gases has been written to permit this change with *no* disruption in the flow of material. It is also possible to treat the balancing of redox equations (Sections 20.1 and 20.2) earlier, after the introduction of redox reactions in Section 4.4. Finally, some instructors like to cover organic chemistry (Chapter 25) right after bonding (Chapter 9). This, too, is a largely seamless move.

We have introduced students to descriptive organic and inorganic chemistry by integrating examples throughout the text. You will find pertinent and relevant examples of "real" chemistry woven into all the chapters as a means to illustrate principles and applications. Some chapters, of course, more directly address the properties of elements and their compounds, especially Chapters 4, 7, 12, 18, and 22–25. We also incorporate descriptive organic and inorganic chemistry in the end-of-chapter exercises.

Changes in This Edition

Some of the changes in the eleventh edition made in individual chapters have already been mentioned. More broadly, we have introduced a number of new features that are general throughout the text. *Chemistry: The Central Science* has traditionally been valued for its clarity of writing, its scientific accuracy and currency, its strong end-of-chapter exercises, and its consistency in level of coverage. In making changes, we have made sure not to compromise these characteristics. At the same time, we have responded to feedback received from the faculty and students who used previous editions. To make the text easier for students to use, we have continued to employ an open, clean design in the layout of the book. Illustrations that lend themselves to a more schematic, bolder presentation of the underlying principles have been introduced or revised from earlier versions. The art program in general has been strengthened, to better convey the beauty, excitement, and concepts of chemistry to students. The chapter-opening photos have been integrated into the introduction to each chapter, and thus made more relevant to the chapter's contents.

We have continued to use the What's Ahead overview at the opening of each chapter, introduced in the ninth edition, but we have changed the format to make the materials more useful to students. *Concept links* (∞) continue to provide easy-to-see cross-references to pertinent material covered earlier in the text. The essays titled *Strategies in Chemistry*, which provide advice to students on problem solving and "thinking like a chemist," continue to be an important feature. The *Give It Some Thought* exercises that we introduced in the tenth edition have proven to be very popular, and we have increased their number. These are informal, rather sharply focused questions that give students opportunities to test whether they are actually "getting it" as they read along. We have continued to emphasize conceptual exercises in the end-of-chapter exercise materials. The *Visualizing Concepts* category of exercise has been continued in this edition. These exercises are designed to facilitate concept understanding through use of models, graphs, and other visual materials. They precede the regular end-of-chapter exercises and are identified in each case with the relevant chapter section number. We continue to use multi-focus graphics to depict topics in macroscopic, microscopic, symbolic, and conceptual representation so students learn to see chemistry the way scientists do, from a variety of perspectives. The *Integrative Exercises*, which give students the opportunity to solve more challenging problems that integrate concepts from the present chapter with those of previous chapters, have also been increased in number.

New essays in our well-received *Chemistry Put to Work* and *Chemistry and Life* series emphasize world events, scientific discoveries, and medical breakthroughs that have occurred since publication of the tenth edition. We maintain our focus on the positive aspects of chemistry, without neglecting the problems that can arise in an increasingly technological world. Our goal is to help students appreciate the real-world perspective of chemistry and the ways in which chemistry affects their lives.

A minor change that you will see throughout the text is the use of condensed structural formulas for simple carboxylic acids. For example, we now write CH_3COOH for acetic acid instead of $HC_2H_3O_2$.

You'll also find that we've

- Revised or replaced some of the end-of-chapter Exercises, with particular focus on the black-numbered exercises (those not answered in the Appendix).

- Integrated more conceptual questions into the end-of-chapter material. For the convenience of instructors, these are identified by the CQ annotation in the Annotated Instructor's Edition, but not in the student edition of the text.

- Carried the stepwise Analyze, Plan, Solve, Check problem-solving strategy into nearly all of the Sample Exercises of the book to provide additional guidance in problem solving.

- Expanded the use of dual-column problem-solving strategies in many Sample Exercises to more clearly outline the process underlying mathematical calculations, thereby helping students to better perform mathematical calculations.

- Added both Key Skills and Key Equations sections to the end of chapter material to help students focus their study.

TO THE STUDENT

Chemistry: The Central Science, Eleventh Edition, has been written to introduce you to modern chemistry. As authors, we have, in effect, been engaged by your instructor to help you learn chemistry. Based on the comments of students and instructors who have used this book in its previous editions, we believe that we have done that job well. Of course, we expect the text to continue to evolve through future editions. We invite you to write to us to tell us what you like about the book so that we will know where we have helped you most. Also, we would like to learn of any shortcomings, so that we might further improve the book in subsequent editions. Our addresses are given at the end of the Preface.

Advice for Learning and Studying Chemistry

Learning chemistry requires both the assimilation of many new concepts and the development of analytical skills. In this text we have provided you with numerous tools to help you succeed in both. If you are going to succeed in your course in chemistry, you will have to develop good study habits. Science courses, and chemistry in particular, make different demands on your learning skills than other types of courses. We offer the following tips for success in your study of chemistry:

Don't fall behind! As your chemistry course moves along, new topics will build on material already presented. If you don't keep up in your reading and problem solving, you will find it much harder to follow the lectures and discussions on current topics. "Cramming" just before an exam has been shown to be an ineffective way to study any subject, chemistry included.

Focus your study. The amount of information you will be expected to learn can sometimes seem overwhelming. It is essential to recognize those concepts and skills that are particularly important. Pay attention to what your instructor is emphasizing. As you work through the Sample Exercises and homework assignments, try to see what general principles and skills they deal with. Use the **What's Ahead** feature at the beginning of each chapter to help orient you to what is important in each chapter. A single reading of a chapter will simply not be enough for successful learning of chapter concepts and problem-solving skills. You will need to go over assigned materials more than once. Don't skip the **Give It Some Thought** features, **Sample Exercises**, and **Practice Exercises**.

List of Resources

For Students

MasteringChemistry: MasteringChemistry is the first adaptive-learning online homework system. It provides selected end-of-chapter problems from the text, as well as hundreds of tutorials with automatic grading, immediate answer-specific feedback, and simpler questions on request. Based on extensive research of precise concepts students struggle with, MasteringChemistry uniquely responds to your immediate learning needs, thereby optimizing your study time.

Solutions to Red Exercises (0-13-600287-0) Prepared by Roxy Wilson of the University of Illinois–Urbana-Champaign. Full solutions to all of the red-numbered exercises in the text are provided. (Short answers to red exercises are found in the appendix of the text).

Solutions to Black Exercises (0-13-600324-9) Prepared by Roxy Wilson of the University of Illinois–Urbana-Champaign. Full solutions to all of the black-numbered exercises in the text are provided.

Student's Guide (0-13-600264-1) Prepared by James C. Hill of California State University. This book assists students through the text material with chapter overviews, learning objectives, a review of key terms, as well as self-tests with answers and explanations. This edition also features the addition of MCAT practice questions.

Laboratory Experiments (0-13-600285-4) Prepared by John H. Nelson and Kenneth C. Kemp, both of the University of Nevada. This manual contains 43 finely tuned experiments chosen to introduce students to basic lab techniques and to illustrate core chemical principles. This new edition has been revised to correlate more tightly with the text and now features a guide on how to keep a lab report notebook. You can also customize these labs through Catalyst, our custom database program. For more information, visit www.prenhall.com/catalyst.

Virtual ChemLab: An easy to use simulation of five different general chemistry laboratories that can be used to supplement a wet lab, for pre-laboratory and post-laboratory activities, for homework or quiz assignments, or for classroom demonstrations.

For Instructors

Annotated Instructor's Edition (0-13-601250-7) Prepared by Linda Brunauer of Santa Clara University. Provides marginal notes and information for instructors and TAs, including transparency icons, suggested lecture demonstrations, teaching tips, and background references from the chemical education literature.

Full Solutions Manual (0-13-600325-7) Prepared by Roxy Wilson of the University of Illinois–Urbana-Champaign. This manual contains all end-of-chapter exercises in the text. With an instructor's permission, this manual may be made available to students.

Instructor's Resource Center on CD-DVD (0-13-600281-1) This resource provides an integrated collection of resources to help you make efficient and effective use of your time. This CD/DVD features most art from the text, including figures and tables in PDF format for high-resolution printing, as well as four pre-built PowerPoint™ presentations. The first presentation contains the images embedded within PowerPoint slides. The second includes a complete lecture outline that is modifiable by the user. The final two presentations contain worked "in chapter" sample exercises and questions to be used with Classroom Response Systems. This CD/DVD also contains movies, animations, and electronic files of the Instructor's Resource Manual.

Test Item File (0-13-601251-5) Prepared by Joseph P. Laurino and Donald Cannon, both of the University of Tampa. The Test Item File now provides a selection of more than 4000 test questions.

Instructor's Resource Manual (0-13-600237-4) Prepared by Linda Brunauer of Santa Clara University and Elizabeth Cook of Louisiana State University. Organized by chapter, this manual offers detailed lecture outlines and complete descriptions of all available lecture demonstrations, the interactive media assets, common student misconceptions, and more.

Transparencies (0-13-601256-6) Approximately 300 full-color transparencies put principles into visual perspective and save you time when preparing lectures.

Annotated Instructor's Edition to *Laboratory Experiments* (0-13-6002862) Prepared by John H. Nelson and Kenneth C. Kemp, both of the University of Nevada. This AIE combines the full student lab manual with appendices covering the proper disposal of chemical waste, safety instructions for the lab, descriptions of standard lab equipment, answers to questions, and more.

BlackBoard and WebCT: Practice and assessment materials are available upon request in these course management platforms.

About the Authors

THEODORE L. BROWN received his Ph.D. from Michigan State University in 1956. Since then, he has been a member of the faculty of the University of Illinois, Urbana-Champaign, where he is now Professor of Chemistry, Emeritus. He served as Vice Chancellor for Research, and Dean, The Graduate College, from 1980 to 1986, and as Founding Director of the Arnold and Mabel Beckman Institute for Advanced Science and Technology from 1987 to 1993. Professor Brown has been an Alfred P. Sloan Foundation Research Fellow and has been awarded a Guggenheim Fellowship. In 1972 he was awarded the American Chemical Society Award for Research in Inorganic Chemistry, and received the American Chemical Society Award for Distinguished Service in the Advancement of Inorganic Chemistry in 1993. He has been elected a Fellow of both the American Association for the Advancement of Science and the American Academy of Arts and Sciences.

H. EUGENE LeMAY, JR., received his B.S. degree in Chemistry from Pacific Lutheran University (Washington) and his Ph.D. in Chemistry in 1966 from the University of Illinois (Urbana). He then joined the faculty of the University of Nevada, Reno, where he is currently Professor of Chemistry, Emeritus. He has enjoyed Visiting Professorships at the University of North Carolina at Chapel Hill, at the University College of Wales in Great Britain, and at the University of California, Los Angeles. Professor LeMay is a popular and effective teacher, who has taught thousands of students during more than 35 years of university teaching. Known for the clarity of his lectures and his sense of humor, he has received several teaching awards, including the University Distinguished Teacher of the Year Award (1991) and the first Regents' Teaching Award given by the State of Nevada Board of Regents (1997).

BRUCE E. BURSTEN received his Ph.D. in Chemistry from the University of Wisconsin in 1978. After two years as a National Science Foundation Postdoctoral Fellow at Texas A&M University, he joined the faculty of The Ohio State University, where he rose to the rank of Distinguished University Professor. In 2005, he moved to his present position at the University of Tennessee, Knoxville as Distinguished Professor of Chemistry and Dean of the College of Arts and Sciences. Professor Bursten has been a Camille and Henry Dreyfus Foundation Teacher-Scholar and an Alfred P. Sloan Foundation Research Fellow, and he has been elected a Fellow of the American Association for the Advancement of Science. At Ohio State he has received the University Distinguished Teaching Award in 1982 and 1996, the Arts and Sciences Student Council Outstanding Teaching Award in 1984, and the University Distinguished Scholar Award in 1990. He received the Spiers Memorial Prize and Medal of the Royal Society of Chemistry in 2003, and the Morley Medal of the Cleveland Section of the American Chemical Society in 2005. He was elected President of the American Chemical Society for 2008. In addition to his teaching and service activities, Professor Bursten's research program focuses on compounds of the transition-metal and actinide elements.

CATHERINE J. MURPHY received two B.S. degrees, one in Chemistry and one in Biochemistry, from the University of Illinois, Urbana-Champaign, in 1986. She received her Ph.D. in Chemistry from the University of Wisconsin in 1990. She was a National Science Foundation and National Institutes of Health Postdoctoral Fellow at the California Institute of Technology from 1990 to 1993. In 1993, she joined the faculty of the University of South Carolina, Columbia, where she is currently the Guy F. Lipscomb Professor of Chemistry. Professor Murphy has been honored for both research and teaching as a Camille Dreyfus Teacher-Scholar, an Alfred P. Sloan Foundation Research Fellow, a Cottrell Scholar of the Research Corporation, a National Science Foundation CAREER Award winner, and a subsequent NSF Award for Special Creativity. She has also received a USC Mortar Board Excellence in Teaching Award, the USC Golden Key Faculty Award for Creative Integration of Research and Undergraduate Teaching, the USC Michael J. Mungo Undergraduate Teaching Award, and the USC Outstanding Undergraduate Research Mentor Award. Since 2006, Professor Murphy has served as a Senior Editor to the *Journal of Physical Chemistry*. Professor Murphy's research program focuses on the synthesis and optical properties of inorganic nanomaterials, and on the local structure and dynamics of the DNA double helix.

Contributing Author

PATRICK M. WOODWARD received B.S. degrees in both Chemistry and Engineering from Idaho State University in 1991. He received a M.S. degree in Materials Science and a Ph.D. in Chemistry from Oregon State University in 1996. He spent two years as a postdoctoral researcher in the Department of Physics at Brookhaven National Laboratory. In 1998, he joined the faculty of the Chemistry Department at The Ohio State University where he currently holds the rank of Associate Professor. He has enjoyed visiting professorships at the University of Bordeaux, in France, and the University of Sydney, in Australia. Professor Woodward has been an Alfred P. Sloan Foundation Research Fellow and a National Science Foundation CAREER Award winner. He currently serves as an Associate Editor to the *Journal of Solid State Chemistry* and as the director of the Ohio REEL program, an NSF funded center that works to bring authentic research experiments into the laboratories of first and second year chemistry classes in 15 colleges and universities across the state of Ohio. Professor Woodward's research program focuses on understanding the links between bonding, structure, and properties of solid state inorganic functional materials.

CHAPTER 1

INTRODUCTION: MATTER AND MEASUREMENT

HUBBLE SPACE TELESCOPE IMAGE of the Crab Nebula, a 6-light-year-wide expanding remnant of a star's supernova explosion. The orange filaments are the tattered remains of the star and consist mostly of hydrogen, the simplest and most plentiful element in the universe. Hydrogen occurs as molecules in cool regions, as atoms in hotter regions, and as ions in the hottest regions. The processes that occur within stars are responsible for creating other chemical elements from hydrogen.

HAVE YOU EVER WONDERED why ice melts and water evaporates? Why do leaves turn colors in the fall, and how does a battery generate electricity? Why does keeping foods cold slow their spoilage, and how do our bodies use food to maintain life?

Chemistry answers these questions and countless others like them. **Chemistry** is the study of materials and the changes that materials undergo. One of the joys of learning chemistry is seeing how chemical principles operate in all aspects of our lives, from everyday activities like lighting a match to more far-reaching matters like the development of drugs to cure cancer. Chemical principles also operate in the far reaches of our galaxy (chapter-opening photo) as well as within and around us.

This first chapter lays a foundation for our study of chemistry by providing an overview of what chemistry is about and dealing with some fundamental concepts of matter and scientific measurements. The list above, entitled "What's Ahead," gives a brief overview of the organization of this chapter and some of the ideas that we will consider. As you study, keep in mind that the chemical facts and concepts you are asked to learn are not ends in themselves; they are tools to help you better understand the world around you.

1.1 THE STUDY OF CHEMISTRY

Before traveling to an unfamiliar city, you might look at a map to get some sense of where you are heading. Because chemistry may be unfamiliar to you, it's useful to get a general idea of what lies ahead before you embark on your journey. In fact, you might even ask why you are taking the trip.

The Atomic and Molecular Perspective of Chemistry

Chemistry is the study of the properties and behavior of matter. **Matter** is the physical material of the universe; it is anything that has mass and occupies space. A **property** is any characteristic that allows us to recognize a particular type of matter and to distinguish it from other types. This book, your body, the clothes you are wearing, and the air you are breathing are all samples of matter. Not all forms of matter are so common or so familiar. Countless experiments have shown that the tremendous variety of matter in our world is due to combinations of only about 100 very basic, or elementary, substances called **elements**. As we proceed through this text, we will seek to relate the properties of matter to its composition, that is, to the particular elements it contains.

Chemistry also provides a background to understanding the properties of matter in terms of **atoms**, the almost infinitesimally small building blocks of matter. Each element is composed of a unique kind of atom. We will see that the properties of matter relate to both the kinds of atoms the matter contains (*composition*) and to the arrangements of these atoms (*structure*).

Atoms can combine to form **molecules** in which two or more atoms are joined together in specific shapes. Throughout this text you will see molecules represented using colored spheres to show how their component atoms connect to each other (Figure 1.1 ▼). The color provides a convenient and easy way to distinguish between the atoms of different elements. For examples, compare the molecules of ethanol and ethylene glycol in Figure 1.1. Notice that these molecules have different compositions and structures. Ethanol contains only one oxygen atom, which is depicted by one red sphere. In contrast, ethylene glycol has two atoms of oxygen.

Even apparently minor differences in the composition or structure of molecules can cause profound differences in their properties. Ethanol, also called grain alcohol, is the alcohol in beverages such as beer and wine. Ethylene glycol, on the other hand, is a viscous liquid used as automobile antifreeze. The properties of these two substances differ in many ways, including the temperatures at which they freeze and boil. The biological activities of the two molecules are also quite different. Ethanol is consumed throughout the world, but you should *never* consume ethylene glycol because it is highly toxic. One of the challenges that chemists undertake is to alter the composition or structure of molecules in a controlled way, creating new substances with different properties.

Every change in the observable world—from boiling water to the changes that occur as our bodies combat invading viruses—has its basis in the world of atoms and molecules. Thus, as we proceed with our study of chemistry, we will find ourselves thinking in two realms: the *macroscopic* realm

▼ **Figure 1.1 Molecular models.** The white, dark gray, and red spheres represent atoms of hydrogen, carbon, and oxygen, respectively.

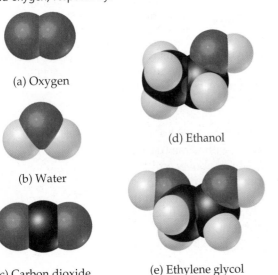

(a) Oxygen

(b) Water

(c) Carbon dioxide

(d) Ethanol

(e) Ethylene glycol

(f) Aspirin

of ordinary-sized objects (*macro* = large) and the *submicroscopic* realm of atoms and molecules. We make our observations in the macroscopic world—in the laboratory and in our everyday surroundings. To understand that world, however, we must visualize how atoms and molecules behave at the submicroscopic level. Chemistry is the science that seeks to understand the properties and behavior of matter by studying the properties and behavior of atoms and molecules.

GIVE IT SOME THOUGHT

(a) In round numbers, about how many elements are there? **(b)** What submicroscopic particles are the building blocks of matter?

Why Study Chemistry?

Chemistry provides important understanding of our world and how it works. It is an extremely practical science that greatly impacts our daily lives. Indeed, chemistry lies near the heart of many matters of public concern: improvement of health care; conservation of natural resources; protection of the environment; and provision of our everyday needs for food, clothing, and shelter. Using chemistry, we have discovered pharmaceutical chemicals that enhance our health and prolong our lives. We have increased food production through the use of fertilizers and pesticides, and we have developed plastics and other materials that are used in almost every facet of our lives. Unfortunately, some chemicals also have the potential to harm our health or the environment. As educated citizens and consumers, it is in our best interest to understand the profound effects, both positive and negative, that chemicals have on our lives and to strike an informed balance about their uses.

Most of you are studying chemistry, however, not merely to satisfy your curiosity or to become more informed consumers or citizens, but because it is an essential part of your curriculum. Your major might be biology, engineering, pharmacy, agriculture, geology, or some other field. Why do so many diverse subjects share an essential tie to chemistry? The answer is that chemistry, by its very nature, is the *central science*, central to a fundamental understanding of other sciences and technologies. For example, our interactions with the material world raise basic questions about the materials around us. What are their compositions and properties? How do they interact with us and our environment? How, why, and when do they undergo change? These questions are important whether the material is part of high-tech computer chips, a pigment used by a Renaissance painter, or the DNA that transmits genetic information in our bodies (Figure 1.2 ▼).

By studying chemistry, you will learn to use the powerful language and ideas that have evolved to describe and enhance our understanding of matter. The language of chemistry is a universal scientific language that is widely used

▼ Figure 1.2 **Chemistry helps us better understand materials.** (a) A microscopic view of an EPROM (Erasable Programmable Read-Only Memory) silicon microchip. (b) A Renaissance painting, *Young Girl Reading*, by Vittore Carpaccio (1472–1526). (c) A long strand of DNA that has spilled out of the damaged cell wall of a bacterium.

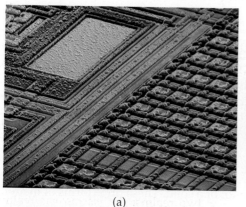
(a)

(b)

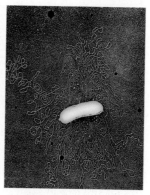
(c)

Chemistry Put to Work   CHEMISTRY AND THE CHEMICAL INDUSTRY

Many people are familiar with common household chemicals such as those shown in Figure 1.3▶, but few realize the size and importance of the chemical industry. Worldwide sales of chemicals and related products manufactured in the United States total approximately $550 billion annually. The chemical industry employs more than 10% of all scientists and engineers and is a major contributor to the US economy.

Vast amounts of chemicals are produced each year and serve as raw materials for a variety of uses, including the manufacture of metals, plastics, fertilizers, pharmaceuticals, fuels, paints, adhesives, pesticides, synthetic fibers, microprocessor chips, and numerous other products. Table 1.1▼ lists the top eight chemicals produced in the United States. We will discuss many of these substances and their uses as the course progresses.

People who have degrees in chemistry hold a variety of positions in industry, government, and academia. Those who work in the chemical industry find positions as laboratory chemists, carrying out experiments to develop new products (research and development), analyzing materials (quality control), or assisting customers in using products (sales and service). Those with more experience or training may work as managers or company directors. A chemistry degree also can prepare you for alternate careers in teaching, medicine, biomedical research, information science, environmental work, technical sales, work with government regulatory agencies, and patent law.

▲ Figure 1.3 **Household chemicals.** Many common supermarket products have very simple chemical compositions.

TABLE 1.1 ■ The Top Eight Chemicals Produced by the Chemical Industry in 2006[a]				
Rank	Chemical	Formula	2006 Production (billions of pounds)	Principal End Uses
1	Sulfuric acid	H_2SO_4	79	Fertilizers, chemical manufacturing
2	Ethylene	C_2H_4	55	Plastics, antifreeze
3	Lime	CaO	45	Paper, cement, steel
4	Propylene	C_3H_6	35	Plastics
5	Phosphoric acid	H_3PO_4	24	Fertilizers
6	Ammonia	NH_3	23	Fertilizers
7	Chlorine	Cl_2	23	Bleaches, plastics, water purification
8	Sodium hydroxide	$NaOH$	18	Aluminum production, soap

[a]Most data from *Chemical and Engineering News*, July 2, 2007, pp. 57, 60.

in other disciplines. Furthermore, an understanding of the behavior of atoms and molecules provides powerful insights into other areas of modern science, technology, and engineering.

1.2 CLASSIFICATIONS OF MATTER

Let's begin our study of chemistry by examining some fundamental ways in which matter is classified and described. Two principal ways of classifying matter are according to its physical state (as a gas, liquid, or solid) and according to its composition (as an element, compound, or mixture).

States of Matter

A sample of matter can be a gas, a liquid, or a solid. These three forms of matter are called the **states of matter**. The states of matter differ in some of their simple observable properties. A **gas** (also known as *vapor*) has no fixed volume or shape; rather, it conforms to the volume and shape of its container. A gas can be compressed to occupy a smaller volume, or it can expand to occupy a larger one. A **liquid** has a distinct volume independent of its container but has no specific shape. A liquid assumes the shape of the portion of the container that it occupies. A **solid** has both a definite shape and a definite volume. Neither liquids nor solids can be compressed to any appreciable extent.

The properties of the states of matter can be understood on the molecular level (Figure 1.4 ▶). In a gas the molecules are far apart and are moving at high speeds, colliding repeatedly with each other and with the walls of the container. Compressing a gas decreases the amount of space between molecules, increases the frequency of collisions between molecules, but does not alter the size or shape of the molecules. In a liquid the molecules are packed closely together but still move rapidly. The rapid movement allows the molecules to slide over each other; thus, a liquid pours easily. In a solid the molecules are held tightly together, usually in definite arrangements in which the molecules can wiggle only slightly in their otherwise fixed positions.

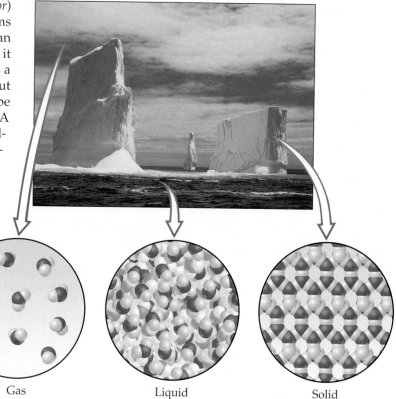

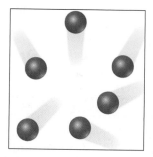  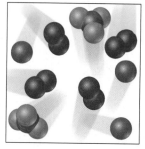

Gas   Liquid   Solid

▲ Figure 1.4 **The three physical states of water—water vapor, liquid water, and ice.** In this photo we see both the liquid and solid states of water. We cannot see water vapor. What we see when we look at steam or clouds is tiny droplets of liquid water dispersed in the atmosphere. The molecular views show that the molecules in the gas are much further apart than those in the liquid or solid. The molecules in the liquid do not have the orderly arrangement seen in the solid.

Pure Substances

Most forms of matter that we encounter—for example, the air we breathe (a gas), gasoline for cars (a liquid), and the sidewalk on which we walk (a solid)—are not chemically pure. We can, however, resolve, or separate, these forms of matter into different pure substances. A **pure substance** (usually referred to simply as a *substance*) is matter that has distinct properties and a composition that does not vary from sample to sample. Water and ordinary table salt (sodium chloride), the primary components of seawater, are examples of pure substances.

All substances are either elements or compounds. **Elements** cannot be decomposed into simpler substances. On the molecular level, each element is composed of only one kind of atom [Figure 1.5(a and b) ▼]. **Compounds** are

(a) Atoms of an element   (b) Molecules of an element   (c) Molecules of a compound   (d) Mixture of elements and a compound

▲ Figure 1.5 **Molecular comparison of element, compounds, and mixtures.** Each element contains a unique kind of atom. Elements might consist of individual atoms, as in (a), or molecules, as in (b). Compounds contain two or more different atoms chemically joined together, as in (c). A mixture contains the individual units of its components, shown in (d) as both atoms and molecules.

◀ **Figure 1.6 Relative abundances of elements.** Elements in percent by mass in (a) Earth's crust (including oceans and atmosphere) and (b) the human body.

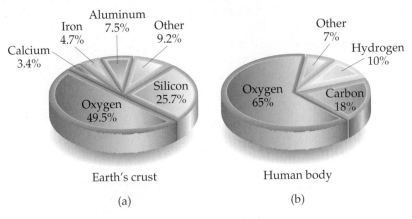

Earth's crust

(a)

Human body

(b)

substances composed of two or more elements; they contain two or more kinds of atoms [Figure 1.5(c)]. Water, for example, is a compound composed of two elements: hydrogen and oxygen. Figure 1.5(d) shows a mixture of substances. **Mixtures** are combinations of two or more substances in which each substance retains its own chemical identity.

Elements

Currently, 117 elements are known. These elements vary widely in their abundance, as shown in Figure 1.6▲. For example, only five elements—oxygen, silicon, aluminum, iron, and calcium—account for over 90% of Earth's crust (including oceans and atmosphere). Similarly, just three elements—oxygen, carbon, and hydrogen—account for over 90% of the mass of the human body.

Some of the more common elements are listed in Table 1.2▼, along with the chemical abbreviations, or chemical *symbols*, used to denote them. The symbol for each element consists of one or two letters, with the first letter capitalized. These symbols are mostly derived from the English name for the element, but sometimes they are derived from a foreign name instead (last column in Table 1.2). You will need to know these symbols and learn others as we encounter them in the text.

All the known elements and their symbols are listed on the front inside cover of this text. The table in which the symbol for each element is enclosed in a box is called the *periodic table*. In the periodic table the elements are arranged in vertical columns so that closely related elements are grouped together. We describe the periodic table in more detail in Section 2.5.

▲ GIVE IT SOME THOUGHT

Which element is most abundant in both Earth's crust and in the human body? What is the symbol for this element?

Compounds

Most elements can interact with other elements to form compounds. For example, consider the fact that when hydrogen gas burns in oxygen gas, the

TABLE 1.2 ■ Some Common Elements and Their Symbols

Carbon	C	Aluminum	Al	Copper	Cu (from *cuprum*)
Fluorine	F	Bromine	Br	Iron	Fe (from *ferrum*)
Hydrogen	H	Calcium	Ca	Lead	Pb (from *plumbum*)
Iodine	I	Chlorine	Cl	Mercury	Hg (from *hydrargyrum*)
Nitrogen	N	Helium	He	Potassium	K (from *kalium*)
Oxygen	O	Lithium	Li	Silver	Ag (from *argentum*)
Phosphorus	P	Magnesium	Mg	Sodium	Na (from *natrium*)
Sulfur	S	Silicon	Si	Tin	Sn (from *stannum*)

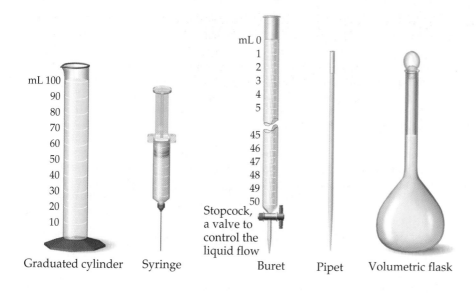

Graduated cylinder   Syringe   Buret   Pipet   Volumetric flask

Stopcock, a valve to control the liquid flow

▲ **GIVE IT SOME THOUGHT**

Which of the following quantities represents a volume measurement: 15 m²; 2.5×10^2 m³; 5.77 L/s? How do you know?

Density

Density is a property of matter that is widely used to characterize a substance. Density is defined as the amount of mass in a unit volume of the substance:

$$\text{Density} = \frac{\text{mass}}{\text{volume}} \qquad [1.3]$$

The densities of solids and liquids are commonly expressed in units of grams per cubic centimeter (g/cm^3) or grams per milliliter (g/mL). The densities of some common substances are listed in Table 1.6▼. It is no coincidence that the density of water is 1.00 g/mL; the gram was originally defined as the mass of 1 mL of water at a specific temperature. Because most substances change volume when they are heated or cooled, densities are temperature dependent. When reporting densities, the temperature should be specified. If no temperature is reported, we usually assume that the temperature is 25 °C, close to normal room temperature.

The terms *density* and *weight* are sometimes confused. A person who says that iron weighs more than air generally means that iron has a higher density than air—1 kg of air has the same mass as 1 kg of iron, but the iron occupies a smaller volume, thereby giving it a higher density. If we combine two liquids that do not mix, the less dense liquid will float on the denser liquid.

TABLE 1.6 ■ Densities of Some Selected Substances at 25 °C	
Substance	**Density (g/cm³)**
Air	0.001
Balsa wood	0.16
Ethanol	0.79
Water	1.00
Ethylene glycol	1.09
Table sugar	1.59
Table salt	2.16
Iron	7.9
Gold	19.32

Chemistry is a very lively, active field of science. Because chemistry is so central to our lives, reports on matters of chemical significance appear in the news nearly every day. Some reports tell of recent breakthroughs in the development of new pharmaceuticals, materials, and processes. Others deal with environmental and public safety issues. As you study chemistry, we hope you will develop the skills to better understand the importance of chemistry in your life. By way of examples, here are summaries of a few recent stories in which chemistry plays a role.

Biofuels Reality Check

With the Energy Policy Act of 2005, the United States Congress has given a big push to fuels derived from biomass as a renewable, homegrown alternative to gasoline. The law requires that 4 billion gallons of the so-called renewable fuel be mixed with gasoline in 2007, increasing to 7.5 billion gallons by 2012. The United States currently consumes about 140 billion gallons of gasoline per year.

Although the Act does not dictate which renewable fuels to use, ethanol derived from corn currently dominates the alternatives with 40% of all gasoline now containing some ethanol. A blend of 10% ethanol and 90% gasoline, called E10, is the most common blend because it can be used in virtually all vehicles. Blends of 85% ethanol and 15% gasoline, called E85, are also available but can be used only with specially modified engines in what are called flexible-fuel vehicles (FFVs) (Figure 1.21 ▼).

▲ **Figure 1.21   A gasoline pump that dispenses E85 ethanol.**

When it comes to ethanol's pros and cons, there is no shortage of disagreement. In 2006, researchers at the University of Minnesota calculated that "Even dedicating all U.S. corn and soybean production to biofuels would meet only 12% of gasoline and 6% of diesel demand." The conversion of a much wider range of plant material, making use of a much greater fraction of the available plant matter, into fuels will be necessary to improve these numbers substantially. Because most cellulose of which plants are formed does not readily convert to ethanol, a great deal of research will be needed to solve this challenging problem. Meanwhile, it is worth reflecting that a 3% improvement in vehicle efficiency of fuel use would displace more gasoline use than the entire 2006 US ethanol production.

New Element Created

A new entry has been made to the list of elements. The production of the newest and heaviest element—element 118—was announced in October 2006. The synthesis of element 118 resulted from studies performed from 2002 to 2006 at the Joint Institute for Nuclear Research (JINR) in Dubna, Russia. JINR scientists and their collaborators from Lawrence Livermore National Laboratory in California announced that they had produced three atoms of the new element, one atom in 2002 and two more in 2005.

The new element was formed by striking a target of californium atoms (element 98) with a highly energetic beam consisting of the nuclei of calcium atoms (element 20) in a device called a particle accelerator. Occasionally, the nuclei from the atoms of the two different elements fused to form the new, superheavy element 118. The 2002 experiment took four months and used a beam of 2.5×10^{19} calcium atoms to produce the single atom of element 118.

The three atoms of element 118 created during these experiments came and went in a literal flash. On the average, the atoms survived for just 0.9 milliseconds before decomposing.

These experimental results were met with praise but also caution from other scientists in the field, particularly given the difficult history of element 118. Another California lab, the Lawrence Berkeley National Laboratory, announced that it discovered element 118 in 1999 but retracted the claim two years later after an investigation found that one of the researchers had fabricated data.

This discovery brings the total number of elements created by the Livermore-Dubna collaboration to five: elements 113, 114, 115, 116, and 118. As of this writing, element 118 has not yet been named.

Important Antibiotic Modified to Combat Bacterial Resistance

Vancomycin is an antibiotic of last resort—used only when other antibacterial agents are ineffective. Some bacteria have developed a resistance to vancomycin, causing researchers to modify the molecular structure of the substance to make it

WHAT'S AHEAD

LOOK AROUND YOU. Notice the great variety of colors, textures, and other properties in the materials that surround you— the colors in a garden scene, the texture of the fabric in your clothes, the solubility of sugar in a cup of coffee, the transparency of a window. The materials in our world exhibit a striking and seemingly infinite variety.

We can classify properties in different ways, but how do we understand and explain them? What makes diamonds transparent and hard, while table salt is brittle and dissolves in water? Why does paper burn, and why does water quench fires? The structure and behavior of atoms are key to understanding both the physical and chemical properties of matter.

Remarkably, the diversity of these properties we see around us results from only about 100 different elements and therefore about 100 chemically different kinds of atoms. In a sense, the atoms are like the 26 letters of the English alphabet that join in different combinations to form the immense number of words in our language. But how do atoms combine with one another? What rules govern the ways in which atoms can combine? How do the properties of a substance relate to the kinds of atoms it contains? Indeed, what is an atom like, and what makes the atoms of one element different from those of another?

The chapter-opening photograph is an image of a circle of 48 iron atoms arranged on a copper metal surface. The diameter of the circle is about 1/20,000 the diameter of a human hair. Atoms are indeed very tiny entities.

This very striking image reveals the power of modern experimental methods to identify individual atoms, but it does not reveal the structures of the atoms themselves. Fortunately, we can use a variety of experimental techniques to probe the atom to gain a clearer understanding of what it is like. In this chapter we begin to explore the fascinating world of atoms that we discover by such experiments. We will examine the basic structure of the atom and briefly discuss the formation of molecules and ions, thereby providing a foundation for exploring chemistry more deeply in later chapters.

2.1 THE ATOMIC THEORY OF MATTER

Philosophers from the earliest times have speculated about the nature of the fundamental "stuff" from which the world is made. Democritus (460–370 BC) and other early Greek philosophers thought that the material world must be made up of tiny indivisible particles that they called *atomos*, meaning "indivisible or uncuttable." Later, Plato and Aristotle formulated the notion that there can be no ultimately indivisible particles. The "atomic" view of matter faded for many centuries during which Aristotelean philosophy dominated Western culture.

The notion of atoms reemerged in Europe during the seventeenth century, when scientists tried to explain the properties of gases. Air is composed of something invisible and in constant motion; we can feel the motion of the wind against us, for example. It is natural to think of tiny invisible particles as giving rise to these familiar effects. Isaac Newton (1642–1727), the most famous scientist of his time, favored the idea of atoms. But thinking of atoms as invisible particles in air is very different from thinking of atoms as the fundamental building blocks of elements.

As chemists learned to measure the amounts of elements that reacted with one another to form new substances, the ground was laid for an atomic theory that linked the idea of elements with the idea of atoms. That theory came from the work of an English schoolteacher, John Dalton (Figure 2.1 ◄), during the period from 1803–1807. Dalton's atomic theory involved the following postulates:

1. Each element is composed of extremely small particles called atoms.

2. All atoms of a given element are identical to one another in mass and other properties, but the atoms of one element are different from the atoms of all other elements.

3. The atoms of one element cannot be changed into atoms of a different element by chemical reactions; atoms are neither created nor destroyed in chemical reactions.

4. Compounds are formed when atoms of more than one element combine; a given compound always has the same relative number and kind of atoms.

According to Dalton's atomic theory, **atoms** are the smallest particles of an element that retain the chemical identity of the element. ∞ (Section 1.1) As noted in the postulates of Dalton's theory, an element is composed of only one kind of atom. A compound, in contrast, contains atoms of two or more elements.

Dalton's theory explains several simple laws of chemical combination that were known during his time. One of these laws was the *law of constant composition*: In a given compound, the relative numbers and kinds of atoms are constant. ∞ (Section 1.2) This law is the basis of Dalton's Postulate 4. Another fundamental chemical law was the *law of conservation of mass* (also known as the *law of conservation of matter*): The total mass of materials present after a chemical reaction is the same as the total mass present before the reaction. This law is the basis for Postulate 3. Dalton proposed that atoms always retain their identities and that atoms taking part in a chemical reaction rearrange to give new chemical combinations.

▲ **Figure 2.1 John Dalton (1766–1844).** Dalton was the son of a poor English weaver. He began teaching at the age of 12. He spent most of his years in Manchester, where he taught both grammar school and college. His lifelong interest in meteorology led him to study gases, then chemistry, and eventually atomic theory.

A good theory should explain the known facts and predict new ones. Dalton used his theory to deduce the *law of multiple proportions*: If two elements A and B combine to form more than one compound, the masses of B that can combine with a given mass of A are in the ratio of small whole numbers. We can illustrate this law by considering the substances water and hydrogen peroxide, both of which consist of the elements hydrogen and oxygen. In forming water, 8.0 g of oxygen combine with 1.0 g of hydrogen. In forming hydrogen peroxide, 16.0 g of oxygen combine with 1.0 g of hydrogen. In other words, the ratio of the mass of oxygen per gram of hydrogen in the two compounds is 2 : 1. Using the atomic theory, we can conclude that hydrogen peroxide contains twice as many atoms of oxygen per hydrogen atom as does water.

GIVE IT SOME THOUGHT

One compound of carbon and oxygen contains 1.333 g of oxygen per gram of carbon, whereas a second compound contains 2.666 g of oxygen per gram of carbon. **(a)** What chemical law do these data illustrate? **(b)** If the first compound has an equal number of oxygen and carbon atoms, what can we conclude about the composition of the second compound?

2.2 THE DISCOVERY OF ATOMIC STRUCTURE

Dalton reached his conclusion about atoms based on chemical observations in the macroscopic world of the laboratory. Neither he nor those who followed him during the century after his work was published had direct evidence for the existence of atoms. Today, however, we can use powerful instruments to measure the properties of individual atoms and even provide images of them (Figure 2.2►).

As scientists began to develop methods for more detailed probing of the nature of matter, the atom, which was supposed to be indivisible, began to show signs of a more complex structure: We now know that the atom is composed of still smaller **subatomic particles**. Before we summarize the current model of atomic structure, we will briefly consider a few of the landmark discoveries that led to that model. We will see that the atom is composed in part of electrically charged particles, some with a positive (+) charge and some with a negative (−) charge. As we discuss the development of our current model of the atom, keep in mind a simple statement of the behavior of charged particles: *Particles with the same charge repel one another, whereas particles with unlike charges attract one another.*

Cathode Rays and Electrons

During the mid-1800s, scientists began to study electrical discharge through partially evacuated tubes (tubes that had been pumped almost empty of air), such as those shown in Figure 2.3▼. When a high voltage was applied to the

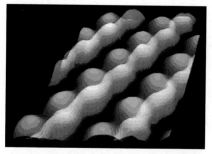

▲ Figure 2.2 **An image of the surface of the semiconductor GaAs (gallium arsenide).** This image was obtained by a technique called scanning tunneling microscopy. The color was added to the image by computer to distinguish the gallium atoms (blue spheres) from the arsenic atoms (red spheres).

▼ Figure 2.3 **Cathode-ray tube.** (a) In a cathode-ray tube, electrons move from the negative electrode (cathode) to the positive electrode (anode). (b) A photo of a cathode-ray tube containing a fluorescent screen to show the path of the cathode rays. (c) The path of the cathode rays is deflected by the presence of a magnet.

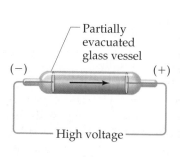

Partially evacuated glass vessel

(−)   (+)

High voltage

(a)

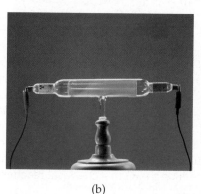

(b)

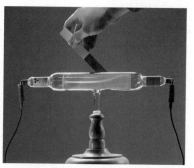

(c)

▶ Figure 2.4 **Cathode-ray tube with perpendicular magnetic and electric fields.** The cathode rays (electrons) originate from the negative plate on the left and are accelerated toward the positive plate on the right, which has a hole in its center. A narrow beam of electrons passes through the hole and is then deflected by the magnetic and electric fields. The three paths result from different strengths of the magnetic and electric fields. The charge-to-mass ratio of the electron can be determined by measuring the effects that the magnetic and electric fields have on the direction of the beam.

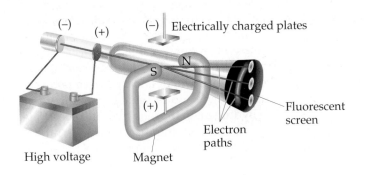

electrodes in the tube, radiation was produced. This radiation, called **cathode rays**, originated from the negative electrode, or cathode. Although the rays themselves could not be seen, their movement was detected because the rays cause certain materials, including glass, to *fluoresce*, or to give off light.

Scientists held conflicting views about the nature of the cathode rays. It was not initially clear whether the rays were an invisible stream of particles or a new form of radiation. Experiments showed that cathode rays are deflected by electric or magnetic fields in a way consistent with their being a stream of negative electrical charge [Figure 2.3(c)]. The British scientist J. J. Thomson observed many properties of the cathode rays, including the fact that they are the same regardless of the identity of the cathode material. In a paper published in 1897, Thomson summarized his observations and concluded that cathode rays are streams of negatively charged particles. Thomson's paper is generally accepted as the "discovery" of what later became known as the *electron*.

Thomson constructed a cathode-ray tube having a fluorescent screen at one end, such as that shown in Figure 2.4 ▲, so that he could quantitatively measure the effects of electric and magnetic fields on the thin stream of electrons passing through a hole in the positively charged electrode. These measurements made it possible to calculate a value of 1.76×10^8 coulombs per gram for the ratio of the electron's electrical charge to its mass.*

Once the charge-to-mass ratio of the electron was known, measuring either the charge or the mass of an electron would yield the value of the other quantity. In 1909, Robert Millikan (1868–1953) of the University of Chicago succeeded in measuring the charge of an electron by performing a series of experiments described in Figure 2.5 ▼. He then calculated the mass of the electron by using

▶ Figure 2.5 **Millikan's oil-drop experiment.** A representation of the apparatus Millikan used to measure the charge of the electron. Small drops of oil, which had picked up extra electrons, were allowed to fall between two electrically charged plates. Millikan monitored the drops, measuring how the voltage on the plates affected their rate of fall. From these data he calculated the charges on the drops. His experiment showed that the charges were always integral multiples of 1.602×10^{-19} C, which he deduced was the charge of a single electron.

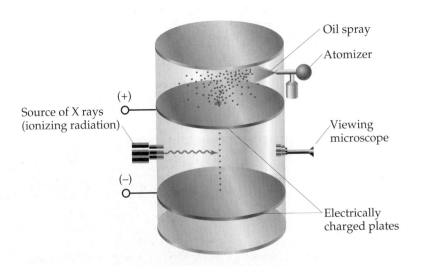

*The coulomb (C) is the SI unit for electrical charge.

his experimental value for the charge, 1.602×10^{-19} C, and Thomson's charge-to-mass ratio, 1.76×10^8 C/g:

$$\text{Electron mass} = \frac{1.602 \times 10^{-19} \text{ C}}{1.76 \times 10^8 \text{ C/g}} = 9.10 \times 10^{-28} \text{ g}$$

This result agrees well with the presently accepted value for the mass of the electron, 9.10938×10^{-28} g. This mass is about 2000 times smaller than that of hydrogen, the lightest atom.

Radioactivity

In 1896 the French scientist Henri Becquerel (1852–1908) was studying a uranium compound when he discovered that it spontaneously emits high-energy radiation. This spontaneous emission of radiation is called **radioactivity**. At Becquerel's suggestion Marie Curie (Figure 2.6▶) and her husband, Pierre, began experiments to isolate the radioactive components of the compound.

Further study of the nature of radioactivity, principally by the British scientist Ernest Rutherford (Figure 2.7▶), revealed three types of radiation: alpha (α), beta (β), and gamma (γ) radiation. Each type differs in its response to an electric field, as shown in Figure 2.8▼. The paths of both α and β radiation are bent by the electric field, although in opposite directions; γ radiation is unaffected.

Rutherford showed that both α and β rays consist of fast-moving particles, which were called α and β particles. In fact, β particles are high-speed electrons and can be considered the radioactive equivalent of cathode rays. They are attracted to a positively charged plate. The α particles have a positive charge and are attracted toward a negative plate. In units of the charge of the electron, β particles have a charge of $1-$ and α particles a charge of $2+$. Each α particle has a mass about 7400 times that of an electron. Gamma radiation is high-energy radiation similar to X-rays; it does not consist of particles and carries no charge. We will discuss radioactivity in greater detail in Chapter 21.

The Nuclear Atom

With the growing evidence that the atom is composed of smaller particles, attention was given to how the particles fit together. During the early 1900s Thomson reasoned that because electrons contribute only a very small fraction of the mass of an atom, they probably were responsible for an equally small fraction of the atom's size. He proposed that the atom consisted of a uniform positive sphere of matter in which the electrons were embedded, as shown in

▲ **Figure 2.6 Marie Sklodowska Curie (1867–1934).** When M. Curie presented her doctoral thesis, it was described as the greatest single contribution of any doctoral thesis in the history of science. Among other things, Curie discovered two new elements, polonium and radium. In 1903 Henri Becquerel, M. Curie, and her husband, Pierre, were jointly awarded the Nobel Prize in physics. In 1911 M. Curie won a second Nobel Prize, this time in chemistry.

▲ **Figure 2.7 Ernest Rutherford (1871–1937).** Rutherford, whom Einstein called "the second Newton," was born and educated in New Zealand. In 1895 he was the first overseas student ever to be awarded a position at the Cavendish Laboratory at Cambridge University in England, where he worked with J. J. Thomson. In 1898 he joined the faculty of McGill University in Montreal. While at McGill, Rutherford did his research on radioactivity that led to his being awarded the 1908 Nobel Prize in chemistry. In 1907 Rutherford moved back to England to be a faculty member at Manchester University, where in 1910 he performed his famous α-particle scattering experiments that led to the nuclear model of the atom. In 1992 his native New Zealand honored Rutherford by putting his likeness, along with his Nobel Prize medal, on their $100 currency note.

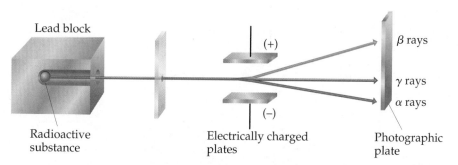

▲ **Figure 2.8 Behavior of alpha (α), beta (β), and gamma (γ) rays in an electric field.** The α rays consist of positively charged particles and are therefore attracted to the negatively charged plate. The β rays consist of negatively charged particles and are attracted to the positively charged plate. The γ rays, which carry no charge, are unaffected by the electric field.

Lead block

Radioactive substance

Electrically charged plates

(+)

(−)

β rays

γ rays

α rays

Photographic plate

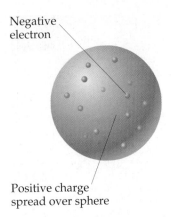

Negative
electron

Positive charge
spread over sphere

▲ **Figure 2.9** **J. J. Thomson's "plum-pudding" model of the atom.** Thomson pictured the small electrons to be embedded in the atom much like raisins in a pudding or seeds in a watermelon. Ernest Rutherford proved this model wrong.

Figure 2.9 ◄. This so-called "plum-pudding" model, named after a traditional English dessert, was very short lived.

In 1910, Rutherford and his coworkers performed an experiment that disproved Thomson's model. Rutherford was studying the angles at which α particles were deflected, or *scattered*, as they passed through a thin gold foil only a few thousand atoms thick (Figure 2.10 ▼). Rutherford and his coworkers discovered that almost all the α particles passed directly through the foil without deflection. A few particles were found to be deflected by approximately 1 degree, consistent with Thomson's plum-pudding model. Just for the sake of completeness, Rutherford suggested that Ernest Marsden, an undergraduate student working in the laboratory, look for evidence of scattering at large angles. To everyone's surprise, a small amount of scattering was observed at large angles. Some particles were even scattered back in the direction from which they had come. The explanation for these results was not immediately obvious, but they were clearly inconsistent with Thomson's plum-pudding model.

By 1911, Rutherford was able to explain these observations. He postulated that most of the mass of each gold atom in his foil and all of its positive charge reside in a very small, extremely dense region, which he called the **nucleus**. He postulated further that most of the total volume of an atom is empty space in which electrons move around the nucleus. In the α-scattering experiment, most α particles passed directly through the foil because they did not encounter the minute nucleus of any gold atom; they merely passed through the empty space making up the greatest part of all the atoms in the foil. Occasionally, however, an α particle came close to a gold nucleus. The repulsion between the highly charged gold nucleus and the α particle was strong enough to deflect the less massive α particle, as shown in Figure 2.11 ▶.

Subsequent experimental studies led to the discovery of both positive particles (*protons*) and neutral particles (*neutrons*) in the nucleus. Protons were discovered in 1919 by Rutherford. In 1932 British scientist James Chadwick (1891–1972) discovered neutrons. We examine these particles more closely in Section 2.3.

▶ **Figure 2.10** **Rutherford's experiment on the scattering of α particles.** The red lines represent the paths of the α particles. When the incoming beam strikes the gold foil, most particles pass straight through the foil, but some are scattered.

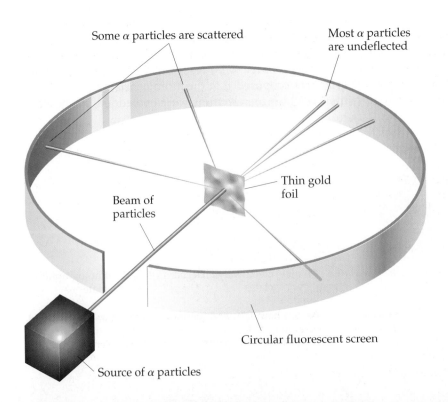

Some α particles are scattered

Most α particles are undeflected

Thin gold foil

Beam of particles

Circular fluorescent screen

Source of α particles

Today we can determine the masses of individual atoms with a high degree of accuracy. For example, we know that the ^{1}H atom has a mass of 1.6735×10^{-24} g and the ^{16}O atom has a mass of 2.6560×10^{-23} g. As we noted in Section 2.3, it is convenient to use the *atomic mass unit* (amu) when dealing with these extremely small masses:

$$1 \text{ amu} = 1.66054 \times 10^{-24} \text{ g and } 1 \text{ g} = 6.02214 \times 10^{23} \text{ amu}$$

The atomic mass unit is presently defined by assigning a mass of exactly 12 amu to an atom of the ^{12}C isotope of carbon. In these units, an ^{1}H atom has a mass of 1.0078 amu and an ^{16}O atom has a mass of 15.9949 amu.

Average Atomic Masses

Most elements occur in nature as mixtures of isotopes. We can determine the *average atomic mass* of an element by using the masses of its various isotopes and their relative abundances. Naturally occurring carbon, for example, is composed of 98.93% ^{12}C and 1.07% ^{13}C. The masses of these isotopes are 12 amu (exactly) and 13.00335 amu, respectively. We calculate the average atomic mass of carbon from the fractional abundance of each isotope and the mass of that isotope:

$$(0.9893)(12 \text{ amu}) + (0.0107)(13.00335 \text{ amu}) = 12.01 \text{ amu}$$

The average atomic mass of each element (expressed in atomic mass units) is also known as its **atomic weight**. Although the term *average atomic mass* is more proper, the term *atomic weight* is more common. The atomic weights of the elements are listed in both the periodic table and the table of elements inside the front cover of this text.

GIVE IT SOME THOUGHT

A particular atom of chromium has a mass of 52.94 amu, whereas the atomic weight of chromium is 51.99 amu. Explain the difference in the two masses.

■ SAMPLE EXERCISE 2.4 | Calculating the Atomic Weight of an Element from Isotopic Abundances

Naturally occurring chlorine is 75.78% ^{35}Cl, which has an atomic mass of 34.969 amu, and 24.22% ^{37}Cl, which has an atomic mass of 36.966 amu. Calculate the average atomic mass (that is, the atomic weight) of chlorine.

SOLUTION

We can calculate the average atomic mass by multiplying the abundance of each isotope by its atomic mass and summing these products. Because 75.78% = 0.7578 and 24.22% = 0.2422, we have

$$\text{Average atomic mass} = (0.7578)(34.969 \text{ amu}) + (0.2422)(36.966 \text{ amu})$$
$$= 26.50 \text{ amu} + 8.953 \text{ amu}$$
$$= 35.45 \text{ amu}$$

This answer makes sense: The average atomic mass of Cl is between the masses of the two isotopes and is closer to the value of ^{35}Cl, which is the more abundant isotope.

■ PRACTICE EXERCISE

Three isotopes of silicon occur in nature: ^{28}Si (92.23%), which has an atomic mass of 27.97693 amu; ^{29}Si (4.68%), which has an atomic mass of 28.97649 amu; and ^{30}Si (3.09%), which has an atomic mass of 29.97377 amu. Calculate the atomic weight of silicon.
Answer: 28.09 amu

The most direct and accurate means for determining atomic and molecular weights is provided by the **mass spectrometer** (Figure 2.13 ▼). A gaseous sample is introduced at *A* and bombarded by a stream of high-energy electrons at *B*. Collisions between the electrons and the atoms or molecules of the gas produce positively charged particles, mostly with a 1+ charge. These charged particles are accelerated toward a negatively charged wire grid (*C*). After the particles pass through the grid, they encounter two slits that allow only a narrow beam of particles to pass. This beam then passes between the poles of a magnet, which deflects the particles into a curved path, much as electrons are deflected by a magnetic field (Figure 2.4). For charged particles with the same charge, the extent of deflection depends on mass—the more massive the particle, the less the deflection. The particles are thereby separated according to their masses. By changing the strength of the magnetic field or the accelerating voltage on the negatively charged grid, charged particles of various masses can be selected to enter the detector at the end of the instrument.

A graph of the intensity of the detector signal versus particle atomic mass is called a *mass spectrum*. The mass spectrum of chlorine atoms, shown in Figure 2.14 ▼, reveals the presence of two isotopes. Analysis of a mass spectrum gives both the masses of the charged particles reaching the detector and their relative abundances. The abundances are obtained from the signal intensities. Knowing the atomic mass and the abundance of each isotope allows us to calculate the atomic weight of an element, as shown in Sample Exercise 2.4.

Mass spectrometers are used extensively today to identify chemical compounds and analyze mixtures of substances. Any molecule that loses electrons can fall apart, forming an array of positively charged fragments. The mass spectrometer measures the masses of these fragments, producing a chemical "fingerprint" of the molecule and providing clues about how the atoms were connected in the original molecule. Thus, a chemist might use this technique to determine the molecular structure of a newly synthesized compound or to identify a pollutant in the environment.

Related Exercises: 2.33, 2.34, 2.35(b), 2.36, 2.93, and 2.94

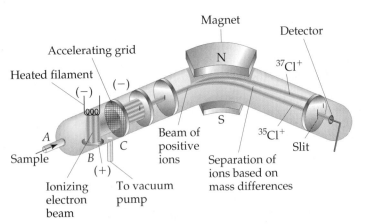

▲ **Figure 2.13 A mass spectrometer.** Cl atoms are introduced on the left side of the spectrometer and are ionized to form Cl$^+$ ions, which are then directed through a magnetic field. The paths of the ions of the two isotopes of Cl diverge as they pass through the magnetic field. As drawn, the spectrometer is tuned to detect ^{35}Cl$^+$ ions. The heavier ^{37}Cl$^+$ ions are not deflected enough for them to reach the detector.

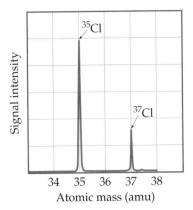

▲ **Figure 2.14 Mass spectrum of atomic chlorine.** The fractional abundances of the ^{35}Cl and ^{37}Cl isotopes of chlorine are indicated by the relative signal intensities of the beams reaching the detector of the mass spectrometer.

2.5 THE PERIODIC TABLE

Dalton's atomic theory set the stage for a vigorous growth in chemical experimentation during the early 1800s. As the body of chemical observations grew and the list of known elements expanded, attempts were made to find regular patterns in chemical behavior. These efforts culminated in the development of the periodic table in 1869. We will have much to say about the periodic table in later chapters, but it is so important and useful that you should become acquainted with it now. You will quickly learn that *the periodic table is the most significant tool that chemists use for organizing and remembering chemical facts.*

Many elements show very strong similarities to one another. The elements lithium (Li), sodium (Na), and potassium (K) are all soft, very reactive metals,

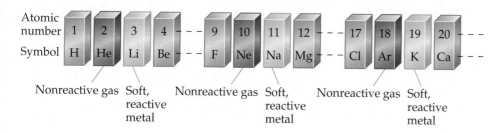

Atomic number | 1 | 2 | 3 | 4 — — | 9 | 10 | 11 | 12 — — | 17 | 18 | 19 | 20 — — —
Symbol | H | He | Li | Be — — | F | Ne | Na | Mg — — | Cl | Ar | K | Ca — — —

Nonreactive gas   Soft, reactive metal   Nonreactive gas   Soft, reactive metal   Nonreactive gas   Soft, reactive metal

◄ **Figure 2.15 Arranging the elements by atomic number reveals a periodic pattern of properties.** This periodic pattern is the basis of the periodic table.

for example. The elements helium (He), neon (Ne), and argon (Ar) are all very nonreactive gases. If the elements are arranged in order of increasing atomic number, their chemical and physical properties show a repeating, or periodic, pattern. For example, each of the soft, reactive metals—lithium, sodium, and potassium—comes immediately after one of the nonreactive gases—helium, neon, and argon—as shown in Figure 2.15▲.

The arrangement of elements in order of increasing atomic number, with elements having similar properties placed in vertical columns, is known as the **periodic table**. The periodic table is shown in Figure 2.16▼ and is also given on the front inside cover of the text. For each element in the table, the atomic number and atomic symbol are given. The atomic weight is often given as well, as in the following typical entry for potassium:

19 ← — atomic number
K ← — atomic symbol
39.0983 ← — atomic weight

You may notice slight variations in periodic tables from one book to another or between those in the lecture hall and in the text. These are simply matters of style, or they might concern the particular information included. There are no fundamental differences.

	1A 1																8A 18
1	1 H	2A 2										3A 13	4A 14	5A 15	6A 16	7A 17	2 He
2	3 Li	4 Be										5 B	6 C	7 N	8 O	9 F	10 Ne
3	11 Na	12 Mg	3B 3	4B 4	5B 5	6B 6	7B 7	8B 8	9	10	1B 11	2B 12	13 Al	14 Si	15 P	16 S	17 Cl	18 Ar
4	19 K	20 Ca	21 Sc	22 Ti	23 V	24 Cr	25 Mn	26 Fe	27 Co	28 Ni	29 Cu	30 Zn	31 Ga	32 Ge	33 As	34 Se	35 Br	36 Kr
5	37 Rb	38 Sr	39 Y	40 Zr	41 Nb	42 Mo	43 Tc	44 Ru	45 Rh	46 Pd	47 Ag	48 Cd	49 In	50 Sn	51 Sb	52 Te	53 I	54 Xe
6	55 Cs	56 Ba	71 Lu	72 Hf	73 Ta	74 W	75 Re	76 Os	77 Ir	78 Pt	79 Au	80 Hg	81 Tl	82 Pb	83 Bi	84 Po	85 At	86 Rn
7	87 Fr	88 Ra	103 Lr	104 Rf	105 Db	106 Sg	107 Bh	108 Hs	109 Mt	110 Ds	111 Rg	112	113	114	115	116		118

Metals

57 La	58 Ce	59 Pr	60 Nd	61 Pm	62 Sm	63 Eu	64 Gd	65 Tb	66 Dy	67 Ho	68 Er	69 Tm	70 Yb
89 Ac	90 Th	91 Pa	92 U	93 Np	94 Pu	95 Am	96 Cm	97 Bk	98 Cf	99 Es	100 Fm	101 Md	102 No

Metalloids

Nonmetals

▲ **Figure 2.16 Periodic table of the elements.** Different colors are used to show the division of the elements into metals, metalloids, and nonmetals.

The horizontal rows of the periodic table are called **periods**. The first period consists of only two elements, hydrogen (H) and helium (He). The second and third periods, which begin with lithium (Li) and sodium (Na), respectively, consist of eight elements each. The fourth and fifth periods contain 18 elements. The sixth period has 32 elements, but for it to fit on a page, 14 of these elements (those with atomic numbers 57–70) appear at the bottom of the table. The seventh and last period is incomplete, but it also has 14 of its members placed in a row at the bottom of the table.

The vertical columns of the periodic table are called **groups**. The way in which the groups are labeled is somewhat arbitrary. Three labeling schemes are in common use, two of which are shown in Figure 2.16. The top set of labels, which have A and B designations, is widely used in North America. Roman numerals, rather than Arabic ones, are often employed in this scheme. Group 7A, for example, is often labeled VIIA. Europeans use a similar convention that numbers the columns from 1A through 8A and then from 1B through 8B, thereby giving the label 7B (or VIIB) instead of 7A to the group headed by fluorine (F). In an effort to eliminate this confusion, the International Union of Pure and Applied Chemistry (IUPAC) has proposed a convention that numbers the groups from 1 through 18 with no A or B designations, as shown in the lower set of labels at the top of the table in Figure 2.16. We will use the traditional North American convention with Arabic numerals.

Elements that belong to the same group often exhibit similarities in physical and chemical properties. For example, the "coinage metals"—copper (Cu), silver (Ag), and gold (Au)— belong to group 1B. As their name suggests, the coinage metals are used throughout the world to make coins. Many other groups in the periodic table also have names, as listed in Table 2.3 ▼.

We will learn in Chapters 6 and 7 that the elements in a group of the periodic table have similar properties because they have the same arrangement of electrons at the periphery of their atoms. However, we need not wait until then to make good use of the periodic table; after all, chemists who knew nothing about electrons developed the table! We can use the table, as they intended, to correlate the behaviors of elements and to aid in remembering many facts. You will find it helpful to refer to the periodic table frequently when studying the remainder of this chapter.

Except for hydrogen, all the elements on the left side and in the middle of the periodic table are **metallic elements**, or **metals**. The majority of elements are metallic; they all share characteristic properties, such as luster and high electrical and heat conductivity. All metals, with the exception of mercury (Hg), are solids at room temperature. The metals are separated from the **nonmetallic elements**, or **nonmetals**, by a diagonal steplike line that runs from boron (B) to astatine (At), as shown in Figure 2.16. Hydrogen, although on the left side of the periodic table, is a nonmetal. At room temperature some of the nonmetals are gaseous, some are solid, and one is liquid. Nonmetals generally differ from the metals in appearance (Figure 2.17 ◄) and in other physical properties. Many of the elements that lie along the line that separates metals from nonmetals, such as antimony (Sb), have properties that fall between those of metals and those of nonmetals. These elements are often referred to as **metalloids**.

▲ Figure 2.17 **Some familiar examples of metals and nonmetals.** The nonmetals (from bottom left) are sulfur (yellow powder), iodine (dark, shiny crystals), bromine (reddish brown liquid and vapor in glass vial), and three samples of carbon (black charcoal powder, diamond, and graphite in the pencil lead). The metals are in the form of an aluminum wrench, copper pipe, lead shot, silver coins, and gold nuggets.

TABLE 2.3 ■ Names of Some Groups in the Periodic Table		
Group	Name	Elements
1A	Alkali metals	Li, Na, K, Rb, Cs, Fr
2A	Alkaline earth metals	Be, Mg, Ca, Sr, Ba, Ra
6A	Chalcogens	O, S, Se, Te, Po
7A	Halogens	F, Cl, Br, I, At
8A	Noble gases (or rare gases)	He, Ne, Ar, Kr, Xe, Rn

Prior to 1940 the periodic table ended at uranium, element number 92. Since that time, no scientist has had a greater effect on the periodic table than Glenn Seaborg. Seaborg (Figure 2.18 ▶) became a faculty member in the chemistry department at the University of California, Berkeley in 1937. In 1940 he and his colleagues Edwin McMillan, Arthur Wahl, and Joseph Kennedy succeeded in isolating plutonium (Pu) as a product of the reaction between uranium and neutrons. We will talk about reactions of this type, called *nuclear reactions*, in Chapter 21.

During the period 1944 through 1958, Seaborg and his coworkers also identified various products of nuclear reactions as being the elements having atomic numbers 95 through 102. All these elements are radioactive and are not found in nature; they can be synthesized only via nuclear reactions. For their efforts in identifying the elements beyond uranium (the *transuranium* elements), McMillan and Seaborg shared the 1951 Nobel Prize in chemistry.

From 1961 to 1971, Seaborg served as the chairman of the U.S. Atomic Energy Commission (now the Department of Energy). In this position he had an important role in establishing international treaties to limit the testing of nuclear weapons. Upon his return to Berkeley, he was part of the team that in 1974 first identified element number 106. Another team at Berkeley corroborated that discovery in 1993. In 1994, to honor Seaborg's many contributions to the discovery of new elements, the American Chemical Society proposed that element

◀ Figure 2.18 **Glenn Seaborg (1912–1999).** The photograph shows Seaborg at Berkeley in 1941 using a Geiger counter to try to detect radiation produced by plutonium. Geiger counters will be discussed in Section 21.5.

number 106 be named "seaborgium," with a proposed symbol of Sg. After several years of controversy about whether an element should be named after a living person, the IUPAC officially adopted the name seaborgium in 1997. Seaborg became the first person to have an element named after him while he was still alive.

Related Exercise: 2.96

▲ **GIVE IT SOME THOUGHT**

Chlorine is a halogen. Locate this element in the periodic table. **(a)** What is its symbol? **(b)** In what period and in what group is the element located? **(c)** What is its atomic number? **(d)** Is chlorine a metal or nonmetal?

■ **SAMPLE EXERCISE 2.5** | **Using the Periodic Table**

Which two of the following elements would you expect to show the greatest similarity in chemical and physical properties: B, Ca, F, He, Mg, P?

SOLUTION

Elements that are in the same group of the periodic table are most likely to exhibit similar chemical and physical properties. We therefore expect that Ca and Mg should be most alike because they are in the same group (2A, the alkaline earth metals).

■ **PRACTICE EXERCISE**

Locate Na (sodium) and Br (bromine) on the periodic table. Give the atomic number of each, and label each a metal, metalloid, or nonmetal.
Answer: Na, atomic number 11, is a metal; Br, atomic number 35, is a nonmetal.

2.6 MOLECULES AND MOLECULAR COMPOUNDS

Even though the atom is the smallest representative sample of an element, only the noble-gas elements are normally found in nature as isolated atoms. Most matter is composed of molecules or ions, both of which are formed from atoms. We examine molecules here and ions in Section 2.7.

▶ Figure 2.19 **Diatomic molecules.** Seven common elements exist as diatomic molecules at room temperature.

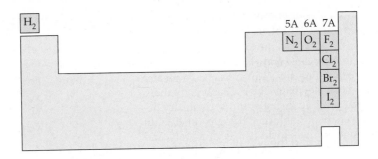

A **molecule** is an assembly of two or more atoms tightly bound together. The resultant "package" of atoms behaves in many ways as a single, distinct object, just as a cell phone composed of many parts can be recognized as a single object. We will discuss the forces that hold the atoms together (the chemical bonds) in Chapters 8 and 9.

Molecules and Chemical Formulas

Many elements are found in nature in molecular form; that is, two or more of the same type of atom are bound together. For example, the oxygen normally found in air consists of molecules that contain two oxygen atoms. We represent this molecular form of oxygen by the **chemical formula** O_2 (read "oh two"). The subscript in the formula tells us that two oxygen atoms are present in each molecule. A molecule that is made up of two atoms is called a **diatomic molecule**. Oxygen also exists in another molecular form known as *ozone*. Molecules of ozone consist of three oxygen atoms, making the chemical formula for this substance O_3. Even though "normal" oxygen (O_2) and ozone (O_3) are both composed only of oxygen atoms, they exhibit very different chemical and physical properties. For example, O_2 is essential for life, but O_3 is toxic; O_2 is odorless, whereas O_3 has a sharp, pungent smell.

The elements that normally occur as diatomic molecules are hydrogen, oxygen, nitrogen, and the halogens. Their locations in the periodic table are shown in Figure 2.19 ▲. When we speak of the substance hydrogen, we mean H_2 unless we explicitly indicate otherwise. Likewise, when we speak of oxygen, nitrogen, or any of the halogens, we are referring to O_2, N_2, F_2, Cl_2, Br_2, or I_2. Thus, the properties of oxygen and hydrogen listed in Table 1.3 are those of O_2 and H_2. Other, less common forms of these elements behave much differently.

Compounds that are composed of molecules contain more than one type of atom and are called **molecular compounds**. A molecule of water, for example, consists of two hydrogen atoms and one oxygen atom and is therefore represented by the chemical formula H_2O. Lack of a subscript on the O indicates one atom of O per water molecule. Another compound composed of these same elements (in different relative proportions) is hydrogen peroxide, H_2O_2. The properties of hydrogen peroxide are very different from the properties of water.

Several common molecules are shown in Figure 2.20 ◀. Notice how the composition of each compound is given by its chemical formula. Notice also that these substances are composed only of nonmetallic elements. *Most molecular substances that we will encounter contain only nonmetals.*

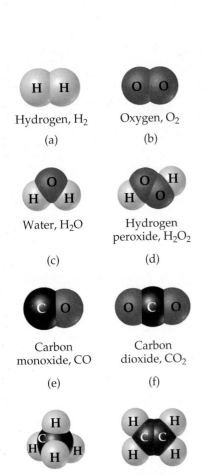

▲ Figure 2.20 **Molecular models of some simple molecules.** Notice how the chemical formulas of these substances correspond to their compositions.

Molecular and Empirical Formulas

Chemical formulas that indicate the actual numbers and types of atoms in a molecule are called **molecular formulas**. (The formulas in Figure 2.20 are molecular formulas.) Chemical formulas that give only the relative number of atoms of each type in a molecule are called **empirical formulas**. The subscripts in an empirical formula are always the smallest possible whole-number ratios. The molecular formula for hydrogen peroxide is H_2O_2, for example, whereas its empirical formula is HO. The molecular formula for ethylene is C_2H_4, and its empirical formula is CH_2. For many substances, the molecular formula and the empirical formula are identical, as in the case of water, H_2O.

Molecular formulas provide more information about molecules than do empirical formulas. Whenever we know the molecular formula of a compound, we can determine its empirical formula. The converse is not true, however. If we know the empirical formula of a substance, we cannot determine its molecular formula unless we have more information. So why do chemists bother with empirical formulas? As we will see in Chapter 3, certain common methods of analyzing substances lead to the empirical formula only. Once the empirical formula is known, additional experiments can give the information needed to convert the empirical formula to the molecular one. In addition, there are substances, such as the most common forms of elemental carbon, that do not exist as isolated molecules. For these substances, we must rely on empirical formulas. Thus, all the common forms of elemental carbon are represented by the element's chemical symbol, C, which is the empirical formula for all the forms.

Structural formula

■ SAMPLE EXERCISE 2.6 | Relating Empirical and Molecular Formulas

Write the empirical formulas for the following molecules: **(a)** glucose, a substance also known as either blood sugar or dextrose, whose molecular formula is $C_6H_{12}O_6$; **(b)** nitrous oxide, a substance used as an anesthetic and commonly called laughing gas, whose molecular formula is N_2O.

SOLUTION

(a) The subscripts of an empirical formula are the smallest whole-number ratios. The smallest ratios are obtained by dividing each subscript by the largest common factor, in this case 6. The resultant empirical formula for glucose is CH_2O.
(b) Because the subscripts in N_2O are already the lowest integral numbers, the empirical formula for nitrous oxide is the same as its molecular formula, N_2O.

■ PRACTICE EXERCISE

Give the empirical formula for the substance called *diborane*, whose molecular formula is B_2H_6.
Answer: BH_3

Perspective drawing

Ball-and-stick model

Picturing Molecules

The molecular formula of a substance summarizes the composition of the substance but does not show how the atoms come together to form the molecule. The **structural formula** of a substance shows which atoms are attached to which within the molecule. For example, the structural formulas for water, hydrogen peroxide, and methane (CH_4) can be written as follows:

Water   Hydrogen peroxide   Methane

The atoms are represented by their chemical symbols, and lines are used to represent the bonds that hold the atoms together.

A structural formula usually does not depict the actual geometry of the molecule, that is, the actual angles at which atoms are joined together. A structural formula can be written as a *perspective drawing*, however, to give some sense of three-dimensional shape, as shown in Figure 2.21 ▶.

Scientists also rely on various models to help visualize molecules. *Ball-and-stick models* show atoms as spheres and bonds as sticks. This type of model has the advantage of accurately representing the angles at which the atoms are attached to one another within the molecule (Figure 2.21). In a ball-and-stick

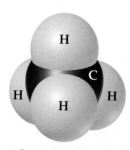

Space-filling model

▲ Figure 2.21 **Different representations of the methane (CH_4) molecule.** Structural formulas, perspective drawings, ball-and-stick models, and space-filling models each help us visualize the ways atoms are attached to each other in molecules. In the perspective drawing, solid lines represent bonds in the plane of the paper, the solid wedge represents a bond that extends out from the plane of the paper, and dashed lines represent bonds behind the paper.

model, balls of the same size may represent all atoms, or the relative sizes of the balls may reflect the relative sizes of the atoms. Sometimes the chemical symbols of the elements are superimposed on the balls, but often the atoms are identified simply by color.

A *space-filling model* depicts what the molecule would look like if the atoms were scaled up in size (Figure 2.21). These models show the relative sizes of the atoms, but the angles between atoms, which help define their molecular geometry, are often more difficult to see than in ball-and-stick models. As in ball-and-stick models, the identities of the atoms are indicated by their colors, but they may also be labeled with the element's symbol.

◢ GIVE IT SOME THOUGHT

The structural formula for the substance ethane is shown here:

$$H-\underset{\underset{H}{|}}{\overset{\overset{H}{|}}{C}}-\underset{\underset{H}{|}}{\overset{\overset{H}{|}}{C}}-H$$

(a) What is the molecular formula for ethane? **(b)** What is its empirical formula? **(c)** Which kind of molecular model would most clearly show the angles between atoms?

2.7 IONS AND IONIC COMPOUNDS

The nucleus of an atom is unchanged by chemical processes, but some atoms can readily gain or lose electrons. If electrons are removed from or added to a neutral atom, a charged particle called an **ion** is formed. An ion with a positive charge is called a **cation** (pronounced CAT-ion); a negatively charged ion is called an **anion** (AN-ion).

To see how ions form, consider the sodium atom, which has 11 protons and 11 electrons. This atom easily loses one electron. The resulting cation has 11 protons and 10 electrons, which means it has a net charge of 1+.

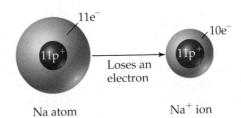

Na atom   Na$^+$ ion

The net charge on an ion is represented by a superscript. The superscripts $+$, $2+$, and $3+$, for instance, mean a net charge resulting from the *loss* of one, two, and three electrons, respectively. The superscripts $-$, $2-$, and $3-$ represent net charges resulting from the *gain* of one, two, and three electrons, respectively. Chlorine, with 17 protons and 17 electrons, for example, can gain an electron in chemical reactions, producing the Cl$^-$ ion:

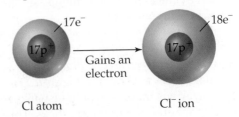

Cl atom   Cl$^-$ ion

In general, metal atoms tend to lose electrons to form cations, whereas nonmetal atoms tend to gain electrons to form anions.

■ **SAMPLE EXERCISE 2.7** | **Writing Chemical Symbols for Ions**

Give the chemical symbol, including mass number, for each of the following ions: **(a)** The ion with 22 protons, 26 neutrons, and 19 electrons; **(b)** the ion of sulfur that has 16 neutrons and 18 electrons.

SOLUTION

(a) The number of protons (22) is the atomic number of the element. By referring to a periodic table or list of elements, we see that the element with atomic number 22 is titanium (Ti). The mass number of this isotope of titanium is $22 + 26 = 48$ (the sum of the protons and neutrons). Because the ion has three more protons than electrons, it has a net charge of 3+. Thus, the symbol for the ion is $^{48}Ti^{3+}$.

(b) By referring to a periodic table or a table of elements, we see that sulfur (S) has an atomic number of 16. Thus, each atom or ion of sulfur must contain 16 protons. We are told that the ion also has 16 neutrons, meaning the mass number of the ion is $16 + 16 = 32$. Because the ion has 16 protons and 18 electrons, its net charge is 2−. Thus, the symbol for the ion is $^{32}S^{2-}$.

In general, we will focus on the net charges of ions and ignore their mass numbers unless the circumstances dictate that we specify a certain isotope.

■ **PRACTICE EXERCISE**

How many protons, neutrons, and electrons does the $^{79}Se^{2-}$ ion possess?
Answer: 34 protons, 45 neutrons, and 36 electrons

In addition to simple ions, such as Na^+ and Cl^-, there are **polyatomic ions**, such as NH_4^+ (ammonium ion) and SO_4^{2-} (sulfate ion). These latter ions consist of atoms joined as in a molecule, but they have a net positive or negative charge. We will consider further examples of polyatomic ions in Section 2.8.

It is important to realize that the chemical properties of ions are very different from the chemical properties of the atoms from which the ions are derived. The difference is like the change from Dr. Jekyll to Mr. Hyde: Although a given atom and its ion may be essentially the same (plus or minus a few electrons), the behavior of the ion is very different from that of the atom.

Predicting Ionic Charges

Many atoms gain or lose electrons to end up with the same number of electrons as the noble gas closest to them in the periodic table. The members of the noble-gas family are chemically very nonreactive and form very few compounds. We might deduce that this is because their electron arrangements are very stable. Nearby elements can obtain these same stable arrangements by losing or gaining electrons. For example, the loss of one electron from an atom of sodium leaves it with the same number of electrons as the neutral neon atom (atomic number 10). Similarly, when chlorine gains an electron, it ends up with 18, the same number of electrons as in argon (atomic number 18). We will use this simple observation to explain the formation of ions until Chapter 8, where we discuss chemical bonding.

■ **SAMPLE EXERCISE 2.8** | **Predicting the Charges of Ions**

Predict the charge expected for the most stable ion of barium and for the most stable ion of oxygen.

SOLUTION

We will assume that these elements form ions that have the same number of electrons as the nearest noble-gas atom. From the periodic table, we see that barium has atomic number 56. The nearest noble gas is xenon, atomic number 54. Barium can attain a stable arrangement of 54 electrons by losing two of its electrons, forming the Ba^{2+} cation.

Oxygen has atomic number 8. The nearest noble gas is neon, atomic number 10. Oxygen can attain this stable electron arrangement by gaining two electrons, thereby forming the O^{2-} anion.

■ **PRACTICE EXERCISE**

Predict the charge expected for the most stable ion of **(a)** aluminum and **(b)** fluorine.
Answer: **(a)** 3+; **(b)** 1−

1A																7A	8A
H^+																	H^-
Li^+	2A											3A	4A	5A	6A		
Na^+	Mg^{2+}													N^{3-}	O^{2-}	F^-	N O B L E G A S E S
K^+	Ca^{2+}		Transition metals									Al^{3+}			S^{2-}	Cl^-	
Rb^+	Sr^{2+}														Se^{2-}	Br^-	
Cs^+	Ba^{2+}														Te^{2-}	I^-	

▲ **Figure 2.22 Charges of some common ions.** Notice that the steplike line that divides metals from nonmetals also separates cations from anions. Hydrogen forms both 1+ and 1− ions.

The periodic table is very useful for remembering the charges of ions, especially those of the elements on the left and right sides of the table. As Figure 2.22▲ shows, the charges of these ions relate in a simple way to their positions in the table. On the left side of the table, for example, the group 1A elements (the alkali metals) form 1+ ions, and the group 2A elements (the alkaline earths) form 2+ ions. On the other side of the table the group 7A elements (the halogens) form 1− ions, and the group 6A elements form 2− ions. As we will see later in the text, many of the other groups do not lend themselves to such simple rules.

Ionic Compounds

A great deal of chemical activity involves the transfer of electrons from one substance to another. As we just saw, ions form when one or more electrons transfer from one neutral atom to another. Figure 2.23▼ shows that when elemental sodium is allowed to react with elemental chlorine, an electron transfers from a neutral sodium atom to a neutral chlorine atom. We are left with a Na^+ ion and a Cl^- ion. Because objects of opposite charge attract, the Na^+ and the Cl^- ions bind together to form the compound sodium chloride (NaCl). Sodium chloride, which we know better as common table salt, is an example of an **ionic compound**, a compound that contains both positively and negatively charged ions.

We can often tell whether a compound is ionic (consisting of ions) or molecular (consisting of molecules) from its composition. In general, cations are metal ions, whereas anions are nonmetal ions. Consequently, *ionic compounds*

▼ **Figure 2.23 The formation of an ionic compound.** (a) The transfer of an electron from a neutral Na atom to a neutral Cl atom leads to the formation of a Na^+ ion and a Cl^- ion. (b) Arrangement of these ions in solid sodium chloride (NaCl). (c) A sample of sodium chloride crystals.

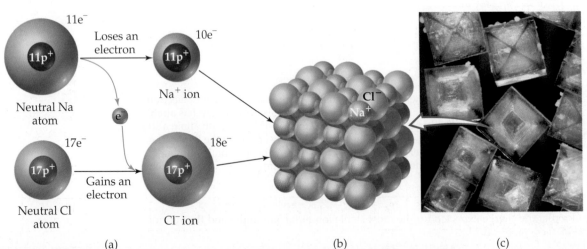

(a) (b) (c)

are generally combinations of metals and nonmetals, as in NaCl. In contrast, molecular compounds are generally composed of nonmetals only, as in H₂O.

■ **SAMPLE EXERCISE 2.9** | **Identifying Ionic and Molecular Compounds**

Which of the following compounds would you expect to be ionic: N_2O, Na_2O, $CaCl_2$, SF_4?

SOLUTION

We would predict that Na_2O and $CaCl_2$ are ionic compounds because they are composed of a metal combined with a nonmetal. The other two compounds, composed entirely of nonmetals, are predicted (correctly) to be molecular compounds.

■ **PRACTICE EXERCISE**

Which of the following compounds are molecular: CBr_4, FeS, P_4O_6, PbF_2?
Answer: CBr_4 and P_4O_6

The ions in ionic compounds are arranged in three-dimensional structures. The arrangement of Na^+ and Cl^- ions in NaCl is shown in Figure 2.23. Because there is no discrete molecule of NaCl, we are able to write only an empirical formula for this substance. In fact, only empirical formulas can be written for most ionic compounds.

Chemistry and Life   ELEMENTS REQUIRED BY LIVING ORGANISMS

Figure 2.24 ▼ shows the elements that are essential for life. More than 97% of the mass of most organisms comprises just six elements—oxygen, carbon, hydrogen, nitrogen, phosphorus, and sulfur. Water (H_2O) is the most common compound in living organisms, accounting for at least 70% of the mass of most cells. Carbon is the most prevalent element (by mass) in the solid components of cells. Carbon atoms are found in a vast variety of organic molecules, in which the carbon atoms are bonded to other carbon atoms or to atoms of other elements, principally H, O, N, P, and S. All proteins, for example, contain the following group of atoms that occurs repeatedly within the molecules:

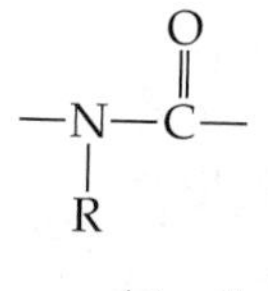

$$-\overset{\displaystyle O}{\underset{\displaystyle R}{\overset{\|}{-N-C-}}}$$

(R is either an H atom or a combination of atoms such as CH_3.)

In addition, 23 more elements have been found in various living organisms. Five are ions that are required by all organisms: Ca^{2+}, Cl^-, Mg^{2+}, K^+, and Na^+. Calcium ions, for example, are necessary for the formation of bone and for the transmission of signals in the nervous system, such as those that trigger the contraction of cardiac muscles, causing the heart to beat. Many other elements are needed in only very small quantities and consequently are called *trace* elements. For example, trace quantities of copper are required in the diet of humans to aid in the synthesis of hemoglobin.

▼ **Figure 2.24 Biologically essential elements.** The elements that are essential for life are indicated by colors. Red denotes the six most abundant elements in living systems (hydrogen, carbon, nitrogen, oxygen, phosphorus, and sulfur). Blue indicates the five next most abundant elements. Green indicates the elements needed in only trace amounts.

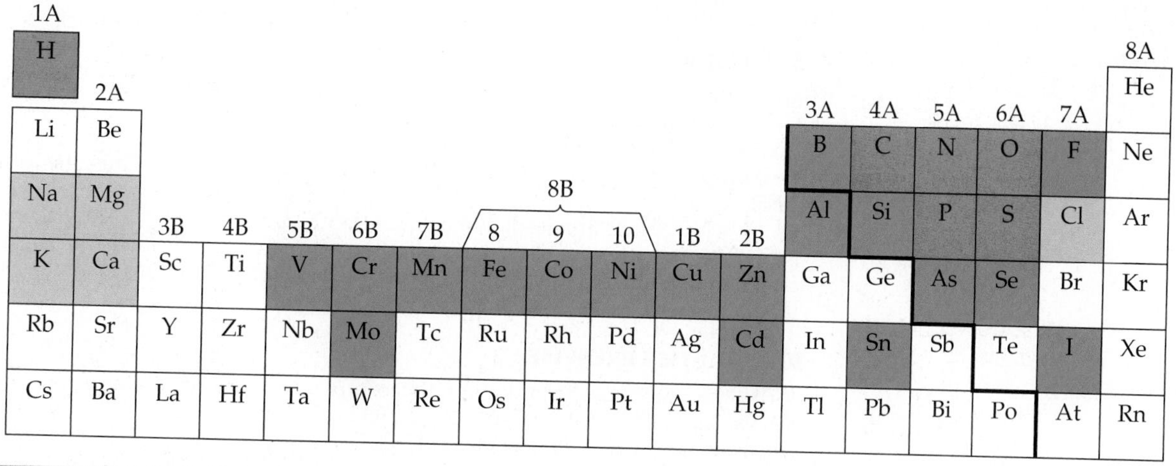

Strategies in Chemistry   PATTERN RECOGNITION

Someone once said that drinking at the fountain of knowledge in a chemistry course is like drinking from a fire hydrant. Indeed, the pace can sometimes seem brisk. More to the point, however, we can drown in the facts if we do not see the general patterns. The value of recognizing patterns and learning rules and generalizations is that the patterns, rules, and generalizations free us from learning (or trying to memorize) many individual facts. The patterns, rules, and generalizations tie ideas together so that we do not get lost in the details.

Many students struggle with chemistry because they do not see how the topics relate to one another, how ideas connect together. They therefore treat every idea and problem as being unique instead of as an example or application of a general rule, procedure, or relationship. You can avoid this pitfall by remembering the following: Begin to notice the structure of the topic you are studying. Pay attention to the trends and rules given to summarize a large body of information. Notice, for example, how atomic structure helps us understand the existence of isotopes (as seen in Table 2.2) and how the periodic table aids us in remembering the charges of ions (as seen in Figure 2.22). You may surprise yourself by observing patterns that are not even explicitly spelled out yet. Perhaps you have even noticed certain trends in chemical formulas. Moving across the periodic table from element 11 (Na), we find that the elements form compounds with F having the following compositions: NaF, MgF_2, and AlF_3. Does this trend continue? Do SiF_4, PF_5, and SF_6 exist? Indeed they do. If you have noticed trends like this from the scraps of information you have seen so far, then you are ahead of the game and you have already prepared yourself for some topics we will address in later chapters.

We can readily write the empirical formula for an ionic compound if we know the charges of the ions of which the compound is composed. Chemical compounds are always electrically neutral. Consequently, the ions in an ionic compound always occur in such a ratio that the total positive charge equals the total negative charge. Thus, there is one Na^+ to one Cl^- (giving NaCl), one Ba^{2+} to two Cl^- (giving $BaCl_2$), and so forth.

As you consider these and other examples, you will see that if the charges on the cation and anion are equal, the subscript on each ion will be 1. If the charges are not equal, the charge on one ion (without its sign) will become the subscript on the other ion. For example, the ionic compound formed from Mg (which forms Mg^{2+} ions) and N (which forms N^{3-} ions) is Mg_3N_2:

$$Mg^{(2)+} \diagdown\!\!\!\diagup N^{(3)-} \longrightarrow Mg_3N_2$$

GIVE IT SOME THOUGHT

Why don't we write the formula for the compound formed by Ca^{2+} and O^{2-} as Ca_2O_2?

■ SAMPLE EXERCISE 2.10 | Using Ionic Charge to Write Empirical Formulas for Ionic Compounds

What are the empirical formulas of the compounds formed by **(a)** Al^{3+} and Cl^- ions, **(b)** Al^{3+} and O^{2-} ions, **(c)** Mg^{2+} and NO_3^- ions?

SOLUTION

(a) Three Cl^- ions are required to balance the charge of one Al^{3+} ion. Thus, the formula is $AlCl_3$.
(b) Two Al^{3+} ions are required to balance the charge of three O^{2-} ions (that is, the total positive charge is 6+, and the total negative charge is 6−). Thus, the formula is Al_2O_3.
(c) Two NO_3^- ions are needed to balance the charge of one Mg^{2+}. Thus, the formula is $Mg(NO_3)_2$. In this case the formula for the entire polyatomic ion NO_3^- must be enclosed in parentheses so that it is clear that the subscript 2 applies to all the atoms of that ion.

■ PRACTICE EXERCISE

Write the empirical formulas for the compounds formed by the following ions:
(a) Na^+ and PO_4^{3-}, **(b)** Zn^{2+} and SO_4^{2-}, **(c)** Fe^{3+} and CO_3^{2-}.
Answers: **(a)** Na_3PO_4, **(b)** $ZnSO_4$, **(c)** $Fe_2(CO_3)_3$

2.8   NAMING INORGANIC COMPOUNDS

To obtain information about a particular substance, you must know its chemical formula and name. The names and formulas of compounds are essential vocabulary in chemistry. The system used in naming substances is called **chemical nomenclature** from the Latin words *nomen* (name) and *calare* (to call).

There are now more than 19 million known chemical substances. Naming them all would be a hopelessly complicated task if each had a special name independent of all others. Many important substances that have been known for a long time, such as water (H_2O) and ammonia (NH_3), do have individual, traditional names (so-called "common" names). For most substances, however, we rely on a systematic set of rules that leads to an informative and unique name for each substance, a name based on the composition of the substance.

The rules for chemical nomenclature are based on the division of substances into categories. The major division is between organic and inorganic compounds. *Organic compounds* contain carbon, usually in combination with hydrogen, oxygen, nitrogen, or sulfur. All others are *inorganic compounds*. Early chemists associated organic compounds with plants and animals, and they associated inorganic compounds with the nonliving portion of our world. Although this distinction between living and nonliving matter is no longer pertinent, the classification between organic and inorganic compounds continues to be useful. In this section we consider the basic rules for naming inorganic compounds, and in Section 2.9 we will introduce the names of some simple organic compounds. Among inorganic compounds, we will consider three categories: ionic compounds, molecular compounds, and acids.

Names and Formulas of Ionic Compounds

Recall from Section 2.7 that ionic compounds usually consist of metal ions combined with nonmetal ions. The metals form the positive ions, and the nonmetals form the negative ions. Let's examine the naming of positive ions, then the naming of negative ones. After that, we will consider how to put the names of the ions together to identify the complete ionic compound.

1. **Positive Ions (Cations)**

   (a) *Cations formed from metal atoms have the same name as the metal:*

   Na^+ sodium ion Zn^{2+} zinc ion Al^{3+} aluminum ion

   Ions formed from a single atom are called *monatomic ions*.

   (b) *If a metal can form different cations, the positive charge is indicated by a Roman numeral in parentheses following the name of the metal:*

   Fe^{2+} iron(II) ion Cu^+ copper(I) ion
   Fe^{3+} iron(III) ion Cu^{2+} copper(II) ion

   Ions of the same element that have different charges exhibit different properties, such as different colors (Figure 2.25▶).

   Most of the metals that can form more than one cation are *transition metals*, elements that occur in the middle block of elements, from group 3B to group 2B in the periodic table. The charges of these ions are indicated by Roman numerals. The metals that form only one cation are those of group 1A (Na^+, K^+, and Rb^+) and group 2A (Mg^{2+}, Ca^{2+}, Sr^{2+}, and Ba^{2+}), as well as Al^{3+} (group 3A) and two transition-metal ions: Ag^+ (group 1B) and Zn^{2+} (group 2B). Charges are not expressed explicitly when naming these ions. However, if there is any doubt in your mind whether a metal forms more than one cation, use a Roman numeral to indicate the charge. It is never wrong to do so, even though it may be unnecessary.

   An older method still widely used for distinguishing between two differently charged ions of a metal is to apply the ending *-ous* or *-ic*.

▲ **Figure 2.25 Ions of the same element with different charges exhibit different properties.** Compounds containing ions of the same element but with different charge can be very different in appearance and properties. Both substances shown are complex compounds of iron that also contain K^+ and CN^- ions. The substance on the left is potassium ferrocyanide, which contains Fe(II) bound to CN^- ions. The substance on the right is potassium ferricyanide, which contains Fe(III) bound to CN^- ions. Both substances are used extensively in blueprinting and other dyeing processes.

These endings represent the lower and higher charged ions, respectively. They are added to the root of the element's Latin name:

Fe^{2+} ferrous ion Cu^+ cuprous ion

Fe^{3+} ferric ion Cu^{2+} cupric ion

Although we will only rarely use these older names in this text, you might encounter them elsewhere.

(c) *Cations formed from nonmetal atoms have names that end in* -ium:

NH_4^+ ammonium ion H_3O^+ hydronium ion

These two ions are the only ions of this kind that we will encounter frequently in the text. They are both polyatomic. The vast majority of cations are monatomic metal ions.

The names and formulas of some common cations are shown in Table 2.4 ▼; they are also included in a table of common ions in the back inside cover of the text. The ions listed on the left side in Table 2.4 are the monatomic ions that do not have variable charges. Those listed on the right side are either polyatomic cations or cations with variable charges. The Hg_2^{2+} ion is unusual because this metal ion is not monatomic. It is called the mercury(I) ion because it can be thought of as two Hg^+ ions bound together. The cations that you will encounter most frequently are shown in boldface. You should learn these cations first.

▲ GIVE IT SOME THOUGHT

Why is CrO named using a Roman numeral, chromium(II) oxide, whereas CaO is named without a Roman numeral in the name, calcium oxide?

2. Negative Ions (Anions)

(a) *The names of monatomic anions are formed by replacing the ending of the name of the element with* -ide:

H^- hydride ion O^{2-} oxide ion N^{3-} nitride ion

TABLE 2.4 ■ Common Cations*

Charge	Formula	Name	Formula	Name
1+	**H^+**	**Hydrogen ion**	**NH_4^+**	**Ammonium ion**
	Li^+	Lithium ion	Cu^+	Copper(I) or cuprous ion
	Na^+	**Sodium ion**		
	K^+	**Potassium ion**		
	Cs^+	Cesium ion		
	Ag^+	**Silver ion**		
2+	**Mg^{2+}**	**Magnesium ion**	Co^{2+}	Cobalt(II) or cobaltous ion
	Ca^{2+}	**Calcium ion**	**Cu^{2+}**	**Copper(II)** or cupric ion
	Sr^{2+}	Strontium ion	**Fe^{2+}**	**Iron(II)** or ferrous ion
	Ba^{2+}	Barium ion	Mn^{2+}	Manganese(II) or manganous ion
	Zn^{2+}	**Zinc ion**	Hg_2^{2+}	Mercury(I) or mercurous ion
	Cd^{2+}	Cadmium ion	**Hg^{2+}**	**Mercury(II)** or mercuric ion
			Ni^{2+}	Nickel(II) or nickelous ion
			Pb^{2+}	**Lead(II)** or plumbous ion
			Sn^{2+}	Tin(II) or stannous ion
3+	**Al^{3+}**	**Aluminum ion**	Cr^{3+}	Chromium(III) or chromic ion
			Fe^{3+}	**Iron(III)** or ferric ion

*The most common ions are in boldface.

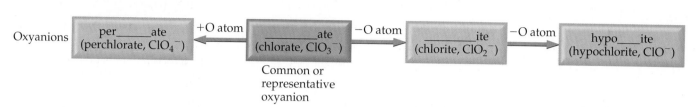

▲ **Figure 2.26 Summary of the procedure for naming anions.** The root of the name (such as "chlor" for chlorine) goes in the blank.

A few simple polyatomic anions also have names ending in *-ide*:

OH^- hydroxide ion CN^- cyanide ion O_2^{2-} peroxide ion

(b) *Polyatomic anions containing oxygen have names ending in* -ate *or* -ite. These anions are called **oxyanions**. The ending *-ate* is used for the most common oxyanion of an element. The ending *-ite* is used for an oxyanion that has the same charge but one O atom fewer:

NO_3^- nitrate ion SO_4^{2-} sulfate ion
NO_2^- nitrite ion SO_3^{2-} sulfite ion

Prefixes are used when the series of oxyanions of an element extends to four members, as with the halogens. The prefix *per-* indicates one more O atom than the oxyanion ending in *-ate*; the prefix *hypo-* indicates one O atom fewer than the oxyanion ending in *-ite*:

ClO_4^- perchlorate ion (one more O atom than chlorate)
ClO_3^- chlorate ion
ClO_2^- chlorite ion (one O atom fewer than chlorate)
ClO^- hypochlorite ion (one O atom fewer than chlorite)

These rules are summarized in Figure 2.26▲.

◢ **GIVE IT SOME THOUGHT**

What information is conveyed by the endings *-ide*, *-ate*, and *-ite* in the name of an anion?

Students often have a hard time remembering the number of oxygen atoms in the various oxyanions and the charges of these ions. Figure 2.27▼ lists the oxyanions of C, N, P, S, and Cl that contain the maximum number of O atoms. The periodic pattern seen in these formulas can help you remember them. Notice that C and N, which are in the second period of the periodic table, have only three O atoms each, whereas P, S, and Cl, which are in the third period, have four O atoms each. If we begin at the lower right side of the figure, with Cl, we see that the charges increase from right to left, from 1− for Cl (ClO_4^-) to 3− for P (PO_4^{3-}). In the second period the charges also increase from right to left, from 1− for N (NO_3^-) to 2− for C (CO_3^{2-}). Each anion

	4A	5A	6A	7A
2	CO_3^{2-} **Carbonate ion**	NO_3^- **Nitrate ion**		
3		PO_4^{3-} **Phosphate ion**	SO_4^{2-} **Sulfate ion**	ClO_4^- **Perchlorate ion**

◀ **Figure 2.27 Common oxyanions.** The composition and charges of common oxyanions are related to their location in the periodic table.

shown in Figure 2.27 has a name ending in -ate. The ClO_4^- ion also has a per- prefix. If you know the rules summarized in Figure 2.26 and the names and formulas of the five oxyanions in Figure 2.27, you can deduce the names for the other oxyanions of these elements.

GIVE IT SOME THOUGHT

Predict the formulas for the borate ion and silicate ion, assuming that they contain a single B and Si atom, respectively, and follow the trends shown in Figure 2.27 ▲.

■■ SAMPLE EXERCISE 2.11 | Determining the Formula of an Oxyanion from Its Name

Based on the formula for the sulfate ion, predict the formula for **(a)** the selenate ion and **(b)** the selenite ion. (Sulfur and selenium are both members of group 6A and form analogous oxyanions.)

SOLUTION
(a) The sulfate ion is SO_4^{2-} The analogous selenate ion is therefore SeO_4^{2-}.
(b) The ending -*ite* indicates an oxyanion with the same charge but one O atom fewer than the corresponding oxyanion that ends in -*ate*. Thus, the formula for the selenite ion is SeO_3^{2-}.

■■ PRACTICE EXERCISE
The formula for the bromate ion is analogous to that for the chlorate ion. Write the formula for the hypobromite and perbromate ions.
Answer: BrO^- and BrO_4^-

(c) *Anions derived by adding H^+ to an oxyanion are named by adding as a prefix the word* hydrogen *or* dihydrogen, *as appropriate:*

CO_3^{2-}	carbonate ion	PO_4^{3-}	phosphate ion
HCO_3^-	hydrogen carbonate ion	$H_2PO_4^-$	dihydrogen phosphate ion

Notice that each H^+ reduces the negative charge of the parent anion by one. An older method for naming some of these ions is to use the prefix *bi-*. Thus, the HCO_3^- ion is commonly called the bicarbonate ion, and HSO_4^- is sometimes called the bisulfate ion.

The names and formulas of the common anions are listed in Table 2.5 ▼ and on the back inside cover of the text. Those anions whose names end in -*ide* are listed on the left portion of Table 2.5, and those

TABLE 2.5 ■ Common Anions[*]

Charge	Formula	Name	Formula	Name
1−	H^-	Hydride ion	CH_3COO^- (or $C_2H_3O_2^-$)	**Acetate ion**
	F^-	**Fluoride ion**	ClO_3^-	Chlorate ion
	Cl^-	**Chloride ion**	ClO_4^-	**Perchlorate ion**
	Br^-	**Bromide ion**	NO_3^-	**Nitrate ion**
	I^-	**Iodide ion**	MnO_4^-	Permanganate ion
	CN^-	Cyanide ion		
	OH^-	**Hydroxide ion**		
2−	O^{2-}	**Oxide ion**	CO_3^{2-}	**Carbonate ion**
	O_2^{2-}	Peroxide ion	CrO_4^{2-}	Chromate ion
	S^{2-}	**Sulfide ion**	$Cr_2O_7^{2-}$	Dichromate ion
			SO_4^{2-}	**Sulfate ion**
3−	N^{3-}	Nitride ion	PO_4^{3-}	**Phosphate ion**

* The most common ions are in boldface.

systematic name: **(a)** saltpeter, KNO_3; **(b)** soda ash, Na_2CO_3; **(c)** lime, CaO; **(d)** muriatic acid, HCl; **(e)** Epsom salts, $MgSO_4$; **(f)** milk of magnesia, $Mg(OH)_2$.

2.104 Many ions and compounds have very similar names, and there is great potential for confusing them. Write the correct chemical formulas to distinguish between **(a)** calcium sulfide and calcium hydrogen sulfide, **(b)** hydrobromic acid and bromic acid, **(c)** aluminum nitride and aluminum nitrite, **(d)** iron(II) oxide and iron(III) oxide, **(e)** ammonia and ammonium ion, **(f)** potassium sulfite and potassium bisulfite, **(g)** mercurous chloride and mercuric chloride, **(h)** chloric acid and perchloric acid.

2.105 The compound *cyclohexane* is an alkane in which six carbon atoms form a ring. The partial structural formula of the compound is as follows:

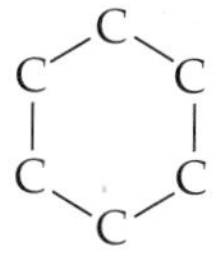

(a) Complete the structural formula for cyclohexane. **(b)** Is the molecular formula for cyclohexane the same as that for *n*-hexane, in which the carbon atoms are in a straight line? If possible, comment on the source of any differences. **(c)** Propose a structural formula for *cyclohexanol*, the alcohol derived from cyclohexane.

2.106 The periodic table helps organize the chemical behaviors of the elements. As a class discussion or as a short essay, describe how the table is organized, and mention as many ways as you can think of in which the position of an element in the table relates to the chemical and physical properties of the element.

CHAPTER 3

STOICHIOMETRY: CALCULATIONS WITH CHEMICAL FORMULAS AND EQUATIONS

SUGAR CARAMELIZING. Major changes in the appearance of compounds are indications of chemical reactions. Here, prolonged heating of sucrose, common table sugar, produces caramel.

Interconverting Masses and Moles

Conversions of mass to moles and of moles to mass are frequently encountered in calculations using the mole concept. These calculations are simplified using dimensional analysis, as shown in Sample Exercises 3.10 and 3.11.

■ SAMPLE EXERCISE 3.10 | Converting Grams to Moles

Calculate the number of moles of glucose ($C_6H_{12}O_6$) in 5.380 g of $C_6H_{12}O_6$.

SOLUTION

Analyze We are given the number of grams of a substance and its chemical formula and asked to calculate the number of moles.

Plan The molar mass of a substance provides the factor for converting grams to moles. The molar mass of $C_6H_{12}O_6$ is 180.0 g/mol (Sample Exercise 3.9).

Solve Using 1 mol $C_6H_{12}O_6$ = 180.0 g $C_6H_{12}O_6$ to write the appropriate conversion factor, we have

$$\text{Moles } C_6H_{12}O_6 = (5.380 \text{ g } C_6H_{12}O_6)\left(\frac{1 \text{ mol } C_6H_{12}O_6}{180.0 \text{ g } C_6H_{12}O_6}\right) = 0.02989 \text{ mol } C_6H_{12}O_6$$

Check Because 5.380 g is less than the molar mass, a reasonable answer is less than one mole. The units of our answer (mol) are appropriate. The original data had four significant figures, so our answer has four significant figures.

■ PRACTICE EXERCISE

How many moles of sodium bicarbonate ($NaHCO_3$) are in 508 g of $NaHCO_3$?
Answer: 6.05 mol $NaHCO_3$

■ SAMPLE EXERCISE 3.11 | Converting Moles to Grams

Calculate the mass, in grams, of 0.433 mol of calcium nitrate.

SOLUTION

Analyze We are given the number of moles and the name of a substance and asked to calculate the number of grams in the sample.

Plan To convert moles to grams, we need the molar mass, which we can calculate using the chemical formula and atomic weights.

Solve Because the calcium ion is Ca^{2+} and the nitrate ion is NO_3^-, calcium nitrate is $Ca(NO_3)_2$. Adding the atomic weights of the elements in the compound gives a formula weight of 164.1 amu. Using 1 mol $Ca(NO_3)_2$ = 164.1 g $Ca(NO_3)_2$ to write the appropriate conversion factor, we have

$$\text{Grams } Ca(NO_3)_2 = (0.433 \text{ mol } Ca(NO_3)_2)\left(\frac{164.1 \text{ g } Ca(NO_3)_2}{1 \text{ mol } Ca(NO_3)_2}\right) = 71.1 \text{ g } Ca(NO_3)_2$$

Check The number of moles is less than 1, so the number of grams must be less than the molar mass, 164.1 g. Using rounded numbers to estimate, we have $0.5 \times 150 = 75$ g. The magnitude of our answer is reasonable. Both the units (g) and the number of significant figures (3) are correct.

■ PRACTICE EXERCISE

What is the mass, in grams, of **(a)** 6.33 mol of $NaHCO_3$ and **(b)** 3.0×10^{-5} mol of sulfuric acid?
Answers: **(a)** 532 g, **(b)** 2.9×10^{-3} g

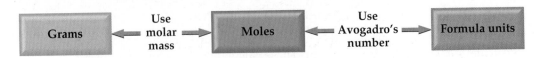

◄ Figure 3.10 Procedure for interconverting the mass and the number of formula units of a substance. The number of moles of the substance is central to the calculation; thus, the mole concept can be thought of as the bridge between the mass of a substance in grams and the number of formula units.

Interconverting Masses and Numbers of Particles

The mole concept provides the bridge between mass and the number of particles. To illustrate how we can interconvert mass and numbers of particles, let's calculate the number of copper atoms in an old copper penny. Such a penny weighs about 3 g, and we will assume that it is 100% copper:

$$\text{Cu atoms} = (3 \text{ g Cu})\left(\frac{1 \text{ mol Cu}}{63.5 \text{ g Cu}}\right)\left(\frac{6.02 \times 10^{23} \text{ Cu atoms}}{1 \text{ mol Cu}}\right)$$
$$= 3 \times 10^{22} \text{ Cu atoms}$$

We have rounded our answer to one significant figure, since we used only one significant figure for the mass of the penny. Notice how dimensional analysis ∞ (Section 1.6) provides a straightforward route from grams to numbers of atoms. The molar mass and Avogadro's number are used as conversion factors to convert grams → moles → atoms. Notice also that our answer is a very large number. Any time you calculate the number of atoms, molecules, or ions in an ordinary sample of matter, you can expect the answer to be very large. In contrast, the number of moles in a sample will usually be much smaller, often less than 1. The general procedure for interconverting mass and number of formula units (atoms, molecules, ions, or whatever is represented by the chemical formula) of a substance is summarized in Figure 3.10 ▲.

■■ **SAMPLE EXERCISE 3.12** | Calculating the Number of Molecules and Number of Atoms from Mass

(a) How many glucose molecules are in 5.23 g of $C_6H_{12}O_6$? **(b)** How many oxygen atoms are in this sample?

SOLUTION

Analyze We are given the number of grams and the chemical formula and asked to calculate (a) the number of molecules and (b) the number of O atoms in the sample.

(a) Plan The strategy for determining the number of molecules in a given quantity of a substance is summarized in Figure 3.10. We must convert 5.23 g $C_6H_{12}O_6$ to moles $C_6H_{12}O_6$, which can then be converted to molecules $C_6H_{12}O_6$. The first conversion uses the molar mass of $C_6H_{12}O_6$: 1 mol $C_6H_{12}O_6$ = 180.0 g $C_6H_{12}O_6$. The second conversion uses Avogadro's number.

Solve

Molecules $C_6H_{12}O_6$

$$= (5.23 \text{ g } C_6H_{12}O_6)\left(\frac{1 \text{ mol } C_6H_{12}O_6}{180.0 \text{ g } C_6H_{12}O_6}\right)\left(\frac{6.02 \times 10^{23} \text{ molecules } C_6H_{12}O_6}{1 \text{ mol } C_6H_{12}O_6}\right)$$
$$= 1.75 \times 10^{22} \text{ molecules } C_6H_{12}O_6$$

Check The magnitude of the answer is reasonable. Because the mass we began with is less than a mole, there should be fewer than 6.02×10^{23} molecules. We can make a ballpark estimate of the answer: $5/200 = 2.5 \times 10^{-2}$ mol; $2.5 \times 10^{-2} \times 6 \times 10^{23} = 15 \times 10^{21} = 1.5 \times 10^{22}$ molecules. The units (molecules) and significant figures (three) are appropriate.

(b) Plan To determine the number of O atoms, we use the fact that there are six O atoms in each molecule of $C_6H_{12}O_6$. Thus, multiplying the number of molecules $C_6H_{12}O_6$ by the factor (6 atoms O/1 molecule $C_6H_{12}O_6$) gives the number of O atoms.

Solve
$$\text{Atoms O} = (1.75 \times 10^{22} \text{ molecules } C_6H_{12}O_6)\left(\frac{6 \text{ atoms O}}{1 \text{ molecule } C_6H_{12}O_6}\right)$$
$$= 1.05 \times 10^{23} \text{ atoms O}$$

Check The answer is simply 6 times as large as the answer to part (a). The number of significant figures (three) and the units (atoms O) are correct.

■ **PRACTICE EXERCISE**

(a) How many nitric acid molecules are in 4.20 g of HNO_3? **(b)** How many O atoms are in this sample?
Answers: **(a)** 4.01×10^{22} molecules HNO_3, **(b)** 1.20×10^{23} atoms O

3.5 EMPIRICAL FORMULAS FROM ANALYSES

As we learned in Section 2.6, the empirical formula for a substance tells us the relative number of atoms of each element it contains. The empirical formula H_2O shows that water contains two H atoms for each O atom. This ratio also applies on the molar level: 1 mol of H_2O contains 2 mol of H atoms and 1 mol of O atoms. Conversely, *the ratio of the number of moles of each element in a compound gives the subscripts in a compound's empirical formula.* In this way, the mole concept provides a way of calculating the empirical formulas of chemical substances, as shown in the following examples.

Mercury and chlorine combine to form a compound that is 73.9% mercury and 26.1% chlorine by mass. This means that if we had a 100.0-g sample of the solid, it would contain 73.9 g of mercury (Hg) and 26.1 g of chlorine (Cl). (Any size sample can be used in problems of this type, but we will generally use 100.0 g to simplify the calculation of mass from percentage.) Using the atomic weights of the elements to give us molar masses, we can calculate the number of moles of each element in the sample:

$$(73.9 \text{ g Hg})\left(\frac{1 \text{ mol Hg}}{200.6 \text{ g Hg}}\right) = 0.368 \text{ mol Hg}$$

$$(26.1 \text{ g Cl})\left(\frac{1 \text{ mol Cl}}{35.5 \text{ g Cl}}\right) = 0.735 \text{ mol Cl}$$

We then divide the larger number of moles (0.735) by the smaller (0.368) to obtain a Cl: Hg mole ratio of 1.99:1:

$$\frac{\text{moles of Cl}}{\text{moles of Hg}} = \frac{0.735 \text{ mol Cl}}{0.368 \text{ mol Hg}} = \frac{1.99 \text{ mol Cl}}{1 \text{ mol Hg}}$$

Because of experimental errors, the results may not lead to exact integers for the ratios of moles. The number 1.99 is very close to 2, so we can confidently conclude that the empirical formula for the compound is $HgCl_2$. The empirical formula is correct because its subscripts are the smallest integers that express the *ratios* of atoms present in the compound. ∞ (Section 2.6) The general procedure for determining empirical formulas is outlined in Figure 3.11▼.

Given:

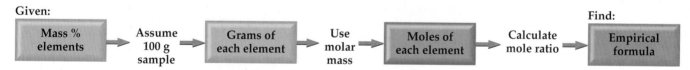

▲ Figure 3.11 **Procedure for calculating an empirical formula from percentage composition.** The central part of the calculation is determining the number of moles of each element in the compound. The procedure is also summarized as "percent to mass, mass to mole, divide by small, multiply 'til whole."

■ **SAMPLE EXERCISE 3.13** | Calculating an Empirical Formula

Ascorbic acid (vitamin C) contains 40.92% C, 4.58% H, and 54.50% O by mass. What is the empirical formula of ascorbic acid?

SOLUTION

Analyze We are to determine an empirical formula of a compound from the mass percentages of its elements.

Plan The strategy for determining the empirical formula involves the three steps given in Figure 3.11.

Solve We *first* assume, for simplicity, that we have exactly 100 g of material (although any mass can be used). In 100 g of ascorbic acid, therefore, we have

40.92 g C, 4.58 g H, and 54.50 g O.

Second, we calculate the number of moles of each element:

$$\text{Moles C} = (40.92 \text{ g C})\left(\frac{1 \text{ mol C}}{12.01 \text{ g C}}\right) = 3.407 \text{ mol C}$$

$$\text{Moles H} = (4.58 \text{ g H})\left(\frac{1 \text{ mol H}}{1.008 \text{ g H}}\right) = 4.54 \text{ mol H}$$

$$\text{Moles O} = (54.50 \text{ g O})\left(\frac{1 \text{ mol O}}{16.00 \text{ g O}}\right) = 3.406 \text{ mol O}$$

Third, we determine the simplest whole-number ratio of moles by dividing each number of moles by the smallest number of moles, 3.406:

$$\text{C:} \frac{3.407}{3.406} = 1.000 \qquad \text{H:} \frac{4.54}{3.406} = 1.33 \qquad \text{O:} \frac{3.406}{3.406} = 1.000$$

The ratio for H is too far from 1 to attribute the difference to experimental error; in fact, it is quite close to $1\frac{1}{3}$. This suggests that if we multiply the ratio by 3, we will obtain whole numbers:

$$\text{C:H:O} = 3(1\text{:}1.33\text{:}1) = 3\text{:}4\text{:}3$$

The whole-number mole ratio gives us the subscripts for the empirical formula:

$$C_3H_4O_3$$

Check It is reassuring that the subscripts are moderately sized whole numbers. Otherwise, we have little by which to judge the reasonableness of our answer.

■ **PRACTICE EXERCISE**

A 5.325-g sample of methyl benzoate, a compound used in the manufacture of perfumes, contains 3.758 g of carbon, 0.316 g of hydrogen, and 1.251 g of oxygen. What is the empirical formula of this substance?
Answer: C_4H_4O

Molecular Formula from Empirical Formula

For any compound, the formula obtained from percentage compositions is always the empirical formula. We can obtain the molecular formula from the empirical formula if we are given the molecular weight or molar mass of the compound. *The subscripts in the molecular formula of a substance are always a whole-number multiple of the corresponding subscripts in its empirical formula.* ∞ (Section 2.6) This multiple can be found by comparing the empirical formula weight with the molecular weight:

$$\text{Whole-number multiple} = \frac{\text{molecular weight}}{\text{empirical formula weight}} \qquad \text{[3.11]}$$

In Sample Exercise 3.13, for example, the empirical formula of ascorbic acid was determined to be $C_3H_4O_3$, giving an empirical formula weight of 3(12.0 amu) + 4(1.0 amu) + 3(16.0 amu) = 88.0 amu. The experimentally determined molecular weight is 176 amu. Thus, the molecular weight is 2 times the empirical formula weight (176/88.0 = 2.00), and the molecular formula must therefore have twice as many of each kind of atom as the empirical formula. Consequently, we multiply the subscripts in the empirical formula by 2 to obtain the molecular formula: $C_6H_8O_6$.

■ **SAMPLE EXERCISE 3.14** | **Determining a Molecular Formula**

Mesitylene, a hydrocarbon that occurs in small amounts in crude oil, has an empirical formula of C_3H_4. The experimentally determined molecular weight of this substance is 121 amu. What is the molecular formula of mesitylene?

SOLUTION

Analyze We are given an empirical formula and a molecular weight and asked to determine a molecular formula.

Plan The subscripts in the molecular formula of a compound are whole-number multiples of the subscripts in its empirical formula. To find the appropriate multiple, we must compare the molecular weight with the formula weight of the empirical formula.

Solve First, we calculate the formula weight of the empirical formula, C_3H_4:

$$3(12.0 \text{ amu}) + 4(1.0 \text{ amu}) = 40.0 \text{ amu}$$

Next, we divide the molecular weight by the empirical formula weight to obtain the multiple used to multiply the subscripts in C_3H_4:

$$\frac{\text{Molecular weight}}{\text{Empirical formula weight}} = \frac{121}{40.0} = 3.02$$

Only whole-number ratios make physical sense because we must be dealing with whole atoms. The 3.02 in this case could result from a small experimental error in the molecular weight. We therefore multiply each subscript in the empirical formula by 3 to give the molecular formula: C_9H_{12}.

Check We can have confidence in the result because dividing the molecular weight by the formula weight yields nearly a whole number.

■ PRACTICE EXERCISE

Ethylene glycol, the substance used in automobile antifreeze, is composed of 38.7% C, 9.7% H, and 51.6% O by mass. Its molar mass is 62.1 g/mol. **(a)** What is the empirical formula of ethylene glycol? **(b)** What is its molecular formula?
Answers: **(a)** CH_3O, **(b)** $C_2H_6O_2$

Combustion Analysis

The empirical formula of a compound is based on experiments that give the number of moles of each element in a sample of the compound. The word "empirical" means "based on observation and experiment." Chemists have devised a number of experimental techniques to determine empirical formulas. One technique is combustion analysis, which is commonly used for compounds containing principally carbon and hydrogen as their component elements.

When a compound containing carbon and hydrogen is completely combusted in an apparatus such as that shown in Figure 3.12▶, the carbon in the compound is converted to CO_2, and the hydrogen is converted to H_2O. ∞ (Section 3.2) The amounts of CO_2 and H_2O produced are determined by measuring the mass increase in the CO_2 and H_2O absorbers. From the masses of CO_2 and H_2O we can calculate the number of moles of C and H in the original compound and thereby the empirical formula. If a third element is present in the compound, its mass can be determined by subtracting the masses of C and H from the compound's original mass. Sample Exercise 3.15 shows how to determine the empirical formula of a compound containing C, H, and O.

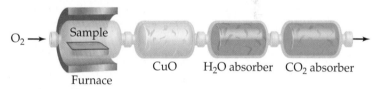

▲ Figure 3.12 **Apparatus to determine percentages of carbon and hydrogen in a compound.** The compound is combusted to form CO_2 and H_2O. Copper oxide helps to oxidize traces of carbon and carbon monoxide to carbon dioxide and to oxidize hydrogen to water.

■ SAMPLE EXERCISE 3.15 | Determining Empirical Formula by Combustion Analysis

Isopropyl alcohol, a substance sold as rubbing alcohol, is composed of C, H, and O. Combustion of 0.255 g of isopropyl alcohol produces 0.561 g of CO_2 and 0.306 g of H_2O. Determine the empirical formula of isopropyl alcohol.

SOLUTION

Analyze We are told that isopropyl alcohol contains C, H, and O atoms and given the quantities of CO_2 and H_2O produced when a given quantity of the alcohol is combusted. We must use this information to determine the empirical formula for isopropyl alcohol, a task that requires us to calculate the number of moles of C, H, and O in the sample.

Plan We can use the mole concept to calculate the number of grams of C present in the CO_2 and the number of grams of H present in the H_2O. These amounts are the quantities of C and H present in the isopropyl alcohol before combustion. The number of grams of O in the compound equals the mass of the isopropyl alcohol minus the sum of the C and H masses. Once we have the number of grams of C, H, and O in the sample, we can then proceed as in Sample Exercise 3.13. We can calculate the number of moles of each element, and determine the mole ratio, which gives the subscripts in the empirical formula.

Solve To calculate the number of grams of C, we first use the molar mass of CO_2, 1 mol CO_2 = 44.0 g CO_2, to convert grams of CO_2 to moles of CO_2. Because each CO_2 molecule has only 1 C atom, there is 1 mol of C atoms per mole of CO_2 molecules. This fact allows us to convert the moles of CO_2 to moles of C. Finally, we use the molar mass of C, 1 mol C = 12.0 g C, to convert moles of C to grams of C. Combining the three conversion factors, we have

$$\text{Grams C} = (0.561 \text{ g } CO_2)\left(\frac{1 \text{ mol } CO_2}{44.0 \text{ g } CO_2}\right)\left(\frac{1 \text{ mol C}}{1 \text{ mol } CO_2}\right)\left(\frac{12.0 \text{ g C}}{1 \text{ mol C}}\right) = 0.153 \text{ g C}$$

The calculation of the number of grams of H from the grams of H_2O is similar, although we must remember that there are 2 mol of H atoms per 1 mol of H_2O molecules:

$$\text{Grams H} = (0.306 \text{ g } H_2O)\left(\frac{1 \text{ mol } H_2O}{18.0 \text{ g } H_2O}\right)\left(\frac{2 \text{ mol H}}{1 \text{ mol } H_2O}\right)\left(\frac{1.01 \text{ g H}}{1 \text{ mol H}}\right) = 0.0343 \text{ g H}$$

The total mass of the sample, 0.255 g, is the sum of the masses of the C, H, and O. Thus, we can calculate the mass of O as follows:

$$\text{Mass of O} = \text{mass of sample} - (\text{mass of C} + \text{mass of H})$$
$$= 0.255 \text{ g} - (0.153 \text{ g} + 0.0343 \text{ g}) = 0.068 \text{ g O}$$

We then calculate the number of moles of C, H, and O in the sample:

$$\text{Moles C} = (0.153 \text{ g C})\left(\frac{1 \text{ mol C}}{12.0 \text{ g C}}\right) = 0.0128 \text{ mol C}$$

$$\text{Moles H} = (0.0343 \text{ g H})\left(\frac{1 \text{ mol H}}{1.01 \text{ g H}}\right) = 0.0340 \text{ mol H}$$

$$\text{Moles O} = (0.068 \text{ g O})\left(\frac{1 \text{ mol O}}{16.0 \text{ g O}}\right) = 0.0043 \text{ mol O}$$

To find the empirical formula, we must compare the relative number of moles of each element in the sample. The relative number of moles of each element is found by dividing each number by the smallest number, 0.0043. The mole ratio of C:H:O so obtained is 2.98:7.91:1.00. The first two numbers are very close to the whole numbers 3 and 8, giving the empirical formula C_3H_8O.

Check The subscripts work out to be moderately sized whole numbers, as expected.

■ **PRACTICE EXERCISE**

(a) Caproic acid, which is responsible for the foul odor of dirty socks, is composed of C, H, and O atoms. Combustion of a 0.225-g sample of this compound produces 0.512 g CO_2 and 0.209 g H_2O. What is the empirical formula of caproic acid? **(b)** Caproic acid has a molar mass of 116 g/mol. What is its molecular formula?
Answers: **(a)** C_3H_6O, **(b)** $C_6H_{12}O_2$

▲ **GIVE IT SOME THOUGHT**

In Sample Exercise 3.15, how do you explain the fact that the ratios C:H:O are 2.98:7.91:1.00, rather than exact integers 3:8:1?

3.6 QUANTITATIVE INFORMATION FROM BALANCED EQUATIONS

The coefficients in a chemical equation represent the relative numbers of molecules in a reaction. The mole concept allows us to convert this information to the masses of the substances. Consider the following balanced equation:

$$2 H_2(g) + O_2(g) \longrightarrow 2 H_2O(l) \qquad [3.12]$$

The coefficients indicate that two molecules of H_2 react with each molecule of O_2 to form two molecules of H_2O. It follows that the relative numbers of moles are identical to the relative numbers of molecules:

$2 H_2(g)$	+	$O_2(g)$	$\longrightarrow$	$2 H_2O(l)$
2 molecules		1 molecule		2 molecules
$2(6.02 \times 10^{23}$ molecules)		$1(6.02 \times 10^{23}$ molecules)		$2(6.02 \times 10^{23}$ molecules)
2 mol		1 mol		2 mol

We can generalize this observation for all balanced chemical equations: *The co-efficients in a balanced chemical equation indicate both the relative numbers of mole-cules (or formula units) in the reaction and the relative numbers of moles.* Table 3.3▼ further summarizes this result and shows how it corresponds to the law of con-servation of mass. Notice that the total mass of the reactants (4.0 g + 32.0 g) equals the total mass of the products (36.0 g).

TABLE 3.3 ■ Information from a Balanced Equation

Equation:	$2 H_2(g)$	$+$	$O_2(g)$	$\longrightarrow$	$2 H_2O(l)$
Molecules:	2 molecules H_2	$+$	1 molecule O_2	$\longrightarrow$	2 molecules H_2O
Mass (amu):	4.0 amu H_2	$+$	32.0 amu O_2	$\longrightarrow$	36.0 amu H_2O
Amount (mol):	2 mol H_2	$+$	1 mol O_2	$\longrightarrow$	2 mol H_2O
Mass (g):	4.0 g H_2	$+$	32.0 g O_2	$\longrightarrow$	36.0 g H_2O

The quantities 2 mol H_2, 1 mol O_2, and 2 mol H_2O, which are given by the coefficients in Equation 3.12, are called *stoichiometrically equivalent quantities.* The relationship between these quantities can be represented as

$$2 \text{ mol } H_2 \simeq 1 \text{ mol } O_2 \simeq 2 \text{ mol } H_2O$$

where the $\simeq$ symbol means "is stoichiometrically equivalent to." In other words, Equation 3.12 shows 2 mol of H_2 and 1 mol of O_2 forming 2 mol of H_2O. These stoichiometric relations can be used to convert between quantities of re-actants and products in a chemical reaction. For example, the number of moles of H_2O produced from 1.57 mol of O_2 can be calculated as follows:

$$\text{Moles } H_2O = (1.57 \text{ mol } O_2)\left(\frac{2 \text{ mol } H_2O}{1 \text{ mol } O_2}\right) = 3.14 \text{ mol } H_2O$$

▲ **GIVE IT SOME THOUGHT**

When 1.57 mol O_2 reacts with H_2 to form H_2O, how many moles of H_2 are consumed in the process?

As an additional example, consider the combustion of butane (C_4H_{10}), the fuel in disposable cigarette lighters:

$$2 C_4H_{10}(l) + 13 O_2(g) \longrightarrow 8 CO_2(g) + 10 H_2O(g) \qquad \text{[3.13]}$$

Let's calculate the mass of CO_2 produced when 1.00 g of C_4H_{10} is burned. The coefficients in Equation 3.13 tell how the amount of C_4H_{10} consumed is related to the amount of CO_2 produced: 2 mol $C_4H_{10} \simeq 8$ mol CO_2. To use this relation-ship we must use the molar mass of C_4H_{10} to convert grams of C_4H_{10} to moles of C_4H_{10}. Because 1 mol $C_4H_{10} = 58.0$ g C_4H_{10}, we have

$$\text{Moles } C_4H_{10} = (1.00 \text{ g } C_4H_{10})\left(\frac{1 \text{ mol } C_4H_{10}}{58.0 \text{ g } C_4H_{10}}\right)$$
$$= 1.72 \times 10^{-2} \text{ mol } C_4H_{10}$$

We can then use the stoichiometric factor from the balanced equation, 2 mol $C_4H_{10} \simeq 8$ mol CO_2, to calculate moles of CO_2:

$$\text{Moles } CO_2 = (1.72 \times 10^{-2} \text{ mol } C_4H_{10})\left(\frac{8 \text{ mol } CO_2}{2 \text{ mol } C_4H_{10}}\right)$$
$$= 6.88 \times 10^{-2} \text{ mol } CO_2$$

Finally, we can calculate the mass of the CO_2, in grams, using the molar mass of CO_2 (1 mol CO_2 = 44.0 g CO_2):

$$\text{Grams } CO_2 = (6.88 \times 10^{-2} \text{ mol } CO_2)\left(\frac{44.0 \text{ g } CO_2}{1 \text{ mol } CO_2}\right)$$

$$= 3.03 \text{ g } CO_2$$

Thus, the conversion sequence is

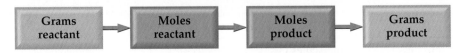

These steps can be combined in a single sequence of factors:

$$\text{Grams } CO_2 = (1.00 \text{ g } C_4H_{10})\left(\frac{1 \text{ mol } C_4H_{10}}{58.0 \text{ g } C_4H_{10}}\right)\left(\frac{8 \text{ mol } CO_2}{2 \text{ mol } C_4H_{10}}\right)\left(\frac{44.0 \text{ g } CO_2}{1 \text{ mol } CO_2}\right)$$

$$= 3.03 \text{ g } CO_2$$

Similarly, we can calculate the amount of O_2 consumed or H_2O produced in this reaction. For example, to calculate the amount of O_2 consumed, we again rely on the coefficients in the balanced equation to give us the appropriate stoichiometric factor: 2 mol $C_4H_{10} \approx 13$ mol O_2:

$$\text{Grams } O_2 = (1.00 \text{ g } C_4H_{10})\left(\frac{1 \text{ mol } C_4H_{10}}{58.0 \text{ g } C_4H_{10}}\right)\left(\frac{13 \text{ mol } O_2}{2 \text{ mol } C_4H_{10}}\right)\left(\frac{32.0 \text{ g } O_2}{1 \text{ mol } O_2}\right)$$

$$= 3.59 \text{ g } O_2$$

Figure 3.13 ▼ summarizes the general approach used to calculate the quantities of substances consumed or produced in chemical reactions. The balanced chemical equation provides the relative numbers of moles of reactants and products in the reaction.

▶ **Figure 3.13 The procedure for calculating amounts of reactants or products in a reaction.** The number of grams of a reactant consumed or of a product formed in a reaction can be calculated, starting with the number of grams of one of the other reactants or products. Notice how molar masses and the coefficients in the balanced equation are used.

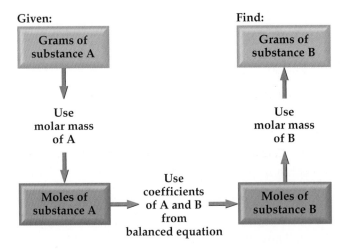

GIVE IT SOME THOUGHT

If 20.00 g of a compound reacts completely with 30.00 g of another compound in a combination reaction, how many grams of product were formed?

■■ **SAMPLE EXERCISE 3.16** | Calculating Amounts of Reactants and Products

How many grams of water are produced in the oxidation of 1.00 g of glucose, $C_6H_{12}O_6$?

$$C_6H_{12}O_6(s) + 6\,O_2(g) \longrightarrow 6\,CO_2(g) + 6\,H_2O(l)$$

SOLUTION

Analyze We are given the mass of a reactant and are asked to determine the mass of a product in the given equation.

Plan The general strategy, as outlined in Figure 3.13, requires three steps. First, the amount of $C_6H_{12}O_6$ must be converted from grams to moles. Second, we can use the balanced equation, which relates the moles of $C_6H_{12}O_6$ to the moles of H_2O: 1 mol $C_6H_{12}O_6 \cong 6$ mol H_2O. Third, we must convert the moles of H_2O to grams.

Solve First, use the molar mass of $C_6H_{12}O_6$ to convert from grams $C_6H_{12}O_6$ to moles $C_6H_{12}O_6$:

$$\text{Moles } C_6H_{12}O_6 = (1.00 \text{ g } C_6H_{12}O_6)\left(\frac{1 \text{ mol } C_6H_{12}O_6}{180.0 \text{ g } C_6H_{12}O_6}\right)$$

Second, use the balanced equation to convert moles of $C_6H_{12}O_6$ to moles of H_2O:

$$\text{Moles } H_2O = (1.00 \text{ g } C_6H_{12}O_6)\left(\frac{1 \text{ mol } C_6H_{12}O_6}{180.0 \text{ g } C_6H_{12}O_6}\right)\left(\frac{6 \text{ mol } H_2O}{1 \text{ mol } C_6H_{12}O_6}\right)$$

Third, use the molar mass of H_2O to convert from moles of H_2O to grams of H_2O:

$$\text{Grams } H_2O = (1.00 \text{ g } C_6H_{12}O_6)\left(\frac{1 \text{ mol } C_6H_{12}O_6}{180.0 \text{ g } C_6H_{12}O_6}\right)\left(\frac{6 \text{ mol } H_2O}{1 \text{ mol } C_6H_{12}O_6}\right)\left(\frac{18.0 \text{ g } H_2O}{1 \text{ mol } H_2O}\right)$$
$$= 0.600 \text{ g } H_2O$$

The steps can be summarized in a diagram like that in Figure 3.13:

Check An estimate of the magnitude of our answer, $18/180 = 0.1$ and $0.1 \times 6 = 0.6$, agrees with the exact calculation. The units, grams H_2O, are correct. The initial data had three significant figures, so three significant figures for the answer is correct.

Comment An average person ingests 2 L of water daily and eliminates 2.4 L. The difference between 2 L and 2.4 L is produced in the metabolism of foodstuffs, such as in the oxidation of glucose. (*Metabolism* is a general term used to describe all the chemical processes of a living animal or plant.) The desert rat (kangaroo rat), on the other hand, apparently never drinks water. It survives on its metabolic water.

▬▬ **PRACTICE EXERCISE**

The decomposition of $KClO_3$ is commonly used to prepare small amounts of O_2 in the laboratory: $2 KClO_3(s) \longrightarrow 2 KCl(s) + 3 O_2(g)$. How many grams of O_2 can be prepared from 4.50 g of $KClO_3$?
Answer: 1.77 g

▬▬ **SAMPLE EXERCISE 3.17** | **Calculating Amounts of Reactants and Products**

Solid lithium hydroxide is used in space vehicles to remove the carbon dioxide exhaled by astronauts. The lithium hydroxide reacts with gaseous carbon dioxide to form solid lithium carbonate and liquid water. How many grams of carbon dioxide can be absorbed by 1.00 g of lithium hydroxide?

SOLUTION

Analyze We are given a verbal description of a reaction and asked to calculate the number of grams of one reactant that reacts with 1.00 g of another.

Plan The verbal description of the reaction can be used to write a balanced equation:

$$2 LiOH(s) + CO_2(g) \longrightarrow Li_2CO_3(s) + H_2O(l)$$

We are given the grams of LiOH and asked to calculate grams of CO_2. We can accomplish this task by using the following sequence of conversions:

$$\text{Grams LiOH} \longrightarrow \text{moles LiOH} \longrightarrow \text{moles } CO_2 \longrightarrow \text{grams } CO_2$$

The conversion from grams of LiOH to moles of LiOH requires the molar mass of LiOH ($6.94 + 16.00 + 1.01 = 23.95$ g/mol). The conversion of moles of LiOH to moles of CO_2 is based on the balanced chemical equation: 2 mol LiOH $\cong$ 1 mol CO_2. To convert the number of moles of CO_2 to grams, we must use the molar mass of CO_2: $12.01 + 2(16.00) = 44.01$ g/mol.

Solve

$$(1.00\text{ g LiOH})\left(\frac{1\text{ mol LiOH}}{23.95\text{ g LiOH}}\right)\left(\frac{1\text{ mol CO}_2}{2\text{ mol LiOH}}\right)\left(\frac{44.01\text{ g CO}_2}{1\text{ mol CO}_2}\right) = 0.919\text{ g CO}_2$$

Check Notice that $23.95 \approx 24$, $24 \times 2 = 48$, and $44/48$ is slightly less than 1. The magnitude of the answer is reasonable based on the amount of starting LiOH; the significant figures and units are appropriate, too.

■ PRACTICE EXERCISE

Propane, C_3H_8, is a common fuel used for cooking and home heating. What mass of O_2 is consumed in the combustion of 1.00 g of propane?
Answer: 3.64 g

Chemistry and Life   GLUCOSE MONITORING

Over 20 million Americans have diabetes. In the world, the number approaches 172 million. Diabetes is a disorder of metabolism in which the body cannot produce or properly use the hormone insulin. One signal that a person is diabetic is that the concentration of glucose in her or his blood is higher than normal. Therefore, people who are diabetic need to measure their blood glucose concentrations regularly. Untreated diabetes can cause severe complications such as blindness and loss of limbs.

How does insulin relate to glucose? The body converts most of the food we eat into glucose. After digestion, glucose is delivered to cells via the bloodstream; cells need glucose to live. Insulin must be present for glucose to enter the cells. Normally, the body adjusts the concentration of insulin automatically, in concert with the glucose concentration after eating. However, in a diabetic person, little or no insulin is produced (Type 1 diabetes), or the cells cannot take up insulin properly (Type 2 diabetes). The result is that the blood glucose concentration is too high. People normally have a range of 70–120 mg glucose per deciliter of blood (about 4–6 mmol glucose per liter of blood). If a person has not eaten for 8 hours or more, he or she would be diagnosed as diabetic if the glucose levels were 126 mg/dL or higher. In the United States, diabetics monitor their blood glucose concentrations in mg/dL; in Europe, they use different units—millimoles glucose per liter of blood.

Glucose monitors work by the introduction of blood from a person, usually by a prick of the finger, onto a small strip of paper that contains numerous chemicals that react specifically with glucose. Insertion of the strip into a small battery-operated reader gives the glucose concentration (Figure 3.14 ▼). The actual mechanism of the readout varies for different devices—it may be a small electrical current or a measure of light produced in a chemical reaction. Depending on the result, a diabetic person may need to receive an injection of insulin or simply stop eating sweets for a while.

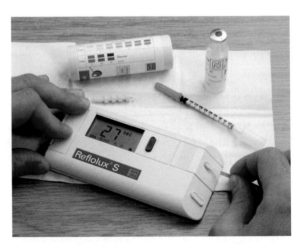

▲ Figure 3.14 **Glucose meter.** This is an example of a commercial glucose meter and its readout.

3.7 LIMITING REACTANTS

Suppose you wish to make several sandwiches using one slice of cheese and two slices of bread for each sandwich. Using Bd = bread, Ch = cheese, and Bd_2Ch = sandwich, the recipe for making a sandwich can be represented like a chemical equation:

$$2\text{ Bd} + \text{Ch} \longrightarrow \text{Bd}_2\text{Ch}$$

If you have 10 slices of bread and 7 slices of cheese, you will be able to make only five sandwiches before you run out of bread. You will have 2 slices of cheese left over. The amount of available bread limits the number of sandwiches.

An analogous situation occurs in chemical reactions when one of the reactants is used up before the others. The reaction stops as soon as any one of the reactants is totally consumed, leaving the excess reactants as leftovers.

Suppose, for example, that we have a mixture of 10 mol H_2 and 7 mol O_2, which react to form water:

$$2\,H_2(g) + O_2(g) \longrightarrow 2\,H_2O(g)$$

Because 2 mol $H_2 \simeq$ 1 mol O_2, the number of moles of O_2 needed to react with all the H_2 is

$$\text{Moles } O_2 = (10\ \cancel{\text{mol } H_2})\left(\frac{1\ \text{mol } O_2}{2\ \cancel{\text{mol } H_2}}\right) = 5\ \text{mol } O_2$$

Because 7 mol O_2 was available at the start of the reaction, 7 mol $O_2 - $ 5 mol O_2 = 2 mol O_2 will still be present when all the H_2 is consumed. The example we have considered is depicted on a molecular level in Figure 3.15▶.

The reactant that is completely consumed in a reaction is called either the **limiting reactant** or *limiting reagent* because it determines, or limits, the amount of product formed. The other reactants are sometimes called either *excess reactants* or *excess reagents*. In our example, H_2 is the limiting reactant, which means that once all the H_2 has been consumed, the reaction stops. O_2 is the excess reactant, and some is left over when the reaction stops.

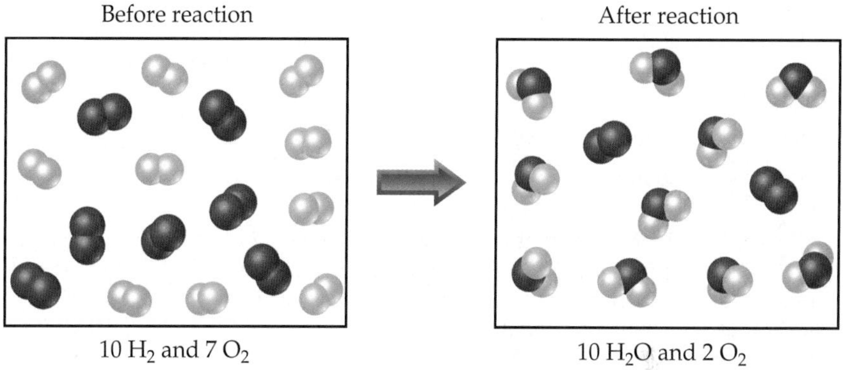

There are no restrictions on the starting amounts of the reactants in any reaction. Indeed, many reactions are carried out using an excess of one reagent. The quantities of reactants consumed and the quantities of products formed, however, are restricted by the quantity of the limiting reactant. When a combustion reaction takes place in the open air, oxygen is plentiful and is therefore the excess reactant. You may have had the unfortunate experience of running out of gasoline while driving. The car stops because you have run out of the limiting reactant in the combustion reaction, the fuel.

Before we leave our present example, let's summarize the data in a tabular form:

Before reaction

10 H_2 and 7 O_2

After reaction

10 H_2O and 2 O_2

▲ Figure 3.15 **Example illustrating a limiting reactant.** Because the H_2 is completely consumed, it is the limiting reagent in this case. Because there is a stoichiometric excess of O_2, some is left over at the end of the reaction. The amount of H_2O formed is related directly to the amount of H_2 consumed.

	$2\,H_2(g)$	$+$	$O_2(g)$	$\longrightarrow$	$2\,H_2O(g)$
Initial quantities:	10 mol		7 mol		0 mol
Change (reaction):	−10 mol		−5 mol		+10 mol
Final quantities:	0 mol		2 mol		10 mol

The initial amounts of the reactants are what we started with (10 mol H_2 and 7 mol O_2). The second line in the table (change) summarizes the amounts of the reactants consumed and the amount of the product formed in the reaction. These quantities are restricted by the quantity of the limiting reactant and depend on the coefficients in the balanced equation. The mole ratio H_2: O_2: H_2O = 10:5:10 conforms to the ratio of the coefficients in the balanced equation, 2:1:2. The changes are negative for the reactants because they are consumed during the reaction and positive for the product because it is formed during the reaction. Finally, the quantities in the third line of the table (final quantities) depend on the initial quantities and their changes, and these entries are found by adding the entries for the initial quantity and change for each column. No amount of the limiting reactant (H_2) remains at the end of the reaction. All that remains is 2 mol O_2 and 10 mol H_2O.

■ SAMPLE EXERCISE 3.18 | Calculating the Amount of Product Formed from a Limiting Reactant

The most important commercial process for converting N_2 from the air into nitrogen-containing compounds is based on the reaction of N_2 and H_2 to form ammonia (NH_3):

$$N_2(g) + 3 H_2(g) \longrightarrow 2 NH_3(g)$$

How many moles of NH_3 can be formed from 3.0 mol of N_2 and 6.0 mol of H_2?

SOLUTION

Analyze We are asked to calculate the number of moles of product, NH_3, given the quantities of each reactant, N_2 and H_2, available in a reaction. Thus, this is a limiting reactant problem.

Plan If we assume that one reactant is completely consumed, we can calculate how much of the second reactant is needed in the reaction. By comparing the calculated quantity with the available amount, we can determine which reactant is limiting. We then proceed with the calculation, using the quantity of the limiting reactant.

Solve The number of moles of H_2 needed for complete consumption of 3.0 mol of N_2 is:

$$\text{Moles } H_2 = (3.0 \text{ mol } N_2)\left(\frac{3 \text{ mol } H_2}{1 \text{ mol } N_2}\right) = 9.0 \text{ mol } H_2$$

Because only 6.0 mol H_2 is available, we will run out of H_2 before the N_2 is gone, and H_2 will be the limiting reactant. We use the quantity of the limiting reactant, H_2, to calculate the quantity of NH_3 produced:

$$\text{Moles } NH_3 = (6.0 \text{ mol } H_2)\left(\frac{2 \text{ mol } NH_3}{3 \text{ mol } H_2}\right) = 4.0 \text{ mol } NH_3$$

Comment The table on the right summarizes this example:

	$N_2(g)$ +	$3 H_2(g)$ $\longrightarrow$	$2 NH_3(g)$
Initial quantities:	3.0 mol	6.0 mol	0 mol
Change (reaction):	−2.0 mol	−6.0 mol	+4.0 mol
Final quantities:	1.0 mol	0 mol	4.0 mol

Notice that we can calculate not only the number of moles of NH_3 formed but also the number of moles of each of the reactants remaining after the reaction. Notice also that although the number of moles of H_2 present at the beginning of the reaction is greater than the number of moles of N_2 present, the H_2 is nevertheless the limiting reactant because of its larger coefficient in the balanced equation.

Check The summarizing table shows that the mole ratio of reactants used and product formed conforms to the coefficients in the balanced equation, 1:3:2. Also, because H_2 is the limiting reactant, it is completely consumed in the reaction, leaving 0 mol at the end. Because 6.0 mol H_2 has two significant figures, our answer has two significant figures.

■ PRACTICE EXERCISE

Consider the reaction $2 Al(s) + 3 Cl_2(g) \longrightarrow 2 AlCl_3(s)$. A mixture of 1.50 mol of Al and 3.00 mol of Cl_2 is allowed to react. **(a)** Which is the limiting reactant? **(b)** How many moles of $AlCl_3$ are formed? **(c)** How many moles of the excess reactant remain at the end of the reaction?
Answers: **(a)** Al, **(b)** 1.50 mol, **(c)** 0.75 mol Cl_2

■ SAMPLE EXERCISE 3.19 | Calculating the Amount of Product Formed from a Limiting Reactant

Consider the following reaction that occurs in a fuel cell:

$$2 H_2(g) + O_2(g) \longrightarrow 2 H_2O(g)$$

This reaction, properly done, produces energy in the form of electricity and water. Suppose a fuel cell is set up with 150 g of hydrogen gas and 1500 grams of oxygen gas (each measurement is given with two significant figures). How many grams of water can be formed?

SOLUTION

Analyze We are asked to calculate the amount of a product, given the amounts of two reactants, so this is a limiting reactant problem.

Plan We must first identify the limiting reagent. To do so, we can calculate the number of moles of each reactant and compare their ratio with that required by the balanced

2. *Calculations in which you must show your work* Your instructor may present you with a numerical problem in which you are to show your work in arriving at a solution. In questions of this kind, you may receive partial credit even if you do not arrive at the correct answer, depending on whether the instructor can follow your line of reasoning. It is important, therefore, to be as neat and organized as you can be, given the pressures of exam taking. It is helpful in approaching such questions to take a few moments to think about the direction you are going to take in solving the problem. You may even want to write a few words or a diagram on the test paper to indicate your approach. Then write out your calculations as neatly as you can. Show the units for every number you write down, and use dimensional analysis as much as you can, showing how units cancel.

3. *Questions requiring drawings* Sometimes a test question will require you to draw a chemical structure, a diagram related to chemical bonding, or a figure showing some kind of chemical process. Questions of this kind will

come later in the course, but it is useful to talk about them here. (You should review this box before each exam you take, to remind yourself of good exam-taking practices.) Be sure to label your drawing as completely as possible.

4. *Other types of questions* Other exam questions you might encounter include true-false questions and ones in which you are given a list and asked to indicate which members of the list match some criterion given in the question. Often students answer such questions incorrectly because, in their haste, they misunderstand the nature of the question. Whatever the form of the question, ask yourself this: What is the instructor testing here? What material am I supposed to know that this question covers?

Finally, if you find that you simply do not understand how to arrive at a reasoned response to a question, do not linger over the question. Put a check next to it and go on to the next one. If time permits, you can come back to the unanswered questions, but lingering over a question when nothing is coming to mind is wasting time you may need to finish the exam.

■■ PRACTICE EXERCISE

Imagine that you are working on ways to improve the process by which iron ore containing Fe_2O_3 is converted into iron. In your tests you carry out the following reaction on a small scale:

$$Fe_2O_3(s) + 3\,CO(g) \longrightarrow 2\,Fe(s) + 3\,CO_2(g)$$

(a) If you start with 150 g of Fe_2O_3 as the limiting reagent, what is the theoretical yield of Fe? **(b)** If the actual yield of Fe in your test was 87.9 g, what was the percent yield? *Answers:* **(a)** 105 g Fe, **(b)** 83.7%

C H A P T E R   R E V I E W

SUMMARY AND KEY TERMS

Introduction and Section 3.1 The study of the quantitative relationships between chemical formulas and chemical equations is known as **stoichiometry**. One of the important concepts of stoichiometry is the law of conservation of mass, which states that the total mass of the products of a chemical reaction is the same as the total mass of the reactants. The same numbers of atoms of each type are present before and after a chemical reaction. A balanced **chemical equation** shows equal numbers of atoms of each element on each side of the equation. Equations are balanced by placing coefficients in front of the chemical formulas for the **reactants** and **products** of a reaction, *not* by changing the subscripts in chemical formulas.

Section 3.2 Among the reaction types described in this chapter are (1) **combination reactions**, in which two reactants combine to form one product; (2) **decomposition reactions**, in which a single reactant forms two or more products; and (3) **combustion reactions** in oxygen, in

which a hydrocarbon or related compound reacts with O_2 to form CO_2 and H_2O.

Section 3.3 Much quantitative information can be determined from chemical formulas and balanced chemical equations by using atomic weights. The **formula weight** of a compound equals the sum of the atomic weights of the atoms in its formula. If the formula is a molecular formula, the formula weight is also called the **molecular weight**. Atomic weights and formula weights can be used to determine the elemental composition of a compound.

Section 3.4 A **mole** of any substance is **Avogadro's number** (6.02×10^{23}) of formula units of that substance. The mass of a mole of atoms, molecules, or ions (the **molar mass**) equals the formula weight of that material expressed in grams. The mass of one molecule of H_2O, for example, is 18 amu, so the mass of 1 mol of H_2O is 18 g. That is, the molar mass of H_2O is 18 g/mol.

Section 3.5 The empirical formula of any substance can be determined from its percent composition by calculating the relative number of moles of each atom in 100 g of the substance. If the substance is molecular in nature, its molecular formula can be determined from the empirical formula if the molecular weight is also known.

Sections 3.6 and 3.7 The mole concept can be used to calculate the relative quantities of reactants and products in chemical reactions. The coefficients in a balanced equation give the relative numbers of moles of the reactants and products. To calculate the number of grams of a product from the number of grams of a reactant, first convert grams of reactant to moles of reactant. Then use the coefficients in the balanced equation to convert the number of moles of reactant to moles of product. Finally, convert moles of product to grams of product.

A **limiting reactant** is completely consumed in a reaction. When it is used up, the reaction stops, thus limiting the quantities of products formed. The **theoretical yield** of a reaction is the quantity of product calculated to form when all of the limiting reagent reacts. The actual yield of a reaction is always less than the theoretical yield. The **percent yield** compares the actual and theoretical yields.

KEY SKILLS

- Balance chemical equations.
- Calculate molecular weights.
- Convert grams to moles and moles to grams using molar masses.
- Convert number of molecules to moles and moles to number of molecules using Avogadro's number.
- Calculate the empirical and molecular formula of a compound from percentage composition and molecular weight.
- Calculate amounts, in grams or moles, of reactants and products for a reaction.
- Calculate the percent yield of a reaction.

KEY EQUATIONS

- $\% \text{ element} = \dfrac{\left(\begin{array}{c}\text{number of atoms}\\\text{of that element}\end{array}\right)\left(\begin{array}{c}\text{atomic weight}\\\text{of element}\end{array}\right)}{\text{formula weight of compound}} \times 100\%$ [3.10]

    This is the formula to calculate the mass percentage of each element in a compound. The sum of all the percentages of all the elements in a compound should add up to 100%.

- $\% \text{ yield} = \dfrac{(\text{actual yield})}{(\text{theoretical yield})} \times 100\%$ [3.14]

    This is the formula to calculate the percent yield of a reaction. The percent yield can never be more than 100%.

VISUALIZING CONCEPTS

3.1 The reaction between reactant A (blue spheres) and reactant B (red spheres) is shown in the following diagram:

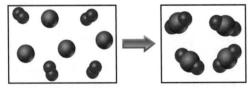

Based on this diagram, which equation best describes the reaction? [Section 3.1]

(a) $A_2 + B \longrightarrow A_2B$

(b) $A_2 + 4 B \longrightarrow 2 AB_2$

(c) $2 A + B_4 \longrightarrow 2 AB_2$

(d) $A + B_2 \longrightarrow AB_2$

3.2 Under appropriate experimental conditions, H_2 and CO undergo a combination reaction to form CH_3OH. The drawing below represents a sample of H_2. Make a corresponding drawing of the CO needed to react completely with the H_2. How did you arrive at the number of CO molecules in your drawing? [Section 3.2]

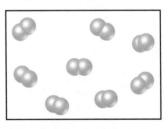

3.3 The following diagram represents the collection of elements formed by a decomposition reaction. **(a)** If the blue spheres represent N atoms and the red ones represent O atoms, what was the empirical formula of the original compound? **(b)** Could you draw a diagram representing the molecules of the compound that had been decomposed? Why or why not? [Section 3.2]

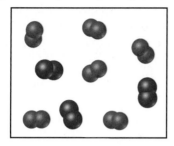

3.4 The following diagram represents the collection of CO_2 and H_2O molecules formed by complete combustion of a hydrocarbon. What is the empirical formula of the hydrocarbon? [Section 3.2]

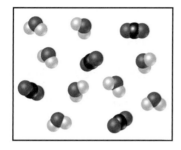

3.5 Glycine, an amino acid used by organisms to make proteins, is represented by the molecular model below.
(a) Write its molecular formula.
(b) Determine its molar mass.
(c) Calculate the mass of 3 moles of glycine.
(d) Calculate the percent nitrogen by mass in glycine. [Sections 3.3 and 3.5]

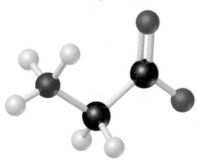

3.6 The following diagram represents a high-temperature reaction between CH_4 and H_2O. Based on this reaction,

how many moles of each product can be obtained starting with 4.0 mol CH_4? [Section 3.6]

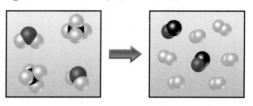

3.7 Nitrogen (N_2) and hydrogen (H_2) react to form ammonia (NH_3). Consider the mixture of N_2 and H_2 shown in the accompanying diagram. The blue spheres represent N, and the white ones represent H. Draw a representation of the product mixture, assuming that the reaction goes to completion. How did you arrive at your representation? What is the limiting reactant in this case? [Section 3.7]

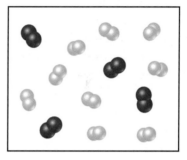

3.8 Nitrogen monoxide and oxygen react to form nitrogen dioxide. Consider the mixture of NO and O_2 shown in the accompanying diagram. The blue spheres represent N, and the red ones represent O. (a) Draw a representation of the product mixture, assuming that the reaction goes to completion. What is the limiting reactant in this case? (b) How many NO_2 molecules would you draw as products if the reaction had a percent yield of 75%? [Section 3.7]

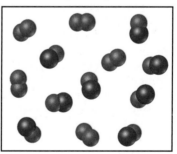

EXERCISES

Balancing Chemical Equations

3.9 (a) What scientific principle or law is used in the process of balancing chemical equations? (b) In balancing equations, why should you not change subscripts in chemical formulas? (c) How would one write out liquid water, water vapor, aqueous sodium chloride, and solid sodium chloride in chemical equations?

3.10 (a) What is the difference between adding a subscript 2 to the end of the formula for CO to give CO_2 and adding a coefficient in front of the formula to give 2 CO?

(b) Is the following chemical equation, as written, consistent with the law of conservation of mass?

$$3 \, Mg(OH)_2 \, (s) + 2 \, H_3PO_4(aq) \longrightarrow Mg_3(PO_4)_2(s) + 6 \, H_2O(l)$$

Why or why not?

3.11 Balance the following equations:
(a) $CO(g) + O_2(g) \longrightarrow CO_2(g)$
(b) $N_2O_5(g) + H_2O(l) \longrightarrow HNO_3(aq)$
(c) $CH_4(g) + Cl_2(g) \longrightarrow CCl_4(l) + HCl(g)$

(d) $Al_4C_3(s) + H_2O(l) \longrightarrow Al(OH)_3(s) + CH_4(g)$

(e) $C_5H_{10}O_2(l) + O_2(g) \longrightarrow CO_2(g) + H_2O(g)$

(f) $Fe(OH)_3(s) + H_2SO_4(aq) \longrightarrow$
$$Fe_2(SO_4)_3(aq) + H_2O(l)$$

(g) $Mg_3N_2(s) + H_2SO_4(aq) \longrightarrow$
$$MgSO_4(aq) + (NH_4)_2SO_4(aq)$$

3.12 Balance the following equations:

(a) $Li(s) + N_2(g) \longrightarrow Li_3N(s)$

(b) $La_2O_3(s) + H_2O(l) \longrightarrow La(OH)_3(aq)$

(c) $NH_4NO_3(s) \longrightarrow N_2(g) + O_2(g) + H_2O(g)$

(d) $Ca_3P_2(s) + H_2O(l) \longrightarrow Ca(OH)_2(aq) + PH_3(g)$

(e) $Ca(OH)_2(aq) + H_3PO_4(aq) \longrightarrow$
$$Ca_3(PO_4)_2(s) + H_2O(l)$$

(f) $AgNO_3(aq) + Na_2SO_4(aq) \longrightarrow$
$$Ag_2SO_4(s) + NaNO_3(aq)$$

(g) $CH_3NH_2(g) + O_2(g) \longrightarrow$
$$CO_2(g) + H_2O(g) + N_2(g)$$

3.13 Write balanced chemical equations to correspond to each of the following descriptions: **(a)** Solid calcium carbide, CaC_2, reacts with water to form an aqueous solution of calcium hydroxide and acetylene gas, C_2H_2. **(b)** When solid potassium chlorate is heated, it decomposes to form solid potassium chloride and oxygen gas. **(c)** Solid zinc metal reacts with sulfuric acid to form hydrogen gas and an aqueous solution of zinc sulfate. **(d)** When liquid phosphorus trichloride is added to water, it reacts to form aqueous phosphorous acid, $H_3PO_3(aq)$, and aqueous hydrochloric acid. **(e)** When hydrogen sulfide gas is passed over solid hot iron(III) hydroxide, the resultant reaction produces solid iron(III) sulfide and gaseous water.

3.14 Write balanced chemical equations to correspond to each of the following descriptions: **(a)** When sulfur trioxide gas reacts with water, a solution of sulfuric acid forms. **(b)** Boron sulfide, $B_2S_3(s)$, reacts violently with water to form dissolved boric acid, H_3BO_3, and hydrogen sulfide gas. **(c)** When an aqueous solution of lead(II) nitrate is mixed with an aqueous solution of sodium iodide, an aqueous solution of sodium nitrate and a yellow solid, lead iodide, are formed. **(d)** When solid mercury(II) nitrate is heated, it decomposes to form solid mercury(II) oxide, gaseous nitrogen dioxide, and oxygen. **(e)** Copper metal reacts with hot concentrated sulfuric acid solution to form aqueous copper(II) sulfate, sulfur dioxide gas, and water.

Patterns of Chemical Reactivity

3.15 **(a)** When the metallic element sodium combines with the nonmetallic element bromine, $Br_2(l)$, how can you determine the chemical formula of the product? How do you know whether the product is a solid, liquid, or gas at room temperature? Write the balanced chemical equation for the reaction. **(b)** When a hydrocarbon burns in air, what reactant besides the hydrocarbon is involved in the reaction? What products are formed? Write a balanced chemical equation for the combustion of benzene, $C_6H_6(l)$, in air.

3.16 **(a)** Determine the chemical formula of the product formed when the metallic element calcium combines with the nonmetallic element oxygen, O_2. Write the balanced chemical equation for the reaction. **(b)** What products form when a compound containing C, H, and O is completely combusted in air? Write a balanced chemical equation for the combustion of acetone, $C_3H_6O(l)$, in air.

3.17 Write a balanced chemical equation for the reaction that occurs when **(a)** Mg(s) reacts with $Cl_2(g)$; **(b)** barium carbonate decomposes into barium oxide and carbon dioxide gas when heated; **(c)** the hydrocarbon styrene, $C_8H_8(l)$, is combusted in air; **(d)** dimethylether, $CH_3OCH_3(g)$, is combusted in air.

3.18 Write a balanced chemical equation for the reaction that occurs when **(a)** aluminum metal undergoes a combination reaction with $O_2(g)$; **(b)** copper(II) hydroxide decomposes into copper(II) oxide and water when heated; **(c)** heptane, $C_7H_{16}(l)$, burns in air; **(d)** the gasoline additive MTBE (methyl tert-butyl ether), $C_5H_{12}O(l)$, burns in air.

3.19 Balance the following equations, and indicate whether they are combination, decomposition, or combustion reactions:

(a) $Al(s) + Cl_2(g) \longrightarrow AlCl_3(s)$

(b) $C_2H_4(g) + O_2(g) \longrightarrow CO_2(g) + H_2O(g)$

(c) $Li(s) + N_2(g) \longrightarrow Li_3N(s)$

(d) $PbCO_3(s) \longrightarrow PbO(s) + CO_2(g)$

(e) $C_7H_8O_2(l) + O_2(g) \longrightarrow CO_2(g) + H_2O(g)$

3.20 Balance the following equations, and indicate whether they are combination, decomposition, or combustion reactions:

(a) $C_3H_6(g) + O_2(g) \longrightarrow CO_2(g) + H_2O(g)$

(b) $NH_4NO_3(s) \longrightarrow N_2O(g) + H_2O(g)$

(c) $C_5H_6O(l) + O_2(g) \longrightarrow CO_2(g) + H_2O(g)$

(d) $N_2(g) + H_2(g) \longrightarrow NH_3(g)$

(e) $K_2O(s) + H_2O(l) \longrightarrow KOH(aq)$

Formula Weights

3.21 Determine the formula weights of each of the following compounds: **(a)** nitric acid, HNO_3; **(b)** $KMnO_4$; **(c)** $Ca_3(PO_4)_2$; **(d)** quartz, SiO_2; **(e)** gallium sulfide, **(f)** chromium(III) sulfate, **(g)** phosphorus trichloride.

3.22 Determine the formula weights of each of the following compounds: **(a)** nitrous oxide, N_2O, known as laughing gas and used as an anesthetic in dentistry; **(b)** benzoic acid, $HC_7H_5O_2$, a substance used as a food preservative; **(c)** $Mg(OH)_2$, the active ingredient in milk of magnesia; **(d)** urea, $(NH_2)_2CO$, a compound used as a nitrogen fertilizer; **(e)** isopentyl acetate, $CH_3CO_2C_5H_{11}$, responsible for the odor of bananas.

WHAT'S AHEAD

THE WATERS OF THE PACIFIC OCEAN, seen in this chapter-opening photograph of the California coast, are part of the World Ocean that covers almost two-thirds of our planet. Water has been the key to much of Earth's evolutionary history. Life itself almost certainly originated in water, and the

need for water by all forms of life has helped determine diverse biological structures. Your own body is about 60% water by mass. We will see repeatedly throughout this text that water possesses many unusual properties essential to supporting life on Earth.

The waters of the World Ocean may not appear to be any different from those of Lake Tahoe or the water that flows from your kitchen faucet, but a taste of seawater is all it takes to demonstrate that there is an important difference. Water has an exceptional ability to dissolve a wide variety of substances. Water on Earth—whether it is drinking water from the tap, water from a clear mountain stream, or seawater—invariably contains a variety of dissolved substances. A solution in which water is the dissolving medium is called an **aqueous solution**. Seawater is different from what we call "freshwater" because it has a much higher total concentration of dissolved ionic substances.

Water is the medium for most of the chemical reactions that take place within us and around us. Nutrients dissolved in blood are carried to our cells, where they enter into reactions that help keep us alive. Automobile parts rust

▲ **Figure 4.1 Limestone cave.** When CO_2 dissolves in water, the resulting solution is slightly acidic. Limestone caves are formed by the dissolving action of this acidic solution acting on $CaCO_3$ in the limestone.

when they come into frequent contact with aqueous solutions that contain various dissolved substances. Spectacular limestone caves (Figure 4.1 ◄) are formed by the dissolving action of underground water containing carbon dioxide, $CO_2(aq)$:

$$CaCO_3(s) + H_2O(l) + CO_2(aq) \longrightarrow Ca(HCO_3)_2(aq) \qquad [4.1]$$

In Chapter 3 we saw a few simple types of chemical reactions and their descriptions. In this chapter we continue to examine chemical reactions by focusing on aqueous solutions. A great deal of important chemistry occurs in aqueous solutions, so we need to learn the vocabulary and concepts used to describe and understand this chemistry. In addition, we will extend the concepts of stoichiometry that we learned in Chapter 3 by considering how solution concentrations are expressed and used.

4.1 GENERAL PROPERTIES OF AQUEOUS SOLUTIONS

Recall that a *solution* is a homogeneous mixture of two or more substances. ∞ (Section 1.2) The substance present in the greatest quantity is usually called the **solvent**. The other substances in the solution are called the **solutes**; they are said to be dissolved in the solvent. When a small amount of sodium chloride (NaCl) is dissolved in a large quantity of water, for example, the water is the solvent and the sodium chloride is the solute.

Electrolytic Properties

Imagine preparing two aqueous solutions—one by dissolving a teaspoon of table salt (sodium chloride) in a cup of water and the other by dissolving a teaspoon of table sugar (sucrose) in a cup of water. Both solutions are clear and colorless. How do they differ? One way, which might not be immediately obvious, is in their electrical conductivity: The salt solution is a good conductor of electricity; the sugar solution is not.

Whether a solution conducts electricity can be determined by using a device such as that shown in Figure 4.2 ▶. To light the bulb, an electric current must flow between the two electrodes that are immersed in the solution. Although water itself is a poor conductor of electricity, the presence of ions causes aqueous solutions to become good conductors. Ions carry electrical charge from one electrode to the other, completing the electrical circuit. Thus, the conductivity of NaCl solutions indicates the presence of ions in the solution. The lack of conductivity of sucrose solutions indicates the absence of ions. When NaCl dissolves in water, the solution contains Na^+ and Cl^- ions, each surrounded by water molecules. When sucrose ($C_{12}H_{22}O_{11}$) dissolves in water, the solution contains only neutral sucrose molecules surrounded by water molecules.

A substance (such as NaCl) whose aqueous solutions contain ions is called an **electrolyte**. A substance (such as $C_{12}H_{22}O_{11}$) that does not form ions in solution is called a **nonelectrolyte**. The difference between NaCl and $C_{12}H_{22}O_{11}$ arises largely because NaCl is ionic, whereas $C_{12}H_{22}O_{11}$ is molecular.

Ionic Compounds in Water

Recall from Section 2.7 and especially Figure 2.23 that solid NaCl consists of an orderly arrangement of Na^+ and Cl^- ions. When NaCl dissolves in water, each ion separates from the solid structure and disperses throughout the solution, as shown in Figure 4.3(a) ▶. The ionic solid *dissociates* into its component ions as it dissolves.

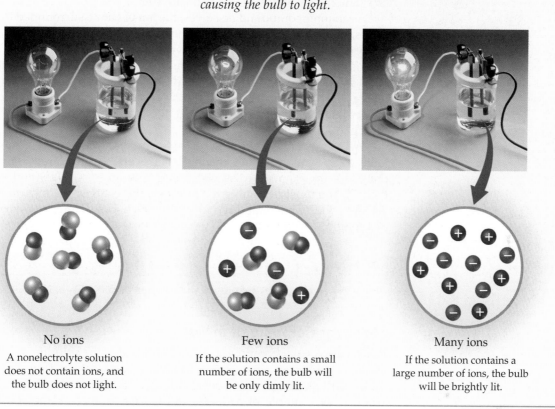

ELECTROLYTIC PROPERTIES

One way to differentiate two aqueous solutions is to employ a device that measures their electrical conductivities. The ability of a solution to conduct electricity depends on the number of ions it contains. An electrolyte solution contains ions that serve as charge carriers, causing the bulb to light.

No ions

A nonelectrolyte solution does not contain ions, and the bulb does not light.

Few ions

If the solution contains a small number of ions, the bulb will be only dimly lit.

Many ions

If the solution contains a large number of ions, the bulb will be brightly lit.

▲ Figure 4.2 **Measuring ion concentrations using conductivity.**

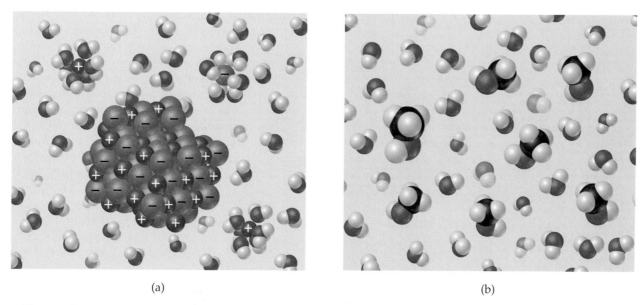

(a)   (b)

▲ Figure 4.3 **Dissolution in water.** (a) When an ionic compound dissolves in water, H_2O molecules separate, surround, and disperse the ions into the liquid. (b) Methanol, CH_3OH, a molecular compound, dissolves without forming ions. The methanol molecules contain black spheres, which represent carbon atoms. In both parts (a) and (b) the water molecules have been moved apart so that the solute particles can be seen more clearly.

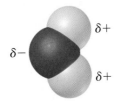

Water is a very effective solvent for ionic compounds. Although water is an electrically neutral molecule, one end of the molecule (the O atom) is rich in electrons and has a partial negative charge, denoted by $\delta-$. The other end (the H atoms) has a partial positive charge, denoted by $\delta+$ as shown in the margin. Positive ions (cations) are attracted by the negative end of H_2O, and negative ions (anions) are attracted by the positive end.

As an ionic compound dissolves, the ions become surrounded by H_2O molecules, as shown in Figure 4.3(a). The ions are said to be solvated. We denote these ions in chemical equations by writing them as $Na^+(aq)$ and $Cl^-(aq)$, where "aq" is an abbreviation for "aqueous." ∞ (Section 3.1) The **solvation** process helps stabilize the ions in solution and prevents cations and anions from recombining. Furthermore, because the ions and their shells of surrounding water molecules are free to move about, the ions become dispersed uniformly throughout the solution.

We can usually predict the nature of the ions present in a solution of an ionic compound from the chemical name of the substance. Sodium sulfate (Na_2SO_4), for example, dissociates into sodium ions (Na^+) and sulfate ions (SO_4^{2-}). You must remember the formulas and charges of common ions (Tables 2.4 and 2.5) to understand the forms in which ionic compounds exist in aqueous solution.

GIVE IT SOME THOUGHT

What dissolved species are present in a solution of **(a)** KCN, **(b)** $NaClO_4$?

Molecular Compounds in Water

When a molecular compound dissolves in water, the solution usually consists of intact molecules dispersed throughout the solution. Consequently, most molecular compounds are nonelectrolytes. As we have seen, table sugar (sucrose) is an example of a nonelectrolyte. As another example, a solution of methanol (CH_3OH) in water consists entirely of CH_3OH molecules dispersed throughout the water [Figure 4.3(b)].

A few molecular substances, however, have aqueous solutions that contain ions. Acids are the most important of these solutions. For example, when $HCl(g)$ dissolves in water to form hydrochloric acid, $HCl(aq)$, it *ionizes*; that is, it dissociates into $H^+(aq)$ and $Cl^-(aq)$ ions.

Strong and Weak Electrolytes

Two categories of electrolytes—strong and weak—differ in the extent to which they conduct electricity. **Strong electrolytes** are those solutes that exist in solution completely or nearly completely as ions. Essentially all soluble ionic compounds (such as NaCl) and a few molecular compounds (such as HCl) are strong electrolytes. **Weak electrolytes** are those solutes that exist in solution mostly in the form of molecules with only a small fraction in the form of ions. For example, in a solution of acetic acid (CH_3COOH) most of the solute is present as $CH_3COOH(aq)$ molecules. Only a small fraction (about 1%) of the CH_3COOH is present as $H^+(aq)$ and $CH_3COO^-(aq)$ ions.*

We must be careful not to confuse the extent to which an electrolyte dissolves with whether it is strong or weak. For example, CH_3COOH is extremely soluble in water but is a weak electrolyte. $Ba(OH)_2$, on the other hand, is not very soluble, but the amount of the substance that does dissolve dissociates almost completely. Thus, $Ba(OH)_2$ is a strong electrolyte.

*The chemical formula of acetic acid is sometimes written as $HC_2H_3O_2$ with the acidic H written in front of the chemical formula, so the formula looks like that of other common acids such as HCl. The formula CH_3COOH conforms to the molecular structure of acetic acid, with the acidic H on the O atom at the end of the formula.

When a weak electrolyte such as acetic acid ionizes in solution, we write the reaction in the following manner:

$$CH_3COOH(aq) \rightleftharpoons CH_3COO^-(aq) + H^+(aq) \qquad [4.2]$$

The half-arrows in both directions mean that the reaction is significant in both directions. At any given moment some CH_3COOH molecules are ionizing to form H^+ and CH_3COO^- ions. At the same time, H^+ and CH_3COO^- ions are recombining to form CH_3COOH. The balance between these opposing processes determines the relative numbers of ions and neutral molecules. This balance produces a state of **chemical equilibrium** in which the relative numbers of each type of ion or molecule in the reaction are constant over time. This equilibrium condition varies from one weak electrolyte to another. Chemical equilibria are extremely important. We will devote Chapters 15–17 to examining them in detail.

Chemists use half-arrows in both directions to represent the ionization of weak electrolytes and a single arrow to represent the ionization of strong electrolytes. Because HCl is a strong electrolyte, we write the equation for the ionization of HCl as follows:

$$HCl(aq) \longrightarrow H^+(aq) + Cl^-(aq) \qquad [4.3]$$

The absence of a reverse arrow indicates that the H^+ and Cl^- ions have no tendency to recombine in water to form HCl molecules.

In the following sections we will look more closely at how we can use the composition of a compound to predict whether it is a strong electrolyte, weak electrolyte, or nonelectrolyte. For the moment, you need only to remember that *soluble ionic compounds are strong electrolytes.* We identify ionic compounds as those composed of metals and nonmetals—such as NaCl, $FeSO_4$, and $Al(NO_3)_3$—or compounds containing the ammonium ion, NH_4^+—such as NH_4Br and $(NH_4)_2CO_3$.

GIVE IT SOME THOUGHT

Which solute will cause the lightbulb in the experiment shown in Figure 4.2 to glow more brightly, CH_3OH or $MgBr_2$?

■ **SAMPLE EXERCISE 4.1** | **Relating Relative Numbers of Anions and Cations to Chemical Formulas**

The diagram on the right represents an aqueous solution of one of the following compounds: $MgCl_2$, KCl, or K_2SO_4. Which solution does the drawing best represent?

SOLUTION

Analyze: We are asked to associate the charged spheres in the diagram with ions present in a solution of an ionic substance.

Plan: We examine the ionic substances given in the problem to determine the relative numbers and charges of the ions that each contains. We then correlate these charged ionic species with the ones shown in the diagram.

Solve: The diagram shows twice as many cations as anions, consistent with the formulation K_2SO_4.

Check: Notice that the total net charge in the diagram is zero, as it must be if it is to represent an ionic substance.

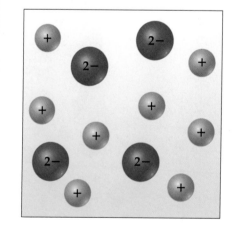

■ **PRACTICE EXERCISE**

If you were to draw diagrams (such as that shown on the right) representing aqueous solutions of each of the following ionic compounds, how many anions would you show if the diagram contained six cations? **(a)** $NiSO_4$, **(b)** $Ca(NO_3)_2$, **(c)** Na_3PO_4, **(d)** $Al_2(SO_4)_3$
Answers: **(a)** 6, **(b)** 12, **(c)** 2, **(d)** 9

4.2 PRECIPITATION REACTIONS

Figure 4.4▼ shows two clear solutions being mixed. One solution contains lead nitrate, $Pb(NO_3)_2$, and the other contains potassium iodide (KI). The reaction between these two solutes produces an insoluble yellow product. Reactions that result in the formation of an insoluble product are called **precipitation reactions**. A **precipitate** is an insoluble solid formed by a reaction in solution. In Figure 4.4 the precipitate is lead iodide (PbI_2), a compound that has a very low solubility in water:

$$Pb(NO_3)_2(aq) + 2\ KI(aq) \longrightarrow PbI_2(s) + 2\ KNO_3(aq) \qquad [4.4]$$

The other product of this reaction, potassium nitrate (KNO_3), remains in solution.

Precipitation reactions occur when certain pairs of oppositely charged ions attract each other so strongly that they form an insoluble ionic solid. To predict whether certain combinations of ions form insoluble compounds, we must consider some guidelines concerning the solubilities of common ionic compounds.

Solubility Guidelines for Ionic Compounds

The **solubility** of a substance at a given temperature is the amount of the substance that can be dissolved in a given quantity of solvent at the given temperature.

▼ Figure 4.4 **A precipitation reaction.**

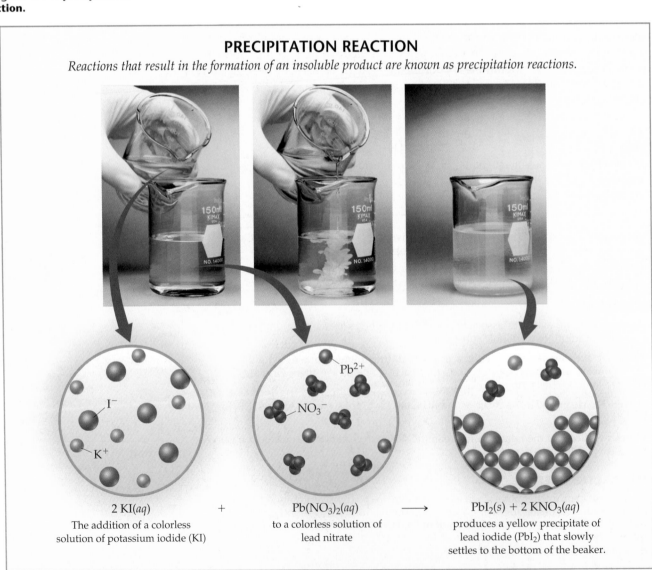

PRECIPITATION REACTION

Reactions that result in the formation of an insoluble product are known as precipitation reactions.

| 2 KI(aq) | + | Pb(NO₃)₂(aq) | ⟶ | PbI₂(s) + 2 KNO₃(aq) |

The addition of a colorless solution of potassium iodide (KI) to a colorless solution of lead nitrate produces a yellow precipitate of lead iodide (PbI₂) that slowly settles to the bottom of the beaker.

TABLE 4.1 ■ Solubility Guidelines for Common Ionic Compounds in Water

Soluble Ionic Compounds		Important Exceptions
Compounds containing	NO_3^-	None
	CH_3COO^-	None
	Cl^-	Compounds of Ag^+, Hg_2^{2+}, and Pb^{2+}
	Br^-	Compounds of Ag^+, Hg_2^{2+}, and Pb^{2+}
	I^-	Compounds of Ag^+, Hg_2^{2+}, and Pb^{2+}
	SO_4^{2-}	Compounds of Sr^{2+}, Ba^{2+}, Hg_2^{2+}, and Pb^{2+}

Insoluble Ionic Compounds		Important Exceptions
Compounds containing	S^{2-}	Compounds of NH_4^+, the alkali metal cations, and Ca^{2+}, Sr^{2+}, and Ba^{2+}
	CO_3^{2-}	Compounds of NH_4^+ and the alkali metal cations
	PO_4^{3-}	Compounds of NH_4^+ and the alkali metal cations
	OH^-	Compounds of the alkali metal cations, and NH_4^+, Ca^{2+}, Sr^{2+}, and Ba^{2+}

For instance, only 1.2×10^{-3} mol of PbI_2 dissolves in a liter of water at 25 °C. In our discussions, any substance with a solubility less than 0.01 mol/L will be referred to as *insoluble*. In those cases the attraction between the oppositely charged ions in the solid is too great for the water molecules to separate the ions to any significant extent; the substance remains largely undissolved.

Unfortunately, there are no rules based on simple physical properties such as ionic charge to guide us in predicting whether a particular ionic compound will be soluble. Experimental observations, however, have led to guidelines for predicting solubility for ionic compounds. For example, experiments show that all common ionic compounds that contain the nitrate anion, NO_3^-, are soluble in water. Table 4.1▲ summarizes the solubility guidelines for common ionic compounds. The table is organized according to the anion in the compound, but it also reveals many important facts about cations. Note that *all common ionic compounds of the alkali metal ions (group 1A of the periodic table) and of the ammonium ion (NH_4^+) are soluble in water.*

■ **SAMPLE EXERCISE 4.2** │ **Using Solubility Rules**

Classify the following ionic compounds as soluble or insoluble in water: **(a)** sodium carbonate (Na_2CO_3), **(b)** lead sulfate ($PbSO_4$).

SOLUTION

Analyze: We are given the names and formulas of two ionic compounds and asked to predict whether they are soluble or insoluble in water.

Plan: We can use Table 4.1 to answer the question. Thus, we need to focus on the anion in each compound because the table is organized by anions.

Solve:
(a) According to Table 4.1, most carbonates are insoluble. But carbonates of the alkali metal cations (such as sodium ion) are an exception to this rule and are soluble. Thus, Na_2CO_3 is soluble in water.
(b) Table 4.1 indicates that although most sulfates are water soluble, the sulfate of Pb^{2+} is an exception. Thus, $PbSO_4$ is insoluble in water.

■ **PRACTICE EXERCISE**

Classify the following compounds as soluble or insoluble in water: **(a)** cobalt(II) hydroxide, **(b)** barium nitrate, **(c)** ammonium phosphate.
Answers: **(a)** insoluble, **(b)** soluble, **(c)** soluble

To predict whether a precipitate forms when we mix aqueous solutions of two strong electrolytes, we must (1) note the ions present in the reactants, (2) consider the possible combinations of the cations and anions, and (3) use Table 4.1 to determine if any of these combinations is insoluble. For example, will a precipitate form when solutions of $Mg(NO_3)_2$ and NaOH are mixed? Both $Mg(NO_3)_2$ and NaOH are soluble ionic compounds and strong electrolytes. Mixing $Mg(NO_3)_2(aq)$ and $NaOH(aq)$ first produces a solution containing Mg^{2+}, NO_3^-, Na^+, and OH^- ions. Will either of the cations interact with either of the anions to form an insoluble compound? In addition to the reactants, the other possible interactions are Mg^{2+} with OH^- and Na^+ with NO_3^-. From Table 4.1 we see that hydroxides are generally insoluble. Because Mg^{2+} is not an exception, $Mg(OH)_2$ is insoluble and will thus form a precipitate. $NaNO_3$, however, is soluble, so Na^+ and NO_3^- will remain in solution. The balanced equation for the precipitation reaction is

$$Mg(NO_3)_2(aq) + 2\,NaOH(aq) \longrightarrow Mg(OH)_2(s) + 2\,NaNO_3(aq) \qquad [4.5]$$

Exchange (Metathesis) Reactions

Notice in Equation 4.5 that the cations in the two reactants exchange anions—Mg^{2+} ends up with OH^-, and Na^+ ends up with NO_3^-. The chemical formulas of the products are based on the charges of the ions—two OH^- ions are needed to give a neutral compound with Mg^{2+}, and one NO_3^- ion is needed to give a neutral compound with Na^+. ∞ (Section 2.7) The equation can be balanced only after the chemical formulas of the products have been determined.

Reactions in which positive ions and negative ions appear to exchange partners conform to the following general equation:

$$AX + BY \longrightarrow AY + BX \qquad [4.6]$$

Example: $AgNO_3(aq) + KCl(aq) \longrightarrow AgCl(s) + KNO_3(aq)$

Such reactions are called **exchange reactions**, or **metathesis reactions** (meh-TATH-eh-sis, which is the Greek word for "to transpose"). Precipitation reactions conform to this pattern, as do many acid–base reactions, as we will see in Section 4.3.

To complete and balance a metathesis equation, we follow these steps:

1. Use the chemical formulas of the reactants to determine the ions that are present.
2. Write the chemical formulas of the products by combining the cation from one reactant with the anion of the other. (Use the charges of the ions to determine the subscripts in the chemical formulas.)
3. Finally, balance the equation.

■■ SAMPLE EXERCISE 4.3 | Predicting a Metathesis Reaction

(a) Predict the identity of the precipitate that forms when solutions of $BaCl_2$ and K_2SO_4 are mixed.
(b) Write the balanced chemical equation for the reaction.

SOLUTION

Analyze: We are given two ionic reactants and asked to predict the insoluble product that they form.

Plan: We need to write down the ions present in the reactants and to exchange the anions between the two cations. Once we have written the chemical formulas for these products, we can use Table 4.1 to determine which is insoluble in water. Knowing the products also allows us to write the equation for the reaction.

Solve:
(a) The reactants contain Ba^{2+}, Cl^-, K^+, and SO_4^{2-} ions. If we exchange the anions, we will have $BaSO_4$ and KCl. According to Table 4.1, most compounds of SO_4^{2-} are soluble but those of Ba^{2+} are not. Thus, $BaSO_4$ is insoluble and will precipitate from solution. KCl, on the other hand, is soluble.

Your stomach secretes acids to help digest foods. These acids, which include hydrochloric acid, contain about 0.1 mol of H^+ per liter of solution. The stomach and digestive tract are normally protected from the corrosive effects of stomach acid by a mucosal lining. Holes can develop in this lining, however, allowing the acid to attack the underlying tissue, causing painful damage. These holes, known as ulcers, can be caused by the secretion of excess acids or by a weakness in the digestive lining. Studies indicate, however, that many ulcers are caused by bacterial infection. Between 10 and 20% of Americans suffer from ulcers at some point in their lives. Many others experience occasional indigestion or heartburn that is due to digestive acids entering the esophagus.

We can address the problem of excess stomach acid in two simple ways: (1) removing the excess acid, or (2) decreasing the production of acid. Those substances that remove excess acid are called *antacids*, whereas those that decrease the production of acid are called *acid inhibitors*. Figure 4.10▼ shows several common, over-the-counter antacids.

Antacids are simple bases that neutralize digestive acids. They are able to neutralize acids because they contain hydroxide, carbonate, or bicarbonate ions. Table 4.4 ◄ lists the active ingredients in some antacids.

The newer generation of antiulcer drugs, such as Tagamet® and Zantac®, are acid inhibitors. They act on acid-producing cells in the lining of the stomach. Formulations that control acid in this way are now available as over-the-counter drugs.

Related Exercise: 4.95

TABLE 4.4 ■ Some Common Antacids

Commercial Name	Acid-Neutralizing Agents
Alka-Seltzer®	$NaHCO_3$
Amphojel®	$Al(OH)_3$
Di-Gel®	$Mg(OH)_2$ and $CaCO_3$
Milk of Magnesia	$Mg(OH)_2$
Maalox®	$Mg(OH)_2$ and $Al(OH)_3$
Mylanta®	$Mg(OH)_2$ and $Al(OH)_3$
Rolaids®	$NaAl(OH)_2CO_3$
Tums®	$CaCO_3$

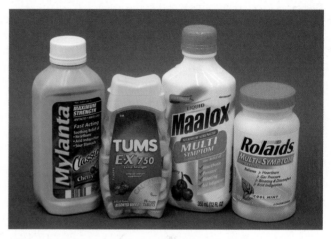

▲ Figure 4.10 **Antacids.** These products all serve as acid-neutralizing agents in the stomach.

Both $NaHCO_3$ and Na_2CO_3 are used as acid neutralizers in acid spills. The bicarbonate or carbonate salt is added until the fizzing due to the formation of $CO_2(g)$ stops. Sometimes sodium bicarbonate is used as an antacid to soothe an upset stomach. In that case the HCO_3^- reacts with stomach acid to form $CO_2(g)$. The fizz when Alka-Seltzer® tablets are added to water arises from the reaction of sodium bicarbonate and citric acid.

GIVE IT SOME THOUGHT

By analogy to examples already given in the text, predict what gas forms when $Na_2SO_3(s)$ is treated with HCl(*aq*).

4.4 OXIDATION-REDUCTION REACTIONS

In precipitation reactions, cations and anions come together to form an insoluble ionic compound. In neutralization reactions H^+ ions and OH^- ions come together to form H_2O molecules. Now let's consider a third important kind of reaction, one in which electrons are transferred between reactants. Such reactions are called **oxidation-reduction**, or *redox*, **reactions**.

▶ Figure 4.11 **Corrosion of iron.**
Corrosion of iron is caused by chemical
attack of oxygen and water on exposed
metal surfaces. Corrosion is even more
rapid in salt water.

Oxidation and Reduction

The corrosion of iron (rusting) and of other metals, such as the corrosion of the
terminals of an automobile battery, are familiar processes. What we call
corrosion is the conversion of a metal into a metal compound by a reaction between the metal and some substance in its environment. Rusting, as shown in
Figure 4.11 ▲, involves the reaction of oxygen with iron in the presence of water.

When a metal corrodes, it loses electrons and forms cations. Calcium, for
example, is vigorously attacked by acids to form calcium ions:

$$Ca(s) + 2\,H^+(aq) \longrightarrow Ca^{2+}(aq) + H_2(g) \qquad [4.23]$$

When an atom, ion, or molecule has become more positively charged (that is,
when it has lost electrons), we say that it has been oxidized. *Loss of electrons by a
substance is called* **oxidation.** Thus, Ca, which has no net charge, is *oxidized* (undergoes oxidation) in Equation 4.23, forming Ca^{2+}.

The term oxidation is used because the first reactions of this sort to be studied thoroughly were reactions with oxygen. Many metals react directly with O_2
in air to form metal oxides. In these reactions the metal loses electrons to oxygen, forming an ionic compound of the metal ion and oxide ion. For example,
when calcium metal is exposed to air, the bright metallic surface of the metal
tarnishes as CaO forms:

$$2\,Ca(s) + O_2(g) \longrightarrow 2\,CaO(s) \qquad [4.24]$$

As Ca is oxidized in Equation 4.24, oxygen is transformed from neutral
O_2 to two O^{2-} ions (Figure 4.12 ▼). When an atom, ion, or molecule has become more negatively charged (gained electrons), we say that it is *reduced*.

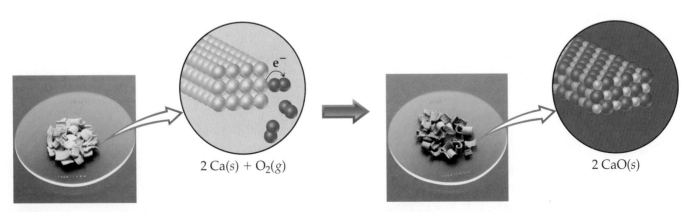

▲ Figure 4.12 **Oxidation of calcium metal by molecular oxygen.** The oxidation involves
transfer of electrons from the metal to O_2, eventually leading to formation of CaO.

TABLE 4.5 ■ Activity Series of Metals in Aqueous Solution

Metal	Oxidation Reaction
Lithium	$Li(s) \longrightarrow Li^+(aq) + e^-$
Potassium	$K(s) \longrightarrow K^+(aq) + e^-$
Barium	$Ba(s) \longrightarrow Ba^{2+}(aq) + 2e^-$
Calcium	$Ca(s) \longrightarrow Ca^{2+}(aq) + 2e^-$
Sodium	$Na(s) \longrightarrow Na^+(aq) + e^-$
Magnesium	$Mg(s) \longrightarrow Mg^{2+}(aq) + 2e^-$
Aluminum	$Al(s) \longrightarrow Al^{3+}(aq) + 3e^-$
Manganese	$Mn(s) \longrightarrow Mn^{2+}(aq) + 2e^-$
Zinc	$Zn(s) \longrightarrow Zn^{2+}(aq) + 2e^-$
Chromium	$Cr(s) \longrightarrow Cr^{3+}(aq) + 3e^-$
Iron	$Fe(s) \longrightarrow Fe^{2+}(aq) + 2e^-$
Cobalt	$Co(s) \longrightarrow Co^{2+}(aq) + 2e^-$
Nickel	$Ni(s) \longrightarrow Ni^{2+}(aq) + 2e^-$
Tin	$Sn(s) \longrightarrow Sn^{2+}(aq) + 2e^-$
Lead	$Pb(s) \longrightarrow Pb^{2+}(aq) + 2e^-$
Hydrogen	$H_2(g) \longrightarrow 2H^+(aq) + 2e^-$
Copper	$Cu(s) \longrightarrow Cu^{2+}(aq) + 2e^-$
Silver	$Ag(s) \longrightarrow Ag^+(aq) + e^-$
Mercury	$Hg(l) \longrightarrow Hg^{2+}(aq) + 2e^-$
Platinum	$Pt(s) \longrightarrow Pt^{2+}(aq) + 2e^-$
Gold	$Au(s) \longrightarrow Au^{3+}(aq) + 3e^-$

Ease of oxidation increases

Thus, copper metal will be oxidized by silver ions, as pictured in Figure 4.14 ▼:

$$Cu(s) + 2Ag^+(aq) \longrightarrow Cu^{2+}(aq) + 2Ag(s) \qquad [4.30]$$

The oxidation of copper to copper ions is accompanied by the reduction of silver ions to silver metal. The silver metal is evident on the surface of the copper wires in Figure 4.14(b) and 4.14(c). The copper(II) nitrate produces a blue color in the solution, which is most evident in part (c).

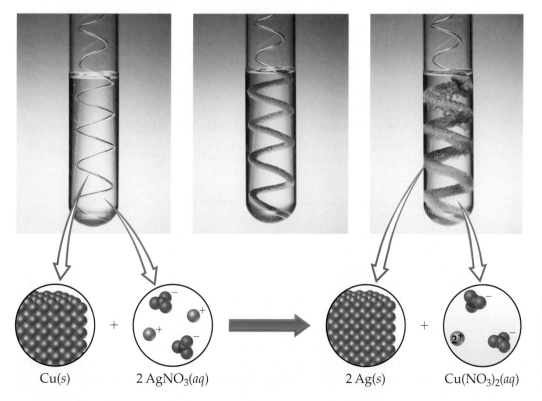

$Cu(s)$ $2 AgNO_3(aq)$ $2 Ag(s)$ $Cu(NO_3)_2(aq)$

◀ Figure 4.14 **Reaction of copper with silver ion.** When copper metal is placed in a solution of silver nitrate, a redox reaction occurs, forming silver metal and a blue solution of copper(II) nitrate.

▲ GIVE IT SOME THOUGHT

Which is the more easily reduced, $Mg^{2+}(aq)$ or $Ni^{2+}(aq)$?

Only those metals above hydrogen in the activity series are able to react with acids to form H_2. For example, Ni reacts with $HCl(aq)$ to form H_2:

$$Ni(s) + 2\,HCl(aq) \longrightarrow NiCl_2(aq) + H_2(g) \qquad [4.31]$$

Because elements below hydrogen in the activity series are not oxidized by H^+, Cu does not react with $HCl(aq)$. Interestingly, copper does react with nitric acid, as shown previously in Figure 1.11. This reaction, however, is not a simple oxidation of Cu by the H^+ ions of the acid. Instead, the metal is oxidized to Cu^{2+} by the nitrate ion of the acid, accompanied by the formation of brown nitrogen dioxide, $NO_2(g)$:

$$Cu(s) + 4\,HNO_3(aq) \longrightarrow Cu(NO_3)_2(aq) + 2\,H_2O(l) + 2\,NO_2(g) \qquad [4.32]$$

What substance is reduced as copper is oxidized in Equation 4.32? In this case the NO_2 results from the reduction of NO_3^-. We will examine reactions of this type in more detail in Chapter 20.

■ **SAMPLE EXERCISE 4.10** | **Determining When an Oxidation-Reduction Reaction Can Occur**

Will an aqueous solution of iron(II) chloride oxidize magnesium metal? If so, write the balanced molecular and net ionic equations for the reaction.

SOLUTION

Analyze: We are given two substances—an aqueous salt, $FeCl_2$, and a metal, Mg—and asked if they react with each other.

Plan: A reaction will occur if Mg is above Fe in the activity series, Table 4.5. If the reaction occurs, the Fe^{2+} ion in $FeCl_2$ will be reduced to Fe, and the elemental Mg will be oxidized to Mg^{2+}.

Solve: Because Mg is above Fe in the table, the reaction will occur. To write the formula for the salt that is produced in the reaction, we must remember the charges on common ions. Magnesium is always present in compounds as Mg^{2+}: the chloride ion is Cl^-. The magnesium salt formed in the reaction is $MgCl_2$, meaning the balanced molecular equation is

$$Mg(s) + FeCl_2(aq) \longrightarrow MgCl_2(aq) + Fe(s)$$

Both $FeCl_2$ and $MgCl_2$ are soluble strong electrolytes and can be written in ionic form. Cl^- then, is a spectator ion in the reaction. The net ionic equation is

$$Mg(s) + Fe^{2+}(aq) \longrightarrow Mg^{2+}(aq) + Fe(s)$$

The net ionic equation shows that Mg is oxidized and Fe^{2+} is reduced in this reaction.

Check: Note that the net ionic equation is balanced with respect to both charge and mass.

■ PRACTICE EXERCISE

Which of the following metals will be oxidized by $Pb(NO_3)_2$: Zn, Cu, Fe?
Answer: Zn and Fe

4.5 CONCENTRATIONS OF SOLUTIONS

The behavior of solutions often depends on the nature of the solutes and their concentrations. Scientists use the term **concentration** to designate the amount of solute dissolved in a given quantity of solvent or quantity of solution. The concept of concentration is intuitive: The greater the amount of solute dissolved in a certain amount of solvent, the more concentrated the resulting solution. In chemistry we often need to express the concentrations of solutions quantitatively.

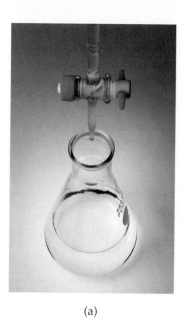

(a)   (b)   (c)

▲ **Figure 4.20 Change in appearance of a solution containing phenolphthalein indicator as base is added.**
Before the end point, the solution is colorless (a). As the end point is approached, a pale pink color forms where the
base is added (b). At the end point, this pale pink color extends throughout the solution after mixing. As even
more base is added, the intensity of the pink color increases (c).

For example, the dye known as phenolphthalein is colorless in acidic solution
but is pink in basic solution. If we add phenolphthalein to an unknown solution
of acid, the solution will be colorless, as seen in Figure 4.20(a) ▲. We can then add
standard base from a buret until the solution barely turns from colorless to pink,
as seen in Figure 4.20(b). This color change indicates that the acid has been neutralized and the drop of base that caused the solution to become colored has no
acid to react with. The solution therefore becomes basic, and the dye turns pink.
The color change signals the *end point* of the titration, which usually coincides
very nearly with the equivalence point. Care must be taken to choose indicators
whose end points correspond to the equivalence point of the titration. We will
consider this matter in Chapter 17. The titration procedure is summarized in
Figure 4.21 ▼.

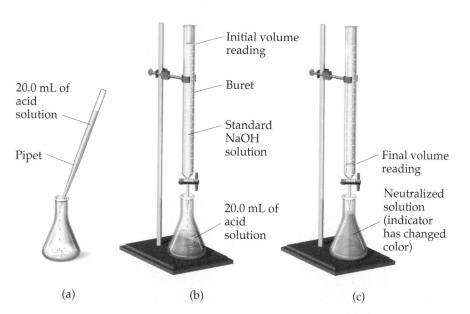

◀ **Figure 4.21 Procedure for
titrating an acid against a
standardized solution of NaOH.**
(a) A known quantity of acid is added
to a flask. (b) An acid–base indicator is
added, and standardized NaOH is
added from a buret. (c) The
equivalence point is signaled by a color
change in the indicator.

20.0 mL of
acid
solution

Pipet

Initial volume
reading

Buret

Standard
NaOH
solution

20.0 mL of
acid
solution

Final volume
reading

Neutralized
solution
(indicator
has changed
color)

(a)   (b)   (c)

■ **SAMPLE EXERCISE 4.16** | Determining the Quantity of Solute by Titration

The quantity of Cl^- in a municipal water supply is determined by titrating the sample with Ag^+. The reaction taking place during the titration is

$$Ag^+(aq) + Cl^-(aq) \longrightarrow AgCl(s)$$

The end point in this type of titration is marked by a change in color of a special type of indicator. **(a)** How many grams of chloride ion are in a sample of the water if 20.2 mL of 0.100 M Ag^+ is needed to react with all the chloride in the sample? **(b)** If the sample has a mass of 10.0 g, what percent Cl^- does it contain?

SOLUTION

Analyze: We are given the volume (20.2 mL) and molarity (0.100 M) of a solution of Ag^+ and the chemical equation for reaction of this ion with Cl^-. We are asked first to calculate the number of grams of Cl^- in the sample and, second, to calculate the mass percent of Cl^- in the sample.

(a) Plan: We begin by using the volume and molarity of Ag^+ to calculate the number of moles of Ag^+ used in the titration. We can then use the balanced equation to determine the moles of Cl^- in the sample and from that the grams of Cl^-.

Solve:

$$\text{moles Ag}^+ = (20.2 \text{ mL soln})\left(\frac{1 \text{ L soln}}{1000 \text{ mL soln}}\right)\left(0.100 \frac{\text{mol Ag}^+}{\text{L soln}}\right)$$

$$= 2.02 \times 10^{-3} \text{ mol Ag}^+$$

From the balanced equation we see that 1 mol $Ag^+ \simeq$ 1 mol Cl^-. Using this information and the molar mass of Cl, we have

$$\text{grams Cl}^- = (2.02 \times 10^{-3} \text{ mol Ag}^+)\left(\frac{1 \text{ mol Cl}^-}{1 \text{ mol Ag}^+}\right)\left(\frac{35.5 \text{ g Cl}^-}{1 \text{ mol Cl}^-}\right)$$

$$= 7.17 \times 10^{-2} \text{ g Cl}^-$$

(b) Plan: To calculate the percentage of Cl^- in the sample, we compare the number of grams of Cl^- in the sample, 7.17×10^{-2} g, with the original mass of the sample, 10.0 g.

Solve: $\text{Percent Cl}^- = \dfrac{7.17 \times 10^{-2} \text{ g}}{10.0 \text{ g}} \times 100\% = 0.717\% \text{ Cl}^-$

Comment: Chloride ion is one of the most common ions in water and sewage. Ocean water contains 1.92% Cl^-. Whether water containing Cl^- tastes salty depends on the other ions present. If the only accompanying ions are Na^+, a salty taste may be detected with as little as 0.03% Cl^-.

■ **PRACTICE EXERCISE**

A sample of an iron ore is dissolved in acid, and the iron is converted to Fe^{2+}. The sample is then titrated with 47.20 mL of 0.02240 M MnO_4^- solution. The oxidation-reduction reaction that occurs during titration is as follows:

$$MnO_4^-(aq) + 5 Fe^{2+}(aq) + 8 H^+(aq) \longrightarrow Mn^{2+}(aq) + 5 Fe^{3+}(aq) + 4 H_2O(l)$$

(a) How many moles of MnO_4^- were added to the solution? **(b)** How many moles of Fe^{2+} were in the sample? **(c)** How many grams of iron were in the sample? **(d)** If the sample had a mass of 0.8890 g, what is the percentage of iron in the sample? *Answers:* **(a)** 1.057×10^{-3} mol MnO_4^- **(b)** 5.286×10^{-3} mol Fe^{2+}, **(c)** 0.2952 g, **(d)** 33.21%

■ **SAMPLE EXERCISE 4.17** | Determining Solution Concentration Via an Acid–Base Titration

One commercial method used to peel potatoes is to soak them in a solution of NaOH for a short time, remove them from the NaOH, and spray off the peel. The concentration of NaOH is normally in the range of 3 to 6 M. The NaOH is analyzed periodically. In one such analysis, 45.7 mL of 0.500 M H_2SO_4 is required to neutralize a 20.0-mL sample of NaOH solution. What is the concentration of the NaOH solution?

SOLUTION

Analyze: We are given the volume (45.7 mL) and molarity (0.500 M) of an H_2SO_4 solution that reacts completely with a 20.0-mL sample of NaOH. We are asked to calculate the molarity of the NaOH solution.

Plan: We can use the volume and molarity of the H_2SO_4 to calculate the number of moles of this substance. Then, we can use this quantity and the balanced equation for the reaction to calculate the number of moles of NaOH. Finally, we can use the moles of NaOH and the volume of this solution to calculate molarity.

Solve: The number of moles of H_2SO_4 is given by the product of the volume and molarity of this solution:

$$\text{moles } H_2SO_4 = (45.7 \text{ mL soln})\left(\frac{1 \text{ L soln}}{1000 \text{ mL soln}}\right)\left(0.500 \frac{\text{mol } H_2SO_4}{\text{L soln}}\right)$$

$$= 2.28 \times 10^{-2} \text{ mol } H_2SO_4$$

Acids react with metal hydroxides to form water and a salt. Thus, the balanced equation for the neutralization reaction is

$$H_2SO_4(aq) + 2\,NaOH(aq) \longrightarrow 2\,H_2O(l) + Na_2SO_4(aq)$$

According to the balanced equation, 1 mol $H_2SO_4 \simeq 2$ mol NaOH. Therefore,

$$\text{moles NaOH} = (2.28 \times 10^{-2} \text{ mol } H_2SO_4)\left(\frac{2 \text{ mol NaOH}}{1 \text{ mol } H_2SO_4}\right)$$

$$= 4.56 \times 10^{-2} \text{ mol NaOH}$$

Knowing the number of moles of NaOH present in 20.0 mL of solution allows us to calculate the molarity of this solution:

$$\text{Molarity NaOH} = \frac{\text{mol NaOH}}{\text{L soln}} = \left(\frac{4.56 \times 10^{-2} \text{ mol NaOH}}{20.0 \text{ mL soln}}\right)\left(\frac{1000 \text{ mL soln}}{1 \text{ L soln}}\right)$$

$$= 2.28 \frac{\text{mol NaOH}}{\text{L soln}} = 2.28 \ M$$

▉ PRACTICE EXERCISE

What is the molarity of an NaOH solution if 48.0 mL is needed to neutralize 35.0 mL of 0.144 M H_2SO_4?
Answers: 0.210 M

▉ SAMPLE INTEGRATIVE EXERCISE │ Putting Concepts Together

Note: Integrative exercises require skills from earlier chapters as well as ones from the present chapter.

A sample of 70.5 mg of potassium phosphate is added to 15.0 mL of 0.050 M silver nitrate, resulting in the formation of a precipitate. **(a)** Write the molecular equation for the reaction. **(b)** What is the limiting reactant in the reaction? **(c)** Calculate the theoretical yield, in grams, of the precipitate that forms.

SOLUTION

(a) Potassium phosphate and silver nitrate are both ionic compounds. Potassium phosphate contains K^+ and PO_4^{3-} ions, so its chemical formula is K_3PO_4. Silver nitrate contains Ag^+ and NO_3^- ions, so its chemical formula is $AgNO_3$. Because both reactants are strong electrolytes, the solution contains K^+, PO_4^{3-}, Ag^+, and NO_3^- ions before the reaction occurs. According to the solubility guidelines in Table 4.1, Ag^+ and PO_4^{3-} form an insoluble compound, so Ag_3PO_4 will precipitate from the solution. In contrast, K^+ and NO_3^- will remain in solution because KNO_3 is water soluble. Thus, the balanced molecular equation for the reaction is

$$K_3PO_4(aq) + 3\,AgNO_3(aq) \longrightarrow Ag_3PO_4(s) + 3\,KNO_3(aq)$$

(b) To determine the limiting reactant, we must examine the number of moles of each reactant. ∞(Section 3.7) The number of moles of K_3PO_4 is calculated from the mass of the sample using the molar mass as a conversion factor. ∞(Section 3.4)

The molar mass of K_3PO_4 is $3(39.1) + 31.0 + 4(16.0) = 212.3$ g/mol. Converting milligrams to grams and then to moles, we have

$$(70.5 \text{ mg K}_3PO_4)\left(\frac{10^{-3} \text{ g K}_3PO_4}{1 \text{ mg K}_3PO_4}\right)\left(\frac{1 \text{ mol K}_3PO_4}{212.3 \text{ g K}_3PO_4}\right) = 3.32 \times 10^{-4} \text{ mol K}_3PO_4$$

We determine the number of moles of $AgNO_3$ from the volume and molarity of the solution. ∞ (Section 4.5) Converting milliliters to liters and then to moles, we have

$$(15.0 \text{ mL})\left(\frac{10^{-3} \text{ L}}{1 \text{ mL}}\right)\left(\frac{0.050 \text{ mol AgNO}_3}{\text{L}}\right) = 7.5 \times 10^{-4} \text{ mol AgNO}_3$$

Comparing the amounts of the two reactants, we find that there are $(7.5 \times 10^{-4})/(3.32 \times 10^{-4}) = 2.3$ times as many moles of $AgNO_3$ as there are moles of K_3PO_4. According to the balanced equation, however, 1 mol K_3PO_4 requires 3 mol of $AgNO_3$. Thus, there is insufficient $AgNO_3$ to consume the K_3PO_4, and $AgNO_3$ is the limiting reactant.

(c) The precipitate is Ag_3PO_4, whose molar mass is $3(107.9) + 31.0 + 4(16.0) = 418.7$ g/mol. To calculate the number of grams of Ag_3PO_4 that could be produced in this reaction (the theoretical yield), we use the number of moles of the limiting reactant, converting mol $AgNO_3 \Rightarrow$ mol $Ag_3PO_4 \Rightarrow$ g Ag_3PO_4. We use the coefficients in the balanced equation to convert moles of $AgNO_3$ to moles Ag_3PO_4, and we use the molar mass of Ag_3PO_4 to convert the number of moles of this substance to grams.

$$(7.5 \times 10^{-4} \text{ mol AgNO}_3)\left(\frac{1 \text{ mol Ag}_3PO_4}{3 \text{ mol AgNO}_3}\right)\left(\frac{418.7 \text{ g Ag}_3PO_4}{1 \text{ mol Ag}_3PO_4}\right) = 0.10 \text{ g Ag}_3PO_4$$

The answer has only two significant figures because the quantity of $AgNO_3$ is given to only two significant figures.

CHAPTER REVIEW

SUMMARY AND KEY TERMS

Introduction and Section 4.1 Solutions in which water is the dissolving medium are called **aqueous solutions**. The component of the solution that is in the greater quantity is the **solvent**. The other components are **solutes**.

Any substance whose aqueous solution contains ions is called an **electrolyte**. Any substance that forms a solution containing no ions is a **nonelectrolyte**. Electrolytes that are present in solution entirely as ions are **strong electrolytes**, whereas those that are present partly as ions and partly as molecules are **weak electrolytes**. Ionic compounds dissociate into ions when they dissolve, and they are strong electrolytes. The solubility of ionic substances is made possible by **solvation**, the interaction of ions with polar solvent molecules. Most molecular compounds are nonelectrolytes, although some are weak electrolytes, and a few are strong electrolytes. When representing the ionization of a weak electrolyte in solution, half-arrows in both directions are used, indicating that the forward and reverse reactions can achieve a chemical balance called a **chemical equilibrium**.

Section 4.2 Precipitation reactions are those in which an insoluble product, called a **precipitate**, forms. Solubility guidelines help determine whether or not an ionic compound will be soluble in water. (The **solubility** of a substance is the amount that dissolves in a given quantity of solvent.) Reactions such as precipitation reactions, in which cations and anions appear to exchange partners, are called **exchange reactions**, or **metathesis reactions**.

Chemical equations can be written to show whether dissolved substances are present in solution predominantly as ions or molecules. When the complete chemical formulas of all reactants and products are used, the equation is called a **molecular equation**. A **complete ionic equation** shows all dissolved strong electrolytes as their component ions. In a **net ionic equation**, those ions that go through the reaction unchanged (**spectator ions**) are omitted.

Section 4.3 Acids and bases are important electrolytes. **Acids** are proton donors; they increase the concentration of $H^+(aq)$ in aqueous solutions to which they are added.

Bases are proton acceptors; they increase the concentration of $OH^-(aq)$ in aqueous solutions. Those acids and bases that are strong electrolytes are called **strong acids** and **strong bases**, respectively. Those that are weak electrolytes are **weak acids** and **weak bases**. When solutions of acids and bases are mixed, a **neutralization reaction** results. The neutralization reaction between an acid and a metal hydroxide produces water and a **salt**. Gases can also be formed as a result of acid–base reactions. The reaction of a sulfide with an acid forms $H_2S(g)$; the reaction between a carbonate and an acid forms $CO_2(g)$.

Section 4.4 **Oxidation** is the loss of electrons by a substance, whereas **reduction** is the gain of electrons by a substance. **Oxidation numbers** keep track of electrons during chemical reactions and are assigned to atoms using specific rules. The oxidation of an element results in an increase in its oxidation number, whereas reduction is accompanied by a decrease in oxidation number. Oxidation is always accompanied by reduction, giving **oxidation-reduction**, or redox, **reactions**.

Many metals are oxidized by O_2, acids, and salts. The redox reactions between metals and acids and between metals and salts are called **displacement reactions**. The products of these displacement reactions are always an element (H_2 or a metal) and a salt. Comparing such reactions allows us to rank metals according to their ease of oxidation. A list of metals arranged in order of decreasing ease of oxidation is called an **activity series**. Any metal on the list can be oxidized by ions of metals (or H^+) below it in the series.

Section 4.5 The composition of a solution expresses the relative quantities of solvent and solutes that it contains. One of the common ways to express the **concentration** of a solute in a solution is in terms of molarity. The **molarity** of a solution is the number of moles of solute per liter of solution. Molarity makes it possible to interconvert solution volume and number of moles of solute. Solutions of known molarity can be formed either by weighing out the solute and diluting it to a known volume or by the **dilution** of a more concentrated solution of known concentration (a stock solution). Adding solvent to the solution (the process of dilution) decreases the concentration of the solute without changing the number of moles of solute in the solution ($M_{conc} \times V_{conc} = M_{dil} \times V_{dil}$).

Section 4.6 In the process called **titration**, we combine a solution of known concentration (a **standard solution**) with a solution of unknown concentration to determine the unknown concentration or the quantity of solute in the unknown. The point in the titration at which stoichiometrically equivalent quantities of reactants are brought together is called the **equivalence point**. An **indicator** can be used to show the end point of the titration, which coincides closely with the equivalence point.

KEY SKILLS

- Recognize compounds as acids or bases, and as strong, weak, or nonelectrolytes.

- Recognize reactions as acid–base, precipitation, metathesis, or redox.

- Be able to calculate moles or grams of substances in solution using molarity.

- Understand how to carry out a dilution to achieve a desired solution concentration.

- Understand how to perform and interpret the results of a titration.

KEY EQUATIONS

- $$\text{Molarity} = \frac{\text{moles solute}}{\text{volume of solution in liters}} \quad [4.33]$$

  Molarity is the most commonly used unit of concentration in chemistry.

- $$M_{conc} \times V_{conc} = M_{dil} \times V_{dil} \quad [4.35]$$

  When adding solvent to a concentrated solution to make a dilute solution, molarities and volumes of both concentrated and dilute solutions can be calculated if three of the quantities are known.

VISUALIZING CONCEPTS

4.1 Which of the following schematic drawings best describes a solution of Li_2SO_4 in water (water molecules not shown for simplicity)? [Section 4.1]

(a)

(b)

(c)

4.2 Methanol, CH_3OH, and hydrogen chloride, HCl, are both molecular substances, yet an aqueous solution of methanol does not conduct an electrical current, whereas a solution of HCl does conduct. Account for this difference. [Section 4.1]

4.3 Aqueous solutions of three different substances, AX, AY, and AZ, are represented by the three diagrams below. Identify each substance as a strong electrolyte, weak electrolyte, or nonelectrolyte. [Section 4.1]

AX

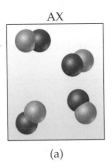
(a)

AY

(b)

AZ

(c)

4.4 A 0.1 M solution of acetic acid, CH_3COOH, causes the lightbulb in the apparatus of Figure 4.2 to glow about as brightly as a 0.001 M solution of HBr. How do you account for this fact? [Section 4.1]

4.5 You are presented with three white solids, A, B, and C, which are glucose (a sugar substance), NaOH, and AgBr. Solid A dissolves in water to form a conducting solution. B is not soluble in water. C dissolves in water to form a nonconducting solution. Identify A, B, and C. [Section 4.2]

4.6 We have seen that ions in aqueous solution are stabilized by the attractions between the ions and the water molecules. Why then do some pairs of ions in solution form precipitates? [Section 4.2]

4.7 Which of the following ions will *always* be a spectator ion in a precipitation reaction? **(a)** Cl^-, **(b)** NO_3^-, **(c)** NH_4^+, **(d)** S^{2-}, **(e)** SO_4^{2-}. Explain briefly. [Section 4.2]

4.8 The labels have fallen off two bottles, one containing $Mg(NO_3)_2$ and the other containing $Pb(NO_3)_2$. You have a bottle of dilute H_2SO_4. How could you use it to test a portion of each solution to identify which solution is which? [Section 4.2]

4.9 Explain how a redox reaction involves electrons in the same way that an acid–base reaction involves protons. [Sections 4.3 and 4.4]

4.10 If you want to double the concentration of a solution, how could you do it? [Section 4.5]

EXERCISES

Electrolytes

4.11 When asked what causes electrolyte solutions to conduct electricity, a student responds that it is due to the movement of electrons through the solution. Is the student correct? If not, what is the correct response?

4.12 When methanol, CH_3OH, is dissolved in water, a nonconducting solution results. When acetic acid, CH_3COOH, dissolves in water, the solution is weakly conducting and acidic in nature. Describe what happens upon dissolution in the two cases, and account for the different results.

4.13 We have learned in this chapter that many ionic solids dissolve in water as strong electrolytes, that is, as separated ions in solution. What properties of water facilitate this process?

4.14 What does it mean to say that ions are hydrated when an ionic substance dissolves in water?

4.15 Specify what ions are present in solution upon dissolving each of the following substances in water: **(a)** $ZnCl_2$, **(b)** HNO_3, **(c)** $(NH_4)_2SO_4$, **(d)** $Ca(OH)_2$.

4.16 Specify what ions are present upon dissolving each of the following substances in water: **(a)** MgI_2, **(b)** $Al(NO_3)_3$, **(c)** $HClO_4$, **(d)** $NaCH_3COO$.

4.17 Formic acid, HCOOH, is a weak electrolyte. What solute particles are present in an aqueous solution of this compound? Write the chemical equation for the ionization of HCOOH.

4.18 Acetone, CH_3COCH_3, is a nonelectrolyte; hypochlorous acid, HClO, is a weak electrolyte; and ammonium chloride, NH_4Cl, is a strong electrolyte. **(a)** What are the solute particles present in aqueous solutions of each compound? **(b)** If 0.1 mol of each compound is dissolved in solution, which one contains 0.2 mol of solute particles, which contains 0.1 mol of solute particles, and which contains somewhere between 0.1 and 0.2 mol of solute particles?

Precipitation Reactions and Net Ionic Equations

4.19 Using solubility guidelines, predict whether each of the following compounds is soluble or insoluble in water: **(a)** $NiCl_2$, **(b)** Ag_2S, **(c)** Cs_3PO_4, **(d)** $SrCO_3$, **(e)** $PbSO_4$.

4.20 Predict whether each of the following compounds is soluble in water: **(a)** $Ni(OH)_2$, **(b)** $PbBr_2$, **(c)** $Ba(NO_3)_2$, **(d)** $AlPO_4$, **(e)** $AgCH_3COO$.

4.21 Will precipitation occur when the following solutions are mixed? If so, write a balanced chemical equation for the reaction. **(a)** Na_2CO_3 and $AgNO_3$, **(b)** $NaNO_3$ and $NiSO_4$, **(c)** $FeSO_4$ and $Pb(NO_3)_2$.

4.22 Identify the precipitate (if any) that forms when the following solutions are mixed, and write a balanced equation for each reaction. **(a)** $Ni(NO_3)_2$ and $NaOH$, **(b)** $NaOH$ and K_2SO_4, **(c)** Na_2S and $Cu(CH_3COO)_2$.

4.23 Name the spectator ions in any reactions that may be involved when each of the following pairs of solutions are mixed.
(a) $Na_2CO_3(aq)$ and $MgSO_4(aq)$
(b) $Pb(NO_3)_2(aq)$ and $Na_2S(aq)$
(c) $(NH_4)_3PO_4(aq)$ and $CaCl_2(aq)$

4.24 Write balanced net ionic equations for the reactions that occur in each of the following cases. Identify the spectator ion or ions in each reaction.

(a) $Cr_2(SO_4)_3(aq) + (NH_4)_2CO_3(aq) \longrightarrow$
(b) $Ba(NO_3)_2(aq) + K_2SO_4(aq) \longrightarrow$
(c) $Fe(NO_3)_2(aq) + KOH(aq) \longrightarrow$

4.25 Separate samples of a solution of an unknown salt are treated with dilute solutions of HBr, H_2SO_4, and $NaOH$. A precipitate forms in all three cases. Which of the following cations could the solution contain: K^+; Pb^{2+}; Ba^{2+}?

4.26 Separate samples of a solution of an unknown ionic compound are treated with dilute $AgNO_3$, $Pb(NO_3)_2$, and $BaCl_2$. Precipitates form in all three cases. Which of the following could be the anion of the unknown salt: Br^-; CO_3^{2-}; NO_3^-?

4.27 You know that an unlabeled bottle contains a solution of one of the following: $AgNO_3$, $CaCl_2$, or $Al_2(SO_4)_3$. A friend suggests that you test a portion of the solution with $Ba(NO_3)_2$ and then with $NaCl$ solutions. Explain how these two tests together would be sufficient to determine which salt is present in the solution.

4.28 Three solutions are mixed together to form a single solution. One contains 0.2 mol $Pb(CH_3COO)_2$, the second contains 0.1 mol Na_2S, and the third contains 0.1 mol $CaCl_2$. **(a)** Write the net ionic equations for the precipitation reaction or reactions that occur. **(b)** What are the spectator ions in the solution?

Acid–Base Reactions

4.29 Which of the following solutions has the largest concentration of solvated protons: **(a)** 0.2 M $LiOH$, **(b)** 0.2 M HI, **(c)** 1.0 M methyl alcohol (CH_3OH)? Explain.

4.30 Which of the following solutions is the most basic? **(a)** 0.6 M NH_3, **(b)** 0.150 M KOH, **(c)** 0.100 M $Ba(OH)_2$. Explain.

4.31 What is the difference between **(a)** a monoprotic acid and a diprotic acid, **(b)** a weak acid and a strong acid, **(c)** an acid and a base?

4.32 Explain the following observations: **(a)** NH_3 contains no OH^- ions, and yet its aqueous solutions are basic; **(b)** HF is called a weak acid, and yet it is very reactive; **(c)** although sulfuric acid is a strong electrolyte, an aqueous solution of H_2SO_4 contains more HSO_4^- ions than SO_4^{2-} ions.

4.33 HCl, HBr, and HI are strong acids, yet HF is a weak acid. What does this mean in terms of the extent to which these substances are ionized in solution?

4.34 What is the relationship between the solubility rules in Table 4.1 and the list of strong bases in Table 4.2? Another way of asking this question is, why is $Cd(OH)_2$, for example, not listed as a strong base in Table 4.2?

4.35 Label each of the following substances as an acid, base, salt, or none of the above. Indicate whether the substance exists in aqueous solution entirely in molecular form, entirely as ions, or as a mixture of molecules and ions. **(a)** HF; **(b)** acetonitrile, CH_3CN; **(c)** $NaClO_4$; **(d)** $Ba(OH)_2$.

4.36 An aqueous solution of an unknown solute is tested with litmus paper and found to be acidic. The solution is weakly conducting compared with a solution of $NaCl$ of the same concentration. Which of the following substances could the unknown be: KOH, NH_3, HNO_3, $KClO_2$, H_3PO_3, CH_3COCH_3 (acetone)?

4.37 Classify each of the following substances as a nonelectrolyte, weak electrolyte, or strong electrolyte in water: **(a)** H_2SO_3, **(b)** C_2H_5OH (ethanol), **(c)** NH_3, **(d)** $KClO_3$, **(e)** $Cu(NO_3)_2$.

4.38 Classify each of the following aqueous solutions as a nonelectrolyte, weak electrolyte, or strong electrolyte: **(a)** $HClO_4$, **(b)** HNO_3, **(c)** NH_4Cl, **(d)** CH_3COCH_3 (acetone), **(e)** $CoSO_4$, **(f)** $C_{12}H_{22}O_{11}$ (sucrose).

4.39 Complete and balance the following molecular equations, and then write the net ionic equation for each:

(a) $HBr(aq) + Ca(OH)_2(aq) \longrightarrow$
(b) $Cu(OH)_2(s) + HClO_4(aq) \longrightarrow$
(c) $Al(OH)_3(s) + HNO_3(aq) \longrightarrow$

4.40 Write the balanced molecular and net ionic equations for each of the following neutralization reactions:

(a) Aqueous acetic acid is neutralized by aqueous potassium hydroxide.
(b) Solid chromium(III) hydroxide reacts with nitric acid.
(c) Aqueous hypochlorous acid and aqueous calcium hydroxide react.

4.41 Write balanced molecular and net ionic equations for the following reactions, and identify the gas formed in each: **(a)** solid cadmium sulfide reacts with an aqueous solution of sulfuric acid; **(b)** solid magnesium carbonate reacts with an aqueous solution of perchloric acid.

4.42 Because the oxide ion is basic, metal oxides react readily with acids. **(a)** Write the net ionic equation for the following reaction:

$$FeO(s) + 2\,HClO_4(aq) \longrightarrow Fe(ClO_4)_2(aq) + H_2O(l)$$

(b) Based on the equation in part (a), write the net ionic equation for the reaction that occurs between $NiO(s)$ and an aqueous solution of nitric acid.

4.43 Write a balanced molecular equation and a net ionic equation for the reaction that occurs when **(a)** solid $CaCO_3$ reacts with an aqueous solution of nitric acid; **(b)** solid iron(II) sulfide reacts with an aqueous solution of hydrobromic acid.

4.44 As K_2O dissolves in water, the oxide ion reacts with water molecules to form hydroxide ions. Write the molecular and net ionic equations for this reaction. Based on the definitions of acid and base, what ion is the base in this reaction? What is the acid? What is the spectator ion in the reaction?

Oxidation-Reduction Reactions

4.45 Define oxidation and reduction in terms of **(a)** electron transfer and **(b)** oxidation numbers.

4.46 Can oxidation occur without accompanying reduction? Explain.

4.47 Which circled region of the periodic table shown here contains the most readily oxidized elements? Which contains the least readily oxidized?

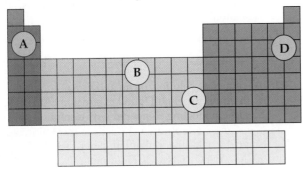

4.48 From the elements listed in Table 4.5, select an element that lies in region A of the periodic table shown above and an element that lies in region C. Write a balanced oxidation-reduction equation that shows the oxidation of one metal and reduction of an ion of the other. You will need to decide which element is oxidized and which is reduced.

4.49 Determine the oxidation number for the indicated element in each of the following substances: **(a)** S in SO_2, **(b)** C in $COCl_2$, **(c)** Mn in MnO_4^-, **(d)** Br in $HBrO$, **(e)** As in As_4, **(f)** O in K_2O_2.

4.50 Determine the oxidation number for the indicated element in each of the following compounds: **(a)** Ti in TiO_2, **(b)** Sn in $SnCl_3^-$, **(c)** C in $C_2O_4^{2-}$, **(d)** N in N_2H_4, **(e)** N in HNO_2, **(f)** Cr in $Cr_2O_7^{2-}$.

4.51 Which element is oxidized and which is reduced in the following reactions?

(a) $N_2(g) + 3\,H_2(g) \longrightarrow 2\,NH_3(g)$

(b) $3\,Fe(NO_3)_2(aq) + 2\,Al(s) \longrightarrow$
$$3\,Fe(s) + 2\,Al(NO_3)_3(aq)$$

(c) $Cl_2(aq) + 2\,NaI(aq) \longrightarrow I_2(aq) + 2\,NaCl(aq)$

(d) $PbS(s) + 4\,H_2O_2(aq) \longrightarrow PbSO_4(s) + 4\,H_2O(l)$

4.52 Which of the following are redox reactions? For those that are, indicate which element is oxidized and which is reduced. For those that are not, indicate whether they are precipitation or acid–base reactions.

(a) $Cu(OH)_2(s) + 2\,HNO_3(aq) \longrightarrow$
$$Cu(NO_3)_2(aq) + 2\,H_2O(l)$$

(b) $Fe_2O_3(s) + 3\,CO(g) \longrightarrow 2\,Fe(s) + 3\,CO_2(g)$

(c) $Sr(NO_3)_2(aq) + H_2SO_4(aq) \longrightarrow$
$$SrSO_4(s) + 2\,HNO_3(aq)$$

(d) $4\,Zn(s) + 10\,H^+(aq) + 2\,NO_3^-(aq) \longrightarrow$
$$4\,Zn^{2+}(aq) + N_2O(g) + 5\,H_2O(l)$$

4.53 Write balanced molecular and net ionic equations for the reactions of **(a)** manganese with dilute sulfuric acid; **(b)** chromium with hydrobromic acid; **(c)** tin with hydrochloric acid; **(d)** aluminum with formic acid, $HCOOH$.

4.54 Write balanced molecular and net ionic equations for the reactions of **(a)** hydrochloric acid with nickel; **(b)** dilute sulfuric acid with iron; **(c)** hydrobromic acid with magnesium; **(d)** acetic acid, CH_3COOH, with zinc.

4.55 Using the activity series (Table 4.5), write balanced chemical equations for the following reactions. If no reaction occurs, simply write NR. **(a)** Iron metal is added to a solution of copper(II) nitrate; **(b)** zinc metal is added to a solution of magnesium sulfate; **(c)** hydrobromic acid is added to tin metal; **(d)** hydrogen gas is bubbled through an aqueous solution of nickel(II) chloride; **(e)** aluminum metal is added to a solution of cobalt(II) sulfate.

4.56 Based on the activity series (Table 4.5), what is the outcome (if any) of each of the following reactions?

(a) $Mn(s) + NiCl_2(aq) \longrightarrow$

(b) $Cu(s) + Cr(CH_3COO)_3(aq) \longrightarrow$

(c) $Cr(s) + NiSO_4(aq) \longrightarrow$

(d) $Pt(s) + HBr(aq) \longrightarrow$

(e) $H_2(g) + CuCl_2(aq) \longrightarrow$

4.57 The metal cadmium tends to form Cd^{2+} ions. The following observations are made: (i) When a strip of zinc metal is placed in $CdCl_2(aq)$, cadmium metal is deposited on

WHAT'S AHEAD

MODERN SOCIETY DEPENDS ON ENERGY for its existence. Energy is used to drive our machinery and appliances, to power our transportation vehicles, and to keep us warm in the winter and cool in the summer. It is not just modern society, however, that depends on energy. Energy is

necessary for all life. Plants, such as those in the chapter-opening photograph, use solar energy to carry out photosynthesis, allowing the plants to grow. The plants, in turn, provide food, from which we humans derive the energy we need to move, to maintain body temperature, and to carry out bodily functions. What exactly is energy, though, and what principles are involved in its many transactions and transformations, such as those from the sun to plants to animals?

In this chapter we begin to explore energy and its changes. We are motivated partly by the fact that energy changes invariably accompany chemical reactions. Indeed, sometimes we use a chemical reaction specifically to obtain energy, as when we burn fuels. Thus, energy is very much a chemical topic. Nearly all of the energy on which we depend is derived from chemical reactions, whether those reactions are associated with the combustion of fuels, the discharge of a battery, or the metabolism of our foods. If we are to properly understand chemistry, we must also understand the energy changes that accompany chemical reactions.

The study of energy and its transformations is known as **thermodynamics** (Greek: *thérme-*, "heat"; *dy′namis*, "power"). In this chapter we will examine an aspect of thermodynamics that involves the relationships between chemical reactions and energy changes involving heat. This portion of thermodynamics is called **thermochemistry**. We will discuss additional aspects of thermodynamics in Chapter 19.

5.1 THE NATURE OF ENERGY

Although the idea of energy is a familiar one, it is a bit challenging to deal with the concept in a precise way. **Energy** is commonly defined as *the capacity to do work or to transfer heat.* This definition requires us to understand the concepts of work and heat. We can think of **work** as *the energy used to cause an object with mass to move against a force* and **heat** as *the energy used to cause the temperature of an object to increase* (Figure 5.1 ◄). We will consider each of these concepts more closely to give them fuller meaning. Let's begin by examining the ways in which matter can possess energy and how that energy can be transferred from one piece of matter to another.

Kinetic Energy and Potential Energy

Objects, whether they are tennis balls or molecules, can possess **kinetic energy**, the energy of *motion*. The magnitude of the kinetic energy, E_k, of an object depends on its mass, m, and speed, v:

$$E_k = \tfrac{1}{2} mv^2 \qquad [5.1]$$

Equation 5.1 shows that the kinetic energy increases as the speed of an object increases. For example, a car moving at 55 miles per hour (mph) has greater kinetic energy than it does at 40 mph. For a given speed the kinetic energy increases with increasing mass. Thus, a large sport-utility vehicle traveling at 55 mph has greater kinetic energy than a small sedan traveling at the same speed because the SUV has greater mass than the sedan. Atoms and molecules have mass and are in motion. They therefore possess kinetic energy.

All other kinds of energy—the energy stored in chemical bonds, the energy of attraction of north and south poles of magnets, for example—are potential energy. An object can possess **potential energy** by virtue of its *position* relative to other objects. Potential energy arises when a force operates on an object. A **force** is any kind of push or pull exerted on an object. The most familiar force is the pull of gravity. Think of a cyclist poised at the top of a hill, as illustrated in Figure 5.2 ▼. Gravity acts upon her and her bicycle, exerting a force directed toward the center of Earth. At the top of the hill the cyclist and her bicycle possess a certain potential energy by virtue of their elevation. The potential energy, E_p,

(a)

(b)

▲ Figure 5.1 **Work and heat.** Energy can be used to achieve two basic types of tasks: (a) Work is energy used to cause an object with mass to move. (b) Heat is energy used to cause the temperature of an object to increase.

► Figure 5.2 **Potential energy and kinetic energy.** (a) A bicycle at the top of a hill has a high potential energy relative to the bottom of the hill. (b) As the bicycle proceeds down the hill, the potential energy is converted into kinetic energy.

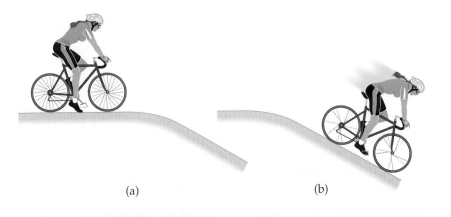

(a)   (b)

is given by the equation $E_p = mgh$, where m is the mass of the object in question (in this case the cyclist and her bicycle), h is the height of the object relative to some reference height, and g is the gravitational constant, 9.8 m/s^2. Once in motion, without any further effort on her part, the cyclist gains speed as the bicycle rolls down the hill. Her potential energy decreases as she moves downward, but the energy does not simply disappear. It is converted to other forms of energy, principally kinetic energy, the energy of motion. This example illustrates that forms of energy are interconvertible.

Gravity is an important force for large objects, such as the cyclist and Earth. Chemistry, however, deals mostly with extremely small objects—atoms and molecules. Gravitational forces play a negligible role in the ways these submicroscopic objects interact with one another. Forces that arise from electrical charges are more important when dealing with atoms and molecules.

One of the most important forms of potential energy in chemistry is *electrostatic potential energy*, which arises from the interactions between charged particles. The electrostatic potential energy, E_{el}, is proportional to the electrical charges on the two interacting objects, Q_1 and Q_2, and is inversely proportional to the distance separating them:

$$E_{el} = \frac{\kappa Q_1 Q_2}{d} \qquad\qquad [5.2]$$

Here κ is simply a constant of proportionality, $8.99 \times 10^9 \text{ J-m/C}^2$. (C is the coulomb, a unit of electrical charge ∞ (Section 2.2), and J is the joule, a unit of energy that we will soon discuss.) When dealing with molecular-level objects, the electrical charges Q_1 and Q_2 are typically on the order of magnitude of the charge of the electron (1.60×10^{-19} C). When Q_1 and Q_2 have the same sign (for example, both are positive), the two charges repel one another, pushing them apart; E_{el} is positive. When they have opposite signs, they attract one another, pulling them toward each other; E_{el} is negative. The lower the energy of a system, the more stable it is. Thus, the more strongly opposite charges interact, the more stable the system.

One of our goals in chemistry is to relate the energy changes that we see in our macroscopic world to the kinetic or potential energy of substances at the atomic or molecular level. Many substances—fuels, for example—release energy when they react. The *chemical energy* of these substances is due to the potential energy stored in the arrangements of their atoms. Likewise, we will see that the energy a substance possesses because of its temperature (its *thermal energy*) is associated with the kinetic energy of the molecules in the substance.

▲ **GIVE IT SOME THOUGHT**

What are the terms for the energy an object possesses **(a)** because of its motion, **(b)** because of its position? What terms are used to describe changes of energy associated with **(c)** temperature changes, **(d)** moving an object against a force?

Units of Energy

The SI unit for energy is the **joule** (pronounced "jool"), J, in honor of James Joule (1818–1889), a British scientist who investigated work and heat: $1 \text{ J} = 1 \text{ kg-m}^2/\text{s}^2$. A mass of 2 kg moving at a speed of 1 m/s possesses a kinetic energy of 1 J:

$$E_k = \tfrac{1}{2} mv^2 = \tfrac{1}{2}(2 \text{ kg})(1 \text{ m/s})^2 = 1 \text{ kg-m}^2/\text{s}^2 = 1 \text{ J}$$

A joule is not a large amount of energy, and we will often use *kilojoules* (kJ) in discussing the energies associated with chemical reactions.

Traditionally, energy changes accompanying chemical reactions have been expressed in calories, a non-SI unit still widely used in chemistry, biology, and biochemistry. A **calorie** (cal) was originally defined as the amount of energy required to raise the temperature of 1 g of water from 14.5 °C to 15.5 °C. A calorie is now defined in terms of the joule:

$$1 \text{ cal} = 4.184 \text{ J (exactly)}$$

A related energy unit used in nutrition is the nutritional *Calorie* (note that this unit is capitalized): 1 Cal = 1000 cal = 1 kcal.

System and Surroundings

When we analyze energy changes, we need to focus our attention on a limited and well-defined part of the universe to keep track of the energy changes that occur. The portion we single out for study is called the **system**; everything else is called the **surroundings**. When we study the energy change that accompanies a chemical reaction in the laboratory, the reactants and products constitute the system. The container and everything beyond it are considered the surroundings.

Systems may be open, closed, or isolated. An *open* system is one in which matter and energy can be exchanged with the surroundings. A boiling pot of water on a stove, without its lid, is an open system: heat comes into the system from the stove, and water is released to the surroundings as steam.

The systems we can most readily study in thermochemistry are called *closed systems*. A closed system can exchange energy but not matter with its surroundings. For example, consider a mixture of hydrogen gas, H_2, and oxygen gas, O_2, in a cylinder, as illustrated in Figure 5.3 ◀. The system in this case is just the hydrogen and oxygen; the cylinder, piston, and everything beyond them (including us) are the surroundings. If the hydrogen and oxygen react to form water, energy is liberated:

$$2 \, H_2(g) + O_2(g) \longrightarrow 2 \, H_2O(g) + \text{energy}$$

Although the chemical form of the hydrogen and oxygen atoms in the system is changed by this reaction, the system has not lost or gained mass; it undergoes no exchange of matter with its surroundings. However, it can exchange energy with its surroundings in the form of *work* and *heat*.

An *isolated* system is one in which neither energy nor matter can be exchanged with the surroundings. An insulated thermos containing hot coffee approximates an isolated system. We know, however, that the coffee eventually cools, so it is not perfectly isolated.

▲ **Figure 5.3 A closed system and its surroundings.** Hydrogen and oxygen gases are confined in a cylinder with a movable piston. If we are interested only in the properties of these gases, the gases are the system and the cylinder and piston are part of the surroundings. Because the system can exchange energy (in the form of heat and work) but not matter with its surroundings, it is a closed system.

GIVE IT SOME THOUGHT

Is a human being an isolated, closed, or open system? Explain your choice.

Transferring Energy: Work and Heat

Figure 5.1 illustrates the two ways that we experience energy changes in our everyday lives—in the form of work or heat. In Figure 5.1(a) energy is transferred from the tennis racquet to the ball, changing the direction and speed of the ball's movement. In Figure 5.1(b) energy is transferred in the form of heat. Indeed, energy is transferred between systems and surroundings in two general ways, as work or heat.

Energy used to cause an object to move against a force is called *work*. Thus, we can define work, w, as the energy transferred when a force moves an object. The magnitude of this work equals the product of the force, F, and the distance, d, that the object is moved:

$$w = F \times d \qquad [5.3]$$

We perform work, for example, when we lift an object against the force of gravity or when we bring two like charges closer together. If we define the object as the system, then we—as part of the surroundings—are performing work on that system, transferring energy to it.

The other way in which energy is transferred is as heat. *Heat* is the energy transferred from a hotter object to a colder one. Or stating this idea in a slightly more abstract but nevertheless useful way, heat is the energy transferred between a system and its surroundings because of their difference in temperature. A combustion reaction, such as the burning of natural gas illustrated in Figure 5.1(b), releases the chemical energy stored in the molecules of the fuel. ∞ (Section 3.2) If we define the substances involved in the reaction as the system and everything else as the surroundings, we find that the released energy causes the temperature of the system to increase. Energy in the form of heat is then transferred from the hotter system to the cooler surroundings.

■ SAMPLE EXERCISE 5.1 | Describing and Calculating Energy Changes

A bowler lifts a 5.4-kg (12-lb) bowling ball from ground level to a height of 1.6 m (5.2 feet) and then drops the ball back to the ground. **(a)** What happens to the potential energy of the bowling ball as it is raised from the ground? **(b)** What quantity of work, in J, is used to raise the ball? **(c)** After the ball is dropped, it gains kinetic energy. If we assume that all of the work done in part (b) has been converted to kinetic energy by the time the ball strikes the ground, what is the speed of the ball at the instant just before it hits the ground? (Note: The force due to gravity is $F = m \times g$, where m is the mass of the object and g is the gravitational constant; $g = 9.8$ m/s^2.)

SOLUTION

Analyze: We need to relate the potential energy of the bowling ball to its position relative to the ground. We then need to establish the relationship between work and the change in potential energy of the ball. Finally, we need to connect the change in potential energy when the ball is dropped with the kinetic energy attained by the ball.

Plan: We can calculate the work done in lifting the ball by using Equation 5.3: $w = F \times d$. The kinetic energy of the ball at the moment of impact equals its initial potential energy. We can use the kinetic energy and Equation 5.1 to calculate the speed, v, at impact.

Solve:

(a) Because the bowling ball is raised to a greater height above the ground, its potential energy increases.

(b) The ball has a mass of 5.4 kg, and it is lifted a distance of 1.6 m. To calculate the work performed to raise the ball, we use both Equation 5.3 and $F = m \times g$ for the force that is due to gravity:

$$w = F \times d = m \times g \times d = (5.4 \text{ kg})(9.8 \text{ m/s}^2)(1.6 \text{ m}) = 85 \text{ kg-m}^2/\text{s}^2 = 85 \text{ J}$$

Thus, the bowler has done 85 J of work to lift the ball to a height of 1.6 m.

(c) When the ball is dropped, its potential energy is converted to kinetic energy. At the instant just before the ball hits the ground, we assume that the kinetic energy is equal to the work done in part (b), 85 J:

$$E_k = \tfrac{1}{2} mv^2 = 85 \text{ J} = 85 \text{ kg-m}^2/\text{s}^2$$

We can now solve this equation for v:

$$v^2 = \left(\frac{2E_k}{m}\right) = \left(\frac{2(85 \text{ kg-m}^2/\text{s}^2)}{5.4 \text{ kg}}\right) = 31.5 \text{ m}^2/\text{s}^2$$

$$v = \sqrt{31.5 \text{ m}^2/\text{s}^2} = 5.6 \text{ m/s}$$

Check: Work must be done in part (b) to increase the potential energy of the ball, which is in accord with our experience. The units are appropriate in both parts (b) and (c). The work is in units of J and the speed in units of m/s. In part (c) we have carried an additional digit in the intermediate calculation involving the square root, but we report the final value to only two significant figures, as appropriate.

Comment: A speed of 1 m/s is roughly 2 mph, so the bowling ball has a speed greater than 10 mph upon impact.

■ PRACTICE EXERCISE

What is the kinetic energy, in J, of **(a)** an Ar atom moving with a speed of 650 m/s, **(b)** a mole of Ar atoms moving with a speed of 650 m/s (Hint: 1 amu $= 1.66 \times 10^{-27}$ kg)
Answers: **(a)** 1.4×10^{-20} J, **(b)** 8.4×10^3 J

5.2 THE FIRST LAW OF THERMODYNAMICS

We have seen that the potential energy of a system can be converted into kinetic energy, and vice versa. We have also seen that energy can be transferred back and forth between a system and its surroundings in the forms of work and heat. In general, energy can be converted from one form to another, and it can be transferred from one place to another. All of these transactions proceed in accord with one of the most important observations in science—that energy can be neither created nor destroyed. A simple statement known as the **first law of thermodynamics** summarizes this simple truth: *Energy is conserved.* Any energy that is lost by the system must be gained by the surroundings, and vice versa. To apply the first law of thermodynamics quantitatively, we must first define the energy of a system more precisely.

Internal Energy

The **internal energy** of a system is the sum of *all* the kinetic and potential energies of all its components. For the system in Figure 5.3, for example, the internal energy includes the motions of the H_2 and O_2 molecules through space, their rotations, and their internal vibrations. It also includes the energies of the nuclei of each atom and of the component electrons. We represent the internal energy with the symbol E. (Some texts, particularly more advanced ones, use the symbol U.) We generally do not know the actual numerical value of E. What we can hope to know, however, is ΔE (read "delta E"),* the change in E that accompanies a change in the system.

Imagine that we start with a system with an initial internal energy, $E_{initial}$. The system then undergoes a change, which might involve work being done or heat being transferred. After the change, the final internal energy of the system is E_{final}. We define the *change* in internal energy, ΔE, as the difference between E_{final} and $E_{initial}$:

$$\Delta E = E_{final} - E_{initial} \qquad [5.4]$$

To apply the first law of thermodynamics, we need only the value of ΔE. We do not really need to know the actual values of E_{final} or $E_{initial}$ for the system.

Thermodynamic quantities such as ΔE have three parts: (1) a number and (2) a unit, that together give the magnitude of the change, and (3) a sign that gives the direction. A *positive* value of ΔE results when $E_{final} > E_{initial}$, indicating the system has gained energy from its surroundings. A *negative* value of ΔE is obtained when $E_{final} < E_{initial}$, indicating the system has lost energy to its surroundings. Notice that we are taking the point of view of the system rather than that of the surroundings in discussing the energy changes. We need to remember, however, that any change in the energy of the system is accompanied by an opposite change in the energy of the surroundings. These features of energy changes are summarized in Figure 5.4▼.

▼ **Figure 5.4 Changes in internal energy.** (a) When a system loses energy, that energy is released to the surroundings. The loss of energy is represented by an arrow that points downward between the initial and final states of the system. In this case, the energy change of the system, $\Delta E = E_{final} - E_{initial}$, is negative. (b) When a system gains energy, that energy is gained from the surroundings. In this case, the gain of energy is represented by an arrow that points upward between the initial and final states of the system, and the energy change of the system is positive. Notice in both (a) and (b) that the vertical arrow originates at the initial state and has its head at the final state.

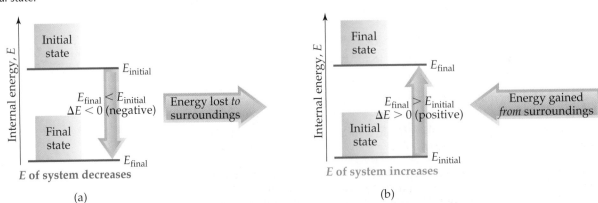

(a)   (b)

*The symbol Δ is commonly used to denote change. For example, a change in height, h, can be represented by Δh.

In a chemical reaction, the initial state of the system refers to the reactants, and the final state refers to the products. When hydrogen and oxygen form water at a given temperature, the system loses energy to the surroundings. Because energy is lost from the system, the internal energy of the products (final state) is less than that of the reactants (initial state), and ΔE for the process is negative. Thus, the *energy diagram* in Figure 5.5▶ shows that the internal energy of the mixture of H_2 and O_2 is greater than that of H_2O.

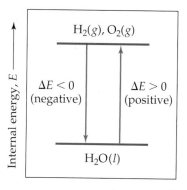

▲ **Figure 5.5 Energy diagram for the interconversion of $H_2(g)$, $O_2(g)$, and $H_2O(l)$.** A system composed of $H_2(g)$ and $O_2(g)$ has a greater internal energy than one composed of $H_2O(l)$. The system loses energy ($\Delta E < 0$) when H_2 and O_2 are converted to H_2O. It gains energy ($\Delta E > 0$) when H_2O is decomposed into H_2 and O_2.

▲ GIVE IT SOME THOUGHT

The internal energy for $Mg(s)$ and $Cl_2(g)$ is greater than that of $MgCl_2(s)$. Sketch an energy diagram that represents the reaction $MgCl_2(s) \longrightarrow Mg(s) + Cl_2(g)$.

Relating ΔE to Heat and Work

As we noted in Section 5.1, a system may exchange energy with its surroundings as heat or as work. The internal energy of a system changes in magnitude as heat is added to or removed from the system or as work is done on it or by it. If we think of internal energy as the system's bank account of energy, we see that deposits or withdrawals can be made either in terms of heat or in terms of work. Deposits increase the energy of the system (positive ΔE), whereas withdrawals decrease the energy of the system (negative ΔE).

We can use these ideas to write a very useful algebraic expression of the first law of thermodynamics. When a system undergoes any chemical or physical change, the magnitude and sign of the accompanying change in internal energy, ΔE, is given by the heat added to or liberated from the system, q, plus the work done on or by the system, w:

$$\Delta E = q + w \qquad [5.5]$$

When heat is added to a system or work is done on a system, its internal energy increases. Therefore, when heat is transferred to the system from the surroundings, q has a positive value. Adding heat to the system is like making a deposit to the energy account—the total amount of energy goes up. Likewise, when work is done on the system by the surroundings, w has a positive value (Figure 5.6▶). Work also is a deposit, increasing the internal energy of the system. Conversely, both the heat lost by the system to the surroundings and the work done by the system on the surroundings have negative values; that is, they lower the internal energy of the system. They are energy withdrawals and as a result, lower the total amount of energy in the energy account. The sign conventions for q, w, and ΔE are summarized in Table 5.1▼. Notice that any energy entering the system as either heat or work carries a positive sign.

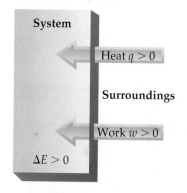

▲ **Figure 5.6 Sign conventions for heat and work.** Heat, q, gained by a system and work, w, done on a system are both positive quantities. Both increase the internal energy, E, of the system, causing ΔE to be a positive quantity.

TABLE 5.1 ■ Sign Conventions for q, w, and ΔE

For q	+ means system *gains* heat	− means system *loses* heat
For w	+ means work done *on* system	− means work done *by* system
For ΔE	+ means *net gain* of energy by system	− means *net loss* of energy by system

■ **SAMPLE EXERCISE 5.2** | **Relating Heat and Work to Changes of Internal Energy**

Two gases, $A(g)$ and $B(g)$, are confined in a cylinder-and-piston arrangement like that in Figure 5.3. Substances A and B react to form a solid product: $A(g) + B(g) \rightarrow C(s)$. As the reaction occurs, the system loses 1150 J of heat to the surroundings. The piston moves downward as the gases react to form a solid. As the volume of the gas decreases under the constant pressure of the atmosphere, the surroundings do 480 J of work on the system. What is the change in the internal energy of the system?

SOLUTION

Analyze: The question asks us to determine ΔE, given information about q and w.

Plan: We first determine the signs of q and w (Table 5.1) and then use Equation 5.5, $\Delta E = q + w$, to calculate ΔE.

Solve: Heat is transferred from the system to the surroundings, and work is done on the system by the surroundings, so q is negative and w is positive: $q = -1150$ J and $w = 480$ kJ. Thus,

$$\Delta E = q + w = (-1150 \text{ J}) + (480 \text{ J}) = -670 \text{ J}$$

The negative value of ΔE tells us that a net quantity of 670 J of energy has been transferred from the system to the surroundings.

Comment: You can think of this change as a decrease of 670 J in the net value of the system's energy bank account (hence the negative sign); 1150 J is withdrawn in the form of heat, while 480 J is deposited in the form of work. Notice that as the volume of the gases decreases, work is being done on the system by the surroundings, resulting in a deposit of energy.

■ PRACTICE EXERCISE

Calculate the change in the internal energy of the system for a process in which the system absorbs 140 J of heat from the surroundings and does 85 J of work on the surroundings.
Answer: +55 J

(a)

(b)

▲ **Figure 5.7 Examples of endothermic and exothermic reactions.** (a) When ammonium thiocyanate and barium hydroxide octahydrate are mixed at room temperature, an endothermic reaction occurs:
$2 \text{ NH}_4\text{SCN}(s) + \text{Ba(OH)}_2 \cdot 8 \text{ H}_2\text{O}(s) \longrightarrow$
$\text{Ba(SCN)}_2(aq) + 2 \text{ NH}_3(aq) + 10 \text{ H}_2\text{O}(l)$.
As a result, the temperature of the system drops from about 20 °C to −9 °C. (b) The reaction of powdered aluminum with Fe_2O_3 (the thermite reaction) is highly exothermic. The reaction proceeds vigorously to form Al_2O_3 and molten iron:
$2 \text{ Al}(s) + \text{Fe}_2\text{O}_3(s) \longrightarrow$
$\text{Al}_2\text{O}_3(s) + 2 \text{ Fe}(l)$.

Endothermic and Exothermic Processes

When a process occurs in which the system absorbs heat, the process is called **endothermic**. (*Endo-* is a prefix meaning "into.") During an endothermic process, such as the melting of ice, heat flows *into* the system from its surroundings. If we, as part of the surroundings, touch a container in which ice is melting, it feels cold to us because heat has passed from our hands to the container.

A process in which the system loses heat is called **exothermic**. (*Exo-* is a prefix meaning "out of.") During an exothermic process, such as the combustion of gasoline, heat *exits* or flows *out* of the system and into the surroundings. Figure 5.7 ◄ shows two examples of chemical reactions: one endothermic and the other highly exothermic. In the endothermic process shown in Figure 5.7(a), the temperature in the beaker decreases. In this example the system consists of the chemical reactants and products. The solvent in which they are dissolved is part of the surroundings. Heat flows from the solvent, as part of the surroundings, into the system as reactants are converted to products. Thus, the temperature of the solution drops.

⚠ GIVE IT SOME THOUGHT

Using Figure 5.5 as a reference, indicate whether the reaction $2 \text{ H}_2\text{O}(l) \longrightarrow 2 \text{ H}_2(g) + \text{O}_2(g)$ is exothermic or endothermic. What feature(s) of the figure indicate whether the reaction is exothermic or endothermic?

State Functions

Although we usually have no way of knowing the precise value of the internal energy of a system, E, it does have a fixed value for a given set of conditions. The conditions that influence internal energy include the temperature and pressure. Furthermore, the total internal energy of a system is proportional to the total quantity of matter in the system because energy is an extensive property. ∞ (Section 1.3)

Suppose we define our system as 50 g of water at 25 °C, as in Figure 5.8 ▶. The system could have arrived at this state by cooling 50 g of water from 100 °C or by melting 50 g of ice and subsequently warming the water to 25 °C.

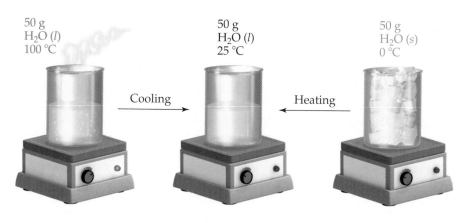

50 g
H₂O (l)
100 °C

Cooling →

50 g
H₂O (l)
25 °C

← Heating

50 g
H₂O (s)
0 °C

◀ **Figure 5.8 Internal energy, E, a state function.** E depends only on the present state of the system and not on the path by which it arrived at that state. The internal energy of 50 g of water at 25 °C is the same whether the water is cooled from a higher temperature to 25 °C or warmed from a lower temperature to 25 °C.

The internal energy of the water at 25 °C is the same in either case. Internal energy is an example of a **state function**, a property of a system that is determined by specifying the system's condition, or state (in terms of temperature, pressure, and so forth). *The value of a state function depends only on the present state of the system, not on the path the system took to reach that state.* Because E is a state function, ΔE depends only on the initial and final states of the system, not on how the change occurs.

An analogy may help to explain the difference between quantities that are state functions and those that are not. Suppose you are traveling between Chicago and Denver. Chicago is 596 ft above sea level; Denver is 5280 ft above sea level. No matter what route you take, the altitude change will be 4684 ft. The distance you travel, however, will depend on your route. Altitude is analogous to a state function because the change in altitude is independent of the path taken. Distance traveled is not a state function.

Some thermodynamic quantities, such as E, are state functions. Other quantities, such as q and w, are not. Although $\Delta E = q + w$ does not depend on how the change occurs, the specific amounts of heat and work produced depend on the way in which the change is carried out, analogous to the choice of travel route between Chicago and Denver. Nevertheless, if changing the path by which a system goes from an initial state to a final state increases the value of q, that path change will also decrease the value of w by exactly the same amount. The result is that the value for ΔE for the two paths will be the same.

We can illustrate this principle with the example of a flashlight battery as our system. In Figure 5.9 ▶, we consider two possible ways of discharging the battery at constant temperature. If a coil of wire shorts out the battery, no work is accomplished because nothing is moved against a force. All the energy is lost from the battery in the form of heat. (The wire coil will get warmer and release heat to the surrounding air.) On the other hand, if the battery is used to make a small motor turn, the discharge of the battery produces work. Some heat will be released as well, although not as much as when the battery is shorted out. The magnitudes of q and w are different for these two cases. If the initial and final states of the battery are identical in both cases, however, then $\Delta E = q + w$ must be the same in both cases because ΔE is a state function. Thus, ΔE depends only on the initial and final states of the system, regardless of how the transfers of energy occur in terms of heat and work.

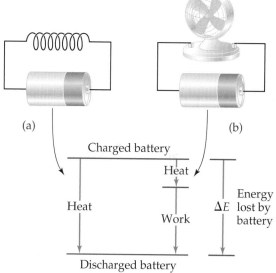

(a)   (b)

Charged battery

Heat

Heat ↓
Work

ΔE Energy lost by battery

Discharged battery

▲ **Figure 5.9 Internal energy is a state function, but heat and work are not.** The amounts of heat and work transferred between the system and the surroundings depend on the way in which the system goes from one state to another. (a) A battery shorted out by a wire loses energy to the surroundings only as heat; no work is performed by the system. (b) A battery discharged through a motor loses energy as work (to make the fan turn) and also loses energy as heat. Now, however, the amount of heat lost is much less than in (a). The value of ΔE is the same for both processes even though the values of q and w in (a) are different from the values of q and w in (b).

▲ GIVE IT SOME THOUGHT

In what ways is the balance in your checkbook a state function?

5.3 ENTHALPY

The chemical and physical changes that occur around us, such as photosynthesis in the leaves of a plant, the evaporation of water from a lake, or a reaction in an open beaker in a laboratory, occur at essentially constant atmospheric pressure. The changes can result in the release or absorption of heat or can be accompanied by work that is done by or on the system. The heat flow is the easiest change to measure, so we will begin to focus on that aspect of reactions. Nevertheless, we still need to account for any work that accompanies the process.

Most commonly, the only kind of work produced by chemical or physical changes open to the atmosphere is the mechanical work associated with a change in the volume of the system. Consider, for example, the reaction of zinc metal with hydrochloric acid solution:

$$Zn(s) + 2\,H^+(aq) \longrightarrow Zn^{2+}(aq) + H_2(g) \qquad [5.6]$$

If we carry out this reaction in the laboratory hood in an open beaker, we can see the evolution of hydrogen gas, but it may not be so obvious that work is being done. Still, the hydrogen gas that is being produced must expand against the existing atmosphere, which requires the system to do work. We can see this better by conducting the reaction in a closed vessel at constant pressure, as illustrated in Figure 5.10▼. In this apparatus the piston moves up or down to maintain a constant pressure in the reaction vessel. If we assume for simplicity that the piston has no mass, the pressure in the apparatus is the same as the atmospheric pressure outside the apparatus. As the reaction proceeds, H_2 gas forms, and the piston rises. The gas within the flask is thus doing work on the surroundings by lifting the piston against the force of atmospheric pressure that presses down on it.

The work involved in the expansion or compression of gases is called **pressure-volume work** (or *P-V* work). When the pressure is constant, as in our example, the sign and magnitude of the pressure-volume work is given by

$$w = -P\,\Delta V \qquad [5.7]$$

where P is pressure and ΔV is the change in volume of the system ($\Delta V = V_{final} - V_{initial}$). The negative sign in Equation 5.7 is necessary to conform to the sign conventions given in Table 5.1. Thus, when the volume expands, ΔV is a positive quantity and w is a negative quantity. That is, energy leaves the system as work, indicating that work is done *by* the system *on* the surroundings. On the other hand, when a gas is compressed, ΔV is a negative quantity

▶ **Figure 5.10 A system that does work on its surroundings.** (a) An apparatus for studying the reaction of zinc metal with hydrochloric acid at constant pressure. The piston is free to move up and down in its cylinder to maintain a constant pressure equal to atmospheric pressure inside the apparatus. Notice the pellets of zinc in the L-shaped arm on the left. When this arm is rotated, the pellets will fall into the main container and the reaction will begin. (b) When zinc is added to the acid solution, hydrogen gas is evolved. The hydrogen gas does work on the surroundings, raising the piston against atmospheric pressure to maintain constant pressure inside the reaction vessel.

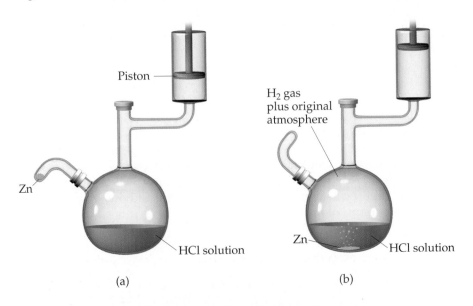

Piston

H_2 gas plus original atmosphere

Zn

Zn

HCl solution

HCl solution

(a)

(b)

(the volume decreases), which makes w a positive quantity. That is, energy enters the system as work, indicating that work is done on the system by the surroundings. The "A Closer Look" box discusses pressure-volume work in more detail, but all you really need to keep in mind for now is Equation 5.7, which applies to processes occurring at constant pressure. We will take up the properties of gases in more detail in Chapter 10.

GIVE IT SOME THOUGHT

If a system does not change its volume during the course of a process, does it do pressure-volume work?

A thermodynamic function called **enthalpy** (from the Greek word *enthalpein*, meaning "to warm") accounts for heat flow in processes occurring at constant pressure when no forms of work are performed other than P-V work. Enthalpy, which we denote by the symbol H, equals the internal energy plus the product of the pressure and volume of the system:

$$H = E + PV \qquad [5.8]$$

Enthalpy is a state function because internal energy, pressure, and volume are all state functions.

When a change occurs at constant pressure, the change in enthalpy, ΔH, is given by the following relationship:

$$
\begin{aligned}
\Delta H &= \Delta(E + PV) \\
&= \Delta E + P\,\Delta V
\end{aligned}
\qquad [5.9]
$$

That is, the change in enthalpy equals the change in internal energy plus the product of the constant pressure times the change in volume.

We can gain further insight into enthalpy change by recalling that $\Delta E = q + w$ (Equation 5.5) and that the work involved in the expansion or compression of gases is $w = -P\,\Delta V$. If we substitute $-w$ for $P\,\Delta V$ and $q + w$ for ΔE into Equation 5.9, we have

$$\Delta H = \Delta E + P\,\Delta V = (q_P + w) - w = q_P \qquad [5.10]$$

where the subscript P on the heat, q, emphasizes changes at constant pressure. Thus, *the change in enthalpy equals the heat gained or lost at constant pressure.* Because q_P is something we can either measure or readily calculate and because so many physical and chemical changes of interest to us occur at constant pressure, enthalpy is a more useful function than internal energy. For most reactions the difference in ΔH and ΔE is small because $P\,\Delta V$ is small.

When ΔH is positive (that is, when q_P is positive), the system has gained heat from the surroundings (Table 5.1), which is an endothermic process. When ΔH is negative, the system has released heat to the surroundings, which is an exothermic process. These cases are diagrammed in Figure 5.11 ▶.

Because H is a state function, ΔH (which equals q_P) depends only on the initial and final states of the system, not on how the change occurs. At first glance this statement might seem to contradict our earlier discussion in Section 5.2, in which we said that q is *not* a state function. There is no contradiction, however, because the relationship between ΔH and heat (q_P) has the special limitations that only P-V work is involved and the pressure is constant.

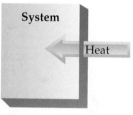

$\Delta H > 0$
(Endothermic)

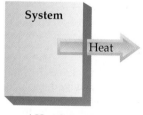

$\Delta H < 0$
(Exothermic)

▲ **Figure 5.11 Endothermic and exothermic processes.** (a) If the system absorbs heat (endothermic process), ΔH will be positive ($\Delta H > 0$). (b) If the system loses heat (exothermic process), ΔH will be negative ($\Delta H < 0$).

GIVE IT SOME THOUGHT

What is the advantage of using enthalpy rather than internal energy to describe energy changes in reactions?

A Closer Look   ENERGY, ENTHALPY, AND *P-V* WORK

In chemistry we are interested mainly in two types of work: electrical work and mechanical work done by expanding gases. We will focus here only on the latter, called pressure-volume, or *P-V*, work. Expanding gases in the cylinder of an automobile engine do *P-V* work on the piston; this work eventually turns the wheels. Expanding gases from an open reaction vessel do *P-V* work on the atmosphere. This work accomplishes nothing in a practical sense, but we must keep track of all work, useful or not, when monitoring the energy changes of a system.

Consider a gas confined to a cylinder with a movable piston of cross-sectional area *A* (Figure 5.12▼). A downward force, *F*, acts on the piston. The *pressure*, *P*, on the gas is the force per area: $P = F/A$. We will assume that the piston is weightless and that the only pressure acting on it is the *atmospheric pressure* that is due to the weight of Earth's atmosphere, which we will assume to be constant.

Suppose the gas in the cylinder expands and the piston moves a distance, Δh. From Equation 5.3, the magnitude of the work done by the system equals the distance moved times the force acting on the piston:

$$\text{Magnitude of work} = \text{force} \times \text{distance} = F \times \Delta h \quad [5.11]$$

We can rearrange the definition of pressure, $P = F/A$, to $F = P \times A$. In addition, the volume change, ΔV, resulting from the movement of the piston, is the product of the cross-sectional area of the piston and the distance it moves: $\Delta V = A \times \Delta h$. Substituting into Equation 5.11,

$$\text{Magnitude of work} = F \times \Delta h = P \times A \times \Delta h$$
$$= P \times \Delta V$$

Because the system (the confined gas) is doing work on the surroundings, the work is a negative quantity:

$$w = -P\,\Delta V \quad [5.12]$$

Now, if *P-V* work is the only work that can be done, we can substitute Equation 5.12 into Equation 5.5 to give

$$\Delta E = q + w = q - P\,\Delta V \quad [5.13]$$

When a reaction is carried out in a constant-volume container ($\Delta V = 0$), the heat transferred equals the change in internal energy:

$$\Delta E = q_V \quad \text{(constant volume)} \quad [5.14]$$

The subscript *V* indicates that the volume is constant.

Most reactions are run under constant-pressure conditions. In this case Equation 5.13 becomes

$$\Delta E = q_P - P\,\Delta V \text{ or}$$
$$q_P = \Delta E + P\,\Delta V \quad \text{(constant pressure)} \quad [5.15]$$

But we see from Equation 5.9 that the right-hand side of Equation 5.15 is just the enthalpy change under constant-pressure conditions. Thus, $\Delta H = q_P$, as we saw earlier in Equation 5.10.

In summary, the change in internal energy is equal to the heat gained or lost at constant volume; the change in enthalpy is equal to the heat gained or lost at constant pressure. The difference between ΔE and ΔH is the amount of *P-V* work done by the system when the process occurs at constant pressure, $-P\,\Delta V$. The volume change accompanying many reactions is close to zero, which makes $P\,\Delta V$, and therefore the difference between ΔE and ΔH, small. It is generally satisfactory to use ΔH as the measure of energy changes during most chemical processes.

Related Exercises: 5.33, 5.34, 5.35, 5.36

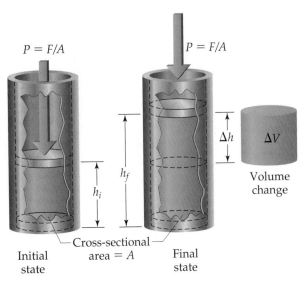

▲ **Figure 5.12 Pressure-volume work.** A piston moving upward, expanding the volume of the system against an external pressure, *P*, does work on the surroundings. The amount of work done by the system on the surroundings is $w = -P\,\Delta V$.

■ **SAMPLE EXERCISE 5.3** | Determining the Sign of ΔH

Indicate the sign of the enthalpy change, ΔH, in each of the following processes carried out under atmospheric pressure, and indicate whether the process is endothermic or exothermic: **(a)** An ice cube melts; **(b)** 1 g of butane (C_4H_{10}) is combusted in sufficient oxygen to give complete combustion to CO_2 and H_2O.

SOLUTION

Analyze: Our goal is to determine whether ΔH is positive or negative for each process. Because each process appears to occur at constant pressure, the enthalpy change of each one equals the amount of heat absorbed or released, $\Delta H = q_P$.

Plan: We must predict whether heat is absorbed or released by the system in each process. Processes in which heat is absorbed are endothermic and have a positive sign for ΔH; those in which heat is released are exothermic and have a negative sign for ΔH.

Solve: In (a) the water that makes up the ice cube is the system. The ice cube absorbs heat from the surroundings as it melts, so ΔH is positive and the process is endothermic. In (b) the system is the 1 g of butane and the oxygen required to combust it. The combustion of butane in oxygen gives off heat, so ΔH is negative and the process is exothermic.

■ PRACTICE EXERCISE

Suppose we confine 1 g of butane and sufficient oxygen to completely combust it in a cylinder like that in Figure 5.12. The cylinder is perfectly insulating, so no heat can escape to the surroundings. A spark initiates combustion of the butane, which forms carbon dioxide and water vapor. If we used this apparatus to measure the enthalpy change in the reaction, would the piston rise, fall, or stay the same?
Answer: The piston must move to maintain a constant pressure in the cylinder. The products contain more molecules of gas than the reactants, as shown by the balanced equation

$$2\,C_4H_{10}(g) + 13\,O_2(g) \longrightarrow 8\,CO_2(g) + 10\,H_2O(g)$$

As a result, the piston would rise to make room for the additional molecules of gas. Heat is given off, so the piston would also rise an additional amount to accommodate the expansion of the gases because of the temperature increase.

5.4 ENTHALPIES OF REACTION

Because $\Delta H = H_{final} - H_{initial}$, the enthalpy change for a chemical reaction is given by the enthalpy of the products minus the enthalpy of the reactants:

$$\Delta H = H_{products} - H_{reactants} \qquad [5.16]$$

The enthalpy change that accompanies a reaction is called the **enthalpy of reaction**, or merely the *heat of reaction*, and is sometimes written ΔH_{rxn}, where "rxn" is a commonly used abbreviation for "reaction."

The combustion of hydrogen is shown in Figure 5.13▼. When the reaction is controlled so that 2 mol $H_2(g)$ burn to form 2 mol $H_2O(g)$ at a constant pressure, the system releases 483.6 kJ of heat. We can summarize this information as

$$2\,H_2(g) + O_2(g) \longrightarrow 2\,H_2O(g) \qquad \Delta H = -483.6 \text{ kJ} \qquad [5.17]$$

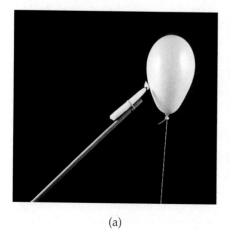  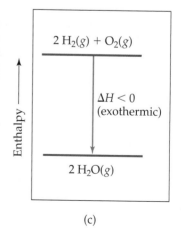

(a) (b) (c)

▲ Figure 5.13 **Exothermic reaction of hydrogen with oxygen.** (a) A candle is held near a balloon filled with hydrogen gas and oxygen gas. (b) The $H_2(g)$ ignites, reacting with $O_2(g)$ to form $H_2O(g)$. The resultant explosion produces a ball of flame. The system gives off heat to its surroundings. (c) The enthalpy diagram for this reaction, showing its exothermic character.

ΔH is negative, so this reaction is exothermic. Notice that ΔH is reported at the end of the balanced equation, without explicitly mentioning the amounts of chemicals involved. In such cases the coefficients in the balanced equation represent the number of moles of reactants and products producing the associated enthalpy change. Balanced chemical equations that show the associated enthalpy change in this way are called *thermochemical equations*.

▲ **GIVE IT SOME THOUGHT**

What information is summarized by the coefficients in a *thermochemical equation*?

▲ **Figure 5.14 The burning of the hydrogen-filled airship** *Hindenburg.* This photograph was taken only 22 seconds after the first explosion occurred. This tragedy, which occurred in Lakehurst, New Jersey, on May 6, 1937, led to the discontinuation of hydrogen as a buoyant gas in such craft. Modern-day blimps are filled with helium, which is not as buoyant as hydrogen but is not flammable.

The enthalpy change accompanying a reaction may also be represented in an *enthalpy diagram* such as that shown in Figure 5.13(c). Because the combustion of $H_2(g)$ is exothermic, the enthalpy of the products in the reaction is lower than the enthalpy of the reactants. The enthalpy of the system is lower after the reaction because energy has been lost in the form of heat released to the surroundings.

The reaction of hydrogen with oxygen is highly exothermic (ΔH is negative and has a large magnitude), and it occurs rapidly once it starts. It can occur with explosive violence, too, as demonstrated by the disastrous explosions of the German airship *Hindenburg* in 1937 (Figure 5.14 ◀) and the space shuttle *Challenger* in 1986.

The following guidelines are helpful when using thermochemical equations and enthalpy diagrams:

1. *Enthalpy is an extensive property.* The magnitude of ΔH, therefore, is directly proportional to the amount of reactant consumed in the process. For the combustion of methane to form carbon dioxide and liquid water, for example, 890 kJ of heat is produced when 1 mol of CH_4 is burned in a constant-pressure system:

$$CH_4(g) + 2\,O_2(g) \longrightarrow CO_2(g) + 2\,H_2O(l) \qquad \Delta H = -890 \text{ kJ} \quad [5.18]$$

Because the combustion of 1 mol of CH_4 with 2 mol of O_2 releases 890 kJ of heat, the combustion of 2 mol of CH_4 with 4 mol of O_2 releases twice as much heat, 1780 kJ.

2. *The enthalpy change for a reaction is equal in magnitude, but opposite in sign, to* ΔH *for the reverse reaction.* For example, if we could reverse Equation 5.18 so that $CH_4(g)$ and $O_2(g)$ formed from $CO_2(g)$ and $H_2O(l)$, ΔH for the process would be +890 kJ:

$$CO_2(g) + 2\,H_2O(l) \longrightarrow CH_4(g) + 2\,O_2(g) \qquad \Delta H = 890 \text{ kJ} \quad [5.19]$$

When we reverse a reaction, we reverse the roles of the products and the reactants. As a result, the reactants in a reaction become the products of the reverse reaction, and so forth. From Equation 5.16, we can see that reversing the products and reactants leads to the same magnitude, but a change in sign for ΔH_{rxn}. This relationship is diagrammed for Equations 5.18 and 5.19 in Figure 5.15 ◀.

3. *The enthalpy change for a reaction depends on the state of the reactants and products.* If the product in the combustion of methane (Equation 5.18) were gaseous H_2O instead of liquid H_2O, ΔH_{rxn} would be -802 kJ instead of

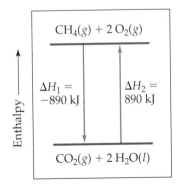

▲ **Figure 5.15 ΔH for a reverse reaction.** Reversing a reaction changes the sign but not the magnitude of the enthalpy change: $\Delta H_2 = -\Delta H_1$.

−890 kJ. Less heat would be available for transfer to the surroundings because the enthalpy of $H_2O(g)$ is greater than that of $H_2O(l)$. One way to see this is to imagine that the product is initially liquid water. The liquid water must be converted to water vapor, and the conversion of 2 mol $H_2O(l)$ to 2 mol $H_2O(g)$ is an endothermic process that absorbs 88 kJ:

$$2\,H_2O(l) \longrightarrow 2\,H_2O(g) \qquad \Delta H = +88\text{ kJ} \qquad\qquad [5.20]$$

Thus, it is important to specify the states of the reactants and products in thermochemical equations. In addition, we will generally assume that the reactants and products are both at the same temperature, 25 °C, unless otherwise indicated.

■ SAMPLE EXERCISE 5.4 | **Relating ΔH to Quantities of Reactants and Products**

How much heat is released when 4.50 g of methane gas is burned in a constant-pressure system? (Use the information given in Equation 5.18.)

SOLUTION

Analyze: Our goal is to use a thermochemical equation to calculate the heat produced when a specific amount of methane gas is combusted. According to Equation 5.18, 890 kJ is released by the system when 1 mol CH_4 is burned at constant pressure ($\Delta H = -890$ kJ).

Plan: Equation 5.18 provides us with a stoichiometric conversion factor: 1 mol $CH_4 \stackrel{\wedge}{=} -890$ kJ. Thus, we can convert moles of CH_4 to kJ of energy. First, however, we must convert grams of CH_4 to moles of CH_4. Thus, the conversion sequence is grams CH_4 (given) → moles CH_4 → kJ (unknown to be found).

Solve: By adding the atomic weights of C and 4 H, we have 1 mol $CH_4 = 16.0$ g CH_4. We can use the appropriate conversion factors to convert grams of CH_4 to moles of CH_4 to kilojoules:

$$\text{Heat} = (4.50\text{ g CH}_4)\left(\frac{1\text{ mol CH}_4}{16.0\text{ g CH}_4}\right)\left(\frac{-890\text{ kJ}}{1\text{ mol CH}_4}\right) = -250\text{ kJ}$$

The negative sign indicates that the system released 250 kJ into the surroundings.

■ PRACTICE EXERCISE

Hydrogen peroxide can decompose to water and oxygen by the following reaction:

$$2\,H_2O_2(l) \longrightarrow 2\,H_2O(l) + O_2(g) \qquad \Delta H = -196\text{ kJ}$$

Calculate the value of q when 5.00 g of $H_2O_2(l)$ decomposes at constant pressure.
Answer: −14.4 kJ

In many situations it is valuable to know the enthalpy change associated with a given chemical process. As we will see in the following sections, ΔH can be determined directly by experiment or calculated from the known enthalpy changes of other reactions by invoking the first law of thermodynamics.

5.5 CALORIMETRY

The value of ΔH can be determined experimentally by measuring the heat flow accompanying a reaction at constant pressure. Typically, we can determine the magnitude of the heat flow by measuring the magnitude of the temperature change the heat flow produces. The measurement of heat flow is **calorimetry**; a device used to measure heat flow is a **calorimeter**.

Heat Capacity and Specific Heat

The more heat an object gains, the hotter it gets. All substances change temperature when they are heated, but the magnitude of the temperature change produced by a given quantity of heat varies from substance to substance.

Strategies in Chemistry   USING ENTHALPY AS A GUIDE

If you hold a brick in the air and let it go, it will fall as the force of gravity pulls it toward Earth. A process that is thermodynamically favored to happen, such as a falling brick, is called a *spontaneous* process. A spontaneous process can be either fast or slow. Speed is not the issue in thermodynamics.

Many chemical processes are thermodynamically favored, or spontaneous, too. By "spontaneous," we do not mean that the reaction will form products without any intervention. That can be the case, but often some energy must be imparted to get the process started. The enthalpy change in a reaction gives one indication as to whether the reaction is likely to be spontaneous. The combustion of $H_2(g)$ and $O_2(g)$, for example, is a highly exothermic process:

$$H_2(g) + \tfrac{1}{2}O_2(g) \longrightarrow H_2O(g) \qquad \Delta H = -242 \text{ kJ}$$

Hydrogen gas and oxygen gas can exist together in a volume indefinitely without noticeable reaction occurring, as in Figure 5.13(a). Once initiated, however, energy is rapidly transferred from the system (the reactants) to the surroundings. As the reaction proceeds, large amounts of heat are released, which greatly increases the temperature of the reactants and the products. The system then loses enthalpy by transferring the heat to the surroundings. (Recall that the first law of thermodynamics indicates that the total energy of the system plus the surroundings will not change; energy is conserved.)

Enthalpy change is not the only consideration in the spontaneity of reactions, however, nor is it a foolproof guide. For example, the melting of ice is an endothermic process:

$$H_2O(s) \longrightarrow H_2O(l) \qquad \Delta H = +6.01 \text{ kJ}$$

Even though this process is endothermic, it is spontaneous at temperatures above the freezing point of water (0 °C). The reverse process, the freezing of water to ice, is spontaneous at temperatures below 0 °C. Thus, we know that ice at room temperature will melt and that water put into a freezer at −20 °C will turn into ice. Both of these processes are spontaneous under different conditions even though they are the reverse of one another. In Chapter 19 we will address the spontaneity of processes more fully. We will see why a process can be spontaneous at one temperature, but not at another, as is the case for the conversion of water to ice.

Despite these complicating factors, however, you should pay attention to the enthalpy changes in reactions. As a general observation, when the enthalpy change is large, it is the dominant factor in determining spontaneity. Thus, reactions for which ΔH is *large* and *negative* tend to be spontaneous. Reactions for which ΔH is *large* and *positive* tend to be spontaneous only in the reverse direction. The enthalpy of a reaction can be estimated in a number of ways. From these estimates, the likelihood of the reaction being thermodynamically favorable can be predicted.

Related Exercises: 5.45, 5.46

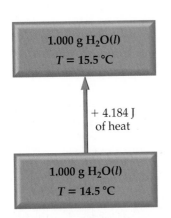

▲ **Figure 5.16 Specific heat of water.** Specific heat indicates the amount of heat that must be added to one gram of a substance to raise its temperature by 1 K (or 1 °C). Specific heats can vary slightly with temperature, so for precise measurements the temperature is specified. The specific heat of $H_2O(l)$ at 14.5 °C is 4.184 J/g-K; the addition of 4.184 J of heat to 1 g of liquid water at this temperature raises the temperature to 15.5 °C. This amount of energy defines the calorie: 1 cal = 4.184 J.

The temperature change experienced by an object when it absorbs a certain amount of heat is determined by its **heat capacity**, C. The heat capacity of an object is the amount of heat required to raise its temperature by 1 K (or 1 °C). The greater the heat capacity, the greater the heat required to produce a given increase in temperature.

For pure substances the heat capacity is usually given for a specified amount of the substance. The heat capacity of one mole of a substance is called its **molar heat capacity**, C_m. The heat capacity of one gram of a substance is called its *specific heat capacity*, or merely its **specific heat** (Figure 5.16 ◀). The specific heat, C_s, of a substance can be determined experimentally by measuring the temperature change, ΔT, that a known mass, m, of the substance undergoes when it gains or loses a specific quantity of heat, q:

$$\text{Specific heat} = \frac{\text{(quantity of heat transferred)}}{\text{(grams of substance)} \times \text{(temperature change)}}$$

$$C_s = \frac{q}{m \times \Delta T} \qquad [5.21]$$

For example, 209 J is required to increase the temperature of 50.0 g of water by 1.00 K. Thus, the specific heat of water is

$$C_s = \frac{209 \text{ J}}{(50.0 \text{ g})(1.00 \text{ K})} = 4.18 \frac{\text{J}}{\text{g-K}}$$

A temperature change in kelvins is equal in magnitude to the temperature change in degrees Celsius: ΔT in K = ΔT in °C. ∞(Section 1.4) When the

TABLE 5.2 ▪ Specific Heats of Some Substances at 298 K

Elements		Compounds	
Substance	Specific Heat (J/g-K)	Substance	Specific Heat (J/g-K)
$N_2(g)$	1.04	$H_2O(l)$	4.18
$Al(s)$	0.90	$CH_4(g)$	2.20
$Fe(s)$	0.45	$CO_2(g)$	0.84
$Hg(l)$	0.14	$CaCO_3(s)$	0.82

sample gains heat (positive q), the temperature of the sample increases (positive ΔT). Rearranging Equation 5.21, we get

$$q = C_s \times m \times \Delta T \qquad [5.22]$$

Thus, we can calculate the quantity of heat that a substance has gained or lost by using its specific heat together with its measured mass and temperature change.

The specific heats of several substances are listed in Table 5.2▲. Notice that the specific heat of liquid water is higher than those of the other substances listed. For example, it is about five times as great as that of aluminum metal. The high specific heat of water affects Earth's climate because it makes the temperatures of the oceans relatively resistant to change. It also is very important in maintaining a constant temperature in our bodies, as we will discuss in the "Chemistry and Life" box later in this chapter.

GIVE IT SOME THOUGHT

Which substance in Table 5.2 will undergo the greatest temperature change when the same mass of each substance absorbs the same quantity of heat?

▪ SAMPLE EXERCISE 5.5 | Relating Heat, Temperature Change, and Heat Capacity

(a) How much heat is needed to warm 250 g of water (about 1 cup) from 22 °C (about room temperature) to near its boiling point, 98 °C? The specific heat of water is 4.18 J/g-K. (b) What is the molar heat capacity of water?

SOLUTION

Analyze: In part (a) we must find the quantity of heat (q) needed to warm the water, given the mass of water (m), its temperature change (ΔT), and its specific heat (C_s). In part (b) we must calculate the molar heat capacity (heat capacity per mole, C_m) of water from its specific heat (heat capacity per gram).

Plan: (a) Given C_s, m, and ΔT, we can calculate the quantity of heat, q, using Equation 5.22. (b) We can use the molar mass of water and dimensional analysis to convert from heat capacity per gram to heat capacity per mole.

Solve:

(a) The water undergoes a temperature change of

$$\Delta T = 98\ °C - 22\ °C = 76\ °C = 76\ K$$

Using Equation 5.22, we have

$$q = C_s \times m \times \Delta T$$
$$= (4.18\ \text{J/g-K})(250\ \text{g})(76\ \text{K}) = 7.9 \times 10^4\ \text{J}$$

(b) The molar heat capacity is the heat capacity of one mole of substance. Using the atomic weights of hydrogen and oxygen, we have

$$1\ \text{mol}\ H_2O = 18.0\ \text{g}\ H_2O$$

From the specific heat given in part (a), we have

$$C_m = \left(4.18\ \frac{\text{J}}{\text{g-K}}\right)\left(\frac{18.0\ \text{g}}{1\ \text{mol}}\right) = 75.2\ \text{J/mol-K}$$

▪ PRACTICE EXERCISE

(a) Large beds of rocks are used in some solar-heated homes to store heat. Assume that the specific heat of the rocks is 0.82 J/g-K. Calculate the quantity of heat absorbed by 50.0 kg of rocks if their temperature increases by 12.0 °C. (b) What temperature change would these rocks undergo if they emitted 450 kJ of heat?
Answers: (a) 4.9×10^5 J, (b) 11 K decrease = 11 °C decrease

Thermometer

Glass stirrer

Cork stopper

Two Styrofoam®
cups nested
together containing
reactants in solution

▲ **Figure 5.17 Coffee-cup
calorimeter.** This simple apparatus is
used to measure heat-accompanying
reactions at constant pressure.

Constant-Pressure Calorimetry

The techniques and equipment employed in calorimetry depend on the nature of the process being studied. For many reactions, such as those occurring in solution, it is easy to control pressure so that ΔH is measured directly. (Recall that $\Delta H = q_p$) Although the calorimeters used for highly accurate work are precision instruments, a very simple "coffee-cup" calorimeter, as shown in Figure 5.17 ◄, is often used in general chemistry labs to illustrate the principles of calorimetry. Because the calorimeter is not sealed, the reaction occurs under the essentially constant pressure of the atmosphere.

In this case there is no physical boundary between the system and the surroundings. The reactants and products of the reaction are the system, and the water in which they dissolve as well as the calorimeter are part of the surroundings. If we assume that the calorimeter perfectly prevents the gain or loss of heat from the solution, the heat gained by the solution must be produced from the chemical reaction under study. In other words, the heat produced by the reaction, q_{rxn}, is entirely absorbed by the solution; it does not escape the calorimeter. (We also assume that the calorimeter itself does not absorb heat. In the case of the coffee-cup calorimeter, this is a reasonable approximation because the calorimeter has a very low thermal conductivity and heat capacity.) For an exothermic reaction, heat is "lost" by the reaction and "gained" by the solution, so the temperature of the solution rises. The opposite occurs for an endothermic reaction. The heat gained by the solution, q_{soln}, is therefore equal in magnitude to q_{rxn} but opposite in sign: $q_{soln} = -q_{rxn}$. The value of q_{soln} is readily calculated from the mass of the solution, its specific heat, and the temperature change:

$$q_{soln} = \text{(specific heat of solution)} \times \text{(grams of solution)} \times \Delta T = -q_{rxn} \quad [5.23]$$

For dilute aqueous solutions the specific heat of the solution will be approximately the same as that of water, 4.18 J/g-K.

Equation 5.23 makes it possible to calculate q_{rxn} from the temperature change of the solution in which the reaction occurs. A temperature increase ($\Delta T > 0$) means the reaction is exothermic ($q_{rxn} < 0$).

▲ GIVE IT SOME THOUGHT

(a) How are the energy changes of a system and its surroundings related? **(b)** How is the heat gained or lost by a system related to the heat gained or lost by its surroundings?

■■ **SAMPLE EXERCISE 5.6** | Measuring ΔH Using a Coffee-Cup Calorimeter

When a student mixes 50 mL of 1.0 M HCl and 50 mL of 1.0 M NaOH in a coffee-cup calorimeter, the temperature of the resultant solution increases from 21.0 °C to 27.5 °C. Calculate the enthalpy change for the reaction in kJ/mol HCl, assuming that the calorimeter loses only a negligible quantity of heat, that the total volume of the solution is 100 mL, that its density is 1.0 g/mL, and that its specific heat is 4.18 J/g-K.

SOLUTION

Analyze: Mixing solutions of HCl and NaOH results in an acid–base reaction:

$$\text{HCl}(aq) + \text{NaOH}(aq) \longrightarrow \text{H}_2\text{O}(l) + \text{NaCl}(aq)$$

We need to calculate the heat produced per mole of HCl, given the temperature increase of the solution, the number of moles of HCl and NaOH involved, and the density and specific heat of the solution.

Plan: The total heat produced can be calculated using Equation 5.23. The number of moles of HCl consumed in the reaction must be calculated from the volume and molarity of this substance, and this amount then used to determine the heat produced per mol HCl.

Solve:

Because the total volume of the solution is 100 mL, its mass is

$$(100 \text{ mL})(1.0 \text{ g/mL}) = 100 \text{ g}$$

The temperature change is

$$\Delta T = 27.5 \,°\text{C} - 21.0 \,°\text{C} = 6.5 \,°\text{C} = 6.5 \text{ K}$$

Using Equation 5.23, we have

$$q_{rxn} = -C_s \times m \times \Delta T$$
$$= -(4.18 \text{ J/g-K})(100 \text{ g})(6.5 \text{ K}) = -2.7 \times 10^3 \text{ J} = -2.7 \text{ kJ}$$

Because the process occurs at constant pressure,

$$\Delta H = q_P = -2.7 \text{ kJ}$$

To express the enthalpy change on a molar basis, we use the fact that the number of moles of HCl is given by the product of the respective solution volumes (50 mL = 0.050 L) and concentrations (1.0 M = 1.0 mol/L):

$$(0.050 \text{ L})(1.0 \text{ mol/L}) = 0.050 \text{ mol}$$

Thus, the enthalpy change per mole of HCl is

$$\Delta H = -2.7 \text{ kJ}/0.050 \text{ mol} = -54 \text{ kJ/mol}$$

Check: ΔH is negative (exothermic), which is expected for the reaction of an acid with a base and evidenced by the fact that the reaction causes the temperature of the solution to increase. The molar magnitude of the heat produced seems reasonable.

▬ PRACTICE EXERCISE

When 50.0 mL of 0.100 M $AgNO_3$ and 50.0 mL of 0.100 M HCl are mixed in a constant-pressure calorimeter, the temperature of the mixture increases from 22.30 °C to 23.11 °C. The temperature increase is caused by the following reaction:

$$AgNO_3(aq) + HCl(aq) \longrightarrow AgCl(s) + HNO_3(aq)$$

Calculate ΔH for this reaction in kJ/mol $AgNO_3$, assuming that the combined solution has a mass of 100.0 g and a specific heat of 4.18 J/g °C.
Answer: −68,000 J/mol = −68 kJ/mol

Bomb Calorimetry (Constant-Volume Calorimetry)

One of the most important types of reactions studied using calorimetry is combustion, in which a compound (usually an organic compound) reacts completely with excess oxygen. ∞(Section 3.2) Combustion reactions are most conveniently studied using a **bomb calorimeter**, a device shown schematically in Figure 5.18▶. The substance to be studied is placed in a small cup within a sealed vessel called a *bomb*. The bomb, which is designed to withstand high pressures, has an inlet valve for adding oxygen and electrical contacts to initiate the combustion. After the sample has been placed in the bomb, the bomb is sealed and pressurized with oxygen. It is then placed in the calorimeter, which is essentially an insulated container, and covered with an accurately measured quantity of water. When all the components within the calorimeter have come to the same temperature, the combustion reaction is initiated by passing an electrical current through a fine wire that is in contact with the sample. When the wire becomes sufficiently hot, the sample ignites.

Heat is released when combustion occurs. This heat is absorbed by the calorimeter contents, causing a rise in the temperature of the water. The temperature of the water is very carefully measured before reaction and then after reaction when the contents of the calorimeter have again arrived at a common temperature.

To calculate the heat of combustion from the measured temperature increase in the bomb calorimeter, we must know the total heat capacity of the calorimeter, C_{cal}. This quantity is determined by combusting a sample that releases a known quantity of heat and measuring the resulting temperature change. For example, the combustion of exactly 1 g of benzoic acid, C_6H_5COOH, in a bomb calorimeter produces 26.38 kJ of heat. Suppose 1.000 g of benzoic acid is combusted in a calorimeter, and it increases the temperature by 4.857 °C. The heat capacity of the calorimeter is then given by C_{cal} = 26.38 kJ/4.857 °C = 5.431 kJ/°C. Once we know the value of C_{cal}, we can measure temperature changes produced by other reactions, and from these we can calculate the heat evolved in the reaction, q_{rxn}:

$$q_{rxn} = -C_{cal} \times \Delta T \qquad [5.24]$$

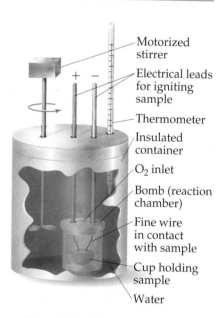

Motorized stirrer

Electrical leads for igniting sample

Thermometer

Insulated container

O_2 inlet

Bomb (reaction chamber)

Fine wire in contact with sample

Cup holding sample

Water

▲ **Figure 5.18 Bomb calorimeter.** This device is used to measure heat accompanying combustion reactions at constant volume.

■ **SAMPLE EXERCISE 5.7** | Measuring q_{rxn} Using a Bomb Calorimeter

Methylhydrazine (CH_6N_2) is used as a liquid rocket fuel. The combustion of methylhydrazine with oxygen produces $N_2(g)$, $CO_2(g)$, and $H_2O(l)$:

$$2\,CH_6N_2(l) + 5\,O_2(g) \longrightarrow 2\,N_2(g) + 2\,CO_2(g) + 6\,H_2O(l)$$

When 4.00 g of methylhydrazine is combusted in a bomb calorimeter, the temperature of the calorimeter increases from 25.00 °C to 39.50 °C. In a separate experiment the heat capacity of the calorimeter is measured to be 7.794 kJ/°C. Calculate the heat of reaction for the combustion of a mole of CH_6N_2.

SOLUTION

Analyze: We are given a temperature change and the total heat capacity of the calorimeter. We are also given the amount of reactant combusted. Our goal is to calculate the enthalpy change per mole for combustion of the reactant.

Plan: We will first calculate the heat evolved for the combustion of the 4.00-g sample. We will then convert this heat to a molar quantity.

Solve:

For combustion of the 4.00-g sample of methylhydrazine, the temperature change of the calorimeter is

$$\Delta T = (39.50 \,°C - 25.00 \,°C) = 14.50 \,°C$$

We can use ΔT and the value for C_{cal} to calculate the heat of reaction (Equation 5.24):

$$q_{rxn} = -C_{cal} \times \Delta T = -(7.794 \text{ kJ/°C})(14.50 \,°C) = -113.0 \text{ kJ}$$

We can readily convert this value to the heat of reaction for a mole of CH_6N_2:

$$\left(\frac{-113.0 \text{ kJ}}{4.00 \text{ g } CH_6N_2}\right) \times \left(\frac{46.1 \text{ g } CH_6N_2}{1 \text{ mol } CH_6N_2}\right) = -1.30 \times 10^3 \text{ kJ/mol } CH_6N_2$$

Check: The units cancel properly, and the sign of the answer is negative as it should be for an exothermic reaction.

■ **PRACTICE EXERCISE**

A 0.5865-g sample of lactic acid ($HC_3H_5O_3$) is burned in a calorimeter whose heat capacity is 4.812 kJ/°C. The temperature increases from 23.10 °C to 24.95 °C. Calculate the heat of combustion of lactic acid **(a)** per gram and **(b)** per mole.
Answers: **(a)** −15.2 kJ/g, **(b)** −1370 kJ/mol

Because the reactions in a bomb calorimeter are carried out under constant-volume conditions, the heat transferred corresponds to the change in internal energy, ΔE, rather than the change in enthalpy, ΔH (Equation 5.14). For most reactions, however, the difference between ΔE and ΔH is very small. For the reaction discussed in Sample Exercise 5.7, for example, the difference between ΔE and ΔH is only about 1 kJ/mol—a difference of less than 0.1%. It is possible to correct the measured heat changes to obtain ΔH values, and these form the basis of the tables of enthalpy change that we will see in the following sections. However, we need not concern ourselves with how these small corrections are made.

5.6 HESS'S LAW

Many enthalpies of reaction have been measured and tabulated. In this section and the next we will see that it is often possible to calculate the ΔH for a reaction from the tabulated ΔH values of other reactions. Thus, it is not necessary to make calorimetric measurements for all reactions.

Because enthalpy is a state function, the enthalpy change, ΔH, associated with any chemical process depends only on the amount of matter that undergoes change and on the nature of the initial state of the reactants and the final state of the products. This means that whether a particular reaction is carried out in one step or in a series of steps, the sum of the enthalpy changes associated with the individual steps must be the same as the enthalpy change associated with the one-step process. As an example, the combustion of methane gas, $CH_4(g)$, to

Chemistry and Life   THE REGULATION OF HUMAN BODY TEMPERATURE

For most of us, the question "Are you running a fever?" was one of our first introductions to medical diagnosis. Indeed, a deviation in body temperature of only a few degrees indicates that something is amiss. In the laboratory you may have tried to maintain a solution at a constant temperature, only to find how difficult it can be. Yet our bodies manage to maintain a near-constant temperature in spite of widely varying weather, levels of physical activity, and periods of high metabolic activity (such as after a meal). How does the human body manage this task, and how does it relate to some of the topics we have discussed in this chapter?

Maintaining a near-constant temperature is one of the primary physiological functions of the human body. Normal body temperature generally ranges from 35.8 °C to 37.2 °C (96.5 °F–99 °F). This very narrow temperature range is essential to proper muscle function and to the control of the rates of the biochemical reactions in the body. You will learn more about the effects of temperature on reaction rates in Chapter 14.

A portion of the human brain stem called the *hypothalamus* regulates the temperature. The hypothalamus acts as a thermostat for body temperature. When body temperature rises above the high end of the normal range, the hypothalamus triggers mechanisms to lower the temperature. It likewise triggers mechanisms to increase the temperature if body temperature drops too low.

To understand qualitatively how the body's heating and cooling mechanisms operate, we can view the body as a thermodynamic system. The body increases its internal energy content by ingesting foods from the surroundings. ∞ (Section 5.8) The foods, such as glucose ($C_6H_{12}O_6$), are metabolized—a process that is essentially controlled oxidation to CO_2 and H_2O:

$$C_6H_{12}O_6(s) + 6\,O_2(g) \longrightarrow 6\,CO_2(g) + 6\,H_2O(l)$$
$$\Delta H = -2803\text{ kJ}$$

Roughly 40% of the energy produced is ultimately used to do work in the form of muscle contractions and nerve cell activities. The remainder of the energy is released as heat, part of which is used to maintain body temperature. When the body produces too much heat, as in times of heavy physical exertion, it dissipates the excess to the surroundings.

Heat is transferred from the body to its surroundings primarily by *radiation, convection,* and *evaporation*. Radiation is the direct loss of heat from the body to cooler surroundings, much as a hot stovetop radiates heat to its surroundings. Convection is heat loss by virtue of heating air that is in contact with the body. The heated air rises and is replaced with cooler air, and the process continues. Warm clothing, which usually consists of insulating layers of material with "dead air" in between, decreases convective heat loss in cold weather. Evaporative cooling occurs when perspiration is generated at the skin surface by the sweat glands. Heat is removed from the body as the perspiration evaporates into the surroundings. Perspiration is predominantly water, so the process involved is the endothermic conversion of liquid water into water vapor:

$$H_2O(l) \longrightarrow H_2O(g) \qquad \Delta H = +44.0\text{ kJ}$$

The speed with which evaporative cooling occurs decreases as the atmospheric humidity increases, which is why people seem to be more sweaty and uncomfortable on hot and humid days.

When the hypothalamus senses that the body temperature has risen too high, it increases heat loss from the body in two principal ways. First, it increases the flow of blood near the surface of the skin, which allows for increased radiational and convective cooling. The reddish "flushed" appearance of a hot individual is the result of this increased subsurface blood flow. Second, the hypothalamus stimulates the secretion of perspiration from the sweat glands, which increases evaporative cooling. During periods of extreme activity, the amount of liquid secreted as perspiration can be as high as 2 to 4 liters per hour. As a result, water must be replenished to the body during these periods (Figure 5.19▼). If the body loses too much fluid through perspiration, it will no longer be able to cool itself and blood volume decreases, which can lead to *heat exhaustion* or the more serious and potentially fatal *heat stroke*, during which the body temperature can rise to as high as 41 °C to 45 °C (106 °F–113 °F). On the other hand, replenishing water without replenishing the electrolytes that are lost during perspiration can also lead to serious problems as pointed out in the "Chemistry in Life" box in Section 4.5.

When body temperature drops too low, the hypothalamus decreases the blood flow to the surface of the skin, thereby decreasing heat loss. It also triggers small involuntary contractions of the muscles; the biochemical reactions that generate the energy to do this work also generate more heat for the body. When these contractions get large enough—as when the body feels a chill—a *shiver* results. If the body is unable to maintain a temperature above 35 °C (95 °F), the very dangerous condition called *hypothermia* can result.

▲ Figure 5.19 **Marathon runner drinking water.** Runners must constantly replenish the water in their bodies that is lost through perspiration.

form $CO_2(g)$ and liquid water can be thought of as occurring in two steps: (1) the combustion of $CH_4(g)$ to form $CO_2(g)$ and gaseous water, $H_2O(g)$ and (2) the condensation of gaseous water to form liquid water, $H_2O(l)$. The enthalpy change for the overall process is simply the sum of the enthalpy changes for these two steps:

$$CH_4(g) + 2\,O_2(g) \longrightarrow CO_2(g) + 2\,H_2O(g) \qquad \Delta H = -802 \text{ kJ}$$

(Add) $\qquad 2\,H_2O(g) \longrightarrow 2\,H_2O(l) \qquad\qquad\qquad\quad \Delta H = -\ 88 \text{ kJ}$

$$CH_4(g) + 2\,O_2(g) + 2\,H_2O(g) \longrightarrow CO_2(g) + 2\,H_2O(l) + 2\,H_2O(g) \qquad \Delta H = -890 \text{ kJ}$$

The net equation is

$$CH_4(g) + 2\,O_2(g) \longrightarrow CO_2(g) + 2\,H_2O(l) \qquad \Delta H = -890 \text{ kJ}$$

To obtain the net equation, the sum of the reactants of the two equations is placed on one side of the arrow and the sum of the products on the other side. Because $2\,H_2O(g)$ occurs on both sides, it can be canceled like an algebraic quantity that appears on both sides of an equal sign. Figure 5.20◄ compares the two-step reaction with the direct one.

Hess's law states that *if a reaction is carried out in a series of steps, ΔH for the overall reaction will equal the sum of the enthalpy changes for the individual steps.* The overall enthalpy change for the process is independent of the number of steps or the particular nature of the path by which the reaction is carried out. This principle is a consequence of the fact that enthalpy is a state function, and ΔH is therefore independent of the path between the initial and final states. We can therefore calculate ΔH for any process, as long as we find a route for which ΔH is known for each step. This means that a relatively small number of experimental measurements can be used to calculate ΔH for a vast number of different reactions.

Hess's law provides a useful means of calculating energy changes that are difficult to measure directly. For instance, it is impossible to measure directly the enthalpy for the combustion of carbon to form carbon monoxide. Combustion of 1 mol of carbon with 0.5 mol of O_2 produces both CO and CO_2, leaving some carbon unreacted. However, solid carbon and carbon monoxide can both be completely burned in O_2 to produce CO_2. We can use the enthalpy changes of these reactions to calculate the heat of combustion of C to CO, as shown in Sample Exercise 5.8.

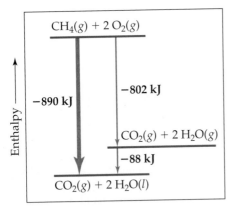

▲ **Figure 5.20 An enthalpy diagram comparing a one-step and a two-step process for a reaction.** The enthalpy change of the direct reaction on the left equals the sum of the two steps on the right. That is, ΔH for the overall reaction equals the sum of the ΔH values for the two steps shown.

GIVE IT SOME THOUGHT

What effect do the following changes have on ΔH for a reaction: **(a)** reversing a reaction, **(b)** multiplying coefficients by 2?

■ **SAMPLE EXERCISE 5.8** | Using Hess's Law to Calculate ΔH

The enthalpy of reaction for the combustion of C to CO_2 is -393.5 kJ/mol C, and the enthalpy for the combustion of CO to CO_2 is -283.0 kJ/mol CO:

(1) $\qquad\qquad C(s) + O_2(g) \longrightarrow CO_2(g) \qquad \Delta H_1 = -393.5 \text{ kJ}$

(2) $\qquad\qquad CO(g) + \tfrac{1}{2}O_2(g) \longrightarrow CO_2(g) \qquad \Delta H_2 = -283.0 \text{ kJ}$

Using these data, calculate the enthalpy for the combustion of C to CO:

(3) $\qquad\qquad C(s) + \tfrac{1}{2}O_2(g) \longrightarrow CO(g) \qquad \Delta H_3 = ?$

SOLUTION

Analyze: We are given two thermochemical equations, and our goal is to combine them in such a way as to obtain the third equation and its enthalpy change.

Plan: We will use Hess's law. In doing so, we first note the numbers of moles of substances among the reactants and products in the target equation, (3). We then manipulate equations (1) and (2) to give the same number of moles of these substances, so that when the resulting equations are added, we obtain the target equation. At the same time, we keep track of the enthalpy changes, which we add.

Solve: To use equations (1) and (2), we arrange them so that C(s) is on the reactant side and CO(g) is on the product side of the arrow, as in the target reaction, equation (3). Because equation (1) has C(s) as a reactant, we can use that equation just as it is. We need to turn equation (2) around, however, so that CO(g) is a product. Remember that when reactions are turned around, the sign of ΔH is reversed. We arrange the two equations so that they can be added to give the desired equation:

$$C(s) + O_2(g) \longrightarrow CO_2(g) \qquad \Delta H_1 = -393.5 \text{ kJ}$$
$$\underline{CO_2(g) \longrightarrow CO(g) + \tfrac{1}{2}O_2(g) \qquad -\Delta H_2 = 283.0 \text{ kJ}}$$
$$C(s) + \tfrac{1}{2}O_2(g) \longrightarrow CO(g) \qquad \Delta H_3 = -110.5 \text{ kJ}$$

When we add the two equations, $CO_2(g)$ appears on both sides of the arrow and therefore cancels out. Likewise, $\tfrac{1}{2}O_2(g)$ is eliminated from each side.

Comment: It is sometimes useful to add subscripts to the enthalpy changes, as we have done here, to keep track of the associations between the chemical reactions and their ΔH values.

■ PRACTICE EXERCISE

Carbon occurs in two forms, graphite and diamond. The enthalpy of the combustion of graphite is -393.5 kJ/mol and that of diamond is -395.4 kJ/mol:

$$C(graphite) + O_2(g) \longrightarrow CO_2(g) \qquad \Delta H_1 = -393.5 \text{ kJ}$$
$$C(diamond) + O_2(g) \longrightarrow CO_2(g) \qquad \Delta H_2 = -395.4 \text{ kJ}$$

Calculate ΔH for the conversion of graphite to diamond:

$$C(graphite) \longrightarrow C(diamond) \qquad \Delta H_3 = ?$$

Answer: $\Delta H_3 = +1.9$ kJ

■ SAMPLE EXERCISE 5.9 | Using Three Equations with Hess's Law to Calculate ΔH

Calculate ΔH for the reaction

$$2\,C(s) + H_2(g) \longrightarrow C_2H_2(g)$$

given the following chemical equations and their respective enthalpy changes:

$$C_2H_2(g) + \tfrac{5}{2}O_2(g) \longrightarrow 2\,CO_2(g) + H_2O(l) \qquad \Delta H = -1299.6 \text{ kJ}$$
$$C(s) + O_2(g) \longrightarrow CO_2(g) \qquad \Delta H = -393.5 \text{ kJ}$$
$$H_2(g) + \tfrac{1}{2}O_2(g) \longrightarrow H_2O(l) \qquad \Delta H = -285.8 \text{ kJ}$$

SOLUTION

Analyze: We are given a chemical equation and asked to calculate its ΔH using three chemical equations and their associated enthalpy changes.

Plan: We will use Hess's law, summing the three equations or their reverses and multiplying each by an appropriate coefficient so that they add to give the net equation for the reaction of interest. At the same time, we keep track of the ΔH values, reversing their signs if the reactions are reversed and multiplying them by whatever coefficient is employed in the equation.

Solve: Because the target equation has C_2H_2 as a product, we turn the first equation around; the sign of ΔH is therefore changed. The desired equation has $2\,C(s)$ as a reactant, so we multiply the second equation and its ΔH by 2. Because the target equation has H_2 as a reactant, we keep the third equation as it is. We then add the three equations and their enthalpy changes in accordance with Hess's law:

$$2\,CO_2(g) + H_2O(l) \longrightarrow C_2H_2(g) + \tfrac{5}{2}O_2(g) \qquad \Delta H = 1299.6 \text{ kJ}$$
$$2\,C(s) + 2\,O_2(g) \longrightarrow 2\,CO_2(g) \qquad \Delta H = -787.0 \text{ kJ}$$
$$\underline{H_2(g) + \tfrac{1}{2}O_2(g) \longrightarrow H_2O(l) \qquad \Delta H = -285.8 \text{ kJ}}$$
$$2\,C(s) + H_2(g) \longrightarrow C_2H_2(g) \qquad \Delta H = 226.8 \text{ kJ}$$

When the equations are added, there are $2\,CO_2$, $\tfrac{5}{2}O_2$, and H_2O on both sides of the arrow. These are canceled in writing the net equation.

Check: The procedure must be correct because we obtained the correct net equation. In cases like this you should go back over the numerical manipulations of the ΔH values to ensure that you did not make an inadvertent error with signs.

■ PRACTICE EXERCISE

Calculate ΔH for the reaction

$$NO(g) + O(g) \longrightarrow NO_2(g)$$

given the following information:

$$
\begin{array}{ll}
NO(g) + O_3(g) \longrightarrow NO_2(g) + O_2(g) & \Delta H = -198.9 \text{ kJ} \\
O_3(g) \longrightarrow \tfrac{3}{2}O_2(g) & \Delta H = -142.3 \text{ kJ} \\
O_2(g) \longrightarrow 2\,O(g) & \Delta H = 495.0 \text{ kJ}
\end{array}
$$

Answer: −304.1 kJ

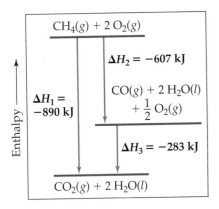

▲ Figure 5.21 **An enthalpy diagram illustrating Hess's law.** Because H is a state function, the enthalpy change for the combustion of 1 mol CH_4 is independent of whether the reaction takes place in one or more steps: $\Delta H_1 = \Delta H_2 + \Delta H_3$.

The key point of these examples is that H is a state function, so *for a particular set of reactants and products, ΔH is the same whether the reaction takes place in one step or in a series of steps.* For example, consider the reaction of methane (CH_4) and oxygen (O_2) to form CO_2 and H_2O. We can envision the reaction forming CO_2 directly or with the initial formation of CO, which is then combusted to CO_2. These two paths are compared in Figure 5.21 ◀. Because H is a state function, both paths *must* produce the same value of ΔH. In the enthalpy diagram, that means $\Delta H_1 = \Delta H_2 + \Delta H_3$.

5.7 ENTHALPIES OF FORMATION

By using the methods we have just discussed, we can calculate the enthalpy changes for a great many reactions from tabulated ΔH values. Many experimental data are tabulated according to the type of process. For example, extensive tables exist of *enthalpies of vaporization* (ΔH for converting liquids to gases), *enthalpies of fusion* (ΔH for melting solids), *enthalpies of combustion* (ΔH for combusting a substance in oxygen), and so forth. A particularly important process used for tabulating thermochemical data is the formation of a compound from its constituent elements. The enthalpy change associated with this process is called the **enthalpy of formation** (or *heat of formation*) and is labeled ΔH_f, where the subscript f indicates that the substance has been *formed* from its component elements.

The magnitude of any enthalpy change depends on the conditions of temperature, pressure, and state (gas, liquid, or solid crystalline form) of the reactants and products. To compare the enthalpies of different reactions, we must define a set of conditions, called a *standard state*, at which most enthalpies are tabulated. The standard state of a substance is its pure form at atmospheric pressure (1 atm; ∞Section 10.2) and the temperature of interest, which we usually choose to be 298 K (25 °C).* The **standard enthalpy change** of a reaction is defined as the enthalpy change when all reactants and products are in their standard states. We denote a standard enthalpy change as $\Delta H°$, where the superscript ° indicates standard-state conditions.

The definition of the standard state for gases has been changed to 1 bar (1 atm = 1.013 bar), a slightly lower pressure than the value of 1 atm that is used for the data in this text. For most purposes, this change makes very little difference in the standard changes.

The **standard enthalpy of formation** of a compound, ΔH_f°, is the change in enthalpy for the reaction that forms one mole of the compound from its elements, with all substances in their standard states:

elements (in standard states) $\longrightarrow$ compound (in standard state) ΔH_f°

We usually report ΔH_f° values at 298 K. If an element exists in more than one form under standard conditions, the most stable form of the element is usually used for the formation reaction. For example, the standard enthalpy of formation for ethanol, C_2H_5OH, is the enthalpy change for the following reaction:

$$2\ C(graphite) + 3\ H_2(g) + \tfrac{1}{2}O_2(g) \longrightarrow C_2H_5OH(l)   \Delta H_f^\circ = -277.7 \text{ kJ}   [5.25]$$

The elemental source of oxygen is O_2, not O or O_3, because O_2 is the stable form of oxygen at 298 K and standard atmospheric pressure. Similarly, the elemental source of carbon is graphite and not diamond, because graphite is more stable (lower energy) at 298 K and standard atmospheric pressure (see Practice Exercise 5.8). Likewise, the most stable form of hydrogen under standard conditions is $H_2(g)$, so this is used as the source of hydrogen in Equation 5.25.

The stoichiometry of formation reactions always indicates that one mole of the desired substance is produced, as in Equation 5.25. As a result, enthalpies of formation are reported in kJ/mol of the substance being formed. Several standard enthalpies of formation are given in Table 5.3▼. A more complete table is provided in Appendix C.

By definition, *the standard enthalpy of formation of the most stable form of any element is zero* because there is no formation reaction needed when the element is already in its standard state. Thus, the values of ΔH_f° for C(graphite), $H_2(g)$, $O_2(g)$, and the standard states of other elements are zero by definition.

GIVE IT SOME THOUGHT

In Table 5.3, the standard enthalpy of formation of $C_2H_2(g)$ is listed as 226.7 kJ/mol. Write the thermochemical equation associated with ΔH_f° for this substance.

TABLE 5.3 ■ Standard Enthalpies of Formation, ΔH_f°, at 298 K

Substance	Formula	ΔH_f° (kJ/mol)	Substance	Formula	ΔH_f° (kJ/mol)
Acetylene	$C_2H_2(g)$	226.7	Hydrogen chloride	$HCl(g)$	−92.30
Ammonia	$NH_3(g)$	−46.19	Hydrogen fluoride	$HF(g)$	−268.60
Benzene	$C_6H_6(l)$	49.0	Hydrogen iodide	$HI(g)$	25.9
Calcium carbonate	$CaCO_3(s)$	−1207.1	Methane	$CH_4(g)$	−74.80
Calcium oxide	$CaO(s)$	−635.5	Methanol	$CH_3OH(l)$	−238.6
Carbon dioxide	$CO_2(g)$	−393.5	Propane	$C_3H_8(g)$	−103.85
Carbon monoxide	$CO(g)$	−110.5	Silver chloride	$AgCl(s)$	−127.0
Diamond	$C(s)$	1.88	Sodium bicarbonate	$NaHCO_3(s)$	−947.7
Ethane	$C_2H_6(g)$	−84.68	Sodium carbonate	$Na_2CO_3(s)$	−1130.9
Ethanol	$C_2H_5OH(l)$	−277.7	Sodium chloride	$NaCl(s)$	−410.9
Ethylene	$C_2H_4(g)$	52.30	Sucrose	$C_{12}H_{22}O_{11}(s)$	−2221
Glucose	$C_6H_{12}O_6(s)$	−1273	Water	$H_2O(l)$	−285.8
Hydrogen bromide	$HBr(g)$	−36.23	Water vapor	$H_2O(g)$	−241.8

■ **SAMPLE EXERCISE 5.10** | **Identifying Equations Associated with Enthalpies of Formation**

For which of the following reactions at 25 °C would the enthalpy change represent a standard enthalpy of formation? For each that does not, what changes are needed to make it an equation whose ΔH is an enthalpy of formation?

(a) $2\,Na(s) + \frac{1}{2}O_2(g) \longrightarrow Na_2O(s)$

(b) $2\,K(l) + Cl_2(g) \longrightarrow 2\,KCl(s)$

(c) $C_6H_{12}O_6(s) \longrightarrow 6\,C(diamond) + 6\,H_2(g) + 3\,O_2(g)$

SOLUTION

Analyze: The standard enthalpy of formation is represented by a reaction in which each reactant is an element in its standard state and the product is one mole of the compound.

Plan: We need to examine each equation to determine, first, whether the reaction is one in which one mole of substance is formed from the elements. Next, we need to determine whether the reactant elements are in their standard states.

Solve: In (a) 1 mol Na_2O is formed from the elements sodium and oxygen in their proper states, solid Na and O_2 gas, respectively. Therefore, the enthalpy change for reaction (a) corresponds to a standard enthalpy of formation.

In (b) potassium is given as a liquid. It must be changed to the solid form, its standard state at room temperature. Furthermore, two moles of product are formed, so the enthalpy change for the reaction as written is twice the standard enthalpy of formation of $KCl(s)$. The equation for the formation reaction of 1 mol of $KCl(s)$ is

$$K(s) + \tfrac{1}{2}Cl(g) \longrightarrow KCl(s)$$

Reaction (c) does not form a substance from its elements. Instead, a substance decomposes to its elements, so this reaction must be reversed. Next, the element carbon is given as diamond, whereas graphite is the standard state of carbon at room temperature and 1 atm pressure. The equation that correctly represents the enthalpy of formation of glucose from its elements is

$$6\,C(graphite) + 6\,H_2(g) + 3\,O_2(g) \longrightarrow C_6H_{12}O_6(s)$$

■ **PRACTICE EXERCISE**

Write the equation corresponding to the standard enthalpy of formation of liquid carbon tetrachloride (CCl_4).
Answer: $C(graphite) + 2\,Cl_2(g) \longrightarrow CCl_4(l)$

Using Enthalpies of Formation to Calculate Enthalpies of Reaction

Tabulations of ΔH_f°, such as those in Table 5.3 and Appendix C, have many important uses. As we will see in this section, we can use Hess's law to calculate the standard enthalpy change for any reaction for which we know the ΔH_f° values for all reactants and products. For example, consider the combustion of propane gas, $C_3H_8(g)$, with oxygen to form $CO_2(g)$ and $H_2O(l)$ under standard conditions:

$$C_3H_8(g) + 5\,O_2(g) \longrightarrow 3\,CO_2(g) + 4\,H_2O(l)$$

We can write this equation as the sum of three formation reactions:

$$
\begin{array}{lll}
C_3H_8(g) \longrightarrow 3\,C(s) + 4\,H_2(g) & \Delta H_1 = -\Delta H_f^\circ[C_3H_8(g)] & [5.26] \\
3\,C(s) + 3\,O_2(g) \longrightarrow 3\,CO_2(g) & \Delta H_2 = 3\Delta H_f^\circ[CO_2(g)] & [5.27] \\
4\,H_2(g) + 2\,O_2(g) \longrightarrow 4\,H_2O(l) & \Delta H_3 = 4\Delta H_f^\circ[H_2O(l)] & [5.28] \\
\hline
C_3H_8(g) + 5\,O_2(g) \longrightarrow 3\,CO_2(g) + 4\,H_2O(l) & \Delta H_{rxn}^\circ = \Delta H_1 + \Delta H_2 + \Delta H_3 & [5.29]
\end{array}
$$

From Hess's law we can write the standard enthalpy change for the overall reaction, Equation 5.29, as the sum of the enthalpy changes for the processes in

Equations 5.26 through 5.28. We can then use values from Table 5.3 to compute a numerical value for $\Delta H°$ for the overall reaction:

$$\Delta H°_{rxn} = \Delta H_1 + \Delta H_2 + \Delta H_3$$

$$= -\Delta H°_f[C_3H_8(g)] + 3\Delta H°_f[CO_2(g)] + 4\Delta H°_f[H_2O(l)] \qquad [5.30]$$

$$= -(-103.85 \text{ kJ}) + 3(-393.5 \text{ kJ}) + 4(-285.8 \text{ kJ}) = -2219.9 \text{ kJ}$$

Several aspects of this calculation depend on the guidelines we discussed in Section 5.4.

1. Equation 5.26 is the reverse of the formation reaction for $C_3H_8(g)$, so the enthalpy change for this reaction is $-\Delta H°_f[C_3H_8(g)]$.

2. Equation 5.27 is the formation reaction for 3 mol of $CO_2(g)$. Because enthalpy is an extensive property, the enthalpy change for this step is $3\Delta H°_f[CO_2(g)]$. Similarly, the enthalpy change for Equation 5.28 is $4\Delta H°_f[H_2O(l)]$. The reaction specifies that $H_2O(l)$, was produced, so be careful to use the value of $\Delta H°_f$ for $H_2O(l)$, not $H_2O(g)$.

3. We assume that the stoichiometric coefficients in the balanced equation represent moles. For Equation 5.29, therefore, the value $\Delta H°_{rxn} = -2220$ kJ represents the enthalpy change for the reaction of 1 mol C_3H_8 and 5 mol O_2 to form 3 mol CO_2 and 4 mol H_2O. The product of the number of moles and the enthalpy change in kJ/mol has the units kJ: (number of moles) × $(\Delta H°_f$ in kJ/mol) = kJ. We therefore report $\Delta H°_{rxn}$ in kJ.

Figure 5.22 ▼ presents an enthalpy diagram for Equation 5.29, showing how it can be broken into steps involving formation reactions.

We can break down any reaction into formation reactions as we have done here. When we do, we obtain the general result that the standard enthalpy change of a reaction is the sum of the standard enthalpies of formation of the products minus the standard enthalpies of formation of the reactants:

$$\Delta H°_{rxn} = \Sigma n \Delta H°_f(\text{products}) - \Sigma m \Delta H°_f(\text{reactants}) \qquad [5.31]$$

The symbol Σ (sigma) means "the sum of," and n and m are the stoichiometric coefficients of the chemical equation. The first term in Equation 5.31 represents the formation reactions of the products, which are written in the "forward" direction, that is, elements reacting to form products. This term is analogous to Equations 5.27 and 5.28 in the previous example. The second term represents the reverse of the formation reactions of the reactants, as in Equation 5.26, which is why the $\Delta H°_f$ values have a minus sign in front of them.

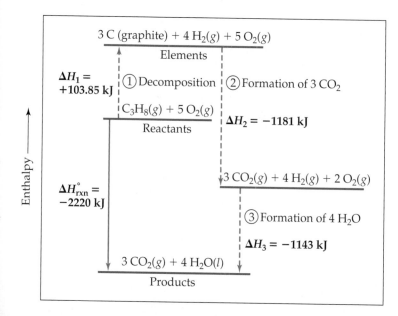

◄ **Figure 5.22 An enthalpy diagram relating the enthalpy change for a reaction to enthalpies of formation.** For the combustion of propane gas, $C_3H_8(g)$, the reaction is $C_3H_8(g) + 5\,O_2(g) \longrightarrow 3\,CO_2(g) + 4\,H_2O(l)$. We can imagine this reaction as occurring in three steps. First, $C_3H_8(g)$ is decomposed to its elements, so $\Delta H_1 = \Delta H°_f[C_3H_8(g)]$. Second, 3 mol $CO_2(g)$ are formed, so $\Delta H_2 = 3\Delta H°_f[CO_2(g)]$. Finally, 4 mol $H_2O(l)$ are formed, so $\Delta H_3 = 4\Delta H°_f[H_2O(l)]$. Hess's law tells us that $\Delta H°_{rxn} = \Delta H_1 + \Delta H_2 + \Delta H_3$. This same result is given by Equation 5.31 because $\Delta H°_f[O_2(g)] = 0$.

■ SAMPLE EXERCISE 5.11 │ Calculating an Enthalpy of Reaction from Enthalpies of Formation

(a) Calculate the standard enthalpy change for the combustion of 1 mol of benzene, $C_6H_6(l)$, to form $CO_2(g)$ and $H_2O(l)$. (b) Compare the quantity of heat produced by combustion of 1.00 g propane to that produced by 1.00 g benzene.

SOLUTION

Analyze: (a) We are given a reaction [combustion of $C_6H_6(l)$ to form $CO_2(g)$ and $H_2O(l)$] and asked to calculate its standard enthalpy change, $\Delta H°$. (b) We then need to compare the quantity of heat produced by combustion of 1.00 g C_6H_6 with that produced by 1.00 g C_3H_8, whose combustion was treated above in the text. (See Equations 5.29 and 5.30.)

Plan: (a) We need to write the balanced equation for the combustion of C_6H_6. We then look up $\Delta H_f°$ values in Appendix C or in Table 5.3 and apply Equation 5.31 to calculate the enthalpy change for the reaction. (b) We use the molar mass of C_6H_6 to change the enthalpy change per mole to that per gram. We similarly use the molar mass of C_3H_8 and the enthalpy change per mole calculated in the text above to calculate the enthalpy change per gram of that substance.

Solve:

(a) We know that a combustion reaction involves $O_2(g)$ as a reactant. Thus, the balanced equation for the combustion reaction of 1 mol $C_6H_6(l)$ is

$$C_6H_6(l) + \tfrac{15}{2}O_2(g) \longrightarrow 6\,CO_2(g) + 3\,H_2O(l)$$

We can calculate $\Delta H°$ for this reaction by using Equation 5.31 and data in Table 5.3. Remember to multiply the $\Delta H_f°$ value for each substance in the reaction by that substance's stoichiometric coefficient. Recall also that $\Delta H_f° = 0$ for any element in its most stable form under standard conditions, so $\Delta H_f°[O_2(g)] = 0$

$$\begin{aligned}
\Delta H_{rxn}° &= [6\Delta H_f°(CO_2) + 3\Delta H_f°(H_2O)] - [\Delta H_f°(C_6H_6) + \tfrac{15}{2}\Delta H_f°(O_2)] \\
&= [6(-393.5\ kJ) + 3(-285.8\ kJ)] - \left[(49.0\ kJ) + \tfrac{15}{2}(0\ kJ)\right] \\
&= (-2361 - 857.4 - 49.0)\ kJ \\
&= -3267\ kJ
\end{aligned}$$

(b) From the example worked in the text, $\Delta H° = -2220$ kJ for the combustion of 1 mol of propane. In part (a) of this exercise we determined that $\Delta H° = -3267$ kJ for the combustion of 1 mol benzene. To determine the heat of combustion per gram of each substance, we use the molar masses to convert moles to grams:

$C_3H_8(g):$ $(-2220\ kJ/mol)(1\ mol/44.1\ g) = -50.3\ kJ/g$

$C_6H_6(l):$ $(-3267\ kJ/mol)(1\ mol/78.1\ g) = -41.8\ kJ/g$

Comment: Both propane and benzene are hydrocarbons. As a rule, the energy obtained from the combustion of a gram of hydrocarbon is between 40 and 50 kJ.

■ PRACTICE EXERCISE

Using the standard enthalpies of formation listed in Table 5.3, calculate the enthalpy change for the combustion of 1 mol of ethanol:

$$C_2H_5OH(l) + 3\,O_2(g) \longrightarrow 2\,CO_2(g) + 3\,H_2O(l)$$

Answer: −1367 kJ

■ SAMPLE EXERCISE 5.12 │ Calculating an Enthalpy of Formation Using an Enthalpy of Reaction

The standard enthalpy change for the reaction

$$CaCO_3(s) \longrightarrow CaO(s) + CO_2(g)$$

is 178.1 kJ. From the values for the standard enthalpies of formation of $CaO(s)$ and $CO_2(g)$ given in Table 5.3, calculate the standard enthalpy of formation of $CaCO_3(s)$.

SOLUTION

Analyze: We need to obtain $\Delta H_f°$ ($CaCO_3$).

Plan: We begin by writing the expression for the standard enthalpy change for the reaction:

$$\Delta H_{rxn}° = [\Delta H_f°(CaO) + \Delta H_f°(CO_2)] - \Delta H_f°(CaCO_3)$$

Solve: Inserting the given $\Delta H_{rxn}°$ and the known $\Delta H_f°$ values from Table 5.3 or Appendix C, we have

$$178.1\ kJ = -635.5\ kJ - 393.5\ kJ - \Delta H_f°(CaCO_3)$$

Solving for $\Delta H_f°$ ($CaCO_3$) gives

$$\Delta H_f° (CaCO_3) = -1207.1\ kJ/mol$$

Check: We expect the enthalpy of formation of a stable solid such as calcium carbonate to be negative, as obtained.

Because it is gaseous, syngas can be easily transported in pipelines. Additionally, because much of the sulfur in coal is removed during the gasification process, combustion of syngas causes less air pollution than burning coal. For these reasons, the economical conversion of coal and petroleum into "cleaner" fuels such as syngas and hydrogen is a very active area of current research in chemistry and engineering.

Other Energy Sources

Nuclear energy is energy that is released in either the splitting or the fusion (combining) of the nuclei of atoms. Nuclear power is currently used to produce about 22% of the electric power in the United States and comprises about 8% of the total U.S. energy production (Figure 5.24). Nuclear energy is, in principle, free of the polluting emissions that are a major problem in the generation of energy from fossil fuels. However, nuclear power plants produce radioactive waste products, and their use has therefore been fraught with controversy. We will discuss issues related to the production of nuclear energy in Chapter 21.

Fossil fuel and nuclear energy are *nonrenewable* sources of energy; they are limited resources that we are consuming at a much greater rate than they are being regenerated. Eventually these fuels will be expended, although estimates vary greatly as to when this will occur. Because nonrenewable sources of energy will eventually be used up, a great deal of research is being conducted into sources of **renewable energy**, energy sources that are essentially inexhaustible. Renewable energy sources include *solar energy* from the Sun, *wind energy* harnessed by windmills, *geothermal energy* from the heat stored in the mass of Earth, *hydroelectric energy* from flowing rivers, and *biomass energy* from crops, such as trees and corn, and from biological waste matter. Currently, renewable sources provide about 6.0% of the U.S. annual energy consumption, with hydroelectric and biomass sources as the major contributors.

Providing our future energy needs will most certainly depend on developing the technology to harness solar energy with greater efficiency. Solar energy is the world's largest energy source. On a clear day about 1 kJ of solar energy

---

car comes to a stop, the engine shuts off. It restarts automatically when the driver presses the accelerator. This feature saves fuel that would otherwise be used to keep the engine idling at traffic lights and other stopping situations.

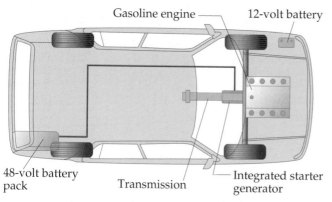

▲ **Figure 5.26   Schematic diagram of a mild hybrid car.**
The 48-volt battery pack provides energy for operating several auxiliary functions. It is recharged from the engine and through the braking system.

The idea is that the added electrical system will improve overall fuel efficiency of the car. The added battery, moreover, is not supposed to need recharging from an external power source. Where, then, can the improved fuel efficiency come from? Clearly, if the battery pack is to continue to operate auxiliary devices such as the water pump, it must be recharged. We can think of it this way: The source of the voltage that the battery develops is a chemical reaction. Recharging the battery thus represents a conversion of mechanical energy into chemical potential energy. The recharging occurs in part through the agency of an alternator, which runs off the engine and provides a recharging voltage. In the mild hybrid car, the braking system serves as an additional source of mechanical energy for recharging. When the brakes are applied in a conventional car, the car's kinetic energy is converted through the brake pads in the wheels into heat, so no useful work is done. In the hybrid car, some of the car's kinetic energy is used to recharge the battery when the brakes are applied. Thus, kinetic energy that would otherwise be dissipated as heat is partially converted into useful work. Overall, the mild hybrid cars are expected to yield 10–20% improvements in fuel economy as compared with similar conventional cars.

reaches each square meter of Earth's surface every second. The average solar energy that falls on only 0.1% of U.S. land area is equivalent to all the energy that this nation currently uses. Harnessing this energy is difficult because it is dilute (it is distributed over a wide area) and it varies with time of day and weather conditions. The effective use of solar energy will depend on the development of some means of storing the collected energy for use at a later time. Any practical means for doing this will almost certainly involve use of an endothermic chemical process that can be later reversed to release heat. One such reaction is the following:

$$CH_4(g) + H_2O(g) + \text{heat} \longleftrightarrow CO(g) + 3\,H_2(g)$$

This reaction proceeds in the forward direction at high temperatures, which can be obtained in a solar furnace. The CO and H_2 formed in the reaction could then be stored and allowed to react later, with the heat released being put to useful work.

A survey taken about 25 years ago at Walt Disney's EPCOT Center revealed that nearly 30% of the visitors expected that solar energy would be the principal source of energy in the United States in the year 2000. The future of solar energy has proven to be a lot like the Sun itself: big and bright but farther away than it seems. Nevertheless, important progress has been made in recent years. Perhaps the most direct way to make use of the Sun's energy is to convert it directly into electricity by use of photovoltaic devices, sometimes called *solar cells*. The efficiencies of solar energy conversion by use of such devices have increased dramatically during the past few years because of intensive research efforts. Photovoltaics are vital to the generation of power for the space station. More significant for our Earth-bound concerns, the unit costs of solar panels have been steadily declining, even as their efficiencies have improved dramatically.

In 2006 construction was started in southern Portugal on what the builders claim will be the world's biggest solar energy power station. The first module of the station is planned to cover about 150 acres and is capable of generating 11 MW (megawatts) of electrical power—enough for 8000 homes. When fully constructed, the plant is projected to cover 620 acres and supply over 100 MW of power. Several other large solar plants with capacities over 100 MW have also been announced in Australia, Israel, and China.

■ **SAMPLE INTEGRATIVE EXERCISE** | **Putting Concepts Together**

Trinitroglycerin, $C_3H_5N_3O_9$ (usually referred to simply as nitroglycerin), has been widely used as an explosive. Alfred Nobel used it to make dynamite in 1866. Rather surprisingly, it also is used as a medication, to relieve angina (chest pains resulting from partially blocked arteries to the heart) by dilating the blood vessels. The enthalpy of decomposition at 1 atm pressure of trinitroglycerin to form nitrogen gas, carbon dioxide gas, liquid water, and oxygen gas at 25 °C is −1541.4 kJ/mol. **(a)** Write a balanced chemical equation for the decomposition of trinitroglycerin. **(b)** Calculate the standard heat of formation of trinitroglycerin. **(c)** A standard dose of trinitroglycerin for relief of angina is 0.60 mg. If the sample is eventually oxidized in the body (not explosively, though!) to nitrogen gas, carbon dioxide gas, and liquid water, what number of calories is released? **(d)** One common form of trinitroglycerin melts at about 3 °C. From this information and the formula for the substance, would you expect it to be a molecular or ionic compound? Explain. **(e)** Describe the various conversions of forms of energy when trinitroglycerin is used as an explosive to break rockfaces in highway construction.

SOLUTION

(a) The general form of the equation we must balance is

$$C_3H_5N_3O_9(l) \longrightarrow N_2(g) + CO_2(g) + H_2O(l) + O_2(g)$$

We go about balancing in the usual way. To obtain an even number of nitrogen atoms on the left, we multiply the formula for $C_3H_5N_3O_9$ by 2. This then gives us 3 mol of N_2, 6 mol of CO_2 and 5 mol of H_2O. Everything is balanced except for oxygen. We have an odd number of oxygen atoms on the right. We can balance the oxygen by adding $\frac{1}{2}$ mol of O_2 on the right:

$$2\,C_3H_5N_3O_9(l) \longrightarrow 3\,N_2(g) + 6\,CO_2(g) + 5\,H_2O(l) + \tfrac{1}{2}\,O_2(g)$$

5.19 (a) What is work? **(b)** How do we determine the amount of work done, given the force associated with the work?

5.20 (a) What is heat? **(b)** Under what conditions is heat transferred from one object to another?

5.21 Identify the force present, and explain whether work is being performed in the following cases: **(a)** You lift a pencil off the top of a desk. **(b)** A spring is compressed to half its normal length.

5.22 Identify the force present, and explain whether work is done when **(a)** a positively charged particle moves in a circle at a fixed distance from a negatively charged particle; **(b)** an iron nail is pulled off a magnet.

The First Law of Thermodynamics

5.23 (a) State the first law of thermodynamics. **(b)** What is meant by the *internal energy* of a system? **(c)** By what means can the internal energy of a closed system increase?

5.24 (a) Write an equation that expresses the first law of thermodynamics in terms of heat and work. **(b)** Under what conditions will the quantities q and w be negative numbers?

5.25 Calculate ΔE, and determine whether the process is endothermic or exothermic for the following cases: **(a)** A system absorbs 105 kJ of heat from its surroundings while doing 29 kJ of work on the surroundings; **(b)** $q = 1.50$ kJ and $w = -657$ J; **(c)** the system releases 57.5 kJ of heat while doing 22.5 kJ of work on the surroundings.

5.26 For the following processes, calculate the change in internal energy of the system and determine whether the process is endothermic or exothermic: **(a)** A balloon is heated by adding 850 J of heat. It expands, doing 382 J of work on the atmosphere. **(b)** A 50-g sample of water is cooled from 30 °C to 15 °C, thereby losing approximately 3140 J of heat. **(c)** A chemical reaction releases 6.47 kJ of heat and does no work on the surroundings.

5.27 A gas is confined to a cylinder fitted with a piston and an electrical heater, as shown in the accompanying illustration. Suppose that current is supplied to the heater so that 100 J of energy is added. Consider two different situations. In case (1) the piston is allowed to move as the energy is added. In case (2) the piston is fixed so that it cannot move. **(a)** In which case does the gas have the higher temperature after addition of the electrical energy? Explain.

(b) What can you say about the values of q and w in each of these cases? **(c)** What can you say about the relative values of ΔE for the system (the gas in the cylinder) in the two cases?

5.28 Consider a system consisting of two oppositely charged spheres hanging by strings and separated by a distance r_1, as shown in the accompanying illustration. Suppose they are separated to a larger distance r_2, by moving them apart along a track. **(a)** What change, if any, has occurred in the potential energy of the system? **(b)** What effect, if any, does this process have on the value of ΔE? **(c)** What can you say about q and w for this process?

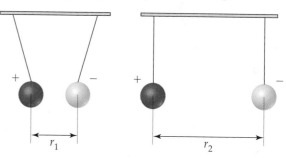

5.29 (a) What is meant by the term *state function?* **(b)** Give an example of a quantity that is a state function and one that is not. **(c)** Is work a state function? Why or why not?

5.30 Indicate which of the following is independent of the path by which a change occurs: **(a)** the change in potential energy when a book is transferred from table to shelf, **(b)** the heat evolved when a cube of sugar is oxidized to $CO_2(g)$ and $H_2O(g)$, **(c)** the work accomplished in burning a gallon of gasoline.

Enthalpy

5.31 (a) Why is the change in enthalpy usually easier to measure than the change in internal energy? **(b)** For a given process at constant pressure, ΔH is negative. Is the process endothermic or exothermic?

5.32 (a) Under what condition will the enthalpy change of a process equal the amount of heat transferred into or out of the system? **(b)** During a constant-pressure process the system absorbs heat from the surroundings. Does the enthalpy of the system increase or decrease during the process?

5.33 You are given ΔH for a process that occurs at constant pressure. What additional information do you need to determine ΔE for the process?

5.34 Suppose that the gas-phase reaction $2\,NO(g) + O_2(g) \longrightarrow 2\,NO_2(g)$ were carried out in a constant-volume container at constant temperature. Would the measured heat change represent ΔH or ΔE? If there is a difference, which quantity is larger for this reaction? Explain.

5.35 A gas is confined to a cylinder under constant atmospheric pressure, as illustrated in Figure 5.3. When the gas undergoes a particular chemical reaction, it releases 79 kJ of heat to its surroundings and does 18 kJ of P-V work on its surroundings. What are the values of ΔH and ΔE for this process?

5.36 A gas is confined to a cylinder under constant atmospheric pressure, as illustrated in Figure 5.3. When 378 J of heat is added to the gas, it expands and does 56 J of work on the surroundings. What are the values of ΔH and ΔE for this process?

5.37 The complete combustion of acetic acid, $CH_3COOH(l)$, to form $H_2O(l)$ and $CO_2(g)$ at constant pressure releases 871.7 kJ of heat per mole of CH_3COOH. **(a)** Write a balanced thermochemical equation for this reaction. **(b)** Draw an enthalpy diagram for the reaction.

5.38 The decomposition of zinc carbonate, $ZnCO_3(s)$, into zinc oxide, $ZnO(s)$, and $CO_2(g)$ at constant pressure requires the addition of 71.5 kJ of heat per mole of $ZnCO_3$. **(a)** Write a balanced thermochemical equation for the reaction. **(b)** Draw an enthalpy diagram for the reaction.

5.39 Consider the following reaction, which occurs at room temperature and pressure:

$$2\,Cl(g) \longrightarrow Cl_2(g) \qquad \Delta H = -243.4 \text{ kJ}$$

Which has the higher enthalpy under these conditions, $2\,Cl(g)$ or $Cl_2(g)$?

5.40 Without referring to tables, predict which of the following has the higher enthalpy in each case: **(a)** 1 mol $CO_2(s)$ or 1 mol $CO_2(g)$ at the same temperature, **(b)** 2 mol of hydrogen atoms or 1 mol of H_2, **(c)** 1 mol $H_2(g)$ and 0.5 mol $O_2(g)$ at 25 °C or 1 mol $H_2O(g)$ at 25 °C, **(d)** 1 mol $N_2(g)$ at 100 °C or 1 mol $N_2(g)$ at 300 °C.

5.41 Consider the following reaction:

$$2\,Mg(s) + O_2(g) \longrightarrow 2\,MgO(s) \qquad \Delta H = -1204 \text{ kJ}$$

(a) Is this reaction exothermic or endothermic? **(b)** Calculate the amount of heat transferred when 2.4 g of $Mg(s)$ reacts at constant pressure. **(c)** How many grams of MgO are produced during an enthalpy change of −96.0 kJ? **(d)** How many kilojoules of heat are absorbed when 7.50 g of $MgO(s)$ is decomposed into $Mg(s)$ and $O_2(g)$ at constant pressure?

5.42 Consider the following reaction:

$$CH_3OH(g) \longrightarrow CO(g) + 2\,H_2(g) \qquad \Delta H = +90.7 \text{ kJ}$$

(a) Is heat absorbed or released in the course of this reaction? **(b)** Calculate the amount of heat transferred when 45.0 g of $CH_3OH(g)$ is decomposed by this reaction at constant pressure. **(c)** For a given sample of CH_3OH, the enthalpy change on reaction is 25.8 kJ. How many grams of hydrogen gas are produced? What is the value of ΔH for the reverse of the previous reaction? **(d)** How

many kilojoules of heat are released when 50.9 g of $CO(g)$ reacts completely with $H_2(g)$ to form $CH_3OH(g)$ at constant pressure?

5.43 When solutions containing silver ions and chloride ions are mixed, silver chloride precipitates:

$$Ag^+(aq) + Cl^-(aq) \longrightarrow AgCl(s) \qquad \Delta H = -65.5 \text{ kJ}$$

(a) Calculate ΔH for production of 0.200 mol of AgCl by this reaction. **(b)** Calculate ΔH for the production of 2.50 g of AgCl. **(c)** Calculate ΔH when 0.150 mmol of AgCl dissolves in water.

5.44 At one time, a common means of forming small quantities of oxygen gas in the laboratory was to heat $KClO_3$:

$$2\,KClO_3(s) \longrightarrow 2\,KCl(s) + 3\,O_2(g) \qquad \Delta H = -89.4 \text{ kJ}$$

For this reaction, calculate ΔH for the formation of **(a)** 0.632 mol of O_2 and **(b)** 8.57 g of KCl. **(c)** The decomposition of $KClO_3$ proceeds spontaneously when it is heated. Do you think that the reverse reaction, the formation of $KClO_3$ from KCl and O_2, is likely to be feasible under ordinary conditions? Explain your answer.

5.45 Consider the combustion of liquid methanol, $CH_3OH(l)$:

$$CH_3OH(l) + \tfrac{3}{2}O_2(g) \longrightarrow CO_2(g) + 2\,H_2O(l)$$
$$\Delta H = -726.5 \text{ kJ}$$

(a) What is the enthalpy change for the reverse reaction? **(b)** Balance the forward reaction with whole-number coefficients. What is ΔH for the reaction represented by this equation? **(c)** Which is more likely to be thermodynamically favored, the forward reaction or the reverse reaction? **(d)** If the reaction were written to produce $H_2O(g)$ instead of $H_2O(l)$, would you expect the magnitude of ΔH to increase, decrease, or stay the same? Explain.

5.46 Consider the decomposition of liquid benzene, $C_6H_6(l)$, to gaseous acetylene, $C_2H_2(g)$:

$$C_6H_6(l) \longrightarrow 3\,C_2H_2(g) \qquad \Delta H = +630 \text{ kJ}$$

(a) What is the enthalpy change for the reverse reaction? **(b)** What is ΔH for the formation of 1 mol of acetylene? **(c)** Which is more likely to be thermodynamically favored, the forward reaction or the reverse reaction? **(d)** If $C_6H_6(g)$ were consumed instead of $C_6H_6(l)$, would you expect the magnitude of ΔH to increase, decrease, or stay the same? Explain.

Calorimetry

5.47 **(a)** What are the units of molar heat capacity? **(b)** What are the units of specific heat? **(c)** If you know the specific heat of copper, what additional information do you need to calculate the heat capacity of a particular piece of copper pipe?

5.48 Two solid objects, A and B, are placed in boiling water and allowed to come to temperature there. Each is then lifted out and placed in separate beakers containing 1000 g water at 10.0 °C. Object A increases the water temperature by 3.50 °C; B increases the water temperature by 2.60 °C. **(a)** Which object has the larger heat capacity? **(b)** What can you say about the specific heats of A and B?

5.49 **(a)** What is the specific heat of liquid water? **(b)** What is the molar heat capacity of liquid water? **(c)** What is the heat capacity of 185 g of liquid water? **(d)** How many kJ of heat are needed to raise the temperature of 10.00 kg of liquid water from 24.6 °C to 46.2 °C?

5.50 **(a)** Which substance in Table 5.2 requires the smallest amount of energy to increase the temperature of 50.0 g of that substance by 10 K? **(b)** Calculate the energy needed for this temperature change.

5.51 The specific heat of iron metal is 0.450 J/g-K. How many J of heat are necessary to raise the temperature of a 1.05-kg block of iron from 25.0 °C to 88.5 °C?

5.52 The specific heat of ethylene glycol is 2.42 J/g-K. How many J of heat are needed to raise the temperature of 62.0 g of ethylene glycol from 13.1 °C to 40.5 °C?

5.53 When a 9.55-g sample of solid sodium hydroxide dissolves in 100.0 g of water in a coffee-cup calorimeter (Figure 5.17), the temperature rises from 23.6 °C to 47.4 °C. Calculate ΔH (in kJ/mol NaOH) for the solution process

$$NaOH(s) \longrightarrow Na^+(aq) + OH^-(aq)$$

Assume that the specific heat of the solution is the same as that of pure water.

5.54 **(a)** When a 3.88-g sample of solid ammonium nitrate dissolves in 60.0 g of water in a coffee-cup calorimeter (Figure 5.17), the temperature drops from 23.0 °C to 18.4 °C. Calculate ΔH (in kJ/mol NH_4NO_3) for the solution process

$$NH_4NO_3(s) \longrightarrow NH_4^+(aq) + NO_3^-(aq)$$

Assume that the specific heat of the solution is the same as that of pure water. **(b)** Is this process endothermic or exothermic?

5.55 A 2.200-g sample of quinone ($C_6H_4O_2$) is burned in a bomb calorimeter whose total heat capacity is 7.854 kJ/°C. The temperature of the calorimeter increases from 23.44 °C to 30.57 °C. What is the heat of combustion per gram of quinone? Per mole of quinone?

5.56 A 1.800-g sample of phenol (C_6H_5OH) was burned in a bomb calorimeter whose total heat capacity is 11.66 kJ/°C. The temperature of the calorimeter plus contents increased from 21.36 °C to 26.37 °C. **(a)** Write a balanced chemical equation for the bomb calorimeter reaction. **(b)** What is the heat of combustion per gram of phenol? Per mole of phenol?

5.57 Under constant-volume conditions the heat of combustion of glucose ($C_6H_{12}O_6$) is 15.57 kJ/g. A 2.500-g sample of glucose is burned in a bomb calorimeter. The temperature of the calorimeter increased from 20.55 °C to 23.25 °C. **(a)** What is the total heat capacity of the calorimeter? **(b)** If the size of the glucose sample had been exactly twice as large, what would the temperature change of the calorimeter have been?

5.58 Under constant-volume conditions the heat of combustion of benzoic acid (C_6H_5COOH) is 26.38 kJ/g. A 1.640-g sample of benzoic acid is burned in a bomb calorimeter. The temperature of the calorimeter increases from 22.25 °C to 27.20 °C. **(a)** What is the total heat capacity of the calorimeter? **(b)** A 1.320-g sample of a new organic substance is combusted in the same calorimeter. The temperature of the calorimeter increases from 22.14 °C to 26.82 °C. What is the heat of combustion per gram of the new substance? **(c)** Suppose that in changing samples, a portion of the water in the calorimeter were lost. In what way, if any, would this change the heat capacity of the calorimeter?

Hess's Law

5.59 What is the connection between Hess's law and the fact that H is a state function?

5.60 Consider the following hypothetical reactions:

$$A \longrightarrow B \qquad \Delta H = +30 \text{ kJ}$$
$$B \longrightarrow C \qquad \Delta H = +60 \text{ kJ}$$

(a) Use Hess's law to calculate the enthalpy change for the reaction $A \longrightarrow C$. **(b)** Construct an enthalpy diagram for substances A, B, and C, and show how Hess's law applies.

5.61 Calculate the enthalpy change for the reaction

$$P_4O_6(s) + 2 O_2(g) \longrightarrow P_4O_{10}(s)$$

given the following enthalpies of reaction:

$$P_4(s) + 3 O_2(g) \longrightarrow P_4O_6(s) \qquad \Delta H = -1640.1 \text{ kJ}$$
$$P_4(s) + 5 O_2(g) \longrightarrow P_4O_{10}(s) \qquad \Delta H = -2940.1 \text{ kJ}$$

5.62 From the enthalpies of reaction

$$2 H_2(g) + O_2(g) \longrightarrow 2 H_2O(g) \qquad \Delta H = -483.6 \text{ kJ}$$
$$3 O_2(g) \longrightarrow 2 O_3(g) \qquad \Delta H = +284.6 \text{ kJ}$$

calculate the heat of the reaction

$$3 H_2(g) + O_3(g) \longrightarrow 3 H_2O(g)$$

5.63 From the enthalpies of reaction

$$H_2(g) + F_2(g) \longrightarrow 2 HF(g) \qquad \Delta H = -537 \text{ kJ}$$
$$C(s) + 2 F_2(g) \longrightarrow CF_4(g) \qquad \Delta H = -680 \text{ kJ}$$
$$2 C(s) + 2 H_2(g) \longrightarrow C_2H_4(g) \qquad \Delta H = +52.3 \text{ kJ}$$

calculate ΔH for the reaction of ethylene with F_2:

$$C_2H_4(g) + 6 F_2(g) \longrightarrow 2 CF_4(g) + 4 HF(g)$$

5.64 Given the data

$$N_2(g) + O_2(g) \longrightarrow 2 NO(g) \qquad \Delta H = +180.7 \text{ kJ}$$
$$2 NO(g) + O_2(g) \longrightarrow 2 NO_2(g) \qquad \Delta H = -113.1 \text{ kJ}$$
$$2 N_2O(g) \longrightarrow 2 N_2(g) + O_2(g) \qquad \Delta H = -163.2 \text{ kJ}$$

use Hess's law to calculate ΔH for the reaction

$$N_2O(g) + NO_2(g) \longrightarrow 3 NO(g)$$

Enthalpies of Formation

5.65 **(a)** What is meant by the term *standard conditions*, with reference to enthalpy changes? **(b)** What is meant by the term *enthalpy of formation*? **(c)** What is meant by the term *standard enthalpy of formation*?

5.66 **(a)** Why are tables of standard enthalpies of formation so useful? **(b)** What is the value of the standard enthalpy of formation of an element in its most stable form? **(c)** Write the chemical equation for the reaction whose enthalpy change is the standard enthalpy of formation of glucose, $C_6H_{12}O_6(s)$, $\Delta H_f^\circ[C_6H_{12}O_6]$.

5.67 For each of the following compounds, write a balanced thermochemical equation depicting the formation of one mole of the compound from its elements in their standard states and use Appendix C to obtain the value of ΔH_f°: **(a)** $NH_3(g)$, **(b)** $SO_2(g)$, **(c)** $RbClO_3(s)$, **(d)** $NH_4NO_3(s)$.

5.68 Write balanced equations that describe the formation of the following compounds from elements in their standard states, and use Appendix C to obtain the values of their standard enthalpies of formation: **(a)** $HBr(g)$, **(b)** $AgNO_3(s)$, **(c)** $Fe_2O_3(s)$, **(d)** $CH_3COOH(l)$.

5.69 The following is known as the thermite reaction [Figure 5.7(b)]:

$$2\,Al(s) + Fe_2O_3(s) \longrightarrow Al_2O_3(s) + 2\,Fe(s)$$

This highly exothermic reaction is used for welding massive units, such as propellers for large ships. Using standard enthalpies of formation in Appendix C, calculate ΔH° for this reaction.

5.70 Many cigarette lighters contain liquid butane, $C_4H_{10}(l)$. Using standard enthalpies of formation, calculate the quantity of heat produced when 5.00 g of butane is completely combusted in air under standard conditions.

5.71 Using values from Appendix C, calculate the standard enthalpy change for each of the following reactions:
(a) $2\,SO_2(g) + O_2(g) \longrightarrow 2\,SO_3(g)$
(b) $Mg(OH)_2(s) \longrightarrow MgO(s) + H_2O(l)$
(c) $N_2O_4(g) + 4\,H_2(g) \longrightarrow N_2(g) + 4\,H_2O(g)$
(d) $SiCl_4(l) + 2\,H_2O(l) \longrightarrow SiO_2(s) + 4\,HCl(g)$

5.72 Using values from Appendix C, calculate the value of ΔH° for each of the following reactions:
(a) $4\,HBr(g) + O_2(g) \longrightarrow 2\,H_2O(l) + 2\,Br_2(l)$
(b) $2\,Na(OH)(s) + SO_3(g) \longrightarrow Na_2SO_4(s) + H_2O(g)$
(c) $CH_4(g) + 4\,Cl_2(g) \longrightarrow CCl_4(l) + 4\,HCl(g)$
(d) $Fe_2O_3(s) + 6\,HCl(g) \longrightarrow 2\,FeCl_3(s) + 3\,H_2O(g)$

5.73 Complete combustion of 1 mol of acetone (C_3H_6O) liberates 1790 kJ:

$$C_3H_6O(l) + 4\,O_2(g) \longrightarrow 3\,CO_2(g) + 3\,H_2O(l)$$
$$\Delta H^\circ = -1790\ kJ$$

Using this information together with data from Appendix C, calculate the enthalpy of formation of acetone.

5.74 Calcium carbide (CaC_2) reacts with water to form acetylene (C_2H_2) and $Ca(OH)_2$. From the following enthalpy of reaction data and data in Appendix C, calculate ΔH_f° for $CaC_2(s)$:

$$CaC_2(s) + 2\,H_2O(l) \longrightarrow Ca(OH)_2(s) + C_2H_2(g)$$
$$\Delta H^\circ = -127.2\ kJ$$

5.75 Gasoline is composed primarily of hydrocarbons, including many with eight carbon atoms, called *octanes*. One of the cleanest-burning octanes is a compound called 2,3,4-trimethylpentane, which has the following structural formula:

$$\begin{array}{ccccc} & CH_3 & CH_3 & CH_3 & \\ & | & | & | & \\ H_3C\!-\!\!&CH\!-\!\!&CH\!-\!\!&CH\!-\!\!&CH_3 \end{array}$$

The complete combustion of one mole of this compound to $CO_2(g)$ and $H_2O(g)$ leads to $\Delta H^\circ = -5064.9$ kJ/mol. **(a)** Write a balanced equation for the combustion of 1 mol of $C_8H_{18}(l)$. **(b)** Write a balanced equation for the formation of $C_8H_{18}(l)$ from its elements. **(c)** By using the information in this problem and data in Table 5.3, calculate ΔH_f° for 2,3,4-trimethylpentane.

5.76 Naphthalene ($C_{10}H_8$) is a solid aromatic compound often sold as mothballs. The complete combustion of this substance to yield $CO_2(g)$ and $H_2O(l)$ at 25 °C yields 5154 kJ/mol. **(a)** Write balanced equations for the formation of naphthalene from the elements and for its combustion. **(b)** Calculate the standard enthalpy of formation of naphthalene.

5.77 Ethanol (C_2H_5OH) is currently blended with gasoline as an automobile fuel. **(a)** Write a balanced equation for the combustion of liquid ethanol in air. **(b)** Calculate the standard enthalpy change for the reaction, assuming $H_2O(g)$ as a product. **(c)** Calculate the heat produced per liter of ethanol by combustion of ethanol under constant pressure. Ethanol has a density of 0.789 g/mL. **(d)** Calculate the mass of CO_2 produced per kJ of heat emitted.

5.78 Methanol (CH_3OH) is used as a fuel in race cars. **(a)** Write a balanced equation for the combustion of liquid methanol in air. **(b)** Calculate the standard enthalpy change for the reaction, assuming $H_2O(g)$ as a product. **(c)** Calculate the heat produced by combustion per liter of methanol. Methanol has a density of 0.791 g/mL. **(d)** Calculate the mass of CO_2 produced per kJ of heat emitted.

Foods and Fuels

5.79 **(a)** What is meant by the term *fuel value*? **(b)** Which is a greater source of energy as food, 5 g of fat or 9 g of carbohydrate?

5.80 **(a)** Why are fats well suited for energy storage in the human body? **(b)** A particular chip snack food is composed of 12% protein, 14% fat, and the rest carbohydrate. What percentage of the calorie content of this food is fat? **(c)** How many grams of protein provide the same fuel value as 25 g of fat?

5.81 A serving of condensed cream of mushroom soup contains 7 g fat, 9 g carbohydrate, and 1 g protein. Estimate the number of Calories in a serving.

5.82 A pound of plain M&M® candies contains 96 g fat, 320 g carbohydrate, and 21 g protein. What is the fuel value in kJ in a 42-g (about 1.5 oz) serving? How many Calories does it provide?

5.83 The heat of combustion of fructose, $C_6H_{12}O_6$, is −2812 kJ/mol. If a fresh golden delicious apple weighing 4.23 oz (120 g) contains 16.0 g of fructose, what caloric content does the fructose contribute to the apple?

5.84 The heat of combustion of ethanol, $C_2H_5OH(l)$, is −1367 kJ/mol. A batch of Sauvignon Blanc wine contains 10.6% ethanol by mass. Assuming the density of

spectrum consists of a continuous range of colors—violet merges into blue, blue into green, and so forth, with no blank spots. This rainbow of colors, containing light of all wavelengths, is called a **continuous spectrum.** The most familiar example of a continuous spectrum is the rainbow produced when raindrops or mist acts as a prism for sunlight.

Not all radiation sources produce a continuous spectrum. When a high voltage is applied to tubes that contain different gases under reduced pressure, the gases emit different colors of light (Figure 6.12▶). The light emitted by neon gas is the familiar red-orange glow of many "neon" lights, whereas sodium vapor emits the yellow light characteristic of some modern streetlights. When light coming from such tubes is passed through a prism, only a few wavelengths are present in the resultant spectra, as shown in Figure 6.13▼. Each wavelength is represented by a colored line in one of these spectra. A spectrum containing radiation of only specific wavelengths is called a **line spectrum.**

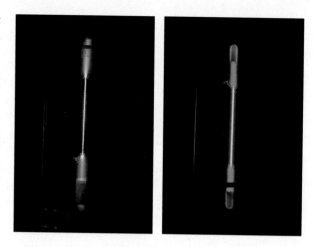

▲ Figure 6.12 **Atomic emission.** Different gases emit light of different characteristic colors upon excitation by an electrical discharge: (a) hydrogen, (b) neon.

When scientists first detected the line spectrum of hydrogen in the mid-1800s, they were fascinated by its simplicity. At that time, only the four lines in the visible portion of the spectrum were observed, as shown in Figure 6.13. These lines correspond to wavelengths of 410 nm (violet), 434 nm (blue), 486 nm (blue-green), and 656 nm (red). In 1885, a Swiss schoolteacher named Johann Balmer showed that the wavelengths of these four visible lines of hydrogen fit an intriguingly simple formula that related the wavelengths of the visible line spectrum to integers. Later, additional lines were found to occur in the ultraviolet and infrared regions of the hydrogen spectrum. Soon Balmer's equation was extended to a more general one, called the *Rydberg equation*, which allowed the calculation of the wavelengths of all the spectral lines of hydrogen:

$$\frac{1}{\lambda} = (R_H)\left(\frac{1}{n_1^2} - \frac{1}{n_2^2}\right) \qquad [6.4]$$

In this formula λ is the wavelength of a spectral line, R_H is the *Rydberg constant* ($1.096776 \times 10^7 \text{ m}^{-1}$), and n_1 and n_2 are positive integers, with n_2 being larger than n_1. How could the remarkable simplicity of this equation be explained? It took nearly 30 more years to answer this question.

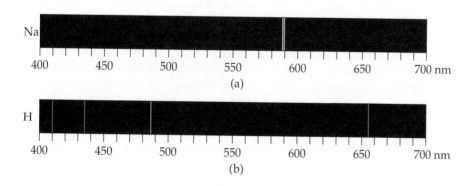

◀ Figure 6.13 **Line spectra.** Spectra obtained from the electrical discharge from (a) Na, (b) H. Light of only a few specific wavelengths is produced, as shown by colored lines in the spectra.

Bohr's Model

Rutherford's discovery of the nuclear nature of the atom ∞∞ (Section 2.2) suggests that the atom can be thought of as a "microscopic solar system" in which electrons orbit the nucleus. To explain the line spectrum of hydrogen, Bohr assumed that electrons move in circular orbits around the nucleus. According to classical physics, however, an electrically charged particle (such as an electron) that moves in a circular path should continuously lose energy by emitting electromagnetic radiation. As the electron loses energy, it should spiral into the positively charged nucleus. This spiraling obviously does not happen since hydrogen atoms are stable. So how can we explain this apparent violation of the laws of physics? Bohr approached this problem in much the same way that Planck had approached the problem of the nature of the radiation emitted by hot objects: Bohr assumed that the prevailing laws of physics were inadequate to describe all aspects of atoms. Furthermore, Bohr adopted Planck's idea that energies are quantized.

Bohr based his model on three postulates:

1. Only orbits of certain radii, corresponding to certain definite energies, are permitted for the electron in a hydrogen atom.

2. An electron in a permitted orbit has a specific energy and is in an "allowed" energy state. An electron in an allowed energy state will not radiate energy and therefore will not spiral into the nucleus.

3. Energy is emitted or absorbed by the electron only as the electron changes from one allowed energy state to another. This energy is emitted or absorbed as a photon, $E = h\nu$.

▲ GIVE IT SOME THOUGHT

Before reading further about the details of Bohr's model, speculate as to how they explain the fact that hydrogen gas emits a line spectrum (Figure 6.13) rather than a continuous spectrum.

The Energy States of the Hydrogen Atom

Starting with his three postulates and using classical equations for motion and for interacting electrical charges, Bohr calculated the energies corresponding to each allowed orbit for the electron in the hydrogen atom. Ultimately, the energies that Bohr calculated fit the formula

$$E = (-hcR_H)\left(\frac{1}{n^2}\right) = (-2.18 \times 10^{-18}\ \text{J})\left(\frac{1}{n^2}\right) \qquad [6.5]$$

In this equation, h, c, and R_H are Planck's constant, the speed of light, and the Rydberg constant, respectively. The product of these three constants equals 2.18×10^{-18} J. The integer n, which can have whole number values of 1, 2, 3, ... to infinity (∞), is called the *principal quantum number*. Each orbit corresponds to a different value of n, and the radius of the orbit gets larger as n increases. Thus, the first allowed orbit (the one closest to the nucleus) has $n = 1$, the next allowed orbit (the one second closest to the nucleus) has $n = 2$, and so forth. The electron in the hydrogen atom can be in any allowed orbit. Equation 6.5 tells us the energy that the electron will have, depending on which orbit it is in.

The energies of the electron of a hydrogen atom given by Equation 6.5 are negative for all values of n. The lower (more negative) the energy is, the more stable the atom will be. The energy is lowest (most negative) for $n = 1$. As n gets larger, the energy becomes successively less negative and therefore increases. We can liken the situation to a ladder in which the rungs are numbered from the bottom rung on up. The higher one climbs the ladder (the greater the value of n), the higher the energy. The lowest energy state ($n = 1$, analogous to the bottom rung) is called the **ground state** of the atom. When the electron is in a higher senergy (less negative) orbit—$n = 2$ or higher—the atom is said to be in an **excited state**. Figure 6.14 ◄ shows the energy of the electron in a hydrogen atom for several values of n.

What happens to the orbit radius and the energy as n becomes infinitely large? The radius increases as n^2, so we reach a point at which the electron is completely separated from the nucleus. When $n = \infty$, the energy is zero:

$$E = (-2.18 \times 10^{-18}\ \text{J})\left(\frac{1}{\infty^2}\right) = 0$$

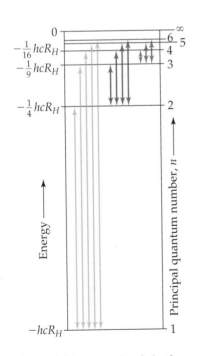

▲ **Figure 6.14 Energy levels in the hydrogen atom from the Bohr model.** The arrows refer to the transitions of the electron from one allowed energy state to another. The states shown are those for which $n = 1$ through $n = 6$ and the state for $n = \infty$ for which the energy, E, equals zero.

Thus, the state in which the electron is removed from the nucleus is the reference, or zero-energy, state of the hydrogen atom. This zero-energy state is *higher* in energy than the states with negative energies.

In his third postulate, Bohr assumed that the electron could "jump" from one allowed energy state to another by either absorbing or emitting photons whose radiant energy corresponds exactly to the energy difference between the two states. Energy must be absorbed for an electron to move to a higher energy state (one with a higher value of n). Conversely, radiant energy is emitted when the electron jumps to a lower energy state (one with a lower value of n). Thus, if the electron jumps from an initial state that has energy E_i to a final state of energy E_f, the change in energy is

$$\Delta E = E_f - E_i = E_{\text{photon}} = h\nu \qquad [6.6]$$

Bohr's model of the hydrogen atom states, therefore, that only the specific frequencies of light that satisfy Equation 6.6 can be absorbed or emitted by the atom.

Substituting the energy expression in Equation 6.5 into Equation 6.6 and recalling that $\nu = c/\lambda$, we have

$$\Delta E = h\nu = \frac{hc}{\lambda} = (-2.18 \times 10^{-18} \text{ J})\left(\frac{1}{n_f^2} - \frac{1}{n_i^2}\right) \qquad [6.7]$$

In this equation n_i and n_f are the principal quantum numbers of the initial and final states of the atom, respectively. If n_f is smaller than n_i, the electron moves closer to the nucleus and ΔE is a negative number, indicating that the atom releases energy. For example, if the electron moves from $n_i = 3$ to $n_f = 1$, we have

$$\Delta E = (-2.18 \times 10^{-18} \text{ J})\left(\frac{1}{1^2} - \frac{1}{3^2}\right) = (-2.18 \times 10^{-18} \text{ J})\left(\frac{8}{9}\right) = -1.94 \times 10^{-18} \text{ J}$$

Knowing the energy for the emitted photon, we can calculate either its frequency or its wavelength. For the wavelength, we have

$$\lambda = \frac{c}{\nu} = \frac{hc}{\Delta E} = \frac{(6.626 \times 10^{-34} \text{ J-s})(3.00 \times 10^8 \text{ m/s})}{1.94 \times 10^{-18} \text{ J}} = 1.03 \times 10^{-7} \text{ m}$$

We have not included the negative sign of the energy in this calculation because wavelength and frequency are always reported as positive quantities. The direction of energy flow is indicated by saying that a photon of wavelength 1.03×10^{-7} m has been *emitted*.

If we solve Equation 6.7 for $1/\lambda$, we find that this equation derived from Bohr's theory corresponds to the Rydberg equation, Equation 6.4, which was obtained using experimental data:

$$\frac{1}{\lambda} = \frac{-hcR_H}{hc}\left(\frac{1}{n_f^2} - \frac{1}{n_i^2}\right) = R_H\left(\frac{1}{n_i^2} - \frac{1}{n_f^2}\right)$$

Thus, the existence of discrete spectral lines can be attributed to the quantized jumps of electrons between energy levels.

GIVE IT SOME THOUGHT

As the electron in a hydrogen atom jumps from the $n = 3$ orbit to the $n = 7$ orbit, does it absorb energy or emit energy?

■ **SAMPLE EXERCISE 6.4** | **Electronic Transitions in the Hydrogen Atom**

Using Figure 6.14, predict which of the following electronic transitions produces the spectral line having the longest wavelength: $n = 2$ to $n = 1$, $n = 3$ to $n = 2$, or $n = 4$ to $n = 3$.

SOLUTION

The wavelength increases as frequency decreases ($\lambda = c/\nu$). Hence the longest wavelength will be associated with the lowest frequency. According to Planck's equation, $E = h\nu$, the lowest frequency is associated with the lowest energy. In Figure 6.14 the shortest vertical line represents the smallest energy change. Thus, the $n = 4$ to $n = 3$ transition produces the longest wavelength (lowest frequency) line.

■ **PRACTICE EXERCISE**

Indicate whether each of the following electronic transitions emits energy or requires the absorption of energy: **(a)** $n = 3$ to $n = 1$; **(b)** $n = 2$ to $n = 4$.
Answers: **(a)** emits energy, **(b)** requires absorption of energy

Limitations of the Bohr Model

While the Bohr model explains the line spectrum of the hydrogen atom, it cannot explain the spectra of other atoms, except in a rather crude way. Bohr also avoided the problem of why the negatively charged electron would not just fall into the positively charged nucleus by simply assuming it would not happen. Therefore, there is a problem with describing an electron merely as a small particle circling about the nucleus. As we will see in Section 6.4, the electron exhibits wavelike properties, a fact that any acceptable model of electronic structure must accommodate. As it turns out, the Bohr model was only an important step along the way toward the development of a more comprehensive model. What is most significant about Bohr's model is that it introduces two important ideas that are also incorporated into our current model: (1) Electrons exist only in certain discrete energy levels, which are described by quantum numbers, and (2) energy is involved in moving an electron from one level to another. We will now start to develop the successor to the Bohr model, which requires that we take a closer look at the behavior of matter.

6.4 THE WAVE BEHAVIOR OF MATTER

In the years following the development of Bohr's model for the hydrogen atom, the dual nature of radiant energy became a familiar concept. Depending on the experimental circumstances, radiation appears to have either a wavelike or a particle-like (photon) character. Louis de Broglie (1892–1987), who was working on his Ph.D. thesis in physics at the Sorbonne in Paris, boldly extended this idea. If radiant energy could, under appropriate conditions, behave as though it were a stream of particles, could matter, under appropriate conditions, possibly show the properties of a wave? Suppose that the electron orbiting the nucleus of a hydrogen atom could be thought of as a wave, with a characteristic wavelength, rather than as a particle. De Broglie suggested that as the electron moves about the nucleus, it is associated with a particular wavelength. He went on to propose that the characteristic wavelength of the electron, or of any other particle, depends on its mass, m, and on its velocity, v, (where h is Planck's constant):

$$\lambda = \frac{h}{mv} \qquad [6.8]$$

The quantity mv for any object is called its **momentum.** De Broglie used the term **matter waves** to describe the wave characteristics of material particles.

Because de Broglie's hypothesis is applicable to all matter, any object of mass m and velocity v would give rise to a characteristic matter wave. However, Equation 6.8 indicates that the wavelength associated with an object of ordinary size, such as a golf ball, is so tiny as to be completely out of the range of any possible observation. This is not so for an electron because its mass is so small, as we see in Sample Exercise 6.5.

■ SAMPLE EXERCISE 6.5 | Matter Waves

What is the wavelength of an electron moving with a speed of 5.97×10^6 m/s? The mass of the electron is 9.11×10^{-31} kg.

SOLUTION

Analyze: We are given the mass, m, and velocity, v, of the electron, and we must calculate its de Broglie wavelength, λ.

Plan: The wavelength of a moving particle is given by Equation 6.8, so λ is calculated by inserting the known quantities h, m, and v. In doing so, however, we must pay attention to units.

Solve: Using the value of Planck's constant, $h = 6.626 \times 10^{-34}$ J-s

and recalling that $1\,J = 1\ \text{kg-m}^2/\text{s}^2$

we have the following:

$$\lambda = \frac{h}{mv}$$

$$= \frac{(6.626 \times 10^{-34}\,\text{J-s})}{(9.11 \times 10^{-31}\,\text{kg})(5.97 \times 10^6\,\text{m/s})}\left(\frac{1\ \text{kg-m}^2/\text{s}^2}{1\,\text{J}}\right)$$

$$= 1.22 \times 10^{-10}\,\text{m} = 0.122\ \text{nm} = 1.22\ \text{Å}$$

Comment: By comparing this value with the wavelengths of electromagnetic radiation shown in Figure 6.4, we see that the wavelength of this electron is about the same as that of X-rays.

■ PRACTICE EXERCISE

Calculate the velocity of a neutron whose de Broglie wavelength is 500 pm. The mass of a neutron is given in the table inside the back cover of the text.
Answer: 7.92×10^2 m/s

Within a few years after de Broglie published his theory, the wave properties of the electron were demonstrated experimentally. As electrons passed through a crystal, they were diffracted by the crystal, just as X-rays are diffracted. Thus, a stream of moving electrons exhibits the same kinds of wave behavior as electromagnetic radiation.

The technique of electron diffraction has been highly developed. In the electron microscope, for instance, the wave characteristics of electrons are used to obtain images at the atomic scale. This microscope is an important tool for studying surface phenomena at very high magnifications. Electron microscopes can magnify objects by 3,000,000 times (x), far more than can be done with visible light (1000x), because the wavelength of the electrons is so small compared to visible light. Figure 6.15▶ is a photograph of an electron microscope image.

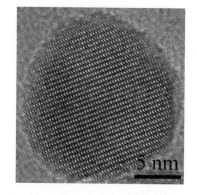

5 nm

▲ **Figure 6.15 Electrons as waves.** The dots you see in this transmission electron micrograph are columns of atoms. Their regular spacing at the atomic level proves that this material is crystalline. Because this crystal is only about 15 nm in diameter, it is a nanocrystal, which has unusual properties that we will discuss in Chapter 12.

△ **GIVE IT SOME THOUGHT**

A baseball pitcher throws a fastball that moves at 95 miles per hour. Does that moving baseball generate matter waves? If so, can we observe them?

The Uncertainty Principle

The discovery of the wave properties of matter raised some new and interesting questions about classical physics. Consider, for example, a ball rolling down a ramp. Using the equations of classical physics, we can calculate the ball's position, direction of motion, and speed at any time, with great accuracy.

▲ **Figure 6.16 Werner Heisenberg (1901–1976).** During his postdoctoral assistantship with Niels Bohr, Heisenberg formulated his famous uncertainty principle. At the age of 25, he became the chair in theoretical physics at the University of Leipzig. At 32 he was one of the youngest scientists to receive the Nobel Prize.

Can we do the same for an electron, which exhibits wave properties? A wave extends in space, and therefore its location is not precisely defined. We might therefore anticipate that it is impossible to determine exactly where an electron is located at a specific time.

The German physicist Werner Heisenberg (Figure 6.16 ◄) proposed that the dual nature of matter places a fundamental limitation on how precisely we can know both the location and the momentum of any object. The limitation becomes important only when we deal with matter at the subatomic level (that is, with masses as small as that of an electron). Heisenberg's principle is called the **uncertainty principle.** When applied to the electrons in an atom, this principle states that it is inherently impossible for us to know simultaneously both the exact momentum of the electron and its exact location in space.

Heisenberg mathematically related the uncertainty of the position (Δx) and the uncertainty in momentum $\Delta(mv)$ to a quantity involving Planck's constant:

$$\Delta x \cdot \Delta(mv) \geq \frac{h}{4\pi} \qquad [6.9]$$

A brief calculation illustrates the dramatic implications of the uncertainty principle. The electron has a mass of 9.11×10^{-31} kg and moves at an average speed of about 5×10^6 m/s in a hydrogen atom. Let's assume that we know the speed to an uncertainty of 1% (that is, an uncertainty of $(0.01)(5 \times 10^6$ m/s$) = 5 \times 10^4$ m/s) and that this is the only important source of uncertainty in the momentum, so that $\Delta(mv) = m\Delta v$. We can then use Equation 6.9 to calculate the uncertainty in the position of the electron:

$$\Delta x \geq \frac{h}{4\pi m \Delta v} = \frac{(6.626 \times 10^{-34} \text{ J-s})}{4\pi(9.11 \times 10^{-31} \text{ kg})(5 \times 10^4 \text{ m/s})} = 1 \times 10^{-9} \text{ m}$$

Because the diameter of a hydrogen atom is only about 1×10^{-10} m, the uncertainty is an order of magnitude greater than the size of the atom. Thus, we have essentially no idea of where the electron is located within the atom. On the other hand, if we were to repeat the calculation with an object of ordinary mass such as a tennis ball, the uncertainty would be so small that it would be inconsequential. In that case, m is large and Δx is out of the realm of measurement and therefore of no practical consequence.

De Broglie's hypothesis and Heisenberg's uncertainty principle set the stage for a new and more broadly applicable theory of atomic structure. In this new approach, any attempt to define precisely the instantaneous location and momentum of the electron is abandoned. The wave nature of the electron is recognized, and its behavior is described in terms appropriate to waves. The result is a model that precisely describes the energy of the electron while describing its location not precisely, but in terms of probabilities.

▲ **GIVE IT SOME THOUGHT**

What is the principal reason that the uncertainty principle should be considered when discussing electrons and other subatomic particles, but is not so necessary when discussing our macroscopic world?

6.5 QUANTUM MECHANICS AND ATOMIC ORBITALS

In 1926 the Austrian physicist Erwin Schrödinger (1887–1961) proposed an equation, now known as Schrödinger's wave equation, that incorporates both the wavelike behavior and the particle-like behavior of the electron. His work opened a new way of dealing with subatomic particles, known as either *quantum mechanics* or *wave mechanics*. The application of Schrödinger's equation

A Closer Look   MEASUREMENT AND THE UNCERTAINTY PRINCIPLE

Whenever any measurement is made, some uncertainty exists. Our experience with objects of ordinary dimensions, such as balls or trains or laboratory equipment, indicates that using more precise instruments can decrease the uncertainty of a measurement. In fact, we might expect that the uncertainty in a measurement can be made indefinitely small. However, the uncertainty principle states that there is an actual limit to the accuracy of measurements. This limit is not a restriction on how well instruments can be made; rather, it is inherent in nature. This limit has no practical consequences when dealing with ordinary-sized objects, but its implications are enormous when dealing with subatomic particles, such as electrons.

To measure an object, we must disturb it, at least a little, with our measuring device. Imagine using a flashlight to locate a large rubber ball in a dark room. You see the ball when the light from the flashlight bounces off the ball and strikes your eyes. When a beam of photons strikes an object of this size, it does not alter its position or momentum to any practical extent. Imagine, however, that you wish to locate an electron by similarly bouncing light off it into some detector. Objects can be located to an accuracy no greater than the wavelength of the radiation used. Thus, if we want an accurate position measurement for an electron, we must use a short wavelength. This means that photons of high energy must be employed. The more energy the photons have, the more momentum they impart to the electron when they strike it, which changes the electron's motion in an unpredictable way. The attempt to measure accurately the electron's position introduces considerable uncertainty in its momentum; the act of measuring the electron's position at one moment makes our knowledge of its future position inaccurate.

Suppose, then, that we use photons of longer wavelength. Because these photons have lower energy, the momentum of the electron is not so appreciably changed during measurement, but its position will be correspondingly less accurately known. This is the essence of the uncertainty principle: *There is an uncertainty in simultaneously knowing either the position or the momentum of the electron that cannot be reduced beyond a certain minimum level.* The more accurately one is known, the less accurately the other is known. Although we can never know the exact position and momentum of the electron, we can talk about the probability of its being at certain locations in space. In Section 6.5 we introduce a model of the atom that provides the probability of finding electrons of specific energies at certain positions in atoms.
Related Exercises: 6.45 and 6.46

---

requires advanced calculus, and we will not be concerned with the details of his approach. We will, however, qualitatively consider the results he obtained, because they give us a powerful new way to view electronic structure. Let's begin by examining the electronic structure of the simplest atom, hydrogen.

In the same way that a plucked guitar string vibrates as a standing wave, Schrödinger treated the electron as a standing circular wave around the nucleus. Just as the plucked guitar string produces a fundamental frequency and higher overtones (harmonics), there is a lowest-energy standing wave, and higher-energy ones, for an electron in an atom. Solving Schrödinger's equation leads to a series of mathematical functions called **wave functions** that describe the electron in an atom. These wave functions are usually represented by the symbol ψ (the lowercase Greek letter *psi*). Although the wave function itself has no direct physical meaning, the square of the wave function, ψ^2, provides information about an electron's location when the electron is in an allowed energy state.

For the hydrogen atom, the allowed energies are the same as those predicted by the Bohr model. However, the Bohr model assumes that the electron is in a circular orbit of some particular radius about the nucleus. In the quantum mechanical model, the electron's location cannot be described so simply. According to the uncertainty principle, if we know the momentum of the electron with high accuracy, our simultaneous knowledge of its location is very uncertain. Thus, we cannot hope to specify the exact location of an individual electron around the nucleus. Rather, we must be content with a kind of statistical knowledge. In the quantum mechanical model, we therefore speak of the *probability* that the electron will be in a certain region of space at a given instant. As it turns out, the square of the wave function, ψ^2, at a given point in space represents the probability that the electron will be found at that location. For this reason, ψ^2 is called either the **probability density** or the **electron density.**

One way of representing the probability of finding the electron in various regions of an atom is shown in Figure 6.17 ▶. In this figure the density of the dots represents the probability of finding the electron. The regions with a high

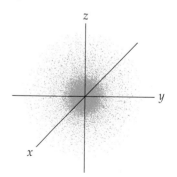

▲ Figure 6.17 **Electron-density distribution.** This rendering represents the probability of where in the space surrounding the nucleus the electron is to be found in a hydrogen atom in its ground state.

density of dots correspond to relatively large values for ψ^2 and are therefore regions where there is a high probability of finding the electron. In Section 6.6 we will say more about the ways in which we can represent electron density.

▲ **GIVE IT SOME THOUGHT**

Is there a difference between stating, "The electron is located at a particular point in space" and "There is a high probability that the electron is located at a particular point in space"?

Orbitals and Quantum Numbers

The solution to Schrödinger's equation for the hydrogen atom yields a set of wave functions and corresponding energies. These wave functions are called **orbitals.** Each orbital describes a specific distribution of electron density in space, as given by the orbital's probability density. Each orbital, therefore, has a characteristic energy and shape. For example, the lowest-energy orbital in the hydrogen atom has an energy of -2.18×10^{-18} J and the shape illustrated in Figure 6.17. Note that an *orbital* (quantum mechanical model) is not the same as an *orbit* (Bohr model). The quantum mechanical model does not refer to orbits, because the motion of the electron in an atom cannot be precisely measured or tracked (Heisenberg uncertainty principle).

The Bohr model introduced a single quantum number, n, to describe an orbit. The quantum mechanical model uses three quantum numbers, n, l, and m_l, which result naturally from the mathematics used, to describe an orbital. Let's consider what information we obtain from each of these quantum numbers and how they are interrelated.

1. The *principal quantum number, n,* can have positive integral values of 1, 2, 3, and so forth. As n increases, the orbital becomes larger, and the electron spends more time farther from the nucleus. An increase in n also means that the electron has a higher energy and is therefore less tightly bound to the nucleus. For the hydrogen atom, $E_n = -(2.18 \times 10^{-18} \text{ J})(1/n^2)$, as in the Bohr model.

2. The second quantum number—the *angular momentum quantum number, l—* can have integral values from 0 to $(n - 1)$ for each value of n. This quantum number defines the shape of the orbital. (We will consider these shapes in Section 6.6.) The value of l for a particular orbital is generally designated by the letters s, p, d, and f,* corresponding to l values of 0, 1, 2, and 3, respectively, as summarized here:

Value of l	0	1	2	3
Letter used	s	p	d	f

3. The *magnetic quantum number, m_l,* can have integral values between $-l$ and l, including zero. This quantum number describes the orientation of the orbital in space, as we will discuss in Section 6.6.

Notice that because the value of n can be any positive integer, an infinite number of orbitals for the hydrogen atom is possible. The electron in a hydrogen atom is described by only one of these orbitals at any given time—we say that the electron *occupies* a certain orbital. The remaining orbitals are *unoccupied* for that particular state of the hydrogen atom. We will see that we are mainly interested in the orbitals of the hydrogen atom with small values of n.

*The letters s, p, d, and f come from the words sharp, principal, diffuse, and fundamental, which were used to describe certain features of spectra before quantum mechanics was developed.

TABLE 6.2 ■ Relationship among Values of *n*, *l*, and m_l through *n* = 4

n	Possible Values of *l*	Subshell Designation	Possible Values of m_l	Number of Orbitals in Subshell	Total Number of Orbitals in Shell
1	0	1*s*	0	1	1
2	0	2*s*	0	1	
	1	2*p*	1, 0, −1	3	4
3	0	3*s*	0	1	
	1	3*p*	1, 0, −1	3	
	2	3*d*	2, 1, 0, −1, −2	5	9
4	0	4*s*	0	1	
	1	4*p*	1, 0, −1	3	
	2	4*d*	2, 1, 0, −1, −2	5	
	3	4*f*	3, 2, 1, 0, −1, −2, −3	7	16

GIVE IT SOME THOUGHT

What is the difference between an *orbit* (Bohr model) and an *orbital* (quantum mechanical model)?

The collection of orbitals with the same value of *n* is called an **electron shell.** All the orbitals that have *n* = 3, for example, are said to be in the third shell. Further, the set of orbitals that have the same *n* and *l* values is called a **subshell.** Each subshell is designated by a number (the value of *n*) and a letter (*s*, *p*, *d*, or *f*, corresponding to the value of *l*). For example, the orbitals that have *n* = 3 and *l* = 2 are called 3*d* orbitals and are in the 3*d* subshell.

Table 6.2▲ summarizes the possible values of the quantum numbers *l* and m_l for values of *n* through *n* = 4. The restrictions on the possible values of the quantum numbers give rise to the following very important observations:

1. The shell with principal quantum number *n* will consist of exactly *n* subshells. Each subshell corresponds to a different allowed value of *l* from 0 to (*n* − 1). Thus, the first shell (*n* = 1) consists of only one subshell, the 1*s* (*l* = 0); the second shell (*n* = 2) consists of two subshells, the 2*s* (*l* = 0) and 2*p* (*l* = 1); the third shell consists of three subshells, 3*s*, 3*p*, and 3*d*, and so forth.

2. Each subshell consists of a specific number of orbitals. Each orbital corresponds to a different allowed value of m_l. For a given value of *l*, there are (2*l* + 1) allowed values of m_l, ranging from −*l* to +*l*. Thus, each *s* (*l* = 0) subshell consists of one orbital, each *p* (*l* = 1) subshell consists of three orbitals, each *d* (*l* = 2) subshell consists of five orbitals, and so forth.

3. The total number of orbitals in a shell is n^2, where *n* is the principal quantum number of the shell. The resulting number of orbitals for the shells—1, 4, 9, 16—is related to a pattern seen in the periodic table: We see that the number of elements in the rows of the periodic table—2, 8, 18, and 32—equals twice these numbers. We will discuss this relationship further in Section 6.9.

Figure 6.18► shows the relative energies of the hydrogen atom orbitals through *n* = 3. Each box represents an orbital; orbitals of the same subshell, such as the 2*p*, are grouped together. When the electron occupies the lowest-energy orbital (1*s*), the hydrogen atom is said to be in its *ground state*. When the

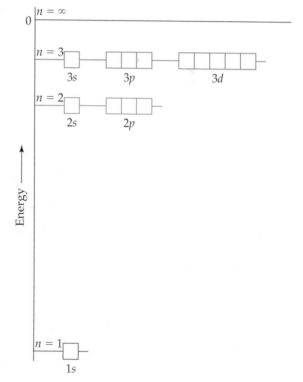

▲ **Figure 6.18 Orbital energy levels in the hydrogen atom.** Each box represents an orbital. Note that all orbitals with the same value for the principal quantum number, *n*, have the same energy. This is true only in one-electron systems, such as the hydrogen atom.

electron occupies any other orbital, the atom is in an *excited state*. At ordinary temperatures, essentially all hydrogen atoms are in the ground state. The electron can be excited to a higher-energy orbital by absorption of a photon of appropriate energy.

GIVE IT SOME THOUGHT

In Figure 6.18, why is the energy difference between the $n = 1$ and $n = 2$ levels so much greater than the energy difference between the $n = 2$ and $n = 3$ levels?

■ SAMPLE EXERCISE 6.6 | Subshells of the Hydrogen Atom

(a) Without referring to Table 6.2, predict the number of subshells in the fourth shell, that is, for $n = 4$. (b) Give the label for each of these subshells. (c) How many orbitals are in each of these subshells?

Analyze and Plan: We are given the value of the principal quantum number, n. We need to determine the allowed values of l and m_l for this given value of n and then count the number of orbitals in each subshell.

SOLUTION

There are four subshells in the fourth shell, corresponding to the four possible values of l (0, 1, 2, and 3).

These subshells are labeled 4s, 4p, 4d, and 4f. The number given in the designation of a subshell is the principal quantum number, n; the letter designates the value of the angular momentum quantum number, l: for $l = 0$, s; for $l = 1$, p; for $l = 2$, d; for $l = 3$, f.

There is one 4s orbital (when $l = 0$, there is only one possible value of m_l: 0). There are three 4p orbitals (when $l = 1$, there are three possible values of m_l: 1, 0, and −1). There are five 4d orbitals (when $l = 2$, there are five allowed values of m_l: 2, 1, 0, −1, −2). There are seven 4f orbitals (when $l = 3$, there are seven permitted values of m_l: 3, 2, 1, 0, −1, −2, −3).

■ PRACTICE EXERCISE

(a) What is the designation for the subshell with $n = 5$ and $l = 1$? (b) How many orbitals are in this subshell? (c) Indicate the values of m_l for each of these orbitals.
Answers: (a) 5p; (b) 3; (c) 1, 0, −1

6.6 REPRESENTATIONS OF ORBITALS

In our discussion of orbitals so far, we have emphasized their energies. But the wave function also provides information about the electron's location in space when it occupies an orbital. Let's examine the ways that we can picture the orbitals. In doing so, we will examine some important aspects of the electron-density distributions of the orbitals. First, we will look at the three-dimensional shape of the orbital—is it spherical, for example, or does it have directionality? Second, we will examine how the probability density changes as we move on a straight line farther and farther from the nucleus. Finally, we will look at the typical three-dimensional sketches that chemists use in describing the orbitals.

The s Orbitals

One representation of the lowest-energy orbital of the hydrogen atom, the 1s, is shown in Figure 6.17. This type of drawing, which shows the distribution of electron density around the nucleus, is one of the several ways we use to help us visualize orbitals. The first thing that we notice about the electron density for the 1s orbital is that it is *spherically symmetric*—in other words, the electron density at a given distance from the nucleus is the same regardless of the direction in which we proceed from the nucleus. All of the other s orbitals (2s, 3s, 4s, and so forth) are spherically symmetric as well. Recall that the l quantum number

With the next element, carbon, we encounter a new situation. We know that the sixth electron must go into a $2p$ orbital. However, does this new electron go into the $2p$ orbital that already has one electron, or into one of the other two $2p$ orbitals? This question is answered by **Hund's rule**, which states that *for degenerate orbitals, the lowest energy is attained when the number of electrons with the same spin is maximized*. This means that electrons will occupy orbitals singly to the maximum extent possible and that these single electrons in a given subshell will all have the same spin magnetic quantum number. Electrons arranged in this way are said to have *parallel spins*. For a carbon atom to achieve its lowest energy, therefore, the two $2p$ electrons will have the same spin. For this to happen, the electrons must be in different $2p$ orbitals, as shown in Table 6.3. Thus, a carbon atom in its ground state has two unpaired electrons. Similarly, for nitrogen in its ground state, Hund's rule requires that the three $2p$ electrons singly occupy each of the three $2p$ orbitals. This is the only way that all three electrons can have the same spin. For oxygen and fluorine, we place four and five electrons, respectively, in the $2p$ orbitals. To achieve this, we pair up electrons in the $2p$ orbitals, as we will see in Sample Exercise 6.7.

Hund's rule is based in part on the fact that electrons repel one another. By occupying different orbitals, the electrons remain as far as possible from one another, thus minimizing electron–electron repulsions.

■■■ **SAMPLE EXERCISE 6.7** | Orbital Diagrams and Electron Configurations

Draw the orbital diagram for the electron configuration of oxygen, atomic number 8. How many unpaired electrons does an oxygen atom possess?

SOLUTION

Analyze and Plan: Because oxygen has an atomic number of 8, each oxygen atom has 8 electrons. Figure 6.25 shows the ordering of orbitals. The electrons (represented as arrows) are placed in the orbitals (represented as boxes) beginning with the lowest-energy orbital, the $1s$. Each orbital can hold a maximum of two electrons (the Pauli exclusion principle). Because the $2p$ orbitals are degenerate, we place one electron in each of these orbitals (spin-up) before pairing any electrons (Hund's rule).

Solve: Two electrons each go into the $1s$ and $2s$ orbitals with their spins paired. This leaves four electrons for the three degenerate $2p$ orbitals. Following Hund's rule, we put one electron into each $2p$ orbital until all three orbitals have one electron each. The fourth electron is then paired up with one of the three electrons already in a $2p$ orbital, so that the representation is

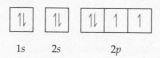

The corresponding electron configuration is written $1s^2 2s^2 2p^4$. The atom has two unpaired electrons.

■■■ **PRACTICE EXERCISE**

(a) Write the electron configuration for phosphorus, element 15. **(b)** How many unpaired electrons does a phosphorus atom possess?
Answers: **(a)** $1s^2 2s^2 2p^6 3s^2 3p^3$, **(b)** three

Condensed Electron Configurations

The filling of the $2p$ subshell is complete at neon (Table 6.3), which has a stable configuration with eight electrons (an *octet*) in the outermost occupied shell. The next element, sodium, atomic number 11, marks the beginning of a new row of the periodic table. Sodium has a single $3s$ electron beyond the stable configuration of neon. We can therefore abbreviate the electron configuration of sodium as

$$\text{Na:} \quad [\text{Ne}]3s^1$$

The symbol [Ne] represents the electron configuration of the ten electrons of neon, $1s^2 2s^2 2p^6$. Writing the electron configuration as $[Ne]3s^1$ helps focus attention on the outermost electrons of the atom, which are the ones largely responsible for the chemical behavior of an element.

We can generalize what we have just done for the electron configuration of sodium. In writing the *condensed electron configuration* of an element, the electron configuration of the nearest noble-gas element of lower atomic number is represented by its chemical symbol in brackets. For example, we can write the electron configuration of lithium as

$$\text{Li: } [\text{He}]2s^1$$

We refer to the electrons represented by the symbol for a noble gas as the *noble-gas core* of the atom. More usually, these inner-shell electrons are referred to as the **core electrons.** The electrons given after the noble-gas core are called the *outer-shell electrons*. The outer-shell electrons include the electrons involved in chemical bonding, which are called the **valence electrons.** For lighter elements (those with atomic number of 30 or less), all of the outer-shell electrons are valence electrons. As we will discuss later, many of the heavier elements have completely filled subshells that are not involved in bonding and are therefore not considered valence electrons.

By comparing the condensed electron configuration of lithium with that of sodium, we can appreciate why these two elements are so similar chemically. They have the same type of electron configuration in the outermost occupied shell. Indeed, all the members of the alkali metal group (1A) have a single *s* valence electron beyond a noble-gas configuration.

Transition Metals

The noble-gas element argon marks the end of the row started by sodium. The configuration for argon is $1s^2 2s^2 2p^6 3s^2 3p^6$. The element following argon in the periodic table is potassium (K), atomic number 19. In all its chemical properties, potassium is clearly a member of the alkali metal group. The experimental facts about the properties of potassium leave no doubt that the outermost electron of this element occupies an *s* orbital. But this means that the electron with the highest energy has *not* gone into a 3*d* orbital, which we might have expected it to do. Here the ordering of energy levels is such that the 4*s* orbital is lower in energy than the 3*d* orbital (Figure 6.25). Hence, the condensed electron configuration of potassium is

$$\text{K: } [\text{Ar}]4s^1$$

Following the complete filling of the 4*s* orbital (this occurs in the calcium atom), the next set of orbitals to be filled is the 3*d* (You will find it helpful as we go along to refer often to the periodic table on the front inside cover.) Beginning with scandium and extending through zinc, electrons are added to the five 3*d* orbitals until they are completely filled. Thus, the fourth row of the periodic table is ten elements wider than the two previous rows. These ten elements are known as either **transition elements** or **transition metals.** Note the position of these elements in the periodic table.

In deriving the electron configurations of the transition elements, the orbitals are filled in accordance with Hund's rule—electrons are added to the 3*d* orbitals singly until all five orbitals have one electron each. Additional electrons are then placed in the 3*d* orbitals with spin pairing until the shell is completely filled.

The condensed electron configurations and the corresponding orbital diagram representations of two transition elements are as follows:

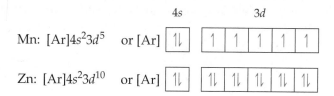

$$\text{Mn: } [\text{Ar}]4s^2 3d^5 \quad \text{or } [\text{Ar}]$$

$$\text{Zn: } [\text{Ar}]4s^2 3d^{10} \quad \text{or } [\text{Ar}]$$

Once all the $3d$ orbitals have been filled with two electrons each, the $4p$ orbitals begin to be occupied until the completed octet of outer electrons ($4s^2 4p^6$) is reached with krypton (Kr), atomic number 36, another of the noble gases. Rubidium (Rb) marks the beginning of the fifth row. Refer again to the periodic table on the front inside cover. Notice that this row is in every respect like the preceding one, except that the value for n is greater by 1.

GIVE IT SOME THOUGHT

Based on the structure of the periodic table, which becomes occupied first, the $6s$ orbital or the $5d$ orbitals?

The Lanthanides and Actinides

The sixth row of the periodic table begins similarly to the preceding one: one electron in the $6s$ orbital of cesium (Cs) and two electrons in the $6s$ orbital of barium (Ba). Notice, however, that the periodic table then has a break, and the subsequent set of elements (elements 57–70) is placed below the main portion of the table. This place is where we begin to encounter a new set of orbitals, the $4f$.

There are seven degenerate $4f$ orbitals, corresponding to the seven allowed values of m_l, ranging from 3 to −3. Thus, it takes 14 electrons to fill the $4f$ orbitals completely. The 14 elements corresponding to the filling of the $4f$ orbitals are known as either the **lanthanide elements** or the **rare earth elements.** These elements are set below the other elements to avoid making the periodic table unduly wide. The properties of the lanthanide elements are all quite similar, and these elements occur together in nature. For many years it was virtually impossible to separate them from one another.

Because the energies of the $4f$ and $5d$ orbitals are very close to each other, the electron configurations of some of the lanthanides involve $5d$ electrons. For example, the elements lanthanum (La), cerium (Ce), and praseodymium (Pr) have the following electron configurations:

$$[\text{Xe}]6s^2\, 5d^1 \qquad [\text{Xe}]6s^2\, 5d^1\, 4f^1 \qquad [\text{Xe}]6s^2\, 4f^3$$
Lanthanum   Cerium   Praseodymium

Because La has a single $5d$ electron, it is sometimes placed below yttrium (Y) as the first member of the third series of transition elements; Ce is then placed as the first member of the lanthanides. Based on their chemistry, however, La can be considered the first element in the lanthanide series. Arranged this way, there are fewer apparent exceptions to the regular filling of the $4f$ orbitals among the subsequent members of the series.

After the lanthanide series, the third transition element series is completed by the filling of the $5d$ orbitals, followed by the filling of the $6p$ orbitals. This brings us to radon (Rn), heaviest of the known noble-gas elements.

The final row of the periodic table begins by filling the 7s orbitals. The **actinide elements,** of which uranium (U, element 92) and plutonium (Pu, element 94) are the best known, are then built up by completing the 5f orbitals. The actinide elements are radioactive, and most of them are not found in nature.

6.9 ELECTRON CONFIGURATIONS AND THE PERIODIC TABLE

Our rather brief survey of electron configurations of the elements has taken us through the periodic table. We have seen that the electron configurations of the elements are related to their locations in the periodic table. The periodic table is structured so that elements with the same pattern of outer-shell (valence) electron configuration are arranged in columns. For example, the electron configurations for the elements in groups 2A and 3A are given in Table 6.4 ◄. We see that all the 2A elements have ns^2 outer configurations, while the all the 3A elements have ns^2np^1 configurations.

Earlier, in Table 6.2, we saw that the total number of orbitals in each shell is equal to n^2: 1, 4, 9, or 16. Because each orbital can hold two electrons, each shell can accommodate up to $2n^2$ electrons: 2, 8, 18, or 32. The structure of the periodic table reflects this orbital structure. The first row has two elements, the second and third rows have eight elements, the fourth and fifth rows have 18 elements, and the sixth row has 32 elements (including the lanthanide metals). Some of the numbers repeat because we reach the end of a row of the periodic table before a shell completely fills. For example, the third row has eight elements, which corresponds to filling the 3s and 3p orbitals. The remaining orbitals of the third shell, the 3d orbitals, do not begin to fill until the fourth row of the periodic table (and after the 4s orbital is filled). Likewise, the 4d orbitals do not begin to fill until the fifth row of the table, and the 4f orbitals don't begin filling until the sixth row.

All these observations are evident in the structure of the periodic table. For this reason, we will emphasize that *the periodic table is your best guide to the order in which orbitals are filled*. You can easily write the electron configuration of an element based on its location in the periodic table. The pattern is summarized in Figure 6.30 ◄. Notice that the elements can be grouped by the *type* of orbital into which the electrons are placed. On the left are *two* columns of elements, depicted in blue. These elements, known as the alkali metals (group 1A) and alkaline earth metals (group 2A), are those in which the valence s orbitals are being filled. On the right is a pink block of *six* columns. These are the elements in which the valence p orbitals are being filled. The s block and the p block of the periodic table together are the **representative elements,** which are sometimes called the **main-group elements.**

In the middle of Figure 6.30 is a gold block of *ten* columns containing the transition metals. These are the elements in which the valence d orbitals are being filled. Below the main portion of the table are two tan rows containing *14* columns. These elements are often referred to as the **f-block metals,** because they are the ones in which the valence f orbitals are being filled. Recall that the numbers 2, 6, 10, and 14 are precisely the number of electrons that can fill the s, p, d, and f subshells, respectively. Recall also that the 1s subshell is the first s subshell, the 2p is the first p subshell, the 3d is the first d subshell, and the 4f is the first f subshell.

TABLE 6.4 ■ Electron Configurations of the Group 2A and 3A Elements	
Group 2A	
Be	$[He]2s^2$
Mg	$[Ne]3s^2$
Ca	$[Ar]4s^2$
Sr	$[Kr]5s^2$
Ba	$[Xe]6s^2$
Ra	$[Rn]7s^2$
Group 3A	
B	$[He]2s^22p^1$
Al	$[Ne]3s^23p^1$
Ga	$[Ar]3d^{10}4s^24p^1$
In	$[Kr]4d^{10}5s^25p^1$
Tl	$[Xe]4f^{14}5d^{10}6s^26p^1$

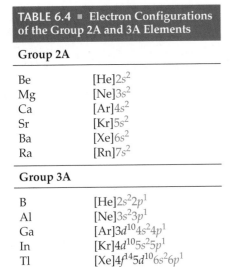

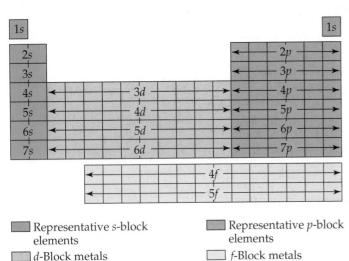

■ Representative s-block elements
■ Representative p-block elements
□ d-Block metals (transition metals)
□ f-Block metals

▲ **Figure 6.30 Regions of the periodic table.** This block diagram of the periodic table shows the order in which electrons are added to orbitals as we move through the table from beginning to end.

■ **SAMPLE EXERCISE 6.8** | **Electron Configurations for a Group**

What is the characteristic valence electron configuration of the group 7A elements, the halogens?

SOLUTION

Analyze and Plan: We first locate the halogens in the periodic table, write the electron configurations for the first two elements, and then determine the general similarity between them.

Solve: The first member of the halogen group is fluorine, atomic number 9. The condensed electron configuration for fluorine is

$$F: \quad [He]2s^2 2p^5$$

Similarly, that for chlorine, the second halogen, is

$$Cl: \quad [Ne]3s^2 3p^5$$

From these two examples, we see that the characteristic valence electron configuration of a halogen is $ns^2 np^5$, where n ranges from 2 in the case of fluorine to 6 in the case of astatine.

■ **PRACTICE EXERCISE**

Which family of elements is characterized by an $ns^2 np^2$ electron configuration in the outermost occupied shell?
Answer: group 4A

■ **SAMPLE EXERCISE 6.9** | **Electron Configurations from the Periodic Table**

(a) Write the electron configuration for bismuth, element number 83. **(b)** Write the condensed electron configuration for this element. **(c)** How many unpaired electrons does each atom of bismuth possess?

SOLUTION

(a) We write the electron configuration by moving across the periodic table one row at a time and writing the occupancies of the orbital corresponding to each row (refer to Figure 6.29).

First row $1s^2$
Second row $2s^2 2p^6$
Third row $3s^2 3p^6$
Fourth row $4s^2 3d^{10} 4p^6$
Fifth row $5s^2 4d^{10} 5p^6$
Sixth row $6s^2 4f^{14} 5d^{10} 6p^3$
Total: $1s^2 2s^2 2p^6 3s^2 3p^6 3d^{10} 4s^2 4p^6 4d^{10} 4f^{14} 5s^2 5p^6 5d^{10} 6s^2 6p^3$

Note that 3 is the lowest possible value that n may have for a d orbital and that 4 is the lowest possible value of n for an f orbital.

The total of the superscripted numbers should equal the atomic number of bismuth, 83. The electrons may be listed, as shown above in the "Total" row, in the order of increasing principal quantum number. However, it is equally correct to list the orbitals in the order in which they are read from Figure 6.30: $1s^2 2s^2 2p^6 3s^2 3p^6 4s^2 3d^{10} 4p^6 5s^2 4d^{10} 5p^6 6s^2 4f^{14} 5d^{10} 6p^3$.

(b) We write the condensed electron configuration by locating bismuth on the periodic table and then moving *backward* to the nearest noble gas, which is Xe, element 54. Thus, the noble-gas core is [Xe]. The outer electrons are then read from the periodic table as before. Moving from Xe to Cs, element 55, we find ourselves in the sixth row. Moving across this row to Bi gives us the outer electrons. Thus, the abbreviated electron configuration is $[Xe]6s^2 4f^{14} 5d^{10} 6p^3$ or $[Xe]4f^{14} 5d^{10} 6s^2 6p^3$.

(c) We can see from the abbreviated electron configuration that the only partially occupied subshell is the $6p$. The orbital diagram representation for this subshell is

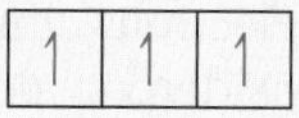

In accordance with Hund's rule, the three $6p$ electrons occupy the three $6p$ orbitals singly, with their spins parallel. Thus, there are three unpaired electrons in each atom of bismuth.

■ **PRACTICE EXERCISE**

Use the periodic table to write the condensed electron configurations for **(a)** Co (atomic number 27), **(b)** Te (atomic number 52).
Answers: **(a)** $[Ar]4s^2 3d^7$ or $[Ar]3d^7 4s^2$, **(b)** $[Kr]5s^2 4d^{10} 5p^4$ or $[Kr]4d^{10} 5s^2 5p^4$

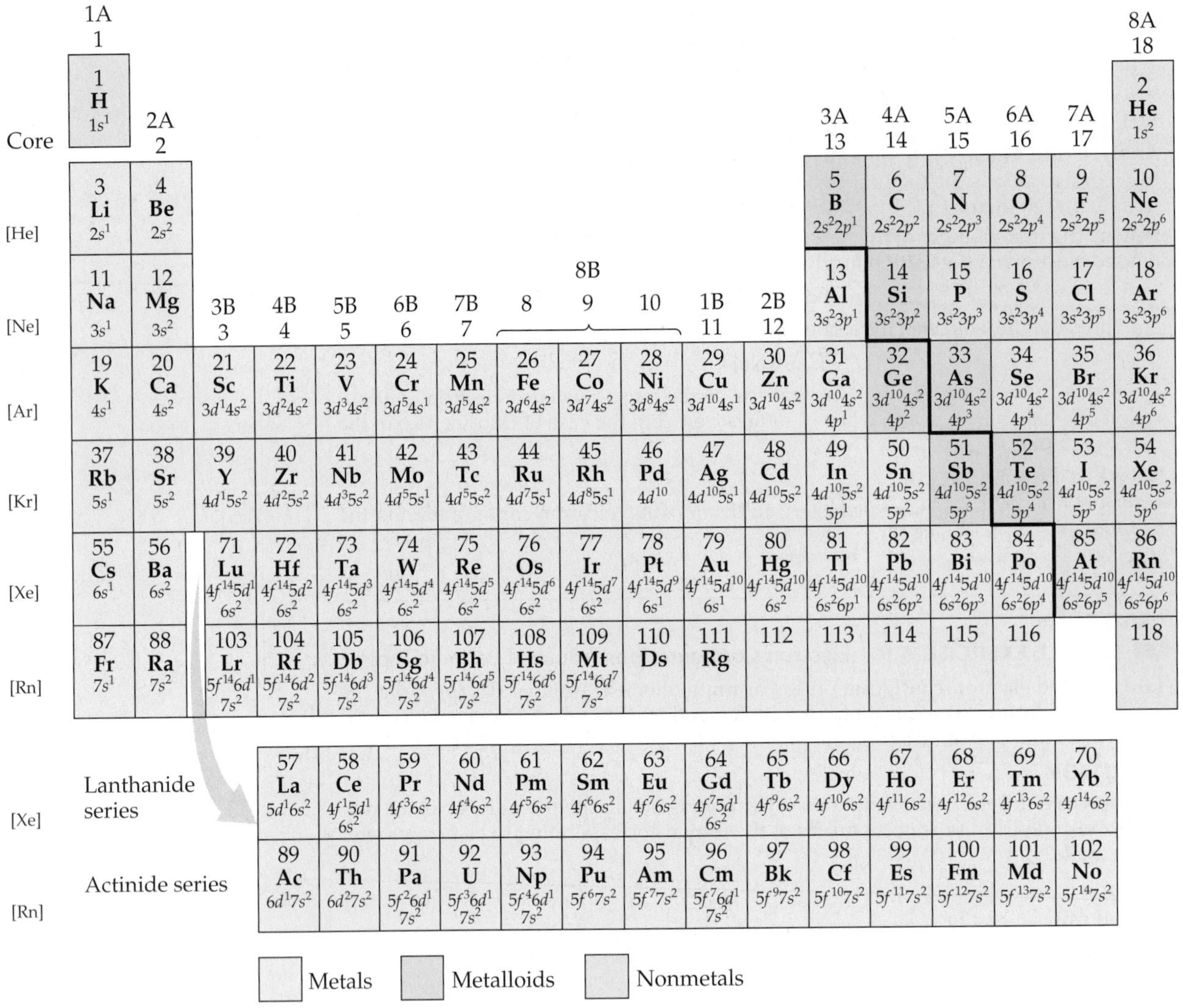

Group	1A 1	2A 2	3B 3	4B 4	5B 5	6B 6	7B 7	8	8B 9	10	1B 11	2B 12	3A 13	4A 14	5A 15	6A 16	7A 17	8A 18
Core	1 H $1s^1$																	2 He $1s^2$
[He]	3 Li $2s^1$	4 Be $2s^2$											5 B $2s^22p^1$	6 C $2s^22p^2$	7 N $2s^22p^3$	8 O $2s^22p^4$	9 F $2s^22p^5$	10 Ne $2s^22p^6$
[Ne]	11 Na $3s^1$	12 Mg $3s^2$											13 Al $3s^23p^1$	14 Si $3s^23p^2$	15 P $3s^23p^3$	16 S $3s^23p^4$	17 Cl $3s^23p^5$	18 Ar $3s^23p^6$
[Ar]	19 K $4s^1$	20 Ca $4s^2$	21 Sc $3d^14s^2$	22 Ti $3d^24s^2$	23 V $3d^34s^2$	24 Cr $3d^54s^1$	25 Mn $3d^54s^2$	26 Fe $3d^64s^2$	27 Co $3d^74s^2$	28 Ni $3d^84s^2$	29 Cu $3d^{10}4s^1$	30 Zn $3d^{10}4s^2$	31 Ga $3d^{10}4s^2 4p^1$	32 Ge $3d^{10}4s^2 4p^2$	33 As $3d^{10}4s^2 4p^3$	34 Se $3d^{10}4s^2 4p^4$	35 Br $3d^{10}4s^2 4p^5$	36 Kr $3d^{10}4s^2 4p^6$
[Kr]	37 Rb $5s^1$	38 Sr $5s^2$	39 Y $4d^15s^2$	40 Zr $4d^25s^2$	41 Nb $4d^35s^2$	42 Mo $4d^55s^1$	43 Tc $4d^55s^2$	44 Ru $4d^75s^1$	45 Rh $4d^85s^1$	46 Pd $4d^{10}$	47 Ag $4d^{10}5s^1$	48 Cd $4d^{10}5s^2$	49 In $4d^{10}5s^2 5p^1$	50 Sn $4d^{10}5s^2 5p^2$	51 Sb $4d^{10}5s^2 5p^3$	52 Te $4d^{10}5s^2 5p^4$	53 I $4d^{10}5s^2 5p^5$	54 Xe $4d^{10}5s^2 5p^6$
[Xe]	55 Cs $6s^1$	56 Ba $6s^2$	71 Lu $4f^{14}5d^1 6s^2$	72 Hf $4f^{14}5d^2 6s^2$	73 Ta $4f^{14}5d^3 6s^2$	74 W $4f^{14}5d^4 6s^2$	75 Re $4f^{14}5d^5 6s^2$	76 Os $4f^{14}5d^6 6s^2$	77 Ir $4f^{14}5d^7 6s^2$	78 Pt $4f^{14}5d^9 6s^1$	79 Au $4f^{14}5d^{10} 6s^1$	80 Hg $4f^{14}5d^{10} 6s^2$	81 Tl $4f^{14}5d^{10} 6s^26p^1$	82 Pb $4f^{14}5d^{10} 6s^26p^2$	83 Bi $4f^{14}5d^{10} 6s^26p^3$	84 Po $4f^{14}5d^{10} 6s^26p^4$	85 At $4f^{14}5d^{10} 6s^26p^5$	86 Rn $4f^{14}5d^{10} 6s^26p^6$
[Rn]	87 Fr $7s^1$	88 Ra $7s^2$	103 Lr $5f^{14}6d^1 7s^2$	104 Rf $5f^{14}6d^2 7s^2$	105 Db $5f^{14}6d^3 7s^2$	106 Sg $5f^{14}6d^4 7s^2$	107 Bh $5f^{14}6d^5 7s^2$	108 Hs $5f^{14}6d^6 7s^2$	109 Mt $5f^{14}6d^7 7s^2$	110 Ds	111 Rg	112	113	114	115	116		118

Lanthanide series [Xe]

57 La $5d^16s^2$	58 Ce $4f^15d^1 6s^2$	59 Pr $4f^36s^2$	60 Nd $4f^46s^2$	61 Pm $4f^56s^2$	62 Sm $4f^66s^2$	63 Eu $4f^76s^2$	64 Gd $4f^75d^1 6s^2$	65 Tb $4f^96s^2$	66 Dy $4f^{10}6s^2$	67 Ho $4f^{11}6s^2$	68 Er $4f^{12}6s^2$	69 Tm $4f^{13}6s^2$	70 Yb $4f^{14}6s^2$

Actinide series [Rn]

89 Ac $6d^17s^2$	90 Th $6d^27s^2$	91 Pa $5f^26d^1 7s^2$	92 U $5f^36d^1 7s^2$	93 Np $5f^46d^1 7s^2$	94 Pu $5f^67s^2$	95 Am $5f^77s^2$	96 Cm $5f^76d^1 7s^2$	97 Bk $5f^97s^2$	98 Cf $5f^{10}7s^2$	99 Es $5f^{11}7s^2$	100 Fm $5f^{12}7s^2$	101 Md $5f^{13}7s^2$	102 No $5f^{14}7s^2$

☐ Metals   ☐ Metalloids   ☐ Nonmetals

▲ Figure 6.31 **Valence electron configurations of the elements.**

Figure 6.31 ▲ gives the valence ground-state electron configurations for all the elements. You can use this figure to check your answers as you practice writing electron configurations. We have written these configurations with orbitals listed in order of increasing principal quantum number. As we saw in Sample Exercise 6.9, the orbitals can also be listed in order of filling, as they would be read off the periodic table.

The electron configurations in Figure 6.31 allow us to reexamine the concept of *valence electrons*. Notice, for example, that as we proceed from Cl ($[Ne]3s^23p^5$) to Br ($[Ar]3d^{10}4s^24p^5$) we have added a complete subshell of $3d$ electrons to the outer-shell electrons beyond the noble-gas core of Ar. Although the $3d$ electrons are outer-shell electrons, they are not involved in chemical bonding and are therefore not considered valence electrons. Thus, we consider only the $4s$ and $4p$ electrons of Br to be valence electrons. Similarly, if we compare the electron configuration of Ag and Au, Au has a completely full $4f^{14}$ subshell beyond its noble-gas core, but those $4f$ electrons are not involved in bonding. In general, *for representative elements we do not consider completely full* d *or* f *subshells to be among the valence electrons*, and *for transition elements we likewise do not consider a completely full* f *subshell to be among the valence electrons*.

Anomalous Electron Configurations

If you inspect Figure 6.31 closely, you will see that the electron configurations of certain elements appear to violate the rules we have just discussed. For example, the electron configuration of chromium is $[Ar]3d^5 4s^1$ rather than the $[Ar]3d^4 4s^2$ configuration we might have expected. Similarly, the configuration of copper is $[Ar]3d^{10}4s^1$ instead of $[Ar]3d^9 4s^2$. This anomalous behavior is largely a consequence of the closeness of the 3d and 4s orbital energies. It frequently occurs when there are enough electrons to lead to precisely half-filled sets of degenerate orbitals (as in chromium) or to completely fill a d subshell (as in copper). There are a few similar cases among the heavier transition metals (those with partially filled 4d or 5d orbitals) and among the f-block metals. Although these minor departures from the expected are interesting, they are not of great chemical significance.

GIVE IT SOME THOUGHT

The elements Ni, Pd, and Pt are all in the same group. By examining the electron configurations for these elements in Figure 6.31, what can you conclude about the relative energies of the nd and $(n + 1) s$ orbitals for this group?

■■ SAMPLE INTEGRATIVE EXERCISE | Putting Concepts Together

Boron, atomic number 5, occurs naturally as two isotopes, ^{10}B and ^{11}B, with natural abundances of 19.9% and 80.1%, respectively. **(a)** In what ways do the two isotopes differ from each other? Does the electronic configuration of ^{10}B differ from that of ^{11}B? **(b)** Draw the orbital diagram for an atom of ^{11}B. Which electrons are the valence electrons? **(c)** Indicate three major ways in which the 1s electrons in boron differ from its 2s electrons. **(d)** Elemental boron reacts with fluorine to form BF_3, a gas. Write a balanced chemical equation for the reaction of solid boron with fluorine gas. **(e)** ΔH_f° for $BF_3(g)$ is -1135.6 kJ mol^{-1}. Calculate the standard enthalpy change in the reaction of boron with fluorine. **(f)** When BCl_3, also a gas at room temperature, comes into contact with water, the two react to form hydrochloric acid and boric acid, H_3BO_3, a very weak acid in water. Write a balanced net ionic equation for this reaction.

SOLUTION

(a) The two isotopes of boron differ in the number of neutrons in the nucleus. ∞ (Sections 2.3 and 2.4) Each of the isotopes contains five protons, but ^{10}B contains five neutrons, whereas ^{11}B contains six neutrons. The two isotopes of boron have identical electron configurations, $1s^2 2s^2 2p^1$, because each has five electrons.
(b) The complete orbital diagram is

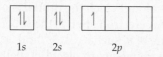

$$1s \qquad 2s \qquad 2p$$

The valence electrons are the ones in the outermost occupied shell, the $2s^2$ and $2p^1$ electrons. The $1s^2$ electrons constitute the core electrons, which we represent as [He] when we write the condensed electron configuration, $[He]2s^2 2p^1$.
(c) The 1s and 2s orbitals are both spherical, but they differ in three important respects: First, the 1s orbital is lower in energy than the 2s orbital. Second, the average distance of the 2s electrons from the nucleus is greater than that of the 1s electrons, so the 1s orbital is smaller than the 2s. Third, the 2s orbital has one node, whereas the 1s orbital has no nodes (Figure 6.19).
(d) The balanced chemical equation is

$$2 \, B(s) + 3 \, F_2(g) \longrightarrow 2 \, BF_3(g)$$

(e) $\Delta H^\circ = 2(-1135.6) - [0 + 0] = -2271.2$ kJ. The reaction is strongly exothermic.
(f) $BCl_3(g) + 3 \, H_2O(l) \longrightarrow H_3BO_3(aq) + 3 \, H^+(aq) + 3 \, Cl^-(aq)$. Note that because H_3BO_3 is a very weak acid, its chemical formula is written in molecular form, as discussed in Section 4.3.

CHAPTER REVIEW

SUMMARY AND KEY TERMS

Introduction and Section 6.1 The **electronic structure** of an atom describes the energies and arrangement of electrons around the atom. Much of what is known about the electronic structure of atoms was obtained by observing the interaction of light with matter. Visible light and other forms of **electromagnetic radiation** (also known as radiant energy) move through a vacuum at the speed of light, $c = 3.00 \times 10^8$ m/s. Electromagnetic radiation has both electric and magnetic components that vary periodically in wavelike fashion. The wave characteristics of radiant energy allow it to be described in terms of **wavelength,** λ and **frequency,** ν, which are interrelated: $c = \lambda\nu$.

Section 6.2 Planck proposed that the minimum amount of radiant energy that an object can gain or lose is related to the frequency of the radiation: $E = h\nu$. This smallest quantity is called a **quantum** of energy. The constant h is called **Planck's constant:** $h = 6.626 \times 10^{-34}$ J-s. In the quantum theory, energy is quantized, meaning that it can have only certain allowed values. Einstein used the quantum theory to explain the **photoelectric effect,** the emission of electrons from metal surfaces by light. He proposed that light behaves as if it consists of quantized energy packets called **photons.** Each photon carries energy, $E = h\nu$.

Section 6.3 Dispersion of radiation into its component wavelengths produces a **spectrum.** If the spectrum contains all wavelengths, it is called a **continuous spectrum;** if it contains only certain specific wavelengths, the spectrum is called a **line spectrum.** The radiation emitted by excited hydrogen atoms forms a line spectrum; the frequencies observed in the spectrum follow a simple mathematical relationship that involves small integers.

Bohr proposed a model of the hydrogen atom that explains its line spectrum. In this model the energy of the electron in the hydrogen atom depends on the value of a number n, called the quantum number. The value of n must be a positive integer (1, 2, 3, ...), and each value of n corresponds to a different specific energy, E_n. The energy of the atom increases as n increases. The lowest energy is achieved for $n = 1$; this is called the **ground state** of the hydrogen atom. Other values of n correspond to **excited states** of the atom. Light is emitted when the electron drops from a higher energy state to a lower energy state; light must be absorbed to excite the electron from a lower energy state to a higher one. The frequency of light emitted or absorbed must be such that $h\nu$ equals the difference in energy between two allowed states of the atom.

Section 6.4 De Broglie proposed that matter, such as electrons, should exhibit wavelike properties. This hypothesis of **matter waves** was proved experimentally by observing the diffraction of electrons. An object has a characteristic wavelength that depends on its **momentum,** mv: $\lambda = h/mv$. Discovery of the wave properties of the electron led to Heisenberg's **uncertainty principle,** which states that there is an inherent limit to the accuracy with which the position and momentum of a particle can be measured simultaneously.

Section 6.5 In the quantum mechanical model of the hydrogen atom, the behavior of the electron is described by mathematical functions called **wave functions,** denoted with the Greek letter ψ. Each allowed wave function has a precisely known energy, but the location of the electron cannot be determined exactly; rather, the probability of it being at a particular point in space is given by the **probability density,** ψ^2. The **electron density** distribution is a map of the probability of finding the electron at all points in space.

The allowed wave functions of the hydrogen atom are called **orbitals.** An orbital is described by a combination of an integer and a letter, corresponding to values of three quantum numbers for the orbital. The principal quantum number, n, is indicated by the integers 1,2,3, ... This quantum number relates most directly to the size and energy of the orbital. The angular momentum quantum number, l, is indicated by the letters s, p, d, f, and so on, corresponding to the values of 0, 1,2,3, ... The l quantum number defines the shape of the orbital. For a given value of n, l can have integer values ranging from 0 to $(n - 1)$. The magnetic quantum number, m_l, relates to the orientation of the orbital in space. For a given value of l, m_l can have integral values ranging from $-l$ to l, including 0. Cartesian labels can be used to label the orientations of the orbitals. For example, the three 3p orbitals are designated $3p_x$, $3p_y$, and $3p_z$, with the subscripts indicating the axis along which the orbital is oriented.

An **electron shell** is the set of all orbitals with the same value of n, such as 3s, 3p, and 3d. In the hydrogen atom all the orbitals in an electron shell have the same energy. A **subshell** is the set of one or more orbitals with the same n and l values; for example, 3s, 3p, and 3d are each subshells of the $n = 3$ shell. There is one orbital in an s subshell, three in a p subshell, five in a d subshell, and seven in an f subshell.

Section 6.6 Contour representations are useful for visualizing the spatial characteristics (shapes) of the orbitals. Represented this way, s orbitals appear as spheres that increase in size as n increases. The **radial probability function** tells us the probability that the electron will be found at a certain distance from the nucleus. The wave function for each p orbital has two lobes on opposite sides of the nucleus. They are oriented along the x-, y-, and z-axes. Four of the d orbitals appear as shapes with four lobes around the nucleus; the fifth one, the d_{z^2} orbital, is represented as two lobes along the z-axis and a "doughnut" in the xy plane. Regions in which the wave function is zero are called **nodes.** There is zero probability that the electron will be found at a node.

Section 6.7 In many-electron atoms, different subshells of the same electron shell have different energies. For a given value of n, the energy of the subshells increases as the value of l increases: $ns < np < nd < nf$. Orbitals within the same subshell are **degenerate,** meaning they have the same energy.

Electrons have an intrinsic property called **electron spin,** which is quantized. The **spin magnetic quantum number,** m_s, can have two possible values, $+\frac{1}{2}$ and $-\frac{1}{2}$, which can be envisioned as the two directions of an electron spinning about an axis. The **Pauli exclusion principle** states that no two electrons in an atom can have the same values for n, l, m_l, and m_s. This principle places a limit of two on the number of electrons that can occupy any one atomic orbital. These two electrons differ in their value of m_s.

Sections 6.8 and 6.9 The **electron configuration** of an atom describes how the electrons are distributed among the orbitals of the atom. The ground-state electron configurations are generally obtained by placing the electrons in the atomic orbitals of lowest possible energy with the restriction that each orbital can hold no more than two electrons. When electrons occupy a subshell with more than one degenerate orbital, such as the $2p$ subshell, **Hund's rule** states that the lowest energy is attained by maximizing the number of electrons with the same electron spin.

For example, in the ground-state electron configuration of carbon, the two $2p$ electrons have the same spin and must occupy two different $2p$ orbitals.

Elements in any given group in the periodic table have the same type of electron arrangements in their outermost shells. For example, the electron configurations of the halogens fluorine and chlorine are $[He]2s^2 2p^5$ and $[Ne]3s^2 3p^5$, respectively. The outer-shell electrons are those that lie outside the orbitals occupied in the next lowest noble-gas element. The outer-shell electrons that are involved in chemical bonding are the **valence electrons** of an atom; for the elements with atomic number 30 or less, all the outer-shell electrons are valence electrons. The electrons that are not valence electrons are called **core electrons.**

The periodic table is partitioned into different types of elements, based on their electron configurations. Those elements in which the outermost subshell is an s or p subshell are called the **representative** (or **main-group**) **elements.** The alkali metals (group 1A), halogens (group 7A), and noble gases (group 8A) are representative elements. Those elements in which a d subshell is being filled are called the **transition elements** (or **transition metals**). The elements in which the $4f$ subshell is being filled are called the **lanthanide** (or **rare earth**) **elements.** The **actinide elements** are those in which the $5f$ subshell is being filled. The lanthanide and actinide elements are collectively referred to as the *f*-block metals. These elements are shown as two rows of 14 elements below the main part of the periodic table. The structure of the periodic table, summarized in Figure 6.30, allows us to write the electron configuration of an element from its position in the periodic table.

KEY SKILLS

- Be able to calculate the wavelength of electromagnetic radiation given its frequency or its frequency given its wavelength.

- Be able to order the common kinds of radiation in the electromagnetic spectrum according to their wavelengths or energy.

- Understand the concept of photons, and be able to calculate their energies given either their frequency or wavelength.

- Be able to explain how line spectra of the elements relate to the idea of quantized energy states of electrons in atoms.

- Be familiar with the wavelike properties of matter.

- Understand how the uncertainty principle limits how precisely we can specify the position and the momentum of subatomic particles such as electrons.

- Know how the quantum numbers relate to the number and type of orbitals, and recognize the different orbital shapes.

- Interpret radial probability function graphs for the orbitals.

- Be able to draw an energy-level diagram for the orbitals in a many-electron atom, and describe how electrons populate the orbitals in the ground-state of an atom, using the Pauli Exclusion Principle and Hund's rule.

- Be able to use the periodic table to write abbreviated electron configurations and determine the number of unpaired electrons in an atom.

KEY EQUATIONS

- $c = \lambda \nu$ [6.1]

  light as a wave: c = speed of light (3.00×10^8 m/s), λ = wavelength in meters, ν = frequency in s^{-1}

- $E = h\nu$ [6.2]

  light as a particle (photon): E = energy of photon in Joules, h = Planck's constant (6.626×10^{-34} J-s), ν = frequency in s^{-1} (same frequency as previous formula)

- $\lambda = h/mv$ [6.8]

  matter as a wave: λ = wavelength, h = Planck's constant, m = mass of object in kg, v = speed of object in m/s

- $\Delta x \cdot \Delta(mv) \geq \dfrac{h}{4\pi}$ [6.9]

  Heisenberg's uncertainty principle. The uncertainty in position (Δx) and momentum ($\Delta(mv)$) of an object cannot be zero; the smallest value of their product is $h/4\pi$

VISUALIZING CONCEPTS

6.1 Consider the water wave shown here. **(a)** How could you measure the speed of this wave? **(b)** How would you determine the wavelength of the wave? **(c)** Given the speed and wavelength of the wave, how could you determine the frequency of the wave? **(d)** Suggest an independent experiment to determine the frequency of the wave. [Section 6.1]

6.2 A popular kitchen appliance produces electromagnetic radiation with a frequency of 2450 MHz. With reference to Figure 6.4, answer the following: **(a)** Estimate the wavelength of this radiation. **(b)** Would the radiation produced by the appliance be visible to the human eye? **(c)** If the radiation is not visible, do photons of this radiation have more or less energy than photons of visible light? **(d)** Propose the identity of the kitchen appliance. [Section 6.1]

6.3 As shown in the accompanying photograph, an electric stove burner on its highest setting exhibits an orange glow. **(a)** When the burner setting is changed to low, the burner continues to produce heat but the orange glow disappears. How can this observation be explained with reference to one of the fundamental observations that led to the notion of quanta? **(b)** Suppose that the energy provided to the burner could be increased beyond the highest setting of the stove. What would we expect to observe with regard to visible light emitted by the burner? [Section 6.2]

6.4 The familiar phenomenon of a rainbow results from the diffraction of sunlight through raindrops. **(a)** Does the wavelength of light increase or decrease as we proceed outward from the innermost band of the rainbow? **(b)** Does the frequency of light increase or decrease as we proceed outward? **(c)** Suppose that instead of sunlight, the visible light from a hydrogen discharge tube (Figure 6.12) was used as the light source. What do you think the resulting "hydrogen discharge rainbow" would look like? [Section 6.3]

SOLUTION

Analyze and Plan: The locations of the elements in the periodic table allow us to predict the electron configurations. The greatest ionization energies involve removal of core electrons. Thus, we should look first for an element with only one electron in the outermost occupied shell.

Solve: The element in group 1A (Na), indicated by the red box, has only one valence electron. The second ionization energy of this element is associated, therefore, with the removal of a core electron. The other elements indicated, S (green box) and Ca (blue box), have two or more valence electrons. Thus, Na should have the largest second ionization energy.

Check: If we consult a chemistry handbook, we find the following values for the second ionization energies (I_2) of the respective elements: Ca (1,145 kJ/mol) < S (2,252 kJ/mol) < Na (4,562 kJ/mol).

■ PRACTICE EXERCISE

Which will have the greater third ionization energy, Ca or S?
Answer: Ca

Periodic Trends in First Ionization Energies

We have seen that the ionization energy for a given element increases as we remove successive electrons. What trends do we observe in ionization energy as we move from one element to another in the periodic table? Figure 7.11 ▶ shows a graph of I_1 versus atomic number for the first 54 elements. The important trends are as follows:

1. Within each row (period) of the table, I_1 generally increases with increasing atomic number. The alkali metals show the lowest ionization energy in each row, and the noble gases show the highest. There are slight irregularities in this trend that we will discuss shortly.

2. Within each column (group) of the table, the ionization energy generally decreases with increasing atomic number. For example, the ionization energies of the noble gases follow the order He > Ne > Ar > Kr > Xe.

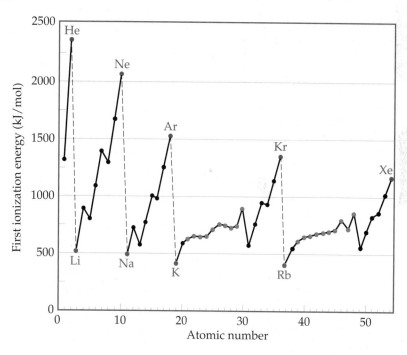

▲ **Figure 7.11 First ionization energy versus atomic number.** The red dots mark the beginning of a period (alkali metals), the blue dots mark the end of a period (noble gases), and the black dots indicate *s*- and *p*-block elements, while green dots are used to represent the transition metals.

3. The *s*- and *p*-block elements show a larger range of values of I_1 than do the transition-metal elements. Generally, the ionization energies of the transition metals increase slowly as we proceed from left to right in a period. The *f*-block metals, which are not shown in Figure 7.11, also show only a small variation in the values of I_1.

The periodic trends in the first ionization energies of the *s*- and *p*-block elements are further illustrated in Figure 7.12 ▼.

In general, smaller atoms have higher ionization energies. The same factors that influence atomic size also influence ionization energies. The energy needed to remove an electron from the outermost occupied shell depends on both the effective nuclear charge and the average distance of the electron from the nucleus. Either increasing the effective nuclear charge or decreasing the distance from the nucleus increases the attraction between the electron and the nucleus.

As this attraction increases, it becomes more difficult to remove the electron and, thus, the ionization energy increases. As we move across a period, there is both an increase in effective nuclear charge and a decrease in atomic radius, causing the ionization energy to increase. As we move down a column, however, the atomic radius increases, while the effective nuclear charge increases rather gradually. Thus, the attraction between the nucleus and the electron decreases, causing the ionization energy to decrease.

The irregularities within a given row are somewhat subtler but still readily explained. For example, the decrease in ionization energy from beryllium ($[He]2s^2$) to boron ($[He]2s^22p^1$), shown in Figures 7.11 and 7.12, occurs because the third valence electron of B must occupy the $2p$ subshell, which is empty for Be. Recall that, as we discussed earlier, the $2p$ subshell is at a higher energy than the $2s$ subshell (Figure 6.23). The decrease in ionization energy when moving from nitrogen ($[He]2s^22p^3$) to oxygen ($[He]2s^22p^4$) is because of the repulsion of paired electrons in the p^4 configuration, as shown in Figure 7.13 ◀. Remember that according to Hund's rule, each electron in the p^3 configuration resides in a different p orbital, which minimizes the electron–electron repulsion among the three $2p$ electrons. ∞ (Section 6.8)

▲ **Figure 7.12 Trends in first ionization energy.** First ionization energies for the *s*- and *p*-block elements in the first six periods. The ionization energy generally increases from left to right and decreases from top to bottom. The ionization energy of astatine has not been determined.

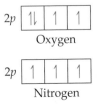

▲ **Figure 7.13 2p orbital filling in nitrogen and oxygen.** The presence of a fourth electron in the $2p$ orbitals of oxygen leads to an extra repulsion associated with putting two electrons in a single orbital. This repulsion is responsible for the lower first ionization energy of oxygen.

■ **SAMPLE EXERCISE 7.6** | Periodic Trends in Ionization Energy

Referring to a periodic table, arrange the following atoms in order of increasing first ionization energy: Ne, Na, P, Ar, K.

SOLUTION

Analyze and Plan: We are given the chemical symbols for five elements. To rank them according to increasing first ionization energy, we need to locate each element in the periodic table. We can then use their relative positions and the trends in first ionization energies to predict their order.

Solve: Ionization energy increases as we move left to right across a row. It decreases as we move from the top of a group to the bottom. Because Na, P, and Ar are in the same row of the periodic table, we expect I_1 to vary in the order Na < P < Ar.

Because Ne is above Ar in group 8A, we expect Ne to have the greater first ionization energy: Ar < Ne. Similarly, K is the alkali metal directly below Na in group 1A, and so we expect I_1 for K to be less than that of Na: K < Na.

From these observations, we conclude that the ionization energies follow the order

$$K < Na < P < Ar < Ne$$

Check: The values shown in Figure 7.12 confirm this prediction.

■ **PRACTICE EXERCISE**

Which has the lowest first ionization energy, B, Al, C, or Si? Which has the highest first ionization energy?
Answer: Al lowest, C highest

Electron Configurations of Ions

When electrons are removed from an atom to form a cation, they are always removed first from the occupied orbitals having the largest principal quantum number, n. For example, when one electron is removed from a lithium atom $(1s^2 2s^1)$, it is the $2s^1$ electron that is removed:

$$\text{Li } (1s^2 2s^1) \Rightarrow \text{Li}^+ (1s^2) + e^-$$

Likewise, when two electrons are removed from Fe ($[\text{Ar}]3d^6 4s^2$), the $4s^2$ electrons are the ones removed:

$$\text{Fe } ([\text{Ar}]3d^6 4s^2) \Rightarrow \text{Fe}^{2+} ([\text{Ar}]3d^6) + 2e^-$$

If an additional electron is removed, forming Fe^{3+}, it now comes from a $3d$ orbital because all the orbitals with $n = 4$ are empty:

$$\text{Fe}^{2+} ([\text{Ar}]3d^6) \Rightarrow \text{Fe}^{3+} ([\text{Ar}]3d^5) + e^-$$

It may seem odd that the $4s$ electrons are removed before the $3d$ electrons in forming transition-metal cations. After all, in writing electron configurations, we added the $4s$ electrons before the $3d$ ones. In writing electron configurations for atoms, however, we are going through an imaginary process in which we move through the periodic table from one element to another. In doing so, we are adding both an electron to an orbital and a proton to the nucleus to change the identity of the element. In ionization, we do not reverse this process because no protons are being removed.

If there is more than one occupied subshell for a given value of n the electrons are first removed from the orbital with the highest value of l. For example a tin atom loses its $5p$ electrons before it loses its $5s$ electrons:

$$\text{Sn } ([\text{Kr}]4d^{10}5s^2 5p^2) \Rightarrow \text{Sn}^{2+} ([\text{Kr}]4d^{10}5s^2) + 2e^- \Rightarrow \text{Sn}^{4+} ([\text{Kr}]4d^{10}) + 4e^-$$

When electrons are added to an atom to form an anion, they are added to the empty or partially filled orbital having the lowest value of n. For example, when an electron is added to a fluorine atom to form the F^- ion, the electron goes into the one remaining vacancy in the $2p$ subshell:

$$\text{F } (1s^2 2s^2 2p^5) + e^- \Rightarrow \text{F}^- (1s^2 2s^2 2p^6)$$

GIVE IT SOME THOUGHT

Would Cr^{3+} and V^{2+} have the same or different electron configurations?

■ SAMPLE EXERCISE 7.7 | Electron Configurations of Ions

Write the electron configuration for (a) Ca^{2+} (b) Co^{3+}, and (c) S^{2-}.

SOLUTION

Analyze and Plan: We are asked to write electron configurations for three ions. To do so, we first write the electron configuration of the parent atom. We then remove electrons to form cations or add electrons to form anions. Electrons are first removed from the orbitals having the highest value of n. They are added to the empty or partially filled orbitals having the lowest value of n.

Solve:

(a) Calcium (atomic number 20) has the electron configuration

$$\text{Ca: } [\text{Ar}]4s^2$$

To form a 2+ ion, the two outer electrons must be removed, giving an ion that is isoelectronic with Ar:

$$\text{Ca}^{2+}: [\text{Ar}]$$

(b) Cobalt (atomic number 27) has the electron configuration

$$\text{Co: } [\text{Ar}]3d^7 4s^2$$

To form a 3+ ion, three electrons must be removed. As discussed in the text preceding this Sample Exercise, the $4s$ electrons are removed before the $3d$ electrons. Consequently, the electron configuration for Co^{3+} is

$$\text{Co}^{3+}: [\text{Ar}]3d^6$$

(c) Sulfur (atomic number 16) has the electron configuration

$$\text{S: [Ne]}3s^2\,3p^4$$

To form a 2− ion, two electrons must be added. There is room for two additional electrons in the 3p orbitals. Thus, the S^{2-} electron configuration is

$$\text{S}^{2-}\text{: [Ne]}3s^2\,3p^6 = \text{[Ar]}$$

Comment: Remember that many of the common ions of the s- and p-block elements, such as Ca^{2+} and S^{2-}, have the same number of electrons as the closest noble gas. ∞ (Section 2.7)

■ PRACTICE EXERCISE

Write the electron configuration for (a) Ga^{3+}, (b) Cr^{3+}, and (c) Br^-.

Answers: (a) $\text{[Ar]}3d^{10}$, (b) $\text{[Ar]}3d^3$, (c) $\text{[Ar]}3d^{10}4s^24p^6 = \text{[Kr]}$

7.5 ELECTRON AFFINITIES

The first ionization energy of an atom is a measure of the energy change associated with removing an electron from the atom to form a positively charged ion. For example, the first ionization energy of Cl(g), 1251 kJ/mol, is the energy change associated with the process

$$\textit{Ionization energy: } \text{Cl}(g) \longrightarrow \text{Cl}^+(g) + e^- \qquad \Delta E = 1251 \text{ kJ/mol} \qquad [7.5]$$
$$\quad\quad\quad [Ne]3s^23p^5 \quad\quad [Ne]3s^23p^4$$

The positive value of the ionization energy means that energy must be put into the atom to remove the electron.

In addition, most atoms can gain electrons to form negatively charged ions. The energy change that occurs when an electron is added to a gaseous atom is called the **electron affinity** because it measures the attraction, or *affinity*, of the atom for the added electron. For most atoms, energy is released when an electron is added. For example, the addition of an electron to a chlorine atom is accompanied by an energy change of −349 kJ/mol, the negative sign indicating that energy is released during the process. We therefore say that the electron affinity of Cl is −349 kJ/mol:*

$$\textit{Electron affinity: } \text{Cl}(g) + e^- \longrightarrow \text{Cl}^-(g) \qquad \Delta E = -349 \text{ kJ/mol} \qquad [7.6]$$
$$\quad\quad\quad\quad [Ne]3s^23p^5 \quad\quad\quad [Ne]3s^23p^6$$

It is important to understand the difference between ionization energy and electron affinity: Ionization energy measures the ease with which an atom *loses* an electron, whereas electron affinity measures the ease with which an atom *gains* an electron.

The greater the attraction between a given atom and an added electron, the more negative the atom's electron affinity will be. For some elements, such as the noble gases, the electron affinity has a positive value, meaning that the anion is higher in energy than are the separated atom and electron:

$$\text{Ar}(g) + e^- \longrightarrow \text{Ar}^-(g)^- \qquad \Delta E > 0 \qquad [7.7]$$
$$\quad [Ne]3s^23p^6 \quad\quad [Ne]3s^23p^64s^1$$

The fact that the electron affinity is a positive number means that an electron will not attach itself to an Ar atom; the Ar− ion is unstable and does not form.

Two sign conventions are used for electron affinity. In most introductory texts, including this one, the thermodynamic sign convention is used: a negative sign indicates that the addition of an electron is an exothermic process, as in the electron affinity given for chlorine, −349 kJ/mol. Historically, however, electron affinity has been defined as the energy released when an electron is added to a gaseous atom or ion. Because 349 kJ/mol is released when an electron is added to Cl(g), the electron affinity by this convention would be +349 kJ/mol.

nonmetals, the metal atoms are oxidized to cations and ionic substances are generally formed. Most metal oxides are basic; they react with acids to form salts and water.

Nonmetals lack metallic luster and are generally poor conductors of heat and electricity. Several are gases at room temperature. Compounds composed entirely of nonmetals are generally molecular. Nonmetals usually form anions in their reactions with metals. Nonmetal oxides are acidic; they react with bases to form salts and water. Metalloids have properties that are intermediate between those of metals and nonmetals.

Section 7.7 The periodic properties of the elements can help us understand the properties of groups of the representative elements. The **alkali metals** (group 1A) are soft metals with low densities and low melting points. They have the lowest ionization energies of the elements. As a result, they are very reactive toward nonmetals, easily losing their outer s electron to form 1+ ions. The **alkaline earth metals** (group 2A) are harder and more dense and have higher melting points than the alkali metals. They are also very reactive toward nonmetals, although not as reactive as the alkali metals. The alkaline earth metals readily lose their two outer s electrons to form 2+ ions. Both alkali and alkaline earth metals react with hydrogen to form ionic substances that contain the **hydride ion**, H^-.

Section 7.8 Hydrogen is a nonmetal with properties that are distinct from any of the groups of the periodic table. It forms molecular compounds with other nonmetals, such as oxygen and the halogens.

Oxygen and sulfur are the most important elements in group 6A. Oxygen is usually found as a diatomic molecule, O_2. **Ozone**, O_3, is an important allotrope of oxygen. Oxygen has a strong tendency to gain electrons from other elements, thus oxidizing them. In combination with metals, oxygen is usually found as the oxide ion, O^{2-}, although salts of the peroxide ion, O_2^{2-}, and superoxide ion, O_2^-, are sometimes formed. Elemental sulfur is most commonly found as S_8 molecules. In combination with metals, it is most often found as the sulfide ion, S^{2-}.

The **halogens** (group 7A) are nonmetals that exist as diatomic molecules. The halogens have the most negative electron affinities of the elements. Thus their chemistry is dominated by a tendency to form 1− ions, especially in reactions with metals.

The **noble gases** (group 8A) are nonmetals that exist as monatomic gases. They are very unreactive because they have completely filled s and p subshells. Only the heaviest noble gases are known to form compounds, and they do so only with very active nonmetals, such as fluorine.

KEY SKILLS

- Understand the meaning of effective nuclear charge, Z_{eff}, and how Z_{eff} depends upon nuclear charge and electron configuration.
- Use the periodic table to predict the trends in atomic radii, ionic radii, ionization energy, and electron affinity.
- Understand how the radius of an atom changes upon losing electrons to form a cation or gaining electrons to form an anion.
- Understand how the ionization energy changes as we remove successive electrons. Recognize the jump in ionization energy that occurs when the ionization corresponds to removing a core electron.
- Be able to write the electron configurations of ions.
- Understand how irregularities in the periodic trends for electron affinity can be related to electron configuration.
- Recognize the differences in chemical and physical properties of metals and nonmetals, including the basicity of metal oxides and the acidity of nonmetal oxides.
- Understand how the atomic properties, such as ionization energy and electron configuration, are related to the chemical reactivity and physical properties of the alkali and alkaline earth metals (groups 1A and 2A).
- Be able to write balanced equations for the reactions of the group 1A and 2A metals with water, oxygen, hydrogen, and the halogens.
- Understand and recognize the unique characteristics of hydrogen.
- Understand how the atomic properties (such as ionization energy, electron configuration, and electron affinity) of group 6A, 7A, and 8A elements are related to their chemical reactivity and physical properties.

KEY EQUATIONS

- $Z_{eff} = Z - S$ [7.1]   Estimating effective nuclear charge

VISUALIZING CONCEPTS

7.1 We can draw an analogy between the attraction of an electron to a nucleus and seeing a lightbulb—in essence, the more nuclear charge the electron "sees," the greater the attraction. **(a)** Within this analogy, discuss how the shielding by core electrons is analogous to putting a frosted-glass lampshade between the lightbulb and your eyes, as shown in the illustration. **(b)** Explain how we could mimic moving to the right in a row of the periodic table by changing the wattage of the lightbulb. **(c)** How would you change the wattage of the bulb and/or the frosted glass to mimic the effect of moving down a column of the periodic table? [Section 7.2]

Observer

Light bulb   Frosted glass

7.2 Fluorine has atomic number 9. If we represent the radius of a fluorine atom with the billiard ball illustrated here, would the analogy be more appropriate for the bonding or nonbonding atomic radius? If we used the same billiard ball to illustrate the concept of fluorine's bonding atomic radius, would we overestimate or underestimate the bonding atomic radius? Explain. [Section 7.3]

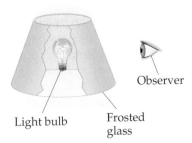

7.3 Consider the A_2X_4 molecule depicted below, where A and X are elements. The A—A bond length in this molecule is d_1, and the four A—X bond lengths are each d_2. **(a)** In terms of d_1 and d_2, how could you define the bonding atomic radii of atoms A and X? **(b)** In terms of d_1 and d_2, what would you predict for the X—X bond length of an X_2 molecule? [Section 7.3]

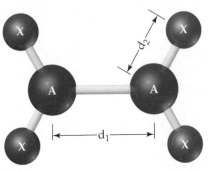

7.4 Make a simple sketch of the shape of the main part of the periodic table, as shown. **(a)** Ignoring H and He, write a single straight arrow from the element with the smallest bonding atomic radius to the element with the largest. **(b)** Ignoring H and He, write a single straight arrow from the element with the smallest first ionization energy to the element with the largest. **(c)** What significant observation can you make from the arrows you drew in parts (a) and (b)? [Sections 7.3 and 7.4]

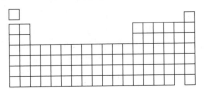

7.5 In the chemical process called *electron transfer*, an electron is transferred from one atom or molecule to another (We will talk about electron transfer extensively in Chapter 20.) A simple electron transfer reaction is

$$A(g) + A(g) \longrightarrow A^+(g) + A^-(g)$$

In terms of the ionization energy and electron affinity of atom A, what is the energy change for this reaction? For a representative nonmetal such as chlorine, is this process exothermic? For a representative metal such as sodium, is this process exothermic? [Sections 7.4 and 7.5]

7.6 An element X reacts with $F_2(g)$ to form the molecular product shown below. **(a)** Write a balanced equation for this reaction (do not worry about the phases for X and the product). **(b)** Do you think that X is a metal or nonmetal? Explain. [Section 7.6]

EXERCISES

Periodic Table; Effective Nuclear Charge

7.7 Why did Mendeleev leave blanks in his early version of the periodic table? How did he predict the properties of the elements that belonged in those blanks?

7.8 The prefix *eka-* comes from the Sanskrit word for one. Mendeleev used this prefix to indicate that the unknown element was one place away from the known element that followed the prefix. For example, *eka-silicon*, which we now call germanium, is one element below silicon. Mendeleev also predicted the existence of *eka-manganese*, which was not experimentally confirmed until 1937 because this element is radioactive and does not occur in nature. Based on the periodic table shown in Figure 7.2, what do we now call the element Mendeleev called *eka-manganese*?

7.9 In Chapter 1 we learned that silicon is the second most abundant element in Earth's crust, accounting for more than one-fourth of the mass of the crust (Figure 1.6). Yet we see that silicon is not among the elements that have been known since ancient times (Figure 7.2), whereas iron, which accounts for less than 5% of Earth's crust, has been known since prehistoric times. Given silicon's abundance how do you account for its relatively late discovery?

7.10 (a) During the period from about 1800 to about 1865, the atomic weights of many elements were accurately measured. Why was this important to Mendeleev's formulation of the periodic table? **(b)** What property of the atom did Moseley associate with the wavelength of X-rays emitted from an element in his experiments? **(c)** Why are chemical and physical properties of the elements more closely related to atomic number than they are to atomic weight?

7.11 (a) What is meant by the term *effective nuclear charge*? **(b)** How does the effective nuclear charge experienced by the valence electrons of an atom vary going from left to right across a period of the periodic table?

7.12 (a) How is the concept of effective nuclear charge used to simplify the numerous electron-electron repulsions in a many-electron atom? **(b)** Which experiences a greater effective nuclear charge in a Be atom, the $1s$ electrons or the $2s$ electrons? Explain.

7.13 Detailed calculations show that the value of Z_{eff} for Na and K atoms is 2.51+ and 3.49+, respectively. **(a)** What value do you estimate for Z_{eff} experienced by the outermost electron in both Na and K by assuming core electrons contribute 1.00 and valence electrons contribute 0.00 to the screening constant? **(b)** What values do you estimate for Z_{eff} using Slater's rules? **(c)** Which approach gives a more accurate estimate of Z_{eff}? **(d)** Does either method of approximation account for the gradual increase in Z_{eff} that occurs upon moving down a group?

7.14 Detailed calculations show that the value of Z_{eff} for Si and Cl atoms is 4.29+ and 6.12+, respectively. **(a)** What value do you estimate for Z_{eff} experienced by the outermost electron in both Si and Cl by assuming core electrons contribute 1.00 and valence electrons contribute 0.00 to the screening constant? **(b)** What values do you estimate for Z_{eff} using Slater's rules? **(c)** Which approach gives a more accurate estimate of Z_{eff}? **(d)** Which method of approximation more accurately accounts for the steady increase in Z_{eff} that occurs upon moving left to right across a period?

7.15 Which will experience the greater effective nuclear charge, the electrons in the $n = 3$ shell in Ar or the $n = 3$ shell in Kr? Which will be closer to the nucleus? Explain.

7.16 Arrange the following atoms in order of increasing effective nuclear charge experienced by the electrons in the $n = 3$ electron shell: K, Mg, P, Rh, and Ti. Explain the basis for your order.

Atomic and Ionic Radii

7.17 (a) Because an exact outer boundary cannot be measured or even calculated for an atom, how are atomic radii determined? **(b)** What is the difference between a bonding radius and a nonbonding radius? **(c)** For a given element, which one is larger?

7.18 (a) Why does the quantum mechanical description of many-electron atoms make it difficult to define a precise atomic radius? **(b)** When nonbonded atoms come up against one another, what determines how closely the nuclear centers can approach?

7.19 The distance between W atoms in tungsten metal is 2.74 Å. What is the atomic radius of a tungsten atom in this environment? (This radius is called the *metallic radius*.)

7.20 Based on the radii presented in Figure 7.7, predict the distance between Si atoms in solid silicon.

7.21 Estimate the As—I bond length from the data in Figure 7.7, and compare your value to the experimental As—I bond length in arsenic triiodide, AsI_3, 2.55 Å.

7.22 The experimental Bi—I bond length in bismuth triiodide, BiI_3, is 2.81 Å. Based on this value and data in Figure 7.7, predict the atomic radius of Bi.

7.23 How do the sizes of atoms change as we move **(a)** from left to right across a row in the periodic table, **(b)** from top to bottom in a group in the periodic table? **(c)** Arrange the following atoms in order of increasing atomic radius: F, P, S, As.

7.24 **(a)** Among the nonmetallic elements, the change in atomic radius in moving one place left or right in a row is smaller than the change in moving one row up or down. Explain these observations. **(b)** Arrange the following atoms in order of increasing atomic radius: Si, Al, Ge, Ga.

7.25 Using only the periodic table, arrange each set of atoms in order of increasing radius: **(a)** Ca, Mg, Be; **(b)** Ga, Br, Ge; **(c)** Al, Tl, Si.

7.26 Using only the periodic table, arrange each set of atoms in order of increasing radius: **(a)** Ba, Ca, Na; **(b)** Sn, Sb, As; **(c)** Al, Be, Si.

7.27 **(a)** Why are monatomic cations smaller than their corresponding neutral atoms? **(b)** Why are monatomic anions larger than their corresponding neutral atoms? **(c)** Why does the size of ions increase as one proceeds down a column in the periodic table?

7.28 Explain the following variations in atomic or ionic radii: **(a)** $I^- > I > I^+$, **(b)** $Ca^{2+} > Mg^{2+} > Be^{2+}$, **(c)** $Fe > Fe^{2+} > Fe^{3+}$.

7.29 Consider a reaction represented by the following spheres:

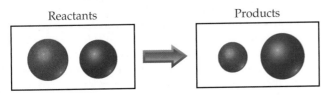

Reactants	Products

Which sphere represents a metal and which a nonmetal? Explain.

7.30 Consider the following spheres:

Which one represents Ca, which Ca^{2+}, and which Mg^{2+}?

7.31 **(a)** What is an isoelectronic series? **(b)** Which neutral atom is isoelectronic with each of the following ions: Al^{3+}, Ti^{4+}, Br^-, Sn^{2+}.

7.32 Some ions do not have a corresponding neutral atom that has the same electron configuration. For each of the following ions identify the neutral atom that has the same number of electrons and determine if this atom has the same electron configuration. If such an atom does not exist explain why: **(a)** Cl^-, **(b)** Sc^{3+}, **(c)** Fe^{2+}, **(d)** Zn^{2+}, **(e)** Sn^{4+}.

7.33 Consider the isoelectronic ions F^- and Na^+. **(a)** Which ion is smaller? **(b)** Using Equation 7.1 and assuming that core electrons contribute 1.00 and valence electrons contribute 0.00 to the screening constant, S, calculate Z_{eff} for the 2p electrons in both ions. **(c)** Repeat this calculation using Slater's rules to estimate the screening constant, S. **(d)** For isoelectronic ions, how are effective nuclear charge and ionic radius related?

7.34 Consider the isoelectronic ions Cl^- and K^+. **(a)** Which ion is smaller? **(b)** Use Equation 7.1 and assuming that core electrons contribute 1.00 and valence electrons contribute nothing to the screening constant, S, calculate Z_{eff} for these two ions. **(c)** Repeat this calculation using Slater's rules to estimate the screening constant, S. **(d)** For isoelectronic ions how are effective nuclear charge and ionic radius related?

7.35 Consider S, Cl, and K and their most common ions. **(a)** List the atoms in order of increasing size. **(b)** List the ions in order of increasing size. **(c)** Explain any differences in the orders of the atomic and ionic sizes.

7.36 For each of the following sets of atoms and ions, arrange the members in order of increasing size: **(a)** Se^{2-}, Te^{2-}, Se; **(b)** Co^{3+}, Fe^{2+}, Fe^{3+}; **(c)** Ca, Ti^{4+}, Sc^{3+}; **(d)** Be^{2+}, Na^+, Ne.

7.37 For each of the following statements, provide an explanation: **(a)** O^{2-} is larger than O; **(b)** S^{2-} is larger than O^{2-}; **(c)** S^{2-} is larger than K^+; **(d)** K^+ is larger than Ca^{2+}.

7.38 In the ionic compounds LiF, NaCl, KBr, and RbI, the measured cation–anion distances are 2.01 Å (Li–F), 2.82 Å (Na–Cl), 3.30 Å (K–Br), and 3.67 Å (Rb–I), respectively. **(a)** Predict the cation–anion distance using the values of ionic radii given in Figure 7.8. **(b)** Is the agreement between the prediction and the experiment perfect? If not, why not? **(c)** What estimates of the cation–anion distance would you obtain for these four compounds using *bonding atomic radii*? Are these estimates as accurate as the estimates using ionic radii?

Ionization Energies; Electron Affinities

7.39 Write equations that show the processes that describe the first, second, and third ionization energies of a boron atom.

7.40 Write equations that show the process for **(a)** the first two ionization energies of tin and **(b)** the fourth ionization energy of titanium.

7.41 **(a)** Why are ionization energies always positive quantities? **(b)** Why does F have a larger first ionization energy than O? **(c)** Why is the second ionization energy of an atom always greater than its first ionization energy?

7.42 **(a)** Why does Li have a larger first ionization energy than Na? **(b)** The difference between the third and fourth ionization energies of scandium is much larger than the difference between the third and fourth ionization energies of titanium. Why? **(c)** Why does Li have a much larger second ionization energy than Be?

7.43 **(a)** What is the general relationship between the size of an atom and its first ionization energy? **(b)** Which element in the periodic table has the largest ionization energy? Which has the smallest?

7.44 **(a)** What is the trend in first ionization energies as one proceeds down the group 7A elements? Explain how this trend relates to the variation in atomic radii. **(b)** What is the trend in first ionization energies as one moves across the fourth period from K to Kr? How does this trend compare with the trend in atomic radii?

7.45 Based on their positions in the periodic table, predict which atom of the following pairs will have the larger first ionization energy: **(a)** Cl, Ar; **(b)** Be, Ca; **(c)** K, Co; **(d)** S, Ge; **(e)** Sn, Te.

7.46 For each of the following pairs, indicate which element has the larger first ionization energy: **(a)** Ti, Ba; **(b)** Ag, Cu; **(c)** Ge, Cl; **(d)** Pb, Sb. (In each case use electron configuration and effective nuclear charge to explain your answer.)

7.47 Write the electron configurations for the following ions: **(a)** In^{3+}, **(b)** Sb^{3+}, **(c)** Te^{2-}, **(d)** Te^{6+}, **(e)** Hg^{2+}, **(f)** Rh^{3+}.

7.48 Write electron configurations for the following ions, and determine which have noble-gas configurations: **(a)** Cr^{3+}, **(b)** N^{3-}, **(c)** Sc^{3+}, **(d)** Cu^{2+}, **(e)** Tl^{+}, **(f)** Au^{+}.

7.49 Write the electron configuration for **(a)** the Ni^{2+} ion and **(b)** the Sn^{2+} ion. How many unpaired electrons does each contain?

7.50 Identify the element whose ions have the following electron configurations: **(a)** a 2+ ion with $[Ar]3d^9$, **(b)** a 1+ ion with $[Xe]4f^{14}5d^{10}6s^2$. How many unpaired electrons does each ion contain?

7.51 The first ionization energy of Ar and the electron affinity of Ar are both positive values. What is the significance of the positive value in each case?

7.52 The electron affinity of lithium is a negative value, whereas the electron affinity of beryllium is a positive value. Use electron configurations to account for this observation.

7.53 While the electron affinity of bromine is a negative quantity, it is positive for Kr. Use the electron configurations of the two elements to explain the difference.

7.54 What is the relationship between the ionization energy of an anion with a 1− charge such as F^- and the electron affinity of the neutral atom, F?

7.55 Consider the first ionization energy of neon and the electron affinity of fluorine. **(a)** Write equations, including electron configurations, for each process. **(b)** These two quantities will have opposite signs. Which will be positive, and which will be negative? **(c)** Would you expect the **magnitudes** of these two quantities to be equal? If not, which one would you expect to be larger? Explain your answer.

7.56 Write an equation for the process that corresponds to the electron affinity of the Mg^+ ion. Also write the electron configurations of the species involved. What is the magnitude of the energy change in the process? [*Hint:* The answer is in Table 7.2.]

Properties of Metals and Nonmetals

7.57 How are metallic character and first ionization energy related?

7.58 Arrange the following pure solid elements in order of increasing electrical conductivity: Ge, Ca, S, and Si. Explain the reasoning you used.

7.59 If we look at groups 3A through 5A, we see two metalloids for groups 4A (Si, Ge) and 5A (As, Sb), but only one metalloid in group 3A (B). To maintain a regular geometric pattern one might expect that aluminum would also be a metalloid, giving group 3A two metalloids. What can you say about the metallic character of aluminum with respect to its neighbors based on its first ionization energy?

7.60 For each of the following pairs, which element will have the greater metallic character: **(a)** Li or Be, **(b)** Li or Na, **(c)** Sn or P, **(d)** Al or B?

7.61 Predict whether each of the following oxides is ionic or molecular: SO_2, MgO, Li_2O, P_2O_5, Y_2O_3, N_2O, and XeO_3. Explain the reasons for your choices.

7.62 Some metal oxides, such as Sc_2O_3, do not react with pure water, but they do react when the solution becomes either acidic or basic. Do you expect Sc_2O_3 to react when the solution becomes acidic or when it becomes basic? Write a balanced chemical equation to support your answer.

7.63 **(a)** What is meant by the terms acidic oxide and basic oxide? **(b)** How can we predict whether an oxide will be acidic or basic, based on its composition?

7.64 Arrange the following oxides in order of increasing acidity: CO_2, CaO, Al_2O_3, SO_3, SiO_2, and P_2O_5.

7.65 Chlorine reacts with oxygen to form Cl_2O_7. **(a)** What is the name of this product (see Table 2.6)? **(b)** Write a balanced equation for the formation of $Cl_2O_7(l)$ from the elements. **(c)** Under usual conditions, Cl_2O_7 is a colorless liquid with a boiling point of 81 °C. Is this boiling point expected or surprising? **(d)** Would you expect Cl_2O_7 to be more reactive toward $H^+(aq)$ or $OH^-(aq)$? Explain.

[7.66] An element X reacts with oxygen to form XO_2 and with chlorine to form XCl_4. XO_2 is a white solid that melts at high temperatures (above 1000 °C). Under usual conditions, XCl_4 is a colorless liquid with a boiling point of 58 °C. **(a)** XCl_4 reacts with water to form XO_2 and another product. What is the likely identity of the other product? **(b)** Do you think that element X is a metal, nonmetal, or metalloid? Explain. **(c)** By using a sourcebook such as the *CRC Handbook of Chemistry and Physics*, try to determine the identity of element X.

7.67 Write balanced equations for the following reactions: **(a)** barium oxide with water, **(b)** iron(II) oxide with perchloric acid, **(c)** sulfur trioxide with water, **(d)** carbon dioxide with aqueous sodium hydroxide.

7.68 Write balanced equations for the following reactions: **(a)** potassium oxide with water, **(b)** diphosphorus trioxide with water, **(c)** chromium(III) oxide with dilute hydrochloric acid, **(d)** selenium dioxide with aqueous potassium hydroxide.

Group Trends in Metals and Nonmetals

7.69 Compare the elements sodium and magnesium with respect to the following properties: **(a)** electron configuration, **(b)** most common ionic charge, **(c)** first ionization energy, **(d)** reactivity toward water, **(e)** atomic radius. Account for the differences between the two elements.

7.70 (a) Compare the electron configurations and atomic radii (see Figure 7.7) of rubidium and silver. In what respects are their electronic configurations similar? Account for the difference in radii of the two elements. **(b)** As with rubidium, silver is most commonly found as the 1+ ion, Ag^+. However, silver is far less reactive. Explain these observations.

7.71 (a) Why is calcium generally more reactive than magnesium? **(b)** Why is calcium generally less reactive than potassium?

7.72 (a) Why is cesium more reactive toward water than is lithium? **(b)** One of the alkali metals reacts with oxygen to form a solid white substance. When this substance is dissolved in water, the solution gives a positive test for hydrogen peroxide, H_2O_2. When the solution is tested in a burner flame, a lilac-purple flame is produced. What is the likely identity of the metal? **(c)** Write a balanced chemical equation for reaction of the white substance with water.

7.73 Write a balanced equation for the reaction that occurs in each of the following cases: **(a)** Potassium metal burns in an atmosphere of chlorine gas. **(b)** Strontium oxide is added to water. **(c)** A fresh surface of lithium metal is exposed to oxygen gas. **(d)** Sodium metal is reacted with molten sulfur.

7.74 Write a balanced equation for the reaction that occurs in each of the following cases: **(a)** Cesium is added to water. **(b)** Stontium is added to water. **(c)** Sodium reacts with oxygen. **(d)** Calcium reacts with iodine.

7.75 (a) If we arrange the elements of the second period (Li–Ne) in order of increasing first ionization energy, where would hydrogen fit into this series? **(b)** If we now arrange the elements of the third period (Na–Ar) in order of increasing first ionization energy, where would lithium fit into this series? **(c)** Are these series consistent with the assignment of hydrogen as a nonmetal and lithium as a metal?

7.76 (a) As described in Section 7.7, the alkali metals react with hydrogen to form hydrides and react with halogens—for example, fluorine—to form halides. Compare the roles of hydrogen and the halogen in these reactions. In what sense are the forms of hydrogen and halogen in the products alike? **(b)** Write balanced equations for the reaction of fluorine with calcium and for the reaction of hydrogen with calcium. What are the similarities among the products of these reactions?

7.77 Compare the elements fluorine and chlorine with respect to the following properties: **(a)** electron configuration, **(b)** most common ionic charge, **(c)** first ionization energy, **(d)** reactivity toward water, **(e)** electron affinity, **(f)** atomic radius. Account for the differences between the two elements.

7.78 Little is known about the properties of astatine, At, because of its rarity and high radioactivity. Nevertheless, it is possible for us to make many predictions about its properties. **(a)** Do you expect the element to be a gas, liquid, or solid at room temperature? Explain. **(b)** What is the chemical formula of the compound it forms with Na?

7.79 Until the early 1960s the group 8A elements were called the inert gases; before that they were called the rare gases. The term rare gases was dropped after it was discovered that argon accounts for roughly 1% of Earth's atmosphere. **(a)** Why was the term inert gases dropped? **(b)** What discovery triggered this change in name? **(c)** What name is applied to the group now?

7.80 Why does xenon react with fluorine, whereas neon does not?

7.81 Write a balanced equation for the reaction that occurs in each of the following cases: **(a)** Ozone decomposes to dioxygen. **(b)** Xenon reacts with fluorine. (Write three different equations.) **(c)** Sulfur reacts with hydrogen gas. **(d)** Fluorine reacts with water.

7.82 Write a balanced equation for the reaction that occurs in each of the following cases: **(a)** Chlorine reacts with water. **(b)** Barium metal is heated in an atmosphere of hydrogen gas. **(c)** Lithium reacts with sulfur. **(d)** Fluorine reacts with magnesium metal.

ADDITIONAL EXERCISES

7.83 Consider the stable elements through lead (Z = 82). In how many instances are the atomic weights of the elements in the reverse order relative to the atomic numbers of the elements? What is the explanation for these cases?

7.84 (a) Which will have the lower energy, a 4s or a 4p electron in an As atom? **(b)** How can we use the concept of effective nuclear charge to explain your answer to part (a)?

7.85 (a) If the core electrons were totally effective at shielding the valence electrons and the valence electrons provided no shielding for each other, what would be the effective nuclear charge acting on the 3s and 3p valence electrons in P? **(b)** Repeat these calculations using Slater's rules. **(c)** Detailed calculations indicate that the effective nuclear charge is 5.6+ for the 3s electrons and 4.9+ for the 3p electrons. Why are the values for the 3s and 3p electrons different? **(d)** If you remove a single electron from a P atom, which orbital will it come from? Explain.

7.86 Nearly all the mass of an atom is in the nucleus, which has a very small radius. When atoms bond together (for example, two fluorine atoms in F_2), why is the distance separating the nuclei so much larger than the radii of the nuclei?

[7.87] Consider the change in effective nuclear charge experienced by a $2p$ electron as we proceed from C to N. **(a)** Based on a simple model in which core electrons screen the valence electrons completely and valence electrons do not screen other valence electrons, what do you predict for the change in Z_{eff} from C to N? **(b)** What change do you predict using Slater's rules? **(c)** The actual change in Z_{eff} from C to N is 0.70+. Which approach to estimating Z_{eff} is more accurate? **(d)** The change in Z_{eff} from N to O is smaller than that from C to N. Can you provide an explanation for this observation?

7.88 As we move across a period of the periodic table, why do the sizes of the transition elements change more gradually than those of the representative elements?

7.89 In the series of group 5A hydrides, of general formula MH_3, the measured bond distances are P—H, 1.419 Å; As—H, 1.519 Å; Sb—H, 1.707 Å. **(a)** Compare these values with those estimated by use of the atomic radii in Figure 7.7. **(b)** Explain the steady increase in M—H bond distance in this series in terms of the electronic configurations of the M atoms.

7.90 It is possible to produce compounds of the form $GeClH_3$, $GeCl_2H_2$, and $GeCl_3H$. What values do you predict for the Ge—H and Ge—Cl bond lengths in these compounds?

7.91 Note from the following table that the increase in atomic radius in moving from Zr to Hf is smaller than in moving from Y to La. Suggest an explanation for this effect.

Atomic Radii (Å)

Sc	1.44	Ti	1.36
Y	1.62	Zr	1.48
La	1.69	Hf	1.50

7.92 The "Chemistry and Life" box on ionic size in Section 7.3 compares the ionic radii of Zn^{2+} and Cd^{2+} **(a)** The 2+ ion of which other element seems the most obvious one to compare to Zn^{2+} and Cd^{2+}? **(b)** With reference to Figure 2.24, is the element in part (a) essential for life? **(c)** Estimate the ionic radius of the 2+ ion of the element in part (a). Explain any assumptions you have made. **(d)** Would you expect the 2+ ion of the element in part (a) to be physiologically more similar to Zn^{2+} or to Cd^{2+}? **(e)** Use a sourcebook or a Web search to determine whether the element in part (a) is toxic to humans.

[7.93] The ionic substance strontium oxide, SrO, forms from the direct reaction of strontium metal with molecular oxygen. The arrangement of the ions in solid SrO is analogous to that in solid NaCl (see Figure 2.23) and is shown here. **(a)** Write a balanced equation for the formation of SrO(s) from the elements. **(b)** Based on the ionic radii in Figure 7.8, predict the length of the side of the

cube in the figure (the distance from the center of an atom at one corner to the center of an atom at a neighboring corner). **(c)** The experimental density of SrO is 5.10 g/cm^3. Given your answer to part (b), what is the number of formula units of SrO that are contained in the cube in the figure? (We will examine structures like those in the figure more closely in Chapter 11.)

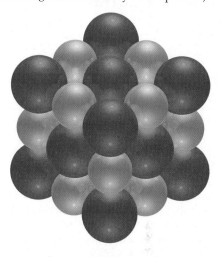

7.94 Explain the variation in ionization energies of carbon, as displayed in the following graph:

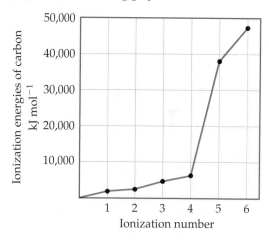

7.95 Do you agree with the following statement? "A negative value for the electron affinity of an atom occurs when the outermost electrons incompletely shield one another from the nucleus." If not, change it to make it more nearly correct in your view. Apply either the statement as given or your revised statement to explain why the electron affinity of bromine is −325 kJ/mol and that for its neighbor Kr is > 0.

7.96 Use orbital diagrams to illustrate what happens when an oxygen atom gains two electrons. Why is it extremely difficult to add a third electron to the atom?

[7.97] Use electron configurations to explain the following observations: **(a)** The first ionization energy of phosphorus is greater than that of sulfur. **(b)** The electron affinity of nitrogen is lower (less negative) than those of both carbon and oxygen. **(c)** The second ionization energy of oxygen is greater than the first ionization energy of fluorine. **(d)** The third ionization energy of manganese is greater than those of both chromium and iron.

7.98 The following table gives the electron affinities, in kJ/mol, for the group 1B and group 2B metals: **(a)** Why are the electron affinities of the group 2B elements greater than zero? **(b)** Why do the electron affinities of the group 1B elements become more negative as we move down the group? [*Hint:* Examine the trends in the electron affinity of other groups as we proceed down the periodic table.]

Cu −119	Zn > 0
Ag −126	Cd > 0
Au −223	Hg > 0

7.99 Hydrogen is an unusual element because it behaves in some ways like the alkali metal elements and in other ways like a nonmetal. Its properties can be explained in part by its electron configuration and by the values for its ionization energy and electron affinity. **(a)** Explain why the electron affinity of hydrogen is much closer to the values for the alkali elements than for the halogens. **(b)** Is the following statement true? "Hydrogen has the smallest bonding atomic radius of any element that forms chemical compounds." If not, correct it. If it is, explain in terms of electron configurations. **(c)** Explain why the ionization energy of hydrogen is closer to the values for the halogens than for the alkali metals.

[7.100] The first ionization energy of the oxygen molecule is the energy required for the following process:

$$O_2(g) \longrightarrow O_2^+(g) + e^-$$

The energy needed for this process is 1175 kJ/mol, very similar to the first ionization energy of Xe. Would you expect O_2 to react with F_2? If so, suggest a product or products of this reaction.

7.101 Based on your reading of this chapter, arrange the following in order of increasing melting point: K, Br_2, Mg, and O_2. Explain the factors that determine the order.

7.102 The element strontium is used in a variety of industrial processes. It is not an extremely hazardous substance, but low levels of strontium ingestion could affect the health of children. Radioactive strontium is very hazardous; it was a by-product of nuclear weapons testing and was found widely distributed following nuclear tests. Calcium is quite common in the environment, including food products, and is frequently present in drinking water. Discuss the similarities and differences between calcium and strontium, and indicate how and why strontium might be expected to accompany calcium in water supplies, uptake by plants, and so on.

[7.103] There are certain similarities in properties that exist between the first member of any periodic family and the element located below it and to the right in the periodic table. For example, in some ways Li resembles Mg, Be resembles Al, and so forth. This observation is called the diagonal relationship. Using what we have learned in this chapter, offer a possible explanation for this relationship.

[7.104] A historian discovers a nineteenth-century notebook in which some observations, dated 1822, on a substance thought to be a new element, were recorded. Here are some of the data recorded in the notebook: Ductile, silver-white, metallic looking. Softer than lead. Unaffected by water. Stable in air. Melting point: 153 °C Density: 7.3 g/cm³. Electrical conductivity: 20% that of copper. Hardness: About 1% as hard as iron. When 4.20 g of the unknown is heated in an excess of oxygen, 5.08 g of a white solid is formed. The solid could be sublimed by heating to over 800 °C. **(a)** Using information in the text and a handbook of chemistry, and making allowances for possible variations in numbers from current values, identify the element reported. **(b)** Write a balanced chemical equation for the reaction with oxygen. **(c)** Judging from Figure 7.2, might this nineteenth-century investigator have been the first to discover a new element?

INTEGRATIVE EXERCISES

[7.105] Moseley established the concept of atomic number by studying X-rays emitted by the elements. The X-rays emitted by some of the elements have the following wavelengths:

Element	Wavelength (Å)
Ne	14.610
Ca	3.358
Zn	1.435
Zr	0.786
Sn	0.491

(a) Calculate the frequency, ν, of the X-rays emitted by each of the elements, in Hz. **(b)** Using graph paper (or

suitable computer software), plot the square root of ν versus the atomic number of the element. What do you observe about the plot? **(c)** Explain how the plot in part (b) allowed Moseley to predict the existence of undiscovered elements. **(d)** Use the result from part (b) to predict the X-ray wavelength emitted by iron. **(e)** A particular element emits X-rays with a wavelength of 0.980 Å. What element do you think it is?

[7.106] **(a)** Write the electron configuration for Li, and estimate the effective nuclear charge experienced by the valence electron. **(b)** The energy of an electron in a one-electron atom or ion equals $(-2.18 \times 10^{-18} \text{ J})\left(\dfrac{Z^2}{n^2}\right)$ where Z is the nuclear charge and n is the principal quantum number of the electron. Estimate the first ionization energy of Li. **(c)** Compare the result of your calculation with the value reported in table 7.4, and explain the difference. **(d)** What value of the effective nuclear charge gives the proper value for the ionization energy? Does this agree with your explanation in (c)?

[**7.107**] One way to measure ionization energies is photoelectron spectroscopy (PES), a technique based on the photoelectric effect. ∞ (Section 6.2) In PES, monochromatic light is directed onto a sample, causing electrons to be emitted. The kinetic energy of the emitted electrons is measured. The difference between the energy of the photons and the kinetic energy of the electrons corresponds to the energy needed to remove the electrons (that is, the ionization energy). Suppose that a PES experiment is performed in which mercury vapor is irradiated with ultraviolet light of wavelength 58.4 nm. **(a)** What is the energy of a photon of this light, in eV? **(b)** Write an equation that shows the process corresponding to the first ionization energy of Hg. **(c)** The kinetic energy of the emitted electrons is measured to be 10.75 eV. What is the first ionization energy of Hg, in kJ/mol? **(d)** With reference to Figure 7.11, determine which of the halogen elements has a first ionization energy closest to that of mercury.

7.108 Consider the gas-phase transfer of an electron from a sodium atom to a chlorine atom:

$$Na(g) + Cl(g) \longrightarrow Na^+(g) + Cl^-(g)$$

(a) Write this reaction as the sum of two reactions, one that relates to an ionization energy and one that relates to an electron affinity. **(b)** Use the result from part (a), data in this chapter, and Hess's law to calculate the enthalpy of the above reaction. Is the reaction exothermic or endothermic? **(c)** The reaction between sodium metal and chlorine gas is highly exothermic and produces NaCl(s), whose structure was discussed in Section 2.7. Comment on this observation relative to the calculated enthalpy for the aforementioned gas-phase reaction.

[**7.109**] When magnesium metal is burned in air (Figure 3.5), two products are produced. One is magnesium oxide, MgO. The other is the product of the reaction of Mg with molecular nitrogen, magnesium nitride. When water is added to magnesium nitride, it reacts to form magnesium oxide and ammonia gas. **(a)** Based on the charge of the nitride ion (Table 2.5), predict the formula of magnesium nitride. **(b)** Write a balanced equation for the reaction of magnesium nitride with water. What is the driving force for this reaction? **(c)** In an experiment a piece of magnesium ribbon is burned in air in a crucible.

The mass of the mixture of MgO and magnesium nitride after burning is 0.470 g. Water is added to the crucible, further reaction occurs, and the crucible is heated to dryness until the final product is 0.486 g of MgO. What was the mass percentage of magnesium nitride in the mixture obtained after the initial burning? **(d)** Magnesium nitride can also be formed by reaction of the metal with ammonia at high temperature. Write a balanced equation for this reaction. If a 6.3-g Mg ribbon reacts with 2.57 g $NH_3(g)$ and the reaction goes to completion, which component is the limiting reactant? What mass of $H_2(g)$ is formed in the reaction? **(e)** The standard enthalpy of formation of solid magnesium nitride is −461.08 kJ/mol. Calculate the standard enthalpy change for the reaction between magnesium metal and ammonia gas.

7.110 **(a)** The experimental Bi—Br bond length in bismuth tribromide, $BiBr_3$, is 2.63 Å. Based on this value and the data in Figure 7.7, predict the atomic radius of Bi. **(b)** Bismuth tribromide is soluble in acidic solution. It is formed by treating solid bismuth(III) oxide with aqueous hydrobromic acid. Write a balanced chemical equation for this reaction. **(c)** While bismuth(III) oxide is soluble in acidic solutions, it is insoluble in basic solutions such as NaOH(aq). Based on these properties, is bismuth characterized as a metallic, metalloid, or nonmetallic element? **(d)** Treating bismuth with fluorine gas forms BiF_5. Use the electron configuration of Bi to explain the formation of a compound with this formulation. **(e)** While it is possible to form BiF_5 in the manner just described, pentahalides of bismuth are not known for the other halogens. Explain why the pentahalide might form with fluorine, but not with the other halogens. How does the behavior of bismuth relate to the fact that xenon reacts with fluorine to form compounds, but not with the other halogens?

7.111 Potassium superoxide, KO_2, is often used in oxygen masks (such as those used by firefighters) because KO_2 reacts with CO_2 to release molecular oxygen. Experiments indicate that 2 mol of $KO_2(s)$ react with each mole of $CO_2(g)$. **(a)** The products of the reaction are $K_2CO_3(s)$ and $O_2(g)$. Write a balanced equation for the reaction between $KO_2(s)$ and $CO_2(g)$. **(b)** Indicate the oxidation number for each atom involved in the reaction in part (a). What elements are being oxidized and reduced? **(c)** What mass of $KO_2(s)$ is needed to consume 18.0 g $CO_2(g)$? What mass of $O_2(g)$ is produced during this reaction?

CHAPTER 8

BASIC CONCEPTS OF CHEMICAL BONDING

THE WHITE CLIFFS OF DOVER in southeastern England are made up largely of chalk, a porous form of limestone. The mineral calcite, with a composition of $CaCO_3$, is the predominant chemical substance in both chalk and limestone. Much of Earth's calcite is produced by marine organisms, which combine Ca^{2+} and CO_3^{2-} ions to form shells of $CaCO_3$. The presence of CO_3^{2-} ions in oceans can be traced to dissolved CO_2 from the atmosphere.

F₂   HF   LiF

▲ Figure 8.7 **Electron density distribution.** This computer-generated rendering shows the calculated electron-density distribution on the surface of the F₂, HF, and LiF molecules. The regions of relatively low electron density (net positive charge) appear blue, those of relatively high electron density (net negative charge) appear red, and regions that are close to electrically neutral appear green.

In F₂ the electrons are shared equally between the fluorine atoms, and thus the covalent bond is *nonpolar*. In general, a nonpolar covalent bond results when the electronegativities of the bonded atoms are equal.

In HF the fluorine atom has a greater electronegativity than the hydrogen atom, with the result that the sharing of electrons is unequal—the bond is polar. In general, a polar covalent bond results when the atoms differ in electronegativity. In HF the more electronegative fluorine atom attracts electron density away from the less electronegative hydrogen atom, leaving a partial positive charge on the hydrogen atom and a partial negative charge on the fluorine atom. We can represent this charge distribution as

$$\overset{\delta+}{\text{H}} - \overset{\delta-}{\text{F}}$$

The δ+ and δ− (read "delta plus" and "delta minus") symbolize the partial positive and negative charges, respectively.

In LiF the electronegativity difference is very large, meaning that the electron density is shifted far toward F. The resultant bond is therefore most accurately described as *ionic*. This shift of electron density toward the more electronegative atom can be seen in the results of calculations of electron density distributions. For the three species in our example, the calculated electron density distributions are shown in Figure 8.7▲. The regions of space that have relatively higher electron density are shown in red, and those with a relatively lower electron density are shown in blue. You can see that in F₂ the distribution is symmetrical, in HF it is clearly shifted toward fluorine, and in LiF the shift is even greater. These examples illustrate, therefore, that *the greater the difference in electronegativity between two atoms, the more polar their bond.*

▲ **GIVE IT SOME THOUGHT**

Based on differences in electronegativity, how would you characterize the bonding in silicon nitride, Si₃N₄? Would you expect the bonds between Si and N to be nonpolar, polar covalent, or ionic?

■■ **SAMPLE EXERCISE 8.4** │ Bond Polarity

In each case, which bond is more polar: **(a)** B—Cl or C—Cl, **(b)** P—F or P—Cl? Indicate in each case which atom has the partial negative charge.

SOLUTION

Analyze: We are asked to determine relative bond polarities, given nothing but the atoms involved in the bonds.

Plan: Because we are not asked for quantitative answers, we can use the periodic table and our knowledge of electronegativity trends to answer the question.

Solve:

(a) The chlorine atom is common to both bonds. Therefore, the analysis reduces to a comparison of the electronegativities of B and C. Because boron is to the left of carbon in the periodic table, we predict that boron has the lower electronegativity. Chlorine, being on the right side of the table, has a higher electronegativity. The more polar bond will be the one between the atoms having the lowest electronegativity (boron) and the highest electronegativity (chlorine). Consequently, the B—Cl bond is more polar; the chlorine atom carries the partial negative charge because it has a higher electronegativity.

(b) In this example phosphorus is common to both bonds, and the analysis reduces to a comparison of the electronegativities of F and Cl. Because fluorine is above chlorine in the periodic table, it should be more electronegative and will form the more polar bond with P. The higher electronegativity of fluorine means that it will carry the partial negative charge.

Check:

(a) Using Figure 8.6: The difference in the electronegativities of chlorine and boron is $3.0 - 2.0 = 1.0$; the difference between chlorine and carbon is $3.0 - 2.5 = 0.5$. Hence the B—Cl bond is more polar, as we had predicted.

(b) Using Figure 8.6: The difference in the electronegativities of chlorine and phosphorus is $3.0 - 2.1 = 0.9$; the difference between fluorine and phosphorus is $4.0 - 2.1 = 1.9$. Hence the P—F bond is more polar, as we had predicted.

■ **PRACTICE EXERCISE**

Which of the following bonds is most polar: S—Cl, S—Br, Se—Cl, or Se—Br?
Answer: Se—Cl

Dipole Moments

The difference in electronegativity between H and F leads to a polar covalent bond in the HF molecule. As a consequence, there is a concentration of negative charge on the more electronegative F atom, leaving the less electronegative H atom at the positive end of the molecule. A molecule such as HF, in which the centers of positive and negative charge do not coincide, is said to be a **polar molecule**. Thus, we describe both bonds and entire molecules as being polar and nonpolar.

We can indicate the polarity of the HF molecule in two ways:

$$\overset{\delta+}{H} - \overset{\delta-}{F} \quad or \quad \overset{\longmapsto}{H - F}$$

Recall from the preceding subsection that "$\delta+$" and "$\delta-$" indicate the partial positive and negative charges on the H and F atoms. In the notation on the right, the arrow denotes the shift in electron density toward the fluorine atom. The crossed end of the arrow can be thought of as a plus sign that designates the positive end of the molecule.

Polarity helps determine many of the properties of substances that we observe at the macroscopic level, in the laboratory and in everyday life. Polar molecules align themselves with respect to one another, with the negative end of one molecule and the positive end of another attracting each other. Polar molecules are likewise attracted to ions. The negative end of a polar molecule is attracted to a positive ion, and the positive end is attracted to a negative ion. These interactions account for many properties of liquids, solids, and solutions, as you will see in Chapters 11, 12, and 13.

How can we quantify the polarity of a molecule? Whenever a distance separates two electrical charges of equal magnitude but opposite sign, a **dipole** is established. The quantitative measure of the magnitude of a dipole is called its **dipole moment**, denoted μ. If a distance r separates two equal and opposite charges $Q+$ and $Q-$, the magnitude of the dipole moment is the product of Q and r (Figure 8.8 ◀):

$$\mu = Qr \qquad\qquad [8.11]$$

▲ Figure 8.8 Dipole and dipole moment. When charges of equal magnitude and opposite sign $Q+$ and $Q-$ are separated by a distance r, a dipole is produced. The size of the dipole is given by the dipole moment, μ, which is the product of the charge separated and the distance of separation between the charge centers: $\mu = Qr$.

The dipole moment increases as the magnitude of charge that is separated increases and as the distance between the charges increases. For a nonpolar molecule, such as F_2, the dipole moment is zero because there is no charge separation.

GIVE IT SOME THOUGHT

The molecules chlorine monofluoride, ClF, and iodine monofluoride, IF, are examples of *interhalogen* compounds—compounds that contain bonds between different halogen elements. Which of these molecules will have the larger dipole moment?

Dipole moments are usually reported in *debyes* (D), a unit that equals 3.34×10^{-30} coulomb-meters (C-m). For molecules, we usually measure charge in units of the electronic charge e, 1.60×10^{-19} C, and distance in units of angstroms. Suppose that two charges $1+$ and $1-$ (in units of e) are separated by a distance of 1.00 Å. The dipole moment produced is

$$\mu = Qr = (1.60 \times 10^{-19}\,\text{C})(1.00\,\text{Å})\left(\frac{10^{-10}\,\text{m}}{1\,\text{Å}}\right)\left(\frac{1\,\text{D}}{3.34 \times 10^{-30}\,\text{C-m}}\right) = 4.79\,\text{D}$$

Measurement of the dipole moments can provide us with valuable information about the charge distributions in molecules, as illustrated in Sample Exercise 8.5.

■ SAMPLE EXERCISE 8.5 | Dipole Moments of Diatomic Molecules

The bond length in the HCl molecule is 1.27 Å. **(a)** Calculate the dipole moment, in debyes, that would result if the charges on the H and Cl atoms were $1+$ and $1-$, respectively. **(b)** The experimentally measured dipole moment of HCl(g) is 1.08 D. What magnitude of charge, in units of e, on the H and Cl atoms would lead to this dipole moment?

SOLUTION

Analyze and Plan: We are asked in (a) to calculate the dipole moment of HCl that would result if there were a full charge transferred from H to Cl. We can use Equation 8.11 to obtain this result. In (b), we are given the actual dipole moment for the molecule and will use that value to calculate the actual partial charges on the H and Cl atoms.

Solve:

(a) The charge on each atom is the electronic charge, $e = 1.60 \times 10^{-19}$ C. The separation is 1.27 Å. The dipole moment is therefore

$$\mu = Qr = (1.60 \times 10^{-19}\,\text{C})(1.27\,\text{Å})\left(\frac{10^{-10}\,\text{m}}{1\,\text{Å}}\right)\left(\frac{1\,\text{D}}{3.34 \times 10^{-30}\,\text{C-m}}\right) = 6.08\,\text{D}$$

(b) We know the value of μ, 1.08 D and the value of r, 1.27 Å. We want to calculate the value of Q:

$$Q = \frac{\mu}{r} = \frac{(1.08\,\text{D})\left(\dfrac{3.34 \times 10^{-30}\,\text{C-m}}{1\,\text{D}}\right)}{(1.27\,\text{Å})\left(\dfrac{10^{-10}\,\text{m}}{1\,\text{Å}}\right)} = 2.84 \times 10^{-20}\,\text{C}$$

We can readily convert this charge to units of e:

$$\text{Charge in } e = (2.84 \times 10^{-20}\,\text{C})\left(\frac{1\,e}{1.60 \times 10^{-19}\,\text{C}}\right) = 0.178e$$

Thus, the experimental dipole moment indicates that the charge separation in the HCl molecule is

$$\overset{0.178+}{\text{H}} - \overset{0.178-}{\text{Cl}}$$

Because the experimental dipole moment is less than that calculated in part (a), the charges on the atoms are much less than a full electronic charge. We could have anticipated this because the H—Cl bond is polar covalent rather than ionic.

■ PRACTICE EXERCISE

The dipole moment of chlorine monofluoride, ClF(g), is 0.88 D. The bond length of the molecule is 1.63 Å. **(a)** Which atom is expected to have the partial negative charge? **(b)** What is the charge on that atom, in units of e?
Answers: **(a)** F, **(b)** 0.11−

TABLE 8.3 ■ Bond Lengths, Electronegativity Differences, and Dipole Moments of the Hydrogen Halides			
Compound	Bond Length (Å)	Electronegativity Difference	Dipole Moment (D)
HF	0.92	1.9	1.82
HCl	1.27	0.9	1.08
HBr	1.41	0.7	0.82
HI	1.61	0.4	0.44

Table 8.3 ◀ presents the bond lengths and dipole moments of the hydrogen halides. Notice that as we proceed from HF to HI, the electronegativity difference decreases and the bond length increases. The first effect decreases the amount of charge separated and causes the dipole moment to decrease from HF to HI, even though the bond length is increasing. Calculations identical to those used in Sample Exercise 8.5 show that the actual charges on the atoms decrease from $0.41+/0.41-$ in HF to $0.057+/0.057-$ in HI. We can "visualize" the varying degree of electronic charge shift in these substances from computer-generated renderings based on calculations of electron distribution, as shown in Figure 8.9 ▼. For these molecules, the change in the electronegativity difference has a greater effect on the dipole moment than does the change in bond length.

▲ GIVE IT SOME THOUGHT

The bond between carbon and hydrogen is one of the most important types of bonds in chemistry. The length of a H—C bond is approximately 1.1 Å. Based on this distance and differences in electronegativity, would you predict the dipole moment of an individual H—C bond to be larger or smaller than the dipole moment of the H—I bond?

Before leaving this section let's return to the LiF molecule pictured in Figure 8.7. Under standard conditions LiF exists as an extended ionic solid with an arrangement of atoms analogous to the sodium chloride structure shown in Figure 8.3. However, it is possible to generate LiF molecules by vaporizing the solid at high temperature. The molecules have a dipole moment of 6.28 D and a bond distance of 1.53 Å. From these values we can calculate the charge on lithium and fluorine to be $0.857+$ and $0.857-$, respectively. This bond is extremely polar, and the presence of such large charges strongly favors the formation of an extended ionic lattice whereby each lithium ion is surrounded by fluoride ions and vice versa.

Differentiating Ionic and Covalent Bonding

To understand the interactions responsible for chemical bonding, it is advantageous to treat ionic and covalent bonding separately. That is the approach taken in this chapter, as well as in most undergraduate-level chemistry texts. The partitioning of bonding into ionic and covalent extremes is considered when we name chemical substances. We saw in Section 2.8 that there are two general approaches

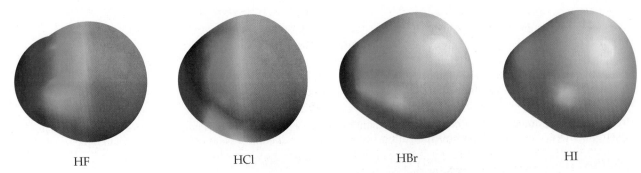

| HF | HCl | HBr | HI |

▲ Figure 8.9 **Charge separation in the hydrogen halides.** Blue represents regions of lowest electron density, red regions of highest electron density. In HF the strongly electronegative F pulls much of the electron density away from H. In HI the I, being much less electronegative than F, does not attract the shared electrons as strongly, and consequently there is far less polarization of the bond.

to naming binary compounds: one used for ionic compounds and the other for molecular ones. However, in reality there is a continuum between the extremes of ionic and covalent bonding. This lack of a well-defined separation between the two types of bonding may seem unsettling or confusing at first.

Fortunately, the simple models of ionic and covalent bonding presented in this chapter go quite a long way toward understanding and predicting the structures and properties of chemical compounds. When covalent bonding is dominant, more often than not we expect compounds to exist as molecules*, with all of the properties we associate with molecular substances, such as relatively low melting and boiling points and non-electrolyte behavior when dissolved in water. Furthermore, we will see later that the polarity of covalent bonds has important consequence for the properties of substances. On the other hand, when ionic bonding is dominant, we expect the compounds to possess very different properties. Ionic compounds tend to be brittle, high-melting solids with extended lattice structures and they exhibit strong electrolyte behavior when dissolved in water.

There are of course exceptions to these general stereotypes, some of which we will examine later in the book. Nonetheless, the ability to quickly categorize the predominant bonding interactions in a substance as covalent or ionic imparts considerable insight into the properties of that substance. The question then becomes what is the best system for recognizing which type of bonding will be dominant?

The simplest approach one can take is to assume that the interaction between a metal and a nonmetal will be ionic, while the interaction between two nonmetals will be covalent. While this classification scheme is reasonably predictive, there are far too many exceptions to use it blindly. For example, tin is a metal and chlorine is a nonmetal, but $SnCl_4$ is a molecular substance that exists as a colorless liquid at room temperature. It freezes at $-33\,°C$ and boils at $114\,°C$. Clearly the bonding in this substance is better described as polar covalent than ionic. A more sophisticated approach, as outlined in the preceding discussion, is to use the difference in electronegativity as the main criterion for determining whether ionic or covalent bonding will be dominant. This approach correctly predicts the bonding in $SnCl_4$ to be polar covalent based on an electronegativity difference of 1.2 and at the same time correctly predicts the bonding in NaCl to be predominantly ionic based on an electronegativity difference of 2.1.

Evaluating the bonding based on electronegativity difference is a useful system, but it has one shortcoming. Our electronegativity scale does not explicitly take into account changes in bonding that accompany changes in the oxidation state of the metal. For example, the electronegativity difference between manganese and oxygen is $3.5 - 1.5 = 2.0$, which falls in the range where the bonding is normally considered to be ionic (the electronegativity difference for NaCl was 2.1). Therefore, it is not surprising to learn that manganese (II) oxide, MnO, is a green solid that melts at $1842\,°C$ and has the same crystal structure as NaCl.

However, it would be incorrect to assume that the bonding between manganese and oxygen is always ionic. Manganese (VII) oxide, which has the formula Mn_2O_7, is a green liquid that freezes at $5.9\,°C$, signaling that covalent rather than ionic bonding is dominant. The change in the oxidation state of manganese is responsible for the change in bonding type. As a general principle, whenever the oxidation state of the metal increases, it will lead to an increase in the degree of covalent character in the bonding. When the oxidation state of the metal becomes highly positive (roughly speaking +4 or larger), we should expect a significant degree of covalency in bonds it forms with nonmetals. In such instances you should not be surprised if a compound or polyatomic ion (such as MnO_4^- or CrO_4^{2-}) exhibits the general properties of molecular, rather than ionic compounds.

*There are some obvious exceptions to this rule, such as the network solids, including diamond, silicon, and germanium, where an extended structure is formed even though the bonding is clearly covalent. These examples are discussed in more detail in Section 11.8.

You encounter two substances: one is a yellow solid that melts at 41 °C and boils at 131 °C. The other is a green solid that melts at 2320 °C. If you are told that one of the compounds is Cr_2O_3 and the other is OsO_4, which one would you expect to be the yellow solid?

8.5 DRAWING LEWIS STRUCTURES

Lewis structures can help us understand the bonding in many compounds and are frequently used when discussing the properties of molecules. For this reason, drawing Lewis structures is an important skill that you should practice. To do so, you should follow a regular procedure. First we will outline the procedure, and then we will go through several examples.

1. *Sum the valence electrons from all atoms.* (Use the periodic table as necessary to help you determine the number of valence electrons in each atom.) For an anion, add one electron to the total for each negative charge. For a cation, subtract one electron from the total for each positive charge. Do not worry about keeping track of which electrons come from which atoms. Only the total number is important.

2. *Write the symbols for the atoms to show which atoms are attached to which, and connect them with a single bond* (a dash, representing *two* electrons). Chemical formulas are often written in the order in which the atoms are connected in the molecule or ion. The formula HCN, for example, tells you that the carbon atom is bonded to the H and to the N. In many polyatomic molecules and ions, the central atom is usually written first, as in CO_3^{2-} and SF_4. Remember that the central atom is generally less electronegative than the atoms surrounding it. In other cases, you may need more information before you can draw the Lewis structure.

3. *Complete the octets around all the atoms bonded to the central atom.* Remember, however, that you use only a single pair of electrons around hydrogen.

4. *Place any leftover electrons on the central atom,* even if doing so results in more than an octet of electrons around the atom. In Section 8.7 we will discuss molecules that do not adhere to the octet rule.

5. *If there are not enough electrons to give the central atom an octet, try multiple bonds.* Use one or more of the unshared pairs of electrons on the atoms bonded to the central atom to form double or triple bonds.

■■ **SAMPLE EXERCISE 8.6** | Drawing Lewis Structures
Draw the Lewis structure for phosphorus trichloride, PCl_3.

SOLUTION
Analyze and Plan: We are asked to draw a Lewis structure from a molecular formula. Our plan is to follow the five-step procedure just described.

Solve:

First, we sum the valence electrons. Phosphorus (group 5A) has five valence electrons, and each chlorine (group 7A) has seven. The total number of valence electrons is therefore

$$5 + (3 \times 7) = 26$$

Second, we arrange the atoms to show which atom is connected to which, and we draw a single bond between them. There are various ways the atoms might be arranged. In binary (two-element) compounds, however, the first element listed in the chemical formula is generally surrounded by the remaining atoms. Thus, we begin with a skeleton structure that shows a single bond between the phosphorus atom and each chlorine atom:

```
Cl—P—Cl
    |
    Cl
```

(It is not crucial to place the atoms in exactly this arrangement.)

Third, we complete the octets on the atoms bonded to the central atom. Placing octets around each Cl atom accounts for 24 electrons (remember, each line in our structure represents *two* electrons):

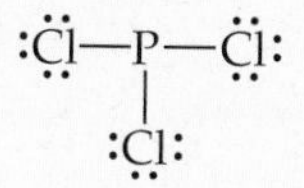

:C̈l—P—C̈l:
         |
       :C̈l:

Fourth, we place the remaining two electrons on the central atom, completing the octet around it:

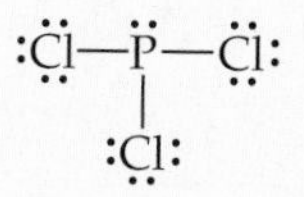

:C̈l—P̈—C̈l:
         |
       :C̈l:

This structure gives each atom an octet, so we stop at this point. (Remember that in achieving an octet, the bonding electrons are counted for both atoms.)

■ PRACTICE EXERCISE

(a) How many valence electrons should appear in the Lewis structure for CH_2Cl_2?
(b) Draw the Lewis structure.

Answers: **(a)** 20, **(b)**

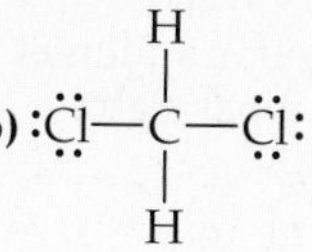

                H
                |
      :C̈l—C—C̈l:
                |
                H

■ SAMPLE EXERCISE 8.7 │ Lewis Structures with Multiple Bonds

Draw the Lewis structure for HCN.

SOLUTION

Hydrogen has one valence electron, carbon (group 4A) has four, and nitrogen (group 5A) has five. The total number of valence electrons is therefore $1 + 4 + 5 = 10$. In principle, there are different ways in which we might choose to arrange the atoms. Because hydrogen can accommodate only one electron pair, it always has only one single bond associated with it in any compound. Therefore, C—H—N is an impossible arrangement. The remaining two possibilities are H—C—N and H—N—C. The first is the arrangement found experimentally. You might have guessed this to be the atomic arrangement because **(a)** the formula is written with the atoms in this order, and **(b)** carbon is less electronegative than nitrogen. Thus, we begin with a skeleton structure that shows single bonds between hydrogen, carbon, and nitrogen:

$$H—C—N$$

These two bonds account for four electrons. If we then place the remaining six electrons around N to give it an octet, we do not achieve an octet on C:

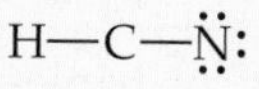

$$H—C—N̈:$$

We therefore try a double bond between C and N, using one of the unshared pairs of electrons we placed on N. Again, there are fewer than eight electrons on C, and so we next try a triple bond. This structure gives an octet around both C and N:

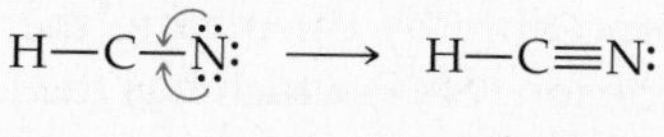

$$H—C⌒N: \longrightarrow H—C≡N:$$

We see that the octet rule is satisfied for the C and N atoms, and the H atom has two electrons around it. This appears to be a correct Lewis structure.

■ PRACTICE EXERCISE

Draw the Lewis structure for **(a)** NO^+ ion, **(b)** C_2H_4.

Answers: **(a)** $[:N≡O:]^+$, **(b)**

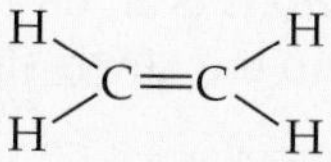

      H   H
        \   /
          C=C
        /   \
      H   H

■ **SAMPLE EXERCISE 8.8** | **Lewis Structure for a Polyatomic Ion**

Draw the Lewis structure for the BrO_3^- ion.

SOLUTION

Bromine (group 7A) has seven valence electrons, and oxygen (group 6A) has six. We must now add one more electron to our sum to account for the 1− charge of the ion. The total number of valence electrons is therefore $7 + (3 \times 6) + 1 = 26$. For oxyanions—$BrO_3^-$, SO_4^{2-}, NO_3^-, CO_3^{2-}, and so forth—the oxygen atoms surround the central nonmetal atoms. After following this format and then putting in the single bonds and distributing the unshared electron pairs, we have

$$\left[\ddot{:}\ddot{O} - \ddot{Br} - \ddot{O}\ddot{:} \atop :\ddot{O}: \right]^-$$

Notice here and elsewhere that the Lewis structure for an ion is written in brackets with the charge shown outside the brackets at the upper right.

■ **PRACTICE EXERCISE**

Draw the Lewis structure for **(a)** ClO_2^- ion, **(b)** PO_4^{3-} ion.

Answers: **(a)** $\left[:\ddot{O} - \ddot{Cl} - \ddot{O}: \right]^-$ **(b)** $\left[:\ddot{O} - \overset{\overset{\textstyle :\ddot{O}:}{|}}{P} - \ddot{O}: \atop :\ddot{O}: \right]^{3-}$

Formal Charge

When we draw a Lewis structure, we are describing how the electrons are distributed in a molecule (or polyatomic ion). In some instances we can draw several different Lewis structures that all obey the octet rule. How do we decide which one is the most reasonable? One approach is to do some "bookkeeping" of the valence electrons to determine the formal charge of each atom in each Lewis structure. The **formal charge** of any atom in a molecule is the charge the atom would have if all the atoms in the molecule had the same electronegativity (that is, if each bonding electron pair in the molecule were shared equally between its two atoms).

To calculate the formal charge on any atom in a Lewis structure, we assign the electrons to the atom as follows:

1. *All* unshared (nonbonding) electrons are assigned to the atom on which they are found.

2. For any bond—single, double, or triple—*half* of the bonding electrons are assigned to each atom in the bond.

The formal charge of each atom is then calculated *by subtracting the number of electrons assigned to the atom from the number of valence electrons in the isolated atom.*

Let's illustrate this procedure by calculating the formal charges on the C and N atoms in the cyanide ion, CN^-, which has the Lewis structure

$$[:C \equiv N:]^-$$

For the C atom, there are 2 nonbonding electrons and 3 electrons from the 6 in the triple bond ($\frac{1}{2} \times 6 = 3$) for a total of 5. The number of valence electrons on a neutral C atom is 4. Thus, the formal charge on C is $4 - 5 = -1$. For N, there are 2 nonbonding electrons and 3 electrons from the triple bond. Because the number of valence electrons on a neutral N atom is 5, its formal charge is $5 - 5 = 0$. Thus, the formal charges on the atoms in the Lewis structure of CN^- are

$$\overset{-1 \quad\quad 0}{[:C \equiv N:]^-}$$

Notice that the sum of the formal charges equals the overall charge on the ion, 1−. The formal charges on a neutral molecule must add to zero, whereas those on an ion add to give the overall charge on the ion.

The concept of formal charge can help us choose between alternative Lewis structures. We will consider the CO_2 molecule to see how this is done. As shown in Section 8.3, CO_2 is represented as having two double bonds. However, we can also satisfy the octet rule by drawing a Lewis structure having one single bond and one triple bond. Calculating the formal charge for each atom in these structures, we have

	Ö=C=Ö			:Ö—C≡O:	
Valence electrons:	6	4	6	6	4	6
−(Electrons assigned to atom):	6	4	6	7	4	5
Formal charge:	0	0	0	−1	0	+1

Note that in both cases the formal charges add up to zero, as they must because CO_2 is a neutral molecule. So, which is the correct structure? As a general rule, when several Lewis structures are possible, we will use the following guidelines to choose the most correct one:

1. We generally choose the Lewis structure in which the atoms bear formal charges closest to zero.

2. We generally choose the Lewis structure in which any negative charges reside on the more electronegative atoms.

Thus, the first Lewis structure of CO_2 is preferred because the atoms carry no formal charges and so satisfy the first guideline.

Although the concept of formal charge helps us choose between alternative Lewis structures, it is very important that you remember that *formal charges do not represent real charges on atoms*. These charges are just a bookkeeping convention. The actual charge distributions in molecules and ions are determined not by formal charges but by a number of factors, including the electronegativity differences between atoms.

GIVE IT SOME THOUGHT

Suppose that a Lewis structure for a neutral fluorine-containing molecule results in a formal charge on the fluorine atom of +1. What conclusion would you draw?

■ SAMPLE EXERCISE 8.9 | Lewis Structures and Formal Charges

The following are three possible Lewis structures for the thiocyanate ion, NCS^-:

$[:\ddot{N}—C≡S:]^-$ $[\ddot{N}=C=\ddot{S}]^-$ $[:N≡C—\ddot{S}:]^-$

(a) Determine the formal charges of the atoms in each structure. (b) Which Lewis structure is the preferred one?

SOLUTION

(a) Neutral N, C, and S atoms have five, four, and six valence electrons, respectively. We can determine the following formal charges in the three structures by using the rules we just discussed:

−2	0	+1		−1	0	0		0	0	−1
$[:\ddot{N}—C≡S:]^-$				$[\ddot{N}=C=\ddot{S}]^-$				$[:N≡C—\ddot{S}:]^-$		

As they must, the formal charges in all three structures sum to 1−, the overall charge of the ion.

(b) We will use the guidelines for the best Lewis structure to determine which of the three structures is likely the most correct. As discussed in Section 8.4, N is more electronegative than C or S. Therefore, we expect that any negative formal charge will reside on the N atom (guideline 2). Further, we usually choose the Lewis structure that produces the formal charges of smallest magnitude (guideline 1). For these two reasons, the middle structure is the preferred Lewis structure of the NCS⁻ ion.

■ PRACTICE EXERCISE

The cyanate ion (NCO⁻), like the thiocyanate ion, has three possible Lewis structures. **(a)** Draw these three Lewis structures, and assign formal charges to the atoms in each structure. **(b)** Which Lewis structure is the preferred one?

$$\begin{array}{ccc} \overset{-2 \quad 0 \quad +1}{[:\ddot{\text{N}}\text{—C}\equiv\text{O}:]^-} & \overset{-1 \quad 0 \quad 0}{[\ddot{\text{N}}\text{=C=}\ddot{\text{O}}]^-} & \overset{0 \quad 0 \quad -1}{[:\text{N}\equiv\text{C—}\ddot{\text{O}}:]^-} \\ \text{(i)} & \text{(ii)} & \text{(iii)} \end{array}$$

Answers: **(a)** (as shown above)

(b) Structure (iii), which places a negative charge on oxygen, the most electronegative of the three elements, is the preferred Lewis structure.

A Closer Look   OXIDATION NUMBERS, FORMAL CHARGES, AND ACTUAL PARTIAL CHARGES

In Chapter 4 we introduced the rules for assigning *oxidation numbers* to atoms. The concept of electronegativity is the basis of these numbers. The oxidation number of an atom is the charge it would have if its bonds were completely ionic. That is, in determining the oxidation number, all shared electrons are counted with the more electronegative atom. For example, consider the Lewis structure of HCl shown in Figure 8.10(a) ▼. To assign oxidation numbers, the pair of electrons in the covalent bond between the atoms is assigned to the more electronegative Cl atom. This procedure gives Cl eight valence-shell electrons, one more than the neutral atom. Thus, its oxidation number is −1. Hydrogen has no valence electrons when they are counted this way, giving it an oxidation number of +1.

In this section we have just considered another way of counting electrons that gives rise to *formal charges*. The formal charge is assigned by ignoring electronegativity and assigning equally the electrons in bonds between the bonded atoms. Consider again the HCl molecule, but this time divide the bonding pair of electrons equally between H and Cl as shown in Figure 8.10(b). In this case Cl has seven assigned electrons, the same as that of the neutral Cl atom. Thus, the formal charge of Cl in this compound is 0. Likewise, the formal charge of H is also 0.

Neither the oxidation number nor the formal charge gives an accurate depiction of the actual charges on atoms. Oxidation numbers overstate the role of electronegativity, and formal charges ignore it completely. It seems reasonable that electrons in covalent bonds should be apportioned according to the relative electronegativities of the bonded atoms. From Figure 8.6 we see that Cl has an electronegativity of 3.0, while that of H is 2.1. The more electronegative Cl atom might therefore be expected to have roughly $3.0/(3.0 + 2.1) = 0.59$ of the electrical charge in the bonding pair, whereas the H atom has $2.1/(3.0 + 2.1) = 0.41$ of the charge. Because the bond consists of two electrons, the Cl atom's share is $0.59 \times 2e = 1.18e$, or $0.18e$ more than the neutral Cl atom. This gives rise to a partial charge of 0.18− on Cl and 0.18+ on H (notice again that we place the + and − signs before the magnitude when speaking about oxidation numbers and formal charges, but after the magnitude when talking about actual charges).

The dipole moment of HCl gives an experimental measure of the partial charges on each atom. In Sample Exercise 8.5 we saw that the dipole moment of HCl indicates a charge separation with a partial charge of 0.178+ on H and 0.178− on Cl, in remarkably good agreement with our simple approximation based on electronegativities. Although that type of calculation provides "ballpark" numbers for the magnitude of charge on atoms, the relationship between electronegativities and charge separation is generally more complicated. As we have already seen, computer programs employing quantum mechanical principles have been developed to obtain more accurate estimates of the partial charges on atoms, even in complex molecules. Figure 8.10(c) shows a graphical representation of the charge distribution in HCl.

Related Exercises: 8.6, 8.47, 8.48, 8.49, 8.50, 8.88, and 8.89

◄ **Figure 8.10 Oxidation number and formal charge.** (a) The oxidation number for any atom in a molecule is determined by assigning all shared electrons to the more electronegative atom (in this case Cl). (b) Formal charges are derived by dividing all shared electron pairs equally between the bonded atoms. (c) The calculated distribution of electron density on an HCl molecule. Regions of relatively more negative charge are red; those of more positive charge are blue. Negative charge is clearly localized on the chlorine atom.

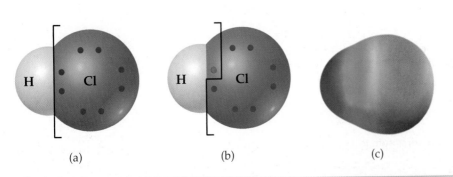

(a)   (b)   (c)

8.6   RESONANCE STRUCTURES

We sometimes encounter molecules and ions in which the experimentally determined arrangement of atoms is not adequately described by a single Lewis structure. Consider a molecule of ozone, O_3, which is a bent molecule with two equal O—O bond lengths (Figure 8.11 ▶). Because each oxygen atom contributes 6 valence electrons, the ozone molecule has 18 valence electrons. In writing the Lewis structure, we find that we must have one O—O single bond and one O—O double bond to attain an octet of electrons about each atom:

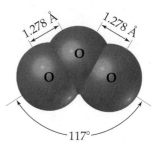

▲ **Figure 8.11   Ozone.** Molecular structure (top) and electron-distribution diagram (bottom) for the ozone molecule, O_3.

However, this structure cannot by itself be correct because it requires that one O—O bond be different from the other, contrary to the observed structure—we would expect the O=O double bond to be shorter than the O—O single bond. ∞ (Section 8.3) In drawing the Lewis structure, however, we could just as easily have put the O=O bond on the left:

The placement of the atoms in these two alternative but completely equivalent Lewis structures for ozone is the same, but the placement of the electrons is different. Lewis structures of this sort are called **resonance structures.** To describe the structure of ozone properly, we write both Lewis structures and use a double-headed arrow to indicate that the real molecule is described by an average of the two resonance structures:

To understand why certain molecules require more than one resonance structure, we can draw an analogy to the mixing of paint (Figure 8.12 ▶). Blue and yellow are both primary colors of paint pigment. An equal blend of blue and yellow pigments produces green pigment. We cannot describe green paint in terms of a single primary color, yet it still has its own identity. Green paint does not oscillate between its two primary colors: It is not blue part of the time and yellow the rest of the time. Similarly, molecules such as ozone cannot be described as oscillating between the two individual Lewis structures shown above.

The true arrangement of the electrons in molecules such as O_3 must be considered as a blend of two (or more) Lewis structures. By analogy to the green paint, the molecule has its own identity separate from the individual resonance structures. For example, the ozone molecule always has two equivalent O—O bonds whose lengths are intermediate between the lengths of an oxygen–oxygen single bond and an oxygen–oxygen double bond. Another way of looking at it is to say that the rules for drawing Lewis structures do not allow us to have a single structure that adequately represents the ozone molecule. For example, there are no rules for drawing half-bonds. We can get around this limitation by drawing two equivalent Lewis structures that, when averaged, amount to something very much like what is observed experimentally.

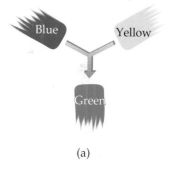

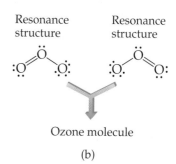

▲ **Figure 8.12   Resonance.** Describing a molecule as a blend of different resonance structures is similar to describing a paint color as a blend of primary colors. (a) Green paint is a blend of blue and yellow. We cannot describe green as a single primary color. (b) The ozone molecule is a blend of two resonance structures. We cannot describe the ozone molecule in terms of a single Lewis structure.

▲

GIVE IT SOME THOUGHT

The O—O bonds in ozone are often described as "one-and-a-half" bonds. Is this description consistent with the idea of resonance?

As an additional example of resonance structures, consider the nitrate ion, NO_3^-, for which three equivalent Lewis structures can be drawn:

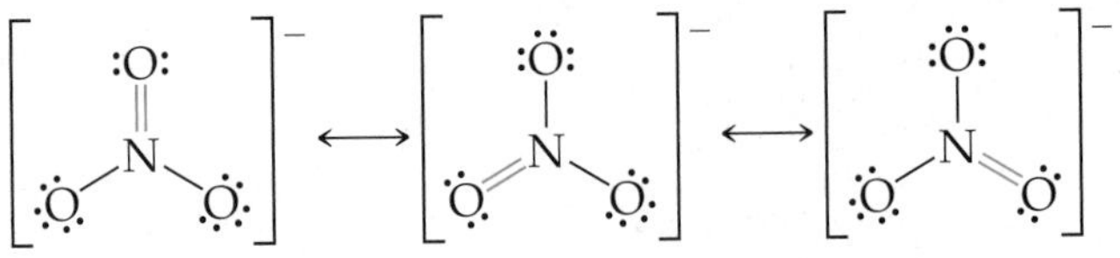

Notice that the arrangement of atoms is the same in each structure—only the placement of electrons differs. In writing resonance structures, the same atoms must be bonded to each other in all structures, so that the only differences are in the arrangements of electrons. All three Lewis structures taken together adequately describe the nitrate ion, in which all three N—O bond lengths are the same.

GIVE IT SOME THOUGHT

In the same sense that we describe the O—O bonds in O_3 as "one-and-a-half" bonds, how would you describe the N—O bonds in NO_3^-?

In some instances all the possible Lewis structures for a species may not be equivalent to one another. Instead, one or more may represent a more stable arrangement than other possibilities. We will encounter examples of this as we proceed.

■■■ SAMPLE EXERCISE 8.10 | Resonance Structures

Which is predicted to have the shorter sulfur–oxygen bonds, SO_3 or SO_3^{2-}?

SOLUTION

The sulfur atom has six valence electrons, as does oxygen. Thus, SO_3 contains 24 valence electrons. In writing the Lewis structure, we see that three equivalent resonance structures can be drawn:

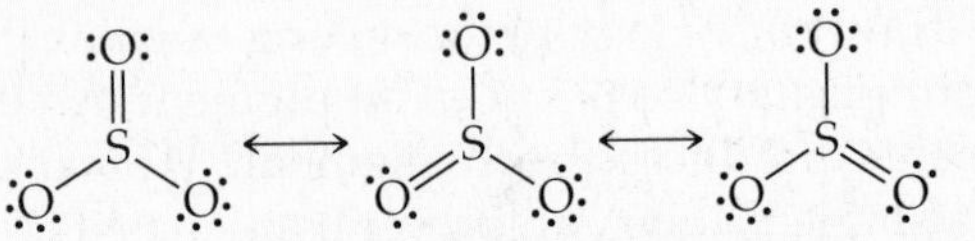

As was the case for NO_3^-, the actual structure of SO_3 is an equal blend of all three. Thus, each S—O bond distance should be about one-third of the way between that of a single and that of a double bond (see the Give It Some Thought exercise above). That is, they should be shorter than single bonds but not as short as double bonds.

The SO_3^{2-} ion has 26 electrons, which leads to a Lewis structure in which all the S—O bonds are single bonds:

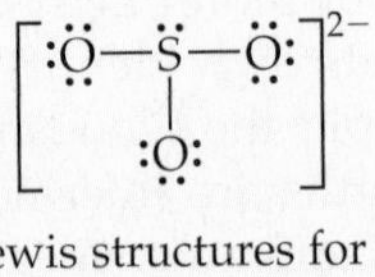

There are no other reasonable Lewis structures for this ion. It can be described quite well by a single Lewis structure rather than by multiple resonance structures.

Our analysis of the Lewis structures leads us to conclude that SO_3 should have the shorter S—O bonds and SO_3^{2-} the longer ones. This conclusion is correct: The experimentally measured S—O bond lengths are 1.42 Å in SO_3 and 1.51 Å in SO_3^{2-}.

■■■ PRACTICE EXERCISE

Draw two equivalent resonance structures for the formate ion, HCO_2^-.

Answer:

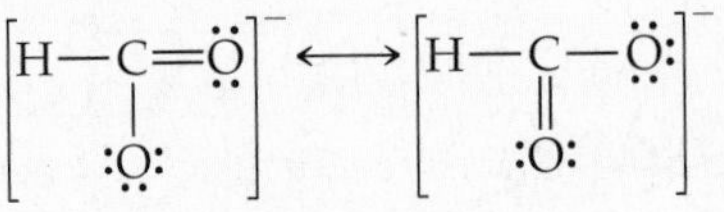

Resonance in Benzene

Resonance is an extremely important concept in describing the bonding in organic molecules, particularly in the ones called *aromatic* molecules. Aromatic organic molecules include the hydrocarbon called *benzene*, which has the molecular formula C_6H_6 (Figure 8.13▶). The six C atoms of benzene are bonded in a hexagonal ring, and one H atom is bonded to each C atom.

We can write two equivalent Lewis structures for benzene, each of which satisfies the octet rule. These two structures are in resonance:

(a)

Each resonance structure shows three C—C single bonds and three C=C double bonds, but the double bonds are in different places in the two structures. The experimental structure of benzene shows that all six C—C bonds are of equal length, 1.40 Å, intermediate between the typical bond lengths for a C—C single bond (1.54 Å) and a C=C double bond (1.34 Å).

Benzene is commonly represented by omitting the hydrogen atoms attached to carbon and showing only the carbon-carbon framework with the vertices unlabeled. In this convention, the resonance in the benzene molecule is represented either by two structures separated by a double-headed arrow, as with our other examples, or by a shorthand notation in which we draw a hexagon with a circle in it:

The shorthand notation on the right reminds us that benzene is a blend of two resonance structures—it emphasizes that the C=C double bonds cannot be assigned to specific edges of the hexagon. Chemists use both representations of benzene interchangeably.

The bonding arrangement in benzene confers special stability to the molecule. As a result, literally millions of organic compounds contain the six-membered rings characteristic of benzene. Many of these compounds are important in biochemistry, in pharmaceuticals, and in the production of modern materials. We will say more about the bonding in benzene in Chapter 9 and about its unusual stability in Chapter 25.

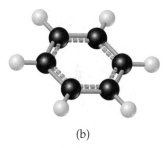

(b)

▲ **Figure 8.13 Benzene, an "aromatic" organic compound.** (a) Benzene is obtained from the distillation of fossil fuels. More than 4 billion pounds of benzene is produced annually in the United States. Because benzene is a carcinogen, its use is closely regulated. (b) The benzene molecule is a regular hexagon of carbon atoms with a hydrogen atom bonded to each one.

GIVE IT SOME THOUGHT

Each Lewis structure of benzene has three C=C double bonds. Another hydrocarbon containing three C=C double bonds is *hexatriene*, C_6H_8. A Lewis structure of hexatriene is

Would you expect hexatriene to have multiple resonance structures like benzene? If not, why is this molecule different from benzene with respect to resonance?

8.7 EXCEPTIONS TO THE OCTET RULE

The octet rule is so simple and useful in introducing the basic concepts of bonding that you might assume it is always obeyed. In Section 8.2, however, we noted its limitation in dealing with ionic compounds of the transition metals. The octet rule also fails in many situations involving covalent bonding. These exceptions to the octet rule are of three main types:

1. Molecules and polyatomic ions containing an odd number of electrons
2. Molecules and polyatomic ions in which an atom has fewer than an octet of valence electrons
3. Molecules and polyatomic ions in which an atom has more than an octet of valence electrons

Odd Number of Electrons

In the vast majority of molecules and polyatomic ions, the total number of valence electrons is even, and complete pairing of electrons occurs. However, in a few molecules and polyatomic ions, such as ClO_2, NO, NO_2, and O_2^-, the number of valence electrons is odd. Complete pairing of these electrons is impossible, and an octet around each atom cannot be achieved. For example, NO contains $5 + 6 = 11$ valence electrons. The two most important Lewis structures for this molecule are

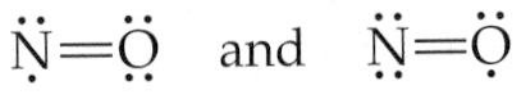

$$\ddot{\ddot{N}}\!=\!\ddot{O} \quad \text{and} \quad \dot{\ddot{N}}\!=\!\ddot{O}$$

⚠ **GIVE IT SOME THOUGHT**

Which of the Lewis structures shown above for NO would be preferred based on analysis of the formal charges?

Less than an Octet of Valence Electrons

A second type of exception occurs when there are fewer than eight valence electrons around an atom in a molecule or polyatomic ion. This situation is also relatively rare (with the exception of hydrogen and helium as we have already discussed), most often encountered in compounds of boron and beryllium. As an example, let's consider boron trifluoride, BF_3. If we follow the first four steps of the procedure at the beginning of Section 8.5 for drawing Lewis structures, we obtain the structure

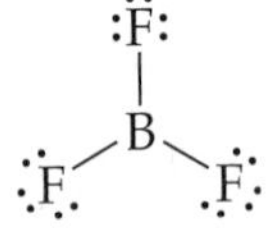

$$
\begin{array}{c}
:\ddot{F}: \\
| \\
\ddot{F}\!-\!B\!-\!\ddot{F}: \\
\end{array}
$$

There are only six electrons around the boron atom. In this Lewis structure the formal charges on both the B and the F atoms are zero. We could complete the octet around boron by forming a double bond (step 5). In so doing, we see that there are three equivalent resonance structures (the formal charges on each atom are shown in red):

$$
\ddot{F}^{+1}\!=\!B^{-1}(\,:\!\ddot{F}:\,)_2 \quad \longleftrightarrow \quad \ddot{F}^{0}\!-\!B^{-1} \quad \longleftrightarrow \quad \ddot{F}^{0}\!-\!B
$$

These Lewis structures force a fluorine atom to share additional electrons with the boron atom, which is inconsistent with the high electronegativity of fluorine. In fact, the formal charges tell us that this is an unfavorable situation.

In each of the Lewis structures, the F atom involved in the B=F double bond has a formal charge of +1, while the less electronegative B atom has a formal charge of −1. Thus, the Lewis structures in which there is a B=F double bond are less important than the one in which there are fewer than an octet of valence electrons around boron:

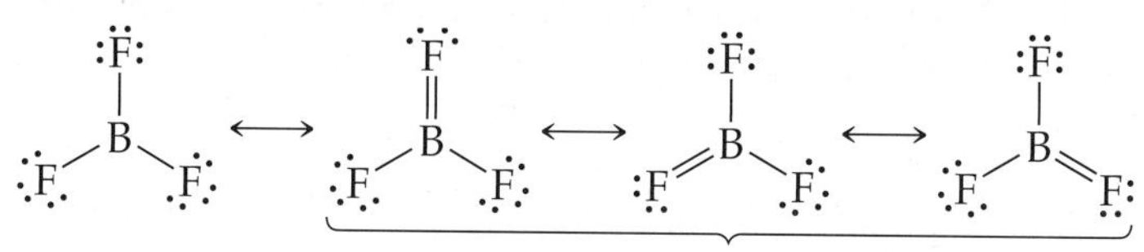

Most important   Less important

We usually represent BF_3 solely by the leftmost resonance structure, in which there are only six valence electrons around boron. The chemical behavior of BF_3 is consistent with this representation. In particular, BF_3 reacts very energetically with molecules having an unshared pair of electrons that can be used to form a bond with boron. For example, BF_3 reacts with ammonia, NH_3, to form the compound NH_3BF_3:

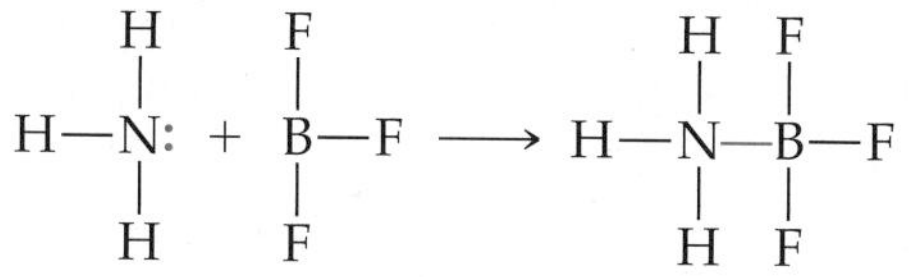

In this stable compound, boron has an octet of valence electrons. We will consider reactions of this type in more detail in Chapter 16 when we study Lewis acids and bases. ∞∞ (Section 16.11)

More than an Octet of Valence Electrons

The third and largest class of exceptions consists of molecules or polyatomic ions in which there are more than eight electrons in the valence shell of an atom. When we draw the Lewis structure for PCl_5, for example, we are forced to "expand" the valence shell and place ten electrons around the central phosphorus atom:

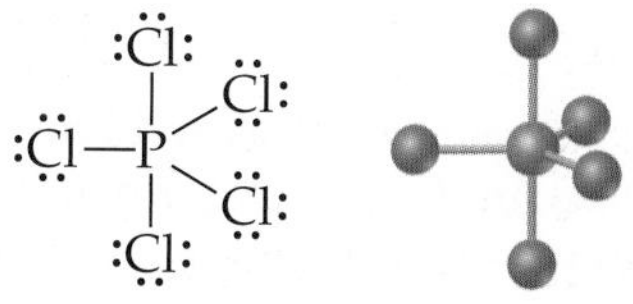

Other examples of molecules and ions with "expanded" valence shells are SF_4, AsF_6^-, and ICl_4^-. The corresponding molecules with a second-period atom as the central atom, such as NCl_5 and OF_4, do *not* exist. Let's take a look at why expanded valence shells are observed only for elements in period 3 and beyond in the periodic table.

Elements of the second period have only the $2s$ and $2p$ valence orbitals available for bonding. Because these orbitals can hold a maximum of eight electrons, we never find more than an octet of electrons around elements from the second period. Elements from the third period and beyond, however, have ns, np, and unfilled nd orbitals that can be used in bonding. For example, the orbital diagram for the valence shell of a phosphorus atom is

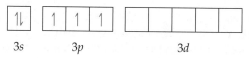

3s   3p   3d

Although third-period elements often satisfy the octet rule, as in PCl_3, they also often exceed an octet by seeming to use their empty d orbitals to accommodate additional electrons.*

Size also plays an important role in determining whether an atom in a molecule or polyatomic ion can accommodate more than eight electrons in its valence shell. The larger the central atom is, the larger the number of atoms that can surround it. The number of molecules and ions with expanded valence shells therefore increases with increasing size of the central atom. The size of the surrounding atoms is also important. Expanded valence shells occur most often when the central atom is bonded to the smallest and most electronegative atoms, such as F, Cl, and O.

■ SAMPLE EXERCISE 8.11 │ Lewis Structure for an Ion with an Expanded Valence Shell

Draw the Lewis structure for ICl_4^-.

SOLUTION

Iodine (group 7A) has seven valence electrons. Each chlorine (group 7A) also has seven. An extra electron is added to account for the 1− charge of the ion. Therefore, the total number of valence electrons is

$$7 + 4(7) + 1 = 36$$

The I atom is the central atom in the ion. Putting eight electrons around each Cl atom (including a pair of electrons between I and each Cl to represent the single bond between these atoms) requires $8 \times 4 = 32$ electrons.

We are thus left with $36 - 32 = 4$ electrons to be placed on the larger iodine:

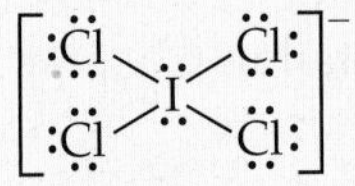

Iodine has 12 valence electrons around it, four more than needed for an octet.

■ PRACTICE EXERCISE

(a) Which of the following atoms is never found with more than an octet of valence electrons around it: S, C, P, Br? (b) Draw the Lewis structure for XeF_2.

Answers: (a) C, (b) $:\!\ddot{F}\!\!-\!\!\ddot{X}\!e\!\!-\!\!\ddot{F}\!:$

At times you may see Lewis structures written with an expanded valence shell even though structures can be written with an octet. For example, consider the following Lewis structures for the phosphate ion, PO_4^{3-}:

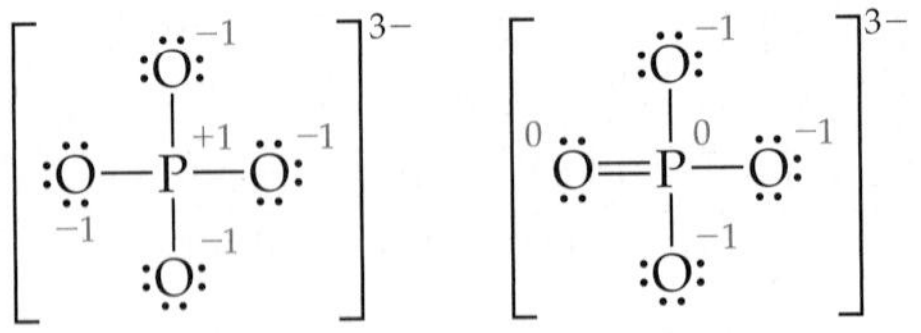

The formal charges on the atoms are shown in red. In the Lewis structure shown on the left, the P atom obeys the octet rule. In the Lewis structure shown on the right, the P atom has an expanded valence shell of five electron pairs† leading to smaller formal charges on the atoms. Which Lewis structure is a better representation of the bonding in PO_4^{3-}? Theoretical calculations based on quantum

---

Based on theoretical calculations, some chemists have questioned whether valence d orbitals are actually used in the bonding of molecules and ions with expanded valence shells. Nevertheless, the presence of valence d orbitals in period 3 and beyond provides the simplest explanation of this phenomenon, especially within the scope of a general chemistry textbook.

†*The Lewis structure shown on the right has four equivalent resonance forms. Only one is shown for clarity.*

mechanics suggest that the structure on the left is the best single Lewis structure for the phosphate ion. In general, when choosing between alternative Lewis structures, if it is possible to draw a Lewis structure where the octet rule is satisfied without using multiple bonds, that structure will be preferred.

8.8   STRENGTHS OF COVALENT BONDS

The stability of a molecule is related to the strengths of the covalent bonds it contains. The strength of a covalent bond between two atoms is determined by the energy required to break that bond. It is easiest to relate bond strength to the enthalpy change in reactions in which bonds are broken. ∞ (Section 5.4) The **bond enthalpy** is the enthalpy change, ΔH, for the breaking of a particular bond in one mole of a gaseous substance. For example, the bond enthalpy for the bond between chlorine atoms in the Cl_2 molecule is the enthalpy change when 1 mol of Cl_2 is dissociated into chlorine atoms:

$$:\ddot{C}l-\ddot{C}l:(g) \longrightarrow 2 :\ddot{C}l\cdot(g)$$

We use the designation D(bond type) to represent bond enthalpies.

It is relatively simple to assign bond enthalpies to bonds that are found in diatomic molecules, such as the Cl—Cl bond in Cl_2, $D(Cl-Cl)$, or the H—Br bond in HBr, $D(H-Br)$. The bond enthalpy is just the energy required to break the diatomic molecule into its component atoms. Many important bonds, such as the C—H bond, exist only in polyatomic molecules. For these types of bonds, we usually use *average* bond enthalpies. For example, the enthalpy change for the following process in which a methane molecule is decomposed to its five atoms (a process called *atomization*) can be used to define an average bond enthalpy for the C—H bond, D (C—H):

$$\underset{\overset{|}{H}}{\overset{\overset{H}{|}}{H-C-H}}(g) \longrightarrow \cdot\ddot{C}\cdot(g) + 4 H\cdot(g) \qquad \Delta H = 1660 \text{ kJ}$$

Because there are four equivalent C—H bonds in methane, the heat of atomization is equal to the sum of the bond enthalpies of the four C—H bonds. Therefore, the average C—H bond enthalpy for CH_4 is $D(C-H) = (1660/4)$ kJ/mol = 415 kJ/mol.

The bond enthalpy for a given set of atoms, say C—H, depends on the rest of the molecule of which the atom pair is a part. However, the variation from one molecule to another is generally small, which supports the idea that bonding electron pairs are localized between atoms. If we consider C—H bond enthalpies in many different compounds, we find that the average bond enthalpy is 413 kJ/mol, which compares closely with the 415 kJ/mol value calculated from CH_4.

▲ GIVE IT SOME THOUGHT

The hydrocarbon *ethane*, C_2H_6, was first introduced in Section 2.9. How could you use the enthalpy of atomization of $C_2H_6(g)$ along with the value of $D(C-H)$ to provide an estimate for $D(C-C)$?

Table 8.4▼ lists several average bond enthalpies. *The bond enthalpy is always a positive quantity*; energy is always required to break chemical bonds. Conversely, energy is always released when a bond forms between two gaseous atoms or molecular fragments. The greater the bond enthalpy is, the stronger the bond.

TABLE 8.4 ■ Average Bond Enthalpies (kJ/mol)							

Single Bonds

C—H	413	N—H	391	O—H	463	F—F	155
C—C	348	N—N	163	O—O	146		
C—N	293	N—O	201	O—F	190	Cl—F	253
C—O	358	N—F	272	O—Cl	203	Cl—Cl	242
C—F	485	N—Cl	200	O—I	234		
C—Cl	328	N—Br	243			Br—F	237
C—Br	276					Br—Cl	218
C—I	240			S—H	339	Br—Br	193
C—S	259	H—H	436	S—F	327		
		H—F	567	S—Cl	253		
		H—Cl	431	S—Br	218	I—Cl	208
Si—H	323	H—Br	366	S—S	266	I—Br	175
Si—Si	226	H—I	299			I—I	151
Si—C	301						
Si—O	368						
Si—Cl	464						

Multiple Bonds

C=C	614	N=N	418	O_2	495
C≡C	839	N≡N	941		
C=N	615	N=O	607	S=O	523
C≡N	891			S=S	418
C=O	799				
C≡O	1072				

A molecule with strong chemical bonds generally has less tendency to undergo chemical change than does one with weak bonds. This relationship between strong bonding and chemical stability helps explain the chemical form in which many elements are found in nature. For example, Si—O bonds are among the strongest ones that silicon forms. It should not be surprising, therefore, that SiO_2 and other substances containing Si—O bonds (silicates) are so common; it is estimated that over 90% of Earth's crust is composed of SiO_2 and silicates.

Bond Enthalpies and the Enthalpies of Reactions

We can use average bond enthalpies to estimate the enthalpies of reactions in which bonds are broken and new bonds are formed. This procedure allows us to estimate quickly whether a given reaction will be endothermic ($\Delta H > 0$) or exothermic ($\Delta H < 0$) even if we do not know ΔH_f° for all the chemical species involved.

Our strategy for estimating reaction enthalpies is a straightforward application of Hess's law. ∞ (Section 5.6) We use the fact that breaking bonds is always an endothermic process, and bond formation is always exothermic. We therefore imagine that the reaction occurs in two steps: (1) We supply enough energy to break those bonds in the reactants that are not present in the products. In this step the enthalpy of the system is increased by the sum of the bond enthalpies of the bonds that are broken. (2) We form the bonds in the products that were not present in the reactants. This step releases energy and therefore lowers the enthalpy of the system by the sum of the bond enthalpies of the bonds that are formed. The enthalpy of the reaction, ΔH_{rxn}, is estimated as the sum of the bond enthalpies of the bonds broken minus the sum of the bond enthalpies of the bonds formed:

$$\Delta H_{rxn} = \Sigma(\text{bond enthalpies of bonds broken}) -$$
$$\Sigma(\text{bond enthalpies of bonds formed}) \qquad [8.12]$$

WE SAW IN CHAPTER 8 THAT LEWIS STRUCTURES help us understand the compositions of molecules and their covalent bonds. However, Lewis structures do not show one of the most important aspects of molecules—their overall shapes. Molecules have shapes and sizes that are defined by the

angles and distances between the nuclei of their component atoms. Indeed, chemists often refer to molecular *architecture* when describing the distinctive shapes and sizes of molecules.

The shape and size of a molecule of a particular substance, together with the strength and polarity of its bonds, largely determine the properties of that substance. Some of the most dramatic examples of the important roles of molecular shape and size are seen in biochemical reactions and in substances produced by living species. For example, the chapter-opening photograph shows a Pacific yew tree, a species that grows along the Pacific coast of the northwestern United States and Canada. In 1967 two chemists isolated from the bark of the Pacific yew small amounts of a molecule that was found to be among the most effective treatments for breast and ovarian cancer. This molecule, now known as the pharmaceutical Taxol®, has a complex molecular architecture that leads to its powerful therapeutic effectiveness. Even a small modification to the shape and size of the molecule decreases its effectiveness and can lead to the formation of a substance toxic to humans. Chemists now know how to synthesize the drug in the laboratory, which has made it more available and has saved the slow-growing Pacific yew tree from possible extinction. Before the drug was synthesized, six trees had to be harvested to provide the Taxol® necessary to treat one cancer patient.

Our first goal in this chapter is to learn the relationship between two-dimensional Lewis structures and three-dimensional molecular shapes. Armed with this knowledge, we can then examine more closely the nature of covalent bonds. The lines that are used to depict bonds in Lewis structures provide important clues about the orbitals that molecules use in bonding. By examining these orbitals, we can gain a greater understanding of the behavior of molecules. You will find that the material in this chapter will help you in later discussions of the physical and chemical properties of substances.

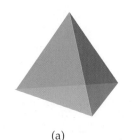

(a)

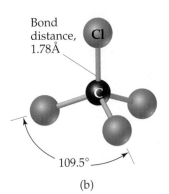

Bond distance, 1.78Å

Cl

C

109.5°

(b)

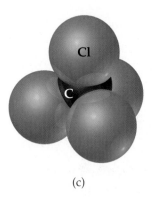

Cl

C

(c)

▲ **Figure 9.1 Tetrahedral geometry.** (a) A tetrahedron is an object with four faces and four vertices. Each face is an equilateral triangle. (b) The geometry of the CCl_4 molecule. Each C—Cl bond in the molecule points toward a vertex of a tetrahedron. All of the C—Cl bonds are the same length, and all of the Cl—C—Cl bond angles are the same. This type of drawing of CCl_4 is called a ball-and-stick model. (c) A representation of CCl_4, called a space-filling model. It shows the relative sizes of the atoms, but the geometry is somewhat harder to see.

9.1 MOLECULAR SHAPES

In Chapter 8 we used Lewis structures to account for the formulas of covalent compounds. ∞ (Section 8.5) Lewis structures, however, do not indicate the shapes of molecules; they simply show the number and types of bonds between atoms. For example, the Lewis structure of CCl_4 tells us only that four Cl atoms are bonded to a central C atom:

The Lewis structure is drawn with the atoms all in the same plane. As shown in Figure 9.1 ◄, however, the actual three-dimensional arrangement of the atoms shows the Cl atoms at the corners of a *tetrahedron*, a geometric object with four corners and four faces, each of which is an equilateral triangle.

The overall shape of a molecule is determined by its **bond angles**, the angles made by the lines joining the nuclei of the atoms in the molecule. The bond angles of a molecule, together with the bond lengths ∞ (Section 8.8), accurately define the shape and size of the molecule. In CCl_4 the bond angles are defined as the angles between the C—Cl bonds. You should be able to see that there are six Cl—C—Cl angles in CCl_4, and they all have the same value—109.5°, which is characteristic of a tetrahedron. In addition, all four C—Cl bonds are the same length (1.78 Å). Thus, the shape and size of CCl_4 are completely described by stating that the molecule is tetrahedral with C—Cl bonds of length 1.78 Å.

In our discussion of the shapes of molecules, we will begin with molecules (and ions) that, like CCl_4, have a single central atom bonded to two or more atoms of the same type. Such molecules conform to the general formula AB_n, in which the central atom A is bonded to n B atoms. Both CO_2 and H_2O are AB_2 molecules, for example, whereas SO_3 and NH_3 are AB_3 molecules, and so on.

The possible shapes of AB_n molecules depend on the value of n. We observe only a few general shapes for a given value of n. Those commonly found for AB_2 and AB_3 molecules are shown in Figure 9.2 ▶. Therefore, an AB_2 molecule must be either linear (bond angle = 180°) or bent (bond angle ≠ 180°). For example, CO_2 is linear, and SO_2 is bent. For AB_3 molecules, the two most common

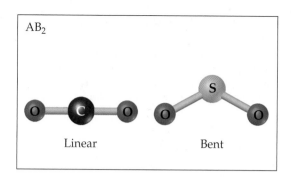

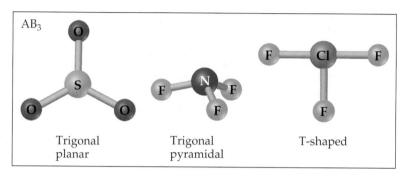

◀ **Figure 9.2 Shapes of AB₂ and AB₃ molecules.** Top: AB₂ molecules can be either linear or bent. Bottom: Three possible shapes for AB₃ molecules.

shapes place the B atoms at the corners of an equilateral triangle. If the A atom lies in the same plane as the B atoms, the shape is called *trigonal planar*. If the A atom lies above the plane of the B atoms, the shape is called *trigonal pyramidal* (a pyramid with an equilateral triangle as its base). For example, SO_3 is trigonal planar, and NF_3 is trigonal pyramidal. Some AB₃ molecules, such as ClF_3, exhibit the more unusual *T shape* shown in Figure 9.2.

The shape of any particular AB_n molecule can usually be derived from one of the five basic geometric structures shown in Figure 9.3 ▶. Starting with a tetrahedron, for example, we can remove atoms successively from the corners as shown in Figure 9.4 ▼. When an atom is removed from one corner of the tetrahedron, the remaining fragment has a trigonal-pyramidal geometry, such as that found for NF_3. When two atoms are removed, a bent geometry results.

Why do so many AB_n molecules have shapes related to the basic structures in Figure 9.3, and can we predict these shapes? When A is a representative element (one of the elements from the *s* block or *p* block of the periodic table), we can answer these questions by using the **valence-shell electron-pair repulsion (VSEPR) model.** Although the name is rather imposing, the model is quite simple. It has useful predictive capabilities, as we will see in Section 9.2.

▼ **Figure 9.3 Shapes of AB_n molecules.** For molecules whose formula is of the general form AB_n, there are five fundamental shapes.

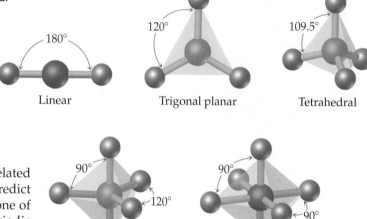

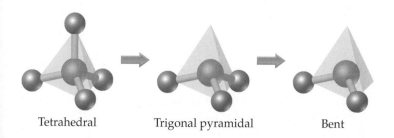

Tetrahedral   Trigonal pyramidal   Bent

◀ **Figure 9.4 Derivatives from the AB_n geometries.** Additional molecular shapes can be obtained by removing corner atoms from the basic shapes shown in Figure 9.3. Here we begin with a tetrahedron and successively remove corners, producing first a trigonal-pyramidal geometry and then a bent geometry, each having ideal bond angles of 109.5°. Molecular shape is meaningful only when there are at least three atoms. If there are only two, they must be arranged next to each other, and no special name is given to describe the molecule.

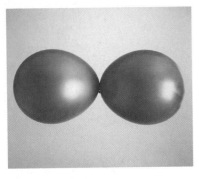

(a) Two balloons adopt a linear arrangement.

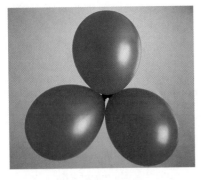

(b) Three balloons adopt a trigonal-planar arrangement.

(c) Four balloons adopt a tetrahedral arrangement.

▲ Figure 9.5 **A balloon analogy for electron domains.** Balloons tied together at their ends naturally adopt their lowest-energy arrangement.

GIVE IT SOME THOUGHT

One of the common shapes for AB_4 molecules is *square planar*: All five atoms lie in the same plane, the B atoms lie at the corners of a square, and the A atom is at the center of the square. Which of the shapes in Figure 9.3 could lead to a square-planar geometry upon the removal of one or more atoms?

9.2 THE VSEPR MODEL

Imagine tying two identical balloons together at their ends. As shown in Figure 9.5(a) ◄, the balloons naturally orient themselves to point away from each other; that is, they try to "get out of each other's way" as much as possible. If we add a third balloon, the balloons orient themselves toward the vertices of an equilateral triangle as shown in Figure 9.5(b). If we add a fourth balloon, they adopt a tetrahedral shape [Figure 9.5(c)]. We see that an optimum geometry exists for each number of balloons.

In some ways the electrons in molecules behave like the balloons shown in Figure 9.5. We have seen that a single covalent bond is formed between two atoms when a pair of electrons occupies the space between the atoms. ∞ (Section 8.3) A **bonding pair** of electrons thus defines a region in which the electrons will most likely be found. We will refer to such a region as an **electron domain**. Likewise, a **nonbonding pair** (or **lone pair**) of electrons defines an electron domain that is located principally on one atom. For example, the Lewis structure of NH_3 has four electron domains around the central nitrogen atom (three bonding pairs and one nonbonding pair):

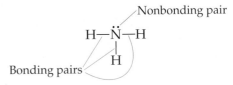

Each multiple bond in a molecule also constitutes a single electron domain. Thus, the following resonance structure for O_3 has three electron domains around the central oxygen atom (a single bond, a double bond, and a nonbonding pair of electrons):

$$:\ddot{O}—\ddot{O}=\ddot{O}$$

In general, *each nonbonding pair, single bond, or multiple bond produces an electron domain around the central atom.*

GIVE IT SOME THOUGHT

An AB_3 molecule has the resonance structure

$$
:\ddot{B}—\overset{\overset{\textstyle :B:}{\|}}{A}—\ddot{B}:
$$

Does this Lewis structure follow the octet rule? How many electron domains are there around the A atom?

The VSEPR model is based on the idea that electron domains are negatively charged and therefore repel one another. Like the balloons in Figure 9.5, electron domains try to stay out of one another's way. *The best arrangement of a given number of electron domains is the one that minimizes the repulsions among them.* In fact, the analogy between electron domains and balloons is so close that the same preferred geometries are found in both cases. Like the balloons in

TABLE 9.1 ■ Electron-Domain Geometries as a Function of the Number of Electron Domains

Number of Electron Domains	Arrangement of Electron Domains	Electron-Domain Geometry	Predicted Bond Angles
2	180°	Linear	180°
3	120°	Trigonal planar	120°
4	109.5°	Tetrahedral	109.5°
5	90° 120°	Trigonal bipyramidal	120° 90°
6	90° 90°	Octahedral	90°

Figure 9.5, two electron domains are arranged *linearly*, three domains are arranged in a *trigonal-planar* fashion, and four are arranged *tetrahedrally*. These arrangements, together with those for five electron domains (*trigonal bipyramidal*) and six electron domains (*octahedral*), are summarized in Table 9.1 ▲. If you compare the geometries in Table 9.1 with those in Figure 9.3, you will see that they are the same. *The shapes of different AB_n molecules or ions depend on the number of electron domains surrounding the central A atom.*

The arrangement of electron domains about the central atom of an AB_n molecule or ion is called its **electron-domain geometry**. In contrast, the **molecular geometry** is the arrangement of *only the atoms* in a molecule or ion—any nonbonding pairs are not part of the description of the molecular geometry. In the VSEPR model, we predict the electron-domain geometry. From knowing how many domains are due to nonbonding pairs, we can then predict the molecular geometry of a molecule or ion from its electron-domain geometry.

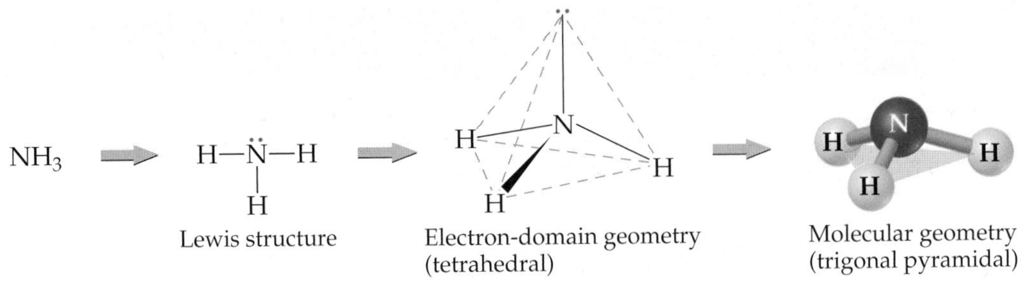

NH_3 ⟹ Lewis structure ⟹ Electron-domain geometry (tetrahedral) ⟹ Molecular geometry (trigonal pyramidal)

▲ **Figure 9.6 The molecular geometry of NH_3.** The geometry is predicted by first drawing the Lewis structure, then using the VSEPR model to determine the electron-domain geometry, and finally focusing on the atoms themselves to describe the molecular geometry.

When all the electron domains in a molecule arise from bonds, the molecular geometry is identical to the electron-domain geometry. When, however, one or more of the domains involve nonbonding pairs of electrons, we must remember to ignore those domains when predicting molecular shape. Consider the NH_3 molecule, which has four electron domains around the nitrogen atom (Figure 9.6 ▲). We know from Table 9.1 that the repulsions among four electron domains are minimized when the domains point toward the vertices of a tetrahedron, so the electron-domain geometry of NH_3 is tetrahedral. We know from the Lewis structure of NH_3 that one of the electron domains is due to a nonbonding pair of electrons, which will occupy one of the four vertices of the tetrahedron. Hence the molecular geometry of NH_3 is trigonal pyramidal, as shown in Figure 9.6. Notice that the tetrahedral arrangement of the four electron domains leads us to predict the trigonal-pyramidal molecular geometry.

We can generalize the steps we follow in using the VSEPR model to predict the shapes of molecules or ions:

1. Draw the *Lewis structure* of the molecule or ion, and count the total number of electron domains around the central atom. Each nonbonding electron pair, each single bond, each double bond, and each triple bond counts as an electron domain.

2. Determine the *electron-domain geometry* by arranging the electron domains about the central atom so that the repulsions among them are minimized, as shown in Table 9.1.

3. Use the arrangement of the bonded atoms to determine the *molecular geometry*.

Figure 9.6 shows how these steps are applied to predict the geometry of the NH_3 molecule. Because the trigonal-pyramidal molecular geometry is based on tetrahedral electron-domain geometry, the *ideal bond angles* are 109.5°. As we will soon see, bond angles deviate from the ideal angles when the surrounding atoms and electron domains are not identical.

Let's apply these steps to determine the shape of the CO_2 molecule. We first draw its Lewis structure, which reveals two electron domains (two double bonds) around the central carbon:

$$\ddot{O}{=}C{=}\ddot{O}$$

Two electron domains will arrange themselves to give a linear electron-domain geometry (Table 9.1). Because neither domain is a nonbonding pair of electrons, the molecular geometry is also linear, and the O—C—O bond angle is 180°.

Table 9.2▶ summarizes the possible molecular geometries when an AB_n molecule has four or fewer electron domains about A. These geometries are important because they include all the commonly occurring shapes found for molecules or ions that obey the octet rule.

TABLE 9.2 ■ **Electron-Domain Geometries and Molecular Shapes for Molecules with Two, Three, and Four Electron Domains around the Central Atom**

Number of Electron Domains	Electron-Domain Geometry	Bonding Domains	Nonbonding Domains	Molecular Geometry	Example
2	 Linear	2	0	 Linear	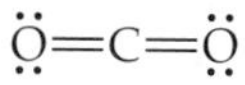 $\ddot{O}=C=\ddot{O}$
3	 Trigonal planar	3	0	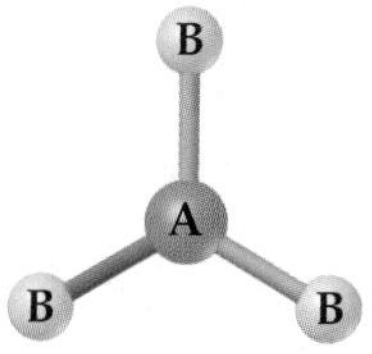 Trigonal planar	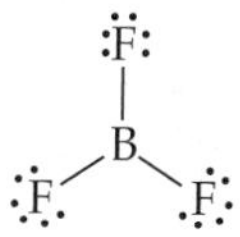 F–B–F (BF₃ structure)
		2	1	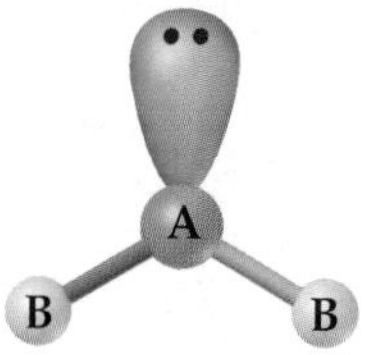 Bent	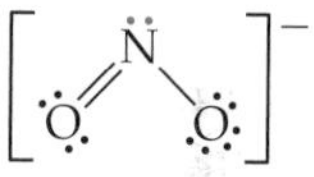 $\left[\ddot{O}-N-\ddot{O} \right]^-$
4	 Tetrahedral	4	0	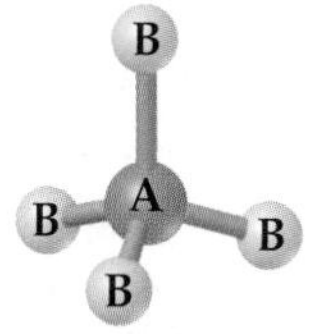 Tetrahedral	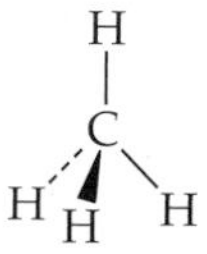 H–C–H (CH₄ structure)
		3	1	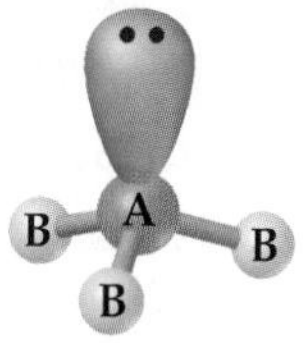 Trigonal pyramidal	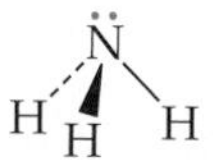 H–N–H (NH₃ structure)
		2	2	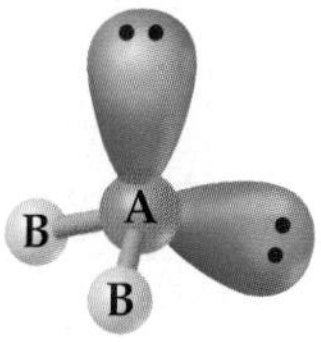 Bent	 H–O–H (H₂O structure)

■ **SAMPLE EXERCISE 9.1** | **Using the VSEPR Model**

Use the VSEPR model to predict the molecular geometry of **(a)** O_3, **(b)** $SnCl_3^-$.

SOLUTION

Analyze: We are given the molecular formulas of a molecule and a polyatomic ion, both conforming to the general formula AB_n and both having a central atom from the p block of the periodic table.

Plan: To predict the molecular geometries of these species, we first draw their Lewis structures and then count the number of electron domains around the central atom. The number of electron domains gives the electron-domain geometry. We then obtain the molecular geometry from the arrangement of the domains that are due to bonds.

Solve:

(a) We can draw two resonance structures for O_3:

$$:\ddot{O}—\ddot{O}{=}\ddot{O} \longleftrightarrow \ddot{O}{=}\ddot{O}—\ddot{O}:$$

Because of resonance, the bonds between the central O atom and the outer O atoms are of equal length. In both resonance structures the central O atom is bonded to the two outer O atoms and has one nonbonding pair. Thus, there are three electron domains about the central O atoms. (Remember that a double bond counts as a single electron domain.) The arrangement of three electron domains is trigonal planar (Table 9.1). Two of the domains are from bonds, and one is due to a nonbonding pair. So, the molecule has a bent shape with an ideal bond angle of 120° (Table 9.2).

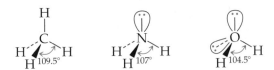

As this example illustrates, when a molecule exhibits resonance, any one of the resonance structures can be used to predict the molecular geometry.

(b) The Lewis structure for the $SnCl_3^-$ ion is

$$\left[:\ddot{C}l—\dot{S}n—\ddot{C}l:\atop :\ddot{C}l:\right]^-$$

The central Sn atom is bonded to the three Cl atoms and has one nonbonding pair. Therefore, the Sn atom has four electron domains around it. The resulting electron-domain geometry is tetrahedral (Table 9.1) with one of the corners occupied by a nonbonding pair of electrons. The molecular geometry is therefore trigonal pyramidal (Table 9.2), like that of NH_3.

■ PRACTICE EXERCISE

Predict the electron-domain geometry and the molecular geometry for **(a)** $SeCl_2$, **(b)** CO_3^{2-}.
Answers: **(a)** tetrahedral, bent; **(b)** trigonal planar, trigonal planar

---

Bonding electron pair

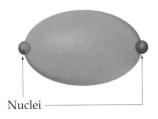

Nuclei

Nonbonding pair

Nucleus

▲ **Figure 9.7 Relative "sizes" of bonding and nonbonding electron domains.**

The Effect of Nonbonding Electrons and Multiple Bonds on Bond Angles

We can refine the VSEPR model to predict and explain slight distortions of molecules from the ideal geometries summarized in Table 9.2. For example, consider methane (CH_4), ammonia (NH_3), and water (H_2O). All three have tetrahedral electron-domain geometries, but their bond angles differ slightly:

Notice that the bond angles decrease as the number of nonbonding electron pairs increases. A bonding pair of electrons is attracted by both nuclei of the bonded atoms. By contrast, a nonbonding pair is attracted primarily by only one nucleus. Because a nonbonding pair experiences less nuclear attraction, its electron domain is spread out more in space than is the electron domain for a bonding pair, as shown in Figure 9.7 ◄. Nonbonding pairs of electrons, therefore, take up more space than bonding pairs. As a result, *the electron domains for nonbonding electron pairs exert greater repulsive forces on adjacent electron domains and tend to compress the bond angles.* Using the analogy in Figure 9.5, we can envision the domains for nonbonding electron pairs as represented by balloons that are slightly larger and slightly fatter than those for bonding pairs.

Because multiple bonds contain a higher electronic-charge density than single bonds, multiple bonds also represent larger electron domains ("fatter balloons"). Consider the Lewis structure of phosgene, $COCl_2$:

$$:\ddot{\underset{..}{Cl}} \diagdown \atop C = \ddot{O}$$

Because three electron domains surround the central carbon atom, we might expect a trigonal-planar geometry with 120° bond angles. The double bond, however, seems to act much like a nonbonding pair of electrons, reducing the Cl—C—Cl bond angle from the ideal angle of 120° to an actual angle of 111.4°:

In general, *electron domains for multiple bonds exert a greater repulsive force on adjacent electron domains than do electron domains for single bonds.*

GIVE IT SOME THOUGHT

One of the resonance structures of the nitrate ion, NO_3^-, is

The bond angles in this ion are exactly 120°. Is this observation consistent with the above discussion of the effect of multiple bonds on bond angles?

Molecules with Expanded Valence Shells

So far, our discussion of the VSEPR model has considered molecules with no more than an octet of electrons around the central atom. Recall, however, that when the central atom of a molecule is from the third period of the periodic table and beyond, that atom may have more than four electron pairs around it. ∞ (Section 8.7) Molecules with five or six electron domains around the central atom display a variety of molecular geometries based on the *trigonal-bipyramidal* (five electron domains) or the *octahedral* (six electron domains) electron-domain geometries, as shown in Table 9.3▼.

The most stable electron-domain geometry for five electron domains is the trigonal bipyramid (two trigonal pyramids sharing a base). Unlike the arrangements we have seen to this point, the electron domains in a trigonal bipyramid can point toward two geometrically distinct types of positions. Two of the five domains point toward *axial positions*, and the remaining three domains point toward *equatorial positions* (Figure 9.8►). Each axial domain makes a 90° angle with any equatorial domain. Each equatorial domain makes a 120° angle with either of the other two equatorial domains and a 90° angle with either axial domain.

Suppose a molecule has five electron domains, one or more of which originates from a nonbonding pair. Will the electron domains from the nonbonding pairs occupy axial or equatorial positions? To answer this question, we must determine which location minimizes the repulsions between the electron domains. Repulsions between domains are much greater when they are situated 90° from each other than when they are at 120°. An equatorial domain is 90° from only two other domains (the two axial domains). By contrast, an axial domain is situated 90° from *three* other domains (the three equatorial domains). Hence, an equatorial domain experiences less repulsion than an axial domain. Because the domains from nonbonding pairs exert larger repulsions than those from bonding pairs, they always occupy the equatorial positions in a trigonal bipyramid.

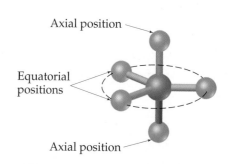

Axial position

Equatorial positions

Axial position

▲ Figure 9.8 **Trigonal-bipyramidal geometry.** Five electron domains arrange themselves around a central atom as a trigonal bipyramid. The three *equatorial* electron domains define an equilateral triangle. The two *axial* domains lie above and below the plane of the triangle. If a molecule has nonbonding electron domains, they will occupy the equatorial positions.

TABLE 9.3 ■ Electron-Domain Geometries and Molecular Shapes for Molecules with Five and Six Electron Domains around the Central Atom

Total Electron Domains	Electron-Domain Geometry	Bonding Domains	Nonbonding Domains	Molecular Geometry	Example
5	Trigonal bipyramidal	5	0	Trigonal bipyramidal	PCl_5
		4	1	Seesaw	SF_4
		3	2	T-shaped	ClF_3
		2	3	Linear	XeF_2
6	Octahedral	6	0	Octahedral	SF_6
		5	1	Square pyramidal	BrF_5
		4	2	Square planar	XeF_4

It might seem that a square planar geometry of four electron domains around a central atom would be more favorable than a tetrahedron. Can you rationalize why the tetrahedron is preferred, based on angles between electron domains?

The most stable electron-domain geometry for six electron domains is the *octahedron*. As shown in Figure 9.9▶, an octahedron is a polyhedron with eight faces and six vertices, each of which is an equilateral triangle. If an atom has six electron domains around it, that atom can be visualized as being at the center of the octahedron with the electron domains pointing toward the six vertices. All the bond angles in an octahedron are 90°, and all six vertices are equivalent. Therefore, if an atom has five bonding electron domains and one nonbonding domain, we can put the nonbonding domain at any of the six vertices of the octahedron. The result is always a *square-pyramidal* molecular geometry. When there are two nonbonding electron domains, however, their repulsions are minimized by pointing them toward opposite sides of the octahedron, producing a *square-planar* molecular geometry, as shown in Table 9.3.

▲ Figure 9.9 **An octahedron.** The octahedron is an object with eight faces and six vertices. Each face is an equilateral triangle.

■■ **SAMPLE EXERCISE 9.2** │ Molecular Geometries of Molecules with Expanded Valence Shells

Use the VSEPR model to predict the molecular geometry of **(a)** SF_4, **(b)** IF_5.

SOLUTION

Analyze: The molecules are of the AB_n type with a central atom from the p block of the periodic table.

Plan: We can predict their structures by first drawing Lewis structures and then using the VSEPR model to determine the electron-domain geometry and molecular geometry.

Solve:

(a) The Lewis structure for SF_4 is

The sulfur has five electron domains around it: four from the S—F bonds and one from the nonbonding pair. Each domain points toward a vertex of a trigonal bipyramid. The domain from the nonbonding pair will point toward an equatorial position. The four bonds point toward the remaining four positions, resulting in a molecular geometry that is described as seesaw-shaped:

Comment: The experimentally observed structure is shown on the right. We can infer that the nonbonding electron domain occupies an equatorial position, as predicted. The axial and equatorial S—F bonds are slightly bent back away from the nonbonding domain, suggesting that the bonding domains are "pushed" by the nonbonding domain, which is larger and has greater repulsion (Figure 9.7).

(b) The Lewis structure of IF_5 is

The iodine has six electron domains around it, one of which is from a nonbonding pair. The electron-domain geometry is therefore octahedral, with one position occupied by the nonbonding pair. The resulting molecular geometry is therefore *square pyramidal* (Table 9.3):

Comment: Because the domain for the nonbonding pair is larger than the other domains, the four F atoms in the base of the pyramid are tipped up slightly toward the F atom on top. Experimentally, we find that the angle between the base and top F atoms is 82°, smaller than the ideal 90° angle of an octahedron.

■■ **PRACTICE EXERCISE**

Predict the electron-domain geometry and molecular geometry of **(a)** ClF_3, **(b)** ICl_4^-.
Answers: **(a)** trigonal bipyramidal, T-shaped; **(b)** octahedral, square planar

Shapes of Larger Molecules

Although the structures of the molecules and ions we have already considered contain only a single central atom, the VSEPR model can be extended to more complex molecules. Consider the acetic acid molecule, with the following Lewis structure:

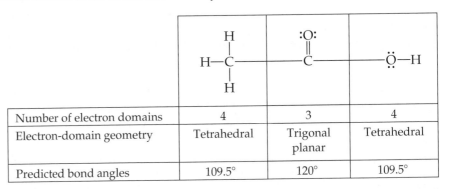

Acetic acid has three interior atoms: the left C atom, the central C atom, and the right-most O atom. We can use the VSEPR model to predict the geometry about each of these atoms individually:

	H—C	:O:‖—C	—Ö—H
Number of electron domains	4	3	4
Electron-domain geometry	Tetrahedral	Trigonal planar	Tetrahedral
Predicted bond angles	109.5°	120°	109.5°

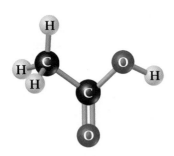

▲ **Figure 9.10 Ball-and-stick (top) and space-filling (bottom) representations of acetic acid, CH₃COOH.**

The leftmost C has four electron domains (all from bonding pairs), and so the geometry around that atom is tetrahedral. The central C has three electron domains (counting the double bond as one domain). Thus, the geometry around that atom is trigonal planar. The O atom has four electron domains (two from bonding pairs and two from nonbonding pairs), so its electron-domain geometry is tetrahedral, and the molecular geometry around O is bent. The bond angles about the central C atom and the O atom are expected to deviate slightly from the ideal values of 120° and 109.5° because of the spatial demands of multiple bonds and nonbonding electron pairs. The structure of the acetic acid molecule is shown in Figure 9.10 ◀.

■ **SAMPLE EXERCISE 9.3 | Predicting Bond Angles**

Eyedrops for dry eyes usually contain a water-soluble polymer called *poly(vinyl alcohol)*, which is based on the unstable organic molecule called *vinyl alcohol*:

$$H—\overset{..}{\underset{..}{O}}—C=C—H$$

Predict the approximate values for the H—O—C and O—C—C bond angles in vinyl alcohol.

SOLUTION

Analyze: We are given a molecular structure and asked to determine two bond angles in the structure.

Plan: To predict a particular bond angle, we consider the middle atom of the angle and determine the number of electron domains surrounding that atom. The ideal angle corresponds to the electron-domain geometry around the atom. The angle will be compressed somewhat by nonbonding electrons or multiple bonds.

Solve: For the H—O—C bond angle, the middle O atom has four electron domains (two bonding and two nonbonding). The electron-domain geometry around O is therefore tetrahedral, which gives an ideal angle of 109.5°. The H—O—C angle will be compressed somewhat by the nonbonding pairs, so we expect this angle to be slightly less than 109.5°.

To predict the O—C—C bond angle, we must examine the leftmost C atom, which is the central atom for this angle. There are three atoms bonded to this C atom and no nonbonding pairs, and so it has three electron domains about it. The predicted electron-domain geometry is trigonal planar, resulting in an ideal bond angle of 120°. Because of the larger size of the C=C domain, however, the O—C=C bond angle should be slightly greater than 120°.

■ PRACTICE EXERCISE

Predict the H—C—H and C—C—C bond angles in the following molecule, called *propyne*:

$$H-\overset{\displaystyle \overset{H}{|}}{\underset{\displaystyle \underset{H}{|}}{C}}-C\equiv C-H$$

Answers: 109.5°, 180°

9.3 MOLECULAR SHAPE AND MOLECULAR POLARITY

We now have a sense of the shapes that molecules adopt and why they do so. We will spend the rest of this chapter looking more closely at the ways in which electrons are shared to form the bonds between atoms in molecules. We will begin by returning to a topic that we first discussed in Section 8.4, namely *bond polarity* and *dipole moments*.

Recall that bond polarity is a measure of how equally the electrons in a bond are shared between the two atoms of the bond: As the difference in electronegativity between the two atoms increases, so does the bond polarity. ∞ (Section 8.4) We saw that the dipole moment of a diatomic molecule is a quantitative measure of the amount of charge separation in the molecule. The charge separation in molecules has a significant effect on physical and chemical properties. We will see in Chapter 11, for example, how molecular polarity affects boiling points, melting points, and other physical properties.

For a molecule that consists of more than two atoms, *the dipole moment depends on both the polarities of the individual bonds and the geometry of the molecule.* For each bond in the molecule, we can consider the **bond dipole**, which is the dipole moment that is due only to the two atoms in that bond. Consider the linear CO_2 molecule, for example. As shown in Figure 9.11(a)▶, each C=O bond is polar, and because the C=O bonds are identical, the bond dipoles are equal in magnitude. A plot of the electron density of the CO_2 molecule, shown in Figure 9.11(b), clearly shows that the bonds are polar: On the oxygen atoms, regions of high electron density (red) are at the ends of the molecule. On the carbon atom, regions of low electron density (blue) are in the center. But what can we say about the *overall* dipole moment of the CO_2 molecule?

Bond dipoles and dipole moments are *vector* quantities; that is, they have both a magnitude and a direction. The *overall* dipole moment of a polyatomic molecule is the vector sum of its bond dipoles. Both the magnitudes *and* the directions of the bond dipoles must be considered when summing these vectors. The two bond dipoles in CO_2, although equal in magnitude, are exactly opposite in direction. Adding them together is the same as adding two numbers that are equal in magnitude but opposite in sign, such as $100 + (-100)$. The bond dipoles, like the numbers, "cancel" each other. Therefore, the overall dipole moment of CO_2 is zero, even though the individual bonds are polar. Thus, the geometry of the molecule dictates that the overall dipole moment be zero, making CO_2 a *nonpolar* molecule.

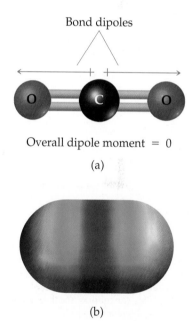

▲ Figure 9.11 **CO₂, a nonpolar molecule.** (a) The overall dipole moment of a molecule is the sum of its bond dipoles. In CO_2 the bond dipoles are equal in magnitude, but exactly oppose each other. The overall dipole moment is zero, therefore, making the molecule nonpolar. (b) The electron-density model shows that the regions of higher electron density (red) are at the ends of the molecule while the region of lower electron density (blue) is at the center.

Bond dipoles

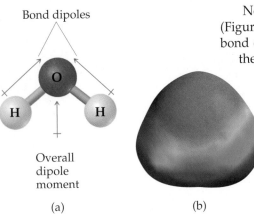

Overall
dipole
moment

(a)   (b)

▲ **Figure 9.12 The dipole moment of a bent molecule.** (a) In H_2O the bond dipoles are equal in magnitude, but do not exactly oppose each other. The molecule has a nonzero dipole moment overall, making the molecule polar. (b) The electron-density model shows that one end of the molecule has more electron density (the oxygen end) while the other end has less electron density (the hydrogens).

Now let's consider H_2O, which is a bent molecule with two polar bonds (Figure 9.12◀). Again, the two bonds in the molecule are identical, and the bond dipoles are equal in magnitude. Because the molecule is bent, however, the bond dipoles do not directly oppose each other and therefore do not cancel each other. Hence, the H_2O molecule has an overall nonzero dipole moment ($\mu = 1.85$ D). Because H_2O has a nonzero dipole moment, it is a *polar* molecule. The oxygen atom carries a partial negative charge, and the hydrogen atoms each have a partial positive charge, as shown by the electron-density model in Figure 9.12(b).

GIVE IT SOME THOUGHT

The molecule O=C=S has a Lewis structure analogous to that of CO_2 and is a linear molecule. Will it necessarily have a zero dipole moment like that of CO_2?

Figure 9.13▼ shows examples of polar and nonpolar molecules, all of which have polar bonds. The molecules in which the central atom is symmetrically surrounded by identical atoms (BF_3 and CCl_4) are nonpolar. For AB_n molecules in which all the B atoms are the same, certain symmetrical shapes—linear (AB_2), trigonal planar (AB_3), tetrahedral and square planar (AB_4), trigonal bipyramidal (AB_5), and octahedral (AB_6)—must lead to nonpolar molecules even though the individual bonds might be polar.

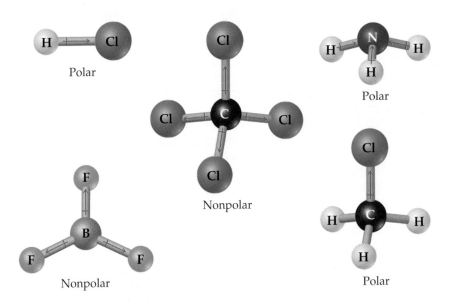

▶ **Figure 9.13 Molecules containing polar bonds.** Two of these molecules have a zero dipole moment because their bond dipoles cancel one another, while the other molecules are polar.

■■ SAMPLE EXERCISE 9.4 | Polarity of Molecules

Predict whether the following molecules are polar or nonpolar: **(a)** BrCl, **(b)** SO_2, **(c)** SF_6.

SOLUTION

Analyze: We are given the molecular formulas of several substances and asked to predict whether the molecules are polar.

Plan: If the molecule contains only two atoms, it will be polar if the atoms differ in electronegativity. If the molecule contains three or more atoms, its polarity depends on both its molecular geometry and the polarity of its bonds. Thus, we must draw a Lewis structure for each molecule containing three or more atoms and determine its molecular geometry. We then use the relative electronegativities of the atoms in each bond to determine the direction of the bond dipoles. Finally, we see if the bond dipoles cancel each other to give a nonpolar molecule or reinforce each other to give a polar one.

Solve:

(a) Chlorine is more electronegative than bromine. All diatomic molecules with polar bonds are polar molecules. Consequently, BrCl will be polar, with chlorine carrying the partial negative charge:

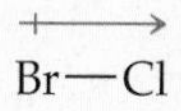

$$\overset{\longrightarrow}{\underset{\text{Br}\,-\,\text{Cl}}{\,\,\,\,\,\,\,\,}}$$

The actual dipole moment of BrCl, as determined by experimental measurement, is $\mu = 0.57\,\text{D}$.

(b) Because oxygen is more electronegative than sulfur, SO_2 has polar bonds. Three resonance forms can be written for SO_2:

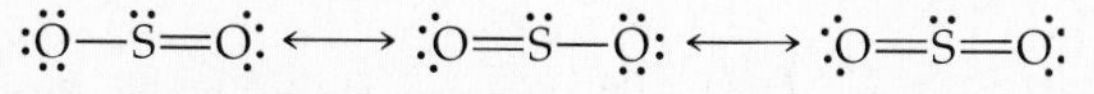

$$:\ddot{\text{O}}-\ddot{\text{S}}=\ddot{\text{O}}: \longleftrightarrow :\ddot{\text{O}}=\ddot{\text{S}}-\ddot{\text{O}}: \longleftrightarrow :\ddot{\text{O}}=\ddot{\text{S}}=\ddot{\text{O}}:$$

For each of these, the VSEPR model predicts a bent geometry. Because the molecule is bent, the bond dipoles do not cancel, and the molecule is polar:

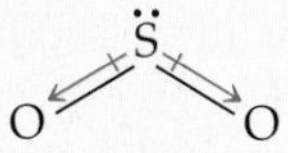

Experimentally, the dipole moment of SO_2 is $\mu = 1.63\,\text{D}$.

(c) Fluorine is more electronegative than sulfur, so the bond dipoles point toward fluorine. The six S—F bonds are arranged octahedrally around the central sulfur:

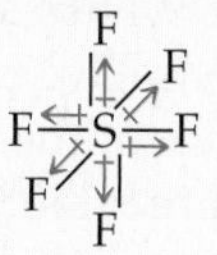

Because the octahedral geometry is symmetrical, the bond dipoles cancel, and the molecule is nonpolar, meaning that $\mu = 0$.

■ PRACTICE EXERCISE
Determine whether the following molecules are polar or nonpolar: **(a)** NF_3, **(b)** BCl_3.
Answers: **(a)** polar because polar bonds are arranged in a trigonal-pyramidal geometry, **(b)** nonpolar because polar bonds are arranged in a trigonal-planar geometry

9.4 COVALENT BONDING AND ORBITAL OVERLAP

The VSEPR model provides a simple means for predicting the shapes of molecules. However, it does not explain why bonds exist between atoms. In developing theories of covalent bonding, chemists have approached the problem from another direction, using quantum mechanics. How can we use atomic orbitals to explain bonding and to account for the geometries of molecules? The marriage of Lewis's notion of electron-pair bonds and the idea of atomic orbitals leads to a model of chemical bonding called **valence-bond theory**. By extending this approach to include the ways in which atomic orbitals can mix with one another, we obtain a picture that corresponds nicely to the VSEPR model.

In the Lewis theory, covalent bonding occurs when atoms share electrons, which concentrates electron density between the nuclei. In the valence-bond theory, we visualize the buildup of electron density between two nuclei as occurring when a valence atomic orbital of one atom shares space, or *overlaps*, with that of another atom. The overlap of orbitals allows two electrons of opposite spin to share the common space between the nuclei, forming a covalent bond.

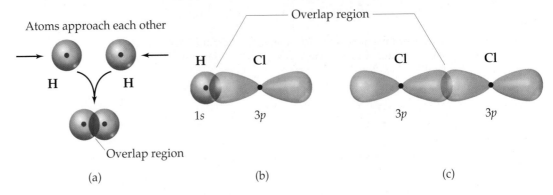

(a)   (b)   (c)

▲ Figure 9.14 The overlap of orbitals to form covalent bonds. (a) The bond in H_2 results from the overlap of two $1s$ orbitals from two H atoms. (b) The bond in HCl results from the overlap of a $1s$ orbital of H and one of the lobes of a $3p$ orbital of Cl. (c) The bond in Cl_2 results from the overlap of two $3p$ orbitals from two Cl atoms.

The coming together of two H atoms to form H_2 is depicted in Figure 9.14(a) ▲. Each atom has a single electron in a $1s$ orbital. As the orbitals overlap, electron density is concentrated between the nuclei. Because the electrons in the overlap region are simultaneously attracted to both nuclei, they hold the atoms together, forming a covalent bond.

The idea of orbital overlap producing a covalent bond applies equally well to other molecules. In HCl, for example, chlorine has the electron configuration $[Ne]3s^23p^5$. All the valence orbitals of chlorine are full except one $3p$ orbital, which contains a single electron. This electron pairs with the single electron of H to form a covalent bond. Figure 9.14(b) shows the overlap of the $3p$ orbital of Cl with the $1s$ orbital of H. Likewise, we can explain the covalent bond in the Cl_2 molecule in terms of the overlap of the $3p$ orbital of one atom with the $3p$ orbital of another, as shown in Figure 9.14(c).

There is always an optimum distance between the two bonded nuclei in any covalent bond. Figure 9.15▼ shows how the potential energy of the system changes as two H atoms come together to form an H_2 molecule. At infinite distance, the atoms do not "feel" each other and so the energy approaches zero. As the distance between the atoms decreases, the overlap between their $1s$ orbitals increases. Because of the resultant increase in electron density between the nuclei, the potential energy of the system decreases. That is, the strength of the bond increases, as shown by the decrease in the energy on the curve. However, the curve also shows that as the atoms come very close together, the energy increases sharply. This increase, which becomes significant at short internuclear distances, is due mainly to the electrostatic repulsion between the nuclei. The internuclear distance, or bond length, is the distance that corresponds to the minimum of the potential-energy curve. The potential energy at this minimum corresponds to the bond strength. Thus, the observed bond length is the distance at which the attractive forces between unlike charges (electrons and nuclei) are balanced by the repulsive forces between like charges (electron–electron and nucleus–nucleus).

▶ Figure 9.15 Formation of the H_2 molecule. Plot of the change in potential energy as two hydrogen atoms come together to form the H_2 molecule. The minimum in the energy, at 0.74 Å, represents the equilibrium bond distance. The energy at that point, −436 kJ/mol, corresponds to the energy change for formation of the H—H bond.

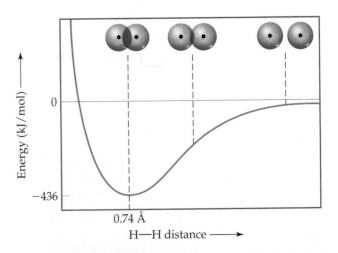

If you could put pressure on the hydrogen molecule so that its bond length decreased, would its bond strength increase or decrease? (Refer to Figure 9.15).

9.5 HYBRID ORBITALS

The VSEPR model, simple as it is, does a surprisingly good job at predicting molecular shape, despite the fact that it has no obvious relationship to the filling and shapes of atomic orbitals. For example, based on the shapes and orientations of the $2s$ and $2p$ orbitals on a carbon atom, it is not obvious why a CH_4 molecule should have a tetrahedral geometry. How can we reconcile the notion that covalent bonds are formed from the overlap of atomic orbitals with the molecular geometries that come from the VSEPR model?

To explain geometries, we assume that the atomic orbitals on an atom (usually the central atom) mix to form new orbitals called **hybrid orbitals**. The shape of any hybrid orbital is different from the shapes of the original atomic orbitals. The process of mixing atomic orbitals is called **hybridization**. The total number of atomic orbitals on an atom remains constant, however, and so the number of hybrid orbitals on an atom equals the number of atomic orbitals that are mixed.

Let's examine the common types of hybridization. As we do so, notice the connection between the type of hybridization and the five basic electron-domain geometries predicted by the VSEPR model: linear, trigonal planar, tetrahedral, trigonal bipyramidal, and octahedral.

sp Hybrid Orbitals

To illustrate the process of hybridization, consider the BeF_2 molecule, which is generated when solid BeF_2 is heated to high temperatures. The Lewis structure of BeF_2 is

$$:\ddot{F}\!-\!Be\!-\!\ddot{F}:$$

The VSEPR model correctly predicts that BeF_2 is linear with two identical Be—F bonds. How can we use valence-bond theory to describe the bonding? The electron configuration of F ($1s^2 2s^2 2p^5$) indicates there is an unpaired electron in a $2p$ orbital. This $2p$ electron can be paired with an unpaired electron from the Be atom to form a polar covalent bond. Which orbitals on the Be atom, however, overlap with those on the F atoms to form the Be—F bonds?

The orbital diagram for a ground-state Be atom is

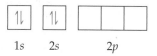

Because it has no unpaired electrons, the Be atom in its ground state is incapable of forming bonds with the fluorine atoms. The Be atom could form two bonds, however, by "promoting" one of the $2s$ electrons to a $2p$ orbital:

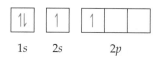

The Be atom now has two unpaired electrons and can therefore form two polar covalent bonds with the F atoms. The two bonds would not be identical, however, because a Be $2s$ orbital would be used to form one of the bonds and a $2p$ orbital would be used for the other. Therefore, although the promotion of an electron allows two Be—F bonds to form, we still have not explained the structure of BeF_2.

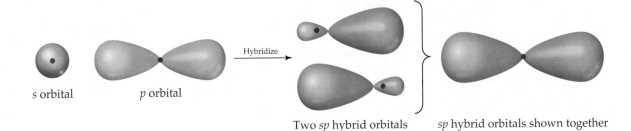

▲ **Figure 9.16 Formation of *sp* hybrid orbitals.** One *s* orbital and one *p* orbital can hybridize to form two equivalent *sp* hybrid orbitals. The two hybrid orbitals have their large lobes pointing in opposite directions, 180° apart.

We can solve this dilemma by "mixing" the 2*s* orbital with one of the 2*p* orbitals to generate two new orbitals, as shown in Figure 9.16▲. Like *p* orbitals, each of the new orbitals has two lobes. Unlike *p* orbitals, however, one lobe is much larger than the other. The two new orbitals are identical in shape, but their large lobes point in opposite directions. These two new orbitals are hybrid orbitals. Because we have hybridized one *s* and one *p* orbital, we call each hybrid an *sp* hybrid orbital. *According to the valence-bond model, a linear arrangement of electron domains implies* sp *hybridization.*

For the Be atom of BeF$_2$, we write the orbital diagram for the formation of two *sp* hybrid orbitals as follows:

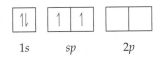

1*s*   *sp*   2*p*

The electrons in the *sp* hybrid orbitals can form two-electron bonds with the two fluorine atoms (Figure 9.17◄). Because the *sp* hybrid orbitals are equivalent but point in opposite directions, BeF$_2$ has two identical bonds and a linear geometry. The remaining two 2*p* orbitals remain unhybridized.

Large lobe of *sp* hybrid orbital

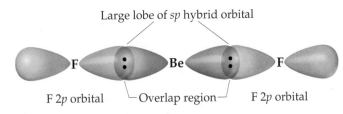

F 2*p* orbital   └─ Overlap region ─┘   F 2*p* orbital

▲ **Figure 9.17 Formation of two equivalent Be—F bonds in BeF$_2$.** Each *sp* hybrid orbital on Be overlaps with a 2*p* orbital on F to form a bond. The two bonds are equivalent to each other and form an angle of 180°.

△ **GIVE IT SOME THOUGHT**

Suppose that the two unhybridized 2*p* orbitals on Be were used to make the Be—F bonds in BeF$_2$. Would the two bonds be equivalent to each other? What would be the expected F—Be—F bond angle?

sp² and *sp³* Hybrid Orbitals

Whenever we mix a certain number of atomic orbitals, we get the same number of hybrid orbitals. Each of these hybrid orbitals is equivalent to the others but points in a different direction. Thus, mixing one 2*s* and one 2*p* orbital yields two equivalent *sp* hybrid orbitals that point in opposite directions (Figure 9.16). Other combinations of atomic orbitals can be hybridized to obtain different geometries. In BF$_3$, for example, mixing the 2*s* and two of the 2*p* orbitals yields three equivalent *sp²* (pronounced "s-p-two") hybrid orbitals (Figure 9.18▶).

The three *sp²* hybrid orbitals lie in the same plane, 120° apart from one another (Figure 9.18). They are used to make three equivalent bonds with the three fluorine atoms, leading to the trigonal-planar geometry of BF$_3$. Notice that an unfilled 2*p* orbital remains unhybridized. This unhybridized orbital will be important when we discuss double bonds in Section 9.6.

△ **GIVE IT SOME THOUGHT**

In an *sp²* hybridized atom, what is the orientation of the unhybridized *p* orbital relative to the three *sp²* hybrid orbitals?

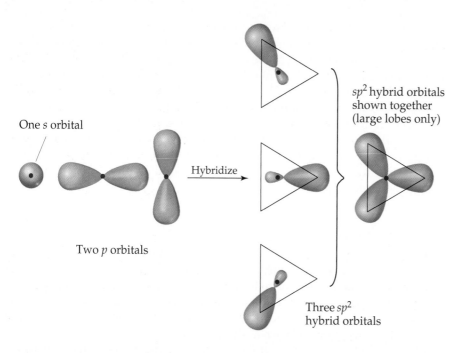

◀ Figure 9.18 **Formation of *sp*²
hybrid orbitals.** One *s* orbital and two
p orbitals can hybridize to form three
equivalent *sp*² hybrid orbitals. The large
lobes of the hybrid orbitals point toward
the corners of an equilateral triangle.

An *s* orbital can also mix with all three *p* orbitals in the same subshell.
For example, the carbon atom in CH₄ forms four equivalent bonds with the four
hydrogen atoms. We envision this process as resulting from the mixing of the 2*s*
and all three 2*p* atomic orbitals of carbon to create four equivalent *sp*³
(pronounced "*s-p*-three") hybrid orbitals. Each *sp*³ hybrid orbital has a large
lobe that points toward a vertex of a tetrahedron, as shown in Figure 9.19▼.

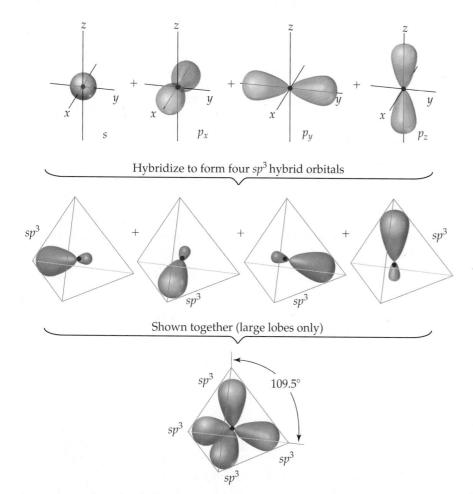

◀ Figure 9.19 **Formation of *sp*³
hybrid orbitals.** One *s* orbital and three
p orbitals can hybridize to form four
equivalent *sp*³ hybrid orbitals. The large
lobes of the hybrid orbitals point toward
the corners of a tetrahedron.

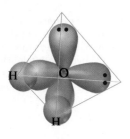

▲ **Figure 9.20 Valence-bond description of H₂O.** The bonding in a water molecule can be envisioned as sp^3 hybridization of the orbitals on O. Two of the four hybrid orbitals overlap with $1s$ orbitals of H to form covalent bonds. The other two hybrid orbitals are occupied by nonbonding pairs of electrons.

These hybrid orbitals can be used to form two-electron bonds by overlap with the atomic orbitals of another atom, such as H. Using valence-bond theory, we can describe the bonding in CH_4 as the overlap of four equivalent sp^3 hybrid orbitals on C with the $1s$ orbitals of the four H atoms to form four equivalent bonds.

The idea of hybridization is used in a similar way to describe the bonding in molecules containing nonbonding pairs of electrons. In H_2O, for example, the electron-domain geometry around the central O atom is approximately tetrahedral. Thus, the four electron pairs can be envisioned as occupying sp^3 hybrid orbitals. Two of the hybrid orbitals contain nonbonding pairs of electrons, while the other two are used to form bonds with hydrogen atoms, as shown in Figure 9.20 ◄.

Hybridization Involving d Orbitals

With the exception of H and He, all atoms have one s and three p orbitals in their valence shell. Because the number of hybrid orbitals must be equal to the number of atomic orbitals that mix to form the hybrids, this fact would seem to limit the maximum number of hybrid orbitals to four. How, then, can we apply the concept of hybridization to molecules where the central atom has more than an octet of electrons around it, such as PF_5 and SF_6? To do so we turn to the unfilled d orbitals with the same value of the principal quantum number, n. Mixing one s orbital, three p orbitals, and one d orbital leads to five sp^3d hybrid orbitals. These hybrid orbitals are directed toward the vertices of a trigonal bipyramid.

Similarly, mixing one s orbital, three p orbitals, and two d orbitals gives six sp^3d^2 hybrid orbitals that are directed toward the vertices of an octahedron. The use of d orbitals in constructing hybrid orbitals nicely corresponds to the notion of an expanded valence shell. ∞(Section 8.7) Keep in mind, however, that only atoms in the third period and beyond (atoms beyond Ne) possess vacant d orbitals that can be used to form hybrid orbitals of this type. The geometric arrangements characteristic of hybrid orbitals are summarized in Table 9.4▶.

Hybrid Orbital Summary

Overall, hybrid orbitals provide a convenient model for using valence-bond theory to describe covalent bonds in molecules with geometries that conform to the electron-domain geometries predicted by the VSEPR model. The picture of hybrid orbitals has limited predictive value. When we know the electron-domain geometry, however, we can employ hybridization to describe the atomic orbitals used by the central atom in bonding.

The following steps allow us to predict the hybrid orbitals used by an atom in bonding:

1. Draw the *Lewis structure* for the molecule or ion.
2. Determine the electron-domain geometry using the *VSEPR model*.
3. Specify the *hybrid orbitals* needed to accommodate the electron pairs based on their geometric arrangement (Table 9.4).

These steps are illustrated in Figure 9.21 ▼, which shows how the hybridization employed by N in NH_3 is determined.

▼ **Figure 9.21 Bonding in NH₃.** The hybrid orbitals used by N in the NH_3 molecule are predicted by first drawing the Lewis structure, then using the VSEPR model to determine the electron-domain geometry, and then specifying the hybrid orbitals that correspond to that geometry. This is essentially the same procedure as that used to determine molecular structure (Figure 9.6), except we focus on the orbitals used to make bonds and to hold nonbonding pairs.

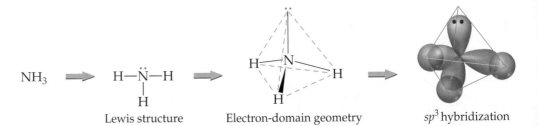

NH_3 ⟹   H—N̈—H   ⟹   ⟹

Lewis structure   Electron-domain geometry sp^3 hybridization

Heteronuclear Diatomic Molecules

The same principles we have used in developing an MO description of homonuclear diatomic molecules can be extended to *heteronuclear* diatomic molecules—those in which the two atoms in the molecule are not the same. We will conclude this section on MO theory with a brief discussion of the MOs of a fascinating heteronuclear diatomic molecule—the nitric oxide, NO, molecule.

The NO molecule controls several important human physiological functions. Our bodies use it, for example, to relax muscles, to kill foreign cells, and to reinforce memory. The 1998 Nobel Prize in Physiology or Medicine was awarded to three scientists for their research that uncovered the importance of NO as a "signalling" molecule in the cardiovascular system. NO also functions as a neurotransmitter and is implicated in many other biological pathways. That NO plays such an important role in human metabolism was unsuspected before 1987 because NO has an odd number of electrons and is highly reactive. The molecule has 11 valence electrons, and two possible Lewis structures can be drawn. The Lewis structure with the lower formal charges places the odd electron on the N atom:

$$\overset{0}{\ddot{N}} = \overset{0}{\ddot{O}} \longleftrightarrow \overset{-1}{\ddot{N}} = \overset{+1}{\ddot{O}}$$

Both structures indicate the presence of a double bond, but when compared with the molecules in Figure 9.46, the experimental bond length of NO (1.15 Å) suggests a bond order greater than two. How do we treat NO using the MO model?

If the atoms in a heteronuclear diatomic molecule do not differ too greatly in their electronegativities, the description of their MOs will resemble those for homonuclear diatomics, with one important modification: The atomic energies of the more electronegative atom will be lower in energy than those of the less electronegative element. The MO diagram for NO is shown in Figure 9.49 ▶. You can see that the 2s and 2p atomic orbitals of oxygen are slightly lower than those of nitrogen because oxygen is more electronegative than nitrogen. We see that the MO energy-level diagram is much like that of a homonuclear diatomic molecule—because the 2s and 2p orbitals on the two atoms interact, the same types of MOs are produced.

There is one other important change in the MOs when we consider heteronuclear molecules. The MOs that result are still a mix of the atomic orbitals from both atoms, but in general *an MO will have a greater contribution from the atomic orbital to which it is closer in energy.* In the case of NO, for example, the σ_{2s} bonding MO is closer in energy to the O 2s atomic orbital than to the N 2s atomic orbital. As a result, the σ_{2s} MO has a slightly greater contribution from O than from N—the orbital is no longer an equal mixture of the two atoms, as was the case for the homonuclear diatomic molecules. Similarly, the σ_{2s}^* antibonding MO is weighted more heavily toward the N atom because that MO is closest in energy to the N 2s atomic orbital.

We complete the MO diagram for NO by filling the MOs in Figure 9.49 with the 11 valence electrons. We see that there are eight bonding and three antibonding electrons, giving a bond order of $\frac{1}{2}(8-3) = 2\frac{1}{2}$, which agrees better with experiment than the Lewis structures do. The unpaired electron resides in one of the π_{2p}^* MOs, which are more heavily weighted toward the N atom. Thus, the Lewis structure that places the unpaired electron on nitrogen (the one preferred on the basis of formal charge) is a more accurate description of the true electron distribution in the molecule.

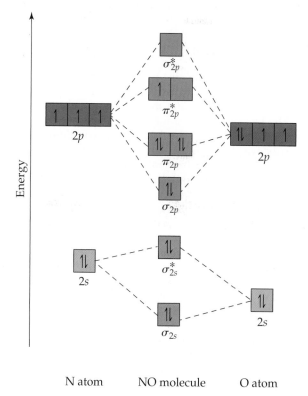

N atom   NO molecule   O atom

▲ Figure 9.49 **The MO energy-level diagram for NO.**

Chemistry Put to Work ORBITALS AND ENERGY

If you were asked to identify the major technological challenge for the twenty-first century, you might say "energy." The development of sustainable energy sources is crucial to meet the needs of future generations of people on our planet. Currently, the majority of the world, in one way or another, relies on exothermic combustion reactions of oil, coal, or natural gas to provide heat and ultimately power. Oil, coal, and natural gas are examples of "fossil fuels"—carbon-containing compounds that are the long-term decomposition products of ancient plants and animals. Fossil fuels are not renewable in the several-hundred-year timeframe in which we need them. But every day our planet receives plenty of energy from the Sun to easily power the world for millions of years. Whereas the combustion of fossil fuels results in release of CO_2 into the atmosphere, solar energy represents a renewable energy source that is potentially less harmful to the environment. One way to utilize solar energy is to convert it into electrical energy using photovoltaic solar cells. The problem with this alternative is that the current efficiency of solar cell devices is low; only about 10–15% of sunlight is converted into useful energy. Furthermore, the cost of manufacturing solar cells is relatively high.

How does solar energy conversion work? Fundamentally, we need to be able to use photons from the Sun to excite electrons in molecules and materials to different energy levels. The brilliant colors around you—those of your clothes, the photographs in this book, the foods you eat—are due to the selective absorption of light by chemicals. Light excites electrons in molecules. In a molecular orbital picture, we can envision light exciting an electron from a filled molecular orbital to an empty one at higher energy. Because the MOs have definite energies, only light of the proper wavelengths can excite electrons. The situation is analogous to that of atomic line spectra. ∞ (Section 6.3) If the appropriate wavelength for exciting electrons is in the visible portion of the electromagnetic spectrum, the substance will appear colored: Certain wavelengths of white light are absorbed; others are not. A green leaf appears green because only green light is reflected by the leaf; other wavelengths of visible light are absorbed by the leaf.

In using molecular orbital theory to discuss the absorptions of light by molecules, we can focus on two MOs in particular. The *highest occupied molecular orbital* (HOMO) is the MO of highest energy that has electrons in it. The *lowest unoccupied molecular orbital* (LUMO) is the MO of lowest energy that does not have electrons in it. In N_2, for example, the HOMO is the π_{2p} MO and the LUMO is the π_{2p}^* MO (Figure 9.46). The energy difference between the HOMO and the LUMO—known as the HOMO–LUMO gap—is related to the minimum energy needed to excite an electron in the molecule. Colorless or white substances usually have such a large HOMO–LUMO gap that visible light is not energetic enough to excite an electron to the higher level. The minimum energy

▲ Figure 9.50 **Light into electricity.** The light from a flashlight, to the left of the photograph frame, is sufficient to excite electrons from one energy level to another in this simple solar cell, producing electricity that powers the small fan. To capture more light, a red ruthenium-containing complex is added to the colorless TiO_2 paste between the glass plates.

needed to excite an electron in N_2 corresponds to light with a wavelength of less than 200 nm, which is far into the ultraviolet part of the spectrum (Figure 6.4). As a result, N_2 cannot absorb any visible light and is therefore colorless.

The magnitude of the energy gap between filled and empty electronic states is critical for solar energy conversion. Ideally, we would like to have a substance that absorbs as many solar photons as possible and then convert the energy of those photons into a useful form of energy such as electricity. Titanium dioxide, for example, is a readily available material that can be reasonably efficient at converting light directly into electricity. However, TiO_2 is white and absorbs only a small amount of the Sun's radiant energy output. Scientists are working to make solar cells in which TiO_2 is mixed with highly colored molecules, whose HOMO–LUMO gaps correspond to visible and near-infrared light. That way, the molecules can absorb more of the solar spectrum. The molecule's HOMO must also be higher in energy than the TiO_2's HOMO so that the excited electrons can flow from the molecules into the TiO_2, thereby generating electricity when the device is illuminated with light and connected to an external circuit.

Figure 9.50 ▲ shows a simple solar cell made from ruthenium-containing molecules, which appear red, mixed with TiO_2 in a paste, sandwiched between two glass plates. Light that shines from a flashlight to the left of the device generates enough current to run the small fan that is connected to it with wires.

Related Exercises: 9.93, 9.104

■ **SAMPLE INTEGRATIVE EXERCISE** │ **Putting Concepts Together**

Elemental sulfur is a yellow solid that consists of S_8 molecules. The structure of the S_8 molecule is a puckered, eight-membered ring (Figure 7.34). Heating elemental sulfur to high temperatures produces gaseous S_2 molecules:

$$S_8 (s) \longrightarrow 4 S_2 (g)$$

(a) With respect to electronic structure, which element in the second row of the periodic table is most similar to sulfur? **(b)** Use the VSEPR model to predict the S—S—S bond angles in S_8 and the hybridization at S in S_8. **(c)** Use MO theory to predict the sulfur–sulfur bond order in S_2. Is the molecule expected to be diamagnetic or paramagnetic? **(d)** Use average bond enthalpies (Table 8.4) to estimate the enthalpy change for the reaction just described. Is the reaction exothermic or endothermic?

SOLUTION

(a) Sulfur is a group 6A element with an $[Ne]3s^23p^4$ electron configuration. It is expected to be most similar electronically to oxygen (electron configuration, $[He]2s^22p^4$), which is immediately above it in the periodic table. **(b)** The Lewis structure of S_8 is

There is a single bond between each pair of S atoms and two nonbonding electron pairs on each S atom. Thus, we see four electron domains around each S atom, and we would expect a tetrahedral electron-domain geometry corresponding to sp^3 hybridization. ∞ (Sections 9.2, 9.5) Because of the nonbonding pairs, we would expect the S—S—S angles to be somewhat less than 109°, the tetrahedral angle. Experimentally, the S—S—S angle in S_8 is 108°, in good agreement with this prediction. Interestingly, if S_8 were a planar ring (like a stop sign), it would have S—S—S angles of 135°. Instead, the S_8 ring puckers to accommodate the smaller angles dictated by sp^3 hybridization. **(c)** The MOs of S_2 are entirely analogous to those of O_2, although the MOs for S_2 are constructed from the 3s and 3p atomic orbitals of sulfur. Further, S_2 has the same number of valence electrons as O_2. Thus, by analogy to our discussion of O_2, we would expect S_2 to have a bond order of 2 (a double bond) and to be paramagnetic with two unpaired electrons in the π^*_{3p} molecular orbitals of S_2. ∞ (Section 9.8) **(d)** We are considering the reaction in which an S_8 molecule falls apart into four S_2 molecules. From parts (b) and (c), we see that S_8 has S—S single bonds and S_2 has S=S double bonds. During the course of the reaction, therefore, we are breaking eight S—S single bonds and forming four S=S double bonds. We can estimate the enthalpy of the reaction by using Equation 8.12 and the average bond enthalpies in Table 8.4:

$$\Delta H_{rxn} = 8\,D(S—S) - 4\,D(S=S) = 8(266\text{ kJ}) - 4(418\text{ kJ}) = +456\text{ kJ}$$

Because $\Delta H_{rxn} > 0$, the reaction is endothermic. ∞ (Section 5.4) The very positive value of ΔH_{rxn} suggests that high temperatures are required to cause the reaction to occur.

CHAPTER REVIEW

SUMMARY AND KEY TERMS

Introduction and Section 9.1 The three-dimensional shapes and sizes of molecules are determined by their **bond angles** and bond lengths. Molecules with a central atom A surrounded by n atoms B, denoted AB_n, adopt a number of different geometric shapes, depending on the value of n and on the particular atoms involved. In the

overwhelming majority of cases, these geometries are related to five basic shapes (linear, trigonal pyramidal, tetrahedral, trigonal bipyramidal, and octahedral).

Section 9.2 The **valence-shell electron-pair repulsion (VSEPR) model** rationalizes molecular geometries based on the repulsions between **electron domains**, which are regions about a central atom in which electrons are likely to be found. **Bonding pairs** of electrons, which are those involved in making bonds, and **nonbonding pairs** of electrons, also called lone pairs, both create electron domains around an atom. According to the VSEPR model, electron domains orient themselves to minimize electrostatic repulsions; that is, they remain as far apart as possible. Electron domains from nonbonding pairs exert slightly greater repulsions than those from bonding pairs, which leads to certain preferred positions for nonbonding pairs and to the departure of bond angles from idealized values. Electron domains from multiple bonds exert slightly greater repulsions than those from single bonds. The arrangement of electron domains around a central atom is called the **electron-domain geometry**; the arrangement of atoms is called the **molecular geometry**.

Section 9.3 The dipole moment of a polyatomic molecule depends on the vector sum of the dipole moments associated with the individual bonds, called the **bond dipoles**. Certain molecular shapes, such as linear AB_2 and trigonal planar AB_3, assure that the bond dipoles cancel, producing a nonpolar molecule, which is one whose dipole moment is zero. In other shapes, such as bent AB_2 and trigonal pyramidal AB_3, the bond dipoles do not cancel and the molecule will be polar (that is, it will have a nonzero dipole moment).

Section 9.4 **Valence-bond theory** is an extension of Lewis's notion of electron-pair bonds. In valence-bond theory, covalent bonds are formed when atomic orbitals on neighboring atoms **overlap** one another. The overlap region is a favorable one for the two electrons because of their attraction to two nuclei. The greater the overlap between two orbitals, the stronger will be the bond that is formed.

Section 9.5 To extend the ideas of valence-bond theory to polyatomic molecules, we must envision mixing s, p, and sometimes d orbitals to form **hybrid orbitals**. The process of **hybridization** leads to hybrid atomic orbitals that have a large lobe directed to overlap with orbitals on another atom to make a bond. Hybrid orbitals can also accommodate nonbonding pairs. A particular mode of hybridization can be associated with each of the five common electron-domain geometries (linear = sp; trigonal planar = sp^2; tetrahedral = sp^3; trigonal bipyramidal = sp^3d; and octahedral = sp^3d^2).

Section 9.6 Covalent bonds in which the electron density lies along the line connecting the atoms (the internuclear axis) are called **sigma (σ) bonds**. Bonds can also be formed from the sideways overlap of p orbitals. Such a bond is called a **pi (π) bond**. A double bond, such as that in C_2H_4, consists of one σ bond and one π bond; a triple bond, such as that in C_2H_2, consists of one σ and two π bonds. The formation of a π bond requires that molecules adopt a specific orientation; the two CH_2 groups in C_2H_4, for example, must lie in the same plane. As a result, the presence of π bonds introduces rigidity into molecules.

In molecules that have multiple bonds and more than one resonance structure, such as C_6H_6, the π bonds are **delocalized**; that is, the π bonds are spread among several atoms.

Section 9.7 **Molecular orbital theory** is another model used to describe the bonding in molecules. In this model the electrons exist in allowed energy states called **molecular orbitals (MOs)**. These orbitals can be spread among all the atoms of a molecule. Like an atomic orbital, a molecular orbital has a definite energy and can hold two electrons of opposite spin. The combination of two atomic orbitals leads to the formation of two MOs, one at lower energy, and one at higher energy relative to the energy of the atomic orbitals. The lower-energy MO concentrates charge density in the region between the nuclei and is called a **bonding molecular orbital**. The higher-energy MO excludes electrons from the region between the nuclei and is called an **antibonding molecular orbital**. Occupation of bonding MOs favors bond formation, whereas occupation of antibonding MOs is unfavorable. The bonding and antibonding MOs formed by the combination of s orbitals are **sigma (σ) molecular orbitals**; like σ bonds, they lie on the internuclear axis.

The combination of atomic orbitals and the relative energies of the molecular orbitals are shown by an **energy-level** (or **molecular orbital**) **diagram**. When the appropriate number of electrons are put into the MOs, we can calculate the **bond order** of a bond, which is half the difference between the number of electrons in bonding MOs and the number of electrons in antibonding MOs. A bond order of 1 corresponds to a single bond, and so forth. Bond orders can be fractional numbers.

Section 9.8 Electrons in core orbitals do not contribute to the bonding between atoms, so a molecular orbital description usually needs to consider only electrons in the outermost electron subshells. In order to describe the MOs of second-row homonuclear diatomic molecules, we need to consider the MOs that can form by the combination of p orbitals. The p orbitals that point directly at one another can form σ bonding and σ^* antibonding MOs. The p orbitals that are oriented perpendicular to the internuclear axis combine to form **pi (π) molecular orbitals**. In diatomic molecules the π molecular orbitals occur as pairs of degenerate (same energy) bonding and antibonding MOs. The σ_{2p} bonding MO is expected to be lower in energy than the π_{2p} bonding MOs because of larger orbital overlap. This ordering is reversed in B_2, C_2, and N_2 because of interaction between the $2s$ and $2p$ atomic orbitals of different atoms.

The molecular orbital description of second-row diatomic molecules leads to bond orders in accord with the Lewis structures of these molecules. Further, the model predicts correctly that O_2 should exhibit **paramagnetism**, an attraction of a molecule by a magnetic field due to unpaired electrons. Those molecules in which all the electrons are paired exhibit **diamagnetism**, a weak repulsion from a magnetic field.

KEY SKILLS

- Be able to describe the three-dimensional shapes of molecules using the VSEPR model.
- Determine whether a molecule is polar or nonpolar based on its geometry and the individual bond dipole moments.
- Be able to identify the hybridization state of atoms in molecules.
- Be able to sketch how orbitals overlap to form sigma (σ) and pi (π) bonds.
- Be able to explain the concept of bonding and antibonding orbitals.
- Be able to draw molecular orbital energy-level diagrams and place electrons into them to obtain the bond orders and electron configurations of diatomic molecules using molecular orbital theory.
- Understand the relationships among bond order, bond strength, and bond length.

KEY EQUATIONS

- Bond order = $\frac{1}{2}$ (no. of bonding electrons − no. of antibonding electrons)

VISUALIZING CONCEPTS

9.1 A certain AB_4 molecule has a "seesaw" shape:

From which of the fundamental geometries shown in Figure 9.3 could you remove one or more atoms to create a molecule having this seesaw shape? [Section 9.1]

9.2 **(a)** If the three balloons shown on the right are all the same size, what angle is formed between the red one and the green one? **(b)** If additional air is added to the blue balloon so that it gets larger, what happens to the angle between the red and green balloons? **(c)** What aspect of the VSEPR model is illustrated by part (b)? [Section 9.2]

9.3 An AB_5 molecule adopts the geometry shown below. **(a)** What is the name of this geometry? **(b)** Do you think there are any nonbonding electron pairs on atom A? Why or why not? **(c)** Suppose the atoms B are halogen atoms. Can you determine uniquely to which group in the periodic table atom A belongs? [Section 9.2]

9.4 The molecule shown here is *difluoromethane* (CH_2F_2), which is used as a refrigerant called R-32. **(a)** Based on the structure, how many electron domains surround the C atom in this molecule? **(b)** Would the molecule have a nonzero dipole moment? **(c)** If the molecule is polar, in what direction will the overall dipole moment vector point in the molecule? [Sections 9.2 and 9.3]

9.5 The plot below shows the potential energy of two Cl atoms as a function of the distance between them. **(a)** To what does an energy of zero correspond in this diagram? **(b)** According to the valence-bond model, why does the energy decrease as the Cl atoms move from a large separation to a smaller one? **(c)** What is the significance of the Cl–Cl distance at the minimum point in the plot? **(d)** Why does the energy rise at Cl–Cl distances less than that at the minimum point in the plot? **(e)** How can you estimate the bond strength of the Cl–Cl bond from the plot? [Section 9.4]

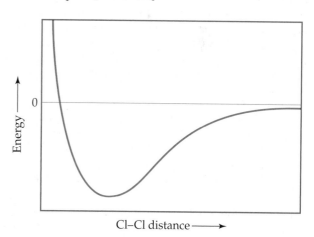

9.6 Shown below are three pairs of hybrid orbitals, with each set at a characteristic angle. For each pair, determine the type or types of hybridization that could lead to hybrid orbitals at the specified angle. [Section 9.5]

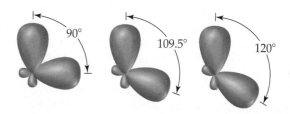

9.7 The orbital diagram below presents the final step in the formation of hybrid orbitals by a silicon atom. What type of hybrid orbitals is produced in this hybridization? [Section 9.5]

3s   3p

9.8 Consider the hydrocarbon drawn below. **(a)** What is the hybridization at each carbon atom in the molecule? **(b)** How many σ bonds are there in the molecule? **(c)** How many π bonds? [Section 9.6]

$$H-\overset{\overset{\displaystyle H}{|}}{C}=\overset{\overset{\displaystyle H}{|}}{C}-\overset{\overset{\displaystyle H}{|}}{\underset{\underset{\displaystyle H}{|}}{C}}-C\equiv C-\overset{\overset{\displaystyle H}{|}}{\underset{\underset{\displaystyle H}{|}}{C}}-H$$

9.9 For each of the following contour representations of molecular orbitals, identify (i) the atomic orbitals (s or p) used to construct the MO, (ii) the type of MO (σ or π), and (iii) whether the MO is bonding or antibonding. [Sections 9.7 and 9.8]

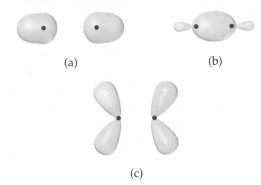

(a)   (b)

(c)

9.10 The diagram below shows the highest occupied MOs of a neutral molecule CX, where element X is in the same row of the periodic table as C. **(a)** Based on the number of electrons, can you determine the identity of X? **(b)** Would the molecule be diamagnetic or paramagnetic? **(c)** Consider the π_{2p} MOs of the molecule. Would you expect them to have a greater atomic orbital contribution from C, have a greater atomic orbital contribution from X, or be an equal mixture of atomic orbitals from the two atoms? [Section 9.8]

σ_{2p}

π_{2p}

EXERCISES

Molecular Shapes; the VSEPR Model

9.11 An AB_2 molecule is described as linear, and the A—B bond length is known. **(a)** Does this information completely describe the geometry of the molecule? **(b)** Can you tell how many nonbonding pairs of electrons are around the A atom from this information?

9.12 **(a)** Methane (CH_4) and the perchlorate ion (ClO_4^-) are both described as tetrahedral. What does this indicate about their bond angles? **(b)** The NH_3 molecule is trigonal pyramidal, while BF_3 is trigonal planar. Which of these molecules is flat?

9.13 **(a)** What is meant by the term *electron domain*? **(b)** Explain in what way electron domains behave like the balloons in Figure 9.5. Why do they do so?

9.14 **(a)** How does one determine the number of electron domains in a molecule or ion? **(b)** What is the difference between a *bonding electron domain* and a *nonbonding electron domain*?

9.15 How many nonbonding electron pairs are there in each of the following molecules: (a) $(CH_3)_2S$; (b) HCN; (c) H_2C_2; (d) CH_3F?

9.16 Describe the characteristic electron-domain geometry of each of the following numbers of electron domains about a central atom: **(a)** 3, **(b)** 4, **(c)** 5, **(d)** 6.

9.17 What is the difference between the electron-domain geometry and the molecular geometry of a molecule? Use the water molecule as an example in your discussion.

9.18 An AB_3 molecule is described as having a trigonal-bipyramidal electron-domain geometry. How many nonbonding domains are on atom A? Explain.

9.19 Give the electron-domain and molecular geometries of a molecule that has the following electron domains on its central atom: **(a)** four bonding domains and no nonbonding domains, **(b)** three bonding domains and two nonbonding domains, **(c)** five bonding domains and one nonbonding domain, **(e)** four bonding domains and two nonbonding domains.

9.20 What are the electron-domain and molecular geometries of a molecule that has the following electron domains on its central atom? **(a)** three bonding domains and no nonbonding domains, **(b)** three bonding domains and one nonbonding domain, **(c)** two bonding domains and two nonbonding domains.

9.21 Give the electron-domain and molecular geometries for the following molecules and ions: **(a)** HCN, **(b)** SO_3^{2-}, **(c)** SF_4, **(d)** PF_6^-, **(e)** NH_3Cl^+, **(f)** N_3^-.

9.22 Draw the Lewis structure for each of the following molecules or ions, and predict their electron-domain and molecular geometries: **(a)** PF_3, **(b)** CH_3^+, **(c)** BrF_3, **(d)** ClO_4^- **(e)** XeF_2, **(f)** BrO_2^-.

9.23 The figure that follows shows ball-and-stick drawings of three possible shapes of an AF_3 molecule. **(a)** For each shape, give the electron-domain geometry on which the molecular geometry is based. **(b)** For each shape, how many nonbonding electron domains are there on atom A? **(c)** Which of the following elements will lead to an AF_3 molecule with the shape in (ii): Li, B, N, Al, P, Cl? **(d)** Name an element A that is expected to lead to the AF_3 structure shown in (iii). Explain your reasoning.

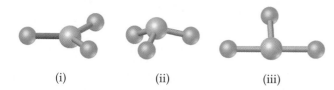

(i)   (ii)   (iii)

9.24 The figure that follows contains ball-and-stick drawings of three possible shapes of an AF_4 molecule. **(a)** For each shape, give the electron-domain geometry on which the molecular geometry is based. **(b)** For each shape, how many nonbonding electron domains are there on atom A? **(c)** Which of the following elements will lead to an AF_4 molecule with the shape in (iii): Be, C, S, Se, Si, Xe? **(d)** Name an element A that is expected to lead to the AF_4 structure shown in (i).

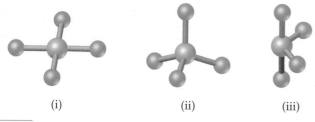

(i)   (ii)   (iii)

9.25 Give the approximate values for the indicated bond angles in the following molecules:

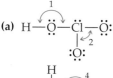

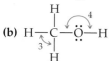

(c) H—C≡C—H

(b) H—C—O—H

(d) H—C—O—C—H

9.26 Give approximate values for the indicated bond angles in the following molecules:

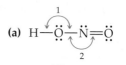

(a) H—Ö—N=Ö

(c) H—N—Ö—H

(b) H—C—C=Ö

(d) H—C—C≡N:

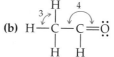

9.27 Predict the trend in the F(axial)—A—F(equatorial) bond angle in the following AF_n molecules: PF_5, SF_4, and ClF_3.

9.28 The three species NH_2^-, NH_3, and NH_4^+ have H—N—H bond angles of 105°, 107°, and 109°, respectively. Explain this variation in bond angles.

9.29 **(a)** Explain why BrF_4^- is square planar, whereas BF_4^- is tetrahedral. **(b)** Water, H_2O, is a bent molecule. Predict the shape of the molecular ion formed from the water molecule if you were able to remove four electrons to make $(H_2O)^{4+}$.

9.30 **(a)** Explain why the following ions have different bond angles: ClO_2^- and NO_2^-. Predict the bond angle in each case. **(b)** Explain why the XeF_2 molecule is linear and not bent.

Polarity of Polyatomic Molecules

9.31 **(a)** Does SCl_2 have a dipole moment? If so, in which direction does the net dipole point? **(b)** Does $BeCl_2$ have a dipole moment? If so, in which direction does the net dipole point?

9.32 **(a)** The PH_3 molecule is polar. How does this offer experimental proof that the molecule cannot be planar? **(b)** It turns out that ozone, O_3, has a small dipole moment. How is this possible, given that all the atoms are the same?

9.33 **(a)** Consider the AF_3 molecules in Exercise 9.23. Which of these will have a nonzero dipole moment? Explain. **(b)** Which of the AF_4 molecules in Exercise 9.24 will have a zero dipole moment?

9.34 **(a)** What conditions must be met if a molecule with polar bonds is nonpolar? **(b)** What geometries will give nonpolar molecules for AB_2, AB_3, and AB_4 geometries?

9.35 Predict whether each of the following molecules is polar or nonpolar: **(a)** IF, **(b)** CS_2, **(c)** SO_3, **(d)** PCl_3, **(e)** SF_6, **(f)** IF_5.

9.36 Predict whether each of the following molecules is polar or nonpolar: **(a)** CCl_4, **(b)** NH_3, **(c)** SF_4, **(d)** XeF_4, **(e)** CH_3Br, **(f)** GaH_3.

9.37 Dichloroethylene ($C_2H_2Cl_2$) has three forms (isomers), each of which is a different substance. **(a)** Draw Lewis structures of the three isomers, all of which have a carbon–carbon double bond. **(b)** Which of these isomers has a zero dipole moment? **(c)** How many isomeric forms can chloroethylene, C_2H_3Cl, have? Would they be expected to have dipole moments?

9.38 Dichlorobenzene, $C_6H_4Cl_2$, exists in three forms (isomers), called *ortho*, *meta*, and *para*:

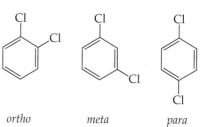

ortho   *meta*   *para*

Which of these would have a nonzero dipole moment? Explain.

Orbital Overlap; Hybrid Orbitals

9.39 **(a)** What is meant by the term *orbital overlap*? **(b)** Describe what a chemical bond is in terms of electron density between two atoms.

9.40 Draw sketches illustrating the overlap between the following orbitals on two atoms: **(a)** the $2s$ orbital on each atom, **(b)** the $2p_z$ orbital on each atom (assume both atoms are on the z-axis), **(c)** the $2s$ orbital on one atom and the $2p_z$ orbital on the other atom.

9.41 Consider the bonding in an MgH_2 molecule. **(a)** Draw a Lewis structure for the molecule, and predict its molecular geometry. **(b)** What hybridization scheme is used in MgH_2? **(c)** Sketch one of the two-electron bonds between an Mg hybrid orbital and an H $1s$ atomic orbital.

9.42 How would you expect the extent of overlap of atomic orbitals to vary in the series IF, ICl, IBr, and I_2?

9.43 Fill in the following chart. If the molecule column is blank, find an example that fulfills the conditions of the rest of the row.

Molecule	Electron-domain Geometry	Hybridization of Central Atom	Dipole moment? Yes or No.
CO_2			
		sp^3	yes
		sp^3	no
	trigonal planar		no
SF_4			
	octahedral		no
		sp^2	yes
	trigonal bipyramidal		no
XeF_2			

9.44 Why are there no sp^4 or sp^5 hybrid orbitals?

9.45 **(a)** Starting with the orbital diagram of a boron atom, describe the steps needed to construct hybrid orbitals appropriate to describe the bonding in BF_3. **(b)** What is the name given to the hybrid orbitals constructed in (a)? **(c)** Sketch the large lobes of the hybrid orbitals constructed in part (a). **(d)** Are there any valence atomic orbitals of B that are left unhybridized? If so, how are they oriented relative to the hybrid orbitals?

9.46 **(a)** Starting with the orbital diagram of a sulfur atom, describe the steps needed to construct hybrid orbitals appropriate to describe the bonding in SF_2. **(b)** What is the name given to the hybrid orbitals constructed in (a)? **(c)** Sketch the large lobes of the hybrid orbitals constructed in part (a). **(d)** Would the hybridization scheme in part (a) be appropriate for SF_4? Explain.

9.47 Indicate the hybridization of the central atom in **(a)** BCl_3, **(b)** $AlCl_4^-$, **(c)** CS_2, **(d)** KrF_2, **(e)** PF_6^-.

9.48 What is the hybridization of the central atom in **(a)** $SiCl_4$, **(b)** HCN, **(c)** SO_3, **(d)** ICl_2^-, **(e)** BrF_4^-?

Multiple Bonds

9.49 **(a)** Draw a picture showing how two p orbitals on two different atoms can be combined to make a sigma bond. **(b)** Sketch a π bond that is constructed from p orbitals. **(c)** Which is generally stronger, a σ bond or a π bond? Explain. **(d)** Can two s orbitals make a π bond? Explain.

9.50 **(a)** If the valence atomic orbitals of an atom are sp hybridized, how many unhybridized p orbitals remain in the valence shell? How many π bonds can the atom form? **(b)** Imagine that you could hold two atoms that are bonded together, twist them, and not change the bond length. Would it be easier to twist (rotate) around a single σ bond or around a double (σ plus π) bond, or would they be the same? Explain.

9.51 **(a)** Draw Lewis structures for ethane (C_2H_6), ethylene (C_2H_4), and acetylene (C_2H_2). **(b)** What is the hybridization of the carbon atoms in each molecule? **(c)** Predict which molecules, if any, are planar. **(d)** How many σ and π bonds are there in each molecule? **(e)** Suppose that silicon could form molecules that are precisely the analogs of ethane, ethylene, and acetylene. How would you describe the bonding about Si in terms of hybrid orbitals? Does it make a difference that Si lies in the row below C in the periodic table? Explain.

9.52 The nitrogen atoms in N_2 participate in multiple bonding, whereas those in hydrazine, N_2H_4, do not. **(a)** Draw Lewis structures for both molecules. **(b)** What is the hybridization of the nitrogen atoms in each molecule? **(c)** Which molecule has a stronger N—N bond?

9.53 Propylene, C_3H_6, is a gas that is used to form the important polymer called polypropylene. Its Lewis structure is

$$\begin{array}{ccccccc} & & H & & H & & H \\ & & | & & | & & | \\ H-&C=&C&-&C&-&H \\ & & & & & & | \\ & & & & & & H \end{array}$$

(a) What is the total number of valence electrons in the propylene molecule? **(b)** How many valence electrons are used to make σ bonds in the molecule? **(c)** How many valence electrons are used to make π bonds in the molecule? **(d)** How many valence electrons remain in nonbonding pairs in the molecule? **(e)** What is the hybridization at each carbon atom in the molecule?

9.54 Ethyl acetate, $C_4H_8O_2$, is a fragrant substance used both as a solvent and as an aroma enhancer. Its Lewis structure is

(a) What is the hybridization at each of the carbon atoms of the molecule? **(b)** What is the total number of valence electrons in ethyl acetate? **(c)** How many of the valence electrons are used to make σ bonds in the molecule? **(d)** How many valence electrons are used to make π bonds? **(e)** How many valence electrons remain in nonbonding pairs in the molecule?

9.55 Consider the Lewis structure for glycine, the simplest amino acid:

(a) What are the approximate bond angles about each of the two carbon atoms, and what are the hybridizations of the orbitals on each of them? **(b)** What are the hybridizations of the orbitals on the two oxygens and the nitrogen atom, and what are the approximate bond angles at the nitrogen? **(c)** What is the total number of σ bonds in the entire molecule, and what is the total number of π bonds?

9.56 The compound with the following Lewis structure is acetylsalicylic acid, better known as aspirin:

(a) What are the approximate values of the bond angles labeled 1, 2, and 3? **(b)** What hybrid orbitals are used about the central atom of each of these angles? **(c)** How many σ bonds are in the molecule?

9.57 **(a)** What is the difference between a localized π bond and a delocalized one? **(b)** How can you determine whether a molecule or ion will exhibit delocalized π bonding? **(c)** Is the π bond in NO_2^- localized or delocalized?

9.58 **(a)** Write a single Lewis structure for SO_3, and determine the hybridization at the S atom. **(b)** Are there other equivalent Lewis structures for the molecule? **(c)** Would you expect SO_3 to exhibit delocalized π bonding? Explain.

Molecular Orbitals

9.59 **(a)** What is the difference between hybrid orbitals and molecular orbitals? **(b)** How many electrons can be placed into each MO of a molecule? **(c)** Can antibonding molecular orbitals have electrons in them?

9.60 **(a)** If you combine two atomic orbitals on two different atoms to make a new orbital, is this a hybrid orbital or a molecular orbital? **(b)** If you combine two atomic orbitals on *one* atom to make a new orbital, is this a hybrid orbital or a molecular orbital? **(c)** Does the Pauli exclusion principle (Section 6.7) apply to MOs? Explain.

9.61 Consider the H_2^+ ion. **(a)** Sketch the molecular orbitals of the ion, and draw its energy-level diagram. **(b)** How many electrons are there in the H_2^+ ion? **(c)** Draw the electron configuration of the ion in terms of its MOs. **(d)** What is the bond order in H_2^+? **(e)** Suppose that the ion is excited by light so that an electron moves from a lower-energy to a higher-energy MO. Would you expect the excited-state H_2^+ ion to be stable or to fall apart? Explain.

9.62 **(a)** Sketch the molecular orbitals of the H_2^- ion, and draw its energy-level diagram. **(b)** Write the electron configuration of the ion in terms of its MOs. **(c)** Calculate the bond order in H_2^- **(d)** Suppose that the ion is excited by light, so that an electron moves from a lower-energy to a higher-energy molecular orbital. Would you expect the excited-state H_2^- ion to be stable? Explain.

9.63 Draw a picture that shows all three $2p$ orbitals on one atom and all three $2p$ orbitals on another atom. **(a)** Imagine the atoms coming close together to bond. How many σ bonds can the two sets of $2p$ orbitals make with each other? **(b)** How many π bonds can the two sets of $2p$ orbitals make with each other? **(c)** How many antibonding orbitals, and of what type, can be made from the two sets of $2p$ orbitals?

9.64 **(a)** What is the probability of finding an electron on the internuclear axis if the electron occupies a π molecular orbital? **(b)** For a homonuclear diatomic molecule, what similarities and differences are there between the π_{2p} MO made from the $2p_x$ atomic orbitals and the π_{2p} MO made from the $2p_y$ atomic orbitals? **(c)** Why are the π_{2p} MOs lower in energy than the π_{2p}^* MOs?

9.65 **(a)** What are the relationships among bond order, bond length, and bond energy? **(b)** According to molecular orbital theory, would either Be_2 or Be_2^+ be expected to exist? Explain.

9.66 Explain the following: **(a)** The *peroxide* ion, O_2^{2-}, has a longer bond length than the *superoxide* ion, O_2^-. **(b)** The magnetic properties of B_2 are consistent with the π_{2p} MOs being lower in energy than the σ_{2p} MO. **(c)** The O_2^{2+} ion has a stronger O—O bond than O_2 itself.

9.67 **(a)** What does the term *diamagnetism* mean? **(b)** How does a diamagnetic substance respond to a magnetic field? **(c)** Which of the following ions would you expect to be diamagnetic: N_2^{2-}, O_2^{2-}, Be_2^{2+}, C_2^-?

9.68 **(a)** What does the term *paramagnetism* mean? **(b)** How can one determine experimentally whether a substance is paramagnetic? **(c)** Which of the following ions would you expect to be paramagnetic: O_2^+, N_2^{2-}, Li_2^+, O_2^{2-}? For those ions that are paramagnetic, determine the number of unpaired electrons.

9.69 Using Figures 9.37 and 9.45 as guides, draw the molecular orbital electron configuration for (a) B_2^+, (b) Li_2^+, (c) N_2^+, (d) Ne_2^{2+}. In each case indicate whether the addition of an electron to the ion would increase or decrease the bond order of the species.

9.70 If we assume that the energy-level diagrams for homonuclear diatomic molecules shown in Figure 9.43 can be applied to heteronuclear diatomic molecules and ions, predict the bond order and magnetic behavior of (a) CO^+, (b) NO^-, (c) OF^+, (d) NeF^+.

9.71 Determine the electron configurations for CN^+, CN, and CN^-. (a) Which species has the strongest C—N bond? (b) Which species, if any, has unpaired electrons?

9.72 (a) The nitric oxide molecule, NO, readily loses one electron to form the NO^+ ion. Why is this consistent with the electronic structure of NO? (b) Predict the order of the N—O bond strengths in NO, NO^+, and NO^-, and describe the magnetic properties of each. (c) With what neutral homonuclear diatomic molecules are the NO^+ and NO^- ions isoelectronic (same number of electrons)?

[9.73] Consider the molecular orbitals of the P_2 molecule. Assume that the MOs of diatomics from the third row of the periodic table are analogous to those from the second row. (a) Which valence atomic orbitals of P are used

to construct the MOs of P_2? (b) The figure below shows a sketch of one of the MOs for P_2. What is the label for this MO? (c) For the P_2 molecule, how many electrons occupy the MO in the figure? (d) Is P_2 expected to be diamagnetic or paramagnetic? Explain.

[9.74] The iodine bromide molecule, IBr, is an *interhalogen compound*. Assume that the molecular orbitals of IBr are analogous to the homonuclear diatomic molecule F_2. (a) Which valence atomic orbitals of I and of Br are used to construct the MOs of IBr? (b) What is the bond order of the IBr molecule? (c) One of the valence MOs of IBr is sketched below. Why are the atomic orbital contributions to this MO different in size? (d) What is the label for the MO? (e) For the IBr molecule, how many electrons occupy the MO?

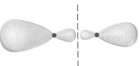

ADDITIONAL EXERCISES

9.75 (a) What is the physical basis for the VSEPR model? (b) When applying the VSEPR model, we count a double or triple bond as a single electron domain. Why is this justified?

9.76 The molecules SiF_4, SF_4, and XeF_4 have molecular formulas of the type AF_4, but the molecules have different molecular geometries. Predict the shape of each molecule, and explain why the shapes differ.

[9.77] The vertices of a tetrahedron correspond to four alternating corners of a cube. By using analytical geometry, demonstrate that the angle made by connecting two of the vertices to a point at the center of the cube is 109.5°, the characteristic angle for tetrahedral molecules.

9.78 Consider the molecule PF_4Cl. (a) Draw a Lewis structure for the molecule, and predict its electron-domain geometry. (b) Which would you expect to take up more space, a P—F bond or a P—Cl bond? Explain. (c) Predict the molecular geometry of PF_4Cl. How did your answer for part (b) influence your answer here in part (c)? (d) Would you expect the molecule to distort from its ideal electron-domain geometry? If so, how would it distort?

9.79 From their Lewis structures, determine the number of σ and π bonds in each of the following molecules or ions: (a) CO_2; (b) thiocyanate ion, NCS^-; (c) formaldehyde, H_2CO; (d) formic acid, HCOOH, which has one H and two O atoms attached to C.

9.80 The lactic acid molecule, $CH_3CH(OH)COOH$, gives sour milk its unpleasant, sour taste. (a) Draw the Lewis structure for the molecule, assuming that carbon always forms four bonds in its stable compounds. (b) How many π and how many σ bonds are in the molecule? (c) Which CO bond is shortest in the molecule? (d) What

is the hybridization of atomic orbitals around each carbon atom associated with that short bond? (e) What are the approximate bond angles around each carbon atom in the molecule?

9.81 The PF_3 molecule has a dipole moment of 1.03 D, but BF_3 has a dipole moment of zero. How can you explain the difference?

9.82 There are two compounds of the formula $Pt(NH_3)_2Cl_2$:

$$\begin{array}{cc} NH_3 & Cl \\ | & | \\ Cl-Pt-Cl & Cl-Pt-NH_3 \\ | & | \\ NH_3 & NH_3 \end{array}$$

The compound on the right, *cisplatin*, is used in cancer therapy. The compound on the left, *transplatin*, is ineffective for cancer therapy. Both compounds have a square-planar geometry. (a) Which compound has a nonzero dipole moment? (b) The reason cisplatin is a good anticancer drug is that it binds tightly to DNA. Cancer cells are rapidly dividing, producing a lot of DNA. Consequently cisplatin kills cancer cells at a faster rate than normal cells. However, since normal cells also are making DNA, cisplatin also attacks healthy cells, which leads to unpleasant side effects. The way both molecules bind to DNA involves the Cl^- ions leaving the Pt ion, to be replaced by two nitrogens in DNA. Draw a picture in which a long vertical line represents a piece of DNA. Draw the $Pt(NH_3)_2$ fragments of cisplatin and transplatin with the proper shape. Also draw them attaching to your DNA line. Can you explain from your drawing why the shape of the cisplatin causes it to bind to DNA more effectively than transplatin?

[9.83] The O—H bond lengths in the water molecule (H_2O) are 0.96 Å, and the H—O—H angle is 104.5°. The dipole moment of the water molecule is 1.85 D. **(a)** In what directions do the bond dipoles of the O—H bonds point? In what direction does the dipole moment vector of the water molecule point? **(b)** Calculate the magnitude of the bond dipole of the O—H bonds. (*Note:* You will need to use vector addition to do this.) **(c)** Compare your answer from part (b) to the dipole moments of the hydrogen halides (Table 8.3). Is your answer in accord with the relative electronegativity of oxygen?

[9.84] The reaction of three molecules of fluorine gas with a Xe atom produces the substance xenon hexafluoride, XeF_6:

$$Xe(g) + 3\ F_2(g) \longrightarrow XeF_6(s)$$

(a) Draw a Lewis structure for XeF_6. **(b)** If you try to use the VSEPR model to predict the molecular geometry of XeF_6, you run into a problem. What is it? **(c)** What could you do to resolve the difficulty in part (b)? **(d)** Suggest a hybridization scheme for the Xe atom in XeF_6. **(e)** The molecule IF_7 has a pentagonal-bipyramidal structure (five equatorial fluorine atoms at the vertices of a regular pentagon and two axial fluorine atoms). Based on the structure of IF_7, suggest a structure for XeF_6.

[9.85] The Lewis structure for allene is

$$\underset{H}{\overset{H}{\diagdown}} C = C = C \underset{H}{\overset{H}{\diagup}}$$

Make a sketch of the structure of this molecule that is analogous to Figure 9.27. In addition, answer the following three questions: **(a)** Is the molecule planar? **(b)** Does it have a nonzero dipole moment? **(c)** Would the bonding in allene be described as delocalized? Explain.

[9.86] The azide ion, N_3^-, is linear with two N—N bonds of equal length, 1.16 Å. **(a)** Draw a Lewis structure for the azide ion. **(b)** With reference to Table 8.5, is the observed N—N bond length consistent with your Lewis structure? **(c)** What hybridization scheme would you expect at each of the nitrogen atoms in N_3^-? **(d)** Show which hybridized and unhybridized orbitals are involved in the formation of σ and π bonds in N_3^-. **(e)** It is often observed that σ bonds that involve an sp hybrid orbital are shorter than those that involve only sp^2 or sp^3 hybrid orbitals. Can you propose a reason for this? Is this observation applicable to the observed bond lengths in N_3^-?

[9.87] In ozone, O_3, the two oxygen atoms on the ends of the molecule are equivalent to one another. **(a)** What is the best choice of hybridization scheme for the atoms of ozone? **(b)** For one of the resonance forms of ozone, which of the orbitals are used to make bonds and which are used to hold nonbonding pairs of electrons? **(c)** Which of the orbitals can be used to delocalize the π electrons? **(d)** How many electrons are delocalized in the π system of ozone?

9.88 Butadiene, C_4H_6, is a planar molecule that has the following carbon—carbon bond lengths:

$$\underset{1.34\ \text{Å}}{H_2C = \!\!=\!\! CH} \underset{1.48\ \text{Å}}{-\!\!\!-\!\!\!-\!\! CH} \underset{1.34\ \text{Å}}{=\!\!\!=\!\! CH_2}$$

(a) Predict the bond angles around each of the carbon atoms, and sketch the molecule. **(b)** Compare the bond lengths to the average bond lengths listed in Table 8.5. Can you explain any differences?

[9.89] The sketches below show the atomic orbital wave functions (with phases) used to construct some of the MOs of a homonuclear diatomic molecule. For each sketch, determine the MO that will result from mixing the atomic orbital wave functions as drawn. Use the same labels for the MOs as in the "Closer Look" box on phases.

(a)   (b)

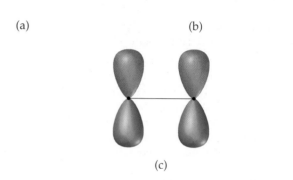

(c)

[9.90] The *cyclopentadienide ion* has the formula $C_5H_5^-$. The ion consists of a regular pentagon of C atoms, each bonded to two C neighbors, with a hydrogen atom bonded to each C atom. All the atoms lie in the same plane. **(a)** Draw a Lewis structure for the ion. According to your structure, do all five C atoms have the same hybridization? Explain. **(b)** Chemists generally view this ion as having sp^2 hybridization at each C atom. Is that view consistent with your answer to part (a)? **(c)** Your Lewis structure should show one nonbonding pair of electrons. Under the assumption of part (b), in what type of orbital must this nonbonding pair reside? **(d)** Are there resonance structures equivalent to the Lewis structure you drew in part (a)? If so, how many? **(e)** The ion is often drawn as a pentagon enclosing a circle. Is this representation consistent with your answer to part (d)? Explain. **(f)** Both benzene and the cyclopentadienide ion are often described as systems containing six π electrons. What do you think is meant by this description?

9.91 Write the electron configuration for the first excited state for N_2—that is, the state with the highest-energy electron moved to the next available energy level. **(a)** Is the nitrogen in its first excited state diamagnetic or paramagnetic? **(b)** Is the N—N bond strength in the first excited state stronger or weaker compared to that in the ground state? Explain.

9.92 Figure 9.47 shows how the magnetic properties of a compound can be measured experimentally. When such measurements are made, the sample is generally covered by an atmosphere of pure nitrogen gas rather than air. Why do you suppose this is done?

9.93 *Azo dyes* are organic dyes that are used for many applications, such as the coloring of fabrics. Many azo dyes are derivatives of the organic substance *azobenzene*, $C_{12}H_{10}N_2$.

A closely related substance is *hydrazobenzene*, $C_{12}H_{12}N_2$. The Lewis structures of these two substances are

Azobenzene   Hydrazobenzene

(Recall the shorthand notation used for benzene.) **(a)** What is the hybridization at the N atom in each of the substances? **(b)** How many unhybridized atomic orbitals are there on the N and the C atoms in each of the substances? **(c)** Predict the N—N—C angles in each of the substances. **(d)** Azobenzene is said to have greater delocalization of its π electrons than hydrazobenzene. Discuss this statement in light of your answers to (a) and (b). **(e)** All the atoms of azobenzene lie in one plane, whereas those of hydrazobenzene do not. Is this observation consistent with the statement in part (d)? **(f)** Azobenzene is an intense red-orange color, whereas hydrazobenzene is nearly colorless. Which molecule would be a better one to use in a solar energy conversion device? (See the "Chemistry Put to Work" box for more information about solar cells.)

[9.94] **(a)** Using only the valence atomic orbitals of a hydrogen atom and a fluorine atom, how many MOs would you expect for the HF molecule? **(b)** How many of the MOs from part (a) would be occupied by electrons? **(c)** Do you think the MO diagram shown in Figure 9.49 could be used to describe the MOs of the HF molecule? Why or why not? **(d)** It turns out that the difference in energies between the valence atomic orbitals of H and F are sufficiently different that we can neglect the interaction of the $1s$ orbital of hydrogen with the 2s orbital of fluorine. The $1s$ orbital of hydrogen will mix only with one $2p$ orbital of fluorine. Draw pictures showing the proper orientation of all three $2p$ orbitals on F interacting with a $1s$ orbital on H. Which of the $2p$ orbitals can actually make a bond with a $1s$ orbital, assuming that the atoms lie on the z-axis? **(e)** In the most accepted picture of HF, all the other atomic orbitals on fluorine move over at the same energy into the molecular orbital energy level diagram for HF. These are called "nonbonding orbitals." Sketch the energy level diagram for HF using this information, and calculate the bond order. (Nonbonding electrons do not contribute to bond order.) **(f)** Look at the Lewis structure for HF. Where are the nonbonding electrons?

[9.95] Carbon monoxide, CO, is isoelectronic to N_2. **(a)** Draw a Lewis structure for CO that satisfies the octet rule. **(b)** Assume that the diagram in Figure 9.49 can be used to describe the MOs of CO. What is the predicted bond order for CO? Is this answer in accord with the Lewis structure you drew in part (a)? **(c)** Experimentally, it is found that the highest-energy electrons in CO reside in a σ-type MO. Is that observation consistent with Figure 9.49? If not, what modification needs to be made to the diagram? How does this modification relate to Figure 9.45? **(d)** Would you expect the π_{2p} MOs of CO to have equal atomic orbital contributions from the C and O atoms? If not, which atom would have the greater contribution?

INTEGRATIVE EXERCISES

9.96 A compound composed of 2.1% H, 29.8% N, and 68.1% O has a molar mass of approximately 50 g/mol. **(a)** What is the molecular formula of the compound? **(b)** What is its Lewis structure if H is bonded to O? **(c)** What is the geometry of the molecule? **(d)** What is the hybridization of the orbitals around the N atom? **(e)** How many σ and how many π bonds are there in the molecule?

9.97 Sulfur tetrafluoride (SF_4) reacts slowly with O_2 to form sulfur tetrafluoride monoxide (OSF_4) according to the following unbalanced reaction:

$$SF_4(g) + O_2(g) \longrightarrow OSF_4(g)$$

The O atom and the four F atoms in OSF_4 are bonded to a central S atom. **(a)** Balance the equation. **(b)** Write a Lewis structure of OSF_4 in which the formal charges of all atoms are zero. **(c)** Use average bond enthalpies (Table 8.4) to estimate the enthalpy of the reaction. Is it endothermic or exothermic? **(d)** Determine the electron-domain geometry of OSF_4, and write two possible molecular geometries for the molecule based on this electron-domain geometry. **(e)** Which of the molecular geometries in part (d) is more likely to be observed for the molecule? Explain.

[9.98] The phosphorus trihalides (PX_3) show the following variation in the bond angle X—P—X: PF_3, 96.3°; PCl_3, 100.3°; PBr_3, 101.0°; PI_3, 102.0°. The trend is generally attributed to the change in the electronegativity of the halogen. **(a)** Assuming that all electron domains are the same size, what value of the X—P—X angle is predicted by the VSEPR model? **(b)** What is the general trend in the X—P—X angle as the electronegativity increases? **(c)** Using the VSEPR model, explain the observed trend in X—P—X angle as the electronegativity of X changes. **(d)** Based on your answer to part (c), predict the structure of $PBrCl_4$.

[9.99] The molecule 2-butene, C_4H_8, can undergo a geometric change called *cis-trans isomerization*:

cis-2-butene   *trans*-2-butene

As discussed in the "Chemistry and Life" box on the chemistry of vision, such transformations can be induced by light and are the key to human vision. **(a)** What is the hybridization at the two central carbon atoms of 2-butene? **(b)** The isomerization occurs by rotation about the central C—C bond. With reference to Figure 9.32, explain why the π bond between the two central carbon atoms is destroyed halfway through the rotation from *cis*- to *trans*-2-butene. **(c)** Based on average bond enthalpies (Table 8.4), how much energy per molecule must be supplied to break the C—C π bond? **(d)** What is the longest wavelength of light that will provide photons of sufficient energy to break the C—C π bond and cause the isomerization? **(e)** Is the wavelength in your answer to part (d) in the visible portion of the electromagnetic spectrum? Comment on the importance of this result for human vision.

9.100 **(a)** Compare the bond enthalpies (Table 8.4) of the carbon–carbon single, double, and triple bonds to deduce an average π-bond contribution to the enthalpy. What fraction of a single bond does this quantity represent? **(b)** Make a similar comparison of nitrogen–nitrogen bonds. What do you observe? **(c)** Write Lewis structures of N_2H_4, N_2H_2, and N_2, and determine the hybridization around nitrogen in each case. **(d)** Propose a reason for the large difference in your observations of parts (a) and (b).

9.101 Use average bond enthalpies (Table 8.4) to estimate ΔH for the atomization of benzene, C_6H_6:

$$C_6H_6(g) \longrightarrow 6\,C(g) + 6\,H(g)$$

Compare the value to that obtained by using ΔH_f° data given in Appendix C and Hess's law. To what do you attribute the large discrepancy in the two values?

9.102 For both atoms and molecules, ionization energies (Section 7.4) are related to the energies of orbitals: The lower the energy of the orbital, the greater the ionization energy. The first ionization energy of a molecule is therefore a measure of the energy of the highest occupied molecular orbital (HOMO). See the "Chemistry Put to Work" box on Orbitals and Energy. The first ionization energies of several diatomic molecules are given in electron-volts in the following table:

Molecule	I_1 (eV)
H_2	15.4
N_2	15.6
O_2	12.1
F_2	15.7

(a) Convert these ionization energies to kJ/mol. **(b)** On the same plot, graph I_1 for the H, N, O, and F atoms (Figure 7.12) and I_1 for the molecules listed. **(c)** Do the ionization energies of the molecules follow the same periodic trends as the ionization energies of the atoms? **(d)** Use molecular orbital energy-level diagrams to explain the trends in the ionization energies of the molecules.

[9.103] Many compounds of the transition-metal elements contain direct bonds between metal atoms. We will assume that the z-axis is defined as the metal–metal bond axis. **(a)** Which of the 3d orbitals (Figure 6.24) can be used to make a σ bond between metal atoms? **(b)** Sketch the σ_{3d} bonding and σ_{3d}^* antibonding MOs. **(c)** With reference to the "Closer Look" box on the phases of orbitals, explain why a node is generated in the σ_{3d}^* MO. **(d)** Sketch the energy-level diagram for the Sc_2 molecule, assuming that only the 3d orbital from part (a) is important. **(e)** What is the bond order in Sc_2?

[9.104] The organic molecules shown below are derivatives of benzene in which additional six-membered rings are "fused" at the edges of the hexagons. The compounds are shown in the usual abbreviated method for organic molecules. **(a)** Determine the empirical formula of benzene and of these three compounds. **(b)** Suppose you are given a sample of one of the compounds. Could combustion analysis be used to determine unambiguously

which of the compounds it is? **(c)** Naphthalene, which is the active ingredient in mothballs, is a white solid. Write a balanced equation for the combustion of naphthalene to $CO_2(g)$ and $H_2O(g)$. **(d)** Using the Lewis structure below for naphthalene and the average bond enthalpies in Table 8.4, estimate the heat of combustion of naphthalene, in kJ/mol. **(e)** Would you expect naphthalene, anthracene, and tetracene to have multiple resonance structures? If so, draw the additional resonance structures for naphthalene. **(f)** Benzene, naphthalene, and anthracene are colorless, but tetracene is orange. What does this imply about the relative HOMO–LUMO energy gaps in these molecules? See the "Chemistry Put to Work" box on Orbitals and Energy.

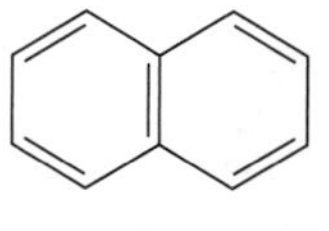

Naphthalene 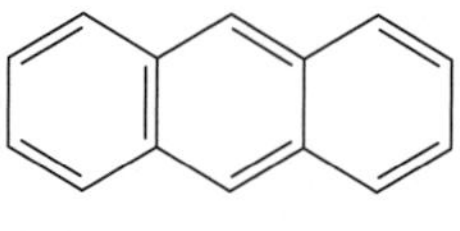   Anthracene

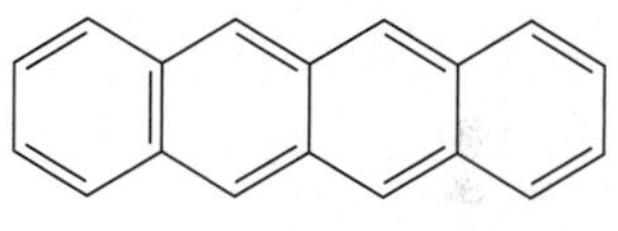

Tetracene

[9.105] Antibonding molecular orbitals can be used to make bonds to other atoms in a molecule. For example, metal atoms can use appropriate d orbitals to overlap with the π_{2p}^* orbitals of the carbon monoxide molecule. This is called d-π backbonding. **(a)** Draw a coordinate axis system in which the y-axis is vertical in the plane of the paper and the x-axis horizontal. Write "M" at the origin to denote a metal atom. **(b)** Now, on the x-axis to the right of M, draw the Lewis structure of a CO molecule, with the carbon nearest the M. The CO bond axis should be on the x-axis. **(c)** Draw the CO π_{2p}^* orbital, with phases (see the Closer Look box on phases) in the plane of the paper. Two lobes should be pointing toward M. **(d)** Now draw the d_{xy} orbital of M, with phases. Can you see how they will overlap with the π_{2p}^* orbital of CO? **(e)** What kind of bond is being made with the orbitals between M and C, σ or π? **(f)** Predict what will happen to the strength of the CO bond in a metal–CO complex compared to CO alone.

[9.106] You can think of the bonding in the Cl_2 molecule in several ways. For example, you can picture the Cl—Cl bond containing two electrons that each come from the 3p orbitals of a Cl atom that are pointing in the appropriate direction. However, you can also think about hybrid orbitals. **(a)** Draw the Lewis structure of the Cl_2 molecule. **(b)** What is the hybridization of each Cl atom? **(c)** What kind of orbital overlap, in this view, makes the Cl—Cl bond? **(d)** Imagine if you could measure the positions of the lone pairs of electrons in Cl_2. How would you distinguish between the atomic orbital and hybrid orbital models of bonding using that knowledge? **(e)** You can also treat Cl_2 using molecular orbital theory to obtain an energy level diagram similar to that for F_2. Design an experiment that could tell you if the MO picture of Cl_2 is the best one, assuming you could easily measure bond lengths, bond energies, and the light absorption properties for any ionized species.

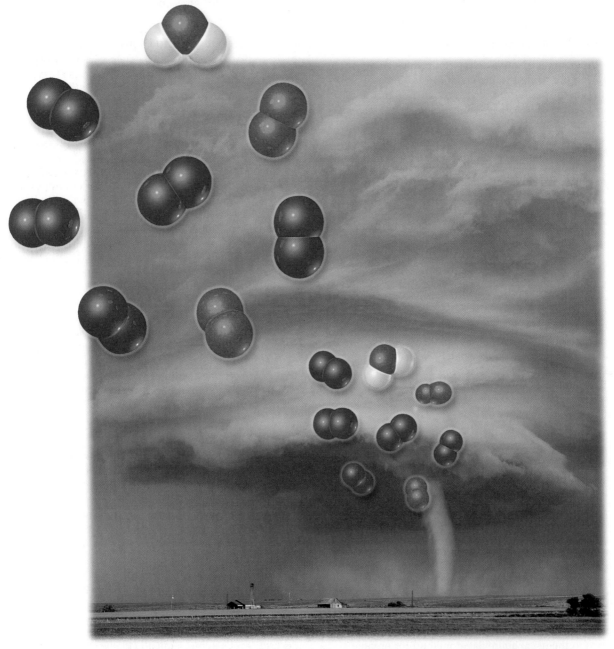

10

C H A P T E R

GASES

A TORNADO IS A VIOLENT rotating column of air characterized by a funnel-shaped cloud.
A tornado can be up to 100 m in diameter with wind speeds approaching 500 km/hr.

WHAT'S AHEAD

IN THE PAST SEVERAL CHAPTERS we have learned about electronic structures of atoms and about how atoms combine to form molecules and ionic substances. In everyday life, however, we do not have direct experiences with atoms. Instead, we encounter matter as collections of enormous numbers of atoms or molecules that make up gases, liquids, and solids. Large collections of atoms and molecules in the atmosphere, for example, are responsible for our weather—the gentle breezes and the gales, the humidity and the rain. Tornados, such as the one shown in the chapter-opening photo, form when moist, warm air at lower elevations converges with cooler, dry air above. The resultant air flows produce winds that can approach speeds up to 500 km/hr (300 mph).

It was John Dalton's interest in the weather that motivated him to study gases and eventually to propose the atomic theory of matter. ∞ (Section 2.1) We now know that the properties of gases, liquids, and solids are readily understood in terms of the behavior of their component atoms, ions, and molecules. In this chapter we will examine the physical properties of gases and consider how we can understand these properties in terms of the behavior of gas molecules. In Chapter 11 we will turn our attention to the physical properties of liquids and solids.

10.1 CHARACTERISTICS OF GASES

In many ways gases are the most easily understood form of matter. Even though different gaseous substances may have very different *chemical* properties, they behave quite similarly as far as their *physical* properties are concerned. For example, we live in an atmosphere composed of a mixture of gases that we refer to as air. Air is a complex mixture of several substances, primarily N_2 (78%) and O_2 (21%), with small amounts of several other gases, including Ar (0.9%). We breathe air to absorb oxygen, O_2, which supports human life. Air also contains nitrogen, N_2, which has very different chemical properties from oxygen, yet this mixture behaves physically as one gaseous material.

Only a few elements exist as gases under ordinary conditions of temperature and pressure: The noble gases (He, Ne, Ar, Kr, and Xe) are all monatomic gases, whereas H_2, N_2, O_2, F_2, and Cl_2 are diatomic gases. Many molecular compounds are also gases. Table 10.1 ▼ lists a few of the more common gaseous compounds. Notice that all of these gases are composed entirely of nonmetallic elements. Furthermore, all have simple molecular formulas and, therefore, low molar masses. Substances that are liquids or solids under ordinary conditions can also exist in the gaseous state, where they are often referred to as **vapors**. The substance H_2O, for example, can exist as liquid water, solid ice, or water vapor.

Gases differ significantly from solids and liquids in several respects. For example, a gas expands spontaneously to fill its container. Consequently, the volume of a gas equals the volume of the container in which it is held. Gases also are highly compressible: When pressure is applied to a gas, its volume readily decreases. Solids and liquids, on the other hand, do not expand to fill their containers, and solids and liquids are not readily compressible.

Gases form homogeneous mixtures with each other regardless of the identities or relative proportions of the component gases. The atmosphere serves as an excellent example. As a further example, when water and gasoline are mixed, the two liquids remain as separate layers. In contrast, the water vapor and gasoline vapors above the liquids form a homogeneous gas mixture.

The characteristic properties of gases arise because the individual molecules are relatively far apart. In the air we breathe, for example, the molecules take up only about 0.1% of the total volume, with the rest being empty space. Thus, each molecule behaves largely as though the others were not present.

TABLE 10.1 ■ Some Common Compounds That Are Gases at Room Temperature		
Formula	**Name**	**Characteristics**
HCN	Hydrogen cyanide	Very toxic, slight odor of bitter almonds
H_2S	Hydrogen sulfide	Very toxic, odor of rotten eggs
CO	Carbon monoxide	Toxic, colorless, odorless
CO_2	Carbon dioxide	Colorless, odorless
CH_4	Methane	Colorless, odorless, flammable
C_2H_4	Ethylene	Colorless, ripens fruit
C_3H_8	Propane	Colorless, odorless, bottled gas
N_2O	Nitrous oxide	Colorless, sweet odor, laughing gas
NO_2	Nitrogen dioxide	Toxic, red-brown, irritating odor
NH_3	Ammonia	Colorless, pungent odor
SO_2	Sulfur dioxide	Colorless, irritating odor

Suppose we have 1.000 mol of an ideal gas at 1.000 atm and 0.00 °C (273.15 K). According to the ideal-gas equation, the volume of the gas is

$$V = \frac{nRT}{P} = \frac{(1.000 \text{ mol})(0.08206 \text{ L-atm/mol-K})(273.15 \text{ K})}{1.000 \text{ atm}} = 22.41 \text{ L}$$

The conditions 0 °C and 1 atm are referred to as the **standard temperature and pressure (STP)**. Many properties of gases are tabulated for these conditions. The volume occupied by one mole of ideal gas at STP, 22.41 L, is known as the *molar volume* of an ideal gas at STP.

GIVE IT SOME THOUGHT

How many molecules are in 22.41 L of an ideal gas at STP?

The ideal-gas equation accounts adequately for the properties of most gases under a wide variety of circumstances. The equation is not exactly correct, however, for any real gas. Thus, the measured volume, V, for given conditions of P, n, and T, might differ from the volume calculated from $PV = nRT$. To illustrate, the measured molar volumes of real gases at STP are compared with the calculated volume of an ideal gas in Figure 10.13▶. While these real gases do not match the ideal gas behavior exactly, the differences are so small that we can ignore them for all but the most accurate work. We will have more to say about the differences between ideal and real gases in Section 10.9.

▼ Figure 10.13 **Comparison of molar volumes at STP.** One mole of an ideal gas at STP occupies a volume of 22.41 L. One mole of various real gases at STP occupies close to this ideal volume.

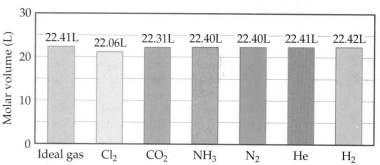

▇ SAMPLE EXERCISE 10.4 | Using the Ideal-Gas Equation

Calcium carbonate, $CaCO_3(s)$, decomposes upon heating to give $CaO(s)$ and $CO_2(g)$. A sample of $CaCO_3$ is decomposed, and the carbon dioxide is collected in a 250-mL flask. After the decomposition is complete, the gas has a pressure of 1.3 atm at a temperature of 31 °C. How many moles of CO_2 gas were generated?

SOLUTION

Analyze: We are given the volume (250 mL), pressure (1.3 atm), and temperature 31 °C of a sample of CO_2 gas and asked to calculate the number of moles of CO_2 in the sample.

Plan: Because we are given V, P, and T, we can solve the ideal-gas equation for the unknown quantity, n.

Solve: In analyzing and solving gas-law problems, it is helpful to tabulate the information given in the problems and then to convert the values to units that are consistent with those for R (0.0821 L-atm/mol-K). In this case the given values are

$$V = 250 \text{ mL} = 0.250 \text{ L}$$
$$P = 1.3 \text{ atm}$$
$$T = 31 \text{ °C} = (31 + 273) \text{ K} = 304 \text{ K}$$

Remember: *Absolute temperature must always be used when the ideal-gas equation is solved.*

We now rearrange the ideal-gas equation (Equation 10.5) to solve for n

$$n = \frac{PV}{RT}$$

$$n = \frac{(1.3 \text{ atm}) (0.250 \text{ L})}{(0.0821 \text{ L-atm/mol-K}) (304 \text{ K})} = 0.013 \text{ mol } CO_2$$

Check: Appropriate units cancel, thus ensuring that we have properly rearranged the ideal-gas equation and have converted to the correct units.

▇ PRACTICE EXERCISE

Tennis balls are usually filled with air or N_2 gas to a pressure above atmospheric pressure to increase their "bounce." If a particular tennis ball has a volume of 144 cm³ and contains 0.33 g of N_2 gas, what is the pressure inside the ball at 24 °C?
Answer: 2.0 atm

In chemistry and throughout your studies of science and math, you may encounter problems that involve several experimentally measured variables as well as several different physical constants. In this chapter we encounter a variety of problems based on the ideal-gas equation, which consists of four experimental quantities—P, V, n, and T—and one constant, R. Depending on the type of problem, we might need to solve for any of the four quantities.

To avoid any difficulty extracting the necessary information from problems when many variables are involved, we suggest you take the following steps as you analyze, plan, and solve such problems:

1. *Tabulate information.* Read the problems carefully to determine which quantity is the unknown and which quantities are given. Every time you encounter a numerical value, jot it down. In many cases, constructing a table of the given information will be useful.

2. *Convert to consistent units.* As you have already seen, we can use several different units to express the same quantity. Make certain that quantities are converted to the proper units by using the correct conversion factors. In using the ideal-gas equation, for example, we usually use the value of R that has units of L-atm/mol-K. If you are given a pressure in torr, you will need to convert it to atmospheres.

3. *If a single equation relates the variables, rearrange the equation to solve for the unknown.* Make certain that you are comfortable using algebra to solve the equation for the desired variable. In the case of the ideal-gas equation the following algebraic rearrangements will all be used at one time or another:

$$P = \frac{nRT}{V}; \quad V = \frac{nRT}{P}; \quad n = \frac{PV}{RT}; \quad T = \frac{PV}{nR}$$

4. *Use dimensional analysis.* Carry the units through your calculation. Use of dimensional analysis enables you to check that you have solved the equation correctly. If the units of the quantities in the equation cancel properly to give the units of the desired variable, you have probably used the equation correctly.

Sometimes you will not be given values for the necessary variables directly. Rather, you will be given the values of other quantities that can be used to determine the needed variables. For example, suppose you are trying to use the ideal-gas equation to calculate the pressure of a gas. You are given the temperature of the gas, but you are not given explicit values for n and V. However, the problem states that "the sample of gas contains 0.15 mol of gas per liter." We can turn this statement into the expression

$$\frac{n}{V} = 0.15 \text{ mol/L}$$

Solving the ideal-gas equation for pressure yields

$$P = \frac{nRT}{V} = \left(\frac{n}{V}\right)RT$$

Thus, we can solve the equation even though we are not given specific values for n and V. We will examine how to use the density and molar mass of a gas in this fashion in Section 10.5.

As we have continuously stressed, the most important thing you can do to become proficient at solving problems is to practice by using practice exercises and assigned exercises at the end of each chapter. By using systematic procedures, such as those described here, you should be able to minimize difficulties in solving problems involving many variables.

Relating the Ideal-Gas Equation and the Gas Laws

The simple gas laws that we discussed in Section 10.3, such as Boyle's law, are special cases of the ideal-gas equation. For example, when the quantity of gas and the temperature are held constant, n and T have fixed values. Therefore, the product nRT is the product of three constants and must itself be a constant.

$$PV = nRT = \text{constant} \quad \text{or} \quad PV = \text{constant} \qquad [10.6]$$

Thus, we have Boyle's law. We see that if n and T are constant, the individual values of P and V can change, but the product PV must remain constant.

We can use Boyle's law to determine how the volume of a gas changes when its pressure changes. For example, if a metal cylinder holds 50.0 L of O_2 gas at 18.5 atm and 21 °C, what volume will the gas occupy if the temperature is maintained at 21 °C while the pressure is reduced to 1.00 atm? Because the product PV is a constant when a gas is held at constant n and T, we know that

$$P_1V_1 = P_2V_2 \qquad [10.7]$$

where P_1 and V_1 are initial values and P_2 and V_2 are final values. Dividing both sides of this equation by P_2 gives the final volume, V_2.

$$V_2 = V_1 \times \frac{P_1}{P_2}$$

Substituting the given quantities into this equation gives

$$V_2 = (50.0 \text{ L})\left(\frac{18.5 \text{ atm}}{1.00 \text{ atm}}\right) = 925 \text{ L}$$

The answer is reasonable because gases expand as their pressures are decreased.

In a similar way we can start with the ideal-gas equation and derive relationships between any other two variables, V and T (Charles's law), n and V (Avogadro's law), or P and T. Sample Exercise 10.5 illustrates how these relationships can be derived and used.

■ SAMPLE EXERCISE 10.5 | Calculating the Effect of Temperature Changes on Pressure

The gas pressure in an aerosol can is 1.5 atm at 25 °C. Assuming that the gas inside obeys the ideal-gas equation, what would the pressure be if the can were heated to 450 °C?

SOLUTION

Analyze: We are given the initial pressure (1.5 atm) and temperature (25 °C) of the gas and asked for the pressure at a higher temperature (450 °C).

Plan: The volume and number of moles of gas do not change, so we must use a relationship connecting pressure and temperature. Converting temperature to the Kelvin scale and tabulating the given information, we have

	P	T
INITIAL	1.5 atm	298 K
FINAL	P_2	723 K

Solve: To determine how P and T are related, we start with the ideal-gas equation and isolate the quantities that do not change (n, V, and R) on one side and the variables (P and T) on the other side.

$$\frac{P}{T} = \frac{nR}{V} = \text{constant}$$

Because the quotient P/T is a constant, we can write

$$\frac{P_1}{T_1} = \frac{P_2}{T_2}$$

(where the subscripts 1 and 2 represent the initial and final states, respectively). Rearranging to solve for P_2 and substituting the given data give

$$P_2 = P_1 \times \frac{T_2}{T_1}$$

$$P_2 = (1.5 \text{ atm})\left(\frac{723 \text{ K}}{298 \text{ K}}\right) = 3.6 \text{ atm}$$

Check: This answer is intuitively reasonable—increasing the temperature of a gas increases its pressure.

Comment: It is evident from this example why aerosol cans carry a warning not to incinerate.

■ PRACTICE EXERCISE
A large natural-gas storage tank is arranged so that the pressure is maintained at 2.20 atm. On a cold day in December when the temperature is −15 °C (4 °F), the volume of gas in the tank is $3.25 \times 10^3 \text{ m}^3$. What is the volume of the same quantity of gas on a warm July day when the temperature is 31 °C (88 °F)?
Answer: $3.83 \times 10^3 \text{ m}^3$

We are often faced with the situation in which P, V, and T all change for a fixed number of moles of gas. Because n is constant under these circumstances, the ideal-gas equation gives

$$\frac{PV}{T} = nR = \text{constant}$$

If we represent the initial and final conditions of pressure, temperature, and volume by subscripts 1 and 2, respectively, we can write

$$\frac{P_1 V_1}{T_1} = \frac{P_2 V_2}{T_2} \qquad\qquad [10.8]$$

This equation is often called the *combined gas law*.

■ **SAMPLE EXERCISE 10.6** | **Calculating the Effect of Changing *P* and *T* on the Volume of a Gas**

An inflated balloon has a volume of 6.0 L at sea level (1.0 atm) and is allowed to ascend in altitude until the pressure is 0.45 atm. During ascent the temperature of the gas falls from 22 °C to −21 °C. Calculate the volume of the balloon at its final altitude.

SOLUTION

Analyze: We need to determine a new volume for a gas sample in a situation where both pressure and temperature change.

Plan: Let's again proceed by converting temperature to the Kelvin scale and tabulating the given information.

	P	*V*	*T*
INITIAL	1.0 atm	6.0 L	295 K
FINAL	0.45 atm	V_2	252 K

Because *n* is constant, we can use Equation 10.8.

Solve: Rearranging Equation 10.8 to solve for V_2 gives

$$V_2 = V_1 \times \frac{P_1}{P_2} \times \frac{T_2}{T_1} = (6.0 \text{ L}) \left(\frac{1.0 \text{ atm}}{0.45 \text{ atm}} \right) \left(\frac{252 \text{ K}}{295 \text{ K}} \right) = 11 \text{ L}$$

Check: The result appears reasonable. Notice that the calculation involves multiplying the initial volume by a ratio of pressures and a ratio of temperatures. Intuitively, we expect that decreasing pressure will cause the volume to increase. Similarly, decreasing temperature should cause the volume to decrease. Note that the difference in pressures is more dramatic than the difference in temperatures. Thus, we should expect the effect of the pressure change to predominate in determining the final volume, as it does.

■ **PRACTICE EXERCISE**

A 0.50-mol sample of oxygen gas is confined at 0 °C in a cylinder with a movable piston, such as that shown in Figure 10.12. The gas has an initial pressure of 1.0 atm. The piston then compresses the gas so that its final volume is half the initial volume. The final pressure of the gas is 2.2 atm. What is the final temperature of the gas in degrees Celsius?
Answer: 27 °C

10.5 FURTHER APPLICATIONS OF THE IDEAL-GAS EQUATION

The ideal-gas equation can be used to determine many relationships involving the physical properties of gases. In this section we use it first to define the relationship between the density of a gas and its molar mass, and then to calculate the volumes of gases formed or consumed in chemical reactions.

Gas Densities and Molar Mass

The ideal-gas equation allows us to calculate gas density from the molar mass, pressure, and temperature of the gas. Recall that density has the units of mass per unit volume ($d = m/V$). ∞ (Section 1.4) We can arrange the gas equation to obtain similar units, moles per unit volume, n/V:

$$\frac{n}{V} = \frac{P}{RT}$$

If we multiply both sides of this equation by the molar mass, $\mathcal{M}$, which is the number of grams in one mole of a substance, we obtain the following relationship:

$$\frac{n\mathcal{M}}{V} = \frac{P\mathcal{M}}{RT}$$

[10.9]

The product of the quantities n/V and $\mathcal{M}$ equals the density in g/L, as seen from their units:

$$\frac{\text{moles}}{\text{liter}} \times \frac{\text{grams}}{\text{mole}} = \frac{\text{grams}}{\text{liter}}$$

Thus, the density, d, of the gas is given by the expression on the right in Equation 10.9:

$$d = \frac{P\mathcal{M}}{RT} \qquad\qquad [10.10]$$

From Equation 10.10 we see that the density of a gas depends on its pressure, molar mass, and temperature. The higher the molar mass and pressure, the more dense the gas. The higher the temperature, the less dense the gas. Although gases form homogeneous mixtures regardless of their identities, a less dense gas will lie above a more dense gas in the absence of mixing. For example, CO_2 has a higher molar mass than N_2 or O_2 and is therefore more dense than air. When CO_2 is released from a CO_2 fire extinguisher, as shown in Figure 10.14▶, it blankets a fire, preventing O_2 from reaching the combustible material. The fact that a hotter gas is less dense than a cooler one explains why hot air rises. The difference between the densities of hot and cold air is responsible for the lift of hot-air balloons. It is also responsible for many phenomena in weather, such as the formation of large thunderhead clouds during thunderstorms.

▲ Figure 10.14 A CO_2 fire extinguisher. The CO_2 gas from a fire extinguisher is denser than air. The CO_2 cools significantly as it emerges from the tank. Water vapor in the air is condensed by the cool CO_2 gas and forms a white fog accompanying the colorless CO_2.

▲ GIVE IT SOME THOUGHT

Is water vapor more or less dense than N_2 under the same conditions of temperature and pressure?

■■ SAMPLE EXERCISE 10.7 | Calculating Gas Density

What is the density of carbon tetrachloride vapor at 714 torr and 125 °C?

SOLUTION

Analyze: We are asked to calculate the density of a gas given its name, its pressure, and its temperature. From the name we can write the chemical formula of the substance and determine its molar mass.

Plan: We can use Equation 10.10 to calculate the density. Before we can use that equation, however, we need to convert the given quantities to the appropriate units. We must convert temperature to the Kelvin scale and pressure to atmospheres. We must also calculate the molar mass of CCl_4.

Solve: The temperature on the Kelvin scale is $125 + 273 = 398$ K.
The pressure in atmospheres is (714 torr)(1 atm/760 torr) = 0.939 atm.
The molar mass of CCl_4 is $12.0 + (4)(35.5) = 154.0$ g/mol.
Using these quantities along with Equation 10.10, we have

$$d = \frac{(0.939 \text{ atm})(154.0 \text{ g/mol})}{(0.0821 \text{ L-atm/mol-K})(398 \text{ K})} = 4.43 \text{ g/L}$$

Check: If we divide the molar mass (g/mol) by the density (g/L), we end up with L/mol. The numerical value is roughly $154/4.4 = 35$. That is in the right ballpark for the molar volume of a gas heated to 125 °C at near atmospheric pressure, so our answer is reasonable.

■■ PRACTICE EXERCISE

The mean molar mass of the atmosphere at the surface of Titan, Saturn's largest moon, is 28.6 g/mol. The surface temperature is 95 K, and the pressure is 1.6 atm. Assuming ideal behavior, calculate the density of Titan's atmosphere.
Answer: 5.9 g/L

Equation 10.10 can be rearranged to solve for the molar mass of a gas:

$$\mathcal{M} = \frac{dRT}{P} \qquad [10.11]$$

Thus, we can use the experimentally measured density of a gas to determine the molar mass of the gas molecules, as shown in Sample Exercise 10.8.

■ **SAMPLE EXERCISE 10.8** | **Calculating the Molar Mass of a Gas**

A series of measurements are made to determine the molar mass of an unknown gas. First, a large flask is evacuated and found to weigh 134.567 g. It is then filled with the gas to a pressure of 735 torr at 31 °C and reweighed. Its mass is now 137.456 g. Finally, the flask is filled with water at 31 °C and found to weigh 1067.9 g. (The density of the water at this temperature is 0.997 g/mL.) Assume that the ideal-gas equation applies, and calculate the molar mass of the unknown gas.

SOLUTION

Analyze: We are given the temperature (31 °C) and pressure (735 torr) for a gas, together with information to determine its volume and mass, and we are asked to calculate its molar mass.

Plan: We need to use the mass information given to calculate the volume of the container and the mass of the gas within it. From this we calculate the gas density and then apply Equation 10.11 to calculate the molar mass of the gas.

Solve: The mass of the gas is the difference between the mass of the flask filled with gas and that of the empty (evacuated) flask:

137.456 g − 134.567 g = 2.889 g

The volume of the gas equals the volume of water that the flask can hold. The volume of water is calculated from its mass and density. The mass of the water is the difference between the masses of the full and empty flask:

1067.9 g − 134.567 g = 933.3 g

By rearranging the equation for density ($d = m/V$), we have

$$V = \frac{m}{d} = \frac{(933.3 \text{ g})}{(0.997 \text{ g/mL})} = 936 \text{ mL} = 0.936 \text{ L}$$

Knowing the mass of the gas (2.889 g) and its volume (936 mL), we can calculate the density of the gas:

2.889 g/0.936 L = 3.09 g/L

After converting pressure to atmospheres and temperature to kelvins, we can use Equation 10.11 to calculate the molar mass:

$$\mathcal{M} = \frac{dRT}{P}$$

$$= \frac{(3.09 \text{ g/L})(0.0821 \text{ L-atm/mol-K})(304 \text{ K})}{(735/760) \text{ atm}}$$

$$= 79.7 \text{ g/mol}$$

Check: The units work out appropriately, and the value of molar mass obtained is reasonable for a substance that is gaseous near room temperature.

■ **PRACTICE EXERCISE**

Calculate the average molar mass of dry air if it has a density of 1.17 g/L at 21 °C and 740.0 torr.
Answer: 29.0 g/mol

Volumes of Gases in Chemical Reactions

We are often concerned with knowing the identity of a gas involved as a reactant or product in a chemical reaction, as well as its quantity. Thus, it is useful to be able to calculate the volumes of gases consumed or produced in reactions. Such calculations are based on the use of the mole concept together with balanced chemical equations. ∞ (Section 3.6) We have seen that the coefficients in balanced chemical equations tell us the relative amounts (in moles) of reactants and products in a reaction. The ideal gas equation relates the number of moles of a gas, to P, V, and T.

Chemistry Put to Work   GAS PIPELINES

Most people are quite unaware of the vast network of underground pipelines that undergirds the developed world. Pipelines are used to move massive quantities of liquids and gases over considerable distances. For example, pipelines move natural gas (methane) from huge natural-gas fields in Siberia to Western Europe. Natural gas from Algeria is moved to Italy through a pipeline 120 cm in diameter and 2500 km in length that stretches across the Mediterranean Sea at depths up to 600 m. In the United States the pipeline systems consist of trunk lines, large-diameter pipes for long-distance transport, with branch lines of lower diameter and lower pressure for local transport to and from the trunk lines.

Essentially all substances that are gases at STP are transported commercially by pipeline, including ammonia, carbon dioxide, carbon monoxide, chlorine, ethane, helium, hydrogen, and methane. The largest volume transport by far, though, is natural gas. (Figure 10.15 ►) The methane-rich gas from oil and gas wells is processed to remove particulates, water, and various gaseous impurities such as hydrogen sulfide and carbon dioxide. The gas is then compressed to pressures ranging from 3.5 MPa (35 atm) to 10 MPa (100 atm), depending on the age and diameter of the pipe. The long-distance pipelines are about 40 cm in diameter and made of steel. Large compressor stations along the pipeline, spaced at 50- to 100-mile intervals, maintain pressure.

Recall from Figure 5.24 that natural gas is a major source of energy for the United States. To meet this demand, methane must be transported from source wells throughout the United

▲ Figure 10.15 **A natural gas pipeline junction.**

States and Canada to all parts of the nation. The total length of pipeline for natural-gas transport in the United States is about 6×10^5 km, and growing. The United States is divided into seven regions. The total deliverability of natural gas to the seven regions exceeds 2.7×10^{12} L (measured at STP), which is almost 100 billion cubic feet per day! The volume of the pipelines themselves would be entirely inadequate for managing the enormous quantities of natural gas that are placed into and taken out of the system on a continuing basis. For this reason, underground storage facilities, such as salt caverns and other natural formations, are employed to hold large quantities of gas.

Related Exercise: 10.117

■ SAMPLE EXERCISE 10.9 | Relating the Volume of a Gas to the Amount of Another Substance in a Reaction

The safety air bags in automobiles are inflated by nitrogen gas generated by the rapid decomposition of sodium azide, NaN_3:

$$2\,NaN_3(s) \longrightarrow 2\,Na(s) + 3\,N_2(g)$$

If an air bag has a volume of 36 L and is to be filled with nitrogen gas at a pressure of 1.15 atm at a temperature of 26.0 °C, how many grams of NaN_3 must be decomposed?

SOLUTION

Analyze: This is a multistep problem. We are given the volume, pressure, and temperature of the N_2 gas and the chemical equation for the reaction by which the N_2 is generated. We must use this information to calculate the number of grams of NaN_3 needed to obtain the necessary N_2.

Plan: We need to use the gas data (P, V, and T) and the ideal-gas equation to calculate the number of moles of N_2 gas that should be formed for the air bag to operate correctly. We can then use the balanced equation to determine the number of moles of NaN_3. Finally, we can convert the moles of NaN_3 to grams.

```
Gas data  →  mol N₂  →  mol NaN₃  →  g NaN₃
```

Solve: The number of moles of N_2 is determined using the ideal-gas equation:

$$n = \frac{PV}{RT} = \frac{(1.15\ \text{atm})(36\ \text{L})}{(0.0821\ \text{L-atm/mol-K})(299\ \text{K})} = 1.7\ \text{mol}\ N_2$$

From here we use the coefficients in the balanced equation to calculate the number of moles of NaN_3.

$$(1.7\ \text{mol}\ N_2)\left(\frac{2\ \text{mol}\ NaN_3}{3\ \text{mol}\ N_2}\right) = 1.1\ \text{mol}\ NaN_3$$

Finally, using the molar mass of NaN_3, we convert moles of NaN_3 to grams:

$$(1.1\ \text{mol}\ NaN_3)\left(\frac{65.0\ \text{g}\ NaN_3}{1\ \text{mol}\ NaN_3}\right) = 72\ \text{g}\ NaN_3$$

Check: The best way to check our approach is to make sure the units cancel properly at each step in the calculation, leaving us with the correct units in the answer, g NaN_3.

■ **PRACTICE EXERCISE**

In the first step in the industrial process for making nitric acid, ammonia reacts with oxygen in the presence of a suitable catalyst to form nitric oxide and water vapor:

$$4\,NH_3(g) + 5\,O_2(g) \longrightarrow 4\,NO(g) + 6\,H_2O(g)$$

How many liters of $NH_3(g)$ at 850 °C and 5.00 atm are required to react with 1.00 mol of $O_2(g)$ in this reaction?
Answer: 14.8 L

10.6 GAS MIXTURES AND PARTIAL PRESSURES

Thus far we have considered mainly the behavior of pure gases—those that consist of only one substance in the gaseous state. How do we deal with gases composed of a mixture of two or more different substances? While studying the properties of air, John Dalton (Section 2.1) made an important observation: The *total pressure of a mixture of gases equals the sum of the pressures that each would exert if it were present alone*. The pressure exerted by a particular component of a mixture of gases is called the **partial pressure** of that gas. Dalton's observation is known as **Dalton's law of partial pressures**.

▲ **GIVE IT SOME THOUGHT**

How is the pressure exerted by N_2 gas affected when some O_2 is introduced into a container if the temperature and volume remain constant?

If we let P_t be the total pressure of a mixture of gases and P_1, P_2, P_3, and so forth be the partial pressures of the individual gases, we can write Dalton's law as follows:

$$P_t = P_1 + P_2 + P_3 + \cdots \qquad [10.12]$$

This equation implies that each gas in the mixture behaves independently of the others, as we can see by the following analysis. Let n_1, n_2, n_3, and so forth be the number of moles of each of the gases in the mixture and n_t be the total number of moles of gas ($n_t = n_1 + n_2 + n_3 + \cdots$).

If each of the gases obeys the ideal-gas equation, we can write

$$P_1 = n_1\!\left(\frac{RT}{V}\right); \quad P_2 = n_2\!\left(\frac{RT}{V}\right); \quad P_3 = n_3\!\left(\frac{RT}{V}\right); \quad \text{and so forth}$$

All the gases in the mixture are at the same temperature and occupy the same volume. Therefore, by substituting into Equation 10.12, we obtain

$$P_t = (n_1 + n_2 + n_3 + \cdots)\frac{RT}{V} = n_t\!\left(\frac{RT}{V}\right) \qquad [10.13]$$

That is, at constant temperature and constant volume the total pressure is determined by the total number of moles of gas present, whether that total represents just one substance or a mixture.

▌▌▌ SAMPLE EXERCISE 10.10 | Applying Dalton's Law of Partial Pressures

A gaseous mixture made from 6.00 g O_2 and 9.00 g CH_4 is placed in a 15.0-L vessel at 0 °C. What is the partial pressure of each gas, and what is the total pressure in the vessel?

SOLUTION

Analyze: We need to calculate the pressure for two different gases in the same volume and at the same temperature.

Plan: Because each gas behaves independently, we can use the ideal-gas equation to calculate the pressure that each would exert if the other were not present. The total pressure is the sum of these two partial pressures.

Solve: We must first convert the mass of each gas to moles:

$$n_{O_2} = (6.00 \text{ g } O_2)\left(\frac{1 \text{ mol } O_2}{32.0 \text{ g } O_2}\right) = 0.188 \text{ mol } O_2$$

$$n_{CH_4} = (9.00 \text{ g } CH_4)\left(\frac{1 \text{ mol } CH_4}{16.0 \text{ g } CH_4}\right) = 0.563 \text{ mol } CH_4$$

We can now use the ideal-gas equation to calculate the partial pressure of each gas:

$$P_{O_2} = \frac{n_{O_2} RT}{V} = \frac{(0.188 \text{ mol})(0.0821 \text{ L-atm/mol-K})(273 \text{ K})}{15.0 \text{ L}} = 0.281 \text{ atm}$$

$$P_{CH_4} = \frac{n_{CH_4} RT}{V} = \frac{(0.563 \text{ mol})(0.0821 \text{ L-atm/mol-K})(273 \text{ K})}{15.0 \text{ L}} = 0.841 \text{ atm}$$

According to Dalton's law (Equation 10.12), the total pressure in the vessel is the sum of the partial pressures:

$$P_t = P_{O_2} + P_{CH_4} = 0.281 \text{ atm} + 0.841 \text{ atm} = 1.122 \text{ atm}$$

Check: Performing rough estimates is good practice, even when you may not feel that you need to do it to check an answer. In this case a pressure of roughly 1 atm seems right for a mixture of about 0.2 mol O_2 (that is, 6/32) and a bit more than 0.5 mol CH_4 (that is, 9/16), together in a 15-L volume, because one mole of an ideal gas at 1 atm pressure and 0 °C occupies about 22 L.

▌▌▌ PRACTICE EXERCISE

What is the total pressure exerted by a mixture of 2.00 g of H_2 and 8.00 g of N_2 at 273 K in a 10.0-L vessel?
Answer: 2.86 atm

Partial Pressures and Mole Fractions

Because each gas in a mixture behaves independently, we can relate the amount of a given gas in a mixture to its partial pressure. For an ideal gas, $P = nRT/V$ and so we can write

$$\frac{P_1}{P_t} = \frac{n_1 RT/V}{n_t RT/V} = \frac{n_1}{n_t} \qquad [10.14]$$

The ratio n_1/n_t is called the mole fraction of gas 1, which we denote X_1. The **mole fraction**, X, is a dimensionless number that expresses the ratio of the number of moles of one component to the total number of moles in the mixture. We can rearrange Equation 10.14 to give

$$P_1 = \left(\frac{n_1}{n_t}\right)P_t = X_1 P_t \qquad [10.15]$$

Thus, the partial pressure of a gas in a mixture is its mole fraction times the total pressure.

The mole fraction of N_2 in air is 0.78 (that is, 78% of the molecules in air are N_2). If the total barometric pressure is 760 torr, then the partial pressure of N_2 is

$$P_{N_2} = (0.78)(760 \text{ torr}) = 590 \text{ torr}$$

This result makes intuitive sense: Because N_2 makes up 78% of the mixture, it contributes 78% of the total pressure.

■■ SAMPLE EXERCISE 10.11 | Relating Mole Fractions and Partial Pessures

A study of the effects of certain gases on plant growth requires a synthetic atmosphere composed of 1.5 mol percent CO_2, 18.0 mol percent O_2, and 80.5 mol percent Ar. **(a)** Calculate the partial pressure of O_2 in the mixture if the total pressure of the atmosphere is to be 745 torr. **(b)** If this atmosphere is to be held in a 121-L space at 295 K, how many moles of O_2 are needed?

SOLUTION

Analyze: **(a)** We first need to calculate the partial pressure of O_2 given its mole percentage and the total pressure of the mixture. **(b)** We need to calculate the number of moles of O_2 in the mixture given its volume (121 L), temperature (745 torr), and partial pressure (from part (a)).

Plan: **(a)** We will calculate the partial pressures using Equation 10.15. **(b)** We will then use P_{O_2}, V, and T together with the ideal-gas equation to calculate the number of moles of O_2, n_{O_2}.

Solve: **(a)** The mole percent is just the mole fraction times 100. Therefore, the mole fraction of O_2 is 0.180. Using Equation 10.15, we have

$$P_{O_2} = (0.180)(745 \text{ torr}) = 134 \text{ torr}$$

(b) Tabulating the given variables and changing them to appropriate units, we have

$$P_{O_2} = (134 \text{ torr})\left(\frac{1 \text{ atm}}{760 \text{ torr}}\right) = 0.176 \text{ atm}$$

$$V = 121 \text{ L}$$

$$n_{O_2} = ?$$

$$R = 0.0821 \frac{\text{L-atm}}{\text{mol-K}}$$

$$T = 295 \text{ K}$$

Solving the ideal-gas equation for n_{O_2}, we have

$$n_{O_2} = P_{O_2}\left(\frac{V}{RT}\right)$$

$$= (0.176 \text{ atm})\frac{121 \text{ L}}{(0.0821 \text{ L-atm/mol-K})(295 \text{ K})} = 0.879 \text{ mol}$$

Check: The units check out satisfactorily, and the answer seems to be the right order of magnitude.

■■ PRACTICE EXERCISE

From data gathered by *Voyager 1*, scientists have estimated the composition of the atmosphere of Titan, Saturn's largest moon. The total pressure on the surface of Titan is 1220 torr. The atmosphere consists of 82 mol percent N_2, 12 mol percent Ar, and 6.0 mol percent CH_4. Calculate the partial pressure of each of these gases in Titan's atmosphere.
Answer: 1.0×10^3 torr N_2, 1.5×10^2 torr Ar, and 73 torr CH_4

Collecting Gases over Water

An experiment that is often encountered in general chemistry laboratories involves determining the number of moles of gas collected from a chemical reaction. Sometimes this gas is collected over water. For example, solid potassium chlorate, $KClO_3$, can be decomposed by heating it in a test tube in an arrangement such as that shown in Figure 10.16 ▶. The balanced equation for the reaction is

$$2 \text{ KClO}_3(s) \longrightarrow 2 \text{ KCl}(s) + 3 \text{ O}_2(g) \qquad [10.16]$$

The oxygen gas is collected in a bottle that is initially filled with water and then inverted in a water pan.

The volume of gas collected is measured by raising or lowering the bottle as necessary until the water levels inside and outside the bottle are the same. When this condition is met, the pressure inside the bottle is equal to the atmospheric pressure outside. The total pressure inside is the sum of the pressure of gas collected and the pressure of water vapor in equilibrium with liquid water.

$$P_{\text{total}} = P_{\text{gas}} + P_{\text{H}_2\text{O}} \qquad [10.17]$$

The pressure exerted by water vapor, $P_{\text{H}_2\text{O}}$, at various temperatures is listed in Appendix B.

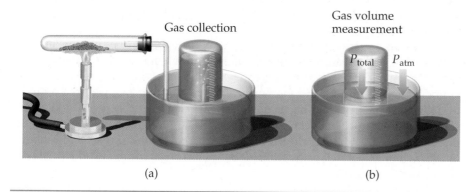

Gas collection

Gas volume measurement

P_total P_atm

(a)   (b)

◀ Figure 10.16 **Collecting a water-insoluble gas over water.** (a) A solid is heated, releasing a gas, which is bubbled through water into a collection bottle. (b) When the gas has been collected, the bottle is raised or lowered so that the water levels inside and outside the bottle are equal. The total pressure of the gases inside the bottle is then equal to the atmospheric pressure.

■■■ **SAMPLE EXERCISE 10.12** | **Calculating the Amount of Gas Collected over Water**

A sample of $KClO_3$ is partially decomposed (Equation 10.16), producing O_2 gas that is collected over water as in Figure 10.16. The volume of gas collected is 0.250 L at 26 °C and 765 torr total pressure. **(a)** How many moles of O_2 are collected? **(b)** How many grams of $KClO_3$ were decomposed?

SOLUTION

(a) Analyze: We need to calculate the number of moles of O_2 gas in a container that also contains water vapor.

Plan: If we tabulate the information presented, we will see that values are given for V and T. To use the ideal-gas equation to calculate the unknown, n_{O_2}, we also must know the partial pressure of O_2 in the system. We can calculate the partial pressure of O_2 from the total pressure (765 torr) and the vapor pressure of water.

Solve: The partial pressure of the O_2 gas is the difference between the total pressure, 765 torr, and the pressure of the water vapor at 26 °C, 25 torr (Appendix B):

$$P_{O_2} = 765 \text{ torr} - 25 \text{ torr} = 740 \text{ torr}$$

We can use the ideal-gas equation to calculate the number of moles of O_2:

$$n_{O_2} = \frac{P_{O_2} V}{RT} = \frac{(740 \text{ torr})(1 \text{ atm}/760 \text{ torr})(0.250 \text{ L})}{(0.0821 \text{ L-atm/mol-K})(299 \text{ K})} = 9.92 \times 10^{-3} \text{ mol } O_2$$

(b) Analyze: We now need to calculate the number of moles of reactant $KClO_3$ decomposed.

Plan: We can use the number of moles of O_2 formed and the balanced chemical equation to determine the number of moles of $KClO_3$ decomposed, which we can then convert to grams of $KClO_3$.

Solve: From Equation 10.16, we have 2 mol $KClO_3 \simeq 3$ mol O_2. The molar mass of $KClO_3$ is 122.6 g/mol. Thus, we can convert the moles of O_2 that we found in part (a) to moles of $KClO_3$ and then to grams of $KClO_3$:

$$(9.92 \times 10^{-3} \text{ mol } O_2)\left(\frac{2 \text{ mol } KClO_3}{3 \text{ mol } O_2}\right)\left(\frac{122.6 \text{ g } KClO_3}{1 \text{ mol } KClO_3}\right) = 0.811 \text{ g } KClO_3$$

Check: As always, we make sure that the units cancel appropriately in the calculations. In addition, the numbers of moles of O_2 and $KClO_3$ seem reasonable, given the small volume of gas collected.

Comment: Many chemical compounds that react with water and water vapor would be degraded by exposure to wet gas. Thus, in research laboratories gases are often dried by passing wet gas over a substance that absorbs water (a *desiccant*), such as calcium sulfate, $CaSO_4$. Calcium sulfate crystals are sold as a desiccant under the trade name Drierite™.

■■■ **PRACTICE EXERCISE**

Ammonium nitrite, NH_4NO_2, decomposes upon heating to form N_2 gas:

$$NH_4NO_2(s) \longrightarrow N_2(g) + 2 H_2O(l)$$

When a sample of NH_4NO_2 is decomposed in a test tube, as in Figure 10.16, 511 mL of N_2 gas is collected over water at 26 °C and 745 torr total pressure. How many grams of NH_4NO_2 were decomposed?
Answer: 1.26 g

10.7 KINETIC-MOLECULAR THEORY

The ideal-gas equation describes *how* gases behave, but it does not explain *why* they behave as they do. Why does a gas expand when heated at constant pressure? Or, why does its pressure increase when the gas is compressed at constant temperature? To understand the physical properties of gases, we need a model that helps us picture what happens to gas particles as experimental conditions such as pressure or temperature change. Such a model, known as the **kinetic-molecular theory**, was developed over a period of about 100 years, culminating in 1857 when Rudolf Clausius (1822–1888) published a complete and satisfactory form of the theory.

The kinetic-molecular theory (the theory of moving molecules) is summarized by the following statements:

1. Gases consist of large numbers of molecules that are in continuous, random motion. (The word *molecule* is used here to designate the smallest particle of any gas; some gases, such as the noble gases, consist of individual atoms.)

2. The combined volume of all the molecules of the gas is negligible relative to the total volume in which the gas is contained.

3. Attractive and repulsive forces between gas molecules are negligible.

4. Energy can be transferred between molecules during collisions, but the *average* kinetic energy of the molecules does not change with time, as long as the temperature of the gas remains constant. In other words, the collisions are perfectly elastic.

5. The average kinetic energy of the molecules is proportional to the absolute temperature. At any given temperature the molecules of all gases have the same average kinetic energy.

The kinetic-molecular theory explains both pressure and temperature at the molecular level. The pressure of a gas is caused by collisions of the molecules with the walls of the container, as shown in Figure 10.17 ◀. The magnitude of the pressure is determined by both how often and how forcefully the molecules strike the walls.

The absolute temperature of a gas is a measure of the *average* kinetic energy of its molecules. If two different gases are at the same temperature, their molecules have the same average kinetic energy (statement 5 of the kinetic-molecular theory). If the absolute temperature of a gas is doubled, the average kinetic energy of its molecules doubles. Thus, molecular motion increases with increasing temperature.

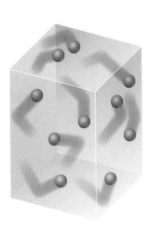

▲ Figure 10.17 **The molecular origin of gas pressure.** The pressure exerted by a gas is caused by collisions of the gas molecules with the walls of their container.

GIVE IT SOME THOUGHT

Consider three samples of gas: HCl at 298 K, H_2 at 298 K, and O_2 at 350 K. Compare the average kinetic energies of the molecules in the three samples.

Distributions of Molecular Speed

Although the molecules in a sample of gas have an *average* kinetic energy and hence an average speed, the individual molecules move at varying speeds. The moving molecules collide frequently with other molecules. Momentum is conserved in each collision, but one of the colliding molecules might be deflected off at high speed while the other is nearly stopped. The result is that the molecules at any instant have a wide range of speeds. Figure 10.18 ▶ illustrates the distribution of molecular speeds for nitrogen gas at 0 °C (blue line) and at 100 °C (red line). The curve shows us the fraction of molecules moving at each speed. At higher temperatures, a larger fraction of molecules moves at greater speeds; the distribution curve has shifted to the right toward higher speeds and hence toward higher average kinetic energy. The peak of each curve represents the most probable speed (the speed of the largest number of molecules). Notice that the blue curve (0 °C) has a peak at about 4×10^2 m/s, whereas the red curve (100 °C) has a peak at a higher speed, about 5×10^2 m/s.

Figure 10.18 also shows the value of the **root-mean-square (rms) speed**, u, of the molecules at each temperature. This quantity is the speed of a molecule possessing average kinetic energy. The rms speed is not quite the same as the average (mean) speed. The difference between the two, however, is small.* Notice that the rms speed is higher at 100 °C than at 0 °C. Notice also that the distribution curve broadens as we go to a higher temperature.

The rms speed is important because the average kinetic energy of the gas molecules in a sample, ε, is related directly to u^2:

$$\varepsilon = \tfrac{1}{2} mu^2 \qquad [10.18]$$

where m is the mass of an individual molecule. Mass does not change with temperature. Thus, the increase in the average kinetic energy as the temperature increases implies that the rms speed (and also the average speed) of molecules likewise increases as temperature increases.

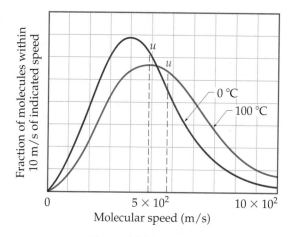

▲ Figure 10.18 **The effect of temperature on molecular speeds.** Distribution of molecular speeds for nitrogen at 0 °C (blue line) and 100 °C (red line). Increasing temperature increases both the most probable speed (curve maximum) and the rms speed, u, which is indicated by the vertical dashed line.

GIVE IT SOME THOUGHT

Consider three samples of gas all at 298 K: HCl, H_2, and O_2. List the molecules in order of increasing average speed.

Application to the Gas Laws

The empirical observations of gas properties as expressed by the various gas laws are readily understood in terms of the kinetic-molecular theory. The following examples illustrate this point:

1. *Effect of a volume increase at constant temperature:* A constant temperature means that the average kinetic energy of the gas molecules remains unchanged. This in turn means that the rms speed of the molecules, u, is unchanged. If the volume is increased, however, the molecules must move a longer distance between collisions. Consequently, there are fewer collisions per unit time with the container walls, and pressure decreases. Thus, the model accounts in a simple way for Boyle's law.

2. *Effect of a temperature increase at constant volume:* An increase in temperature means an increase in the average kinetic energy of the molecules and thus an increase in u. If there is no change in volume, there will be more collisions with the walls per unit time. Furthermore, the change in momentum in each collision increases (the molecules strike the walls more forcefully). Hence, the model explains the observed pressure increase.

---

*To illustrate the difference between rms speed and average speed, suppose that we have four objects with speeds of 4.0, 6.0, 10.0, and 12.0 m/s. Their average speed is $\tfrac{1}{4}$ (4.0 + 6.0 + 10.0 + 12.0) = 8.0 m/s. The rms speed, u, however, is the square root of the average squared speeds of the molecules:

$$\sqrt{\tfrac{1}{4}(4.0^2 + 6.0^2 + 10.0^2 + 12.0^2)} = \sqrt{74.0} = 8.6 \ m/s$$

For an ideal gas the average speed equals 0.921 × u. Thus, the average speed is directly proportional to the rms speed, and the two are in fact nearly equal.

A Closer Look   THE IDEAL-GAS EQUATION

Beginning with the five statements given in the text for the kinetic-molecular theory, it is possible to derive the ideal-gas equation. Rather than proceed through a derivation, let's consider in somewhat qualitative terms how the ideal-gas equation might follow. As we have seen, pressure is force per unit area. ∞ (Section 10.2) The total force of the molecular collisions on the walls and hence the pressure produced by these collisions depend both on how strongly the molecules strike the walls (impulse imparted per collision) and on the rate at which these collisions occur:

$$P \propto \text{impulse imparted per collision} \times \text{rate of collisions}$$

For a molecule traveling at the rms speed, u, the impulse imparted by a collision with a wall depends on the momentum of the molecule; that is, it depends on the product of its mass and speed, mu. The rate of collisions is proportional to both the number of molecules per unit volume, n/V, and their speed, u. If there are more molecules in a container, there will be more frequent collisions with the container walls. As the molecular speed increases or the volume of the container decreases, the time required for molecules to traverse the distance from one wall to another is reduced, and the molecules collide more frequently with the walls. Thus, we have

$$P \propto mu \times \frac{n}{V} \times u \propto \frac{nmu^2}{V} \qquad [10.19]$$

Because the average kinetic energy, $\frac{1}{2}mu^2$, is proportional to temperature, we have $mu^2 \propto T$. Making this substitution into Equation 10.19 gives

$$P \propto \frac{n(mu^2)}{V} \propto \frac{nT}{V} \qquad [10.20]$$

Let's now convert the proportionality sign to an equal sign by expressing n as the number of moles of gas. We then insert a proportionality constant, R, the gas constant:

$$P = \frac{nRT}{V} \qquad [10.21]$$

This expression is the ideal-gas equation.

An eminent Swiss mathematician, Daniel Bernoulli (1700–1782), conceived of a model for gases that was, for all practical purposes, the same as the kinetic theory model. From this model, Bernoulli derived Boyle's law and the ideal-gas equation. His was one of the first examples in science of developing a mathematical model from a set of assumptions, or hypothetical statements. However, Bernoulli's work on this subject was completely ignored, only to be rediscovered a hundred years later by Clausius and others. It was ignored because it conflicted with popular beliefs and was in conflict with Isaac Newton's incorrect model for gases. Those idols of the times had to fall before the way was clear for the kinetic-molecular theory. As this story illustrates, science is not a straight road running from here to the "truth." The road is built by humans, so it zigs and zags.

Related Exercises: 10.71, 10.72, 10.73, and 10.74

■ SAMPLE EXERCISE 10.13 │ Applying the Kinetic-Molecular Theory

A sample of O_2 gas initially at STP is compressed to a smaller volume at constant temperature. What effect does this change have on **(a)** the average kinetic energy of O_2 molecules, **(b)** the average speed of O_2 molecules, **(c)** the total number of collisions of O_2 molecules with the container walls in a unit time, **(d)** the number of collisions of O_2 molecules with a unit area of container wall per unit time?

SOLUTION

Analyze: We need to apply the concepts of the kinetic-molecular theory to a situation in which a gas is compressed at constant temperature.

Plan: We will determine how each of the quantities in (a)–(d) is affected by the change in volume at constant temperature.

Solve: **(a)** The average kinetic energy of the O_2 molecules is determined only by temperature. Thus the average kinetic energy is unchanged by the compression of O_2 at constant temperature. **(b)** If the average kinetic energy of O_2 molecules does not change, the average speed remains constant. **(c)** The total number of collisions with the container walls per unit time must increase because the molecules are moving within a smaller volume but with the same average speed as before. Under these conditions they must encounter a wall more frequently. **(d)** The number of collisions with a unit area of wall per unit time increases because the total number of collisions with the walls per unit time increases and the area of the walls decreases.

Check: In a conceptual exercise of this kind, there is no numerical answer to check. All we can check in such cases is our reasoning in the course of solving the problem.

■ PRACTICE EXERCISE

How is the rms speed of N_2 molecules in a gas sample changed by **(a)** an increase in temperature, **(b)** an increase in volume, **(c)** mixing with a sample of Ar at the same temperature?
Answers: **(a)** increases, **(b)** no effect, **(c)** no effect

10.8 MOLECULAR EFFUSION AND DIFFUSION

According to the kinetic-molecular theory, the average kinetic energy of *any* collection of gas molecules, $\frac{1}{2}mu^2$, has a specific value at a given temperature. Thus, a gas composed of lightweight particles, such as He, will have the same average kinetic energy as one composed of much heavier particles, such as Xe, provided the two gases are at the same temperature. The mass, m, of the particles in the lighter gas is smaller than that in the heavier gas. Consequently, the particles of the lighter gas must have a higher rms speed, u, than the particles of the heavier one. The following equation, which expresses this fact quantitatively, can be derived from kinetic-molecular theory:

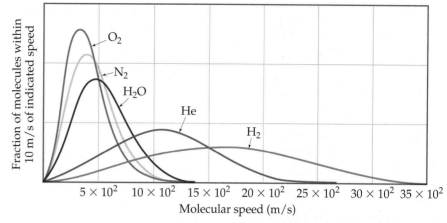

▲ Figure 10.19 **The effect of molecular mass on molecular speeds.** The distributions of molecular speeds for different gases are compared at 25 °C. The molecules with lower molecular masses have higher rms speeds.

$$u = \sqrt{\frac{3RT}{\mathcal{M}}} \qquad [10.22]$$

Because the molar mass, $\mathcal{M}$, appears in the denominator, the less massive the gas molecules, the higher the rms speed, u.

Figure 10.19 ▲ shows the distribution of molecular speeds for several gases at 25 °C. Notice how the distributions are shifted toward higher speeds for gases of lower molar masses.

■ **SAMPLE EXERCISE 10.14** | Calculating a Root-Mean-Square Speed

Calculate the rms speed, u, of an N_2 molecule at 25 °C.

SOLUTION

Analyze: We are given the identity of the gas and the temperature, the two quantities we need to calculate the rms speed.

Plan: We will calculate the rms speed using Equation 10.22.

Solve: In using Equation 10.22, we should convert each quantity to SI units so that all the units are compatible. We will also use R in units of J/mol-K (Table 10.2) to make the units cancel correctly.

$T = 25 + 273 = 298$ K

$\mathcal{M} = 28.0$ g/mol $= 28.0 \times 10^{-3}$ kg/mol

$R = 8.314$ J/mol-K $= 8.314$ kg-m^2/s^2-mol-K   (These units follow from the fact that 1 J $= 1$ kg-m^2/s^2)

$$u = \sqrt{\frac{3(8.314 \text{ kg-m}^2/\text{s}^2\text{-mol-K})(298 \text{ K})}{28.0 \times 10^{-3} \text{ kg/mol}}} = 5.15 \times 10^2 \text{ m/s}$$

Comment: This corresponds to a speed of 1150 mi/hr. Because the average molecular weight of air molecules is slightly greater than that of N_2, the rms speed of air molecules is a little slower than that for N_2. The speed at which sound propagates through air is about 350 m/s, a value about two-thirds the average rms speed for air molecules.

■ **PRACTICE EXERCISE**

What is the rms speed of an He atom at 25 °C?
Answer: 1.36×10^3 m/s

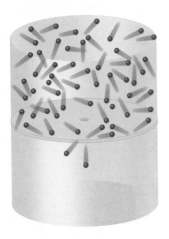

The dependence of molecular speeds on mass has several interesting consequences. The first phenomenon is **effusion**, which is the escape of gas molecules through a tiny hole into an evacuated space, as shown in Figure 10.20 ◀. The second is **diffusion**, which is the spread of one substance throughout a space or throughout a second substance. For example, the molecules of a perfume diffuse throughout a room.

Graham's Law of Effusion

In 1846 Thomas Graham (1805–1869) discovered that the effusion rate of a gas is inversely proportional to the square root of its molar mass. Assume that we have two gases at the same temperature and pressure in containers with identical pinholes. If the rates of effusion of the two substances are r_1 and r_2 and their respective molar masses are $\mathcal{M}_1$ and $\mathcal{M}_2$, **Graham's law** states

$$\frac{r_1}{r_2} = \sqrt{\frac{\mathcal{M}_2}{\mathcal{M}_1}} \qquad [10.23]$$

Equation 10.23 compares the *rates* of effusion of two different gases under identical conditions, and it indicates that the lighter gas effuses more rapidly.

▲ **Figure 10.20 Effusion.** The top half of this cylinder is filled with a gas, and the bottom half is an evacuated space. Gas molecules effuse through a pinhole in the partitioning wall only when they happen to hit the hole.

GRAHAM'S LAW OF EFFUSION

The effusion rate of a gas is inversely proportional to the square root of its molar mass.
Gas effuses through pores of a balloon. At identical pressure and temperature,
the lighter gas effuses more rapidly.

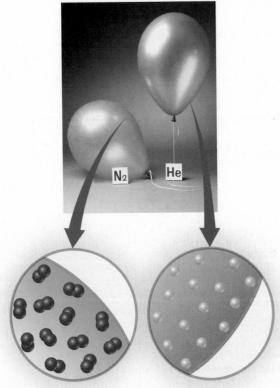

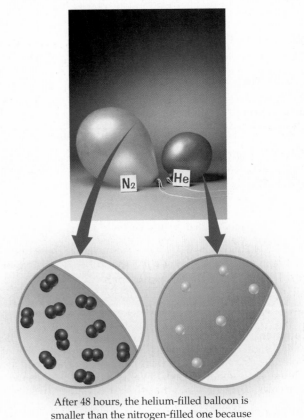

Two balloons are filled to the same volume,
one with nitrogen and one with helium.

After 48 hours, the helium-filled balloon is
smaller than the nitrogen-filled one because
helium escapes faster than nitrogen.

▲ **Figure 10.21 An illustration of Graham's law.**

Figure 10.20 illustrates the basis of Graham's law. The only way for a molecule to escape from its container is for it to "hit" the hole in the partitioning wall. The faster the molecules are moving, the greater is the likelihood that a molecule will hit the hole and effuse. This implies that the rate of effusion is directly proportional to the rms speed of the molecules. Because R and T are constant, we have, from Equation 10.22

$$\frac{r_1}{r_2} = \frac{u_1}{u_2} = \sqrt{\frac{3RT/\mathcal{M}_1}{3RT/\mathcal{M}_2}} = \sqrt{\frac{\mathcal{M}_2}{\mathcal{M}_1}} \qquad [10.24]$$

As expected from Graham's law, helium escapes from containers through tiny pinhole leaks more rapidly than other gases of higher molecular weight (Figure 10.21 ◄).

■ SAMPLE EXERCISE 10.15 | Applying Graham's Law

An unknown gas composed of homonuclear diatomic molecules effuses at a rate that is only 0.355 times that of O_2 at the same temperature. Calculate the molar mass of the unknown, and identify it.

SOLUTION

Analyze: We are given the rate of effusion of an unknown gas relative to that of O_2, and we are asked to find the molar mass and identity of the unknown. Thus, we need to connect relative rates of effusion to relative molar masses.

Plan: We can use Graham's law of effusion, Equation 10.23, to determine the molar mass of the unknown gas. If we let r_x and $\mathcal{M}_x$ represent the rate of effusion and molar mass of the unknown gas, Equation 10.23 can be written as follows:

$$\frac{r_x}{r_{O_2}} = \sqrt{\frac{\mathcal{M}_{O_2}}{\mathcal{M}_x}}$$

Solve: From the information given,

$$r_x = 0.355 \times r_{O_2}$$

Thus,

$$\frac{r_x}{r_{O_2}} = 0.355 = \sqrt{\frac{32.0\ \text{g/mol}}{\mathcal{M}_x}}$$

We now solve for the unknown molar mass, $\mathcal{M}_x$

$$\frac{32.0\ \text{g/mol}}{\mathcal{M}_x} = (0.355)^2 = 0.126$$

$$\mathcal{M}_x = \frac{32.0\ \text{g/mol}}{0.126} = 254\ \text{g/mol}$$

Because we are told that the unknown gas is composed of homonuclear diatomic molecules, it must be an element. The molar mass must represent twice the atomic weight of the atoms in the unknown gas. We conclude that the unknown gas is I_2.

■ PRACTICE EXERCISE

Calculate the ratio of the effusion rates of N_2 and O_2, r_{N_2}/r_{O_2}.
Answer: $r_{N_2}/r_{O_2} = 1.07$

Diffusion and Mean Free Path

Diffusion, like effusion, is faster for lower mass molecules than for higher mass ones. In fact, Graham's law, Equation 10.23, approximates the ratio of rates of diffusion of two gases under identical experimental conditions. Nevertheless, molecular collisions make diffusion more complicated than effusion.

We can see from the horizontal scale in Figure 10.19 that the speeds of molecules are quite high. For example, the average speed of N_2 at room temperature is 515 m/s (1150 mi/hr). In spite of this high speed, if someone opens a vial of perfume at one end of a room, some time elapses—perhaps a few minutes—before the scent is detected at the other end of the room. The diffusion of gases is much slower than molecular speeds because of molecular collisions.* These

---

The rate at which the perfume moves across the room also depends on how well stirred the air is from temperature gradients and the movement of people. Nevertheless, even with the aid of these factors, it still takes much longer for the molecules to traverse the room than one would expect from the rms speed alone.

Chemistry Put to Work   GAS SEPARATIONS

The fact that lighter molecules move at higher average speeds than more massive ones has many interesting consequences and applications. For example, the effort to develop the atomic bomb during World War II required scientists to separate the relatively low-abundance uranium isotope ^{235}U (0.7%) from the much more abundant ^{238}U (99.3%). This separation was accomplished by converting the uranium into a volatile compound, UF_6, that was then allowed to pass through porous barriers. Because of the diameters of the pores, this process is not a simple effusion. Nevertheless, the dependence on molar mass is essentially the same. The slight difference in molar mass between the two hexafluorides, $^{235}UF_6$ and $^{238}UF_6$, caused the molecules to move at slightly different rates:

$$\frac{r_{235}}{r_{238}} = \sqrt{\frac{352.04}{349.03}} = 1.0043$$

Thus, the gas initially appearing on the opposite side of the barrier was very slightly enriched in the lighter molecule. The effusion process was repeated thousands of times, leading to a nearly complete separation of the two isotopes of uranium.

Separation of uranium isotopes by effusion has been largely replaced by a technique that uses centrifuges. In this procedure, cylindrical rotors containing UF_6 vapor spin at high speed inside an evacuated casing. Molecules containing the heavier ^{238}U isotope move closer to the spinning walls, whereas the molecules containing the lighter ^{235}U isotope remain in the middle of the cylinders. A stream of gas moves the UF_6 from the center of one centrifuge into another. Plants that use centrifuges consume less energy and can be constructed in a more compact, modular fashion than those that rely on effusion. Such plants are frequently in the news as countries such as Iran and North Korea enrich uranium in the ^{235}U isotope for both nuclear power and nuclear weaponry.
Related Exercises: 10.79 and 10.80

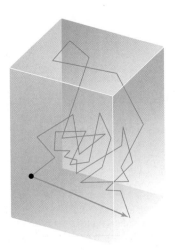

▲ **Figure 10.22 Diffusion of a gas molecule.** For clarity, no other gas molecules in the container are shown. The path of the molecule of interest begins at the dot. Each short segment of line represents travel between collisions. The blue arrow indicates the net distance traveled by the molecule.

collisions occur quite frequently for a gas at atmospheric pressure—about 10^{10} times per second for each molecule. Collisions occur because real gas molecules have finite volumes.

Because of molecular collisions, the direction of motion of a gas molecule is constantly changing. Therefore, the diffusion of a molecule from one point to another consists of many short, straight-line segments as collisions buffet it around in random directions, as depicted in Figure 10.22 ◄. First the molecule moves in one direction, then in another; one instant at high speed, the next at low speed.

The average distance traveled by a molecule between collisions is called the **mean free path** of the molecule. The mean free path varies with pressure as the following analogy illustrates. Imagine walking through a shopping mall. When the mall is very crowded (high pressure), the average distance you can walk before bumping into someone is short (short mean free path). When the mall is empty (low pressure), you can walk a long way (long mean free path) before bumping into someone. The mean free path for air molecules at sea level is about 60 nm (6×10^{-8} m). At about 100 km in altitude, where the air density is much lower, the mean free path is about 10 cm, over 1 million times longer than at Earth's surface.

▲ **GIVE IT SOME THOUGHT**

Will the following changes increase, decrease, or have no effect on the mean free path of the gas molecules in a sample of gas? **(a)** Increasing pressure, **(b)** increasing temperature?

10.9 REAL GASES: DEVIATIONS FROM IDEAL BEHAVIOR

Although the ideal-gas equation is a very useful description of gases, all real gases fail to obey the relationship to some degree. The extent to which a real gas departs from ideal behavior can be seen by rearranging the ideal-gas equation to solve for n:

$$\frac{PV}{RT} = n$$

[10.25]

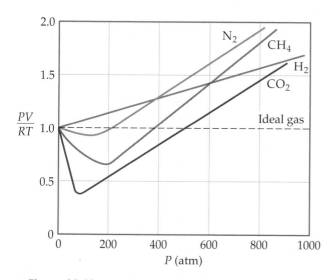

▲ **Figure 10.23 The effect of pressure on the behavior of several gases.** The ratios of PV/RT versus pressure are compared for one mole of several gases at 300 K. The data for CO_2 are at 313 K because under high pressure CO_2 liquefies at 300 K. The dashed horizontal line shows the behavior of an ideal gas.

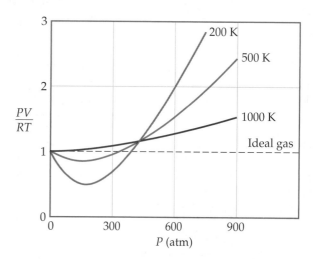

▲ **Figure 10.24 The effect of temperature and pressure on the behavior of nitrogen gas.** The ratios of PV/RT versus pressure are shown for 1 mol of nitrogen gas at three temperatures. As temperature increases, the gas more closely approaches ideal behavior, which is represented by the dashed horizontal line.

For one mole of ideal gas ($n = 1$) the quantity PV/RT equals 1 at all pressures. In Figure 10.23 ▲ PV/RT is plotted as a function of P for one mole of several different gases. At high pressures the deviation from ideal behavior ($PV/RT = 1$) is large and is different for each gas. *Real gases, therefore, do not behave ideally at high pressure.* At lower pressures (usually below 10 atm), however, the deviation from ideal behavior is small, and we can use the ideal-gas equation without generating serious error.

The deviation from ideal behavior also depends on temperature. Figure 10.24 ▲ shows graphs of PV/RT versus P for 1 mol of N_2 at three temperatures. As temperature increases, the behavior of the gas more nearly approaches that of the ideal gas. In general, *the deviations from ideal behavior increase as temperature decreases*, becoming significant near the temperature at which the gas is converted into a liquid.

▼ **Figure 10.25 Comparing the volume of gas molecules to the container volume.** In (a), at low pressure, the combined volume of the gas molecules is small relative to the container volume, and we can approximate the empty space between molecules as being equal to the container volume. In (b), at high pressure, the combined volume of the gas molecules is a larger fraction of the total space available. Now we must account for the volume of the molecules themselves in determining the empty space available for the motion of the gas molecules.

▲ **GIVE IT SOME THOUGHT**

Would you expect helium gas to deviate from ideal behavior more at **(a)** 100 K and 1 atm, **(b)** 100 K and 5 atm, or **(c)** 300 K and 2 atm?

The basic assumptions of the kinetic-molecular theory give us insight into why real gases deviate from ideal behavior. The molecules of an ideal gas are assumed to occupy no space and have no attractions for one another. *Real molecules, however, do have finite volumes, and they do attract one another.* As shown in Figure 10.25 ▶, the free, unoccupied space in which molecules can move is somewhat less than the container volume. At relatively low pressures the volume of the gas molecules is negligible relative to the container volume. Thus, the free volume available to the molecules is essentially the entire volume of the container. As the pressure increases, however, the free space in which the molecules can move becomes a smaller fraction of the container volume. Under these conditions, therefore, gas volumes tend to be slightly greater than those predicted by the ideal-gas equation.

(a)   (b)

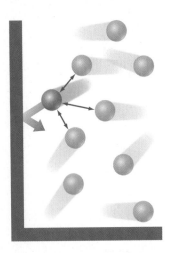

▲ Figure 10.26 **The effect of intermolecular forces on gas pressure.** The molecule that is about to strike the wall experiences attractive forces from nearby gas molecules, and its impact on the wall is thereby lessened. The lessened impact means the molecule exerts a lower-than-expected pressure on the wall. The attractive forces become significant only under high-pressure conditions, when the average distance between molecules is small.

In addition, the attractive forces between molecules come into play at short distances, as when molecules are crowded together at high pressures. Because of these attractive forces, the impact of a given molecule with the wall of the container is lessened. If we could stop the action in a gas, the positions of the molecules might resemble the illustration in Figure 10.26 ◄. The molecule about to make contact with the wall experiences the attractive forces of nearby molecules. These attractions lessen the force with which the molecule hits the wall. As a result, the pressure is less than that of an ideal gas. This effect serves to decrease PV/RT below its ideal value, as seen in Figure 10.23. When the pressure is sufficiently high, however, the volume effects dominate and PV/RT increases to above the ideal value.

Temperature determines how effective attractive forces between gas molecules are. As a gas is cooled, the average kinetic energy of the molecules decreases, but intermolecular attractions remain constant. In a sense, cooling a gas deprives molecules of the energy they need to overcome their mutual attractive influence. The effects of temperature shown in Figure 10.24 illustrate this point very well. As temperature increases, the negative departure of PV/RT from ideal-gas behavior disappears. The difference that remains at high temperature stems mainly from the effect of the finite volumes of the molecules.

> ⚠ **GIVE IT SOME THOUGHT**
>
> List two reasons why gases deviate from ideal behavior.

The van der Waals Equation

Engineers and scientists who work with gases at high pressures often cannot use the ideal-gas equation to predict the pressure-volume properties of gases because departures from ideal behavior are too large. One useful equation developed to predict the behavior of real gases was proposed by the Dutch scientist Johannes van der Waals (1837–1923).

Van der Waals recognized that the ideal gas equation could be corrected to account for the effects of attractive forces between gas molecules and for molecular volumes. He introduced two constants, a and b, to make these corrections. The constant a is a measure of how strongly the gas molecules attract each other. The constant b is a measure of the small but finite volume occupied by the gas molecules themselves. His description of gas behavior is known as the **van der Waals equation**:

$$\left(P + \frac{n^2 a}{V^2} \right)(V - nb) = nRT \qquad [10.26]$$

In this equation the factor $n^2 a/V^2$ accounts for the attractive forces. The van der Waals equation adjusts the pressure, P, upward by adding $n^2 a/V^2$ because attractive forces between molecules tend to reduce the pressure (Figure 10.26). That is, a correction must be added to give the pressure that an ideal gas would have. The form of the correction factor, $n^2 a/V^2$, results because the attractive forces between pairs of molecules increase as the square of the number of molecules per unit volume, $(n/V)^2$.

The factor nb accounts for the small but finite volume occupied by the gas molecules themselves (Figure 10.25). The van der Waals equation adjusts volume, V, downward (subtracting nb), to give the free volume available to the gas molecules. That is, the particles of an ideal gas have the full volume, V, as free space in which to move, whereas in a real gas only the volume $V - nb$ is available as free space.

The constants a and b, which are called *van der Waals constants*, are experimentally determined positive quantities that differ for each gas. Values of these constants for several gases are listed in Table 10.3 ►. Notice that the values of

TABLE 10.3 ■ van der Waals Constants for Gas Molecules		
Substance	a (L^2-atm/mol^2)	b (L/mol)
He	0.0341	0.02370
Ne	0.211	0.0171
Ar	1.34	0.0322
Kr	2.32	0.0398
Xe	4.19	0.0510
H_2	0.244	0.0266
N_2	1.39	0.0391
O_2	1.36	0.0318
Cl_2	6.49	0.0562
H_2O	5.46	0.0305
CH_4	2.25	0.0428
CO_2	3.59	0.0427
CCl_4	20.4	0.1383

both a and b generally increase with an increase in mass of the molecule and with an increase in the complexity of its structure. Larger, more massive molecules have larger volumes and tend to have greater intermolecular attractive forces. As we will see in the next chapter, substances with large intermolecular attractive forces are relatively easy to liquefy.

■ **SAMPLE EXERCISE 10.16** | **Using the van der Waals Equation**

If 1.000 mol of an ideal gas were confined to 22.41 L at 0.0 °C, it would exert a pressure of 1.000 atm. Use the van der Waals equation and the constants in Table 10.3 to estimate the pressure exerted by 1.000 mol of $Cl_2(g)$ in 22.41 L at 0.0 °C.

SOLUTION

Analyze: The quantity we need to solve for is pressure. Because we will use the van der Waals equation, we must identify the appropriate values for the constants that appear there.

Plan: Solving Equation 10.26 for P, we have

$$P = \frac{nRT}{V - nb} - \frac{n^2a}{V^2}$$

Solve: Substituting $n = 1.000$ mol, $R = 0.08206$ L-atm/mol-K, $T = 273.2$ K, $V = 22.41$ L, $a = 6.49$ L^2-atm/mol^2, and $b = 0.0562$ L/mol:

$$P = \frac{(1.000 \text{ mol})(0.08206 \text{ L-atm/mol-K})(273.2 \text{ K})}{22.41 \text{ L} - (1.000 \text{ mol})(0.0562 \text{ L/mol})} - \frac{(1.000 \text{ mol})^2(6.49 \text{ L}^2\text{-atm/mol}^2)}{(22.14 \text{ L})^2}$$

$$= 1.003 \text{ atm} - 0.013 \text{ atm} = 0.990 \text{ atm}$$

Check: We expect a pressure not far from 1.000 atm, which would be the value for an ideal gas, so our answer seems very reasonable.

Comment: Notice that the first term, 1.003 atm, is the pressure corrected for molecular volume. This value is higher than the ideal value, 1.000 atm, because the volume in which the molecules are free to move is smaller than the container volume, 22.41 L. Thus, the molecules must collide more frequently with the container walls. The second factor, 0.013 atm, corrects for intermolecular forces. The intermolecular attractions between molecules reduce the pressure to 0.990 atm. We can conclude, therefore, that the intermolecular attractions are the main cause of the slight deviation of $Cl_2(g)$ from ideal behavior under the stated experimental conditions.

■ **PRACTICE EXERCISE**

Consider a sample of 1.000 mol of $CO_2(g)$ confined to a volume of 3.000 L at 0.0 °C. Calculate the pressure of the gas using **(a)** the ideal-gas equation and **(b)** the van der Waals equation.
Answers: **(a)** 7.473 atm, **(b)** 7.182 atm

■ SAMPLE INTEGRATIVE EXERCISE | Putting Concepts Together

Cyanogen, a highly toxic gas, is composed of 46.2% C and 53.8% N by mass. At 25 °C and 751 torr, 1.05 g of cyanogen occupies 0.500 L. **(a)** What is the molecular formula of cyanogen? **(b)** Predict its molecular structure. **(c)** Predict the polarity of the compound.

SOLUTION

Analyze: First we need to determine the molecular formula of a compound from elemental analysis data and data on the properties of the gaseous substance. Thus, we have two separate calculations to do.

(a) Plan: We can use the percentage composition of the compound to calculate its empirical formula. ∞ (Section 3.5) Then we can determine the molecular formula by comparing the mass of the empirical formula with the molar mass. ∞ (Section 3.5)

Solve: To determine the empirical formula, we assume that we have a 100-g sample of the compound and then calculate the number of moles of each element in the sample:

$$\text{Moles C} = (46.2 \text{ g C})\left(\frac{1 \text{ mol C}}{12.01 \text{ g C}}\right) = 3.85 \text{ mol C}$$

$$\text{Moles N} = (53.8 \text{ g N})\left(\frac{1 \text{ mol N}}{14.01 \text{ g N}}\right) = 3.84 \text{ mol N}$$

Because the ratio of the moles of the two elements is essentially 1:1, the empirical formula is CN.

To determine the molar mass of the compound, we use Equation 10.11.

$$\mathcal{M} = \frac{dRT}{p} = \frac{(1.05 \text{ g}/0.500 \text{ L}) (0.0821 \text{ L-atm/mol-K}) (298 \text{ K})}{(751/760) \text{ atm}} = 52.0 \text{ g/mol}$$

The molar mass associated with the empirical formula, CN, is 12.0 + 14.0 = 26.0 g/mol. Dividing the molar mass of the compound by that of its empirical formula gives (52.0 g/mol)/(26.0 g/mol) = 2.00. Thus, the molecule has twice as many atoms of each element as the empirical formula, giving the molecular formula C_2N_2.

(b) Plan: To determine the molecular structure of the molecule, we must first determine its Lewis structure. ∞ (Section 8.5) We can then use the VSEPR model to predict the structure. ∞ (Section 9.2)

Solve: The molecule has 2(4) + 2(5) = 18 valence-shell electrons. By trial and error, we seek a Lewis structure with 18 valence electrons in which each atom has an octet and in which the formal charges are as low as possible. The following structure meets these criteria:

$$:N\equiv C-C\equiv N:$$

(This structure has zero formal charge on each atom.)

The Lewis structure shows that each atom has two electron domains. (Each nitrogen has a nonbonding pair of electrons and a triple bond, whereas each carbon has a triple bond and a single bond.) Thus the electron-domain geometry around each atom is linear, causing the overall molecule to be linear.

(c) Plan: To determine the polarity of the molecule, we must examine the polarity of the individual bonds and the overall geometry of the molecule.

Solve: Because the molecule is linear, we expect the two dipoles created by the polarity in the carbon–nitrogen bond to cancel each other, leaving the molecule with no dipole moment.

WHAT'S AHEAD

SITTING IN A HOT SPRING ON A SNOWY day is not something many of us have experienced. If we were in the hot spring shown in the chapter-opening photo, however, we would be surrounded simultaneously by all three phases of water—gas, liquid, and solid. The water vapor—

or humidity—in the air, the water in the hot spring, and the surrounding snow are all forms of the same substance, H_2O. They all have the same chemical properties. Their physical properties differ greatly, however, because the physical properties of a substance depend on its physical state. In Chapter 10 we discussed the gaseous state in some detail. In this chapter we turn our attention to the physical properties of liquids and solids and to the phase changes that occur between the three states of matter.

Many of the substances that we will consider in this chapter are molecular. In fact, virtually all substances that are liquids at room temperature are molecular substances. The intramolecular forces *within* molecules that give rise to covalent bonding influence molecular shape, bond energies, and many aspects of chemical behavior. The physical properties of molecular liquids and solids, however, are due largely to **intermolecular forces**, the forces that exist *between* molecules. We learned in Section 10.9 that attractions between gas molecules lead to deviations from ideal-gas behavior. But how do these intermolecular attractions arise? By understanding the nature and strength of intermolecular forces, we can begin to relate the composition and structure of molecules to their physical properties.

TABLE 11.1 ■ Some Characteristic Properties of the States of Matter	
Gas	Assumes both the volume and shape of its container
	Is compressible
	Flows readily
	Diffusion within a gas occurs rapidly
Liquid	Assumes the shape of the portion of the container it occupies
	Does not expand to fill container
	Is virtually incompressible
	Flows readily
	Diffusion within a liquid occurs slowly
Solid	Retains its own shape and volume
	Is virtually incompressible
	Does not flow
	Diffusion within a solid occurs extremely slowly

11.1 A MOLECULAR COMPARISON OF GASES, LIQUIDS, AND SOLIDS

Some of the characteristic properties of gases, liquids, and solids are listed in Table 11.1 ▲. These properties can be understood in terms of the energy of motion (kinetic energy) of the particles (atoms, molecules, or ions) of each state, compared to the energy of the intermolecular interactions between those particles. As we learned from the kinetic-molecular theory of gases in Chapter 10, the average kinetic energy, which is related to the particle's average speed, is proportional to the absolute temperature.

Gases consist of a collection of widely separated particles in constant, chaotic motion. The average energy of the attractions between the particles is much smaller than their average kinetic energy. The lack of strong attractive forces between particles allows a gas to expand to fill its container.

In liquids the intermolecular attractive forces are stronger than in gases and are strong enough to hold particles close together. Thus, liquids are much denser and far less compressible than gases. Unlike gases, liquids have a definite volume, independent of the size and shape of their container. The attractive forces in liquids are not strong enough, however, to keep the particles from moving past one another. Thus, any liquid can be poured, and it assumes the shape of whatever portion of its container it occupies.

In solids the intermolecular attractive forces are strong enough to hold particles close together and to lock them virtually in place. Solids, like liquids, are not very compressible because the particles have little free space between them. Because the particles in a solid or liquid are fairly close together compared with those of a gas, we often refer to solids and liquids as *condensed phases*. Often the particles of a solid take up positions in a highly regular three-dimensional pattern. Solids that possess highly ordered three-dimensional structures are said to be *crystalline*. Because the particles of a solid are not free to undergo long-range movement, solids are rigid. Keep in mind, however, that the units that form the solid, whether ions or molecules, possess thermal energy and vibrate in place. This vibrational motion increases in amplitude as a solid is heated. In fact, the energy may increase to the point that the solid either melts or sublimes.

Figure 11.1 ▶ compares the three states of matter. The particles that compose the substance can be individual atoms, as in Ar; molecules, as in H_2O; or ions, as in NaCl. *The state of a substance depends largely on the balance between the kinetic energies of the particles and the interparticle energies of attraction.* The kinetic energies, which depend on temperature, tend to keep the particles apart and moving. The interparticle attractions tend to draw the particles together.

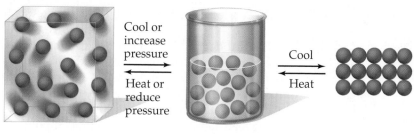

Gas	Liquid	Crystalline solid
Total disorder; much empty space; particles have complete freedom of motion; particles far apart	Disorder; particles or clusters of particles are free to move relative to each other; particles close together	Ordered arrangement; particles are essentially in fixed positions; particles close together

◀ Figure 11.1 **Molecular-level comparison of gases, liquids, and solids.** The particles can be atoms, ions, or molecules. The density of particles in the gas phase is exaggerated compared with most real situations.

Substances that are gases at room temperature have weaker interparticle attractions than those that are liquids; substances that are liquids have weaker interparticle attractions than those that are solids.

We can change a substance from one state to another by heating or cooling, which changes the average kinetic energy of the particles. NaCl, for example, which is a solid at room temperature, melts at 801 °C and boils at 1413 °C under 1 atm pressure. N_2O, on the other hand, which is a gas at room temperature, liquefies at −88.5 °C and solidifies at −90.8 °C under 1 atm pressure. As the temperature of a gas decreases, the average kinetic energy of its particles decreases, allowing the attractions between the particles to first draw the particles close together, forming a liquid, and then virtually locking them in place, forming a solid.

Increasing the pressure on a gas forces the molecules closer together, which in turn increases the strength of the intermolecular forces of attraction. Propane (C_3H_8) is a gas at room temperature and 1 atm pressure, whereas liquefied propane (LP) gas is a liquid at room temperature because it is stored under much higher pressure.

GIVE IT SOME THOUGHT

How does the energy of attraction between particles compare with their kinetic energies in **(a)** a gas, **(b)** a solid?

11.2 INTERMOLECULAR FORCES

The strengths of intermolecular forces of different substances vary over a wide range, but they are generally much weaker than ionic or covalent bonds (Figure 11.2▶). Less energy, therefore, is required to vaporize, or evaporate, a liquid or to melt a solid than to break covalent bonds in molecules. For example, only 16 kJ/mol is required to overcome the intermolecular attractions between HCl molecules in liquid HCl to vaporize it. In contrast, the energy required to break the covalent bond to dissociate HCl into H and Cl atoms is 431 kJ/mol. Thus, when a molecular substance such as HCl changes from solid to liquid to gas, the molecules themselves remain intact.

Many properties of liquids, including their *boiling points*, reflect the strengths of the intermolecular forces. For example, because the forces between HCl molecules are so weak, HCl boils at a very low temperature, −85 °C at atmospheric pressure. A liquid boils when bubbles of its vapor form within the liquid.

▼ Figure 11.2 **Intermolecular attraction.** Comparison of a covalent bond (an intramolecular force) and an intermolecular attraction. Because intermolecular attractions are weaker than covalent bonds, they are usually represented by dashes or dots.

Covalent bond (strong)

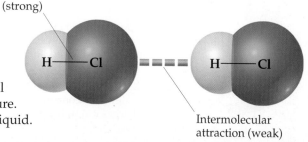

Intermolecular attraction (weak)

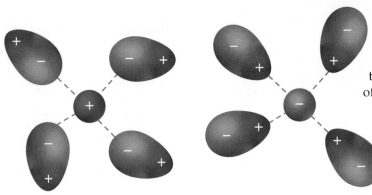

Cation–dipole attractions

(a)

Anion–dipole attractions

(b)

▲ **Figure 11.3 Ion–dipole attractions.** Illustration of the preferred orientations of polar molecules toward ions. The negative end of the dipoles is oriented toward a cation (a), and the positive end of the dipoles is oriented toward an anion (b).

The molecules of a liquid must overcome their attractive forces to separate and form a vapor. The stronger the attractive forces are, the higher the temperature at which the liquid boils. Similarly, the *melting points* of solids increase as the strengths of the intermolecular forces increase.

Three types of intermolecular attractions exist between neutral molecules: dipole–dipole attractions, London dispersion forces, and hydrogen bonding. The first two forms of attraction are collectively called *van der Waals forces* after Johannes van der Waals, who developed the equation for predicting the deviation of gases from ideal behavior. ∞ (Section 10.9) Another kind of attractive force, the ion–dipole force, is important in solutions. All of these intermolecular interactions are electrostatic in nature, involving attractions between positive and negative species. Even at their strongest, these interactions are much weaker than covalent or ionic bonds (<15% as strong).

Ion–Dipole Forces

An **ion–dipole force** exists between an ion and the partial charge on the end of a polar molecule. Polar molecules are dipoles; they have a positive end and a negative end. ∞ (Section 9.3) HCl is a polar molecule, for example, because the electronegativities of the H and Cl atoms differ.

Positive ions are attracted to the negative end of a dipole, whereas negative ions are attracted to the positive end, as shown in Figure 11.3 ▲. The magnitude of the attraction increases as either the charge of the ion or the magnitude of the dipole moment increases. Ion–dipole forces are especially important for solutions of ionic substances in polar liquids, such as a solution of NaCl in water. ∞ (Section 4.1) We will discuss these solutions in more detail in Section 13.1.

GIVE IT SOME THOUGHT

In which of the following mixtures do you encounter ion–dipole forces: CH_3OH in water or $Ca(NO_3)_2$ in water?

▼ **Figure 11.4 Dipole–dipole attractions.** The interaction of many dipoles in a condensed state. There are both repulsive interactions between like charges and attractive interactions between unlike charges, but the attractive interactions predominate.

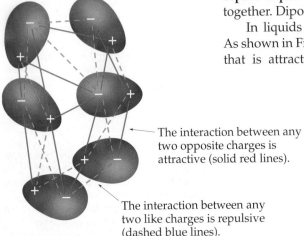

The interaction between any two opposite charges is attractive (solid red lines).

The interaction between any two like charges is repulsive (dashed blue lines).

Dipole–Dipole Forces

Neutral polar molecules attract each other when the positive end of one molecule is near the negative end of another, as shown in Figure 11.4 ◄. These **dipole–dipole forces** are effective only when polar molecules are very close together. Dipole–dipole forces are generally weaker than ion–dipole forces.

In liquids polar molecules are free to move with respect to one another. As shown in Figure 11.4, the polar molecules will sometimes be in an orientation that is attractive (red solid lines) and sometimes in an orientation that is repulsive (blue dashed lines). Two molecules that are attracting each other spend more time near each other than do two that are repelling each other. Thus, the overall effect is a net attraction. When we examine various liquids, we find that *for molecules of approximately equal mass and size, the strengths of intermolecular attractions increase with increasing polarity.* We can see this trend in Table 11.2 ▶, which lists several substances with similar molecular weights but different dipole moments. Notice that the boiling point increases as the dipole moment increases. For dipole–dipole forces to operate, the molecules must be able to get close together in the correct orientation.

■ **SAMPLE EXERCISE 11.3** | Predicting the Types and Relative Strengths of Intermolecular Attractions

List the substances $BaCl_2$, H_2, CO, HF, and Ne in order of increasing boiling points.

SOLUTION

Analyze: We need to relate the properties of the listed substances to boiling point.

Plan: The boiling point depends in part on the attractive forces in the liquid. We need to order these according to the relative strengths of the different kinds of intermolecular attractions.

Solve: The attractive forces are stronger for ionic substances than for molecular ones, so $BaCl_2$ should have the highest boiling point. The intermolecular forces of the remaining substances depend on molecular weight, polarity, and hydrogen bonding. The molecular weights are H_2 (2), CO (28), HF (20), and Ne (20). The boiling point of H_2 should be the lowest because it is nonpolar and has the lowest molecular weight. The molecular weights of CO, HF, and Ne are roughly the same. Because HF can hydrogen bond, however, it should have the highest boiling point of the three. Next is CO, which is slightly polar and has the highest molecular weight. Finally, Ne, which is nonpolar, should have the lowest boiling point of these three. The predicted order of boiling points is therefore

$$H_2 < Ne < CO < HF < BaCl_2$$

Check: The actual normal boiling points are H_2 (20 K), Ne (27 K), CO (83 K), HF (293 K), and $BaCl_2$ (1813 K)—in agreement with our predictions.

■ **PRACTICE EXERCISE**

(a) Identify the intermolecular attractions present in the following substances, and (b) select the substance with the highest boiling point: CH_3CH_3, CH_3OH, and CH_3CH_2OH.
Answers: (a) CH_3CH_3 has only dispersion forces, whereas the other two substances have both dispersion forces and hydrogen bonds; (b) CH_3CH_2OH

11.3 SOME PROPERTIES OF LIQUIDS

The intermolecular attractions we have just discussed can help us understand many familiar properties of liquids and solids. In this section we examine two important properties of liquids: viscosity and surface tension.

Viscosity

Some liquids, such as molasses and motor oil, flow very slowly; others, such as water and gasoline, flow easily. The resistance of a liquid to flow is called its **viscosity**. The greater a liquid's viscosity, the more slowly it flows. Viscosity can be measured by timing how long it takes a certain amount of the liquid to flow through a thin tube under gravitational force. More viscous liquids take longer (Figure 11.13 ▶). Viscosity can also be determined by measuring the rate at which steel balls fall through the liquid. The balls fall more slowly as the viscosity increases.

Viscosity is related to the ease with which individual molecules of the liquid can move with respect to one another. It thus depends on the attractive forces between molecules, and on whether structural features exist that cause the molecules to become entangled (for example, long molecules might become tangled like spaghetti). For a series of related compounds, therefore, viscosity increases with molecular weight, as illustrated in Table 11.4 ▼. The SI units for viscosity are kg/m-s. For any given substance, viscosity decreases with increasing temperature. Octane, for example, has a viscosity of 7.06×10^{-4} kg/m-s at 0 °C, and of 4.33×10^{-4} kg/m-s at 40 °C. At higher temperatures the greater average kinetic energy of the molecules more easily overcomes the attractive forces between molecules.

▲ Figure 11.13 **Comparing viscosities.** The Society of Automotive Engineers (SAE) has established numbers to indicate the viscosity of motor oils. The higher the number, the greater the viscosity is at any given temperature. The SAE 40 motor oil on the left is more viscous and flows more slowly than the less viscous SAE 10 oil on the right.

▲ Figure 11.14 Surface tension. Surface tension permits an insect such as the water strider to "walk" on water.

TABLE 11.4 ■ Viscosities of a Series of Hydrocarbons at 20 °C		
Substance	**Formula**	**Viscosity (kg/m-s)**
Hexane	$CH_3CH_2CH_2CH_2CH_2CH_3$	3.26×10^{-4}
Heptane	$CH_3CH_2CH_2CH_2CH_2CH_2CH_3$	4.09×10^{-4}
Octane	$CH_3CH_2CH_2CH_2CH_2CH_2CH_2CH_3$	5.42×10^{-4}
Nonane	$CH_3CH_2CH_2CH_2CH_2CH_2CH_2CH_2CH_3$	7.11×10^{-4}
Decane	$CH_3CH_2CH_2CH_2CH_2CH_2CH_2CH_2CH_2CH_3$	1.42×10^{-3}

Surface Tension

The surface of water behaves almost as if it had an elastic skin, as evidenced by the ability of certain insects to "walk" on water (Figure 11.14 ◀). This behavior is due to an imbalance of intermolecular forces at the surface of the liquid, as shown in Figure 11.15 ◀. Notice that molecules in the interior are attracted equally in all directions, whereas those at the surface experience a net inward force. The resultant inward force pulls molecules from the surface into the interior, thereby reducing the surface area and making the molecules at the surface pack closely together. Because spheres have the smallest surface area for their volume, water droplets assume an almost spherical shape. Similarly, water tends to "bead up" on a newly waxed car because there is little or no attraction between the polar water molecules and the nonpolar wax molecules.

A measure of the inward forces that must be overcome to expand the surface area of a liquid is given by its surface tension. **Surface tension** is the energy required to increase the surface area of a liquid by a unit amount. For example, the surface tension of water at 20 °C is 7.29×10^{-2} J/m^2, which means that an energy of 7.29×10^{-2} J must be supplied to increase the surface area of a given amount of water by 1 m^2. Water has a high surface tension because of its strong hydrogen bonds. The surface tension of mercury is even higher (4.6×10^{-1} J/m^2) because of even stronger metallic bonds between the atoms of mercury. ∞ (Section 11.8)

▲ Figure 11.15 Molecular-level view of surface and interior intermolecular forces in a liquid. Molecules at the surface are attracted only by other surface molecules and by molecules below the surface. The result is a net downward attraction into the interior of the liquid. Molecules in the interior experience attractions in all directions, resulting in no net attraction in any direction.

GIVE IT SOME THOUGHT

How do viscosity and surface tension change **(a)** as temperature increases, **(b)** as intermolecular forces of attraction become stronger?

Intermolecular forces that bind similar molecules to one another, such as the hydrogen bonding in water, are also called *cohesive forces*. Intermolecular forces that bind a substance to a surface are called *adhesive forces*. Water placed in a glass tube adheres to the glass because the adhesive forces between the water and glass are even greater than the cohesive forces between water molecules. The curved upper surface, or *meniscus*, of the water is therefore U-shaped (Figure 11.16 ◀). For mercury, however, the meniscus is curved downward where the mercury contacts the glass. In this case the cohesive forces between the mercury atoms are much greater than the adhesive forces between the mercury atoms and the glass.

When a small-diameter glass tube, or capillary, is placed in water, water rises in the tube. The rise of liquids up very narrow tubes is called **capillary action**. The adhesive forces between the liquid and the walls of the tube tend to increase the surface area of the liquid. The surface tension of the liquid tends to reduce the area, thereby pulling the liquid up the tube. The liquid climbs until the force of gravity on the liquid balances the adhesive and cohesive forces. Capillary action helps water and dissolved nutrients move upward through plants.

▲ Figure 11.16 Two meniscus shapes. The water meniscus in a glass tube compared with the mercury meniscus in a similar tube. Water wets the glass, and the bottom of the meniscus is below the level of the water–glass contact line, giving a U-shape to the water surface. Mercury does not wet glass and the meniscus is above the mercury–glass contact line, giving an inverted U-shape to the mercury surface.

GIVE IT SOME THOUGHT

If a liquid in a thin tube has no meniscus (in other words, the top of the liquid looks completely flat), what does that imply about the relative strengths of cohesive and adhesive forces?

Chemistry Put to Work SUPERCRITICAL FLUID EXTRACTION

At ordinary pressures, a substance above its critical temperature behaves as an ordinary gas. However, as pressure increases up to several hundred atmospheres, its character changes. Like a gas, the substance still expands to fill the confines of its container, but its density approaches that of a liquid. (For example, the critical temperature of water is 647.6 K, and its critical pressure is 217.7 atm. At this temperature and pressure, the density of water is 0.4 g/mL.) A substance at temperatures and pressures higher than its critical temperature and pressure is better considered a *supercritical fluid* rather than a gas.

Like liquids, supercritical fluids can behave as solvents, dissolving a wide range of substances. Using *supercritical fluid extraction*, the components of mixtures can be separated. The solvent power of a supercritical fluid increases as its density increases. Conversely, lowering its density (by either decreasing pressure or increasing temperature) causes the supercritical fluid and the dissolved material to separate. By appropriate manipulation of pressure, supercritical fluid extraction has been used successfully to separate complex mixtures in the chemical, food, pharmaceutical, and energy industries. Supercritical carbon dioxide, for example, is environmentally benign

because there are no problems disposing of solvent and there are no toxic residues resulting from the process. In addition, supercritical CO_2 is inexpensive compared to solvents other than water. Figure 11.20▼ shows what supercritical CO_2 looks like through a window in a high-pressure vessel.

A process for removing caffeine from green coffee beans by extraction with supercritical CO_2, diagrammed in Figure 11.21▼, has been in commercial operation for several years. At the proper temperature and pressure the supercritical CO_2 removes caffeine from the beans by dissolution, but leaves the flavor and aroma components, producing decaffeinated coffee. Supercritical CO_2 is also now used as a solvent in dry cleaning. In 2007, the state of California banned the most common dry-cleaning solvent, perchloroethylene ($Cl_2C{=}CCl_2$), which is an environmental hazard and a suspected human carcinogen. Supercritical CO_2 is a more sustainable alternative.

Related Exercises: 11.41, 11.42, 11.87

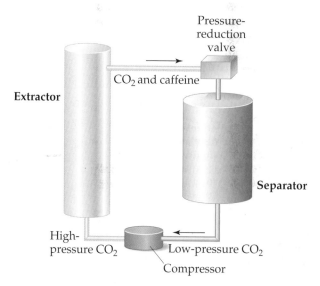

▲ Figure 11.21 **Diagram of a supercritical fluid extraction process.** The material to be processed is placed in the extractor. The desired material dissolves in supercritical CO_2 at high pressure, then is precipitated in the separator when the CO_2 pressure is reduced. The carbon dioxide is then recycled through the compressor with a fresh batch of material in the extractor.

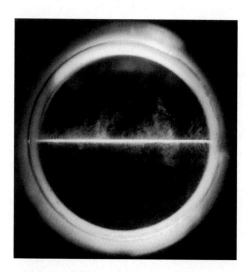

▲ Figure 11.20 Photograph of carbon dioxide under temperature and pressure conditions so that it is a supercritical fluid.

11.5 VAPOR PRESSURE

Molecules can escape from the surface of a liquid into the gas phase by evaporation. Suppose we conduct an experiment in which we place a quantity of ethanol (CH_3CH_2OH) in an evacuated, closed container such as that in Figure 11.22▼. The ethanol will quickly begin to evaporate. As a result, the pressure exerted by the vapor in the space above the liquid will begin to increase. After a short time the pressure of the vapor will attain a constant value, which we call the **vapor pressure** of the substance.

▶ Figure 11.22 **Illustration of the equilibrium vapor pressure over a liquid.** In (a) we imagine that no molecules of the liquid are in the gas phase initially; there is zero vapor pressure in the vessel. In (b), after equilibrium is reached, the rate at which molecules leave the surface equals the rate at which gas molecules return to the liquid phase. These equal rates produce a stable vapor pressure that does not change as long as the temperature remains constant.

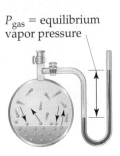

P_{gas} = equilibrium vapor pressure

Liquid ethanol

Liquid before any evaporation

At equilibrium, molecules enter and leave liquid at the same rate.

(a)

(b)

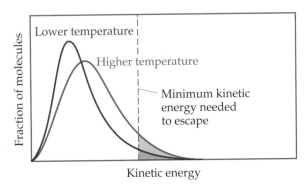

▲ Figure 11.23 **The effect of temperature on the distribution of kinetic energies in a liquid.** The distribution of kinetic energies of surface molecules of a hypothetical liquid are shown at two temperatures. Only the fastest molecules have sufficient kinetic energy to escape the liquid and enter the vapor, as shown by the shaded areas. The higher the temperature, the larger is the fraction of molecules with enough energy to escape from the liquid into the vapor phase.

Explaining Vapor Pressure on the Molecular Level

The molecules of a liquid move at various speeds. Figure 11.23 ◀ shows the distribution of kinetic energies of the particles at the surface of a liquid at two temperatures. The distribution curves are like those shown earlier for gases. ∞ (Section 10.7) At any instant some of the molecules on the surface of the liquid possess sufficient kinetic energy to overcome the attractive forces of their neighbors and escape into the gas phase. The weaker the attractive forces, the larger is the number of molecules that are able to escape and therefore the higher the vapor pressure.

At any particular temperature the movement of molecules from the liquid to the gas phase goes on continuously. As the number of gas-phase molecules increases, however, the probability increases that a molecule in the gas phase will strike the liquid surface and be recaptured by the liquid, as shown in Figure 11.22(b). Eventually, the rate at which molecules return to the liquid exactly equals the rate at which they escape. The number of molecules in the gas phase then reaches a steady value, and the pressure of the vapor at this stage becomes constant.

The condition in which two opposing processes are occurring simultaneously at equal rates is called a **dynamic equilibrium**, but is usually referred to merely as *equilibrium*. A liquid and its vapor are in dynamic equilibrium when evaporation and condensation occur at equal rates. It may appear that nothing is occurring at equilibrium because there is no net change in the system. In fact, a great deal is happening: molecules continuously pass from the liquid state to the gas state and from the gas state to the liquid state. All equilibria between different states of matter possess this dynamic character. *The vapor pressure of a liquid is the pressure exerted by its vapor when the liquid and vapor states are in dynamic equilibrium.*

Volatility, Vapor Pressure, and Temperature

When vaporization occurs in an open container, as when water evaporates from a bowl, the vapor spreads away from the liquid. Little, if any, is recaptured at the surface of the liquid. Equilibrium never occurs, and the vapor continues to form until the liquid evaporates to dryness. Substances with high vapor pressure (such as gasoline) evaporate more quickly than substances with low vapor pressure (such as motor oil). Liquids that evaporate readily are said to be **volatile**.

(a) Pyrite (fool's gold)

(b) Fluorite

(c) Amethyst

▲ Figure 11.29 **Crystalline solids.** Crystalline solids come in a variety of forms and colors: (a) pyrite (fool's gold), (b) fluorite, (c) amethyst.

These solids usually have flat surfaces, or *faces*, that make definite angles with one another. The orderly stacks of particles that produce these faces also cause the solids to have highly regular shapes (Figure 11.29▲). Quartz and diamond are crystalline solids.

An **amorphous solid** (from the Greek words for "without form") is a solid in which particles have no orderly structure. These solids lack well-defined faces and shapes. Many amorphous solids are mixtures of particles that do not stack together well. Most others are composed of large, complicated molecules. Familiar amorphous solids include rubber and glass.

Quartz (SiO_2) is a crystalline solid with a three-dimensional structure like that shown in Figure 11.30(a)▼. When quartz melts (at about 1600 °C), it becomes a viscous, tacky liquid. Although the silicon–oxygen network remains largely intact, many Si—O bonds are broken, and the rigid order of the quartz is lost. If the melt is rapidly cooled, the atoms are unable to return to an orderly arrangement. As a result, an amorphous solid known either as quartz glass or as silica glass results [Figure 11.30(b)].

▼ Figure 11.30 **Schematic comparisons of (a) crystalline SiO_2 (quartz) and (b) amorphous SiO_2 (quartz glass).** The structures are actually three-dimensional and not planar as drawn. The two-dimensional unit shown as the basic building block of the structure (silicon and three oxygens) actually has four oxygens, the fourth coming out of the plane of the paper and capable of bonding to other silicon atoms. The actual three-dimensional building block is shown.

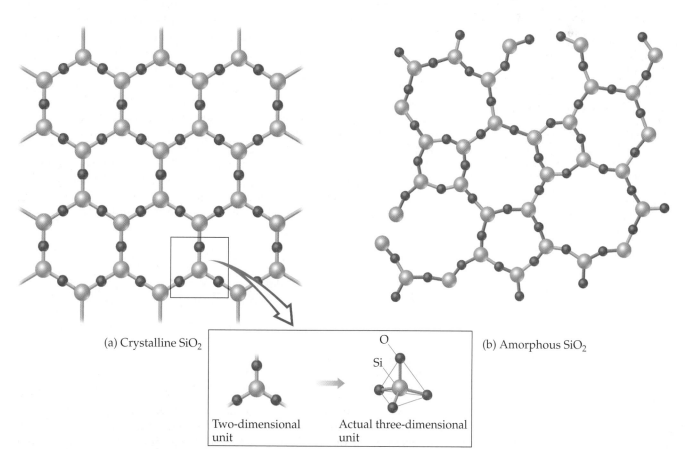

(a) Crystalline SiO_2

(b) Amorphous SiO_2

O

Si

Two-dimensional unit

Actual three-dimensional unit

Because the particles of an amorphous solid lack any long-range order, intermolecular forces vary in strength throughout a sample. Thus, amorphous solids do not melt at specific temperatures. Instead, they soften over a temperature range as intermolecular forces of various strengths are overcome. A crystalline solid, in contrast, melts at a specific temperature.

▲ **GIVE IT SOME THOUGHT**

What is the general difference in the melting behaviors of crystalline and amorphous solids?

Unit Cells

The characteristic order of crystalline solids allows us to convey a picture of an entire crystal by looking at only a small part of it. We can think of the solid as being built by stacking together identical building blocks, much as stacking rows of individual "identical" bricks forms a brick wall. The repeating unit of a solid, the crystalline "brick," is known as the **unit cell**. A simple two-dimensional example appears in the sheet of wallpaper shown in Figure 11.31 ◄. There are several ways of choosing a unit cell, but the choice is usually the smallest unit cell that shows clearly the symmetry characteristic of the entire pattern.

A crystalline solid can be represented by a three-dimensional array of points called a **crystal lattice**. Each point in the lattice is called a *lattice point*, and it represents an identical environment within the solid. The crystal lattice is, in effect, an abstract scaffolding for the crystal structure. We can imagine forming the entire crystal structure by arranging the contents of the unit cell repeatedly on the crystal lattice. In the simplest case the crystal structure would consist of identical atoms, and each atom would be centered on a lattice point. This is the case for most metals.

Figure 11.32 ◄ shows a crystal lattice and its associated unit cell. In general, unit cells are parallelepipeds (six-sided figures whose faces are parallelograms). Each unit cell can be described by the lengths of the edges of the cell and by the angles between these edges. Seven basic types of unit cells can describe the lattices of all crystalline compounds. The simplest of these is the cubic unit cell, in which all the sides are equal in length and all the angles are 90°.

Three kinds of cubic unit cells are illustrated in Figure 11.33 ▼. When lattice points are at the corners only, the unit cell is called **primitive cubic** (or *simple cubic*). When a lattice point also occurs at the center of the unit cell, the cell is **body-centered cubic**. When the cell has lattice points at the center of each face, as well as at each corner, it is **face-centered cubic**.

The simplest crystal structures are cubic unit cells with only one atom centered at each lattice point. Most metals have such structures. Nickel, for example, has a face-centered cubic unit cell, whereas sodium has a body-centered cubic one. Figure 11.34 ▶ shows how atoms fill the cubic unit cells. Notice that

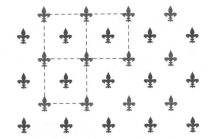

▲ **Figure 11.31 A two-dimensional analog of a lattice and its unit cell.** The wallpaper design shows a characteristic repeat pattern. Each dashed blue square denotes a unit cell of the pattern. The unit cell could equally well be selected with red figures at the corners.

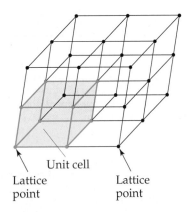

▲ **Figure 11.32 Part of a simple crystal lattice and its associated unit cell.** A lattice is an array of points that define the positions of particles in a crystalline solid. Each lattice point represents an identical environment in the solid. The points here are shown connected by lines to help convey the three-dimensional character of the lattice and to help us see the unit cell.

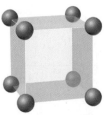 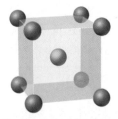 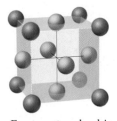

Primitive cubic   Body-centered cubic   Face-centered cubic

▲ **Figure 11.33 The three types of unit cells found in cubic lattices.** For clarity, the corner spheres are red and the body-centered and face-centered ones are yellow. Each sphere represents a lattice point (an identical environment in the solid).

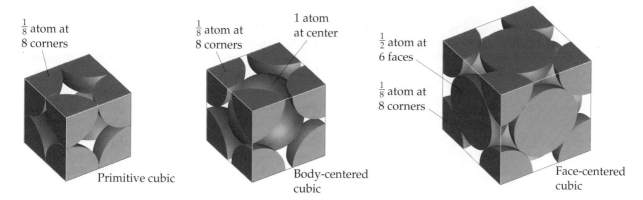

$\frac{1}{8}$ atom at 8 corners

Primitive cubic

$\frac{1}{8}$ atom at 8 corners

1 atom at center

Body-centered cubic

$\frac{1}{2}$ atom at 6 faces

$\frac{1}{8}$ atom at 8 corners

Face-centered cubic

▲ Figure 11.34 **Space-filling view of cubic unit cells.** Only the portion of each atom that belongs to the unit cell is shown.

the atoms on the corners and faces do not lie wholly within the unit cell. Instead, these atoms are shared between unit cells. As an example, let's look at the primitive cubic structure in Figure 11.34. In an actual solid, this primitive cubic structure has other primitive cubic unit cells next to it in all directions, on top of it, and underneath it. If you look at any one corner of the primitive cubic unit cell, you will see that is shared by 8 unit cells. Therefore, in an individual primitive cubic unit cell, each corner contains only one-eighth of an atom. Because a cube has eight corners, each primitive cubic unit cell has a total of $1/8 \times 8 = 1$ atom. Similarly, each body-centered cubic unit cell shown in Figure 11.34 contains two atoms ($1/8 \times 8 = 1$ from the corners, and 1 totally inside the cube). Two unit cells share equally atoms that are on the faces of a face-centered cubic unit cell so that only one-half of the atom belongs to each unit cell. Therefore, the total number of atoms in the face-centered cubic unit cell shown in Figure 11.34 is four (that is, $1/8 \times 8 = 1$ from the corners and $1/2 \times 6 = 3$ from the faces). Table 11.6 ▶ summarizes the fraction of an atom that occupies a unit cell when atoms are shared between unit cells.

TABLE 11.6 ■ Fraction of an Atom That Occupies a Unit Cell for Various Positions in the Unit Cell	
Position in Unit Cell	**Fraction in Unit Cell**
Center	1
Face	$\frac{1}{2}$
Edge	$\frac{1}{4}$
Corner	$\frac{1}{8}$

△ **GIVE IT SOME THOUGHT**

If you know the unit cell dimensions for a solid, the number of atoms per unit cell, and the mass of the atoms, show how you can calculate the density of the solid.

The Crystal Structure of Sodium Chloride

In the crystal structure of NaCl (Figure 11.35 ▼) we can center either the Na$^+$ ions or the Cl$^-$ ions on the lattice points of a face-centered cubic unit cell. Thus, we can describe the structure as being face-centered cubic.

▼ Figure 11.35 **Two ways of defining the unit cell of NaCl.** A representation of an NaCl crystal lattice can show either (a) Cl$^-$ ions (green spheres) or (b) Na$^+$ ions (purple spheres) at the lattice points of the unit cell. In both cases, the red lines define the unit cell. Both of these choices for the unit cell are acceptable; both have the same volume, and in both cases identical points are arranged in a face-centered cubic fashion.

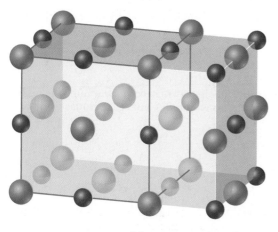

(a)

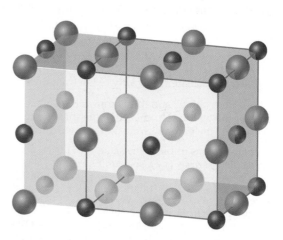

(b)

▶ **Figure 11.36**
Relative size of ions in an NaCl unit cell.
As in Figure 11.35, purple represents Na⁺ ions and green represents Cl⁻ ions. Only portions of most of the ions lie within the boundaries of the single unit cell.

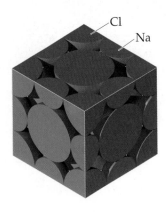

In Figure 11.35 the Na^+ and Cl^- ions have been moved apart so the symmetry of the structure can be seen more clearly. In this representation no attention is paid to the relative sizes of the ions. The representation in Figure 11.36 ◀, on the other hand, shows the relative sizes of the ions and how they fill the unit cell. Notice that other unit cells share the particles at corners, edges, and faces.

The total cation-to-anion ratio of a unit cell must be the same as that for the entire crystal. Therefore, within the unit cell of NaCl there must be an equal number of Na^+ and Cl^- ions. Similarly, the unit cell for $CaCl_2$ would have one Ca^{2+} for every two Cl^-, and so forth.

■■ **SAMPLE EXERCISE 11.7** | **Determining the Contents of a Unit Cell**

Determine the net number of Na^+ and Cl^- ions in the NaCl unit cell (Figure 11.36).

SOLUTION

Analyze: We must sum the various contributing elements to determine the number of Na^+ and Cl^- ions within the unit cell.

Plan: To find the total number of ions of each type, we must identify the different locations within the unit cell and determine the fraction of the ion that lies within the unit cell boundaries.

Solve: There is one-fourth of an Na^+ on each edge, a whole Na^+ in the center of the cube (refer also to Figure 11.35), one-eighth of a Cl^- on each corner, and one-half of a Cl^- on each face. Thus, we have the following:

$$Na^+: \left(\tfrac{1}{4}\,Na^+ \text{ per edge}\right)(12 \text{ edges}) = 3\,Na^+$$
$$(1\,Na^+ \text{ per center})(1 \text{ center}) = 1\,Na^+$$
$$Cl^-: \left(\tfrac{1}{8}\,Cl^- \text{ per corner}\right)(8 \text{ corners}) = 1\,Cl^-$$
$$\left(\tfrac{1}{2}\,Cl^- \text{ per face}\right)(6 \text{ faces}) = 3\,Cl^-$$

Thus, the unit cell contains

$$4\,Na^+ \text{ and } 4\,Cl^-$$

Check: Since individually the Cl^- ions form a face-centered cubic lattice [see Figure 11.35(a)], as do the Na^+ ions [see Figure 11.35(b)], we would expect there to be four ions of each type in the unit cell. More important, the presence of equal amounts of the two ions agree with the compound's stoichiometry:

$$1\,Na^+ \text{ for each } Cl^-$$

■■ **PRACTICE EXERCISE**

The element iron crystallizes in a form called α-iron, which has a body-centered cubic unit cell. How many iron atoms are in the unit cell?
Answer: two

■■ **SAMPLE EXERCISE 11.8** | **Using the Contents and Dimensions of a Unit Cell to Calculate Density**

The geometric arrangement of ions in crystals of LiF is the same as that in NaCl. The unit cell of LiF is 4.02 Å on an edge. Calculate the density of LiF.

SOLUTION

Analyze: We are asked to calculate the density of LiF from the size of the unit cell.

Plan: Density is mass per volume, and this is true at the unit cell level as well as the bulk level. We need to determine the number of formula units of LiF within the unit cell. From that, we can calculate the total mass within the unit cell. Because we know the mass and can calculate the volume of the unit cell, we can then calculate density.

Solve: The arrangement of ions in LiF is the same as that in NaCl (Sample Exercise 11.7), so a unit cell of LiF contains

$$4\,Li^+ \text{ ions and } 4\,F^- \text{ ions}$$

Density is mass per unit volume. Thus, we can calculate the density of LiF from the mass contained in a unit cell and the volume of the unit cell. The mass contained in one unit cell is

$$4(6.94 \text{ amu}) + 4(19.0 \text{ amu}) = 103.8 \text{ amu}$$

The volume of a cube of length a on an edge is a^3, so the volume of the unit cell is $(4.02 \text{ Å})^3$. We can now calculate the density, converting to the common units of g/cm^3:

$$\text{Density} = \frac{(103.8 \text{ amu})}{(4.02 \text{ Å})^3} \left(\frac{1 \text{ g}}{6.02 \times 10^{23} \text{ amu}}\right) \left(\frac{1 \text{ Å}}{10^{-8} \text{ cm}}\right)^3 = 2.65 \text{ g/cm}^3$$

Check: This value agrees with that found by simple density measurements, 2.640 g/cm^3 at 20 °C. The size and contents of the unit cell are therefore consistent with the macroscopic density of the substance.

■ **PRACTICE EXERCISE**

The body-centered cubic unit cell of a particular crystalline form of iron is 2.8664 Å on each side. Calculate the density of this form of iron.
Answer: 7.8753 g/cm^3

Close Packing of Spheres

The structures adopted by crystalline solids are those that bring particles in closest contact to maximize the attractive forces between them. In many cases the particles that make up the solids are spherical or approximately so. Such is the case for atoms in metallic solids. It is therefore instructive to consider how equal-sized spheres can pack most efficiently (that is, with the minimum amount of empty space).

The most efficient arrangement of a layer of equal-sized spheres is shown in Figure 11.37(a) ▼. Each sphere is surrounded by six others in the layer. A second layer of spheres can be placed in the depressions on top of the first layer. A third layer can then be added above the second with the spheres sitting in the depressions of the second layer. However, there are two types of depressions for this third layer, and they result in different structures, as shown in Figure 11.37(b) and (c).

If the spheres of the third layer are placed in line with those of the first layer, as shown in Figure 11.37(b), the structure is known as **hexagonal close packing**. The third layer repeats the first layer, the fourth layer repeats the second layer, and so forth, giving a layer sequence that we denote ABAB.

The spheres of the third layer, however, can be placed so they do not sit above the spheres in the first layer. The resulting structure, shown in Figure 11.37(c), is known as **cubic close packing**. In this case it is the fourth layer that repeats the first layer, and the layer sequence is ABCA. Although it cannot be seen in Figure 11.37(c), the unit cell of the cubic close-packed structure is face-centered cubic.

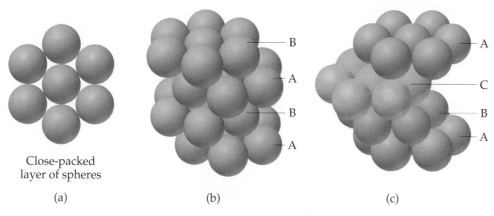

Close-packed
layer of spheres

(a)   (b)   (c)

▲ **Figure 11.37 Close packing of equal-sized spheres.** (a) Close packing of a single layer of equal-sized spheres. (b) In the hexagonal close-packed structure the atoms in the third layer lie directly over those in the first layer. The order of layers is ABAB. (c) In the cubic close-packed structure the atoms in the third layer are not over those in the first layer. Instead, they are offset a bit, and it is the fourth layer that lies directly over the first. Thus, the order of layers is ABCA.

In both of the close-packed structures, each sphere has 12 equidistant nearest neighbors: six in one plane, three above that plane, and three below. We say that each sphere has a **coordination number** of 12. The coordination number is the number of particles immediately surrounding a particle in the crystal structure. In both types of close packing, spheres occupy 74% of the total volume of the structure; 26% is empty space between the spheres. By comparison, each sphere in the body-centered cubic structure has a coordination number of 8, and only 68% of the space is occupied. In the primitive cubic structure the coordination number is 6, and only 52% of the space is occupied.

When unequal-sized spheres are packed in a lattice, the larger particles sometimes assume one of the close-packed arrangements, with smaller particles occupying the holes between the large spheres. In Li_2O, for example, the larger oxide ions assume a cubic close-packed structure, and the smaller Li^+ ions occupy small cavities that exist between oxide ions.

> ▲ **GIVE IT SOME THOUGHT**
>
> Based on the information given above for close-packed structures and structures with cubic unit cells, what qualitative relationship exists between coordination numbers and packing efficiencies?

11.8 BONDING IN SOLIDS

The physical properties of crystalline solids, such as melting point and hardness, depend both on the arrangements of particles (atoms, ions, or molecules) and on the attractive forces between them. Table 11.7 ▼ classifies solids according to the types of forces between particles in solids.

Molecular Solids

Molecular solids consist of atoms or molecules held together by intermolecular forces (dipole–dipole forces, London dispersion forces, and hydrogen bonds). Because these forces are weak, molecular solids are soft. Furthermore, they normally have relatively low melting points (usually below 200 °C). Most substances that are gases or liquids at room temperature form molecular solids at low temperature. Examples include Ar, H_2O, and CO_2.

TABLE 11.7 ■ Types of Crystalline Solids

Type of Solid	Form of Unit Particles	Forces Between Particles	Properties	Examples
Molecular	Atoms or molecules	London dispersion forces, dipole–dipole forces, hydrogen bonds	Fairly soft, low to moderately high melting point, poor thermal and electrical conduction	Argon, Ar; methane, CH_4; sucrose, $C_{12}H_{22}O_{11}$; Dry Ice, CO_2
Covalent-network	Atoms connected in a network of covalent bonds	Covalent bonds	Very hard, very high melting point, variable thermal and electrical conduction	Diamond, C; quartz, SiO_2
Ionic	Positive and negative ions	Electrostatic attractions	Hard and brittle, high melting point, poor thermal and electrical conduction	Typical salts—for example, NaCl, $Ca(NO_3)_2$
Metallic	Atoms	Metallic bonds	Soft to very hard, low to very high melting point, excellent thermal and electrical conduction, malleable and ductile	All metallic elements—for example, Cu, Fe, Al, Pt

Metals vary greatly in the strength of their bonding, as shown by their wide range of physical properties such as hardness and melting point. In general, however, the strength of the bonding increases as the number of electrons available for bonding increases. Thus, sodium, which has only one valence electron per atom, melts at 97.5 °C, whereas chromium, with six electrons beyond the noble-gas core, melts at 1890 °C. The mobility of the electrons explains why metals are good conductors of heat and electricity. The bonding and properties of metals will be examined more closely in Chapter 23.

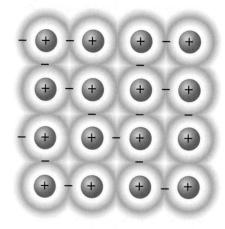

▲ Figure 11.45 **Representation of a cross section of a metal.** Each sphere represents the nucleus and inner-core electrons of a metal atom. The surrounding blue "fog" represents the mobile sea of electrons that binds the atoms together.

■ **SAMPLE INTEGRATIVE EXERCISE** | Putting Concepts Together

The substance CS_2 has a melting point of −110.8 °C and a boiling point of 46.3 °C. Its density at 20 °C is 1.26 g/cm³. It is highly flammable. **(a)** What is the name of this compound? **(b)** List the intermolecular forces that CS_2 molecules would have with each other. **(c)** Predict what type of crystalline solid $CS_2(s)$ would form. **(d)** Write a balanced equation for the combustion of this compound in air. (You will have to decide on the most likely oxidation products.) **(e)** The critical temperature and pressure for CS_2 are 552 K and 78 atm, respectively. Compare these values with those for CO_2 (Table 11.5), and discuss the possible origins of the differences. **(f)** Would you expect the density of CS_2 at 40 °C to be greater or less than at 20 °C? What accounts for the difference?

SOLUTION

(a) The compound is named carbon disulfide, in analogy with the naming of other binary molecular compounds such as carbon dioxide. ∞ (Section 2.8)
(b) Only London dispersion forces affect CS_2; it does not have a dipole moment, based upon its molecular shape, and obviously cannot undergo hydrogen bonding.
(c) Because $CS_2(s)$ consists of individual CS_2 molecules, it will be a molecular solid.
(d) The most likely products of the combustion will be CO_2 and SO_2. ∞ (Sections 3.2 and 7.8) Under some conditions SO_3 might be formed, but this would be the less likely outcome. Thus, we have the following equation for combustion:

$$CS_2(l) + 3\,O_2(g) \longrightarrow CO_2(g) + 2\,SO_2(g)$$

(e) The critical temperature and pressure of CS_2 (552 K and 78 atm) are both higher than those given for CO_2 in Table 11.5 (304 K and 73 atm). The difference in critical temperatures is especially notable. The higher values for CS_2 arise from the greater London dispersion attractions between the CS_2 molecules compared with CO_2. These greater attractions are due to the larger size of the sulfur compared to oxygen and therefore its greater polarizability.
(f) The density would be lower at the higher temperature. Density decreases with increasing temperature because the molecules possess higher kinetic energies. Their more energetic movements result in larger average distances between molecules, which translate into lower densities.

CHAPTER REVIEW

SUMMARY AND KEY TERMS

Introduction and Section 11.1 Substances that are gases or liquids at room temperature are usually composed of molecules. In gases the intermolecular attractive forces are negligible compared to the kinetic energies of the molecules; thus, the molecules are widely separated and undergo constant, chaotic motion. In liquids the **intermolecular forces** are strong enough to keep the molecules in close proximity; nevertheless, the molecules are free to move with respect to one another. In solids the interparticle attractive forces are strong enough to restrain

molecular motion and to force the particles to occupy specific locations in a three-dimensional arrangement.

Section 11.2 Three types of intermolecular forces exist between neutral molecules: **dipole–dipole forces**, **London dispersion forces**, and **hydrogen bonding**. **Ion–dipole forces** are important in solutions in which ionic compounds are dissolved in polar solvents. London dispersion forces operate between all molecules (and atoms, for atomic substances such as He, Ne, Ar, and so forth). The relative strengths of the dipole–dipole and dispersion forces depend on the polarity, **polarizability**, size, and shape of the molecule. Dipole–dipole forces increase in strength with increasing polarity. Dispersion forces increase in strength with increasing molecular weight, although molecular shape is also an important factor. Hydrogen bonding occurs in compounds containing O—H, N—H, and F—H bonds. Hydrogen bonds are generally stronger than dipole–dipole or dispersion forces.

Section 11.3 The stronger the intermolecular forces, the greater is the **viscosity**, or resistance to flow, of a liquid. The surface tension of a liquid also increases as intermolecular forces increase in strength. **Surface tension** is a measure of the tendency of a liquid to maintain a minimum surface area. The adhesion of a liquid to the walls of a narrow tube and the cohesion of the liquid account for **capillary action** and the formation of a meniscus at the surface of a liquid.

Section 11.4 A substance may exist in more than one state of matter, or phase. **Phase changes** are transformations from one phase to another. Changes of a solid to liquid (melting), solid to gas (sublimation), and liquid to gas (vaporization) are all endothermic processes. Thus, the **heat of fusion** (melting), the **heat of sublimation**, and the **heat of vaporization** are all positive quantities. The reverse processes are exothermic. A gas cannot be liquefied by application of pressure if the temperature is above its **critical temperature**. The pressure required to liquefy a gas at its critical temperature is called the **critical pressure**.

Section 11.5 The **vapor pressure** of a liquid indicates the tendency of the liquid to evaporate. The vapor pressure is the partial pressure of the vapor when it is in **dynamic equilibrium** with the liquid. At equilibrium the rate of transfer of molecules from the liquid to the vapor equals the rate of transfer from the vapor to the liquid. The higher the vapor pressure of a liquid, the more readily it evaporates and the more **volatile** it is. Vapor pressure increases nonlinearly with temperature. Boiling occurs when the vapor pressure equals the external pressure.

The **normal boiling point** is the temperature at which the vapor pressure equals 1 atm.

Section 11.6 The equilibria between the solid, liquid, and gas phases of a substance as a function of temperature and pressure are displayed on a **phase diagram**. A line indicates equilibria between any two phases. The line through the melting point usually slopes slightly to the right as pressure increases, because the solid is usually more dense than the liquid. The melting point at 1 atm is the **normal melting point**. The point on the diagram at which all three phases coexist in equilibrium is called the **triple point**.

Section 11.7 In a **crystalline solid**, particles are arranged in a regularly repeating pattern. An **amorphous solid** is one whose particles show no such order. The essential structural features of a crystalline solid can be represented by its **unit cell**, the smallest part of the crystal that can, by simple displacement, reproduce the three-dimensional structure. The three-dimensional structures of a crystal can also be represented by its **crystal lattice**. The points in a crystal lattice represent positions in the structure where there are identical environments. The simplest unit cells are cubic. There are three kinds of cubic unit cells: **primitive cubic, body-centered cubic**, and **face-centered cubic**. Many solids have a close-packed structure in which spherical particles are arranged so as to leave the minimal amount of empty space. Two closely related forms of close packing, **cubic close packing** and **hexagonal close packing**, are possible. In both, each sphere has a **coordination number** of 12.

Section 11.8 The properties of solids depend both on the arrangements of particles and on the attractive forces between them. **Molecular solids**, which consist of atoms or molecules held together by intermolecular forces, are soft and low melting. **Covalent-network solids**, which consist of atoms held together by covalent bonds that extend throughout the solid, are hard and high melting. **Ionic solids** are hard and brittle and have high melting points. **Metallic solids**, which consist of metal cations held together by a sea of electrons, exhibit a wide range of properties.

KEY SKILLS

- Understand and be able to describe the intermolecular attractive interactions (ion–dipole, dipole–dipole, London dispersion, hydrogen bonding) that exist between molecules or ions, and be able to compare the relative strengths of intermolecular attractions in substances based on their molecular structure, or physical properties.

- Understand the concept of polarizability.

- Understand the concepts of viscosity and surface tension in liquids.

- Know the names of the various phase changes for a pure substance.

- Interpret heating curves and be able to calculate quantities related to temperature and enthalpies of phase changes.

- Define critical pressure, critical temperature, vapor pressure, normal boiling point, normal melting point, critical point, triple point.

- Be able to interpret and sketch phase diagrams; know how water's phase diagram differs from most other substances, and why.

- Know the difference between crystalline and amorphous solids, and be able to explain the differences between primitive cubic, body-centered cubic, and face-centered cubic unit cells.

- Classify solids based on their bonding/intermolecular forces and understand how difference in bonding relates to physical properties.

VISUALIZING CONCEPTS

11.1 Does the following diagram best describe a crystalline solid, liquid, or gas? Explain. [Section 11.1]

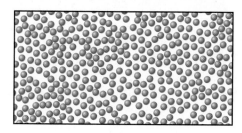

11.2 (a) What kind of intermolecular attractive force is shown in each of the following cases? (b) Predict which two interactions are stronger than the other two. [Section 11.2]

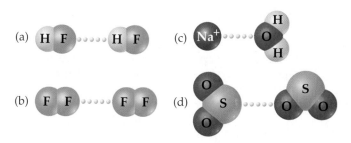

11.3 The molecular models of glycerol and 1-propanol are given here.

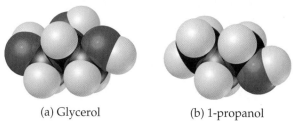

(a) Glycerol   (b) 1-propanol

Do you expect the viscosity of glycerol to be larger or smaller than that of 1-propanol? Explain. [Section 11.3]

11.4 Using the following graph of CS_2 data, determine (a) the approximate vapor pressure of CS_2 at 30 °C, (b) the temperature at which the vapor pressure equals 300 torr, (c) the normal boiling point of CS_2. [Section 11.5]

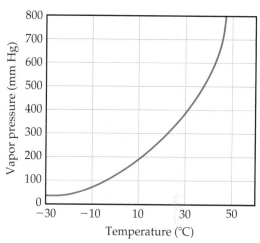

11.5 The following molecules have the same molecular formula (C_3H_8O), yet they have different normal boiling points, as shown. Rationalize the difference in boiling points. [Sections 11.2 and 11.5]

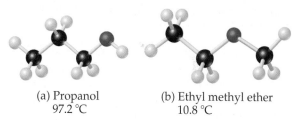

(a) Propanol   (b) Ethyl methyl ether
97.2 °C   10.8 °C

11.6 The phase diagram of a hypothetical substance is shown below.

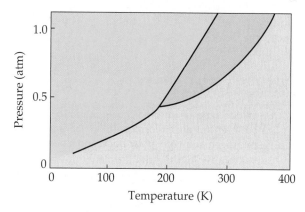

(a) Estimate the normal boiling point and freezing point of the substance.

(b) What is the physical state of the substance under the following conditions?
(i) $T = 150$ K, $P = 0.2$ atm
(ii) $T = 100$ K, $P = 0.8$ atm
(iii) $T = 300$ K, $P = 1.0$ atm

(c) What is the triple point of the substance? [Section 11.6]

11.7 Niobium(II) oxide crystallizes in the following cubic unit cell.

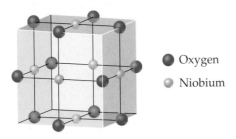

Oxygen

Niobium

(a) How many niobium atoms and how many oxygen atoms are within the unit cell?

(b) What is the empirical formula of niobium oxide?

(c) Is this a molecular, covalent-network, or ionic solid? [Sections 11.7 and 11.8]

11.8 (a) What kind of packing arrangement is seen in the accompanying photo? (b) What is the coordination number of each orange in the interior of the stack? (c) If each orange represents an argon atom, what category of solid is represented? [Sections 11.7 and 11.8]

EXERCISES

Molecular Comparisons of Gases, Liquids, and Solids

11.9 List the three states of matter in order of (a) increasing molecular disorder and (b) increasing intermolecular attractions. (c) Which state of matter is most easily compressed?

11.10 (a) How does the average kinetic energy of molecules compare with the average energy of attraction between molecules in solids, liquids, and gases? (b) Why does increasing the temperature cause a solid substance to change in succession from a solid to a liquid to a gas? (c) What happens to a gas if you put it under extremely high pressure?

11.11 If you mix olive oil with water, the olive oil will float on top of the water. The density of water is 1.00 g/cm^3 at room temperature. (a) Is the density of olive oil more or less than 1.00 g/cm^3? (b) The density of olive oil in its liquid phase does vary with temperature. Do you think olive oil would be more dense or less dense at higher temperatures? Explain.

11.12 Benzoic acid, C_6H_5COOH, melts at 122 °C. The density in the liquid state at 130 °C is 1.08 g/cm^3. The density of solid benzoic acid at 15 °C is 1.266 g/cm^3. (a) In which of these two states is the average distance between molecules greater? (b) Explain the difference in densities at the two temperatures in terms of the relative kinetic energies of the molecules.

Intermolecular Forces

11.13 Which type of intermolecular attractive force operates between (a) all molecules, (b) polar molecules, (c) the hydrogen atom of a polar bond and a nearby small electronegative atom?

11.14 Based on what you have learned about intermolecular forces, would you say that matter is fundamentally attracted or repulsed by other matter?

11.15 Describe the intermolecular forces that must be overcome to convert each of the following from a liquid or solid to a gas: (a) I_2, (b) CH_3CH_2OH, (c) H_2Se.

11.16 What type of intermolecular force accounts for the following differences in each case? (a) CH_3OH boils at 65 °C, CH_3SH boils at 6 °C. (b) Xe is liquid at atmospheric pressure and 120 K, whereas Ar is a gas. (c) Kr, atomic weight 84, boils at 120.9 K, whereas Cl_2, molecular weight about 71, boils at 238 K. (d) Acetone boils at 56 °C, whereas 2-methylpropane boils at −12 °C.

$$CH_3-\overset{\overset{\displaystyle O}{\|}}{C}-CH_3 \qquad CH_3-\overset{\overset{\displaystyle CH_3}{|}}{CH}-CH_3$$

Acetone   2-Methylpropane

11.17 (a) What is meant by the term *polarizability*? (b) Which of the following atoms would you expect to be most polarizable: N, P, As, Sb? Explain. (c) Put the following molecules in order of increasing polarizability: $GeCl_4$, CH_4, $SiCl_4$, SiH_4, and $GeBr_4$. (d) Predict the order of boiling points of the substances in part (c).

11.18 True or false:

(a) The more polarizable the molecules, the stronger the dispersion forces between them.

(b) The boiling points of the noble gases decrease as you go down the column in the periodic table.

(c) In general, the smaller the molecule, the stronger the dispersion forces.

(d) All other factors being the same, dispersion forces between molecules increase with the number of electrons in the molecules.

11.19 Which member of the following pairs has the larger London dispersion forces: (a) H_2O or H_2S, (b) CO_2 or CO, (c) SiH_4 or GeH_4?

11.20 Which member of the following pairs has the stronger intermolecular dispersion forces: (a) Br_2 or O_2, (b) $CH_3CH_2CH_2CH_2SH$ or $CH_3CH_2CH_2CH_2CH_2SH$, (c) $CH_3CH_2CH_2Cl$ or $(CH_3)_2CHCl$?

11.21 Butane and 2-methylpropane, whose space-filling models are shown, are both nonpolar and have the same molecular formula, yet butane has the higher boiling point ($-0.5\,°C$ compared to $-11.7\,°C$). Explain.

(a) Butane   (b) 2-Methylpropane

11.22 Propyl alcohol ($CH_3CH_2CH_2OH$) and isopropyl alcohol [$(CH_3)_2CHOH$], whose space-filling models are shown, have boiling points of $97.2\,°C$ and $82.5\,°C$, respectively. Explain why the boiling point of propyl alcohol is higher, even though both have the molecular formula of C_3H_8O.

(a) Propyl alcohol   (b) Isopropyl alcohol

11.23 (a) What atoms must a molecule contain to participate in hydrogen bonding with other molecules of the same kind? (b) Which of the following molecules can form hydrogen bonds with other molecules of the same kind: CH_3F, CH_3NH_2, CH_3OH, CH_3Br?

11.24 Rationalize the difference in boiling points between the members of the following pairs of substances: (a) HF ($20\,°C$) and HCl ($-85\,°C$), (b) $CHCl_3$ ($61\,°C$) and $CHBr_3$ ($150\,°C$), (c) Br_2 ($59\,°C$) and ICl ($97\,°C$).

11.25 Ethylene glycol ($HOCH_2CH_2OH$), the major substance in antifreeze, has a normal boiling point of $198\,°C$. By comparison, ethyl alcohol (CH_3CH_2OH) boils at $78\,°C$ at atmospheric pressure. Ethylene glycol dimethyl ether ($CH_3OCH_2CH_2OCH_3$) has a normal boiling point of $83\,°C$, and ethyl methyl ether ($CH_3CH_2OCH_3$) has a normal boiling point of $11\,°C$. (a) Explain why replacement of a hydrogen on the oxygen by CH_3 generally results in a lower boiling point. (b) What are the major factors responsible for the difference in boiling points of the two ethers?

11.26 Identify the types of intermolecular forces present in each of the following substances, and select the substance in each pair that has the higher boiling point: (a) C_6H_{14} or C_8H_{18}, (b) C_3H_8 or CH_3OCH_3, (c) HOOH or HSSH, (d) NH_2NH_2 or CH_3CH_3.

11.27 Look up and compare the normal boiling points and normal melting points of H_2O and H_2S. (a) Based on these physical properties, which substance has stronger intermolecular forces? What kind of intermolecular forces exist for each molecule? (b) Predict whether solid H_2S is more or less dense than liquid H_2S. How does this compare to H_2O? Explain. (c) Water has an unusually high specific heat. Is this related to its intermolecular forces? Explain.

11.28 The following quote about ammonia (NH_3) is from a textbook of inorganic chemistry: "It is estimated that 26% of the hydrogen bonding in NH_3 breaks down on melting, 7% on warming from the melting to the boiling point, and the final 67% on transfer to the gas phase at the boiling point." From the standpoint of the kinetic energy of the molecules, explain (a) why there is a decrease of hydrogen-bonding energy on melting and (b) why most of the loss in hydrogen bonding occurs in the transition from the liquid to the vapor state.

Viscosity and Surface Tension

11.29 (a) Explain why surface tension and viscosity decrease with increasing temperature. (b) Why do substances with high surface tensions also tend to have high viscosities?

11.30 (a) Distinguish between adhesive forces and cohesive forces. (b) What adhesive and cohesive forces are involved when a paper towel absorbs water? (c) Explain the cause for the U-shaped meniscus formed when water is in a glass tube.

11.31 Explain the following observations: (a) The surface tension of $CHBr_3$ is greater than that of $CHCl_3$. (b) As tem-

perature increases, oil flows faster through a narrow tube. (c) Raindrops that collect on a waxed automobile hood take on a nearly spherical shape. (d) Oil droplets that collect on a waxed automobile hood take on a flat shape.

11.32 Hydrazine (H_2NNH_2), hydrogen peroxide (HOOH), and water (H_2O) all have exceptionally high surface tensions compared with other substances of comparable molecular weights. (a) Draw the Lewis structures for these three compounds. (b) What structural property do these substances have in common, and how might that account for the high surface tensions?

Phase Changes

11.33 Name the phase transition in each of the following situations, and indicate whether it is exothermic or endothermic: **(a)** When ice is heated, it turns to water. **(b)** Wet clothes dry on a warm summer day. **(c)** Frost appears on a window on a cold winter day. **(d)** Droplets of water appear on a cold glass of beer.

11.34 Name the phase transition in each of the following situations, and indicate whether it is exothermic or endothermic: **(a)** Bromine vapor turns to bromine liquid as it is cooled. **(b)** Crystals of iodine disappear from an evaporating dish as they stand in a fume hood. **(c)** Rubbing alcohol in an open container slowly disappears. **(d)** Molten lava from a volcano turns into solid rock.

11.35 Explain why the heat of fusion of any substance is generally lower than its heat of vaporization.

11.36 Ethyl chloride (C_2H_5Cl) boils at 12 °C. When liquid C_2H_5Cl under pressure is sprayed on a room-temperature (25 °C) surface in air, the surface is cooled considerably. **(a)** What does this observation tell us about the specific heat of $C_2H_5Cl(g)$ as compared with $C_2H_5Cl(l)$? **(b)** Assume that the heat lost by the surface is gained by ethyl chloride. What enthalpies must you consider if you were to calculate the final temperature of the surface?

11.37 For many years drinking water has been cooled in hot climates by evaporating it from the surfaces of canvas bags or porous clay pots. How many grams of water can be cooled from 35 °C to 20 °C by the evaporation of 60 g of water? (The heat of vaporization of water in this temperature range is 2.4 kJ/g. The specific heat of water is 4.18 J/g-K.)

11.38 Compounds like CCl_2F_2 are known as chlorofluorocarbons, or CFCs. These compounds were once widely used as refrigerants but are now being replaced by compounds that are believed to be less harmful to the environment. The heat of vaporization of CCl_2F_2 is 289 J/g. What mass of this substance must evaporate to freeze 200 g of water initially at 15 °C? (The heat of fusion of water is 334 J/g; the specific heat of water is 4.18 J/g-K.)

11.39 Ethanol (C_2H_5OH) melts at −114 °C and boils at 78 °C. Its density is 0.789 g/mL. The enthalpy of fusion of ethanol is 5.02 kJ/mol, and its enthalpy of vaporization is 38.56 kJ/mol. The specific heats of solid and liquid ethanol are 0.97 J/g-K and 2.3 J/g-K, respectively. **(a)** How much heat is required to convert 25.0 g of ethanol at 25 °C to the vapor phase at 78 °C? **(b)** How much heat is required to convert 5.00 L of ethanol at −140 °C to the vapor phase at 78 °C?

11.40 The fluorocarbon compound $C_2Cl_3F_3$ has a normal boiling point of 47.6 °C. The specific heats of $C_2Cl_3F_3(l)$ and $C_2Cl_3F_3(g)$ are 0.91 J/g-K and 0.67 J/g-K, respectively. The heat of vaporization for the compound is 27.49 kJ/mol. Calculate the heat required to convert 50.0 g of $C_2Cl_3F_3$ from a liquid at 10.00 °C to a gas at 85.00 °C.

11.41 **(a)** What is the significance of the critical pressure of a substance? **(b)** What happens to the critical temperature of a series of compounds as the force of attraction between molecules increases? **(c)** Which of the substances listed in Table 11.5 can be liquefied at the temperature of liquid nitrogen (−196 °C)?

11.42 The critical temperatures (K) and pressures (atm) of a series of halogenated methanes are as follows:

Compound	CCl_3F	CCl_2F_2	$CClF_3$	CF_4
Critical Temperature	471	385	302	227
Critical Pressure	43.5	40.6	38.2	37.0

(a) List the intermolecular forces that occur for each compound. **(b)** Predict the order of increasing intermolecular attraction, from least to most, for this series of compounds. **(c)** Predict the critical temperature and pressure for CCl_4 based on the trends in this table. Look up the experimentally determined critical temperatures and pressures for CCl_4, using a source such as the *CRC Handbook of Chemistry and Physics*, and suggest a reason for any discrepancies.

Vapor Pressure and Boiling Point

11.43 Explain how each of the following affects the vapor pressure of a liquid: **(a)** volume of the liquid, **(b)** surface area, **(c)** intermolecular attractive forces, **(d)** temperature, **(e)** density of the liquid.

11.44 A liquid that has an equilibrium vapor pressure of 130 torr at 25 °C is placed into a 1-L vessel like that shown in Figure 11.22. What is the pressure difference shown on the manometer, and what is the composition of the gas in the vessel, under each of the following conditions: **(a)** Two hundred mL of the liquid is introduced into the vessel and frozen at the bottom. The vessel is evacuated and sealed, and the liquid is allowed to warm to 25 °C. **(b)** Two hundred milliliters of the liquid is added to the vessel at 25 °C under atmospheric pressure, and after a

few minutes the vessel is closed off. **(c)** A few mL of the liquid is introduced into the vessel at 25 °C while it has a pressure of 1 atm of air in it, without allowing any of the air to escape. After a few minutes a few drops of liquid remain in the vessel.

11.45 **(a)** Place the following substances in order of increasing volatility: CH_4, CBr_4, CH_2Cl_2, CH_3Cl, $CHBr_3$, and CH_2Br_2. Explain. **(b)** How do the boiling points vary through this series?

11.46 True or false:
(a) CBr_4 is more volatile than CCl_4.
(b) CBr_4 has a higher boiling point than CCl_4.
(c) CBr_4 has weaker intermolecular forces than CCl_4.
(d) CBr_4 has a higher vapor pressure at the same temperature than CCl_4.

WHAT'S AHEAD

13.1 The Solution Process

We begin by considering what happens at a molecular level when a substance dissolves, paying particular attention to the role of *intermolecular forces* in the process. Two important aspects of the solution process are the changes in *energy* and the changes in how particles are distributed in space as a result of the solution process.

13.2 Saturated Solutions and Solubility

We will see that in *saturated solutions* the dissolved and undissolved solutes are in *equilibrium*. The amount of solute in a saturated solution defines its *solubility*, the extent to which a particular solute dissolves in a particular solvent.

13.3 Factors Affecting Solubility

We next consider the major factors affecting solubility. The nature of the solute and solvent determines the kinds of intermolecular forces between and within them and strongly influences solubility. Temperature also influences solubility: Most solids are more soluble in water at higher temperatures, whereas gases are less soluble in water at higher temperatures. In addition, the solubility of gases increases with increasing pressure.

13.4 Ways of Expressing Concentration

We observe that many physical properties of solutions depend on their concentration, and we examine several common ways of expressing concentration.

13.5 Colligative Properties

We observe that solutes affect the properties of solutions. The physical properties of solutions that depend only on concentration and not on the identity of the solute are called *colligative properties*. These properties include the extent to which the solute lowers the vapor pressure, increases the boiling point, and decreases the freezing point of the solvent. The osmotic pressure of a solution is also a colligative property.

13.6 Colloids

We close the chapter by investigating *colloids*, mixtures in which particles larger than typical molecular sizes are dispersed in another component.

ON A WARM DAY AT THE BEACH, we are unlikely to consider chemistry while we enjoy the water and warmth of the sun. But as we breathe the air, swim in the water, and walk on the sand, we are experiencing the three states of matter. In Chapter 10 and 11, we explored the properties

of gases, liquids, and solids. Most of the discussion focused on pure substances. However, the matter that we encounter in our daily lives, such as air, seawater, and sand, is usually composed of mixtures. In this chapter we examine mixtures, although we limit ourselves to those that are homogeneous. As we have noted in earlier chapters, a homogeneous mixture is called a *solution*. ∞ (Sections 1.2 and 4.1)

When we think of solutions, we usually first think about liquids, such as a solution of salt in water, like the seawater shown in this chapter's opening photo. Sterling silver, which is used in jewelry, is also a solution—a homogeneous distribution of about 7% copper in silver. Sterling silver is an example of a solid solution. Numerous examples of solutions abound in the world around us—some solid, some liquid, and some gas. For example, the air we breathe is a solution of several gases; brass is a solid solution of zinc in copper; and the fluids that run through our bodies are solutions that carry a variety of essential nutrients, salts, and other materials.

Each of the substances in a solution is called a *component* of the solution. As we saw in Chapter 4, the *solvent* is normally the component present in the greatest amount. Other components are called *solutes*. Because liquid solutions are the most common, we will focus our attention on them in this chapter. Our primary goal is to examine the physical properties of solutions, comparing them with the properties of their components. We will be particularly concerned with *aqueous solutions*, which contain water as the solvent and a gas, liquid, or solid as a solute.

13.1 THE SOLUTION PROCESS

A solution is formed when one substance disperses uniformly throughout another. As we noted in the introduction, solutions may be gases, liquids, or solids. Each of these possibilities is listed in Table 13.1 ▼.

The ability of substances to form solutions depends on two general factors: (1) the types of intermolecular interactions involved in the solution process, and (2) the natural tendency of substances to spread into larger volumes when not restrained in some way. We begin our discussion of the solution process by examining the role of intermolecular interactions.

The Effect of Intermolecular Forces

Any of the various kinds of intermolecular forces that we discussed in Chapter 11 can operate between solute and solvent particles in a solution. Ion–dipole forces, for example, dominate in solutions of ionic substances in water. Dispersion forces, on the other hand, dominate when a nonpolar substance such as C_6H_{14} dissolves in another nonpolar one like CCl_4. Indeed, a major factor determining whether a solution forms is the relative strengths of intermolecular forces between and among the solute and solvent particles. That is, the extent to which one substance is able to dissolve in another depends on the relative magnitudes of the solute–solvent, solute–solute, and solvent–solvent interactions involved in the solution process.

Solutions form when the magnitudes of the attractive forces between solute and solvent particles are comparable to or greater than those that exist between the solute particles themselves or between the solvent particles themselves. For example, the ionic substance NaCl dissolves readily in water because the attractive interactions between the ions and the polar H_2O molecules (solute–solvent interactions) overcome the attraction between the ions in the solid NaCl

TABLE 13.1 ■ Examples of Solutions			
State of Solution	**State of Solvent**	**State of Solute**	**Example**
Gas	Gas	Gas	Air
Liquid	Liquid	Gas	Oxygen in water
Liquid	Liquid	Liquid	Alcohol in water
Liquid	Liquid	Solid	Salt in water
Solid	Solid	Gas	Hydrogen in palladium
Solid	Solid	Liquid	Mercury in silver
Solid	Solid	Solid	Silver in gold

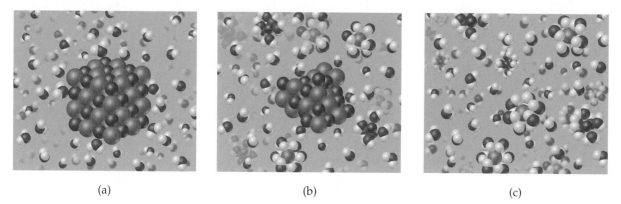

(a)   (b)   (c)

▲ **Figure 13.1 Dissolution of an ionic solid in water.** (a) A crystal of the ionic solid is hydrated by water molecules, with the oxygen atoms of the water molecules oriented toward the cations (purple) and the hydrogens oriented toward the anions (green). (b, c) As the solid dissolves, the individual ions are removed from the solid surface and become completely separate hydrated species in solution.

(solute–solute interactions) and between H_2O molecules in the solvent (solvent–solvent interactions). Let's examine this solution process more closely, paying attention to these various attractive forces.

When NaCl is added to water (Figure 13.1▲), the water molecules orient themselves on the surface of the NaCl crystals. The positive end of the water dipole is oriented toward the Cl^- ions, and the negative end of the water dipole is oriented toward the Na^+ ions. The ion–dipole attractions between the ions and water molecules are strong enough to pull the ions from their positions in the crystal.

Once separated from the crystal, the Na^+ and Cl^- ions are surrounded by water molecules, as shown in Figure 13.1(b and c) and Figure 13.2▶. We learned in Section 4.1 that interactions such as this between solute and solvent molecules are known as **solvation**. When the solvent is water, the interactions are also referred to as **hydration**.

In addition to the solvent–solute interactions (the ion–dipole attractions between H_2O molecules and the Na^+ and Cl^- ions) and the solute–solute interactions (between the Na^+ and Cl^- ions in the solid), we must consider one other interaction: the solvent–solvent interaction (in this case the hydrogen-bonding attractions between H_2O molecules). In forming the solution, the water molecules must make room for the hydrated Na^+ and Cl^- ions in their midst, causing some water molecules to move apart.

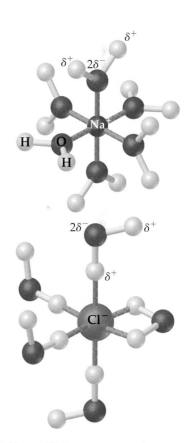

▲ **Figure 13.2 Hydrated Na^+ and Cl^- ions.** The negative ends of the water dipoles point toward the positive ion, and the positive ends point toward the negative ion.

▲ **GIVE IT SOME THOUGHT**

Why doesn't NaCl dissolve in nonpolar solvents such as hexane, C_6H_{14}?

Energy Changes and Solution Formation

We can analyze the roles played by the solute–solvent, solute–solute, and solvent–solvent interactions by examining the energy changes associated with each. Let's continue to analyze the process of dissolving NaCl in water as an example of how energy considerations provide insight into the solution process.

We have observed that sodium chloride dissolves in water because the water molecules have a strong enough attraction for the Na^+ and Cl^- ions to overcome the attraction of these two ions for one another in the crystal. In addition, water molecules must separate from one another to form spaces in the solvent that the Na^+ and Cl^- ions will occupy. Thus, we can think of the overall energetics of solution formation as having three components—associated

▶ Figure 13.3 **Enthalpy contributions to ΔH_{soln}.** The enthalpy changes ΔH_1 and ΔH_2 represent endothermic processes, requiring an input of energy, whereas ΔH_3 represents an exothermic process.

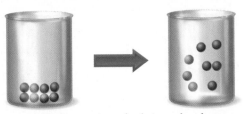

ΔH_1: Separation of solute molecules

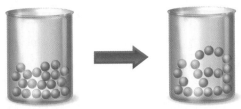

ΔH_2: Separation of solvent molecules

ΔH_3: Formation of solute–solvent interactions

with breaking the solute–solute and the solvent–solvent interactions and forming the solute–solvent interactions—as illustrated schematically in Figure 13.3▲. The overall enthalpy change in forming a solution, ΔH_{soln}, is the sum of three terms associated with these three processes:

$$\Delta H_{\text{soln}} = \Delta H_1 + \Delta H_2 + \Delta H_3 \qquad [13.1]$$

Regardless of the particular solute being considered, separation of the solute particles from one another requires an input of energy to overcome their attractive interactions. The process is therefore endothermic ($\Delta H_1 > 0$). Separation of solvent molecules to accommodate the solute also always requires energy ($\Delta H_2 > 0$). The third component, which arises from the attractive interactions between solute and solvent, is always exothermic ($\Delta H_3 < 0$).

As shown in Figure 13.4▶, the three enthalpy terms in Equation 13.1 can be added together to give either a negative or a positive sum, depending on the relative magnitudes of the terms. Thus, the formation of a solution can be either exothermic or endothermic. For example, when magnesium sulfate, $MgSO_4$, is added to water, the resultant solution gets quite warm: $\Delta H_{\text{soln}} = -91.2$ kJ/mol. In contrast, the dissolution of ammonium nitrate (NH_4NO_3) is endothermic: $\Delta H_{\text{soln}} = 26.4$ kJ/mol. These particular substances have been used to make the instant heat packs and ice packs that are used to treat athletic injuries (Figure 13.5▶). The packs consist of a pouch of water and a dry chemical, $MgSO_4$ for hot packs and NH_4NO_3 for cold packs. When the pack is squeezed, the seal separating the solid from the water is broken and a solution forms, either increasing or decreasing the temperature.

In Chapter 5 we learned that the enthalpy change in a process can provide information about the extent to which a process will occur. ∞ (Section 5.4) Processes that are exothermic tend to proceed spontaneously. A solution will not form if ΔH_{soln} is too endothermic. The solvent–solute interaction must be

(a) A seed crystal of NaCH₃COO being added to the supersaturated solution.

(b) Excess NaCH₃COO crystallizes from the solution.

(c) The solution arrives at saturation.

When the rates of these opposing processes become equal, there is no further net increase in the amount of solute in solution. A dynamic equilibrium is established similar to the one between evaporation and condensation discussed in Section 11.5.

▲ **Figure 13.10 Sodium acetate readily forms a supersaturated solution in water.**

A solution that is in equilibrium with undissolved solute is **saturated**. Additional solute will not dissolve if added to a saturated solution. The amount of solute needed to form a saturated solution in a given quantity of solvent is known as the **solubility** of that solute. That is, *the solubility is the maximum amount of solute that will dissolve in a given amount of solvent at a specified temperature, given that excess solute is present*. For example, the solubility of NaCl in water at 0 °C is 35.7 g per 100 mL of water. This is the maximum amount of NaCl that can be dissolved in water to give a stable equilibrium solution at that temperature.

If we dissolve less solute than that needed to form a saturated solution, the solution is **unsaturated**. Thus, a solution containing only 10.0 g of NaCl per 100 mL of water at 0 °C is unsaturated because it has the capacity to dissolve more solute.

Under suitable conditions it is sometimes possible to form solutions that contain a greater amount of solute than that needed to form a saturated solution. Such solutions are **supersaturated**. For example, considerably more sodium acetate (NaCH₃COO) can dissolve in water at high temperatures than at low temperatures. When a saturated solution of sodium acetate is made at a high temperature and then slowly cooled, all of the solute may remain dissolved even though the solubility decreases as the temperature decreases. Because the solute in a supersaturated solution is present in a concentration higher than the equilibrium concentration, supersaturated solutions are unstable. Supersaturated solutions result for much the same reason as supercooled liquids (Section 11.4). For crystallization to occur, the molecules or ions of solute must arrange themselves properly to form crystals. The addition of a small crystal of the solute (a seed crystal) provides a template for crystallization of the excess solute, leading to a saturated solution in contact with excess solid (Figure 13.10 ▲).

GIVE IT SOME THOUGHT

Is a supersaturated solution of sodium acetate a stable equilibrium solution?

13.3 FACTORS AFFECTING SOLUBILITY

The extent to which one substance dissolves in another depends on the nature of both the solute and the solvent. ⇔ (Section 13.1) It also depends on temperature and, at least for gases, on pressure. Let's consider these factors more closely.

Solute–Solvent Interactions

One factor determining solubility is the natural tendency of substances to mix (the tendency of systems to move toward a more dispersed, or random, state). ∞ (Section 13.2) If this were the only factor involved, however, we would expect all substances to be completely soluble in one another. This is clearly not the case. So what other factors are involved? As we saw in Section 13.1, the relative forces of attraction among the solute and solvent molecules also play very important roles in the solution process.

Although the tendency toward dispersal and the various interactions among solute and solvent particles are all involved in determining the solubilities, considerable insight can often be gained by focusing on the interaction between the solute and solvent. The data in Table 13.2 ◄ show, for example, that the solubilities of various simple gases in water increase with increasing molecular mass or polarity. The attractive forces between the gas and solvent molecules are mainly of the London dispersion type, which increase with increasing size and mass of the gas molecules. ∞ (Section 11.2) Thus, the data indicate that the solubilities of gases in water increase as the attraction between the solute (gas) and solvent (water) increases. In general, when other factors are comparable, *the stronger the attractions are between solute and solvent molecules, the greater the solubility.*

Because of favorable dipole–dipole attractions between solvent molecules and solute molecules, *polar liquids tend to dissolve readily in polar solvents.* Water is both polar and able to form hydrogen bonds. ∞ (Section 11.2) Thus, polar molecules, especially those that can form hydrogen bonds with water molecules, tend to be soluble in water. For example, acetone, a polar molecule with the structural formula shown in the margin, mixes in all proportions with water. Acetone has a strongly polar $C=O$ bond and pairs of nonbonding electrons on the O atom that can form hydrogen bonds with water.

Pairs of liquids such as acetone and water that mix in all proportions are **miscible**, whereas those that do not dissolve in one another are **immiscible**. Gasoline, which is a mixture of hydrocarbons, is immiscible with water. Hydrocarbons are nonpolar substances because of several factors: The C—C bonds are nonpolar, the C—H bonds are nearly nonpolar, and the shapes of the molecules are symmetrical enough to cancel much of the weak C—H bond dipoles. The attraction between the polar water molecules and the nonpolar hydrocarbon molecules is not sufficiently strong to allow the formation of a solution. *Nonpolar liquids tend to be insoluble in polar liquids.* As a result, hexane (C_6H_{14}) does not dissolve in water, as the photo in the margin shows.

The series of compounds in Table 13.3 ▼ demonstrates that polar liquids tend to dissolve in other polar liquids and nonpolar liquids in nonpolar ones. These organic compounds all contain the OH group attached to a C atom. Organic compounds with this molecular feature are called *alcohols.* The O—H bond is polar and is able to form hydrogen bonds. For example, CH_3CH_2OH molecules can form hydrogen bonds with water molecules as well as with each other (Figure 13.11 ▶). As a result, the solute–solute, solvent–solvent, and solute–solvent forces

TABLE 13.2 ■ Solubilities of Gases in Water at 20 °C, with 1 atm Gas Pressure	
Gas	**Solubility (M)**
N_2	0.69×10^{-3}
CO	1.04×10^{-3}
O_2	1.38×10^{-3}
Ar	1.50×10^{-3}
Kr	2.79×10^{-3}

$$:\overset{\displaystyle :O:}{\underset{\displaystyle }{CH_3\overset{\|}{C}CH_3}}$$

Acetone

Hexane is insoluble in water. Hexane is the top layer because it is less dense than water.

TABLE 13.3 ■ Solubilities of Some Alcohols in Water and in Hexane*		
Alcohol	**Solubility in H_2O**	**Solubility in C_6H_{14}**
CH_3OH (methanol)	∞	0.12
CH_3CH_2OH (ethanol)	∞	∞
$CH_3CH_2CH_2OH$ (propanol)	∞	∞
$CH_3CH_2CH_2CH_2OH$ (butanol)	0.11	∞
$CH_3CH_2CH_2CH_2CH_2OH$ (pentanol)	0.030	∞
$CH_3CH_2CH_2CH_2CH_2CH_2OH$ (hexanol)	0.0058	∞

*Expressed in mol alcohol/100 g solvent at 20 °C. The infinity symbol (∞) indicates that the alcohol is completely miscible with the solvent.

Hence, the boiling and freezing points of the solution are

$$\text{Boiling point} = (\text{normal bp of solvent}) + \Delta T_b$$
$$= 100.0\,°\text{C} + 2.7\,°\text{C} = 102.7\,°\text{C}$$

$$\text{Freezing point} = (\text{normal fp of solvent}) - \Delta T_f$$
$$= 0.0\,°\text{C} - 10.0\,°\text{C} = -10.0\,°\text{C}$$

Comment: Notice that the solution is a liquid over a larger temperature range than the pure solvent.

■ PRACTICE EXERCISE

Calculate the freezing point of a solution containing 0.600 kg of $CHCl_3$ and 42.0 g of eucalyptol ($C_{10}H_{18}O$), a fragrant substance found in the leaves of eucalyptus trees. (See Table 13.4.)
Answer: $-65.6\,°\text{C}$

■ SAMPLE EXERCISE 13.10 | **Freezing-Point Depression in Aqueous Solutions**

List the following aqueous solutions in order of their expected freezing point: $0.050\ m$ $CaCl_2$, $0.15\ m$ NaCl, $0.10\ m$ HCl, $0.050\ m$ CH_3COOH, $0.10\ m$ $C_{12}H_{22}O_{11}$.

SOLUTION

Analyze: We must order five aqueous solutions according to expected freezing points, based on molalities and the solute formulas.

Plan: The lowest freezing point will correspond to the solution with the greatest concentration of solute particles. To determine the total concentration of solute particles in each case, we must determine whether the substance is a nonelectrolyte or an electrolyte and consider the number of ions formed when an electrolyte ionizes.

Solve: $CaCl_2$, NaCl, and HCl are strong electrolytes, CH_3COOH (acetic acid) is a weak electrolyte, and $C_{12}H_{22}O_{11}$ is a nonelectrolyte. The molality of each solution in total particles is as follows:

$0.050\ m$ $CaCl_2 \Rightarrow 0.050\ m$ in Ca^{2+} and $0.10\ m$ in $Cl^- \Rightarrow 0.15\ m$ in particles

$0.15\ m$ NaCl $\Rightarrow 0.15\ m$ in Na^+ and $0.15\ m$ in $Cl^- \Rightarrow 0.30\ m$ in particles

$0.10\ m$ HCl $\Rightarrow 0.10\ m$ in H^+ and $0.10\ m$ in $Cl^- \Rightarrow 0.20\ m$ in particles

$0.050\ m$ $CH_3COOH \Rightarrow$ weak electrolyte $\Rightarrow$ between $0.050\ m$ and $0.10\ m$ in particles

$0.10\ m$ $C_{12}H_{22}O_{11} \Rightarrow$ nonelectrolyte $\Rightarrow 0.10\ m$ in particles

Because the freezing points depend on the total molality of particles in solution, the expected ordering is $0.15\ m$ NaCl (lowest freezing point), $0.10\ m$ HCl, $0.050\ m$ $CaCl_2$, $0.10\ m$ $C_{12}H_{22}O_{11}$, and $0.050\ m$ CH_3COOH (highest freezing point).

■ PRACTICE EXERCISE

Which of the following solutes will produce the largest increase in boiling point upon addition to 1 kg of water: 1 mol of $Co(NO_3)_2$, 2 mol of KCl, 3 mol of ethylene glycol ($C_2H_6O_2$)?
Answer: 2 mol of KCl because it contains the highest concentration of particles, $2\ m$ K^+ and $2\ m$ Cl^-, giving $4\ m$ in all

---

Osmosis

Certain materials, including many membranes in biological systems and synthetic substances such as cellophane, are *semipermeable*. When in contact with a solution, they allow some molecules to pass through their network of tiny pores but not others. Most importantly, semipermeable membranes generally allow small solvent molecules such as water to pass through but block larger solute molecules or ions. This selectivity gives rise to some interesting and important applications.

Consider a situation in which only solvent molecules are able to pass through a membrane. If such a membrane is placed between two solutions of different concentration, solvent molecules move in both directions through the membrane. The concentration of *solvent* is higher in the solution containing less solute, however, so the rate with which solvent passes from the less concentrated (lower solute concentration) to the more concentrated solution (higher solute concentration) is greater than the rate in the opposite direction. Thus, there is a net movement of solvent molecules from the less concentrated solution into the more concentrated one. In this process, called **osmosis**, *the net movement of solvent is always toward the solution with the higher solute concentration.*

Osmosis is illustrated in Figure 13.23▼. Let's begin with two solutions of different concentration separated by a semipermeable membrane. Because the solution on the left is more concentrated than the one on the right, there is a net movement of *solvent* through the membrane from right to left, as if the solutions

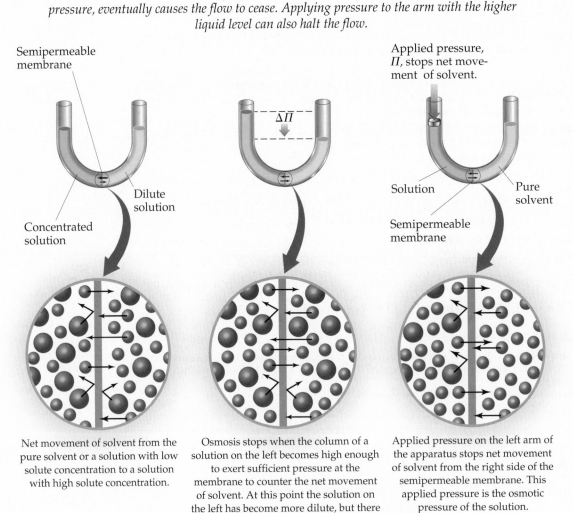

OSMOSIS

In osmosis, the net movement of solvent is always toward the solution with the higher solute concentration. There is a net movement of solvent through the semipermeable membrane, as if the solutions were driven to attain equal concentrations. The difference in liquid level, and thus pressure, eventually causes the flow to cease. Applying pressure to the arm with the higher liquid level can also halt the flow.

Semipermeable membrane

Dilute solution

Concentrated solution

$\Delta \Pi$

Applied pressure, Π, stops net movement of solvent.

Solution

Pure solvent

Semipermeable membrane

Net movement of solvent from the pure solvent or a solution with low solute concentration to a solution with high solute concentration.

Osmosis stops when the column of a solution on the left becomes high enough to exert sufficient pressure at the membrane to counter the net movement of solvent. At this point the solution on the left has become more dilute, but there still exists a difference in concentrations between the two solutions.

Applied pressure on the left arm of the apparatus stops net movement of solvent from the right side of the semipermeable membrane. This applied pressure is the osmotic pressure of the solution.

▲ **Figure 13.23 Osmosis.**

were driven to attain equal concentrations. As a result, the liquid levels in the two arms become unequal. Eventually, the pressure difference resulting from the unequal heights of the liquid in the two arms becomes so large that the net flow of solvent ceases, as shown in the center panel. Alternatively, we may apply pressure to the left arm of the apparatus, as shown in the panel on the right, to halt the net flow of solvent. The pressure required to prevent osmosis by pure solvent is the **osmotic pressure**, Π of the solution. The osmotic pressure obeys a law similar in form to the ideal-gas law, $\Pi V = nRT$ where V is the volume of the solution, n is the number of moles of solute, R is the ideal-gas constant, and T is the temperature on the Kelvin scale. From this equation, we can write

$$\Pi = \left(\frac{n}{V}\right)RT = MRT \qquad [13.13]$$

where M is the molarity of the solution.

If two solutions of identical osmotic pressure are separated by a semipermeable membrane, no osmosis will occur. The two solutions are *isotonic*. If one solution is of lower osmotic pressure, it is *hypotonic* with respect to the more concentrated solution. The more concentrated solution is *hypertonic* with respect to the dilute solution.

GIVE IT SOME THOUGHT

Of two KBr solutions, one 0.5 m and the other 0.20 m, which is hypotonic with respect to the other?

Osmosis plays a very important role in living systems. The membranes of red blood cells, for example, are semipermeable. Placing a red blood cell in a solution that is *hyper*tonic relative to the intracellular solution (the solution within the cells) causes water to move out of the cell, as shown in Figure 13.24(a)▶. This causes the cell to shrivel, a process called *crenation*. Placing the cell in a solution that is *hypotonic* relative to the intracellular fluid causes water to move into the cell, as illustrated in Figure 13.24(b). This may cause the cell to rupture, a process called *hemolysis*. People who need body fluids or nutrients replaced but cannot be fed orally are given solutions by intravenous (IV) infusion, which feeds nutrients directly into the veins. To prevent crenation or hemolysis of red blood cells, the IV solutions must be isotonic with the intracellular fluids of the cells.

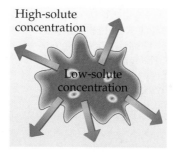

(a) Crenation

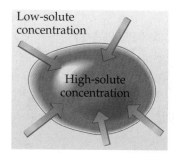

(b) Hemolysis

▲ Figure 13.24 **Osmosis through red blood cell wall.** The blue arrows represent the net movement of water molecules.

◼◼ SAMPLE EXERCISE 13.11 | Calculations Involving Osmotic Pressure

The average osmotic pressure of blood is 7.7 atm at 25 °C. What molarity of glucose ($C_6H_{12}O_6$) will be isotonic with blood?

SOLUTION

Analyze: We are asked to calculate the concentration of glucose in water that would be isotonic with blood, given that the osmotic pressure of blood at 25 °C is 7.7 atm.

Plan: Because we are given the osmotic pressure and temperature, we can solve for the concentration, using Equation 13.13.

Solve:

$$\Pi = MRT$$

$$M = \frac{\Pi}{RT} = \frac{7.7 \text{ atm}}{\left(0.0821 \dfrac{\text{L-atm}}{\text{mol-K}}\right)(298 \text{ K})} = 0.31 \, M$$

Comment: In clinical situations the concentrations of solutions are generally expressed as mass percentages. The mass percentage of a 0.31 M solution of glucose is 5.3%. The concentration of NaCl that is isotonic with blood is 0.16 M, because NaCl ionizes to form two particles, Na^+ and Cl^- (a 0.155 M solution of NaCl is 0.310 M in particles). A 0.16 M solution of NaCl is 0.9 mass % in NaCl. This kind of solution is known as a physiological saline solution.

■ PRACTICE EXERCISE

What is the osmotic pressure at 20 °C of a 0.0020 M sucrose ($C_{12}H_{22}O_{11}$) solution?
Answer: 0.048 atm, or 37 torr

A Closer Look   COLLIGATIVE PROPERTIES OF ELECTROLYTE SOLUTIONS

The colligative properties of solutions depend on the total concentration of solute particles, regardless of whether the particles are ions or molecules. Thus, we would expect a 0.100 m solution of NaCl to have a freezing-point depression of $(0.200\ m)(1.86\ °C/m) = 0.372\ °C$ because it is 0.100 m in $Na^+(aq)$ and 0.100 m in $Cl^-(aq)$. The measured freezing-point depression is only 0.348 °C, however, and the situation is similar for other strong electrolytes. A 0.100 m solution of KCl, for example, freezes at −0.344 °C.

The difference between the expected and observed colligative properties for strong electrolytes is due to electrostatic attractions between ions. As the ions move about in solution, ions of opposite charge collide and "stick together" for brief moments. While they are together, they behave as a single particle called an *ion pair* (Figure 13.25 ▼). The number of independent particles is thereby reduced, causing a reduction in the freezing-point depression (as well as in the boiling-point elevation, the vapor-pressure reduction, and the osmotic pressure).

One measure of the extent to which electrolytes dissociate is the *van't Hoff factor, i*. This factor is the ratio of the actual value of a colligative property to the value calculated, assuming the substance to be a nonelectrolyte. Using the freezing-point depression, for example, we have

$$i = \frac{\Delta T_f\ (\text{measured})}{\Delta T_f\ (\text{calculated for nonelectrolyte})} \quad [13.14]$$

The ideal value of i can be determined for a salt from the number of ions per formula unit. For NaCl, for example, the ideal van't Hoff factor is 2 because NaCl consists of one Na^+ and one Cl^- per formula unit; for K_2SO_4 it is 3 because K_2SO_4 consists of two K^+ and one SO_4^{2-}. In the absence of any information about the actual value of i for a solution, we will use the ideal value in calculations.

Table 13.5 ▼ gives the observed van't Hoff factors for several substances at different dilutions. Two trends are evident in these data. First, dilution affects the value of i for electrolytes; the more dilute the solution, the more closely i approaches the ideal or limiting value. Thus, the extent of ion pairing in electrolyte solutions decreases upon dilution. Second, the lower the charges on the ions, the less i departs from the limiting value because the extent of ion pairing decreases as the ionic charges decrease. Both trends are consistent with simple electrostatics: The force of interaction between charged particles decreases as their separation increases and as their charges decrease.
Related Exercises: 13.79, 13.80, 13.99, 13.102

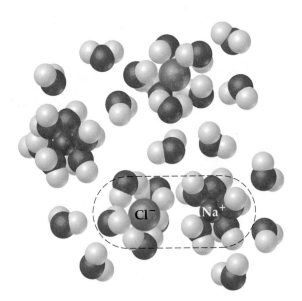

▲ **Figure 13.25 Ion pairing and colligative properties.** A solution of NaCl contains not only separated $Na^+(aq)$ and $Cl^-(aq)$ ions but ion pairs as well. Ion pairing becomes more prevalent as the solution concentration increases and has an effect on all the colligative properties of the solution.

TABLE 13.5 ■ van't Hoff Factors for Several Substances at 25 °C			
	Concentration		
Compound	0.100 m	0.0100 m	0.00100 m	Limiting Value
Sucrose	1.00	1.00	1.00	1.00
NaCl	1.87	1.94	1.97	2.00
K_2SO_4	2.32	2.70	2.84	3.00
$MgSO_4$	1.21	1.53	1.82	2.00

There are many interesting biological examples of osmosis. A cucumber placed in concentrated brine loses water via osmosis and shrivels into a pickle. If a carrot that has become limp because of water loss to the atmosphere is placed in water, the water moves into the carrot through osmosis, making it firm once again. People who eat a lot of salty food retain water in tissue cells and intercellular space because of osmosis. The resultant swelling or puffiness is called *edema*. Water moves from soil into plant roots and subsequently into the upper portions of the plant at least in part because of osmosis. Bacteria on salted meat or candied fruit lose water through osmosis, shrivel, and die—thus preserving the food.

The movement of a substance from an area where its concentration is high to an area where it is low is spontaneous. Biological cells transport water and other select materials through their membranes, permitting nutrients to enter and waste materials to exit. In some cases substances must be moved across the cell membrane from an area of low concentration to one of high concentration. This movement—called *active transport*—is not spontaneous, so cells must expend energy to do it.

▲ GIVE IT SOME THOUGHT

Is the osmotic pressure of a 0.10 *M* solution of NaCl greater than, less than, or equal to that of a 0.10 *M* solution of KBr?

Determination of Molar Mass

The colligative properties of solutions provide a useful means of experimentally determining molar mass. Any of the four colligative properties can be used, as shown in Sample Exercises 13.12 and 13.13.

■ SAMPLE EXERCISE 13.12 | Molar Mass from Freezing-Point Depression

A solution of an unknown nonvolatile nonelectrolyte was prepared by dissolving 0.250 g of the substance in 40.0 g of CCl_4. The boiling point of the resultant solution was 0.357 °C higher than that of the pure solvent. Calculate the molar mass of the solute.

SOLUTION

Analyze: Our goal is to calculate the molar mass of a solute based on knowledge of the boiling-point elevation of its solution in CCl_4, $\Delta T_b = 0.357$ °C, and the masses of solute and solvent. Table 13.4 gives K_b for the solvent (CCl_4), $K_b = 5.02$ °C/*m*.

Plan: We can use Equation 13.11, $\Delta T_b = K_b m$, to calculate the molality of the solution. Then we can use molality and the quantity of solvent (40.0 g CCl_4) to calculate the number of moles of solute. Finally, the molar mass of the solute equals the number of grams per mole, so we divide the number of grams of solute (0.250 g) by the number of moles we have just calculated.

Solve: From Equation 13.11 we have

$$\text{Molality} = \frac{\Delta T_b}{K_b} = \frac{0.357 \text{ °C}}{5.02 \text{ °C/}m} = 0.0711 \ m$$

Thus, the solution contains 0.0711 mol of solute per kilogram of solvent. The solution was prepared using 40.0 g = 0.0400 kg of solvent (CCl_4). The number of moles of solute in the solution is therefore

$$(0.0400 \text{ kg } CCl_4)\left(0.0711 \ \frac{\text{mol solute}}{\text{kg } CCl_4}\right) = 2.84 \times 10^{-3} \text{ mol solute}$$

The molar mass of the solute is the number of grams per mole of the substance:

$$\text{Molar mass} = \frac{0.250 \text{ g}}{2.84 \times 10^{-3} \text{ mol}} = 88.0 \text{ g/mol}$$

■ PRACTICE EXERCISE

Camphor ($C_{10}H_{16}O$) melts at 179.8 °C, and it has a particularly large freezing-point-depression constant, $K_f = 40.0$ °C/*m*. When 0.186 g of an organic substance of unknown molar mass is dissolved in 22.01 g of liquid camphor, the freezing point of the mixture is found to be 176.7 °C. What is the molar mass of the solute?
Answer: 110 g/mol

■ **SAMPLE EXERCISE 13.13** | Molar Mass from Osmotic Pressure

The osmotic pressure of an aqueous solution of a certain protein was measured to determine the protein's molar mass. The solution contained 3.50 mg of protein dissolved in sufficient water to form 5.00 mL of solution. The osmotic pressure of the solution at 25 °C was found to be 1.54 torr. Treating the protein as a nonelectrolyte, calculate its molar mass.

SOLUTION

Analyze: Our goal is to calculate the molar mass of a high-molecular-mass protein, based on its osmotic pressure and a knowledge of the mass of protein and solution volume.

Plan: The temperature ($T = 25$ °C) and osmotic pressure ($\Pi = 1.54$ torr) are given, and we know the value of R so we can use Equation 13.13 to calculate the molarity of the solution, M. In doing so, we must convert temperature from °C to K and the osmotic pressure from torr to atm. We then use the molarity and the volume of the solution (5.00 mL) to determine the number of moles of solute. Finally, we obtain the molar mass by dividing the mass of the solute (3.50 mg) by the number of moles of solute.

Solve: Solving Equation 13.13 for molarity gives

$$\text{Molarity} = \frac{\Pi}{RT} = \frac{(1.54 \text{ torr})\left(\dfrac{1 \text{ atm}}{760 \text{ torr}}\right)}{\left(0.0821 \dfrac{\text{L-atm}}{\text{mol-K}}\right)(298 \text{ K})} = 8.28 \times 10^{-5} \frac{\text{mol}}{\text{L}}$$

Because the volume of the solution is 5.00 ml = 5.00×10^{-3} L, the number of moles of protein must be

$$\text{Moles} = (8.28 \times 10^{-5} \text{ mol/L})(5.00 \times 10^{-3} \text{ L}) = 4.14 \times 10^{-7} \text{ mol}$$

The molar mass is the number of grams per mole of the substance. The sample has a mass of 3.50 mg = 3.50×10^{-3} g. The molar mass is the number of grams divided by the number of moles:

$$\text{Molar mass} = \frac{\text{grams}}{\text{moles}} = \frac{3.50 \times 10^{-3} \text{ g}}{4.14 \times 10^{-7} \text{ mol}} = 8.45 \times 10^{3} \text{ g/mol}$$

Comment: Because small pressures can be measured easily and accurately, osmotic pressure measurements provide a useful way to determine the molar masses of large molecules.

■ **PRACTICE EXERCISE**

A sample of 2.05 g of polystyrene of uniform polymer chain length was dissolved in enough toluene to form 0.100 L of solution. The osmotic pressure of this solution was found to be 1.21 kPa at 25 °C. Calculate the molar mass of the polystyrene.
Answer: 4.20×10^{4} g/mol

13.6 COLLOIDS

When finely divided clay particles are dispersed throughout water, they eventually settle out of the water because of gravity. The dispersed clay particles are much larger than most molecules and consist of many thousands or even millions of atoms. In contrast, the dispersed particles of a solution are of molecular size. Between these extremes lie dispersed particles that are larger than typical molecules, but not so large that the components of the mixture separate under the influence of gravity. These intermediate types of dispersions or suspensions are called **colloidal dispersions**, or simply **colloids**. Colloids form the dividing line between solutions and heterogeneous mixtures. Like solutions, colloids can be gases, liquids, or solids. Examples of each are listed in Table 13.6▶.

TABLE 13.6 ■ Types of Colloids

Phase of Colloid	Dispersing (solutelike) Substance	Dispersed (solventlike) Substance	Colloid Type	Example
Gas	Gas	Gas	—	None (all are solutions)
Gas	Gas	Liquid	Aerosol	Fog
Gas	Gas	Solid	Aerosol	Smoke
Liquid	Liquid	Gas	Foam	Whipped cream
Liquid	Liquid	Liquid	Emulsion	Milk
Liquid	Liquid	Solid	Sol	Paint
Solid	Solid	Gas	Solid foam	Marshmallow
Solid	Solid	Liquid	Solid emulsion	Butter
Solid	Solid	Solid	Solid sol	Ruby glass

The size of the dispersed particles is used to classify a mixture as a colloid. Colloid particles range in diameter from approximately 5 to 1000 nm. Solute particles are smaller. The colloid particle may consist of many atoms, ions, or molecules, or it may even be a single giant molecule. The hemoglobin molecule, for example, which carries oxygen in blood, has molecular dimensions of 65 Å × 55 Å × 50 Å and a molar mass of 64,500 g/mol.

Although colloid particles may be so small that the dispersion appears uniform even under a microscope, they are large enough to scatter light very effectively. Consequently, most colloids appear cloudy or opaque unless they are very dilute. (Homogenized milk is a colloid.) Furthermore, because they scatter light, a light beam can be seen as it passes through a colloidal suspension, as shown in Figure 13.26 ▶. This scattering of light by colloidal particles, known as the **Tyndall effect**, makes it possible to see the light beam of an automobile on a dusty dirt road or the sunlight coming through a forest canopy [Figure 13.27(a) ▼]. Not all wavelengths are scattered to the same extent. As a result, brilliant red sunsets are seen when the sun is near the horizon and the air contains dust, smoke, or other particles of colloidal size [Figure 13.27(b)].

▲ Figure 13.26 **Tyndall effect in the laboratory.** The glass on the left contains a colloidal suspension; that on the right contains a solution. The path of the beam through the colloidal suspension is visible because the light is scattered by the colloidal particles. Light is not scattered by the individual solute molecules in the solution.

Hydrophilic and Hydrophobic Colloids

The most important colloids are those in which the dispersing medium is water. These colloids may be **hydrophilic** (water loving) or **hydrophobic** (water fearing). Hydrophilic colloids are most like the solutions that we have previously examined. In the human body the extremely large molecules that make up such important substances as enzymes and antibodies are kept in suspension by interaction with surrounding water molecules. The molecules fold in such a way that the hydrophobic groups are away from the water molecules,

◀ Figure 13.27 **Tyndall effect in nature.** (a) Scattering of sunlight by colloidal particles in the misty air of a forest. (b) The scattering of light by smoke or dust particles produces a rich red sunset.

▲ **Figure 13.28 Hydrophilic colloids.** Examples of hydrophilic groups on the surface of a giant molecule (macromolecule) that help to keep the molecule suspended in water.

on the "inside" of the folded molecule, while the hydrophilic, polar groups are on the surface, interacting with the water molecules. These hydrophilic groups generally contain oxygen or nitrogen and often carry a charge. Some examples are shown in Figure 13.28 ◄.

Hydrophobic colloids can be prepared in water only if they are stabilized in some way. Otherwise, their natural lack of affinity for water causes them to separate from the water. Hydrophobic colloids can be stabilized by adsorption of ions on their surface, as shown in Figure 13.29 ▼. (*Adsorption* means to adhere to a surface. It differs from *absorption*, which means to pass into the interior, as when a sponge absorbs water.) These adsorbed ions can interact with water, thereby stabilizing the colloid. At the same time, the mutual repulsion between colloid particles with adsorbed ions of the same charge keeps the particles from colliding and getting larger.

Hydrophobic colloids can also be stabilized by the presence of hydrophilic groups on their surfaces. Small droplets of oil are hydrophobic, for example, so they do not remain suspended in water. Instead, they aggregate, forming an oil slick on the surface of the water. Sodium stearate (Figure 13.30 ◄), or any similar substance having one end that is hydrophilic (polar, or charged) and one that is hydrophobic (nonpolar), will stabilize a suspension of oil in water. Stabilization results from the interaction of the hydrophobic ends of the stearate ions with the oil droplet and the hydrophilic ends with the water as shown in Figure 13.31 ►.

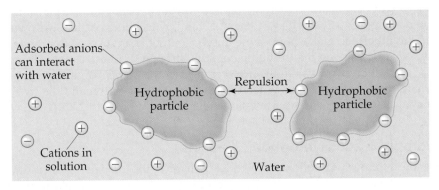

▲ **Figure 13.29 Hydrophobic colloids.** Schematic illustration of how adsorbed ions stabilize a hydrophobic colloid in water.

▲ **GIVE IT SOME THOUGHT**

Why don't the oil droplets emulsified by sodium stearate coagulate to form larger oil droplets?

The stabilization of colloids has an interesting application in our own digestive system. When fats in our diet reach the small intestine, a hormone causes the gallbladder to excrete a fluid called bile. Among the components of bile are compounds that have chemical structures similar to sodium stearate; that is, they have a hydrophilic (polar) end and a hydrophobic (nonpolar) end. These compounds emulsify the fats present in the intestine and thus permit digestion and absorption of fat-soluble vitamins through the intestinal wall. The term *emulsify* means "to form an emulsion," a suspension of one liquid in another, as in milk, for example (Table 13.6). A substance that aids in the formation of an emulsion is called an emulsifying agent. If you read the labels on foods and other materials, you will find that a variety of chemicals are used as emulsifying agents. These chemicals typically have a hydrophilic end and a hydrophobic end.

Sodium stearate

▲ **Figure 13.30 Sodium stearate.**

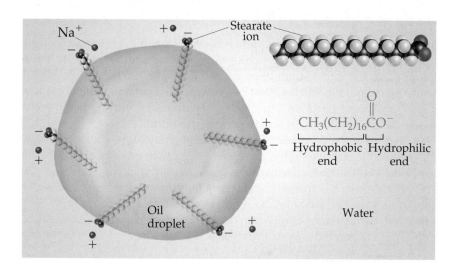

◀ Figure 13.31 **Stabilization of an emulsion of oil in water by stearate ions.**

$$CH_3(CH_2)_{16}CO^-$$

Hydrophobic end   Hydrophilic end

Water

Na⁺ — Stearate ion — Oil droplet

Chemistry and Life   SICKLE-CELL ANEMIA

Our blood contains a complex protein called *hemoglobin* that carries oxygen from our lungs to other parts of our body. In the genetic disease known as *sickle-cell anemia*, hemoglobin molecules are abnormal and have a lower solubility, especially in their unoxygenated form. Consequently, as much as 85% of the hemoglobin in red blood cells crystallizes from solution.

The reason for the insolubility of hemoglobin in sickle-cell anemia can be traced to a structural change in one part of an amino acid side chain. Normal hemoglobin molecules have an amino acid in their makeup that has the following side chain protruding from the main body of the molecule:

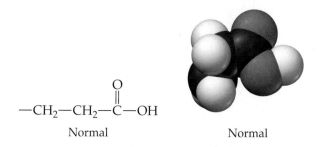

$$-CH_2-CH_2-\overset{\overset{\displaystyle O}{\|}}{C}-OH$$

Normal   Normal

This side chain terminates in a polar group, which contributes to the solubility of the hemoglobin molecule in water. In the hemoglobin molecules of persons suffering from sickle-cell anemia, the side chain is of a different type:

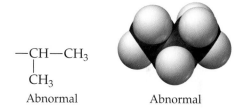

$$-CH-CH_3$$
$$\quad|$$
$$\ CH_3$$

Abnormal   Abnormal

This abnormal group of atoms is nonpolar (hydrophobic), and its presence leads to the aggregation of this defective form of hemoglobin into particles too large to remain suspended in biological fluids. It also causes the cells to distort into a sickle shape, as shown in Figure 13.32▼. The sickled cells tend to clog the capillaries, causing severe pain, physical weakness, and the gradual deterioration of the vital organs. The disease is hereditary, and if both parents carry the defective genes, it is likely that their children will possess only abnormal hemoglobin.

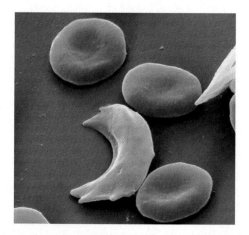

◀ Figure 13.32 **Normal and sickled red blood cells.** Normal red blood cells are about 1×10^{-3} mm in diameter.

Removal of Colloidal Particles

Colloidal particles frequently must be removed from a dispersing medium, as in the removal of smoke from smokestacks or butterfat from milk. Because colloidal particles are so small, they cannot be separated by simple filtration. Instead, the colloidal particles must be enlarged in a process called *coagulation*. The resultant larger particles can then be separated by filtration or merely by allowing them to settle out of the dispersing medium.

Heating the mixture or adding an electrolyte may bring about coagulation. Heating the colloidal dispersion increases the particle motion and so the number of collisions. The particles increase in size as they stick together after colliding. The addition of electrolytes neutralizes the surface charges of the particles, thereby removing the electrostatic repulsions that prevent them from coming together. Wherever rivers empty into oceans or other salty bodies of water, for example, the suspended clay in the river is deposited as a delta when it mixes with the electrolytes in the salt water.

Semipermeable membranes can also be used to separate ions from colloidal particles because the ions can pass through the membrane but the colloidal particles cannot. This type of separation is known as *dialysis* and is used to purify blood in artificial kidney machines. Our kidneys normally remove the waste products of metabolism from blood. In a kidney machine, blood is circulated through a dialyzing tube immersed in a washing solution. The washing solution contains the same concentrations and kinds of ions as blood but is lacking the molecules and ions that are waste products. Wastes therefore dialyze out of the blood, but the ions and large colloidal particles such as proteins do not.

▇ SAMPLE INTEGRATIVE EXERCISE │ Putting Concepts Together

A 0.100-L solution is made by dissolving 0.441 g of $CaCl_2(s)$ in water. **(a)** Calculate the osmotic pressure of this solution at 27 °C, assuming that it is completely dissociated into its component ions. **(b)** The measured osmotic pressure of this solution is 2.56 atm at 27 °C. Explain why it is less than the value calculated in (a), and calculate the van't Hoff factor, i, for the solute in this solution. (See the "A Closer Look" box on Colligative Properties of Electrolyte Solutions in Section 13.5.) **(c)** The enthalpy of solution for $CaCl_2$ is $\Delta H = -81.3$ kJ/mol. If the final temperature of the solution is 27.0 °C, what was its initial temperature? (Assume that the density of the solution is 1.00 g/mL, that its specific heat is 4.18 J/g-K, and that the solution loses no heat to its surroundings.)

SOLUTION

(a) The osmotic pressure is given by Equation 13.13, $\Pi = MRT$. We know the temperature, $T = 27$ °C = 300 K, and the gas constant, $R = 0.0821$ L-atm/mol-K. We can calculate the molarity of the solution from the mass of $CaCl_2$ and the volume of the solution:

$$\text{Molarity} = \left(\frac{0.441 \text{ g CaCl}_2}{0.100 \text{ L}}\right)\left(\frac{1 \text{ mol CaCl}_2}{111.0 \text{ g CaCl}_2}\right) = 0.0397 \text{ mol CaCl}_2/\text{L}$$

Soluble ionic compounds are strong electrolytes. ∞ (Sections 4.1 and 4.3) Thus, $CaCl_2$ consists of metal cations (Ca^{2+}) and nonmetal anions (Cl^-). When completely dissociated, each $CaCl_2$ unit forms three ions (one Ca^{2+} and two Cl^-). Hence the total concentration of ions in the solution is (3)(0.0397 M) = 0.119 M, and the calculated osmotic pressure is

$$\Pi = MRT = (0.119 \text{ mol/L})(0.0821 \text{ L-atm/mol-K})(300 \text{ K}) = 2.93 \text{ atm}$$

(b) The actual values of colligative properties of electrolytes are less than those calculated, because the electrostatic interactions between ions limit their independent movements. In this case the van't Hoff factor, which measures the extent to which electrolytes actually dissociate into ions, is given by

$$i = \frac{\Pi(\text{measured})}{\Pi(\text{calculated for nonelectrolyte})}$$

$$= \frac{2.56 \text{ atm}}{(0.0397 \text{ mol/L})(0.0821 \text{ L-atm/mol-K})(300 \text{ K})} = 2.62$$

Thus, the solution behaves as if the $CaCl_2$ has dissociated into 2.62 particles instead of the ideal 3.

(c) If the solution is 0.0397 M in $CaCl_2$ and has a total volume of 0.100 L, the number of moles of solute is (0.100 L)(0.0397 mol/L) = 0.00397 mol. Hence the quantity of heat generated in forming the solution is (0.00397 mol)(−81.3 kJ/mol) = −0.323 kJ. The solution absorbs this heat, causing its temperature to increase. The relationship between temperature change and heat is given by Equation 5.22:

$$q = (\text{specific heat})(\text{grams})(\Delta T)$$

The heat absorbed by the solution is $q = +0.323$ kJ = 323 J. The mass of the 0.100 L of solution is (100 mL)(1.00 g/mL) = 100 g (to 3 significant figures). Thus the temperature change is

$$\Delta T = \frac{q}{(\text{specific heat of solution})(\text{grams of solution})}$$

$$= \frac{323 \text{ J}}{(4.18 \text{ J/g-K})(100 \text{ g})} = 0.773 \text{ K}$$

A kelvin has the same size as a degree Celsius. ∞ (Section 1.4) Because the solution temperature increases by 0.773 °C, the initial temperature was 27.0 °C − 0.773 °C = 26.2 °C.

C H A P T E R   R E V I E W

SUMMARY AND KEY TERMS

Section 13.1 Solutions form when one substance disperses uniformly throughout another. The attractive interaction of solvent molecules with solute is called **solvation**. When the solvent is water, the interaction is called **hydration**. The dissolution of ionic substances in water is promoted by hydration of the separated ions by the polar water molecules. The overall enthalpy change upon solution formation may be either positive or negative. Solution formation is favored both by a negative enthalpy change (exothermic process) and by an increased dispersal in space of the components of the solution, corresponding to a positive **entropy** change.

Section 13.2 The equilibrium between a saturated solution and undissolved solute is dynamic; the process of solution and the reverse process, **crystallization**, occur simultaneously. In a solution in equilibrium with undissolved solute, the two processes occur at equal rates, giving a **saturated** solution. If there is less solute present than is needed to saturate the solution, the solution is **unsaturated**. When solute concentration is greater than the equilibrium concentration value, the solution is **supersaturated**. This is an unstable condition, and separation of some solute from the solution will occur if the process is initiated with a solute seed crystal. The amount of solute needed to form a saturated solution at any particular temperature is the **solubility** of that solute at that temperature.

Section 13.3 The solubility of one substance in another depends on the tendency of systems to become more random, by becoming more dispersed in space, and on the relative intermolecular solute–solute and solvent–solvent energies compared with solute–solvent interactions. Polar and ionic solutes tend to dissolve in polar solvents, and nonpolar solutes tend to dissolve in nonpolar solvents ("like dissolves like"). Liquids that mix in all proportions are **miscible**; those that do not dissolve significantly in one another are **immiscible**. Hydrogen-bonding interactions between solute and solvent often play an important role in determining solubility; for example, ethanol and water, whose molecules form hydrogen bonds with each other, are miscible. The solubilities of gases in a liquid are generally proportional to the pressure of the gas over the solution, as expressed by **Henry's law**: $S_g = kP_g$. The solubilities of most solid solutes in water increase as the temperature of the solution increases. In contrast, the solubilities of gases in water generally decrease with increasing temperature.

Section 13.4 Concentrations of solutions can be expressed quantitatively by several different measures, including **mass percentage** [(mass solute/mass solution) $\times 10^2$], **parts per million (ppm)** [(mass solute/mass solution) $\times 10^6$], **parts per billion (ppb)** [(mass solute/mass solution) $\times 10^9$], and mole fraction [mol solute/(mol solute + mol solvent)]. Molarity, M, is defined as moles of solute per liter of solution; **molality**, m, is defined as moles of solute per kg of solvent. Molarity can be converted to these other concentration units if the density of the solution is known.

Section 13.5 A physical property of a solution that depends on the concentration of solute particles present, regardless of the nature of the solute, is a **colligative property**. Colligative properties include vapor-pressure lowering, freezing-point lowering, boiling-point elevation, and osmotic pressure. **Raoult's law** expresses the lowering of vapor pressure. An **ideal solution** obeys Raoult's law. Differences in solvent–solute as compared with solvent–solvent and solute–solute intermolecular forces cause many solutions to depart from ideal behavior.

A solution containing a nonvolatile solute possesses a higher boiling point than the pure solvent. The **molal boiling-point-elevation constant**, K_b, represents the increase in boiling point for a 1 m solution of solute particles as compared with the pure solvent. Similarly, the **molal freezing-point-depression constant**, K_f, measures the lowering of the freezing point of a solution for a 1 m solution of solute particles. The temperature changes are given by the equations $\Delta T_b = K_b m$ and $\Delta T_f = K_f m$.

When NaCl dissolves in water, two moles of solute particles are formed for each mole of dissolved salt. The boiling point or freezing point is thus elevated or depressed, respectively, approximately twice as much as that of a nonelectrolyte solution of the same concentration. Similar considerations apply to other strong electrolytes.

Osmosis is the movement of solvent molecules through a semipermeable membrane from a less concentrated to a more concentrated solution. This net movement of solvent generates an **osmotic pressure**, Π, which can be measured in units of gas pressure, such as atm. The osmotic pressure of a solution as compared with pure solvent is proportional to the solution molarity: $\Pi = MRT$. Osmosis is a very important process in living systems, in which cell walls act as semipermeable membranes, permitting the passage of water, but restricting the passage of ionic and macromolecular components.

Section 13.6 Particles that are large on the molecular scale but still small enough to remain suspended indefinitely in a solvent system form **colloids**, or **colloidal dispersions**. Colloids, which are intermediate between solutions and heterogeneous mixtures, have many practical applications. One useful physical property of colloids, the scattering of visible light, is referred to as the **Tyndall effect**. Aqueous colloids are classified as **hydrophilic** or **hydrophobic**. Hydrophilic colloids are common in living organisms, in which large molecular aggregates (enzymes, antibodies) remain suspended because they have many polar, or charged, atomic groups on their surfaces that interact with water. Hydrophobic colloids, such as small droplets of oil, may remain in suspension through adsorption of charged particles on their surfaces.

KEY SKILLS

- Understand how enthalpy and entropy changes affect solution formation.

- Understand the relationship between intermolecular forces and solubility, including use of the "like dissolves like" rule.

- Describe the effect of temperature on the solubility of solids and gases.

- Describe the relationship between the partial pressure of a gas and its solubility.

- Be able to calculate the concentration of a solution in terms of molarity, molality, mole fraction, percent composition, and parts per million and be able to interconvert between them.

- Describe what a colligative property is and explain the difference between the effects of nonelectrolytes and electrolyes on colligative properties.

- Be able to calculate the vapor pressure of a solvent over a solution.

- Be able to calculate the boiling point elevation and freezing point depression of a solution.

- Be able to calculate the osmotic pressure of a solution.

KEY EQUATIONS

- $S_g = kP_g$ [13.4]   Henry's law, relating gas solubility to partial pressure

- Mass % of component $= \dfrac{\text{mass of component in soln}}{\text{total mass of soln}} \times 100$ [13.5]   Defining concentration in terms of mass percent

- ppm of component $= \dfrac{\text{mass of component in soln}}{\text{total mass of soln}} \times 10^6$ [13.6]   Defining concentration in terms of parts per million (ppm)

- Mole fraction of component $= \dfrac{\text{moles of component}}{\text{total moles of all components}}$ [13.7]   Defining concentration in terms of mole fraction

- Molarity $= \dfrac{\text{moles solute}}{\text{liters soln}}$ [13.8]   Defining concentration in terms of molarity

- Molality $= \dfrac{\text{moles of solute}}{\text{kilograms of solvent}}$ [13.9]   Defining concentration in terms of molality

- $P_A = X_A P_A^\circ$ [13.10]   Raoult's law, calculating vapor pressure of solvent above a solution

- $\Delta T_b = K_b m$ [13.11]   Calculating the boiling point elevation of a solution

- $\Delta T_f = K_f m$ [13.12]   Calculating the freezing point depression of a solution

- $\Pi = \left(\dfrac{n}{V}\right) RT = MRT$ [13.13]   Calculating the osmotic pressure of a solution

VISUALIZING CONCEPTS

13.1 This figure shows the interaction of a cation with surrounding water molecules.

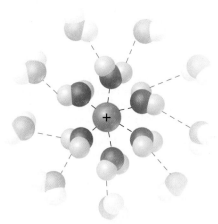

Would you expect the energy of ion–solvent interaction to be greater for Na^+ or Li^+? Explain. [Section 13.1]

13.2 Why do ionic substances with higher lattice energies tend to be less soluble in water than those with lower lattice energies? [Section 13.1]

13.3 Rank the contents of the following containers in order of increasing entropy: [Section 13.1]

(a)   (b)   (c)

13.4 A quantity of the pink solid on the left in Figure 13.8 is placed in a warming oven and heated for a time. It slowly turns from pink to the deep blue color of the solid on the right. What has occurred? [Section 13.1]

13.5 Which of the following is the best representation of a saturated solution? Explain your reasoning. [Section 13.2]

(a)   (b)   (c)

13.6 The solubility of Xe in water at 20 °C is approximately 5×10^{-3} M. Compare this with the solubilities of Ar and Kr in water (Table 13.2) and explain what properties of the rare gas atoms account for the variation in solubility. [Section 13.3]

13.7 The structures of vitamins E and B_6 are shown below. Predict which is largely water soluble and which is largely fat soluble. Explain. [Section 13.3]

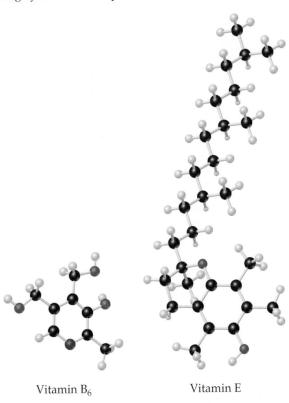

Vitamin B_6 Vitamin E

13.8 If you wanted to prepare a solution of CO in water at 25 °C in which the CO concentration was 2.5 mM, what pressure of CO would you need to use? (See Figure 13.18.) [Section 13.3]

13.9 The figure shows two identical volumetric flasks containing the same solution at two temperatures.
 (a) Does the molarity of the solution change with the change in temperature? Explain.
 (b) Does the molality of the solution change with the change in temperature? Explain. [Section 13.4]

25 °C   55 °C

13.10 The following diagram shows the vapor pressure curves of a volatile solvent and a solution of that solvent containing a nonvolatile solute. (a) Which line represents the solution? (b) What are the normal boiling points of the solvent and the solution? [Section 13.5]

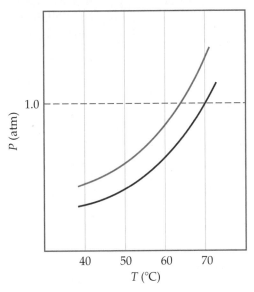

13.11 Suppose you had a balloon made of some highly flexible semipermeable membrane. The balloon is filled completely with a 0.2 M solution of some solute and is submerged in a 0.1 M solution of the same solute:

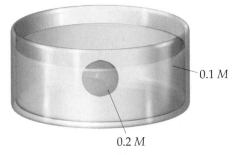

0.1 M

0.2 M

Initially, the volume of solution in the balloon is 0.25 L. Assuming the volume outside the semipermeable membrane is large, as the illustration shows, what would you expect for the solution volume inside the balloon once the system has come to equilibrium through osmosis? [Section 13.5]

13.12 The molecule *n*-octylglucoside, shown here, is widely used in biochemical research as a nonionic detergent for "solubilizing" large hydrophobic protein molecules. What characteristics of this molecule are important for its use in this way? [Section 13.6]

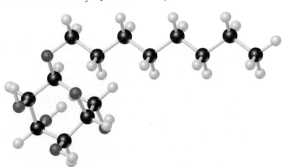

EXERCISES

The Solution Process

13.13 In general, the attractive intermolecular forces between solvent and solute particles must be comparable or greater than solute–solute interactions for significant solubility to occur. Explain this statement in terms of the overall energetics of solution formation.

13.14 **(a)** Considering the energetics of solute–solute, solvent–solvent, and solute–solvent interactions, explain why NaCl dissolves in water but not in benzene (C_6H_6). **(b)** What factors cause a cation to be strongly hydrated?

13.15 Indicate the type of solute–solvent interaction (Section 11.2) that should be most important in each of the following solutions: **(a)** CCl_4 in benzene (C_6H_6), **(b)** methanol (CH_3OH) in water, **(c)** KBr in water, **(d)** HCl in acetonitrile (CH_3CN).

13.16 Indicate the principal type of solute–solvent interaction in each of the following solutions, and rank the solutions from weakest to strongest solute–solvent interaction: **(a)** KCl in water, **(b)** CH_2Cl_2 in benzene (C_6H_6), **(c)** methanol (CH_3OH) in water.

13.17 **(a)** In Equation 13.1 which of the energy terms for dissolving an ionic solid would correspond to the lattice energy? **(b)** Which energy terms in this equation are always exothermic?

13.18 The schematic diagram of the solution process as the net sum of three steps in Figure 13.4 does not show the relative magnitudes of the three components because these will vary from case to case. For the dissolution of NH_4NO_3 in water, which of the three enthalpy changes would you expect to be much smaller than the other two? Explain.

13.19 When two nonpolar organic liquids such as hexane (C_6H_{14}) and heptane (C_7H_{16}) are mixed, the enthalpy change that occurs is generally quite small. **(a)** Use the energy diagram in Figure 13.4 to explain why. **(b)** Given that $\Delta H_{soln} \approx 0$, explain why hexane and heptane spontaneously form a solution.

13.20 The enthalpy of solution of KBr in water is about +198 kJ/mol. Nevertheless, the solubility of KBr in water is relatively high. Why does the solution process occur even though it is endothermic?

Saturated Solutions; Factors Affecting Solubility

13.21 The solubility of $Cr(NO_3)_3 \cdot 9\ H_2O$ in water is 208 g per 100 g of water at 15 °C. A solution of $Cr(NO_3)_3 \cdot 9\ H_2O$ in water at 35 °C is formed by dissolving 324 g in 100 g water. When this solution is slowly cooled to 15 °C, no precipitate forms. **(a)** What term describes this solution? **(b)** What action might you take to initiate crystallization? Use molecular-level processes to explain how your suggested procedure works.

13.22 The solubility of $MnSO_4 \cdot H_2O$ in water at 20 °C is 70 g per 100 mL of water. **(a)** Is a 1.22 M solution of $MnSO_4 \cdot H_2O$ in water at 20 °C saturated, supersaturated, or unsaturated? **(b)** Given a solution of $MnSO_4 \cdot H_2O$ of unknown concentration, what experiment could you perform to determine whether the new solution is saturated, supersaturated, or unsaturated?

13.23 By referring to Figure 13.17, determine whether the addition of 40.0 g of each of the following ionic solids to 100 g of water at 40 °C will lead to a saturated solution: **(a)** $NaNO_3$, **(b)** KCl, **(c)** $K_2Cr_2O_7$, **(d)** $Pb(NO_3)_2$.

13.24 By referring to Figure 13.17, determine the mass of each of the following salts required to form a saturated solution in 250 g of water at 30 °C: **(a)** $KClO_3$, **(b)** $Pb(NO_3)_2$, **(c)** $Ce_2(SO_4)_3$.

13.25 Water and glycerol, $CH_2(OH)CH(OH)CH_2OH$, are miscible in all proportions. What does this mean? How do the OH groups of the alcohol molecule contribute to this miscibility?

13.26 Oil and water are immiscible. What does this mean? Explain in terms of the structural features of their respective molecules and the forces between them.

13.27 **(a)** Would you expect stearic acid, $CH_3(CH_2)_{16}COOH$, to be more soluble in water or in carbon tetrachloride? Explain. **(b)** Which would you expect to be more soluble in water, cyclohexane or dioxane? Explain.

Dioxane   Cyclohexane

13.28 Consider a series of carboxylic acids whose general formula is $CH_3(CH_2)_nCOOH$. How would you expect the solubility of these compounds in water and in hexane to change as n increases? Explain.

13.29 Which of the following in each pair is likely to be more soluble in hexane, C_6H_{14}: **(a)** CCl_4 or $CaCl_2$; **(b)** benzene (C_6H_6) or glycerol, $CH_2(OH)CH(OH)CH_2OH$; **(c)** octanoic acid, $CH_3CH_2CH_2CH_2CH_2CH_2CH_2COOH$, or acetic acid, CH_3COOH. Explain your answer in each case.

13.30 Which of the following in each pair is likely to be more soluble in water: **(a)** cyclohexane (C_6H_{12}) or glucose $(C_6H_{12}O_6)$ (Figure 13.12); **(b)** propionic acid (CH_3CH_2COOH) or sodium propionate (CH_3CH_2COONa); **(c)** HCl or ethyl chloride (CH_3CH_2Cl)? Explain in each case.

13.31 (a) Explain why carbonated beverages must be stored in sealed containers. (b) Once the beverage has been opened, why does it maintain more carbonation when refrigerated than at room temperature?

13.32 Explain why pressure affects the solubility of O_2 in water, but not the solubility of NaCl in water.

13.33 The Henry's law constant for helium gas in water at 30 °C is 3.7×10^{-4} M/atm and the constant for N_2 at 30 °C is 6.0×10^{-4} M/atm. If the two gases are each present at 1.5 atm pressure, calculate the solubility of each gas.

13.34 The partial pressure of O_2 in air at sea level is 0.21 atm. Using the data in Table 13.2, together with Henry's law, calculate the molar concentration of O_2 in the surface water of a mountain lake saturated with air at 20 °C and an atmospheric pressure of 650 torr.

Concentrations of Solutions

13.35 (a) Calculate the mass percentage of Na_2SO_4 in a solution containing 10.6 g Na_2SO_4 in 483 g water. (b) An ore contains 2.86 g of silver per ton of ore. What is the concentration of silver in ppm?

13.36 (a) What is the mass percentage of iodine (I_2) in a solution containing 0.035 mol I_2 in 115 g of CCl_4? (b) Seawater contains 0.0079 g Sr^{2+} per kilogram of water. What is the concentration of Sr^{2+} measured in ppm?

13.37 A solution is made containing 14.6 g of CH_3OH in 184 g H_2O. Calculate (a) the mole fraction of CH_3OH, (b) the mass percent of CH_3OH, (c) the molality of CH_3OH.

13.38 A solution is made containing 25.5 g phenol (C_6H_5OH) in 425 g ethanol (C_2H_5OH). Calculate (a) the mole fraction of phenol, (b) the mass percent of phenol, (c) the molality of phenol.

13.39 Calculate the molarity of the following aqueous solutions: (a) 0.540 g $Mg(NO_3)_2$ in 250.0 mL of solution, (b) 22.4 g $LiClO_4 \cdot 3 H_2O$ in 125 mL of solution, (c) 25.0 mL of 3.50 M HNO_3 diluted to 0.250 L.

13.40 What is the molarity of each of the following solutions: (a) 15.0 g $Al_2(SO_4)_3$ in 0.350 L solution, (b) 5.25 g $Mn(NO_3)_2 \cdot 2 H_2O$ in 175 mL of solution, (c) 35.0 mL of 9.00 M H_2SO_4 diluted to 0.500 L?

13.41 Calculate the molality of each of the following solutions: (a) 8.66 g benzene (C_6H_6) dissolved in 23.6 g carbon tetrachloride (CCl_4), (b) 4.80 g NaCl dissolved in 0.350 L of water.

13.42 (a) What is the molality of a solution formed by dissolving 1.25 mol of KCl in 16.0 mol of water? (b) How many grams of sulfur (S_8) must be dissolved in 100.0 g naphthalene ($C_{10}H_8$) to make a 0.12 m solution?

13.43 A sulfuric acid solution containing 571.6 g of H_2SO_4 per liter of solution has a density of 1.329 g/cm³. Calculate (a) the mass percentage, (b) the mole fraction, (c) the molality, (d) the molarity of H_2SO_4 in this solution.

13.44 Ascorbic acid (vitamin C, $C_6H_8O_6$) is a water-soluble vitamin. A solution containing 80.5 g of ascorbic acid dissolved in 210 g of water has a density of 1.22 g/mL at 55 °C. Calculate (a) the mass percentage, (b) the mole fraction, (c) the molality, (d) the molarity of ascorbic acid in this solution.

13.45 The density of acetonitrile (CH_3CN) is 0.786 g/mL and the density of methanol (CH_3OH) is 0.791 g/mL. A solution is made by dissolving 22.5 mL CH_3OH in 98.7 mL CH_3CN. (a) What is the mole fraction of methanol in the solution? (b) What is the molality of the solution?

(c) Assuming that the volumes are additive, what is the molarity of CH_3OH in the solution?

13.46 The density of toluene (C_7H_8) is 0.867 g/mL, and the density of thiophene (C_4H_4S) is 1.065 g/mL. A solution is made by dissolving 9.08 g of thiophene in 250.0 mL of toluene. (a) Calculate the mole fraction of thiophene in the solution. (b) Calculate the molality of thiophene in the solution. (c) Assuming that the volumes of the solute and solvent are additive, what is the molarity of thiophene in the solution?

13.47 Calculate the number of moles of solute present in each of the following aqueous solutions: (a) 600 mL of 0.250 M $SrBr_2$, (b) 86.4 g of 0.180 m KCl, (c) 124.0 g of a solution that is 6.45% glucose ($C_6H_{12}O_6$) by mass.

13.48 Calculate the number of moles of solute present in each of the following solutions: (a) 185 mL of 1.50 M $HNO_3(aq)$, (b) 50.0 mg of an aqueous solution that is 1.25 m NaCl, (c) 75.0 g of an aqueous solution that is 1.50% sucrose ($C_{12}H_{22}O_{11}$) by mass.

13.49 Describe how you would prepare each of the following aqueous solutions, starting with solid KBr: (a) 0.75 L of 1.5×10^{-2} M KBr, (b) 125 g of 0.180 m KBr, (c) 1.85 L of a solution that is 12.0% KBr by mass (the density of the solution is 1.10 g/mL), (d) a 0.150 M solution of KBr that contains just enough KBr to precipitate 16.0 g of AgBr from a solution containing 0.480 mol of $AgNO_3$.

13.50 Describe how you would prepare each of the following aqueous solutions: (a) 1.50 L of 0.110 M $(NH_4)_2SO_4$ solution, starting with solid $(NH_4)_2SO_4$; (b) 120 g of a solution that is 0.65 m in Na_2CO_3, starting with the solid solute; (c) 1.20 L of a solution that is 15.0% $Pb(NO_3)_2$ by mass (the density of the solution is 1.16 g/mL), starting with solid solute; (d) a 0.50 M solution of HCl that would just neutralize 5.5 g of $Ba(OH)_2$ starting with 6.0 M HCl.

13.51 Commercial aqueous nitric acid has a density of 1.42 g/mL and is 16 M. Calculate the percent HNO_3 by mass in the solution.

13.52 Commercial concentrated aqueous ammonia is 28% NH_3 by mass and has a density of 0.90 g/mL. What is the molarity of this solution?

13.53 Brass is a substitutional alloy consisting of a solution of copper and zinc. A particular sample of red brass consisting of 80.0% Cu and 20.0% Zn by mass has a density of 8750 kg/m³. (a) What is the molality of Zn in the solid solution? (b) What is the molarity of Zn in the solution?

13.54 Caffeine ($C_8H_{10}N_4O_2$) is a stimulant found in coffee and tea. If a solution of caffeine in chloroform ($CHCl_3$) as a solvent has a concentration of 0.0750 m, calculate **(a)** the percent caffeine by mass, **(b)** the mole fraction of caffeine.

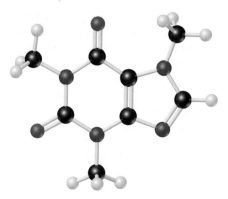

13.55 During a typical breathing cycle the CO_2 concentration in the expired air rises to a peak of 4.6% by volume. Calculate the partial pressure of the CO_2 at this point, assuming 1 atm pressure. What is the molarity of the CO_2 in air at this point, assuming a body temperature of 37 °C?

13.56 Breathing air that contains 4.0% by volume CO_2 over time causes rapid breathing, throbbing headache, and nausea, among other symptoms. What is the concentration of CO_2 in such air in terms of **(a)** mol percentage, **(b)** molarity, assuming 1 atm pressure, and a body temperature of 37 °C?

Colligative Properties

13.57 List four properties of a solution that depend on the total concentration but not the type of particle or particles present as solute. Write the mathematical expression that describes how each of these properties depends on concentration.

13.58 How does increasing the concentration of a nonvolatile solute in water affect the following properties: **(a)** vapor pressure, **(b)** freezing point, **(c)** boiling point; **(d)** osmotic pressure?

13.59 Consider two solutions, one formed by adding 10 g of glucose ($C_6H_{12}O_6$) to 1 L of water and the other formed by adding 10 g of sucrose ($C_{12}H_{22}O_{11}$) to 1 L of water. Are the vapor pressures over the two solutions the same? Why or why not?

13.60 **(a)** What is an *ideal solution*? **(b)** The vapor pressure of pure water at 60 °C is 149 torr. The vapor pressure of water over a solution at 60 °C containing equal numbers of moles of water and ethylene glycol (a nonvolatile solute) is 67 torr. Is the solution ideal according to Raoult's law? Explain.

13.61 **(a)** Calculate the vapor pressure of water above a solution prepared by adding 22.5 g of lactose ($C_{12}H_{22}O_{11}$) to 200.0 g of water at 338 K. (Vapor-pressure data for water are given in Appendix B.) **(b)** Calculate the mass of propylene glycol ($C_3H_8O_2$) that must be added to 0.340 kg of water to reduce the vapor pressure by 2.88 torr at 40 °C.

[13.62] **(a)** Calculate the vapor pressure of water above a solution prepared by dissolving 32.5 g of glycerin ($C_3H_8O_3$) in 125 g of water at 343 K. (The vapor pressure of water is given in Appendix B.) **(b)** Calculate the mass of ethylene glycol ($C_2H_6O_2$) that must be added to 1.00 kg of ethanol (C_2H_5OH) to reduce its vapor pressure by 10.0 torr at 35 °C. The vapor pressure of pure ethanol at 35 °C is 1.00×10^2 torr.

[13.63] At 63.5 °C the vapor pressure of H_2O is 175 torr, and that of ethanol (C_2H_5OH) is 400 torr. A solution is made by mixing equal masses of H_2O and C_2H_5OH. **(a)** What is the mole fraction of ethanol in the solution? **(b)** Assuming ideal-solution behavior, what is the vapor pressure of the solution at 63.5 °C? **(c)** What is the mole fraction of ethanol in the vapor above the solution?

[13.64] At 20 °C the vapor pressure of benzene (C_6H_6) is 75 torr, and that of toluene (C_7H_8) is 22 torr. Assume that benzene and toluene form an ideal solution. **(a)** What is the composition in mole fractions of a solution that has a vapor pressure of 35 torr at 20 °C? **(b)** What is the mole fraction of benzene in the vapor above the solution described in part (a)?

13.65 **(a)** Why does a 0.10 m aqueous solution of NaCl have a higher boiling point than a 0.10 m aqueous solution of $C_6H_{12}O_6$? **(b)** Calculate the boiling point of each solution. **(c)** The experimental boiling point of the NaCl solution is lower than that calculated, assuming that NaCl is completely dissociated in solution. Why is this the case?

13.66 Arrange the following aqueous solutions, each 10% by mass in solute, in order of increasing boiling point: glucose ($C_6H_{12}O_6$), sucrose ($C_{12}H_{22}O_{11}$), sodium nitrate (NaNO$_3$).

13.67 List the following aqueous solutions in order of increasing boiling point: 0.120 m glucose, 0.050 m LiBr, 0.050 m Zn(NO$_3$)$_2$.

13.68 List the following aqueous solutions in order of decreasing freezing point: 0.040 m glycerin ($C_3H_8O_3$), 0.020 m KBr, 0.030 m phenol (C_6H_5OH).

13.69 Using data from Table 13.4, calculate the freezing and boiling points of each of the following solutions: **(a)** 0.22 m glycerol ($C_3H_8O_3$) in ethanol, **(b)** 0.240 mol of naphthalene ($C_{10}H_8$) in 2.45 mol of chloroform, **(c)** 2.04 g KBr and 4.82 g glucose ($C_6H_{12}O_6$) in 188 g of water.

13.70 Using data from Table 13.4, calculate the freezing and boiling points of each of the following solutions: **(a)** 0.30 m glucose in ethanol; **(b)** 20.0 g of decane, $C_{10}H_{22}$, in 45.5 g CHCl$_3$; **(c)** 0.45 mol ethylene glycol and 0.15 mol KBr in 150 g H_2O.

13.71 How many grams of ethylene glycol ($C_2H_6O_2$) must be added to 1.00 kg of water to produce a solution that freezes at $-5.00\,°C$?

13.72 What is the freezing point of an aqueous solution that boils at $105.0\,°C$?

13.73 What is the osmotic pressure formed by dissolving 44.2 mg of aspirin ($C_9H_8O_4$) in 0.358 L of water at 25 °C?

13.74 Seawater contains 3.4 g of salts for every liter of solution. Assuming that the solute consists entirely of NaCl (over 90% is), calculate the osmotic pressure of seawater at 20 °C.

13.75 Adrenaline is the hormone that triggers the release of extra glucose molecules in times of stress or emergency. A solution of 0.64 g of adrenaline in 36.0 g of CCl_4 elevates the boiling point by 0.49 °C. Is the molar mass of adrenaline calculated from the boiling point elevation in agreement with the following structural formula?

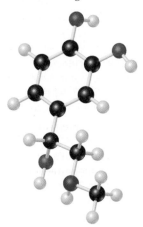

13.76 Lauryl alcohol is obtained from coconut oil and is used to make detergents. A solution of 5.00 g of lauryl alcohol in 0.100 kg of benzene freezes at 4.1 °C. What is the approximate molar mass of lauryl alcohol?

13.77 Lysozyme is an enzyme that breaks bacterial cell walls. A solution containing 0.150 g of this enzyme in 210 mL of solution has an osmotic pressure of 0.953 torr at 25 °C. What is the molar mass of lysozyme?

13.78 A dilute aqueous solution of an organic compound soluble in water is formed by dissolving 2.35 g of the compound in water to form 0.250 L solution. The resulting solution has an osmotic pressure of 0.605 atm at 25 °C. Assuming that the organic compound is a nonelectrolyte, what is its molar mass?

[13.79] The osmotic pressure of a 0.010 *M* aqueous solution of $CaCl_2$ is found to be 0.674 atm at 25 °C. **(a)** Calculate the van't Hoff factor, *i*, for the solution. **(b)** How would you expect the value of *i* to change as the solution becomes more concentrated? Explain.

[13.80] Based on the data given in Table 13.5, which solution would give the larger freezing-point lowering, a 0.030 *m* solution of NaCl or a 0.020 *m* solution of K_2SO_4? How do you explain the departure from ideal behavior and the differences observed between the two salts?

Colloids

13.81 **(a)** Why is there no colloid in which both the dispersed substance and the dispersing substance are gases? **(b)** Michael Faraday first prepared ruby-red colloids of gold particles in water that were stable for indefinite times. ∞ (Section 12.6) To the unaided eye these brightly colored colloids are not distinguishable from solutions. How could you determine whether a given colored preparation is a solution or colloid?

13.82 **(a)** Many proteins that remain homogeneously distributed in water have molecular masses in the range of 30,000 amu and larger. In what sense is it appropriate to consider such suspensions to be colloids rather than solutions? Explain. **(b)** What general name is given to a colloidal dispersion of one liquid in another? What is an emulsifying agent?

13.83 Indicate whether each of the following is a hydrophilic or a hydrophobic colloid: **(a)** butterfat in homogenized milk, **(b)** hemoglobin in blood, **(c)** vegetable oil in a salad dressing, **(d)** colloidal gold particles in water.

13.84 Explain how each of the following factors helps determine the stability or instability of a colloidal dispersion: **(a)** particulate mass, **(b)** hydrophobic character, **(c)** charges on colloidal particles.

13.85 Colloidal suspensions of proteins, such as a gelatin, can often be caused to separate into two layers by addition of a solution of an electrolyte. Given that protein molecules may carry electrical charges on their outer surface as illustrated in Figure 13.28, what do you believe happens when the electrolyte solution is added?

13.86 Explain how **(a)** a soap such as sodium stearate stabilizes a colloidal dispersion of oil droplets in water; **(b)** milk curdles upon addition of an acid.

WHAT'S AHEAD

CHEMISTRY IS, BY ITS VERY NATURE, CONCERNED WITH CHANGE.

Chemical reactions convert substances with well-defined properties into other materials with different properties. Much of our study of chemical reactions concerns the formation of new substances from a given set

of reactants. It is equally important to understand how rapidly chemical reactions occur.

The rates of reactions span an enormous range, from those that are complete within fractions of seconds, such as explosions, to those that take thousands or even millions of years, such as the formation of diamonds or other minerals in Earth's crust (Figure 14.1 ▼). The fireworks shown in this chapter-opening photograph require very rapid reactions, both to propel them skyward and to produce their colorful bursts of light. The chemicals used in the fireworks are chosen both to give the desired colors and to do so very rapidly. The characteristic red, blue, and green colors are produced by salts of strontium, copper, and barium, respectively.

▲ **Figure 14.1 Reaction rates.** The rates of chemical reactions span a range of time scales. For example, explosions are rapid, occurring in seconds or fractions of seconds; corrosion can take years; and the weathering of rocks takes place over thousands or even millions of years.

The area of chemistry that is concerned with the speeds, or rates, of reactions is called **chemical kinetics**. Chemical kinetics is a subject of broad importance. It relates, for example, to how quickly a medicine is able to work, to whether the formation and depletion of ozone in the upper atmosphere are in balance, and to industrial challenges such as the development of catalysts to synthesize new materials.

Our goal in this chapter is to understand how to determine the rates at which reactions occur and to consider the factors that control these rates. For example, what factors determine how rapidly food spoils? How does one design a fast-setting material for dental fillings? What determines the rate at which steel rusts? What controls the rate at which fuel burns in an automobile engine? Although we will not address these specific questions, we will see that the rates of all chemical reactions are subject to the same basic principles.

14.1 FACTORS THAT AFFECT REACTION RATES

Before we examine the quantitative aspects of chemical kinetics, such as how rates are measured, let's examine the key factors that influence the rates of reactions. Because reactions involve the breaking and forming of bonds, the speeds of reactions depend on the nature of the reactants themselves. Four factors allow us to change the rates at which particular reactions occur:

1. *The physical state of the reactants.* Reactants must come together to react. The more readily molecules collide with each other, the more rapidly they react. Most of the reactions we consider are homogeneous, involving either gases or liquid solutions. When reactants are in different phases, as when one is a gas and another a solid, the reaction is limited to their area of contact. Thus, reactions that involve solids tend to proceed faster if the surface area of the solid is increased. For example, a medicine in the form of a fine powder will dissolve in the stomach and enter the bloodstream more quickly than the same medicine in the form of a tablet.

2. *The concentrations of the reactants.* Most chemical reactions proceed faster if the concentration of one or more of the reactants is increased. For example, steel wool burns with difficulty in air, which contains 20% O_2, but bursts into a brilliant white flame in pure oxygen (Figure 14.2 ▶). As concentration increases, the frequency with which the reactant molecules collide increases, leading to increased rates.

3. *The temperature at which the reaction occurs.* The rates of chemical reactions increase as temperature is increased. We refrigerate perishable foods such as milk for this reason. The bacterial reactions that lead to the spoiling of milk proceed much more rapidly at room temperature than they do at the lower temperature of a refrigerator. Increasing temperature increases the kinetic energies of molecules. ∞ (Section 10.7) As molecules move more rapidly, they collide more frequently and also with higher energy, leading to increased reaction rates.

Box 2 contains 7 red spheres and 3 purple spheres:

$$\text{Box 2: Rate} = k(7)(3)^2 = 63k$$

Box 3 contains 3 red spheres and 7 purple spheres:

$$\text{Box 3: Rate} = k(3)(7)^2 = 147k$$

The slowest rate is $63k$ (box 2), and the highest is $147k$ (box 3). Thus, the rates vary in the order $2 < 1 < 3$.

Check: Each box contains 10 spheres. The rate law indicates that in this case [B] has a greater influence on rate than [A] because B has a higher reaction order. Hence, the mixture with the highest concentration of B (most purple spheres) should react fastest. This analysis confirms the order $2 < 1 < 3$.

■ **PRACTICE EXERCISE**

Assuming that rate $= k$[A][B], rank the mixtures represented in this Sample Exercise in order of increasing rate.
Answer: $2 = 3 < 1$

Units of Rate Constants

The units of the rate constant depend on the overall reaction order of the rate law. In a reaction that is second order overall, for example, the units of the rate constant must satisfy the equation:

$$\text{Units of rate} = (\text{units of rate constant})(\text{units of concentration})^2$$

Hence, in our usual units of concentration and time

$$\text{Units of rate constant} = \frac{\text{units of rate}}{(\text{units of concentration})^2} = \frac{M/s}{M^2} = M^{-1}\,\text{s}^{-1}$$

■ **SAMPLE EXERCISE 14.5** | **Determining Reaction Orders and Units for Rate Constants**

(a) What are the overall reaction orders for the reactions described in Equations 14.9 and 14.10? **(b)** What are the units of the rate constant for the rate law in Equation 14.9?

SOLUTION

Analyze: We are given two rate laws and asked to express **(a)** the overall reaction order for each and **(b)** the units for the rate constant for the first reaction.

Plan: The overall reaction order is the sum of the exponents in the rate law. The units for the rate constant, k, are found by using the normal units for rate (M/s) and concentration (M) in the rate law and applying algebra to solve for k.

Solve: (a) The rate of the reaction in Equation 14.9 is first order in N_2O_5 and first order overall. The reaction in Equation 14.10 is first order in $CHCl_3$ and one-half order in Cl_2. The overall reaction order is three halves.
(b) For the rate law for Equation 14.9, we have

$$\text{Units of rate} = (\text{units of rate constant})(\text{units of concentration})$$

So

$$\text{Units of rate constant} = \frac{\text{units of rate}}{\text{units of concentration}} = \frac{M/s}{M} = \text{s}^{-1}$$

Notice that the units of the rate constant change as the overall order of the reaction changes.

■ **PRACTICE EXERCISE**

(a) What is the reaction order of the reactant H_2 in Equation 14.11? **(b)** What are the units of the rate constant for Equation 14.11?
Answers: **(a)** 1, **(b)** $M^{-1}\text{s}^{-1}$

Using Initial Rates to Determine Rate Laws

The rate law for any chemical reaction must be determined experimentally; it cannot be predicted by merely looking at the chemical equation. We often determine the rate law for a reaction by the same method we applied to the data in Table 14.2: We observe the effect of changing the initial concentrations of the reactants on the initial rate of the reaction.

We have seen that the rate laws for most reactions have the general form

$$\text{Rate} = k[\text{reactant 1}]^m[\text{reactant 2}]^n \ldots$$

Thus, the task of determining the rate law becomes one of determining the reaction orders, m and n. In most reactions the reaction orders are 0, 1, or 2. If a reaction is zero order in a particular reactant, changing its concentration will have no effect on rate (as long as some of the reactant is present) because any concentration raised to the zero power equals 1. On the other hand, we have seen that when a reaction is first order in a reactant, changes in the concentration of that reactant will produce proportional changes in the rate. Thus, doubling the concentration will double the rate, and so forth. Finally, when the rate law is second order in a particular reactant, doubling its concentration increases the rate by a factor of $2^2 = 4$, tripling its concentration causes the rate to increase by a factor of $3^2 = 9$, and so forth.

In working with rate laws, it is important to realize that the *rate* of a reaction depends on concentration, but the *rate constant* does not. As we will see later in this chapter, the rate constant (and hence the reaction rate) is affected by temperature and by the presence of a catalyst.

■■ **SAMPLE EXERCISE 14.6** | **Determining a Rate Law from Initial Rate Data**

The initial rate of a reaction A + B $\longrightarrow$ C was measured for several different starting concentrations of A and B, and the results are as follows:

Experiment Number	[A] (M)	[B] (M)	Initial Rate (M/s)
1	0.100	0.100	4.0×10^{-5}
2	0.100	0.200	4.0×10^{-5}
3	0.200	0.100	16.0×10^{-5}

Using these data, determine **(a)** the rate law for the reaction, **(b)** the rate constant, **(c)** the rate of the reaction when [A] = 0.050 M and [B] = 0.100 M.

SOLUTION

Analyze: We are given a table of data that relates concentrations of reactants with initial rates of reaction and asked to determine **(a)** the rate law, **(b)** the rate constant, and **(c)** the rate of reaction for a set of concentrations not listed in the table.

Plan: (a) We assume that the rate law has the following form: Rate = $k[\text{A}]^m[\text{B}]^n$ so we must use the given data to deduce the reaction orders m and n. We do so by determining how changes in the concentration change the rate. **(b)** Once we know m and n, we can use the rate law and one of the sets of data to determine the rate constant k. **(c)** Now that we know both the rate constant and the reaction orders, we can use the rate law with the given concentrations to calculate rate.

Solve: (a) As we move from experiment 1 to experiment 2, [A] is held constant and [B] is doubled. Thus, this pair of experiments shows how [B] affects the rate, allowing us to deduce the order of the rate law with respect to B. Because the rate remains the same when [B] is doubled, the concentration of B has no effect on the reaction rate. The rate law is therefore zero order in B (that is, $n = 0$).

In experiments 1 and 3, [B] is held constant so these data show how [A] affects rate. Holding [B] constant while doubling [A] increases the rate fourfold. This result indicates that rate is proportional to $[\text{A}]^2$ (that is, the reaction is second order in A). Hence, the rate law is

$$\text{Rate} = k[\text{A}]^2[\text{B}]^0 = k[\text{A}]^2$$

This rate law could be reached in a more formal way by taking the ratio of the rates from two experiments:

$$\frac{\text{Rate 2}}{\text{Rate 1}} = \frac{4.0 \times 10^{-5}\ M/s}{4.0 \times 10^{-5}\ M/s} = 1$$

Using the rate law, we have

$$1 = \frac{\text{rate 2}}{\text{rate 1}} = \frac{k[\cancel{0.100\ M}]^m[0.200\ M]^n}{k[\cancel{0.100\ M}]^m[0.100\ M]^n} = \frac{[0.200]^n}{[0.100]^n} = 2^n$$

2^n equals 1 under only one condition:

$$n = 0$$

We can deduce the value of m in a similar fashion:

$$\frac{\text{Rate 3}}{\text{Rate 1}} = \frac{16.0 \times 10^{-5}\ M/s}{4.0 \times 10^{-5}\ M/s} = 4$$

Using the rate law gives

$$4 = \frac{\text{rate 3}}{\text{rate 1}} = \frac{k[0.200\ M]^m[\cancel{0.100\ M}]^n}{k[0.100\ M]^m[\cancel{0.100\ M}]^n} = \frac{[0.200]^m}{[0.100]^m} = 2^m$$

Because $2^m = 4$, we conclude that

$$m = 2$$

(b) Using the rate law and the data from experiment 1, we have

$$k = \frac{\text{rate}}{[A]^2} = \frac{4.0 \times 10^{-5}\ M/s}{(0.100\ M)^2} = 4.0 \times 10^{-3}\ M^{-1}\,s^{-1}$$

(c) Using the rate law from part (a) and the rate constant from part (b), we have

$$\text{Rate} = k[A]^2 = (4.0 \times 10^{-3}\ M^{-1}\,s^{-1})(0.050\ M)^2 = 1.0 \times 10^{-5}\ M/s$$

Because [B] is not part of the rate law, it is irrelevant to the rate, if there is at least some B present to react with A.

Check: A good way to check our rate law is to use the concentrations in experiment 2 or 3 and see if we can correctly calculate the rate. Using data from experiment 3, we have

$$\text{Rate} = k[A]^2 = (4.0 \times 10^{-3}\ M^{-1}\,s^{-1})(0.200\ M)^2 = 1.6 \times 10^{-4}\ M/s$$

Thus, the rate law correctly reproduces the data, giving both the correct number and the correct units for the rate.

■ **PRACTICE EXERCISE**

The following data were measured for the reaction of nitric oxide with hydrogen:

$$2\ NO(g) + 2\ H_2(g) \longrightarrow N_2(g) + 2\ H_2O(g)$$

Experiment Number	[NO] (M)	[H$_2$] (M)	Initial Rate (M/s)
1	0.10	0.10	1.23×10^{-3}
2	0.10	0.20	2.46×10^{-3}
3	0.20	0.10	4.92×10^{-3}

(a) Determine the rate law for this reaction. **(b)** Calculate the rate constant. **(c)** Calculate the rate when [NO] = 0.050 M and [H$_2$] = 0.150 M

Answers: **(a)** rate = $k[NO]^2[H_2]$; **(b)** $k = 1.2\ M^{-2}\,s^{-1}$; **(c)** rate = $4.5 \times 10^{-4}\ M/s$

14.4 THE CHANGE OF CONCENTRATION WITH TIME

The rate laws that we have examined so far enable us to calculate the rate of a reaction from the rate constant and reactant concentrations. These rate laws can also be converted into equations that show the relationship between the concentrations of the reactants or products and time. The mathematics required to accomplish this conversion involves calculus. We do not expect you to be able to perform the calculus operations; however, you should be able to use the resulting equations. We will apply this conversion to two of the simplest rate laws: those that are first order overall and those that are second order overall.

First-Order Reactions

A **first-order reaction** is one whose rate depends on the concentration of a single reactant raised to the first power. For a reaction of the type A $\longrightarrow$ products the rate law may be first order:

$$\text{Rate} = -\frac{\Delta[A]}{\Delta t} = k[A]$$

This form of a rate law, which expresses how rate depends on concentration, is called the *differential rate law*. Using an operation from calculus called integration, this relationship can be transformed into an equation that relates the concentration of A at the start of the reaction, $[A]_0$, to its concentration at any other time t, $[A]_t$:

$$\ln[A]_t - \ln[A]_0 = -kt \qquad \text{or} \qquad \ln\frac{[A]_t}{[A]_0} = -kt \qquad [14.12]$$

This form of the rate law is called the *integrated rate law*. The function "ln" in Equation 14.12 is the natural logarithm (Appendix A.2). Equation 14.12 can also be rearranged and written as follows:

$$\ln[A]_t = -kt + \ln[A]_0 \qquad [14.13]$$

Equations 14.12 and 14.13 can be used with any concentration units, as long as the units are the same for both $[A]_t$ and $[A]_0$.

For a first-order reaction, Equation 14.12 or 14.13 can be used in several ways. Given any three of the following quantities, we can solve for the fourth: k, t, $[A]_0$, and $[A]_t$. Thus, you can use these equations, for example, to determine (1) the concentration of a reactant remaining at any time after the reaction has started, (2) the time required for a given fraction of a sample to react, or (3) the time required for a reactant concentration to fall to a certain level.

■■■ **SAMPLE EXERCISE 14.7** | **Using the Integrated First-Order Rate Law**

The decomposition of a certain insecticide in water follows first-order kinetics with a rate constant of 1.45 yr^{-1} at 12 °C. A quantity of this insecticide is washed into a lake on June 1, leading to a concentration of 5.0×10^{-7} g/cm^3. Assume that the average temperature of the lake is 12 °C. **(a)** What is the concentration of the insecticide on June 1 of the following year? **(b)** How long will it take for the concentration of the insecticide to decrease to 3.0×10^{-7} g/cm^3?

SOLUTION

Analyze: We are given the rate constant for a reaction that obeys first-order kinetics, as well as information about concentrations and times, and asked to calculate how much reactant (insecticide) remains after one year. We must also determine the time interval needed to reach a particular insecticide concentration. Because the exercise gives time in (a) and asks for time in (b), we know that the integrated rate law, Equation 14.13, is required.

Plan: **(a)** We are given $k = 1.45$ yr^{-1}, $t = 1.00$ yr and $[\text{insecticide}]_0 = 5.0 \times 10^{-7}$ g/cm^3, and so Equation 14.13 can be solved for $[\text{insecticide}]_t$. **(b)** We have $k = 1.45$ yr^{-1}, $[\text{insecticide}]_0 = 5.0 \times 10^{-7}$ g/cm^3, and $[\text{insecticide}]_t = 3.0 \times 10^{-7}$ g/cm^3, and so we can solve Equation 14.13 for time, t.

Solve: (a) Substituting the known quantities into Equation 14.13, we have

$$\ln[\text{insecticide}]_{t=1\ \text{yr}} = -(1.45\ \text{yr}^{-1})(1.00\ \text{yr}) + \ln(5.0 \times 10^{-7})$$

We use the ln function on a calculator to evaluate the second term on the right, giving

$$\ln[\text{insecticide}]_{t=1\ \text{yr}} = -1.45 + (-14.51) = -15.96$$

To obtain $[\text{insecticide}]_{t=1\ \text{yr}}$, we use the inverse natural logarithm, or e^x, function on the calculator:

$$[\text{insecticide}]_{t=1\ \text{yr}} = e^{-15.96} = 1.2 \times 10^{-7}\ \text{g/cm}^3$$

Note that the concentration units for $[A]_t$ and $[A]_0$ must be the same.

(b) Again substituting into Equation 14.13, with $[\text{insecticide}]_t = 3.0 \times 10^{-7}$ g/cm^3, gives

$$\ln(3.0 \times 10^{-7}) = -(1.45\ \text{yr}^{-1})(t) + \ln(5.0 \times 10^{-7})$$

Solving for t gives

$$t = -[\ln(3.0 \times 10^{-7}) - \ln(5.0 \times 10^{-7})]/1.45\ \text{yr}^{-1}$$
$$= -(-15.02 + 14.51)/1.45\ \text{yr}^{-1} = 0.35\ \text{yr}$$

Check: In part (a) the concentration remaining after 1.00 yr (that is, $1.2 \times 10^{-7} \text{ g/cm}^3$) is less than the original concentration ($5.0 \times 10^{-7} \text{ g/cm}^3$), as it should be. In (b) the given concentration ($3.0 \times 10^{-7} \text{ g/cm}^3$) is greater than that remaining after 1.00 yr, indicating that the time must be less than a year. Thus, $t = 0.35$ yr is a reasonable answer.

■ PRACTICE EXERCISE

The decomposition of dimethyl ether, $(CH_3)_2O$, at 510 °C is a first-order process with a rate constant of $6.8 \times 10^{-4} \text{ s}^{-1}$:

$$(CH_3)_2 O(g) \longrightarrow CH_4(g) + H_2(g) + CO(g)$$

If the initial pressure of $(CH_3)_2O$ is 135 torr, what is its pressure after 1420 s?
Answer: 51 torr

Equation 14.13 can be used to verify whether a reaction is first order and to determine its rate constant. This equation has the form of the general equation for a straight line, $y = mx + b$, in which m is the slope and b is the y-intercept of the line (Appendix A.4):

$$\ln[A]_t = -k \cdot t + \ln[A]_0$$

$$y \quad = \quad m \cdot x + \quad b$$

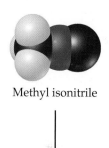

Methyl isonitrile

For a first-order reaction, therefore, a graph of $\ln[A]_t$ versus time gives a straight line with a slope of $-k$ and a y-intercept of $\ln[A]_0$. A reaction that is not first order will not yield a straight line.

As an example, consider the conversion of methyl isonitrile (CH_3NC) to acetonitrile (CH_3CN) (Figure 14.6►). Because experiments show that the reaction is first order, we can write the rate equation:

$$\ln[CH_3NC]_t = -kt + \ln[CH_3NC]_0$$

Acetonitrile

Figure 14.7(a)▼ shows how the pressure of methyl isonitrile varies with time as it rearranges in the gas phase at 198.9 °C. We can use pressure as a unit of concentration for a gas because from the ideal-gas law the pressure is directly proportional to the number of moles per unit volume. Figure 14.7(b) shows a plot of the natural logarithm of the pressure versus time, a plot that yields a straight line. The slope of this line is $-5.1 \times 10^{-5} \text{ s}^{-1}$. (You should verify this for yourself, remembering that your result may vary slightly from ours because of inaccuracies associated with reading the graph.) Because the slope of the line equals $-k$, the rate constant for this reaction equals $5.1 \times 10^{-5} \text{ s}^{-1}$.

▲ **Figure 14.6 A first-order reaction.** The transformation of methyl isonitrile (CH_3NC) to acetonitrile (CH_3CN) is a first-order process. Methyl isonitrile and acetonitrile are isomers, molecules that have the same atoms arranged differently. This reaction is called an isomerization reaction.

▲ GIVE IT SOME THOUGHT

What do the y-intercepts in Figure 14.7(a) and (b) represent?

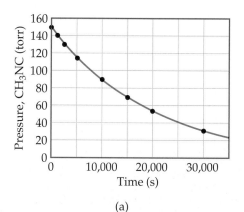

(a)

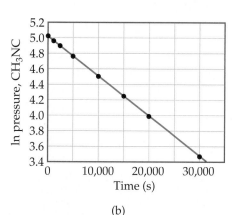

(b)

◄ **Figure 14.7 Kinetic data for conversion of methyl isonitrile.** (a) Variation in the partial pressure of methyl isonitrile (CH_3NC) with time during the reaction $CH_3NC \longrightarrow CH_3CN$ at 198.9 °C. (b) A plot of the natural logarithm of the CH_3NC pressure as a function of time. The fact that a straight line fits the data confirms that the rate law is first order.

Second-Order Reactions

A **second-order reaction** is one whose rate depends on the reactant concentration raised to the second power or on the concentrations of two different reactants, each raised to the first power. For simplicity, let's consider reactions of the type A $\longrightarrow$ products or A + B $\longrightarrow$ products that are second order in just one reactant, A:

$$\text{Rate} = -\frac{\Delta[A]}{\Delta t} = k[A]^2$$

With the use of calculus, this differential rate law can be used to derive the following integrated rate law:

$$\frac{1}{[A]_t} = kt + \frac{1}{[A]_0} \qquad [14.14]$$

This equation, like Equation 14.13, has four variables, k, t, $[A]_0$, and $[A]_t$, and any one of these can be calculated knowing the other three. Equation 14.14 also has the form of a straight line ($y = mx + b$). If the reaction is second order, a plot of $1/[A]_t$ versus t will yield a straight line with a slope equal to k and a y-intercept equal to $1/[A]_0$. One way to distinguish between first- and second-order rate laws is to graph both $\ln[A]_t$ and $1/[A]_t$ against t. If the $\ln[A]_t$ plot is linear, the reaction is first order; if the $1/[A]_t$ plot is linear, the reaction is second order.

■ SAMPLE EXERCISE 14.8 | **Determining Reaction Order from the Integrated Rate Law**

The following data were obtained for the gas-phase decomposition of nitrogen dioxide at 300 °C, $NO_2(g) \longrightarrow NO(g) + \frac{1}{2}O_2(g)$:

Time (s)	[NO$_2$] (M)
0.0	0.01000
50.0	0.00787
100.0	0.00649
200.0	0.00481
300.0	0.00380

Is the reaction first or second order in NO_2?

SOLUTION

Analyze: We are given the concentrations of a reactant at various times during a reaction and asked to determine whether the reaction is first or second order.

Plan: We can plot $\ln[NO_2]$ and $1/[NO_2]$ against time. One or the other will be linear, indicating whether the reaction is first or second order.

Solve: To graph $\ln[NO_2]$ and $1/[NO_2]$ against time, we will first prepare the following table from the data given:

Time (s)	[NO$_2$] (M)	ln[NO$_2$]	1/[NO$_2$]
0.0	0.01000	−4.605	100
50.0	0.00787	−4.845	127
100.0	0.00649	−5.037	154
200.0	0.00481	−5.337	208
300.0	0.00380	−5.573	263

As Figure 14.8 ▶ shows, only the plot of $1/[NO_2]$ versus time is linear. Thus, the reaction obeys a second-order rate law: Rate = $k[NO_2]^2$. From the slope of this straight-line graph, we determine that $k = 0.543 \ M^{-1} \ s^{-1}$ for the disappearance of NO_2.

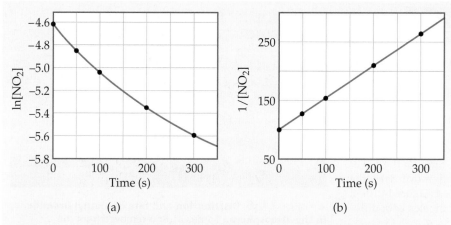

(a)   (b)

▲ **Figure 14.8 Kinetic data for decomposition of NO₂.** The reaction is $NO_2(g) \longrightarrow$ $NO(g) + \frac{1}{2} O_2(g)$, and the data were collected at 300 °C. (a) A plot of $\ln[NO_2]$ versus time is not linear, indicating that the reaction is not first order in NO_2. (b) A plot of $1/[NO_2]$ versus time is linear, indicating that the reaction is second order in NO_2.

■■ PRACTICE EXERCISE

Consider again the decomposition of NO_2 discussed in the Sample Exercise. The reaction is second order in NO_2 with $k = 0.543 \ M^{-1} \ s^{-1}$. If the initial concentration of NO_2 in a closed vessel is 0.0500 M, what is the remaining concentration after 0.500 h? *Answer:* Using Equation 14.14, we find $[NO_2] = 1.00 \times 10^{-3} \ M$

Half-life

The **half-life** of a reaction, $t_{1/2}$, is the time required for the concentration of a reactant to reach one-half of its initial value, $[A]_{t_{1/2}} = \frac{1}{2}[A]_0$. The half-life is a convenient way to describe how fast a reaction occurs, especially if it is a first-order process. A fast reaction will have a short half-life.

We can determine the half-life of a first-order reaction by substituting $[A]_{t_{1/2}}$ into Equation 14.12:

$$\ln \frac{\frac{1}{2}[A]_0}{[A]_0} = -kt_{1/2}$$

$$\ln \frac{1}{2} = -kt_{1/2}$$

$$t_{1/2} = -\frac{\ln \frac{1}{2}}{k} = \frac{0.693}{k} \qquad [14.15]$$

From Equation 14.15, we see that $t_{1/2}$ for a first-order rate law does not depend on the starting concentration. Consequently, the half-life remains constant throughout the reaction. If, for example, the concentration of the reactant is 0.120 M at some moment in the reaction, it will be $\frac{1}{2}(0.120 \ M) = 0.060 \ M$ after one half-life. After one more half-life passes, the concentration will drop to 0.030 M, and so on. Equation 14.15 also indicates that we can calculate $t_{1/2}$ for a first-order reaction if k is known, or k if $t_{1/2}$ is known.

The change in concentration over time for the first-order rearrangement of methyl isonitrile at 198.9 °C is graphed in Figure 14.9▶. The first half-life is shown at 13,600 s (that is, 3.78 h). At a time 13,600 s later, the isonitrile concentration has decreased to one-half of one-half, or one-fourth the original concentration. *In a first-order reaction, the concentration of the reactant decreases by $\frac{1}{2}$ in each of a series of regularly spaced time intervals, namely, $t_{1/2}$.* The concept of half-life is widely used in describing radioactive decay, a first-order process that we will discuss in detail in Section 21.4.

▼ **Figure 14.9 Half-life of a first-order reaction.** Pressure of methyl isonitrile as a function of time showing two successive half-lives of the isomerization reaction depicted in Figure 14.6.

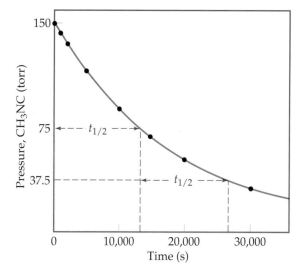

Chemistry Put to Work   METHYL BROMIDE IN THE ATMOSPHERE

Several small molecules containing carbon–chlorine or carbon–bromine bonds, when present in the stratosphere, are capable of reacting with ozone (O_3) and thus contributing to the destruction of Earth's ozone layer. Whether a halogen-containing molecule contributes significantly to destruction of the ozone layer depends in part on the molecule's average lifetime in the atmosphere. It takes quite a long time for molecules formed at Earth's surface to diffuse through the lower atmosphere (called the troposphere) and move into the stratosphere, where the ozone layer is located (Figure 14.10▶). Decomposition in the lower atmosphere competes with diffusion into the stratosphere.

The much-discussed chlorofluorocarbons, or CFCs, contribute to the destruction of the ozone layer because they have long lifetimes in the troposphere. Thus, they persist long enough for a substantial fraction of the molecules to find their way to the stratosphere.

Another simple molecule that has the potential to destroy the stratospheric ozone layer is methyl bromide (CH_3Br). This substance has a wide range of uses, including antifungal treatment of plant seeds, and has therefore been produced in large quantities in the past (about 150 million pounds per year worldwide in 1997). In the stratosphere, the C—Br bond is broken through absorption of short-wavelength radiation. The resultant Br atoms then catalyze decomposition of O_3.

Methyl bromide is removed from the lower atmosphere by a variety of mechanisms, including a slow reaction with ocean water:

$$CH_3Br(g) + H_2O(l) \longrightarrow CH_3OH(aq) + HBr(aq) \qquad [14.16]$$

To determine the potential importance of CH_3Br in destruction of the ozone layer, it is important to know how rapidly the reaction in Equation 14.16 and all other reactions together remove CH_3Br from the atmosphere before it can diffuse into the stratosphere.

Scientists have carried out research to estimate the average lifetime of CH_3Br in Earth's atmosphere. Such an estimate is difficult to make. It cannot be done in laboratory-based experiments because the conditions that exist in the atmosphere above the planet are too complex to be simulated in the laboratory. Instead, scientists gathered nearly 4000 samples of the

▲ Figure 14.10 **Distribution and fate of methyl bromide in the atmosphere.** Some CH_3Br is removed from the atmosphere by decomposition, and some diffuses upward into the stratosphere, where it contributes to destruction of the ozone layer. The relative rates of decomposition and diffusion determine how extensively methyl bromide is involved in destruction of the ozone layer.

atmosphere during aircraft flights all over the Pacific Ocean and analyzed them for the presence of several trace organic substances, including methyl bromide. From a detailed analysis of the concentrations, it was possible to estimate the *atmospheric residence time* for CH_3Br.

The atmospheric residence time is related to the half-life for CH_3Br in the lower atmosphere, assuming that it decomposes by a first-order process. From the experimental data, the half-life for methyl bromide in the lower atmosphere is estimated to be 0.8 ± 0.1 yr. That is, a collection of CH_3Br molecules present at any given time will, on average, be 50% decomposed after 0.8 years, 75% decomposed after 1.6 years, and so on. A half-life of 0.8 years, while comparatively short, is still sufficiently long so that CH_3Br contributes significantly to the destruction of the ozone layer. In 1997 an international agreement was reached to phase out use of methyl bromide in developed countries by 2005. However, in recent years exemptions for critical agricultural use have been requested and granted. Nevertheless, worldwide production was down to 30 million pounds worldwide in 2005, two-thirds of which is used in the United States.

Related Exercise: 14.111

◢ GIVE IT SOME THOUGHT

If a solution containing 10.0 g of a substance reacts by first-order kinetics, how many grams remain after 3 half-lives?

■ **SAMPLE EXERCISE 14.9** | **Determining the Half-life of a First-Order Reaction**

The reaction of C_4H_9Cl with water is a first-order reaction. Figure 14.4 shows how the concentration of C_4H_9Cl changes with time at a particular temperature. **(a)** From that graph, estimate the half-life for this reaction. **(b)** Use the half-life from (a) to calculate the rate constant.

SOLUTION

Analyze: We are asked to estimate the half-life of a reaction from a graph of concentration versus time and then to use the half-life to calculate the rate constant for the reaction.

Plan: **(a)** To estimate a half-life, we can select a concentration and then determine the time required for the concentration to decrease to half of that value. **(b)** Equation 14.15 is used to calculate the rate constant from the half-life.

Solve: **(a)** From the graph, we see that the initial value of $[C_4H_9Cl]$ is 0.100 M. The half-life for this first-order reaction is the time required for $[C_4H_9Cl]$ to decrease to 0.050 M, which we can read off the graph. This point occurs at approximately 340 s. **(b)** Solving Equation 14.15 for k, we have

$$k = \frac{0.693}{t_{1/2}} = \frac{0.693}{340 \text{ s}} = 2.0 \times 10^{-3} \text{ s}^{-1}$$

Check: At the end of the second half-life, which should occur at 680 s, the concentration should have decreased by yet another factor of 2, to 0.025 M. Inspection of the graph shows that this is indeed the case.

■ PRACTICE EXERCISE

(a) Using Equation 14.15, calculate $t_{1/2}$ for the decomposition of the insecticide described in Sample Exercise 14.7. **(b)** How long does it take for the concentration of the insecticide to reach one-quarter of the initial value?
Answers: **(a)** 0.478 yr = 1.51×10^7 s; **(b)** it takes two half-lives, 2(0.478 yr) = 0.956 yr

---

In contrast to the behavior of first-order reactions, the half-life for second-order and other reactions depends on reactant concentrations and therefore changes as the reaction progresses. Using Equation 14.14, we find that the half-life of a second-order reaction is

$$t_{1/2} = \frac{1}{k[A]_0} \qquad [14.17]$$

In this case the half-life depends on the initial concentration of reactant—the lower the initial concentration, the greater the half-life.

GIVE IT SOME THOUGHT

How does the half-life of a second-order reaction change as the reaction proceeds?

14.5 TEMPERATURE AND RATE

The rates of most chemical reactions increase as the temperature rises. For example, dough rises faster at room temperature than when refrigerated, and plants grow more rapidly in warm weather than in cold. We can literally see the effect of temperature on reaction rate by observing a chemiluminescence reaction (one that produces light). The characteristic glow of fireflies is a familiar example of chemiluminescence. Another is the light produced by Cyalume® light sticks, which contain chemicals that produce chemiluminescence when mixed. As seen in Figure 14.11 ▶, these light sticks produce a brighter light at higher temperature. The amount of light produced is greater because the rate of the reaction is faster at the higher temperature. Although the light stick glows more brightly initially, its luminescence also dies out more rapidly.

How is this experimentally observed temperature effect reflected in the rate expression? The faster rate at higher temperature is due to an increase in the rate constant with increasing temperature. For example, let's reconsider the first-order reaction $CH_3NC \longrightarrow CH_3CN$

▼ Figure 14.11 **Temperature affects the rate of the chemiluminescence reaction in Cyalume® light sticks.** The light stick in hot water (left) glows more brightly than the one in cold water (right); at the higher temperature, the reaction is initially faster and produces a brighter light.

Higher temperature   Lower temperature

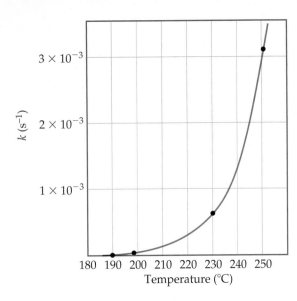

▲ Figure 14.12 Dependence of rate constant on temperature. The data show the variation in the first-order rate constant for the rearrangement of methyl isonitrile as a function of temperature. The four points indicated are used in connection with Sample Exercise 14.11.

(Figure 14.6). Figure 14.12 ◄ shows the rate constant for this reaction as a function of temperature. The rate constant, and hence the rate of the reaction, increases rapidly with temperature, approximately doubling for each 10 °C rise.

The Collision Model

We have seen that reaction rates are affected both by the concentrations of reactants and by temperature. The **collision model**, which is based on the kinetic-molecular theory (Section 10.7), accounts for both of these effects at the molecular level. The central idea of the collision model is that molecules must collide to react. The greater the number of collisions occurring per second, the greater is the reaction rate. As the concentration of reactant molecules increases, therefore, the number of collisions increases, leading to an increase in reaction rate. According to the kinetic-molecular theory of gases, increasing the temperature increases molecular speeds. As molecules move faster, they collide more forcefully (with more energy) and more frequently, increasing reaction rates.

For a reaction to occur, though, more is required than simply a collision. For most reactions, only a tiny fraction of the collisions leads to a reaction. For example, in a mixture of H_2 and I_2 at ordinary temperatures and pressures, each molecule undergoes about 10^{10} collisions per second. If every collision between H_2 and I_2 resulted in the formation of HI, the reaction would be over in much less than a second. Instead, at room temperature the reaction proceeds very slowly. Only about one in every 10^{13} collisions produces a reaction. What keeps the reaction from occurring more rapidly?

▲ GIVE IT SOME THOUGHT

What is the central idea of the collision model?

The Orientation Factor

In most reactions, molecules must be oriented in a certain way during collisions for a reaction to occur. The relative orientations of the molecules during their collisions determine whether the atoms are suitably positioned to form new bonds. For example, consider the reaction of Cl atoms with NOCl:

$$Cl + NOCl \longrightarrow NO + Cl_2$$

The reaction will take place if the collision brings Cl atoms together to form Cl_2 as shown in Figure 14.13(a) ▶. In contrast, the collision shown in Figure 14.13(b) will be ineffective and will not yield products. Indeed, a great many collisions do not lead to reaction, merely because the molecules are not suitably oriented. Another factor, however, is usually even more important in determining whether particular collisions result in reaction.

Activation Energy

In 1888 the Swedish chemist Svante Arrhenius suggested that molecules must possess a certain minimum amount of energy to react. According to the collision model, this energy comes from the kinetic energies of the colliding molecules. Upon collision, the kinetic energy of the molecules can be used to stretch, bend, and ultimately break bonds, leading to chemical reactions. That is, the kinetic energy is used to change the potential energy of the molecule. If molecules are moving too slowly, with too little kinetic energy, they merely bounce off one another without changing. To react, colliding molecules must have a total kinetic energy equal to or greater than some minimum value. The minimum energy required to initiate a chemical reaction is called the **activation energy**, E_a. The value of E_a varies from reaction to reaction.

14.7 CATALYSIS

A **catalyst** is a substance that changes the speed of a chemical reaction without undergoing a permanent chemical change itself in the process. Catalysts are very common; most reactions in the body, the atmosphere, and the oceans occur with the help of catalysts. Much industrial chemical research is devoted to the search for new and more effective catalysts for reactions of commercial importance. Extensive research efforts also are devoted to finding means of inhibiting or removing certain catalysts that promote undesirable reactions, such as those that corrode metals, age our bodies, and cause tooth decay.

Homogeneous Catalysis

A catalyst that is present in the same phase as the reacting molecules is called a **homogeneous catalyst**. Examples abound both in solution and in the gas phase. Consider, for example, the decomposition of aqueous hydrogen peroxide, $H_2O_2(aq)$, into water and oxygen:

$$2 H_2O_2(aq) \longrightarrow 2 H_2O(l) + O_2(g) \qquad [14.29]$$

In the absence of a catalyst, this reaction occurs extremely slowly.

Many different substances are capable of catalyzing the reaction represented by Equation 14.29, including bromide ion, $Br^-(aq)$, as shown in Figure 14.19▼.

▼ Figure 14.19 **Effect of catalyst.** (H_2O molecules and Na^+ ions are omitted from the molecular art for clarity.)

HOMOGENEOUS CATALYSIS

A catalyst that is present in the same phase as the reacting molecules is a homogeneous catalyst.

In the absence of a catalyst, $H_2O_2(aq)$ decomposes very slowly.

Shortly after the addition of a small amount of NaBr(aq) to $H_2O_2(aq)$, the solution turns brown because Br_2 is generated (Equation 14.30). The buildup of Br_2 leads to rapid evolution of O_2 according to Equation 14.31.

After all of the H_2O_2 has decomposed, a colorless solution of NaBr(aq) remains. Thus, NaBr has catalyzed the reaction even though it is not consumed during the reaction.

The bromide ion reacts with hydrogen peroxide in acidic solution, forming aqueous bromine and water:

$$2\,Br^-(aq) + H_2O_2(aq) + 2\,H^+ \longrightarrow Br_2(aq) + 2\,H_2O(l) \qquad [14.30]$$

The brown color observed in the middle photograph of Figure 14.19 indicates the formation of $Br_2(aq)$. If this were the complete reaction, bromide ion would not be a catalyst, because it undergoes chemical change during the reaction. However, hydrogen peroxide also reacts with the $Br_2(aq)$ generated in Equation 14.30:

$$Br_2(aq) + H_2O_2(aq) \longrightarrow 2\,Br^-(aq) + 2\,H^+(aq) + O_2(g) \qquad [14.31]$$

The bubbling evident in Figure 14.19(b) is due to the formation of $O_2(g)$.
    The sum of Equations 14.30 and 14.31 is just Equation 14.29:

$$2\,H_2O_2(aq) \longrightarrow 2\,H_2O(l) + O_2(g)$$

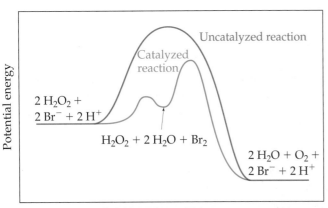

▲ Figure 14.20 **Energy profiles for uncatalyzed and catalyzed reactions.** The energy profiles for the uncatalyzed decomposition of hydrogen peroxide and for the reaction as catalyzed by Br^- are compared. The catalyzed reaction involves two successive steps, each of which has a lower activation energy than the uncatalyzed reaction. Notice that the energies of reactants and products are unchanged by the catalyst.

When H_2O_2 has been completely decomposed, we are left with a colorless solution of $Br^-(aq)$, as seen in the photograph on the right in Figure 14.19. Bromide ion, therefore, is indeed a catalyst of the reaction because it speeds the overall reaction without itself undergoing any net change. It is added at the start of the reaction, reacts, and then reforms at the end. In contrast, Br_2 is an intermediate because it is first formed (Equation 14.30) and then consumed (Equation 14.31). Neither the catalyst nor the intermediate appears in the chemical equation for the overall reaction. Notice, however, that *the catalyst is there at the start of the reaction, whereas the intermediate is formed during the course of the reaction.*
    On the basis of the Arrhenius equation (Equation 14.19), the rate constant (k) is determined by the activation energy (E_a) and the frequency factor (A). A catalyst may affect the rate of reaction by altering the value of either E_a or A. The most dramatic catalytic effects come from lowering E_a. As a general rule, *a catalyst lowers the overall activation energy for a chemical reaction.*
    A catalyst usually lowers the overall activation energy for a reaction by providing a different mechanism for the reaction. In the decomposition of hydrogen peroxide, for example, two successive reactions of H_2O_2, with bromide and then with bromine, take place. Because these two reactions together serve as a catalytic pathway for hydrogen peroxide decomposition, *both* of them must have significantly lower activation energies than the uncatalyzed decomposition, as shown schematically in Figure 14.20 ◄.

▲ GIVE IT SOME THOUGHT

How does a catalyst increase the rate of a reaction?

Heterogeneous Catalysis

A **heterogeneous catalyst** exists in a different phase from the reactant molecules, usually as a solid in contact with either gaseous reactants or with reactants in a liquid solution. Many industrially important reactions are catalyzed by the surfaces of solids. For example, hydrocarbon molecules are rearranged to form gasoline with the aid of what are called "cracking" catalysts (see the "Chemistry Put to Work" box in Section 25.3). Heterogeneous catalysts are often composed of metals or metal oxides. Because the catalyzed reaction occurs on the surface, special methods are often used to prepare catalysts so that they have very large surface areas.
    The initial step in heterogeneous catalysis is usually **adsorption** of reactants. *Adsorption* refers to the binding of molecules to a surface, whereas

absorption refers to the uptake of molecules into the interior of another substance. ∞ (Section 13.6) Adsorption occurs because the atoms or ions at the surface of a solid are extremely reactive. Unlike their counterparts in the interior of the substance, surface atoms and ions have unused bonding capacity. This unused bonding capability may be used to bond molecules from the gas or solution phase to the surface of the solid.

The reaction of hydrogen gas with ethylene gas to form ethane gas provides an example of heterogeneous catalysis:

$$C_2H_4(g) + H_2(g) \longrightarrow C_2H_6(g) \quad \Delta H° = -137 \text{ kJ/mol} \qquad [14.32]$$

Ethylene   Ethane

Even though this reaction is exothermic, it occurs very slowly in the absence of a catalyst. In the presence of a finely powdered metal, however, such as nickel, palladium, or platinum, the reaction occurs rather easily at room temperature. The mechanism by which the reaction occurs is diagrammed in Figure 14.21 ▼. Both ethylene and hydrogen are adsorbed on the metal surface [Figure 14.21(a)]. Upon adsorption the H—H bond of H_2 breaks, leaving two H atoms that are bonded to the metal surface, as shown in Figure 14.21(b). The hydrogen atoms are relatively free to move about the surface. When a hydrogen encounters an adsorbed ethylene molecule, it can form a σ bond to one of the carbon atoms, effectively destroying the C—C π bond and leaving an *ethyl group* (C_2H_5) bonded to the surface via a metal-to-carbon σ bond [Figure 14.21(c)]. This σ bond is relatively weak, so when the other carbon atom also encounters a hydrogen atom, a sixth C—H σ bond is readily formed and an ethane molecule is released from the metal surface [Figure 14.21(d)]. The site is ready to adsorb another ethylene molecule and thus begin the cycle again.

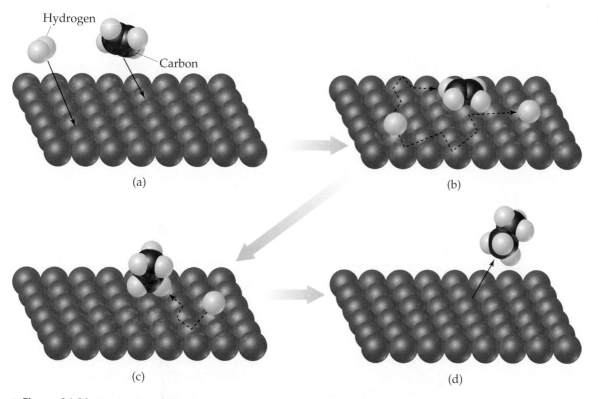

▲ **Figure 14.21 Mechanism for reaction of ethylene with hydrogen on a catalytic surface.** (a) The hydrogen and ethylene are adsorbed at the metal surface. (b) The H—H bond is broken to give adsorbed hydrogen atoms. (c) These migrate to the adsorbed ethylene and bond to the carbon atoms. (d) As C—H bonds are formed, the adsorption of the molecule to the metal surface is decreased and ethane is released.

Chemistry Put to Work   CATALYTIC CONVERTERS

Heterogeneous catalysis plays a major role in the fight against urban air pollution. Two components of automobile exhausts that help form photochemical smog are nitrogen oxides and unburned hydrocarbons of various types (Section 18.4). In addition, automobile exhausts may contain considerable quantities of carbon monoxide. Even with the most careful attention to engine design, it is impossible under normal driving conditions to reduce the quantity of these pollutants to an acceptable level in the exhaust gases. It is therefore necessary to remove them from the exhaust before they are vented to the air. This removal is accomplished in the *catalytic converter*.

The catalytic converter, which is part of the exhaust system, must perform two distinct functions: (1) oxidation of CO and unburned hydrocarbons (C_xH_y) to carbon dioxide and water, and (2) reduction of nitrogen oxides to nitrogen gas:

$$CO, C_xH_y \xrightarrow{O_2} CO_2 + H_2O$$
$$NO, NO_2 \longrightarrow N_2$$

These two functions require two distinctly different catalysts, so the development of a successful catalyst system is a difficult challenge. The catalysts must be effective over a wide range of operating temperatures. They must continue to be active despite the fact that various components of the exhaust can block the active sites of the catalyst. And the catalysts must be sufficiently rugged to withstand exhaust gas turbulence and the mechanical shocks of driving under various conditions for thousands of miles.

Catalysts that promote the combustion of CO and hydrocarbons are, in general, the transition-metal oxides and the noble metals, such as platinum. A mixture of two different metal oxides, CuO and Cr_2O_3, might be used, for example. These materials are supported on a structure (Figure 14.22▶) that allows the best possible contact between the flowing exhaust gas and the catalyst surface. A honeycomb structure made from alumina (Al_2O_3) and impregnated with the catalyst is employed. Such catalysts operate by first adsorbing oxygen gas, also present in the exhaust gas. This adsorption weakens the O—O bond in O_2, so that oxygen atoms are available for reaction with adsorbed CO to form CO_2. Hydrocarbon oxidation probably proceeds somewhat similarly, with the hydrocarbons first being adsorbed followed by rupture of a C—H bond.

The most effective catalysts for reduction of NO to yield N_2 and O_2 are transition-metal oxides and noble metals, the same kinds of materials that catalyze the oxidation of CO and hydrocarbons. The catalysts that are most effective in one reaction, however, are usually much less effective in the other. It is therefore necessary to have two different catalytic components.

Catalytic converters are remarkably efficient heterogeneous catalysts. The automotive exhaust gases are in contact with the catalyst for only 100 to 400 ms. In this very short time, 96% of the hydrocarbons and CO is converted to CO_2 and H_2O, and the emission of nitrogen oxides is reduced by 76%.

There are costs as well as benefits associated with the use of catalytic converters. Some of the metals used in the converters are very expensive. Catalytic converters currently account for about 35% of the platinum, 65% of the palladium, and 95% of the rhodium used annually. All of these metals, which come mainly from Russia and South Africa, are far more expensive than gold.

Related Exercises: 14.56, 14.75, and 14.76

▲ **Figure 14.22 Cross section of a catalytic converter.** Automobiles are equipped with catalytic converters, which are part of their exhaust systems. The exhaust gases contain CO, NO, NO_2, and unburned hydrocarbons that pass over surfaces impregnated with catalysts. The catalysts promote the conversion of the exhaust gases into CO_2, H_2O, and N_2.

GIVE IT SOME THOUGHT

How does a homogeneous catalyst compare with a heterogeneous one regarding the ease of recovery of the catalyst from the reaction mixture?

Enzymes

Many of the most interesting and important examples of catalysis involve reactions within living systems. The human body is characterized by an extremely complex system of interrelated chemical reactions. All these reactions must occur at carefully controlled rates to maintain life. A large number of marvelously efficient biological catalysts known as **enzymes** are necessary for many of these reactions to occur at suitable rates. Most enzymes are large protein molecules with molecular weights ranging from about 10,000 to about 1 million amu. They are very selective in the reactions that they catalyze, and some are absolutely specific, operating for only one substance in only one reaction. The decomposition of hydrogen peroxide, for example, is an important biological process. Because hydrogen peroxide is strongly oxidizing, it can be physiologically harmful. For this reason, the blood and livers of mammals contain an enzyme, *catalase*, which catalyzes the decomposition of hydrogen peroxide into water and oxygen (Equation 14.29). Figure 14.23▶ shows the dramatic acceleration of this chemical reaction by the catalase in beef liver.

Although an enzyme is a large molecule, the reaction is catalyzed at a very specific location in the enzyme, called the **active site**. The substances that undergo reaction at this site are called **substrates**. The **lock-and-key model**, illustrated in Figure 14.24▼, provides a simple explanation for the specificity of an enzyme. The substrate is pictured as fitting neatly into a special place on the enzyme (the active site), much like a specific key fits into a lock. The active site is created by coiling and folding of the long protein molecule to form a space, something like a pocket, into which the substrate molecule fits. Figure 14.25▶ shows a model of the enzyme *lysozyme* with and without a bound substrate molecule.

The combination of the enzyme and the substrate is called the *enzyme-substrate complex*. Although Figure 14.24 shows both the active site and its complementary substrate as having rigid shapes, the active site is often fairly flexible. Thus, the active site may change shape as it binds the substrate. The binding between the substrate and the active site involves intermolecular forces such as dipole–dipole attractions, hydrogen bonds, and London dispersion forces. ∞∞ (Section 11.2)

As the substrate molecules enter the active site, they are somehow activated, so that they are capable of extremely rapid reaction. This activation may result from the withdrawal or donation of electron density at a particular bond by the enzyme. In addition, in the process of fitting into the active site, the substrate molecule may be distorted and thus made more reactive. Once the reaction occurs, the products then depart, allowing another substrate molecule to enter.

▲ Figure 14.23 **Effect of an enzyme.** Ground-up beef liver causes hydrogen peroxide to decompose rapidly into water and oxygen. The decomposition is catalyzed by the enzyme *catalase*. Grinding the liver breaks open the cells, so that the reaction takes place more rapidly. The frothing is due to escape of oxygen gas from the reaction mixture.

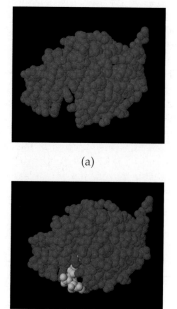

(a)

(b)

▲ Figure 14.25 **Molecular model of an enzyme.** (a) A molecular model of the enzyme *lysozyme*. Note the characteristic cleft, which is the location of the active site. (b) Lysozyme with a bound substrate molecule.

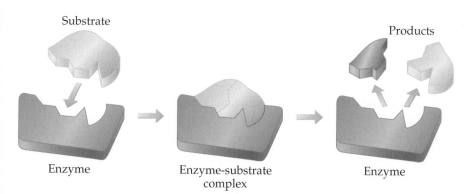

▲ Figure 14.24 **The lock-and-key model for enzyme action.** The correct substrate is recognized by its ability to fit the active site of the enzyme, forming the enzyme-substrate complex. After the reaction of the substrate is complete, the products separate from the enzyme.

Chemistry and Life NITROGEN FIXATION AND NITROGENASE

Nitrogen is one of the most essential elements in living organisms. It is found in many compounds that are vital to life, including proteins, nucleic acids, vitamins, and hormones. Plants use very simple nitrogen-containing compounds, especially NH_3, NH_4^+, and NO_3^-, as starting materials from which such complex, biologically necessary compounds are formed. Animals are unable to synthesize the complex nitrogen compounds they require from the simple substances used by plants. Instead, they rely on more complicated precursors present in vitamin- and protein-rich foods.

Nitrogen is continually cycling through this biological arena in various forms, as shown in the simplified nitrogen cycle in Figure 14.26▼. For example, certain microorganisms convert the nitrogen in animal waste and dead plants and animals into molecular nitrogen, $N_2(g)$, which returns to the atmosphere. For the food chain to be sustained, there must be a means of reincorporating this atmospheric N_2 in a form that plants can utilize. The process of converting N_2 into compounds that plants can use is called *nitrogen fixation*. Fixing nitrogen is difficult; N_2 is an exceptionally unreactive molecule, in large part because of its very strong $N\equiv N$ triple bond. ∞ (Section 8.3) Some fixed nitrogen results from the action of lightning on the atmosphere, and some is produced industrially using a process we will discuss in Chapter 15. About 60% of fixed nitrogen, however, is a consequence of the action of a remarkable and complex enzyme called *nitrogenase*. This enzyme

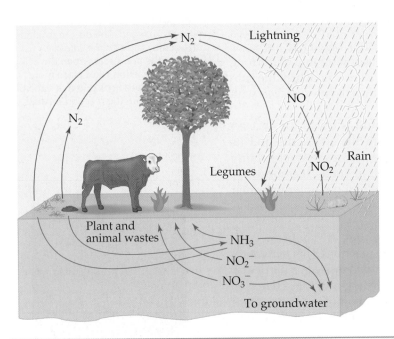

◀ **Figure 14.26 Simplified picture of the nitrogen cycle.** The compounds of nitrogen in the soil are water-soluble species, such as NH_3, NO_2^-, and NO_3^-, which can be washed out of the soil by groundwater. These nitrogen compounds are converted into biomolecules by plants and are incorporated into animals that eat the plants. Certain bacteria that release N_2 to the atmosphere attack animal waste and dead plants and animals. Atmospheric N_2 is fixed in the soil predominantly by the action of certain plants that contain the enzyme nitrogenase, thereby completing the cycle.

The activity of an enzyme is destroyed if some molecule in the solution is able to bind strongly to the active site and block the entry of the substrate. Such substances are called *enzyme inhibitors*. Nerve poisons and certain toxic metal ions such as lead and mercury are believed to act in this way to inhibit enzyme activity. Some other poisons act by attaching elsewhere on the enzyme, thereby distorting the active site so that the substrate no longer fits.

Enzymes are enormously more efficient than ordinary nonbiochemical catalysts. The number of individual catalyzed reaction events occurring at a particular active site, called the *turnover number*, is generally in the range of 10^3 to 10^7 per second. Such large turnover numbers correspond to very low activation energies.

GIVE IT SOME THOUGHT

What names are given to the following aspects of enzymes and enzyme catalysis: **(a)** the place on the enzyme where catalysis occurs, **(b)** the substances that undergo catalysis?

Third, we use the stoichiometry of the reaction to determine the changes in concentration that occur as the reaction proceeds to equilibrium. The concentrations of H_2 and I_2 will decrease as equilibrium is established and that of HI will increase. Let's represent the change in concentration of H_2 by the variable x. The balanced chemical equation tells us the relationship between the changes in the concentrations of the three gases:

For each x mol of H_2 that reacts, x mol of I_2 are consumed and $2x$ mol of HI are produced:

	$H_2(g)$	+	$I_2(g)$	$\rightleftharpoons$	2 HI(g)
Initial	1.000 M		2.000 M		0 M
Change	$-x$		$-x$		$+2x$
Equilibrium					

Fourth, we use the initial concentrations and the changes in concentrations, as dictated by stoichiometry, to express the equilibrium concentrations. With all our entries, our table now looks like this:

	$H_2(g)$	+	$I_2(g)$	$\rightleftharpoons$	2 HI(g)
Initial	1.000 M		2.000 M		0 M
Change	$-x$		$-x$		$+2x$
Equilibrium	$(1.000 - x)$ M		$(2.000 - x)$ M		$2x$ M

Fifth, we substitute the equilibrium concentrations into the equilibrium-constant expression and solve for the unknown, x:

$$K_c = \frac{[\text{HI}]^2}{[\text{H}_2][\text{I}_2]} = \frac{(2x)^2}{(1.000 - x)(2.000 - x)} = 50.5$$

If you have an equation-solving calculator, you can solve this equation directly for x. If not, expand this expression to obtain a quadratic equation in x:

$$4x^2 = 50.5(x^2 - 3.000x + 2.000)$$
$$46.5x^2 - 151.5x + 101.0 = 0$$

Solving the quadratic equation (Appendix A.3) leads to two solutions for x:

$$x = \frac{-(-151.5) \pm \sqrt{1(-151.5)^2 - 4(46.5)(101.0)}}{2(46.5)} = 2.323 \text{ or } 0.935$$

When we substitute $x = 2.323$ into the expressions for the equilibrium concentrations, we find *negative* concentrations of H_2 and I_2. Because a negative concentration is not chemically meaningful, we reject this solution. We then use $x = 0.935$ to find the equilibrium concentrations:

$$[\text{H}_2] = 1.000 - x = 0.065 \ M$$
$$[\text{I}_2] = 2.000 - x = 1.065 \ M$$
$$[\text{HI}] = 2x = 1.87 \ M$$

Check: We can check our solution by putting these numbers into the equilibrium-constant expression to assure that we correctly calculate the equilibrium constant:

$$K_c = \frac{[\text{HI}]^2}{[\text{H}_2][\text{I}_2]} = \frac{(1.87)^2}{(0.065)(1.065)} = 51$$

Comment: Whenever you use a quadratic equation to solve an equilibrium problem, one of the solutions will not be chemically meaningful and should be rejected.

■ PRACTICE EXERCISE

For the equilibrium $PCl_5(g) \rightleftharpoons PCl_3(g) + Cl_2(g)$, the equilibrium constant K_p has the value 0.497 at 500 K. A gas cylinder at 500 K is charged with $PCl_5(g)$ at an initial pressure of 1.66 atm. What are the equilibrium pressures of PCl_5, PCl_3, and Cl_2 at this temperature?
Answer: $P_{PCl_5} = 0.967$ atm; $P_{PCl_3} = P_{Cl_2} = 0.693$ atm

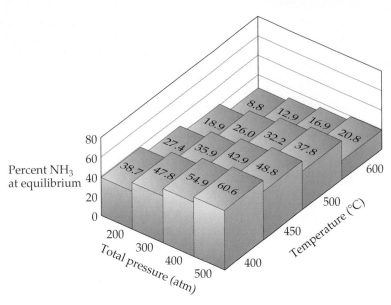

15.7 LE CHÂTELIER'S PRINCIPLE

When Haber developed his process for making ammonia from N_2 and H_2, he sought the factors that might be varied to increase the yield of NH_3. Using the values of the equilibrium constant at various temperatures, he calculated the equilibrium amounts of NH_3 formed under a variety of conditions. Some of Haber's results are shown in Figure 15.10 ◀. Notice that the percent of NH_3 present at equilibrium decreases with increasing temperature and increases with increasing pressure. We can understand these effects in terms of a principle first put forward by Henri-Louis Le Châtelier* (1850–1936), a French industrial chemist. **Le Châtelier's principle** can be stated as follows: *If a system at equilibrium is disturbed by a change in temperature, pressure, or the concentration of one of the components, the system will shift its equilibrium position so as to counteract the effect of the disturbance.*

In this section we will use Le Châtelier's principle to make qualitative predictions about how a system at equilibrium responds to various changes in external conditions. We will consider three ways that a chemical equilibrium can be disturbed: (1) adding or removing a reactant or product, (2) changing the pressure by changing the volume, and (3) changing the temperature.

▲ **Figure 15.10 Effect of temperature and pressure on the percentage of NH₃ in an equilibrium mixture of N₂, H₂, and NH₃.** Each mixture was produced by starting with a 3 : 1 molar mixture of H_2 and N_2. The yield of NH_3 is greatest at the lowest temperature and at the highest pressure.

Change in Reactant or Product Concentrations

A system at equilibrium is in a dynamic state of balance. When the conditions of the equilibrium are altered, the equilibrium shifts until a new state of balance is attained. Le Châtelier's principle states that the shift will be in the direction that minimizes or reduces the effect of the change. Therefore, *if a chemical system is at equilibrium and we increase the concentration of a substance (either a reactant or a product), the system reacts to consume some of the substance. Conversely, if we decrease the concentration of a substance, the system reacts to produce some of the substance.*

As an example, consider an equilibrium mixture of N_2, H_2, and NH_3:

$$N_2(g) + 3\,H_2(g) \rightleftharpoons 2\,NH_3(g)$$

Adding H_2 would cause the system to shift so as to reduce the newly increased concentration of H_2. This change can occur only by consuming H_2 and simultaneously consuming N_2 to form more NH_3. This situation is illustrated in Figure 15.11 ◀. Adding more N_2 to the equilibrium mixture would likewise cause the direction of the reaction to shift toward forming more NH_3. Removing NH_3 would also cause a shift toward producing more NH_3, whereas *adding* NH_3 to the system at equilibrium would cause the concentrations to shift in the direction that reduces the newly increased NH_3 concentration. Some of the added ammonia would decompose to form N_2 and H_2.

In the Haber reaction, therefore, removing NH_3 from an equilibrium mixture of N_2, H_2, and NH_3 causes the reaction to shift from left to right to form more NH_3. If the NH_3 can be removed continuously, the yield of NH_3 can be increased dramatically. In the industrial production of ammonia, the NH_3 is continuously

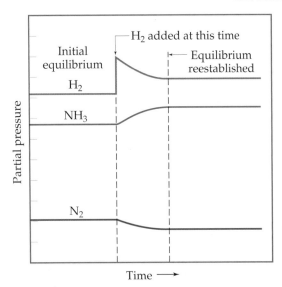

▲ **Figure 15.11 Effect of adding H₂ to an equilibrium mixture of N₂, H₂, and NH₃.** When H_2 is added, a portion of the H_2 reacts with N_2 to form NH_3, thereby establishing a new equilibrium position that has the same equilibrium constant. The results shown are in accordance with Le Châtelier's principle.

*Pronounced "le-SHOT-lee-ay."

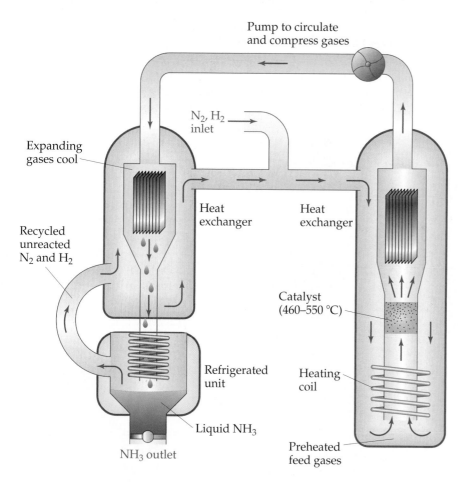

Pump to circulate
and compress gases

N₂, H₂
inlet

Expanding
gases cool

Heat
exchanger

Heat
exchanger

Recycled
unreacted
N₂ and H₂

Catalyst
(460–550 °C)

Refrigerated
unit

Heating
coil

Liquid NH₃

NH₃ outlet

Preheated
feed gases

▲ **Figure 15.12 Schematic diagram summarizing the industrial production of ammonia.** Incoming N_2 and H_2 gases are heated to approximately 500 °C and passed over a catalyst. The resultant gas mixture is allowed to expand and cool, causing NH_3 to liquefy. Unreacted N_2 and H_2 gases are recycled.

removed by selectively liquefying it; the boiling point of NH_3 ($-33\,°C$) is much higher than that of N_2 ($-196\,°C$) and H_2 ($-253\,°C$). The liquid NH_3 is removed, and the N_2 and H_2 are recycled to form more NH_3, as diagrammed in Figure 15.12▲. By continuously removing the product, the reaction is driven essentially to completion.

GIVE IT SOME THOUGHT

What happens to the equilibrium $2\,NO(g) + O_2(g) \rightleftharpoons 2\,NO_2(g)$ if **(a)** O_2 is added to the system, **(b)** NO is removed?

Effects of Volume and Pressure Changes

If a system is at equilibrium and its volume is decreased, thereby increasing its total pressure, Le Châtelier's principle indicates that the system will respond by shifting its equilibrium position to reduce the pressure. A system can reduce its pressure by reducing the total number of gas molecules (fewer molecules of gas exert a lower pressure). Thus, at constant temperature, *reducing the volume of a gaseous equilibrium mixture causes the system to shift in the direction that reduces the number of moles of gas.* Conversely, increasing the volume causes a shift in the direction that produces more gas molecules.

For example, let's again consider the equilibrium $N_2O_4(g) \rightleftharpoons 2\,NO_2(g)$. What happens if the total pressure of an equilibrium mixture is increased by decreasing the volume as shown in the sequential photos in Figure 15.13▼? According to Le Châtelier's principle, we expect the equilibrium to shift to the side that reduces the total number of moles of gas, which is the reactant side in this case. (Notice the coefficients in the chemical equation; 1 mol of N_2O_4 appears on the reactant side and 2 mol NO_2 appears on the product side.) We therefore expect the equilibrium to shift to the left, so that NO_2 is

LE CHÂTELIER'S PRINCIPLE

If a system at equilibrium is disturbed by a change in temperature, pressure, or the concentration of one of the components, the system will shift its equilibrium position so as to counteract the effect of the disturbance. The equilibrium shown is $N_2O_4(g) \rightleftharpoons 2\,NO_2(g)$.

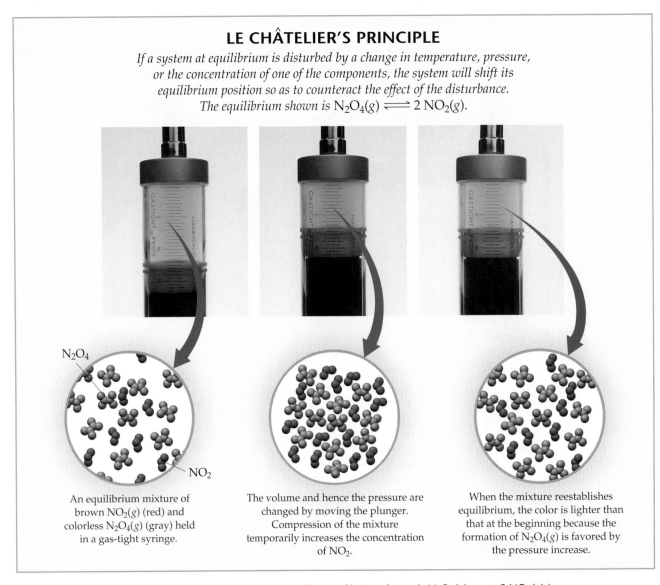

An equilibrium mixture of brown $NO_2(g)$ (red) and colorless $N_2O_4(g)$ (gray) held in a gas-tight syringe.

The volume and hence the pressure are changed by moving the plunger. Compression of the mixture temporarily increases the concentration of NO_2.

When the mixture reestablishes equilibrium, the color is lighter than that at the beginning because the formation of $N_2O_4(g)$ is favored by the pressure increase.

▲ Figure 15.13 **Effect of pressure on an equilibrium.** (The equilibrium shown is $N_2O_4(g) \rightleftharpoons 2\,NO_2(g)$.)

converted into N_2O_4 as equilibrium is reestablished. In Figure 15.13, compressing the gas mixture initially causes the color to darken as the concentration of NO_2 increases. The color then fades as equilibrium is reestablished. The color fades because the pressure increase causes the equilibrium to shift in favor of colorless N_2O_4.

GIVE IT SOME THOUGHT

What happens to the equilibrium $2\,SO_2(g) + O_2(g) \rightleftharpoons 2\,SO_3(g)$ if the volume of the system is increased?

For the reaction $N_2(g) + 3\,H_2(g) \rightleftharpoons 2\,NH_3(g)$, four molecules of reactant are consumed for every two molecules of product produced. Consequently, an increase in pressure (decrease in volume) causes a shift toward the side with fewer gas molecules, which leads to the formation of more NH_3, as indicated in Figure 15.10. In the case of the reaction $H_2(g) + I_2(g) \rightleftharpoons 2\,HI(g)$, the number of molecules of gaseous products (two) equals the number of molecules of gaseous reactants; therefore, changing the pressure will not influence the position of the equilibrium.

Keep in mind that pressure-volume changes do *not* change the value of K as long as the temperature remains constant. Rather, they change the partial pressures of the gaseous substances. In Sample Exercise 15.8 we calculated K_p for an equilibrium mixture at 472 °C that contained 7.38 atm H_2, 2.46 atm N_2, and 0.166 atm NH_3. The value of K_p is 2.79×10^{-5}. Consider what happens when we suddenly reduce the volume of the system by one-half. If there were no shift in equilibrium, this volume change would cause the partial pressures of all substances to double, giving $P_{H_2} = 14.76$ atm, $P_{N_2} = 4.92$ atm, and $P_{NH_3} = 0.332$ atm. The reaction quotient would then no longer equal the equilibrium constant.

$$Q_p = \frac{(P_{NH_3})^2}{P_{N_2}(P_{H_2})^3} = \frac{(0.332)^2}{(4.92)(14.76)^3} = 6.97 \times 10^{-6} \neq K_p$$

Because $Q_p < K_p$, the system is no longer at equilibrium. Equilibrium will be reestablished by increasing P_{NH_3} and decreasing P_{N_2} and P_{H_2} until $Q_p = K_p = 2.79 \times 10^{-5}$. Therefore, the equilibrium shifts to the right as Le Châtelier's principle predicts.

It is possible to change the total pressure of the system without changing its volume. For example, pressure increases if additional amounts of any of the reacting components are added to the system. We have already seen how to deal with a change in concentration of a reactant or product. The total pressure within the reaction vessel might also be increased by adding a gas that is not involved in the equilibrium. For example, argon might be added to the ammonia equilibrium system. The argon would not alter the partial pressures of any of the reacting components and therefore would not cause a shift in equilibrium.

Effect of Temperature Changes

Changes in concentrations or partial pressures cause shifts in equilibrium without changing the value of the equilibrium constant. In contrast, almost every equilibrium constant changes in value as the temperature changes. For example, consider the equilibrium established when cobalt(II) chloride ($CoCl_2$) is dissolved in hydrochloric acid, $HCl(aq)$:

$$\underset{\text{Pale pink}}{Co(H_2O)_6{}^{2+}(aq)} + 4\,Cl^-(aq) \rightleftharpoons \underset{\text{Deep blue}}{CoCl_4{}^{2-}(aq)} + 6\,H_2O(l) \qquad \Delta H > 0 \quad [15.23]$$

The formation of $CoCl_4{}^{2-}$ from $Co(H_2O)_6{}^{2+}$ is an endothermic process. We will discuss the significance of this enthalpy change shortly. Because $Co(H_2O)_6{}^{2+}$ is pink and $CoCl_4{}^{2-}$ is blue, the position of this equilibrium is readily apparent from the color of the solution. Figure 15.14(left) ▼ shows a room-temperature solution of $CoCl_2$ in $HCl(aq)$. Both $Co(H_2O)_6{}^{2+}$ and $CoCl_4{}^{2-}$ are present in significant amounts in the solution; the violet color results from the presence of both the pink and blue ions. When the solution is heated [Figure 15.14(middle)], it becomes intensely blue in color, indicating that the equilibrium has shifted to form more $CoCl_4{}^{2-}$. Cooling the solution, as in Figure 15.14(right), leads to a pink solution, indicating that the equilibrium has shifted to produce more $Co(H_2O)_6{}^{2+}$. How can we explain the dependence of this equilibrium on temperature?

We can deduce the rules for the temperature dependence of the equilibrium constant by applying Le Châtelier's principle. A simple way to do this is to treat heat as if it were a chemical reagent. In an *endothermic* (heat-absorbing) reaction we can consider heat as a *reactant*, whereas in an *exothermic* (heat-releasing) reaction we can consider heat as a *product*.

Endothermic: Reactants + *heat* $\rightleftharpoons$ products

Exothermic: Reactants $\rightleftharpoons$ products + *heat*

When the temperature of a system at equilibrium is increased, the system reacts as if we added a reactant to an endothermic reaction or a product to an exothermic reaction. The equilibrium shifts in the direction that consumes the excess reactant (or product), namely heat.

EFFECT OF TEMPERATURE CHANGES

Almost every equilibrium constant changes in value as the temperature changes. In an endothermic reaction, such as the one shown, heat is absorbed as reactants are converted to products. Increasing the temperature causes the equilibrium to shift to the right and K to increase. Lowering the temperature shifts the equilibrium in the direction that produces heat, to the left, decreasing K.

$$Co(H_2O)_6^{2+}(aq) + 4\,Cl^-(aq) \rightleftharpoons CoCl_4^{2-}(aq) + 6\,H_2O(l)$$

$Co(H_2O)_6^{2+}$

$CoCl_4^{2-}$

At room temperature both the pink $Co(H_2O)_6^{2+}$ and blue $CoCl_4^{2-}$ ions are present in significant amounts, giving a violet color to the solution.

Heating the solution shifts the equilibrium to the right, forming more blue $CoCl_4^{2-}$.

Cooling the solution shifts the equilibrium to the left, toward pink $Co(H_2O)_6^{2+}$.

▲ **Figure 15.14 Temperature and equilibrium.** (The reaction shown is $Co(H_2O)_6^{2+}(aq) + 4\,Cl^-(aq) \rightleftharpoons CoCl_4^{2-}(aq) + 6\,H_2O(l)$.)

GIVE IT SOME THOUGHT

Use Le Châtelier's principle to explain why the equilibrium vapor pressure of a liquid increases with increasing temperature.

In an endothermic reaction, such as Equation 15.23, heat is absorbed as reactants are converted to products. Thus, increasing the temperature causes the equilibrium to shift to the right, in the direction of products, and *K* increases. For Equation 15.23, increasing the temperature leads to the formation of more $CoCl_4^{2-}$, as observed in Figure 15.14(b).

In an exothermic reaction the opposite occurs. Heat is absorbed as products are converted to reactants; therefore the equilibrium shifts to the left and *K* decreases. We can summarize these results as follows:

Endothermic: Increasing *T* results in an increase in *K*.

Exothermic: Increasing *T* results in a decrease in *K*.

Cooling a reaction has the opposite effect. As we lower the temperature, the equilibrium shifts to the side that produces heat. Thus, cooling an endothermic reaction shifts the equilibrium to the left, decreasing K. We observed this effect in Figure 15.14(c). Cooling an exothermic reaction shifts the equilibrium to the right, increasing K.

■ **SAMPLE EXERCISE 15.13** | **Using Le Châtelier's Principle to Predict Shifts in Equilibrium**

Consider the equilibrium

$$N_2O_4(g) \rightleftharpoons 2\,NO_2(g) \qquad \Delta H° = 58.0\ kJ$$

In which direction will the equilibrium shift when **(a)** N_2O_4 is added, **(b)** NO_2 is removed, **(c)** the total pressure is increased by addition of $N_2(g)$, **(d)** the volume is increased, **(e)** the temperature is decreased?

SOLUTION

Analyze: We are given a series of changes to be made to a system at equilibrium and are asked to predict what effect each change will have on the position of the equilibrium.

Plan: Le Châtelier's principle can be used to determine the effects of each of these changes.

Solve:

(a) The system will adjust to decrease the concentration of the added N_2O_4, so the equilibrium shifts to the right, in the direction of products.
(b) The system will adjust to the removal of NO_2 by shifting to the side that produces more NO_2; thus, the equilibrium shifts to the right.
(c) Adding N_2 will increase the total pressure of the system, but N_2 is not involved in the reaction. The partial pressures of NO_2 and N_2O_4 are therefore unchanged, and there is no shift in the position of the equilibrium.
(d) If the volume is increased, the system will shift in the direction that occupies a larger volume (more gas molecules); thus, the equilibrium shifts to the right. (This is the opposite of the effect observed in Figure 15.13, where the volume was decreased.)
(e) The reaction is endothermic, so we can imagine heat as a reagent on the reactant side of the equation. Decreasing the temperature will shift the equilibrium in the direction that produces heat, so the equilibrium shifts to the left, toward the formation of more N_2O_4. Note that only this last change also affects the value of the equilibrium constant, K.

■ **PRACTICE EXERCISE**

For the reaction

$$PCl_5(g) \rightleftharpoons PCl_3(g) + Cl_2(g) \qquad \Delta H° = 87.9\ kJ$$

in which direction will the equilibrium shift when **(a)** $Cl_2(g)$ is removed, **(b)** the temperature is decreased, **(c)** the volume of the reaction system is increased, **(d)** $PCl_3(g)$ is added?
Answers: **(a)** right, **(b)** left, **(c)** right, **(d)** left

---

■ **SAMPLE EXERCISE 15.14** | **Predicting the Effect of Temperature on K**

(a) Using the standard heat of formation data in Appendix C, determine the standard enthalpy change for the reaction

$$N_2(g) + 3\,H_2(g) \rightleftharpoons 2\,NH_3(g)$$

(b) Determine how the equilibrium constant for this reaction should change with temperature.

SOLUTION

Analyze: We are asked to determine the standard enthalpy change of a reaction and how the equilibrium constant for the reaction varies with temperature.

Plan: **(a)** We can use standard enthalpies of formation to calculate $\Delta H°$ for the reaction. **(b)** We can then use Le Châtelier's principle to determine what effect temperature will have on the equilibrium constant.

TABLE 15.2 ■ Variation in K_p for the Equilibrium $N_2 + 3 H_2 \rightleftharpoons 2 NH_3$ as a Function of Temperature

Temperature (°C)	K_p
300	4.34×10^{-3}
400	1.64×10^{-4}
450	4.51×10^{-5}
500	1.45×10^{-5}
550	5.38×10^{-6}
600	2.25×10^{-6}

Solve:

(a) Recall that the standard enthalpy change for a reaction is given by the sum of the standard molar enthalpies of formation of the products, each multiplied by its coefficient in the balanced chemical equation, less the same quantities for the reactants. At 25 °C, ΔH_f° for $NH_3(g)$ is -46.19 kJ/mol. The ΔH_f° values for $H_2(g)$ and $N_2(g)$ are zero by definition because the enthalpies of formation of the elements in their normal states at 25 °C are defined as zero (Section 5.7). Because 2 mol of NH_3 is formed, the total enthalpy change is

$$(2 \text{ mol})(-46.19 \text{ kJ/mol}) - 0 = -92.38 \text{ kJ}$$

(b) Because the reaction in the forward direction is exothermic, we can consider heat a product of the reaction. An increase in temperature causes the reaction to shift in the direction of less NH_3 and more N_2 and H_2. This effect is seen in the values for K_p presented in Table 15.2 ◄. Notice that K_p changes markedly with changes in temperature and that it is larger at lower temperatures.

Comment: The fact that K_p for the formation of NH_3 from N_2 and H_2 decreases with increasing temperature is a matter of great practical importance. To form NH_3 at a reasonable rate requires higher temperatures. At higher temperatures, however, the equilibrium constant is smaller, and so the percentage conversion to NH_3 is smaller. To compensate for this, higher pressures are needed because high pressure favors NH_3 formation.

■■ PRACTICE EXERCISE

Using the thermodynamic data in Appendix C, determine the enthalpy change for the reaction

$$2 POCl_3(g) \rightleftharpoons 2 PCl_3(g) + O_2(g)$$

Use this result to determine how the equilibrium constant for the reaction should change with temperature.

Answer: $\Delta H^\circ = 508.3$ kJ; the equilibrium constant will increase with increasing temperature

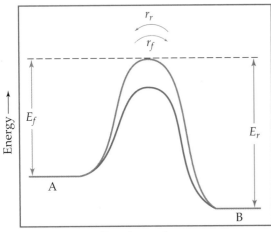

▲ Figure 15.15 **Effect of a catalyst on equilibrium.** At equilibrium for the hypothetical reaction A $\rightleftharpoons$ B, the forward reaction rate, r_f, equals the reverse reaction rate, r_r. The violet curve represents the path over the transition state in the absence of a catalyst. A catalyst lowers the energy of the transition state, as shown by the green curve. Thus, the activation energy is lowered for both the forward and the reverse reactions. As a result, the rates of forward and reverse reactions in the catalyzed reaction are increased.

The Effect of Catalysts

What happens if we add a catalyst to a chemical system that is at equilibrium? As shown in Figure 15.15 ◄, a catalyst lowers the activation barrier between the reactants and products. The activation energy of the forward reaction is lowered to the same extent as that for the reverse reaction. The catalyst thereby increases the rates of both the forward and reverse reactions. As a result, *a catalyst increases the rate at which equilibrium is achieved, but it does not change the composition of the equilibrium mixture.* The value of the equilibrium constant for a reaction is not affected by the presence of a catalyst.

The rate at which a reaction approaches equilibrium is an important practical consideration. As an example, let's again consider the synthesis of ammonia from N_2 and H_2. In designing a process for ammonia synthesis, Haber had to deal with a rapid decrease in the equilibrium constant with increasing temperature, as shown in Table 15.2. At temperatures sufficiently high to give a satisfactory reaction rate, the amount of ammonia formed was too small. The solution to this dilemma was to develop a catalyst that would produce a reasonably rapid approach to equilibrium at a sufficiently low temperature, so that the equilibrium constant was still reasonably large. The development of a suitable catalyst thus became the focus of Haber's research efforts.

After trying different substances to see which would be most effective, Haber finally settled on iron mixed with metal oxides. Variants of the original catalyst formulations are still used. These catalysts make it possible to obtain a reasonably rapid approach to equilibrium at temperatures around 400 °C to 500 °C and with gas pressures of 200 to 600 atm. The high pressures are needed to obtain a satisfactory degree of conversion at equilibrium. You can see from

Likewise, for the reaction between NH_3 and H_2O (Equation 16.5), we have

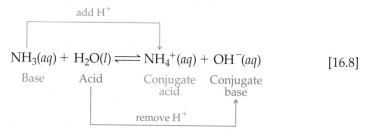

$$NH_3(aq) + H_2O(l) \rightleftharpoons NH_4^+(aq) + OH^-(aq) \qquad [16.8]$$

Base   Acid   Conjugate   Conjugate
                 acid   base

■ SAMPLE EXERCISE 16.1 | Identifying Conjugate Acids and Bases

(a) What is the conjugate base of each of the following acids: $HClO_4$, H_2S, PH_4^+, HCO_3^-? **(b)** What is the conjugate acid of each of the following bases: CN^-, SO_4^{2-}, H_2O, HCO_3^-?

SOLUTION

Analyze: We are asked to give the conjugate base for each of a series of species and to give the conjugate acid for each of another series of species.

Plan: The conjugate base of a substance is simply the parent substance minus one proton, and the conjugate acid of a substance is the parent substance plus one proton.

Solve: (a) $HClO_4$ less one proton (H^+) is ClO_4^-. The other conjugate bases are HS^-, PH_3, and CO_3^{2-}. **(b)** CN^- plus one proton (H^+) is HCN. The other conjugate acids are HSO_4^-, H_3O^+, and H_2CO_3.
  Notice that the hydrogen carbonate ion (HCO_3^-) is amphiprotic. It can act as either an acid or a base.

■ PRACTICE EXERCISE

Write the formula for the conjugate acid of each of the following: HSO_3^-, F^-, PO_4^{3-}, CO.
Answers: H_2SO_3, HF, HPO_4^{2-}, HCO^+

■ SAMPLE EXERCISE 16.2 | Writing Equations for Proton-Transfer Reactions

The hydrogen sulfite ion (HSO_3^-) is amphiprotic. **(a)** Write an equation for the reaction of HSO_3^- with water, in which the ion acts as an acid. **(b)** Write an equation for the reaction of HSO_3^- with water, in which the ion acts as a base. In both cases identify the conjugate acid–base pairs.

SOLUTION

Analyze and Plan: We are asked to write two equations representing reactions between HSO_3^- and water, one in which HSO_3^- should donate a proton to water, thereby acting as a Brønsted–Lowry acid, and one in which HSO_3^- should accept a proton from water, thereby acting as a base. We are also asked to identify the conjugate pairs in each equation.

Solve:

(a)
$$HSO_3^-(aq) + H_2O(l) \rightleftharpoons SO_3^{2-}(aq) + H_3O^+(aq)$$

The conjugate pairs in this equation are HSO_3^- (acid) and SO_3^{2-} (conjugate base); and H_2O (base) and H_3O^+ (conjugate acid).

(b)
$$HSO_3^-(aq) + H_2O(l) \rightleftharpoons H_2SO_3(aq) + OH^-(aq)$$

The conjugate pairs in this equation are H_2O (acid) and OH^- (conjugate base), and HSO_3^- (base) and H_2SO_3 (conjugate acid).

■ PRACTICE EXERCISE

When lithium oxide (Li_2O) is dissolved in water, the solution turns basic from the reaction of the oxide ion (O^{2-}) with water. Write the reaction that occurs, and identify the conjugate acid–base pairs.
Answer: $O^{2-}(aq) + H_2O(l) \longrightarrow OH^-(aq) + OH^-(aq)$. OH^- is the conjugate acid of the base O^{2-}. OH^- is also the conjugate base of the acid H_2O.

Relative Strengths of Acids and Bases

Some acids are better proton donors than others; likewise, some bases are better proton acceptors than others. If we arrange acids in order of their ability to donate a proton, we find that the more easily a substance gives up a proton, the less easily its conjugate base accepts a proton. Similarly, the more easily a base accepts a proton, the less easily its conjugate acid gives up a proton. In other words, *the stronger an acid, the weaker is its conjugate base; the stronger a base, the weaker is its conjugate acid.* Thus, if we know something about the strength of an acid (its ability to donate protons), we also know something about the strength of its conjugate base (its ability to accept protons).

The inverse relationship between the strengths of acids and the strengths of their conjugate bases is illustrated in Figure 16.4 ◀. Here we have grouped acids and bases into three broad categories based on their behavior in water.

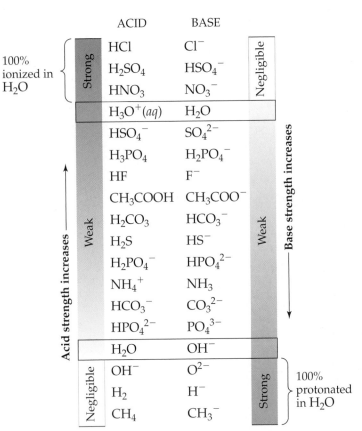

▲ **Figure 16.4 Relative strengths of some conjugate acid–base pairs.** The two members of each pair are listed opposite each other in the two columns. The acids decrease in strength from top to bottom, whereas their conjugate bases increase in strength from top to bottom.

1. A *strong acid* completely transfers its protons to water, leaving no undissociated molecules in solution. ∞∞(Section 4.3) Its conjugate base has a negligible tendency to be protonated (to abstract protons) in aqueous solution.

2. A *weak acid* only partially dissociates in aqueous solution and therefore exists in the solution as a mixture of acid molecules and their constituent ions. The conjugate base of a weak acid shows a slight ability to remove protons from water. (*The conjugate base of a weak acid is a weak base.*)

3. A substance with *negligible acidity*, such as CH_4, contains hydrogen but does not demonstrate any acidic behavior in water. Its conjugate base is a strong base, reacting completely with water, abstracting protons to form OH^- ions.

GIVE IT SOME THOUGHT

Using the three categories above, specify the strength of HNO_3 and the strength of its conjugate base, NO_3^-.

We can think of proton-transfer reactions as being governed by the relative abilities of two bases to abstract protons. For example, consider the proton transfer that occurs when an acid HX dissolves in water:

$$HX(aq) + H_2O(l) \rightleftharpoons H_3O^+(aq) + X^-(aq) \qquad [16.9]$$

If H_2O (the base in the forward reaction) is a stronger base than X^- (the conjugate base of HX), then H_2O will abstract the proton from HX to produce H_3O^+ and X^-. As a result, the equilibrium will lie to the right. This describes the behavior of a strong acid in water. For example, when HCl dissolves in water, the solution consists almost entirely of H_3O^+ and Cl^- ions with a negligible concentration of HCl molecules.

$$HCl(g) + H_2O(l) \longrightarrow H_3O^+(aq) + Cl^-(aq) \qquad [16.10]$$

H_2O is a stronger base than Cl^- (Figure 16.4), so H_2O acquires the proton to become the hydronium ion.

When X^- is a stronger base than H_2O, the equilibrium will lie to the left. This situation occurs when HX is a weak acid. For example, an aqueous solution of acetic acid (CH_3COOH) consists mainly of CH_3COOH molecules with only a relatively few H_3O^+ and CH_3COO^- ions.

$$CH_3COOH(aq) + H_2O(l) \rightleftharpoons H_3O^+(aq) + CH_3COO^-(aq) \quad [16.11]$$

CH_3COO^- is a stronger base than H_2O (Figure 16.4) and therefore abstracts the proton from H_3O^+.

From these examples, we conclude that *in every acid–base reaction the position of the equilibrium favors transfer of the proton from the stronger acid to the stronger base to form the weaker acid and the weaker base.* As a result, the equilibrium mixture contains more of the weaker acid and weaker base and less of the stronger acid and stronger base.

■ **SAMPLE EXERCISE 16.3** | **Predicting the Position of a Proton-Transfer Equilibrium**

For the following proton-transfer reaction, use Figure 16.4 to predict whether the equilibrium lies predominantly to the left (that is, $K_c < 1$) or to the right ($K_c > 1$):

$$HSO_4^-(aq) + CO_3^{2-}(aq) \rightleftharpoons SO_4^{2-}(aq) + HCO_3^-(aq)$$

SOLUTION

Analyze: We are asked to predict whether the equilibrium shown lies to the right, favoring products, or to the left, favoring reactants.

Plan: This is a proton-transfer reaction, and the position of the equilibrium will favor the proton going to the stronger of two bases. The two bases in the equation are CO_3^{2-}, the base in the forward reaction as written, and SO_4^{2-}, the conjugate base of HSO_4^-. We can find the relative positions of these two bases in Figure 16.4 to determine which is the stronger base.

Solve: CO_3^{2-} appears lower in the right-hand column in Figure 16.4 and is therefore a stronger base than SO_4^{2-}. CO_3^{2-}, therefore, will get the proton preferentially to become HCO_3^-, while SO_4^{2-} will remain mostly unprotonated. The resulting equilibrium will lie to the right, favoring products (that is, $K_c > 1$).

$$\underset{\text{Acid}}{HSO_4^-(aq)} + \underset{\text{Base}}{CO_3^{2-}(aq)} \rightleftharpoons \underset{\text{Conjugate base}}{SO_4^{2-}(aq)} + \underset{\text{Conjugate acid}}{HCO_3^-(aq)} \quad K_c > 1$$

Comment: Of the two acids in the equation, HSO_4^- and HCO_3^-, the stronger one gives up a proton more readily while the weaker one tends to retain its proton. Thus, the equilibrium favors the direction in which the proton moves from the stronger acid and becomes bonded to the stronger base.

■ **PRACTICE EXERCISE**

For each of the following reactions, use Figure 16.4 to predict whether the equilibrium lies predominantly to the left or to the right:
(a) $HPO_4^{2-}(aq) + H_2O(l) \rightleftharpoons H_2PO_4^-(aq) + OH^-(aq)$
(b) $NH_4^+(aq) + OH^-(aq) \rightleftharpoons NH_3(aq) + H_2O(l)$
Answers: (a) left, (b) right

16.3 THE AUTOIONIZATION OF WATER

One of the most important chemical properties of water is its ability to act as either a Brønsted acid or a Brønsted base, depending on the circumstances. In the presence of an acid, water acts as a proton acceptor; in the presence of a base, water acts as a proton donor. In fact, one water molecule can donate a proton to another water molecule:

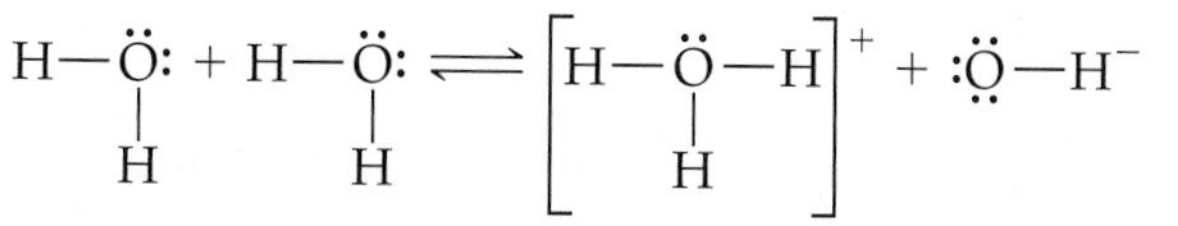

$$H\!-\!\ddot{O}\!: + H\!-\!\ddot{O}\!: \rightleftharpoons \left[H\!-\!\overset{}{\underset{H}{\ddot{O}}}\!-\!H\right]^+ + :\!\ddot{O}\!-\!H^- \quad [16.12]$$

We call this process the **autoionization** of water. No individual molecule remains ionized for long; the reactions are extremely rapid in both directions.

At room temperature only about two out of every 10^9 molecules are ionized at any given instant. Thus, pure water consists almost entirely of H_2O molecules and is an extremely poor conductor of electricity. Nevertheless, the autoionization of water is very important, as we will soon see.

The Ion Product of Water

Because the autoionization of water (Equation 16.12) is an equilibrium process, we can write the following equilibrium-constant expression for it:

$$K_c = [H_3O^+][OH^-] \qquad [16.13]$$

The term $[H_2O]$ is excluded from the equilibrium-constant expression because we exclude the concentrations of pure solids and liquids. ∞ (Section 15.4) Because this equilibrium-constant expression refers specifically to the autoionization of water, we use the symbol K_w to denote the equilibrium constant, which we call the **ion-product constant** for water. At 25 °C, K_w equals 1.0×10^{-14}. Thus, we have

$$K_w = [H_3O^+][OH^-] = 1.0 \times 10^{-14} \quad \text{(at 25 °C)} \qquad [16.14]$$

Because we use $H^+(aq)$ and $H_3O^+(aq)$ interchangeably to represent the hydrated proton, the autoionization reaction for water can also be written as

$$H_2O(l) \rightleftharpoons H^+(aq) + OH^-(aq) \qquad [16.15]$$

Likewise, the expression for K_w can be written in terms of either H_3O^- or H^+, and K_w has the same value in either case:

$$K_w = [H_3O^+][OH^-] = [H^+][OH^-] = 1.0 \times 10^{-14} \quad \text{(at 25 °C)} \qquad [16.16]$$

This equilibrium-constant expression and the value of K_w at 25 °C are extremely important, and you should commit them to memory.

What makes Equation 16.16 particularly useful is that it is applicable to pure water and to any aqueous solution. Although the equilibrium between $H^+(aq)$ and $OH^-(aq)$ as well as other ionic equilibria are affected somewhat by the presence of additional ions in solution, it is customary to ignore these ionic effects except in work requiring exceptional accuracy. Thus, Equation 16.16 is taken to be valid for any dilute aqueous solution, and it can be used to calculate either $[H^+]$ (if $[OH^-]$ is known) or $[OH^-]$ (if $[H^+]$ is known).

A solution in which $[H^+] = [OH^-]$ is said to be *neutral*. In most solutions H^+ and OH^- concentrations are not equal. As the concentration of one of these ions increases, the concentration of the other must decrease, so that the product of their concentrations equals 1.0×10^{-14}. In acidic solutions $[H^+]$ exceeds $[OH^-]$. In basic solutions $[OH^-]$ exceeds $[H^+]$.

■■ **SAMPLE EXERCISE 16.4** | Calculating $[H^+]$ for Pure Water

Calculate the values of $[H^+]$ and $[OH^-]$ in a neutral solution at 25 °C.

SOLUTION

Analyze: We are asked to determine the concentrations of H^+ and OH^- ions in a neutral solution at 25 °C.

Plan: We will use Equation 16.16 and the fact that, by definition, $[H^+] = [OH^-]$ in a neutral solution.

Solve: We will represent the concentration of $[H^+]$ and $[OH^-]$ in neutral solution with x. This gives

$$[H^+][OH^-] = (x)(x) = 1.0 \times 10^{-14}$$
$$x^2 = 1.0 \times 10^{-14}$$
$$x = 1.0 \times 10^{-7} \, M = [H^+] = [OH^-]$$

In an acid solution $[H^+]$ is greater than $1.0 \times 10^{-7} \, M$; in a basic solution $[H^+]$ is less than $1.0 \times 10^{-7} \, M$.

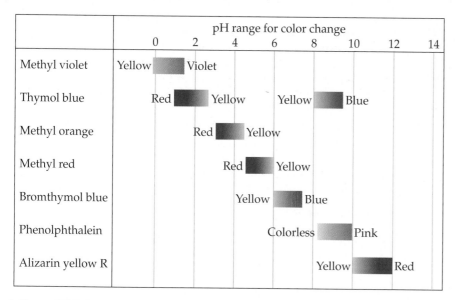

▲ Figure 16.7 Some common acid–base indicators. The pH ranges for the color changes of some common acid–base indicators. Most indicators have a useful range of about 2 pH units.

16.5 STRONG ACIDS AND BASES

The chemistry of an aqueous solution often depends critically on the pH of the solution. It is therefore important to examine how the pH of solutions relates to the concentrations of acids and bases. The simplest cases are those involving strong acids and strong bases. Strong acids and bases are *strong electrolytes*, existing in aqueous solution entirely as ions. There are relatively few common strong acids and bases, and we listed these substances in Table 4.2.

Strong Acids

The seven most common strong acids include six monoprotic acids (HCl, HBr, HI, HNO$_3$, HClO$_3$, and HClO$_4$), and one diprotic acid (H$_2$SO$_4$). Nitric acid (HNO$_3$) exemplifies the behavior of the monoprotic strong acids. For all practical purposes, an aqueous solution of HNO$_3$ consists entirely of H$_3$O$^+$ and NO$_3^-$ ions.

$$HNO_3(aq) + H_2O(l) \longrightarrow H_3O^+(aq) + NO_3^-(aq) \text{ (complete ionization)} \quad [16.21]$$

We have not used equilibrium arrows for Equation 16.21 because the reaction lies entirely to the right, the side with the ions. ∞ (Section 4.1) As noted in Section 16.3, we use H$_3$O$^+$(aq) and H$^+$(aq) interchangeably to represent the hydrated proton in water. Thus, we often simplify the equations for the ionization reactions of acids as follows:

$$HNO_3(aq) \longrightarrow H^+(aq) + NO_3^-(aq)$$

In an aqueous solution of a strong acid, the acid is normally the only significant source of H$^+$ ions.* As a result, calculating the pH of a solution of a strong monoprotic acid is straightforward because [H$^+$] equals the original concentration of acid. In a 0.20 M solution of HNO$_3$(aq), for example, [H$^+$] = [NO$_3^-$] = 0.20 M. The situation with the diprotic acid H$_2$SO$_4$ is more complex, as we will see in Section 16.6.

---

*If the concentration of the acid is 10^{-6} M or less, we also need to consider H$^+$ ions that result from the autoionization of H$_2$O. Normally, the concentration of H$^+$ from H$_2$O is so small that it can be neglected.

■ SAMPLE EXERCISE 16.8 | Calculating the pH of a Strong Acid

What is the pH of a 0.040 M solution of $HClO_4$?

SOLUTION

Analyze and Plan: Because $HClO_4$ is a strong acid, it is completely ionized, giving $[H^+] = [ClO_4^-] = 0.040\ M$.

Solve: The pH of the solution is given by

$$pH = -\log(0.040) = 1.40.$$

Check: Because $[H^+]$ lies between 1×10^{-2} and 1×10^{-1}, the pH will be between 2.0 and 1.0. Our calculated pH falls within the estimated range. Furthermore, because the concentration has two significant figures, the pH has two decimal places.

■ PRACTICE EXERCISE

An aqueous solution of HNO_3 has a pH of 2.34. What is the concentration of the acid?
Answer: 0.0046 M

Strong Bases

There are relatively few common strong bases. The most common soluble strong bases are the ionic hydroxides of the alkali metals (group 1A) and the heavier alkaline earth metals (group 2A), such as NaOH, KOH, and $Ca(OH)_2$. These compounds completely dissociate into ions in aqueous solution. Thus, a solution labeled 0.30 M NaOH consists of 0.30 M $Na^+(aq)$ and 0.30 M $OH^-(aq)$; there is essentially no undissociated NaOH.

■ SAMPLE EXERCISE 16.9 | Calculating the pH of a Strong Base

What is the pH of **(a)** a 0.028 M solution of NaOH, **(b)** a 0.0011 M solution of $Ca(OH)_2$?

SOLUTION

Analyze: We are asked to calculate the pH of two solutions of strong bases.

Plan: We can calculate each pH by either of two equivalent methods. First, we could use Equation 16.16 to calculate $[H^+]$ and then use Equation 16.17 to calculate the pH. Alternatively, we could use $[OH^-]$ to calculate pOH and then use Equation 16.20 to calculate the pH.

Solve:

(a) NaOH dissociates in water to give one OH^- ion per formula unit. Therefore, the OH^- concentration for the solution in (a) equals the stated concentration of NaOH, namely 0.028 M.

Method 1:

$$[H^+] = \frac{1.0 \times 10^{-14}}{0.028} = 3.57 \times 10^{-13}\ M \qquad pH = -\log(3.57 \times 10^{-13}) = 12.45$$

Method 2:

$$pOH = -\log(0.028) = 1.55 \qquad pH = 14.00 - pOH = 12.45$$

(b) $Ca(OH)_2$ is a strong base that dissociates in water to give two OH^- ions per formula unit. Thus, the concentration of $OH^-(aq)$ for the solution in part (b) is $2 \times (0.0011\ M) = 0.0022\ M$.

Method 1:

$$[H^+] = \frac{1.0 \times 10^{-14}}{0.0022} = 4.55 \times 10^{-12}\ M \qquad pH = -\log(4.55 \times 10^{-12}) = 11.34$$

Method 2:

$$pOH = -\log(0.0022) = 2.66 \qquad pH = 14.00 - pOH = 11.34$$

■ PRACTICE EXERCISE

What is the concentration of a solution of **(a)** KOH for which the pH is 11.89; **(b)** $Ca(OH)_2$ for which the pH is 11.68?
Answers: **(a)** $7.8 \times 10^{-3}\ M$, **(b)** $2.4 \times 10^{-3}\ M$

This expression leads to a quadratic equation in x, which we can solve by using an equation-solving calculator or by using the quadratic formula. We can also simplify the problem, however, by noting that the value of K_a is quite small. As a result, we anticipate that the equilibrium will lie far to the left and that x will be very small compared to the initial concentration of acetic acid. Thus, we will *assume* that x is negligible compared to 0.30, so that $0.30 - x$ is essentially equal to 0.30.

$$0.30 - x \simeq 0.30$$

As we will see, we can (and should!) check the validity of this assumption when we finish the problem. By using this assumption, Equation 16.30 now becomes

$$K_a = \frac{x^2}{0.30} = 1.8 \times 10^{-5}$$

Solving for x, we have

$$x^2 = (0.30)(1.8 \times 10^{-5}) = 5.4 \times 10^{-6}$$

$$x = \sqrt{5.4 \times 10^{-6}} = 2.3 \times 10^{-3}$$

$$[H^+] = x = 2.3 \times 10^{-3}\ M$$

$$pH = -\log(2.3 \times 10^{-3}) = 2.64$$

We should now go back and check the validity of our simplifying assumption that $0.30 - x \simeq 0.30$. The value of x we determined is so small that, for this number of significant figures, the assumption is entirely valid. We are thus satisfied that the assumption was a reasonable one to make. Because x represents the moles per liter of acetic acid that ionize, we see that, in this particular case, less than 1% of the acetic acid molecules ionize:

$$\text{Percent ionization of } CH_3COOH = \frac{0.0023\ M}{0.30\ M} \times 100\% = 0.77\%$$

As a general rule, if the quantity x is more than about 5% of the initial value, it is better to use the quadratic formula. You should always check the validity of any simplifying assumptions after you have finished solving a problem.

GIVE IT SOME THOUGHT

Why can we generally assume that the equilibrium concentration of a weak acid equals its initial concentration?

Finally, we can compare the pH value of this weak acid to a solution of a strong acid of the same concentration. The pH of the 0.30 M solution of acetic acid is 2.64. By comparison, the pH of a 0.30 M solution of a strong acid such as HCl is $-\log(0.30) = 0.52$. As expected, the pH of a solution of a weak acid is higher than that of a solution of a strong acid of the same molarity.

SAMPLE EXERCISE 16.12 | Using K_a to Calculate pH

Calculate the pH of a 0.20 M solution of HCN. (Refer to Table 16.2 or Appendix D for the value of K_a.)

SOLUTION

Analyze: We are given the molarity of a weak acid and are asked for the pH. From Table 16.2, K_a for HCN is 4.9×10^{-10}.

Plan: We proceed as in the example just worked in the text, writing the chemical equation and constructing a table of initial and equilibrium concentrations in which the equilibrium concentration of H^+ is our unknown.

Solve: Writing both the chemical equation for the ionization reaction that forms $H^+(aq)$ and the equilibrium-constant (K_a) expression for the reaction:

$$HCN(aq) \rightleftharpoons H^+(aq) + CN^-(aq)$$

$$K_a = \frac{[H^+][CN^-]}{[HCN]} = 4.9 \times 10^{-10}$$

Next, we tabulate the concentration of the species involved in the equilibrium reaction, letting $x = [H^+]$ at equilibrium:

	$HCN(aq)$ $\rightleftharpoons$	$H^+(aq)$ $+$	$CN^-(aq)$
Initial	0.20 M	0	0
Change	$-x$ M	$+x$ M	$+x$ M
Equilibrium	$(0.20 - x)$ M	x M	x M

Substituting the equilibrium concentrations from the table into the equilibrium-constant expression yields

$$K_a = \frac{(x)(x)}{0.20 - x} = 4.9 \times 10^{-10}$$

We next make the simplifying approximation that x, the amount of acid that dissociates, is small compared with the initial concentration of acid; that is,

$$0.20 - x \simeq 0.20$$

Thus,

$$\frac{x^2}{0.20} = 4.9 \times 10^{-10}$$

Solving for x, we have

$$x^2 = (0.20)(4.9 \times 10^{-10}) = 0.98 \times 10^{-10}$$

$$x = \sqrt{0.98 \times 10^{-10}} = 9.9 \times 10^{-6} \ M = [H^+]$$

A concentration of $9.9 \times 10^{-6} \ M$ is much smaller than 5% of 0.20, the initial HCN concentration. Our simplifying approximation is therefore appropriate. We now calculate the pH of the solution:

$$pH = -\log[H^+] = -\log(9.9 \times 10^{-6}) = 5.00$$

█ PRACTICE EXERCISE

The K_a for niacin (Practice Exercise 16.10) is 1.5×10^{-5}. What is the pH of a 0.010 M solution of niacin?
Answer: 3.41

The properties of the acid solution that relate directly to the concentration of $H^+(aq)$, such as electrical conductivity and rate of reaction with an active metal, are much less evident for a solution of a weak acid than for a solution of a strong acid of the same concentration. Figure 16.8▼ presents an experiment that demonstrates this difference by comparing the behavior of 1 M CH_3COOH and 1 M HCl. The 1 M CH_3COOH contains only 0.004 M $H^+(aq)$, whereas the 1 M HCl solution contains 1 M $H^+(aq)$. As a result, the rate of reaction with the metal is much faster for the solution of HCl.

As the concentration of a weak acid increases, the equilibrium concentration of $H^+(aq)$ increases, as expected. However, as shown in Figure 16.9▶, *the percent ionization decreases as the concentration increases*. Thus, the concentration of $H^+(aq)$ is not directly proportional to the concentration of the weak acid. For example, doubling the concentration of a weak acid does not double the concentration of $H^+(aq)$. This lack of proportionality between the concentration of a weak acid and the concentration of $H^+(aq)$ is demonstrated in Sample Exercise 16.13.

▶ **Figure 16.8 Reaction rates for weak and strong acids.** (a) The flask on the left contains 1 M CH_3COOH; the one on the right contains 1 M HCl. Each balloon contains the same amount of magnesium metal. (b) When the Mg metal is dropped into the acid, H_2 gas is formed. The rate of H_2 formation is higher for the 1 M HCl solution on the right as evidenced by more gas in the balloon. Eventually, the same amount of H_2 forms in both cases.

(a)

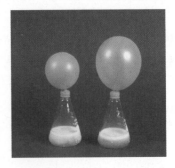

(b)

Chemistry and Life   THE AMPHIPROTIC BEHAVIOR OF AMINO ACIDS

*A*mino acids are the building blocks of proteins. The general structure of amino acids is shown here, where different amino acids have different R groups attached to the central carbon atom:

Amine group   Carboxyl group
(basic)   (acidic)

For example, in *glycine*, which is the simplest amino acid, R is a hydrogen atom, whereas in *alanine*, R is a CH₃ group.

$H_2N-C-COOH$ $H_2N-C-COOH$

Glycine   Alanine

Amino acids contain a carboxyl group and can therefore serve as acids. They also contain an NH₂ group, characteristic of amines (Section 16.7), and thus they can also act as bases. Amino acids, therefore, are amphiprotic. For glycine, we might expect that the acid and the base reactions with water would be as follows:

Acid: $H_2N-CH_2-COOH(aq) + H_2O(l) \rightleftharpoons$
$\quad H_2N-CH_2-COO^-(aq) + H_3O^+(aq)$ [16.47]

Base: $H_2N-CH_2-COOH(aq) + H_2O(l) \rightleftharpoons$
$\quad {}^+H_3N-CH_2-COOH(aq) + OH^+(aq)$ [16.48]

The pH of a solution of glycine in water is about 6.0, indicating that it is a slightly stronger acid than a base.

The acid–base chemistry of amino acids is somewhat more complicated than shown in Equations 16.47 and 16.48, however. Because the COOH can act as an acid and the NH₂ group can act as a base, amino acids undergo a "self-contained" Brønsted–Lowry acid–base reaction in which the proton of the carboxyl group is transferred to the basic nitrogen atom:

proton transfer

Neutral molecule   Zwitterion   [16.49]

Although the form of the amino acid on the right side of Equation 16.49 is electrically neutral overall, it has a positively charged end and a negatively charged end. A molecule of this type is called a *zwitterion* (German for "hybrid ion").

Do amino acids exhibit any properties indicating that they behave as zwitterions? If so, they should behave similar to ionic substances. ∞ (Section 8.2) Crystalline amino acids (Figure 16.14 ▼) have relatively high melting points, usually above 200 °C, which is characteristic of ionic solids. Amino acids are far more soluble in water than in nonpolar solvents. In addition, the dipole moments of amino acids are large, consistent with a large separation of charge in the molecule. Thus, the ability of amino acids to act simultaneously as acids and bases has important effects on their properties.

Related Exercise: 16.119

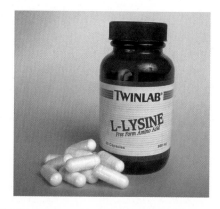

▲ **Figure 16.14 Lysine.** One of the amino acids found in proteins, lysine is available as a dietary supplement. The L on the label refers to a specific arrangement of atoms that is found in naturally occurring amino acids. Molecules with the L arrangement are mirror images of molecules with the D arrangement, much like our left hand is a mirror image of our right hand.

Second, the conjugate base of a carboxylic acid (a *carboxylate anion*) can exhibit resonance (Section 8.6), which contributes further to the stability of the anion by spreading the negative charge over several atoms:

resonance

GIVE IT SOME THOUGHT

What group of atoms is present in all carboxylic acids?

16.11 LEWIS ACIDS AND BASES

For a substance to be a proton acceptor (a Brønsted–Lowry base), it must have an unshared pair of electrons for binding the proton. NH_3, for example, acts as a proton acceptor. Using Lewis structures, we can write the reaction between H^+ and NH_3 as follows:

$$H^+ + :\overset{\displaystyle H}{\underset{\displaystyle H}{N}}-H \longrightarrow \left[H-\overset{\displaystyle H}{\underset{\displaystyle H}{N}}-H \right]^+$$

G. N. Lewis was the first to notice this aspect of acid–base reactions. He proposed a definition of acid and base that emphasizes the shared electron pair: A **Lewis acid** is an electron-pair acceptor, and a **Lewis base** is an electron-pair donor.

Every base that we have discussed thus far—whether it be OH^-, H_2O, an amine, or an anion—is an electron-pair donor. Everything that is a base in the Brønsted–Lowry sense (a proton acceptor) is also a base in the Lewis sense (an electron-pair donor). In the Lewis theory, however, a base can donate its electron pair to something other than H^+. The Lewis definition therefore greatly increases the number of species that can be considered acids; H^+ is a Lewis acid, but not the only one. For example, consider the reaction between NH_3 and BF_3. This reaction occurs because BF_3 has a vacant orbital in its valence shell. ∞ (Section 8.7) It therefore acts as an electron-pair acceptor (a Lewis acid) toward NH_3, which donates the electron pair. The curved arrow shows the donation of a pair of electrons from N to B to form a covalent bond:

$$H-\overset{\displaystyle H}{\underset{\displaystyle H}{N}}: + \overset{\displaystyle F}{\underset{\displaystyle F}{B}}-F \longrightarrow H-\overset{\displaystyle H}{\underset{\displaystyle H}{N}}-\overset{\displaystyle F}{\underset{\displaystyle F}{B}}-F$$

Lewis   Lewis
base   acid

▲ GIVE IT SOME THOUGHT

What feature must any molecule or ion have to act as a Lewis base?

Our emphasis throughout this chapter has been on water as the solvent and on the proton as the source of acidic properties. In such cases we find the Brønsted–Lowry definition of acids and bases to be the most useful. In fact, when we speak of a substance as being acidic or basic, we are usually thinking of aqueous solutions and using these terms in the Arrhenius or Brønsted–Lowry sense. The advantage of the Lewis theory is that it allows us to treat a wider variety of reactions, including those that do not involve proton transfer, as acid–base reactions. To avoid confusion, a substance such as BF_3 is rarely called an acid unless it is clear from the context that we are using the term in the sense of the Lewis definition. Instead, substances that function as electron-pair acceptors are referred to explicitly as "Lewis acids."

Lewis acids include molecules that, like BF_3, have an incomplete octet of electrons. In addition, many simple cations can function as Lewis acids. For example, Fe^{3+} interacts strongly with cyanide ions to form the ferricyanide ion, $Fe(CN)_6^{3-}$.

$$Fe^{3+} + 6[:C{\equiv}N:]^- \longrightarrow [Fe(C{\equiv}N:)_6]^{3-}$$

The Fe^{3+} ion has vacant orbitals that accept the electron pairs donated by the cyanide ions; we will learn more in Chapter 24 about just which orbitals are used by the Fe^{3+} ion. The metal ion is highly charged, too, which contributes to the interaction with CN^- ions.

- $pH + pOH = 14.00$ \quad [16.20] \hfill Relationship between pH and pOH

- $K_a = \dfrac{[H_3O^+][A^-]}{[HA]}$ or $K_a = \dfrac{[H^+][A^-]}{[HA]}$ \quad [16.25] \hfill The acid dissociation constant for a weak acid, HA

- Percent ionization $= \dfrac{[H^+]_{\text{equilibrium}}}{[HA]_{\text{initial}}} \times 100\%$ \quad [16.27] \hfill Percent ionization of a weak acid

- $K_b = \dfrac{[BH^+][OH^-]}{[B]}$ \quad [16.34] \hfill The base dissociation constant for a weak base, B

- $K_a \times K_b = K_w$ \quad [16.40] \hfill The relationship between the acid and base dissociation constants of a conjugate acid–base pair

VISUALIZING CONCEPTS

16.1 **(a)** Identify the Brønsted–Lowry acid and the Brønsted–Lowry base in the following reaction:

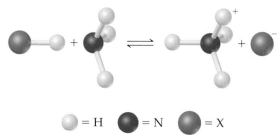

$$\bigcirc = H \qquad \bullet = N \qquad \bullet = X$$

(b) Identify the Lewis acid and the Lewis base in the reaction. [Sections 16.2 and 16.11]

16.2 The following diagrams represent aqueous solutions of two monoprotic acids, HA (A = X or Y). The water molecules have been omitted for clarity. **(a)** Which is the stronger acid, HX or HY? **(b)** Which is the stronger base, X^- or Y^-? **(c)** If you mix equal concentrations of HX and NaY, will the equilibrium

$$HX(aq) + Y^-(aq) \rightleftharpoons HY(aq) + X^-(aq)$$

lie mostly to the right ($K_c > 1$) or to the left ($K_c < 1$)? [Section 16.2]

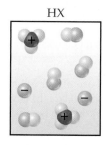 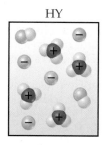

16.3 The following diagrams represent aqueous solutions of three acids, HX, HY, and HZ. The water molecules have been omitted for clarity, and the hydrated proton is represented as a simple sphere rather than as a hydronium ion. **(a)** Which of the acids is a strong acid? Explain.

(b) Which acid would have the smallest acid-dissociation constant, K_a? **(c)** Which solution would have the highest pH? [Sections 16.5 and 16.6]

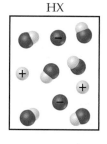 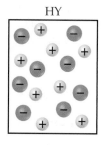 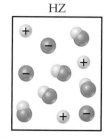

16.4 In which of the following cases is the approximation that the equilibrium concentration of $H^+(aq)$ is small relative to the initial concentration of HA likely to be most valid: **(a)** initial [HA] = 0.100 M and $K_a = 1.0 \times 10^{-6}$, **(b)** initial [HA] = 0.100 M and $K_a = 1.0 \times 10^{-4}$, **(c)** initial [HA] = 0.100 M and $K_a = 1.0 \times 10^{-3}$? [Section 16.6]

16.5 **(a)** Which of these three lines represents the effect of concentration on the percent ionization of a weak acid? **(b)** Explain in qualitative terms why the curve you choose has the shape it does. [Section 16.6]

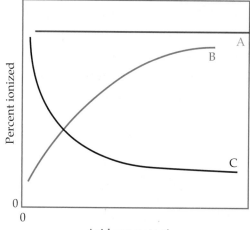

16.6 Refer to the diagrams accompanying Exercise 16.3. **(a)** Rank the anions, X^-, Y^-, and Z^-, in order of increasing basicity. **(b)** Which of the ions would have the largest base-dissociation constant, K_b? [Sections 16.2 and 16.8]

16.7 **(a)** Draw the Lewis structure for the following molecule and explain why it is able to act as a base. **(b)** To what class of organic compounds does this substance belong? (See the color key in Exercise 16.1.) [Section 16.7]

16.8 The following diagram represents an aqueous solution formed by dissolving a sodium salt of a weak acid in water. The diagram shows only the Na^+ ions, the X^- ions, and the HX molecules. What ion is missing from the diagram? If the drawing is completed by drawing all the ions, how many of the missing ions should be shown? [Section 16.9]

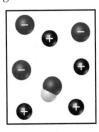

16.9 **(a)** What kinds of acids are represented by the following molecular models? **(b)** Indicate how the acidity of each molecule is affected by increasing the electronegativity of the atom X, and explain the origin of the effect. [Section 16.10]

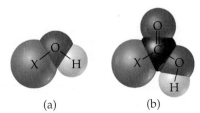

(a)   (b)

16.10 In this model of acetylsalicylic acid (aspirin), identify the carboxyl group in the molecule. [Section 16.10]

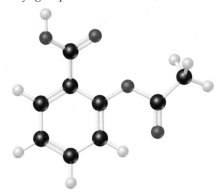

16.11 Rank the following acids in order of increasing acidity: CH_3COOH, $CH_2ClCOOH$, $CHCl_2COOH$, CCl_3COOH, CF_3COOH. [Section 16.10]

16.12 **(a)** The following diagram represents the reaction of PCl_4^+ with Cl^-. Draw the Lewis structures for the reactants and products, and identify the Lewis acid and the Lewis base in the reaction.

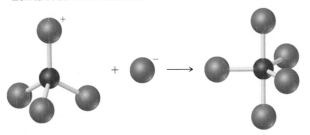

(b) The following reaction represents the acidity of a hydrated cation. How does the equilibrium constant for the reaction change as the charge of the cation increases? [Section 16.11]

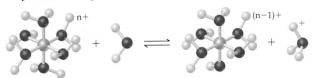

EXERCISES

Arrhenius and Brønsted–Lowry Acids and Bases

16.13 Although HCl and H_2SO_4 have very different properties as pure substances, their aqueous solutions possess many common properties. List some general properties of these solutions, and explain their common behavior in terms of the species present.

16.14 Although pure NaOH and NH_3 have very different properties, their aqueous solutions possess many common properties. List some general properties of these solutions, and explain their common behavior in terms of the species present.

16.15 **(a)** What is the difference between the Arrhenius and the Brønsted–Lowry definitions of an acid? **(b)** $NH_3(g)$ and $HCl(g)$ react to form the ionic solid $NH_4Cl(s)$ (Figure 16.3). Which substance is the Brønsted–Lowry acid in this reaction? Which is the Brønsted–Lowry base?

16.16 **(a)** What is the difference between the Arrhenius and the Brønsted–Lowry definitions of a base? **(b)** When ammonia is dissolved in water, it behaves both as an Arrhenius base and as a Brønsted–Lowry base. Explain.

16.17 **(a)** Give the conjugate base of the following Brønsted–Lowry acids: **(i)** HIO_3, **(ii)** NH_4^+. **(b)** Give the conjugate acid of the following Brønsted–Lowry bases: **(i)** O^{2-}, **(ii)** $H_2PO_4^-$.

16.18 **(a)** Give the conjugate base of the following Brønsted–Lowry acids: **(i)** C_6H_5COOH. **(ii)** HPO_4^{2-}. **(b)** Give the conjugate acid of the following Brønsted–Lowry bases: **(i)** CO_3^{2-}, **(ii)** $C_2H_5NH_2$.

16.19 Designate the Brønsted–Lowry acid and the Brønsted–Lowry base on the left side of each of the following equations, and also designate the conjugate acid and conjugate base on the right side:

(a) $NH_4^+(aq) + CN^-(aq) \rightleftharpoons HCN(aq) + NH_3(aq)$

(b) $(CH_3)_3N(aq) + H_2O(l) \rightleftharpoons$
$(CH_3)_3NH^+(aq) + OH^-(aq)$

(c) $HCOOH(aq) + PO_4^{3-}(aq) \rightleftharpoons$
$HCOO^-(aq) + HPO_4^{2-}(aq)$

16.20 Designate the Brønsted–Lowry acid and the Brønsted–Lowry base on the left side of each equation, and also designate the conjugate acid and conjugate base on the right side.

(a) $HBrO(aq) + H_2O(l) \rightleftharpoons H_3O^+(aq) + BrO^-(aq)$

(b) $HSO_4^-(aq) + HCO_3^-(aq) \rightleftharpoons$
$SO_4^{2-}(aq) + H_2CO_3(aq)$

(c) $HSO_3^-(aq) + H_3O^+(aq) \rightleftharpoons H_2SO_3(aq) + H_2O(l)$

16.21 (a) The hydrogen oxalate ion ($HC_2O_4^-$) is amphiprotic. Write a balanced chemical equation showing how it acts as an acid toward water and another equation showing how it acts as a base toward water. (b) What is the conjugate acid of $HC_2O_4^-$? What is its conjugate base?

16.22 (a) Write an equation for the reaction in which $H_2C_6H_7O_5^-(aq)$ acts as a base in $H_2O(l)$. (b) Write an equation for the reaction in which $H_2C_6H_7O_5^-(aq)$ acts as an acid in $H_2O(l)$. (c) What is the conjugate acid of $H_2C_6H_7O_5^-$? What is its conjugate base?

16.23 Label each of the following as being a strong base, a weak base, or a species with negligible basicity. In each case write the formula of its conjugate acid, and indicate whether the conjugate acid is a strong acid, a weak acid,

or a species with negligible acidity: (a) CH_3COO^-, (b) HCO_3^-, (c) O^{2-}, (d) Cl^-, (e) NH_3.

16.24 Label each of the following as being a strong acid, a weak acid, or a species with negligible acidity. In each case write the formula of its conjugate base, and indicate whether the conjugate base is a strong base, a weak base, or a species with negligible basicity: (a) HNO_2, (b) H_2SO_4, (c) HPO_4^{2-}, (d) CH_4, (e) $CH_3NH_3^+$ (an ion related to NH_4^+).

16.25 (a) Which of the following is the stronger Brønsted–Lowry acid, HBrO or HBr? (b) Which is the stronger Brønsted–Lowry base, F^- or Cl^-? Briefly explain your choices.

16.26 (a) Which of the following is the stronger Brønsted–Lowry acid, HNO_3 or HNO_2? (b) Which is the stronger Brønsted–Lowry base, NH_3 or H_2O? Briefly explain your choices.

16.27 Predict the products of the following acid–base reactions, and predict whether the equilibrium lies to the left or to the right of the equation:

(a) $O^{2-}(aq) + H_2O(l) \rightleftharpoons$

(b) $CH_3COOH(aq) + HS^-(aq) \rightleftharpoons$

(c) $NO_2^-(aq) + H_2O(l) \rightleftharpoons$

16.28 Predict the products of the following acid–base reactions, and predict whether the equilibrium lies to the left or to the right of the equation:

(a) $NH_4^+(aq) + OH^-(aq) \rightleftharpoons$

(b) $CH_3COO^-(aq) + H_3O^+(aq) \rightleftharpoons$

(c) $HCO_3^-(aq) + F^-(aq) \rightleftharpoons$

Autoionization of Water

16.29 (a) What does the term *autoionization* mean? (b) Explain why pure water is a poor conductor of electricity. (c) You are told that an aqueous solution is acidic. What does this statement mean?

16.30 (a) Write a chemical equation that illustrates the autoionization of water. (b) Write the expression for the ion-product constant for water, K_w. Why is $[H_2O]$ absent from this expression? (c) A solution is described as basic. What does this statement mean?

16.31 Calculate $[H^+]$ for each of the following solutions, and indicate whether the solution is acidic, basic, or neutral: (a) $[OH^-] = 0.00045 \ M$; (b) $[OH^-] = 8.8 \times 10^{-9} \ M$; (c) a solution in which $[OH^-]$ is 100 times greater than $[H^+]$.

16.32 Calculate $[OH^-]$ for each of the following solutions, and indicate whether the solution is acidic, basic, or neutral: (a) $[H^+] = 0.0045 \ M$; (b) $[H^+] = 1.5 \times 10^{-9} \ M$; (c) a solution in which $[H^+]$ is 10 times greater than $[OH^-]$.

16.33 At the freezing point of water (0 °C), $K_w = 1.2 \times 10^{-15}$. Calculate $[H^+]$ and $[OH^-]$ for a neutral solution at this temperature.

16.34 Deuterium oxide (D_2O, where D is deuterium, the hydrogen-2 isotope) has an ion-product constant, K_w, of 8.9×10^{-16} at 20 °C. Calculate $[D^+]$ and $[OD^-]$ for pure (neutral) D_2O at this temperature.

The pH Scale

16.35 By what factor does $[H^+]$ change for a pH change of (a) 2.00 units, (b) 0.50 units?

16.36 Consider two solutions, solution A and solution B. $[H^+]$ in solution A is 500 times greater than that in solution B. What is the difference in the pH values of the two solutions?

16.37 (a) If NaOH is added to water, how does $[H^+]$ change? How does pH change? (b) Use the pH values in Figure 16.5 to estimate the pH of a solution with $[H^+] = 0.0006 \ M$. Is the solution acidic or basic? (c) If the pH of a solution is 5.2, first estimate and then calculate the molar concentrations of $H^+(aq)$ and $OH^-(aq)$ in the solution.

16.38 **(a)** If HNO_3 is added to water, how does $[OH^-]$ change? How does pH change? **(b)** Use the pH values in Figure 16.5 to estimate the pH of a solution with $[OH^-] = 0.014 \, M$. Is the solution acidic or basic? **(c)** If pH = 6.6, first estimate and then calculate the molar concentrations of $H^+(aq)$ and $OH^-(aq)$ in the solution.

16.39 Complete the following table by calculating the missing entries and indicating whether the solution is acidic or basic.

$[H^+]$	$OH^-(aq)$	pH	pOH	Acidic or basic?
$7.5 \times 10^{-3} \, M$				
	$3.6 \times 10^{-10} \, M$			
		8.25		
			5.70	

16.40 Complete the following table by calculating the missing entries. In each case indicate whether the solution is acidic or basic.

pH	pOH	$[H^+]$	$[OH^-]$	Acidic or basic?
11.25				
	6.02			
		$4.4 \times 10^{-4} \, M$		
			$8.5 \times 10^{-3} \, M$	

16.41 The average pH of normal arterial blood is 7.40. At normal body temperature (37 °C), $K_w = 2.4 \times 10^{-14}$. Calculate $[H^+]$, $[OH^-]$, and pOH for blood at this temperature.

16.42 Carbon dioxide in the atmosphere dissolves in raindrops to produce carbonic acid (H_2CO_3), causing the pH of clean, unpolluted rain to range from about 5.2 to 5.6. What are the ranges of $[H^+]$ and $[OH^-]$ in the raindrops?

Strong Acids and Bases

16.43 **(a)** What is a strong acid? **(b)** A solution is labeled 0.500 M HCl. What is $[H^+]$ for the solution? **(c)** Which of the following are strong acids: HF, HCl, HBr, HI?

16.44 **(a)** What is a strong base? **(b)** A solution is labeled 0.035 M $Sr(OH)_2$. What is $[OH^-]$ for the solution? **(c)** Is the following statement true or false? Because $Mg(OH)_2$ is not very soluble, it cannot be a strong base. Explain.

16.45 Calculate the pH of each of the following strong acid solutions: **(a)** $8.5 \times 10^{-3} \, M$ HBr, **(b)** 1.52 g of HNO_3 in 575 mL of solution, **(c)** 5.00 mL of 0.250 M $HClO_4$ diluted to 50.0 mL, **(d)** a solution formed by mixing 10.0 mL of 0.100 M HBr with 20.0 mL of 0.200 M HCl.

16.46 Calculate the pH of each of the following strong acid solutions: **(a)** 0.00135 M HNO_3, **(b)** 0.425 g of $HClO_4$ in 2.00 L of solution, **(c)** 5.00 mL of 1.00 M HCl diluted to 0.500 L, **(d)** a mixture formed by adding 50.0 mL of 0.020 M HCl to 150 mL of 0.010 M HI.

16.47 Calculate $[OH^-]$ and pH for **(a)** $1.5 \times 10^{-3} \, M$ $Sr(OH)_2$, **(b)** 2.250 g of LiOH in 250.0 mL of solution, **(c)** 1.00 mL of 0.175 M NaOH diluted to 2.00 L, **(d)** a solution formed by adding 5.00 mL of 0.105 M KOH to 15.0 mL of $9.5 \times 10^{-2} \, M$ $Ca(OH)_2$.

16.48 Calculate $[OH^-]$ and pH for each of the following strong base solutions: **(a)** 0.082 M KOH, **(b)** 1.065 g of KOH in 500.0 mL of solution, **(c)** 10.0 mL of 0.0105 M $Ca(OH)_2$ diluted to 500.0 mL, **(d)** a solution formed by mixing 10.0 mL of 0.015 M $Ba(OH)_2$ with 40.0 mL of $7.5 \times 10^{-3} \, M$ NaOH.

16.49 Calculate the concentration of an aqueous solution of NaOH that has a pH of 11.50.

16.50 Calculate the concentration of an aqueous solution of $Ca(OH)_2$ that has a pH of 12.05.

Weak Acids

16.51 Write the chemical equation and the K_a expression for the ionization of each of the following acids in aqueous solution. First show the reaction with $H^+(aq)$ as a product and then with the hydronium ion: **(a)** $HBrO_2$, **(b)** C_2H_5COOH.

16.52 Write the chemical equation and the K_a expression for the acid dissociation of each of the following acids in aqueous solution. First show the reaction with $H^+(aq)$ as a product and then with the hydronium ion: **(a)** C_6H_5COOH, **(b)** HCO_3^-.

16.53 Lactic acid ($CH_3CH(OH)COOH$) has one acidic hydrogen. A 0.10 M solution of lactic acid has a pH of 2.44. Calculate K_a.

16.54 Phenylacetic acid ($C_6H_5CH_2COOH$) is one of the substances that accumulates in the blood of people with phenylketonuria, an inherited disorder that can cause mental retardation or even death. A 0.085 M solution of $C_6H_5CH_2COOH$ has a pH of 2.68. Calculate the K_a value for this acid.

16.55 A 0.100 M solution of chloroacetic acid (ClCH$_2$COOH) is 11.0% ionized. Using this information, calculate [ClCH$_2$COO$^-$], [H$^+$], [ClCH$_2$COOH)], and K_a for chloroacetic acid.

16.56 A 0.100 M solution of bromoacetic acid (BrCH$_2$COOH) is 13.2% ionized. Calculate [H$^+$], [BrCH$_2$COO$^-$], and [BrCH$_2$COOH].

16.57 A particular sample of vinegar has a pH of 2.90. If acetic acid is the only acid that vinegar contains ($K_a = 1.8 \times 10^{-5}$), calculate the concentration of acetic acid in the vinegar.

16.58 How many moles of HF ($K_a = 6.8 \times 10^{-4}$) must be present in 0.200 L to form a solution with a pH of 3.25?

16.59 The acid-dissociation. constant for benzoic acid (C$_6$H$_5$COOH) is 6.3×10^{-5}. Calculate the equilibrium concentrations of H$_3$O$^+$, C$_6$H$_5$COO$^-$, and C$_6$H$_5$COOH in the solution if the initial concentration of C$_6$H$_5$COOH is 0.050 M.

16.60 The acid-dissociation constant for hypochlorous acid (HClO) is 3.0×10^{-8}. Calculate the concentrations of H$_3$O$^+$, ClO$^-$, and HClO at equilibrium if the initial concentration of HClO is 0.0090 M.

16.61 Calculate the pH of each of the following solutions (K_a and K_b values are given in Appendix D): **(a)** 0.095 M propionic acid (C$_2$H$_5$COOH), **(b)** 0.100 M hydrogen chromate ion (HCrO$_4^-$), **(c)** 0.120 M pyridine (C$_5$H$_5$N).

16.62 Determine the pH of each of the following solutions (K_a and K_b values are given in Appendix D): **(a)** 0.095 M hypochlorous acid, **(b)** 0.0085 M phenol, **(c)** 0.095 M hydroxylamine.

16.63 Saccharin, a sugar substitute, is a weak acid with $pK_a = 2.32$ at 25 °C. It ionizes in aqueous solution as follows:

$$HNC_7H_4SO_3(aq) \rightleftharpoons H^+(aq) + NC_7H_4SO_3^-(aq)$$

What is the pH of a 0.10 M solution of this substance?

16.64 The active ingredient in aspirin is acetylsalicylic acid (HC$_9$H$_7$O$_4$), a monoprotic acid with $K_a = 3.3 \times 10^{-4}$ at 25 °C. What is the pH of a solution obtained by dissolving two extra-strength aspirin tablets, containing 500 mg of acetylsalicylic acid each, in 250 mL of water?

16.65 Calculate the percent ionization of hydrazoic acid (HN$_3$) in solutions of each of the following concentrations (K_a is given in Appendix D): **(a)** 0.400 M, **(b)** 0.100 M, **(c)** 0.0400 M.

16.66 Calculate the percent ionization of propionic acid (C$_2$H$_5$COOH) in solutions of each of the following concentrations (K_a is given in Appendix D): **(a)** 0.250 M, **(b)** 0.0800 M, **(c)** 0.0200 M.

[16.67] Show that for a weak acid, the percent ionization should vary as the inverse square root of the acid concentration.

[16.68] For solutions of a weak acid, a graph of pH versus the log of the initial acid concentration should be a straight line. What is the magnitude of the slope of that line?

[16.69] Citric acid, which is present in citrus fruits, is a triprotic acid (Table 16.3). Calculate the pH and the citrate ion (C$_6$H$_5$O$_7^{3-}$) concentration for a 0.050 M solution of citric acid. Explain any approximations or assumptions that you make in your calculations.

[16.70] Tartaric acid is found in many fruits, including grapes, and is partially responsible for the dry texture of certain wines. Calculate the pH and the tartarate ion (C$_4$H$_4$O$_6^{2-}$) concentration for a 0.250 M solution of tartaric acid, for which the acid-dissociation constants are listed in Table 16.3. Explain any approximations or assumptions that you make in your calculation.

Weak Bases

16.71 What is the essential structural feature of all Brønsted–Lowry bases?

16.72 What are two kinds of molecules or ions that commonly function as weak bases?

16.73 Write the chemical equation and the K_b expression for the ionization of each of the following bases in aqueous solution: **(a)** dimethylamine, (CH$_3$)$_2$NH; **(b)** carbonate ion, CO$_3^{2-}$; **(c)** formate ion, CHO$_2^-$.

16.74 Write the chemical equation and the K_b expression for the reaction of each of the following bases with water: **(a)** propylamine, C$_3$H$_7$NH$_2$; **(b)** monohydrogen phosphate ion, HPO$_4^{2-}$; **(c)** benzoate ion, C$_6$H$_5$CO$_2^-$.

16.75 Calculate the molar concentration of OH$^-$ ions in a 0.075 M solution of ethylamine (C$_2$H$_5$NH$_2$; $K_b = 6.4 \times 10^{-4}$). Calculate the pH of this solution.

16.76 Calculate the molar concentration of OH$^-$ ions in a 0.550 M solution of hypobromite ion (BrO$^-$; $K_b = 4.0 \times 10^{-6}$). What is the pH of this solution?

16.77 Ephedrine, a central nervous system stimulant, is used in nasal sprays as a decongestant. This compound is a weak organic base:

$$C_{10}H_{15}ON(aq) + H_2O(l) \rightleftharpoons C_{10}H_{15}ONH^+(aq) + OH^-(aq)$$

A 0.035 M solution of ephedrine has a pH of 11.33. **(a)** What are the equilibrium concentrations of C$_{10}$H$_{15}$ON, C$_{10}$H$_{15}$ONH$^+$, and OH$^-$? **(b)** Calculate K_b for ephedrine.

16.78 Codeine (C$_{18}$H$_{21}$NO$_3$) is a weak organic base. A $5.0 \times 10^{-3} M$ solution of codeine has a pH of 9.95. Calculate the value of K_b for this substance. What is the pK_b for this base?

The K_a–K_b Relationship; Acid–Base Properties of Salts

16.79 Although the acid-dissociation constant for phenol (C_6H_5OH) is listed in Appendix D, the base-dissociation constant for the phenolate ion ($C_6H_5O^-$) is not. **(a)** Explain why it is not necessary to list both K_a for phenol and K_b for the phenolate ion. **(b)** Calculate K_b for the phenolate ion. **(c)** Is the phenolate ion a weaker or stronger base than ammonia?

16.80 We can calculate K_b for the carbonate ion if we know the K_a values of carbonic acid (H_2CO_3). **(a)** Is K_{a1} or K_{a2} of carbonic acid used to calculate K_b for the carbonate ion? Explain. **(b)** Calculate K_b for the carbonate ion. **(c)** Is the carbonate ion a weaker or stronger base than ammonia?

16.81 **(a)** Given that K_a for acetic acid is 1.8×10^{-5} and that for hypochlorous acid is 3.0×10^{-8}, which is the stronger acid? **(b)** Which is the stronger base, the acetate ion or the hypochlorite ion? **(c)** Calculate K_b values for CH_3COO^- and ClO^-.

16.82 **(a)** Given that K_b for ammonia is 1.8×10^{-5} and that for hydroxylamine is 1.1×10^{-8}, which is the stronger base? **(b)** Which is the stronger acid, the ammonium ion or the hydroxylammonium ion? **(c)** Calculate K_a values for NH_4^+ and H_3NOH^+.

16.83 Using data from Appendix D, calculate $[OH^-]$ and pH for each of the following solutions: **(a)** 0.10 M NaCN, **(b)** 0.080 M Na_2CO_3, **(c)** a mixture that is 0.10 M in $NaNO_2$ and 0.20 M in $Ca(NO_2)_2$.

16.84 Using data from Appendix D, calculate $[OH^-]$ and pH for each of the following solutions: **(a)** 0.105 M NaF, **(b)** 0.035 M Na_2S, **(c)** a mixture that is 0.045 M in CH_3COONa and 0.055 M in $(CH_3COO)_2Ba$.

16.85 Predict whether aqueous solutions of the following compounds are acidic, basic, or neutral: **(a)** NH_4Br, **(b)** $FeCl_3$, **(c)** Na_2CO_3, **(d)** $KClO_4$, **(e)** $NaHC_2O_4$.

16.86 Predict whether aqueous solutions of the following substances are acidic, basic, or neutral: **(a)** $CrBr_3$, **(b)** LiI, **(c)** K_3PO_4, **(d)** $[CH_3NH_3]Cl$, **(e)** $KHSO_4$.

16.87 An unknown salt is either NaF, NaCl, or NaOCl. When 0.050 mol of the salt is dissolved in water to form 0.500 L of solution, the pH of the solution is 8.08. What is the identity of the salt?

16.88 An unknown salt is either KBr, NH_4Cl, KCN, or K_2CO_3. If a 0.100 M solution of the salt is neutral, what is the identity of the salt?

16.89 Sorbic acid (C_5H_7COOH) is a weak monoprotic acid with $K_a = 1.7 \times 10^{-5}$. Its salt (potassium sorbate) is added to cheese to inhibit the formation of mold. What is the pH of a solution containing 11.25 g of potassium sorbate in 1.75 L of solution?

16.90 Trisodium phosphate (Na_3PO_4) is available in hardware stores as TSP and is used as a cleaning agent. The label on a box of TSP warns that the substance is very basic (caustic or alkaline). What is the pH of a solution containing 35.0 g of TSP in a liter of solution?

Acid–Base Character and Chemical Structure

16.91 How does the acid strength of an oxyacid depend on **(a)** the electronegativity of the central atom; **(b)** the number of nonprotonated oxygen atoms in the molecule?

16.92 **(a)** How does the strength of an acid vary with the polarity and strength of the H—X bond? **(b)** How does the acidity of the binary acid of an element vary as a function of the electronegativity of the element? How does this relate to the position of the element in the periodic table?

16.93 Explain the following observations: **(a)** HNO_3 is a stronger acid than HNO_2; **(b)** H_2S is a stronger acid than H_2O; **(c)** H_2SO_4 is a stronger acid than HSO_4^-; **(d)** H_2SO_4 is a stronger acid than H_2SeO_4; **(e)** CCl_3COOH is a stronger acid than CH_3COOH.

16.94 Explain the following observations: **(a)** HCl is a stronger acid than H_2S; **(b)** H_3PO_4 is a stronger acid than H_3AsO_4; **(c)** $HBrO_3$ is a stronger acid than $HBrO_2$; **(d)** $H_2C_2O_4$ is a stronger acid than $HC_2O_4^-$; **(e)** benzoic acid (C_6H_5COOH) is a stronger acid than phenol (C_6H_5OH).

16.95 Based on their compositions and structures and on conjugate acid–base relationships, select the stronger base in each of the following pairs: **(a)** BrO^- or ClO^-, **(b)** BrO^- or BrO_2^-, **(c)** HPO_4^{2-} or $H_2PO_4^-$.

16.96 Based on their compositions and structures and on conjugate acid–base relationships, select the stronger base in each of the following pairs: **(a)** NO_3^- or NO_2^-, **(b)** PO_4^{3-} or AsO_4^{3-}, **(c)** HCO_3^- or CO_3^{2-}.

16.97 Indicate whether each of the following statements is true or false. For each statement that is false, correct the statement to make it true. **(a)** In general, the acidity of binary acids increases from left to right in a given row of the periodic table. **(b)** In a series of acids that have the same central atom, acid strength increases with the number of hydrogen atoms bonded to the central atom. **(c)** Hydrotelluric acid (H_2Te) is a stronger acid than H_2S because Te is more electronegative than S.

WHAT'S AHEAD

WATER IS THE MOST COMMON AND MOST IMPORTANT SOLVENT ON EARTH. In a sense, it is the solvent of life. It is difficult to imagine how living matter in all its complexity could exist with any liquid other than water as the solvent. Water occupies its position of importance because of its abundance

and its exceptional ability to dissolve a wide variety of substances. For example, the chapter-opening photograph shows a hot spring; this water contains a high concentration of ions (especially Mg^{2+}, Ca^{2+}, Fe^{2+}, CO_3^{2-}, and SO_4^{2-}). The ions are dissolved as the hot water, initially underground, passes through various rocks on its way to the surface and dissolves minerals in the rocks. When the solution reaches the surface and cools, the minerals deposit and make the terracelike formations seen in the photograph.

The various aqueous solutions encountered in nature typically contain many solutes. For example, the aqueous solutions in hot springs and oceans, as well as those in biological fluids, contain a variety of dissolved ions and molecules. Consequently, many equilibria can occur simultaneously in these solutions.

In this chapter we take a step toward understanding such complex solutions by looking first at further applications of acid–base equilibria. The idea is to consider not only solutions in which there is a single solute but also those containing a mixture of solutes. We then broaden our discussion to include two additional types of aqueous equilibria: those involving slightly soluble salts and those involving the formation of metal complexes in solution. For the most part, the discussions and calculations in this chapter are an extension of those in Chapters 15 and 16.

17.1 THE COMMON-ION EFFECT

In Chapter 16 we examined the equilibrium concentrations of ions in solutions containing a weak acid or a weak base. We now consider solutions that contain a weak acid, such as acetic acid (CH_3COOH), and a soluble salt of that acid, such as sodium acetate (CH_3COONa). Notice that these solutions contain two substances that share a *common ion* CH_3COO^-. It is instructive to view these solutions from the perspective of Le Châtelier's principle. ∞ (Section 15.7) Sodium acetate is a soluble ionic compound and is therefore a strong electrolyte. ∞ (Section 4.1) Consequently, it dissociates completely in aqueous solution to form Na^+ and CH_3COO^- ions:

$$CH_3COONa(aq) \longrightarrow Na^+(aq) + CH_3COO^-(aq)$$

In contrast, CH_3COOH is a weak electrolyte that ionizes as follows:

$$CH_3COOH(aq) \rightleftharpoons H^+(aq) + CH_3COO^-(aq) \qquad [17.1]$$

The CH_3COO^- from CH_3COONa causes this equilibrium to shift to the left, thereby decreasing the equilibrium concentration of $H^+(aq)$.

$$CH_3COOH(aq) \rightleftharpoons H^+(aq) + CH_3COO^-(aq)$$

Addition of CH_3COO^- shifts equilibrium, reducing $[H^+]$

In other words, the presence of the added acetate ion causes the acetic acid to ionize less than it normally would.

Whenever a weak electrolyte and a strong electrolyte contain a common ion, the weak electrolyte ionizes less than it would if it were alone in solution. We call this observation the **common-ion effect**. Sample Exercises 17.1 and 17.2 illustrate how equilibrium concentrations may be calculated when a solution contains a mixture of a weak electrolyte and a strong electrolyte that have a common ion. The procedures are similar to those encountered for weak acids and weak bases in Chapter 16.

SAMPLE EXERCISE 17.1 | Calculating the pH When a Common Ion Is Involved

What is the pH of a solution made by adding 0.30 mol of acetic acid and 0.30 mol of sodium acetate to enough water to make 1.0 L of solution?

SOLUTION

Analyze: We are asked to determine the pH of a solution of a weak electrolyte (CH_3COOH) and a strong electrolyte (CH_3COONa) that share a common ion, CH_3COO^-.

Plan: In any problem in which we must determine the pH of a solution containing a mixture of solutes, it is helpful to proceed by a series of logical steps:

1. Consider which solutes are strong electrolytes and which are weak electrolytes, and identify the major species in solution.
2. Identify the important equilibrium that is the source of H^+ and therefore determines pH.
3. Tabulate the concentrations of ions involved in the equilibrium.
4. Use the equilibrium-constant expression to calculate $[H^+]$ and then pH.

Solve: First, because CH_3COOH is a weak electrolyte and CH_3COONa is a strong electrolyte, the major species in the solution are CH_3COOH (a weak acid), Na^+ (which is neither acidic nor basic and is therefore a spectator in the acid–base chemistry), and CH_3COO^- (which is the conjugate base of CH_3COOH).

Second, $[H^+]$ and, therefore, the pH are controlled by the dissociation equilibrium of CH_3COOH:

$$CH_3COOH(aq) \rightleftharpoons H^+(aq) + CH_3COO^-(aq)$$

(We have written the equilibrium using $H^+(aq)$ rather than $H_3O^+(aq)$ but both representations of the hydrated hydrogen ion are equally valid.)

Third, we tabulate the initial and equilibrium concentrations as we did in solving other equilibrium problems in Chapters 15 and 16:

	$CH_3COOH(aq)$	$\rightleftharpoons$	$H^+(aq)$	$+$	$CH_3COO^-(aq)$
Initial	0.30 M		0		0.30 M
Change	$-x$ M		$+x$ M		$+x$ M
Equilibrium	$(0.30 - x)$ M		x M		$(0.30 + x)$ M

The equilibrium concentration of CH_3COO^- (the common ion) is the initial concentration that is due to CH_3COONa (0.30 M) plus the change in concentration (x) that is due to the ionization of CH_3COOH.

Now we can use the equilibrium-constant expression:

$$K_a = 1.8 \times 10^{-5} = \frac{[H^+][CH_3COO^-]}{[CH_3COOH]}$$

(The dissociation constant for CH_3COOH at 25 °C is from Appendix D; addition of CH_3COONa does not change the value of this constant.) Substituting the equilibrium-constant concentrations from our table into the equilibrium expression gives

$$K_a = 1.8 \times 10^{-5} = \frac{x(0.30 + x)}{0.30 - x}$$

Because K_a is small, we assume that x is small compared to the original concentrations of CH_3COOH and CH_3COO^- (0.30 M each). Thus, we can ignore the very small x relative to 0.30 M, giving

$$K_a = 1.8 \times 10^{-5} = \frac{x(0.30)}{0.30}$$

$$x = 1.8 \times 10^{-5} M = [H^+]$$

The resulting value of x is indeed small relative to 0.30, justifying the approximation made in simplifying the problem.

Finally, we calculate the pH from the equilibrium concentration of $H^+(aq)$:

$$pH = -\log(1.8 \times 10^{-5}) = 4.74$$

Comment: In Section 16.6 we calculated that a 0.30 M solution of CH_3COOH has a pH of 2.64, corresponding to $[H^+] = 2.3 \times 10^{-3}$ M. Thus, the addition of CH_3COONa has substantially decreased $[H^+]$, as we would expect from Le Châtelier's principle.

■ **PRACTICE EXERCISE**

Calculate the pH of a solution containing 0.085 M nitrous acid (HNO_2; $K_a = 4.5 \times 10^{-4}$) and 0.10 M potassium nitrite (KNO_2).
Answer: 3.42

■■ **SAMPLE EXERCISE 17.2** | Calculating Ion Concentrations When a Common Ion Is Involved

Calculate the fluoride ion concentration and pH of a solution that is 0.20 M in HF and 0.10 M in HCl.

SOLUTION

Analyze: We are asked to determine the concentration of F^- and the pH in a solution containing the weak acid HF and the strong acid HCl. In this case the common ion is H^+.

Plan: We can again use the four steps outlined in Sample Exercise 17.1.

Solve: Because HF is a weak acid and HCl is a strong acid, the major species in solution are HF, H^+, and Cl^-. The Cl^-, which is the conjugate base of a strong acid, is merely a spectator ion in any acid–base chemistry. The problem asks for $[F^-]$, which is formed by ionization of HF. Thus, the important equilibrium is

$$HF(aq) \rightleftharpoons H^+(aq) + F^-(aq)$$

The common ion in this problem is the hydrogen (or hydronium) ion. Now we can tabulate the initial and equilibrium concentrations of each species involved in this equilibrium:

	HF(aq)	$\rightleftharpoons$	$H^+(aq)$	+	$F^-(aq)$
Initial	0.20 M		0.10 M		0
Change	$-x$ M		$+x$ M		$+x$ M
Equilibrium	$(0.20 - x)$ M		$(0.10 + x)$ M		x M

The equilibrium constant for the ionization of HF, from Appendix D, is 6.8×10^{-4}. Substituting the equilibrium-constant concentrations into the equilibrium expression gives

$$K_a = 6.8 \times 10^{-4} = \frac{[H^+][F^-]}{[HF]} = \frac{(0.10 + x)(x)}{0.20 - x}$$

If we assume that x is small relative to 0.10 or 0.20 M, this expression simplifies to

$$\frac{(0.10)(x)}{0.20} = 6.8 \times 10^{-4}$$

$$x = \frac{0.20}{0.10}(6.8 \times 10^{-4}) = 1.4 \times 10^{-3} \ M = [F^-]$$

This F^- concentration is substantially smaller than it would be in a 0.20 M solution of HF with no added HCl. The common ion, H^+, suppresses the ionization of HF. The concentration of $H^+(aq)$ is

$$[H^+] = (0.10 + x) \ M \simeq 0.10 \ M$$

Thus,

$$pH = 1.00$$

Comment: Notice that for all practical purposes, $[H^+]$ is due entirely to the HCl; the HF makes a negligible contribution by comparison.

■■ **PRACTICE EXERCISE**

Calculate the formate ion concentration and pH of a solution that is 0.050 M in formic acid (HCOOH; $K_a = 1.8 \times 10^{-4}$) and 0.10 M in HNO_3.
Answer: $[HCOO^-] = 9.0 \times 10^{-5}$; pH = 1.00

Sample Exercises 17.1 and 17.2 both involve weak acids. The ionization of a weak base is also decreased by the addition of a common ion. For example, the addition of NH_4^+ (as from the strong electrolyte NH_4Cl) causes the base-dissociation equilibrium of NH_3 to shift to the left, decreasing the equilibrium concentration of OH^- and lowering the pH:

$$NH_3(aq) + H_2O(l) \rightleftharpoons NH_4^+(aq) + OH^-(aq) \qquad [17.2]$$

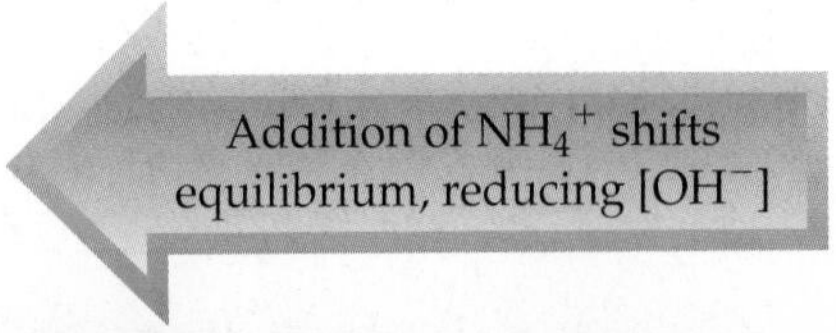

Addition of NH_4^+ shifts equilibrium, reducing $[OH^-]$

A mixture of 0.10 mol of NH_4Cl and 0.12 mol of NH_3 is added to enough water to make 1.0 L of solution. **(a)** What are the initial concentrations of the major species in the solution? **(b)** Which of the ions in this solution is a spectator ion in any acid–base chemistry occurring in the solution? **(c)** What equilibrium reaction determines $[OH^-]$ and therefore the pH of the solution?

17.2 | BUFFERED SOLUTIONS

Solutions such as those discussed in Section 17.1, which contain a weak conjugate acid–base pair, can resist drastic changes in pH upon the addition of small amounts of strong acid or strong base. These solutions are called **buffered solutions** (or merely **buffers**). Human blood, for example, is a complex aqueous mixture with a pH buffered at about 7.4 (see the "Chemistry and Life" box near the end of this section). Much of the chemical behavior of seawater is determined by its pH, buffered at about 8.1 to 8.3 near the surface. Buffered solutions find many important applications in the laboratory and in medicine (Figure 17.1▶).

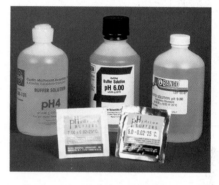

▲ **Figure 17.1 Buffer solutions.** Prepackaged buffer solutions and ingredients for making up buffer solutions of predetermined pH can be purchased.

Composition and Action of Buffered Solutions

A buffer resists changes in pH because it contains both an acid to neutralize OH^- ions and a base to neutralize H^+ ions. The acid and base that make up the buffer, however, must not consume each other through a neutralization reaction. These requirements are fulfilled by a weak acid–base conjugate pair such as CH_3COOH–CH_3COO^- or NH_4^+–NH_3. Thus, buffers are often prepared by mixing a weak acid or a weak base with a salt of that acid or base. The CH_3COOH–CH_3COO^- buffer can be prepared, for example, by adding CH_3COONa to a solution of CH_3COOH. The NH_4^+–NH_3 buffer can be prepared by adding NH_4Cl to a solution of NH_3. By choosing appropriate components and adjusting their relative concentrations, we can buffer a solution at virtually any pH.

Which of the following conjugate acid–base pairs will *not* function as a buffer: C_2H_5COOH and $C_2H_5COO^-$; HCO_3^- and CO_3^{2-}; HNO_3 and NO_3^-? Explain.

To understand better how a buffer works, let's consider a buffer composed of a weak acid (HX) and one of its salts (MX, where M^+ could be Na^+, K^+, or another cation). The acid-dissociation equilibrium in this buffered solution involves both the acid and its conjugate base:

$$HX(aq) \rightleftharpoons H^+(aq) + X^-(aq) \qquad [17.3]$$

The corresponding acid-dissociation-constant expression is

$$K_a = \frac{[H^+][X^-]}{[HX]} \qquad [17.4]$$

Solving this expression for $[H^+]$, we have

$$[H^+] = K_a\frac{[HX]}{[X^-]} \qquad [17.5]$$

We see from this expression that $[H^+]$, and thus the pH, is determined by two factors: the value of K_a for the weak-acid component of the buffer and the ratio of the concentrations of the conjugate acid–base pair, $[HX]/[X^-]$.

▶ **Figure 17.2 Buffer action.** When a small portion of OH⁻ is added to a buffer consisting of a mixture of the weak acid HF and its conjugate base (left), the OH⁻ reacts with the HF, decreasing [HF] and increasing [F⁻] in the buffer. Conversely, when a small portion of H⁺ is added to the buffer (right), the H⁺ reacts with the F⁻, decreasing [F⁻] and increasing [HF] in the buffer. Because pH depends on the ratio of F⁻ to HF, the resulting pH change is small.

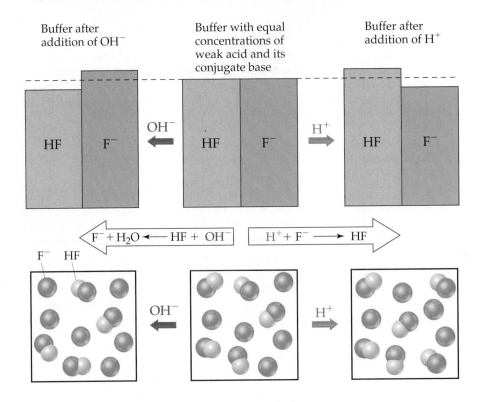

If OH⁻ ions are added to the buffered solution, they react with the acid component of the buffer to produce water and X⁻:

$$OH^-(aq) + HX(aq) \longrightarrow H_2O(l) + X^-(aq) \qquad [17.6]$$

added base   weak acid in buffer

This reaction causes [HX] to decrease and [X⁻] to increase. As long as the amounts of HX and X⁻ in the buffer are large compared to the amount of OH⁻ added, however, the ratio [HX]/[X⁻] does not change much, and thus the change in pH is small. A specific example of such a buffer, the HF/F⁻ buffer, is shown in Figure 17.2 ▲.

If H⁺ ions are added, they react with the base component of the buffer:

$$H^+(aq) + X^-(aq) \longrightarrow HX(aq) \qquad [17.7]$$

added base   weak acid in buffer

This reaction can also be represented using H_3O^+:

$$H_3O^+(aq) + X^-(aq) \longrightarrow HX(aq) + H_2O(l)$$

Using either equation, we see that the reaction causes [X⁻] to decrease and [HX] to increase. As long as the change in the ratio [HX]/[X⁻] is small, the change in pH will be small.

Figure 17.2 shows a buffer consisting of equal concentrations of hydrofluoric acid and fluoride ion (center). The addition of OH⁻ (left) reduces [HF] and increases [F⁻]. The addition of H⁺ (right) reduces [F⁻] and increases [HF].

◢ **GIVE IT SOME THOUGHT**

(a) What happens when NaOH is added to a buffer composed of CH_3COOH and CH_3COO^-? **(b)** What happens when HCl is added to this buffer?

Calculating the pH of a Buffer

Because conjugate acid–base pairs share a common ion, we can use the same procedures to calculate the pH of a buffer that we used to treat the common-ion effect (see Sample Exercise 17.1). However, we can sometimes take an alternate approach that is based on an equation derived from Equation 17.5.

Taking the negative log of both sides of Equation 17.5, we have

$$-\log[H^+] = -\log\left(K_a \frac{[HX]}{[X^-]}\right) = -\log K_a - \log \frac{[HX]}{[X^-]}$$

Because $-\log[H^+] = pH$ and $-\log K_a = pK_a$, we have

$$pH = pK_a - \log\frac{[HX]}{[X^-]} = pK_a + \log\frac{[X^-]}{[HX]} \qquad [17.8]$$

In general,

$$pH = pK_a + \log\frac{[\text{base}]}{[\text{acid}]} \qquad [17.9]$$

where [acid] and [base] refer to the equilibrium concentrations of *the conjugate acid–base pair*. Note that when [base] = [acid], pH = pK_a.

Equation 17.9 is known as the **Henderson–Hasselbalch equation**. Biologists, biochemists, and others who work frequently with buffers often use this equation to calculate the pH of buffers. In doing equilibrium calculations, we have seen that we can normally neglect the amounts of the acid and base of the buffer that ionize. Therefore, we can usually use the starting concentrations of the acid and base components of the buffer directly in Equation 17.9.

■ SAMPLE EXERCISE 17.3 | Calculating the pH of a Buffer

What is the pH of a buffer that is 0.12 *M* in lactic acid [$CH_3CH(OH)COOH$, or $HC_3H_5O_3$] and 0.10 *M* in sodium lactate [$CH_3CH(OH)COONa$ or $NaC_3H_5O_3$]? For lactic acid, $K_a = 1.4 \times 10^{-4}$.

SOLUTION

Analyze: We are asked to calculate the pH of a buffer containing lactic acid $HC_3H_5O_3$ and its conjugate base, the lactate ion ($C_3H_5O_3^-$).

Plan: We will first determine the pH using the method described in Section 17.1. Because $HC_3H_5O_3$ is a weak electrolyte and $NaC_3H_5O_3$ is a strong electrolyte, the major species in solution are $HC_3H_5O_3$, Na^+, and $C_3H_5O_3^-$. The Na^+ ion is a spectator ion. The $HC_3H_5O_3$–$C_3H_5O_3^-$ conjugate acid–base pair determines [H^+] and thus pH; [H^+] can be determined using the acid-dissociation equilibrium of lactic acid.

Solve: The initial and equilibrium concentrations of the species involved in this equilibrium are

	$HC_3H_5O_3(aq)$	$\rightleftharpoons$	$H^+(aq)$	+	$C_3H_5O_3^-(aq)$
Initial	0.12 M		0		0.10 M
Change	−x M		+x M		+x M
Equilibrium	(0.12 − x) M		x M		(0.10 + x) M

The equilibrium concentrations are governed by the equilibrium expression:

$$K_a = 1.4 \times 10^{-4} = \frac{[H^+][C_3H_5O_3^-]}{[HC_3H_5O_3]} = \frac{x(0.10+x)}{(0.12-x)}$$

Because K_a is small and a common ion is present, we expect x to be small relative to either 0.12 or 0.10 *M*. Thus, our equation can be simplified to give

$$K_a = 1.4 \times 10^{-4} = \frac{x(0.10)}{0.12}$$

Solving for x gives a value that justifies our approximation:

$$[H^+] = x = \left(\frac{0.12}{0.10}\right)(1.4 \times 10^{-4}) = 1.7 \times 10^{-4}\ M$$

$$pH = -\log(1.7 \times 10^{-4}) = 3.77$$

Alternatively, we could have used the Henderson–Hasselbalch equation to calculate pH directly:

$$pH = pK_a + \log\left(\frac{[\text{base}]}{[\text{acid}]}\right) = 3.85 + \log\left(\frac{0.10}{0.12}\right)$$

$$= 3.85 + (-0.08) = 3.77$$

■ PRACTICE EXERCISE

Calculate the pH of a buffer composed of 0.12 *M* benzoic acid and 0.20 *M* sodium benzoate. (Refer to Appendix D.)
Answer: 4.42

■ SAMPLE EXERCISE 17.4 | Preparing a Buffer

How many moles of NH_4Cl must be added to 2.0 L of 0.10 M NH_3 to form a buffer whose pH is 9.00? (Assume that the addition of NH_4Cl does not change the volume of the solution.)

SOLUTION

Analyze: Here we are asked to determine the amount of NH_4^+ ion required to prepare a buffer of a specific pH.

Plan: The major species in the solution will be NH_4^+, Cl^-, and NH_3. Of these, the Cl^- ion is a spectator (it is the conjugate base of a strong acid). Thus, the NH_4^+–NH_3 conjugate acid–base pair will determine the pH of the buffer solution. The equilibrium relationship between NH_4^+ and NH_3 is given by the base-dissociation constant for NH_3:

$$NH_3(aq) + H_2O(l) \rightleftharpoons NH_4^+(aq) + OH^-(aq) \qquad K_b = \frac{[NH_4^+][OH^-]}{[NH_3]} = 1.8 \times 10^{-5}$$

The key to this exercise is to use this K_b expression to calculate $[NH_4^+]$.

Solve: We obtain $[OH^-]$ from the given pH:

$$pOH = 14.00 - pH = 14.00 - 9.00 = 5.00$$

and so

$$[OH^-] = 1.0 \times 10^{-5} \, M$$

Because K_b is small and the common ion NH_4^+ is present, the equilibrium concentration of NH_3 will essentially equal its initial concentration:

$$[NH_3] = 0.10 \, M$$

We now use the expression for K_b to calculate $[NH_4^+]$:

$$[NH_4^+] = K_b \frac{[NH_3]}{[OH^-]} = (1.8 \times 10^{-5}) \frac{(0.10 \, M)}{(1.0 \times 10^{-5} \, M)} = 0.18 \, M$$

Thus, for the solution to have pH = 9.00, $[NH_4^+]$ must equal 0.18 M. The number of moles of NH_4Cl needed to produce this concentration is given by the product of the volume of the solution and its molarity:

$$(2.0 \, L)(0.18 \, mol \, NH_4Cl/L) = 0.36 \, mol \, NH_4Cl$$

Comment: Because NH_4^+ and NH_3 are a conjugate acid–base pair, we could use the Henderson–Hasselbalch equation (Equation 17.9) to solve this problem. To do so requires first using Equation 16.41 to calculate pK_a for NH_4^+ from the value of pK_b for NH_3. We suggest you try this approach to convince yourself that you can use the Henderson–Hasselbalch equation for buffers for which you are given K_b for the conjugate base rather than K_a for the conjugate acid.

■ PRACTICE EXERCISE

Calculate the concentration of sodium benzoate that must be present in a 0.20 M solution of benzoic acid (C_6H_5COOH) to produce a pH of 4.00.
Answer: 0.13 M

Buffer Capacity and pH Range

Two important characteristics of a buffer are its capacity and its effective pH range. **Buffer capacity** is the amount of acid or base the buffer can neutralize before the pH begins to change to an appreciable degree. The buffer capacity depends on the amount of acid and base from which the buffer is made. The pH of the buffer depends on the K_a for the acid and on the relative concentrations of the acid and base that comprise the buffer. According to Equation 17.5, for example, $[H^+]$ for a 1-L solution that is 1 M in CH_3COOH and 1 M in CH_3COONa will be the same as for a 1-L solution that is 0.1 M in CH_3COOH and 0.1 M in CH_3COONa. The first solution has a greater buffering capacity, however, because it contains more CH_3COOH and CH_3COO^-. The greater the amounts of the conjugate acid–base pair, the more resistant is the ratio of their concentrations, and hence the pH, is to change.

The **pH range** of any buffer is the pH range over which the buffer acts effectively. Buffers most effectively resist a change in pH in *either* direction when the concentrations of weak acid and conjugate base are about the same. From Equation 17.9 we see that when the concentrations of weak acid and conjugate base are equal, pH = pK_a. This relationship gives the optimal pH of any buffer. Thus, we usually try to select a buffer whose acid form has a pK_a close to the desired pH. In practice, we find that if the concentration of one component of the buffer is more than 10 times the concentration of the other component, the buffering action is poor. Because log 10 = 1, *buffers usually have a usable range within ±1 pH unit of* pK_a (that is, a range of pH = pK_a ± 1).

◢ **GIVE IT SOME THOUGHT**

What is the optimal pH buffered by a solution containing CH₃COOH and CH₃COONa? (K_a for CH₃COOH is 1.8×10^{-5}.)

Addition of Strong Acids or Bases to Buffers

Let's now consider in a more quantitative way the response of a buffered solution to the addition of a strong acid or base. In solving these problems, it is important to understand that reactions between strong acids and weak bases proceed essentially to completion, as do those between strong bases and weak acids. Thus, as long as we do not exceed the buffering capacity of the buffer, we can assume that the strong acid or strong base is completely consumed by reaction with the buffer.

Consider a buffer that contains a weak acid HX and its conjugate base X⁻. When a strong acid is added to this buffer, the added H⁺ is consumed by X⁻ to produce HX; thus, [HX] increases and [X⁻] decreases. (See Equation 17.7.) When a strong base is added to the buffer, the added OH⁻ is consumed by HX to produce X⁻; in this case [HX] decreases and [X⁻] increases. (See Equation 17.6.) These two situations are summarized in Figure 17.2.

To calculate how the pH of the buffer responds to the addition of a strong acid or a strong base, we follow the strategy outlined in Figure 17.3 ▼:

1. Consider the acid–base neutralization reaction, and determine its effect on [HX] and [X⁻]. This step of the procedure is a *stoichiometry calculation*.

2. Use K_a and the new concentrations of [HX] and [X⁻] from step 1 to calculate [H⁺]. This second step of the procedure is a standard *equilibrium calculation* and is most easily done using the Henderson–Hasselbalch equation.

The complete procedure is illustrated in Sample Exercise 17.5.

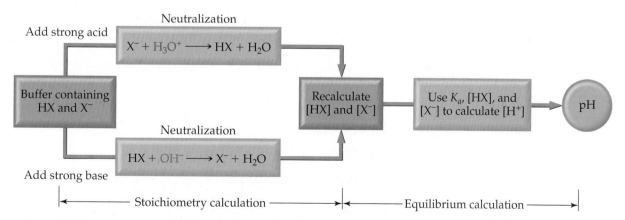

▲ **Figure 17.3   Calculation of the pH of a buffer after the addition of acid or base.** First consider how the neutralization reaction between the added strong acid or strong base and the buffer affects the composition of the buffer (stoichiometry calculation). Then calculate the pH of the remaining buffer (equilibrium calculation). As long as the amount of added acid or base does not exceed the buffer capacity, the Henderson–Hasselbalch equation, Equation 17.9, can be used for the equilibrium calculation.

■ SAMPLE EXERCISE 17.5 | Calculating pH Changes in Buffers

A buffer is made by adding 0.300 mol CH_3COOH and 0.300 mol CH_3COONa to enough water to make 1.00 L of solution. The pH of the buffer is 4.74 (Sample Exercise 17.1). **(a)** Calculate the pH of this solution after 0.020 mol of NaOH is added. **(b)** For comparison, calculate the pH that would result if 0.020 mol of NaOH were added to 1.00 L of pure water (neglect any volume changes).

SOLUTION

Analyze: We are asked to determine the pH of a buffer after addition of a small amount of strong base and to compare the pH change to the pH that would result if we were to add the same amount of strong base to pure water.

Plan: **(a)** Solving this problem involves the two steps outlined in Figure 17.3. Thus, we must first do a stoichiometry calculation to determine how the added OH^- reacts with the buffer and affects its composition. Then we can use the resultant composition of the buffer and either the Henderson–Hasselbalch equation or the equilibrium-constant expression for the buffer to determine the pH.

Solve: *Stoichiometry Calculation:* The OH^- provided by NaOH reacts with CH_3COOH, the weak acid component of the buffer. Prior to this neutralization reaction, there are 0.300 mol each of CH_3COOH and CH_3COO^-. Neutralizing the 0.020 mol OH^- requires 0.020 mol of CH_3COOH. Consequently, the amount of CH_3COOH *decreases* by 0.020 mol, and the amount of the product of the neutralization, CH_3COO^-, *increases* by 0.020 mol. We can create a table to see how the composition of the buffer changes as a result of its reaction with OH^-:

$$CH_3COOH(aq) + OH^-(aq) \longrightarrow H_2O(l) + CH_3COO^-(aq)$$

	CH_3COOH	OH^-	H_2O	CH_3COO^-
Buffer before addition	0.300 mol	0	—	0.300 mol
Addition	—	0.020 mol	—	—
Buffer after addition	0.280 mol	0	—	0.320 mol

Equilibrium Calculation: We now turn our attention to the equilibrium that will determine the pH of the buffer, namely the ionization of acetic acid.

$$CH_3COOH(aq) \rightleftharpoons H^+(aq) + CH_3COO^-(aq)$$

Using the quantities of CH_3COOH and CH_3COO^- remaining in the buffer, we can determine the pH using the Henderson–Hasselbalch equation.

$$pH = 4.74 + \log \frac{0.320 \text{ mol}/1.00 \text{ L}}{0.280 \text{ mol}/1.00 \text{ L}} = 4.80$$

Comment Notice that we could have used mole amounts in place of concentrations in the Henderson–Hasselbalch equation and gotten the same result. The volumes of the acid and base are equal and cancel.

If 0.020 mol of H^+ was added to the buffer, we would proceed in a similar way to calculate the resulting pH of the buffer. In this case the pH decreases by 0.06 units, giving pH = 4.68, as shown in the figure in the margin.

(b) To determine the pH of a solution made by adding 0.020 mol of NaOH to 1.00 L of pure water, we can first determine pOH using Equation 16.18 and subtracting from 14.

$$pH = 14 - (-\log 0.020) = 12.30$$

Note that although the small amount of NaOH changes the pH of water significantly, the pH of the buffer changes very little.

■ PRACTICE EXERCISE

Determine **(a)** the pH of the original buffer described in Sample Exercise 17.5 after the addition of 0.020 mol HCl and **(b)** the pH of the solution that would result from the addition of 0.020 mol HCl to 1.00 L of pure water.
Answers: **(a)** 4.68, **(b)** 1.70

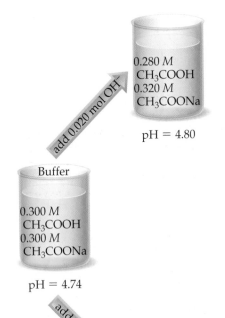

add 0.020 mol OH^-

0.280 M
CH_3COOH
0.320 M
CH_3COONa

pH = 4.80

Buffer

0.300 M
CH_3COOH
0.300 M
CH_3COONa

pH = 4.74

add 0.020 mol H^+

0.320 M
CH_3COOH
0.280 M
CH_3COONa

pH = 4.68

in this region is therefore like that for the strong acid–strong base titration illustrated in Sample Exercise 17.6(b). Thus, the addition of 51.0 mL of 0.100 M NaOH to 50.0 mL of either 0.100 M HCl or 0.100 M CH$_3$COOH yields the same pH, 11.00. Notice in Figures 17.6 and 17.9 that the titration curves for the titrations of both the strong acid and the weak acid are the same after the equivalence point.

■ **SAMPLE EXERCISE 17.7** | **Calculating pH for a Weak Acid–Strong Base Titration**

Calculate the pH of the solution formed when 45.0 mL of 0.100 M NaOH is added to 50.0 mL of 0.100 M CH$_3$COOH ($K_a = 1.8 \times 10^{-5}$).

SOLUTION

Analyze: We are asked to calculate the pH before the equivalence point of the titration of a weak acid with a strong base.

Plan: We first must determine the number of moles of CH$_3$COOH and CH$_3$COO$^-$ that are present after the neutralization reaction. We then calculate pH using K_a together with [CH$_3$COOH] and [CH$_3$COO$^-$].

Solve: *Stoichiometry Calculation:* The product of the volume and concentration of each solution gives the number of moles of each reactant present before the neutralization:

$$(0.0500 \text{ L soln})\left(\frac{0.100 \text{ mol CH}_3\text{COOH}}{1 \text{ L soln}}\right) = 5.00 \times 10^{-3} \text{ mol CH}_3\text{COOH}$$

$$(0.0450 \text{ L soln})\left(\frac{0.100 \text{ mol NaOH}}{1 \text{ L soln}}\right) = 4.50 \times 10^{-3} \text{ mol NaOH}$$

The 4.50×10^{-3} mol of NaOH consumes 4.50×10^{-3} mol of CH$_3$COOH:

	CH$_3$COOH(aq) +	OH$^-$(aq) $\longrightarrow$	CH$_3$COO$^-$(aq) +	H$_2$O(l)
Before addition	5.00×10^{-3} mol	0	0	—
Addition		4.50×10^{-3} mol		
After addition	0.50×10^{-3} mol	0	4.50×10^{-3} mol	—

The total volume of the solution is

45.0 mL + 50.0 mL = 95.0 mL = 0.0950 L

The resulting molarities of CH$_3$COOH and CH$_3$COO$^-$ after the reaction are therefore

$$[\text{CH}_3\text{COOH}] = \frac{0.50 \times 10^{-3} \text{ mol}}{0.0950 \text{ L}} = 0.0053 \ M$$

$$[\text{CH}_3\text{COO}^-] = \frac{4.50 \times 10^{-3} \text{ mol}}{0.0950 \text{ L}} = 0.0474 \ M$$

Equilibrium Calculation: The equilibrium between CH$_3$COOH and CH$_3$COO$^-$ must obey the equilibrium-constant expression for CH$_3$COOH

$$K_a = \frac{[\text{H}^+][\text{CH}_3\text{COO}^-]}{[\text{CH}_3\text{COOH}]} = 1.8 \times 10^{-5}$$

Solving for [H$^+$] gives

$$[\text{H}^+] = K_a \times \frac{[\text{CH}_3\text{COOH}]}{[\text{CH}_3\text{COO}^-]} = (1.8 \times 10^{-5}) \times \left(\frac{0.0053}{0.0474}\right) = 2.0 \times 10^{-6} \ M$$

$$\text{pH} = -\log(2.0 \times 10^{-6}) = 5.70$$

Comment: We could have solved for pH equally well using the Henderson–Hasselbalch equation.

■ **PRACTICE EXERCISE**

(a) Calculate the pH in the solution formed by adding 10.0 mL of 0.050 M NaOH to 40.0 mL of 0.0250 M benzoic acid (C$_6$H$_5$COOH, $K_a = 6.3 \times 10^{-5}$). **(b)** Calculate the pH in the solution formed by adding 10.0 mL of 0.100 M HCl to 20.0 mL of 0.100 M NH$_3$.

Answers: **(a)** 4.20, **(b)** 9.26

■ **SAMPLE EXERCISE 17.8** | **Calculating the pH at the Equivalence Point**

Calculate the pH at the equivalence point in the titration of 50.0 mL of 0.100 M CH$_3$COOH with 0.100 M NaOH.

SOLUTION

Analyze: We are asked to determine the pH at the equivalence point of the titration of a weak acid with a strong base. Because the neutralization of a weak acid produces its anion, which is a weak base, we expect the pH at the equivalence point to be greater than 7.

Plan: The initial number of moles of acetic acid will equal the number of moles of acetate ion at the equivalence point. We use the volume of the solution at the equivalence point to calculate the concentration of acetate ion. Because the acetate ion is a weak base, we can calculate the pH using K_b and $[CH_3COO^-]$.

Solve: The number of moles of acetic acid in the initial solution is obtained from the volume and molarity of the solution:

$$\text{Moles} = M \times L = (0.100 \text{ mol/L})(0.0500 \text{ L}) = 5.00 \times 10^{-3} \text{ mol } CH_3COOH$$

Hence 5.00×10^{-3} mol of CH_3COO^- is formed. It will take 50.0 mL of NaOH to reach the equivalence point (Figure 17.9). The volume of this salt solution at the equivalence point is the sum of the volumes of the acid and base, 50.0 mL + 50.0 mL = 100.0 mL = 0.1000 L. Thus, the concentration of CH_3COO^- is

$$[CH_3COO^-] = \frac{5.00 \times 10^{-3} \text{ mol}}{0.1000 \text{ L}} = 0.0500 \ M$$

The CH_3COO^- ion is a weak base.

$$CH_3COO^-(aq) + H_2O(l) \rightleftharpoons CH_3COOH(aq) + OH^-(aq)$$

The K_b for CH_3COO^- can be calculated from the K_a value of its conjugate acid, $K_b = K_w/K_a = (1.0 \times 10^{-14})/(1.8 \times 10^{-5}) = 5.6 \times 10^{-10}$. Using the K_b expression, we have

$$K_b = \frac{[CH_3COOH][OH^-]}{[CH_3COO^-]} = \frac{(x)(x)}{0.0500 - x} = 5.6 \times 10^{-10}$$

Making the approximation that $0.0500 - x \simeq 0.0500$, and then solving for x, we have $x = [OH^-] = 5.3 \times 10^{-6} \ M$, which gives pOH = 5.28 and pH = 8.72.

Check: The pH is above 7, as expected for the salt of a weak acid and strong base.

■■ PRACTICE EXERCISE

Calculate the pH at the equivalence point when **(a)** 40.0 mL of 0.025 M benzoic acid (C_6H_5COOH, $K_a = 6.3 \times 10^{-5}$) is titrated with 0.050 M NaOH; **(b)** 40.0 mL of 0.100 M NH_3 is titrated with 0.100 M HCl.
Answers: **(a)** 8.21, **(b)** 5.28

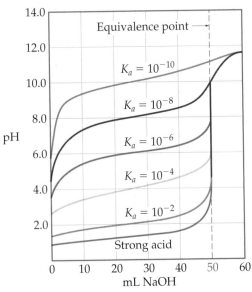

▲ **Figure 17.11 Effect of K_a on titration curves.** This set of curves shows the influence of acid strength (K_a) on the shape of the curve for titration with NaOH. Each curve represents titration of 50.0 mL of 0.10 M acid with 0.10 M NaOH. The weaker the acid, the higher the initial pH and the smaller the pH change at the equivalence point.

The pH titration curves for weak acid–strong base titrations differ from those for strong acid–strong base titrations in three noteworthy ways:

1. The solution of the weak acid has a higher initial pH than a solution of a strong acid of the same concentration.

2. The pH change at the rapid-rise portion of the curve near the equivalence point is smaller for the weak acid than it is for the strong acid.

3. The pH at the equivalence point is above 7.00 for the weak acid–strong base titration.

To illustrate these differences further, consider the family of titration curves shown in Figure 17.11 ◀. Notice that the initial pH increases as the acid becomes weaker (that is, as K_a becomes smaller), and that the pH change near the equivalence point becomes less marked. Notice also that the pH at the equivalence point steadily increases as K_a decreases. It is virtually impossible to determine the equivalence point when pK_a is 10 or higher because the pH change is too small and gradual.

Because the pH change near the equivalence point becomes smaller as K_a decreases, the choice of indicator for a weak acid–strong base titration is more critical than it is for a strong acid–strong base titration. When 0.100 M CH_3COOH ($K_a = 1.8 \times 10^{-5}$) is titrated with 0.100 M NaOH, for example, as shown in Figure 17.9, the pH increases rapidly only over the pH range of about 7 to 10. Phenolphthalein is therefore an ideal indicator because it changes color from pH 8.3 to 10.0, close to the pH at the equivalence point. Methyl red is a poor choice, however, because its color change occurs from 4.2 to 6.0, which begins well before the equivalence point is reached.

Titration of a weak base (such as 0.100 M NH$_3$) with a strong acid solution (such as 0.100 M HCl) leads to the titration curve shown in Figure 17.12▶. In this particular example the equivalence point occurs at pH 5.28. Thus, methyl red would be an ideal indicator, but phenolphthalein would be a poor choice.

GIVE IT SOME THOUGHT

Why is the choice of indicator more crucial for a weak acid–strong base titration than for a strong acid–strong base titration?

Titrations of Polyprotic Acids

When weak acids contain more than one ionizable H atom, as in phosphorous acid (H$_3$PO$_3$), reaction with OH$^-$ occurs in a series of steps. Neutralization of H$_3$PO$_3$ proceeds in two stages. ∞∞ (Chapter 16 Sample Integrative Exercise)

$$H_3PO_3(aq) + OH^-(aq) \longrightarrow H_2PO_3^-(aq) + H_2O(l) \quad [17.13]$$

$$H_2PO_3^-(aq) + OH^-(aq) \longrightarrow HPO_3^{2-}(aq) + H_2O(l) \quad [17.14]$$

When the neutralization steps of a polyprotic acid or polybasic base are sufficiently separated, the substance exhibits a titration curve with multiple equivalence points. Figure 17.13▶ shows the two distinct equivalence points in the titration curve for the H$_3$PO$_3$–H$_2$PO$_3^-$–HPO$_3^{2-}$ system.

GIVE IT SOME THOUGHT

Sketch the titration curve for the titration of Na$_2$CO$_3$ with HCl.

17.4 | SOLUBILITY EQUILIBRIA

The equilibria that we have considered thus far in this chapter have involved acids and bases. Furthermore, they have been homogeneous; that is, all the species have been in the same phase. Through the rest of this chapter we will consider the equilibria involved in the dissolution or precipitation of ionic compounds. These reactions are heterogeneous.

The dissolving and precipitating of compounds are phenomena that occur both within us and around us. Tooth enamel dissolves in acidic solutions, for example, causing tooth decay. The precipitation of certain salts in our kidneys produces kidney stones. The waters of Earth contain salts dissolved as water passes over and through the ground. Precipitation of CaCO$_3$ from groundwater is responsible for the formation of stalactites and stalagmites within limestone caves (Figure 4.1).

In our earlier discussion of precipitation reactions, we considered some general rules for predicting the solubility of common salts in water. ∞∞ (Section 4.2) These rules give us a qualitative sense of whether a compound will have a low or high solubility in water. By considering solubility equilibria, in contrast, we can make quantitative predictions about the amount of a given compound that will dissolve. We can also use these equilibria to analyze the factors that affect solubility.

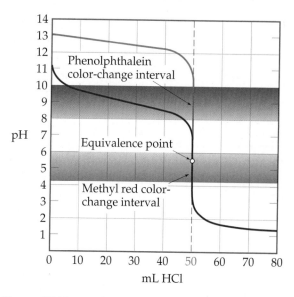

▲ **Figure 17.12 Adding a strong acid to a base.** The blue curve shows pH versus volume of added HCl in the titration of 50.0 mL of 0.10 M ammonia (weak base) with 0.10 M HCl. The red curve shows pH versus added acid for the titration of 0.10 M NaOH (strong base). Both phenolphthalein and methyl red change color at the equivalence point in the titration of the strong base. Phenolphthalein changes color before the equivalence point in the titration of the weak base.

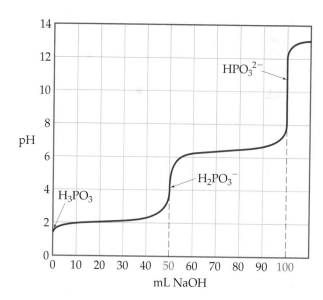

▲ **Figure 17.13 Diprotic acid.** Titration curve for the reaction of 50.0 mL of 0.10 M H$_3$PO$_3$ with 0.10 M NaOH.

The Solubility-Product Constant, K_{sp}

Recall that a *saturated solution* is one in which the solution is in contact with undissolved solute. ⚬⚬ (Section 13.2) Consider, for example, a saturated aqueous solution of $BaSO_4$ that is in contact with solid $BaSO_4$. Because the solid is an ionic compound, it is a strong electrolyte and yields $Ba^{2+}(aq)$ and $SO_4^{2-}(aq)$ ions upon dissolving. The following equilibrium is readily established between the undissolved solid and hydrated ions in solution:

$$BaSO_4(s) \rightleftharpoons Ba^{2+}(aq) + SO_4^{2-}(aq) \qquad [17.15]$$

As with any other equilibrium, the extent to which this dissolution reaction occurs is expressed by the magnitude of its equilibrium constant. Because this equilibrium equation describes the dissolution of a solid, the equilibrium constant indicates how soluble the solid is in water and is referred to as the **solubility-product constant** (or simply the **solubility product**). It is denoted K_{sp}, where sp stands for solubility product.

The equilibrium-constant expression for the equilibrium between a solid and an aqueous solution of its component ions is written according to the rules that apply to any equilibrium-constant expression. Remember, however, that solids do not appear in the equilibrium-constant expressions for heterogeneous equilibria. ⚬⚬ (Section 15.4) Thus, the solubility-product expression for $BaSO_4$, which is based on Equation 17.15, is

$$K_{sp} = [Ba^{2+}][SO_4^{2-}] \qquad [17.16]$$

In general, *the solubility product of a compound equals the product of the concentration of the ions involved in the equilibrium, each raised to the power of its coefficient in the equilibrium equation.* The coefficient for each ion in the equilibrium equation also equals its subscript in the compound's chemical formula.

The values of K_{sp} at 25 °C for many ionic solids are tabulated in Appendix D. The value of K_{sp} for $BaSO_4$ is 1.1×10^{-10}, a very small number, indicating that only a very small amount of the solid will dissolve in water.

■ SAMPLE EXERCISE 17.9 | Writing Solubility-Product (K_{sp}) Expressions

Write the expression for the solubility-product constant for CaF_2, and look up the corresponding K_{sp} value in Appendix D.

SOLUTION

Analyze: We are asked to write an equilibrium-constant expression for the process by which CaF_2 dissolves in water.

Plan: We apply the same rules for writing any equilibrium-constant expression, excluding the solid reactant from the expression. We assume that the compound dissociates completely into its component ions.

$$CaF_2(s) \rightleftharpoons Ca^{2+}(aq) + 2 F^-(aq)$$

Solve: Following the italicized rule stated previously, the expression for K_{sp} is

$$K_{sp} = [Ca^{2+}][F^-]^2$$

In Appendix D we see that this K_{sp} has a value of 3.9×10^{-11}.

■ PRACTICE EXERCISE

Give the solubility-product-constant expressions and the values of the solubility-product constants (from Appendix D) for the following compounds: **(a)** barium carbonate, **(b)** silver sulfate.
Answers: **(a)** $K_{sp} = [Ba^{2+}][CO_3^{2-}] = 5.0 \times 10^{-9}$; **(b)** $K_{sp} = [Ag^+]^2[SO_4^{2-}] = 1.5 \times 10^{-5}$

Solubility and K_{sp}

It is important to distinguish carefully between solubility and the solubility-product constant. The solubility of a substance is the quantity that dissolves to form a saturated solution. ⚬⚬ (Section 13.2) Solubility is often expressed as grams of solute per liter of solution (g/L). *Molar solubility* is the number of moles of the solute that dissolve in forming a liter of saturated solution of the solute (mol/L). The solubility-product constant (K_{sp}) is the equilibrium constant for the equilibrium between an ionic solid and its saturated solution and is a unitless number. Thus, the magnitude of K_{sp} is a measure of how much of the solid dissolves to form a saturated solution.

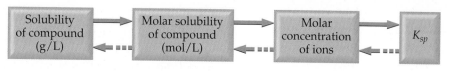

▲ Figure 17.14 **Relationships between solubility and K_{sp}.** The solubility of any compound in grams per liter can be converted to molar solubility. The molar solubility can be used to determine the concentrations of ions in solution. The concentration of ions can be used to calculate K_{sp}. The steps can be reversed, and solubility calculated from K_{sp}.

▲ GIVE IT SOME THOUGHT

Without doing a calculation, predict which of the following compounds will have the greatest molar solubility in water: AgCl ($K_{sp} = 1.8 \times 10^{-10}$), AgBr ($K_{sp} = 5.0 \times 10^{-13}$), or AgI ($K_{sp} = 8.3 \times 10^{-17}$).

The solubility of a substance can change considerably as the concentrations of other solutes change. The solubility of $Mg(OH)_2$, for example, depends highly on pH. The solubility is also affected by the concentrations of other ions in solution, especially Mg^{2+}. In contrast, the solubility-product constant, K_{sp}, has only one value for a given solute at any specific temperature.*

In principle, it is possible to use the K_{sp} value of a salt to calculate solubility under a variety of conditions. In practice, great care must be taken in doing so for the reasons indicated in "A Closer Look: Limitations of Solubility Products" at the end of this section. Agreement between measured solubility and that calculated from K_{sp} is usually best for salts whose ions have low charges (1+ and 1−) and do not hydrolyze. Figure 17.14▲ summarizes the relationships among various expressions of solubility and K_{sp}.

■ SAMPLE EXERCISE 17.10 | Calculating K_{sp} from Solubility

Solid silver chromate is added to pure water at 25 °C. Some of the solid remains undissolved at the bottom of the flask. The mixture is stirred for several days to ensure that equilibrium is achieved between the undissolved $Ag_2CrO_4(s)$ and the solution. Analysis of the equilibrated solution shows that its silver ion concentration is 1.3×10^{-4} M. Assuming that Ag_2CrO_4 dissociates completely in water and that there are no other important equilibria involving the Ag^+ or CrO_4^{2-} ions in the solution, calculate K_{sp} for this compound.

SOLUTION

Analyze: We are given the equilibrium concentration of Ag^+ in a saturated solution of Ag_2CrO_4. From this information, we are asked to determine the value of the solubility-product constant, K_{sp}, for Ag_2CrO_4.

Plan: The equilibrium equation and the expression for K_{sp} are

$$Ag_2CrO_4(s) \rightleftharpoons 2\, Ag^+(aq) + CrO_4^{2-}(aq) \qquad K_{sp} = [Ag^+]^2[CrO_4^{2-}]$$

To calculate K_{sp}, we need the equilibrium concentrations of Ag^+ and CrO_4^{2-}. We know that at equilibrium $[Ag^+] = 1.3 \times 10^{-4}$ M. All the Ag^+ and CrO_4^{2-} ions in the solution come from the Ag_2CrO_4 that dissolves. Thus, we can use $[Ag^+]$ to calculate $[CrO_4^{2-}]$.

Solve: From the chemical formula of silver chromate, we know that there must be 2 Ag^+ ions in solution for each CrO_4^{2-} ion in solution. Consequently, the concentration of CrO_4^{2-} is half the concentration of Ag^+:

$$[CrO_4^{2-}] = \left(\frac{1.3 \times 10^{-4} \text{ mol } Ag^+}{L}\right)\left(\frac{1 \text{ mol } CrO_4^{2-}}{2 \text{ mol } Ag^+}\right) = 6.5 \times 10^{-5} \text{ M}$$

We can now calculate the value of K_{sp}.

$$K_{sp} = [Ag^+]^2[CrO_4^{2-}] = (1.3 \times 10^{-4})^2(6.5 \times 10^{-5}) = 1.1 \times 10^{-12}$$

Check: We obtain a small value, as expected for a slightly soluble salt. Furthermore, the calculated value agrees well with the one given in Appendix D, 1.2×10^{-12}.

---

*This is strictly true only for very dilute solutions. The values of equilibrium constants are somewhat altered when the total concentration of ionic substances in water is increased. However, we will ignore these effects, which are taken into consideration only for work that requires exceptional accuracy.

A saturated solution of $Mg(OH)_2$ in contact with undissolved solid is prepared at 25 °C. The pH of the solution is found to be 10.17. Assuming that $Mg(OH)_2$ dissociates completely in water and that there are no other simultaneous equilibria involving the Mg^{2+} or OH^- ions in the solution, calculate K_{sp} for this compound.
Answer: 1.6×10^{-12}

■ SAMPLE EXERCISE 17.11 | Calculating Solubility from K_{sp}

The K_{sp} for CaF_2 is 3.9×10^{-11} at 25 °C. Assuming that CaF_2 dissociates completely upon dissolving and that there are no other important equilibria affecting its solubility, calculate the solubility of CaF_2 in grams per liter.

SOLUTION

Analyze: We are given K_{sp} for CaF_2 and are asked to determine solubility. Recall that the *solubility* of a substance is the quantity that can dissolve in solvent, whereas the *solubility-product constant*, K_{sp}, is an equilibrium constant.

Plan: We can approach this problem by using our standard techniques for solving equilibrium problems. We write the chemical equation for the dissolution process and set up a table of the initial and equilibrium concentrations. We then use the equilibrium-constant expression. In this case we know K_{sp}, and so we solve for the concentrations of the ions in solution.

Solve: Assume initially that none of the salt has dissolved, and then allow x moles/liter of CaF_2 to dissociate completely when equilibrium is achieved.

	$CaF_2(s)$	$\rightleftharpoons$	Ca^{2+}	+	$2\ F^-(aq)$
Initial	—		0		0
Change	—		$+x\ M$		$+2x\ M$
Equilibrium	—		$x\ M$		$2x\ M$

The stoichiometry of the equilibrium dictates that $2x$ moles/liter of F^- are produced for each x moles/liter of CaF_2 that dissolve. We now use the expression for K_{sp} and substitute the equilibrium concentrations to solve for the value of x:

$$K_{sp} = [Ca^{2+}][F^-]^2 = (x)(2x)^2 = 4x^3 = 3.9 \times 10^{-11}$$

$$x = \sqrt[3]{\frac{3.9 \times 10^{-11}}{4}} = 2.1 \times 10^{-4}\ M$$

(Remember that $\sqrt[3]{y} = y^{1/3}$; to calculate the cube root of a number, you can use the y^x function on your calculator, with $x = \frac{1}{3}$.) Thus, the molar solubility of CaF_2 is 2.1×10^{-4} mol/L. The mass of CaF_2 that dissolves in water to form a liter of solution is

$$\left(\frac{2.1 \times 10^{-4}\ mol\ CaF_2}{1\ L\ soln}\right)\left(\frac{78.1\ g\ CaF_2}{1\ mol\ CaF_2}\right) = 1.6 \times 10^{-2}\ g\ CaF_2/L\ soln$$

Check: We expect a small number for the solubility of a slightly soluble salt. If we reverse the calculation, we should be able to recalculate the solubility product: $K_{sp} = (2.1 \times 10^{-4})(4.2 \times 10^{-4})^2 = 3.7 \times 10^{-11}$, close to the starting value for K_{sp}, 3.9×10^{-11}.

Comment: Because F^- is the anion of a weak acid, you might expect that the hydrolysis of the ion would affect the solubility of CaF_2. The basicity of F^- is so small ($K_b = 1.5 \times 10^{-11}$), however, that the hydrolysis occurs to only a slight extent and does not significantly influence the solubility. The reported solubility is 0.017 g/L at 25 °C, in good agreement with our calculation.

The K_{sp} for LaF_3 is 2×10^{-19}. What is the solubility of LaF_3 in water in moles per liter?
Answer: 9×10^{-6} mol/L

A Closer Look   LIMITATIONS OF SOLUBILITY PRODUCTS

The concentrations of ions calculated from K_{sp} sometimes deviate appreciably from those found experimentally. In part, these deviations are due to electrostatic interactions between ions in solution, which can lead to ion pairs. (See Section 13.5, "A Closer Look: Colligative Properties of Electrolyte Solutions.") These interactions increase in magnitude both as the concentrations of the ions increase and as their charges increase. The solubility calculated from K_{sp} tends to be low unless it is corrected to account for these interactions between ions. Chemists have developed procedures for correcting for these "ionic-strength" or "ionic-activity" effects, and these procedures are examined in more advanced chemistry courses. As an example of the effect of these interionic interactions, consider $CaCO_3$ (calcite), whose solubility product, $K_{sp} = 4.5 \times 10^{-9}$, gives a calculated solubility of 6.7×10^{-5} mol/L. Making corrections for the interionic interactions in the solution yields a higher solubility, 7.3×10^{-5} mol/L. The reported solubility, however, is twice as high (1.4×10^{-4} mol/L), so there must be one or more additional factors involved.

Another common source of error in calculating ion concentrations from K_{sp} is ignoring other equilibria that occur simultaneously in the solution. It is possible, for example, that acid–base equilibria take place simultaneously with solubility equilibria. In particular, both basic anions and cations with high charge-to-size ratios undergo hydrolysis reactions that can measurably increase the solubilities of their salts. For example, $CaCO_3$ contains the basic carbonate ion ($K_b = 1.8 \times 10^{-4}$), which hydrolyzes in water: $CO_3^{2-}(aq) + H_2O(l) \rightleftharpoons HCO_3^{-}(aq) + OH^{-}(aq)$. If we consider both the effect of the interionic interactions in the solution and the effect of the simultaneous solubility and hydrolysis equilibria, we calculate a solubility of 1.4×10^{-4} mol/L, in agreement with the measured value.

Finally, we generally assume that ionic compounds dissociate completely into their component ions when they dissolve. This assumption is not always valid. When MgF_2 dissolves, for example, it yields not only Mg^{2+} and F^{-} ions but also MgF^{+} ions in solution. Thus, we see that calculating solubility using K_{sp} can be more complicated than it first appears and it requires considerable knowledge of the equilibria occurring in solution.

17.5 FACTORS THAT AFFECT SOLUBILITY

The solubility of a substance is affected by temperature as well as by the presence of other solutes. The presence of an acid, for example, can have a major influence on the solubility of a substance. In Section 17.4 we considered the dissolving of ionic compounds in pure water. In this section we examine three factors that affect the solubility of ionic compounds: (1) the presence of common ions, (2) the pH of the solution, and (3) the presence of complexing agents. We will also examine the phenomenon of *amphoterism*, which is related to the effects of both pH and complexing agents.

Common-Ion Effect

The presence of either $Ca^{2+}(aq)$ or $F^{-}(aq)$ in a solution reduces the solubility of CaF_2, shifting the solubility equilibrium of CaF_2 to the left.

$$CaF_2(s) \rightleftharpoons Ca^{2+}(aq) + 2\,F^{-}(aq)$$

Addition of Ca^{2+} or F^{-} shifts equilibrium, reducing solubility

This reduction in solubility is another application of the common-ion effect. ∞ (Section 17.1) In general, *the solubility of a slightly soluble salt is decreased by the presence of a second solute that furnishes a common ion.* Figure 17.15 ▶ shows how the solubility of CaF_2 decreases as NaF is added to the solution. Sample Exercise 17.12 shows how the K_{sp} can be used to calculate the solubility of a slightly soluble salt in the presence of a common ion.

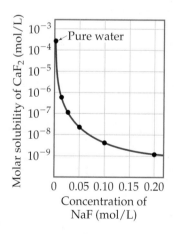

▲ **Figure 17.15 Common-ion effect.** The way in which NaF concentration affects the solubility of CaF_2 demonstrates the common-ion effect. Notice that the CaF_2 solubility is on a logarithmic scale.

■■■ **SAMPLE EXERCISE 17.12** | **Calculating the Effect of a Common Ion on Solubility**

Calculate the molar solubility of CaF_2 at 25 °C in a solution that is **(a)** 0.010 M in $Ca(NO_3)_2$, **(b)** 0.010 M in NaF.

SOLUTION

Analyze: We are asked to determine the solubility of CaF_2 in the presence of two strong electrolytes, each of which contains an ion common to CaF_2. In (a) the common ion is Ca^{2+}, and NO_3^- is a spectator ion. In (b) the common ion is F^-, and Na^+ is a spectator ion.

Plan: Because the slightly soluble compound is CaF_2, we need to use the K_{sp} for this compound, which is available in Appendix D:

$$K_{sp} = [Ca^{2+}][F^-]^2 = 3.9 \times 10^{-11}$$

The value of K_{sp} is unchanged by the presence of additional solutes. Because of the common-ion effect, however, the solubility of the salt will decrease in the presence of common ions. We can again use our standard equilibrium techniques of starting with the equation for CaF_2 dissolution, setting up a table of initial and equilibrium concentrations, and using the K_{sp} expression to determine the concentration of the ion that comes only from CaF_2.

Solve: (a) In this instance the initial concentration of Ca^{2+} is 0.010 M because of the dissolved $Ca(NO_3)_2$:

	$CaF_2(s)$	$\rightleftharpoons$	$Ca^{2+}(aq)$	+	$2\,F^-(aq)$
Initial	—		0.010 M		0
Change	—		$+x\ M$		$+2x\ M$
Equilibrium	—		$(0.010 + x)\ M$		$2x\ M$

Substituting into the solubility-product expression gives

$$K_{sp} = 3.9 \times 10^{-11} = [Ca^{2+}][F^-]^2 = (0.010 + x)(2x)^2$$

This would be a messy problem to solve exactly, but fortunately it is possible to simplify matters greatly. Even without the common-ion effect, the solubility of CaF_2 is very small $(2.1 \times 10^{-4}\ M)$. Thus, we assume that the 0.010 M concentration of Ca^{2+} from $Ca(NO_3)_2$ is very much greater than the small additional concentration resulting from the solubility of CaF_2; that is, x is small compared to 0.010 M, and $0.010 + x \simeq 0.010$. We then have

$$3.9 \times 10^{-11} = (0.010)(2x)^2$$

$$x^2 = \frac{3.9 \times 10^{-11}}{4(0.010)} = 9.8 \times 10^{-10}$$

$$x = \sqrt{9.8 \times 10^{-10}} = 3.1 \times 10^{-5}\ M$$

The very small value for x validates the simplifying assumption we have made. Our calculation indicates that 3.1×10^{-5} mol of solid CaF_2 dissolves per liter of the 0.010 M $Ca(NO_3)_2$ solution.

(b) In this case the common ion is F^-, and at equilibrium we have

$$[Ca^{2+}] = x \quad \text{and} \quad [F^-] = 0.010 + 2x$$

Assuming that $2x$ is small compared to 0.010 M (that is, $0.010 + 2x \simeq 0.010$), we have

$$3.9 \times 10^{-11} = x(0.010)^2$$

$$x = \frac{3.9 \times 10^{-11}}{(0.010)^2} = 3.9 \times 10^{-7}\ M$$

Thus, 3.9×10^{-7} mol of solid CaF_2 should dissolve per liter of 0.010 M NaF solution.

Comment: The molar solubility of CaF_2 in pure water is $2.1 \times 10^{-4}\ M$ (Sample Exercise 17.11). By comparison, our calculations above show that the solubility of CaF_2 in the presence of 0.010 M Ca^{2+} is $3.1 \times 10^{-5}\ M$, and in the presence of 0.010 M F^- ion it is $3.9 \times 10^{-7}\ M$. Thus, the addition of either Ca^{2+} or F^- to a solution of CaF_2 decreases the solubility. However, the effect of F^- on the solubility is more pronounced than that of Ca^{2+} because $[F^-]$ appears to the second power in the K_{sp} expression for CaF_2, whereas Ca^{2+} appears to the first power.

■■■ **PRACTICE EXERCISE**

The value for K_{sp} for manganese(II) hydroxide, $Mn(OH)_2$, is 1.6×10^{-13}. Calculate the molar solubility of $Mn(OH)_2$ in a solution that contains 0.020 M NaOH.
Answer: $4.0 \times 10^{-10}\ M$

Solubility and pH

The pH of a solution will affect the solubility of any substance whose anion is basic. Consider $Mg(OH)_2$, for example, for which the solubility equilibrium is

$$Mg(OH)_2(s) \rightleftharpoons Mg^{2+}(aq) + 2\,OH^-(aq) \quad K_{sp} = 1.8 \times 10^{-11} \quad [17.17]$$

17.107 Excess $Ca(OH)_2$ is shaken with water to produce a saturated solution. The solution is filtered, and a 50.00-mL sample titrated with HCl requires 11.23 mL of 0.0983 M HCl to reach the end point. Calculate K_{sp} for $Ca(OH)_2$. Compare your result with that in Appendix D. Do you think the solution was kept at 25 °C?

17.108 The osmotic pressure of a saturated solution of strontium sulfate at 25 °C is 21 torr. What is the solubility product of this salt at 25 °C?

17.109 A concentration of 10–100 parts per billion (by mass) of Ag^+ is an effective disinfectant in swimming pools. However, if the concentration exceeds this range, the Ag^+ can cause adverse health effects. One way to maintain an appropriate concentration of Ag^+ is to add a slightly soluble salt to the pool. Using K_{sp} values from Appendix D, calculate the equilibrium concentration of Ag^+ in parts per billion that would exist in equilibrium with **(a)** AgCl, **(b)** AgBr, **(c)** AgI.

[17.110] Fluoridation of drinking water is employed in many places to aid in the prevention of tooth decay. Typically the F^- ion concentration is adjusted to about 1 ppb. Some water supplies are also "hard"; that is, they contain certain cations such as Ca^{2+} that interfere with the action of soap. Consider a case where the concentration of Ca^{2+} is 8 ppb. Could a precipitate of CaF_2 form under these conditions? (Make any necessary approximations.)

18 CHEMISTRY OF THE ENVIRONMENT

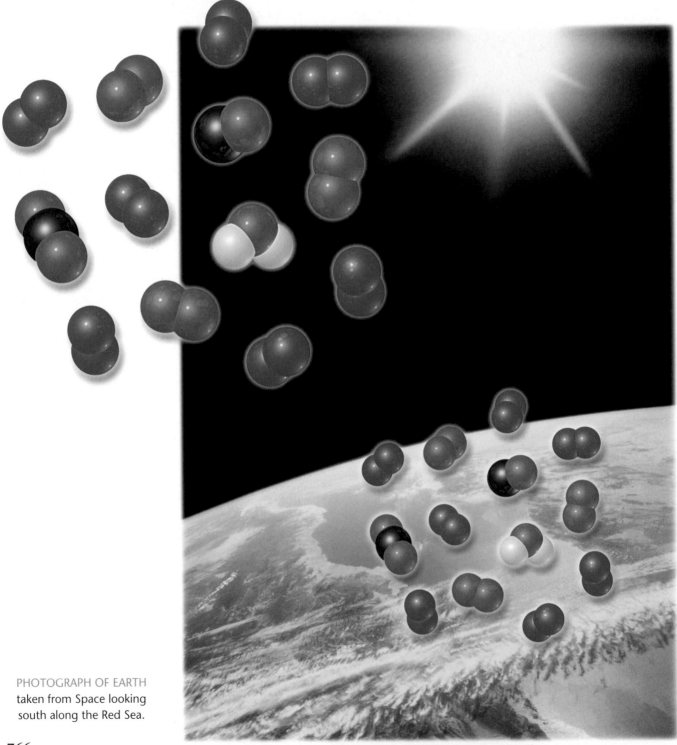

PHOTOGRAPH OF EARTH
taken from Space looking
south along the Red Sea.

What is the enthalpy change for the overall reaction that results from these two steps?

18.75 The main reason that distillation is a costly method for purifying water is the high energy required to heat and vaporize water. **(a)** Using the density, specific heat, and heat of vaporization of water from Appendix B, calculate the amount of energy required to vaporize 1.00 gal of water beginning with water at 20 °C. **(b)** If the energy is provided by electricity costing $0.085/kWh, calculate its cost. **(c)** If distilled water sells in a grocery store for $1.26 per gal, what percentage of the sales price is represented by the cost of the energy?

[18.76] A reaction that contributes to the depletion of ozone in the stratosphere is the direct reaction of oxygen atoms with ozone:

$$O(g) + O_3(g) \longrightarrow 2\,O_2(g)$$

At 298 K the rate constant for this reaction is $4.8 \times 10^5\,M^{-1}\,s^{-1}$. **(a)** Based on the units of the rate constant, write the likely rate law for this reaction. **(b)** Would you expect this reaction to occur via a single elementary process? Explain why or why not. **(c)** From the magnitude of the rate constant, would you expect the activation energy of this reaction to be large or small? Explain. **(d)** Use ΔH_f° values from Appendix C to estimate the enthalpy change for this reaction. Would this reaction raise or lower the temperature of the stratosphere?

18.77 Nitrogen dioxide (NO_2) is the only important gaseous species in the lower atmosphere that absorbs visible light. **(a)** Write the Lewis structure(s) for NO_2. **(b)** How does this structure account for the fact that NO_2 dimerizes to form N_2O_4? Based on what you can find about this dimerization reaction in the text, would you expect to find the NO_2 that forms in an urban environment to be in the form of dimer? Explain. **(c)** What would you expect as products, if any, for the reaction of NO_2 with CO? **(d)** Would you expect NO_2 generated in an urban environment to migrate to the stratosphere? Explain.

18.78 The following data was collected for the destruction of O_3 by H ($O_3 + H \rightarrow O_2 + OH$) at very low concentrations:

Experiment	$[O_3]$, M	$[H]$, M	Initial Rate, M/s
1	5.17×10^{-33}	3.22×10^{-26}	1.88×10^{-14}
2	2.59×10^{-33}	3.25×10^{-26}	9.44×10^{-15}
3	5.19×10^{-33}	6.46×10^{-26}	3.77×10^{-14}

(a) Write the rate law for the reaction.
(b) Calculate the rate constant.

18.79 The degradation of CF_3CH_2F (an HFC) by OH radicals in the troposphere is first order in each reactant and has a rate constant of $k = 1.6 \times 10^8\,M^{-1}\,s^{-1}$ at 4 °C. If the tropospheric concentrations of OH and CF_3CH_2F are 8.1×10^5 and 6.3×10^8 molecules cm^{-3}, respectively, what is the rate of reaction at this temperature in M/s?

[18.80] The Henry's law constant for CO_2 in water at 25 °C is $3.1 \times 10^{-2}\,M\,atm^{-1}$. **(a)** What is the solubility of CO_2 in water at this temperature if the solution is in contact with air at normal atmospheric pressure? **(b)** Assume that all of this CO_2 is in the form of H_2CO_3 produced by the reaction between CO_2 and H_2O:

$$CO_2(aq) + H_2O(l) \longrightarrow H_2CO_3(aq)$$

What is the pH of this solution?

[18.81] If the pH of a 1.0-in. rainfall over 1500 mi^2 is 3.5, how many kilograms of H_2SO_4 are present, assuming that it is the only acid contributing to the pH?

[18.82] The precipitation of $Al(OH)_3$ ($K_{sp} = 1.3 \times 10^{-33}$) is sometimes used to purify water. **(a)** Estimate the pH at which precipitation of $Al(OH)_3$ will begin if 5.0 lb of $Al_2(SO_4)_3$ is added to 2000 gal of water. **(b)** Approximately how many pounds of CaO must be added to the water to achieve this pH?

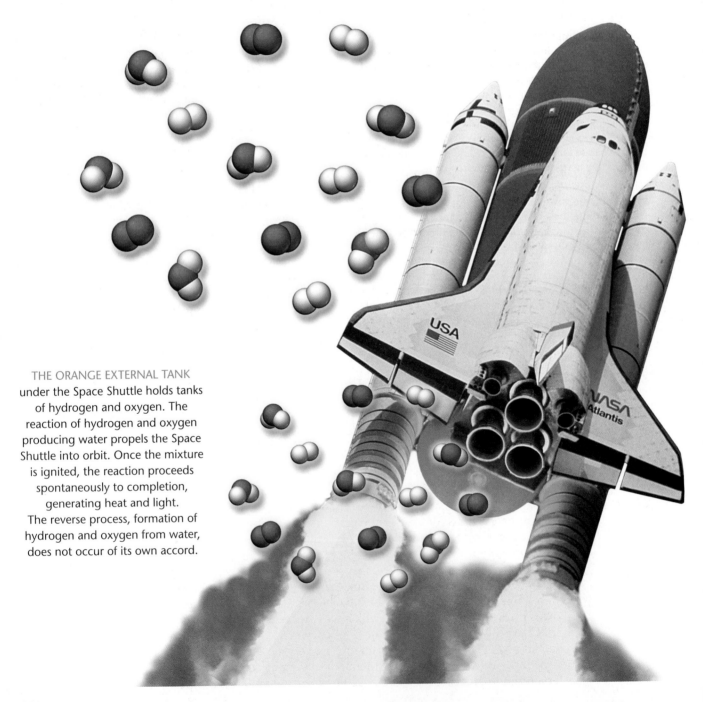

THE ORANGE EXTERNAL TANK under the Space Shuttle holds tanks of hydrogen and oxygen. The reaction of hydrogen and oxygen producing water propels the Space Shuttle into orbit. Once the mixture is ignited, the reaction proceeds spontaneously to completion, generating heat and light. The reverse process, formation of hydrogen and oxygen from water, does not occur of its own accord.

WHAT'S AHEAD

THE ENERGY REQUIRED TO PROPEL THE SPACE SHUTTLE INTO SPACE

is obtained from two solid-fuel booster rockets and a rocket engine that relies on the combustion of hydrogen and oxygen to form water. The hydrogen and oxygen are stored as liquids at very low temperatures in tanks mounted below the

Space Shuttle. As the hydrogen and oxygen vapors are ingnited, they react very rapidly and virtually completely, producing enormous quantities of water vapor and heat. Two of the most important questions chemists ask when designing and using chemical reactions are "How fast is the reaction?" and "How far does it proceed?" The first question is addressed by the study of chemical kinetics, which we discussed in Chapter 14. The second question involves the equilibrium constant, which was the focus of Chapter 15.

In Chapter 14 we learned that the rates of chemical reactions are controlled largely by a factor related to energy, namely the activation energy of the reaction. ∞ (Section 14.5) In general, the lower the activation energy, the faster a reaction proceeds. In Chapter 15 we saw that equilibrium depends on the rates of the forward and reverse reactions: Equilibrium is reached when the opposing reactions occur at equal rates. ∞ (Section 15.1) Because reaction rates are closely tied to energy, it is logical that equilibrium also depends in some way on energy.

In this chapter we will explore the connection between energy and the extent of a reaction. Doing so requires us to take a deeper look at *chemical thermodynamics*, the area of chemistry that deals with energy relationships. We first encountered thermodynamics in Chapter 5, where we discussed the nature of energy, the first law of thermodynamics, and the concept of enthalpy. Recall that the enthalpy change is the heat transferred between the system and its surroundings during a constant-pressure process. ∞ (Section 5.3)

Now we will see that reactions involve not only changes in enthalpy but also changes in *entropy*—another important thermodynamic quantity. Our discussion of entropy will lead us to the second law of thermodynamics, which provides insight into why physical and chemical changes tend to favor one direction over another. We drop a brick, for example, and it falls to the ground. We do not expect bricks to spontaneously rise from the ground to our outstretched hand. We light a candle, and it burns down. We do not expect a half-consumed candle to regenerate itself spontaneously, even if we have kept all the gases produced when the candle burned. Thermodynamics helps us understand the significance of this directional character of processes, whether they are exothermic or endothermic.

19.1 SPONTANEOUS PROCESSES

The first law of thermodynamics states that *energy is conserved.* ∞ (Section 5.2) In other words, energy is neither created nor destroyed in any process, whether it is the falling of a brick, the burning of a candle, or the melting of an ice cube. Energy can be transferred between a system and the surroundings or can be converted from one form to another, but the total energy remains constant. We expressed the first law of thermodynamics mathematically as $\Delta E = q + w$, where ΔE is the change in the internal energy of a system, q is the heat absorbed by the system from the surroundings, and w is the work done on the system by the surroundings.

The first law helps us balance the books, so to speak, on the heat transferred between a system and its surroundings and the work done by a particular process or reaction. But the first law does not address another important feature of reactions—the extent to which they occur. As we noted in the introduction, our experience tells us that physical and chemical processes have a directional character. For instance, sodium metal and chlorine gas combine readily to form sodium chloride, which we also know as table salt. We never find table salt decomposing of its own accord to form sodium and chlorine. (Have you ever smelled chlorine gas in the kitchen or seen sodium metal on your table salt?) In both processes—the formation of sodium chloride from sodium and chlorine and the decomposition of sodium chloride into sodium and chlorine—energy is conserved, as it must be according to the first law of thermodynamics. Yet one process occurs, and the other does not. A process that occurs of its own accord without any ongoing outside intervention is said to be spontaneous. A **spontaneous process** is one that proceeds on its own without any outside assistance.

A spontaneous process occurs in a definite direction. Imagine you were to see a video clip in which a brick rises from the ground. You would conclude that the video is running in reverse—bricks do not magically rise from the ground! A brick falling is a spontaneous process, whereas the reverse process is *nonspontaneous*.

A gas will expand into a vacuum as shown in Figure 19.1 ◄, but the process will never reverse itself. The expansion of the gas is spontaneous. Likewise, a nail left out in the weather will rust (Figure 19.2►). In this process the iron in the nail reacts with oxygen from the air to form an iron oxide. We would never expect the rusty nail to reverse this process and become shiny. The rusting process

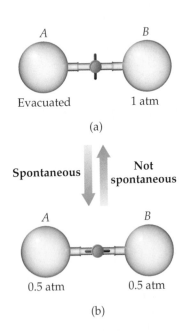

▲ Figure 19.1 **Spontaneous expansion of an ideal gas into an evacuated space.** In (a) flask *B* holds an ideal gas at 1 atm pressure and flask *A* is evacuated. In (b) the stopcock connecting the flasks has been opened. The ideal gas expands to occupy both flasks *A* and *B* at a pressure of 0.5 atm. The reverse process—all the gas molecules moving back into flask *B*— is not spontaneous.

is spontaneous, whereas the reverse process is nonspontaneous. There are countless other examples we could cite that illustrate the same idea: *Processes that are spontaneous in one direction are nonspontaneous in the opposite direction.*

Experimental conditions, such as temperature and pressure, are often important in determining whether a process is spontaneous. Consider, for example, the melting of ice. When the temperature of the surroundings is above 0 °C at ordinary atmospheric pressures, ice melts spontaneously and the reverse process—liquid water turning into ice—is not spontaneous. However, when the surroundings are below 0 °C, the opposite is true. Liquid water converts into ice spontaneously, and the conversion of ice into water is *not* spontaneous (Figure 19.3▼).

What happens at $T = 0$ °C, the normal melting point of water, when the flask of Figure 19.3 contains both water and ice? At the normal melting point of a substance, the solid and liquid phases are in equilibrium. ∞ (Section 11.5) At this temperature the two phases are interconverting at the same rate and there is no preferred direction for the process.

It is important to realize that the fact that a process is spontaneous does not necessarily mean that it will occur at an observable rate. A chemical reaction is spontaneous if it occurs on its own accord, regardless of its speed. A spontaneous reaction can be very fast, as in the case of acid–base neutralization, or very slow, as in the rusting of iron. Thermodynamics can tell us the *direction* and *extent* of a reaction but tells us nothing about the *speed* of the reaction.

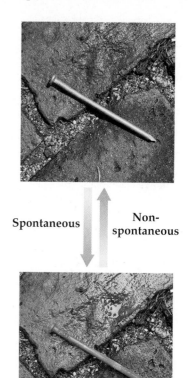

Spontaneous   Non-
                  spontaneous

▲ Figure 19.2 **A spontaneous process.** Elemental iron in the shiny nail in the top photograph spontaneously combines with H_2O and O_2 in the surrounding air to form a layer of rust—Fe_2O_3—on the nail surface.

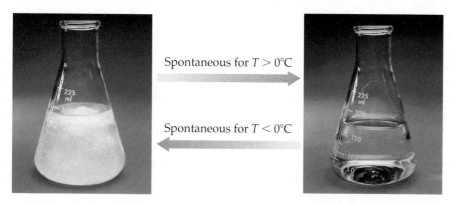

Spontaneous for $T > 0$°C

Spontaneous for $T < 0$°C

▲ Figure 19.3 **Spontaneity can depend on the temperature.** At $T > 0$ °C ice melts spontaneously to liquid water. At $T < 0$ °C the reverse process, water freezing to ice, is spontaneous. At $T = 0$ °C the two states are in equilibrium.

■ SAMPLE EXERCISE 19.1 | Identifying Spontaneous Processes

Predict whether the following processes are spontaneous as described, spontaneous in the reverse direction, or in equilibrium: **(a)** When a piece of metal heated to 150 °C is added to water at 40 °C, the water gets hotter. **(b)** Water at room temperature decomposes into $H_2(g)$ and $O_2(g)$, **(c)** Benzene vapor, $C_6H_6(g)$, at a pressure of 1 atm condenses to liquid benzene at the normal boiling point of benzene, 80.1 °C.

SOLUTION

Analyze: We are asked to judge whether each process will proceed spontaneously in the direction indicated, in the reverse direction, or in neither direction.

Plan: We need to think about whether each process is consistent with our experience about the natural direction of events or whether we expect the reverse process to occur.

Solve: (a) This process is spontaneous. Whenever two objects at different temperatures are brought into contact, heat is transferred from the hotter object to the colder one. Thus, heat is transferred from the hot metal to the cooler water. The final temperature, after the metal and water achieve the same temperature (thermal equilibrium), will be somewhere between the initial temperatures of the metal and the water. **(b)** Experience tells us that this process is not spontaneous—we certainly have never seen hydrogen and oxygen gases spontaneously bubbling up out of water! Rather, the *reverse* process—the reaction of H_2 and O_2 to form H_2O—is spontaneous. **(c)** By definition, the normal boiling point is the temperature at which a vapor at 1 atm is in equilibrium with its liquid. Thus, this is an equilibrium situation. If the temperature were below 80.1 °C, condensation would be spontaneous.

■ PRACTICE EXERCISE

Under 1 atm pressure $CO_2(s)$ sublimes at −78 °C. Is the transformation of $CO_2(s)$ to $CO_2(g)$ a spontaneous process at −100 °C and 1 atm pressure?
Answer: No, the reverse process is spontaneous at this temperature.

Seeking a Criterion for Spontaneity

A marble rolling down an incline or a brick falling from your hand loses energy. The loss of energy is a common feature of spontaneous change in mechanical systems. During the 1870s Marcellin Bertholet (1827–1907), a famous chemist of that era, suggested that the direction of spontaneous changes in chemical systems was also determined by the loss of energy. He proposed that all spontaneous chemical and physical changes were exothermic. It takes only a few moments, however, to find exceptions to this generalization. For example, the melting of ice at room temperature is spontaneous even though melting is an endothermic process. Similarly, many spontaneous solution processes, such as the dissolving of NH_4NO_3, are endothermic, as we discovered in Section 13.1. We conclude therefore that, although the majority of spontaneous reactions are exothermic, there are spontaneous endothermic ones as well. Clearly, some other factor must be at work in determining the natural direction of processes. What is this factor?

To understand why certain processes are spontaneous, we need to consider more closely the ways in which the state of a system can change. Recall that quantities such as temperature, internal energy, and enthalpy are *state functions*, properties that define a state and do not depend on how we reach that state. ∞ (Section 5.2) The heat transferred between a system and its surroundings, q, and the work done by or on the system, w, are *not* state functions. The values of q and w depend on the specific path taken from one state to another. One of the keys to understanding spontaneity is distinguishing between reversible and irreversible paths between states.

▲ GIVE IT SOME THOUGHT

If a process is nonspontaneous, does that mean the process cannot occur under any circumstances?

Reversible and Irreversible Processes

In 1824 a 28-year-old French engineer named Sadi Carnot (1796–1832) published an analysis of the factors that determine how efficiently a steam engine can convert heat to work. Carnot considered what an ideal engine, one with the highest possible efficiency, would be like. He observed that it is impossible to convert the energy content of a fuel completely to work because a significant amount of heat is always lost to the surroundings. Carnot's analysis gave insight into how to build better, more efficient engines, and it was one of the earliest studies in what has developed into the discipline of thermodynamics.

About 40 years later, Rudolph Clausius (1822–1888), a German physicist, extended Carnot's work in an important way. Clausius concluded that a special significance could be ascribed to the ratio of the heat delivered to an ideal engine and the temperature at which it is delivered, q/T. He was so convinced of the importance of this ratio that he gave it a special name, *entropy*. He deliberately selected the name to sound like energy to emphasize his belief that the importance of entropy was comparable to that of energy.

An ideal engine, one with the maximum efficiency, operates under an ideal set of conditions in which all the processes are reversible. In a **reversible process**, a system is changed in such a way that the system and surroundings can be restored to their original state by *exactly* reversing the change. In other words, we can completely restore the system to its original condition with no net change to either the system or its surroundings. An **irreversible process** is one that cannot simply be reversed to restore the system and its surroundings to their original states. What Carnot discovered is that the amount of work we can extract from any spontaneous process depends on the manner in which the process is carried out. *A reversible change produces the maximum amount of work that can be achieved by the system on the surroundings* ($w_{rev} = w_{max}$).

GIVE IT SOME THOUGHT

If you evaporate water and then condense it, have you necessarily performed a reversible process?

Let's examine some examples of reversible and irreversible processes. When two objects at different temperatures are in contact, heat will flow spontaneously from the hotter object to the colder one. Because it is impossible to make heat flow in the opposite direction, the flow of heat is irreversible. Given these facts, can we imagine any conditions under which heat transfer can be made reversible? Consider two objects or a system and its surroundings that are at essentially the same temperature, with just an infinitesimal difference (an extremely small temperature difference, ΔT) to make heat flow in the desired direction (Figure 19.4▶). We can then reverse the direction of heat flow by making an infinitesimal change of temperature in the opposite direction. *Reversible processes are those that reverse direction whenever an infinitesimal change is made in some property of the system.*

Now consider another example, the expansion of an ideal gas at constant temperature. A constant-temperature process such as this is said to be **isothermal**. To keep the example simple, consider the gas in the cylinder-and-piston arrangement shown in Figure 19.5▼. When the partition is removed, the gas expands spontaneously to fill the evacuated space. Because the gas is expanding into a vacuum with no external pressure, it does no *P-V* work on the surroundings ($w = 0$). ∞ (Section 5.3) We can use the piston to compress the gas back to its original state, but doing so requires that the surroundings do work on the system ($w > 0$). That is, reversing the process has produced a change in the surroundings as energy is used to do work on the system. The fact that the system and the surroundings are not both returned to their original conditions indicates that the process is irreversible.

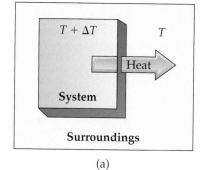

(a)

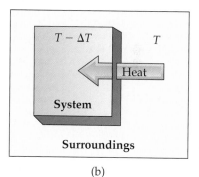

(b)

▲ **Figure 19.4 Reversible flow of heat.** Heat can flow reversibly between a system and its surroundings if the two have only an infinitesimally small difference in temperature, ΔT. The direction of heat flow can be changed by increasing or decreasing the temperature of the system by ΔT. (a) Increasing the temperature of the system by ΔT causes heat to flow from the system to the surroundings. (b) Decreasing the temperature of the system by ΔT causes heat to flow from the surroundings into the system.

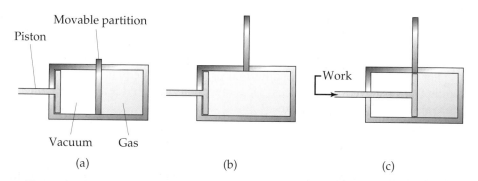

(a)   (b)   (c)

▲ **Figure 19.5 An irreversible process.** Restoring the system to its original state after an irreversible process changes the surroundings. In (a) the gas is confined to the right half of the cylinder by a partition. When the partition is removed (b), the gas spontaneously (irreversibly) expands to fill the whole cylinder. No work is done by the system during this expansion. In (c) we can use the piston to compress the gas back to its original state. Doing so requires that the surroundings do work on the system, which changes the surroundings forever.

What might a reversible, isothermal expansion of an ideal gas be like? It will occur only if the external pressure acting on the piston exactly balances the pressure exerted by the gas. Under these conditions, the piston will not move unless the external pressure is reduced infinitely slowly, allowing the pressure of the confined gas to readjust to maintain a balance in the two pressures. This gradual, infinitely slow process in which the external pressure and internal pressure are always in equilibrium is reversible. If we reverse the process and compress the gas in the same infinitely slow manner, we can return the gas to its original volume. The complete cycle of expansion and compression in this hypothetical process, moreover, is accomplished without any net change to the surroundings.

Because real processes can at best only approximate the slow, ever-in-equilibrium change associated with reversible processes, all real processes are irreversible. Further, the reverse of any spontaneous process is a nonspontaneous process. A nonspontaneous process can occur only if the surroundings do work on the system. Thus, *any spontaneous process is irreversible*. Even if we return the system to the original condition, the surroundings will have changed.

19.2 ENTROPY AND THE SECOND LAW OF THERMODYNAMICS

We are now closer to understanding spontaneity because we know that any spontaneous process is irreversible. But how can we use this idea to make predictions about the spontaneity of an unfamiliar process? Understanding spontaneity requires us to examine the thermodynamic quantity called **entropy**. Entropy has been variously associated with the extent of *randomness* in a system or with the extent to which energy is distributed or dispersed among the various motions of the molecules of the system. In fact, entropy is a multifaceted concept whose interpretations are not so quickly summarized by a simple definition. In this section we consider how we can relate entropy changes to heat transfer and temperature. Our analysis will bring us to a profound statement about spontaneity that we call the second law of thermodynamics. In Section 19.3 we examine the molecular significance of entropy.

Entropy Change

The entropy, S, of a system is a state function just like the internal energy, E, and enthalpy, H. As with these other quantities, the value of S is a characteristic of the state of a system. ∞ (Section 5.2) Thus, the change in entropy, ΔS, in a system depends only on the initial and final states of the system and not on the path taken from one state to the other:

$$\Delta S = S_{\text{final}} - S_{\text{initial}} \qquad [19.1]$$

For the special case of an isothermal process, ΔS is equal to the heat that would be transferred if the process were reversible, q_{rev}, divided by the temperature at which the process occurs:

$$\Delta S = \frac{q_{\text{rev}}}{T} \qquad (\text{constant } T) \qquad [19.2]$$

Because S is a state function, we can use Equation 19.2 to calculate ΔS for *any* isothermal process, not just those that are reversible. If a change between two states is irreversible, we calculate ΔS by using a reversible path between the states.

How do we reconcile the fact that S is a state function but that ΔS depends on q, which is not a state function?

ΔS for Phase Changes

The melting of a substance at its melting point and the vaporization of a substance at its boiling point are isothermal processes. Consider the melting of ice. At 1 atm pressure, ice and liquid water are in equilibrium with each other at 0 °C. Imagine that we melt one mole of ice at 0 °C, 1 atm to form one mole of liquid water at 0 °C, 1 atm. We can achieve this change by adding a certain amount of heat to the system from the surroundings: $q = \Delta H_{fusion}$. Now imagine that we carry out the change by adding the heat infinitely slowly, raising the temperature of the surroundings only infinitesimally above 0 °C. When we make the change in this fashion, the process is reversible. We can reverse the process simply by infinitely slowly removing the same amount of heat, ΔH_{fusion}, from the system, using immediate surroundings that are infinitesimally below 0 °C. Thus, $q_{rev} = \Delta H_{fusion}$ and $T = 0$ °C = 273 K.

The enthalpy of fusion for H_2O is $\Delta H_{fusion} = 6.01$ kJ/mol. (The melting is an endothermic process, and so the sign of ΔH is positive.) Thus, we can use Equation 19.2 to calculate ΔS_{fusion} for melting one mole of ice at 273 K:

$$\Delta S_{fusion} = \frac{q_{rev}}{T} = \frac{\Delta H_{fusion}}{T} = \frac{(1 \text{ mol})(6.01 \times 10^3 \text{ J/mol})}{273 \text{ K}} = 22.0 \frac{\text{J}}{\text{K}}$$

Notice that the units for ΔS, J/K, are energy divided by absolute temperature, as we expect from Equation 19.2.

■ **SAMPLE EXERCISE 19.2** | Calculating ΔS for a Phase Change

The element mercury, Hg, is a silvery liquid at room temperature. The normal freezing point of mercury is −38.9 °C, and its molar enthalpy of fusion is $\Delta H_{fusion} = 2.29$ kJ/mol. What is the entropy change of the system when 50.0 g of Hg(l) freezes at the normal freezing point?

SOLUTION

Analyze: We first recognize that freezing is an *exothermic* process; heat is transferred from the system to the surroundings when a liquid freezes ($q < 0$). The enthalpy of fusion is ΔH for the melting process. Because freezing is the reverse of melting, the enthalpy change that accompanies the freezing of 1 mol of Hg is $-\Delta H_{fusion} = -2.29$ kJ/mol.

Plan: We can use $-\Delta H_{fusion}$ and the atomic weight of Hg to calculate q for freezing 50.0 g of Hg:

$$q = (50.0 \text{ g Hg})\left(\frac{1 \text{ mol Hg}}{200.59 \text{ g Hg}}\right)\left(\frac{-2.29 \text{ kJ}}{1 \text{ mol Hg}}\right)\left(\frac{1000 \text{ J}}{1 \text{ kJ}}\right) = -571 \text{ J}$$

We can use this value of q as q_{rev} in Equation 19.2. We must first, however, convert the temperature to K:

$$-38.9 \text{ °C} = (-38.9 + 273.15) \text{ K} = 234.3 \text{ K}$$

Solve: We can now calculate the value of ΔS_{sys}

$$\Delta S_{sys} = \frac{q_{rev}}{T} = \frac{-571 \text{ J}}{234.3 \text{ K}} = -2.44 \text{ J/K}$$

Check: The entropy change is negative because heat flows from the system, making q_{rev} negative.

Comment: The procedure we have used here can be used to calculate ΔS for other isothermal phase changes, such as the vaporization of a liquid at its boiling point.

■ **PRACTICE EXERCISE**

The normal boiling point of ethanol, C_2H_5OH, is 78.3 °C, and its molar enthalpy of vaporization is 38.56 kJ/mol. What is the change in entropy in the system when 68.3 g of $C_2H_5OH(g)$ at 1 atm condenses to liquid at the normal boiling point?
Answer: −163 J/K

A Closer Look   THE ENTROPY CHANGE WHEN A GAS EXPANDS ISOTHERMALLY

In general, we will see that if a system becomes more spread out, or more random, the system's entropy increases. Thus, we expect the spontaneous expansion of a gas to result in an increase in entropy. To illustrate how the entropy change associated with an expanding gas can be calculated, consider the expansion of an ideal gas that is initially constrained by a piston, as in Figure 19.5(c). If the gas undergoes a reversible isothermal expansion, the work done on the surroundings by the moving piston can be calculated with the aid of calculus:

$$w_{rev} = -nRT \ln \frac{V_2}{V_1}$$

In this equation, n is the number of moles of gas, R is the gas constant, T is the absolute temperature, V_1 is the initial volume, and V_2 is the final volume. Notice that if $V_2 > V_1$, as it must be in our expansion, then $w_{rev} < 0$, meaning that the expanding gas does work on the surroundings.

One of the characteristics of an ideal gas is that its internal energy depends only on temperature, not on pressure. Thus, when an ideal gas expands at a constant temperature, $\Delta E = 0$. Because $\Delta E = q_{rev} + w_{rev} = 0$, we see that $q_{rev} = -w_{rev} = nRT \ln(V_2/V_1)$. Then, using Equation 19.2, we can calculate the entropy change in the system:

$$\Delta S_{sys} = \frac{q_{rev}}{T} = \frac{nRT \ln \dfrac{V_2}{V_1}}{T} = nR \ln \frac{V_2}{V_1} \qquad [19.3]$$

For 1.00 L of an ideal gas at 1.00 atm and 0 °C, we can calculate the number of moles, $n = 4.46 \times 10^{-2}$ mol. The gas constant, R, can be expressed in units of J/mol-K, 8.314 J/mol-K (Table 10.2). Thus, for the expansion of the gas from 1.00 L to 2.00 L, we have

$$\Delta S_{sys} = (4.46 \times 10^{-2} \text{ mol})\left(8.314 \frac{J}{\text{mol-K}}\right)\left(\ln \frac{2.00 \text{ L}}{1.00 \text{ L}}\right)$$

$$= 0.26 \text{ J/K}$$

In Section 19.3 we will see that this increase in entropy is a measure of the increased randomness of the molecules because of the expansion.

Related Exercises: 19.27 and 19.28

The Second Law of Thermodynamics

The key idea of the first law of thermodynamics is that energy is conserved in any process. Thus, the quantity of energy lost by a system equals the quantity gained by its surroundings. ∞ (Section 5.1) We will see, however, that entropy is different because it actually increases in any spontaneous process. Thus, the sum of the entropy change of the system and surroundings for any spontaneous process is always greater than zero. Entropy change is like a signpost indicating whether a process is spontaneous. Let's illustrate this generalization by again considering the melting of ice, designating the ice and water as our system.

Let's calculate the entropy change of the system and the entropy change of the surroundings when a mole of ice (a piece roughly the size of an ordinary ice cube) melts in the palm of your hand. The process is not reversible because the system and surroundings are at different temperatures. Nevertheless, because ΔS is a state function, the entropy change of the system is the same regardless of whether the process is reversible or irreversible. We calculated the entropy change of the system just before Sample Exercise 19.2:

$$\Delta S_{sys} = \frac{q_{rev}}{T} = \frac{(1 \text{mol})(6.01 \times 10^3 \text{ J/mol})}{273 \text{ K}} = 22.0 \frac{J}{K}$$

The surroundings immediately in contact with the ice are your hand, which we will assume is at body temperature, 37 °C = 310 K. The heat lost by your hand is equal in magnitude to the heat gained by the ice but has the opposite sign, -6.01×10^3 J/mol. Hence the entropy change of the surroundings is

$$\Delta S_{surr} = \frac{q_{rev}}{T} = \frac{(1 \text{ mol})(-6.01 \times 10^3 \text{ J/mol})}{310 \text{ K}} = -19.4 \frac{J}{K}$$

Thus, the total entropy change is positive:

$$\Delta S_{total} = \Delta S_{sys} + \Delta S_{surr} = \left(22.0 \frac{J}{K}\right) + \left(-19.4 \frac{J}{K}\right) = 2.6 \frac{J}{K}$$

Now imagine that we could take a "snapshot" of the positions and speeds of all of the molecules at a given instant. That particular set of 6×10^{23} positions and energies of the individual gas molecules is what we call a **microstate** of the thermodynamic system. A microstate is a single possible arrangement of the positions and kinetic energies of the gas molecules when the gas is in a specific thermodynamic state. We could envision continuing to take snapshots of our system to see other possible microstates. In fact, as you no doubt see, there would be such a staggeringly large number of microstates that taking individual snapshots of all of them is not feasible. Because we are examining such a large number of particles, however, we can use the tools of statistics and probability to determine the total number of microstates for the thermodynamic state. (That is where the *statistical* part of statistical thermodynamics comes in.) Each thermodynamic state has a characteristic number of microstates associated with it, and we will use the symbol W for that number.

The connection between the number of microstates of a system, W, and its entropy, S, is expressed in a beautifully simple equation developed by Boltzmann:

$$S = k \ln W \qquad [19.5]$$

In this equation, k is Boltzmann's constant, 1.38×10^{-23} J/K. Thus, *entropy is a measure of how many microstates are associated with a particular macroscopic state.* Equation 19.5 appears on Boltzmann's gravestone (Figure 19.7▶).

▲ Figure 19.7 **Ludwig Boltzmann's gravestone.** Boltzmann's gravestone in Vienna is inscribed with his famous relationship between the entropy of a state and the number of available microstates. (In Boltzmann's time, "log" was used to represent the natural logarithm.)

> ### GIVE IT SOME THOUGHT
>
> What is the entropy of a system that has only a single microstate?

The entropy change accompanying any process is

$$\Delta S = k \ln W_{\text{final}} - k \ln W_{\text{initial}} = k \ln \frac{W_{\text{final}}}{W_{\text{initial}}} \qquad [19.6]$$

Thus, any change in the system that leads to an increase in the number of microstates leads to a positive value of ΔS: *Entropy increases with the number of microstates of the system.*

Let's briefly consider two simple changes to our ideal-gas sample and see how the entropy changes in each case. First, suppose we increase the volume of the system, which is analogous to allowing the gas to expand isothermally. A greater volume means that there are a greater number of positions available to the gas atoms. Thus, there will be a greater number of microstates for the system after the increase in volume. The entropy therefore increases as the volume increases, as we saw in the "A Closer Look" box in Section 19.2. Second, suppose we keep the volume fixed but increase the temperature. How will this change affect the entropy of the system? Recall the distribution of molecular speeds presented in Figure 10.18. An increase in temperature increases the average (rms) speed of the molecules and broadens the distribution of speeds. Hence, the molecules have a greater number of possible kinetic energies, and the number of microstates will once again increase. The entropy of the system will therefore increase with increasing temperature.

If we consider real molecules instead of ideal-gas particles, we must also consider the different amounts of vibrational and rotational energies the molecules have in addition to their kinetic energies. A collection of real molecules therefore has a greater number of microstates available than does the same number of ideal-gas particles. In general, *the number of microstates available to a system increases with an increase in volume, an increase in temperature, or an increase in the number of molecules because any of these changes increases the possible positions and energies of the molecules of the system.*

A Closer Look   ENTROPY AND PROBABILITY

The game of poker is sometimes used as an analogy to explore the idea of the microstates associated with a particular state. There are about 2.6 million different five-card poker hands that can be dealt, and each of these hands can be viewed as a possible "microstate" for the hand dealt to any one player in a game. Table 19.1▼ shows two poker hands. The probability that a particular hand will contain five *specific* cards is the same regardless of which five cards are specified. Thus, there is an equal probability of dealing either of the hands shown in Table 19.1. However, the first hand, a royal flush (the ten through ace of a single suit), strikes us as much more highly ordered than the second hand, a "nothing." The reason for this is clear if we compare the number of five-card arrangements that correspond to a royal flush to the number corresponding to a nothing: only four hands (microstates) for a royal flush but more than 1.3 million for a nothing hand. The nothing state has a higher probability of being dealt from a shuffled deck than the royal-flush state because there are so many more arrangements of cards that correspond to the nothing state. In other words, the value of W in Boltzmann's equation (Equation 19.5) is much greater for a nothing than for a royal flush. This example teaches us that there is a connection between probability and entropy.

The entropy of any system has a natural tendency to increase, because increased entropy represents a movement toward a state of higher probability. Let's use this reasoning to explain the isothermal expansion of a gas, such as that depicted in Figure 19.1. When the stopcock is opened, the gas molecules are less constrained, and there are more possible arrangements for them (more microstates) in the larger volume. The various microstates are depicted in a schematic way in Figure 19.8▼. In this figure, we make no attempt to describe the motion of the particles, focusing instead only on their locations. The spreading of the molecules over the larger volume represents movement to the more probable state.

When we use the terms randomness and disorder to describe entropy, we have to be careful not to carry an aesthetic sense of what we mean. What we must remember is that the fundamental connection to entropy is not tied directly with randomness, disorder, or energy dispersal, but with the number of available microstates.

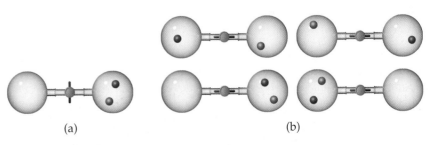

(a)   (b)

▲ **Figure 19.8 Probability and the locations of gas molecules.** The two molecules are colored red and blue to keep track of them. (a) Before the stopcock is opened, both molecules are in the right-hand flask. (b) After the stopcock is opened, there are four possible arrangements of the two molecules. Only one of the four arrangements corresponds to both molecules being in the right-hand flask. The greater number of possible arrangements corresponds to greater disorder in the system. In general, the probability that the molecules will stay in the original flask is $\left(\frac{1}{2}\right)^n$, where n is the number of molecules.

TABLE 19.1 ■ A Comparison of the Number of Combinations that Can Lead to a Royal Flush and to a "Nothing" Hand in Poker		
Hand	**State**	**Number of Hands that Lead to This State**
	Royal flush	4
	"Nothing"	1,302,540

Chemists use several different ways to describe an increase in the number of microstates and therefore an increase in the entropy for a system. Each of these ways seeks to capture a sense of the increased freedom of motion that causes molecules to spread out if not restrained by physical barriers or chemical bonds.

Some say the increase in entropy represents an increase in the *randomness* or *disorder* of the system. Others liken an increase in entropy to an increased *dispersion (spreading out) of energy* because there is an increase in the number of ways the positions and energies of the molecules can be distributed throughout the system. Each of these descriptions (randomness, disorder, and energy dispersal) is conceptually helpful if applied correctly. Indeed, you will find it useful to keep these descriptions in mind as you evaluate entropy changes.

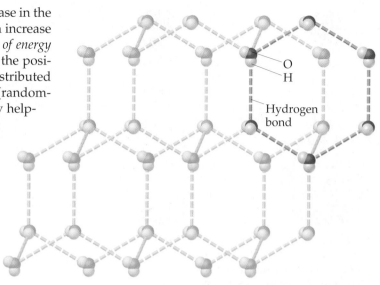

▲ Figure 19.9 **Structure of ice.** The intermolecular attractions in the three-dimensional lattice restrict the molecules to vibrational motion only.

Making Qualitative Predictions About ΔS

It is usually not difficult to construct a mental picture to estimate qualitatively how the entropy of a system changes during a simple process. In most instances, an increase in the number of microstates, and hence an increase in entropy, parallels an increase in

1. temperature
2. volume
3. number of independently moving particles

Thus, we can usually make qualitative predictions about entropy changes by focusing on these factors. For example, when water vaporizes, the molecules spread out into a larger volume. Because they occupy a larger space, there is an increase in their freedom of motion, giving rise to more accessible microstates and hence to an increase in entropy.

Consider the melting of ice. The rigid structure of the water molecules, shown in Figure 19.9 ▲, restricts motion to only tiny vibrations throughout the crystal. In contrast, the molecules in liquid water are free to move about with respect to one another (translation) and to tumble around (rotation) as well as vibrate. During melting, therefore, the number of accessible microstates increases and so does the entropy.

When an ionic solid, such as KCl, dissolves in water, a mixture of water and ions replaces the pure solid and pure water (Figure 19.10 ▼). The ions now move in a larger volume and possess more motional energy than in the rigid solid. We have to be careful, however, because water molecules are held around the ions as water of hydration. ∞ (Section 13.1) These water molecules have less motional energy than before because they are now confined to the immediate environment of the ions. The greater the charge of an ion, the greater are the ion–dipole attractions that hold the ion and the water together, thereby restricting motions. Thus, even though the solution process is normally accompanied by a net increase in entropy, the dissolving of salts with highly charged ions can result in a net *decrease* in entropy.

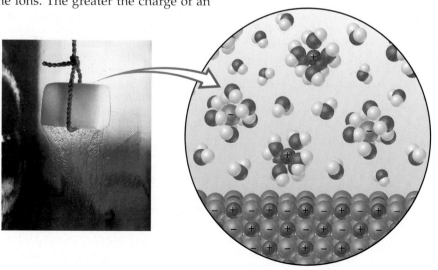

▶ Figure 19.10 **Dissolving an ionic solid in water.** The ions become more spread out and random in their motions, but the water molecules that hydrate the ions become less random.

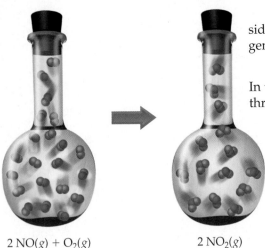

$$2\,NO(g) + O_2(g) \qquad\qquad 2\,NO_2(g)$$

▲ **Figure 19.11 Entropy change for a reaction.** A decrease in the number of gaseous molecules leads to a decrease in the entropy of the system. When the $NO(g)$ and $O_2(g)$ (left) react to form the $NO_2(g)$ (right), the number of gaseous molecules decreases. The atoms have fewer degrees of freedom because new N—O bonds form and the entropy decreases.

The same ideas apply to systems involving chemical reactions. Consider the reaction between nitric oxide gas and oxygen gas to form nitrogen dioxide gas:

$$2\,NO(g) + O_2(g) \longrightarrow 2\,NO_2(g) \qquad\qquad [19.7]$$

In this case the reaction results in a decrease in the number of molecules—three molecules of gaseous reactants form two molecules of gaseous products (Figure 19.11 ◀). The formation of new N—O bonds reduces the motions of the atoms in the system. The formation of new bonds decreases the *number of degrees of freedom*, or forms of motion, available to the atoms. That is, the atoms are less free to move in random fashion because of the formation of new bonds. The decrease in the number of molecules and the resultant decrease in motion result in fewer accessible microstates and therefore a decrease in the entropy of the system.

In summary, we generally expect the entropy of the system to increase for processes in which

1. Gases are formed from either solids or liquids.
2. Liquids or solutions are formed from solids.
3. The number of gas molecules increases during a chemical reaction.

■ SAMPLE EXERCISE 19.3 | Predicting the Sign of ΔS

Predict whether ΔS is positive or negative for each of the following processes, assuming each occurs at constant temperature:

(a) $H_2O(l) \longrightarrow H_2O(g)$
(b) $Ag^+(aq) + Cl^-(aq) \longrightarrow AgCl(s)$
(c) $4\,Fe(s) + 3\,O_2(g) \longrightarrow 2\,Fe_2O_3(s)$
(d) $N_2(g) + O_2(g) \longrightarrow 2\,NO(g)$

SOLUTION

Analyze: We are given four equations and asked to predict the sign of ΔS for each chemical reaction.

Plan: The sign of ΔS will be positive if there is an increase in temperature, an increase in the volume in which the molecules move, or an increase in the number of gas particles in the reaction. The question states that the temperature is constant. Thus, we need to evaluate each equation with the other two factors in mind.

Solve:

(a) The evaporation of a liquid is accompanied by a large increase in volume. One mole of water (18 g) occupies about 18 mL as a liquid and if it could exist as a gas at STP it would occupy 22.4 L. Because the molecules are distributed throughout a much larger volume in the gaseous state than in the liquid state, an increase in motional freedom accompanies vaporization. Therefore, ΔS is positive.

(b) In this process the ions, which are free to move throughout the volume of the solution, form a solid in which they are confined to a smaller volume and restricted to more highly constrained positions. Thus, ΔS is negative.

(c) The particles of a solid are confined to specific locations and have fewer ways to move (fewer microstates) than do the molecules of a gas. Because O_2 gas is converted into part of the solid product Fe_2O_3, ΔS is negative.

(d) The number of moles of gases is the same on both sides of the equation, and so the entropy change will be small. The sign of ΔS is impossible to predict based on our discussions thus far, but we can predict that ΔS will be close to zero.

■ PRACTICE EXERCISE

Indicate whether each of the following processes produces an increase or decrease in the entropy of the system:

(a) $CO_2(s) \longrightarrow CO_2(g)$
(b) $CaO(s) + CO_2(g) \longrightarrow CaCO_3(s)$
(c) $HCl(g) + NH_3(g) \longrightarrow NH_4Cl(s)$
(d) $2\,SO_2(g) + O_2(g) \longrightarrow 2\,SO_3(g)$

Answers: **(a)** increase, **(b)** decrease, **(c)** decrease, **(d)** decrease

■ **SAMPLE EXERCISE 19.4** | **Predicting Which Sample of Matter Has the Higher Entropy**

Choose the sample of matter that has greater entropy in each pair, and explain your choice: **(a)** 1 mol of NaCl(s) or 1 mol of HCl(g) at 25 °C, **(b)** 2 mol of HCl(g) or 1 mol of HCl(g) at 25 °C, **(c)** 1 mol of HCl(g) or 1 mol of Ar(g) at 298 K.

SOLUTION

Analyze: We need to select the system in each pair that has the greater entropy.

Plan: To do this, we examine the state of the system and the complexity of the molecules it contains.

Solve: **(a)** Gaseous HCl has the higher entropy because gases have more available motions than solids. **(b)** The sample containing 2 mol of HCl has twice the number of molecules as the sample containing 1 mol. Thus, the 2-mol sample has twice the number of microstates and twice the entropy when they are at the same pressure. **(c)** The HCl sample has the higher entropy because the HCl molecule is capable of storing energy in more ways than is Ar. HCl molecules can rotate and vibrate; Ar atoms cannot.

■ **PRACTICE EXERCISE**

Choose the substance with the greater entropy in each case: **(a)** 1 mol of $H_2(g)$ at STP or 1 mol of $H_2(g)$ at 100 °C and 0.5 atm, **(b)** 1 mol of $H_2O(s)$ at 0 °C or 1 mol of $H_2O(l)$ at 25 °C, **(c)** 1 mol of $H_2(g)$ at STP or 1 mol of $SO_2(g)$ at STP, **(d)** 1 mol of $N_2O_4(g)$ at STP or 2 mol of $NO_2(g)$ at STP.
Answers: **(a)** 1 mol of $H_2(g)$ at 100 °C and 0.5 atm, **(b)** 1 mol of $H_2O(l)$ at 25 °C, **(c)** 1 mol of $SO_2(g)$ at STP, **(d)** 2 mol of $NO_2(g)$ at STP

Chemistry and Life   ENTROPY AND LIFE

The ginkgo leaf shown in Figure 19.12(a)▶ reveals beautiful patterns of form and color. Both plant systems and animal systems, including those of humans, are incredibly complex structures in which a host of substances come together in organized ways to form cells, tissue, organ systems, and so on. These various components must operate in synchrony for the organism as a whole to be viable. If even one key system strays far from its optimal state, the organism as a whole may die.

To make a living system from its component molecules—such as a ginkgo leaf from sugar molecules, cellulose molecules, and the other substances present in the leaf—requires a very large reduction in entropy. It would seem, then, that living systems might violate the second law of thermodynamics. They seem spontaneously to become more, not less, organized as they develop. To get the full picture, however, we must take into account the surroundings.

We know that a system can move toward lower entropy if we do work on it. (That is, if we supply energy to the system in a very specific way.) When we do work on a gas, for example, by compressing it isothermally, the entropy of the gas is lowered. The energy for the work done is provided by the surroundings, and in the process the net entropy change in the universe is positive.

The striking thing about living systems is that they are organized to recruit energy from their surroundings spontaneously. Some single-celled organisms, called *autotrophs*, capture energy from sunlight and store it in molecules such as sugars and fats [Figure 19.12(b)]. Others, called *heterotrophs*, absorb food molecules from their surroundings and then break down the molecules to provide needed energy. Whatever their mode of existence, however, living systems gain their order at the expense of the surroundings. Each cell exists at the expense of an increase in the entropy of the universe.

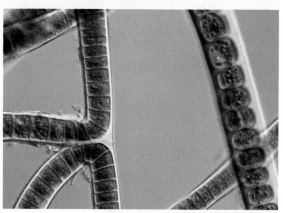

▲ **Figure 19.12 Entropy and life.** (a) This ginkgo leaf represents a highly organized living system. (b) Cyanobacteria absorb light energy and utilize it to synthesize the substances needed for growth.

▶ Figure 19.13 **A perfectly ordered crystalline solid at and above 0 K.** At absolute zero (left), all lattice units are in their lattice sites, devoid of thermal motion. As the temperature rises above 0 K (right), the atoms or molecules gain energy and their vibrational motion increases.

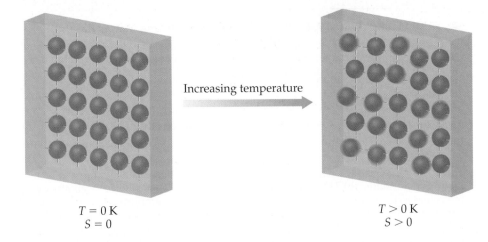

Increasing temperature

$T = 0\,K$
$S = 0$

$T > 0\,K$
$S > 0$

The Third Law of Thermodynamics

If we decrease the thermal energy of a system by lowering the temperature, the energy stored in translational, vibrational, and rotational forms of motion decreases. As less energy is stored, the entropy of the system decreases. If we keep lowering the temperature, do we reach a state in which these motions are essentially shut down, a point described by a single microstate? This question is addressed by the **third law of thermodynamics**, which states that *the entropy of a pure crystalline substance at absolute zero is zero*: $S(0\,K) = 0$.

Figure 19.13 ▲ shows schematically a pure crystalline solid. At absolute zero all the units of the lattice have no thermal motion. There is, therefore, only one microstate. As a result $S = k \ln W = k \ln 1 = 0$. As the temperature is increased from absolute zero, the atoms or molecules in the crystal gain energy in the form of vibrational motion about their lattice positions. Thus, the degrees of freedom of the crystal increase. The entropy of the lattice therefore increases with temperature because vibrational motion causes the atoms or molecules to have a greater number of accessible microstates.

What happens to the entropy of the substance as we continue to heat it? Figure 19.14 ◀ is a plot of how the entropy of a typical substance varies with temperature. We see that the entropy of the solid continues to increase steadily with increasing temperature up to the melting point of the solid. When the solid melts, the bonds holding the atoms or molecules are broken and the particles are free to move about the entire volume of the substance. The added degrees of freedom for the individual molecules allow greater dispersal of the substance's energy thereby increasing its entropy. We therefore see a sharp increase in the entropy at the melting point. After all the solid has melted to liquid, the temperature again increases and with it, the entropy.

At the boiling point of the liquid, another abrupt increase in entropy occurs. We can understand this increase as resulting from the increased volume in which the molecules may be found. When the gas is heated further, the entropy increases steadily as more energy is stored in the translational motion of the gas molecules. At higher temperatures, the distribution of molecular speeds is spread out toward higher values. ∞(Figure 10.18) More of the molecules have speeds that differ greatly from the most probable value. The expansion of the range of speeds of the gas molecules leads to an increased entropy.

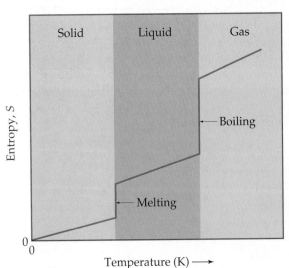

▲ Figure 19.14 **Entropy as a function of temperature.** Entropy increases as the temperature of a crystalline solid is increased from absolute zero. The vertical jumps in entropy correspond to phase changes.

The general conclusions we reach in examining Figure 19.14 are consistent with what we noted earlier: Entropy generally increases with increasing temperature because the increased motional energy can be dispersed in more ways. Further, the entropies of the phases of a given substance follow the order $S_{solid} < S_{liquid} < S_{gas}$. This ordering fits in nicely with our picture of the number of microstates available to solids, liquids, and gases.

◢ **GIVE IT SOME THOUGHT**

If you are told that the entropy of a certain system is zero, what do you know about the system?

19.4 ENTROPY CHANGES IN CHEMICAL REACTIONS

In Section 5.5 we discussed how calorimetry can be used to measure ΔH for chemical reactions. No comparable, easy method exists for measuring ΔS for a reaction. By using experimental measurements of the variation of heat capacity with temperature, however, we can determine the absolute value of the entropy, S, for many substances at any temperature. (The theory and the methods used for these measurements and calculations are beyond the scope of this text.) Absolute entropies are based on the reference point of zero entropy for perfect crystalline solids at 0 K (the third law). Entropies are usually tabulated as molar quantities, in units of joules per mole-kelvin (J/mol-K).

The molar entropy values of substances in their standard states are known as **standard molar entropies** and are denoted $S°$. The standard state for any substance is defined as the pure substance at 1 atm pressure.* Table 19.2▶ lists the values of $S°$ for several substances at 298 K; Appendix C gives a more extensive list.

We can make several observations about the $S°$ values in Table 19.2:

1. Unlike enthalpies of formation, the standard molar entropies of elements at the reference temperature of 298 K are *not* zero.

2. The standard molar entropies of gases are greater than those of liquids and solids, consistent with our interpretation of experimental observations, as represented in Figure 19.14

3. Standard molar entropies generally increase with increasing molar mass. [Compare Li(s), Na(s), and K(s).]

4. Standard molar entropies generally increase with an increasing number of atoms in the formula of a substance.

Point 4 is related to molecular motion (Section 19.3). In general, the number of degrees of freedom for a molecule increases with increasing number of atoms, and thus the number of accessible microstates also increases. Figure 19.15▼ compares the standard molar entropies of three hydrocarbons. Notice how the entropy increases as the number of atoms in the molecule increases.

The entropy change in a chemical reaction equals the sum of the entropies of the products less the sum of the entropies of the reactants:

$$\Delta S° = \sum nS°(\text{products}) - \sum mS°(\text{reactants})\qquad[19.8]$$

As in Equation 5.31, the coefficients n and m are the coefficients in the chemical equation, as illustrated in Sample Exercise 19.5.

TABLE 19.2 ■ Standard Molar Entropies of Selected Substances at 298 K	
Substance	$S°$, J/mol-K
Gases	
$H_2(g)$	130.6
$N_2(g)$	191.5
$O_2(g)$	205.0
$H_2O(g)$	188.8
$NH_3(g)$	192.5
$CH_3OH(g)$	237.6
$C_6H_6(g)$	269.2
Liquids	
$H_2O(l)$	69.9
$CH_3OH(l)$	126.8
$C_6H_6(l)$	172.8
Solids	
$Li(s)$	29.1
$Na(s)$	51.4
$K(s)$	64.7
$Fe(s)$	27.23
$FeCl_3(s)$	142.3
$NaCl(s)$	72.3

▼ **Figure 19.15 Molar entropies.** In general, the more complex a molecule (that is, the greater the number of atoms present), the greater the molar entropy of the substance, as illustrated here by the molar entropies of three simple hydrocarbons.

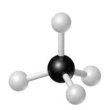

Methane, CH_4
$S° = 186.3\,\text{J mol}^{-1}\,\text{K}^{-1}$

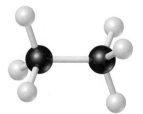

Ethane, C_2H_6
$S° = 229.6\,\text{J mol}^{-1}\,\text{K}^{-1}$

Propane, C_3H_8
$S° = 270.3\,\text{J mol}^{-1}\,\text{K}^{-1}$

*The standard pressure used in thermodynamics is no longer 1 atm but is based on the SI unit for pressure, the pascal (Pa). The standard pressure is 10^5 Pa, a quantity known as a **bar**: 1 bar = 10^5 Pa = 0.987 atm. Because 1 bar differs from 1 atm by only 1.3%, we will continue to refer to the standard pressure as 1 atm.

■ **SAMPLE EXERCISE 19.5** | **Calculating ΔS from Tabulated Entropies**

Calculate $\Delta S°$ for the synthesis of ammonia from $N_2(g)$ and $H_2(g)$ at 298 K:

$$N_2(g) + 3 H_2(g) \longrightarrow 2 NH_3(g)$$

SOLUTION

Analyze: We are asked to calculate the entropy change for the synthesis of $NH_3(g)$ from its constituent elements.

Plan: We can make this calculation using Equation 19.8 and the standard molar entropy values for the reactants and the products that are given in Table 19.2 and in Appendix C.

Solve: Using Equation 19.8, we have

$$\Delta S° = 2S°(NH_3) - [S°(N_2) + 3S°(H_2)]$$

Substituting the appropriate $S°$ values from Table 19.2 yields

$$\Delta S° = (2\ mol)(192.5\ J/mol\text{-}K) - [(1\ mol)(191.5\ J/mol\text{-}K) + (3\ mol)(130.6\ J/mol\text{-}K)]$$
$$= -198.3\ J/K$$

Check: The value for $\Delta S°$ is negative, in agreement with our qualitative prediction based on the decrease in the number of molecules of gas during the reaction.

■ **PRACTICE EXERCISE**

Using the standard entropies in Appendix C, calculate the standard entropy change, $\Delta S°$, for the following reaction at 298 K:

$$Al_2O_3(s) + 3 H_2(g) \longrightarrow 2 Al(s) + 3 H_2O(g)$$

Answer: 180.39 J/K

Entropy Changes in the Surroundings

We can use tabulated absolute entropy values to calculate the standard entropy change in a system, such as a chemical reaction, as just described. But what about the entropy change in the surroundings? We encountered this situation in Section 19.2, but it is good to revisit it now that we are examining chemical reactions.

We should recognize that the surroundings serve essentially as a large, constant-temperature heat source (or heat sink if the heat flows from the system to the surroundings). The change in entropy of the surroundings will depend on how much heat is absorbed or given off by the system. For an isothermal process, the entropy change of the surroundings is given by

$$\Delta S_{surr} = \frac{-q_{sys}}{T}$$

For a reaction occurring at constant pressure, q_{sys} is simply the enthalpy change for the reaction, ΔH. Thus, we can write

$$\Delta S_{surr} = \frac{-\Delta H_{sys}}{T} \qquad [19.9]$$

For the reaction in Sample Exercise 19.5, the formation of ammonia from $H_2(g)$ and $N_2(g)$ at 298 K, q_{sys} is the enthalpy change for reaction under standard conditions, $\Delta H°$. ∞ (Section 5.7) Using the procedures described in Section 5.7, we have

$$\Delta H°_{rxn} = 2\Delta H°_f[NH_3(g)] - 3\Delta H°_f[H_2(g)] - \Delta H°_f[N_2(g)]$$
$$= 2(-46.19\ kJ) - 3(0\ kJ) - (0\ kJ) = -92.38\ kJ$$

Thus at 298 K the formation of ammonia from $H_2(g)$ and $N_2(g)$ is exothermic. Absorption of the heat given off by the system results in an increase in the entropy of the surroundings:

$$\Delta S°_{surr} = \frac{92.38\ kJ}{298\ K} = 0.310\ kJ/K = 310\ J/K$$

Notice that the magnitude of the entropy gained by the surroundings is greater than that lost by the system (as calculated in Sample Exercise 19.5):

$$\Delta S^{\circ}_{\text{univ}} = \Delta S^{\circ}_{\text{sys}} + \Delta S^{\circ}_{\text{surr}} = -198.3\,\text{J/K} + 310\,\text{J/K} = 112\,\text{J/K}$$

Because $\Delta S^{\circ}_{\text{univ}}$ is positive for any spontaneous reaction, this calculation indicates that when $NH_3(g)$, $H_2(g)$, and $N_2(g)$ are together at 298 K in their standard states (each at 1 atm pressure), the reaction system will move spontaneously toward formation of $NH_3(g)$. Keep in mind that while the thermodynamic calculations indicate that formation of ammonia is spontaneous, they do not tell us anything about the rate at which ammonia is formed. Establishing equilibrium in this system within a reasonable period requires a catalyst, as discussed in Section 15.7.

GIVE IT SOME THOUGHT

If a process is exothermic, does the entropy of the surroundings (1) always increase, (2) always decrease, or (3) sometimes increase and sometimes decrease, depending on the process?

19.5 GIBBS FREE ENERGY

We have seen examples of endothermic processes that are spontaneous, such as the dissolution of ammonium nitrate in water. ∞ (Section 13.1) We learned in our discussion of the solution process that a spontaneous, endothermic process must be accompanied by an increase in the entropy of the system. However, we have also encountered processes that are spontaneous and yet proceed with a *decrease* in the entropy of the system, such as the highly exothermic formation of sodium chloride from its constituent elements. ∞ (Section 8.2) Spontaneous processes that result in a decrease in the system's entropy are always exothermic. Thus, the spontaneity of a reaction seems to involve two thermodynamic concepts, enthalpy and entropy.

There should be a way to use ΔH and ΔS to predict whether a given reaction occurring at constant temperature and pressure will be spontaneous. The means for doing so was first developed by the American mathematician J. Willard Gibbs (1839–1903). Gibbs (Figure 19.16▶) proposed a new state function, now called the **Gibbs free energy** (or just **free energy**). The Gibbs free energy, G, of a state is defined as

$$G = H - TS \qquad [19.10]$$

where T is the absolute temperature. For a process occurring at constant temperature, the change in free energy of the system, ΔG, is given by the expression

$$\Delta G = \Delta H - T\Delta S \qquad [19.11]$$

Under standard conditions, this equation becomes

$$\Delta G^{\circ} = \Delta H^{\circ} - T\Delta S^{\circ} \qquad [19.12]$$

To see how the state function G relates to reaction spontaneity, recall that for a reaction occurring at constant temperature and pressure

$$\Delta S_{\text{univ}} = \Delta S_{\text{sys}} + \Delta S_{\text{surr}} = \Delta S_{\text{sys}} + \left(\frac{-\Delta H_{\text{sys}}}{T}\right)$$

Multiplying both sides by $(-T)$ gives us

$$-T\Delta S_{\text{univ}} = \Delta H_{\text{sys}} - T\Delta S_{\text{sys}} \qquad [19.13]$$

▲ **Figure 19.16 Josiah Willard Gibbs (1839–1903).** Gibbs was the first person to be awarded a Ph.D. in science from an American university (Yale, 1863). From 1871 until his death, he held the chair of mathematical physics at Yale. He developed much of the theoretical foundation that led to the development of chemical thermodynamics.

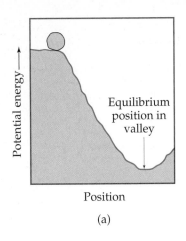

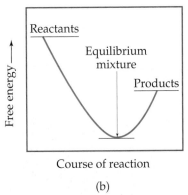

▲ **Figure 19.17 Potential energy and free energy.** An analogy is shown between the gravitational potential-energy change of a boulder rolling down a hill (a) and the free-energy change in a spontaneous reaction (b). The equilibrium position in (a) is given by the minimum gravitational potential energy available to the system. The equilibrium position in (b) is given by the minimum free energy available to the system.

Comparing Equation 19.13 with Equation 19.11, we see that the free-energy change in a process occurring at constant temperature and pressure, ΔG, is equal to $-T\Delta S_{univ}$. We know that for spontaneous processes, ΔS_{univ} is always positive, and therefore $-T\Delta S_{univ}$ will be negative. Thus, the sign of ΔG provides us with extremely valuable information about the spontaneity of processes that occur at constant temperature and pressure. If both T and P are constant, the relationship between the sign of ΔG and the spontaneity of a reaction is as follows:

1. If ΔG is negative, the reaction is spontaneous in the forward direction.

2. If ΔG is zero, the reaction is at equilibrium.

3. If ΔG is positive, the reaction in the forward direction is nonspontaneous; work must be supplied from the surroundings to make it occur. However, the reverse reaction will be spontaneous.

It is more convenient to use ΔG as a criterion for spontaneity than to use ΔS_{univ}, because ΔG relates to the system alone and avoids the complication of having to examine the surroundings.

An analogy is often drawn between the free-energy change during a spontaneous reaction and the potential-energy change when a boulder rolls down a hill. Potential energy in a gravitational field "drives" the boulder until it reaches a state of minimum potential energy in the valley [Figure 19.17(a) ◀]. Similarly, the free energy of a chemical system decreases until it reaches a minimum value [Figure 19.17(b)]. When this minimum is reached, a state of equilibrium exists. *In any spontaneous process at constant temperature and pressure, the free energy always decreases.*

As a specific illustration of these ideas, let's return to the Haber process for the synthesis of ammonia from nitrogen and hydrogen, which we discussed extensively in Chapter 15:

$$N_2(g) + 3\,H_2(g) \rightleftharpoons 2\,NH_3(g)$$

Imagine that we have a reaction vessel that allows us to maintain a constant temperature and pressure and that we have a catalyst that allows the reaction to proceed at a reasonable rate. What will happen if we charge the vessel with a certain number of moles of N_2 and three times that number of moles of H_2? As we saw in Figure 15.3(a), the N_2 and H_2 will react spontaneously to form NH_3 until equilibrium is achieved. Similarly, Figure 15.3(b) demonstrates that if we charge the vessel with pure NH_3, it will decompose spontaneously to form N_2 and H_2 until equilibrium is reached. In each case the free energy of the system is lowered on the way to equilibrium, which represents a minimum in the free energy. We illustrate these cases in Figure 19.18 ▶.

GIVE IT SOME THOUGHT

Give the criterion for spontaneity first in terms of entropy and then in terms of free energy.

This is a good time to remind ourselves of the significance of the reaction quotient, Q, for a system that is not at equilibrium. ∞ (Section 15.6) Recall that when $Q < K$, there is an excess of reactants relative to products. The reaction will proceed spontaneously in the forward direction to reach equilibrium. When $Q > K$, the reaction will proceed spontaneously in the reverse direction. At equilibrium $Q = K$. We have illustrated these points in Figure 19.18. In Section 19.7 we will see how to use the value of Q to calculate the value of ΔG for systems that are not at equilibrium.

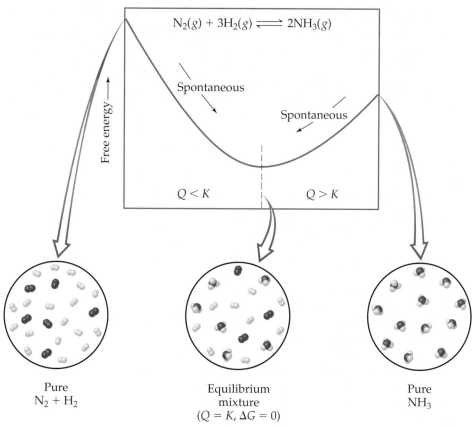

◀ Figure 19.18 **Free energy and equilibrium.** In the reaction $N_2(g) + 3\,H_2(g) \rightleftharpoons 2\,NH_3(g)$, if the reaction mixture has too much N_2 and H_2 relative to NH_3 (left), the equilibrium lies too far to the left ($Q < K$) and NH_3 forms spontaneously. If there is too much NH_3 in the mixture (right), the equilibrium lies too far to the right ($Q > K$) and the NH_3 decomposes spontaneously into N_2 and H_2. Both of these spontaneous processes are "downhill" in free energy. At equilibrium (center), $Q = K$ and the free energy is at a minimum ($\Delta G = 0$).

Pure
$N_2 + H_2$

Equilibrium
mixture
($Q = K, \Delta G = 0$)

Pure
NH_3

■■ **SAMPLE EXERCISE 19.6** | **Calculating Free-Energy Change from $\Delta H°$, T, and $\Delta S°$**

Calculate the standard free energy change for the formation of $NO(g)$ from $N_2(g)$ and $O_2(g)$ at 298 K:

$$N_2(g) + O_2(g) \longrightarrow 2\,NO(g)$$

given that $\Delta H° = 180.7$ kJ and $\Delta S° = 24.7$ J/K. Is the reaction spontaneous under these circumstances?

SOLUTION

Analyze: We are asked to calculate $\Delta G°$ for the indicated reaction (given $\Delta H°$, $\Delta S°$, and T) and to predict whether the reaction is spontaneous under standard conditions at 298 K.

Plan: To calculate $\Delta G°$, we use Equation 19.12, $\Delta G° = \Delta H° - T\Delta S°$. To determine whether the reaction is spontaneous under standard conditions, we look at the sign of $\Delta G°$.

Solve:

$$\Delta G° = \Delta H° - T\Delta S°$$

$$= 180.7 \text{ kJ} - (298 \text{ K})(24.7 \text{ J/K})\left(\frac{1 \text{ kJ}}{10^3 \text{ J}}\right)$$

$$= 180.7 \text{ kJ} - 7.4 \text{ kJ}$$

$$= 173.3 \text{ kJ}$$

Because $\Delta G°$ is positive, the reaction is not spontaneous under standard conditions at 298 K.

Comment: Notice that we had to convert the units of the $T\Delta S°$ term to kJ so that they could be added to the $\Delta H°$ term, whose units are kJ.

■■ **PRACTICE EXERCISE**

A particular reaction has $\Delta H° = 24.6$ kJ and $\Delta S° = 132$ J/K at 298 K. Calculate $\Delta G°$. Is the reaction spontaneous under these conditions?
Answer: $\Delta G° = -14.7$ kJ; the reaction is spontaneous.

TABLE 19.3 ■ Conventions Used in Establishing Standard Free Energies	
State of Matter	**Standard State**
Solid	Pure solid
Liquid	Pure liquid
Gas	1 atm pressure
Solution	1 M concentration
Elements	Standard free energy of formation of an element in its standard state is defined as zero

Standard Free Energy of Formation

Free energy is a state function, like enthalpy. We can tabulate **standard free energies of formation** for substances, just as we can tabulate standard enthalpies of formation. ∞ (Section 5.7) It is important to remember that standard values for these functions imply a particular set of conditions, or standard states. The standard state for gaseous substances is 1 atm pressure. For solid substances, the standard state is the pure solid; for liquids, the pure liquid. For substances in solution, the standard state is normally a concentration of 1 M. (In very accurate work it may be necessary to make certain corrections, but we need not worry about these.) The temperature usually chosen for purposes of tabulating data is 25 °C, but we will calculate $\Delta G°$ at other temperatures as well. Just as for the standard heats of formation, the free energies of elements in their standard states are set to zero. This arbitrary choice of a reference point has no effect on the quantity in which we are interested, namely, the *difference* in free energy between reactants and products. The rules about standard states are summarized in Table 19.3 ◄. A listing of standard free energies of formation, denoted $\Delta G_f°$, appears in Appendix C.

▲ **GIVE IT SOME THOUGHT**

What does the superscript ° indicate when associated with a thermodynamic quantity, as in $\Delta H°$, $\Delta S°$, or $\Delta G°$?

The standard free energies of formation are useful in calculating the *standard free-energy change* for chemical processes. The procedure is analogous to the calculation of $\Delta H°$ (Equation 5.31) and $\Delta S°$ (Equation 19.8):

$$\Delta G° = \sum n\Delta G_f°(\text{products}) - \sum m\Delta G_f°(\text{reactants}) \qquad [19.14]$$

A Closer Look   WHAT'S "FREE" ABOUT FREE ENERGY?

The Gibbs free energy is a remarkable thermodynamic quantity. Because so many chemical reactions are carried out under conditions of near-constant pressure and temperature, chemists, biochemists, and engineers use the sign and magnitude of ΔG as exceptionally useful tools in the design and implementation of chemical and biochemical reactions. We will see examples of the usefulness of ΔG throughout the remainder of this chapter and this text. But what is "free" about free energy?

We have seen that we can use the sign of ΔG to conclude whether a reaction is spontaneous, nonspontaneous, or at equilibrium. The magnitude of ΔG is also significant. A reaction for which ΔG is large and negative, such as the burning of gasoline, is much more capable of doing work on the surroundings than is a reaction for which ΔG is small and negative, such as ice melting at room temperature. In fact, thermodynamics tells us that *the change in free energy for a process, ΔG, equals the maximum useful work that can be done by the system on its surroundings in a spontaneous process occurring at constant temperature and pressure:*

$$\Delta G = -w_{max} \qquad [19.15]$$

In other words, ΔG gives the theoretical limit to how much work can be done by a process. This relationship explains why ΔG is called the *free* energy. It is the portion of the energy change of a spontaneous reaction that is free to do useful work. The remainder of the energy enters the environment as heat.

For example, when we burn gasoline to move a car, only part of the energy of the gasoline is used to drive the car forward, performing useful work. The rest of the energy is dissipated to the surroundings as heat, accomplishing no useful work, as illustrated in Figure 19.19 ▼. The efficiency of energy conversion is given by the ratio of the work accomplished compared to the total energy used.

For processes that are not spontaneous ($\Delta G > 0$), the free-energy change is a measure of the *minimum* amount of work that must be done to cause the process to occur. In actual cases we always need to do more than this theoretical minimum amount because of the inefficiencies in the way the changes occur.

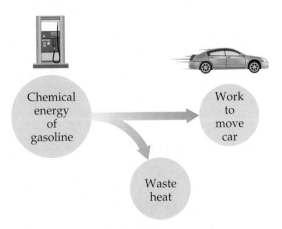

▲ **Figure 19.19 Energy conversion.** All conversions of energy are accompanied by production of heat, which enters the surroundings without accomplishing useful work.

SAMPLE EXERCISE 19.7 | Calculating Standard Free-Energy Change from Free Energies of Formation

(a) Use data from Appendix C to calculate the standard free-energy change for the following reaction at 298 K:

$$P_4(g) + 6\,Cl_2(g) \longrightarrow 4\,PCl_3(g)$$

(b) What is $\Delta G°$ for the reverse of the above reaction?

SOLUTION

Analyze: We are asked to calculate the free-energy change for the indicated reaction and then to determine the free-energy change of its reverse.

Plan: To accomplish our task, we look up the free-energy values for the products and reactants and use Equation 19.14: We multiply the molar quantities by the coefficients in the balanced equation, and subtract the total for the reactants from that for the products.

Solve:

(a) $Cl_2(g)$ is in its standard state, so $\Delta G_f°$ is zero for this reactant. $P_4(g)$, however, is not in its standard state, so $\Delta G_f°$ is not zero for this reactant. From the balanced equation and using Appendix C, we have:

$$\Delta G_{rxn}° = 4\,\Delta G_f°[PCl_3(g)] - \Delta G_f°[P_4(g)] - 6\,\Delta G_f°[Cl_2(g)]$$
$$= (4\,mol)(-269.6\,kJ/mol) - (1\,mol)(24.4\,kJ/mol) - 0$$
$$= -1102.8\,kJ$$

The fact that $\Delta G°$ is negative tells us that a mixture of $P_4(g)$, $Cl_2(g)$, and $PCl_3(g)$ at 25 °C, each present at a partial pressure of 1 atm, would react spontaneously in the forward direction to form more PCl_3. Remember, however, that the value of $\Delta G°$ tells us nothing about the rate at which the reaction occurs.

(b) Remember that $\Delta G = G$ (products) $- G$ (reactants). If we reverse the reaction, we reverse the roles of the reactants and products. Thus, reversing the reaction changes the sign of ΔG, just as reversing the reaction changes the sign of ΔH ∞∞ (Section 5.4) Hence, using the result from part (a):

$$4\,PCl_3(g) \longrightarrow P_4(g) + 6\,Cl_2(g) \quad \Delta G° = +1102.8\,kJ$$

PRACTICE EXERCISE

By using data from Appendix C, calculate $\Delta G°$ at 298 K for the combustion of methane: $CH_4(g) + 2\,O_2(g) \longrightarrow CO_2(g) + 2\,H_2O(g)$.
Answer: $-800.7\,kJ$

SAMPLE EXERCISE 19.8 | Estimating and Calculating $\Delta G°$

In Section 5.7 we used Hess's law to calculate $\Delta H°$ for the combustion of propane gas at 298 K:

$$C_3H_8(g) + 5\,O_2(g) \longrightarrow 3\,CO_2(g) + 4\,H_2O(l) \quad \Delta H° = -2220\,kJ$$

(a) *Without using data from Appendix C*, predict whether $\Delta G°$ for this reaction is more negative or less negative than $\Delta H°$. (b) Use data from Appendix C to calculate the standard free-energy change for the reaction at 298 K. Is your prediction from part (a) correct?

SOLUTION

Analyze: In part (a) we must predict the value for $\Delta G°$ relative to that for $\Delta H°$ on the basis of the balanced equation for the reaction. In part (b) we must calculate the value for $\Delta G°$ and compare with our qualitative prediction.

Plan: The free-energy change incorporates both the change in enthalpy and the change in entropy for the reaction (Equation 19.11), so under standard conditions:

$$\Delta G° = \Delta H° - T\Delta S°$$

To determine whether $\Delta G°$ is more negative or less negative than $\Delta H°$, we need to determine the sign of the term $T\Delta S°$. T is the absolute temperature, 298 K, so it is a positive number. We can predict the sign of $\Delta S°$ by looking at the reaction.

Solve:

(a) We see that the reactants consist of six molecules of gas, and the products consist of three molecules of gas and four molecules of liquid. Thus, the number of molecules of gas has decreased significantly during the reaction. By using the general rules we discussed in Section 19.3, we would expect a decrease in the number of gas molecules to lead to a decrease in the entropy of the system—the products have fewer accessible microstates than the reactants. We therefore expect $\Delta S°$ and therefore $T\Delta S°$ to be negative numbers. Because we are subtracting $T\Delta S°$, which is a negative number, we would predict that $\Delta G°$ is *less negative* than $\Delta H°$.

(b) Using Equation 19.14 and values from Appendix C, we can calculate the value of $\Delta G°$

$$\Delta G° = 3\Delta G_f°[CO_2(g)] + 4\Delta G_f°[H_2O(l)] - \Delta G_f°[C_3H_8(g)] - 5\Delta G_f°[O_2(g)]$$

$$= 3\text{ mol}(-394.4\text{ kJ/mol}) + 4\text{ mol}(-237.13\text{ kJ/mol}) -$$

$$1\text{ mol}(-23.47\text{ kJ/mol}) - 5\text{ mol}(0\text{ kJ/mol}) = -2108\text{ kJ}$$

Notice that we have been careful to use the value of $\Delta G_f°$ for $H_2O(l)$, as in the calculation of ΔH values, the phases of the reactants and products are important. As we predicted, $\Delta G°$ is less negative than $\Delta H°$ because of the decrease in entropy during the reaction.

■ PRACTICE EXERCISE

Consider the combustion of propane to form $CO_2(g)$ and $H_2O(g)$ at 298 K: $C_3H_8(g) + 5\,O_2(g) \longrightarrow 3\,CO_2(g) + 4\,H_2O(g)$. Would you expect $\Delta G°$ to be more negative or less negative than $\Delta H°$?
Answer: more negative

19.6 FREE ENERGY AND TEMPERATURE

We have seen that tabulations of $\Delta G_f°$, such as those in Appendix C, make it possible to calculate $\Delta G°$ for reactions at the standard temperature of 25° C. However, we are often interested in examining reactions at other temperatures. How is the change in free energy affected by the change in temperature? Let's look again at Equation 19.11:

$$\Delta G = \Delta H - T\Delta S = \underset{\substack{\text{Enthalpy} \\ \text{term}}}{\Delta H} + \underset{\substack{\text{Entropy} \\ \text{term}}}{(-T\Delta S)}$$

Notice that we have written the expression for ΔG as a sum of two contributions, an enthalpy term, ΔH, and an entropy term, $-T\Delta S$. Because the value of $-T\Delta S$ depends directly on the absolute temperature T, ΔG will vary with temperature. T is a positive number at all temperatures other than absolute zero. We know that the enthalpy term, ΔH, can be positive or negative. The entropy term, $-T\Delta S$, can also be positive or negative. When ΔS is positive, which means that the final state has greater randomness (a greater number of microstates) than the initial state, the term $-T\Delta S$ is negative. When ΔS is negative, the term $-T\Delta S$ is positive.

The sign of ΔG, which tells us whether a process is spontaneous, will depend on the signs and magnitudes of ΔH and $-T\Delta S$. When both ΔH and $-T\Delta S$ are negative, ΔG will always be negative and the process will be spontaneous at all temperatures. Likewise, when both ΔH and $-T\Delta S$ are positive, ΔG will always be positive and the process will be nonspontaneous at all temperatures (the reverse process will be spontaneous at all temperatures). When ΔH and $-T\Delta S$ have opposite signs, however, the sign of ΔG will depend on the magnitudes of these two terms. In these instances temperature is an important consideration. Generally, ΔH and ΔS change very little with temperature.

■ SAMPLE INTEGRATIVE EXERCISE | Putting Concepts Together

Consider the simple salts NaCl(s) and AgCl(s). We will examine the equilibria in which these salts dissolve in water to form aqueous solutions of ions:

$$NaCl(s) \rightleftharpoons Na^+(aq) + Cl^-(aq)$$
$$AgCl(s) \rightleftharpoons Ag^+(aq) + Cl^-(aq)$$

(a) Calculate the value of $\Delta G°$ at 298 K for each of the preceding reactions. (b) The two values from part (a) are very different. Is this difference primarily due to the enthalpy term or the entropy term of the standard free-energy change? (c) Use the values of $\Delta G°$ to calculate the K_{sp} values for the two salts at 298 K. (d) Sodium chloride is considered a soluble salt, whereas silver chloride is considered insoluble. Are these descriptions consistent with the answers to part (c)? (e) How will $\Delta G°$ for the solution process of these salts change with increasing T? What effect should this change have on the solubility of the salts?

SOLUTION

(a) We will use Equation 19.14 along with $\Delta G_f°$ values from Appendix C to calculate the $\Delta G_{soln}°$ values for each equilibrium. (As we did in Section 13.1, we use the subscript "soln" to indicate that these are thermodynamic quantities for the formation of a solution.) We find

$$\Delta G_{soln}°(NaCl) = (-261.9 \text{ kJ/mol}) + (-131.2 \text{ kJ/mol}) - (-384.0 \text{ kJ/mol})$$
$$= -9.1 \text{ kJ/mol}$$

$$\Delta G_{soln}°(AgCl) = (+77.11 \text{ kJ/mol}) + (-131.2 \text{ kJ/mol}) - (-109.70 \text{ kJ/mol})$$
$$= +55.6 \text{ kJ/mol}$$

(b) We can write $\Delta G_{soln}°$ as the sum of an enthalpy term, $\Delta H_{soln}°$, and an entropy term, $-T\Delta S_{soln}°$: $\Delta G_{soln}° = \Delta H_{soln}° + (-T\Delta S_{soln}°)$. We can calculate the values of $\Delta H_{soln}°$ and $\Delta S_{soln}°$ by using Equations 5.31 and 19.8. We can then calculate $-T\Delta S_{soln}°$ at $T = 298K$. All these calculations are now familiar to us. The results are summarized in the following table:

Salt	$\Delta H_{soln}°$	$\Delta S_{soln}°$	$-T\Delta S_{soln}°$
NaCl	+3.6 kJ/mol	+43.2 J/mol-K	-12.9 kJ/mol
AgCl	+65.7 kJ/mol	+34.3 J/mol-K	-10.2 kJ/mol

The entropy terms for the solution of the two salts are very similar. That seems sensible because each solution process should lead to a similar increase in randomness as the salt dissolves, forming hydrated ions. ∞ (Section 13.1) In contrast, we see a very large difference in the enthalpy term for the solution of the two salts. The difference in the values of $\Delta G_{soln}°$ is dominated by the difference in the values of $\Delta H_{soln}°$.

(c) The solubility product, K_{sp}, is the equilibrium constant for the solution process. ∞ (Section 17.4) As such, we can relate K_{sp} directly to $\Delta G_{soln}°$ by using Equation 19.18:

$$K_{sp} = e^{-\Delta G_{soln}°/RT}$$

We can calculate the K_{sp} values in the same way we applied Equation 19.18 in Sample Exercise 19.12. We use the $\Delta G_{soln}°$ values we obtained in part (a), remembering to convert them from kJ/mol to J/mol:

NaCl: $K_{sp} = [Na^+(aq)][Cl^-(aq)] = e^{-(-9100)/[(8.314)(298)]} = e^{+3.7} = 40$

AgCl: $K_{sp} = [Ag^+(aq)][Cl^-(aq)] = e^{-(+55,600)/[(8.314)(298)]} = e^{-22.4} = 1.9 \times 10^{-10}$

The value calculated for the K_{sp} of AgCl is very close to that listed in Appendix D.

(d) A soluble salt is one that dissolves appreciably in water. ∞ (Section 4.2) The K_{sp} value for NaCl is greater than 1, indicating that NaCl dissolves to a great extent. The K_{sp} value for AgCl is very small, indicating that very little dissolves in water. Silver chloride should indeed be considered an insoluble salt.

(e) As we expect, the solution process has a positive value of ΔS for both salts (see the table in part b). As such, the entropy term of the free-energy change, $-T\Delta S_{soln}°$, is negative. If we assume that $\Delta H_{soln}°$ and $\Delta S_{soln}°$ do not change much with temperature, then an increase in T will serve to make $\Delta G_{soln}°$ more negative. Thus, the driving force for dissolution of the salts will increase with increasing T, and we therefore expect the solubility of the salts to increase with increasing T. In Figure 13.17 we see that the solubility of NaCl (and that of nearly any salt) increases with increasing temperature. ∞ (Section 13.3)

CHAPTER REVIEW

SUMMARY AND KEY TERMS

Section 19.1 Most reactions and chemical processes have an inherent directionality: They are **spontaneous** in one direction and nonspontaneous in the reverse direction. The spontaneity of a process is related to the thermodynamic path the system takes from the initial state to the final state. In a **reversible process**, both the system and its surroundings can be restored to their original state by exactly reversing the change. In an **irreversible process** the system cannnot return to its original state without there being a permanent change in the surroundings. Any spontaneous process is irreversible. A process that occurs at a constant temperature is said to be **isothermal**.

Section 19.2 The spontaneous nature of processes is related to a thermodynamic state function called **entropy**, denoted S. For a process that occurs at constant temperature, the entropy change of the system is given by the heat absorbed by the system along a reversible path, divided by the temperature: $\Delta S = q_{rev}/T$. The way entropy controls the spontaneity of processes is given by the **second law of thermodynamics**, which governs the change in the entropy of the universe, $\Delta S_{univ} = \Delta S_{sys} + \Delta S_{surr}$. The second law states that in a reversible process $\Delta S_{univ} = 0$; in an irreversible (spontaneous) process $\Delta S_{univ} > 0$. Entropy values are usually expressed in units of joules per kelvin, J/K.

Section 19.3 Molecules can undergo three kinds of motion: In **translational motion** the entire molecule moves in space. Molecules can also undergo **vibrational motion**, in which the atoms of the molecule move toward and away from one another in periodic fashion, and **rotational motion**, in which the entire molecule spins like a top. A particular combination of motions and locations of the atoms and molecules of a system at a particular instant is called a **microstate**. Entropy is a measure of the number of microstates, W, over which the energy of the system is distributed: $S = k \ln W$. The number of available microstates, and therefore the entropy, increases with an increase in volume, temperature, or motion of molecules because any of these changes increases the possible motions and locations of the molecules. As a result, entropy generally increases when liquids or solutions are formed from solids, gases are formed from either solids or liquids, or the number of molecules of gas increases during a chemical reaction. The **third law of**

thermodynamics states that the entropy of a pure crystalline solid at 0 K is zero.

Section 19.4 The third law allows us to assign entropy values for substances at different temperatures. Under standard conditions the entropy of a mole of a substance is called its **standard molar entropy**, denoted $S°$. From tabulated values of $S°$, we can calculate the entropy change for any process under standard conditions. For an isothermal process, the entropy change in the surroundings is equal to $-\Delta H/T$.

Section 19.5 The **Gibbs free energy** (or just **free energy**), G, is a thermodynamic state function that combines the two state functions enthalpy and entropy: $G = H - TS$. For processes that occur at constant temperature, $\Delta G = \Delta H - T\Delta S$. For a process occurring at constant temperature and pressure, the sign of ΔG relates to the spontaneity of the process. When ΔG is negative, the process is spontaneous. When ΔG is positive, the process is nonspontaneous but the reverse process is spontaneous. At equilibrium the process is reversible and ΔG is zero. The free energy is also a measure of the maximum useful work that can be performed by a system in a spontaneous process. The standard free-energy change, $\Delta G°$, for any process can be calculated from tabulations of **standard free energies of formation**, $\Delta G_f°$, which are defined in a fashion analogous to standard enthalpies of formation, $\Delta H_f°$. The value of $\Delta G_f°$ for a pure element in its standard state is defined to be zero.

Sections 19.6 and 19.7 The values of ΔH and ΔS generally do not vary much with temperature. Therefore, the dependence of ΔG with temperature is governed mainly by the value of T in the expression $\Delta G = \Delta H - T\Delta S$. The entropy term $-T\Delta S$ has the greater effect on the temperature dependence of ΔG and, hence, on the spontaneity of the process. For example, a process for which $\Delta H > 0$ and $\Delta S > 0$, such as the melting of ice, can be nonspontaneous ($\Delta G > 0$) at low temperatures and spontaneous ($\Delta G < 0$) at higher temperatures. Under nonstandard conditions ΔG is related to $\Delta G°$ and the value of the reaction quotient, Q: $\Delta G = \Delta G° + RT \ln Q$. At equilibrium ($\Delta G = 0, Q = K$), $\Delta G° = -RT \ln K$. Thus, the standard free-energy change is directly related to the equilibrium constant for the reaction. This relationship expresses the temperature dependence of equilibrium constants.

KEY SKILLS

- Understand the meaning of *spontaneous process, reversible process, irreversible process,* and *isothermal process.*
- State the second law of thermodynamics.
- Describe the kinds of molecular motion that a molecule can possess.

19.45 Use Appendix C to compare the standard entropies at 25 °C for the following pairs of substances: **(a)** Sc(s) and Sc(g); **(b)** $NH_3(g)$ and $NH_3(aq)$; **(c)** 1 mol $P_4(g)$ and 2 mol $P_2(g)$; **(d)** C(graphite) and C(diamond). In each case explain the difference in the entropy values.

19.46 Using Appendix C, compare the standard entropies at 25 °C for the following pairs of substances: **(a)** CuO(s) and $Cu_2O(s)$; **(b)** 1 mol $N_2O_4(g)$ and 2 mol $NO_2(g)$; **(c)** $SiO_2(s)$ and $CO_2(g)$; **(d)** CO(g) and $CO_2(g)$. For each pair, explain the difference in the entropy values.

[19.47] The standard entropies at 298 K for certain of the group 4A elements are as follows: C(s, diamond) = 2.43 J/mol-K; Si(s) = 18.81 J/mol-K; Ge(s) = 31.09 J/mol-K; and Sn(s) = 51.18 J/mol-K. All but Sn have the diamond structure. How do you account for the trend in the $S°$ values?

[19.48] Three of the forms of elemental carbon are graphite, diamond, and buckminsterfullerene. The entropies at 298 K for graphite and diamond are listed in Appendix C.

(a) Account for the difference in the $S°$ values of graphite and diamond in light of their structures (Figure 11.41). **(b)** What would you expect for the $S°$ value of buckminsterfullerene (Figure 11.43) relative to the values for graphite and diamond? Explain.

19.49 Using $S°$ values from Appendix C, calculate $\Delta S°$ values for the following reactions. In each case account for the sign of $\Delta S°$.

(a) $C_2H_4(g) + H_2(g) \longrightarrow C_2H_6(g)$
(b) $N_2O_4(g) \longrightarrow 2 NO_2(g)$
(c) $Be(OH)_2(s) \longrightarrow BeO(s) + H_2O(g)$
(d) $2 CH_3OH(g) + 3 O_2(g) \longrightarrow 2 CO_2(g) + 4 H_2O(g)$

19.50 Calculate $\Delta S°$ values for the following reactions by using tabulated $S°$ values from Appendix C. In each case explain the sign of $\Delta S°$.

(a) $N_2H_4(g) + H_2(g) \longrightarrow 2 NH_3(g)$
(b) $K(s) + O_2(g) \longrightarrow KO_2(s)$
(c) $Mg(OH)_2(s) + 2 HCl(g) \longrightarrow MgCl_2(s) + 2 H_2O(l)$
(d) $CO(g) + 2 H_2(g) \longrightarrow CH_3OH(g)$

Gibbs Free Energy

19.51 **(a)** For a process that occurs at constant temperature, express the change in Gibbs free energy in terms of changes in the enthalpy and entropy of the system. **(b)** For a certain process that occurs at constant T and P, the value of ΔG is positive. What can you conclude? **(c)** What is the relationship between ΔG for a process and the rate at which it occurs?

19.52 **(a)** What is the meaning of the standard free-energy change, $\Delta G°$, as compared with ΔG? **(b)** For any process that occurs at constant temperature and pressure, what is the significance of $\Delta G = 0$? **(c)** For a certain process, ΔG is large and negative. Does this mean that the process necessarily occurs rapidly?

19.53 For a certain chemical reaction, $\Delta H° = -35.4$ kJ and $\Delta S° = -85.5$ J/K. **(a)** Is the reaction exothermic or endothermic? **(b)** Does the reaction lead to an increase or decrease in the randomness or disorder of the system? **(c)** Calculate $\Delta G°$ for the reaction at 298 K. **(d)** Is the reaction spontaneous at 298 K under standard conditions?

19.54 A certain reaction has $\Delta H° = -19.5$ kJ and $\Delta S° = +42.7$ J/K. **(a)** Is the reaction exothermic or endothermic? **(b)** Does the reaction lead to an increase or decrease in the randomness or disorder of the system? **(c)** Calculate $\Delta G°$ for the reaction at 298 K. **(d)** Is the reaction spontaneous at 298 K under standard conditions?

19.55 Using data in Appendix C, calculate $\Delta H°$, $\Delta S°$, and $\Delta G°$ at 298 K for each of the following reactions. In each case show that $\Delta G° = \Delta H° - T\Delta S°$.

(a) $H_2(g) + F_2(g) \longrightarrow 2 HF(g)$
(b) C(s, graphite) + 2 $Cl_2(g) \longrightarrow CCl_4(g)$
(c) $2 PCl_3(g) + O_2(g) \longrightarrow 2 POCl_3(g)$
(d) $2 CH_3OH(g) + H_2(g) \longrightarrow C_2H_6(g) + 2 H_2O(g)$

19.56 Use data in Appendix C to calculate $\Delta H°$, $\Delta S°$, and $\Delta G°$ at 25 °C for each of the following reactions. In each case show that $\Delta G° = \Delta H° - T\Delta S°$.

(a) $2 Cr(s) + 3 O_2(g) \longrightarrow 2 Cr_2O_3(s)$
(b) $BaCO_3(s) \longrightarrow BaO(s) + CO_2(g)$
(c) $2 P(s) + 10 HF(g) \longrightarrow 2 PF_5(g) + 5 H_2(g)$
(d) $K(s) + O_2(g) \longrightarrow KO_2(s)$

19.57 Using data from Appendix C, calculate $\Delta G°$ for the following reactions. Indicate whether each reaction is spontaneous under standard conditions.

(a) $2 SO_2(g) + O_2(g) \longrightarrow 2 SO_3(g)$
(b) $NO_2(g) + N_2O(g) \longrightarrow 3 NO(g)$
(c) $6 Cl_2(g) + 2 Fe_2O_3(s) \longrightarrow 4 FeCl_3(s) + 3 O_2(g)$
(d) $SO_2(g) + 2 H_2(g) \longrightarrow S(s) + 2 H_2O(g)$

19.58 Using data from Appendix C, calculate the change in Gibbs free energy for each of the following reactions. In each case indicate whether the reaction is spontaneous under standard conditions.

(a) $H_2(g) + Cl_2(g) \longrightarrow 2 HCl(g)$
(b) $MgCl_2(s) + H_2O(l) \longrightarrow MgO(s) + 2 HCl(g)$
(c) $2 NH_3(g) \longrightarrow N_2H_4(g) + H_2(g)$
(d) $2 NOCl(g) \longrightarrow 2 NO(g) + Cl_2(g)$

19.59 Cyclohexane (C_6H_{12}) is a liquid hydrocarbon at room temperature. **(a)** Write a balanced equation for the combustion of $C_6H_{12}(l)$ to form $CO_2(g)$ and $H_2O(l)$. **(b)** Without using thermochemical data, predict whether $\Delta G°$ for this reaction is more negative or less negative than $\Delta H°$.

19.60 Sulfur dioxide reacts with strontium oxide as follows:

$$SO_2(g) + SrO(s) \longrightarrow SrSO_3(s)$$

(a) Without using thermochemical data, predict whether $\Delta G°$ for this reaction is more negative or less negative than $\Delta H°$. **(b)** If you had only standard enthalpy data for this reaction, how would you go about making a rough estimate of the value of $\Delta G°$ at 298 K, using data from Appendix C on other substances?

19.61 Classify each of the following reactions as one of the four possible types summarized in Table 19.4:
(a) $N_2(g) + 3 F_2(g) \longrightarrow 2 NF_3(g)$
$$\Delta H° = -249 \text{ kJ}; \Delta S° = -278 \text{ J/K}$$
(b) $N_2(g) + 3 Cl_2(g) \longrightarrow 2 NCl_3(g)$
$$\Delta H° = 460 \text{ kJ}; \Delta S° = -275 \text{ J/K}$$
(c) $N_2F_4(g) \longrightarrow 2 NF_2(g)$
$$\Delta H° = 85 \text{ kJ}; \Delta S° = 198 \text{ J/K}$$

19.62 From the values given for $\Delta H°$ and $\Delta S°$, calculate $\Delta G°$ for each of the following reactions at 298 K. If the reaction is not spontaneous under standard conditions at 298 K, at what temperature (if any) would the reaction become spontaneous?
(a) $2 PbS(s) + 3 O_2(g) \longrightarrow 2 PbO(s) + 2 SO_2(g)$
$$\Delta H° = -844 \text{ kJ}; \Delta S° = -165 \text{ J/K}$$
(b) $2 POCl_3(g) \longrightarrow 2 PCl_3(g) + O_2(g)$
$$\Delta H° = 572 \text{ kJ}; \Delta S° = 179 \text{ J/K}$$

19.63 A particular reaction is spontaneous at 450 K. The enthalpy change for the reaction is +34.5 kJ. What can you conclude about the sign and magnitude of ΔS for the reaction?

19.64 A certain reaction is nonspontaneous at -25 °C. The entropy change for the reaction is 95 J/K. What can you conclude about the sign and magnitude of ΔH?

19.65 For a particular reaction, $\Delta H = -32 \text{ kJ}$ and $\Delta S = -98 \text{ J/K}$. Assume that ΔH and ΔS do not vary with temperature. **(a)** At what temperature will the reaction have $\Delta G = 0$? **(b)** If T is increased from that in part (a), will the reaction be spontaneous or nonspontaneous?

19.66 Reactions in which a substance decomposes by losing CO are called *decarbonylation* reactions. The decarbonylation of acetic acid proceeds as follows:

$$CH_3COOH(l) \longrightarrow CH_3OH(g) + CO(g)$$

By using data from Appendix C, calculate the minimum temperature at which this process will be spontaneous under standard conditions. Assume that $\Delta H°$ and $\Delta S°$ do not vary with temperature.

19.67 Consider the following reaction between oxides of nitrogen:

$$NO_2(g) + N_2O(g) \longrightarrow 3 NO(g)$$

(a) Use data in Appendix C to predict how $\Delta G°$ for the reaction varies with increasing temperature. **(b)** Calculate $\Delta G°$ at 800 K, assuming that $\Delta H°$ and $\Delta S°$ do not change with temperature. Under standard conditions is the reaction spontaneous at 800 K? **(c)** Calculate $\Delta G°$ at 1000 K. Is the reaction spontaneous under standard conditions at this temperature?

19.68 Methanol (CH_3OH) can be made by the controlled oxidation of methane:

$$CH_4(g) + \tfrac{1}{2} O_2(g) \longrightarrow CH_3OH(g)$$

(a) Use data in Appendix C to calculate $\Delta H°$ and $\Delta S°$ for this reaction. **(b)** How is $\Delta G°$ for the reaction expected to vary with increasing temperature? **(c)** Calculate $\Delta G°$ at 298 K. Under standard conditions, is the reaction spontaneous at this temperature? **(d)** Is there a temperature at which the reaction would be at equilibrium under standard conditions and that is low enough so that the compounds involved are likely to be stable?

[19.69] **(a)** Use data in Appendix C to estimate the boiling point of benzene, $C_6H_6(l)$. **(b)** Use a reference source, such as the *CRC Handbook of Chemistry and Physics*, to find the experimental boiling point of benzene. How do you explain any deviation between your answer in part (a) and the experimental value?

[19.70] **(a)** Using data in Appendix C, estimate the temperature at which the free-energy change for the transformation from $I_2(s)$ to $I_2(g)$ is zero. What assumptions must you make in arriving at this estimate? **(b)** Use a reference source, such as WebElements (www.webelements.com), to find the experimental melting and boiling points of I_2. **(c)** Which of the values in part (b) is closer to the value you obtained in part (a)? Can you explain why this is so?

19.71 Acetylene gas, $C_2H_2(g)$, is used in welding. **(a)** Write a balanced equation for the combustion of acetylene gas to $CO_2(g)$ and $H_2O(l)$. **(b)** How much heat is produced in burning 1 mol of C_2H_2 under standard conditions if both reactants and products are brought to 298 K? **(c)** What is the maximum amount of useful work that can be accomplished under standard conditions by this reaction?

19.72 **(a)** How much heat is produced in burning 1 mol of ethane (C_2H_6) under standard conditions if reactants are brought to 298 K and $H_2O(l)$ is formed? **(b)** What is the maximum amount of useful work that can be accomplished under standard conditions by this system?

Free Energy and Equilibrium

19.73 Explain qualitatively how ΔG changes for each of the following reactions as the partial pressure of O_2 is increased:
(a) $2 CO(g) + O_2(g) \longrightarrow 2 CO_2(g)$
(b) $2 H_2O_2(l) \longrightarrow 2 H_2O(l) + O_2(g)$
(c) $2 KClO_3(s) \longrightarrow 2 KCl(s) + 3 O_2(g)$

19.74 Indicate whether ΔG increases, decreases, or does not change when the partial pressure of H_2 is increased in each of the following reactions:

(a) $N_2(g) + 3 H_2(g) \longrightarrow 2 NH_3(g)$
(b) $2 HBr(g) \longrightarrow H_2(g) + Br_2(g)$
(c) $2 H_2(g) + C_2H_2(g) \longrightarrow C_2H_6(g)$

19.75 Consider the reaction $2 NO_2(g) \longrightarrow N_2O_4(g)$. **(a)** Using data from Appendix C, calculate $\Delta G°$ at 298 K. **(b)** Calculate ΔG at 298 K if the partial pressures of NO_2 and N_2O_4 are 0.40 atm and 1.60 atm, respectively.

19.76 Consider the reaction $6 H_2(g) + P_4(g) \longrightarrow 4 PH_3(g)$. **(a)** Using data from Appendix C, calculate $\Delta G°$ at 298 K. **(b)** Calculate ΔG at 298 K if the reaction mixture consists of 8.0 atm of H_2, 0.050 atm of P_4, and 0.22 atm of PH_3.

19.77 Use data from Appendix C to calculate the equilibrium constant, K, at 298 K for each of the following reactions:
(a) $H_2(g) + I_2(g) \rightleftharpoons 2 HI(g)$
(b) $C_2H_5OH(g) \rightleftharpoons C_2H_4(g) + H_2O(g)$
(c) $3 C_2H_2(g) \rightleftharpoons C_6H_6(g)$

19.78 Write the equilibrium-constant expression and calculate the value of the equilibrium constant for each of the following reactions at 298 K, using data from Appendix C:
(a) $NaHCO_3(s) \rightleftharpoons NaOH(s) + CO_2(g)$
(b) $2 HBr(g) + Cl_2(g) \rightleftharpoons 2 HCl(g) + Br_2(g)$
(c) $2 SO_2(g) + O_2(g) \rightleftharpoons 2 SO_3(g)$

19.79 Consider the decomposition of barium carbonate:

$$BaCO_3(s) \rightleftharpoons BaO(s) + CO_2(g)$$

Using data from Appendix C, calculate the equilibrium pressure of CO_2 at **(a)** 298 K and **(b)** 1100 K.

19.80 Consider the following reaction:

$$PbCO_3(s) \rightleftharpoons PbO(s) + CO_2(g)$$

Using data in Appendix C, calculate the equilibrium pressure of CO_2 in the system at **(a)** 400 °C and **(b)** 180 °C.

19.81 The value of K_a for nitrous acid (HNO_2) at 25 °C is given in Appendix D. **(a)** Write the chemical equation for the equilibrium that corresponds to K_a. **(b)** By using the value of K_a, calculate $\Delta G°$ for the dissociation of nitrous acid in aqueous solution. **(c)** What is the value of ΔG at equilibrium? **(d)** What is the value of ΔG when $[H^+] = 5.0 \times 10^{-2}\ M$, $[NO_2^-] = 6.0 \times 10^{-4}\ M$, and $[HNO_2] = 0.20\ M$?

19.82 The K_b for methylamine (CH_3NH_2) at 25 °C is given in Appendix D. **(a)** Write the chemical equation for the equilibrium that corresponds to K_b. **(b)** By using the value of K_b, calculate $\Delta G°$ for the equilibrium in part (a). **(c)** What is the value of ΔG at equilibrium? **(d)** What is the value of ΔG when $[CH_3NH_3^+] = [H^+] = 1.5 \times 10^{-8}\ M$, $[CH_3NH_3^+] = 5.5 \times 10^{-4}\ M$, and $[CH_3NH_2] = 0.120\ M$?

ADDITIONAL EXERCISES

19.83 Indicate whether each of the following statements is true or false. If it is false, correct it. **(a)** The feasibility of manufacturing NH_3 from N_2 and H_2 depends entirely on the value of ΔH for the process $N_2(g) + 3 H_2(g) \longrightarrow 2 NH_3(g)$. **(b)** The reaction of $Na(s)$ with $Cl_2(g)$ to form $NaCl(s)$ is a spontaneous process. **(c)** A spontaneous process can in principle be conducted reversibly. **(d)** Spontaneous processes in general require that work be done to force them to proceed. **(e)** Spontaneous processes are those that are exothermic and that lead to a higher degree of order in the system.

19.84 For each of the following processes, indicate whether the signs of ΔS and ΔH are expected to be positive, negative, or about zero. **(a)** A solid sublimes. **(b)** The temperature of a sample of $Co(s)$ is lowered from 60 °C to 25 °C. **(c)** Ethyl alcohol evaporates from a beaker. **(d)** A diatomic molecule dissociates into atoms. **(e)** A piece of charcoal is combusted to form $CO_2(g)$ and $H_2O(g)$.

19.85 The reaction $2 Mg(s) + O_2(g) \longrightarrow 2 MgO(s)$ is highly spontaneous and has a negative value for $\Delta S°$. The second law of thermodynamics states that in any spontaneous process there is always an increase in the entropy of the universe. Is there an inconsistency between the above reaction and the second law?

19.86 Ammonium nitrate dissolves spontaneously and endothermally in water at room temperature. What can you deduce about the sign of ΔS for this solution process?

[19.87] *Trouton's rule* states that for many liquids at their normal boiling points, the standard molar entropy of vaporization is about 88 J/mol-K. **(a)** Estimate the normal boiling point of bromine, Br_2, by determining $\Delta H°_{vap}$ for Br_2 using data from Appendix C. Assume that $\Delta H°_{vap}$ remains constant with temperature and that Trouton's rule holds. **(b)** Look up the normal boiling point of Br_2 in a chemistry handbook or at the WebElements web site (www.webelements.com).

[19.88] For the majority of the compounds listed in Appendix C, the value of $\Delta G_f°$ is more positive (or less negative) than the value of $\Delta H_f°$. **(a)** Explain this observation, using $NH_3(g)$, $CCl_4(l)$, and $KNO_3(s)$ as examples. **(b)** An exception to this observation is $CO(g)$. Explain the trend in the $\Delta H_f°$ and $\Delta G_f°$ values for this molecule.

19.89 Consider the following three reactions:
(i) $Ti(s) + 2 Cl_2(g) \longrightarrow TiCl_4(g)$
(ii) $C_2H_6(g) + 7 Cl_2(g) \longrightarrow 2 CCl_4(g) + 6 HCl(g)$
(iii) $BaO(s) + CO_2(g) \longrightarrow BaCO_3(s)$

(a) For each of the reactions, use data in Appendix C to calculate $\Delta H°$, $\Delta G°$, and $\Delta S°$ at 25 °C. **(b)** Which of these reactions are spontaneous under standard conditions at 25 °C? **(c)** For each of the reactions, predict the manner in which the change in free energy varies with an increase in temperature.

19.90 Using the data in Appendix C and given the pressures listed, calculate ΔG for each of the following reactions:
(a) $N_2(g) + 3 H_2(g) \longrightarrow 2 NH_3(g)$
   $P_{N_2} = 2.6$ atm, $P_{H_2} = 5.9$ atm, $P_{NH_3} = 1.2$ atm
(b) $2 N_2H_4(g) + 2 NO_2(g) \longrightarrow 3 N_2(g) + 4 H_2O(g)$
   $P_{N_2H_4} = P_{NO_2} = 5.0 \times 10^{-2}$ atm, $P_{N_2} = 0.5$ atm, $P_{H_2O} = 0.3$ atm
(c) $N_2H_4(g) \longrightarrow N_2(g) + 2 H_2(g)$
   $P_{N_2H_4} = 0.5$ atm, $P_{N_2} = 1.5$ atm, $P_{H_2} = 2.5$ atm

19.91 **(a)** For each of the following reactions, predict the sign of $\Delta H°$ and $\Delta S°$ and discuss briefly how these factors determine the magnitude of K. **(b)** Based on your general chemical knowledge, predict which of these reactions will have $K > 0$. **(c)** In each case indicate whether K should increase or decrease with increasing temperature.
(i) $2 Mg(s) + O_2(g) \rightleftharpoons 2 MgO(s)$
(ii) $2 KI(s) \rightleftharpoons 2 K(g) + I_2(g)$
(iii) $Na_2(g) \rightleftharpoons 2 Na(g)$
(iv) $2 V_2O_5(s) \rightleftharpoons 4 V(s) + 5 O_2(g)$

19.92 Acetic acid can be manufactured by combining methanol with carbon monoxide, an example of a *carbonylation* reaction:

$$CH_3OH(l) + CO(g) \longrightarrow CH_3COOH(l)$$

(a) Calculate the equilibrium constant for the reaction at 25 °C. **(b)** Industrially, this reaction is run at temperatures above 25 °C. Will an increase in temperature produce an increase or decrease in the mole fraction of acetic acid at equilibrium? Why are elevated temperatures used? **(c)** At what temperature will this reaction have an equilibrium constant equal to 1? (You may assume that $\Delta H°$ and $\Delta S°$ are temperature independent, and you may ignore any phase changes that might occur.)

19.93 The oxidation of glucose ($C_6H_{12}O_6$) in body tissue produces CO_2 and H_2O. In contrast, anaerobic decomposition, which occurs during fermentation, produces ethanol (C_2H_5OH) and CO_2. **(a)** Using data given in Appendix C, compare the equilibrium constants for the following reactions:

$$C_6H_{12}O_6(s) + 6\,O_2(g) \rightleftharpoons 6\,CO_2(g) + 6\,H_2O(l)$$
$$C_6H_{12}O_6(s) \rightleftharpoons 2\,C_2H_5OH(l) + 2\,CO_2(g)$$

(b) Compare the maximum work that can be obtained from these processes under standard conditions.

[19.94] The conversion of natural gas, which is mostly methane, into products that contain two or more carbon atoms, such as ethane (C_2H_6), is a very important industrial chemical process. In principle, methane can be converted into ethane and hydrogen:

$$2\,CH_4(g) \longrightarrow C_2H_6(g) + H_2(g)$$

In practice, this reaction is carried out in the presence of oxygen:

$$2\,CH_4(g) + \tfrac{1}{2}O_2(g) \longrightarrow C_2H_6(g) + H_2O(g)$$

(a) Using the data in Appendix C, calculate K for these reactions at 25 °C and 500 °C. **(b)** Is the difference in $\Delta G°$ for the two reactions due primarily to the enthalpy term (ΔH) or the entropy term ($-T\Delta S$)? **(c)** Explain how the preceding reactions are an example of driving a nonspontaneous reaction, as discussed in the "Chemistry and Life" box in Section 19.7. **(d)** The reaction of CH_4 and O_2 to form C_2H_6 and H_2O must be carried out carefully to avoid a competing reaction. What is the most likely competing reaction?

[19.95] Cells use the hydrolysis of adenosine triphosphate (ATP) as a source of energy (Figure 19.20). The conversion of ATP to ADP has a standard free-energy change of -30.5 kJ/mol. If all the free energy from the metabolism of glucose,

$$C_6H_{12}O_6(s) + 6\,O_2(g) \longrightarrow 6\,CO_2(g) + 6\,H_2O(l)$$

goes into the conversion of ADP to ATP, how many moles of ATP can be produced for each mole of glucose?

[19.96] The potassium-ion concentration in blood plasma is about 5.0×10^{-3} M, whereas the concentration in muscle-cell fluid is much greater (0.15 M). The plasma and intracellular fluid are separated by the cell membrane, which we assume is permeable only to K^+. **(a)** What is ΔG for the transfer of 1 mol of K^+ from blood plasma to the cellular fluid at body temperature 37 °C? **(b)** What is the minimum amount of work that must be used to transfer this K^+?

[19.97] The relationship between the temperature of a reaction, its standard enthalpy change, and the equilibrium constant at that temperature can be expressed as the following linear equation:

$$\ln K = \frac{-\Delta H°}{RT} + \text{constant}$$

(a) Explain how this equation can be used to determine $\Delta H°$ experimentally from the equilibrium constants at several different temperatures. **(b)** Derive the preceding equation using relationships given in this chapter. To what is the constant equal?

[19.98] One way to derive Equation 19.3 depends on the observation that at constant T the number of ways, W, of arranging m ideal-gas particles in a volume V is proportional to the volume raised to the m power:

$$W \propto V^m$$

Use this relationship and Boltzmann's relationship between entropy and number of arrangements (Equation 19.5) to derive the equation for the entropy change for the isothermal expansion or compression of n moles of an ideal gas.

[19.99] About 86% of the world's electrical energy is produced by using steam turbines, a form of heat engine. In his analysis of an ideal heat engine, Sadi Carnot concluded that the maximum possible efficiency is defined by the total work that could be done by the engine, divided by the quantity of heat available to do the work (for example from hot steam produced by combustion of a fuel such as coal or methane). This efficiency is given by the ratio $(T_{high} - T_{low})/T_{high}$, where T_{high} is the temperature of the heat going into the engine and T_{low} is that of the heat leaving the engine. **(a)** What is the maximum possible efficiency of a heat engine operating between an input temperature of 700 K and an exit temperature of 288 K? **(b)** Why is it important that electrical power plants be located near bodies of relatively cool water? **(c)** Under what conditions could a heat engine operate at or near 100% efficiency? **(d)** It is often said that if the energy of combustion of a fuel such as methane were captured in an electrical fuel cell instead of by burning the fuel in a heat engine, a greater fraction of the energy could be put to useful work. Make a qualitative drawing like that in Figure 5.10 that illustrates the fact that in principle the fuel cell route will produce more useful work than the heat engine route from combustion of methane.

INTEGRATIVE EXERCISES

19.100 Most liquids follow Trouton's rule, which states that the molar entropy of vaporization lies in the range of 88 ± 5 J/mol-K. The normal boiling points and enthalpies of vaporization of several organic liquids are as follows:

Substance	Normal Boiling Point (°C)	ΔH_{vap} (kJ/mol)
Acetone, $(CH_3)_2CO$	56.1	29.1
Dimethyl ether, $(CH_3)_2O$	-24.8	21.5
Ethanol, C_2H_5OH	78.4	38.6
Octane, C_8H_{18}	125.6	34.4
Pyridine, C_5H_5N	115.3	35.1

(a) Calculate ΔS_{vap} for each of the liquids. Do all of the liquids obey Trouton's rule? (b) With reference to intermolecular forces (Section 11.2), can you explain any exceptions to the rule? (c) Would you expect water to obey Trouton's rule? By using data in Appendix B, check the accuracy of your conclusion. (d) Chlorobenzene (C_6H_5Cl) boils at 131.8 °C. Use Trouton's rule to estimate ΔH_{vap} for this substance.

19.101 Consider the polymerization of ethylene to polyethylene. ∞ (Section 12.6) (a) What would you predict for the sign of the entropy change during polymerization (ΔS_{poly})? Explain your reasoning. (b) The polymerization of ethylene is a spontaneous process at room temperature. What can you conclude about the enthalpy change during polymerization (ΔH_{poly})? (c) Use average bond enthalpies (Table 8.4) to estimate the value of ΔH_{poly} per ethylene monomer added. (d) Polyethylene is an *addition polymer*. By comparison, Nylon 66 is a *condensation polymer*. How would you expect ΔS_{poly} for a condensation polymer to compare to that for an addition polymer? Explain.

19.102 In chemical kinetics the *entropy of activation* is the entropy change for the process in which the reactants reach the activated complex. The entropy of activation for bimolecular processes is usually negative. Explain this observation with reference to Figure 14.15.

19.103 The following processes were all discussed in Chapter 18, "Chemistry of the Environment." Estimate whether the entropy of the system increases or decreases during each process: (a) photodissociation of $O_2(g)$, (b) formation of ozone from oxygen molecules and oxygen atoms, (c) diffusion of CFCs into the stratosphere, (d) desalination of water by reverse osmosis.

19.104 Carbon disulfide (CS_2) is a toxic, highly flammable substance. The following thermodynamic data are available for $CS_2(l)$ and $CS_2(g)$ at 298 K:

	ΔH_f° (kJ/mol)	ΔG_f° (kJ/mol)
$CS_2(l)$	89.7	65.3
$CS_2(g)$	117.4	67.2

(a) Draw the Lewis structure of the molecule. What do you predict for the bond order of the C—S bonds? (b) Use the VSEPR method to predict the structure of the CS_2 molecule. (c) Liquid CS_2 burns in O_2 with a blue flame, forming $CO_2(g)$ and $SO_2(g)$. Write a balanced equation for this reaction. (d) Using the data in the preceding table and in Appendix C, calculate ΔH° and ΔG° for the reaction in part (c). Is the reaction exothermic? Is it spontaneous at 298 K? (e) Use the data in the preceding table to calculate ΔS° at 298 K for the vaporization of $CS_2(l)$. Is the sign of ΔS° as you would expect for a vaporization? (f) Using data in the preceding table and your answer to part (e), estimate the boiling point of $CS_2(l)$. Do you predict that the substance will be a liquid or a gas at 298 K and 1 atm?

[19.105] The following data compare the standard enthalpies and free energies of formation of some crystalline ionic substances and aqueous solutions of the substances:

Substance	ΔH_f° (kJ/mol)	ΔG_f° (kJ/mol)
$AgNO_3(s)$	−124.4	−33.4
$AgNO_3(aq)$	−101.7	−34.2
$MgSO_4(s)$	−1283.7	−1169.6
$MgSO_4(aq)$	−1374.8	−1198.4

(a) Write the formation reaction for $AgNO_3(s)$. Based on this reaction, do you expect the entropy of the system to increase or decrease upon the formation of $AgNO_3(s)$? (b) Use ΔH_f° and ΔG_f° of $AgNO_3(s)$ to determine the entropy change upon formation of the substance. Is your answer consistent with your reasoning in part (a)? (c) Is dissolving $AgNO_3$ in water an exothermic or endothermic process? What about dissolving $MgSO_4$ in water? (d) For both $AgNO_3$ and $MgSO_4$, use the data to calculate the entropy change when the solid is dissolved in water. (e) Discuss the results from part (d) with reference to material presented in this chapter and in the second "Closer Look" box in Section 13.5.

[19.106] Consider the following equilibrium:

$$N_2O_4(g) \rightleftharpoons 2\,NO_2(g)$$

Thermodynamic data on these gases are given in Appendix C. You may assume that ΔH° and ΔS° do not vary with temperature. (a) At what temperature will an equilibrium mixture contain equal amounts of the two gases? (b) At what temperature will an equilibrium mixture of 1 atm total pressure contain twice as much NO_2 as N_2O_4? (c) At what temperature will an equilibrium mixture of 10 atm total pressure contain twice as much NO_2 as N_2O_4? (d) Rationalize the results from parts (b) and (c) by using Le Châtelier's principle. ∞ (Section 15.7)

[19.107] The reaction

$$SO_2(g) + 2\,H_2S(g) \rightleftharpoons 3\,S(s) + 2\,H_2O(g)$$

is the basis of a suggested method for removal of SO_2 from power-plant stack gases. The standard free energy of each substance is given in Appendix C. (a) What is the equilibrium constant for the reaction at 298 K? (b) In principle, is this reaction a feasible method of removing SO_2? (c) If $P_{SO_2} = P_{H_2S}$ and the vapor pressure of water is 25 torr, calculate the equilibrium SO_2 pressure in the system at 298 K. (d) Would you expect the process to be more or less effective at higher temperatures?

19.108 When most elastomeric polymers (e.g., a rubber band) are stretched, the molecules become more ordered, as illustrated here:

Suppose you stretch a rubber band. (a) Do you expect the entropy of the system to increase or decrease? (b) If the rubber band were stretched isothermally, would heat need to be absorbed or emitted to maintain constant temperature?

20

ELECTROCHEMISTRY

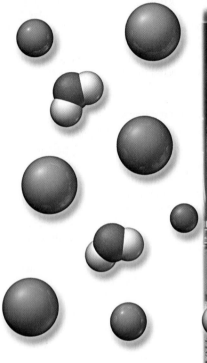

A VARIETY OF BATTERIES of different sizes, composition, and voltages.

we usually do not need to assign oxidation numbers unless we are unsure whether the reaction actually involves oxidation-reduction. We will find that H^+ (for acidic solutions), OH^- (for basic solutions), and H_2O are often involved as reactants or products in redox reactions. Unless H^+, OH^-, or H_2O are being oxidized or reduced, they do not appear in the skeleton equation. Their presence, however, can be deduced during the course of balancing the equation.

For balancing a redox reaction that occurs in acidic aqueous solution, the procedure is as follows:

1. Divide the equation into two half-reactions, one for oxidation and the other for reduction.

2. Balance each half-reaction.
   (a) First, balance the elements other than H and O.
   (b) Next, balance the O atoms by adding H_2O as needed.
   (c) Then, balance the H atoms by adding H^+ as needed.
   (d) Finally, balance the charge by adding e^- as needed.
   This specific sequence is important, and it is summarized in the diagram in the margin. At this point, you can check whether the number of electrons in each half-reaction corresponds to the changes in oxidation state.

3. Multiply the half-reactions by integers, if necessary, so that the number of electrons lost in one half-reaction equals the number of electrons gained in the other.

4. Add the two half-reactions and, if possible, simplify by canceling species appearing on both sides of the combined equation.

5. Check to make sure that atoms and charges are balanced.

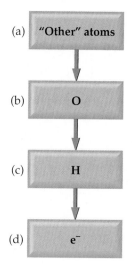

(a) "Other" atoms

(b) O

(c) H

(d) e^-

As an example, let's consider the reaction between permanganate ion (MnO_4^-) and oxalate ion ($C_2O_4^{2-}$) in acidic aqueous solution. When MnO_4^- is added to an acidified solution of $C_2O_4^{2-}$, the deep purple color of the MnO_4^- ion fades, as illustrated in Figure 20.2▼. Bubbles of CO_2 form, and the solution takes on the pale pink color of Mn^{2+}. We can therefore write the skeleton equation as

$$MnO_4^-(aq) + C_2O_4^{2-}(aq) \longrightarrow Mn^{2+}(aq) + CO_2(aq) \qquad [20.6]$$

Experiments show that H^+ is consumed and H_2O is produced in the reaction. We will see that their involvement in the reaction is deduced in the course of balancing the equation.

To complete and balance this equation, we first write the two half-reactions (step 1). One half-reaction must have Mn on both sides of the arrow, and the other must have C on both sides of the arrow:

$$MnO_4^-(aq) \longrightarrow Mn^{2+}(aq)$$
$$C_2O_4^{2-}(aq) \longrightarrow CO_2(g)$$

(a)   (b)   (c)

◀ Figure 20.2 **Titration of an acidic solution of $Na_2C_2O_4$ with $KMnO_4(aq)$.** (a) As it moves from the buret to the reaction flask, the deep purple MnO_4^- is rapidly reduced to extremely pale pink Mn^{2+} by $C_2O_4^{2-}$. (b) Once all the $C_2O_4^{2-}$ in the flask has been consumed, any MnO_4^- added to the flask retains its purple color, and the end point corresponds to the faintest discernible purple color in the solution. (c) Beyond the end point the solution in the flask becomes deep purple because of excess MnO_4^-.

We next complete and balance each half-reaction. First, we balance all the atoms except for H and O (step 2a). In the permanganate half-reaction we already have one manganese atom on each side of the equation and so need to do nothing. In the oxalate half-reaction we need to add a coefficient 2 to the right to balance the two carbons on the left:

$$MnO_4^-(aq) \longrightarrow Mn^{2+}(aq)$$

$$C_2O_4^{2-}(aq) \longrightarrow 2\,CO_2(g)$$

Next we balance O (step 2b). The permanganate half-reaction has four oxygens on the left and none on the right; therefore four H_2O molecules are needed as product to balance the four oxygen atoms in MnO_4^-:

$$MnO_4^-(aq) \longrightarrow Mn^{2+}(aq) + 4\,H_2O(l)$$

The eight hydrogen atoms now in the products must be balanced by adding $8\,H^+$ to the reactants (step 2c):

$$8\,H^+(aq) + MnO_4^-(aq) \longrightarrow Mn^{2+}(aq) + 4\,H_2O(l)$$

There are now equal numbers of each type of atom on the two sides of the equation, but the charge still needs to be balanced. The total charge of the reactants is $8(1+) + (1-) = 7+$, and that of the products is $(2+) + 4(0) = 2+$. To balance the charge, we must add five electrons to the reactant side (step 3d):

$$5\,e^- + 8\,H^+(aq) + MnO_4^-(aq) \longrightarrow Mn^{2+}(aq) + 4\,H_2O(l)$$

We can check our result using oxidation states. In this half-reaction Mn goes from the +7 oxidation state in MnO_4^- to the +2 oxidation state in Mn^{2+}. Therefore, each Mn atom gains five electrons, in agreement with our balanced half-reaction.

Now that the permanganate half-reaction is balanced, let's return to the oxalate half-reaction. We already balanced the C and O atoms in step 2a. We can balance the charge (step 2d) by adding two electrons to the products:

$$C_2O_4^{2-}(aq) \longrightarrow 2\,CO_2(g) + 2\,e^-$$

We can check this result using oxidation states. Carbon goes from the +3 oxidation state in $C_2O_4^{2-}$ to the +4 oxidation state in CO_2. Thus, each C atom loses one electron, and therefore the two C atoms in $C_2O_4^{2-}$ lose two electrons, in agreement with our balanced half-reaction.

Now we need to multiply each half-reaction by an appropriate integer so that the number of electrons gained in one half-reaction equals the number of electrons lost in the other (step 3). We must multiply the MnO_4^- half-reaction by 2 and the $C_2O_4^{2-}$ half-reaction by 5 so that the same number of electrons (10) appears in both equations:

$$10\,e^- + 16\,H^+(aq) + 2\,MnO_4^-(aq) \longrightarrow 2\,Mn^{2+}(aq) + 8\,H_2O(l)$$

$$\underline{5\,C_2O_4^{2-}(aq) \longrightarrow 10\,CO_2(g) + 10\,e^-}$$

$$16\,H^+(aq) + 2\,MnO_4^-(aq) + 5\,C_2O_4^{2-}(aq) \longrightarrow$$
$$2\,Mn^{2+}(aq) + 8\,H_2O(l) + 10\,CO_2(g)$$

The balanced equation is the sum of the balanced half-reactions (step 4). Note that the electrons on the reactant and product sides of the equation cancel each other.

We can check the balanced equation by counting atoms and charges (step 5): There are 16 H, 2 Mn, 28 O, 10 C, and a net charge of 4+ on each side of the equation, confirming that the equation is correctly balanced.

▲ GIVE IT SOME THOUGHT

If the equation for a redox reaction is balanced, will free electrons appear in the equation as either reactants or products?

20.4 CELL EMF UNDER STANDARD CONDITIONS

Why do electrons transfer spontaneously from a Zn atom to a Cu^{2+} ion, either directly as in the reaction of Figure 20.3 or through an external circuit as in the voltaic cell of Figure 20.4? In a simple sense, we can compare the electron flow to the flow of water in a waterfall (Figure 20.9▶). Water flows spontaneously over a waterfall because of a difference in potential energy between the top of the falls and the stream below. ∞∞ (Section 5.1) In a similar fashion, electrons flow from the anode of a voltaic cell to the cathode because of a difference in potential energy. The potential energy of electrons is higher in the anode than in the cathode, and they spontaneously flow through an external circuit from the anode to the cathode. That is, electrons flow spontaneously toward the electrode with the more positive electrical potential.

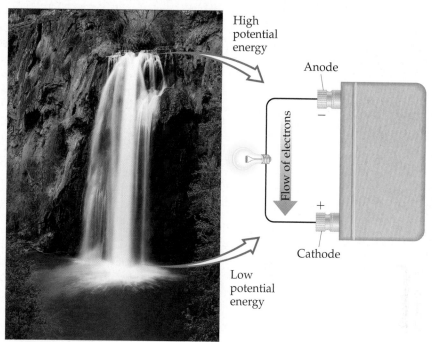

▲ Figure 20.9 **Water analogy for electron flow.** The flow of electrons from the anode to the cathode of a voltaic cell can be likened to the flow of water over a waterfall. Water flows over the waterfall because its potential energy is lower at the bottom of the falls than at the top. Likewise, if there is an electrical connection between the anode and cathode of a voltaic cell, electrons flow from the anode to the cathode to lower their potential energy.

The difference in potential energy per electrical charge (the *potential difference*) between two electrodes is measured in units of volts. One volt (V) is the potential difference required to impart 1 joule (J) of energy to a charge of 1 coulomb (C).

$$1 \text{ V} = 1 \frac{\text{J}}{\text{C}}$$

Recall that one electron has a charge of 1.60×10^{-19} C. ∞∞ (Section 2.2)

The potential difference between the two electrodes of a voltaic cell provides the driving force that pushes electrons through the external circuit. Therefore, we call this potential difference the **electromotive** ("causing electron motion") **force**, or **emf**. The emf of a cell, denoted E_{cell}, is also called the **cell potential**. Because E_{cell} is measured in volts, we often refer to it as the *cell voltage*. For any cell reaction that proceeds spontaneously, such as that in a voltaic cell, the cell potential will be *positive*.

The emf of a particular voltaic cell depends on the specific reactions that occur at the cathode and anode, the concentrations of reactants and products, and the temperature, which we will assume to be 25 °C unless otherwise noted. In this section we will focus on cells that are operated at 25 °C under *standard conditions*. Recall from Section 19.5 that standard conditions include 1 *M* concentrations for reactants and products in solution and 1 atm pressure for those that are gases (Table 19.3). Under standard conditions the emf is called the **standard emf**, or the **standard cell potential**, and is denoted $E°_{cell}$. For the Zn-Cu voltaic cell in Figure 20.5, for example, the standard cell potential at 25 °C is +1.10 V.

$$Zn(s) + Cu^{2+}(aq, 1\ M) \longrightarrow Zn^{2+}(aq, 1\ M) + Cu(s) \qquad E°_{cell} = +1.10 \text{ V}$$

Recall that the superscript ° indicates standard-state conditions. ∞∞ (Section 5.7)

GIVE IT SOME THOUGHT

If a standard cell potential is +0.85 V at 25 °C, is the redox reaction of the cell spontaneous?

Standard Reduction (Half-Cell) Potentials

The emf, or cell potential, of a voltaic cell, $E°_{cell}$, depends on the particular cathode and anode half-cells involved. We could, in principle, tabulate the standard cell potentials for all possible cathode/anode combinations. However, it is not necessary to undertake this arduous task. Rather, we can assign a standard potential to each individual half-cell and then use these half-cell potentials to determine $E°_{cell}$.

The cell potential is the difference between two electrode potentials, one associated with the cathode and the other associated with the anode. By convention, the potential associated with each electrode is chosen to be the potential for reduction to occur at that electrode. Thus, standard electrode potentials are tabulated for reduction reactions; they are **standard reduction potentials**, denoted $E°_{red}$. The cell potential, $E°_{cell}$, is given by the standard reduction potential of the cathode reaction, $E°_{red}$ (cathode), *minus* the standard reduction potential of the anode reaction, $E°_{red}$ (anode):

$$E°_{cell} = E°_{red} \text{ (cathode)} - E°_{red} \text{ (anode)} \qquad [20.8]$$

For all spontaneous reactions at standard conditions, $E°_{cell} > 0$.

Because every voltaic cell involves two half-cells, it is not possible to measure the standard reduction potential of a half-reaction directly. If we assign a standard reduction potential to a certain reference half-reaction, however, we can then determine the standard reduction potentials of other half-reactions relative to that reference. The reference half-reaction is the reduction of $H^+(aq)$ to $H_2(g)$ under standard conditions, which is assigned a standard reduction potential of exactly 0 V.

$$2\,H^+(aq, 1\,M) + 2\,e^- \longrightarrow H_2(g, 1\,atm) \qquad E°_{red} = 0\,V \qquad [20.9]$$

An electrode designed to produce this half-reaction is called a **standard hydrogen electrode** (SHE), or the normal hydrogen electrode (NHE). An SHE consists of a platinum wire connected to a piece of platinum foil covered with finely divided platinum that serves as an inert surface for the reaction. The electrode is encased in a glass tube so that hydrogen gas under standard conditions (1 atm) can bubble over the platinum, and the solution contains $H^+(aq)$ under standard (1 M) conditions (Figure 20.10▼).

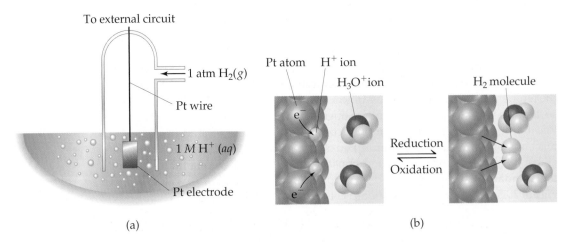

▲ **Figure 20.10 The standard hydrogen electrode (SHE) used as a reference electrode.** (a) An SHE consists of an electrode with finely divided Pt in contact with $H_2(g)$ at 1 atm pressure and an acidic solution with $[H^+] = 1\,M$. (b) Molecular depiction of the processes that occur at the SHE. When the SHE is the cathode of a cell, two H^+ ions each accept an electron from the Pt electrode and are reduced to H atoms. The H atoms bond together to form H_2. When the SHE is the anode of a cell, the reverse process occurs: An H_2 molecule at the electrode surface loses two electrons and is oxidized to H^+. The H^+ ions in solution are hydrated.

Figure 20.11▶ shows a voltaic cell using an SHE and a standard electrode. The spontaneous reaction is the one shown in Figure 20.1, namely, the oxidation of Zn and the reduction of H^+:

$$Zn(s) + 2\,H^+(aq) \longrightarrow Zn^{2+}(aq) + H_2(g)$$

Notice that the Zn^{2+}/Zn electrode is the anode and the SHE is the cathode and that the cell voltage is +0.76 V. By using the defined standard reduction potential of H^+ ($E^\circ_{red} = 0$) and Equation 20.8, we can determine the standard reduction potential for the Zn^{2+}/Zn half-reaction:

$$E^\circ_{cell} = E^\circ_{red}\,(\text{cathode}) - E^\circ_{red}\,(\text{anode})$$

$$+0.76\text{ V} = 0\text{ V} - E^\circ_{red}\,(\text{anode})$$

$$E^\circ_{red}\,(\text{anode}) = -0.76\text{ V}$$

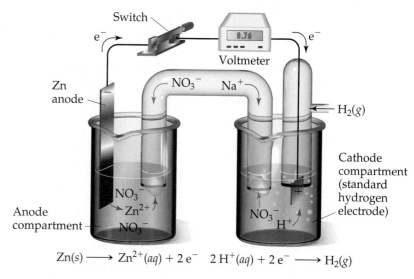

▲ Figure 20.11 **A voltaic cell using a standard hydrogen electrode.**

Thus, a standard reduction potential of −0.76 V can be assigned to the reduction of Zn^{2+} to Zn.

$$Zn^{2+}(aq, 1\text{ }M) + 2\,e^- \longrightarrow Zn(s) \qquad E^\circ_{red} = -0.76\text{ V}$$

We write the reaction as a reduction even though it is "running in reverse" as an oxidation in the cell in Figure 20.11. *Whenever we assign an electrical potential to a half-reaction, we write the reaction as a reduction.*

The standard reduction potentials for other half-reactions can be established from other cell potentials in a fashion analogous to that used for the Zn^{2+}/Zn half-reaction. Table 20.1▼ lists some standard reduction potentials; a more complete list is found in Appendix E. These standard reduction potentials, often called *half-cell potentials*, can be combined to calculate the emfs of a large variety of voltaic cells.

TABLE 20.1 ■ Standard Reduction Potentials in Water at 25 °C

Potential (V)	Reduction Half-Reaction
+2.87	$F_2(g) + 2\,e^- \longrightarrow 2\,F^-(aq)$
+1.51	$MnO_4^-(aq) + 8\,H^+(aq) + 5\,e^- \longrightarrow Mn^{2+}(aq) + 4\,H_2O(l)$
+1.36	$Cl_2(g) + 2\,e^- \longrightarrow 2\,Cl^-(aq)$
+1.33	$Cr_2O_7^{2-}(aq) + 14\,H^+(aq) + 6\,e^- \longrightarrow 2\,Cr^{3+}(aq) + 7\,H_2O(l)$
+1.23	$O_2(g) + 4\,H^+(aq) + 4\,e^- \longrightarrow 2\,H_2O(l)$
+1.06	$Br_2(l) + 2\,e^- \longrightarrow 2\,Br^-(aq)$
+0.96	$NO_3^-(aq) + 4\,H^+(aq) + 3\,e^- \longrightarrow NO(g) + 2\,H_2O(l)$
+0.80	$Ag^+(aq) + e^- \longrightarrow Ag(s)$
+0.77	$Fe^{3+}(aq) + e^- \longrightarrow Fe^{2+}(aq)$
+0.68	$O_2(g) + 2\,H^+(aq) + 2\,e^- \longrightarrow H_2O_2(aq)$
+0.59	$MnO_4^-(aq) + 2\,H_2O(l) + 3\,e^- \longrightarrow MnO_2(s) + 4\,OH^-(aq)$
+0.54	$I_2(s) + 2\,e^- \longrightarrow 2\,I^-(aq)$
+0.40	$O_2(g) + 2\,H_2O(l) + 4\,e^- \longrightarrow 4\,OH^-(aq)$
+0.34	$Cu^{2+}(aq) + 2\,e^- \longrightarrow Cu(s)$
0 [defined]	$2\,H^+(aq) + 2\,e^- \longrightarrow H_2(g)$
−0.28	$Ni^{2+}(aq) + 2\,e^- \longrightarrow Ni(s)$
−0.44	$Fe^{2+}(aq) + 2\,e^- \longrightarrow Fe(s)$
−0.76	$Zn^{2+}(aq) + 2\,e^- \longrightarrow Zn(s)$
−0.83	$2\,H_2O(l) + 2\,e^- \longrightarrow H_2(g) + 2\,OH^-(aq)$
−1.66	$Al^{3+}(aq) + 3\,e^- \longrightarrow Al(s)$
−2.71	$Na^+(aq) + e^- \longrightarrow Na(s)$
−3.05	$Li^+(aq) + e^- \longrightarrow Li(s)$

> ◢ GIVE IT SOME THOUGHT

For the half-reaction $Cl_2(g) + 2e^- \longrightarrow 2Cl^-(aq)$, what are the standard conditions for the reactant and product?

Because electrical potential measures potential energy per electrical charge, standard reduction potentials are intensive properties. ∞ (Section 1.3). In other words, if we increased the amount of substances in a redox reaction, we would increase both the energy and charges involved, but the ratio of energy (joules) to electrical charge (coulombs) would remain constant ($V = J/C$). Thus, *changing the stoichiometric coefficient in a half-reaction does not affect the value of the standard reduction potential.* For example, E°_{red} for the reduction of 10 mol Zn^{2+} is the same as that for the reduction of 1 mol Zn^{2+}:

$$10\,Zn^{2+}(aq, 1\,M) + 20\,e^- \longrightarrow 10\,Zn(s) \qquad E^\circ_{red} = -0.76\,V$$

◼ SAMPLE EXERCISE 20.5 | Calculating E°_{red} from E°_{cell}

For the Zn-Cu^{2+} voltaic cell shown in Figure 20.5, we have

$$Zn(s) + Cu^{2+}(aq, 1\,M) \longrightarrow Zn^{2+}(aq, 1\,M) + Cu(s) \qquad E^\circ_{cell} = 1.10\,V$$

Given that the standard reduction potential of Zn^{2+} to $Zn(s)$ is -0.76 V, calculate the E°_{red} for the reduction of Cu^{2+} to Cu:

$$Cu^{2+}(aq, 1\,M) + 2e^- \longrightarrow Cu(s)$$

SOLUTION

Analyze: We are given E°_{cell} and E°_{red} for Zn^{2+} and asked to calculate E°_{red} for Cu^{2+}.

Plan: In the voltaic cell, Zn is oxidized and is therefore the anode. Thus, the given E°_{red} for Zn^{2+} is E°_{red} (anode). Because Cu^{2+} is reduced, it is in the cathode half-cell. Thus, the unknown reduction potential for Cu^{2+} is E°_{red} (cathode). Knowing E°_{cell} and E°_{red} (anode), we can use Equation 20.8 to solve for E°_{red} (cathode).

Solve:

$$E^\circ_{cell} = E^\circ_{red} (\text{cathode}) - E^\circ_{red} (\text{anode})$$
$$1.10\,V = E^\circ_{red} (\text{cathode}) - (-0.76\,V)$$
$$E^\circ_{red} (\text{cathode}) = 1.10\,V - 0.76\,V = 0.34\,V$$

Check: This standard reduction potential agrees with the one listed in Table 20.1.

Comment: The standard reduction potential for Cu^{2+} can be represented as $E^\circ_{Cu^{2+}} = 0.34$ V, and that for Zn^{2+} as $E^\circ_{Zn^{2+}} = -0.76$ V. The subscript identifies the ion that is reduced in the reduction half-reaction.

◼ PRACTICE EXERCISE

A voltaic cell is based on the half-reactions

$$In^+(aq) \longrightarrow In^{3+}(aq) + 2e^-$$
$$Br_2(l) + 2e^- \longrightarrow 2Br^-(aq)$$

The standard emf for this cell is 1.46 V. Using the data in Table 20.1, calculate E°_{red} for the reduction of In^{3+} to In^+.
Answer: -0.40 V

◼ SAMPLE EXERCISE 20.6 | Calculating E°_{cell} from E°_{red}

Using the standard reduction potentials listed in Table 20.1, calculate the standard emf for the voltaic cell described in Sample Exercise 20.4, which is based on the reaction

$$Cr_2O_7^{2-}(aq) + 14\,H^+(aq) + 6\,I^-(aq) \longrightarrow 2\,Cr^{3+}(aq) + 3\,I_2(s) + 7\,H_2O(l)$$

SOLUTION

Analyze: We are given the equation for a redox reaction and asked to use data in Table 20.1 to calculate the standard emf (standard potential) for the associated voltaic cell.

Plan: Our first step is to identify the half-reactions that occur at the cathode and the anode, which we did in Sample Exercise 20.4. Then we can use data from Table 20.1 and Equation 20.8 to calculate the standard emf.

Solve: The half-reactions are

Cathode: $Cr_2O_7^{2-}(aq) + 14 H^+(aq) + 6 e^- \longrightarrow 2 Cr^{3+}(aq) + 7 H_2O(l)$

Anode: $6 I^-(aq) \longrightarrow 3 I_2(s) + 6 e^-$

According to Table 20.1, the standard reduction potential for the reduction of $Cr_2O_7^{2-}$ to Cr^{3+} is +1.33 V, and the standard reduction potential for the reduction of I_2 to I^- (the reverse of the oxidation half-reaction) is +0.54 V. We then use these values in Equation 20.8.

$$E_{cell}^\circ = E_{red}^\circ \text{ (cathode)} - E_{red}^\circ \text{ (anode)} = 1.33 \text{ V} - 0.54 \text{ V} = 0.79 \text{ V}$$

Although we must multiply the iodide half-reaction at the anode by 3 to obtain a balanced equation for the reaction, the value of E_{red}° is *not* multiplied by 3. As we have noted, the standard reduction potential is an intensive property, so it is independent of the specific stoichiometric coefficients.

Check: The cell potential, 0.79 V, is a positive number. As noted earlier, a voltaic cell must have a positive emf in order to operate.

■ PRACTICE EXERCISE

Using data in Table 20.1, calculate the standard emf for a cell that employs the following overall cell reaction:

$$2 Al(s) + 3 I_2(s) \longrightarrow 2 Al^{3+}(aq) + 6 I^-(aq)$$

Answer: $0.54 \text{ V} - (-1.66 \text{ V}) = 2.20 \text{ V}$

For each of the half-cells in a voltaic cell, the standard reduction potential provides a measure of the driving force for reduction to occur: *The more positive the value of* E_{red}°, *the greater the driving force for reduction under standard conditions.* In any voltaic cell operating under standard conditions, the reaction at the cathode has a more positive value of E_{red}° than does the reaction at the anode.

Equation 20.8, which indicates that the standard cell potential is the difference between the standard reduction potential of the cathode and the standard reduction potential of the anode, is illustrated graphically in Figure 20.12▶. The standard reduction potentials of the cathode and anode are shown on a scale. The more positive E_{red}° value identifies the cathode, and the difference between the two standard reduction potentials is the standard cell potential. Figure 20.13▶ shows the specific values of E_{red}° for the two half-reactions in the Zn-Cu voltaic cell illustrated in Figure 20.5.

▲ **GIVE IT SOME THOUGHT**

Is the following statement true or false? The smaller the difference is between the standard reduction potentials of the cathode and anode, the smaller the driving force for the overall redox reaction.

■ SAMPLE EXERCISE 20.7 | Determining Half-Reactions at Electrodes and Calculating Cell EMF

A voltaic cell is based on the following two standard half-reactions:

$$Cd^{2+}(aq) + 2 e^- \longrightarrow Cd(s)$$
$$Sn^{2+}(aq) + 2 e^- \longrightarrow Sn(s)$$

By using the data in Appendix E, determine **(a)** the half-reactions that occur at the cathode and the anode, and **(b)** the standard cell potential.

SOLUTION

Analyze: We have to look up E_{red}° for two half-reactions and use these values to predict the cathode and anode of the cell and to calculate its standard cell potential, E_{cell}°.

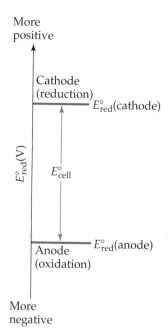

▲ **Figure 20.12 Standard cell potential of a voltaic cell.** The cell potential measures the difference in the standard reduction potentials of the cathode and the anode reactions: $E_{cell}^\circ = E_{red}^\circ$ (cathode) $- E_{red}^\circ$ (anode). In a voltaic cell the cathode reaction is always the one that has the more positive (or less negative) value for E_{red}°.

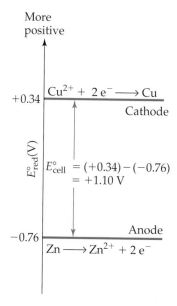

▲ **Figure 20.13 Half-cell potentials.** The half-cell potentials for the voltaic cell in Figure 20.5, diagrammed in the style of Figure 20.12.

Plan: The cathode will have the reduction with the more positive $E°_{red}$ value. The anode will have the less positive $E°_{red}$. To write the half-reaction at the anode, we reverse the half-reaction written for the reduction, so that the half-reaction is written as an oxidation.

Solve:

(a) According to Appendix E, $E°_{red}(Cd^{2+}/Cd) = -0.403$ V and $E°_{red}(Sn^{2+}/Sn) = -0.136$ V. The standard reduction potential for Sn^{2+} is more positive (less negative) than that for Cd^{2+}; hence, the reduction of Sn^{2+} is the reaction that occurs at the cathode.

$$\text{Cathode:} \qquad Sn^{2+}(aq) + 2\,e^- \longrightarrow Sn(s)$$

The anode reaction therefore is the loss of electrons by Cd.

$$\text{Anode:} \qquad Cd(s) \longrightarrow Cd^{2+}(aq) + 2\,e^-$$

(b) The cell potential is given by Equation 20.8.

$$E°_{cell} = E°_{red} \text{ (cathode)} - E°_{red} \text{ (anode)} = (-0.136 \text{ V}) - (-0.403 \text{ V}) = 0.267 \text{ V}$$

Notice that it is unimportant that the $E°_{red}$ values of both half-reactions are negative; the negative values merely indicate how these reductions compare to the reference reaction, the reduction of $H^+(aq)$.

Check: The cell potential is positive, as it must be for a voltaic cell.

■ PRACTICE EXERCISE

A voltaic cell is based on a Co^{2+}/Co half-cell and an $AgCl/Ag$ half-cell.
(a) What half-reaction occurs at the anode? **(b)** What is the standard cell potential?
Answers: **(a)** $Co \longrightarrow Co^{2+} + 2\,e^-$; **(b)** $+0.499$ V

Strengths of Oxidizing and Reducing Agents

We have thus far used the tabulation of standard reduction potentials to examine voltaic cells. We can also use $E°_{red}$ values to understand aqueous reaction chemistry. Recall, for example, the reaction between $Zn(s)$ and $Cu^{2+}(aq)$ shown in Figure 20.3.

$$Zn(s) + Cu^{2+}(aq) \longrightarrow Zn^{2+}(aq) + Cu(s)$$

Zinc metal is oxidized, and $Cu^{2+}(aq)$ is reduced in this reaction. These substances are in direct contact, however, so we are not producing usable electrical work; the direct contact essentially "short-circuits" the cell. Nevertheless, the driving force for the reaction is the same as that in a voltaic cell, as in Figure 20.5. Because the $E°_{red}$ value for the reduction of $Cu^{2+}(0.34$ V) is more positive than the $E°_{red}$ value for the reduction of $Zn^{2+}(-0.76$ V), the reduction of $Cu^{2+}(aq)$ by $Zn(s)$ is a spontaneous process.

We can generalize the relationship between the value of $E°_{red}$ and the spontaneity of redox reactions: *The more positive the E$°_{red}$ value for a half-reaction, the greater the tendency for the reactant of the half-reaction to be reduced and, therefore, to oxidize another species.* In Table 20.1, for example, F_2 is the most easily reduced species, so it is the strongest oxidizing agent listed.

$$F_2(g) + 2\,e^- \longrightarrow 2\,F^-(aq) \qquad E°_{red} = 2.87 \text{ V}$$

Among the most frequently used oxidizing agents are the halogens, O_2, and oxyanions such as MnO_4^-, $Cr_2O_7^{2-}$, and NO_3^-, whose central atoms have high positive oxidation states. According to Table 20.1, all these species undergo reduction with large positive values of $E°_{red}$.

Lithium ion (Li^+) is the most difficult species to reduce and is therefore the poorest oxidizing agent:

$$Li^+(aq) + e^- \longrightarrow Li(s) \qquad E°_{red} = -3.05 \text{ V}$$

Because Li^+ is so difficult to reduce, the reverse reaction, the oxidation of $Li(s)$ to $Li^+(aq)$, is a highly favorable reaction. *The half-reaction with the smallest reduction potential is most easily reversed as an oxidation.* Thus, lithium metal has a great tendency to transfer electrons to other species. In water, Li is the strongest reducing agent among the substances listed in Table 20.1. Because Table 20.1 lists half-reactions as reductions, only the substances on the reactant side of these equations can serve as oxidizing agents; only those on the product side can serve as reducing agents.

Commonly used reducing agents include H_2 and the active metals such as the alkali metals and the alkaline earth metals. Other metals whose cations have negative $E°_{red}$ values—Zn and Fe, for example—are also used as reducing agents. Solutions of reducing agents are difficult to store for extended periods because of the ubiquitous presence of O_2, a good oxidizing agent. For example, developer solutions used in film photography are mild reducing agents; they have only a limited shelf life because they are readily oxidized by O_2 from the air.

The list of $E°_{red}$ values in Table 20.1 orders the ability of substances to act as oxidizing or reducing agents and is summarized in Figure 20.14▶. The substances that are most readily reduced (strong oxidizing agents) are the reactants on the top left of the table. Their products, on the top right of the table, are oxidized with difficulty (weak reducing agents). The substances on the bottom left of the table are reduced with difficulty, but their products are readily oxidized. This inverse relationship between oxidizing and reducing strength is similar to the inverse relationship between the strengths of conjugate acids and bases. ∞∞ (Section 16.2 and Figure 16.4)

To help you remember the relationships between the strengths of oxidizing and reducing agents, recall the very exothermic reaction between sodium metal and chlorine gas to form sodium chloride (Figure 8.2). In this reaction $Cl_2(g)$ is reduced (it serves as a strong oxidizing agent) and Na(s) is oxidized (it serves as a strong reducing agent). The products of this reaction—Na^+ and Cl^- ions—are very weak oxidizing and reducing agents, respectively.

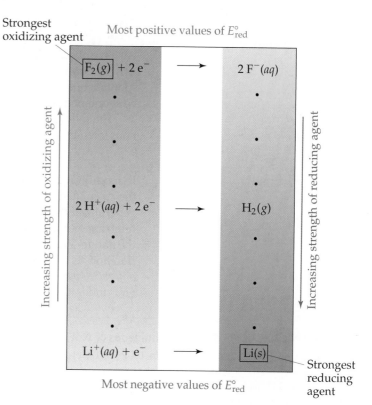

▲ Figure 20.14 **Relative strengths of oxidizing agents.** The standard reduction potentials, $E°_{red}$, listed in Table 20.1 are related to the ability of substances to serve as oxidizing or reducing agents. Species on the left side of the half-reactions can act as oxidizing agents, and those on the right side can act as reducing agents. As $E°_{red}$ becomes more positive, the species on the left become stronger and stronger oxidizing agents. As $E°_{red}$ becomes more negative, the species on the right become stronger and stronger reducing agents.

■ **SAMPLE EXERCISE 20.8** | Determining the Relative Strengths of Oxidizing Agents

Using Table 20.1, rank the following ions in order of increasing strength as oxidizing agents: $NO_3^-(aq)$, $Ag^+(aq)$, $Cr_2O_7^{2-}(aq)$.

SOLUTION

Analyze: We are given several ions and asked to rank their abilities to act as oxidizing agents.

Plan: The more readily an ion is reduced (the more positive its $E°_{red}$ value), the stronger it is as an oxidizing agent.

Solve: From Table 20.1, we have

$$NO_3^-(aq) + 4\,H^+(aq) + 3\,e^- \longrightarrow NO(g) + 2\,H_2O(l) \qquad E°_{red} = +0.96\text{ V}$$

$$Ag^+(aq) + e^- \longrightarrow Ag(s) \qquad E°_{red} = +0.80\text{ V}$$

$$Cr_2O_7^{2-}(aq) + 14\,H^+(aq) + 6\,e^- \longrightarrow 2\,Cr^{3+}(aq) + 7\,H_2O(l) \qquad E°_{red} = +1.33\text{ V}$$

Because the standard reduction potential of $Cr_2O_7^{2-}$ is the most positive, $Cr_2O_7^{2-}$ is the strongest oxidizing agent of the three. The rank order is $Ag^+ < NO_3^- < Cr_2O_7^{2-}$.

■ **PRACTICE EXERCISE**

Using Table 20.1, rank the following species from the strongest to the weakest reducing agent: $I^-(aq)$, Fe(s), Al(s).
Answer: Al(s) > Fe(s) > $I^-(aq)$

20.5 FREE ENERGY AND REDOX REACTIONS

We have observed that voltaic cells use redox reactions that proceed spontaneously. Any reaction that can occur in a voltaic cell to produce a positive emf must be spontaneous. Consequently, it is possible to decide whether a redox reaction will be spontaneous by using half-cell potentials to calculate the emf associated with it.

The following discussion will pertain to general redox reactions, not just reactions in voltaic cells. Thus, we will make Equation 20.8 more general by writing it as

$$E° = E°_{red} \text{ (reduction process)} - E°_{red} \text{ (oxidation process)} \qquad [20.10]$$

In modifying Equation 20.8, we have dropped the subscript "cell" to indicate that the calculated emf does not necessarily refer to a voltaic cell. Similarly, we have generalized the standard reduction potentials on the right side of the equation by referring to the reduction and oxidation processes, rather than the cathode and the anode. We can now make a general statement about the spontaneity of a reaction and its associated emf, E: *A positive value of* E *indicates a spontaneous process; a negative value of* E *indicates a nonspontaneous one.* We will use E to represent the emf under nonstandard conditions and $E°$ to indicate the standard emf.

■ SAMPLE EXERCISE 20.9 | Spontaneous or Not?

Using standard reduction potentials in Table 20.1, determine whether the following reactions are spontaneous under standard conditions.

(a) $Cu(s) + 2 H^+(aq) \longrightarrow Cu^{2+}(aq) + H_2(g)$
(b) $Cl_2(g) + 2 I^-(aq) \longrightarrow 2 Cl^-(aq) + I_2(s)$

SOLUTION

Analyze: We are given two equations and must determine whether each is spontaneous.

Plan: To determine whether a redox reaction is spontaneous under standard conditions, we first need to write its reduction and oxidation half-reactions. We can then use the standard reduction potentials and Equation 20.10 to calculate the standard emf, $E°$, for the reaction. If a reaction is spontaneous, its standard emf must be a positive number.

Solve:

(a) In this reaction Cu is oxidized to Cu^{2+} and H^+ is reduced to H_2. The corresponding half-reactions and associated standard reduction potentials are

Reduction:	$2 H^+(aq) + 2 e^- \longrightarrow H_2(g)$	$E°_{red} = 0 \text{ V}$
Oxidation:	$Cu(s) \longrightarrow Cu^{2+}(aq) + 2 e^-$	$E°_{red} = +0.34 \text{ V}$

Notice that for the oxidation, we use the standard reduction potential from Table 20.1 for the reduction of Cu^{2+} to Cu. We now calculate $E°$ by using Equation 20.10:

$$E° = E°_{red} \text{ (reduction process)} - E°_{red} \text{ (oxidation process)}$$
$$= (0 \text{ V}) - (0.34 \text{ V}) = -0.34 \text{ V}$$

Because $E°$ is negative, the reaction is not spontaneous in the direction written. Copper metal does not react with acids in this fashion. The reverse reaction, however, *is* spontaneous and would have an $E°$ of +0.34V.

$$Cu^{2+}(aq) + H_2(g) \longrightarrow Cu(s) + 2 H^+(aq) \quad E° = +0.34 \text{ V}$$

Cu^{2+} can be reduced by H_2.

(b) We follow a procedure analogous to that in (a):

Reduction:	$Cl_2(g) + 2 e^- \longrightarrow 2 Cl^-(aq)$	$E°_{red} = +1.36 \text{ V}$
Oxidation:	$2 I^-(aq) \longrightarrow I_2(s) + 2 e^-$	$E°_{red} = +0.54 \text{ V}$

In this case

$$E° = (1.36 \text{ V}) - (0.54 \text{ V}) = +0.82 \text{ V}$$

Because the value of $E°$ is positive, this reaction is spontaneous and could be used to build a voltaic cell.

■ PRACTICE EXERCISE

Using the standard reduction potentials listed in Appendix E, determine which of the following reactions are spontaneous under standard conditions:

(a) $I_2(s) + 5 Cu^{2+}(aq) + 6 H_2O(l) \longrightarrow 2 IO_3^-(aq) + 5 Cu(s) + 12 H^+(aq)$
(b) $Hg^{2+}(aq) + 2 I^-(aq) \longrightarrow Hg(l) + I_2(s)$
(c) $H_2SO_3(aq) + 2 Mn(s) + 4 H^+(aq) \longrightarrow S(s) + 2 Mn^{2+}(aq) + 3 H_2O(l)$

Answer: Reactions (b) and (c) are spontaneous.

We can use standard reduction potentials to understand the activity series of metals. ∞ (Section 4.4) Recall that any metal in the activity series will be oxidized by the ions of any metal below it. We can now recognize the origin of this rule based on standard reduction potentials. The activity series, tabulated in Table 4.5, consists of the oxidation reactions of the metals, ordered from the strongest reducing agent at the top to the weakest reducing agent at the bottom. (Thus, the ordering is "flipped over" relative to that in Table 20.1.) For example, nickel lies above silver in the activity series. We therefore expect nickel to displace silver, according to the net reaction

$$Ni(s) + 2\,Ag^+(aq) \longrightarrow Ni^{2+}(aq) + 2\,Ag(s)$$

In this reaction Ni is oxidized and Ag^+ is reduced. Therefore, using data from Table 20.1, the standard emf for the reaction is

$$E° = E°_{red}\,(Ag^+/Ag) - E°_{red}\,(Ni^{2+}/Ni)$$
$$= (+0.80\text{ V}) - (-0.28\text{ V}) = +1.08\text{ V}$$

The positive value of $E°$ indicates that the displacement of silver by nickel is a spontaneous process. Remember that although we multiply the silver half-reaction by 2, the reduction potential is not multiplied.

GIVE IT SOME THOUGHT

Based on Table 4.5, which is the stronger reducing agent, $Hg(l)$ or $Pb(s)$?

EMF and ΔG

The change in the Gibbs free energy, ΔG, is a measure of the spontaneity of a process that occurs at constant temperature and pressure. ∞ (Section 19.5) The emf, E, of a redox reaction also indicates whether the reaction is spontaneous. The relationship between emf and the free-energy change is

$$\Delta G = -nFE \qquad [20.11]$$

In this equation n is a positive number without units that represents the number of electrons transferred in the reaction. The constant F is called *Faraday's constant*, named after Michael Faraday (Figure 20.15▶). Faraday's constant is the quantity of electrical charge on one mole of electrons. This quantity of charge is called a **faraday** (F).

$$1\,F = 96{,}485\text{ C/mol} = 96{,}485\text{ J/V-mol}$$

The units of ΔG calculated by using Equation 20.11 are J/mol; as in Equation 19.16, we use "per mole" to mean "per mole of reaction as written." ∞ (Section 19.7)

Both n and F are positive numbers. Thus, a positive value of E in Equation 20.11 leads to a negative value of ΔG. Remember: *A positive value of* E *and a negative value of* ΔG *both indicate that a reaction is spontaneous.* When the reactants and products are all in their standard states, Equation 20.11 can be modified to relate $\Delta G°$ and $E°$.

$$\Delta G° = -nFE° \qquad [20.12]$$

Equation 20.12 is very important. It relates the standard emf, $E°$, of an electrochemical reaction to the standard free-energy change, $\Delta G°$, for the reaction. Because $\Delta G°$ is related to the equilibrium constant, K, for a reaction by the expression $\Delta G° = -RT \ln K$ ∞ (Section 19.7), we can relate the standard emf to the equilibrium constant for the reaction.

▲ Figure 20.15 **Michael Faraday.** Faraday (1791–1867) was born in England, a child of a poor blacksmith. At the age of 14 he was apprenticed to a bookbinder who gave Faraday time to read and to attend lectures. In 1812 he became an assistant in Humphry Davy's laboratory at the Royal Institution. He succeeded Davy as the most famous and influential scientist in England, making an amazing number of important discoveries, including his formation of the quantitative relationships between electrical current and the extent of chemical reaction in electrochemical cells.

■ **SAMPLE EXERCISE 20.10** | Determining ΔG° and K

(a) Use the standard reduction potentials listed in Table 20.1 to calculate the standard free-energy change, ΔG°, and the equilibrium constant, K, at 298 K for the reaction

$$4\,Ag(s) + O_2(g) + 4\,H^+(aq) \longrightarrow 4\,Ag^+(aq) + 2\,H_2O(l)$$

(b) Suppose the reaction in part (a) was written

$$2\,Ag(s) + \tfrac{1}{2}O_2(g) + 2\,H^+(aq) \longrightarrow 2\,Ag^+(aq) + H_2O(l)$$

What are the values of E°, ΔG°, and K when the reaction is written in this way?

SOLUTION

Analyze: We are asked to determine ΔG° and K for a redox reaction, using standard reduction potentials.

Plan: We use the data in Table 20.1 and Equation 20.10 to determine E° for the reaction and then use E° in Equation 20.12 to calculate ΔG°. We will then use Equation 19.17, $\Delta G^\circ = -RT \ln K$, to calculate K.

Solve:

(a) We first calculate E° by breaking the equation into two half-reactions, as we did in Sample Exercise 20.9, and then obtain E°_{red} values from Table 20.1 (or Appendix E):

Reduction:	$O_2(g) + 4\,H^+(aq) + 4\,e^- \longrightarrow 2\,H_2O(l)$	$E^\circ_{red} = +1.23$ V
Oxidation:	$4\,Ag(s) \longrightarrow 4\,Ag^+(aq) + 4\,e^-$	$E^\circ_{red} = +0.80$ V

Even though the second half-reaction has 4 Ag, we use the E°_{red} value directly from Table 20.1 because emf is an intensive property.

Using Equation 20.10, we have

$$E^\circ = (1.23\text{ V}) - (0.80\text{ V}) = 0.43\text{ V}$$

The half-reactions show the transfer of four electrons. Thus, for this reaction $n = 4$. We now use Equation 20.12 to calculate ΔG°:

$$\Delta G^\circ = -nFE^\circ$$
$$= -(4)(96{,}485\text{ J/V-mol})(+0.43)\text{ V}$$
$$= -1.7 \times 10^5\text{ J/mol} = -170\text{ kJ/mol}$$

The positive value of E° leads to a negative value of ΔG°.

Now we need to calculate the equilibrium constant, K, using $\Delta G^\circ = -RT \ln K$. Because ΔG° is a large negative number, which means the reaction is thermodynamically very favorable, we expect K to be large.

$$\Delta G^\circ = -RT \ln K$$
$$-1.7 \times 10^5\text{ J/mol} = -(8.314\text{ J/K mol})(298\text{ K})\ln K$$
$$\ln K = \frac{-1.7 \times 10^5\text{ J/mol}}{-(8.314\text{ J/K mol})(298\text{ K})}$$
$$\ln K = 69$$
$$K = 9 \times 10^{29}$$

K is indeed very large! This means that we expect silver metal to oxidize in acidic aqueous environments, in air, to Ag^+.

Notice that the voltage calculated for the reaction was 0.43 V, which is easy to measure. Directly measuring such a large equilibrium constant by measuring reactant and product concentrations at equilibrium, on the other hand, would be very difficult.

(b) The overall equation is the same as that in part (a), multiplied by $\tfrac{1}{2}$. The half-reactions are

Reduction:	$\tfrac{1}{2}O_2(g) + 2\,H^+(aq) + 2\,e^- \longrightarrow H_2O(l)$	
Oxidation:	$2\,Ag(s) \longrightarrow 2\,Ag^+(aq) + 2\,e^-$	$E^\circ_{red} = +0.80$ V

The values of E°_{red} are the same as they were in part (a); they are not changed by multiplying the half-reactions by $\tfrac{1}{2}$. Thus, E° has the same value as in part (a):

$$E^\circ = +0.43\text{ V}$$

Notice, though, that the value of n has changed to $n = 2$, which is $\tfrac{1}{2}$ the value in part (a). Thus, ΔG° is half as large as in part (a).

$$\Delta G^\circ = -(2)(96{,}485\text{ J/V-mol})(+0.43\text{ V}) = -83\text{ kJ/mol}$$

Now we can calculate K as before:

$$-8.3 \times 10^4\text{ J/mol} = -(8.314\text{ J/K mol})(298\text{ K})\ln K$$
$$K = 4 \times 10^{14}$$

Comment: E° is an *intensive* quantity, so multiplying a chemical equation by a certain factor will not affect the value of E°. Multiplying an equation will change the value of n, however, and hence the value of ΔG°. The change in free energy, in units of J/mol of reaction as written, is an *extensive* quantity. The equilibrium constant is also an extensive quantity.

■ **PRACTICE EXERCISE**

For the reaction

$$3\,Ni^{2+}(aq) + 2\,Cr(OH)_3(s) + 10\,OH^-(aq) \longrightarrow 3\,Ni(s) + 2\,CrO_4^{2-}(aq) + 8\,H_2O(l)$$

(a) What is the value of n? **(b)** Use the data in Appendix E to calculate ΔG°. **(c)** Calculate K at $T = 298$ K.

Answers: **(a)** 6, **(b)** +87 kJ/mol, **(c)** $K = 6 \times 10^{-16}$

anode and reduced by the cathode determine the emf of a battery, and the usable life of the battery depends on the quantities of these substances packaged in the battery. Usually a barrier analogous to the porous barrier of Figure 20.6 separates the anode and the cathode compartments.

Different applications require batteries with different properties. The battery required to start a car, for example, must be capable of delivering a large electrical current for a short time period. The battery that powers a heart pacemaker, on the other hand, must be very small and capable of delivering a small but steady current over an extended time period. Some batteries are *primary* cells, meaning that they cannot be recharged. A primary cell must be discarded or recycled after its emf drops to zero. A *secondary* cell can be recharged from an external power source after its emf has dropped.

In this section we will briefly discuss some common batteries. As we do so, notice how the principles we have discussed so far in this chapter help us understand these important sources of portable electrical energy.

▲ Figure 20.19 **Combining batteries.** When batteries are connected in series, as in most flashlights, the total emf is the sum of the individual emfs.

Lead-Acid Battery

A 12-V lead-acid automotive battery consists of six voltaic cells in series, each producing 2 V. The cathode of each cell consists of lead dioxide (PbO_2) packed on a metal grid. The anode of each cell is composed of lead. Both electrodes are immersed in sulfuric acid. The electrode reactions that occur during discharge are

Cathode: $\quad PbO_2(s) + HSO_4^-(aq) + 3\,H^+(aq) + 2\,e^- \longrightarrow PbSO_4(s) + 2\,H_2O(l)$

Anode: $\quad\quad\quad\quad\quad\quad Pb(s) + HSO_4^-(aq) \longrightarrow PbSO_4(s) + H^+(aq) + 2\,e^-$

$$PbO_2(s) + Pb(s) + 2\,HSO_4^-(aq) + 2\,H^+(aq) \longrightarrow 2\,PbSO_4(s) + 2\,H_2O(l)$$

The standard cell potential can be obtained from the standard reduction potentials in Appendix E:

$$E^\circ_{cell} = E^\circ_{red}\,(\text{cathode}) - E^\circ_{red}\,(\text{anode}) = (+1.685\ \text{V}) - (-0.356\ \text{V}) = +2.041\ \text{V}$$

The reactants Pb and PbO_2 serve as the electrodes. Because the reactants are solids, there is no need to separate the cell into anode and cathode compartments; the Pb and PbO_2 cannot come into direct physical contact unless one electrode plate touches another. To keep the electrodes from touching, wood or glass-fiber spacers are placed between them (Figure 20.20 ▶).

Using a reaction whose reactants and products are solids has another benefit. Because solids are excluded from the reaction quotient Q, the relative amounts of Pb(s), $PbO_2(s)$, and $PbSO_4(s)$ have no effect on the emf of the lead storage battery, helping the battery maintain a relatively constant emf during discharge. The emf does vary somewhat with use because the concentration of H_2SO_4 varies with the extent of cell discharge. As the equation for the overall cell reaction indicates, H_2SO_4 is consumed during the discharge.

One advantage of a lead-acid battery is that it can be recharged. During recharging, an external source of energy is used to reverse the direction of the overall cell reaction, regenerating Pb(s) and $PbO_2(s)$.

$$2\,PbSO_4(s) + 2\,H_2O(l) \longrightarrow PbO_2(s) + Pb(s) + 2\,HSO_4^-(aq) + 2\,H^+(aq)$$

In an automobile the alternator, driven by the engine, provides the energy necessary for recharging the battery. Recharging is possible because $PbSO_4$ formed during discharge adheres to the electrodes. As the external source forces electrons from one electrode to another, the $PbSO_4$ is converted to Pb at one electrode and to PbO_2 at the other.

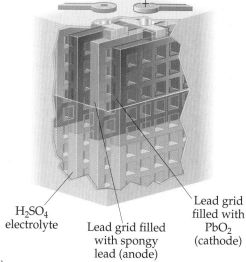

H_2SO_4 electrolyte

Lead grid filled with spongy lead (anode)

Lead grid filled with PbO_2 (cathode)

▲ Figure 20.20 **A 12-V automotive lead-acid battery.** Each anode/cathode pair of electrodes in this schematic cutaway produces a potential of about 2 V. Six pairs of electrodes are connected in series, producing the desired battery voltage.

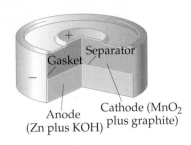

▲ **Figure 20.21 Cutaway view of a miniature alkaline battery.**

Alkaline Battery

The most common primary (nonrechargeable) battery is the alkaline battery. More than 10^{10} alkaline batteries are produced annually. The anode of this battery consists of powdered zinc metal immobilized in a gel in contact with a concentrated solution of KOH (hence the name *alkaline* battery). The cathode is a mixture of $MnO_2(s)$ and graphite, separated from the anode by a porous fabric. The battery is sealed in a steel can to reduce the risk of leakage of the concentrated KOH. A schematic view of an alkaline battery is shown in Figure 20.21 ◀. The cell reactions are complex, but can be approximately represented as follows:

Cathode: $2\,MnO_2(s) + 2\,H_2O(l) + 2\,e^- \longrightarrow 2\,MnO(OH)(s) + 2\,OH^-(aq)$

Anode: $Zn(s) + 2\,OH^-(aq) \longrightarrow Zn(OH)_2(s) + 2\,e^-$

The emf of an alkaline battery is 1.55 V at room temperature. The alkaline battery provides far superior performance over the older "dry cells" that were also based on MnO_2 and Zn as the electrochemically active substances.

Nickel-Cadmium, Nickel-Metal-Hydride, and Lithium-Ion Batteries

The tremendous growth in high-power-demand portable electronic devices, such as cell phones, notebook computers, and video recorders, has increased the demand for lightweight, readily recharged batteries. One of the most common rechargeable batteries is the nickel-cadmium (nicad) battery. During discharge, cadmium metal is oxidized at the anode of the battery while nickel oxyhydroxide $[NiO(OH)(s)]$ is reduced at the cathode.

Cathode: $2\,NiO(OH)(s) + 2\,H_2O(l) + 2\,e^- \longrightarrow 2\,Ni(OH)_2(s) + 2\,OH^-(aq)$

Anode: $Cd(s) + 2\,OH^-(aq) \longrightarrow Cd(OH)_2(s) + 2\,e^-$

As in the lead-acid battery, the solid reaction products adhere to the electrodes, which permits the electrode reactions to be reversed during charging. A single nicad voltaic cell has an emf of 1.30 V. Nicad battery packs typically contain three or more cells in series to produce the higher emfs needed by most electronic devices.

There are drawbacks to nickel-cadmium batteries. Cadmium is a toxic heavy metal. Its use increases the weight of batteries and provides an environmental hazard—roughly 1.5 billion nickel-cadmium batteries are produced annually, and these must eventually be recycled as they lose their ability to be recharged. Some of these problems have been alleviated by the development of nickel-metal-hydride (NiMH) batteries. The cathode reaction of NiMH batteries is the same as that for nickel-cadmium batteries, but the anode reaction is very different. The anode consists of a metal *alloy*, such as $ZrNi_2$, that has the ability to absorb hydrogen atoms (we will discuss alloys in Section 23.6). During the oxidation at the anode, the hydrogen atoms lose electrons, and the resultant H^+ ions react with OH^- ions to form H_2O, a process that is reversed during charging. The current generation of hybrid gas-electric automobiles, which are powered by both a gasoline engine and an electric motor, use NiMH batteries to store the electrical power. The batteries are recharged by the electric motor while braking. Due to the robustness of the batteries toward discharge and recharge, the batteries can last up to 8 years.

The newest rechargeable battery to receive large use in consumer electronic devices is the lithium-ion (Li-ion) battery. You will find this battery in cell phones and laptop computers. Because lithium is a very light element, Li-ion batteries achieve a greater *energy density*—the amount of energy stored per unit mass—than nickel-based batteries. The technology of Li-ion batteries is very different from that of the other batteries we have described here; it is based on the ability of Li^+ ions to be inserted into and removed from certain layered solids.

For example, Li^+ ions can be inserted reversibly into layers of graphite (Figure 11.41). In most commercial cells, one electrode is graphite or some other carbon-based material, and the other is usually made of lithium cobalt oxide ($LiCoO_2$). When the cell is charged, cobalt ions are oxidized, and Li^+ ions migrate into the graphite. During discharge, when the battery is producing electricity for use, the Li^+ ions spontaneously migrate from the graphite anode to the cathode, enabling electrons to flow through the external circuit. An Li-ion battery produces a maximum voltage of 3.7 V, considerably higher than typical 1.5-V alkaline batteries.

Hydrogen Fuel Cells

The thermal energy released by the combustion of fuels can be converted to electrical energy. The heat may convert water to steam, which drives a turbine that in turn drives a generator. Typically, a maximum of only 40% of the energy from combustion is converted to electricity; the remainder is lost as heat. The direct production of electricity from fuels by a voltaic cell could, in principle, yield a higher rate of conversion of the chemical energy of the reaction. Voltaic cells that perform this conversion using conventional fuels, such as H_2 and CH_4, are called **fuel cells**. Strictly speaking, fuel cells are *not* batteries because they are not self-contained systems—the fuel must be continuously supplied to generate electricity.

The most promising fuel-cell system involves the reaction of $H_2(g)$ and $O_2(g)$ to form $H_2O(l)$ as the only product. These cells can generate electricity twice as efficiently as the best internal combustion engine. Under acidic conditions, the electrode reactions are

Cathode:	$O_2(g) + 4 H^+ + 4 e^- \longrightarrow 2 H_2O(l)$
Anode:	$2 H_2(g) \longrightarrow 4 H^+ + 4 e^-$
Overall:	$2 H_2(g) + O_2(g) \longrightarrow 2 H_2O(l)$

The standard emf of an H_2-O_2 fuel cell is +1.23 V, reflecting the large driving force for the reaction of H_2 and O_2 to form H_2O.

In this fuel cell (known as the PEM fuel cell, for "proton-exchange membrane"), the anode and cathode are separated by a thin polymer membrane that is permeable to protons but not to electrons. The polymer membrane, therefore, acts as a salt bridge. The electrodes are typically made from graphite. A PEM cell operates at a temperature of around 80 °C. At this low temperature the electrochemical reactions would normally occur very slowly, and so a thin layer of platinum on each electrode catalyzes the reactions.

Under basic conditions the electrode reactions in the hydrogen fuel cell are

Cathode:	$4 e^- + O_2(g) + 2 H_2O(l) \longrightarrow 4 OH^-(aq)$
Anode:	$2 H_2(g) + 4 OH^-(aq) \longrightarrow 4 H_2O(l) + 4 e^-$
	$2 H_2(g) + O_2(g) \longrightarrow 2 H_2O(l)$

NASA has used this basic hydrogen fuel cell as the energy source for its spacecraft. Liquid hydrogen and oxygen are stored as fuel, and water, the product of the reaction, is drunk by the spacecraft crew.

A schematic drawing of a low-temperature H_2-O_2 fuel cell is shown in Figure 20.22 ▶. This technology is the basis for fuel cell–powered vehicles that are under study by major automobile manufacturers. Currently a great deal of research is going into improving fuel cells. Much effort is being directed toward developing fuel cells that use conventional fuels such as hydrocarbons and alcohols, which are not as difficult to handle and distribute as hydrogen gas.

▼ Figure 20.22 **A low-temperature H_2-O_2 fuel cell.** The porous membrane allows the H^+ ions generated by the oxidation of H_2 at the anode to migrate to the cathode, where H_2O is formed.

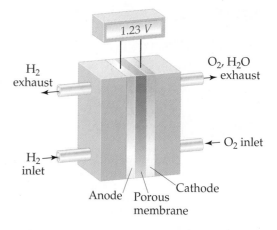

Chemistry Put to Work   DIRECT METHANOL FUEL CELLS

While the hydrogen fuel cell has been widely proposed as a clean and efficient alternative to gasoline-powered internal combustion engines, liquid methanol, CH_3OH, is a far more attractive fuel to store and transport than hydrogen gas. Furthermore, methanol is a clean-burning liquid, and its use would require only minor modifications to existing engines and to fuel-delivery infrastructure.

One of the intriguing aspects of methanol as a fuel is that manufacturing it could make use of carbon dioxide, a source of global warming. ∞ (Section 18.4) Methanol can be made by combining CO_2 and H_2, although the process is presently costly. Imagine, though, that the synthesis can be improved and that the CO_2 used in the synthesis is captured from exhaust gases from power plants or even directly from the atmosphere. In such cases, the CO_2 released by subsequently burning the methanol would be cancelled by the carbon dioxide captured to make it. Thus, the process would be carbon neutral, meaning that it would not increase the concentration of CO_2 in the atmosphere. The prospect of a liquid fuel that could replace conventional fuels without contributing to the greenhouse effect has spurred considerable research to reduce the cost of methanol synthesis and to develop and improve methanol fuel cell technology.

A direct methanol fuel cell has been developed that is similar to the PEM hydrogen fuel cell. The reactions in the cell are

$Cathode: \frac{3}{2} O_2(g) + 6 H^+ + 6 e^- \longrightarrow 3 H_2O(g)$

$Anode:\quad CH_3OH(l) + H_2O(g) \longrightarrow CO_2(g) + 6 H^+ + 6 e^-$

$Overall:\quad CH_3OH(g) + \frac{3}{2} O_2(g) \longrightarrow CO_2(g) + 2 H_2O(g)$

The direct methanol fuel cell is currently too expensive to be used in passenger cars because of the quantity of platinum catalyst it requires to operate. Nevertheless, small methanol fuel cells could appear in mobile devices such as computers or cell phones in the near future.

20.8 CORROSION

Batteries are examples of how spontaneous redox reactions can be used productively. In this section we will examine the undesirable redox reactions that lead to the **corrosion** of metals. Corrosion reactions are spontaneous redox reactions in which a metal is attacked by some substance in its environment and converted to an unwanted compound.

For nearly all metals, oxidation is a thermodynamically favorable process in air at room temperature. When the oxidation process is not inhibited in some way, it can be very destructive to whatever object is made from the metal. Oxidation can form an insulating protective oxide layer, however, that prevents further reaction of the underlying metal. Based on the standard reduction potential for Al^{3+}, for example, we would expect aluminum metal to be very readily oxidized. The many aluminum soft-drink and beer cans that litter the environment are ample evidence, however, that aluminum undergoes only very slow chemical corrosion. The exceptional stability of this active metal in air is due to the formation of a thin protective coat of oxide—a hydrated form of Al_2O_3—on the surface of the metal. The oxide coat is impermeable to O_2 or H_2O and so protects the underlying metal from further corrosion. Magnesium metal is similarly protected. Some metal alloys, such as stainless steel, likewise form protective impervious oxide coats. The semiconductor silicon, as we saw in Chapter 12, also readily forms a protective SiO_2 coating that is important to its use in electronic circuits.

Corrosion of Iron

The rusting of iron (Figure 20.23 ◄) is a familiar corrosion process that carries a significant economic impact. Up to 20% of the iron produced annually in the United States is used to replace iron objects that have been discarded because of rust damage.

The rusting of iron requires both oxygen and water. Other factors—such as the pH of the solution, the presence of salts, contact with metals more difficult to oxidize than iron, and stress on the iron—can accelerate rusting.

The corrosion of iron is electrochemical in nature. The corrosion process involves oxidation and reduction, and the metal itself conducts electricity. Thus, electrons can move through the metal from a region where oxidation occurs to another region where reduction occurs, as in voltaic cells.

▲ **Figure 20.23 Corrosion.** The corrosion of iron is an electrochemical process of great economic importance. The annual cost of metallic corrosion in the United States is estimated to be $70 billion.

Because the standard reduction potential for the reduction of $Fe^{2+}(aq)$ is less positive than that for the reduction of O_2, $Fe(s)$ can be oxidized by $O_2(g)$.

Cathode: $O_2(g) + 4\,H^+(aq) + 4\,e^- \longrightarrow 2\,H_2O(l)$ $\qquad E^\circ_{red} = 1.23\text{ V}$

Anode: $\qquad\qquad\qquad\qquad Fe(s) \longrightarrow Fe^{2+}(aq) + 2\,e^-$ $\quad E^\circ_{red} = -0.44\text{ V}$

A portion of the iron can serve as an anode at which the oxidation of Fe to Fe^{2+} occurs. The electrons produced migrate through the metal to another portion of the surface that serves as the cathode, at which O_2 is reduced. The reduction of O_2 requires H^+, so lowering the concentration of H^+ (increasing the pH) makes the reduction of O_2 less favorable. Iron in contact with a solution whose pH is greater than 9 does not corrode.

The Fe^{2+} formed at the anode is eventually oxidized further to Fe^{3+}, which forms the hydrated iron(III) oxide known as rust:*

$$4\,Fe^{2+}(aq) + O_2(g) + 4\,H_2O(l) + 2\,xH_2O(l) \longrightarrow 2\,Fe_2O_3 \cdot xH_2O(s) + 8\,H^+(aq)$$

Because the cathode is generally the area having the largest supply of O_2, rust often deposits there. If you look closely at a shovel after it has stood outside in the moist air with wet dirt adhered to its blade, you may notice that pitting has occurred under the dirt but that rust has formed elsewhere, where O_2 is more readily available. The corrosion process is summarized in Figure 20.24 ▶.

The enhanced corrosion caused by the presence of salts is usually evident on autos in areas where roads are heavily salted during winter. Like a salt bridge in a voltaic cell, the ions of the salt provide the electrolyte necessary to complete the electrical circuit.

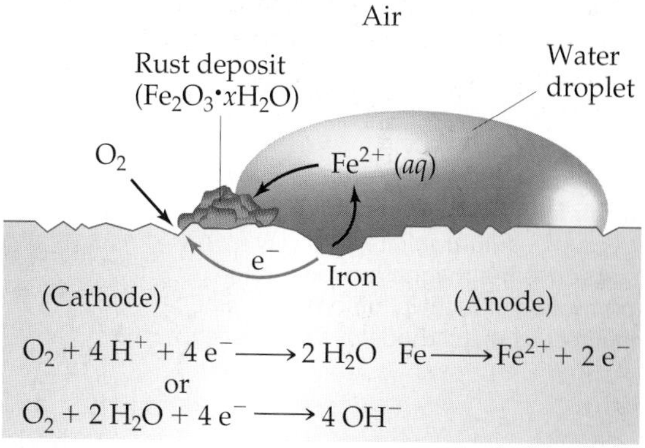

Preventing the Corrosion of Iron

Iron is often covered with a coat of paint or another metal such as tin or zinc to protect its surface against corrosion. Covering the surface with paint or tin is simply a means of preventing oxygen and water from reaching the iron surface. If the coating is broken and the iron is exposed to oxygen and water, corrosion will begin.

Galvanized iron, which is iron coated with a thin layer of zinc, uses the principles of electrochemistry to protect the iron from corrosion even after the surface coat is broken. The standard reduction potentials for iron and zinc are

$$Fe^{2+}(aq) + 2\,e^- \longrightarrow Fe(s) \qquad E^\circ_{red} = -0.44\text{ V}$$
$$Zn^{2+}(aq) + 2\,e^- \longrightarrow Zn(s) \qquad E^\circ_{red} = -0.76\text{ V}$$

Because the E°_{red} value for the reduction of Fe^{2+} is less negative (more positive) than that for the reduction of Zn^{2+}, Fe^{2+} is easier to reduce than Zn^{2+}. Conversely, $Zn(s)$ is easier to oxidize than $Fe(s)$. Thus, even if the zinc coating is broken and the galvanized iron is exposed to oxygen and water, the zinc, which is most easily oxidized, serves as the anode and is corroded instead of the iron. The iron serves as the cathode at which O_2 is reduced, as shown in Figure 20.25 ▶.

Protecting a metal from corrosion by making it the cathode in an electrochemical cell is known as **cathodic protection**. The metal that is oxidized while protecting the cathode is called the *sacrificial anode*. Underground pipelines are often protected against corrosion by making the pipeline the

Air

Rust deposit
$(Fe_2O_3 \cdot xH_2O)$

Water droplet

O_2

$Fe^{2+}(aq)$

e^- Iron

(Cathode)   (Anode)

$O_2 + 4\,H^+ + 4\,e^- \longrightarrow 2\,H_2O$ $Fe \longrightarrow Fe^{2+} + 2\,e^-$
or
$O_2 + 2\,H_2O + 4\,e^- \longrightarrow 4\,OH^-$

▲ **Figure 20.24 Corrosion of iron in contact with water.**

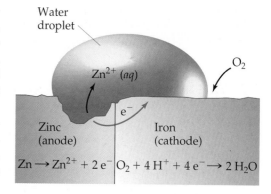

Water droplet

$Zn^{2+}(aq)$

O_2

e^-

Zinc (anode)   Iron (cathode)

$Zn \longrightarrow Zn^{2+} + 2\,e^-$ $O_2 + 4\,H^+ + 4\,e^- \longrightarrow 2\,H_2O$

▲ **Figure 20.25 Cathodic protection of iron in contact with zinc.**

Frequently, metal compounds obtained from aqueous solution have water associated with them. For example, copper(II) sulfate crystallizes from water with five moles of water per mole of $CuSO_4$. We represent this formula as $CuSO_4 \cdot 5H_2O$. Such compounds are called hydrates. ∞ (Section 13.1) Rust is a hydrate of iron(III) oxide with a variable amount of water of hydration. We represent this variable water content by writing the formula as $Fe_2O_3 \cdot xH_2O$.

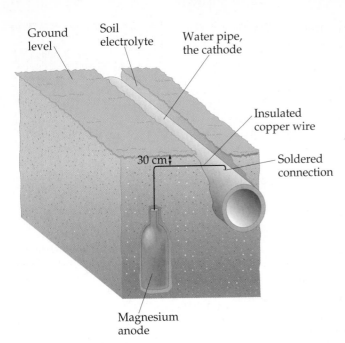

▲ Figure 20.26 Cathodic protection of an iron water pipe. A mixture of gypsum, sodium sulfate, and clay surrounds the magnesium anode to promote conductivity of ions. The pipe, in effect, is the cathode of a voltaic cell.

cathode of a voltaic cell. Pieces of an active metal such as magnesium are buried along the pipeline and connected to it by wire, as shown in Figure 20.26 ◀. In moist soil, where corrosion can occur, the active metal serves as the anode, and the pipe experiences cathodic protection.

GIVE IT SOME THOUGHT

Based on the standard reduction potentials in Table 20.1, which of the following metals could provide cathodic protection to iron: Al, Cu, Ni, Zn?

20.9 ELECTROLYSIS

Voltaic cells are based on spontaneous oxidation-reduction reactions. Conversely, it is possible to use electrical energy to cause nonspontaneous redox reactions to occur. For example, electricity can be used to decompose molten sodium chloride into its component elements:

$$2\,NaCl(l) \longrightarrow 2\,Na(l) + Cl_2(g)$$

Such processes, which are driven by an outside source of electrical energy, are called **electrolysis reactions** and take place in **electrolytic cells**.

An electrolytic cell consists of two electrodes in a molten salt or a solution. A battery or some other source of direct electrical current acts as an electron pump, pushing electrons into one electrode and pulling them from the other. Just as in voltaic cells, the electrode at which the reduction occurs is called the cathode, and the electrode at which oxidation occurs is called the anode.

In the electrolysis of molten NaCl, shown in Figure 20.27 ▼, Na^+ ions pick up electrons and are reduced to Na at the cathode. As the Na^+ ions near the cathode are depleted, additional Na^+ ions migrate in. Similarly, there is net movement of Cl^- ions to the anode, where they are oxidized. The electrode reactions for the electrolysis of molten NaCl are summarized as follows:

Cathode: $2\,Na^+(l) + 2\,e^- \longrightarrow 2\,Na(l)$

Anode: $2\,Cl^-(l) \longrightarrow Cl_2(g) + 2\,e^-$

$$\overline{2\,Na^+(l) + 2\,Cl^-(l) \longrightarrow 2\,Na(l) + Cl_2(g)}$$

► Figure 20.27 Electrolysis of molten sodium chloride. Cl^- ions are oxidized to $Cl_2(g)$ at the anode, and Na^+ ions are reduced to $Na(l)$ at the cathode. Pure NaCl melts at 801 °C.

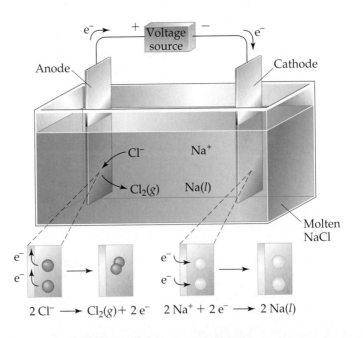

Notice the manner in which the voltage source is connected to the electrodes in Figure 20.27. In a voltaic cell (or any other source of direct current) the electrons move from the negative terminal (Figure 20.6). Thus, the electrode of the electrolytic cell that is connected to the negative terminal of the voltage source is the cathode of the cell; it receives electrons that are used to reduce a substance. The electrons that are removed during the oxidation process at the anode travel to the positive terminal of the voltage source, thus completing the circuit of the cell.

The electrolysis of molten salts is an important industrial process for the production of active metals such as magnesium, sodium, and aluminum. We will have more to say about it in Chapter 23, when we discuss how ores are refined into metals.

Because of the high melting points of ionic substances, the electrolysis of molten salts requires very high temperatures. ∞ (Section 11.8) Do we obtain the same products if we electrolyze the aqueous solution of a salt instead of the molten salt? Frequently the answer is no; the electrolysis of an aqueous solution is complicated by the presence of water, because we must consider whether the water is oxidized to form O_2 or reduced to form H_2 rather than the ions of the salt. These reactions also depend on pH.

So far in our discussion of electrolysis, we have encountered only electrodes that were *inert*; they did not undergo reaction but merely served as the surface where oxidation and reduction occurred. Several practical applications of electrochemistry, however, are based on *active* electrodes—electrodes that participate in the electrolysis process. *Electroplating*, for example, uses electrolysis to deposit a thin layer of one metal on another metal to improve beauty or resistance to corrosion (Figure 20.28 ▲). We can illustrate the principles of electrolysis with active electrodes by describing how to electroplate nickel on a piece of steel.

Figure 20.29 ▶ illustrates the electrolytic cell for our electroplating experiment. The anode of the cell is a strip of nickel metal, and the cathode is the piece of steel that will be electroplated. The electrodes are immersed in a solution of $NiSO_4(aq)$. What happens at the electrodes when the external voltage source is turned on? Reduction will occur at the cathode. The standard reduction potential of Ni^{2+} ($E°_{red} = -0.28$ V) is less negative than that of H_2O ($E°_{red} = -0.83$ V), so Ni^{2+} will be preferentially reduced at the cathode.

At the anode we need to consider which substances can be oxidized. For the $NiSO_4(aq)$ solution, only the H_2O solvent is readily oxidized because neither Ni^{2+} nor the SO_4^{2-} can be oxidized (both already have their elements in their highest possible oxidation state). The Ni atoms in the anode, however, can undergo oxidation. Thus, the two possible oxidation processes are

$$2\,H_2O(l) \longrightarrow O_2(g) + 4\,H^+(aq) + 4\,e^- \qquad E°_{red} = +1.23\text{ V}$$
$$Ni(s) \longrightarrow Ni^{2+}(aq) + 2\,e^- \qquad E°_{red} = -0.28\text{ V}$$

where the potentials are the standard *reduction* potentials of these reactions. Because this is an oxidation, the half-reaction with the more negative value of $E°_{red}$ is favored. (Remember the behavior summarized in Figure 20.14: The strongest reducing agents, which are the substances oxidized most readily, have the most negative values of $E°_{red}$.) We can summarize the electrode reactions as

Cathode (steel strip): $\ Ni^{2+}(aq) + 2\,e^- \longrightarrow Ni(s) \qquad E°_{red} = -0.28$ V

Anode (nickel strip): $\qquad\qquad Ni(s) \longrightarrow Ni^{2+}(aq) + 2\,e^- \quad E°_{red} = -0.28$ V

If we look at the overall reaction, it appears as if nothing has been accomplished. During the electrolysis, however, we are transferring Ni atoms from the Ni anode to the steel cathode, plating the steel electrode with a thin layer of nickel atoms. The standard emf for the overall reaction is $E°_{cell} = E°_{red}$ (cathode) $- E°_{red}$ (anode) $= 0$.

(a)

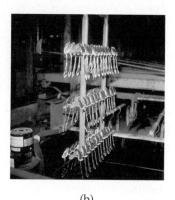
(b)

▲ Figure 20.28 **Electroplating of silverware.** (a) The silverware is being withdrawn from the electroplating bath. (b) The polished final product.

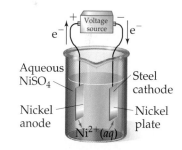

▲ Figure 20.29 **Electrolytic cell with an active metal electrode.** Nickel dissolves from the anode to form $Ni^{2+}(aq)$. At the cathode $Ni^{2+}(aq)$ is reduced and forms a nickel "plate" on the cathode.

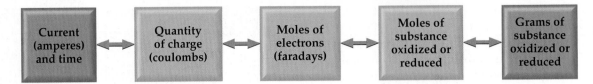

▲ Figure 20.30 Relationship between charge and amount of reactant and product in electrolysis reactions. This flowchart shows the steps relating the quantity of electrical charge used in electrolysis to the amounts of substances oxidized or reduced.

Only a small emf is needed to provide the "push" to transfer the nickel atoms from one electrode to the other. In Chapter 23 we will explore further the utility of electrolysis with active electrodes as a means of purifying crude metals.

Quantitative Aspects of Electrolysis

The stoichiometry of a half-reaction shows how many electrons are needed to achieve an electrolytic process. For example, the reduction of Na^+ to Na is a one-electron process:

$$Na^+ + e^- \longrightarrow Na$$

Thus, one mole of electrons will plate out 1 mol of Na metal, two moles of electrons will plate out 2 mol of Na metal, and so forth. Similarly, two moles of electrons are required to produce 1 mol of copper from Cu^{2+}, and three moles of electrons are required to produce 1 mol of aluminum from Al^{3+}.

$$Cu^{2+} + 2\,e^- \longrightarrow Cu$$

$$Al^{3+} + 3\,e^- \longrightarrow Al$$

For any half-reaction, the amount of a substance that is reduced or oxidized in an electrolytic cell is directly proportional to the number of electrons passed into the cell.

The quantity of charge passing through an electrical circuit, such as that in an electrolytic cell, is generally measured in *coulombs*. As noted in Section 20.5, the charge on one mole of electrons is 96,485 C (1 faraday). A coulomb is the quantity of charge passing a point in a circuit in 1 s when the current is 1 ampere (A). Therefore, the number of coulombs passing through a cell can be obtained by multiplying the amperage and the elapsed time in seconds.

$$\text{Coulombs} = \text{amperes} \times \text{seconds} \qquad [20.18]$$

Figure 20.30▲ shows how the quantities of substances produced or consumed in electrolysis are related to the quantity of electrical charge that is used. The same relationships can also be applied to voltaic cells. In other words, electrons can be thought of as reagents in electrolysis reactions.

■■ **SAMPLE EXERCISE 20.14** | Relating Electrical Charge and Quantity of Electrolysis

Calculate the number of grams of aluminum produced in 1.00 h by the electrolysis of molten $AlCl_3$ if the electrical current is 10.0 A.

SOLUTION

Analyze: We are told that $AlCl_3$ is electrolyzed to form Al and asked to calculate the number of grams of Al produced in 1.00 h with 10.0 A.

Plan: Figure 20.30 provides a road map of the problem. First, the product of the amperage and the time in seconds gives the number of coulombs of electrical charge being used (Equation 20.18). Second, the coulombs can be converted with the Faraday constant ($F = 96,485$ C/mole electrons) to tell us the number of moles of electrons being supplied. Third, reduction of 1 mol of Al^{3+} to Al requires three moles of electrons. Hence we can use the number of moles of electrons to calculate the number of moles of Al metal it produces. Finally, we convert moles of Al into grams.

Solve: First, we calculate the coulombs of electrical charge that are passed into the electrolytic cell:

$$\text{Coulombs} = \text{amperes} \times \text{seconds} = (10.0\ \text{A})(1.00\ \text{h})\frac{(3600\ \text{s})}{\text{h}} = 3.60 \times 10^4\,\text{C}$$

Second, we calculate the number of moles of electrons that pass into the cell:

$$\text{Moles e}^- = (3.60 \times 10^4\,\text{C})\left(\frac{1\ \text{mol e}^-}{96,485\ \text{C}}\right) = 0.373\ \text{mol e}^-$$

Third, we relate the number of moles of electrons to the number of moles of aluminum being formed, using the half-reaction for the reduction of Al^{3+}:

$$Al^{3+} + 3\,e^- \longrightarrow Al$$

Thus, three moles of electrons (3 F of electrical charge) are required to form 1 mol of Al:

$$\text{Moles Al} = (0.373 \text{ mol e}^-)\left(\frac{1 \text{ mol Al}}{3 \text{ mol e}^-}\right) = 0.124 \text{ mol Al}$$

Finally, we convert moles to grams:

$$\text{Grams Al} = (0.124 \text{ mol Al})\left(\frac{27.0 \text{ g Al}}{1 \text{ mol Al}}\right) = 3.36 \text{ g Al}$$

Because each step involves a multiplication by a new factor, the steps can be combined into a single sequence of factors:

$$\text{Grams Al} = (3.60 \times 10^4\,\text{C})\left(\frac{1 \text{ mole e}^-}{96{,}485 \text{ C}}\right)\left(\frac{1 \text{ mol Al}}{3 \text{ mol e}^-}\right)\left(\frac{27.0 \text{ g Al}}{1 \text{ mol Al}}\right) = 3.36 \text{ g Al}$$

■ PRACTICE EXERCISE

(a) The half-reaction for formation of magnesium metal upon electrolysis of molten $MgCl_2$ is $Mg^{2+} + 2\,e^- \longrightarrow Mg$. Calculate the mass of magnesium formed upon passage of a current of 60.0 A for a period of 4.00×10^3 s.
(b) How many seconds would be required to produce 50.0 g of Mg from $MgCl_2$ if the current is 100.0 A?
Answers: **(a)** 30.2 g of Mg, **(b)** 3.97×10^3 s

Electrical Work

We have already seen that a positive value of E is associated with a negative value for the free-energy change and, thus, with a spontaneous process. We also know that for any spontaneous process, ΔG is a measure of the maximum useful work, w_{max}, that can be extracted from the process: $\Delta G = w_{max}$. ∞ (Section 5.2) Because $\Delta G = -nFE$, the maximum useful electrical work obtainable from a voltaic cell is

$$w_{max} = -nFE \qquad [20.19]$$

The cell emf, E, is a positive number for a voltaic cell, so w_{max} will be a negative number for a voltaic cell. Work done *by* a system *on* its surroundings is indicated by a negative sign for w. ∞ (Section 5.2) Thus, the negative value for w_{max} means that a voltaic cell does work on its surroundings.

In an electrolytic cell we use an external source of energy to bring about a nonspontaneous electrochemical process. In this case ΔG is positive and E_{cell} is negative. To force the process to occur, we need to apply an external potential, E_{ext}, which must be larger in magnitude than E_{cell} : $E_{ext} > -E_{cell}$. For example, if a nonspontaneous process has $E_{cell} = -0.9$ V, then the external potential E_{ext} must be greater than 0.9 V in order for the process to occur.

When an external potential E_{ext} is applied to a cell, the surroundings are doing work on the system. The amount of work performed is given by

$$w = nFE_{ext} \qquad [20.20]$$

Unlike Equation 20.19, there is no minus sign in Equation 20.20. The work calculated in Equation 20.20 will be a positive number because the surroundings are doing work on the system. The quantity n in Equation 20.20 is the number of moles of electrons forced into the system by the external potential. The product $n \times F$ is the total electrical charge supplied to the system by the external source of electricity.

Electrical work can be expressed in energy units of watts times time. The **watt** (W) is a unit of electrical power (that is, the rate of energy expenditure).

$$1 \text{ W} = 1 \text{ J/s}$$

Thus, a watt-second is a joule. The unit employed by electric utilities is the kilowatt-hour (kWh), which equals 3.6×10^6 J.

$$1 \text{ kWh} = (1000 \text{ W})(1 \text{ hr})\left(\frac{3600 \text{ s}}{1 \text{ hr}}\right)\left(\frac{1 \text{ J/s}}{1 \text{ W}}\right) = 3.6 \times 10^6 \text{ J} \qquad [20.21]$$

Using these considerations, we can calculate the maximum work obtainable from the voltaic cells and the minimum work required to bring about desired electrolysis reactions.

■ **SAMPLE EXERCISE 20.15** | **Calculating Energy in Kilowatt-hours**

Calculate the number of kilowatt-hours of electricity required to produce 1.0×10^3 kg of aluminum by electrolysis of Al^{3+} if the applied voltage is 4.50 V.

SOLUTION

Analyze: We are given the mass of Al produced from Al^{3+} and the applied voltage and asked to calculate the energy, in kilowatt-hours, required for the reduction.

Plan: From the mass of Al, we can calculate first the number of moles of Al and then the number of coulombs required to obtain that mass. We can then use Equation 20.20, $w = nFE_{ext}$, where nF is the total charge in coulombs and E_{ext} is the applied potential, 4.50 V.

Solve: First, we need to calculate nF, the number of coulombs required:

$$\text{Coulombs} = (1.00 \times 10^3 \text{ kg Al})\left(\frac{1000 \text{ g Al}}{1 \text{ kg Al}}\right)\left(\frac{1 \text{ mol Al}}{27.0 \text{ g Al}}\right)\left(\frac{3 \text{ mol e}^-}{1 \text{ mol Al}}\right)\left(\frac{96{,}485 \text{ C}}{1 \text{ mole e}^-}\right)$$

$$= 1.07 \times 10^{10} \text{ C}$$

We can now calculate w. In doing so, we must apply several conversion factors, including Equation 20.21, which gives the conversion between kilowatt-hours and joules:

$$\text{Kilowatt-hours} = (1.07 \times 10^{10} \text{ C})(4.50 \text{ V})\left(\frac{1 \text{ J}}{1 \text{ C-V}}\right)\left(\frac{1 \text{ kWh}}{3.6 \times 10^6 \text{ J}}\right)$$

$$= 1.34 \times 10^4 \text{ kWh}$$

Comment: This quantity of energy does not include the energy used to mine, transport, and process the aluminum ore, and to keep the electrolysis bath molten during electrolysis. A typical electrolytic cell used to reduce aluminum ore to aluminum metal is only 40% efficient, with 60% of the electrical energy being dissipated as heat. It therefore requires approximately 33 kWh of electricity to produce 1 kg of aluminum. The aluminum industry consumes about 2% of the electrical energy generated in the United States. Because this energy is used mainly to reduce aluminum, recycling this metal saves large quantities of energy.

■ **PRACTICE EXERCISE**

Calculate the number of kilowatt-hours of electricity required to produce 1.00 kg of Mg from electrolysis of molten $MgCl_2$ if the applied emf is 5.00 V. Assume that the process is 100% efficient.
Answer: 11.0 kWh

■ **SAMPLE INTEGRATIVE EXERCISE** | **Putting Concepts Together**

The K_{sp} at 298 K for iron(II) fluoride is 2.4×10^{-6}. **(a)** Write a half-reaction that gives the likely products of the two-electron reduction of $FeF_2(s)$ in water. **(b)** Use the K_{sp} value and the standard reduction potential of Fe^{2+} (aq) to calculate the standard reduction potential for the half-reaction in part (a). **(c)** Rationalize the difference in the reduction potential for the half-reaction in part (a) with that for Fe^{2+} (aq).

SOLUTION

Analyze: We are going to have to combine what we know about equilibrium constants and electrochemistry to obtain reduction potentials.

Plan: For (a) we need to determine which ion, Fe^{2+} or F^-, is more likely to be reduced by 2 electrons and write the overall reaction for $FeF_2 + 2 e^- \longrightarrow$? For (b) we need to write the K_{sp} reaction and manipulate it to get $E°$ for the reaction in (a). For (c) we need to see what we get for (a) and (b).

Solve:

(a) Iron(II) fluoride is an ionic substance that consists of Fe^{2+} and F^- ions. We are asked to predict where two electrons could be added to FeF_2. We can't envision adding the electrons to the F^- ions to form F^{2-}, so it seems likely that we could reduce the Fe^{2+} ions to $Fe(s)$. We therefore predict the half-reaction

$$FeF_2(s) + 2 e^- \longrightarrow Fe(s) + 2 F^-(aq)$$

(b) The K_{sp} value refers to the following equilibrium ∞ (Section 17.4):

$$FeF_2(s) \rightleftharpoons Fe^{2+}(aq) + 2 F^-(aq) \quad K_{sp} = [Fe^{2+}][F^-]^2 = 2.4 \times 10^{-6}$$

We were also asked to use the standard reduction potential of Fe^{2+}, whose half-reaction and standard voltage are listed in Appendix E:

$$Fe^{2+}(aq) + 2 e^- \longrightarrow Fe(s) \quad E° = -0.440 \text{ V}$$

Recall that according to Hess's law, we can add reactions to get the one we want and we can add thermodynamic quantities like ΔH and ΔG to solve for the enthalpy or free energy of the reaction we want. ∞ (Section 5.6) In this case notice that if we add the K_{sp} reaction to the standard reduction half-reaction for Fe^{2+}, we get the half-reaction we want:

1. $FeF_2(s) \longrightarrow Fe^{2+}(aq) + 2\,F^-(aq)$

2. $Fe^{2+}(aq) + 2\,e^- \longrightarrow Fe(s)$

Overall: _____

3. $FeF_2(s) + 2\,e^- \longrightarrow Fe(s) + 2\,F^-(aq)$

Reaction 3 is still a half-reaction, so we do see the free electrons.

If we knew $\Delta G°$ for reactions 1 and 2, we could add them to get $\Delta G°$ for reaction 3. Recall that we can relate $\Delta G°$ to $E°$ by $\Delta G° = -nFE°$ and to K by $\Delta G° = -RT \ln K$. We know K for reaction 1; it is K_{sp}. We know $E°$ for reaction 2. Therefore we can calculate $\Delta G°$ for reactions 1 and 2:

Reaction 1:

$$\Delta G° = -RT \ln K = -(8.314 \text{ J/K mol})(298 \text{ K}) \ln(2.4 \times 10^{-6}) = 3.21 \times 10^4 \text{ J/mol}$$

Reaction 2:

$$\Delta G° = -nFE° = -(2 \text{ mol})(96{,}485 \text{ C/mol})(-0.440 \text{ J/C}) = 8.49 \times 10^4 \text{ J}$$

(Recall that 1 volt is 1 joule per coulomb.)

Then, $\Delta G°$ for reaction 3, the one we want, is 3.21×10^4 J (for one mole of FeF_2) + 8.49×10^4 J = 1.17×10^5 J. We can convert this to $E°$ easily from the relationship $\Delta G° = -nFE°$:

$$1.17 \times 10^5 \text{ J} = -(2 \text{ mol})(96{,}485 \text{ C/mol})\, E°$$

$$E° = -0.606 \text{ J/C} = -0.606 \text{ V}.$$

(c) The standard reduction potential for FeF_2 (-0.606 V) is more negative than that for Fe^{2+} (-0.440 V), telling us that the reduction of FeF_2 is the less favorable process. When FeF_2 is reduced, we not only reduce the Fe^{2+} ions but also break up the ionic solid. Because this additional energy must be overcome, the reduction of FeF_2 is less favorable than the reduction of Fe^{2+}.

CHAPTER REVIEW

SUMMARY AND KEY TERMS

Introduction and Section 20.1 In this chapter we have focused on **electrochemistry**, the branch of chemistry that relates electricity and chemical reactions. Electrochemistry involves oxidation-reduction reactions, also called redox reactions. These reactions involve a change in the oxidation state of one or more elements. In every oxidation-reduction reaction one substance is oxidized (its oxidation state, or number, increases) and one substance is reduced (its oxidation state, or number, decreases). The substance that is oxidized is referred to as a **reducing agent**, or **reductant**, because it causes the reduction of some other substance. Similarly, the substance that is reduced is referred to as an **oxidizing agent**, or **oxidant**, because it causes the oxidation of some other substance.

Section 20.2 An oxidization-reduction reaction can be balanced by dividing the reaction into two **half-reactions**, one for oxidation and one for reduction. A half-reaction is a balanced chemical equation that includes electrons. In oxidation half-reactions the electrons are on the product (right) side of the reaction; we can envision that these electrons are transferred from a substance when it is oxidized. In reduction half-reactions the electrons are on the reactant (left) side of the reaction. Each half-reaction is balanced separately, and the two are brought together with proper coefficients to balance the electrons on each side of the equation.

Section 20.3 A **voltaic** (or **galvanic**) **cell** uses a spontaneous oxidation-reduction reaction to generate electricity. In a voltaic cell the oxidation and reduction half-reactions often occur in separate compartments. Each compartment has a solid surface called an electrode, where the half-reaction occurs. The electrode where oxidation occurs is called the **anode**; reduction occurs at the **cathode**. The electrons released at the anode flow through an external circuit (where they do electrical work) to the cathode. Electrical neutrality in the solution is maintained by the migration of ions between the two compartments through a device such as a salt bridge.

Section 20.4 A voltaic cell generates an **electromotive force (emf)** that moves the electrons from the anode to the cathode through the external circuit. The origin of emf is a difference in the electrical potential energy of the two electrodes in the cell. The emf of a cell is called its **cell potential**, E_{cell}, and is measured in volts. The cell potential under standard conditions is called the **standard emf**, or the **standard cell potential**, and is denoted $E°_{cell}$.

A **standard reduction potential**, $E°_{red}$, can be assigned for an individual half-reaction. This is achieved by comparing the potential of the half-reaction to that of the **standard hydrogen electrode** (SHE), which is defined to have $E°_{red} = 0$ V and is based on the following half-reaction:

$$2\,H^+(aq, 1\,M) + 2\,e^- \longrightarrow H_2(g, 1\,atm) \qquad E°_{red} = 0\,V$$

The standard cell potential of a voltaic cell is the difference between the standard reduction potentials of the half-reactions that occur at the cathode and the anode: $E°_{cell} = E°_{red}$ (cathode) $- E°_{red}$ (anode). The value of $E°_{cell}$ is positive for a voltaic cell.

For a reduction half-reaction, $E°_{red}$ is a measure of the tendency of the reduction to occur; the more positive the value for $E°_{red}$, the greater the tendency of the substance to be reduced. Thus, $E°_{red}$ provides a measure of the oxidizing strength of a substance. Fluorine (F_2) has the most positive value for $E°_{red}$ and is the strongest oxidizing agent. Substances that are strong oxidizing agents produce products that are weak reducing agents, and vice versa.

Section 20.5 The emf, E, is related to the change in the Gibbs free energy, ΔG: $\Delta G = -nFE$, where n is the number of electrons transferred during the redox process and F is *Faraday's constant*, defined as the quantity of electrical charge on one mole of electrons. This amount of charge is 1 **faraday** (F): $1\,F = 96{,}485$ C/mol. Because E is related to ΔG, the sign of E indicates whether a redox process is spontaneous: $E > 0$ indicates a spontaneous process, and $E < 0$ indicates a nonspontaneous one. Because ΔG is also related to the equilibrium constant for a reaction ($\Delta G = -RT \ln K$), we can relate E to K as well.

Section 20.6 The emf of a redox reaction varies with temperature and with the concentrations of reactants and products. The **Nernst equation** relates the emf under nonstandard conditions to the standard emf and the reaction quotient Q:

$$E = E° - (RT/nF) \ln Q = E° - (0.0592/n) \log Q$$

The factor 0.0592 is valid when $T = 298$ K. A **concentration cell** is a voltaic cell in which the same half-reaction occurs at both the anode and cathode but with different concentrations of reactants in each compartment.

At equilibrium, $Q = K$ and $E = 0$. The standard emf is therefore related to the equilibrium constant.

Section 20.7 A **battery** is a self-contained electrochemical power source that contains one or more voltaic cells. Batteries are based on a variety of different redox reactions. Several common batteries were discussed. The lead-acid battery, the nickel-cadmium battery, the nickel-metal-hydride battery, and the lithium-ion battery are examples of rechargeable batteries. The common alkaline dry cell is not rechargeable. **Fuel cells** are voltaic cells that utilize redox reactions in which reactants such as H_2 have to be continuously supplied to the cell to generate voltage.

Section 20.8 Electrochemical principles help us understand **corrosion**, undesirable redox reactions in which a metal is attacked by some substance in its environment. The corrosion of iron into rust is caused by the presence of water and oxygen, and it is accelerated by the presence of electrolytes, such as road salt. The protection of a metal by putting it in contact with another metal that more readily undergoes oxidation is called **cathodic protection**. Galvanized iron, for example, is coated with a thin layer of zinc; because zinc is oxidized more readily than iron, the zinc serves as a sacrificial anode in the redox reaction.

Section 20.9 An **electrolysis reaction**, which is carried out in an **electrolytic cell**, employs an external source of electricity to drive a nonspontaneous electrochemical reaction. The negative terminal of the external source is connected to the cathode of the cell, and the positive terminal to the anode. The current-carrying medium within an electrolytic cell may be either a molten salt or an electrolyte solution. The products of electrolysis can generally be predicted by comparing the reduction potentials associated with possible oxidation and reduction processes. The electrodes in an electrolytic cell can be active, meaning that the electrode can be involved in the electrolysis reaction. Active electrodes are important in electroplating and in metallurgical processes.

The quantity of substances formed during electrolysis can be calculated by considering the number of electrons involved in the redox reaction and the amount of electrical charge that passes into the cell. The maximum amount of electrical work produced by a voltaic cell is given by the product of the total charge delivered, nF, and the emf, E: $w_{max} = -nFE$. The work performed in an electrolysis is given by $w = nFE_{ext}$, where E_{ext} is the applied external potential. The **watt** is a unit of power: $1\,W = 1\,J/s$. Electrical work is often measured in kilowatt-hours.

KEY SKILLS

- Identify oxidation, reduction, oxidizing agent, and reducing agent in a chemical equation.
- Complete and balance redox equations using the method of half-reactions.
- Sketch a voltaic cell and identify its cathode, anode, and the directions that electrons and ions move.
- Calculate standard emfs (cell potentials), $E°_{cell}$, from standard reduction potentials.

- Use reduction potentials to predict whether a redox reaction is spontaneous.
- Relate $E°_{cell}$ to $\Delta G°$ and equilibrium constants.
- Calculate emf under nonstandard conditions.
- Describe the reactions in electrolytic cells.
- Relate amounts of products and reactants in redox reactions to electrical charge.

KEY EQUATIONS

- $E°_{cell} = E°_{red}$ (cathode) $- E°_{red}$ (anode)   [20.8]   Relating standard emf to standard reduction potentials of the reduction (cathode) and oxidation (anode) half reactions

- $\Delta G = -nFE$ [20.11]   Relating free energy change and emf

- $E = E° - \dfrac{0.0592 \text{ V}}{n} \log Q$ (at 298 K)   [20.16]   The Nernst equation, expressing the effect of concentration on cell potential

VISUALIZING CONCEPTS

20.1 In the Brønsted-Lowry concept of acids and bases, acid–base reactions are viewed as proton-transfer reactions. The stronger the acid, the weaker is its conjugate base. In what ways are redox reactions analogous? [Sections 20.1 and 20.2]

20.2 Consider the reaction in Figure 20.3. Describe what would happen if **(a)** the solution contained cadmium(II) sulfate and the metal was zinc, **(b)** the solution contained silver nitrate and the metal was copper. [Section 20.3]

20.3 The diagram below represents a molecular view of a process occurring at an electrode in a voltaic cell.

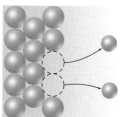

(a) Does the process represent oxidation or reduction? **(b)** Is the electrode the anode or cathode? **(c)** Why are the atoms in the electrode represented by larger spheres than the ions in the solution? [Section 20.3]

20.4 Assume that you want to construct a voltaic cell that uses the following half reactions:

$$A^{2+}(aq) + 2 e^- \longrightarrow A(s) \quad E°_{red} = -0.10 \text{ V}$$
$$B^{2+}(aq) + 2 e^- \longrightarrow B(s) \quad E°_{red} = -1.10 \text{ V}$$

You begin with the incomplete cell pictured below, in which the electrodes are immersed in water.

(a) What additions must you make to the cell for it to generate a standard emf? **(b)** Which electrode functions as the cathode? **(c)** Which direction do electrons move through the external circuit? **(d)** What voltage will the cell generate under standard conditions? [Sections 20.3 and 20.4]

20.5 Where on Figure 20.14 would you find **(a)** the chemical species that is the easiest to oxidize, and **(b)** the chemical species that is the easiest to reduce? [Section 20.4]

20.6 For the generic reaction $A(aq) + B(aq) \longrightarrow A^-(aq) + B^+(aq)$ for which $E°$ is a positive number, answer the following questions:
   (a) What is being oxidized, and what is being reduced?
   (b) If you made a voltaic cell out of this reaction, what half-reaction would be occurring at the cathode, and what half-reaction would be occurring at the anode?
   (c) Which half-reaction from (b) is higher in potential energy?
   (d) What is the sign of the free energy change for the reaction? [Sections 20.4 and 20.5]

20.7 Consider the half reaction $Ag^+(aq) + e^- \longrightarrow Ag(s)$. **(a)** Which of the lines in the following diagram indicates how the reduction potential varies with the concentration of Ag^+? **(b)** What is the value of E_{red} when $\log[Ag^+] = 0$? [Section 20.6]

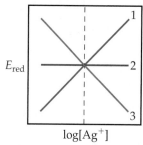

20.8 Draw a generic picture of a fuel cell. What is the main difference between it and a battery, regardless of the redox reactions that occur inside? [Section 20.7]

20.9 How does a zinc coating on iron protect the iron from unwanted oxidation? [Section 20.8]

20.10 You may have heard that "antioxidants" are good for your health. Based on what you have learned in this chapter, what do you deduce an "antioxidant" is? [Sections 20.1 and 20.2]

EXERCISES

Oxidation-Reduction Reactions

20.11 (a) What is meant by the term *oxidation*? (b) On which side of an oxidation half-reaction do the electrons appear? (c) What is meant by the term *oxidant*? (d) What is meant by the term *oxidizing agent*?

20.12 (a) What is meant by the term *reduction*? (b) On which side of a reduction half-reaction do the electrons appear? (c) What is meant by the term *reductant*? (d) What is meant by the term *reducing agent*?

20.13 Indicate whether each of the following statements is true or false:
(a) If something is oxidized, it is formally losing electrons.
(b) For the reaction $Fe^{3+}(aq) + Co^{2+}(aq) \longrightarrow Fe^{2+}(aq) + Co^{3+}(aq)$, $Fe^{3+}(aq)$ is the reducing agent and $Co^{2+}(aq)$ is the oxidizing agent.
(c) If there are no changes in the oxidation state of the reactants or products of a particular reaction, that reaction is not a redox reaction.

20.14 Indicate whether each of the following statements is true or false:
(a) If something is reduced, it is formally losing electrons.
(b) A reducing agent gets oxidized as it reacts.
(c) Oxidizing agents can convert CO into CO_2.

20.15 In each of the following balanced oxidation-reduction equations, identify those elements that undergo changes in oxidation number and indicate the magnitude of the change in each case.
(a) $I_2O_5(s) + 5\,CO(g) \longrightarrow I_2(s) + 5\,CO_2(g)$
(b) $2\,Hg^{2+}(aq) + N_2H_4(aq) \longrightarrow$
$\qquad\qquad\qquad 2\,Hg(l) + N_2(g) + 4\,H^+(aq)$
(c) $3\,H_2S(aq) + 2\,H^+(aq) + 2\,NO_3^-(aq) \longrightarrow$
$\qquad\qquad\qquad 3\,S(s) + 2\,NO(g) + 4\,H_2O(l)$
(d) $Ba^{2+}(aq) + 2\,OH^-(aq) +$
$\qquad H_2O_2(aq) + 2\,ClO_2(aq) \longrightarrow$
$\qquad\qquad Ba(ClO_2)_2(s) + 2\,H_2O(l) + O_2(g)$

20.16 Indicate whether the following balanced equations involve oxidation-reduction. If they do, identify the elements that undergo changes in oxidation number.
(a) $PBr_3(l) + 3\,H_2O(l) \longrightarrow H_3PO_3(aq) + 3\,HBr(aq)$
(b) $NaI(aq) + 3\,HOCl(aq) \longrightarrow NaIO_3(aq) + 3\,HCl(aq)$
(c) $3\,SO_2(g) + 2\,HNO_3(aq) + 2\,H_2O(l) \longrightarrow$
$\qquad\qquad\qquad 3\,H_2SO_4(aq) + 2\,NO(g)$
(d) $2\,H_2SO_4(aq) + 2\,NaBr(s) \longrightarrow$
$\qquad Br_2(l) + SO_2(g) + Na_2SO_4(aq) + 2\,H_2O(l)$

Balancing Oxidation-Reduction Reactions

20.17 At 900 °C titanium tetrachloride vapor reacts with molten magnesium metal to form solid titanium metal and molten magnesium chloride. (a) Write a balanced equation for this reaction. (b) What is being oxidized, and what is being reduced? (c) Which substance is the reductant, and which is the oxidant?

20.18 Hydrazine (N_2H_4) and dinitrogen tetroxide (N_2O_4) form a self-igniting mixture that has been used as a rocket propellant. The reaction products are N_2 and H_2O. (a) Write a balanced chemical equation for this reaction. (b) What is being oxidized, and what is being reduced? (c) Which substance serves as the reducing agent, and which as the oxidizing agent?

20.19 Complete and balance the following half-reactions. In each case indicate whether the half-reaction is an oxidation or a reduction.
(a) $Sn^{2+}(aq) \longrightarrow Sn^{4+}(aq)$ (acidic or basic solution)
(b) $TiO_2(s) \longrightarrow Ti^{2+}(aq)$ (acidic solution)
(c) $ClO_3^-(aq) \longrightarrow Cl^-(aq)$ (acidic solution)
(d) $N_2(g) \longrightarrow NH_4^+(aq)$ (acidic solution)
(e) $OH^-(aq) \longrightarrow O_2(g)$ (basic solution)
(f) $SO_3^{2-}(aq) \longrightarrow SO_4^{2-}(aq)$ (basic solution)
(g) $N_2(g) \longrightarrow NH_3(g)$ (basic solution)

20.20 Complete and balance the following half-reactions. In each case indicate whether the half-reaction is an oxidation or a reduction.
(a) $Mo^{3+}(aq) \longrightarrow Mo(s)$ (acidic or basic solution)
(b) $H_2SO_3(aq) \longrightarrow SO_4^{2-}(aq)$ (acidic solution)
(c) $NO_3^-(aq) \longrightarrow NO(g)$ (acidic solution)
(d) $O_2(g) \longrightarrow H_2O(l)$ (acidic solution)
(e) $Mn^{2+}(aq) \longrightarrow MnO_2(s)$ (basic solution)
(f) $Cr(OH)_3(s) \longrightarrow CrO_4^{2-}(aq)$ (basic solution)
(g) $O_2(g) \longrightarrow H_2O(l)$ (basic solution)

20.21 Complete and balance the following equations, and identify the oxidizing and reducing agents:
(a) $Cr_2O_7^{2-}(aq) + I^-(aq) \longrightarrow Cr^{3+}(aq) + IO_3^-(aq)$
$\qquad\qquad\qquad\qquad\qquad\qquad$ (acidic solution)
(b) $MnO_4^-(aq) + CH_3OH(aq) \longrightarrow$
$\qquad Mn^{2+}(aq) + HCO_2H(aq)$ (acidic solution)
(c) $I_2(s) + OCl^-(aq) \longrightarrow IO_3^-(aq) + Cl^-(aq)$
$\qquad\qquad\qquad\qquad\qquad\qquad$ (acidic solution)
(d) $As_2O_3(s) + NO_3^-(aq) \longrightarrow$
$\qquad H_3AsO_4(aq) + N_2O_3(aq)$ (acidic solution)
(e) $MnO_4^-(aq) + Br^-(aq) \longrightarrow MnO_2(s) + BrO_3^-(aq)$
$\qquad\qquad\qquad\qquad\qquad\qquad$ (basic solution)
(f) $Pb(OH)_4^{2-}(aq) + ClO^-(aq) \longrightarrow PbO_2(s) + Cl^-(aq)$
$\qquad\qquad\qquad\qquad\qquad\qquad$ (basic solution)

20.22 Complete and balance the following equations, and identify the oxidizing and reducing agents. Recall that the O atoms in hydrogen peroxide, H_2O_2, have an atypical oxidation state. ∞ (Table 2.5)
(a) $NO_2^-(aq) + Cr_2O_7^{2-}(aq) \longrightarrow$
$\qquad Cr^{3+}(aq) + NO_3^-(aq)$ (acidic solution)
(b) $S(s) + HNO_3(aq) \longrightarrow H_2SO_3(aq) + N_2O(g)$
$\qquad\qquad\qquad\qquad\qquad\qquad$ (acidic solution)

(c) $Cr_2O_7^{2-}(aq) + CH_3OH(aq) \longrightarrow$
$\qquad HCO_2H(aq) + Cr^{3+}(aq)$ (acidic solution)

(d) $MnO_4^-(aq) + Cl^-(aq) \longrightarrow Mn^{2+}(aq) + Cl_2(aq)$
$\qquad$ (acidic solution)

(e) $NO_2^-(aq) + Al(s) \longrightarrow NH_4^+(aq) + AlO_2^-(aq)$
$\qquad$ (basic solution)

(f) $H_2O_2(aq) + ClO_2(aq) \longrightarrow ClO_2^-(aq) + O_2(g)$
$\qquad$ (basic solution)

Voltaic Cells

20.23 (a) What are the similarities and differences between Figure 20.3 and Figure 20.4? (b) Why are Na^+ ions drawn into the cathode compartment as the voltaic cell shown in Figure 20.5 operates?

20.24 (a) What is the role of the porous glass disc shown in Figure 20.4? (b) Why do NO_3^- ions migrate into the anode compartment as the voltaic cell shown in Figure 20.5 operates?

20.25 A voltaic cell similar to that shown in Figure 20.5 is constructed. One electrode compartment consists of a silver strip placed in a solution of $AgNO_3$, and the other has an iron strip placed in a solution of $FeCl_2$. The overall cell reaction is

$$Fe(s) + 2\,Ag^+(aq) \longrightarrow Fe^{2+}(aq) + 2\,Ag(s)$$

(a) What is being oxidized, and what is being reduced? (b) Write the half-reactions that occur in the two electrode compartments. (c) Which electrode is the anode, and which is the cathode? (d) Indicate the signs of the electrodes. (e) Do electrons flow from the silver electrode to the iron electrode, or from the iron to the silver? (f) In which directions do the cations and anions migrate through the solution?

20.26 A voltaic cell similar to that shown in Figure 20.5 is constructed. One electrode compartment consists of an aluminum strip placed in a solution of $Al(NO_3)_3$, and the other has a nickel strip placed in a solution of $NiSO_4$. The overall cell reaction is

$$2\,Al(s) + 3\,Ni^{2+}(aq) \longrightarrow 2\,Al^{3+}(aq) + 3\,Ni(s)$$

(a) What is being oxidized, and what is being reduced? (b) Write the half-reactions that occur in the two electrode compartments. (c) Which electrode is the anode, and which is the cathode? (d) Indicate the signs of the electrodes. (e) Do electrons flow from the aluminum electrode to the nickel electrode, or from the nickel to the aluminum? (f) In which directions do the cations and anions migrate through the solution? Assume the Al is not coated with its oxide.

Cell EMF under Standard Conditions

20.27 (a) What does the term *electromotive force* mean? (b) What is the definition of the *volt*? (c) What does the term *cell potential* mean?

20.28 (a) Which electrode of a voltaic cell, the cathode or the anode, corresponds to the higher potential energy for the electrons? (b) What are the units for electrical potential? How does this unit relate to energy expressed in joules? (c) What is special about a *standard* cell potential?

20.29 (a) Write the half-reaction that occurs at a hydrogen electrode in acidic aqueous solution when it serves as the cathode of a voltaic cell. (b) What is *standard* about the standard hydrogen electrode? (c) What is the role of the platinum foil in a standard hydrogen electrode?

20.30 (a) Write the half-reaction that occurs at a hydrogen electrode in acidic aqueous solution when it serves as the anode of a voltaic cell. (b) The platinum electrode in a standard hydrogen electrode is specially prepared to have a large surface area. Why is this important? (c) Sketch a standard hydrogen electrode.

20.31 (a) What is a *standard reduction potential*? (b) What is the standard reduction potential of a standard hydrogen electrode?

20.32 (a) Why is it impossible to measure the standard reduction potential of a single half-reaction? (b) Describe how the standard reduction potential of a half-reaction can be determined.

20.33 A voltaic cell that uses the reaction

$$Tl^{3+}(aq) + 2\,Cr^{2+}(aq) \longrightarrow Tl^+(aq) + 2\,Cr^{3+}(aq)$$

has a measured standard cell potential of $+1.19$ V.

(a) Write the two half-cell reactions. (b) By using data from Appendix E, determine E_{red}° for the reduction of $Tl^{3+}(aq)$ to $Tl^+(aq)$. (c) Sketch the voltaic cell, label the anode and cathode, and indicate the direction of electron flow.

20.34 A voltaic cell that uses the reaction

$$PdCl_4^{2-}(aq) + Cd(s) \longrightarrow Pd(s) + 4\,Cl^-(aq) + Cd^{2+}(aq)$$

has a measured standard cell potential of $+1.03$ V. (a) Write the two half-cell reactions. (b) By using data from Appendix E, determine E_{red}° for the reaction involving Pd. (c) Sketch the voltaic cell, label the anode and cathode, and indicate the direction of electron flow.

20.35 Using standard reduction potentials (Appendix E), calculate the standard emf for each of the following reactions:

(a) $Cl_2(g) + 2\,I^-(aq) \longrightarrow 2\,Cl^-(aq) + I_2(s)$

(b) $Ni(s) + 2\,Ce^{4+}(aq) \longrightarrow Ni^{2+}(aq) + 2\,Ce^{3+}(aq)$

(c) $Fe(s) + 2\,Fe^{3+}(aq) \longrightarrow 3\,Fe^{2+}(aq)$

(d) $2\,Al^{3+}(aq) + 3\,Ca(s) \longrightarrow 2\,Al(s) + 3\,Ca^{2+}(aq)$

20.36 Using data in Appendix E, calculate the standard emf for each of the following reactions:

(a) $H_2(g) + F_2(g) \longrightarrow 2\,H^+(aq) + 2\,F^-(aq)$

(b) $Cu^{2+}(aq) + Ca(s) \longrightarrow Cu(s) + Ca^{2+}(aq)$

(c) $3\,Fe^{2+}(aq) \longrightarrow Fe(s) + 2\,Fe^{3+}(aq)$

(d) $Hg_2^{2+}(aq) + 2\,Cu^+(aq) \longrightarrow 2\,Hg(l) + 2\,Cu^{2+}(aq)$

20.37 The standard reduction potentials of the following half-reactions are given in Appendix E:

$$Ag^+(aq) + e^- \longrightarrow Ag(s)$$
$$Cu^{2+}(aq) + 2\,e^- \longrightarrow Cu(s)$$
$$Ni^{2+}(aq) + 2\,e^- \longrightarrow Ni(s)$$
$$Cr^{3+}(aq) + 3\,e^- \longrightarrow Cr(s)$$

(a) Determine which combination of these half-cell reactions leads to the cell reaction with the largest positive cell emf, and calculate the value. (b) Determine which combination of these half-cell reactions leads to the cell reaction with the smallest positive cell emf, and calculate the value.

20.38 Given the following half-reactions and associated standard reduction potentials:

$$AuBr_4^-(aq) + 3 e^- \longrightarrow Au(s) + 4 Br^-(aq)$$
$$E_{red}^\circ = -0.858 \text{ V}$$

$$Eu^{3+}(aq) + e^- \longrightarrow Eu^{2+}(aq)$$
$$E_{red}^\circ = -0.43 \text{ V}$$

$$IO^-(aq) + H_2O(l) + 2 e^- \longrightarrow I^-(aq) + 2 OH^-(aq)$$
$$E_{red}^\circ = +0.49 \text{ V}$$

$$Sn^{2+}(aq) + 2 e^- \longrightarrow Sn(s)$$
$$E_{red}^\circ = -0.14 \text{ V}$$

(a) Write the cell reaction for the combination of these half-cell reactions that leads to the largest positive cell emf, and calculate the value. (b) Write the cell reaction for the combination of half-cell reactions that leads to the smallest positive cell emf, and calculate that value.

Strengths of Oxidizing and Reducing Agents

20.41 From each of the following pairs of substances, use data in Appendix E to choose the one that is the stronger reducing agent:
(a) Fe(s) or Mg(s)
(b) Ca(s) or Al(s)
(c) $H_2(g$, acidic solution) or $H_2S(g)$
(d) $H_2SO_3(aq)$ or $H_2C_2O_4(aq)$

20.42 From each of the following pairs of substances, use data in Appendix E to choose the one that is the stronger oxidizing agent:
(a) $Cl_2(g)$ or $Br_2(l)$
(b) $Zn^{2+}(aq)$ or $Cd^{2+}(aq)$
(c) $BrO_3^-(aq)$ or $IO_3^-(aq)$
(d) $H_2O_2(aq)$ or $O_3(g)$

20.43 By using the data in Appendix E, determine whether each of the following substances is likely to serve as an oxidant or a reductant: (a) $Cl_2(g)$, (b) $MnO_4^-(aq$, acidic solution), (c) Ba(s), (d) Zn(s).

20.44 Is each of the following substances likely to serve as an oxidant or a reductant: (a) $Ce^{3+}(aq)$, (b) Ca(s), (c) $ClO_3^-(aq)$, (d) $N_2O_5(g)$?

Free Energy and Redox Reactions

20.49 Given the following reduction half-reactions:

$$Fe^{3+}(aq) + e^- \longrightarrow Fe^{2+}(aq)$$
$$E_{red}^\circ = +0.77 \text{ V}$$

$$S_2O_6^{2-}(aq) + 4 H^+(aq) + 2 e^- \longrightarrow 2 H_2SO_3(aq)$$
$$E_{red}^\circ = +0.60 \text{ V}$$

$$N_2O(g) + 2 H^+(aq) + 2 e^- \longrightarrow N_2(g) + H_2O(l)$$
$$E_{red}^\circ = -1.77 \text{ V}$$

$$VO_2^+(aq) + 2 H^+(aq) + e^- \longrightarrow VO^{2+}(aq) + H_2O(l)$$
$$E_{red}^\circ = +1.00 \text{ V}$$

20.39 A 1 M solution of $Cu(NO_3)_2$ is placed in a beaker with a strip of Cu metal. A 1 M solution of $SnSO_4$ is placed in a second beaker with a strip of Sn metal. A salt bridge connects the two beakers, and wires to a voltmeter link the two metal electrodes. (a) Which electrode serves as the anode, and which as the cathode? (b) Which electrode gains mass and which loses mass as the cell reaction proceeds? (c) Write the equation for the overall cell reaction. (d) What is the emf generated by the cell under standard conditions?

20.40 A voltaic cell consists of a strip of cadmium metal in a solution of $Cd(NO_3)_2$ in one beaker, and in the other beaker a platinum electrode is immersed in a NaCl solution, with Cl_2 gas bubbled around the electrode. A salt bridge connects the two beakers. (a) Which electrode serves as the anode, and which as the cathode? (b) Does the Cd electrode gain or lose mass as the cell reaction proceeds? (c) Write the equation for the overall cell reaction. (d) What is the emf generated by the cell under standard conditions?

20.45 (a) Assuming standard conditions, arrange the following in order of increasing strength as oxidizing agents in acidic solution: $Cr_2O_7^{2-}$, H_2O_2, Cu^{2+}, Cl_2, O_2. (b) Arrange the following in order of increasing strength as reducing agents in acidic solution: Zn, I^-, Sn^{2+}, H_2O_2, Al.

20.46 Based on the data in Appendix E, (a) which of the following is the strongest oxidizing agent and which is the weakest in acidic solution: Ce^{4+}, Br_2, H_2O_2, Zn? (b) Which of the following is the strongest reducing agent, and which is the weakest in acidic solution: F^-, Zn, $N_2H_5^+$, I_2, NO?

20.47 The standard reduction potential for the reduction of $Eu^{3+}(aq)$ to $Eu^{2+}(aq)$ is -0.43 V. Using Appendix E, which of the following substances is capable of reducing $Eu^{3+}(aq)$ to $Eu^{2+}(aq)$ under standard conditions: Al, Co, H_2O_2, $N_2H_5^+$, $H_2C_2O_4$?

20.48 The standard reduction potential for the reduction of $RuO_4^-(aq)$ to $RuO_4^{2-}(aq)$ is $+0.59$ V. By using Appendix E, which of the following substances can oxidize $RuO_4^{2-}(aq)$ to $RuO_4^-(aq)$ under standard conditions: $Br_2(l)$, $BrO_3^-(aq)$, $Mn^{2+}(aq)$, $O_2(g)$, $Sn^{2+}(aq)$?

(a) Write balanced chemical equations for the oxidation of $Fe^{2+}(aq)$ by $S_2O_6^{2-}(aq)$, by $N_2O(aq)$, and by $VO_2^+(aq)$. (b) Calculate ΔG° for each reaction at 298 K. (c) Calculate the equilibrium constant K for each reaction at 298 K.

20.50 For each of the following reactions, write a balanced equation, calculate the standard emf, calculate ΔG° at 298 K, and calculate the equilibrium constant K at 298 K. (a) Aqueous iodide ion is oxidized to $I_2(s)$ by $Hg_2^{2+}(aq)$. (b) In acidic solution, copper(I) ion is oxidized to copper(II) ion by nitrate ion. (c) In basic solution, $Cr(OH)_3(s)$ is oxidized to $CrO_4^{2-}(aq)$ by $ClO^-(aq)$.

Recall also that all atoms of a given element have the same number of protons; this number is the element's *atomic number*. The atoms of a given element can have different numbers of neutrons, however, so they can have different *mass numbers*; the mass number is the total number of nucleons in the nucleus. Atoms with the same atomic number but different mass numbers are known as *isotopes*.

The different isotopes of an element are distinguished by their mass numbers. For example, the three naturally occurring isotopes of uranium are uranium-234, uranium-235, and uranium-238, where the numerical suffixes represent the mass numbers. These isotopes are also labeled, using chemical symbols, as $^{234}_{92}U$, $^{235}_{92}U$, and $^{238}_{92}U$. The superscript is the mass number; the subscript is the atomic number.

Different isotopes have different natural abundances. For example, 99.3% of naturally occurring uranium is uranium-238, 0.7% is uranium-235, and only a trace is uranium-234. Different nuclei also have different stabilities. Indeed, the nuclear properties of an atom depend on the number of protons and neutrons in its nucleus. A *nuclide* is a nucleus with a specified number of protons and neutrons. Nuclei that are radioactive are called **radionuclides**, and atoms containing these nuclei are called **radioisotopes**.

Nuclear Equations

Most nuclei found in nature are stable and remain intact indefinitely. Radionuclides, however, are unstable and spontaneously emit particles and electromagnetic radiation. Emission of radiation is one of the ways in which an unstable nucleus is transformed into a more stable one with less energy. The emitted radiation is the carrier of the excess energy. Uranium-238, for example, is radioactive, undergoing a nuclear reaction in which helium-4 nuclei are spontaneously emitted. The helium-4 particles are known as **alpha (α) particles**, and a stream of these particles is called *alpha radiation*. When a uranium-238 nucleus loses an alpha particle, the remaining fragment has an atomic number of 90 and a mass number of 234. If you look at the periodic table, you will find that the element with atomic number 90 is Th, thorium. Therefore, the products of uranium-238 decomposition are an alpha particle and a thorium-234 nucleus. We represent this reaction by the following *nuclear equation*:

$$^{238}_{92}U \longrightarrow {}^{234}_{90}Th + {}^{4}_{2}He \qquad [21.1]$$

When a nucleus spontaneously decomposes in this way, it is said to have decayed, or to have undergone *radioactive decay*. Because an alpha particle is involved in this reaction, scientists also describe the process as alpha decay.

GIVE IT SOME THOUGHT

What change in the mass number of a nucleus occurs when the nucleus emits an alpha particle?

In Equation 21.1 the sum of the mass numbers is the same on both sides of the equation (238 = 234 + 4). Likewise, the sum of the atomic numbers on both sides of the equation is equal (92 = 90 + 2). Mass numbers and atomic numbers must be balanced in all nuclear equations.

The radioactive properties of the nucleus are independent of the chemical state of the atom. In writing nuclear equations, therefore, we are not concerned with the chemical form (element or compound) of the atom in which the nucleus resides.

■■ **SAMPLE EXERCISE 21.1** | **Predicting the Product of a Nuclear Reaction**

What product is formed when radium-226 undergoes alpha decay?

SOLUTION

Analyze: We are asked to determine the nucleus that results when radium-226 loses an alpha particle.

Plan: We can best do this by writing a balanced nuclear reaction for the process.

Solve: The periodic table shows that radium has an atomic number of 88. The complete chemical symbol for radium-226 is therefore $^{226}_{88}\text{Ra}$. An alpha particle is a helium-4 nucleus, and so its symbol is $^{4}_{2}\text{He}$ (sometimes written as $^{4}_{2}\alpha$). The alpha particle is a product of the nuclear reaction, and so the equation is of the form

$$^{226}_{88}\text{Ra} \longrightarrow ^{A}_{Z}\text{X} + ^{4}_{2}\text{He}$$

where A is the mass number of the product nucleus and Z is its atomic number. Mass numbers and atomic numbers must balance, so

$$226 = A + 4$$

and

$$88 = Z + 2$$

Hence,

$$A = 222 \quad \text{and} \quad Z = 86$$

Again, from the periodic table, the element with $Z = 86$ is radon (Rn). The product, therefore, is $^{222}_{86}\text{Rn}$, and the nuclear equation is

$$^{226}_{88}\text{Ra} \longrightarrow ^{222}_{86}\text{Rn} + ^{4}_{2}\text{He}$$

■■ **PRACTICE EXERCISE**

Which element undergoes alpha decay to form lead-208?

Answer: $^{212}_{84}\text{Po}$

Types of Radioactive Decay

The three most common kinds of radioactive decay are alpha (α), beta (β), and gamma (γ) radiation. ∞∞ (Section 2.2) Table 21.1 ▼ summarizes some of the important properties of these kinds of radiation. As we have just discussed, alpha radiation consists of a stream of helium-4 nuclei known as alpha particles, which we denote as $^{4}_{2}\text{He}$ or $^{4}_{2}\alpha$.

Beta radiation consists of streams of **beta (β) particles**, which are high-speed electrons emitted by an unstable nucleus. Beta particles are represented in nuclear equations by the symbol $^{0}_{-1}\text{e}$ or sometimes $^{0}_{-1}\beta$. The superscript zero indicates that the mass of the electron is exceedingly small compared to the mass of a nucleon. The subscript -1 represents the negative charge of the particle, which is opposite that of the proton. Iodine-131 is an isotope that undergoes decay by beta emission:

$$^{131}_{53}\text{I} \longrightarrow ^{131}_{54}\text{Xe} + ^{0}_{-1}\text{e} \qquad\qquad [21.2]$$

TABLE 21.1 ■ **Properties of Alpha, Beta, and Gamma Radiation**

Property	Type of Radiation		
	α	β	γ
Charge	2+	1−	0
Mass	$6.64 \times 10^{-24}\,\text{g}$	$9.11 \times 10^{-28}\,\text{g}$	0
Relative penetrating power	1	100	10,000
Nature of radiation	$^{4}_{2}\text{He}$ nuclei	Electrons	High-energy photons

Further Observations

Two further observations can help you predict nuclear stability:

- Nuclei with 2, 8, 20, 28, 50, or 82 protons or 2, 8, 20, 28, 50, 82, or 126 neutrons are generally more stable than nuclei that do not contain these numbers of nucleons. These numbers of protons and neutrons are called **magic numbers**.

- Nuclei with even numbers of both protons and neutrons are generally more stable than those with odd numbers of nucleons, as shown in Table 21.3▶.

These observations can be understood in terms of the *shell model of the nucleus*, in which nucleons are described as residing in shells analogous to the shell structure for electrons in atoms. Just as certain numbers of electrons (2, 8, 18, 36, 54, and 86) correspond to stable closed-shell electron configurations, so also the magic numbers of nucleons represent closed shells in nuclei. As an example of the stability of nuclei with magic numbers of nucleons, note that the radioactive series depicted in Figure 21.5 ends with formation of the stable $^{206}_{82}$Pb nucleus, which has a magic number of protons (82).

Evidence also suggests that pairs of protons and pairs of neutrons have a special stability, analogous to the pairs of electrons in molecules. Thus, stable nuclei with an even number of protons and an even number of neutrons are far more numerous than those with odd numbers (Table 21.3).

TABLE 21.3 ■ The Number of Stable Isotopes with Even and Odd Numbers of Protons and Neutrons		
Number of Stable Isotopes	Protons	Neutrons
157	Even	Even
53	Even	Odd
50	Odd	Even
5	Odd	Odd

▮ SAMPLE EXERCISE 21.4 | Predicting Nuclear Stability

Predict which of these nuclei are especially stable: $^4_2$He, $^{40}_{20}$Ca, $^{98}_{43}$Tc?

SOLUTION

Analyze: We are asked to identify especially stable nuclei, given their mass numbers and atomic numbers.

Plan: We look to see whether the numbers of protons and neutrons correspond to magic numbers.

Solve: The $^4_2$He nucleus (the alpha particle) has a magic number of both protons (2) and neutrons (2) and is very stable. The $^{40}_{20}$Ca nucleus also has a magic number of both protons (20) and neutrons (20) and is especially stable.

The $^{98}_{43}$Tc nucleus does not have a magic number of either protons or neutrons. In fact, it has an odd number of both protons (43) and neutrons (55). There are very few stable nuclei with odd numbers of both protons and neutrons. Indeed, technetium-98 is radioactive.

▮ PRACTICE EXERCISE

Which of the following nuclei would you expect to exhibit a special stability: $^{118}_{50}$Sn, $^{210}_{85}$At, $^{208}_{82}$Pb?

Answer: $^{118}_{50}$Sn, $^{208}_{82}$Pb

21.3 NUCLEAR TRANSMUTATIONS

Thus far we have examined nuclear reactions in which a nucleus spontaneously decays. A nucleus can also change identity if it is struck by a neutron or by another nucleus. Nuclear reactions that are induced in this way are known as **nuclear transmutations**.

In 1919, Ernest Rutherford performed the first conversion of one nucleus into another. He succeeded in converting nitrogen-14 into oxygen-17, plus a proton, using the high-velocity alpha particles emitted by radium. The reaction is

$$^{14}_{7}\text{N} + ^4_2\text{He} \longrightarrow ^{17}_{8}\text{O} + ^1_1\text{H} \qquad [21.8]$$

This reaction demonstrated that striking nuclei with particles such as alpha particles could induce nuclear reactions. Such reactions made it possible to synthesize hundreds of radioisotopes in the laboratory.

Nuclear transmutations are sometimes represented by listing, in order, the target nucleus, the bombarding particle, the ejected particle, and the product nucleus. Written in this fashion, Equation 21.8 is $^{14}_{7}\text{N}(\alpha, \text{p})^{17}_{8}\text{O}$. The alpha particle, proton, and neutron are abbreviated as α, p, and n, respectively.

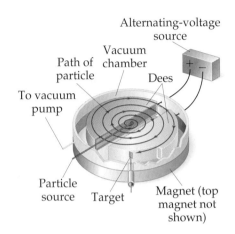

Alternating-voltage source

Vacuum chamber

Path of particle

Dees

To vacuum pump

Particle source   Target

Magnet (top magnet not shown)

▲ **Figure 21.6 Schematic drawing of a cyclotron.** Charged particles are accelerated around the ring by applying alternating voltage to the dees.

■ SAMPLE EXERCISE 21.5 | Writing a Balanced Nuclear Equation

Write the balanced nuclear equation for the process summarized as $^{27}_{13}\text{Al}(\text{n}, \alpha)^{24}_{11}\text{Na}$.

SOLUTION

Analyze: We must go from the condensed descriptive form of the nuclear reaction to the balanced nuclear equation.

Plan: We arrive at the full nuclear equation by writing n and α, each with its associated subscripts and superscripts.

Solve: The n is the abbreviation for a neutron ($^{1}_{0}\text{n}$), and α represents an alpha particle ($^{4}_{2}\text{He}$). The neutron is the bombarding particle, and the alpha particle is a product. Therefore, the nuclear equation is

$$^{27}_{13}\text{Al} + ^{1}_{0}\text{n} \longrightarrow ^{24}_{11}\text{Na} + ^{4}_{2}\text{He}$$

■ PRACTICE EXERCISE

Using a shorthand notation, write the nuclear reaction

$$^{16}_{8}\text{O} + ^{1}_{1}\text{H} \longrightarrow ^{13}_{7}\text{N} + ^{4}_{2}\text{He}$$

Answer: $^{16}_{8}\text{O}(\text{p}, \alpha)^{13}_{7}\text{N}$

▲ **Figure 21.7 CERN (Conseil Européen pour la Recherche Nucléaire), Geneva, Switzerland.** Particles are accelerated to very high energies by circulating them through magnets in the ring, which has a circumference of 27 km.

Accelerating Charged Particles

Charged particles, such as alpha particles, must be moving very fast to overcome the electrostatic repulsion between them and the target nucleus. The higher the nuclear charge on either the projectile or the target, the faster the projectile must be moving to bring about a nuclear reaction. Many methods have been devised to accelerate charged particles, using strong magnetic and electrostatic fields. These **particle accelerators**, popularly called "atom smashers," bear such names as *cyclotron* and *synchrotron*. The cyclotron is illustrated in Figure 21.6 ◄. The hollow D-shaped electrodes are called "dees." The projectile particles are introduced into a vacuum chamber within the cyclotron. The particles are then accelerated by making the dees alternately positively and negatively charged. Magnets placed above and below the dees keep the particles moving in a spiral path until they are finally deflected out of the cyclotron and emerge to strike a target substance. Particle accelerators are used to synthesize heavy elements, to investigate the fundamental structure of matter, and ultimately answer questions about the beginning of the universe. Figure 21.7 ◄ shows an aerial view of CERN (Conseil Européen pour la Recherche Nucléaire), the European Organization for Nuclear Research, near Geneva, Switzerland.

Using Neutrons

Most synthetic isotopes used in medicine and scientific research are made using neutrons as projectiles. Because neutrons are neutral, they are not repelled by the nucleus. Consequently, they do not need to be accelerated, as do charged particles, to cause nuclear reactions. The necessary neutrons are produced by the reactions that occur in nuclear reactors. For example, cobalt-60, which is used in radiation therapy for cancer, is produced by neutron capture. Iron-58 is placed in a nuclear reactor, where neutrons bombard it. The following sequence of reactions takes place:

$$\isotope[58][26]{Fe} + \isotope[1][0]{n} \longrightarrow \isotope[59][26]{Fe} \qquad [21.9]$$

$$\isotope[59][26]{Fe} \longrightarrow \isotope[59][27]{Co} + \isotope[0][-1]{e} \qquad [21.10]$$

$$\isotope[59][27]{Co} + \isotope[1][0]{n} \longrightarrow \isotope[60][27]{Co} \qquad [21.11]$$

▲ GIVE IT SOME THOUGHT

Can neutrons be accelerated in a particle accelerator, using electrostatic or magnetic fields? Why or why not?

Transuranium Elements

Artificial transmutations have been used to produce the elements with atomic number above 92. These elements are known as the **transuranium elements** because they occur immediately following uranium in the periodic table. Elements 93 (neptunium, Np) and 94 (plutonium, Pu) were discovered in 1940. They were produced by bombarding uranium-238 with neutrons:

$$\isotope[238][92]{U} + \isotope[1][0]{n} \longrightarrow \isotope[239][92]{U} \longrightarrow \isotope[239][93]{Np} + \isotope[0][-1]{e} \qquad [21.12]$$

$$\isotope[239][93]{Np} \longrightarrow \isotope[239][94]{Pu} + \isotope[0][-1]{e} \qquad [21.13]$$

Elements with still larger atomic numbers are normally formed in small quantities in particle accelerators. Curium-242, for example, is formed when a plutonium-239 target is struck with accelerated alpha particles:

$$\isotope[239][94]{Pu} + \isotope[4][2]{He} \longrightarrow \isotope[242][96]{Cm} + \isotope[1][0]{n} \qquad [21.14]$$

In 1994 a team of European scientists synthesized element 111 by bombarding a bismuth target for several days with a beam of nickel atoms:

$$\isotope[209][83]{Bi} + \isotope[64][28]{Ni} \longrightarrow \isotope[272][111]{X} + \isotope[1][0]{n}$$

Amazingly, their discovery was based on the detection of only three atoms of the new element. The nuclei are very short lived, and they undergo alpha decay within milliseconds of their synthesis. In 2004 scientists reported the synthesis of elements 113 and 115. As of this writing, these results have yet to be confirmed, although the results look promising. Evidence for element 118 was reported in 2006. Names and symbols have not yet been chosen for these new elements.

21.4 RATES OF RADIOACTIVE DECAY

Some radioisotopes, such as uranium-238, are found in nature, although they are not stable. Other radioisotopes do not exist in nature, even though they can be synthesized in nuclear reactions. To understand this distinction, we must realize that different nuclei undergo radioactive decay at different rates. Many radioisotopes decay essentially completely in a matter of seconds or less, so we do not find them in nature. Uranium-238, on the other hand, decays very slowly. Therefore, despite its instability, we can still observe what remains from its formation in the early history of the universe.

TABLE 21.4 ▪ The Half-lives and Type of Decay for Several Radioisotopes

	Isotope	Half-life (yr)	Type of Decay
Natural radioisotopes	$^{238}_{92}U$	4.5×10^9	Alpha
	$^{235}_{92}U$	7.0×10^8	Alpha
	$^{232}_{90}Th$	1.4×10^{10}	Alpha
	$^{40}_{19}K$	1.3×10^9	Beta
	$^{14}_{6}C$	5715	Beta
Synthetic radioisotopes	$^{239}_{94}Pu$	24,000	Alpha
	$^{137}_{55}Cs$	30	Beta
	$^{90}_{38}Sr$	28.8	Beta
	$^{131}_{53}I$	0.022	Beta

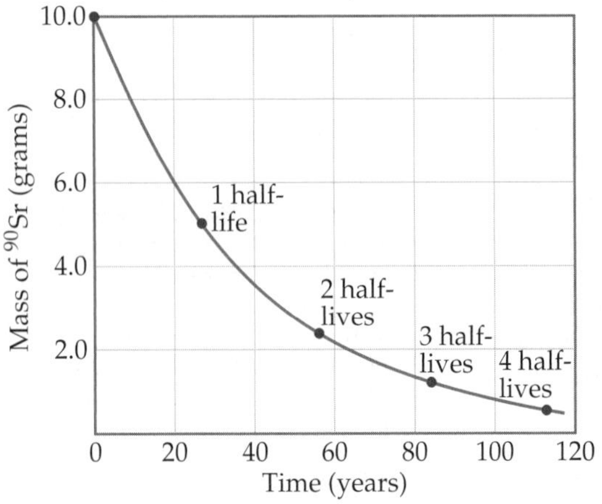

▲ Figure 21.8 **Decay of a 10.0-g sample of $^{90}_{38}Sr$ ($t_{1/2}$ = 28.8 yr).**

Radioactive decay is a first-order kinetic process. Recall that a first-order process has a characteristic **half-life**, which is the time required for half of any given quantity of a substance to react. ∞ (Section 14.4) The rates of decay of nuclei are commonly expressed in terms of their half-lives. Each isotope has its own characteristic half-life. For example, the half-life of strontium-90 is 28.8 yr. If we started with 10.0 g of strontium-90, only 5.0 g of that isotope would remain after 28.8 yr, 2.5 g would remain after another 28.8 yr, and so on. Strontium-90 decays to yttrium-90:

$$^{90}_{38}Sr \longrightarrow {}^{90}_{39}Y + {}^{0}_{-1}e \qquad [21.15]$$

The loss of strontium-90 as a function of time is shown in Figure 21.8 ◄.

Half-lives as short as millionths of a second and as long as billions of years are known. The half-lives of some radioisotopes are listed in Table 21.4 ▲. One important feature of half-lives for nuclear decay is that they are unaffected by external conditions such as temperature, pressure, or state of chemical combination. Unlike toxic chemicals, therefore, radioactive atoms cannot be rendered harmless by chemical reaction or by any other practical treatment. At this point we can do nothing but allow these nuclei to lose radioactivity at their characteristic rates. In the meantime, we must take precautions to prevent radioisotopes, such as those produced in nuclear power plants ∞ (Section 21.7), from entering the environment because of the damage radiation can cause.

■ **SAMPLE EXERCISE 21.6** | Calculation Involving Half-Lives

The half-life of cobalt-60 is 5.3 yr. How much of a 1.000-mg sample of cobalt-60 is left after a 15.9-yr period?

SOLUTION

Analyze: We are given the half-life for cobalt-60 and asked to calculate the amount of cobalt-60 remaining from an initial 1.000-mg sample after a 15.9-yr period.

Plan: We will use the fact that the half-life of a first-order decay process is a constant.

Solve: We notice that $5.3 \times 3 = 15.9$. Therefore, a period of 15.9 yr is three half-lives for cobalt-60. At the end of one half-life, 0.500 mg of cobalt-60 remains, 0.250 mg at the end of two half-lives, and 0.125 mg at the end of three half-lives.

■ **PRACTICE EXERCISE**

Carbon-11, used in medical imaging, has a half-life of 20.4 min. The carbon-11 nuclides are formed, and the carbon atoms are then incorporated into an appropriate compound. The resulting sample is injected into a patient, and the medical image is obtained. If the entire process takes five half-lives, what percentage of the original carbon-11 remains at this time?
Answer: 3.12%

[21.38] Cobalt-60, which undergoes beta decay, has a half-life of 5.26 yr. (a) How many beta particles are emitted in 180 s by a 3.75-mg sample of ^{60}Co? (b) What is the activity of the sample in Bq?

21.39 The cloth shroud from around a mummy is found to have a ^{14}C activity of 9.7 disintegrations per minute per gram of carbon as compared with living organisms that undergo 16.3 disintegrations per minute per gram of carbon. From the half-life for ^{14}C decay, 5715 yr, calculate the age of the shroud.

21.40 A wooden artifact from a Chinese temple has a ^{14}C activity of 38.0 counts per minute as compared with an activity of 58.2 counts per minute for a standard of zero age. From the half-life for ^{14}C decay, 5715 yr, determine the age of the artifact.

21.41 Potassium-40 decays to argon-40 with a half-life of 1.27×10^9 yr. What is the age of a rock in which the mass ratio of ^{40}Ar to ^{40}K is 4.2?

21.42 The half-life for the process $^{238}\text{U} \longrightarrow ^{206}\text{Pb}$ is 4.5×10^9 yr. A mineral sample contains 75.0 mg of ^{238}U and 18.0 mg of ^{206}Pb. What is the age of the mineral?

Energy Changes

21.43 The thermite reaction, $Fe_2O_3(s) + 2\,Al(s) \longrightarrow 2\,Fe(s) + Al_2O_3(s)$, is one of the most exothermic reactions known. The heat released is sufficient to melt the iron product; consequently, the thermite reaction is used to weld metal under the ocean. $\Delta H°$ for the thermite reaction is -851.5 kJ/mole. What is the mass change per mole of Fe_2O_3 that accompanies this reaction?

21.44 An analytical laboratory balance typically measures mass to the nearest 0.1 mg. What energy change would accompany the loss of 0.1 mg in mass?

21.45 How much energy must be supplied to break a single aluminum-27 nucleus into separated protons and neutrons if an aluminum-27 atom has a mass of 26.9815386 amu? How much energy is required for 100.0 grams of aluminum-27? (The mass of an electron is given on the inside back cover.)

21.46 How much energy must be supplied to break a single ^{21}Ne nucleus into separated protons and neutrons if the nucleus has a mass of 20.98846 amu? What is the nuclear binding energy for 1 mol of ^{21}Ne?

21.47 Calculate the binding energy per nucleon for the following nuclei: (a) $^{12}_{6}$C (nuclear mass, 11.996708 amu); (b) ^{37}Cl (nuclear mass, 36.956576 amu); (c) rhodium-103 (atomic mass, 102.905504 amu).

21.48 Calculate the binding energy per nucleon for the following nuclei: (a) $^{14}_{7}$N (nuclear mass, 13.999234 amu); (b) ^{48}Ti (nuclear mass, 47.935878 amu); (c) xenon-129 (atomic mass, 128.904779 amu).

21.49 The energy from solar radiation falling on Earth is 1.07×10^{16} kJ/min. (a) How much loss of mass from the Sun occurs in one day from just the energy falling on Earth? (b) If the energy released in the reaction

$$^{235}\text{U} + ^{1}_{0}\text{n} \longrightarrow ^{141}_{56}\text{Ba} + ^{92}_{36}\text{Kr} + 3\,^{1}_{0}\text{n}$$

(^{235}U nuclear mass, 234.9935 amu; ^{141}Ba nuclear mass, 140.8833 amu; ^{92}Kr nuclear mass, 91.9021 amu) is taken as typical of that occurring in a nuclear reactor, what mass of uranium-235 is required to equal 0.10% of the solar energy that falls on Earth in 1.0 day?

21.50 Based on the following atomic mass values—^{1}H, 1.00782 amu; ^{2}H, 2.01410 amu; ^{3}H, 3.01605 amu; ^{3}He, 3.01603 amu; ^{4}He, 4.00260 amu—and the mass of the neutron given in the text, calculate the energy released per mole in each of the following nuclear reactions, all of which are possibilities for a controlled fusion process:

(a) $^{2}_{1}\text{H} + ^{3}_{1}\text{H} \longrightarrow ^{4}_{2}\text{He} + ^{1}_{0}\text{n}$

(b) $^{2}_{1}\text{H} + ^{2}_{1}\text{H} \longrightarrow ^{3}_{2}\text{He} + ^{1}_{0}\text{n}$

(c) $^{2}_{1}\text{H} + ^{3}_{2}\text{He} \longrightarrow ^{4}_{2}\text{He} + ^{1}_{1}\text{H}$

21.51 Which of the following nuclei is likely to have the largest mass defect per nucleon: (a) ^{59}Co, (b) ^{11}B, (c) ^{118}Sn, (d) ^{243}Cm? Explain your answer.

21.52 Based on Figure 21.13, what is the most stable nucleus in the periodic table?

Effects and Uses of Radioisotopes

21.53 Iodine-131 is a convenient radioisotope to monitor thyroid activity in humans. It is a beta emitter with a half-life of 8.02 days. The thyroid is the only gland in the body that uses iodine. A person undergoing a test of thyroid activity drinks a solution of NaI, in which only a small fraction of the iodide is radioactive. (a) Why is NaI a good choice for the source of iodine? (b) If a Geiger counter is placed near the person's thyroid (which is near the neck) right after the sodium iodide solution is taken, what will the data look like as a function of time? (c) A normal thyroid will take up about 12% of the ingested iodide in a few hours. How long will it take for the radioactive iodide taken up and held by the thyroid to decay to 0.01% of the original amount?

21.54 Chlorine-36 is a convenient radiotracer. It is a weak beta emitter, with $t_{1/2} = 3 \times 10^5$ yr. Describe how you would use this radiotracer to carry out each of the following experiments. (a) Determine whether trichloroacetic acid, CCl_3COOH, undergoes any ionization of its chlorines as chloride ion in aqueous solution. (b) Demonstrate that the equilibrium between dissolved $BaCl_2$ and solid $BaCl_2$ in a saturated solution is a dynamic process. (c) Determine the effects of soil pH on the uptake of chloride ion from the soil by soybeans.

21.55 Explain the following terms that apply to fission reactions: (a) chain reaction, (b) critical mass.

21.56 Explain the function of the following components of a nuclear reactor: (a) control rods, (b) moderator.

21.57 Complete and balance the nuclear equations for the following fission or fusion reactions:

(a) $^2_1H + ^2_1H \longrightarrow ^3_2He + \underline{}$

(b) $^{233}_{92}U + ^1_0n \longrightarrow ^{133}_{51}Sb + ^{98}_{41}Nb + \underline{} ^1_0n$

21.58 Complete and balance the nuclear equations for the following fission reactions:

(a) $^{235}_{92}U + ^1_0n \longrightarrow ^{160}_{62}Sm + ^{72}_{30}Zn + \underline{} ^1_0n$

(b) $^{239}_{94}Pu + ^1_0n \longrightarrow ^{144}_{58}Ce + \underline{} + 2 ^1_0n$

21.59 A portion of the Sun's energy comes from the reaction

$$4 ^1_1H \longrightarrow ^4_2He + 2 ^0_1e$$

This reaction requires a temperature of about 10^6 to 10^7K. **(a)** Why is such a high temperature required? **(b)** Is the Sun solid?

[21.60] The spent fuel rods from a fission reactor are much more intensely radioactive than the original fuel rods. **(a)** What does this tell you about the products of the fission process in relationship to the belt of stability, Figure 21.3? **(b)** Given that only two or three neutrons are released per fission event and knowing that the nucleus undergoing fission has a neutron-to-proton ratio characteristic of a heavy nucleus, what sorts of decay would you expect to be dominant among the fission products?

21.61 Hydroxyl radicals can pluck hydrogen atoms from molecules ("hydrogen abstraction"), and hydroxide ions can pluck protons from molecules ("deprotonation"). Write the reaction equations and Lewis dot structures for the hydrogen abstraction and deprotonation reactions for the generic carboxylic acid R–COOH with hydroxyl radical and hydroxide ion, respectively. Why is hydroxyl radical more toxic to living systems than hydroxide ion?

21.62 Use Lewis structures to represent the reactants and products in Equation 21.31. Why is the H_2O^+ ion a free radical species?

21.63 A laboratory rat is exposed to an alpha-radiation source whose activity is 14.3 mCi. **(a)** What is the activity of the radiation in disintegrations per second? In becquerels? **(b)** The rat has a mass of 385 g and is exposed to the radiation for 14.0 s, absorbing 35% of the emitted alpha particles, each having an energy of 9.12×10^{-13} J. Calculate the absorbed dose in millirads and grays. **(c)** If the RBE of the radiation is 9.5, calculate the effective absorbed dose in mrem and Sv.

21.64 A 65-kg person is accidentally exposed for 240 s to a 15-mCi source of beta radiation coming from a sample of ^{90}Sr. **(a)** What is the activity of the radiation source in disintegrations per second? In becquerels? **(b)** Each beta particle has an energy of 8.75×10^{-14} J, and 7.5% of the radiation is absorbed by the person. Assuming that the absorbed radiation is spread over the person's entire body, calculate the absorbed dose in rads and in grays. **(c)** If the RBE of the beta particles is 1.0, what is the effective dose in mrem and in sieverts? **(d)** How does the magnitude of this dose of radiation compare with that of a mammogram (300 mrem)?

ADDITIONAL EXERCISES

21.65 Radon-222 decays to a stable nucleus by a series of three alpha emissions and two beta emissions. What is the stable nucleus that is formed?

21.66 A free neutron is unstable and decays into a proton with a half-life of 10.4 min. **(a)** What other particle forms? **(b)** Why don't neutrons in atomic nuclei decay at the same rate?

21.67 Americium-241 is an alpha emitter used in smoke detectors. The alpha radiation ionizes molecules in an air-filled gap between two electrodes in the smoke detector, leading to current. When smoke is present, the ionized molecules bind to smoke particles and the current decreases; when the current is reduced sufficiently, an alarm sounds. **(a)** Write the nuclear equation corresponding to the alpha decay of americium-241. **(b)** Why is an alpha emitter a better choice than a gamma emitter for a smoke detector? **(c)** In a commercial smoke detector, only 0.2 micrograms of americium are present. Calculate the energy that is equivalent to the mass loss of this amount of americium due to alpha radiation. The atomic mass of americium-241 is 241.056829 amu. **(d)** The half-life of americium-241 is 432 years; the half life of americium-240 is 2.12 days. Why is the 241 isotope a better choice for a smoke detector?

21.68 Chlorine has two stable nuclides, ^{35}Cl and ^{37}Cl. In contrast, ^{36}Cl is a radioactive nuclide that decays by beta emission. **(a)** What is the product of decay of ^{36}Cl? **(b)** Based on the empirical rules about nuclear stability, explain why the nucleus of ^{36}Cl is less stable than either ^{35}Cl or ^{37}Cl.

21.69 Nuclear scientists have synthesized approximately 1600 nuclei not known in nature. More might be discovered with heavy-ion bombardment using high-energy particle accelerators. Complete and balance the following reactions, which involve heavy-ion bombardments:

(a) $^6_3Li + ^{56}_{28}Ni \longrightarrow ?$

(b) $^{40}_{20}Ca + ^{248}_{96}Cm \longrightarrow ^{147}_{62}Sm + ?$

(c) $^{88}_{38}Sr + ^{84}_{36}Kr \longrightarrow ^{116}_{46}Pd + ?$

(d) $^{40}_{20}Ca + ^{238}_{92}U \longrightarrow ^{70}_{30}Zn + 4 ^1_0n + 2?$

[21.70] The synthetic radioisotope technetium-99, which decays by beta emission, is the most widely used isotope in nuclear medicine. The following data were collected on a sample of ^{99}Tc:

Disintegrations per Minute	Time (h)
180	0
130	2.5
104	5.0
77	7.5
59	10.0
46	12.5
24	17.5

Using these data, make an appropriate graph and curve fit to determine the half-life.

[21.71] According to current regulations, the maximum permissible dose of strontium-90 in the body of an adult is $1 \mu Ci$ (1×10^{-6} Ci). Using the relationship rate = kN, calculate the number of atoms of strontium-90 to which this dose corresponds. To what mass of strontium-90 does this correspond? The half-life for strontium-90 is 28.8 yr.

[21.72] Suppose you had a detection device that could count every decay event from a radioactive sample of plutonium-239 ($t_{1/2}$ is 24,000 yr). How many counts per second would you obtain from a sample containing 0.385 g of plutonium-239?

21.73 Methyl acetate (CH_3COOCH_3) is formed by the reaction of acetic acid with methyl alcohol. If the methyl alcohol is labeled with oxygen-18, the oxygen-18 ends up in the methyl acetate:

$$CH_3\overset{\overset{O}{\|}}{C}OH + H^{18}OCH_3 \longrightarrow CH_3\overset{\overset{O}{\|}}{C}{}^{18}OCH_3 + H_2O$$

Do the C—OH bond of the acid and the O—H bond of the alcohol break in the reaction, or do the O—H bond of the acid and the C—OH bond of the alcohol break? Explain.

21.74 An experiment was designed to determine whether an aquatic plant absorbed iodide ion from water. Iodine-131 ($t_{1/2}$ = 8.02 days) was added as a tracer, in the form of iodide ion, to a tank containing the plants. The initial activity of a $1.00\text{-}\mu L$ sample of the water was 214 counts per minute. After 30 days the level of activity in a $1.00\text{-}\mu L$ sample was 15.7 counts per minute. Did the plants absorb iodide from the water? Explain.

21.75 The nuclear masses of ^7Be, ^9Be, and ^{10}Be are 7.0147, 9.0100, and 10.0113 amu, respectively. Which of these nuclei has the largest binding energy per nucleon?

[21.76] A 26.00-g sample of water containing tritium, ^3_1H, emits 1.50×10^3 beta particles per second. Tritium is a weak beta emitter, with a half-life of 12.3 yr. What fraction of all the hydrogen in the water sample is tritium?

21.77 The Sun radiates energy into space at the rate of 3.9×10^{26} J/s. (a) Calculate the rate of mass loss from the Sun in kg/s. (b) How does this mass loss arise? (c) It is estimated that the Sun contains 9×10^{56} free protons. How many protons per second are consumed in nuclear reactions in the Sun?

[21.78] The average energy released in the fission of a single uranium-235 nucleus is about 3×10^{-11} J. If the conversion of this energy to electricity in a nuclear power plant is 40% efficient, what mass of uranium-235 undergoes fission in a year in a plant that produces 1000 MW (megawatts)? Recall that a watt is 1 J/s.

[21.79] Tests on human subjects in Boston in 1965 and 1966, following the era of atomic bomb testing, revealed average quantities of about 2 pCi of plutonium radioactivity in the average person. How many disintegrations per second does this level of activity imply? If each alpha particle deposits 8×10^{-13} J of energy and if the average person weighs 75 kg, calculate the number of rads and rems of radiation in 1 yr from such a level of plutonium.

INTEGRATIVE EXERCISES

21.80 A 53.8-mg sample of sodium perchlorate contains radioactive chlorine-36 (whose atomic mass is 36.0 amu). If 29.6% of the chlorine atoms in the sample are chlorine-36 and the remainder is naturally occurring nonradioactive chlorine atoms, how many disintegrations per second are produced by this sample? The half-life of chlorine-36 is 3.0×10^5 yr.

21.81 Calculate the mass of octane, $C_8H_{18}(l)$, that must be burned in air to evolve the same quantity of energy as produced by the fusion of 1.0 g of hydrogen in the following fusion reaction:

$$4\,^1_1H \longrightarrow \,^4_2He + 2\,^0_1e$$

Assume that all the products of the combustion of octane are in their gas phases. Use data from Exercise 21.50, Appendix C, and the inside covers of the text. The standard enthalpy of formation of octane is −250.1 kJ/mol.

21.82 A sample of an alpha emitter having an activity of 0.18 Ci is stored in a 25.0-mL sealed container at 22 °C for 245 days. (a) How many alpha particles are formed during this time? (b) Assuming that each alpha particle is converted to a helium atom, what is the partial pressure of helium gas in the container after this 245-day period?

[21.83] Charcoal samples from Stonehenge in England were burned in O_2, and the resultant CO_2 gas bubbled into a solution of $Ca(OH)_2$ (limewater), resulting in the precipitation of $CaCO_3$. The $CaCO_3$ was removed by filtration and dried. A 788-mg sample of the $CaCO_3$ had a radioactivity of 1.5×10^{-2} Bq due to carbon-14. By comparison, living organisms undergo 15.3 disintegrations per minute per gram of carbon. Using the half-life of carbon-14, 5715 yr, calculate the age of the charcoal sample.

21.84 When a positron is annihilated by combination with an electron, two photons of equal energy result. What is the wavelength of these photons? Are they gamma ray photons?

21.85 A 25.0-mL sample of 0.050 M barium nitrate solution was mixed with 25.0 mL of 0.050 M sodium sulfate solution labeled with radioactive sulfur-35. The activity of the initial sodium sulfate solution was 1.22×10^6 Bq/mL. After the resultant precipitate was removed by filtration, the remaining filtrate was found to have an activity of 250 Bq/mL. (a) Write a balanced chemical equation for the reaction that occurred. (b) Calculate the K_{sp} for the precipitate under the conditions of the experiment.

CHEMISTRY OF THE NONMETALS

A MODERN LIVING SPACE

SAMPLE EXERCISE 3 | Using the Quadratic Formula

Find the values of x that satisfy the equation $2x^2 + 4x = 1$.

SOLUTION

To solve the given equation for x, we must first put it in the form

$$ax^2 + bx + c = 0$$

and then use the quadratic formula. If

$$2x^2 + 4x = 1$$

then

$$2x^2 + 4x - 1 = 0$$

Using the quadratic formula, where $a = 2$, $b = 4$, and $c = -1$, we have

$$x = \frac{-4 \pm \sqrt{(4)(4) - 4(2)(-1)}}{2(2)}$$

$$= \frac{-4 \pm \sqrt{16 + 8}}{4} = \frac{-4 \pm \sqrt{24}}{4} = \frac{-4 \pm 4.899}{4}$$

The two solutions are

$$x = \frac{0.899}{4} = 0.225 \quad \text{and} \quad x = \frac{-8.899}{4} = -2.225$$

Often in chemical problems the negative solution has no physical meaning, and only the positive answer is used.

A.4 GRAPHS

Often the clearest way to represent the interrelationship between two variables is to graph them. Usually, the variable that is being experimentally varied, called the *independent variable*, is shown along the horizontal axis (x-axis). The variable that responds to the change in the independent variable, called the *dependent variable*, is then shown along the vertical axis (y-axis). For example, consider an experiment in which we vary the temperature of an enclosed gas and measure its pressure. The independent variable is temperature, and the dependent variable is pressure. The data shown in Table A-1▶ can be obtained by means of this experiment. These data are shown graphically in Figure A.1▶. The relationship between temperature and pressure is linear. The equation for any straight-line graph has the form

$$y = mx + b$$

where m is the slope of the line and b is the intercept with the y-axis. In the case of Figure 1, we could say that the relationship between temperature and pressure takes the form

$$P = mT + b$$

where P is pressure in atm and T is temperature in °C. As shown in Figure 1, the slope is 4.10×10^{-4} atm/°C, and the intercept—the point where the line crosses the y-axis—is 0.112 atm. Therefore, the equation for the line is

$$P = \left(4.10 \times 10^{-4}\, \frac{\text{atm}}{\text{°C}}\right)T + 0.112\ \text{atm}$$

TABLE A-1 ■ Interrelation between Pressure and Temperature	
Temperature (°C)	Pressure (atm)
20.0	0.120
30.0	0.124
40.0	0.128
50.0	0.132

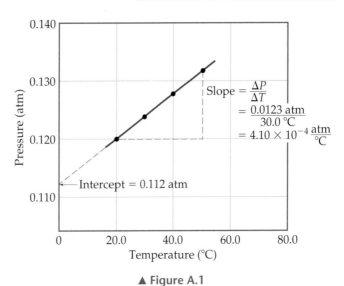

▲ Figure A.1

A.5 STANDARD DEVIATION

The standard deviation from the mean, s, is a common method from describing precision. We define the standard deviation as follows:

$$s = \sqrt{\dfrac{\sum\limits_{i=1}^{N}(x_i - \bar{x})^2}{N - 1}}$$

where N is the number of measurements, $\bar{x}$ is the average (also called the mean), and x_i represents the individual measurements. Electronic calculators with built-in statistical functions can calculate s directly by inputting the individual measurements.

A smaller value of s indicates a higher precision, meaning that the data is more closely clustered around the average. The standard deviation has a statistical significance. Thus, if a large number of measurements is made, 68% of the measured values is expected to be within one standard deviation of the average, assuming only random errors are associated with the measurements.

▣ SAMPLE EXERCISE 4 | Calculating an Average and Standard Deviation

The percent carbon in a sugar is measured four times: 42.01%, 42.28%, 41.79%, and 42.25%. Calculate **(a)** the average and **(b)** the standard deviation for these measurements.

SOLUTION

(a) The average is found by adding the quantities and dividing by the number of measurements:

$$\bar{x} = \frac{42.01 + 42.28 + 41.79 + 42.25}{4} = \frac{168.33}{4} = 42.08$$

(b) The standard deviation is found using the equation above:

$$s = \sqrt{\dfrac{\sum\limits_{i=1}^{N}(x_i - \bar{x})^2}{N - 1}}$$

Let's tabulate the data so the calculation of $\sum\limits_{i=1}^{N}(x_i - \bar{x})^2$ can be seen clearly.

Percent C	Difference between Measurement and Average, $(x_i - \bar{x})$	Square of Difference, $(x_i - \bar{x})^2$
42.01	$42.01 - 42.08 = -0.07$	$(-0.07)^2 = 0.005$
42.28	$42.28 - 42.08 = 0.20$	$(0.20)^2 = 0.040$
41.79	$41.79 - 42.08 = -0.29$	$(-0.29)^2 = 0.084$
42.25	$42.25 - 42.08 = 0.17$	$(0.17)^2 = 0.029$

The sum of the quantities in the last column is

$$\sum_{i=1}^{N}(x_i - \bar{x})^2 = 0.005 + 0.040 + 0.084 + 0.029 = 0.16$$

Thus, the standard deviation is

$$s = \sqrt{\dfrac{\sum\limits_{i=1}^{N}(x_i - \bar{x})^2}{N - 1}} = \sqrt{\frac{0.16}{4 - 1}} = \sqrt{\frac{0.16}{3}} = \sqrt{0.053} = 0.23$$

Based on these measurements, it would be appropriate to represent the measured percent carbon as 42.08 ± 0.23.

B

Properties of Water

Density:	0.99987 g/mL at 0 °C
	1.00000 g/mL at 4 °C
	0.99707 g/mL at 25 °C
	0.95838 g/mL at 100 °C
Heat of fusion:	6.008 kJ/mol at 0 °C
Heat of vaporization:	44.94 kJ/mol at 0 °C
	44.02 kJ/mol at 25 °C
	40.67 kJ/mol at 100 °C
Ion-product constant, K_w:	1.14×10^{-15} at 0 °C
	1.01×10^{-14} at 25 °C
	5.47×10^{-14} at 50 °C
Specific heat:	Ice (at −3 °C) 2.092 J/g-K
	Water (at 14.5 °C) 4.184 J/g-K
	Steam (at 100 °C) 1.841 J/g-K

Vapor Pressure (torr)

T (°C)	P	T (°C)	P	T (°C)	P	T (°C)	P
0	4.58	21	18.65	35	42.2	92	567.0
5	6.54	22	19.83	40	55.3	94	610.9
10	9.21	23	21.07	45	71.9	96	657.6
12	10.52	24	22.38	50	92.5	98	707.3
14	11.99	25	23.76	55	118.0	100	760.0
16	13.63	26	25.21	60	149.4	102	815.9
17	14.53	27	26.74	65	187.5	104	875.1
18	15.48	28	28.35	70	233.7	106	937.9
19	16.48	29	30.04	80	355.1	108	1004.4
20	17.54	30	31.82	90	525.8	110	1074.6

Substance	ΔH_f° (kJ/mol)	ΔG_f° (kJ/mol)	S° (J/mol-K)	Substance	ΔH_f° (kJ/mol)	ΔG_f° (kJ/mol)	S° (J/mol-K)
Aluminum				$C_2H_4(g)$	52.30	68.11	219.4
$Al(s)$	0	0	28.32	$C_2H_6(g)$	−84.68	−32.89	229.5
$AlCl_3(s)$	−705.6	−630.0	109.3	$C_3H_8(g)$	−103.85	−23.47	269.9
$Al_2O_3(s)$	−1669.8	−1576.5	51.00	$C_4H_{10}(g)$	−124.73	−15.71	310.0
Barium				$C_4H_{10}(l)$	−147.6	−15.0	231.0
$Ba(s)$	0	0	63.2	$C_6H_6(g)$	82.9	129.7	269.2
$BaCO_3(s)$	−1216.3	−1137.6	112.1	$C_6H_6(l)$	49.0	124.5	172.8
$BaO(s)$	−553.5	−525.1	70.42	$CH_3OH(g)$	−201.2	−161.9	237.6
Beryllium				$CH_3OH(l)$	−238.6	−166.23	126.8
$Be(s)$	0	0	9.44	$C_2H_5OH(g)$	−235.1	−168.5	282.7
$BeO(s)$	−608.4	−579.1	13.77	$C_2H_5OH(l)$	−277.7	−174.76	160.7
$Be(OH)_2(s)$	−905.8	−817.9	50.21	$C_6H_{12}O_6(s)$	−1273.02	−910.4	212.1
Bromine				$CO(g)$	−110.5	−137.2	197.9
$Br(g)$	111.8	82.38	174.9	$CO_2(g)$	−393.5	−394.4	213.6
$Br^-(aq)$	−120.9	−102.8	80.71	$CH_3COOH(l)$	−487.0	−392.4	159.8
$Br_2(g)$	30.71	3.14	245.3	**Cesium**			
$Br_2(l)$	0	0	152.3	$Cs(g)$	76.50	49.53	175.6
$HBr(g)$	−36.23	−53.22	198.49	$Cs(l)$	2.09	0.03	92.07
Calcium				$Cs(s)$	0	0	85.15
$Ca(g)$	179.3	145.5	154.8	$CsCl(s)$	−442.8	−414.4	101.2
$Ca(s)$	0	0	41.4	**Chlorine**			
$CaCO_3(s, calcite)$	−1207.1	−1128.76	92.88	$Cl(g)$	121.7	105.7	165.2
$CaCl_2(s)$	−795.8	−748.1	104.6	$Cl^-(aq)$	−167.2	−131.2	56.5
$CaF_2(s)$	−1219.6	−1167.3	68.87	$Cl_2(g)$	0	0	222.96
$CaO(s)$	−635.5	−604.17	39.75	$HCl(aq)$	−167.2	−131.2	56.5
$Ca(OH)_2(s)$	−986.2	−898.5	83.4	$HCl(g)$	−92.30	−95.27	186.69
$CaSO_4(s)$	−1434.0	−1321.8	106.7	**Chromium**			
Carbon				$Cr(g)$	397.5	352.6	174.2
$C(g)$	718.4	672.9	158.0	$Cr(s)$	0	0	23.6
$C(s, diamond)$	1.88	2.84	2.43	$Cr_2O_3(s)$	−1139.7	−1058.1	81.2
$C(s, graphite)$	0	0	5.69	**Cobalt**			
$CCl_4(g)$	−106.7	−64.0	309.4	$Co(g)$	439	393	179
$CCl_4(l)$	−139.3	−68.6	214.4	$Co(s)$	0	0	28.4
$CF_4(g)$	−679.9	−635.1	262.3	**Copper**			
$CH_4(g)$	−74.8	−50.8	186.3	$Cu(g)$	338.4	298.6	166.3
$C_2H_2(g)$	226.77	209.2	200.8	$Cu(s)$	0	0	33.30

Substance	ΔH_f° (kJ/mol)	ΔG_f° (kJ/mol)	S° (J/mol-K)	Substance	ΔH_f° (kJ/mol)	ΔG_f° (kJ/mol)	S° (J/mol-K)
$CuCl_2(s)$	−205.9	−161.7	108.1	$MgO(s)$	−601.8	−569.6	26.8
$CuO(s)$	−156.1	−128.3	42.59	$Mg(OH)_2(s)$	−924.7	−833.7	63.24
$Cu_2O(s)$	−170.7	−147.9	92.36	**Manganese**			
Fluorine				$Mn(g)$	280.7	238.5	173.6
$F(g)$	80.0	61.9	158.7	$Mn(s)$	0	0	32.0
$F^-(aq)$	−332.6	−278.8	−13.8	$MnO(s)$	−385.2	−362.9	59.7
$F_2(g)$	0	0	202.7	$MnO_2(s)$	−519.6	−464.8	53.14
$HF(g)$	−268.61	−270.70	173.51	$MnO_4^-(aq)$	−541.4	−447.2	191.2
Hydrogen				**Mercury**			
$H(g)$	217.94	203.26	114.60	$Hg(g)$	60.83	31.76	174.89
$H^+(aq)$	0	0	0	$Hg(l)$	0	0	77.40
$H^+(g)$	1536.2	1517.0	108.9	$HgCl_2(s)$	−230.1	−184.0	144.5
$H_2(g)$	0	0	130.58	$Hg_2Cl_2(s)$	−264.9	−210.5	192.5
Iodine				**Nickel**			
$I(g)$	106.60	70.16	180.66	$Ni(g)$	429.7	384.5	182.1
$I^-(aq)$	−55.19	−51.57	111.3	$Ni(s)$	0	0	29.9
$I_2(g)$	62.25	19.37	260.57	$NiCl_2(s)$	−305.3	−259.0	97.65
$I_2(s)$	0	0	116.73	$NiO(s)$	−239.7	−211.7	37.99
$HI(g)$	25.94	1.30	206.3	**Nitrogen**			
Iron				$N(g)$	472.7	455.5	153.3
$Fe(g)$	415.5	369.8	180.5	$N_2(g)$	0	0	191.50
$Fe(s)$	0	0	27.15	$NH_3(aq)$	−80.29	−26.50	111.3
$Fe^{2+}(aq)$	−87.86	−84.93	113.4	$NH_3(g)$	−46.19	−16.66	192.5
$Fe^{3+}(aq)$	−47.69	−10.54	293.3	$NH_4^+(aq)$	−132.5	−79.31	113.4
$FeCl_2(s)$	−341.8	−302.3	117.9	$N_2H_4(g)$	95.40	159.4	238.5
$FeCl_3(s)$	−400	−334	142.3	$NH_4CN(s)$	0.0	—	—
$FeO(s)$	−271.9	−255.2	60.75	$NH_4Cl(s)$	−314.4	−203.0	94.6
$Fe_2O_3(s)$	−822.16	−740.98	89.96	$NH_4NO_3(s)$	−365.6	−184.0	151
$Fe_3O_4(s)$	−1117.1	−1014.2	146.4	$NO(g)$	90.37	86.71	210.62
$FeS_2(s)$	−171.5	−160.1	52.92	$NO_2(g)$	33.84	51.84	240.45
Lead				$N_2O(g)$	81.6	103.59	220.0
$Pb(s)$	0	0	68.85	$N_2O_4(g)$	9.66	98.28	304.3
$PbBr_2(s)$	−277.4	−260.7	161	$NOCl(g)$	52.6	66.3	264
$PbCO_3(s)$	−699.1	−625.5	131.0	$HNO_3(aq)$	−206.6	−110.5	146
$Pb(NO_3)_2(aq)$	−421.3	−246.9	303.3	$HNO_3(g)$	−134.3	−73.94	266.4
$Pb(NO_3)_2(s)$	−451.9	—	—	**Oxygen**			
$PbO(s)$	−217.3	−187.9	68.70	$O(g)$	247.5	230.1	161.0
Lithium				$O_2(g)$	0	0	205.0
$Li(g)$	159.3	126.6	138.8	$O_3(g)$	142.3	163.4	237.6
$Li(s)$	0	0	29.09	$OH^-(aq)$	−230.0	−157.3	−10.7
$Li^+(aq)$	−278.5	−273.4	12.2	$H_2O(g)$	−241.82	−228.57	188.83
$Li^+(g)$	685.7	648.5	133.0	$H_2O(l)$	−285.83	−237.13	69.91
$LiCl(s)$	−408.3	−384.0	59.30	$H_2O_2(g)$	−136.10	−105.48	232.9
Magnesium				$H_2O_2(g)$	−187.8	−120.4	109.6
$Mg(g)$	147.1	112.5	148.6	**Phosphorus**			
$Mg(s)$	0	0	32.51	$P(g)$	316.4	280.0	163.2
$MgCl_2(s)$	−641.6	−592.1	89.6	$P_2(g)$	144.3	103.7	218.1

Substance	ΔH_f° (kJ/mol)	ΔG_f° (kJ/mol)	S° (J/mol-K)	Substance	ΔH_f° (kJ/mol)	ΔG_f° (kJ/mol)	S° (J/mol-K)
Phosphorus (cont.)				AgCl(s)	−127.0	−109.70	96.11
$P_4(g)$	58.9	24.4	280	$Ag_2O(s)$	−31.05	−11.20	121.3
$P_4(s, red)$	−17.46	−12.03	22.85	$AgNO_3(s)$	−124.4	−33.41	140.9
$P_4(s, white)$	0	0	41.08	Sodium			
$PCl_3(g)$	−288.07	−269.6	311.7	Na(g)	107.7	77.3	153.7
$PCl_3(l)$	−319.6	−272.4	217	Na(s)	0	0	51.45
$PF_5(g)$	−1594.4	−1520.7	300.8	$Na^+(aq)$	−240.1	−261.9	59.0
$PH_3(g)$	5.4	13.4	210.2	$Na^+(g)$	609.3	574.3	148.0
$P_4O_6(s)$	−1640.1	—	—	NaBr(aq)	−360.6	−364.7	141.00
$P_4O_{10}(s)$	−2940.1	−2675.2	228.9	NaBr(s)	−361.4	−349.3	86.82
$POCl_3(g)$	−542.2	−502.5	325	$Na_2CO_3(s)$	−1130.9	−1047.7	136.0
$POCl_3(l)$	−597.0	−520.9	222	NaCl(aq)	−407.1	−393.0	115.5
$H_3PO_4(aq)$	−1288.3	−1142.6	158.2	NaCl(g)	−181.4	−201.3	229.8
				NaCl(s)	−410.9	−384.0	72.33
Potassium				$NaHCO_3(s)$	−947.7	−851.8	102.1
K(g)	89.99	61.17	160.2	$NaNO_3(aq)$	−446.2	−372.4	207
K(s)	0	0	64.67	$NaNO_3(s)$	−467.9	−367.0	116.5
KCl(s)	−435.9	−408.3	82.7	NaOH(aq)	−469.6	−419.2	49.8
$KClO_3(s)$	−391.2	−289.9	143.0	NaOH(s)	−425.6	−379.5	64.46
$KClO_3(aq)$	−349.5	−284.9	265.7	$Na_2OH_4(s)$	−1387.1	−1270.2	149.6
$K_2CO_3(s)$	−1150.18	−1064.58	155.44				
$KNO_3(s)$	−492.70	−393.13	132.9	Strontium			
$K_2O(s)$	−363.2	−322.1	94.14	SrO(s)	−592.0	561.9	54.9
$KO_2(s)$	−284.5	−240.6	122.5	Sr(g)	164.4	110.0	164.6
$K_2O_2(s)$	−495.8	−429.8	113.0	Sulfur			
KOH(s)	−424.7	−378.9	78.91	S(s, rhombic)	0	0	31.88
KOH(aq)	−482.4	−440.5	91.6	$S_8(g)$	102.3	49.7	430.9
				$SO_2(g)$	−296.9	−300.4	248.5
Rubidium				$SO_3(g)$	−395.2	−370.4	256.2
Rb(g)	85.8	55.8	170.0	$SO_4^{2-}(aq)$	−909.3	−744.5	20.1
Rb(s)	0	0	76.78	$SOCl_2(l)$	−245.6	—	—
RbCl(s)	−430.5	−412.0	92	$H_2S(g)$	−20.17	−33.01	205.6
$RbClO_3(s)$	−392.4	−292.0	152	$H_2SO_4(aq)$	−909.3	−744.5	20.1
				$H_2SO_4(l)$	−814.0	−689.9	156.1
Scandium				Titanium			
Sc(g)	377.8	336.1	174.7	Ti(g)	468	422	180.3
Sc(s)	0	0	34.6	Ti(s)	0	0	30.76
				$TiCl_4(g)$	−763.2	−726.8	354.9
Selenium				$TiCl_4(l)$	−804.2	−728.1	221.9
$H_2Se(g)$	29.7	15.9	219.0	$TiO_2(s)$	−944.7	−889.4	50.29
Silicon				Vanadium			
Si(g)	368.2	323.9	167.8	V(g)	514.2	453.1	182.2
Si(s)	0	0	18.7	V(s)	0	0	28.9
SiC(s)	−73.22	−70.85	16.61	Zinc			
$SiCl_4(l)$	−640.1	−572.8	239.3	Zn(g)	130.7	95.2	160.9
$SiO_2(s, quartz)$	−910.9	−856.5	41.84	Zn(s)	0	0	41.63
Silver				$ZnCl_2(s)$	−415.1	−369.4	111.5
Ag(s)	0	0	42.55	ZnO(s)	−348.0	−318.2	43.9
$Ag^+(aq)$	105.90	77.11	73.93				

Aqueous Equilibrium Constants

TABLE D-1 ■ Dissociation Constants for Acids at 25 °C				
Name	**Formula**	K_{a1}	K_{a2}	K_{a3}
Acetic	CH_3COOH (or $HC_2H_3O_2$)	1.8×10^{-5}		
Arsenic	H_3AsO_4	5.6×10^{-3}	1.0×10^{-7}	3.0×10^{-12}
Arsenous	H_3AsO_3	5.1×10^{-10}		
Ascorbic	$H_2C_6H_6O_6$	8.0×10^{-5}	1.6×10^{-12}	
Benzoic	C_6H_5COOH (or $HC_7H_5O_2$)	6.3×10^{-5}		
Boric	H_3BO_3	5.8×10^{-10}		
Butanoic	C_3H_7COOH (or $HC_4H_7O_2$)	1.5×10^{-5}		
Carbonic	H_2CO_3	4.3×10^{-7}	5.6×10^{-11}	
Chloroacetic	$CH_2ClCOOH$ (or $HC_2H_2O_2Cl$)	1.4×10^{-3}		
Chlorous	$HClO_2$	1.1×10^{-2}		
Citric	$HOOCC(OH)(CH_2COOH)_2$ (or $H_3C_6H_5O_7$)	7.4×10^{-4}	1.7×10^{-5}	4.0×10^{-7}
Cyanic	$HCNO$	3.5×10^{-4}		
Formic	$HCOOH$ (or $HCHO_2$)	1.8×10^{-4}		
Hydroazoic	HN_3	1.9×10^{-5}		
Hydrocyanic	HCN	4.9×10^{-10}		
Hydrofluoric	HF	6.8×10^{-4}		
Hydrogen chromate ion	$HCrO_4^-$	3.0×10^{-7}		
Hydrogen peroxide	H_2O_2	2.4×10^{-12}		
Hydrogen selenate ion	$HSeO_4^-$	2.2×10^{-2}		
Hydrosulfuric	H_2S	9.5×10^{-8}	1×10^{-19}	
Hypobromous	$HBrO$	2.5×10^{-9}		
Hypochlorous	$HClO$	3.0×10^{-8}		
Hypoiodous	HIO	2.3×10^{-11}		
Iodic	HIO_3	1.7×10^{-1}		
Lactic	$CH_3CH(OH)COOH$ (or $HC_3H_5O_3$)	1.4×10^{-4}		
Malonic	$CH_2(COOH)_2$ (or $H_2C_3H_2O_4$)	1.5×10^{-3}	2.0×10^{-6}	
Nitrous	HNO_2	4.5×10^{-4}		
Oxalic	$(COOH)_2$ (or $H_2C_2O_4$)	5.9×10^{-2}	6.4×10^{-5}	
Paraperiodic	H_5IO_6	2.8×10^{-2}	5.3×10^{-9}	
Phenol	C_6H_5OH (or HC_6H_5O)	1.3×10^{-10}		
Phosphoric	H_3PO_4	7.5×10^{-3}	6.2×10^{-8}	4.2×10^{-13}
Propionic	C_2H_5COOH (or $HC_3H_5O_2$)	1.3×10^{-5}		
Pyrophosphoric	$H_4P_2O_7$	3.0×10^{-2}	4.4×10^{-3}	2.1×10^{-7}
Selenous	H_2SeO_3	2.3×10^{-3}	5.3×10^{-9}	
Sulfuric	H_2SO_4	Strong acid	1.2×10^{-2}	
Sulfurous	H_2SO_3	1.7×10^{-2}	6.4×10^{-8}	
Tartaric	$HOOC(CHOH)_2COOH$ (or $H_2C_4H_4O_6$)	1.0×10^{-3}	4.6×10^{-5}	

TABLE D-2 ■ Dissociation Constants for Bases at 25 °C

Name	Formula	K_b
Ammonia	NH_3	1.8×10^{-5}
Aniline	$C_6H_5NH_2$	4.3×10^{-10}
Dimethylamine	$(CH_3)_2NH$	5.4×10^{-4}
Ethylamine	$C_2H_5NH_2$	6.4×10^{-4}
Hydrazine	H_2NNH_2	1.3×10^{-6}
Hydroxylamine	$HONH_2$	1.1×10^{-8}
Methylamine	CH_3NH_2	4.4×10^{-4}
Pyridine	C_5H_5N	1.7×10^{-9}
Trimethylamine	$(CH_3)_3N$	6.4×10^{-5}

TABLE D-3 ■ Solubility-Product Constants for Compounds at 25 °C

Name	Formula	K_{sp}	Name	Formula	K_{sp}
Barium carbonate	$BaCO_3$	5.0×10^{-9}	Lead(II) fluoride	PbF_2	3.6×10^{-8}
Barium chromate	$BaCrO_4$	2.1×10^{-10}	Lead(II) sulfate	$PbSO_4$	6.3×10^{-7}
Barium fluoride	BaF_2	1.7×10^{-6}	Lead(II) sulfide*	PbS	3×10^{-28}
Barium oxalate	BaC_2O_4	1.6×10^{-6}	Magnesium hydroxide	$Mg(OH)_2$	1.8×10^{-11}
Barium sulfate	$BaSO_4$	1.1×10^{-10}	Magnesium carbonate	$MgCO_3$	3.5×10^{-8}
Cadmium carbonate	$CdCO_3$	1.8×10^{-14}	Magnesium oxalate	MgC_2O_4	8.6×10^{-5}
Cadmium hydroxide	$Cd(OH)_2$	2.5×10^{-14}	Manganese(II) carbonate	$MnCO_3$	5.0×10^{-10}
Cadmium sulfide*	CdS	8×10^{-28}	Manganese(II) hydroxide	$Mn(OH)_2$	1.6×10^{-13}
Calcium carbonate (calcite)	$CaCO_3$	4.5×10^{-9}	Manganese(II) sulfide*	MnS	2×10^{-53}
Calcium chromate	$CaCrO_4$	7.1×10^{-4}	Mercury(I) chloride	Hg_2Cl_2	1.2×10^{-18}
Calcium fluoride	CaF_2	3.9×10^{-11}	Mercury(I) iodide	Hg_2I_2	1.1×10^{-28}
Calcium hydroxide	$Ca(OH)_2$	6.5×10^{-6}	Mercury(II) sulfide*	HgS	2×10^{-53}
Calcium phosphate	$Ca_3(PO_4)_2$	2.0×10^{-29}	Nickel(II) carbonate	$NiCO_3$	1.3×10^{-7}
Calcium sulfate	$CaSO_4$	2.4×10^{-5}	Nickel(II) hydroxide	$Ni(OH)_2$	6.0×10^{-16}
Chromium(III) hydroxide	$Cr(OH)_3$	1.6×10^{-30}	Nickel(II) sulfide*	NiS	3×10^{-20}
Cobalt(II) carbonate	$CoCO_3$	1.0×10^{-10}	Silver bromate	$AgBrO_3$	5.5×10^{-5}
Cobalt(II) hydroxide	$Co(OH)_2$	1.3×10^{-15}	Silver bromide	$AgBr$	5.0×10^{-13}
Cobalt(II) sulfide*	CoS	5×10^{-22}	Silver carbonate	Ag_2CO_3	8.1×10^{-12}
Copper(I) bromide	$CuBr$	5.3×10^{-9}	Silver chloride	$AgCl$	1.8×10^{-10}
Copper(II) carbonate	$CuCO_3$	2.3×10^{-10}	Silver chromate	Ag_2CrO_4	1.2×10^{-12}
Copper(II) hydroxide	$Cu(OH)_2$	4.8×10^{-20}	Silver iodide	AgI	8.3×10^{-17}
Copper(II) sulfide*	CuS	6×10^{-37}	Silver sulfate	Ag_2SO_4	1.5×10^{-5}
Iron(II) carbonate	$FeCO_3$	2.1×10^{-11}	Silver sulfide*	Ag_2S	6×10^{-51}
Iron(II) hydroxide	$Fe(OH)_2$	7.9×10^{-16}	Strontium carbonate	$SrCO_3$	9.3×10^{-10}
Lanthanum fluoride	LaF_3	2×10^{-19}	Tin(II) sulfide*	SnS	1×10^{-26}
Lanthanum iodate	$La(IO_3)_3$	6.1×10^{-12}	Zinc carbonate	$ZnCO_3$	1.0×10^{-10}
Lead(II) carbonate	$PbCO_3$	7.4×10^{-14}	Zinc hydroxide	$Zn(OH)_2$	3.0×10^{-16}
Lead(II) chloride	$PbCl_2$	1.7×10^{-5}	Zinc oxalate	ZnC_2O_4	2.7×10^{-8}
Lead(II) chromate	$PbCrO_4$	2.8×10^{-13}	Zinc sulfide*	ZnS	2×10^{-25}

*For a solubility equilibrium of the type $MS(s) + H_2O(l) \rightleftharpoons M^{2+}(aq) + HS^-(aq) + OH^-(aq)$

Standard Reduction Potentials at 25 °C

Half-Reaction	$E°$(V)	Half-Reaction	$E°$(V)
$Ag^+(aq) + e^- \longrightarrow Ag(s)$	+0.799	$2\,H_2O(l) + 2\,e^- \longrightarrow H_2(g) + 2\,OH^-(aq)$	−0.83
$AgBr(s) + e^- \longrightarrow Ag(s) + Br^-(aq)$	+0.095	$HO_2^-(aq) + H_2O(l) + 2\,e^- \longrightarrow 3\,OH^-(aq)$	+0.88
$AgCl(s) + e^- \longrightarrow Ag(s) + Cl^-(aq)$	+0.222	$H_2O_2(aq) + 2\,H^+(aq) + 2\,e^- \longrightarrow 2\,H_2O(l)$	+1.776
$Ag(CN)_2^-(aq) + e^- \longrightarrow Ag(s) + 2\,CN^-(aq)$	−0.31	$Hg_2^{2+}(aq) + 2\,e^- \longrightarrow 2\,Hg(l)$	+0.789
$Ag_2CrO_4(s) + 2\,e^- \longrightarrow 2\,Ag(s) + CrO_4^{2-}(aq)$	+0.446	$2\,Hg^{2+}(aq) + 2\,e^- \longrightarrow Hg_2^{2+}(aq)$	+0.920
$AgI(s) + e^- \longrightarrow Ag(s) + I^-(aq)$	−0.151	$Hg^{2+}(aq) + 2\,e^- \longrightarrow Hg(l)$	+0.854
$Ag(S_2O_3)_2^{3-}(aq) + e^- \longrightarrow Ag(s) + 2\,S_2O_3^{2-}(aq)$	+0.01	$I_2(s) + 2\,e^- \longrightarrow 2\,I^-(aq)$	+0.536
$Al^{3+}(aq) + 3\,e^- \longrightarrow Al(s)$	−1.66	$2\,IO_3^-(aq) + 12\,H^+(aq) + 10\,e^- \longrightarrow$ $I_2(s) + 6\,H_2O(l)$	+1.195
$H_3AsO_4(aq) + 2\,H^+(aq) + 2\,e^- \longrightarrow$ $H_3AsO_3(aq) + H_2O(l)$	+0.559	$K^+(aq) + e^- \longrightarrow K(s)$	−2.925
$Ba^{2+}(aq) + 2\,e^- \longrightarrow Ba(s)$	−2.90	$Li^+(aq) + e^- \longrightarrow Li(s)$	−3.05
$BiO^+(aq) + 2\,H^+(aq) + 3\,e^- \longrightarrow Bi(s) + H_2O(l)$	+0.32	$Mg^{2+}(aq) + 2\,e^- \longrightarrow Mg(s)$	−2.37
$Br_2(l) + 2\,e^- \longrightarrow 2\,Br^-(aq)$	+1.065	$Mn^{2+}(aq) + 2\,e^- \longrightarrow Mn(s)$	−1.18
$2\,BrO_3^-(aq) + 12\,H^+(aq) + 10\,e^- \longrightarrow$ $Br_2(l) + 6\,H_2O(l)$	+1.52	$MnO_2(s) + 4\,H^+(aq) + 2\,e^- \longrightarrow$ $Mn^{2+}(aq) + 2\,H_2O(l)$	+1.23
$2\,CO_2(g) + 2\,H^+(aq) + 2\,e^- \longrightarrow H_2C_2O_4(aq)$	−0.49	$MnO_4^-(aq) + 8\,H^+(aq) + 5\,e^- \longrightarrow$ $Mn^{2+}(aq) + 4\,H_2O(l)$	+1.51
$Ca^{2+}(aq) + 2\,e^- \longrightarrow Ca(s)$	−2.87	$MnO_4^-(aq) + 2\,H_2O(l) + 3\,e^- \longrightarrow$ $MnO_2(s) + 4\,OH^-(aq)$	+0.59
$Cd^{2+}(aq) + 2\,e^- \longrightarrow Cd(s)$	−0.403	$HNO_2(aq) + H^+(aq) + e^- \longrightarrow NO(g) + H_2O(l)$	+1.00
$Ce^{4+}(aq) + e^- \longrightarrow Ce^{3+}(aq)$	+1.61	$N_2(g) + 4\,H_2O(l) + 4\,e^- \longrightarrow 4\,OH^-(aq) + N_2H_4(aq)$	−1.16
$Cl_2(g) + 2\,e^- \longrightarrow 2\,Cl^-(aq)$	+1.359	$N_2(g) + 5\,H^+(aq) + 4\,e^- \longrightarrow N_2H_5^+(aq)$	−0.23
$2\,HClO(aq) + 2\,H^+(aq) + 2\,e^- \longrightarrow$ $Cl_2(g) + 2\,H_2O(l)$	+1.63	$NO_3^-(aq) + 4\,H^+(aq) + 3\,e^- \longrightarrow NO(g) + 2\,H_2O(l)$	+0.96
$ClO^-(aq) + H_2O(l) + 2\,e^- \longrightarrow Cl^-(aq) + 2\,OH^-(aq)$	+0.89	$Na^+(aq) + e^- \longrightarrow Na(s)$	−2.71
$2\,ClO_3^-(aq) + 12\,H^+(aq) + 10\,e^- \longrightarrow$ $Cl_2(g) + 6\,H_2O(l)$	+1.47	$Ni^{2+}(aq) + 2\,e^- \longrightarrow Ni(s)$	−0.28
$Co^{2+}(aq) + 2\,e^- \longrightarrow Co(s)$	−0.277	$O_2(g) + 4\,H^+(aq) + 4\,e^- \longrightarrow 2\,H_2O(l)$	+1.23
$Co^{3+}(aq) + e^- \longrightarrow Co^{2+}(aq)$	+1.842	$O_2(g) + 2\,H_2O(l) + 4\,e^- \longrightarrow 4\,OH^-(aq)$	+0.40
$Cr^{3+}(aq) + 3\,e^- \longrightarrow Cr(s)$	−0.74	$O_2(g) + 2\,H^+(aq) + 2\,e^- \longrightarrow H_2O_2(aq)$	+0.68
$Cr^{3+}(aq) + e^- \longrightarrow Cr^{2+}(aq)$	−0.41	$O_3(g) + 2\,H^+(aq) + 2\,e^- \longrightarrow O_2(g) + H_2O(l)$	+2.07
$CrO_7^{2-}(aq) + 14\,H^+(aq) + 6\,e^- \longrightarrow$ $2\,Cr^{3+}(aq) + 7\,H_2O(l)$	+1.33	$Pb^{2+}(aq) + 2\,e^- \longrightarrow Pb(s)$	−0.126
$CrO_4^{2-}(aq) + 4\,H_2O(l) + 3\,e^- \longrightarrow$ $Cr(OH)_3(s) + 5\,OH^-(aq)$	−0.13	$PbO_2(s) + HSO_4^-(aq) + 3\,H^+(aq) + 2\,e^- \longrightarrow$ $PbSO_4(s) + 2\,H_2O(l)$	+1.685
$Cu^{2+}(aq) + 2\,e^- \longrightarrow Cu(s)$	+0.337	$PbSO_4(s) + H^+(aq) + 2\,e^- \longrightarrow Pb(s) + HSO_4^-(aq)$	−0.356
$Cu^{2+}(aq) + e^- \longrightarrow Cu^+(aq)$	+0.153	$PtCl_4^{2-}(aq) + 2\,e^- \longrightarrow Pt(s) + 4\,Cl^-(aq)$	+0.73
$Cu^+(aq) + e^- \longrightarrow Cu(s)$	+0.521	$S(s) + 2\,H^+(aq) + 2\,e^- \longrightarrow H_2S(g)$	+0.141
$CuI(s) + e^- \longrightarrow Cu(s) + I^-(aq)$	−0.185	$H_2SO_3(aq) + 4\,H^+(aq) + 4\,e^- \longrightarrow S(s) + 3\,H_2O(l)$	+0.45
$F_2(g) + 2\,e^- \longrightarrow 2\,F^-(aq)$	+2.87	$HSO_4^-(aq) + 3\,H^+(aq) + 2\,e^- \longrightarrow$ $H_2SO_3(aq) + H_2O(l)$	+0.17
$Fe^{2+}(aq) + 2\,e^- \longrightarrow Fe(s)$	−0.440	$Sn^{2+}(aq) + 2\,e^- \longrightarrow Sn(s)$	−0.136
$Fe^{3+}(aq) + e^- \longrightarrow Fe^{2+}(aq)$	+0.771	$Sn^{4+}(aq) + 2\,e^- \longrightarrow Sn^{2+}(aq)$	+0.154
$Fe(CN)_6^{3-}(aq) + e^- \longrightarrow Fe(CN)_6^{4-}(aq)$	+0.36	$VO_2^+(aq) + 2\,H^+(aq) + e^- \longrightarrow VO^{2+}(aq) + H_2O(l)$	+1.00
$2\,H^+(aq) + 2\,e^- \longrightarrow H_2(g)$	0.000	$Zn^{2+}(aq) + 2\,e^- \longrightarrow Zn(s)$	−0.763

Expt. 4: $2 Ag^+(aq) + C_2O_4^{2-}(aq) \longrightarrow Ag_2C_2O_4(s)$ white precipitate; Expt. 5: $Ca^{2+}(aq) + C_2O_4^{2-}(aq) \longrightarrow CaC_2O_4(s)$ white precipitate; Expt. 6: $Ag^+(aq) + Cl^-(aq) \longrightarrow AgCl(s)$ white precipitate. (c) Chromate salts appear to be more soluble than oxalate salts. **4.100** 1.42 M KBr **4.104** 0.496 M H_2O_2 **4.106** (a) The molar mass of the acid is 136 g/mol. (b) The molecular formula is $C_8H_8O_2$. **4.109** (a) $Mg(OH)_2(s) + 2 HNO_3(aq) \longrightarrow Mg(NO_3)_2(aq) + 2 H_2O(l)$ (b) HNO_3 is the limiting reactant. (c) 0.0923 mol $Mg(OH)_2$, 0 mol HNO_3, and 0.00250 mol $Mg(NO_3)_2$ are present. **4.113** 1.766% Cl^- by mass **4.115** 2.8×10^{-5} g Na_3AsO_4 in 1.00 L H_2O

Chapter 5

5.1 As the book falls, potential energy decreases and kinetic energy increases. At the instant before impact, all potential energy has been converted to kinetic energy, so the book's total kinetic energy is 85 J, assuming no transfer of energy as heat. **5.4** (a) No. The distance traveled to the top of a mountain depends on the path taken by the hiker. Distance is a path function, not a state function. (b) Yes. Change in elevation depends only on the location of the base camp and the height of the mountain, not on the path to the top. Change in elevation is a state function, not a path function. **5.6** (a) The temperatures of the system and surroundings will equalize, so the temperature of the hotter system will decrease and the temperature of the colder surroundings will increase. The sign of q is $(-)$; the process is exothermic. (b) If neither volume nor pressure of the system changes, $w = 0$ and $\Delta E = q = \Delta H$. The change in internal energy is equal to the change in enthalpy. **5.9** (a) $\Delta H_A = \Delta H_B + \Delta H_C$. The diagram and equation both show that the net enthalpy change for a process is independent of path, that ΔH is a state function. (b) $\Delta H_Z = \Delta H_X + \Delta H_Y$. (c) Hess's law states that the enthalpy change for net reaction Z is the sum of the enthalpy changes for steps X and Y, regardless of whether the reaction actually occurs via this path. The diagrams are a visual statement of Hess's law. **5.11** An object can possess energy by virtue of its motion or position. Kinetic energy depends on the mass of the object and its velocity. Potential energy depends on the position of the object relative to the body with which it interacts. **5.13** (a) 84 J (b) 20 cal (c) As the ball hits the sand, its speed (and hence its kinetic energy) drops to zero. Most of the kinetic energy is transferred to the sand, which deforms when the ball lands. Some energy is released as heat through friction between the ball and the sand. **5.15** 1 Btu = 1054 J **5.17** (a) The *system* is the well-defined part of the universe whose energy changes are being studied. (b) A *closed system* can exchange heat but not mass with its surroundings. **5.19** (a) Work is a force applied over a distance. (b) The amount of work done is the magnitude of the force times the distance over which it is applied. $w = F \times d$. **5.21** (a) Gravity; work is done because the force of gravity is opposed and the pencil is lifted. (b) Mechanical force; work is done because the force of the coiled spring is opposed as the spring is compressed over a distance. **5.23** (a) In any chemical or physical change, energy can be neither created nor destroyed; energy is conserved. (b) The *internal energy (E)* of a system is the sum of all the kinetic and potential energies of the system components. (c) Internal energy of a closed system increases when work is done on the system and when heat is transferred to the system. **5.25** (a) $\Delta E = 76$ kJ, endothermic (b) $\Delta E = 0.84$ kJ, endothermic (c) $\Delta E = -80.0$ kJ, exothermic **5.27** (a) Since no work is done by the system in case (2), the gas will absorb most of the energy as heat; the case (2) gas will have the higher temperature. (b) In case (2) $w = 0$ and $q = 100$ J. In case (1) energy will be used to do work on the surroundings $(-w)$, but some will be absorbed as heat $(+q)$. (c) ΔE is greater for case (2) because the entire 100 J increases the internal energy of the system, rather than a part of the energy

doing work on the surroundings. **5.29** (a) A *state function* is a property that depends only on the physical state (pressure, temperature, etc.) of the system, not on the route used to get to the current state. (b) Internal energy is a state function; heat is not a state function. (c) Work is not a state function. The amount of work required to move from one state to another depends of the specific series of processes or path used to accomplish the change. **5.31** (a) ΔH is usually easier to measure than ΔE because at constant pressure $\Delta H = q$. The heat flow associated with a process at constant pressure can easily be measured as a change in temperature, while measuring ΔE requires a means to measure both q and w. (b) The process is exothermic. **5.33** At constant pressure, $\Delta E = \Delta H - P\Delta V$. The values of either P and ΔV or T and Δn must be known to calculate ΔE from ΔH. **5.35** $\Delta E = -97$ kJ; $\Delta H = -79$ kJ **5.37** (a) $CH_3COOH(l) + 2 O_2(g) \longrightarrow 2 H_2O(l) + 2 CO_2(g)$, $\Delta H = -871.7$ kJ

(b) $CH_3COOH(l) + 2 O_2(g)$

$\Delta H = -871.7$ kJ

$2 H_2O(l) + 2 CO_2(g)$

5.39 The reactant, 2 Cl(g), has the higher enthalpy. **5.41** (a) Exothermic (b) -59 kJ heat transferred (c) 6.43 g MgO produced (d) 112 kJ heat absorbed **5.43** (a) -13.1 kJ (b) -1.14 kJ (c) 9.83 J **5.45** (a) $\Delta H = 726.5$ kJ (b) $\Delta H = -1453$ kJ (c) The exothermic forward reaction is more likely to be thermodynamically favored. (d) Vaporization is endothermic. If the product were $H_2O(g)$, the reaction would be more endothermic and would have a smaller negative ΔH. **5.47** (a) J/mol-°C or J/mol-K (b) J/g-°C or J/g-K (c) To calculate heat capacity from specific heat, the mass of the particular piece of copper pipe must be known. **5.49** (a) 4.184 J/g-K (b) 75.40 J/mol-°C (c) 774 J/°C (d) 904 kJ **5.51** 3.00×10^4 J **5.53** $\Delta H = -45.7$ kJ/mol NaOH **5.55** $\Delta E_{rxn} = -25.5$ kJ/g $C_6H_4O_2$ or -2.75×10^3 kJ/mol $C_6H_4O_2$ **5.57** (a) Heat capacity of the complete calorimeter = 14.4 kJ/°C (b) 5.40 °C **5.59** Hess's law is a consequence of the fact that enthalpy is a state function. Since ΔH is independent of path, we can describe a process by any series of steps that add up to the overall process. ΔH for the process is the sum of ΔH values for the steps. **5.61** $\Delta H = -1300.0$ kJ **5.63** $\Delta H = -2.49 \times 10^3$ kJ **5.65** (a) *Standard conditions* for enthalpy changes are $P = 1$ atm and some common temperature, usually 298 K. (b) *Enthalpy of formation* is the enthalpy change that occurs when a compound is formed from its component elements. (c) *Standard enthalpy of formation* ΔH_f° is the enthalpy change that accompanies formation of one mole of a substance from elements in their standard states. **5.67** (a) $\frac{1}{2} N_2(g) + \frac{3}{2} H_2(g) \longrightarrow NH_3(g)$, $\Delta H_f^\circ = -46.19$ kJ (b) $S(s) + O_2(g) \longrightarrow SO_2(g)$, $\Delta H_f^\circ = -296.9$ kJ (c) $Rb(s) + \frac{1}{2} Cl_2(g) + \frac{3}{2} O_2(g) \longrightarrow RbClO_3(s)$, $\Delta H_f^\circ = -392.4$ kJ (d) $N_2(g) + 2 H_2(g) + \frac{3}{2} O_2(g) \longrightarrow NH_4NO_3(s)$, $\Delta H_f^\circ = -365.6$ kJ **5.69** $\Delta H_{rxn}^\circ = -847.6$ kJ **5.71** (a) $\Delta H_{rxn}^\circ = -196.6$ kJ (b) $\Delta H_{rxn}^\circ = 37.1$ kJ (c) $\Delta H_{rxn}^\circ = -976.94$ kJ (d) $\Delta H_{rxn}^\circ = -68.3$ kJ **5.73** $\Delta H_f^\circ = -248$ kJ **5.75** (a) $C_8H_{18}(l) + \frac{25}{2} O_2(g) \longrightarrow 8 CO_2(g) + 9 H_2O(g)$, $\Delta H = -5064.9$ kJ (b) $8 C(s, g) + 9 H_2(g) \longrightarrow C_8H_{18}(l)$ (c) $\Delta H_f^\circ = -259.5$ kJ **5.77** (a) $C_2H_5OH(l) + 3 O_2(g) \longrightarrow 2 CO_2(g) + 3 H_2O(g)$ (b) $\Delta H_{rxn}^\circ = -1234.8$ kJ (c) 2.11×10^4 kJ/L heat produced (d) 0.071284 g CO_2/kJ heat emitted **5.79** (a) *Fuel value* is the amount of heat produced when 1 g of a substance (fuel) is combusted. (b) 5 g of fat **5.81** 104 or 1×10^2 Cal/serving

5.83 59.7 Cal   **5.85** (a) $\Delta H_{comb} = -1850$ kJ/mol C_3H_4, -1926 kJ/mol C_3H_6, -2044 kJ/mol C_3H_8 (b) $\Delta H_{comb} = -4.616 \times 10^4$ kJ/kg C_3H_4, -4.578×10^4 kJ/kg C_3H_6, -4.635×10^4 kJ/kg C_3H_8 (c) These three substances yield nearly identical quantities of heat per unit mass, but propane is marginally higher than the other two.   **5.87** (a) 469.4 m/s (b) 5.124×10^{-21} J (c) 3.086 kJ/mol   **5.90** The spontaneous air bag reaction is probably exothermic, with $-\Delta H$ and thus $-q$. When the bag inflates, work is done by the system, so the sign of w is also negative.   **5.93** $\Delta H = 38.95$ kJ; $\Delta E = 36.48$ kJ   **5.96** (a) 8.0×10^{10} kJ energy released (b) 1.9×10^4 ton dynamite   **5.100** 4.90 g CH_4 **5.103** (a) $\Delta H_f^\circ = 35.4$ kJ (b) We need to measure the heat of combustion of $B_5H_9(l)$.   **5.105** (a) $\Delta H^\circ = -631.3$ kJ (b) 3 mol of acetylene gas has greater enthalpy. (c) Fuel values are 50 kJ/g $C_2H_2(g)$, 42 kJ/g $C_6H_6(l)$.   **5.109** If all work is used to increase the man's potential energy, the stair-climbing uses 58 Cal and will not compensate for the extra order of 245 Cal fries. (More than 58 Cal will be required to climb the stairs, because some energy is used to move limbs and some will be lost as heat.)   **5.112** (a) 1.479×10^{-18} J/molecule (b) 1×10^{-15} J/photon. The X-ray has approximately 1000 times more energy than is produced by the combustion of 1 molecule of $CH_4(g)$.   **5.115** (a) ΔH° for neutralization of the acids is HNO_3, -55.8 kJ; HCl, -56.1 kJ; NH_4^+, -4.1 kJ. (b) $H^+(aq) + OH^-(aq) \longrightarrow H_2O(l)$ is the net ionic equation for the first two reactions. $NH_4^+(aq) + OH^-(aq) \longrightarrow NH_3(aq) + H_2O(l)$ (c) The ΔH° values for the first two reactions are nearly identical, -55.9 kJ and -56.2 kJ. Since spectator ions do not change during a reaction and these two reactions have the same net ionic equation, it is not surprising that they have the same ΔH°. (d) Strong acids are more likely than weak acids to donate H^+. Neutralization of the two strong acids is energetically favorable, while the third reaction is barely so. NH_4^+ is likely a weak acid.   **5.117** (a) $\Delta H^\circ = -65.7$ kJ (b) ΔH° for the complete molecular equation will be the same as ΔH° for the net ionic equation. Since the overall enthalpy change is the enthalpy of products minus the enthalpy of reactants, the contributions of spectator ions cancel. (c) ΔH_f° for $AgNO_3(aq)$ is -100.4 kJ/mol.

Chapter 6

6.2 (a) 0.1 m or 10 cm (b) No. Visible radiation has wavelengths much shorter than 0.1 m. (c) Energy and wavelength are inversely proportional. Photons of the longer 0.1 m radiation have less energy than visible photons. (d) Radiation with $\lambda = 0.1$ m is in the low energy portion of the microwave region. The appliance is probably a microwave oven.   **6.5** (a) $n = 1, n = 4$ (b) $n = 1, n = 2$ (c) In order of increasing wavelength and decreasing energy: (iii) < (iv) < (ii) < (i)   **6.8** (a) In the left-most box, the two electrons cannot have the same spin. (b) Flip one of the arrows in the left-most box, so that one points up and the other down. (c) Group 6A   **6.9** (a) Meters (b) 1/second (c) meters/second   **6.11** (a) True (b) False. The frequency of radiation decreases as the wavelength increases. (c) False. Ultraviolet light has shorter wavelengths than visible light. (d) False. X-rays travel at the same speed as microwaves. (e) False. Electromagnetic radiation and sound waves travel at different speeds.   **6.13** Wavelength of X-rays < ultraviolet < green light < red light < infrared < radio waves   **6.15** (a) 3.0×10^{13} s^{-1} (b) 5.45×10^{-7} m = 545 nm (c) The radiation in (b) is visible, the radiation in (a) is not. (d) 1.50×10^4 m   **6.17** 5.64×10^{14} s^{-1}; green.   **6.19** Quantization means that energy changes can happen only in certain allowed increments. If the human growth quantum is one foot, growth occurs instantaneously in one-foot increments. The child experiences growth spurts of one foot; her height can change only by one-foot increments.

6.21 (a) 4.61×10^{14} s^{-1} (b) 1.84×10^5 J (c) $\Delta E = 3.06 \times 10^{-19}$ J   **6.23** (a) $\lambda = 3.3$ μm, $E = 6.0 \times 10^{-20}$ J; $\lambda = 0.154$ nm, $E = 1.29 \times 10^{-15}$ J (b) The 3.3 μm photon is in the infrared and the 0.154 nm photon is in the X-ray region; the X-ray photon has the greater energy.   **6.25** (a) 6.11×10^{-19} J/photon (b) 368 kJ/mol (c) 1.64×10^{15} photons (d) 368 kJ/mol   **6.27** (a) The $\sim 1 \times 10^{-6}$ m radiation is in the infrared portion of the spectrum. (b) 8.1×10^{16} photons/s   **6.29** (a) $E_{min} = 7.22 \times 10^{-19}$ J (b) $\lambda = 275$ nm (c) $E_{120} = 1.66 \times 10^{-18}$ J. The excess energy of the 120 nm photon is converted into the kinetic energy of the emitted electron. $E_k = 9.3 \times 10^{-19}$ J/electron.   **6.31** When applied to atoms, the notion of quantized energies means that only certain values of ΔE are allowed. These are represented by the lines in the emission spectra of excited atoms.   **6.33** (a) Emitted (b) absorbed (c) emitted   **6.35** (a) $E_2 = -5.45 \times 10^{-19}$ J; $E_6 = -0.606 \times 10^{-19}$ J; $\Delta E = 4.84 \times 10^{-19}$ J; $\lambda = 410$ nm; visible, violet. (b) $E_1 = -2.18 \times 10^{-18}$ J; $E_\infty = 0$ J; $\Delta E = 2.18 \times 10^{-18}$ J/electron = 1.31×10^3 kJ/mol (c) The ionization energy of hydrogen calculated from the Bohr model agrees with the experimental result to three significant figures.   **6.37** (a) Only lines with $n_f = 2$ represent ΔE values and wavelengths that lie in the visible portion of the spectrum. Lines with $n_f = 1$ have shorter wavelengths and lines with $n_f > 2$ have longer wavelengths than visible radiation. (b) $n_i = 3, n_f = 2; \lambda = 6.56 \times 10^{-7}$ m; this is the red line at 656 nm. $n_i = 4, n_f = 2; \lambda = 4.86 \times 10^{-7}$ m; this is the blue line at 486 nm. $n_i = 5, n_f = 2; \lambda = 4.34 \times 10^{-7}$ m; this is the violet line at 434 nm.   **6.39** (a) Ultraviolet region (b) $n_i = 6, n_f = 1$ **6.41** (a) $\lambda = 5.6 \times 10^{-37}$ m (b) $\lambda = 2.65 \times 10^{-34}$ m (c) $\lambda = 2.3 \times 10^{-13}$ m (d) $\lambda = 1.51 \times 10^{-11}$ m   **6.43** 4.14×10^3 m/s   **6.45** (a) $\Delta x \geq 4 \times 10^{-27}$ m (b) $\Delta x \geq 3 \times 10^{-10}$ m   **6.47** (a) The uncertainty principle states that there is a limit to how precisely we can simultaneously know the position and momentum (a quantity related to energy) of an electron. The Bohr model states that electrons move about the nucleus in precisely circular orbits of known radius and energy. This violates the uncertainty principle. (b) De Broglie stated that electrons demonstrate the properties of both particles and waves, that each particle has a wave associated with it. A wave function is the mathematical description of the matter wave of an electron. (c) Although we cannot predict the exact location of an electron in an allowed energy state, we can determine the probability of finding an electron at a particular position. This statistical knowledge of electron location is the *probability density* and is a function of Ψ^2, the square of the wave function Ψ.   **6.49** (a) $n = 4, l = 3, 2, 1, 0$ (b) $l = 2, m_l = -2, -1, 0, 1, 2$ (c) $m_l = 2, l \geq 2$ or $l = 2, 3$ or 4   **6.51** (a) $3p$: $n = 3, l = 1$ (b) $2s$: $n = 2, l = 0$ (c) $4f$: $n = 4, l = 3$ (d) $5d$: $n = 5, l = 2$ **6.53** (a) impossible, $1p$ (b) possible (c) possible (d) impossible, $2d$

6.55 (a)   (b)   (c)

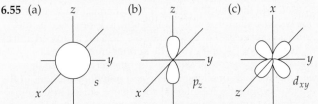

6.57 (a) The hydrogen atom $1s$ and $2s$ orbitals have the same overall spherical shape, but the $2s$ orbital has a larger radial extension and one more node than the $1s$ orbital. (b) A single $2p$ orbital is directional in that its electron density is concentrated along one of the three Cartesian axes of the atom. The $d_{x^2-y^2}$ orbital has electron density along both the x- and y-axes, while the p_x orbital has density only along the x-axis. (c) The average distance of an electron from the nucleus in a $3s$ orbital is greater than for an electron in a $2s$ orbital.

(d) $1s < 2p < 3d < 4f < 6s$ **6.59** (a) In the hydrogen atom, orbitals with the same principal quantum number, n, have the same energy. (b) In a many-electron atom, for a given n value, orbital energy increases with increasing l value: $s < p < d < f$. **6.61** (a) There are two main pieces of experimental evidence for electron "spin." The Stern-Gerlach experiment shows that atoms with a single unpaired electron interact differently with an inhomogeneous magnetic field. Examination of the fine details of emission line spectra of multi-electron atoms reveals that each line is really a close pair of lines. Both observations can be rationalized if electrons have the property of spin.

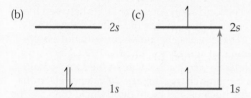

6.63 (a) 6 (b) 10 (c) 2 (d) 14 **6.65** (a) "Valence electrons" are those involved in chemical bonding. They are part or all of the outer-shell electrons listed after the core. (b) "Core electrons" are inner shell electrons that have the electron configuration of the nearest noble-gas element. (c) Each box represents an orbital. (d) Electron spin is represented by the direction of the half-arrows. **6.67** (a) Cs, [Xe]$6s^1$ (b) Ni, [Ar]$4s^23d^8$ (c) Se, [Ar]$4s^23d^{10}4p^4$ (d) Cd, [Kr]$5s^24d^{10}$ (e) U, [Rn]$5f^36d^17s^2$ (f) Pb, [Xe]$6s^24f^{14}5d^{10}6p^2$ **6.69** (a) F$^-$, [He]$2s^22p^6$ or [Ne] (b) I$^-$, [Kr]$5s^25p^6$ or [Xe] (c) O^{2-}, [He]$2s^22p^6$ or [Ne] (d) K$^+$, [Ne]$3s^23p^6$ or [Ar] (e) Mg^{2+}, [He]$2s^22p^6$ or [Ne] (f) Al^{3+}, [He]$2s^22p^6$ or [Ne] **6.71** (a) He (b) O (c) Cr (d) Te (e) H **6.73** (a) The fifth electron would fill the $2p$ subshell before the $3s$. (b) Either the core is [He], or the outer electron configuration should be $3s^23p^3$. (c) The $3p$ subshell would fill before the $3d$. **6.75** (a) $\lambda_A = 3.6 \times 10^{-8}$ m, $\lambda_B = 8.0 \times 10^{-8}$ m (b) $\nu_A = 8.4 \times 10^{15}$ s^{-1}, $\nu_B = 3.7 \times 10^{15}$ s^{-1} (c) A, ultraviolet; B, ultraviolet **6.77** 66.7 min **6.80** 430–490 nm **6.84** (a) The Paschen series lies in the infrared. (b) $n_i = 4$, $\lambda = 1.87 \times 10^{-6}$ m; $n_i = 5$, $\lambda = 1.28 \times 10^{-6}$ m; $n_i = 6$, $\lambda = 1.09 \times 10^{-6}$ m **6.87** $\nu = 1.02 \times 10^7$ m/s **6.90** (a) l (b) n and l (c) m_s (d) m_l **6.96** If m_s had three allowed values instead of two, each orbital would hold three electrons instead of two. Assuming that there is no change in the n, l, and m_l values, the number of elements in each of the first four rows would be: 1st row, 3 elements; 2nd row, 12 elements; 3rd row, 12 elements; 4th row, 27 elements **6.99** (a) 1.7×10^{28} photons (b) 34 s **6.103** (a) Bohr's theory was based on the Rutherford nuclear model of the atom: a dense positive charge at the center and a diffuse negative charge surrounding it. Bohr's theory then specified the nature of the diffuse negative charge. The prevailing theory before the nuclear model was Thomson's plum pudding model: discrete electrons scattered about a diffuse positive charge cloud. Bohr's theory could not have been based on the Thomson model of the atom. (b) De Broglie's hypothesis is that electrons exhibit both particle and wave properties. Thomson's conclusion that electrons have mass is a particle property, while the nature of cathode rays is a wave property. De Broglie's hypothesis actually rationalizes these two seemingly contradictory observations about the properties of electrons.

Chapter 7

7.2 The billiard ball is a more appropriate analogy for the nonbonding atomic radius. The billiard ball has a definite "hard" boundary, and can be used to model nonbonding interactions in which there is no penetration of electron clouds. If we use the billiard ball to represent the bonding atomic radius of a fluorine atom, we overestimate this radius. When atoms bond, attractive interactions cause their electron clouds to penetrate

each other, bringing the nuclei closer together than during a nonbonding (billiard ball) collision. **7.5** The energy change for the reaction is the ionization energy of A plus the electron affinity of A. The process is endothermic for both chlorine and sodium. **7.7** Mendeleev placed elements with similar chemical and physical properties within a family or column of his table. For undiscovered elements, he left blanks. He predicted properties for the "blanks" based on properties of other elements in the family and on either side. **7.9** Even though Si is the second most abundant element in Earth's crust, its abundant forms are compounds. In order to be "discovered," elemental Si had to be chemically removed from one of its compounds. Discovery awaited more sophisticated chemical techniques available in the nineteenth century.
7.11 (a) *Effective nuclear charge*, Z_{eff}, is a representation of the average electrical field experienced by a single electron. It is the average environment created by the nucleus and the other electrons in the molecule, expressed as a net positive charge at the nucleus. (b) Going from left to right across a period, effective nuclear charge increases. **7.13** (a) For both Na and K, $Z_{\text{eff}} = 1$. (b) For both Na and K, $Z_{\text{eff}} = 2.2$. (c) Slater's rules give values closer to the detailed calculations: Na, 2.51; K, 3.49. (d) Both approximations give the same value of Z_{eff} for Na and K; neither accounts for the gradual increase in Z_{eff} moving down a group. **7.15** The $n = 3$ electrons in Kr experience a greater effective nuclear charge and thus have a greater probability of being closer to the nucleus. **7.17** (a) Atomic radii are determined by measuring distances between atoms in various situations. (b) Bonding radii are calculated from the internuclear separation of two atoms joined by a chemical bond. Nonbonding radii are calculated from the internuclear separation between two gaseous atoms that collide and move apart but do not bond. (c) For a given element, the nonbonding radius is always larger than the bonding radius. **7.19** 1.37 Å **7.21** From the sum of the atomic radii, As—I = 2.52 Å. This is very close to the experimental value of 2.55 Å. **7.23** (a) Decrease (b) increase (c) F < S < P < As **7.25** (a) Be < Mg < Ca (b) Br < Ge < Ga (c) Si < Al < Tl **7.27** (a) Electrostatic repulsions are reduced by removing an electron from a neutral atom, effective nuclear charge increases, and the cation is smaller. (b) The additional electrostatic repulsion produced by adding an electron to a neutral atom decreases the effective nuclear charge experienced by the valence electrons, and increases the size of the anion. (c) Going down a column, valence electrons are further from the nucleus, and they experience greater shielding by core electrons. The greater radial extent of the valence electrons outweighs the increase in Z. **7.29** The red sphere is a metal; its size decreases on reaction, characteristic of the change in radius when a metal atom forms a cation. The blue sphere is a nonmetal; its size increases on reaction, characteristic of the change in radius when a nonmetal atom forms an anion. **7.31** (a) An isoelectronic series is a group of atoms or ions that have the same number of electrons and the same electron configuration. (b) (i) Al^{3+} : Ne (ii) Ti^{4+} : Ar (iii) Br$^-$: Kr (iv) Sn^{2+} : Cd **7.33** (a) Na$^+$ (b) Assume a He core of 2 electrons. F$^-$: $Z_{\text{eff}} = 7$; Na$^+$: $Z_{\text{eff}} = 9$. (c) F$^-$: $Z_{\text{eff}} = 4.85$; Na$^+$: $Z_{\text{eff}} = 6.85$. (d) For isoelectronic ions, electron configurations and therefore shielding values (S) are the same. As nuclear charge (Z) increases, effective nuclear charge (Z_{eff}) increases and ionic radius decreases. **7.35** Cl < S < K (b) K$^+$ < Cl$^-$ < S^{2-} (c) In the neutral atoms, the n-value of the outer electron in K is larger than the n-value of valence electrons in S and Cl, so K atoms are largest. When the $4s$ electron is removed, K$^+$ is isoelectronic with Cl$^-$ and S^{2-}, so the ion with the largest Z value, K$^+$, is smallest. **7.37** (a) O^{2-} is larger than O because increased repulsions that accompany addition of electrons cause the electron cloud to expand. (b) S^{2-} is larger than O^{2-}, because for particles with like charges, size increases going down a family. (c) S^{2-} is larger than K$^+$ because the two

ions are isoelectronic and K^+ has the larger Z and Z_{eff}. (d) K^+ is larger than Ca^{2+}, because for isoelectronic particles, the ion with the smaller Z has the larger radius.   **7.39** $B(g) \longrightarrow$ $B^+(g) + e^-$; $B^+(g) \longrightarrow B^{2+}(g) + e^-$; $B^{2+}(g) \longrightarrow B^{3+}(g) + e^-$ **7.41** (a) The electrons in any atom are bound to the atom by their electrostatic attraction to the nucleus. Therefore, energy must be added in order to remove an electron from an atom. The ionization energy, ΔE for this process, is thus positive. (b) F has a greater first ionization energy than O because F has a greater Z_{eff} and the outer electrons in both elements are approximately the same distance from the nucleus. (c) The second ionization energy of an element is greater than the first because more energy is required to overcome the larger Z_{eff} of the 1+ cation than that of the neutral atom.   **7.43** (a) The smaller the atom, the larger its first ionization energy. (b) Of the nonradioactive elements, He has the largest, and Cs the smallest first ionization energy.   **7.45** (a) Ar (b) Be (c) Co (d) S (e) Te   **7.47** (a) In^{3+}, $[Kr]4d^{10}$ (b) Sb^{3+}, $[Kr]5s^24d^{10}$ (c) Te^{2-}, $[Kr]5s^24d^{10}5p^6$ or [Xe] (d) Te^{6+}, $[Kr]4d^{10}$ (e) Hg^{2+}, $[Xe]4f^{14}5d^{10}$ (f) Rh^{3+}, $[Kr]4d^6$ **7.49** (a) Ni^{2+}, $[Ar]3d^8$, 2 unpaired electrons (b) Sn^{2+}, $[Kr]5s^24d^{10}$, 0 unpaired electrons   **7.51** Positive, endothermic, values for ionization energy and electron affinity mean that energy is required to either remove or add electrons. Valence electrons in Ar experience the largest Z_{eff} of any element in the third row, resulting in a large, positive ionization energy. When an electron is added to Ar, the n = 3 electrons become core electrons which screen the extra electron so effectively that Ar^- has a higher energy than an Ar atom and a free electron. This results in a large positive electron affinity.   **7.53** Electron affinity of Br: $Br(g) + 1 e^- \longrightarrow Br^-(g)$; $[Ar]4s^23d^{10}4p^5 \longrightarrow [Ar]4s^23d^{10}4p^6$; electron affinity of Kr: $Kr(g) + 1 e^- \longrightarrow Kr^-(g)$; $[Ar]4s^23d^{10}4p^6 \longrightarrow [Ar]4s^23d^{10}4p^65s^1$. Br^- adopts the stable electron configuration of Kr; the added electron experiences essentially the same Z_{eff} and stabilization as the other valence electrons and electron affinity is negative. In Kr^- ion, the added electron occupies the higher energy 5s orbital. A 5s electron is farther from the nucleus, effectively shielded by the spherical Kr core and not stabilized by the nucleus; electron affinity is positive.   **7.55** (a) Ionization energy (I_1) of Ne: $Ne(g) \longrightarrow Ne^+(g) + 1 e^-$; $[He]2s^22p^6 \longrightarrow [He]2s^22p^5$; electron affinity ($E_1$) of F: $F(g) + 1 e^- \longrightarrow F^-(g)$; $[He]2s^22p^5 \longrightarrow [He]2s^22p^6$. (b) I_1 of Ne is positive; E_1 of F is negative. (c) One process is apparently the reverse of the other, with one important difference. Ne has a greater Z and Z_{eff}, so we expect I_1 for Ne to be somewhat greater in magnitude and opposite in sign to E_1 for F.   **7.57** The smaller the first ionization energy of an element, the greater the metallic character of that element.   **7.59** Based on ionization energies, the metallic character of Al is similar to that of Ca and Sr; it is clearly more metallic than the metalloids in groups 4A and 5A.   **7.61** Ionic: MgO, Li_2O, Y_2O_3; molecular: SO_2, P_2O_5, N_2O, XeO_3. Ionic compounds are formed by combining a metal and a nonmetal; molecular compounds are formed by two or more nonmetals. **7.61** Ionic: MgO, Li_2O, Y_2O_3; molecular: SO_2, P_2O_5, N_2O, XeO_3. Ionic compounds are formed by combining a metal and a nonmetal; molecular compounds are formed by two or more nonmetals.   **7.63** (a) An acidic oxide dissolved in water produces an acidic solution; a basic oxide dissolved in water produces a basic solution. (b) Oxides of nonmetals, such as SO_3, are acidic; oxides of metals, such as CaO, are basic.   **7.65** (a) Dichlorineseptoxide (b) $2 Cl_2(g) + 7 O_2(g) \longrightarrow 2 Cl_2O_7(l)$ (c) While most nonmetal oxides we have seen, such as CO_2 or SO_2, are gases, a boiling point of 81 °C is not totally unexpected for a large molecule like Cl_2O_7. (d) Cl_2O_7 is an acidic oxide, so it will be more reactive to base, OH^-.   **7.67** (a) $BaO(s) + H_2O(l) \longrightarrow$ $Ba(OH)_2(aq)$ (b) $FeO(s) + 2 HClO_4(aq) \longrightarrow Fe(ClO_4)_2(aq) +$ $H_2O(l)$ (c) $SO_3(g) + H_2O(l) \longrightarrow H_2SO_4(aq)$ (d) $CO_2(g) +$ $2 NaOH(aq) \longrightarrow Na_2CO_3(aq) + H_2O(l)$ **7.69** (a) Na, $[Ne]3s^1$;

Mg, $[Ne]3s^2$ (b) When forming ions, both adopt the stable configuration of Ne; Na loses one electron and Mg two electrons to achieve this configuration. (c) The effective nuclear charge of Mg is greater, so its ionization energy is greater. (d) Mg is less reactive because it has a higher ionization energy. (e) The atomic radius of Mg is smaller because its effective nuclear charge is greater.   **7.71** (a) Ca is more reactive because it has a lower ionization energy than Mg. (b) K is more reactive because it has a lower ionization energy than Ca.   **7.73** (a) $2 K(s) +$ $Cl_2(g) \longrightarrow 2 KCl(s)$ (b) $SrO(s) + H_2O(l) \longrightarrow Sr(OH)_2(aq)$ (c) $4 Li(s) + O_2(g) \longrightarrow 2 Li_2O(s)$ (d) $2 Na(s) + S(l) \longrightarrow$ $Na_2S(s)$ **7.75** (a) The ionization energy of H fits between those of C and N. (b) The ionization energy of Li fits between those of Na and Mg. (c) These series are consistent with the assignment of H as a nonmetal and Li as a metal.   **7.77** (a) F, $[He]2s^22p^5$; Cl, $[Ne]3s^23p^5$ (b) F and Cl are in the same group, and both adopt a 1− ionic charge. (c) The 2p valence electrons in F are closer to the nucleus and more tightly held than are the 3p electrons of Cl, so the ionization energy of F is greater. (d) The high ionization energy of F coupled with a relatively large exothermic electron affinity makes it more reactive than Cl toward H_2O. (e) While F has approximately the same effective nuclear charge as Cl, its small atomic radius gives rise to large repulsions when an extra electron is added, so the overall electron affinity of F is less exothermic than that of Cl. (f) The 2p valence electrons in F are closer to the nucleus so the atomic radius is smaller than that of Cl.   **7.79** (a) The term "inert" was dropped because it no longer described all the Group 8A elements. (b) In the 1960s, scientists discovered that Xe would react with substances having a strong tendency to remove electrons, such as F_2. Thus, Xe could not be categorized as an "inert" gas. (c) The group is now called the noble gases. **7.81** (a) $2 O_3(g) \longrightarrow 3 O_2(g)$ (b) $Xe(g) + F_2(g) \longrightarrow XeF_2(g)$; $Xe(g) + 2 F_2(g) \longrightarrow XeF_4(s)$; $Xe(g) + 3 F_2(g) \longrightarrow XeF_6(s)$ (c) $S(s) + H_2(g) \longrightarrow H_2S(g)$ (d) $2 F_2(g) + 2 H_2O(l) \longrightarrow$ $4 HF(aq) + O_2(g)$ **7.83** Up to Z = 82, there are three instances where atomic weights are reversed relative to atomic numbers: Ar and K; Co and Ni; Te and I. In each case the most abundant isotope of the element with the larger atomic number has one more proton, but fewer neutrons than the element with the smaller atomic number. The smaller number of neutrons causes the element with the larger Z to have a smaller than expected atomic weight.   **7.85** (a) 5+ (b) 4.8+ (c) Shielding is greater for 3p electrons, owing to penetration by 3s electrons, so Z_{eff} for 3p electrons is less than that for 3s electrons. (d) The first electron lost is a 3p electron, because it has a smaller Z_{eff} and experiences less attraction for the nucleus than a 3s electron does. **7.88** Moving across the representative elements, electrons added to ns or np valence orbitals do not effectively screen each other. The increase in Z is not accompanied by a similar increase in S. Z_{eff} increases and atomic size decreases. Moving across the transition elements, electrons are added to $(n - 1)d$ orbitals, which do significantly screen the ns valence electrons. The increase in Z is accompanied by a corresponding increase in S. Z_{eff} increases more slowly and atomic size decreases more slowly.   **7.91** The completed 4f subshell in Hf leads to a much larger change in Z and Z_{eff} going from Zr to Hf than in going from Y to La. This larger increase in Z_{eff} going from Zr to Hf leads to a smaller increase in atomic radius than in going from Y to La.   **7.94** I_1 through I_4 represent loss of the 2p and 2s electrons from the outer shell of the atom. Z is constant while removal of each electron reduces repulsion between the remaining electrons, so Z_{eff} increases and I increases. I_5 and I_6 represent loss of the 1s core electrons. These electrons are closer to the nucleus and experience the full nuclear charge, so the values of I_5 and I_6 are significantly greater than $I_1 - I_4$. I_6 is larger than I_5 because all electron–electron repulsion has been eliminated.

9.45 (a) B, $[He]2s^2 2p^1$. One $2s$ electron is "promoted" to an empty $2p$ orbital. The $2s$ and two $2p$ orbitals that each contain one electron are hybridized to form three equivalent hybrid orbitals in a trigonal planar arrangement. (b) sp^2 (d) A single $2p$ orbital is unhybridized. It lies perpendicular to the trigonal plane of the sp^2 hybrid orbitals.   **9.47** (a) sp^2 (b) sp^3 (c) sp (d) sp^3d (e) sp^3d^2

9.49 (a)

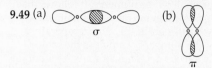

σ

(b)

π

(c) A σ bond is generally stronger than a π bond because there is more extensive orbital overlap. (d) No. Overlap of two s orbitals results in electron density along the internuclear axis, while a π bond has none.   **9.51** (a)

H—C—C—H (with H above and below each C)   C=C (with H above and below)   H—C≡C—H

(b) sp^3, sp^2, sp (c) nonplanar, planar, planar (d) 7 σ, 0 π; 5 σ, 1 π; 3 σ, 2 π (e) The Si analogs would have the same hybridization as the C compounds given in part (b). That Si is in the row below C means it has a larger bonding atomic radius and atomic orbitals than C. The close approach of Si atoms required for π bond formation is unlikely; Si_2H_4 and Si_2H_2 probably do not exist under standard conditions.   **9.53** (a) 18 valence electrons (b) 16 valence electrons form σ bonds (c) 2 valence electrons form π bonds (d) no valence electrons are nonbonding (e) The left and central C atoms are sp^2 hybridized; the right C atom is sp^3 hybridized.   **9.55** (a) ~109° about the leftmost C, sp^3, ~120° about the right-hand C, sp^2 (b) The doubly bonded O can be viewed as sp^2, and the other as sp^3; the nitrogen is sp^3 with approximately 109° bond angles. (c) nine σ bonds, one π bond   **9.57** (a) In a localized π bond, the electron density is concentrated between the two atoms forming the bond. In a delocalized π bond, the electron density is spread over all the atoms that contribute p orbitals to the network. (b) The existence of more than one resonance form is a good indication that a molecule will have delocalized π bonding. (c) delocalized   **9.59** (a) Hybrid orbitals are mixtures of atomic orbitals from a single atom and remain localized on that atom. Molecular orbitals are combinations of atomic orbitals from two or more atoms and are delocalized over at least two atoms. (b) Each MO can hold a maximum of two electrons. (c) Antibonding molecular orbitals can have electrons in them.

9.61 (a)

σ^*_{1s}

$1s$ ----- $1s$

σ_{1s}

σ^*_{1s}

σ_{1s}

H_2^+

(b) There is one electron in H_2^+. (c) σ_{1s}^1 (d) BO = $\frac{1}{2}$ (e) Fall apart. If the single electron in H_2^+ is excited to the σ^*_{1s} orbital, its energy is higher than the energy of an H $1s$ atomic orbital and H_2^+ will decompose into a hydrogen atom and a hydrogen ion.

9.63

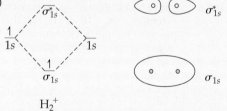

(a) 1 σ bond (b) 2 π bonds (c) 1 σ^* and 2 π^* **9.65** (a) When comparing the same two bonded atoms, bond order and bond energy are directly related, while bond order and bond length

are inversely related. When comparing different bonded nuclei, there are no simple relationships. (b) Be_2 is not expected to exist; it has a bond order of zero and is not energetically favored over isolated Be atoms. Be_2^+ has a bond order of 0.5 and is slightly lower in energy than isolated Be atoms. It will probably exist under special experimental conditions.
9.67 (a, b) Substances with no unpaired electrons are weakly repelled by a magnetic field. This property is called *diamagnetism*. (c) O_2^{2-}, Be_2^{2+} **9.69** (a) B_2^+, $\sigma_{2s}^2 \sigma_{2s}^{*2} \pi_{2p}^1$, increase (b) Li_2^+, $\sigma_{1s}^2 \sigma_{1s}^{*2} \sigma_{2s}^1$, increase (c) N_2^+, $\sigma_{2s}^2 \sigma_{2s}^{*2} \pi_{2p}^4 \sigma_{2p}^1$, increase (d) Ne_2^{2+}, $\sigma_{2s}^2 \sigma_{2s}^{*2} \sigma_{2p}^2 \pi_{2p}^4 \pi_{2p}^{*4}$, decrease   **9.71** CN, $\sigma_{2s}^2 \sigma_{2s}^{*2} \sigma_{2p}^2 \pi_{2p}^3$, bond order = 2.5; CN^+, $\sigma_{2s}^2 \sigma_{2s}^{*2} \sigma_{2p}^2 \pi_{2p}^2$, bond order = 2.0; CN^-, $\sigma_{2s}^2 \sigma_{2s}^{*2} \sigma_{2p}^2 \pi_{2p}^4$, bond order = 3.0. (a) CN^- (b) CN, CN^+ **9.73** (a) $3s$, $3p_x$, $3p_y$, $3p_z$ (b) π_{3p} (c) 2 (d) If the MO diagram for P_2 is similar to that of N_2, P_2 will have no unpaired electrons and be diamagnetic.   **9.76** SiF_4 is tetrahedral, SF_4 is seesaw, XeF_4 is square planar. The shapes are different because the number of nonbonding electron domains is different in each molecule, even though all have four bonding electron domains. Bond angles and thus molecular shape are determined by the total number of electron domains.
9.79 (a) 2 σ bonds, 2 π bonds (b) 2 σ bonds, 2 π bonds (c) 3 σ bonds, 1 π bond (d) 4 σ bonds, 1 π bond   **9.81** BF_3 is trigonal planar, the B—F bond dipoles cancel and the molecule is nonpolar. PF_3 has a tetrahedral electron domain geometry with one position occupied by a nonbonding electron pair. The nonbonding electron pair ensures an asymmetrical electron distribution and the molecule is polar.

9.85

H—C=C=C—H (with H atoms above and below the end carbons, orbitals shown)

(a) The molecule is nonplanar. (b) Allene has no dipole moment. (c) The bonding in allene would not be described as delocalized. The π electron clouds of the two adjacent C=C are mutually perpendicular, so there is no overlap and no delocalization of π electrons.   **9.87** (a) All O atoms have sp^2 hybridization. (b) The two σ bonds are formed by overlap of sp^2 hybrid orbitals, the π bond is formed by overlap of atomic p orbitals, one nonbonded pair is in a p atomic orbital and the other five nonbonded pairs are in sp^2 hybrid orbitals. (c) unhybridized p atomic orbitals (d) four, two from the π bond and two from the nonbonded pair in the p atomic orbital   **9.91** $\sigma_{2s}^2 \sigma_{2s}^{*2} \pi_{2p}^4 \sigma_{2p}^1 \pi_{2p}^{*1}$ (a) Paramagnetic (b) The bond order of N_2 in the ground state is 3; in the first excited state it has a bond order of 2. Owing to the reduction in bond order, N_2 in the first excited state has a weaker N—N bond.
9.97 (a) $2 SF_4(g) + O_2(g) \longrightarrow 2 OSF_4(g)$

(b)

:O:
‖
:F—S—F:
| |
:F: :F:

(c) $\Delta H = -551$ kJ, exothermic (d) The electron domain geometry is trigonal bipyramidal. The O atom can be either equatorial or axial. (e) Since F is more electronegative than O, the structure that minimizes 90° F—S—F angles, the one with O axial, is preferred.   **9.99** (a) sp^2 hybridization at the two central C atoms (b) Isomerization requires 180° rotation around the C=C double bond. A 90° rotation eliminates all overlap of the p orbitals that form the π bond and it is broken. (c) 4.42×10^{-19} J/molecule (d) $\lambda = 450$ nm (e) Yes, 450 nm light is in the visible portion of the spectrum. A cis-trans isomerization in the retinal portion of the large molecule rhodopsin is the first step in a sequence of molecular transformations in the eye that leads to vision. The sequence of events enables the eye to detect visible photons, in other words, to see.   **9.101** From bond enthalpies, $\Delta H = 5364$ kJ;

according to Hess's law, $\Delta H° = 5535$ kJ. The difference in the two results, 171 kJ, is due to the resonance stabilization in benzene. The amount of energy actually required to decompose 1 mol of $C_6H_6(g)$ is greater than the sum of the localized bond enthalpies.   **9.103** (a) $3d_{z^2}$
(b)

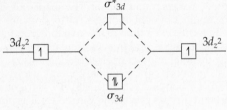

$3d_{z^2}$ $3d_{z^2}$ σ_{3d} σ^*_{3d}

The "donuts" of the $3d_{z^2}$ orbitals have been omitted from the diagram for clarity. (c) A node is generated in σ^*_{3d} because antibonding MOs are formed when atomic orbital lobes with opposite phases interact. Electron density is excluded from the internuclear region and a node is formed in the MO.
(d)

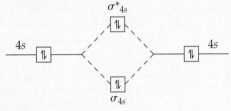

(e) The bond order of Sc_2 is 1.0.

Chapter 10

10.2

(a) $V_2 = \frac{5}{3} V_1$ (b) $V_2 = \frac{1}{2} V_1$

300 K, V_1 500 K, V_2 1 atm, V_1 2 atm, V_2

10.5 Over time, the gases will mix perfectly. Each bulb will contain 4 blue and 3 red atoms. The "blue" gas has the greater partial pressure after mixing, because it has the greater number of particles at the same T and V as the "red" gas.   **10.8** (a) Curve A is $O_2(g)$ and curve B is $He(g)$. (b) For the same gas at different temperatures, curve A represents the lower temperature and curve B the higher temperature.   **10.11** (a) A gas is much less dense than a liquid. (b) A gas is much more compressible than a liquid. (c) All mixtures of gases are homogenous. Similar liquid molecules form homogeneous mixtures, while very dissimilar molecules form heterogeneous mixtures.   **10.13** 1.8×10^3 kPa   **10.15** (a) 10.3 m (b) 2.1 atm   **10.17** (a) The tube can have any cross-sectional area. (b) At equilibrium the force of gravity per unit area acting on the mercury column at the level of the outside mercury is not equal to the force of gravity per unit area acting on the atmosphere. (c) The column of mercury is held up by the pressure of the atmosphere applied to the exterior pool of mercury.   **10.19** (a) 0.349 atm (b) 265 mm Hg (c) 3.53×10^4 Pa (d) 0.353 bar
10.21 (a) $P = 773.4$ torr (b) The pressure in Chicago is greater than standard atmospheric pressure, and so it makes sense to classify this weather system as a "high-pressure system."

10.23 (i) 0.30 atm (ii) 1.073 atm (iii) 0.136 atm   **10.23** (a) If V decreases by a factor of 4, P increases by a factor of 4.
(b) If T decreases by a factor of 2, P decreases by a factor of 2.
(c) If n decreases by a factor of 2, P decreases by a factor of 2.
10.27 (a) If equal volumes of gases at the same temperature and pressure contain equal numbers of molecules and molecules react in the ratios of small whole numbers, it follows that the volumes of reacting gases are in the ratios of small whole numbers. (b) Since the two gases are at the same temperature and pressure, the ratio of the numbers of atoms is the same as the ratio of volumes. There are 1.5 times as many Xe atoms as Ne atoms.   **10.29** (a) $PV = nRT$; P in atmospheres, V in liters, n in moles, T in kelvins. (b) An ideal gas exhibits pressure, volume, and temperature relationships described by the equation $PV = nRT$.   **10.31** Flask A contains the gas with $\mathcal{M} = 30$ g/mol, and flask B contains the gas with $\mathcal{M} = 60$ g/mol.

10.33

P	V	n	T
2.00 atm	1.00 L	0.500 mol	48.7 K
0.300 atm	0.250 L	3.05×10^{-3} mol	27 °C
650 torr	11.2 L	0.333 mol	350 K
10.3 atm	585 mL	0.250 mol	295 K

10.35 8.2×10^2 kg He   **10.37** 5.15×10^{22} molecules
10.39 (a) 91 atm (b) 2.3×10^2 L   **10.41** (a) 29.8 g Cl_2
(b) 9.42 L (c) 501 K (d) 1.90 atm   **10.43** (a) $n = 2 \times 10^{-4}$ mol O_2
(b) The roach needs 8×10^{-3} mol O_2 in 48 h, more than 100% of the O_2 in the jar.   **10.45** For gas samples at the same conditions, molar mass determines density. Of the three gases listed, (c) Cl_2 has the largest molar mass.   **10.47** (c) Because the helium atoms are of lower mass than the average air molecule, the helium gas is less dense than air. The balloon thus weighs less than the air displaced by its volume.   **10.49** (a) $d = 1.77$ g/L
(b) $\mathcal{M} = 80.1$ g/mol   **10.51** $\mathcal{M} = 89.4$ g/mol
10.53 3.5×10^{-9} g Mg   **10.55** 21.4 L CO_2 **10.57** 0.402 g Zn
10.59 (a) When the stopcock is opened, the volume occupied by $N_2(g)$ increases from 2.0 L to 5.0 L. $P_{N_2} = 0.40$ atm (b) When the gases mix, the volume of $O_2(g)$ increases from 3.0 L to 5.0 L. $P_{O_2} = 1.2$ atm (c) $P_t = 1.6$ atm   **10.61** (a) $P_{He} = 1.67$ atm, $P_{Ne} = 0.978$ atm, $P_{Ar} = 0.384$ atm, (b) $P_t = 3.03$ atm
10.63 $P_{CO_2} = 0.305$ atm, $P_t = 1.232$ atm   **10.65** $P_{N_2} = 0.98$ atm, $P_{O_2} = 0.39$ atm, $P_{CO_2} = 0.20$ atm   **10.67** 2.5 mole % O_2
10.69 $P_t = 3.04$ atm   **10.71** (a) Increase in temperature at constant volume or decrease in volume or increase in pressure (b) decrease in temperature (c) increase in volume, decrease in pressure (d) increase in temperature   **10.73** The fact that gases are readily compressible supports the assumption that most of the volume of a gas sample is empty space.   **10.75** (a) Average kinetic energy of the molecules increases.
(b) Average speed of the molecules increases. (c) Strength of an average impact with the container walls increases. (d) Total collisions of molecules with walls per second increases.
10.77 (a) In order of increasing speed and decreasing molar mass: HBr < NF_3 < SO_2 < CO < Ne (b) $u_{NF_3} = 324$ m/s
10.79 The order of increasing rate of effusion is
$^2H^{37}Cl < {}^1H^{37}Cl < {}^2H^{35}Cl < {}^1H^{35}Cl$.   **10.81** As_4S_6 **10.83** (a) Non-ideal-gas behavior is observed at very high pressures and low temperatures. (b) The real volumes of gas molecules and attractive intermolecular forces between molecules cause gases to behave nonideally. (c) According to the ideal-gas law, the ratio PV/RT should be constant for a given gas sample at all combinations of pressure, volume, and temperature. If this ratio changes with increasing pressure, the gas sample is not behaving ideally.   **10.85** Ar ($a = 1.34$, $b = 0.0322$) will behave more like an ideal gas than CO_2 ($a = 3.59$, $b = 0.427$) at high pressures.   **10.87** (a) $P = 4.89$ atm (b) $P = 4.69$ atm

(c) Qualitatively, molecular attractions are more important as the amount of free space decreases and the number of molecular collisions increases. Molecular volume is a larger part of the total volume as the container volume decreases.   **10.89** A mercury barometer with water trapped in its tip will not read the correct pressure. Water at the top of the Hg column establishes a vapor pressure that exerts downward pressure in addition to gravity and partially counterbalances the pressure of the atmosphere.   **10.92** 742 balloons can be filled completely, with a bit of He left over.   **10.95** (a) 13.4 mol $C_3H_8(g)$ (b) 1.47×10^3 mol $C_3H_8(l)$ (c) The ratio of moles liquid to moles gas is 110. Many more molecules and moles of liquid fit in a container of fixed volume because there is much less space between molecules in the liquid phase.   **10.98** $P_t = 5.3 \times 10^2$ torr **10.101** 42.2 g O_2 **10.104** $X_{Ne} = 0.6482$ **10.107** (a) As a gas is compressed at constant temperature, the number of intermolecular collisions increases. Intermolecular attraction causes some of these collisions to be inelastic, which amplifies the deviation from ideal behavior. (b) As the temperature of a gas is increased at constant volume, a larger fraction of the molecules has sufficient kinetic energy to overcome intermolecular attractions and the effect of intermolecular attraction becomes less significant.   **10.110** (a) 0.036% of the total volume is occupied by Ar atoms. (b) 3.6% of the total volume is occupied by Ar atoms.   **10.112** (a) The molecular formula is C_3H_6. (b) Ar and C_3H_6 are nonpolar, have similar molar masses, and experience London disperson forces. We expect the effect of both volume and intermolecular attractions to be more significant for the structurally more complex C_3H_6. Cyclopropane will deviate more from ideal behavior at the specified conditions. **10.114** (a) 44.58% C, 6.596% H, 16.44% Cl, 32.38% N (b) $C_8H_{14}N_5Cl$ **10.117** $\Delta H = -1.1 \times 10^{14}$ kJ (assuming $H_2O(l)$ is a product)   **10.120** (a) 5.02×10^8 L $CH_3OH(l)$ (b) $CH_4(g) + 2\,O_2(g) \longrightarrow CO_2(g) + 2\,H_2O(l),\ \Delta H^\circ = -890.4$ kJ; ΔH for combustion of the methane is -1.10×10^{13} kJ. $CH_3OH(l) + 3/2\,O_2(g) \longrightarrow CO_2(g) + 2\,H_2O(l),\ \Delta H^\circ = -726.6$ kJ; ΔH for combustion of the methanol is -9.00×10^{12} kJ.

Chapter 11

11.1 The diagram best describes a liquid. The particles are close together, mostly touching, but there is no regular arrangement or order. This rules out a gaseous sample, where the particles are far apart, and a crystalline solid, which has a regular repeating structure in all three directions.   **11.4** (a) 385 mm Hg (b) 22 °C (c) 47 °C   **11.7** (a) 3 Nb atoms, 3 O atoms (b) NbO (c) This is primarily an ionic solid, because Nb is a metal and O is a nonmetal. There may be some covalent character to the $Nb \cdots O$ bonds.   **11.9** (a) Solid < liquid < gas (b) gas < liquid < solid (c) Matter in the gaseous state is most easily compressed, because particles are far apart and there is much empty space.   **11.11** (a) The density of olive oil is less than 1.00 g/cm³. (b) At higher temperature, greater molecular motion and collisions cause the volume of the liquid to increase and the density to decrease. Olive oil is less dense at higher temperature.   **11.13** (a) London dispersion forces (b) dipole–dipole and London dispersion forces (c) dipole–dipole forces and in certain cases hydrogen bonding **11.15** (a) Nonpolar covalent molecule; London dispersion forces only (b) polar covalent molecule with O—H bonds; hydrogen bonding, dipole–dipole forces and London dispersion forces (c) polar covalent molecule; dipole–dipole and London dispersion forces (but not hydrogen bonding) **11.17** (a) Polarizability is the ease with which the charge distribution in a molecule can be distorted to produce a transient dipole. (b) Sb is most polarizable because its valence electrons are farthest from the nucleus and least tightly held. (c) in order of increasing polarizability: $CH_4 < SiH_4 < SiCl_4 < GeCl_4 < GeBr_4$ (d) The magnitudes of London dispersion forces and thus the boiling points of molecules increase as polarizability increases.

The order of increasing boiling points is the order of increasing polarizability given in (c).   **11.19** (a) H_2S (b) CO_2 (c) GeH_4 **11.21** Both rodlike butane molecules and spherical 2-methylpropane molecules experience dispersion forces. The larger contact surface between butane molecules facilitates stronger forces and produces a higher boiling point.   **11.23** (a) A molecule must contain H atoms, bound to either N, O or F atoms, in order to participate in hydrogen bonding with like molecules. (b) CH_3NH_2 and CH_3OH.   **11.25** (a) Replacing a hydroxyl hydrogen with a CH_3 group eliminates hydrogen bonding in that part of the molecule. This reduces the strength of intermolecular forces and leads to a lower boiling point. (b) $CH_3OCH_2CH_2OCH_3$ is a larger, more polarizable molecule with stronger London dispersion forces and thus a higher boiling point. **11.27**

Physical Property	H_2O	H_2S
Normal boiling point, °C	100.00	−60.7
Normal melting point, °C	0.00	−85.5

(a) Based on its much higher normal melting point and boiling point, H_2O has much stronger intermolecular forces. H_2O has hydrogen bonding, while H_2S has dipole–dipole forces. (b) H_2S is probably a typical compound with less empty space in the ordered solid than the liquid, so that the solid is denser than the liquid. For H_2O, maximizing the number of hydrogen bonds to each molecule in the solid requires more empty space than in the liquid, and the solid is less dense. (c) Specific heat is the energy required to raise the temperature of one gram of the substance one degree celsius. Hydrogen bonding in water is such a strong attractive interaction that the energy required to disrupt it and increase molecular motion is large.   **11.29** (a) As temperature increases, the number of molecules with sufficient kinetic energy to overcome intermolecular attractive forces increases, and viscosity and surface tension decrease. (b) The same attractive forces that cause surface molecules to be difficult to separate (high surface tension) cause molecules elsewhere in the sample to resist movement relative to each other (high viscosity).   **11.31** (a) $CHBr_3$ has a higher molar mass, is more polarizable, and has stronger dispersion forces, so the surface tension is greater. (b) As temperature increases, the viscosity of the oil decreases because the average kinetic energy of the molecules increases. (c) Adhesive forces between polar water and nonpolar car wax are weak, so the large surface tension of water draws the liquid into the shape with the smallest surface area, a sphere. (d) Adhesive forces between nonpolar oil and nonpolar car wax are similar to cohesive forces in oil, so the oil drops spread out on the waxed car hood.   **11.33** (a) Melting, endothermic (b) evaporation, endothermic (c) deposition, exothermic (d) condensation, exothermic   **11.35** Melting does not require separation of molecules, so the energy requirement is smaller than for vaporization, where molecules must be separated.   **11.37** 2.3×10^3 g H_2O **11.39** (a) 24.0 kJ (b) 5.57×10^3 kJ   **11.41** (a) The critical pressure is the pressure required to cause liquefaction at the critical temperature. (b) As the force of attraction between molecules increases, the critical temperature of the compound increases. (c) All the gases in Table 11.5 can be liquefied at the temperature of liquid nitrogen, given sufficient pressure.   **11.43** (a) No effect (b) no effect (c) Vapor pressure decreases with increasing intermolecular attractive forces because fewer molecules have sufficient kinetic energy to overcome attractive forces and escape to the vapor phase. (d) Vapor pressure increases with increasing temperature because average kinetic energies of molecules increase. (e) Vapor pressure decreases with increasing density because attractive intermolecular forces increase.   **11.45** (a) $CBr_4 < CHBr_3 < CH_2Br_2 < CH_2Cl_2 < CH_3Cl < CH_4$. The trend is dominated by dispersion forces even though four of the molecules are polar. The order of increasing volatility is the

order of increasing vapor pressure, decreasing molar mass, and decreasing strength of dispersion forces. (b) Boiling point increases as the strength of intermolecular forces increases; this is the order of decreasing volatility and the reverse of the order in part (a).
$CH_4 < CH_3Cl < CH_2Cl_2 < CH_2Br_2 < CHBr_3 < CBr_4$
11.47 (a) The temperature of the water in the two pans is the same. (b) Vapor pressure does not depend on either volume or surface area of the liquid. At the same temperature, the vapor pressures of water in the two containers are the same.
11.49 (a) Approximately 48 °C (b) approximately 340 torr (c) approximately 16 °C (d) approximately 1000 torr **11.51** (a) The critical point is the temperature and pressure beyond which the gas and liquid phases are indistinguishable. (b) The line that separates the gas and liquid phases ends at the critical point because at conditions beyond the critical temperature and pressure, there is no distinction between gas and liquid. In experimental terms a gas cannot be liquefied at temperatures higher than the critical temperature, regardless of pressure.
11.53 (a) $H_2O(g)$ will condense to $H_2O(s)$ at approximately 4 torr; at a higher pressure, perhaps 5 atm or so, $H_2O(s)$ will melt to form $H_2O(l)$. (b) At 100 °C and 0.50 atm, water is in the vapor phase. As it cools, water vapor condenses to the liquid at approximately 82 °C, the temperature where the vapor pressure of liquid water is 0.50 atm. Further cooling results in freezing at approximately 0 °C. The freezing point of water increases with decreasing pressure, so at 0.50 atm the freezing temperature is very slightly above 0 °C.
11.55

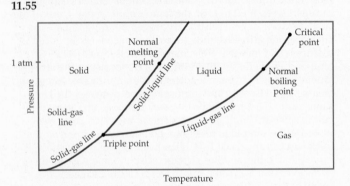

11.57

Crystalline   Amorphous

11.59 (a) $SrTiO_3$ (b) Each Sr atom is coordinated to six O atoms, three in this unit cell and three in adjacent unit cells. **11.61** (a) $r = 1.355$ Å (b) density = 22.67 g/cm³
11.63 Atomic weight = 55.8 g/mol **11.65** (a) $a = 4.70$ Å (b) 2.69 g/cm³ **11.67** $a = 6.13$ Å **11.69** (a) Intermolecular (really interparticle) forces among Ar atoms are dispersion forces. (b) Solid Ar is not a covalent network solid. Atoms in a covalent network solid are joined by strong covalent bonds, whereas atoms in Ar(s) are held in place by weak dispersion forces. **11.71** (a) Hydrogen bonding, dipole-dipole forces, London dispersion forces (b) covalent chemical bonds (c) ionic bonds (d) metallic bonds **11.73** In molecular solids relatively weak intermolecular forces bind the molecules in the lattice, so relatively little energy is required to disrupt these forces. In co-valent-network solids, covalent bonds join atoms into an extended network. Melting or deforming a covalent-network solid means breaking covalent bonds, which requires a large amount of energy. **11.75** Because of its relatively high melting point and properties as a conducting solution, the solid must be ionic. **11.77** (a) Xe, greater atomic weight,

stronger dispersion forces (b) SiO_2, covalent-network lattice versus weak dispersion forces (c) KBr, strong ionic versus weak dispersion forces (d) C_6Cl_6, both are influenced by dispersion forces, C_6Cl_6 has the higher molar mass **11.79** (a) Decrease (b) increase (c) increase (d) increase (e) increase (f) increase (g) increase **11.83** When a halogen is substituted for H in benzene, molar mass, polarizability and strength of dispersion forces increase; the order of increasing molar mass is the order of increasing boiling points for the first three compounds. C_6H_5OH experiences hydrogen bonding, the strongest force between neutral molecules, so it has the highest boiling point. **11.88** (a) Evaporation is an endothermic process. The heat required to vaporize sweat is absorbed from your body, helping to keep it cool. (b) The vacuum pump reduces the pressure of the atmosphere above the water until atmospheric pressure equals the vapor pressure of water and the water boils. Boiling is an endothermic process, and the temperature drops if the system is not able to absorb heat from the sur-roundings fast enough. As the temperature of the water de-creases, the water freezes. **11.92** The large difference in melting points is due to the very different forces imposing atomic order in the solid state. Much more kinetic energy is re-quired to disrupt the delocalized metallic bonding in gold than to overcome the relatively weak London dispersion forces in Xe. **11.95** Diffraction, the phenomenon that enables us to measure interatomic distances in crystals, is most efficient when the wavelength of light is similar to or smaller than the size of the object doing the diffracting. Atom sizes are on the order of 1–10 Å, and the wavelengths of x-rays are also in this range. Visible light, 400–700 nm or 4000–7000 Å, is too long to be diffracted effectively by atoms (electrons) in crystals.
11.98 16 Al atoms, 8 Mg atoms, 32 O atoms
11.101

(i) $M = 44$ (ii) $M = 72$ (iii) $M = 123$

(iv) $M = 58$ (v) $M = 123$ (vi) $M = 60$

(a) Molar mass: Compounds (i) and (ii) have similar rodlike structures. The longer chain in (ii) leads to greater molar mass, stronger London-dispersion forces, and higher heat of vapor-ization. (b) Molecular shape: Compounds (iii) and (v) have the same chemical formula and molar mass but different molecular shapes. The more rodlike shape of (v) leads to more contact be-tween molecules, stronger dispersion forces, and higher heat of vaporization. (c) Molecular polarity: Compound (iv) has a smaller molar mass than (ii) but a larger heat of vaporization, which must be due to the presence of dipole-dipole forces. (d) Hydrogen bonding interactions: Molecules (v) and (vi) have similar structures. Even though (v) has larger molar mass and dispersion forces, hydrogen bonding causes (vi) to have the higher heat of vaporization.
11.105 P(benzene vapor) = 98.6 torr.

Chapter 12

12.1 The band structure of material A is that of a metal.
12.3 Polymer (a), with ordered regions, is denser than branched polymer (b). The ordered regions in polymer (a) also indicate that it has stronger intermolecular forces and higher melting point than polymer (b). **12.5** (a) Molecule (i), with a terminal C=C, is the only monomer shown that is capable of

addition polymerization. (b) Molecule (iii) contains both a carboxyl group and an amine group; it can "condense" with like monomers to form a polymer and NH_3. (c) Molecule (ii), with a —CN group, a rodlike 5 C chain and a planar benzenelike (phenyl) ring, has both dipole–dipole and dispersion forces that are likely to encourage the long range order required to form a liquid crystal   **12.7** (a) Semiconductor (b) insulator (c) semiconductor (d) metal

12.9

(a) Six AOs require six MOs (b) Zero nodes in the lowest energy orbital (c) Five nodes in highest energy orbital (d) Two nodes in the HOMO (e) Three nodes in the LUMO.   **12.11** (a) False. Semiconductors have a smaller band gap; they conduct some electricity, while insulators do not. (b) True. Dopants create either more electrons or more "holes," both of which increase the conductivity of the semiconductor. (c) True. Metals conduct electricity because delocalized electrons in the lattice provide a mechanism for charge mobility. (d) True. Metal oxides are ionic substances with essentially localized electrons. This barrier to charge mobility renders them insulators. **12.13** (a) CdS (b) GaN (c) GaAs   **12.15** Ge or Si (Ge is closer to Ga in bonding atomic radius.)   **12.17** As a semiconductor material for integrated circuits, silicon has the advantages that it is abundant, cheap, nontoxic; can be highly purified; and grows nearly perfect enormous crystals.   **12.19** Traditionally, the insulator silicon dioxide, SiO_2, is the material in a MOSFET gate. The next-generation material is HfO_2.   **12.21** (a) A 1.1 eV photon corresponds to a wavelength of 1.1×10^{-6} m. (b) According to the figure, Si can absorb a portion of the visible light that comes from the sun.   **12.23** $\lambda = 560$ nm   **12.25** The band gap is approximately 1.85 eV, which corresponds to a wavelength of 672 nm.   **12.27** Ceramics are not readily recyclable because of their extremely high melting points and rigid ionic or covalent-network structures.   **12.29** Very small, uniformly sized and shaped particles are required for the production of a strong ceramic object by sintering. Upon heating to initiate condensation reactions, the more uniform the particle size and the greater the total surface area of the solid, the more chemical bonds are formed and the stronger the ceramic object. **12.31** The ceramics are MgO, soda-lime glass, ZrB_2, Al_2O_3, and TaC. The criteria are a combination of chemical formula (with corresponding bonding characteristics) and Knoop values. Ceramics are ionic or covalent-network solids with fairly large hardness values. Hardness alone is not a sufficient criterion for classification as a ceramic. A metal, Cr, lies in the middle of the hardness range for ceramics. Bonding characteristics as well as hardness must be taken into account when classifying materials as ceramics.   **12.33** A superconducting material offers no resistance to the flow of electrical current. Superconductive materials could transmit electricity with much greater efficiency than current carriers.   **12.35** The sharp drop in resistivity of MgB_2 near 39 K is the superconducting transition temperature,

T_c.   **12.37** The phenomenon that superconductors exclude all magnetic fields from their volume is the Meisner effect. It can be used to levitate trains by having either the tracks or the train wheels made from a magnetic material, and the other from a superconductor, with the superconductor cooled below its transition temperature. It is more practical, and therefore more likely, that the train wheels are made of the superconductor and cooled.   **12.39** Monomers are small molecules with low molecular mass that are joined together to form polymers. Three monomers mentioned in this chapter are

Propylene   Styrene   Isoprene
(propene)   (phenyl ethene)   (2-methyl-1,3-butadiene)

12.41

If a dicarboxylic acid and a dialcohol are combined, there is the potential for propagation of the polymer chain at both ends of both monomers.

12.43 (a)

(b)

(c)

12.45

12.47 Flexibility of molecular chains causes flexibility of the bulk polymer. Flexibility is enhanced by molecular features that inhibit order, such as branching, and diminished by features that encourage order, such as cross-linking or delocalized π electron density. Cross-linking, the formation of chemical bonds between polymer chains, reduces flexibility of the molecular chains, increases the hardness of the material, and decreases the chemical reactivity of the polymer.   **12.49** The function of the polymer determines whether high molecular mass and high degree of crystallinity are desirable properties. If the polymer will be used as a flexible wrapping or fiber, rigidity that is due to high molecular mass is an undesirable property.   **12.51** Is the neoprene biocompatible? Does it provoke inflammatory reactions? Does neoprene meet the physical requirements of a flexible lead? Will it remain resistant to degradation and maintain elasticity? Can neoprene be prepared in sufficiently pure form so that it can be classified as medical grade? **12.53** Current vascular graft materials cannot be lined with cells similar to those in the native artery. The body detects that the graft is "foreign," and platelets attach to the inside surfaces, causing blood clots. The inside surfaces of future vascular implants need to accommodate a lining of cells that do not attract or attach to platelets. **12.55** In order for skin cells in a culture medium to develop into synthetic skin, a mechanical matrix that holds the cells in contact with one another must be present. The matrix must be strong, biocompatible, and biodegradable. It probably has polar functional groups that form hydrogen bonds with biomolecules in the tissue cells. **12.57** Both an ordinary liquid and a nematic liquid crystal phase are fluids; they are converted directly to the solid phase upon cooling. The nematic phase is cloudy and more viscous than an ordinary liquid. Upon heating, the nematic phase is converted to an ordinary liquid. **12.59** In the solid state the relative orientation of molecules is fixed and repeating in all three dimensions. When a substance changes to the nematic liquid crystalline phase, the molecules remain aligned in one dimension; translational motion is allowed, but rotational motion is restricted. Transformation to the isotropic liquid phase destroys the one-dimensional order, resulting in free translational and rotational motion. **12.61** The presence of polar groups or nonbonded electron pairs leads to relatively strong dipole–dipole interactions between molecules. These are a significant part of the orienting forces necessary for liquid crystal formation. **12.63** In the nematic phase there is one-dimensional order, while in a smectic phase there is two-dimensional order. In a smectic phase the long directions of the molecules and the ends of the molecules are aligned. **12.65** A nematic phase is composed of sheets of molecules aligned along their lengths, with no additional order within the sheet or between sheets. A cholesteric phase also contains this kind of sheet, but with some ordering between sheets. **12.67** If a solid has nanoscale dimensions of 1–10 nm, there may not be enough atoms contributing atomic orbitals to produce continuous energy bands of molecular orbitals. **12.69** (a) False. As particle size decreases, the band gap increases. (b) False. As particle size decreases, wavelength decreases. **12.71** 2.47×10^5 Au atoms **12.73** Semiconductors have a difference in energy, the band gap, between a filled valence band and an empty conduction bond. When a semiconductor is heated, more electrons have sufficient energy to jump the band gap, and conductivity increases. Metals have a partially-filled continuous energy band. Heating a metal increases the average kinetic energy, including vibrational energy, of the metal atoms. The greater vibrational energy of the atoms leads to imperfections in the lattice and discontinuities in the energy band. This creates barriers to electron delocalization and reduces the conductivity of the metal.

12.75

Teflon™ is formed by addition polymerization. **12.79** At the temperature where a substance changes from the solid to the liquid crystalline phase, kinetic energy sufficient to overcome most of the long-range order in the solid has been supplied. A relatively small increase in temperature is required to overcome the remaining aligning forces and produce an isotropic liquid. **12.83** $TiCl_4(g) + 2\,SiH_4(g) \longrightarrow TiSi_2(s) + 4\,HCl(g) + 2\,H_2(g)$. As a ceramic, $TiSi_2$ will have a three-dimensional network structure similar to that of Si. At the surface of the thin film, there will be Ti and Si atoms with incomplete valences that will chemically bond with Si atoms on the surface of the substrate. This kind of bonding would not be possible with a Cu thin film. **12.84** (a) $\Delta H = -82$ kJ/mol (b) $\Delta H = -14$ kJ/mol (of either reactant) (c) $\Delta H = 0$ kJ **12.87** (a) $x = 0.22$ (b) Hg and Cu both have more than one stable oxidation state. If different ions in the solid lattice have different charges, the average charge is a noninteger value. Ca and Ba are stable only in the +2 oxidation state and are unlikely to have a noninteger average charge. (c) Ba^{2+} is largest; Cu^{2+} is smallest.

Chapter 13

13.1 The ion-solvent interaction should be greater for Li^+. The smaller ionic radius of Li^+ means that the ion–dipole interactions with polar water molecules are stronger. **13.5** Diagram (b) is the best representation of a saturated solution. There is some undissolved solid with particles that are close together and ordered, in contact with a solution containing mobile, separated solute particles. As much solute has dissolved as can dissolve, leaving some undissolved solid in contact with the saturated solution. **13.9** (a) Yes, the *molarity* changes with a change in temperature. Molarity is defined as moles solute per unit volume of solution. A change of temperature changes solution volume and molarity. (b) No, *molality* does not change with change in temperature. Molality is defined as moles solute per kilogram of solvent. Temperature affects neither mass nor moles. **13.13** If the magnitude of ΔH_3 is small relative to the magnitude of ΔH_1, ΔH_{soln} will be large and endothermic (energetically unfavorable) and not much solute will dissolve. **13.15** (a) Dispersion (b) hydrogen bonding (c) ion–dipole (d) dipole–dipole **13.17** (a) ΔH_1 (b) ΔH_3 **13.19** (a) Since the solute and solvent experience very similar London dispersion forces, the energy required to separate them individually and the energy released when they are mixed are approximately equal. $\Delta H_1 + \Delta H_2 \approx -\Delta H_3$. Thus, ΔH_{soln} is nearly zero. (b) Since no strong intermolecular forces prevent the molecules from mixing, they do so spontaneously because of the increase in randomness. **13.21** (a) Supersaturated (b) Add a seed crystal. A seed crystal provides a nucleus of prealigned molecules, so that ordering of the dissolved particles (crystallization) is more facile. **13.23** (a) Unsaturated (b) saturated (c) saturated (d) unsaturated **13.25** The liquids water and glycerol form homogenous mixtures (solutions) regardless of the relative amounts of the two components. The —OH groups of glycerol facilitate strong hydrogen bonding similar to that in water; like dissolves like. **13.27** (a) Dispersion interactions among nonpolar $CH_3(CH_2)_{16}$— chains dominate the properties of stearic acid, causing it to be more soluble in nonpolar CCl_4. (b) Dioxane can act as a hydrogen bond acceptor, so it will be more soluble than cyclohexane in water. **13.29** (a) CCl_4 is more soluble because dispersion forces among nonpolar CCl_4 molecules are similar to dispersion forces in hexane. (b) C_6H_6 is a nonpolar hydrocarbon and will be more soluble in the similarly nonpolar hexane. (c) The long, rodlike hydrocarbon chain of octanoic acid forms strong dispersion interactions and causes it to be more soluble in hexane. **13.31** (a) A sealed container is required to maintain a partial pressure of $CO_2(g)$ greater than 1 atm above the beverage. (b) Since the solubility of gases increases with decreasing temperature, some $CO_2(g)$ will remain dissolved in the beverage if it is kept cool. **13.33** $S_{He} = 5.6 \times 10^{-4}$ M, $S_{N_2} = 9.0 \times 10^{-4}$ M **13.35** (a) 2.15% Na_2SO_4

23.23 Sodium is metallic; each atom is bonded to many others. When the metal lattice is distorted, many bonds remain intact. In NaCl the ionic forces are strong, and the ions are arranged in very regular arrays. The ionic forces tend to be broken along certain cleavage planes in the solid, and the substance does not tolerate much distortion before cleaving.   **23.25** In the electron-sea model, valence electrons move about the metallic lattice, while metal atoms remain more or less fixed in position. Under the influence of an applied potential, the electrons are free to move throughout the structure, giving rise to thermal and electrical conductivity.   **23.27** Moving left to right in the period, atomic mass and Z_{eff} increase. The increase in Z_{eff} leads to smaller bonding atomic radii and shorter metal-metal bond distances. It seems that the extent of metal-metal bonding increases in the series, which is consistent with greater occupancy of the bonding band as the number of valence electrons increases up to 6. The increasing metal-metal bond strength in the series is probably the most important factor influencing the increase in density.   **23.29** (a) Ag (b) Zn. Ductility decreases as the strength of metal-metal bonding increases, producing a stiffer lattice, less susceptible to distortion.   **23.31** White tin has a structure characteristic of a metal, while gray tin has the diamond structure characteristic of group 4A semiconductors. Metallic white tin has the longer bond distance because the valence electrons are shared with twelve nearest neighbors rather than being localized in four bonds as in gray tin.
23.33 An *alloy* contains atoms of more than one element and has the properties of a metal. In a solution alloy the components are randomly dispersed. In a heterogeneous alloy the components are not evenly dispersed and can be distinguished at a macroscopic level. In an intermetallic compound the components have interacted to form a compound substance, as in Cu_3As.   **23.35** (a) Interstitial alloy (b) solution alloy (c) intermetallic compound   **23.37** Isolated atoms: (b) and (f); bulk metal: (a), (c), (d), and (e). Although it seems that atomic radius is a property of isolated atoms, it can only be measured on a bulk sample.   **23.39** Hf has a completed $4f$ subshell, while Zr does not. The build-up in Z that accompanies the filling of the $4f$ orbitals, along with additional shielding of valence electrons, offsets the typical effect of the larger n value for the valence electrons of Hf. Thus, the atomic radius of Hf is about the same as that of Zr, the element above it in group 4B.   **23.41** (a) ScF_3 (b) CoF_3 (c) ZnF_2 (d) MoF_6 **23.43** Chromium, $[Ar]4s^1 3d^5$, has six valence electrons, some or all of which can be involved in bonding, leading to multiple stable oxidation states. Al, $[Ne]3s^2 3p^1$, has only three valence electrons, which are all lost or shared during bonding, producing the +3 state exclusively.   **23.45** (a) Cr^{3+}, $[Ar]3d^3$ (b) Au^{3+}, $[Xe]4f^{14}5d^8$ (c) Ru^{2+}, $[Kr]4d^6$ (d) Cu^+, $[Ar]3d^{10}$ (e) Mn^{4+}, $[Ar]3d^3$ (f) Ir^+, $[Xe]4f^{14}5d^8$ **23.47** Ti^{2+} **23.49** Fe^{2+} is a reducing agent that is readily oxidized to Fe^{3+} in the presence of O_2 from air.   **23.51** (a) $Fe(s) + 2 HCl(aq) \longrightarrow$ $FeCl_2(aq) + H_2(g)$ (b) $Fe(s) + 4 HNO_3(g) \longrightarrow$ $Fe(NO_3)_3(aq) + NO(g) + 2 H_2O(l)$ **23.53** The unpaired electrons in a paramagnetic material cause it to be weakly attracted into a magnetic field. A diamagnetic material, where all electrons are paired, is very weakly repelled by a magnetic field.   **23.55** (a) In ferromagnetic materials, coupled electron spins are aligned in the same direction. In antiferromagnetic materials, coupled spins are aligned in opposite directions and the opposing spins exactly cancel. In ferrimagnetic materials coupled spins are aligned in opposite directions but the opposing spins do not cancel. (b) Antiferromagnetic materials have no net electron spin and cannot be used to make permanent magnets.
23.57 $PbS(s) + O_2(g) \longrightarrow Pb(l) + SO_2(g)$. $SO_2(g)$ is a product of roasting sulfide ores. In an oxygen-rich environment, $SO_2(g)$ is oxidized to $SO_3(g)$, which dissolves in $H_2O(l)$ to form sulfuric acid, $H_2SO_4(aq)$. A sulfuric acid plant near a roasting plant would provide a means for disposing of hazardous $SO_2(g)$ that would also generate a profit.   **23.59** $CO(g)$: $Pb(s)$; $H_2(g)$: $Fe(s)$;

$Zn(s)$: $Au(s)$ **23.62** Based on its reduction potential, Te is less active and more difficult to oxidize than Cu. While Cu is oxidized from the crude anode during electrorefining, Te will not be oxidized. It is likely to accumulate, along with other impurities less active than Cu, in the so-called anode sludge.   **23.67** $E°$ will become more negative as the stability (K_f value) of the complex increases.   **23.71** (a) $Mn(s) + 2 HNO_3(aq) \longrightarrow$ $Mn(NO_3)_2(aq) + H_2(g)$ (b) $Mn(NO_3)_2(s) \xrightarrow{\Delta} MnO_2(s) +$ $2 NO_2(g)$ (c) $MnO_2(s) \xrightarrow{\Delta} Mn_3O_4(s) + O_2(g)$ (d) $2 MnCl_2(s) + 9 F_2(g) \longrightarrow 2 MnF_3(s) + 4 ClF_3(g)$ **23.73** (a) Insulator (b) semiconductor (c) metallic conductor (d) metallic conductor (e) insulator (f) metallic conductor   **23.74** (a) 6.7×10^8 g SO_2 (b) 2.3 mol Cu/mol Fe (c) CuO and Fe_2O_3 (d) $Cu_2S(s) + 2 O_2(g) \longrightarrow 2 CuO(s) + SO_2(g)$; $4 FeS(s) +$ $7 O_2(g) \longrightarrow 2 Fe_2O_3(s) + 4 SO_2(g)$ **23.76** 7.3×10^2 g $Ni^{2+}(aq)$ **23.79** $K = 1.6 \times 10^6$ **23.82** (a) The standard reduction potential for $H_2O(l)$ is much greater than that of $Mg^{2+}(aq)$ (−0.83 V vs. −2.37 V). In aqueous solution $H_2O(l)$ would be preferentially reduced and no $Mg(s)$ would be obtained. (b) 1.0×10^3 kg Mg   **23.85** The density of pure Ni is 8.86 g/cm^3; the density of Ni_3Al is 7.47 g/cm^3. In Ni_3Al, one of every four Ni atoms is replaced with a lighter Al atom. The mass of the unit cell contents of Ni_3Al is ~85% of that of pure Ni, and the densities show the same relationship.

Chapter 24

24.1 (a)

(b) coordination number = 4, coordination geometry = square planar (c) oxidation number = +2   **24.4** Structures (3) and (4) are identical to (1); (2) and (5) are geometric isomers of (1).   **24.6** The yellow-orange solution absorbs blue-violet; the blue-green solution absorbs orange-red.   **24.9** (a) In Werner's theory, *primary valence* is the charge of the metal cation at the center of the complex. *Secondary valence* is the number of atoms bound or coordinated to the central metal ion. The modern terms for these concepts are oxidation state and coordination number, respectively. (b) Ligands are the Lewis base in metal-ligand interactions. As such, they must possess at least one unshared electron pair. NH_3 has an unshared electron pair but BH_3, with less than 8 electrons about B, has no unshared electron pair and cannot act as a ligand.   **24.11** (a) +2 (b) 6 (c) 2 mol $AgBr(s)$ will precipitate per mole of complex.
24.13 (a) Coordination number = 4, oxidation number = +2 (b) 5, +4 (c) 6, +3 (d) 5, +2 (e) 6, +3 (f) 4, +2   **24.15** (a) 4 Cl$^-$ (b) 4 Cl$^-$, 1 O^{2-} (c) 4 N, 2 Cl$^-$ (d) 5 C (e) 6 O (f) 4 N   **24.17** (a) A monodentate ligand binds to a metal via one atom, a bidentate ligand binds through two atoms. (b) Three bidentate ligands fill the coordination sphere of a six-coordinate complex. (c) A tridentate ligand has at least three atoms with unshared electron pairs in the correct orientation to simultaneously bind one or more metal ions.   **24.19** (a) *Ortho*-phenanthroline, o-phen, is bidentate (b) oxalate, $C_2O_4^{2-}$, is bidentate (c) ethylenedi-aminetetraacetate, EDTA, is pentadentate (d) ethylenediamine, en, is bidentate.   **24.21** (a) The term *chelate effect* refers to the special stability associated with formation of a metal complex containing a polydentate (chelate) ligand relative to a complex containing only monodentate ligands. (b) The increase in entropy, $+\Delta S$, associated with the substitution of a chelating ligand for two or more monodentate ligands generally gives rise to the *chelate effect*. Chemical reactions with $+\Delta S$ tend to be spontaneous, have negative ΔG and large values of K. (c) Polydentate ligands are used as *sequestering agents* to bind metal ions and prevent them from undergoing unwanted chemical reactions without removing them from solution.
24.23 (a) $[Cr(NH_3)_6](NO_3)_3$ (b) $[Co(NH_3)_4CO_3]_2SO_4$

(c) [Pt(en)₂Cl₂]Br₂ (d) K[V(H₂O)₂Br₄] (e) [Zn(en)₂][HgI₄]
24.25 (a) tetraamminedichlororhodium(III) chloride (b) potassium hexachlorotitanate(IV) (c) tetrachlorooxomolybdenum(VI) (d) tetraaqua(oxalato)platinum (IV) bromide

24.27 (a)

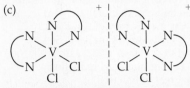

cis   trans

(b) [Pd(NH₃)₂(ONO)₂], [Pd(NH₃)₂(NO₂)₂]

(c)

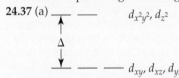

(d) [Co(NH₃)₄Br₂]Cl, [Co(NH₃)₄BrCl]Br   **24.29** Yes. No structural or stereoisomers are possible for a tetrahedral complex of the form MA₂B₂. The complex must be square planar with cis and trans geometric isomers.   **24.31** (a) One isomer (b) trans and cis isomers with 180° and 90° Cl—Ir—Cl angles, respectively (c) trans and cis isomers with 180° and 90° Cl—Fe—Cl angles, respectively. The cis isomer is optically active.
24.33 (a) Visible light has wavelengths between 400 and 700 nm. (b) *Complementary* colors are opposite each other on an artist's color wheel. (c) A colored metal complex absorbs visible light of its complementary color. (d) 196 kJ/mol
24.35 Most of the attraction between a metal ion and a ligand is electrostatic. Whether the interaction is ion-ion or ion-dipole, the ligand is strongly attracted to the metal center and can be modeled as a point negative charge.

24.37 (a)

$$\underline{\quad}\ \underline{\quad} \qquad d_{x^2-y^2},\, d_{z^2}$$

$$\Delta$$

$$\underline{\quad}\ \underline{\quad}\ \underline{\quad} \qquad d_{xy},\, d_{xz},\, d_{yz}$$

(b) The magnitude of Δ and the energy of the d-d transition for a d^1 complex are equal. (c) $\Delta = 203$ kJ/mol   **24.39** A yellow color is due to absorption of light around 400 to 430 nm, a blue color to absorption near 620 nm. The shorter wavelength corresponds to a higher-energy electron transition and larger Δ value. Cyanide is a stronger-field ligand, and its complexes are expected to have larger Δ values than aqua complexes.

24.41 (a) Ti³⁺, d^1 (b) Co³⁺, d^6 (c) Ru³⁺, d^5 (d) Mo⁵⁺, d^1, (e) Re³⁺, d^4 **24.43** (a) Mn, [Ar]4s²3d⁵; Mn²⁺, [Ar]3d⁵; 1 unpaired electron (b) Ru, [Kr]5s¹4d⁷; Ru²⁺, [Kr]4d⁶; 0 unpaired electrons (c) Rh, [Kr]5s¹4d⁸; Rh²⁺, [Kr]4d⁷; 1 unpaired electron   **24.45** All complexes in this exercise are six-coordinate octahedral.

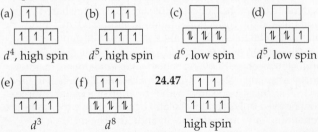

24.49 [Pt(NH₃)₆]Cl₄; [Pt(NH₃)₄Cl₂]Cl₂; [Pt(NH₃)₃Cl₃]Cl; [Pt(NH₃)₂Cl₄]; K[Pt(NH₃)Cl₅]   **24.52** (a) [24.51(a)] *cis*-tetraamminediaquacobalt(II) nitrate; [24.51(b)] sodium aquapentachlororuthenate(III); [24.51(c)] ammonium *trans*-diaquabisoxalatocobaltate(III); [24.51(d)] *cis*-dichlorobisethylenediamineruthenium(II) (b) Only the complex in 24.51(d) is optically active. The mirror images of (a)–(c) can be superimposed on the original structure. The

chelating ligands in (d) prevent its enantiomers from being superimposable.   **24.54** (a) In a square-planar complex, if one pair of ligands is trans, the remaining two coordination sites are also trans to each other. The bidentate ethylenediamine ligand is too short to occupy trans coordination sites, so the trans isomer of [Pt(en)Cl₂] is unknown. (b) The minimum steric requirement for a trans-bidentate ligand is a medium-length chain between the two coordinating atoms that will occupy the trans positions. A polydentate ligand such as EDTA is much more likely to occupy trans positions because it locks the metal ion in place with multiple coordination sites and shields the metal ion from competing ligands present in the solution.
24.57 (a) AgCl(s) + 2 NH₃(aq) ⟶ [Ag(NH₃)₂]⁺(aq) + Cl⁻(aq)
(b) [Cr(en)₂Cl₂]Cl(aq) + 2 H₂O(l) ⟶
[Cr(en)₂(H₂O)₂]³⁺(aq) + 3 Cl⁻(aq); 3 Ag⁺(aq) + 3 Cl⁻(aq) ⟶
3 AgCl(s) (c) Zn(NO₃)₂(aq) + 2 NaOH(aq) ⟶ Zn(OH)₂(s) +
2 NaNO₃(aq); Zn(OH)₂(s) + 2 NaOH(aq) ⟶
[Zn(OH)₄]²⁻(aq) + 2 Na⁺(aq) (d) Co²⁺(aq) + 4 Cl⁻(aq) ⟶
[CoCl₄]²⁻(aq)

24.60 (a)

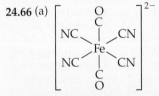

(b) Visible light with $\lambda = hc/\Delta$ is absorbed by the complex, promoting one of the d electrons into a higher energy d orbital. The remaining wavelengths are reflected or transmitted; the combination of these wavelengths is the color we see. (c) [V(H₂O)₆]³⁺ will absorb light with higher energy because it has a larger Δ than [VF₆]³⁻. H₂O is in the middle of the spectrochemical series and causes a larger Δ than F⁻, a weak-field ligand.
24.62 [Co(NH₃)₆]³⁺, yellow; [Co(H₂O)₆]²⁺, pink; [CoCl₄]²⁻, blue
24.64 (a) The term isoelectronic means that the three ions have the same number of valence electrons and the same electron configuration. (b) The three metal atoms are in their maximum oxidation states and have no d-electrons, so there should be no d-d transitions. (c) A ligand-to-metal charge transfer transition occurs when an electron in a filled ligand orbital is excited to an empty d-orbital of the metal. (d) Compounds appear the complementary color of the light they absorb. Permanganate appears purple because it is absorbing 565 nm yellow light. Chromate appears yellow because it is absorbing violet light of approximately 420 nm. The wavelength of the LMCT transition for chromate is smaller than that in permanganate. (e) Yes. A white compound indicates that no visible light is absorbed. Moving left on the periodic chart from Mn to Cr, the wavelength of the LMCT decreases. It is consistent that the ion containing V, further left on the chart, has a LMCT at an even shorter wavelength in the ultraviolet region of the spectrum.

24.66 (a)

$$\left[\begin{array}{c} \text{structure} \end{array}\right]^{2-}$$

(b) sodium dicarbonyltetracyanoferrate(II) (c) +2, 6d electrons (d) We expect the complex to be low spin. Cyanide (and carbonyl) are high on the spectrochemical series, which means the complex will have a large Δ splitting, characteristic of low-spin complexes.   **24.71** In carbonic anhydrase, Zn²⁺ is the Lewis acid, withdrawing electron density from H₂O, the Lewis base. The O—H bond is polarized and H becomes more ionizable, more acidic than the bulk solvent.   **24.73** K₄[Mn(ox)₂Br₂]
24.75 The chemical formula is [Pd(NC₅H₅)₂Br₂]. This is an

electrically neutral square-planar complex of Pd(II), a nonelectrolyte whose solutions do not conduct electricity. Because the dipole moment is zero, it must be the trans isomer.   **24.77** 47.3 mg Mg^{2+}/L, 53.4 mg Ca^{2+}/L
24.80 $\Delta E = 3.02 \times 10^{-19}$ J/photon, $\lambda = 657$ nm. The complex will absorb in the visible around 660 nm and appear blue-green.

Chapter 25

25.1 Molecules (c) and (d) are unsaturated.   **25.3** Compound (b), which has hydrogen bonding, has the highest boiling point.   **25.5** (a) Molecule (i), disaccharide (b) molecule (iv), amino acid (c) molecule (iii), organic base (d) molecule (v), alcohol (e) molecule (ii), fatty acid   **25.7** Numbering from the right on the condensed structural formula, C1 has trigonal planar electron domain geometry, 120° bond angles and sp^2 hybridization; C2 and C5 have tetrahedral electron-domain geometry, 109° bond angles, and sp^3 hybridization; C3 and C4 have linear electron domain geometry, 180° bond angles and sp hybridization.   **25.9** Neither NH_3 nor CO are typical organic molecules. NH_3 contains no carbon atoms. Carbon monoxide contains a C atom that does not form four bonds.
25.11 (a) A straight-chain hydrocarbon has all carbon atoms connected in a continuous chain. A branched-chain hydrocarbon has a branch; at least one carbon atom is bound to three or more carbon atoms. (b) An alkane is a complete molecule composed of carbon and hydrogen in which all bonds are σ bonds. An alkyl group is a substituent formed by removing a hydrogen atom from an alkane. (c) Alkanes are said to be saturated because they cannot undergo addition reactions, such as those characteristic of carbon-carbon double bonds. (d) Ethylene (or ethene), $CH_2{=}CH_2$, is unsaturated.
25.13 (a) C_5H_{12} (b) C_5H_{10} (c) C_5H_{10} (d) C_5H_8; saturated: (a), (b); unsaturated: (c), (d)   **25.15** One possible structure is $CH{\equiv}C{-}CH{=}CH{-}C{\equiv}CH$ **25.17** There are at least 46 structural isomers with the formula C_6H_{10}. A few of them are

$$CH_3CH_2CH_2CH_2C{\equiv}CH \qquad CH_3CH_2CH_2C{\equiv}CCH_3$$

25.19 (a) sp^3 (b) sp^2 (c) sp^2 (d) sp **25.21** (a) 2-methylhexane (b) 4-ethyl-2,4-dimethyldecane

(c) $CH_3CH_2CH_2CH_2CH_2\overset{\overset{\displaystyle CH_3}{|}}{CH}{-}CH_3$

(d) $CH_3{-}CH_2{-}CH_2{-}CH_2{-}CH_2{-}CH{-}CH{-}CH{-}CH_2{-}CH_3$

25.23 (a) 2,3-dimethylheptane (b) *cis*-6-methyl-3-octene (c) *para*-dibromobenzene (d) 4,4-dimethyl-1-hexyne (e) methylcyclobutane   **25.25** Geometric isomerism in alkenes is the result of restricted rotation about the double bond. In alkanes bonding sites are interchangeable by free rotation about the C—C single bonds. In alkynes there is only one additional bonding site on a triply bound carbon, so no isomerism results.
25.27 (a) No

(b)

(c) no (d) no   **25.29** 65   **25.31** (a) An addition reaction is the addition of some reagent to the two atoms that form a multiple bond. In a substitution reaction one atom or group of atoms replaces another atom. Alkenes typically undergo addition, while aromatic hydrocarbons usually undergo substitution.

(b) $CH_3CH_2CH{=}CH{-}CH_3 + Br_2 \longrightarrow$
$\quad$ 2-pentene

$\qquad\qquad\qquad CH_3CH_2CH(Br)CH(Br)CH_3$
$\qquad\qquad\qquad$ 2, 3-dibromopentane

(c)

$$C_6H_6 + Cl_2 \xrightarrow{FeCl_3} C_6H_4Cl_2$$

25.33 (a) The 60° C—C—C angles in the cyclopropane ring cause strain that provides a driving force for reactions that result in ring opening. There is no comparable strain in the five- or six-membered rings. (b) $C_2H_4(g) + HBr(g) \longrightarrow$
$CH_3CH_2Br(l)$; $C_6H_6(l) + CH_3CH_2Br(l) \xrightarrow{AlCl_3}$
$C_6H_5CH_2CH_3(l) + HBr(g)$ **25.35** Not necessarily. That the two rate laws are first order in both reactants and second order overall indicates that the activated complex in the rate-determining step in each mechanism is bimolecular and contains one molecule of each reactant. This is usually an indication that the mechanisms are the same, but it does not rule out the possibility of different fast steps, or a different order of elementary steps.   **25.37** ΔH_{comb}/mol CH_2 for cyclopropane = 696.3 kJ, for cyclopentane = 663.4 kJ. $\Delta H_{comb}/CH_2$ group for cyclopropane is greater because C_3H_6 contains a strained ring. When combustion occurs, the strain is relieved and the stored energy is released.   **25.39** (a) Alcohol (b) amine, alkene (c) ether (d) ketone, alkene (e) aldehyde (f) carboxylic acid, alkyne   **25.41** (a) Propionaldehyde (or propanal):

(b) ethylmethyl ether:

25.43 (a) $H{-}\overset{\overset{\displaystyle O}{\|}}{C}{-}OH$

(b)
$$CH_3CH_2CH_2CH_2\overset{O}{\overset{\|}{C}}-OH$$

or

(c)
$$CH_3CH_2CH_2CH_2CH_2CH_2CH_2\overset{CH_3}{\underset{}{CH}}-\overset{Cl}{\underset{}{C}}-\overset{O}{\overset{\|}{C}}-OH$$

25.45

(a)
$$CH_3CH_2O-\overset{O}{\overset{\|}{C}}-\bigcirc$$

Ethylbenzoate

(b)
$$CH_3\overset{H}{\underset{}{N}}-\overset{O}{\overset{\|}{C}}CH_3$$

N-methylethanamide or
N-methylacetamide

(c)
$$\bigcirc-O-\overset{O}{\overset{\|}{C}}CH_3$$

Phenylacetate

25.47

(a)
$$CH_3CH_2\overset{O}{\overset{\|}{C}}-O-CH_3 + NaOH \longrightarrow \left[CH_3CH_2\overset{O}{\overset{\diagup}{C}}\overset{O}{\diagdown}\right]^-$$
$$+ Na^+ + CH_3OH$$

(b)
$$CH_3\overset{O}{\overset{\|}{C}}-O-\bigcirc + NaOH \longrightarrow \left[CH_3\overset{O}{\overset{\diagup}{C}}\overset{O}{\diagdown}\right]^- + Na^+$$
$$+ \bigcirc^{OH}$$

25.49 The presence of both —OH and —C=O groups in pure acetic acid leads us to conclude that it will be a strongly hydrogen-bonded substance. That the melting and boiling points of pure acetic acid are both higher than those of water, a substance we know to be strongly hydrogen-bonded, supports this conclusion.   **25.51** (a) $CH_3CH_2CH_2CH(OH)CH_3$
(b) $CH_3CH(OH)CH_2OH$

(c)
$$CH_3\overset{O}{\overset{\|}{C}}OCH_2CH_3$$

(d)
$$\bigcirc-\overset{O}{\overset{\|}{C}}-\bigcirc$$

(e) $CH_3OCH_2CH_3$

25.53
$$H-\overset{H}{\underset{H}{C}}-\overset{H}{\underset{H}{C}}-\overset{CH_3}{\underset{H}{\overset{*}{C}}}-\overset{Br}{\underset{Cl}{\overset{*}{C}}}-\overset{H}{\underset{H}{C}}-H \quad \text{*chiral C atoms}$$

25.55 (a) An α-amino acid contains an NH_2 group attached to the carbon adjacent to the carboxylic acid function. (b) In protein formation, amino acids undergo a condensation reaction between the amino group of one molecule and the carboxylic

acid group of another to form the amide linkage. (c) The bond that links amino acids in proteins is called the peptide bond.

$$-\overset{O}{\overset{\|}{C}}\blacksquare\overset{}{\underset{H}{N}}-$$

25.57
$$CH_3-\overset{NH_3^+}{\underset{CH_3}{CH}}-CH_2-CH_2-\overset{O}{\overset{\|}{C}}-\overset{H}{\underset{}{N}}-CH-\overset{O}{\overset{\|}{C}}-O^-$$

25.59 (a)
$$H_3\overset{+}{N}CH_2\overset{O}{\overset{\|}{C}}NHCH_2\overset{O}{\overset{\|}{C}}NHCH\overset{O}{\overset{\|}{C}}O^-$$

(b) Three tripeptides ar possible: Gly-Gly-His, GGH; Gly-His-Gly, GHG; His-Gly-Gly, HGG   **25.61** The primary structure of a protein refers to the sequence of amino acids in the chain. The secondary structure is the configuration (helical, folded, open) of the protein chain. The tertiary structure is the overall shape of the protein determined by the way the segments fold together (b) X-ray crystallography is the primary and preferred technique for determining protein structure.   **25.63** (a) Carbohydrates, or sugars, are polyhydroxyaldehydes or ketones composed of carbon, hydrogen, and oxygen. They are derived primarily from plants and are a major food source for animals. (b) A monosaccharide is a simple sugar molecule that cannot be decomposed into smaller sugar molecules by hydrolysis. (c) A disaccharide is a carbohydrate composed of two simple sugar units. Hydrolysis breaks a disaccharide into two monosaccharides. (d) A polysaccharide is a polymer composed of many simple sugar units.   **25.65** The empirical formula of cellulose is $C_6H_{10}O_5$. As in glycogen, the six-membered ring form of glucose forms the monomer unit that is the basis of the polymer cellulose. In cellulose, glucose monomer units are joined by β linkages.   **25.67** (a) In the linear form of mannose, the aldehydic carbon is C1. Carbon atoms 2, 3, 4, and 5 are chiral because they each carry four different groups. (b) Both the α (left) and β (right) forms are possible.

25.69 Two important kinds of lipids are fats and fatty acids. Structurally, fatty acids are carboxylic acids with a hydrocarbon chain of more than four carbon atoms (typically 16–20 carbon atoms). Fats are esters formed by condensation of an alcohol, often glycerol, and a fatty acid. Phospholipids are glycerol esters formed from one phosphoric acid $[RPO(OH)_2]$ and two fatty acid (RCOOH) molecules. At body pH, the phosphate group is depronated and has a negative charge. The long, nonpolar hydrocarbon chains do not readily mix with water, but they do interact with the nonpolar chains of other phospholipid molecules to form the inside of a bilayer. The charged phosphate heads interact with polar water molecules on the outsides of the bilayer.   **25.71** *Purines*, with the larger electron cloud and molar mass, will have larger dispersion forces than *pyrimidines* in aqueous solution.
25.73 5′–TACG–3′   **25.75** The complimentary strand for 5′–GCATTGGC–3′ is 3′–CGTAACCG–5′.

25.77

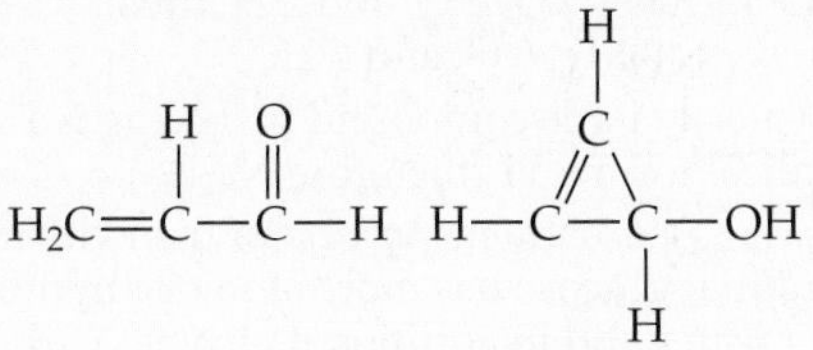

25.80

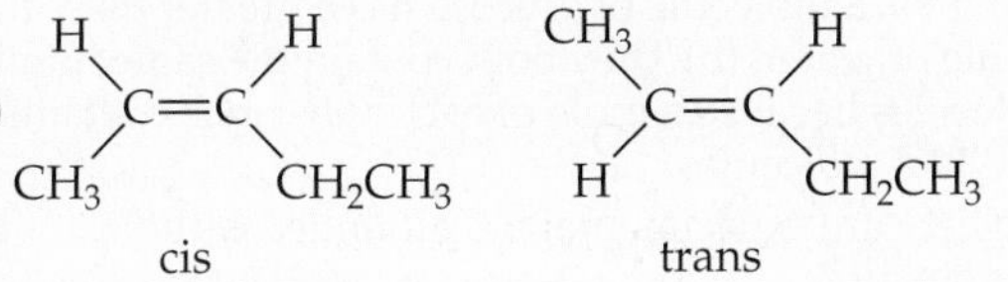

Cyclopentene does not show cis-trans isomerism because the existence of the ring demands that the C—C bonds be cis to one another.

25.83

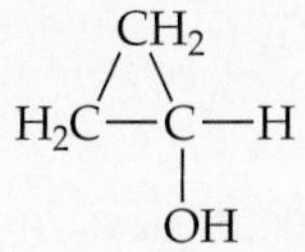

(Structures with the —OH group attached to an alkene carbon atom are called "vinyl alcohols" and are not the major form at equilibrium.)   **25.85** (a) Aldehyde, trans-alkene, cis-alkene (b) ether, alcohol, alkene, amine (two of these, one aliphatic and one aromatic) (c) ketone (two of these), amine (two of these) (d) amide, alcohol (aromatic)   **25.91** Glu-Cys-Gly is the only possible order. Glutamic acid has two carboxyl groups that can form a peptide bond with cysteine, so there are two possible structures for glutathione.

25.97 $CH_3\overset{\overset{\textstyle O}{\|}}{C}CH_2CH_3$

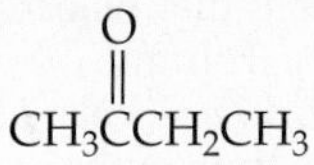

Answers to Give It Some Thought

Chapter 1

page 3 (a) about 100 elements, (b) atoms and molecules

page 6 oxygen, O

page 8 The water molecule contains atoms of two different elements, hydrogen and oxygen. A compound consists of two or more different elements.

page 11 (a) is a chemical change because a new substance is being formed. (b) is a physical change because the water merely changes its physical state and not its composition.

page 14 1 pg, which equals 10^{-12} g.

page 17 2.5×10^2 m^3. The volume of a rectangular object is length $\times$ width $\times$ height. The units for volume, based on the SI unit of length, m, are m^3. 5.77 L/s is a different derived unit because it contains time in the denominator.

page 20 (b) is inexact because it is a measured quantity. Both (a) and (c) are exact; (a) involves counting; and (c) is a defined value.

page 26 Whenever possible, we must avoid using a conversion factor that has fewer significant figures than the data whose units are being converted. It is best to use at least one more significant figure in the conversion factor than in the data, which is what was done in Sample Exercise 1.9.

Chapter 2

page 39 (a) the law of multiple proportions. (b) The second compound must contain two oxygen atoms for each carbon atom (that is, twice as many carbon atoms as the first compound).

page 43 (top) Most α particles pass through the foil without being deflected because most of the volume of the atoms that comprise the foil is empty space.

page 43 (bottom) (a) The atom has 15 electrons because atoms have equal numbers of electrons and protons. (b) The protons reside in the nucleus of the atom.

page 47 Any single atom of chromium must be one of the isotopes of that element. The isotope mentioned has a mass of 52.94 amu and is probably ^{53}Cr. The atomic weight differs from the mass of any particular atom because it is the average atomic mass of the naturally occurring isotopes of the element.

page 51 (a) Cl, (b) third period and group 7A, (c) 17, (d) nonmetal

page 54 (a) C_2H_6, (b) CH_3, (c) probably the ball-and-stick model because the angles between the sticks indicate the angles between the atoms.

page 58 We write the empirical formulas for ionic compounds. Thus, the formula is CaO.

page 60 The transition metals can form more than one type of cation, and the charges of these ions are therefore indicated explicitly with Roman numerals: Chromium(II) ion is Cr^{2+}. Calcium, on the other hand, always forms the Ca^{2+} ion, so there is no need to distinguish it from other calcium ions with different charges.

page 61 An *-ide* ending usually means a monatomic anion, although there are some anions with two atoms that are also named this way. An *-ate* ending indicates an oxyanion. The most common oxyanions have the *-ate* ending. An *-ite* end-

ing also indicates an oxyanion, but one having less O than the anion whose name ends in *-ate*.

page 62 BO_3^{3-} and SiO_4^{4-}. The borate has three O atoms, like the other oxyanions of the second period in Figure 2.27, and its charge is $3-$, following the trend of increasing negative charge as you move to the left in the period. The silicate has four O atoms, as do the other oxyanions in the third period in Figure 2.27, and its charge is $4-$, also following the trend of increasing charge moving to the left.

Chapter 3

page 80 Each $Mg(OH)_2$ has 1 Mg, 2 O, and 2 H; thus, 3 $Mg(OH)_2$ represents 3 Mg, 6 O, and 6 H.

page 84 The product is an ionic compound involving Na^+ and S^{2-}, and its chemical formula is therefore Na_2S.

page 91 (a) A mole of glucose. By inspection of their chemical formulas we find that glucose has more atoms of hydrogen and oxygen than water and in addition it also has carbon atoms; thus, a molecule of glucose has a greater mass than a molecule of water. (b) They both contain the same number of molecules because a mole of each substance contains 6.02×10^{23} molecules.

page 98 There are experimental uncertainties in the measurements.

page 99 3.14 mol because 2 mol $H_2 \cong 1$ mol O_2 based on the stoichiometry of the chemical reaction.

page 100 The number of grams of product formed is the sum of the masses of the two reactants, 50 g. When two substances react in a combination reaction only one substance is formed as a product. According to the law of conservation of mass, the mass of the product must equal the masses of the two reactants.

Chapter 4

page 122 (a) $K^+(aq)$ and $CN^-(aq)$, (b) $Na^+(aq)$ and $ClO_4^-(aq)$

page 123 $MgBr_2$, because it leads to ions in solution.

page 127 Yes, the Na^+ ion. It appears both a reactant and a product in the same state and does change to form a new substance.

page 129 Three. Each COOH group will partially ionize in water to form $H^+(aq)$.

page 130 HBr

page 135 $SO_2(g)$

page 137 (a) Ne, (b) 0

page 142 $Ni^{2+}(aq)$. In Table 4.5 the ease of reduction of ions increases down the table.

page 144 1.00×10^{-2} M solution of sucrose is more concentrated; that is, it has the larger value of molarity. The smaller the value of x in 10^{-x}, the larger the value of 10^{-x}.

page 148 The molarity decreases to 0.25 M. Molarity is directly proportional to the number of moles of solute (not changed) and inversely proportional to the volume of the solution in liters. Doubling the volume changes moles/V to moles/$2V$ and the molarity is reduced by one half.

page 150 12.50 mL. The stoichiometry of the reaction between HBr and NaOH shows a 1 : 1 mole ratio. The given concentration of NaOH is twice that of HBr and, thus, a given volume of NaOH contains twice as many moles of solute than an equivalent volume of HBr. Therefore, the volume of NaOH required to reach the equivalence point is half of the original volume of HBr.

Chapter 5

page 167 (a) kinetic energy, (b) potential energy, (c) heat, (d) work

page 168 Open system. Humans exchange matter and energy with their surroundings.

page 171

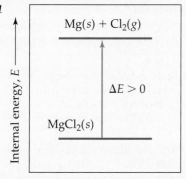

page 172 Endothermic. In Figure 5.5, the final state has a higher internal energy than the initial state and this is a characteristic of an endothermic process. Also, the figure shows $\Delta E > 0$ which means energy flows into the system from the surroundings.

page 173 The balance (current state) does not depend on the ways the money may have been transferred into the account or on the particular expenditures made in withdrawing money from the account. It depends only on the net total of all the transactions.

page 175 (top) No. If ΔV is zero then the expression $w = -P\Delta V$ is also zero.

page 175 (bottom) It provides us with a state function that allows us to focus on heat flow, which is easier to measure than the work that accompanies a process.

page 178 The coefficients indicate the numbers of moles of reactants and products that give rise to the stated enthalpy change.

page 181 Hg(l). Rearranging equation 5.22 gives $\Delta T = \dfrac{q}{C_s \times m}$. When q and m are constant for a series of substances then $\Delta T = \dfrac{constant}{C_s}$. Therefore, the element with the smallest C_s in Table 5.2 has the largest ΔT, Hg(l).

page 182 (a) The energy lost by a system is gained by its surroundings. (b) $q_{system} = -q_{surroundings}$

page 186 (a) The sign of ΔH changes. (b) The magnitude of ΔH doubles.

page 189 $2\,C(s) + H_2(g) \longrightarrow C_2H_2(g)$ $\Delta H_f^\circ = 226.7$ kJ

page 194 Fats, because they have the largest fuel value of the three.

Chapter 6

page 215 No. Both visible light and X-rays are forms of electromagnetic radiation. They therefore both travel at the speed of light, c. The differing ability to penetrate skin is due to the different energies of visible light and X-rays, which we will discuss in the next section.

page 216 As temperature increases, the average energy of the emitted radiation increases. Blue-white light is at the short end of the visible spectrum (at about 400 nm), whereas red light is closer to the other end of the visible spectrum (about 700 nm). Thus, the blue-white light has a higher

frequency, is more energetic, and is consistent with higher temperatures.

page 218 Ultraviolet. Figure 6.4 shows that a photon in the ultraviolet region of electromagnetic radiation has a higher frequency and greater energy than a photon in the infrared.

page 220 According to the third postulate, photons of only certain allowed frequencies can be absorbed or emitted as the electron changes energy state. The lines in the spectrum correspond to the allowed frequencies.

page 221 Absorb, because it is moving from a lower-energy state ($n = 3$) to a higher-energy state ($n = 7$).

page 223 Yes, all moving objects produce matter waves, but the wavelengths associated with macroscopic objects, such as the baseball, are too small to allow for any way of observing them.

page 224 The small size and mass of a subatomic particle. The term $h/4\pi$ in the uncertainty principle is a very small number that becomes important only when considering extremely small objects, such as electrons.

page 226 Yes, there is a difference. The first statement says that the electron's position is known exactly, which violates the uncertainty principle. The second statement says that there is a high probability of where the electron is, but there is still uncertainty in its position.

page 227 Bohr proposed that the electron in the hydrogen atom moves in a well-defined circular orbit about the nucleus, which violates the uncertainty principle. An orbital is a wave function that gives the probability of finding the electron at any point in space, in accord with the uncertainty principle.

page 228 The energy of an orbital is proportional to $-1/n^2$. The difference between $-1/(2)^2$ and $-1/(1)^2$ is much greater than the difference between $-1/(3)^2$ and $-1/(2)^2$.

page 230 The radial probability function for the $4s$ orbital will have four maxima and three nodes.

page 232 The probability of finding the electron when it is in this p orbital is greater in the interior of the lobe than on the edges, which corresponds to changes in intensity of the pink color.

page 233 No. We know that the $4s$ orbital is higher in energy than the $3s$ orbital. Likewise, we know that the $3d$ orbitals are higher in energy than the $3s$ orbital. But, without more information, we do not know whether the $4s$ orbital is higher or lower in energy than the $3d$ orbitals.

page 239 The $6s$ orbital, which starts to hold electrons at element 55, Cs.

page 243 We can't conclude anything! Each of the three elements has a different valence electron configuration for its nd and $(n + 1)s$ subshells: For Ni, $3d^84s^2$; for Pd, $4d^{10}$; and for Pt, $5d^96s^1$.

Chapter 7

page 257 The atomic number of an element depends on the number of protons in the nucleus, whereas the atomic weight depends (mainly) on the number of protons and the number of neutrons in the nucleus. Another example: Co has a lower atomic number (27) than that of Ni (28) but Co has a larger atomic weight (58.933 amu) than that of Ni (58.693 amu).

page 259 The $2p$ electron of an Ne atom experiences a greater Z_{eff}. The atomic number of Na is greater than that of Ne, but an electron in the $3s$ orbital of Na is farther from the nucleus and therefore more screened than is an electron in the $2p$ orbital of Ne.

page 262 The trends work against each other. Atomic radii tend to increase down a column in the periodic table. Atomic radius is determined by the distribution of the electrons in an atom and the volume they occupy in space. The effective nuclear charge experienced by outer electrons increases slightly down a column and this would tend to reduce orbital "size" and determines the trend in atomic radii of atoms in a column.

page 266 (top) The process in [7.4] requires energy with a shorter wavelength. The second ionization energy is associated with the process in [7.4] and it is a greater endothermic quantity than the first ionization energy associated with the process in [7.3]. An inverse relationship exists between energy of electromagnetic radiation and wavelength: the larger the energy, the smaller the wavelength.

page 266 (bottom) I_2 for a carbon atom. In each process an electron is being removed from an atom or ion with five electrons, either $B(g)$ or $C^+(g)$. The higher nuclear charge of the carbon nucleus makes I_2 for carbon greater than I_1 for boron.

page 269 The same: $[Ar]3d^3$. The $4s$ electrons are removed before the $3d$ electrons in forming transition metal ions.

page 271 The first ionization energy of $Cl^-(g)$ is the energy needed to remove an electron from Cl^-, forming $Cl(g) + e^-$. That is the reverse process of Equation 7.6, so the first ionization energy of $Cl^-(g)$ is +349 kJ/mol.

page 273 In general, increasing ionization energy correlates with decreasing metallic character.

page 275 Molecular, because it has a relatively low melting point. P, because it is a nonmetallic element.

page 278 Cs has the lowest ionization energy among the alkali metals.

page 281 Gastric fluids in the stomach are very acidic (see the "Chemistry at Work" box on antacids in Section 4.3). Metal carbonates are soluble in acidic solution, where they react with the acid to form $CO_2(g)$ and soluble salts, as in Equations 4.19 and 4.20.

page 284 We can extrapolate the data in the table to make intelligent guesses for these numbers. Notice that the atomic radii increase by 0.15 Å and 0.19 Å, respectively, from Cl to Br and from Br to I. We might therefore expect an increase of 0.15–0.2 Å from I to At, leading to an estimate of roughly 1.5 Å for the atomic radius of At. Similarly, we might expect I_1 for At to be about 900 kJ/mol.

Chapter 8

page 299 No. Cl has seven valence electrons. The first and second Lewis symbols are both correct—they both show seven valence electrons, and it doesn't matter which of the four sides has the single electron. The third symbol shows only five electrons and is incorrect.

page 301 (top) CaO is an ionic compound consisting of Ca^{2+} and O^{2-} ions. When Ca and O_2 react to form CaO, two Ca atoms lose two electrons each to form two Ca^{2+} ions and each oxygen atom in O_2 takes up two electrons to form two O^{2-} ions. Thus, we can say that each Ca atom transfers two electrons to each oxygen atom.

page 301 (bottom) No. Figure 7.11 shows that the alkali metal with the smallest first ionization energy is Cs with a value of +376 kJ/mol. Figure 7.12 shows that the halogen with the largest electron affinity is Cl with a value of −349 kJ/mol. The sum of the two energies gives a positive energy (endothermic). Therefore, all other combinations of alkali metals with halogens will also have positive values.

page 305 (top) Palladium, Pd

page 305 (bottom) Weaker. In both H_2 and H_2^+ the two H atoms are principally held together by the electrostatic attractions between the nuclei and the electron(s) concentrated between them. H_2^+ has only one electron between the nuclei whereas H_2 has two and this results in the H—H bond in H_2 being stronger.

page 307 Triple bond. CO_2 has two C—O double bonds. Because the C—O bond in carbon monoxide is shorter, it is likely to be a triple bond.

page 308 Electron affinity measures the energy released when an isolated atom gains an electron to form a 1− ion. The electronegativity measures the ability of the atom to hold on to its own electrons and attract electrons from other atoms in compounds.

page 309 Polar covalent. The difference in electronegativity between N and Si is 3.0 − 1.8 = 1.2. Based on the examples of F_2, HF, and LiF, the difference in electronegativity is great enough to introduce some polarity to the bond, but not sufficient to cause a complete electron transfer from one atom to the other.

page 311 IF. Because the difference in electronegativity between I and F is greater than that between Cl and F, the magnitude of Q should be greater for IF. In addition, because I has a larger atomic radius than Cl, the bond length in IF is longer than that in ClF. Thus, both Q and r are larger for IF, and therefore $\mu = Qr$ will be larger for IF.

page 312 Smaller dipole moment for C—H. The magnitude of Q should be similar for C—H and H—I bonds because the difference in electronegativity for each bond is 0.4. The C—H bond length is 1.1 Å and the H—I bond length is 1.6 Å. Therefore $\mu = Qr$ will be greater for H—I because it has a larger bond length (larger r).

page 314 OsO_4. The data suggests that the yellow substance is a molecular species with its low melting and boiling points. Os in OsO_4 has an oxidation number of +8 and Cr in Cr_2O_3 has an oxidation number of +3. In Section 8.4, we learn that a compound with a metal in a high oxidation state should show a high degree of covalence and OsO_4 fits this situation.

page 317 There is probably a better choice of Lewis structure than the one chosen. Because the formal charges must add up to 0 and the formal charge on the F atom is +1, there must be an atom that has a formal charge of −1. Because F is the most electronegative element, we don't expect it to carry a positive formal charge.

page 319 Yes. There are two resonance structures for ozone that each contribute equally to the overall description of the molecule. Each O—O bond is therefore an average of a single bond and a double bond, which is a "one-and-a-half" bond.

page 320 As "one-and-a-third" bonds. There are three resonance structures, and each of the three N—O bonds is single in two of those structures and double in the third. Each bond in the actual ion is an average of these: $(1 + 1 + 2)/3 = 1\frac{1}{3}$.

page 321 No, it will not have multiple resonance structures. We can't "move" the double bonds, as we did in benzene, because the positions of the hydrogen atoms dictate specific positions for the double bonds. We can't write any other reasonable Lewis structures for the molecule.

page 322 The formal charge of each atom is shown below:

$$\ddot{N}\!=\!\ddot{O} \qquad \ddot{\ddot{N}}\!=\!\ddot{O}$$

F.C. 0   0   −1   +1

The first structure shows each atom with a zero formal charge and therefore it is the preferred Lewis structure. The second one shows a positive formal charge for an oxygen atom, which is a highly electronegative atom, and this is not a favorable situation.

page 325 The atomization of ethane produces $2\,C(g) + 6\,H(g)$. In this process, six C—H bonds and one C—C bond are broken. We can use $6D(C—H)$ to estimate the amount of enthalpy needed to break the six C—H bonds. The difference between that number and the enthalpy of atomization is an estimate of the bond enthalpy of the C—C bond, $D(C—C)$.

Chapter 9

page 344 (top) Octahedral. Removing two atoms that are opposite each other leads to a square planar geometry.

page 344 (bottom) The molecule does not follow the octet rule because it has ten electrons around the central A atom. There are four electron domains around A: two single bonds, one double bond, and one nonbonding pair.

page 349 Yes. Based on one resonance structure, we might expect the electron domain that is due to the double bond to "push" the domains that are due to the single bonds, leading to angles slightly different from 120°. However, we must remember that there are two other equivalent resonance structures—each of the three O atoms has a double bond to N in one of the three resonance structures (Section 8.6). Because of resonance, all three O atoms are equivalent, and they will experience the same amount of repulsion, which leads to bond angles equal to 120°.

page 351 A tetrahedral arrangement of electron domains is preferred because the bond angles are 109.5° compared to 90° bond angles in a square planar arrangement of electron domains. The larger bond angles result in smaller repulsions among electron domains and a more stable structure.

page 354 No. The C—O and C—S bond dipoles exactly oppose each other, like in CO_2, but because O and S have different electronegativities, the magnitudes of the bond dipoles will be different. As a consequence, the bond dipoles will not cancel each other and the OCS molecule has a nonzero dipole moment.

page 357 Decrease. Figure 9.15 shows the potential energy of the system increasing when the H—H bond length is shorter than the equilibrium H—H bond position. The equilibrium H—H bond length corresponds to the system in its lowest energy state and any other H—H bond lengths correspond to weaker H—H bond strengths.

page 358 (top) The three $2p$ orbitals are equivalent to one another; they differ only in their orientation. Thus, the two Be—F bonds would be equivalent to each other. Because p orbitals are perpendicular to one another, we would expect an F—Be—F bond angle of 90°. Experimentally, the bond angle is 180°.

page 358 (bottom) The unhybridized p orbital is oriented perpendicular to the plane defined by the three sp^2 hybrids (trigonal planar array of lobes), with one lobe on each side of the plane.

page 363 The molecule should not be linear. Because there are three electron domains around each N atom, we expect sp^2 hybridization and H—N—N angles of approximately 120°.

The molecule is expected to be planar; the unhybridized $2p$ orbitals on the N atoms can form a π bond only if all four atoms lie in the same plane. You might notice that there are two ways in which the H atoms can be arranged: They can be both on the same side of the N=N bond or on opposite sides of the N=N bond.

page 370 The molecule would fall apart. With one electron in the bonding MO and one in the antibonding MO, there is no net stabilization of the electrons relative to two separate H atoms.

page 372 Yes. In Be_2^+ there would be two electrons in the σ_{2s} MO but only one electron in the σ_{2s}^* MO, and therefore the ion is predicted to have a bond order of $\frac{1}{2}$. It should (and does) exist.

page 377 No. If the σ_{2p} MO were lower in energy than the π_{2p} MOs, we would expect the σ_{2p} MO to hold two electrons and the π_{2p} MOs to hold one electron each, with the same spin. The molecule would therefore be paramagnetic.

Chapter 10

page 395 The major reason is the relatively large distance between molecules of gases. Each molecule is acting almost independently from the other molecules.

page 396 The height of the column decreases because atmospheric pressure decreases with increasing altitude.

page 400 (top) As the pressure increases, the volume decreases. Doubling the pressure causes the volume to decrease to half its original value.

page 400 (bottom) The volume decreases, but it doesn't decrease to half because the volume is proportional to the temperature on the Kelvin scale but not on the Celsius scale.

page 403 Because 22.41 L is the volume of one mole of the gas at STP, it contains Avogadro's number of molecules, 6.022×10^{23}.

page 407 Because water has a lower molar mass (18.0 g/mol) than N_2 (28.0 g/mol), the water vapor is less dense. Note that density is proportional to the molar mass of a gas as shown in Equation 10.10.

page 410 According to Dalton's law of partial pressures, the pressure that is due to N_2 (its partial pressure) does not change. However, the total pressure that is due to the partial pressures of both N_2 and O_2 increases.

page 414 The average kinetic energies depend only on temperature and not on the identity of the gas. Thus, the trend in average kinetic energies is HCl (298 K) = H_2 (298 K) < O_2 (350 K).

page 415 Average speed: HCl < O_2 < H_2. The average kinetic energy (ε) of gas molecules in a sample is $\varepsilon = \frac{1}{2}m\mu^2$, where μ is the root mean square speed (rms) and m is the mass of a molecule. Rms is not the same as average speed, but it is very close. Thus, the rms of a sample of a gas is inversely proportional to the square root of m, $\mu = \sqrt{\dfrac{2}{m}\varepsilon}$.

The greater the mass of a gas particle, the smaller the rms, and average speed. At the same temperature, all gases have the same average kinetic energy and ε is a constant for the three gases. The gases are listed in order of increasing average speed (decreasing m).

page 420 (a) Mean free path decreases because the molecules are crowded closer together. (b) There is no effect. Although the molecules are moving faster at the higher temperature, they are not crowded any closer together.

page 421 (b) Gases deviate from ideality most at low temperatures and high pressures. Thus, the helium gas would deviate most from ideal behavior at 100 K (the lowest temperature listed) and 5 atm (the highest pressure listed).

page 422 The fact that real gases deviate from ideal behavior can be attributed to the finite sizes of the molecules and to the attractions that exist between molecules.

Chapter 11

page 439 (a) In a gas the energy of attraction is less than the average kinetic energy. (b) In a solid, the energy of attraction is greater than the average kinetic energy.

page 440 $Ca(NO_3)_2$ in water. CH_3OH is a molecular substance and a nonelectrolyte. When it dissolves in water, no ions are present. $Ca(NO_3)_2$ is an ionic compound and a strong electrolyte. When it dissolves in water, the Ca^{2+} ions and the NO_3^- ions interact with the polar water molecules by ion–dipole attractive forces.

page 441 The magnitude of the dipole–dipole force depends on both the magnitude of the dipoles and the distance between the dipoles. We cannot judge the distance from Table 11.2, but we see that acetonitrile has the largest dipole moment and the highest boiling point, suggesting that the dipole–dipole attractions are greatest for that substance.

page 442 (a) Polarizability increases in order of increasing molecular size and molecular weight: $CH_4 < CCl_4 < CBr_4$. (b) The strength of the dispersion forces follows the same order: $CH_4 < CCl_4 < CBr_4$.

page 446 For nearly all substances, the solid phase is more dense than the liquid phase. For water, however, the solid is less dense than the liquid.

page 448 (top) (a) Both viscosity and surface tension decrease with increasing temperature because of the increased molecular motion. (b) Both properties increase as the strength of intermolecular forces increases.

page 448 (bottom) The strengths of the cohesive and adhesive forces are equal.

page 450 Melting (or fusion), endothermic

page 455 CCl_4. Both compounds are nonpolar. Consequently, only dispersion forces exist between the molecules. Because dispersion forces are stronger for the larger, heavier CBr_4 than for CCl_4, CBr_4 has a lower vapor pressure than CCl_4. The substance with the larger vapor pressure at a given temperature is more volatile. Thus, CCl_4 is more volatile than CBr_4.

page 457 The line slopes to the right with increasing pressure because a liquid is more dense than a gas.

page 460 Crystalline solids melt at a specific temperature, whereas amorphous ones tend to melt over a temperature range.

page 461 Density is the mass of the unit cell in grams divided by the volume of the unit cell in cm^3. Calculate the total mass of the unit cell by summing the atomic masses (amu) of the net number of atoms contained within the unit cell. This mass is converted to grams using the equivalence of 1 gram equals 6.02×10^{23} amu. The volume of the unit cell is the length × width × height. Assuming a cubic unit cell, the length of an edge is cubed. Volume is converted to units of cm^3. Density is then calculated.

page 464 The higher the coordination number of the particles in a crystal, the greater the packing efficiency.

page 466 C_6H_6. Molecular solids are composed of molecules or nonmetal atoms. Because Co is a metal and K_2O is an ionic substance, they do not form molecular solids. C_6H_6, however, is a molecular substance and forms a molecular solid.

Chapter 12

page 502 Yes, the molecule has both the $—NH_2$ and $—COOH$ groups in it, which can react as in nylon to make a polymer.

page 503 Vinyl acetate interferes with intermolecular interactions between adjacent ethylene chains, and so reduces crystallinity and melting point.

Chapter 13

page 529 The lattice energy of NaCl(s) must be overcome to separate Na^+ and Cl^- ions and disperse them into a solvent. C_6H_{14} is a nonpolar hydrocarbon and C_6H_{14} molecules are held together by London dispersion forces. An ion is normally not attracted to a nonpolar molecule. (In some situations a weak ion-induced dipole interaction can exist.) Thus, the energy required to separate the ions in NaCl is not recovered in the form of ion–C_6H_{14} interactions and prevents NaCl from dissolving in C_6H_{14}.

page 531 **(a)** exothermic, **(b)** endothermic

page 532 No, because the AgCl is not dispersed throughout the liquid phase.

page 535 No. The concentration of sodium acetate is higher than the stable equilibrium value, so some of the dissolved solute comes out of solution when a seed crystal initiates the process. The concentration of sodium acetate eventually reaches its equilibrium value.

page 538 Considerably lower because there would no longer be hydrogen bonding with water.

page 541 Dissolved gases are less soluble as temperature increases and they begin to escape below the boiling point of water. Also, adsorbed oxygen on the surface of the cooking pot begins to escape with increasing temperature.

page 542 230 ppm (1 ppm is 1 part in 10^6). 2.30×10^5 ppb (1 ppb is 1 part in 10^9).

page 544 For dilute solutions the two concentration units are approximately the same numerically. Molarity is the number of moles of solute per liter of solution. Molality is the number of moles of solute per kilogram of solvent. In a liter of solution there will generally be less than 1 kg of water because the solute takes up some of the volume. However, in dilute solutions the two ratios are essentially the same.

page 547 NaCl. Raoult's law is $P_A = X_A P_A^\circ$. From this relationship we see that as the mole fraction of solvent, X_A, decreases (increasing mole fraction of solute), the partial pressure exerted by the solvent vapor, P_A, decreases. The solute with the greater mole fraction will cause a larger reduction in P_A. When 1 mole of NaCl dissolves in water it forms one mole each of Na^+ and Cl^- ions whereas 1 mole of $C_6H_{12}O_6$ does not dissociate because it is a nonelectrolyte. Thus, the mole fraction of NaCl is twice that of $C_6H_{12}O_6$ and the NaCl solution has a greater vapor pressure lowering. A useful relationship can be derived from Raoult's law: $\Delta P_A = X_B P_A^\circ$ where ΔP_A is the vapor pressure lowering of the solvent and X_B is the mole fraction of solute.

page 548 P_A° is the vapor pressure of pure solvent and P_A is the vapor pressure of the solvent when a solute is present.

page 549 Not necessarily; if the solute dissociates into particles, it could have a lower molality and still cause an increase of 0.51 °C. The total molality of all the particles in the solution is 1 m.

page 553 The 0.20 *m* solution is hypotonic with respect to the 0.5 *m* solution. A hypotonic solution has the lower osmotic pressure of two solutions.

page 555 They would have the same osmotic pressure because they would have the same total concentration of dissolved particles.

page 558 The smaller droplets carry negative charges because of the embedded stearate ions and thus repel one another.

Chapter 14

page 575 Increasing the partial pressure of a gas increases the number of gas molecules in a given volume and therefore increases the concentration of the gas. Rates normally increase with increasing reactant concentrations.

page 577 The rate of a reaction is measured by the change in concentration of a reactant in a given unit of time. As a reaction proceeds, the concentration of a reactant decreases. As the concentration of a reactant decreases, the frequency with which the reactant particles collide with one another decreases, resulting in a smaller change in reactant concentration, and thus a decreased reaction rate.

page 578 The size of the triangle is mostly a matter of convenience. Drawing a larger triangle will give larger values of both $\Delta[C_4H_9Cl]$ and Δt, but their ratio, $\Delta[C_4H_9Cl]/\Delta t$, remains constant. Thus, the calculated slope is independent of the size of the triangle.

page 581 (a) The rate law for any chemical reaction is the equation that relates the concentrations of reactants to the rate of the reaction. The general form for a rate law is given in Equation 14.7. (b) The quantity *k* in any rate law is the rate constant.

page 582 (a) The rate law is second order in NO, first order in H_2, and third order overall. (b) No. Doubling [NO] will cause the rate to increase fourfold, whereas doubling [H_2] will merely double the rate.

page 587 In (a) the intercept is the initial partial pressure of the CH_3NC, 150 torr. In (b) it is the natural logarithm of this pressure, $\ln(150) = 5.01$.

page 590 As the reaction proceeds, the concentration of the reactant decreases. At the end of each half-life the substance loses half of its initial amount at the start of each half-life. At the end of the first half-life, the substance loses 5.0 g and 5.0 g remains. At the end of the second half-life, 2.5 g remains, and at the end of the third half-life, 1.3 g remains (rounded value). In general, the amount of a substance remaining after *n* half-lives, is: (initial amount)$\left(\frac{1}{2^n}\right)$.

page 591 According to Equation 14.17 the half-life of a second order reaction depends inversely on the concentration of the reactant at the start of each half-life reaction. At the end of each half-life the concentration of the reactant is reduced and thus the half-life is larger for the next half-life reaction. That is, the half-life of a second-order reaction increases during the course of the reaction.

page 592 Molecules must collide in order to react.

page 594 The molecules must not merely collide in order to react, but they must collide in the proper orientation and with an energy greater than the activation energy for the reaction.

page 598 Because the elementary reaction involves two molecules, it is bimolecular.

page 601 The rate law depends not on the overall reaction, but on the slowest step in the mechanism.

page 606 Generally, a catalyst lowers the activation energy by providing a different, lower-energy pathway (different mechanism) for a reaction.

page 608 A heterogeneous catalyst is more easily removed. A heterogeneous catalyst is in a different phase from the reactants and therefore a heterogeneous mixture exists. Typically a heterogeneous catalyst is a solid and the reactants are either in a liquid or gas phase. A heterogeneous catalyst is identifiable as a separate phase in the mixture and an experimental method, such as filtration, can be designed to remove it. In a homogenous mixture, a one phase system, the catalyst is uniformly dispersed throughout the mixture, and its identification and removal is a more complex process.

page 610 (a) active site, (b) substrate

Chapter 15

page 630 (top) (a) The rates of opposing reactions are equal. (b) If the forward step is faster than the reverse step, $k_f > k_r$ and the constant, which equals k_f/k_r, will be greater than 1.

page 630 (bottom) The fact that concentrations no longer change with time indicates that equilibrium has been reached.

page 633 (top) It is independent of the starting concentrations of reactants and products.

page 633 (bottom) They represent equilibrium constants. K_c is obtained when equilibrium concentrations expressed in molarity are substituted into the equilibrium-constant expression. K_p is obtained when equilibrium partial pressures expressed in atmospheres are substituted into the expression.

page 635 $0.00140\ M/1\ M = 0.00140$ (no units)

page 638 Because the coefficients in the equation have been multiplied by 3, the exponents in K_p are also multiplied by 3, so that the magnitude of the equilibrium constant will be $(K_p)^3$.

page 639 Because the pure H_2O liquid is omitted from the equilibrium-constant expression, $K_p = P_{H_2O}$. Thus, at any particular temperature, the equilibrium vapor pressure is a constant.

page 641 $K_c = \dfrac{[NH_4^+][OH^-]}{[NH_3]}$. Water is the solvent and is excluded from the equilibrium-constant expression.

page 649 (a) The equilibrium shifts to the right, using up some of the added O_2 and forming NO_2. (b) The equilibrium shifts to the left, forming more NO to replace some of the NO that was removed.

page 650 Increasing the volume of the system decreases the total gas pressure. The system is no longer at equilibrium and it responds to this stress by favoring the side of the equilibrium which counteracts the effect of the change. The total gas pressure is directly related to the total number of gas molecules in the system. Because there are three gas molecules on the left in the equation and only two on the right, the equilibrium position shifts to the left. This change increases the total number of gas molecules by converting SO_3 into SO_2 and O_2 and also increases the total gas pressure until equilibrium is restored.

page 652 Evaporation is an endothermic process. Increasing the temperature of an endothermic process shifts the equilibrium to the right, forming more product. Because the product of the evaporation is the vapor, the vapor pressure increases.

page 655 No; catalysts have no effect on the position of an equilibrium, although they do affect how quickly equilibrium is reached.

Chapter 16

page 668 The H^+ ion for acids and the OH^- ion for bases.

page 670 NH_3 is the base because it accepts a H^+ from HSO_4^- as the reaction moves from the left side of the equation to the right side.

page 672 HNO_3 is a strong acid, which means that NO_3^- has negligible basicity. In most questions involving the conjugate base of a strong acid we assume it does affect the concentration of hydrogen or hydroxide ions of a solution.

page 676 (a) The solution is neutral, $[H^+] = [OH^-]$. (b) The pH increases as $[OH^-]$ increases.

page 678 (top) pH = 14.00 − 3.00 = 11.00. The solution is basic because pH > 7.

page 678 (bottom) From Figure 16.7, we see that the pH must be above about 8, meaning that the solution is basic.

page 681 Because CH_3^- is the conjugate base of a substance that has negligible acidity, CH_3^- must be a strong base. Bases stronger than OH^- abstract H^+ from water molecules: $CH_3^- + H_2O \longrightarrow CH_4 + OH^-$.

page 685 Because weak acids typically undergo very little ionization, often less than 1%. Normally we make the assumption and then check its validity based on the concentration of conjugate based formed in the calculation. If it is ≤5% of the initial concentration of the weak acid, we will use the assumption. If not, we have to do an exact calculation.

page 688 This is the acid-dissociation constant for the loss of the third and final proton from H_3PO_4: $HPO_4^{2-}(aq) \rightleftharpoons H^+(aq) + PO_4^{3-}(aq)$.

page 696 Because the NO_3^- ion is the conjugate base of a strong acid, it will not affect pH. (NO_3^- has negligible basicity.) Because the CO_3^{2-} ion is the conjugate base of a weak acid, it will affect pH, increasing the pH.

page 697 K^+, an alkali metal cation, does not affect pH. Most transition metal ions with a 2+ charge or higher form acidic solutions.

page 700 The increasing acidity down a column is due mainly to decreasing H—X bond strength. The trend across a period is due mainly to the increasing electronegativity of X, which weakens the H—X bond.

page 703 The carboxyl group, —COOH.

page 704 It must have an unshared pair of electrons which can be shared with another atom.

page 706 Fe^{3+}, because it has the highest charge. The ratio $\dfrac{Z_+}{r_+}$

is an indicator we can use to compare relative abilities of cations to form acidic solutions. The greater the ratio for a cation, the greater is its tendency to react with water and form an acidic solution. Note that a large radius and a small positive charge for an ion, such as for Na^+, results in a low value for the ratio. Na^+ exhibits no reaction with water to form an acidic solution. Fe^{3+} has a large charge and a relatively small ion size; thus, it will have a high value for the ratio.

Chapter 17

page 723 (top) (a) $[NH_4^+] = 0.10$ M; $[Cl^-] = 0.10$ M; $[NH_3] = 0.12$ M. (b) Cl^-, (c) Equation 17.2.

page 723 (bottom) HNO_3 and NO_3^-. This is a strong acid and its conjugate base. Buffers are composed of weak acids and their conjugate bases. The NO_3^- ion is merely a spectator in any acid–base chemistry and is therefore ineffective in helping control the pH of a solution.

page 724 (a) The OH^- of NaOH (a strong base) reacts with the acid member of the buffer ($HC_2H_3O_2$), abstracting a proton. Thus, $[HC_2H_3O_2]$ decreases and $[C_2H_3O_2^-]$ increases. (b) The H^+ of HCl (a strong acid) reacts with the base member of the buffer ($C_2H_3O_2^-$). Thus, $[C_2H_3O_2^-]$ decreases and $[HC_2H_3O_2]$ increases.

page 727 The solution will most effectively resist a change in either direction when its pH = pK_a. Thus, the optimal pH is pH = pK_a = $-\log(1.8 \times 10^{-5})$ = 4.74, and the pH range of the buffer is about 4.7 ± 1.

page 730 pH increases. When NaOH, the titrant, is added to the HCl solution, a strong acid-strong base neutralization reaction occurs. The amount of hydrogen ion decreases and pH increases.

page 733 pH = 7. The neutralization of a strong acid and a strong base at the equivalence point gives a solution of a salt and water. The salt contains ions which do not change the pH of water.

page 737 (top) The nearly vertical part of the titration curve at the equivalence point is smaller for the weak acid–strong base titration, and fewer indicators undergo their color change within this narrow range.

page 737 (bottom) The following titration curve shows the titration of 25 mL of Na_2CO_3 with HCl, both with 0.1 M concentrations. The overall reaction between the two is

$$Na_2CO_3(aq) + 2 HCl(aq) \longrightarrow 2 NaCl(aq) + CO_2(g) + H_2O(l)$$

The initial pH [sodium carbonate in water only] is near 11 because CO_3^{2-} is a weak base in water. The graph shows two equivalence points, **A** and **B**. The first point, **A**, is reached at a pH of about 9:

$$Na_2CO_3(aq) + HCl(aq) \longrightarrow NaCl(aq) + NaHCO_3(aq)$$

HCO_3^- is weakly basic in water, and is a weaker base than the carbonate ion.

The second point, **B**, is reached at a pH of about 4:

$$NaHCO_3(aq) + HCl(aq) \longrightarrow NaCl(aq) + CO_2(g) + H_2O(l)$$

H_2CO_3, a weak acid, forms and decomposes to carbon dioxide and water.

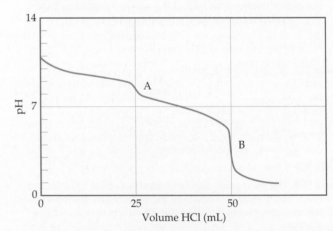

page 739 Because all three compounds produce the same number of ions, their relative solubilities correspond directly to their K_{sp} values, with the compound with the largest K_{sp} value being most soluble, AgCl.

page 750 They are insoluble in water but dissolve in the presence of either an acid or a base.

page 753 A high concentration of H_2S and a low concentration of H^+ (that is, high pH) will shift the equilibrium to the right, reducing $[Cu^{2+}]$.

page 754 The solution must contain one or more of the cations in group 1 of the qualitative analysis scheme shown in Figure 17.22: Ag^+, Pb^{2+}, or Hg_2^{2+}.

Chapter 18

page 773 It looks like the area of the upper curve to the left of the visible portion is about twice as large as the area of the lower curve. The upper curve corresponds to radiation at the "top" of the atmosphere, and the bottom curve corresponds to radiation at sea level; therefore, we estimate about half of the ultraviolet light that arrives at Earth from the Sun gets absorbed by the upper atmosphere and does not make it to the ground.

page 775 Atomic Cl is the catalyst. In Equation 18.6, atomic Cl is produced by the reaction of CFCs with solar radiation with wavelengths in the range of 190 to 225 nm. Atomic Cl is a catalyst for the overall reaction shown in Equation 18.10. The sequence of reactions above Equation 18.10 shows atomic Cl reacting and reforming, which is characteristic of a catalyst.

page 778 SO_2 in the atmosphere reacts with oxygen to form SO_3. SO_3 reacts with water in the atmosphere to form H_2SO_4. Air containing sulfuric acid is referred to as "acid rain" because the presence of sulfuric acid lowers the pH to about 4.

page 780 Equation 18.13

page 783 The higher the humidity of air, the higher the quantity of water vapor in the atmosphere. Water vapor absorbs infrared radiation and at night it radiates part of the absorbed infrared energy back to the surface of the Earth. This warms the surface and helps to reduce cooling at night.

page 786 Biodegradable organic materials consume oxygen in water. A decrease in oxygen concentration in water stored in a closed container over five days shows a significant presence of these materials.

page 790 As with so many other things, there are trade-offs in selecting processes for green chemistry. Yes, increasing CO_2 is expected to lead to global warming; however, the main source of CO_2 is from combustion of fossil fuels. If we can reduce the amount of CO_2 entering the atmosphere from that source, perhaps we can afford to use supercritical or liquid CO_2 in industrial processes, which are safer for workers than other chemicals and form less harmful by-products. Supercritical (or just liquid) water would be a better choice environmentally if the industrial process you want to change still works with water as a solvent.

Chapter 19

page 804 No, nonspontaneous processes can occur so long as they receive some continuous outside assistance. Examples of nonspontaneous processes with which we may be familiar include the building of a brick wall and the electrolysis of water to form hydrogen gas and oxygen gas.

page 805 No. Just because the system is restored to its original condition doesn't mean that the surroundings have likewise been restored to their original condition.

page 807 ΔS depends not merely on q but on q_{rev}. Although there are many possible paths that could take a system from its initial to final state, there is always only one reversible isothermal path between two states. Thus, ΔS has only one particular value regardless of the path taken between states.

page 809 Because rusting is a spontaneous process, ΔS_{univ} must be positive. Therefore the entropy of the surroundings must increase, and that increase must be larger than the entropy decrease of the system.

page 810 A molecule can vibrate (atoms moving relative to one another) and rotate (tumble), whereas a single atom cannot undergo these motions.

page 811 $S = 0$, based on Equation 19.5 and the fact that $\ln 1 = 0$.

page 817 It must be a perfect crystal at 0 K (third law of thermodynamics), which means it has only a single accessible microstate.

page 819 Depends on whether the system is open, closed, or isolated. For an open or closed system, ΔS_{surr} always increases. The change in entropy of the surroundings in an isothermal process is $\Delta S_{surr} = \dfrac{-q_{sys}}{T}$. The energy evolved by an open or closed system is transferred to the surroundings and $-q_{sys}$ is a positive number. Thus ΔS_{surr} is a positive number and the entropy of the surroundings increases. If it is an isolated system, then energy is not transferred to the surroundings and the entropy of the surroundings does not change.

page 820 In any spontaneous process the entropy of the universe increases. In any spontaneous process operating at constant temperature, the free energy of the system decreases.

page 822 It indicates that the process to which the thermodynamic quantity refers has taken place under standard conditions, as summarized in Table 19.3.

page 825 Above the boiling point, vaporization is spontaneous, and $\Delta G < 0$. Therefore, $\Delta H - T\Delta S < 0$, and $\Delta H < T\Delta S$.

Chapter 20

page 845 Oxygen is first assigned a -2 oxidation number. Nitrogen must have a $+3$ oxidation number for the sum of oxidation numbers to equal -1, the charge of the ion.

page 848 No. Electrons should appear in the two half-reactions but cancel when the half-reactions are added properly. That is, the oxidation half-reaction and the reduction half-reaction must show the same number of electrons, but on different sides of the arrow. The electrons cancel when the two half-reactions are added. So, when you are balancing a redox equation and find yourself with e^-'s on either side of the reaction arrow when you are done, you know you should go back and check your work.

page 853 The anode is where oxidation takes place. Because electrons are being removed from the anode, negatively charged anions must migrate to the anode to maintain charge balance.

page 854 The zinc atoms on the surface lose two electrons, forming Zn^{2+} ions, which leave and go into the solution. The surface of the electrode becomes pitted and the size of the electrode diminishes as the reaction proceeds.

page 855 Yes. A redox reaction in a cell with a positive potential is spontaneous.

page 858 1 atm pressure of $Cl_2(g)$ and 1 M solution of $Cl^-(aq)$.

page 859 True. $E°_{cell} = E°_{red}$ (cathode) $- E°_{red}$ (anode) for a cell at standard-state conditions. $E°_{cell}$ is a measure of the net driving force for the overall redox reaction; thus, the smaller the number, the smaller is the net driving force for the overall redox reaction.

page 863 Pb(s) is stronger because it lies above Hg(l) in the activity series, which means that it more readily loses electrons.

page 876 Al, Zn. Both are easier to oxidize than Fe.

Chapter 21

page 895 The mass number decreases by 4.

page 897 Only the neutron, as it is the only neutral particle listed.

page 898 From Figure 21.2, we see that the center of the belt of stability for a nucleus containing 70 protons lies at about 102 neutrons.

page 903 Particle accelerators are designed to accelerate particles with a charge. Normal particle accelerators cannot accelerate neutrons, which are not charged particles. Fast-moving neutrons are typically formed by high-energy protons crashing into a nucleus, resulting in the emission of a number of fast-moving particles, including neutrons.

page 906 (top) Spontaneous radioactive decay is a unimolecular process: A $\longrightarrow$ Products. The rate law that fits this observation is a first-order kinetic rate law, rate = k[A]. A second-order kinetic process has rate = k[A]^2 and the elementary reaction is bimolecular: A + A $\longrightarrow$ Products. A zero-order kinetic process has rate = k, and the rate does not change until the limiting reactant is entirely consumed. The latter two rate laws do not fit a unimolecular process.

page 906 (bottom) (a) Yes; doubling the mass would double the amount of radioactivity of the sample as shown in equation 21.18. (b) No; changing the mass would not change the half-life as shown in equation 21.20.

page 909 No. Alpha particles are more readily absorbed by matter than beta or gamma rays. Geiger counters must be calibrated for the radiation they are being used to detect.

page 913 No. Stable nuclei having mass numbers around 100 are the most stable nuclei. They could not form a still more stable nucleus with an accompanying release of energy.

Chapter 22

page 933 No. Phosphorus, being a third-row element, does not have a capacity for forming strong π bonds. Instead, it exists as a solid in which the phosphorus atoms are singly bonded to one another.

page 938 No. As shown in Figure 22.7, the free energy of formation of H$_2$Se(g) is positive, indicating that the equilibrium constant for the reaction will be small. (Section 19.7)

page 943 NaBrO$_3$ and NaClO$_3$ should be strong oxidizing agents because the halogen in each is in the +5 oxidation state and readily reducible to a lower oxidation state such as 0 or −1. In the Appendix, we find the standard reduction potential in acid solution for BrO$_3^-$ is +1.52 V and for ClO$_3^-$ it is +1.47 V. At standard state conditions, the bromate ion is a slightly better oxidizing agent than the chlorate ion.

page 946 HIO$_3$. Note that the iodine remains in the +5 oxidation state.

page 951 No; the oxidation number of sulfur is the same in both reactants and products.

page 956 The nitrogen atom in nitric acid has an oxidation number of +5 and that in nitrous acid has an oxidation number of +3.

page 963 MgCO$_3$(s). The bicarbonate ion of washing soda ionizes to form a proton and CO$_3^{2-}$ ion. Mg^{2+} reacts with CO$_3^{2-}$ to precipitate MgCO$_3$

Chapter 23

page 984 No. CaO contains a metal which is too active to be reduced with CO. Yes. Ag$_2$O should reduce readily with CO because Ag is not an active metal.

page 987 Gold is the reducing agent, oxidized from 0 to +1 oxidation state. Dissolved oxygen is the oxidizing agent, reduced from 0 to −2 oxidation state.

page 988 Al$_2$O$_3$

page 989 Na$^+$ and Cl$^-$

page 990 Ionic conductivity. Charles Hall needed an ionic salt that melted to form a conducting medium, dissolved aluminum oxide and did not interfere with electrolysis. Ions move toward the anode and cathode in the molten salt solution and electrons in the outer circuit of the cell.

page 991 Cu^{2+} and H$^+$ as cations, and SO$_4^{2-}$ as the anion

page 995 Hg. Hg has more valence electron per atom than W and also lies to the right of the elements in the middle of the transition columns. Thus, Hg has more antibonding orbitals occupied. W is to the left of the elements in middle and has no antibonding orbitals occupied. Hg, with antibonding orbitals occupied, should have weaker bonding between atoms compared to the bonding structure in W. Hg is a liquid at room temperature and has a melting point of −38.8 °C and W is a solid at room temperature and has a melting point of 3422 °C.

page 997 Interstitial, because B is so much smaller than Pd.

page 999 Cr has a smaller bonding atomic radius than Mn as shown in Table 23.4. From Figure 23.19, we see in the group 7B metals that the elements of the third series have greater bonding atomic radii than those of the first series. Therefore, Re, which is in the third series, is larger than either Cr or Mn. Cr has the smallest bonding atomic radius.

page 1002 Yes. From Section 6.9 we expect Cr to have an outer $4s^2 3d^4$ valence electron configuration and Cr^{3+} to have a $3d^3$ configuration. Cr^{3+} would possess three unpaired electrons. Note: even if we wrote $4s^2 3d^1$ instead of $3d^3$ it would still have one unpaired electron.

Chapter 24

page 1016 [Fe(H$_2$O)$_6$]$^{3+}$(aq) + SCN$^-$(aq) $\longrightarrow$
[Fe(H$_2$O)$_5$ NCS]$^{2+}$(aq) + H$_2$O(l)

page 1018 (a) tetrahedral and square planar; (b) octahedral

page 1021 Each NH$_3$ has one donor atom. Consequently, the CO$_3^{2-}$ ion must have two donor atoms to give the cobalt atom a coordination number of 6. Thus, CO$_3^{2-}$ is acting as a bidentate ligand.

page 1023 The porphine ligand has conjugated double bonds which permit it to strongly absorb light in the visible region.

page 1031 The two compounds have the same composition and bonds, but they are optical isomers of each other (nonsuperimposable mirror images). The d isomer rotates plane-polarized light to the right (dextrorotatory), whereas the l isomer rotates plane-polarized light to the left (levorotatory).

page 1033 (a) [Ar]$4s^2 3d^7$, three unpaired electrons; (b) [Ar]$3d^6$, four unpaired electrons

page 1035 The d_{z^2} and $d_{x^2-y^2}$ orbitals

page 1036 The Ti(IV) ion has no *d* electrons, so there can be no *d-d* transitions, which are the ones usually responsible for the color of transition-metal compounds.

page 1039 The d_{xy} orbital, which has electron density in the *xy* plane, strongly interacts with the four ligands which are along the *x* and *y* axes. The d_{xz} and d_{yz} orbitals interact less strongly with the ligands in a tetrahedral complex compared to an octahedral complex because the two ligands along the vertical *z*-axis are removed. (Note that the two orbitals have a significant *z*-component of electron density.) These differences result in the d_{xy} orbital having a higher energy than that of the d_{xz} or d_{yz} orbitals.

Chapter 25

page 1053 C=N, because it is a polar double bond. C—H and C—C bonds are relatively unreactive.

page 1056 Two C—H bonds and two C—C bonds

page 1059 C_3H_7. The propyl group is formed by removing one hydrogen atom from propane, C_3H_8.

page 1063 Only two of the four possible C=C bond sites are distinctly different in a linear chain of five carbon atoms with one double bond.

page 1069

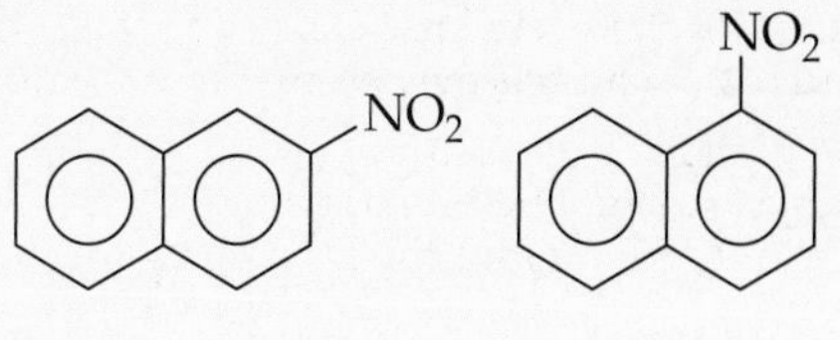

page 1074

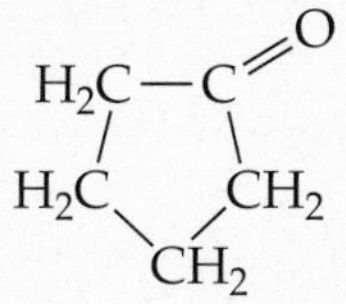

page 1079 All four groups must be different from one another.

page 1085 No. Breaking the hydrogen bonds between N—H and O=C groups in a protein by heating causes the α-helix structure to unwind and the β-sheet structure to separate.

page 1089 The α form of the C—O—C linkage. Glycogen serves as a source of energy in the body, which means that the body's enzymes must be able to hydrolyze it to sugars. The enzymes work only on polysaccharides having the α linkage.

Glossary

absorption spectrum A pattern of variation in the amount of light absorbed by a sample as a function of wavelength. (Section 24.5)

accuracy A measure of how closely individual measurements agree with the correct value. (Section 1.5)

acid A substance that is able to donate a H^+ ion (a proton) and hence increases the concentration of $H^+(aq)$ when it dissolves in water. (Section 4.3)

acid-dissociation constant (K_a) An equilibrium constant that expresses the extent to which an acid transfers a proton to solvent water. (Section 16.6)

acidic anhydride (acidic oxide) An oxide that forms an acid when added to water; soluble nonmetal oxides are acidic anhydrides. (Section 22.5)

acidic oxide (acidic anhydride) An oxide that either reacts with a base to form a salt or with water to form an acid. (Section 22.5)

acid rain Rainwater that has become excessively acidic because of absorption of pollutant oxides, notably SO_3, produced by human activities. (Section 18.4)

actinide element Element in which the $5f$ orbitals are only partially occupied. (Section 6.8)

activated complex (transition state) The particular arrangement of atoms found at the top of the potential-energy barrier as a reaction proceeds from reactants to products. (Section 14.5)

activation energy (E_a) The minimum energy needed for reaction; the height of the energy barrier to formation of products. (Section 14.5)

active site Specific site on a heterogeneous catalyst or an enzyme where catalysis occurs. (Section 14.7)

activity The decay rate of a radioactive material, generally expressed as the number of disintegrations per unit time. (Section 21.4)

activity series A list of metals in order of decreasing ease of oxidation. (Section 4.4)

addition polymerization Polymerization that occurs through coupling of monomers with one another, with no other products formed in the reaction. (Section 12.6)

addition reaction A reaction in which a reagent adds to the two carbon atoms of a carbon–carbon multiple bond. (Section 25.3)

adsorption The binding of molecules to a surface. (Section 14.7)

alcohol An organic compound obtained by substituting a hydroxyl group ($-OH$) for a hydrogen on a hydrocarbon. (Sections 2.9 and 25.4)

aldehyde An organic compound that contains a carbonyl group ($C=O$) to which at least one hydrogen atom is attached. (Section 25.4)

alkali metals Members of group 1A in the periodic table. (Section 7.7)

alkaline earth metals Members of group 2A in the periodic table. (Section 7.7)

alkanes Compounds of carbon and hydrogen containing only carbon–carbon single bonds. (Sections 2.9 and 25.2)

alkenes Hydrocarbons containing one or more carbon–carbon double bonds. (Section 25.2)

alkyl group A group that is formed by removing a hydrogen atom from an alkane. (Section 25.3)

alkynes Hydrocarbons containing one or more carbon–carbon triple bonds. (Section 25.2)

alloy A substance that has the characteristic properties of a metal and contains more than one element. Often there is one principal metallic component, with other elements present in smaller amounts. Alloys may be homogeneous or heterogeneous in nature. (Section 23.6)

alpha (α) helix A protein structure in which the protein is coiled in the form of a helix, with hydrogen bonds between $C=O$ and $N-H$ groups on adjacent turns. (Section 25.7)

alpha particles Particles that are identical to helium-4 nuclei, consisting of two protons and two neutrons, symbol ^4_2He or $^4_2\alpha$. (Section 21.1)

amide An organic compound that has an NR_2 group attached to a carbonyl. (Section 25.4)

amine A compound that has the general formula R_3N, where R may be H or a hydrocarbon group. (Section 16.7)

amino acid A carboxylic acid that contains an amino ($-NH_2$) group attached to the carbon atom adjacent to the carboxylic acid ($-COOH$) functional group. (Section 25.7)

amorphous solid A solid whose molecular arrangement lacks a regular, long-range pattern. (Section 11.7)

amphiprotic Refers to the capacity of a substance to either add or lose a proton (H^+). (Section 16.2)

amphoteric Capable of behaving as either an acid or a base. (Section 17.5)

amphoteric oxides and hydroxides Oxides and hydroxides that are only slightly soluble in water, but which dissolve on addition of either acid or base. (Section 17.5)

angstrom A common non-SI unit of length, denoted Å, that is used to measure atomic dimensions: $1 \text{ Å} = 10^{-10} \text{ m}$. (Section 2.3)

anion A negatively charged ion. (Section 2.7)

anode An electrode at which oxidation occurs. (Section 20.3)

antibonding molecular orbital A molecular orbital in which electron density is concentrated outside the region between the two nuclei of bonded atoms. Such orbitals, designated as σ^* or π^*, are less stable (of higher energy) than bonding molecular orbitals. (Section 9.7)

antiferromagnetism A form of magnetism in which unpaired electron spins on adjacent sites point in opposite directions and cancel each other's effects. (Section 23.8)

aqueous solution A solution in which water is the solvent. (Chapter 4: Introduction)

aromatic hydrocarbons Hydrocarbon compounds that contain a planar, cyclic arrangement of carbon atoms linked by both σ and delocalized π bonds. (Section 25.2)

Arrhenius equation An equation that relates the rate constant for a reaction to the frequency factor, A, the activation energy, E_a, and the temperature, T: $k = Ae^{-E_a/RT}$. In its logarithmic form it is written $\ln k = -E_a/RT + \ln A$. (Section 14.5)

atmosphere (atm) A unit of pressure equal to 760 torr; $1 \text{ atm} = 101.325 \text{ kPa}$. (Section 10.2)

atom The smallest representative particle of an element. (Sections 1.1 and 2.1)

atomic mass unit (amu) A unit based on the value of exactly 12 amu for the mass of the isotope of carbon that has six protons and six neutrons in the nucleus. (Sections 2.3 and 3.3)

atomic number The number of protons in the nucleus of an atom of an element. (Section 2.3)

atomic radius An estimate of the size of an atom. See **bonding atomic radius**. (Section 7.3)

atomic weight The average mass of the atoms of an element in atomic mass units (amu); it is numerically equal to the mass in grams of one mole of the element. (Section 2.4)

autoionization The process whereby water spontaneously forms low concentrations of $H^+(aq)$ and $OH^-(aq)$ ions by proton transfer from one water molecule to another. (Section 16.3)

Avogadro's hypothesis A statement that equal volumes of gases at the same temperature and pressure contain equal numbers of molecules. (Section 10.3)

Avogadro's law A statement that the volume of a gas maintained at constant temperature and pressure is directly proportional to the number of moles of the gas. (Section 10.3)

Avogadro's number The number of ^{12}C atoms in exactly 12 g of ^{12}C; it equals 6.022×10^{23}. (Section 3.4)

band An array of closely spaced molecular orbitals occupying a discrete range of energy. (Section 12.2)

band gap The energy gap between an occupied valence band and a vacant band called the conduction band. (Section 12.2)

bar A unit of pressure equal to 10^5 Pa. (Section 10.2)

base A substance that is an H^+ acceptor; a base produces an excess of $OH^-(aq)$ ions when it dissolves in water. (Section 4.3)

base-dissociation constant (K_b) An equilibrium constant that expresses the extent to which a base reacts with solvent water, accepting a proton and forming $OH^-(aq)$. (Section 16.7)

basic anhydride (basic oxide)   An oxide that forms a base when added to water; soluble metal oxides are basic anhydrides. (Section 22.5)

basic oxide (basic anhydride)   An oxide that either reacts with water to form a base or reacts with an acid to form a salt and water. (Section 22.5)

battery   A self-contained electrochemical power source that contains one or more voltaic cells. (Section 20.7)

Bayer process   A hydrometallurgical procedure for purifying bauxite in the recovery of aluminum from bauxite-containing ores. (Section 23.3)

becquerel   The SI unit of radioactivity. It corresponds to one nuclear disintegration per second. (Section 21.4)

Beer's law   The light absorbed by a substance (A) equals the product of its molar absorptivity constant (a), the path length through which the light passes (b), and the molar concentration of the substance (c): $A = abc$. (Section 14.2)

beta particles   Energetic electrons emitted from the nucleus, symbol $_{-1}^{0}e$. (Section 21.1)

beta sheet   A structural form of protein in which two stands of amino acids are hydrogen-bonded together in a zipperlike configuration. (Section 25.7)

bidentate ligand   A ligand in which two linked coordinating atoms are bound to a metal. (Section 24.2)

bimolecular reaction   An elementary reaction that involves two molecules. (Section 14.6)

biochemistry   The study of the chemistry of living systems. (Chapter 25: Introduction)

biocompatible   Any substance or material that can be compatibly placed within living systems. (Section 12.7)

biodegradable   Organic material that bacteria are able to oxidize. (Section 18.6)

biomaterial   Any material that has a biomedical application. (Section 12.7)

biopolymer   A polymeric molecule of high molecular weight found in living systems. The three major classes of biopolymers are proteins, carbohydrates, and nucleic acids. (Section 25.6)

body-centered cubic cell   A cubic unit cell in which the lattice points occur at the corners and at the center. (Section 11.7)

bomb calorimeter   A device for measuring the heat evolved in the combustion of a substance under constant-volume conditions. (Section 5.5)

bond angles   The angles made by the lines joining the nuclei of the atoms in a molecule. (Section 9.1)

bond dipole   The dipole moment that is due to unequal electron sharing between two atoms in a covalent bond. (Section 9.3)

bond enthalpy   The enthalpy change, ΔH, required to break a particular bond when the substance is in the gas phase. (Section 8.8)

bonding atomic radius   The radius of an atom as defined by the distances separating it from other atoms to which it is chemically bonded. (Section 7.3)

bonding molecular orbital   A molecular orbital in which the electron density is concentrated in the internuclear region. The energy of a bonding molecular orbital is lower than the energy of the separate atomic orbitals from which it forms. (Section 9.7)

bonding pair   In a Lewis structure a pair of electrons that is shared by two atoms. (Section 9.2)

bond length   The distance between the centers of two bonded atoms. (Section 8.8)

bond order   The number of bonding electron pairs shared between two atoms, minus the number of antibonding electron pairs: bond order = (number of bonding electrons − number of antibonding electrons)/2. (Section 9.7)

bond polarity   A measure of the degree to which the electrons are shared unequally between two atoms in a chemical bond. (Section 8.4)

boranes   Covalent hydrides of boron. (Section 22.11)

Born–Haber cycle   A thermodynamic cycle based on Hess's law that relates the lattice energy of an ionic substance to its enthalpy of formation and to other measurable quantities. (Section 8.2)

Boyle's law   A law stating that at constant temperature, the product of the volume and pressure of a given amount of gas is a constant. (Section 10.3)

Brønsted–Lowry acid   A substance (molecule or ion) that acts as a proton donor. (Section 16.2)

Brønsted–Lowry base   A substance (molecule or ion) that acts as a proton acceptor. (Section 16.2)

buffer capacity   The amount of acid or base a buffer can neutralize before the pH begins to change appreciably. (Section 17.2)

buffered solution (buffer)   A solution that undergoes a limited change in pH upon addition of a small amount of acid or base. (Section 17.2)

calcination   The heating of an ore to bring about its decomposition and the elimination of a volatile product. For example, a carbonate ore might be calcined to drive off CO_2. (Section 23.2)

calorie   A unit of energy, it is the amount of energy needed to raise the temperature of 1 g of water by 1 °C from 14.5 °C to 15.5 °C. A related unit is the joule: 1 cal = 4.184 J. (Section 5.1)

calorimeter   An apparatus that measures the evolution of heat. (Section 5.5)

calorimetry   The experimental measurement of heat produced in chemical and physical processes. (Section 5.5)

capillary action   The process by which a liquid rises in a tube because of a combination of adhesion to the walls of the tube and cohesion between liquid particles. (Section 11.3)

carbide   A binary compound of carbon with a metal or metalloid. (Section 22.9)

carbohydrates   A class of substances formed from polyhydroxy aldehydes or ketones. (Section 25.8)

carbon black   A microcrystalline form of carbon. (Section 22.9)

carbonyl group   The $C{=}O$ double bond, a characteristic feature of several organic functional groups, such as ketones and aldehydes. (Section 25.4)

carboxylic acid   A compound that contains the —COOH functional group. (Sections 16.10 and 25.4)

catalyst   A substance that changes the speed of a chemical reaction without itself undergoing a permanent chemical change in the process. (Section 14.7)

cathode   An electrode at which reduction occurs. (Section 20.3)

cathode rays   Streams of electrons that are produced when a high voltage is applied to electrodes in an evacuated tube. (Section 2.2)

cathodic protection   A means of protecting a metal against corrosion by making it the cathode in a voltaic cell. This can be achieved by attaching a more easily oxidized metal, which serves as an anode, to the metal to be protected. (Section 20.8)

cation   A positively charged ion. (Section 2.7)

cell potential   A measure of the driving force, or "electrical pressure," for an electrochemical reaction; it is measured in volts: 1 V = 1 J/C. Also called electromotive force. (Section 20.4)

cellulose   A polysaccharide of glucose; it is the major structural element in plant matter. (Section 25.8)

Celsius scale   A temperature scale on which water freezes at 0° and boils at 100° at sea level. (Section 1.4)

ceramic   A solid inorganic material, either crystalline (oxides, carbides, silicates) or amorphous (glasses). Most ceramics melt at high temperatures. (Section 12.1)

chain reaction   A series of reactions in which one reaction initiates the next. (Section 21.7)

changes of state   Transformations of matter from one state to a different one, for example, from a gas to a liquid. (Section 1.3)

charcoal   A form of carbon produced when wood is heated strongly in a deficiency of air. (Section 22.9)

Charles's law   A law stating that at constant pressure, the volume of a given quantity of gas is proportional to absolute temperature. (Section 10.3)

chelate effect   The generally larger formation constants for polydentate ligands as compared with the corresponding *monodentate* ligands. (Section 24.2)

chelating agent   A polydentate ligand that is capable of occupying two or more sites in the coordination sphere. (Section 24.2)

chemical bond   A strong attractive force that exists between atoms in a molecule. (Section 8.1)

chemical changes   Processes in which one or more substances are converted into other substances; also called **chemical reactions**. (Section 1.3)

chemical equation A representation of a chemical reaction using the chemical formulas of the reactants and products; a balanced chemical equation contains equal numbers of atoms of each element on both sides of the equation. (Section 3.1)

chemical equilibrium A state of dynamic balance in which the rate of formation of the products of a reaction from the reactants equals the rate of formation of the reactants from the products; at equilibrium the concentrations of the reactants and products remain constant. (Section 4.1; Chapter 15: Introduction)

chemical formula A notation that uses chemical symbols with numerical subscripts to convey the relative proportions of atoms of the different elements in a substance. (Section 2.6)

chemical kinetics The area of chemistry concerned with the speeds, or rates, at which chemical reactions occur. (Chapter 14: Introduction)

chemical nomenclature The rules used in naming substances. (Section 2.8)

chemical properties Properties that describe a substance's composition and its reactivity; how the substance reacts or changes into other substances. (Section 1.3)

chemical reactions Processes in which one or more substances are converted into other substances; also called **chemical changes**. (Section 1.3)

chemistry The scientific discipline that treats the composition, properties, and transformations of matter. (Chapter 1: Introduction)

chiral A term describing a molecule or an ion that cannot be superimposed on its mirror image. (Sections 24.4 and 25.5)

chlorofluorocarbons Compounds composed entirely of chlorine, fluorine, and carbon. (Section 18.3)

chlorophyll A plant pigment that plays a major role in conversion of solar energy to chemical energy in photosynthesis. (Section 24.2)

cholesteric liquid crystalline phase A liquid crystal formed from flat, disc-shaped molecules that align through a stacking of the molecular discs. (Section 12.8)

coal A naturally occurring solid containing hydrocarbons of high molecular weight, as well as compounds containing sulfur, oxygen, and nitrogen. (Section 5.8)

coke An impure form of carbon, formed when coal is heated strongly in the absence of air. (Section 22.9)

colligative properties Those properties of a solvent (vapor-pressure lowering, freezing-point lowering, boiling-point elevation, osmotic pressure) that depend on the total concentration of solute particles present. (Section 13.5)

collision model A model of reaction rates based on the idea that molecules must collide to react; it explains the factors influencing reaction rates in terms of the frequency of collisions, the number of collisions with energies exceeding the activation energy, and the probability that the collisions occur with suitable orientations. (Section 14.5)

colloids (colloidal dispersions) Mixtures containing particles larger than normal solutes but small enough to remain suspended in the dispersing medium. (Section 13.6)

combination reaction A chemical reaction in which two or more substances combine to form a single product. (Section 3.2)

combustion reaction A chemical reaction that proceeds with evolution of heat and usually also a flame; most combustion involves reaction with oxygen, as in the burning of a match. (Section 3.2)

common-ion effect A shift of an equilibrium induced by an ion common to the equilibrium. For example, added Na_2SO_4 decreases the solubility of the slightly soluble salt $BaSO_4$, or added NaF decreases the percent ionization of HF. (Section 17.1)

complementary colors Colors that, when mixed in proper proportions, appear white or colorless. (Section 24.5)

complete ionic equation A chemical equation in which dissolved strong electrolytes (such as dissolved ionic compounds) are written as separate ions. (Section 4.2)

complex ion (complex) An assembly of a metal ion and the Lewis bases (ligands) bonded to it. (Sections 17.5 and 24.1)

compound A substance composed of two or more elements united chemically in definite proportions. (Section 1.2)

compound semiconductor A semiconducting material formed from two or more elements. (Section 12.3)

concentration The quantity of solute present in a given quantity of solvent or solution. (Section 4.5)

concentration cell A voltaic cell containing the same electrolyte and the same electrode materials in both the anode and cathode compartments. The emf of the cell is derived from a difference in the concentrations of the same electrolyte solutions in the compartments. (Section 20.6)

condensation polymerization Polymerization in which molecules are joined together through condensation reactions. (Section 12.6)

condensation reaction A chemical reaction in which a small molecule (such as a molecule of water) is split out from between two reacting molecules. (Sections 12.6 and 22.8)

conduction band A band of molecular orbitals lying higher in energy than the occupied valence band, and distinctly separated from it. (Section 12.2)

conjugate acid A substance formed by addition of a proton to a Brønsted–Lowry base. (Section 16.2)

conjugate acid–base pair An acid and a base, such as H_2O and OH^-, that differ only in the presence or absence of a proton. (Section 16.2)

conjugate base A substance formed by the loss of a proton from a Brønsted–Lowry acid. (Section 16.2)

continuous spectrum A spectrum that contains radiation distributed over all wavelengths. (Section 6.3)

conversion factor A ratio relating the same quantity in two systems of units that is used to convert the units of measurement. (Section 1.6)

coordination compound or complex A compound containing a metal ion bonded to a group of surrounding molecules or ions that act as ligands. (Section 24.1)

coordination number The number of adjacent atoms to which an atom is directly bonded. In a complex the coordination number of the metal ion is the number of donor atoms to which it is bonded. (Sections 11.7 and 24.1)

coordination sphere The metal ion and its surrounding ligands. (Section 24.1)

coordination-sphere isomers Structural isomers of coordination compounds in which the ligands within the coordination sphere differ. (Section 24.4)

copolymer A complex polymer resulting from the polymerization of two or more chemically different monomers. (Section 12.6)

core electrons The electrons that are not in the outermost shell of an atom. (Section 6.8)

corrosion The process by which a metal is oxidized by substances in its environment. (Section 20.8)

covalent bond A bond formed between two or more atoms by a sharing of electrons. (Section 8.1)

covalent-network solids Solids in which the units that make up the three-dimensional network are joined by covalent bonds. (Section 11.8)

critical mass The amount of fissionable material necessary to maintain a nuclear chain reaction. (Section 21.7)

critical pressure The pressure at which a gas at its critical temperature is converted to a liquid state. (Section 11.4)

critical temperature The highest temperature at which it is possible to convert the gaseous form of a substance to a liquid. The critical temperature increases with an increase in the magnitude of intermolecular forces. (Section 11.4)

cross-linking The formation of bonds between polymer chains. (Section 12.6)

crystal-field theory A theory that accounts for the colors and the magnetic and other properties of transition-metal complexes in terms of the splitting of the energies of metal ion d orbitals by the electrostatic interaction with the ligands. (Section 24.6)

crystal lattice An imaginary network of points on which the repeating unit of the structure of a solid (the contents of the unit cell) may be imagined to be laid down so that the structure of the crystal is obtained. Each point represents an identical environment in the crystal. (Section 11.7)

crystalline solid (crystal) A solid whose internal arrangement of atoms, molecules, or ions shows a regular repetition in any direction through the solid. (Section 11.7)

crystallinity A measure of the extent of crystalline character (order) in a polymer. (Section 12.6)

crystallization The process in which a dissolved solute comes out of solution and forms a crystalline solid. (Section 13.2)

cubic close packing A close-packing arrangement in which the atoms of the third layer of a solid are not directly over those in the first layer. (Section 11.7)

curie A measure of radioactivity: 1 curie = 3.7×10^{10} nuclear disintegrations per second. (Section 21.4)

cycloalkanes Saturated hydrocarbons of general formula C_nH_{2n} in which the carbon atoms form a closed ring. (Section 25.3)

Dalton's law of partial pressures A law stating that the total pressure of a mixture of gases is the sum of the pressures that each gas would exert if it were present alone. (Section 10.6)

d-d transition The transition of an electron in a transition metal compound from a lower-energy *d* orbital to a higher-energy *d* orbital. (Section 24.6)

decomposition reaction A chemical reaction in which a single compound reacts to give two or more products. (Section 3.2)

degenerate A situation in which two or more orbitals have the same energy. (Section 6.7)

delocalized electrons Electrons that are spread over a number of atoms in a molecule rather than localized between a pair of atoms. (Section 9.6)

density The ratio of an object's mass to its volume. (Section 1.4)

deoxyribonucleic acid (DNA) A polynucleotide in which the sugar component is deoxyribose. (Section 25.10)

desalination The removal of salts from seawater, brine, or brackish water to make it fit for human consumption. (Section 18.5)

deuterium The isotope of hydrogen whose nucleus contains a proton and a neutron: ^2_1H. (Section 22.2)

dextrorotatory, or merely dextro or *d* A term used to label a chiral molecule that rotates the plane of polarization of plane-polarized light to the right (clockwise). (Section 24.4)

diamagnetism A type of magnetism that causes a substance with no unpaired electrons to be weakly repelled from a magnetic field. (Section 9.8)

diatomic molecule A molecule composed of only two atoms. (Section 2.6)

diffusion The spreading of one substance through a space occupied by one or more other substances. (Section 10.8)

dilution The process of preparing a less concentrated solution from a more concentrated one by adding solvent. (Section 4.5)

dimensional analysis A method of problem solving in which units are carried through all calculations. Dimensional analysis ensures that the final answer of a calculation has the desired units. (Section 1.6)

dipole A molecule with one end having a partial negative charge and the other end having a partial positive charge; a polar molecule. (Section 8.4)

dipole–dipole force The force that exists because of the interactions of dipoles on polar molecules in close contact. (Section 11.2)

dipole moment A measure of the separation and magnitude of the positive and negative charges in polar molecules. (Section 8.4)

displacement reaction A reaction in which an element reacts with a compound, displacing an element from it. (Section 4.4)

disproportionation A reaction in which a species undergoes simultaneous oxidation and reduction [as in $N_2O_3(g) \longrightarrow NO(g) + NO_2(g)$.] (Section 22.5)

donor atom The atom of a ligand that bonds to the metal. (Section 24.1)

doping Incorporation of a hetero atom into a solid to change its electrical properties. For example, incorporation of P into Si. (Section 12.3)

double bond A covalent bond involving two electron pairs. (Section 8.3)

double helix The structure for DNA that involves the winding of two DNA polynucleotide chains together in a helical arrangement. The two strands of the double helix are complementary in that the organic bases on the two strands are paired for optimal hydrogen bond interaction. (Section 25.10)

Downs cell A cell used to obtain sodium metal by electrolysis of molten NaCl. (Section 23.4)

dynamic equilibrium A state of balance in which opposing processes occur at the same rate. (Section 11.5)

effective nuclear charge The net positive charge experienced by an electron in a many-electron atom; this charge is not the full nuclear charge because there is some shielding of the nucleus by the other electrons in the atom. (Section 7.2)

effusion The escape of a gas through an orifice or hole. (Section 10.8)

elastomer A material that can undergo a substantial change in shape via stretching, bending, or compression and return to its original shape upon release of the distorting force. (Section 12.6)

electrochemistry The branch of chemistry that deals with the relationships between electricity and chemical reactions. (Chapter 20: Introduction)

electrolysis reaction A reaction in which a nonspontaneous redox reaction is brought about by the passage of current under a sufficient external electrical potential. The devices in which electrolysis reactions occur are called electrolytic cells. (Section 20.9)

electrolyte A solute that produces ions in solution; an electrolytic solution conducts an electric current. (Section 4.1)

electrolytic cell A device in which a nonspontaneous oxidation-reduction reaction is caused to occur by passage of current under a sufficient external electrical potential. (Section 20.9)

electromagnetic radiation (radiant energy) A form of energy that has wave characteristics and that propagates through a vacuum at the characteristic speed of 3.00×10^8 m/s. (Section 6.1)

electrometallurgy The use of electrolysis to reduce or refine metals. (Section 23.4)

electromotive force (emf) A measure of the driving force, or *electrical pressure*, for the completion of an electrochemical reaction. Electromotive force is measured in volts: 1 V = 1 J/C. Also called the cell potential. (Section 20.4)

electron A negatively charged subatomic particle found outside the atomic nucleus; it is a part of all atoms. An electron has a mass 1/1836 times that of a proton. (Section 2.3)

electron affinity The energy change that occurs when an electron is added to a gaseous atom or ion. (Section 7.5)

electron capture A mode of radioactive decay in which an inner-shell orbital electron is captured by the nucleus. (Section 21.1)

electron configuration A particular arrangement of electrons in the orbitals of an atom. (Section 6.8)

electron density The probability of finding an electron at any particular point in an atom; this probability is equal to ψ^2, the square of the wave function. (Section 6.5)

electron domain In the VSEPR model, a region about a central atom in which an electron pair is concentrated. (Section 9.2)

electron-domain geometry The three-dimensional arrangement of the electron domains around an atom according to the VSEPR model. (Section 9.2)

electronegativity A measure of the ability of an atom that is bonded to another atom to attract electrons to itself. (Section 8.4)

electronic charge The negative charge carried by an electron; it has a magnitude of 1.602×10^{-19} C. (Section 2.3)

electronic structure The arrangement of electrons in an atom or molecule. (Chapter 6: Introduction)

electron-sea model A model for the behavior of electrons in metals. (Section 23.5)

electron shell A collection of orbitals that have the same value of *n*. For example, the orbitals with *n* = 3 (the 3*s*, 3*p*, and 3*d* orbitals) comprise the third shell. (Section 6.5)

electron spin A property of the electron that makes it behave as though it were a tiny magnet. The electron behaves as if it were spinning on its axis; electron spin is quantized. (Section 6.7)

element A substance that cannot be separated into simpler substances by chemical means. (Sections 1.1 and 1.2)

elemental semiconductor A semiconducting material composed of just one element. (Section 12.3)

elementary reaction A process in a chemical reaction that occurs in a single event or step. An overall chemical reaction consists of one or more elementary reactions or steps. (Section 14.6)

empirical formula (simplest formula) A chemical formula that shows the kinds of atoms and their relative numbers in a substance in the smallest possible whole-number ratios. (Section 2.6)

enantiomers Two mirror-image molecules of a chiral substance. The enantiomers are non-superimposable. (Section 24.4)

endothermic process A process in which a system absorbs heat from its surroundings. (Section 5.2)

energy The capacity to do work or to transfer heat. (Section 5.1)

energy band A band of allowed energy states of electrons in metals and semiconductors. (Section 23.5)

energy-level diagram A diagram that shows the energies of molecular orbitals relative to the atomic orbitals from which they are derived. Also called a **molecular-orbital diagram**. (Section 9.7)

enthalpy A quantity defined by the relationship $H = E + PV$; the enthalpy change, ΔH, for a reaction that occurs at constant pressure is the heat evolved or absorbed in the reaction: $\Delta H = q_p$. (Section 5.3)

enthalpy (heat) of formation The enthalpy change that accompanies the formation of a substance from the most stable forms of its component elements. (Section 5.7)

enthalpy of reaction The enthalpy change associated with a chemical reaction. (Section 5.4)

entropy A thermodynamic function associated with the number of different equivalent energy states or spatial arrangements in which a system may be found. It is a thermodynamic state function, which means that once we specify the conditions for a system—that is, the temperature, pressure, and so on—the entropy is defined. (Sections 13.1 and 19.2)

enzyme A protein molecule that acts to catalyze specific biochemical reactions. (Section 14.7)

equilibrium constant The numerical value of the equilibrium-constant expression for a system at equilibrium. The equilibrium constant is most usually denoted by K_p for gas-phase systems or K_c for solution-phase systems. (Section 15.2)

equilibrium-constant expression The expression that describes the relationship among the concentrations (or partial pressures) of the substances present in a system at equilibrium. The numerator is obtained by multiplying the concentrations of the substances on the product side of the equation, each raised to a power equal to its coefficient in the chemical equation. The denominator similarly contains the concentrations of the substances on the reactant side of the equation. (Section 15.2)

equivalence point The point in a titration at which the added solute reacts completely with the solute present in the solution. (Section 4.6)

ester An organic compound that has an OR group attached to a carbonyl; it is the product of a reaction between a carboxylic acid and an alcohol. (Section 25.4)

ether A compound in which two hydrocarbon groups are bonded to one oxygen. (Section 25.4)

exchange (metathesis) reaction A reaction between compounds that when written as a molecular equation appears to involve the exchange of ions between the two reactants. (Section 4.2)

excited state A higher energy state than the ground state. (Section 6.3)

exothermic process A process in which a system releases heat to its surroundings. (Section 5.2)

extensive property A property that depends on the amount of material considered; for example, mass or volume. (Section 1.3)

face-centered cubic cell A cubic unit cell that has lattice points at each corner as well as at the center of each face. (Section 11.7)

faraday A unit of charge that equals the total charge of one mole of electrons: $1\ F = 96,500$ C. (Section 20.5)

f-block metals Lanthanide and actinide elements in which the $4f$ or $5f$ orbitals are partially occupied. (Section 6.9)

ferrimagnetism A form of magnetism in which electron spins on different kinds of sites point in opposite directions but do not fully cancel out. (Section 23.8)

ferromagnetism A form of magnetism in which unpaired electron spins at lattice sites are permanently aligned. (Section 23.7)

first law of thermodynamics A statement of our experience that energy is conserved in any process. We can express the law in many ways. One of the more useful expressions is that the change in internal energy, ΔE, of a system in any process is equal to the heat, q, added to the system, plus the work, w, done on the system by its surroundings: $\Delta E = q + w$. (Section 5.2)

first-order reaction A reaction in which the reaction rate is proportional to the concentration of a single reactant, raised to the first power. (Section 14.4)

fission The splitting of a large nucleus into two smaller ones. (Section 21.6)

folding The process by which a protein adopts its biologically active shape. (Section 25.7)

force A push or a pull. (Section 5.1)

formal charge The number of valence electrons in an isolated atom minus the number of electrons assigned to the atom in the Lewis structure. (Section 8.5)

formation constant For a metal ion complex, the equilibrium constant for formation of the complex from the metal ion and base species present in solution. It is a measure of the tendency of the complex to form. (Section 17.5)

formula weight The mass of the collection of atoms represented by a chemical formula. For example, the formula weight of NO_2 (46.0 amu) is the sum of the masses of one nitrogen atom and two oxygen atoms. (Section 3.3)

fossil fuels Coal, oil, and natural gas, which are presently our major sources of energy. (Section 5.8)

free energy (Gibbs free energy, G) A thermodynamic state function that gives a criterion for spontaneous change in terms of enthalpy and entropy: $G = H - TS$. (Section 19.5)

free radical A substance with one or more unpaired electrons. (Section 21.9)

frequency The number of times per second that one complete wavelength passes a given point. (Section 6.1)

frequency factor (A) A term in the Arrhenius equation that is related to the frequency of collision and the probability that the collisions are favorably oriented for reaction. (Section 14.5)

fuel cell A voltaic cell that utilizes the oxidation of a conventional fuel, such as H_2 or CH_4, in the cell reaction. (Section 20.7)

fuel value The energy released when 1 g of a substance is combusted. (Section 5.8)

functional group An atom or group of atoms that imparts characteristic chemical properties to an organic compound. (Section 25.1)

fusion The joining of two light nuclei to form a more massive one. (Section 21.6)

galvanic cell See **voltaic cell**. (Section 20.3)

gamma radiation Energetic electromagnetic radiation emanating from the nucleus of a radioactive atom. (Section 21.1)

gas Matter that has no fixed volume or shape; it conforms to the volume and shape of its container. (Section 1.2)

gas constant (R) The constant of proportionality in the ideal-gas equation. (Section 10.4)

Geiger counter A device that can detect and measure radioactivity. (Section 21.5)

geometric isomers Compounds with the same type and number of atoms and the same chemical bonds but different spatial arrangements of these atoms and bonds. (Sections 24.4 and 25.4)

Gibbs free energy A thermodynamic state function that combines enthalpy and entropy, in the form $G = H - TS$. For a change occurring at constant temperature and pressure, the change in free energy is $\Delta G = \Delta H - T\Delta S$. (Section 19.5)

glass An amorphous solid formed by fusion of SiO_2, CaO, and Na_2O. Other oxides may also be used to form glasses with differing characteristics. (Section 22.10)

glucose A polyhydroxy aldehyde whose formula is $CH_2OH(CHOH)_4CHO$; it is the most important of the monosaccharides. (Section 25.8)

glycogen The general name given to a group of polysaccharides of glucose that are synthesized in mammals and used to store energy from carbohydrates. (Section 25.8)

Graham's law A law stating that the rate of effusion of a gas is inversely proportional to the square root of its molecular weight. (Section 10.8)

gray (Gy) The SI unit for radiation dose corresponding to the absorption of 1 J of energy per kilogram of biological material; 1 Gy $= 100$ rads. (Section 21.9)

green chemistry Chemistry that promotes the design and application of chemical products and processes that are compatible with human health and that preserve the environment. (Section 18.7)

ground state The lowest-energy, or most stable, state. (Section 6.3)

group Elements that are in the same column of the periodic table; elements within the same group or family exhibit similarities in their chemical behavior. (Section 2.5)

Haber process   The catalyst system and conditions of temperature and pressure developed by Fritz Haber and coworkers for the formation of NH_3 from H_2 and N_2. (Section 15.1)

half-life   The time required for the concentration of a reactant substance to decrease to half its initial value; the time required for half of a sample of a particular radioisotope to decay. (Sections 14.4 and 21.4)

half-reaction   An equation for either an oxidation or a reduction that explicitly shows the electrons involved, for example, $Zn^{2+}(aq) + 2\ e^- \longrightarrow Zn(s)$. (Section 20.2)

Hall process   A process used to obtain aluminum by electrolysis of Al_2O_3 dissolved in molten cryolite, Na_3AlF_6. (Section 23.4)

halogens   Members of group 7A in the periodic table. (Sections 7.8 and 22.4)

hard water   Water that contains appreciable concentrations of Ca^{2+} and Mg^{2+}; these ions react with soaps to form an insoluble material. (Section 18.6)

heat   The flow of energy from a body at higher temperature to one at lower temperature when they are placed in thermal contact. (Section 5.1)

heat capacity   The quantity of heat required to raise the temperature of a sample of matter by 1 °C (or 1 K). (Section 5.5)

heat of fusion   The enthalpy change, ΔH, for melting a solid. (Section 11.4)

heat of sublimation   The enthalpy change, ΔH, for vaporization of a solid. (Section 11.4)

heat of vaporization   The enthalpy change, ΔH, for vaporization of a liquid. (Section 11.4)

hemoglobin   An iron-containing protein responsible for oxygen transport in the blood. (Section 18.4)

Henderson–Hasselbalch equation   The relationship among the pH, pK_a, and the concentrations of acid and conjugate base in an aqueous solution: $pH = pK_a + \log \dfrac{[base]}{[acid]}$. (Section 17.2)

Henry's law   A law stating that the concentration of a gas in a solution, C_g, is proportional to the pressure of gas over the solution: $C_g = kP_g$. (Section 13.3)

Hess's law   The heat evolved in a given process can be expressed as the sum of the heats of several processes that, when added, yield the process of interest. (Section 5.6)

heterogeneous alloy   An alloy in which the components are not distributed uniformly; instead, two or more distinct phases with characteristic compositions are present. (Section 23.6)

heterogeneous catalyst   A catalyst that is in a different phase from that of the reactant substances. (Section 14.7)

heterogeneous equilibrium   The equilibrium established between substances in two or more different phases, for example, between a gas and a solid or between a solid and a liquid. (Section 15.4)

hexagonal close packing   A close-packing arrangement in which the atoms of the third layer of a solid lie directly over those in the first layer. (Section 11.7)

high-spin complex   A complex whose electrons populate the d orbitals to give the maximum number of unpaired electrons. (Section 24.6)

high-temperature superconductivity   The "frictionless" flow of electrical current (superconductivity) at temperatures above 30 K in certain complex metal oxides. (Section 12.1)

hole   A vacancy in the valence band of a semiconductor, created by doping. (Section 12.3)

homogeneous catalyst   A catalyst that is in the same phase as the reactant substances. (Section 14.7)

homogeneous equilibrium   The equilibrium established between reactant and product substances that are all in the same phase. (Section 15.4)

Hund's rule   A rule stating that electrons occupy degenerate orbitals in such a way as to maximize the number of electrons with the same spin. In other words, each orbital has one electron placed in it before pairing of electrons in orbitals occurs. Note that this rule applies only to orbitals that are degenerate, which means that they have the same energy. (Section 6.8)

hybridization   The mixing of different types of atomic orbitals to produce a set of equivalent hybrid orbitals. (Section 9.5)

hybrid orbital   An orbital that results from the mixing of different kinds of atomic orbitals on the same atom. For example, an sp^3 hybrid results from the mixing, or hybridizing, of one s orbital and three p orbitals. (Section 9.5)

hydration   Solvation when the solvent is water. (Section 13.1)

hydride ion   An ion formed by the addition of an electron to a hydrogen atom: H^-. (Section 7.7)

hydrocarbons   Compounds composed of only carbon and hydrogen. (Section 2.9)

hydrogen bonding   Bonding that results from intermolecular attractions between molecules containing hydrogen bonded to an electronegative element. The most important examples involve OH, NH, and HF. (Section 11.2)

hydrolysis   A reaction with water. When a cation or anion reacts with water, it changes the pH. (Section 16.9)

hydrometallurgy   Aqueous chemical processes for recovery of a metal from an ore. (Section 23.3)

hydronium ion (H_3O^+)   The predominant form of the proton in aqueous solution. (Section 16.2)

hydrophilic   Water-attracting. The term is often used to describe a type of colloid. (Section 13.6)

hydrophobic   Water-repelling. The term is often used to describe a type of colloid. (Section 13.6)

hypothesis   A tentative explanation of a series of observations or of a natural law. (Section 1.3)

ideal gas   A hypothetical gas whose pressure, volume, and temperature behavior is completely described by the ideal-gas equation. (Section 10.4)

ideal-gas equation   An equation of state for gases that embodies Boyle's law, Charles's law, and Avogadro's hypothesis in the form $PV = nRT$. (Section 10.4)

ideal solution   A solution that obeys Raoult's law. (Section 13.5)

immiscible liquids   Liquids that do not dissolve in one another to a significant extent. (Section 13.3)

indicator   A substance added to a solution that changes color when the added solute has reacted with all the solute present in solution. (Section 4.6)

instantaneous rate   The reaction rate at a particular time as opposed to the average rate over an interval of time. (Section 14.2)

insulator   A solid with extremely low electrical conductivity. (Section 12.1)

intensive property   A property that is independent of the amount of material considered, for example, density. (Section 1.3)

interhalogens   Compounds formed between two different halogen elements. Examples include IBr and BrF_3. (Section 22.4)

intermediate   A substance formed in one elementary step of a multistep mechanism and consumed in another; it is neither a reactant nor an ultimate product of the overall reaction. (Section 14.6)

intermetallic compound   A homogeneous alloy with definite properties and composition. Intermetallic compounds are stoichiometric compounds, but their compositions are not readily explained in terms of ordinary chemical bonding theory. (Section 23.6)

intermolecular forces   The short-range attractive forces operating between the particles that make up the units of a liquid or solid substance. These same forces also cause gases to liquefy or solidify at low temperatures and high pressures. (Chapter 11: Introduction)

internal energy   The total energy possessed by a system. When a system undergoes a change, the change in internal energy, ΔE, is defined as the heat, q, added to the system, plus the work, w, done on the system by its surroundings: $\Delta E = q + w$. (Section 5.2)

ion   Electrically charged atom or group of atoms (polyatomic ion); ions can be positively or negatively charged, depending on whether electrons are lost (positive) or gained (negative) by the atoms. (Section 2.7)

ion–dipole force   The force that exists between an ion and a neutral polar molecule that possesses a permanent dipole moment. (Section 11.2)

ion exchange   A process by which ions in solution are exchanged for other ions held on the surface of an ion-exchange resin; the exchange of a hard-water cation such as Ca^{2+} for a soft-water cation such as Na^+ is used to soften water. (Section 18.6)

ionic bond   A bond between oppositely charged ions. The ions are formed from atoms by transfer of one or more electrons. (Section 8.1)

ionic compound   A compound composed of cations and anions. (Section 2.7)

salt An ionic compound formed by replacing one or more hydrogens of an acid by other cations. (Section 4.3)

saponification Hydrolysis of an ester in the presence of a base. (Section 25.4)

saturated solution A solution in which undissolved solute and dissolved solute are in equilibrium. (Section 13.2)

scientific law A concise verbal statement or a mathematical equation that summarizes a wide range of observations and experiences. (Section 1.3)

scientific method The general process of advancing scientific knowledge by making experimental observations and by formulating hypotheses, theories, and laws. (Section 1.3)

scintillation counter An instrument that is used to detect and measure radiation by the fluorescence it produces in a fluorescing medium. (Section 21.5)

secondary structure The manner in which a protein is coiled or stretched. (Section 25.7)

second law of thermodynamics A statement of our experience that there is a direction to the way events occur in nature. When a process occurs spontaneously in one direction, it is nonspontaneous in the reverse direction. It is possible to state the second law in many different forms, but they all relate back to the same idea about spontaneity. One of the most common statements found in chemical contexts is that in any spontaneous process the entropy of the universe increases. (Section 19.2)

second-order reaction A reaction in which the overall reaction order (the sum of the concentration-term exponents) in the rate law is 2. (Section 14.4)

semiconductor A solid with limited electrical conductivity. (Section 12.1)

sigma (σ) bond A covalent bond in which electron density is concentrated along the internuclear axis. (Section 9.6)

sigma (σ) molecular orbital A molecular orbital that centers the electron density about an imaginary line passing through two nuclei. (Section 9.7)

significant figures The digits that indicate the precision with which a measurement is made; all digits of a measured quantity are significant, including the last digit, which is uncertain. (Section 1.5)

silicates Compounds containing silicon and oxygen, structurally based on SiO_4 tetrahedra. (Section 22.10)

single bond A covalent bond involving one electron pair. (Section 8.3)

SI units The preferred metric units for use in science. (Section 1.4)

slag A mixture of molten silicate minerals. Slags may be acidic or basic, according to the acidity or basicity of the oxide added to silica. (Section 23.2)

smectic liquid crystalline phase A liquid crystal in which the molecules are aligned along their long axes and arranged in sheets, with the ends of the molecules aligned. There are several different kinds of smectic phases. (Section 12.8)

smelting A melting process in which the materials formed in the course of the chemical reactions that occur separate into two or more layers. For example, the layers might be slag and molten metal. (Section 23.2)

solar cell An electronic device composed of doped semiconductors in which radiant energy can be converted into electrical energy. (Section 12.3)

sol-gel process A process in which extremely small particles (0.003 to 0.1 μm in diameter) of uniform size are produced in a series of chemical steps, followed by controlled heating. (Section 12.4)

solid Matter that has both a definite shape and a definite volume. (Section 1.2)

solubility The amount of a substance that dissolves in a given quantity of solvent at a given temperature to form a saturated solution. (Sections 4.2 and 13.2)

solubility-product constant (solubility product) (K_{sp}) An equilibrium constant related to the equilibrium between a solid salt and its ions in solution. It provides a quantitative measure of the solubility of a slightly soluble salt. (Section 17.4)

solute A substance dissolved in a solvent to form a solution; it is normally the component of a solution present in the smaller amount. (Section 4.1)

solution A mixture of substances that has a uniform composition; a homogeneous mixture. (Section 1.2)

solution alloy A homogeneous alloy, with the components distributed uniformly throughout. (Section 23.6)

solvation The clustering of solvent molecules around a solute particle. (Section 13.1)

solvent The dissolving medium of a solution; it is normally the component of a solution present in the greater amount. (Section 4.1)

specific heat (C_s) The heat capacity of 1 g of a substance; the heat required to raise the temperature of 1 g of a substance by 1 °C. (Section 5.5)

spectator ions Ions that go through a reaction unchanged and that appear on both sides of the complete ionic equation. (Section 4.2)

spectrochemical series A list of ligands arranged in order of their abilities to split the d-orbital energies (using the terminology of the crystal-field model). (Section 24.6)

spectrum The distribution among various wavelengths of the radiant energy emitted or absorbed by an object. (Sections 6.3 and 24.6)

spin magnetic quantum number (m_s) A quantum number associated with the electron spin; it may have values of $+\frac{1}{2}$ or $-\frac{1}{2}$. (Section 6.7)

spin-pairing energy The energy required to pair an electron with another electron occupying an orbital. (Section 24.6)

spontaneous process A process that is capable of proceeding in a given direction, as written or described, without needing to be driven by an outside source of energy. A process may be spontaneous even though it is very slow. (Section 19.1)

standard atmospheric pressure Defined as 760 torr or, in SI units, 101.325 kPa. (Section 10.2)

standard electrode potential See **standard reduction potential**. (Section 20.4)

standard emf, also called the standard cell potential ($E°$) The emf of a cell when all reagents are at standard conditions. (Section 20.4)

standard enthalpy change ($\Delta H°$) The change in enthalpy in a process when all reactants and products are in their stable forms at 1 atm pressure and a specified temperature, commonly 25 °C. (Section 5.7)

standard enthalpy of formation ($\Delta H_f°$) The change in enthalpy that accompanies the formation of one mole of a substance from its elements, with all substances in their standard states. (Section 5.7)

standard free energy of formation ($\Delta G_f°$) The change in free energy associated with the formation of a substance from its elements under standard conditions. (Section 19.5)

standard hydrogen electrode (SHE) An electrode based on the half-reaction $2\,H^+(1\,M) + 2\,e^- \longrightarrow H_2(1\,\text{atm})$. The standard electrode potential of the standard hydrogen electrode is defined as 0 V. (Section 20.4)

standard molar entropy ($S°$) The entropy value for a mole of a substance in its standard state. (Section 19.4)

standard reduction potential ($E°_{red}$) The potential of a reduction half-reaction under standard conditions, measured relative to the standard hydrogen electrode. A standard reduction potential is also called a **standard electrode potential**. (Section 20.4)

standard solution A solution of known concentration. (Section 4.6)

standard temperature and pressure (STP) Defined as 0 °C and 1 atm pressure; frequently used as reference conditions for a gas. (Section 10.4)

starch The general name given to a group of polysaccharides that acts as energy-storage substances in plants. (Section 25.8)

state function A property of a system that is determined by the state or condition of the system and not by how it got to that state; its value is fixed when temperature, pressure, composition, and physical form are specified; $P, V, T, E,$ and H are state functions. (Section 5.2)

states of matter The three forms that matter can assume: solid, liquid, and gas. (Section 1.2)

stereoisomers Compounds possessing the same formula and bonding arrangement but differing in the spatial arrangements of the atoms. (Section 24.4)

stoichiometry The relationships among the quantities of reactants and products involved in chemical reactions. (Chapter 3: Introduction)

stratosphere The region of the atmosphere directly above the troposphere. (Section 18.1)

strong acid An acid that ionizes completely in water. (Section 4.3)

strong base A base that ionizes completely in water. (Section 4.3)

strong electrolyte A substance (strong acids, strong bases, and most salts) that is completely ionized in solution. (Section 4.1)

structural formula A formula that shows not only the number and kinds of atoms in the molecule but also the arrangement (connections) of the atoms. (Section 2.6)

structural isomers Compounds possessing the same formula but differing in the bonding arrangements of the atoms. (Sections 24.4 and 25.3)

subatomic particles Particles such as protons, neutrons, and electrons that are smaller than an atom. (Section 2.2)

subshell One or more orbitals with the same set of quantum numbers n and l. For example, we speak of the $2p$ subshell ($n = 2$, $l = 1$), which is composed of three orbitals ($2p_x$, $2p_y$, and $2p_z$). (Section 6.5)

substitutional alloy A homogeneous (solution) alloy in which atoms of different elements randomly occupy sites in the lattice. (Section 23.6)

substitution reactions Reactions in which one atom (or group of atoms) replaces another atom (or group) within a molecule; substitution reactions are typical for alkanes and aromatic hydrocarbons. (Section 25.4)

substrate A substance that undergoes a reaction at the active site in an enzyme. (Section 14.7)

superconductor A material capable of carrying an electrical current without apparent resistance when cooled below a transition temperature, T_c. (Section 12.50)

superconducting ceramic A complex metal oxide that undergoes a transition to a superconducting state at a low temperature. (Section 12.1)

superconducting transition temperature (T_c) The temperature below which a substance exhibits superconductivity. (Section 12.1)

superconductivity The "frictionless" flow of electrons that occurs when a substance loses all resistance to the flow of electrical current. (Section 12.1)

supercritical mass An amount of fissionable material larger than the critical mass. (Section 21.7)

supersaturated solutions Solutions containing more solute than an equivalent saturated solution. (Section 13.2)

surface tension The intermolecular, cohesive attraction that causes a liquid to minimize its surface area. (Section 11.3)

surroundings In thermodynamics, everything that lies outside the system that we study. (Section 5.1)

system In thermodynamics, the portion of the universe that we single out for study. We must be careful to state exactly what the system contains and what transfers of energy it may have with its surroundings. (Section 5.1)

termolecular reaction An elementary reaction that involves three molecules. Termolecular reactions are rare. (Section 14.6)

tertiary structure The overall shape of a large protein, specifically, the manner in which sections of the protein fold back upon themselves or intertwine. (Section 25.9)

theoretical yield The quantity of product that is calculated to form when all of the limiting reagent reacts. (Section 3.7)

theory A tested model or explanation that satisfactorily accounts for a certain set of phenomena. (Section 1.3)

thermochemistry The relationship between chemical reactions and energy changes. (Chapter 5: Introduction)

thermodynamics The study of energy and its transformation. (Chapter 5: Introduction)

thermonuclear reaction Another name for fusion reactions; reactions in which two light nuclei are joined to form a more massive one. (Section 21.8)

thermoplastic A polymeric material that can be readily reshaped by application of heat and pressure. (Section 12.6)

thermosetting plastic A plastic that, once formed in a particular mold, is not readily reshaped by application of heat and pressure. (Section 12.2)

third law of thermodynamics A law stating that the entropy of a pure, crystalline solid at absolute zero temperature is zero: $S(0 \text{ K}) = 0$. (Section 19.3)

titration The process of reacting a solution of unknown concentration with one of known concentration (a standard solution). (Section 4.6)

titration curve A graph of pH as a function of added titrant. (Section 17.3)

torr A unit of pressure (1 torr = 1 mm Hg). (Section 10.2)

transistor An electrical device that forms the heart of an integrated circuit. (Section 12.4)

transition elements (transition metals) Elements in which the d orbitals are partially occupied. (Section 6.8)

transition state (activated complex) The particular arrangement of reactant and product molecules at the point of maximum energy in the rate-determining step of a reaction. (Section 14.5)

translational motion Movement in which an entire molecule moves in a definite direction. (Section 19.3)

transuranium elements Elements that follow uranium in the periodic table. (Section 21.3)

triple bond A covalent bond involving three electron pairs. (Section 8.3)

triple point The temperature at which solid, liquid, and gas phases coexist in equilibrium. (Section 11.6)

tritium The isotope of hydrogen whose nucleus contains a proton and two neutrons. (Section 22.2)

troposphere The region of Earth's atmosphere extending from the surface to about 12 km altitude. (Section 18.1)

Tyndall effect The scattering of a beam of visible light by the particles in a colloidal dispersion. (Section 13.6)

uncertainty principle A principle stating there is an inherent uncertainty in the precision with which we can simultaneously specify the position and momentum of a particle. This uncertainty is significant only for particles of extremely small mass, such as electrons. (Section 6.4)

unimolecular reaction An elementary reaction that involves a single molecule. (Section 14.6)

unit cell The smallest portion of a crystal that reproduces the structure of the entire crystal when repeated in different directions in space.

It is the repeating unit or building block of the crystal lattice. (Section 11.7)

unsaturated solutions Solutions containing less solute than a saturated solution. (Section 13.2)

valence band A band of closely spaced molecular orbitals that is essentially fully occupied by electrons. (Section 12.2)

valence-bond theory A model of chemical bonding in which an electron-pair bond is formed between two atoms by the overlap of orbitals on the two atoms. (Section 9.4)

valence electrons The outermost electrons of an atom; those that occupy orbitals not occupied in the nearest noble-gas element of lower atomic number. The valence electrons are the ones the atom uses in bonding. (Section 6.8)

valence orbitals Orbitals that contain the outer-shell electrons of an atom. (Chapter 7: Introduction)

valence-shell electron-pair repulsion (VSEPR) model A model that accounts for the geometric arrangements of shared and unshared electron pairs around a central atom in terms of the repulsions between electron pairs. (Section 9.2)

van der Waals equation An equation of state for nonideal gases that is based on adding corrections to the ideal-gas equation. The correction terms account for intermolecular forces of attraction and for the volumes occupied by the gas molecules themselves. (Section 10.9)

vapor Gaseous state of any substance that normally exists as a liquid or solid. (Section 10.1)

vapor pressure The pressure exerted by a vapor in equilibrium with its liquid or solid phase. (Section 11.5)

vibrational motion Movement of the atoms within a molecule in which they move periodically toward and away from one another. (Section 19.3)

viscosity A measure of the resistance of fluids to flow. (Section 11.3)

volatile Tending to evaporate readily. (Section 11.5)

voltaic (galvanic) cell A device in which a spontaneous oxidation-reduction reaction occurs with the passage of electrons through an external circuit. (Section 20.3)

vulcanization The process of cross-linking polymer chains in rubber. (Section 12.6)

watt A unit of power; 1 W = 1 J/s. (Section 20.9)

wave function A mathematical description of an allowed energy state (an orbital) for an electron in the quantum mechanical model of the atom; it is usually symbolized by the Greek letter ψ. (Section 6.5)

wavelength The distance between identical points on successive waves. (Section 6.1)

weak acid An acid that only partly ionizes in water. (Section 4.3)

weak base A base that only partly ionizes in water. (Section 4.3)

weak electrolyte A substance that only partly ionizes in solution. (Section 4.1)

work The movement of an object against some force. (Section 5.1)

Photo/Art Credits

Chapter 1: CO01 NASA, ESA and J. Hester and A. Loll (Arizona State University) **1.2a** Dr. Jeremy Burgess/Science Photo Library/Photo Researchers, Inc. **1.2b** Francis G. Mayer/Corbis/Bettmann **1.2c** G. Murti/Photo Researchers, Inc. **1.3** Richard Megna/Fundamental Photographs, NYC **1.4** Dale Wilson/Green Stock/Corbis/Bettmann **1.7** Charles D. Winters/Photo Researchers, Inc. **1.8a** M. Angelo/Corbis/Bettmann **1.8b** Richard Megna/Fundamental Photographs, NYC **1.11a–c** Donald Clegg and Roxy Wilson/Pearson Education/PH College **1.12a–b** Donald Clegg and Roxy Wilson/Pearson Education/PH College **1.14a–c** Richard Megna/Fundamental Photographs, NYC **1.16** Richard Megna/Fundamental Photographs, NYC **1.17** Australian Postal Service/National Standards Commission **1.21** David Frazier/PhotoEdit Inc. **1.23c** Phil Degginger/Color-Pic, Inc. **1.25.1UN** ScienceCartoonsPlus.com

Chapter 2: CO02 IBM Research, Almaden Research Center **2.1** Corbis/Bettmann **2.2** IBMRL/Visuals Unlimited **2.3b–c** Richard Megna/Fundamental Photographs, NYC **2.6** Radium Institute, Courtesy AIP Emilio Segre Visual Archives **2.7** G.R. "Dick" Roberts Photo Library/The Natural Sciences Image Library (NSIL) **2.12** Stephen Frisch/Stock Boston **2.17** Richard Megna/Fundamental Photographs, NYC **2.18** Ernest Orlando Lawrence Berkeley National Laboratory, Courtesy AIP Emilio Segre Visual Archives **2.23c** Ed Degginger/Color-Pic, Inc. **2.25** Richard Megna/Fundamental Photographs, NYC

Chapter 3: CO03 Winfried Heinze/StockFood America **3.1** Jean-Loup Charmet/Science Photo Library/Photo Researchers, Inc. **3.3** Charles D. Winters/ Photo Researchers, Inc. **3.3.1UN** Dave Carpenter **3.5a–c** Richard Megna/ Fundamental Photographs, NYC **3.6** Donald Johnston/Getty Images Inc. - Stone Allstock **3.7** Richard Megna/Fundamental Photographs, NYC **3.9** Richard Megna/Fundamental Photographs, NYC **3.14** Saturn Stills/Photo Researchers, Inc. **p. 113** Carey B. Van Loon **p. 114** Paul Silverman/Fundamental Photographs, NYC

Chapter 4: CO04 Everton, Macduff/Getty Images Inc. - Image Bank **4.1** Richard Megna/Fundamental Photographs, NYC **4.1.1** Richard Megna/Fundamental Photographs, NYC **4.2a–c** Richard Megna/Fundamental Photographs, NYC **4.4** Richard Megna/Fundamental Photographs, NYC **4.5** Tom Pantages **4.7** Richard Megna/Fundamental Photographs, NYC **4.8a–c** Richard Megna/ Fundamental Photographs, NYC **4.9** Richard Megna/Fundamental Photographs, NYC **4.10** Tom Pantages **4.11** Jorg Heimann/Bilderberg/Peter Arnold, Inc. **4.12** Richard Megna/Fundamental Photographs, NYC **4.13** Richard Megna/ Fundamental Photographs, NYC **4.14a–c** Peticolas/Megna/Fundamental Photographs, NYC **4.15** Erich Lessing/Art Resource, N.Y. **4.16a–d** Donald Clegg and Roxy Wilson/Pearson Education/PH College **4.17** Al Bello/Getty Images, Inc - Liaison **4.18a–c** Richard Megna/Fundamental Photographs, NYC **4.20a–c** Richard Megna/Fundamental Photographs, NYC **p. 161** Tom Pantages

Chapter 5: CO05 Adam Jones/Dembinsky Photo Associates **5.1a** Amoz Eckerson/Visuals Unlimited **5.1b** Tom Pantages **5.8a–b** Richard Megna/Fundamental Photographs, NYC **5.14a–b** Donald Clegg and Roxy Wilson/Pearson Education/ PH College **5.15** UPI/Corbis/Bettmann **5.19** Nick Laham/Getty Images **5.23** Phil Degginger/Color-Pic, Inc. **5.25** Toyota Motor Sales, USA, Inc.

Chapter 6: CO06 Chad Ehlers/The Stock Connection **6.1** Pal Hermansen/Getty Images Inc. - Stone Allstock **6.5** Alpine Aperture/Will and Lissa Funk **6.6** AGE/ Peter Arnold, Inc. **6.7a** Laura Martin/Visuals Unlimited **6.7b** PhotoDisc/Getty Images, Inc. - PhotoDisc **6.9** Photograph by Paul Ehrenfest, courtesy AIP Emilio Segre Visual Archives, Ehrenfest Collection **6.10** Getty Images - Digital Vision **6.12a–b** Tom Pantages **6.14** Image courtesy of Nicola Pinna. Version published in: N. Pinna, S. Grancharov, P. Beato, P. Bonville, M. Antonietti, M. Niedereberger *Chem. Mater.* 2005, 17, 3044. **6.16** AIP Emilio Segre Visual Archives **6.29** Alfred Pasieka/Science Photo Library/Photo Researchers, Inc. **p. 246(left)** E.R. Degginger/Color-Pic, Inc. **p. 246(top right)** Getty Images - Photodisc **p. 246(bottom right)** E.R. Degginger/Color-Pic, Inc.

Chapter 7: CO07 Claude Monet (1840–1926) "Rue Montorgueil in Paris, Festival of 30 June 1878" 1878. Herve Lewandowski/Reunion des Musees Nationaux/Art Resource, NY. **7.1** Richard Megna/Fundamental Photographs, NYC **7.9** 1ca2: A.E. Eriksson, T.A. Jones, A. Liljas: Refined structure of human anhydrase II at 2.0 Angstrom resolution. Proteins 4 pp. 274 (1988). PDB: H.M. Berman, J. Westbrook, Z. Feng, G. Gilliland, T.N. Bhat, H. Weissig, I.N. Shindyalov, P.E. Bourne: The Protein Data Bank. Nucleic Acids Research, 28 pp. 235242 (2000). Protein Data Bank (PDB) ID 1ca2 from *www.pdb.org.* **7.14** © Judith Miller/Dorling Kindersley/ Freeman's **7.16a–b** Richard Megna/Fundamental Photographs, NYC **7.17** Ed Degginger/Color-Pic, Inc. **7.18a–b** Richard Megna/Fundamental Photographs, NYC **7.19** Richard Megna/Fundamental Photographs, NYC **7.20** Richard Megna/Fundamental Photographs, NYC **7.21** Jeff Daly/Visuals Unlimited **7.22a–c** Richard Megna/Fundamental Photographs, NYC **7.26a–c** H. Eugene LeMay, Jr. **7.27** Phil Degginger/Color-Pic, Inc. **7.28** Paparazzi Photography Studio - Dr. Pepper/Seven Up and Jeffrey L. Rodengen, Write Stuff Syndicate, Inc. **7.29** Tom Pantages **7.30** Benelux/Photo Researchers, Inc. **7.31** RNHRD NHS Trust/Getty Images Inc. - Stone Allstock **7.32** JPL/Space Science Institute/NASA Headquarters **7.33** Ed Degginger/Color-Pic, Inc. **7.35** Richard Megna/Fundamental Photographs, NYC **7.36** Ed Degginger/Color-Pic, Inc. **7.37** 1ca2: A.E. Eriksson, T.A. Jones, A. Liljas: Refined structure of human anhydrase II at 2.0 Angstrom resolution. Proteins 4 pp. 274 (1988). PDB: H.M. Berman, J. Westbrook, Z. Feng, G. Gilliland, T.N. Bhat, H. Weissig, I.N. Shindyalov, P.E. Bourne: The Protein Data Bank. Nucleic Acids Research, 28 pp. 235–242 (2000). Protein Data Bank (PDB) ID 1ca2 from www.pdb.org. **p. 272** Tom McHugh/Photo Researchers, Inc. **p. 274** Andrew Lambert Photography/Photo Researchers, Inc. **p. 288** Phil Degginger/ Color-Pic, Inc.

Chapter 8: CO08 JON ARNOLD/Getty Images, Inc. - Taxi **8.1a–c** Richard Megna/Fundamental Photographs, NYC **8.2a–c** Donald Clegg and Roxy Wilson/ Pearson Education/PH College **8.13a** Tom Pantages **8.15** Corbis/Bettmann

Chapter 9: CO09 Inga Spence/Visuals Unlimited **9.5a–c** Kristen Brochmann/ Fundamental Photographs, NYC **9.31** Bill Longcore/Photo Researchers, Inc. **9.48** Richard Megna/Fundamental Photographs, NYC **9.50** Courtesy of Prof. Michael GRÄTZEL/Laboratory of Photonics and Interfaces

Chapter 10: CO10 A. T. Willett/Alamy Images **10.4** Michal Heron/Pearson Education/PH College **10.5** Roland Seitre/Peter Arnold, Inc. **10.8a–b** Richard Megna/Fundamental Photographs, NYC **10.14** Glen E. Ellman/911pictures.com **10.15** Lowell Georgia/Corbis/Bettmann **10.21a–b** Richard Megna/Fundamental Photographs, NYC

Chapter 11: CO11 Altrendo Images/Getty Images, Inc. Altrendo Images **11.9** Richard Megna/Fundamental Photographs, NYC **p. 445** Calvin and Hobbes © Watterson. Dist. by Universal Press Syndicate. Reprinted with permission. All rights reserved. **11.10c** Ted Kinsman/Photo Researchers, Inc. **11.11** Richard Megna/Fundamental Photographs, NYC **11.13** Kristen Brochmann/ Fundamental Photographs, NYC **11.14** Hermann Eisenbeiss/Photo Researchers, Inc. **11.16** Richard Megna/Fundamental Photographs, NYC **11.20** Clean Technology Group, University of Nottingham (Brian Case) **11.29a** Dan McCoy/Rainbow **11.29b** Herve Berthoule/Jacana Scientific Control/Photo Researchers, Inc. **11.29c** Michael Dalton/Fundamental Photographs, NYC **11.39** Science Source/ Photo Researchers, Inc. **11.43** Phil Degginger/Merck/Color-Pic, Inc. **11.44** Robert L. Whetten, University of California at Los Angeles **p. 472** Tony Mendoza/ Stock Boston

Chapter 12: CO12 Corbis Royalty Free **12.8** Intel Corporation Pressroom Photo Archives **12.9** Courtesy of International Business Machines Corporation. Unauthorized use not permitted. **12.13** Marvin Rand/PUGH + SCARPA Architecture **12.14** Rimmington CE **12.15** Professor Charles Zukoski, Department of Chemical Engineering, University of Illinois/Urbana-Champaign, Illinois **12.17** David Parker/IMI/University of Birmingham High TC Consortium/Science Photo Library/Photo Researchers, Inc. **12.18** National Railway Japan/Phototake NYC **12.19** Michael Ventura/Alamy Images **12.21** Darren McCollester/Getty Images, Inc - Liaison **12.22** © Copyright and courtesy Superconductor Technologies Inc. **12.23** Richard Megna/Fundamental Photographs, NYC **12.26a–b** Richard Megna/Fundamental Photographs, NYC **12.29** Tom Pantages **12.30** Leonard Lessin/Peter Arnold, Inc. **12.31** Copyright 2004 General Motors Corp. Used with permission of GM Media Archives. **12.33** SJM is a registered trademark of St. Jude Medical, Inc. Copyright St. Jude Medical, Inc. 2002. This image is provided courtesy of St. Jude Medical, Inc. All rights reserved. **12.34** Southern Illinois University/Photo Researchers, Inc. **12.35** Advanced Tissue Sciences, Inc **12.36a–b** Richard Megna/Fundamental Photographs, NYC **12.37** Courtesy of Research In Motion (RIM). Research In Motion, the RIM logo, BlackBerry, the BlackBerry logo and SureType are registered with the U.S. Patent and Trademark Office and may be pending or registered in other countries - these and other marks of Research In Motion Limited are used under license. **12.41** Richard Megna/Fundamental Photographs, NYC **12.43** Prof. Dr. Horst Weller from H. Weller, *Angew. Chem. Int. Ed. Engl.* 1993, 32, 41–53, Fig. 1. **12.44** Prof. Dr. Horst Weller, Weller Group at the Institute of Physical Chemistry. **12.46** Fototeca della Veneranda Fabbrica del Duomo di Milano **12.47** Reproduced by courtesy of The Royal Institution of Great Britain. **12.48** Erik T. Thostenson, "Carbon Nanotube-Reinforced Composites: Processing, Characterization and Modeling" Ph.D. Dissertation, University of Delaware, 2004. **p. 515** Reproduced by courtesy of The Royal Institution of Great Britain. Bridgeman Art Library International Ltd. New York **p. 521** Courtesy Earth Observatory/ NASA and Nicholas M. Short, Sr.

Chapter 13: CO13 Dana Edmunds/PacificStock.com **13.5** Tom Bochsler/Pearson Education/PH College **13.7a–c** Richard Megna/Fundamental Photographs, NYC **13.8** Ed Degginger/Color-Pic, Inc. **13.10a–c** Richard Megna/Fundamental Photographs, NYC **p. 536** Richard Megna/Fundamental Photographs, NYC **13.15** Charles D. Winters/Photo Researchers, Inc. **13.16** Doug Perrine/Pacific-Stock.com **13.21** Grant Heilman/Grant Heilman Photography, Inc. **p. 550** Lon C. Diehl/PhotoEdit Inc. **13.26** Leonard Lessin/Peter Arnold, Inc. **13.27a** E.R. Degginger/Color-Pic, Inc. **13.27b** Gene Rhoden/Visuals Unlimited **13.32** Oliver Meckes & Nicole Ottawa/Photo Researchers, Inc.

Chapter 14: **CO14** Hunter, Jeff/Getty Images Inc. - Image Bank **14.1a** Michael S. Yamashita/Corbis/Bettmann **14.1b** S.C. Fried/Photo Researchers, Inc. **14.1c** David N. Davis/Photo Researchers, Inc. **14.2a** Michael Dalton/Fundamental Photographs, NYC **14.2b** Richard Megna/Fundamental Photographs, NYC **14.11** Richard Megna/Fundamental Photographs, NYC **14.19a–c** Richard Megna/Fundamental Photographs, NYC **14.22** Delphi Energy & Chassis, Troy, Michigan **14.23** Richard Megna/Fundamental Photographs, NYC **14.27a** Science Photo Library/Photo Researchers, Inc.

Chapter 15: **CO15** Mira.com/Ron Niebrugge **15.1a–c** Richard Megna/Fundamental Photographs, NYC **15.5** Ed Degginger/Color Pic, Inc. Courtesy Farmland Industries, Inc. **15.13a–c** Richard Megna/Fundamental Photographs, NYC **15.14a–c** Richard Megna/Fundamental Photographs, NYC **p. 631** Grant Heilman Photography, Inc.

Chapter 16: **CO16** Rosemary Calvert/Getty Images Inc. - Photographer's Choice Royalty Free **16.3** Richard Megna/Fundamental Photographs, NYC **16.6** Yoav Levy/Phototake NYC **16.8a–b** Donald Clegg and Roxy Wilson/Pearson Education/PH College **16.10** Michael Dalton/Fundamental Photographs, NYC **16.11a–c** Richard Megna/Fundamental Photographs, NYC **16.14** Frank LaBua/Pearson Education/PH College **16.16** Tom Pantages

Chapter 17: **CO17** Russ Bishop/Alamy Images **17.1** Donald Clegg & Roxy Wilson/Pearson Education/PH College **17.4** Profs. P. Motta and S. Correr/Science Photo Library/Photo Researchers, Inc. **17.7a–b** Richard Megna/Fundamental Photographs, NYC **17.16a–b** Richard Megna/Fundamental Photographs, NYC **17.17b** Gerry Davis/Phototake NYC **17.19a–c** Richard Megna/Fundamental Photographs, NYC **17.20a–c** Richard Megna/Fundamental Photographs, NYC **17.21a–c** Richard Megna/Fundamental Photographs, NYC **p. 757** Richard Megna/Fundamental Photographs, NYC

Chapter 18: **CO18** SPL/Photo Researchers, Inc. **18.2** Jorma Luhta/Nature Picture Library **18.3** Courtesy Earth Observatory/NASA and Nicholas M. Short, Sr. **18.5** NASA Headquarters **18.5** National Atmospheric Deposition Program/National Trends Network (http://nadp.sws.uiuc.edu) **18.7a–b** Don and Pat Valenti **18.9a** Dennis Kunkel/Phototake NYC **18.10** Tom Pantages **18.11** Ulf E. Wallin/Ulf Wallin Photography **18.13** C.D. Keeling and T.P Whorf, Carbon Dioxide Research Group, Scripps Institution of Oceanography, University of California, La Jolla, CA 92093-0444. **18.14** Australia Picture Library/Corbis/Bettmann **18.15L-R** Windows to the Universe, of the University Corporation for Atmospheric Research. Copyright © 2004 University Corporation for Atmospheric Research. All rights reserved. **18.16a** DuPont **18.17** © Katadyn North America. Used by permission. **18.18** John Sohlden/Visuals Unlimited **18.20** LifeStraw courtesy of Vestergaards Frandsen, Inc. **18.21** Sheila Terry/Science Photo Library **18.22** Kim Fennema/Visuals Unlimited **18.23** PPG Industries Inc. **p. 797** Reprinted with permission from Walter Leitner, "Supercritical Carbon Dioxide as a Green Reaction Medium for Catalysis", *Acc. Chem Res.*, 35 (9), 746–756, 2002. Copyright 2002 American Chemical Society.

Chapter 19: **CO19** NASA/Photo Researchers, Inc. **19.2a–b** Richard Megna/Fundamental Photographs, NYC **19.3.1–2** Michael Dalton/Fundamental Photographs, NYC **19.7** Austrian Central Library for Physics, Vienna, Austria **19.10(left)** Richard Megna/Fundamental Photographs, NYC **19.12a** Klaus Pavsan/Peter Arnold, Inc. **19.12b** Biophoto Associates/Photo Researchers, Inc. **19.16** Library of Congress

Chapter 20: **CO20** Roy Langstaff Photography **20.1a–b** Richard Megna/Fundamental Photographs, NYC **20.2a–c** Richard Megna/Fundamental Photographs, NYC **20.3a–b** Richard Megna/Fundamental Photographs, NYC **20.4** Richard Megna/Fundamental Photographs, NYC **20.9(left)** Jeff Gnass/Corbis/Stock Market **20.15** The Burndy Library, Dibner Institute for the History of Science and Technology, Cambridge, Massachusetts **20.23** John Mead/Science Photo Library/Photo Researchers, Inc. **20.28a–b** Reed Barton/Tom Pantages **p. 855** Jeff Gnass/GEOLIGHT

Chapter 21: **CO21** NOVASTOCK/PhotoEdit Inc. **21.1** CNRI/Photo Researchers, Inc. **21.7** CERN/European Organization for Nuclear Research **21.9** Photo Researchers, Inc. **21.10** Terence Kearey Photography **21.12** Kevin Schafer/Peter Arnold, Inc. **21.18** Archival Photofiles, [apf2-00502], Special Collections Research Center, University of Chicago Library. **21.18** Gary Sheahan "Birth of the Atomic Age" Chicago (Illinois); 1957. Chicago Historical Society, ICHi-33305. **21.20b** Ed Degginger/Color-Pic, Inc. **21.24** Figure 9 from P. W. Swarzenski, "U/Th Radionuclides as Coastal Groundwater Tracers," *Chem. Rev. 2007*, 107, 663–674. Courtesy of Peter W. Swarzenski, PhD, Coastal Marine Geology Program, U.S. Geological Survey **21.25** Richard Megna/Fundamental Photographs, NYC

Chapter 22: **CO22** © Dan Forer/Beateworks/CORBIS. All Rights Reserved **22.5** © Russell Curtis/Photo Researchers, Inc. **22.6a–b** Richard Megna/Fundamental Photographs, NYC **22.9** Donald Clegg and Roxy Wilson/Pearson Education/PH College **22.11** Paul Silverman/Fundamental Photographs, NYC **22.12a–b** Richard Megna/Fundamental Photographs, NYC **22.13** Beth Plowes - Proteapix **22.14** NASA/Johnson Space Center **22.16** Joseph Priestley (1733–1804): colored English engraving, 19th Century. The Granger Collection, New York. **22.16** John Hill/Getty Images Inc. - Image Bank **22.18a–c** Richard Megna/Fundamental Photographs, NYC **22.19** Courtesy of DuPont Nomex® **22.21a** Jeffrey A. Scovil/Jeffrey A. Scovil **22.22** Lawrence Migdale/Science Source/Photo Researchers, Inc. **22.24** Dan McCoy/Rainbow **22.25a–c** Kristen Brochmann/Fundamental Photographs, NYC **22.29a–c** Donald Clegg and Roxy Wilson/Pearson Education/PH College **22.31** Michael Dalton/Fundamental Photographs, NYC **22.33** Richard Megna/Fundamental Photographs, NYC **22.37** © Mufty Munir/epa/CORBIS All Rights Reserved **22.38** General Electric Corporate Research & Development Center **22.40** AP Wide World Photos **22.41** Chip Clark **22.42** David Muench/Corbis/Bettmann **22.43** Photo Courtesy of Texas Instruments Incorporated **22.47** National Institute for Occupational Safety & Health

Chapter 23: **CO23** Frank Micelotta/Getty Images, Inc - Liaison **23.1b** Brownie Harris/Corbis/Stock Market **23.2a–b** Karl Hartmann/Traudel Sachs/Phototake NYC **23.2c** Jeffrey A. Scovil/Jeffrey A. Scovil **23.3** The Cleveland-Cliffs Iron Company **23.5** Robin Smith/Getty Images Inc. - Stone Allstock **23.10** Oberlin College Archives, Oberlin, Ohio **23.12** Richard Megna/Fundamental Photographs, NYC **23.14a** Peter Christopher/Masterfile Corporation **23.14b** IT Stock International/Index Stock Imagery, Inc. **23.15** Magneti Ljubljana, d.d. **23.19** Donald Clegg and Roxy Wilson/Pearson Education/PH College **23.22** Michael Dalton/Fundamental Photographs, NYC **23.23** Donald Clegg and Roxy Wilson/Pearson Education/PH College **23.24** Richard Megna/Fundamental Photographs, NYC **23.25** Donald Clegg and Roxy Wilson/Pearson Education/PH College **23.26** Paul Silverman/Fundamental Photographs, NYC **23.27** Donald Clegg and Roxy Wilson/Pearson Education/PH College

Chapter 24: **CO24** Max Alexander © Dorling Kindersley **24.2a–b** Richard Megna/Fundamental Photographs, NYC **24.7** Gary C. Will/Visuals Unlimited **24.14** Kim Heacox Photography/DRK Photo **24.18L–R** Richard Megna/Fundamental Photographs, NYC **24.22** Richard Megna/Fundamental Photographs, NYC **24.26c** Nigel Forrow Photography, photographersdirect.com **24.36a–c** Tom Pantages **p. 1043** Carey B. Van Loon

Chapter 25: **CO25** Sergio Piumatti **25.8** Ed Degginger/Color-Pic, Inc. **25.9** Wes Thompson/Corbis/Stock Market **25.15** Richard Megna/Fundamental Photographs, NYC **25.16a** Richard Megna/Fundamental Photographs, NYC **25.16b** Beth Plowes - Proteapix **25.18** Richard Megna/Fundamental Photographs, NYC **25.19** Culver Pictures, Inc. **25.25** Richard Megna/Fundamental Photographs, NYC **25.27** Oxford Molecular Biophysics Laboratory/Science Photo Library/Photo Researchers, Inc.

Index

AB$_n$ molecules, 342–43
Absolute entropy, 817, 818
Absolute temperature, 595
Absorption, 558, 607
Absorption spectrum, 1033
Accuracy, 21
Acetaldehyde (ethanal), 570, 1071, 1073, 1075
  properties of, 441
Acetaminophen, 1102
Acetic acid (ethanoic acid), 129, 682, 702–3, 716, 720, 1071, 1074, 1076
  decarbonylation of, 838
  glacial, 1076
  in green chemistry, 790
  ionization of, 122–23
  pH of, 684–85
  production of, 1075
  properties of, 682
  shape of, 352
  titration with caustic soda (NaOH), 733–37
Acetic anhydride, 1100
Acetone (propanone), 478, 536, 570, 571, 1071, 1073, 1074
Acetonitrile, 443, 566, 569, 1052
  methyl isonitrate converted to, 587
  properties of, 441
Acetylene, 838, 945, 964, 1055, 1064, 1071
  production of, 430
  triple bonds in, 364
Acetylide ion, 964
Acetylsalicylic acid (aspirin), 2, 132, 387, 710, 713, 764, 1074, 1076
Acid(s), 129
  adipic, 106, 501–2
  Arrhenius, 668
  binary, 699–70
  carboxylic, 702–3
  conjugate, 670
  defined, 64
  diprotic, 129, 679
  as electron acceptor, 704
  factors affecting strength of, 699
  household, 128
  ionic properties of, 129
  Lewis, 704–7
  metal oxides reacting with, 274
  monoprotic, 129, 679
  names and formulas of, 64–65
  oxidation of metals by, 138–40
  oxyacids, 700–2, 943
  properties of, 129
  reactions of. *See also* Acid–base reactions
    with magnesium, 138–39
    with magnesium hydroxide, 133
  relating to anions, 64–65
  relative strengths of, 672–73
  strong, 130–31, 672, 679–80
    in buffered solutions, 727–28
  titrating, 150–53
  weak, 130–31, 672, 681–90
    acid-dissociation constant (K_a), 681–83, 684–88, 693–95
    common-ion effect on, 720–23
    percent ionization of, 683–84
    polyprotic, 688–90, 737

Acid–base equilibria, 666–717. *See also* Aqueous equilibria
  acid-dissociation constant and base-dissociation constant relationship, 693–95
  Arrhenius definitions, 668
  autoionization of water, 673–75
  Brønsted–Lowry acids and bases, 668–73
    conjugate acid–base pairs, 670–71
    H$^+$ ions in water and, 669
    proton-transfer reactions, 669–70
    relative strengths, 672–73
  chemical structure and, 699–703
    binary acids, 699–700
    carboxylic acids, 702–3
    factors affecting acid strength, 699
    oxyacids, 700–2
  ion product, 674–75
  Lewis acids and bases, 704–7
    electron-pair acceptor/donor concept, 704–5
    metal ions and, 705–7
  in organic substances, 703
  pH scale, 675–79
    measuring, 678–79
    other "p" scales, 678
  of salt solutions, 695–99
    anion reaction with water, 696
    cation reaction with water, 696–97
    combined cation-anion effect, 697–99
  solubility equilibria and, 741
  strong acids and bases, 679–81
    in buffered solutions, 727–28
  weak acids and bases, 681–93
    acid-dissociation constant, 681–83, 684–88, 693–95
    common-ion effect on, 720–23
    percent ionization of, 683–84
    polyprotic acids, 688–90
    types of, 692–93
Acid–base indicators, 150–51, 678, 679
Acid–base properties, of organic substances, 1054
Acid–base reactions, 128–35. *See also* Acid–base equilibria
  electrolytes, 131–32
  with gas formation, 134–35
  gas-phase, 669–70
  neutralization reactions and salts, 132–34
Acid–base titrations, 730–37
  of polyprotic acids, 737
  strong, 730–33
  weak, 733–37
Acid-dissociation constant (K_a), 681
  base-dissociation constant (K_b) and, 693–95
  calculating from pH, 682–83
  calculating pH from, 684–88
  for hydrolysis reactions, 705
  for polyprotic acids, 689
Acidic anhydrides (acidic oxides), 946
Acidic solutions, 697–98
Acid inhibitors, 135
Acid-insoluble sulfides, 754
Acidosis, 729
Acid rain, 275, 491, 776–77, 946

Acid salts, 694
Acid spills, 135
Actinides, electron configurations of, 239–40
Activated complex (transition state), 593
Activation, entropy of, 841
Activation energy, 592–94
  catalysis and, 610, 654
  determining, 595–97
Active metals, 140
Active site, 609
Active transport, 555
Activity, 906
Activity series, 140–42, 863
Actual yield, 105
Addition, significant figures in, 23
Addition polymerization, 499–500
Addition polymers, 500, 841
Addition reactions
  of alkenes and alkynes, 1065–66
  mechanism of, 1066–68
Adenine, 477, 1091, 1092
Adenosine diphosphate (ADP), 830, 960
Adenosine monophosphate (AMP), 1103
Adenosine triphosphate (ATP), 830, 840, 959, 1103
Adhesive forces, 448
Adipic acid, 106, 501–502
ADP (adenosine diphosphate), 830, 960
Adrenaline, 568
Adsorption, 558, 606–607
Air
  combustion in, 86–87
  composition of, 394
Air bags, automobile, 409
Alanine, 703, 1081, 1082, 1083
Alanylglycylserine, 1083
R-Albuterol, 1079
Alchemy, 143
Alcohol(s), 66–67, 1070–71
  condensation reactions with, 1075
  as functional groups, 1072–73
  oxidation of, 1074
  solubilities of, 536–37
Aldehydes, 1073–74
Alizarin yellow R, 679
Alkali (group 1A) metals, 50, 140, 240, 276–79
  group trends for, 276–79
  in ionic hydrides, 937
  ionic hydroxides of, 680–81
  oxidation number of, 137
  as reducing agent, 861
Alkali metal ions, 754
Alkaline battery, 872
Alkaline earth (group 2A) metals, 50, 140, 240, 279–81
  group trends for, 279–81
  in ionic hydrides, 937
  ionic hydroxides of, 680–81
  oxidation number of, 137
  as reducing agent, 861
Alkalosis, 729
Alkanes, 66–67, 1054, 1055–62
  cycloalkanes, 1060–61
  derivatives of, 66–67

  nomenclature of, 1058–60
  reactions of, 1061
  structural isomers of, 1057–58
  structures of, 1056–57
Alka-Seltzer, 135
Alkenes, 1054, 1055, 1062–64
  addition reactions of, 1065–66
Alkyl groups, 1059, 1070–71
  in Friedel-Crafts reaction, 1069
Alkynes, 1054, 1055, 1064–65
  addition reactions of, 1065–66
Allene, 389
Allotropes, 282
Alloys, 981, 983, 995–98
  defined, 995
  heterogeneous, 995, 996
  intermetallic compounds, 996–97
  interstitial, 995, 996
  shape-memory, 997–98
  solution, 995
  steels, 995–96
  substitutional, 995, 996
Alloy steels, 995
Al_2O_3, 484
α-helix, 1084
α radiation, 41, 895, 896, 897, 919–20
Aluminates, 493
Aluminum (Al), 6, 50, 992
  electrometallurgy of, 989–90
  electron configuration of, 240
  electronic properties of, 484
  hydrometallurgy of, 988
  Lewis symbol for, 299
  oxidation number of, 137
  oxidation of, 874
  purification of ore, 750
  recycling, 989–90
  specific heat of, 181
Aluminum hydroxide, 750
Aluminum oxide, 989
American Chemical Society, 51
Americium-241, 623, 928
Amethyst, 459
Amides, 1077–78
Amine hydrochlorides, 694
Amines, 692, 694, 1054, 1077–78
Amino acids, 1080–82
  amphiprotic behavior of, 703
  chiral, 1085
  essential, 1081
  side chain, 1081–82
Ammeter, 891
Ammonia, 129, 394, 452, 754, 953
  as Arrhenius and Brønsted–Lowry base, 670
  bond angles, 348
  bonding in, 360
  critical temperature and pressure of, 452
  in fertilizers, 631
  formation of, 818–19
  Haber (Haber-Bosch) process for synthesizing, 630–31, 890
  free energy changes in, 826, 828
  hydrogen and, 937
  nitrogen and, 953
  temperature effects on, 642
  volume and pressure effects on, 646

Common Ions

Positive Ions (Cations)

1+
Ammonium (NH_4^+)
Cesium (Cs^+)
Copper(I) or cuprous (Cu^+)
Hydrogen (H^+)
Lithium (Li^+)
Potassium (K^+)
Silver (Ag^+)
Sodium (Na^+)

2+
Barium (Ba^{2+})
Cadmium (Cd^{2+})
Calcium (Ca^{2+})
Chromium(II) or chromous (Cr^{2+})
Cobalt(II) or cobaltous (Co^{2+})
Copper(II) or cupric (Cu^{2+})
Iron(II) or ferrous (Fe^{2+})
Lead(II) or plumbous (Pb^{2+})
Magnesium (Mg^{2+})
Manganese(II) or manganous (Mn^{2+})
Mercury(I) or mercurous (Hg_2^{2+})
Mercury(II) or mercuric (Hg^{2+})
Strontium (Sr^{2+})
Nickel(II) (Ni^{2+})
Tin(II) or stannous (Sn^{2+})
Zinc (Zn^{2+})

3+
Aluminum (Al^{3+})
Chromium(III) or chromic (Cr^{3+})
Iron(III) or ferric (Fe^{3+})

Negative Ions (Anions)

1−
Acetate (CH_3COO^- or $C_2H_3O_2^-$)
Bromide (Br^-)
Chlorate (ClO_3^-)
Chloride (Cl^-)
Cyanide (CN^-)
Dihydrogen phosphate ($H_2PO_4^-$)
Fluoride (F^-)
Hydride (H^-)
Hydrogen carbonate or
  bicarbonate (HCO_3^-)
Hydrogen sulfite or bisulfite (HSO_3^-)
Hydroxide (OH^-)
Iodide (I^-)
Nitrate (NO_3^-)
Nitrite (NO_2^-)
Perchlorate (ClO_4^-)
Permanganate (MnO_4^-)
Thiocyanate (SCN^-)

2−
Carbonate (CO_3^{2-})
Chromate (CrO_4^{2-})
Dichromate ($Cr_2O_7^{2-}$)
Hydrogen phosphate (HPO_4^{2-})
Oxide (O^{2-})
Peroxide (O_2^{2-})
Sulfate (SO_4^{2-})
Sulfide (S^{2-})
Sulfite (SO_3^{2-})

3−
Arsenate (AsO_4^{3-})
Phosphate (PO_4^{3-})

Fundamental Constants*

Atomic mass unit	1 amu	= $1.660538782 \times 10^{-27}$ kg
	1 g	= $6.02214179 \times 10^{23}$ amu
Avogadro's number	N	= $6.02214179 \times 10^{23}$/mol
Boltzmann's constant	k	= $1.3806504 \times 10^{-23}$ J/K
Electron charge	e	= $1.602176487 \times 10^{-19}$ C
Faraday's constant	F	= 9.64853399×10^4 C/mol
Gas constant	R	= 0.082058205 L-atm/mol-K
		= 8.314472 J/mol-K
Mass of electron	m_e	= $5.48579909 \times 10^{-4}$ amu
		= $9.10938215 \times 10^{-31}$ kg
Mass of neutron	m_n	= 1.008664916 amu
		= $1.674927211 \times 10^{-27}$ kg
Mass of proton	m_p	= 1.007276467 amu
		= $1.672621637 \times 10^{-27}$ kg
Pi	π	= 3.1415927
Planck's constant	h	= $6.62606896 \times 10^{-34}$ J-s
Speed of light	c	= 2.99792458×10^8 m/s

*Fundamental constants are listed at the National Institute of Standards and Technology Web site:
http://physics.nist.gov/PhysRefData/contents.html

Useful Conversion Factors and Relationships

Length
SI unit: meter (m)

$$1 \text{ km} = 0.62137 \text{ mi}$$
$$1 \text{ mi} = 5280 \text{ ft}$$
$$= 1.6093 \text{ km}$$
$$1 \text{ m} = 1.0936 \text{ yd}$$
$$1 \text{ in.} = 2.54 \text{ cm (exactly)}$$
$$1 \text{ cm} = 0.39370 \text{ in.}$$
$$1 \text{ Å} = 10^{-10} \text{ m}$$

Mass
SI unit: kilogram (kg)

$$1 \text{ kg} = 2.2046 \text{ lb}$$
$$1 \text{ lb} = 453.59 \text{ g}$$
$$= 16 \text{ oz}$$
$$1 \text{ amu} = 1.660538782 \times 10^{-24} \text{ g}$$

Temperature
SI unit: Kelvin (K)

$$0 \text{ K} = -273.15 \text{ °C}$$
$$= -459.67 \text{ °F}$$
$$\text{K} = \text{°C} + 273.15$$
$$\text{°C} = \tfrac{5}{9} (\text{°F} - 32°)$$
$$\text{°F} = \tfrac{9}{5} \text{°C} + 32°$$

Energy (derived)
SI unit: Joule (J)

$$1 \text{ J} = 1 \text{ kg-m}^2/\text{s}^2$$
$$1 \text{ J} = 0.2390 \text{ cal}$$
$$= 1 \text{ C} \times 1 \text{ V}$$
$$1 \text{ cal} = 4.184 \text{ J}$$
$$1 \text{ eV} = 1.602 \times 10^{-19} \text{ J}$$

Pressure (derived)
SI unit: Pascal (Pa)

$$1 \text{ Pa} = 1 \text{ N/m}^2$$
$$= 1 \text{ kg/m-s}^2$$
$$1 \text{ atm} = 101{,}325 \text{ Pa}$$
$$= 760 \text{ torr}$$
$$= 14.70 \text{ lb/in}^2$$
$$1 \text{ bar} = 10^5 \text{ Pa}$$
$$1 \text{ torr} = 1 \text{ mm Hg}$$

Volume (derived)
SI unit: cubic meter (m^3)

$$1 \text{ L} = 10^{-3} \text{ m}^3$$
$$= 1 \text{ dm}^3$$
$$= 10^3 \text{ cm}^3$$
$$= 1.0567 \text{ qt}$$
$$1 \text{ gal} = 4 \text{ qt}$$
$$= 3.7854 \text{ L}$$
$$1 \text{ cm}^3 = 1 \text{ mL}$$
$$1 \text{ in}^3 = 16.4 \text{ cm}^3$$

Index of Useful Tables and Figures